Boolean Functions for Cryptography and Coding Theory

Boolean functions are essential to systems for secure and reliable communication. This comprehensive survey of Boolean functions for cryptography and coding covers the whole domain and all important results, building on the authors influential articles with additional topics and recent results. A useful resource for researchers and graduate students, the book balances detailed discussions of properties and parameters with examples of various types of cryptographic attacks that motivate the consideration of these parameters. It provides all the necessary background on mathematics, cryptography, and coding and an overview of recent applications, such as side-channel attacks on smart cards and hardware, cloud computing through fully homomorphic encryption, and local pseudorandom generators. The result is a complete and accessible text on the state of the art in single- and multiple-output Boolean functions that illustrates the interaction among mathematics, computer science, and telecommunications.

CLAUDE CARLET is Professor Emeritus of Mathematics at the University of Paris 8, France, and member of the Bergen University Department of Computer Science. He has contributed to 16 books, and published more than 130 papers in international journals and more than 70 papers in international proceedings. He has been a member of 80 program committees of international conferences and served as cochair for 10 of them. He has overseen the research group Codage-Cryptographie, which gathers all French researchers in coding and cryptography, and is editor-in-chief of the journal *Cryptography and Communications*. He has been an invited plenary speaker at 20 international conferences and the invited speaker at 30 other international conferences and workshops.

Boolean Functions for Cryptography and Coding Theory

Claude Carlet

University of Bergen, Norway, and University of Paris 8, France

CAMBRIDGE
UNIVERSITY PRESS

Shaftesbury Road, Cambridge CB2 8EA, United Kingdom

One Liberty Plaza, 20th Floor, New York, NY 10006, USA

477 Williamstown Road, Port Melbourne, VIC 3207, Australia

314–321, 3rd Floor, Plot 3, Splendor Forum, Jasola District Centre, New Delhi – 110025, India

103 Penang Road, #05–06/07, Visioncrest Commercial, Singapore 238467

Cambridge University Press is part of Cambridge University Press & Assessment,
a department of the University of Cambridge.

We share the University's mission to contribute to society through the pursuit of
education, learning and research at the highest international levels of excellence.

www.cambridge.org
Information on this title: www.cambridge.org/9781108473804

DOI: 10.1017/9781108606806

First published 2020

A catalogue record for this publication is available from the British Library

Library of Congress Cataloging-in-Publication data
Names: Carlet, Claude, author.
Title: Boolean functions for cryptography and coding theory / Claude Carlet.
Description: Cambridge ; New York, NY : Cambridge University Press, 2020. |
Includes bibliographical references and index.
Identifiers: LCCN 2020002605 (print) | LCCN 2020002606 (ebook) |
ISBN 9781108473804 (hardback) | ISBN 9781108606806 (epub)
Subjects: LCSH: Algebra, Boolean. | Cryptography. | Coding theory.
Classification: LCC QA10.3 .C37 2020 (print) | LCC QA10.3 (ebook) |
DDC 003/.5401511324–dc23
LC record available at https://lccn.loc.gov/2020002605
LC ebook record available at https://lccn.loc.gov/2020002606

ISBN   978-1-108-47380-4   Hardback

Contents

Preface

The present monograph is a merged, reorganized, significantly revised, and extensively completed version of two chapters, entitled "Boolean Functions for Cryptography and Error Correcting Codes" [236] and "Vectorial Boolean Functions for Cryptography" [237], which appeared in 2010 as parts of the book *Boolean Models and Methods in Mathematics, Computer Science, and Engineering* [394] (editors, Yves Crama and Peter Hammer). It is meant for researchers but is accessible to anyone who knows basics in linear algebra and general mathematics. All the other notions needed are introduced and studied (even finite fields are, in the Appendix).

Since these chapters were written in 2009, about 1,500 papers have been published that deal with this twofold topic (which is broad, as we see), and this version is updated with the main references and their main results (with corrections in the rare cases where they were needed). It also contains original results.

New notions on Boolean and vectorial functions and new ways of using them have also emerged. A chapter devoted to these recent and/or not enough studied directions of research has been included.

In the limit of a book, we tried to be as complete as possible. Of course, we could not go into details as much as do papers, but we made our best to ensure a good trade-off between completeness in scope and in depth. The choice of those papers that are referred to and of those results that are developed may seem subjective; it has been difficult, given the large number of papers. We tried, within the imposed length limit, to give the proof of a result each time it was short and simple enough, and when it provided a vision (we tried to avoid giving too technical proofs whose only – but of course important – value would have been to convince the reader that the result is true). We would have liked to avoid, when presenting arguments and observations, to refer to results (and concepts) to come later in the text, but the large number of results has made this necessary; otherwise, it would have been impossible to gather in a same place all the facts related to a same notion.

We have limited ourselves to Boolean and vectorial functions in characteristic 2, since these fit better with applications in coding and cryptography, and since dealing with p-ary and generalized functions would have reduced the description of the results on binary functions.

Acknowledgments

The author wishes to thank Cambridge University Press for publishing this monograph, and in particular Kaitlin Leach, Amy He, and Mark Fox for their kind help. He deeply thanks Lilya Budaghyan, from the Selmer Center, University of Bergen, for her kind support and her precious and numerous bits of information, in particular on almost perfect nonlinear (APN) functions, which allowed me to improve several chapters, making them more accurate, complete, and up-to-date, and Sihem Mesnager, from the University of Paris 8 and the Laboratoire Analyse, Géométrie et Applications (LAGA), for her careful reading of the whole book during the time it was written, for her supporting advice, and for her detailed additive proposals, which improved the completeness. I also thank very much Victor Chen, Sylvain Guilley, Pierrick Méaux, Lauren De Meyer, Stjepan Picek, Emmanuel Prouff, Sondre Rønjom, and Deng Tang, each of whom helped with completing and correcting a part of a section of the book or even several. Many thanks also to the anonymous reviewers invited by Cambridge University Press, whose comments have been helpful.

Research is a collective action and a too-long list of names should be cited to acknowledge all the stimulating discussions, collaborations, and information that contributed to this book. A few names are the 10 previously mentioned and Kanat Abdukhalikov, Benny Applebaum, Thierry Berger, Marco Calderini, Xi Chen, Robert Coulter, Diana Davidova, Ulrich Dempwolff, John Dillon, Cunsheng Ding, the late Hans Dobbertin, Yves Edel, Keqin Feng, Caroline Fontaine, Rafael Fourquet, Philippe Gaborit, Faruk Göloglu, Guang Gong, Aline Gouget, Cem Güneri, Tor Helleseth, Xiang-dong Hou, Nikolay Kaleyski, William Kantor, Selçuk Kavut, Jenny Key, Alexander Kholosha, Andrew Klapper, Nicholas Kolokotronis, Gohar Kyureghyan, Philippe Langevin, Gregor Leander, Alla Levina, Chunlei Li, Nian Li, Konstantinos Limniotis, Mikhail Lobanov, Luca Mariot, Subhamoy Maitra, the late James Massey, Gary McGuire, Wilfried Meidl, Willi Meier, Harald Niederreiter, Svetla Nikova, Kaisa Nyberg, Ferruh Özbudak, Daniel Panario, Matthew Parker, Enes Pasalic, George Petrides, Alexander Pott, Mathieu Rivain, Thomas Roche, François Rodier, Neil Sloane, François-Xavier Standaert, Henning Stichtenoth, Yin Tan, Chunming Tang, Horacio Tapia-Recillas, Faina Solov'eva, Pante Stănică, Yuriy Tarannikov, Cédric Tavernier, Alev Topuzoğlu, Irene Villa, Arne Winterhof, Satoshi Yoshiara, Xiangyong Zeng, Fengrong Zhang, and Victor Zinoviev, as well as the members of the National Institute for Research in Computer Science and Automation (INRIA) team, whose CODES project (now called SECRET) has been a nice research environment and has supported me during my thesis and many years after, and the Bergen Selmer Center team, which does the same now, with a spirit of kindness and generosity, for my great scientific benefit.

I also wish to acknowledge that gathering the bibliography has been considerably eased by websites such as dblp: computer science bibliography (https://dblp.uni-trier.de), Research-Gate (www.researchgate.net), and Google Scholar (https://scholar.google.fr/schhp?hl=fr &tab=Xs).

Last but not least, I am so grateful to my wife Madeleine and my family for their support, patience, and understanding of what a researcher's work is. This is even more true for the last three years, during which the writing of this book, the reviewing of the numerous published papers, and the copyediting took so much of my time. I dedicate my book to them, with a special thought for my children and grandchildren, who will have to face the world we leave them.

Notation

$\lvert I \rvert$	size of a set I,
$\lfloor u \rfloor$	integer part (floor) of a real number u,
$\lceil u \rceil$	ceiling of u (the smallest integer larger than or equal to u),
$\phi^{-1}(u)$	preimage of u by a function ϕ,
1_E	indicator (or characteristic) function of a set E: $1_E(x) = \begin{cases} 1 \text{ if } x \in E \\ 0 \text{ otherwise,} \end{cases}$
δ_a	the Dirac (or Kronecker) symbol at a (*i.e.* the indicator of $\{a\}$),
$\mathbb{F}_2$	the finite field with two elements $0, 1$ (bits),
$\mathbb{F}_2^n$	the n-dimensional vector space over $\mathbb{F}_2$ (sometimes identified with $\mathbb{F}_{2^n}$),
$\mathcal{L}_{n,m}$	the vector space of linear (n, m)-functions,
0_n	zero vector in $\mathbb{F}_2^n$ or in $\mathbb{F}_q^n$, $n > 1$ (in other groups, we just write 0),
1_n	vector $(1, \dots, 1)$ in $\mathbb{F}_2^n$,
$+$	addition in characteristic 0 (*e.g.*, in $\mathbb{R}$), and in $\mathbb{F}_2^n$ and $\mathbb{F}_{2^n}$ for $n > 1$,
$\sum_i$	multiple sum of $+$,
$\oplus$	addition in $\mathbb{F}_2$ (*i.e.*, modulo 2); direct sum of two vector spaces,
$\bigoplus_i$	multiple sum of $\oplus$,
$\overline{x}$	$x + 1_n$, where $x \in \mathbb{F}_2^n$,
$a \cdot x$	inner product in $\mathbb{F}_2^n$,
$\ell_a(x), t_a(x)$	$= a \cdot x$, resp. $x + a$, where "$\cdot$" is an inner product in $\mathbb{F}_2^n$,
$\mathbb{F}_2^I$	the vector space over $\mathbb{F}_2$ of all binary vectors whose indices range in I,
$\mathbb{F}_{2^n}$	the finite (Galois) field of order 2^n, identified with $\mathbb{F}_2^n$ as a vector space,
$tr_m^n(x)$	$= x + x^{2^m} + x^{2^{2m}} + \cdots + x^{2^{n-m}}$, trace function from $\mathbb{F}_{2^n}$ to $\mathbb{F}_{2^m}$ ($m \mid n$),
$tr_n(x)$	$= tr_1^n(x) = \sum_{i=0}^{n-1} x^{2^i}$ the absolute trace function,
$\mathbb{F}_{2^n}^*$	$\mathbb{F}_{2^n} \setminus \{0\}$, where 0 denotes the zero element of $\mathbb{F}_{2^n}$,
α	primitive element of $\mathbb{F}_{2^n}$,
$\otimes$	convolutional product of two functions over $\mathbb{F}_2^n$ (see page 60),
$f, g, h, \dots$	Boolean functions,
$\mathcal{BF}_n$	the $\mathbb{F}_2$-vector space of all n-variable Boolean functions $f : \mathbb{F}_2^n \to \mathbb{F}_2$,
$F, G, H, \dots$	vectorial functions,
$\mathcal{G}_F$	graph of a vectorial function: $\mathcal{G}_F = \{(x, F(x)); \ x \in \mathbb{F}_2^n\}$,
$w_H()$	Hamming weight (of a vector, of a function),
$d_H(,)$	Hamming distance (between two vectors, two functions),
$d(C)$	minimum (Hamming) distance of code C,

$supp()$	the support (of a vector, of a function),
$x \preceq y$	"x is covered by y" (*i.e.*, $supp(x) \subseteq supp(y)$),
$x \vee y$	vector such that $supp(x \vee y) = supp(x) \cup supp(y)$,
$x \wedge y$	vector such that $supp(x \wedge y) = supp(x) \cap supp(y)$,
e_i	ith vector of the canonical basis of $\mathbb{F}_2^n$,
x^I, x^u	$\prod_{i \in I} x_i, I \subseteq \{1, \ldots, n\}, \prod_{i=1}^n x_i^{u_i}, u \in \mathbb{F}_2^n$,
$f \mapsto f^\circ$	binary Möbius transform ($f^\circ : u \mapsto a_u$, coef. of x^u in the ANF of f),
$\widehat{\varphi}$	Fourier–Hadamard transform of a real-valued function φ over $\mathbb{F}_2^n$,
f_χ	sign function of a Boolean function f, that is, $x \mapsto (-1)^{f(x)}$,
$W_f()$	Walsh transform of a Boolean function f (*i.e.*, $\widehat{f_\chi}$),
$W_F(,)$	Walsh transform of a vectorial function F,
$supp(W_f)$	support of W_f: $\{u \in \mathbb{F}_2^n; W_f(u) \neq 0\}$,
N_{W_f}	cardinality of the support of W_f,
$\mathcal{F}(f)$	$\sum_{x \in \mathbb{F}_2^n} (-1)^{f(x)} (= W_f(0_n))$,
$nl()$	nonlinearity of a Boolean or vectorial function,
$nl_r()$	r-th order nonlinearity of a Boolean function,
$\ln, \log_2$	natural (Neperian) logarithm, base 2 logarithm,
$d_{alg}(f)$	the algebraic degree of f (*i.e.*, the degree of its ANF),
$d_{num}(f)$	the numerical degree of f (*i.e.*, the degree of its NNF),
$w_2(j)$	2-weight of integer j (see page 45),
(n, m, t)-function	t-resilient (n, m)-function,
$AI()$	algebraic immunity of a function,
$M_{f,d}$	matrix of the system of equations $\bigoplus_{\substack{I \subseteq \{1, \ldots, n\} \\ |I| \leq d}} a_I u^I = 0, u \in supp(f)$,
$rk(M)$	the rank of a matrix M,
$FAC()$	fast algebraic complexity of a function,
$FAI()$	fast algebraic immunity of a function,
$D_a f, D_a F$	derivatives in the direction a: $x \mapsto f(x) \oplus f(x + a), F(x) + F(x + a)$,
Δ	the symmetric difference between two sets,
$\Delta_f(a)$	autocorrelation function $\Delta_f(a) = \sum_{x \in \mathbb{F}_2^n} (-1)^{D_a f(x)}$,
Δ_f	absolute indicator of f: $\Delta_f = \max_{a \in \mathbb{F}_2^n \setminus \{0_n\}} |\Delta_f(a)|$,
$\mathcal{V}(f)$	sum-of-squares indicator of f: $\sum_{e \in \mathbb{F}_2^n} \mathcal{F}^2(D_e f)$,
$\mathcal{E}_f$	linear kernel of a Boolean function f,
$RM(r, n)$	Reed–Muller code of order r and length 2^n,
$\rho(r, n)$	covering radius of $RM(r, n)$,
β_f	the symplectic form associated to a quadratic function f,
$\widetilde{f}$	dual of a bent Boolean function (Definition 51, page 197),
$\mathcal{M}$	Maiorana–McFarland's class,
$\mathcal{PS}$	partial spread class,
L^*	adjoint operator of a linear automorphism L,
$Im(F)$	the range (*i.e.*, image set) $F(\mathbb{F}_2^n)$ of an (n, m)-function,
$An(f)$	the $\mathbb{F}_2$-vector space of annihilators of a Boolean function f,
$An_d(f)$	restriction of $An(f)$ to those functions of algebraic degree at most d,
$B_{k,l}(f)$	$- \{g \in \mathcal{BJ}_n; d_{alg}(g) \leq k$ and $d_{alg}(fg) \leq l\}$,

f   defined by $f(x) = \mathrm{f}(w_H(x))$, when f is symmetric,

$\sigma_i(x)$ elementary symmetric Boolean fct., of ANF: $\bigoplus_{I \subseteq \{1,\dots,n\}/\ |I|=i} x^I$,

$S_i(x)$ elementary symmetric pseudo-Boolean fct. NNF: $\sum_{I \subseteq \{1,\dots,n\}/\ |I|=i} x^I$,

δ_F differential uniformity of an (n,m)-function F,

Nb_F imbalance of an (n,m)-function (see page 113),

NB_F derivative imbalance of an (n,m)-function (see page 138),

x   a sharing of x (see page 436),

F   a threshold implementation of function F (see page 436),

$E_{n,k}$ $= \{x \in \mathbb{F}_2^n;\ w_H(x) = k\}$,

$w_H(f)_k$ Hamming weight of the restriction of function f to $E_{n,k}$,

1

Introduction to cryptography, codes, Boolean, and vectorial functions

1.1 Cryptography

A fundamental objective of *cryptography* is to enable two persons to communicate over an insecure channel (a public channel such as the internet) in such a way that any other person is unable to recover their messages (constituting the *plaintext*) from what is sent in its place over the channel (the *ciphertext*). The transformation of the plaintext into the ciphertext is called *encryption*, or enciphering. It is ensured by a *cryptosystem*. Encryption–decryption is the most ancient cryptographic activity (ciphers already existed in the fourth century BC) but its nature has deeply changed with the invention of computers, because the *cryptanalysis* (the activity of the third person, the eavesdropper, who aims at recovering the message, or better, the secret data used by the algorithm – which is assumed to be public) can use their power. Another important change will occur (see *e.g.*, [70, 360, 832]), at least for public-key cryptography (see the definition below), when quantum computers become operational.

The encryption algorithm takes as input the plaintext and an encryption key K_E, and it outputs the ciphertext. The *decryption* (or deciphering) algorithm takes as input the ciphertext and a private[1] decryption key K_D. It outputs the plaintext.

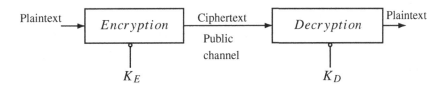

For being considered robust, a cryptosystem should not be cryptanalyzed by an attack needing less than 2^{80} elementary operations (which represent thousands of centuries of computation with a modern computer) and less than billions of plaintext–ciphertext pairs. In particular, an exhaustive search of the secret parameters of the cryptosystem (consisting in trying every possible value of them until the data given to the attacker match the computed data) should not be feasible in less than 2^{80} elementary operations. In fact, we most often even want that there is no faster cryptanalysis than exhaustive search.

---

[1] According to principles already stated in 1883 by A. Kerckhoffs [688], who cited a still more ancient manuscript by R. du Carlet [207], only the key(s) need absolutely to be kept secret – the confidentiality should not rely on the secrecy of the encryption method – and a cipher cannot be considered secure if it can be decrypted by the designer himself without using the decryption key.

1

Note that the term of cryptography is often used indifferently for naming the two activities of designing cryptosystems and of cryptanalyzing them, while the correct term when dealing with both is *cryptology*.

1.1.1 Symmetric versus public-key cryptosystems

If the encryption key is supposed to be secret, then we speak of *conventional cryptography* or of *private-key cryptography*. We also speak of *symmetric cryptography* since the same key can then be used for K_E and K_D. In practice, the principle of conventional cryptography relies then on the sharing of a private key between the sender of a message (often called Alice) and its receiver (often called Bob). Until the late 1970s, only symmetric ciphers existed.

If the encryption key can be public, then we speak of *public-key cryptography* (or *asymmetric cryptography*), which is preferable to conventional cryptography, since it makes it possible to securely communicate without having previously shared keys in a secure way: every person who wants to receive secret messages can keep secret a decryption key and publish an encryption key; if n persons want to secretly communicate pairwise using a public-key cryptosystem, they need n encryption keys and n decryption keys, when conventional cryptosystems will need $\binom{n}{2} = \frac{n(n-1)}{2}$ keys. Of course, it must be impossible to deduce in reasonable time, even with huge computational power, the private decryption key from the public encryption key. Such requirement is related to the problem of building *one-way functions*, that is, functions such that computing the image of an element is fast (*i.e.*, is a problem of polynomial complexity), while the problem of computing the preimage of an element has exponential complexity.

All known public-key cryptosystems, such as RSA, which uses operations in large rings [846], allow a much lower data throughput; they also need keys of sizes 10 times larger than symmetric ciphers for ensuring the same level of security. Some public-key cryptosystems, such as those of McEliece and Niederreiter (based on codes) [846], are faster, but have drawbacks, because the ciphertext and the plaintext have quite different lengths, and the keys are still larger than for other public-key cryptosystems.[2] Private-key cryptosystems are then still needed nowadays for ensuring the confidential transfer of large data. In practice, they are widely used for confidentiality in the internet, banking, mobile communications, etc., and their study and design are still an active domain of research. Thanks to public-key cryptosystems, the share-out of the necessary secret keys for the symmetric cipher can be done without using a secure channel (the secret keys for conventional cryptosystems are strings of a few hundreds of bits only and can then be encrypted by public-key cryptosystems). The protagonists can then exchange safely, over a public channel such as the internet, their common private encryption–decryption key, called a *session key*. Protocols specially devoted to key exchange can also be used.

The change caused by the intervention of quantum computers will be probably much less important for symmetric than for public-key cryptography. Most current symmetric ciphers

---

[2] Code-based, lattice-based, and other "postquantum" cryptosystems are, however, actively studied, mainly because they would be alternatives to RSA and to the cryptosystems based on the discrete logarithm, in case an efficient quantum computer could be built in the future, which would break them.

seem secure against attacks by quantum computers (Grover's algorithm [576], which, given a black box with N possible inputs and some output, deduces with high probability from the results of $\mathcal{O}(\sqrt{N})$ evaluations the supposedly unique input,[3] will probably have as an impact the necessity to double the length of the keys).

1.1.2 Block ciphers versus stream ciphers

The encryption in a symmetric cipher can be treated block by block in a so-called *block cipher* (such as the Advanced Encryption Standard, AES [403, 404]). The binary plaintext is then divided into blocks of the same size, several blocks being encrypted with the same key (and a public data called initial vector being changed more often). It can also be treated in a *stream cipher* [463], through the addition, most often mod 2, of a *keystream* of the same size as the plaintext, output by a pseudorandom generator (PRG) parameterized by a secret key (the keystream can be produced symbol by symbol, or block by block when the PRG uses a block cipher in a proper mode[4]). A quality of stream ciphers is to avoid error propagation, which gives them an advantage in applications where errors may occur during the transmission.

The ciphertext can be decrypted in the case of block ciphers by inverting the process and in the case of stream ciphers by the same bitwise addition of the keystream, which gives back the plaintext. Stream ciphers are also meant to be faster and to consume less electric power (which makes them adapted to cheap embedded devices). The triple constraint of being lightweight and fast while ensuring security is a difficult challenge for stream ciphers, all the more since they do not have the advantage of involving several rounds like block ciphers (their security is dependent on the PRG only). And the situation is nowadays still more difficult because modern block ciphers such as the AES are very fast. This difficulty has been illustrated by the failure of all six stream ciphers submitted to the 2000–2003 NESSIE project (New European Schemes for Signatures, Integrity and Encryption) [901], whose purpose was to identify secure cryptographic primitives. NESSIE has then been followed by the contest eSTREAM [495] organized later, between 2004 and 2008, by the European Union (EU) ECRYPT network.

As mentioned in [242], the price to pay for these three constraints described above is that security proofs hardly exist for efficient stream ciphers as they do for block ciphers. This is a drawback of stream ciphers, compared to block ciphers.[5] The only practical possibility for verifying the security of efficient stream ciphers (in particular, the unpredictability of the keystream they generate) is to prove that they resist the known attacks. It is then advisable to include some amount of randomness in them, so as to increase the probability of resisting future attacks.[6]

---

[3] Or equivalently finds with high probability a specific entry in an unsorted database of N entries.

[4] Note, however, that stream ciphers are often supposed to be used on lighter devices than block ciphers (typically not needing cryptoprocessors, for instance).

[5] However, the security of block ciphers is actually proved under simplifying hypotheses, and it has been said by Lars Knudsen that "what is provably secure is probably not."

[6] Some stream cipher proposals, such as the Toyocrypt, LILI-128 and SFINKS ciphers, learned this at their own expense; see [387].

Proving the security of a cipher consists of reducing it to the intractability of a hard problem (a problem that has been extensively addressed by the academic community, and for which only algorithms of exponential or subexponential complexity could be found), implying that any potential attack on it could be used for designing an efficient algorithm (whose worst-case complexity would be polynomial in the size of its input) solving the hard problem.

Note that provably secure stream ciphers do exist (some proposals are even unconditionally secure, that is, are secure even if the attacker has unlimited computational power, but limited storage or access); see for instance the proposals by Alexi–Chor–Goldreich–Schnorr (whose security is reducible to the intractability of the RSA problem) or Blum–Blum–Shub [98] (whose security is reducible to the intractability of the quadratic residue problem modulo pq, where p and q are large primes), or the stream cipher QUAD [61] (based on the iteration of a multivariate quadratic system over a finite field, and whose security is reducible to the intractability of the so-called multivariate quadratic (MQ) polynomial problem). But they are too slow and too heavy for being used in practice. Even in the case of QUAD, which is the fastest, the encryption speed is lower than for the AES. And this is still worse when security is ensured unconditionally. This is why the stream ciphers using Boolean functions (see below) are still much used and studied.

1.2 Error-correcting codes

The objective of error-detecting/-correcting codes in *coding theory* is to enable digital communication over a noisy channel, in such a way that the errors of transmission can be detected by the receiver and, in the case of error correcting codes, corrected. General references are [63, 780, 809]. Shannon's paper [1033] is also prominent.

Without correction, when an error is detected, the information needs to be requested again by the receiver and sent again by the sender (such procedure is called an Automatic Repeat reQuest, ARQ). This is what happened with the first computers: working with binary words, they could detect only one error (one bit) in the transmission of $(x_1, \ldots, x_k)$, by adding a parity bit $x_{k+1} = \bigoplus_{i=1}^{k} x_i$ (this transformed the word of length k into a word of length $k+1$ having even *Hamming weight*, *i.e.*, an even number of nonzero coordinates, which was then sent over the noisy channel; if an error occurred in the transmission, then, assuming that only one could occur, this was detected by the fact that the received word had odd Hamming weight).

With correction, the ARQ is not necessary, but this requires in practice that fewer errors have occurred than for detection (see below). Hybrid coding techniques exist then that make a trade-off between the two approaches.

The aim of error detection/correction is achieved by using an encoding algorithm that transforms the information (assumed to be a sequence over some alphabet $\mathcal{A}$) before sending it over the channel. In the case of block coding,[7] the original sequence (the *message*) is treated as a list of vectors (words) of the same length – say k – called *source vectors* which are encoded into *codewords* of a larger length – say[8] n. If the alphabet with which the words

---

[7] We shall not address convolutional coding here.
[8] When dealing with Boolean functions, the symbol n will be often devoted to their number of variables; the length of the codes they will constitute will then not be n but $N = 2^n$. See Section 1.3.

are built is the field $\mathbb{F}_2$ of order 2, we say that the code is binary. If the code is not binary, then the symbols of the alphabet will have to be transformed into binary vectors before being sent over a binary channel.

Thanks to the length extension, called *redundancy*, the codewords sent over the channel are some of all possible vectors of length n. The set C of all codewords is called the *code* (for instance, in the case of the detecting codes using a parity bit as indicated above, the code is made of all binary words of length $n = k + 1$ and of even Hamming weights; it is called the *parity code*). The only information the receiver has, concerning the sent word, is that it belongs to C.

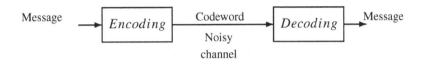

1.2.1 Detecting and correcting capacities of a code

The decoding algorithm of an error-detecting code is able to recognize if a received vector is a codeword. This makes possible to detect errors of transmission if (see [585]) denoting by d the minimum *Hamming distance* between codewords, *i.e.*, the minimum number of positions at which codewords differ (called the *minimum distance* of the code), no more than $d - 1$ coordinates of the received vector differ from those of the sent codeword (condition for having no risk that a codeword different from the sent one can be received and then accepted). In the case of an error-correcting code, the decoding algorithm can additionally correct the errors of transmission, if their number is smaller than or equal to the so-called *correction capacity* of the code. This capacity equals $e = \left\lfloor \frac{d-1}{2} \right\rfloor$, where "$\lfloor \ \rfloor$" denotes the integer part (and so, roughly, a code can detect twice as many errors than it can correct), since the condition for having no risk that a vector corresponds, as received vector, to more than one sent codeword with at most t errors of transmission in each case is that $2t < d$. Indeed, in order to be always able (theoretically) to recover the correct codeword, we need that, for every word y at distance at most t from a codeword x, there does not exist another codeword x' at distance at most t from y, and this is equivalent to saying that the Hamming distance between any two different codewords is larger than or equal to $2t + 1$:

- If there exist a vector y and two codewords x and x' at Hamming distance at most t from y, then we have $d \leq 2t$ by the triangular inequality on distances.
- Conversely, if there exist two codewords x and x' at Hamming distance $\delta \leq 2t$ from each other, then there exists a vector y such that $d_H(x, y) \leq t$ and $d_H(x', y) \leq t$ (let I be the set of positions where x and x' coincide; take $y_i = x_i$ when $i \in I$ and among the δ others, take for instance $\left\lfloor \frac{\delta}{2} \right\rfloor$ coordinates of y equal to those of x and the $\left\lceil \frac{\delta}{2} \right\rceil$ others equal to those of x').

In practice, determining d and then $e = \left\lfloor \frac{d-1}{2} \right\rfloor$ and showing that they are large is not sufficient. We still need to have an efficient decoding algorithm to recover the sent codeword. The naive method consisting in visiting all codewords and keeping the nearest one from the received word is inefficient because the number 2^k of codewords is too large, in general.

Determining the nearest codeword from a received vector is called *maximum likelihood decoding*.

The correction capacity e is limited by the *Hamming bound* (or *sphere-packing bound*): since all the balls $B(x, e) = \{y \in \mathcal{A}^n; d_H(x, y) \leq e\}$, of radius e and centered in codewords are pairwise disjoint, and since there are $|C|$ of them, the size of their union equals $|C| \sum_{i=0}^e \binom{n}{i}(q - 1)^i$, where q is the size of the alphabet. This union is a subset of $\mathcal{A}^n$. This implies the following:

$$|C| \sum_{i=0}^e \binom{n}{i}(q - 1)^i \leq q^n.$$

The codes that achieve this bound with equality are called *perfect codes*.

Puncturing, shortening, and extending codes

The *punctured code* of a code C is the set of vectors obtained by deleting the coordinate at some fixed position i in each codeword of C; we shall call such transformation *puncturing at position i*. This operation can be iterated, and we shall still speak of puncturing a code when deleting the codeword coordinates at several positions.

The *shortened code* of a code C is the set of vectors obtained by keeping only those codewords whose ith coordinate is null and deleting this ith coordinate.

The *extended code* of a code C over an additive group is the set of vectors, say, $(c_0, c_1, \ldots, c_n)$, where $(c_1, \ldots, c_n) \in C$ and $c_0 = -(c_1 + \cdots + c_n)$. Note that the extended code of C equals the intersection of the code $\{(c_0, c_1, \ldots, c_n) \in \mathbb{F}_q; (c_1, \ldots, c_n) \in C\}$ and of the parity code $(c_0, c_1, \ldots, c_n) \in \mathbb{F}_q; \sum_{i=0}^n x_i = 0\}$.

1.2.2 Parameters of a code

Sending words of length n over the channel instead of words of length k slows down the transmission of information in the ratio of $\frac{k}{n}$. This ratio, called the *transmission rate*, must be as high as possible, for a given correction capacity, to make possible fast communication. As we see, the three important parameters of a code C are n, k, d (or equivalently $n, |C|, d$ since if q is the alphabet's size, we have $|C| = q^k$), and the first aim[9] of algebraic coding is to find codes minimizing n, maximizing k, and maximizing d, for diverse ranges of parameters corresponding to the needs of communication (see tables of best-known codes in [570]). It is easily seen that $k \leq n - d + 1$ (this inequality, valid for any code over any alphabet, is called the *Singleton bound*) since erasing the coordinates of all codewords at $d - 1$ fixed positions gives a set of q^k distinct vectors of length $n - d + 1$, where q is the size of the alphabet, and the number of all vectors of length $n - d + 1$ equals q^{n-d+1}. Codes achieving the Singleton bound with equality are called *maximum distance separable* (MDS). In the case of binary linear codes (see below), it can be shown by using the Pless identities (see, *e.g.*, [348]) that MDS codes have dimension at most 1 or at least $n - 1$ and, except for such codes, the bound becomes then $k \leq n - d$.

Another important parameter is the *covering radius*, which is the smallest integer ρ such that the spheres of (Hamming) radius ρ centered at the codewords cover the whole space. In

---

[9] The second aim is to find decoding algorithms for the codes found.

other words, it is the minimal integer ρ such that every vector of length n lies at Hamming distance at most ρ from at least one codeword, that is, the maximum number of errors to be corrected when maximum likelihood decoding (see page 6) is used. The book [375] is devoted to its study.

The sphere-covering bound is the lower bound on the covering radius ρ, which expresses that, by definition, the balls $B(x, \rho) = \{y \in \mathcal{A}^n; d_H(x, y) \leq \rho\}$, of radius ρ and centered in codewords, cover the whole space $\mathcal{A}^n$:

$$|C| \sum_{i=0}^{\rho} \binom{n}{i} (q - 1)^i \geq q^n.$$

1.2.3 Linear codes

The general class of linear codes gives a simple and wide example of codes and how they can be used in error correction.

Definition 1 *A code is called a* linear code *if its alphabet is a finite field* $\mathbb{F}_q$ *(where q is the power of a prime) and if it has the structure of an* $\mathbb{F}_q$*-linear subspace of* $\mathbb{F}_q^n$*, where n is its length (see [809]).*

A code that is not necessarily linear is called an *unrestricted code*. The minimum distance of a linear code equals the minimum Hamming weight of all nonzero codewords, since the Hamming distance between two vectors equals the Hamming weight of their difference. We shall write that a linear code[10] over $\mathbb{F}_q$ is an $[n, k, d]_q$-*code* (and if the value of q is clear from the context, an $[n, k, d]$-*code*) if it has length n, dimension k, and minimum distance d. The translates of a linear code are called its *cosets* and the elements of minimum Hamming weights in these cosets are called *coset leaders* (there may exist several in some cosets).

Generator matrix

Any linear code can be described by a *generator matrix* G, obtained by choosing a basis of this vector space and writing its elements as the rows of this matrix. The code equals the set of all the vectors of the form $u \times G$, where u ranges over $\mathbb{F}_q^k$ (and $\times$ is the matrix product) and a possible encoding algorithm is therefore the mapping $u \in \mathbb{F}_q^k \mapsto u \times G \in \mathbb{F}_q^n$. When the codeword corresponding to a given source vector u is obtained by inserting so-called *parity check coordinates* in the source vector (whose coordinates are then called *information coordinates*), the code is called *systematic* (it equals then the *graph* $\{(x, F(x), x \in \mathbb{F}_q^k\}$ of a function, up to coordinate permutation). The corresponding generator matrix is then called a *systematic generator matrix* and has the form $[I_k : M]$, where I_k is the $k \times k$ identity matrix, up to column permutation. It is easily seen that every linear code has such a generator matrix: any generator matrix (of rank k) has k linearly independent columns, and if we place these columns at the k first positions, we obtain $G = [A : M]$, where A is a nonsingular $k \times k$ matrix; then $A^{-1} \times G = [I_k : A^{-1} \times M]$ is a systematic generator matrix of the permuted

---

[10] The square brackets around n, k, d specify that the code is linear, contrary to standard parentheses.

code (since the multiplication by A^{-1} transforms a basis of the permuted code into another basis of the permuted code).

Dual code and parity check matrix

The generator matrix is well suited for generating the codewords, but it is not for checking if a received word of length n is a codeword or not. A characterization of the codewords is obtained thanks to the generator matrix H of the *dual code* $C^\perp = \{x \in \mathbb{F}_q^n; \forall y \in C, x \cdot y = \sum_{i=1}^n x_i y_i = 0\}$ (such a matrix is called a *parity check matrix* and "$\cdot$" is called the *usual inner product*, or scalar product, in $\mathbb{F}_q^n$): we have $x \in C$ if and only if $x \times H^t$ is the null vector. Consequently, the minimum distance of any linear code equals the minimum number of $\mathbb{F}_q$-linearly dependent columns in one of its parity check matrices (any one). For instance, the binary *Hamming code* of length $n = 2^m - 1$, which has by definition for parity check matrix the $m \times (2^m - 1)$ binary matrix whose columns are all the nonzero vectors of $\mathbb{F}_2^m$ in some order, has minimum distance 3. This code, which by definition is unique up to equivalence, has played an important historical role since it is the first perfect code found. It still plays a role since many computers use it to detect errors in their internal communications. It is the basis on which BCH and Reed–Muller codes were built (see pages 10 and 151). It depends on the choice of the order, but we say that two codes over $\mathbb{F}_q$ are *equivalent codes* if they are equal, up to some permutation of the coordinates of their codewords (and, for nonbinary codes, to the multiplication of each coordinate in each codeword by a nonzero element of $\mathbb{F}_q$ depending only on the position of this coordinate). Note that such codes have the same parameters.

The dual of the binary Hamming code is called the *simplex code*. A generator matrix of this code being the parity check matrix of the Hamming code described above, and the rows of this matrix representing then the *coordinate functions* in $\mathbb{F}_2^m$ (sometimes called dictator functions), on which the order chosen for listing the values is given by the columns of the matrix, the codewords of the simplex code are the lists of values taken on $\mathbb{F}_2^m \setminus \{0_m\}$ by all linear functions.

Note that the dual of a linear code C permuted by some bijection over the indices equals $C^\perp$ permuted by this same bijection, and that, if $G = [I_k : M]$ is a systematic generator matrix of a linear code C, then $[-M^t : I_{n-k}]$ is a parity check matrix of C, where M^t is the transposed matrix of M.

The linear codes that are supplementary with their duals (or equivalently that have trivial intersection with their duals since the dimensions of a code and of its dual are complementary to n) are called complementary dual codes (LCD) and will play an important role in Subsection 12.1.5.

The advantages of linearity

Linearity allows considerably simplifying some main issues about codes. Firstly, the minimum distance being equal to the minimum nonzero Hamming weight, computing it (if it cannot be determined mathematically) needs only to visit $q^k - 1$ codewords instead of $\frac{q^k(q^k-1)}{2}$ pairs of codewords. Secondly, the knowledge of the code is provided by a $k \times n$ generator matrix and needs then the description of k codewords instead of all q^k codewords.

Thirdly, a general decoding algorithm is valid for every linear code. This algorithm is not efficient in general, but it gives a framework for the efficient decoding algorithms that will have to be found for each class of linear codes. The principle of this algorithm is as follows: let y be the (known) received vector corresponding to the (unknown) sent codeword x. We assume that there has been at most $d - 1$ errors of transmission, where d is the minimum distance, if the code is used for error detection, and at most e errors of transmission, where $e = \lfloor (d-1)/2 \rfloor$ is the correcting capacity of the code, if the code is used for error correction. The error detection is made by checking if the so-called *syndrome* $s = y \times H^t$ is the zero vector. If it is not, then denoting by ϵ the so-called (unknown) *error vector* $\epsilon = y - x$, correcting the errors of transmission is equivalent to determining ϵ. This can be done by visiting all vectors z of Hamming weight at most e in $\mathbb{F}_q^n$ and checking if $z \times H^t = s$ (indeed, by linearity of matrix multiplication, the syndrome of the error vector equals the syndrome of the received vector, which is known). There exists a unique z of Hamming weight at most e in $\mathbb{F}_q^n$ such that $z \times H^t = s$; this unique z equals ϵ.

Concatenating codes

Given an $\mathbb{F}_q$-linear $[n, k, d]$ code C (where n is the length, k is the dimension, and d is the minimum distance), where $q = 2^e$, $e \geq 2$, a binary $[n', e, d']$ code C' and an $\mathbb{F}_2$-isomorphism $\phi : \mathbb{F}_q \mapsto C'$, the *concatenated code* C'' equals the $[nn', ke, d'' \geq dd']$ binary code $\{(\phi(c_1), \ldots, \phi(c_n)); (c_1, \ldots, c_n) \in C\}$. Codes C and C' are respectively called outer code and inner code for this construction.

MDS linear codes

Let C be an $[n, k, d]$ code over a field K, let H be its parity check matrix, and G its generator matrix. Then $n - k$ is the rank of H, and we have then $d \leq n - k + 1$ since $n - k + 1$ columns of H are always linearly dependent and therefore any set of indices of size $n - k + 1$ contains the support of a nonzero codeword. This proves again the Singleton bound: $d \leq n - k + 1$.

Recall that C is called *MDS* if $d = n - k + 1$. The following are the properties of MDS linear codes:

1. C is MDS if and only if each set of $n - k$ columns of H has rank $n - k$.
2. If C is MDS, then $C^\perp$ is MDS.
3. C is MDS if and only if each set of k columns of G has rank k (and their positions constitute then an information set; see page 161).

Other properties of linear codes

Puncturing, shortening, and extending codes preserve their linearity. Puncturing preserves the MDS property (if $n > k$).

The following lemma will be useful when dealing with Reed–Muller codes in Chapter 4.

Lemma 1 *Let C be a linear code of length n over $\mathbb{F}_q$ and $\hat{C}$ its extended code. We have* $\hat{C}^\perp = \{(y_0, \ldots, y_n) \in \mathbb{F}_q^{n+1}; (y_1 - y_0, \ldots, y_n - y_0) \in C^\perp\}$.

Proof We have $\hat{C}^{\perp} = \{(y_0, \ldots, y_n) \in \mathbb{F}_q^{n+1}; \forall (x_1, \ldots, x_n) \in C, y_0(-\sum_{i=1}^n x_i) + \sum_{i=1}^n x_i y_i = 0\} = \{(y_0, \ldots, y_n) \in \mathbb{F}_q^{n+1}; \forall (x_1, \ldots, x_n) \in C, \sum_{i=1}^n x_i(y_i - y_0) = 0\} = \{(y_0, \ldots, y_n) \in \mathbb{F}_q^{n+1}; (y_1 - y_0, \ldots, y_n - y_0) \in C^{\perp}\}$. □

Uniformly packed codes: These codes will play a role with respect to almost perfect nonlinear (APN) functions, at page 381.

Definition 2 *[50] Let C be any binary code of length N, with minimum distance $d = 2e+1$ and covering radius ρ. For any $x \in \mathbb{F}_2^N$, let us denote by $\zeta_j(x)$ the number of codewords of C at distance j from x. The code C is called a* uniformly packed code, *if there exist real numbers $h_0, h_1, \ldots, h_\rho$ such that, for any $x \in \mathbb{F}_2^N$, the following equality holds:*

$$\sum_{j=0}^{\rho} h_j \, \zeta_j(x) = 1.$$

As shown in [51], this is equivalent to saying that the covering radius of the code equals its external distance (*i.e.*, the number of different nonzero distances between the codewords of its dual).

1.2.4 Cyclic codes

Two-error correcting Bose–Chaudhuri–Hocquenghem (BCH) codes

The binary Hamming code of length $n = 2^m - 1$ has dimension $n - m$ and needs m parity check bits for being able to correct 1 error. It happens that 2-error binary correcting codes can be built with $2m$ parity check bits. Let us denote by $W_1, \ldots, W_n$ the nonzero binary vectors of length m written as columns in some order. The parity check matrix of the Hamming code of length $n = 2^m - 1$ is as follows:

$$H = [W_1, \ldots, W_n].$$

To find a 2-error correcting code C of the same length, we consider the codes whose parity check matrices H' are the $2m \times n$ matrices whose m first rows are those of H. These codes being subcodes of the binary Hamming code, they are at least 1-error correcting. For each such matrix H', there exists a function F from $\mathbb{F}_2^m$ to itself such that:

$$H' = \begin{bmatrix} W_1 & W_2 & \cdots & W_n \\ F(W_1) & F(W_2) & \cdots & F(W_n) \end{bmatrix}.$$

Note that, when F is a *permutation* (*i.e.*, is bijective), the code of generator matrix H' is a so-called *double simplex code* (and plays a central role in [136]); it is the direct sum of two simplex codes: the standard one and its permutation by F.

Going back to general F, assume that two errors are made in the transmission of a codeword of C, at indices $i \neq j$. The *syndrome* of the received vector equals that of the error vector, that is,

$$\begin{bmatrix} S_1 \\ S_2 \end{bmatrix} = \begin{bmatrix} W_i \\ F(W_i) \end{bmatrix} + \begin{bmatrix} W_j \\ F(W_j) \end{bmatrix},$$

with $S_1 \neq 0_m$ (where 0_m is the length m all-zero vector) since $i \neq j$. We have then the following:

$$\begin{cases} W_i + W_j & = S_1 \neq 0_m \\ F(W_i) + F(W_j) = & S_2 \end{cases}.$$

The code is then 2-error correcting if and only if, for every $S_1, S_2 \in \mathbb{F}_2^m$ such that $S_1 \neq 0_m$, this system of equations has either no solution (i, j) (which happens when $\begin{bmatrix} S_1 \\ S_2 \end{bmatrix}$ is not the syndrome of an error vector of Hamming weight 2) or only two solutions (one solution if we impose $i < j$).

Note that since $\{W_1, \ldots, W_n\}$ equals $\mathbb{F}_2^m \setminus \{0_m\}$ and these vectors are all distinct, it is equivalent to consider the system

$$\begin{cases} x + y & = S_1 \neq 0_m \\ F(x) + F(y) = & S_2 \end{cases},$$

where x and y range over $\mathbb{F}_2^m \setminus \{0_m\}$. This is where finite fields of orders larger than 2 played a historical role in coding theory (see Appendix, page 480, for a description of finite fields): considering such functions F and such systems of equations is easier when we have a structure of field (even though the equations do not involve multiplications). This allows us indeed to take $F(x)$ in a polynomial form, and the first polynomials to be tried are of course monomials. The monomials x and x^2, being linear functions, do not satisfy the condition needed for the code to be 2-error correcting, but the next monomial x^3 does satisfy it (this is easily seen since $x^3 + y^3 = (x + y)^3 + x y (x + y)$ implies that the system is equivalent to $\begin{cases} x + y = S_1 \neq 0 \\ x y & = \frac{S_2 + S_1^3}{S_1} \end{cases}$ and such an equation results in an equation of degree 2, which has at most two solutions over a finite field).

The condition on F (or more precisely on its extension by taking $F(0) = 0$) is equivalent to saying that it is an APN function. This notion plays a very important role in cryptography; see Chapter 11, page 369.

We need here the notion of *primitive element*; see page 487. Such element α satisfies that $\mathbb{F}_{2^n} = \{0, 1, \alpha, \alpha^2, \ldots, \alpha^{2^n - 2}\}$ and exists for every n.

Definition 3 *Let α be a primitive element of $\mathbb{F}_{2^m}$. The binary 2-error correcting BCH code of length $n = 2^m - 1$ is the $[n, n - 2m, 5]$ code due to Bose, Chaudhuri, and Hocquenghem, of the following parity check matrix:*

$$H' = \begin{bmatrix} \alpha & \alpha^2 & \cdots & \alpha^n \\ \alpha^3 & \alpha^6 & \cdots & \alpha^{3n} \end{bmatrix}.$$

Ordering the elements of $\mathbb{F}_{2^n}^*$ as $\alpha, \alpha^2, \ldots, \alpha^{n-1}, \alpha^n = 1$ (we could have also chosen $1, \alpha, \alpha^2, \ldots, \alpha^{n-1}$) implies a property that does not seem so important at first glance but which played a central role in the history of codes and still plays such role nowadays: the code is (globally) invariant under cyclic permutations of the codeword coordinates. This property, when added to the linearity of the code, confers to them a structure of principal ideal, with very nice theoretical and practical consequences.

General cyclic codes

A linear code C of length n is a *cyclic code* if it is (globally) invariant under cyclic shifts of the codeword coordinates (see [809, page 188]). For this, it is enough that it is invariant under one of the primitive cyclic shifts, for instance:

$$(c_0, \ldots, c_{n-1}) \mapsto (c_{n-1}, c_0, \ldots, c_{n-2}).$$

Cyclic codes have been extensively studied in coding theory, because of their strong properties.

Representation of codewords

Each codeword $(c_0, \ldots, c_{n-1})$ is represented by the polynomial $c_0 + c_1 X + \cdots + c_{n-1} X^{n-1}$, viewed as an element of the quotient algebra $A = \mathbb{F}_q[X]/(X^n - 1)$ (each element of this algebra is an equivalence class modulo $X^n - 1$, which will be always represented by its unique element of degree at most $n - 1$, equal to the common rest in the division by $X^n - 1$ of the polynomials constituting the class). We shall call $c_0 + c_1 X + \cdots + c_{n-1} X^{n-1}$ the *polynomial representation of codeword* $(c_0, \ldots, c_{n-1})$. Then it is easily shown that C is cyclic if and only if it is an ideal of $\mathbb{F}_q[X]/(X^n - 1)$, that is, it satisfies $fC \subseteq C$ for every nonzero $f \in A$ (C being assumed linear, it is a subgroup of A).

Generator polynomial

The algebra $\mathbb{F}_q[X]/(X^n - 1)$ is a principal domain. It is easily shown that any (linear) cyclic nontrivial[11] code has a unique monic element $g(X)$ (whose leading coefficient equals 1) having minimal degree, which generates the ideal and is called the *generator polynomial* of the code. In fact, $g(X)$ is a generator of the code in the strong sense that every polynomial of degree at most $n - 1$ is a codeword if and only if it is a multiple of $g(X)$ in $\mathbb{F}_q[X]$ (which implies that it is a multiple of $g(X)$ in $\mathbb{F}_q[X]/(X^n - 1)$). The code equals then the set of all those polynomials that include the zeros of $g(X)$ (in the splitting field of $g(X)$) among their own zeros. It is also easily seen that $g(X)$ is a divisor of $X^n - 1$.

Zeros of the code

In our framework, the length will have the form $n = q^m - 1$ (we call such length a *primitive length*). In such a case, since $g(X)$ divides $X^n - 1$, the zeros of $g(X)$ all belong to $\mathbb{F}_{q^m}^*$. The generator polynomial having all its coefficients in $\mathbb{F}_q$, its zeros are of the form $\{\alpha^i, i \in I\}$ (where α is a primitive element of $\mathbb{F}_{q^m}$), where $I \subseteq \mathbb{Z}/n\mathbb{Z}$ is a union of cyclotomic classes of q modulo $n = q^m - 1$ (and vice versa). The set I is called the *defining set* of the code. The elements $\alpha^i, i \in I$ are called the *zeros of the cyclic code*, which has dimension $n - |I|$. The elements $\alpha^i, i \in \mathbb{Z}/n\mathbb{Z} \setminus I$ are called the *nonzeros of the cyclic code*. The generator polynomial of $C^\perp$ is the reciprocal of the quotient of $X^n - 1$ by $g(X)$, and its defining set therefore equals $\{n - i; i \in \mathbb{Z}/n\mathbb{Z} \setminus I\}$.

---

[11] That is, it is different from $\{0_n\}$; in fact, we shall consider that the trivial cyclic code has also a generator polynomial: $X^n - 1$ itself.

McEliece's theorem [833] states that a binary cyclic code is exactly 2^l-divisible (that is, l is the maximum such that all codeword Hamming weights are divisible by 2^l) if and only if l is the smallest number such that $l + 1$ nonzeros of C (with repetitions allowed) have product 1 (and recall that $\alpha^j = 1$ if and only if $2^n - 1$ divides j).

Generating all cyclic codes of some primitive length

Since a polynomial over $\mathbb{F}_q$ is the generator polynomial of a cyclic code of length n if and only if it divides $X^n - 1$, we obtain all cyclic codes from all the divisors of $X^n - 1$ in $\mathbb{F}_q$. Any such divisor is the product of some irreducible factors of $X^n - 1$ in $\mathbb{F}_q$. These irreducible factors are the polynomials of the form $\prod_{j \in \mathcal{C}}(X - \alpha^j)$, where $\mathcal{C}$ is a cyclotomic class of q modulo n. The number of cyclic codes of length n over $\mathbb{F}_q$ is then 2^r, where r is the number of these cyclotomic classes (including the trivial cyclic code $\{0_n\}$ and the full one $\mathbb{F}_q^n$). The *Hamming code* has for generator polynomial the irreducible polynomial corresponding to the cyclotomic class containing 1. Its dual, the *simplex code*, has then for generator polynomial the polynomial corresponding to all cyclotomic classes except that of $n - 1$.

Nonprimitive length

If the length is not primitive, the zeros of $X^n - 1$ live in its *splitting field* $\mathbb{F}_{q^m}$ (where n divides $q^m - 1$, and m is minimal). If n and q are coprime, the zeros of $X^n - 1$ are simple since the derivative nX^{n-1} of this polynomial does not vanish on them, and the same theory applies by replacing $\mathbb{F}_{q^m}$ by the group of nth roots of unity in $\mathbb{F}_{q^m}$ and α by a primitive nth root of unity.

BCH bound

A very efficient bound on the minimum distance of cyclic codes is the *BCH bound* [809, page 201]: if I contains a "string" $\{l + 1, \ldots, l + \delta - 1\}$ of length $\delta - 1$ of consecutive[12] elements of $\mathbb{Z}/n\mathbb{Z}$, then the cyclic code has minimum distance larger than or equal to δ (which is then called the *designed distance* of the cyclic code). A proof of this bound (in the framework of Boolean functions) is given in the proof of Theorem 23, page 337.

BCH codes

Let n be coprime with q and $\delta < n$, the BCH codes of length n and designed distance δ are the cyclic codes that have such string of length $\delta - 1$ in their zeros (and have then minimum distance at least δ, according to the BCH bound) and maximal dimension (*i.e.*, minimal number of zeros) with such constraint.

Reed–Solomon codes

When $n = q - 1$, the cyclotomic classes of q modulo n are singletons and the set of zeros of a cyclic code can then be any set of nonzero elements of the field (the generator polynomial

---

[12] Considering of course that 0 is the successor of $n - 1$ in $\mathbb{Z}/n\mathbb{Z}$.

can be any divisor of $X^n - 1$); when it is constituted of consecutive powers of a primitive element, this particular case of a BCH code is called a *Reed–Solomon (RS) code*. Such codes are important because they achieve the Singleton bound with equality (*i.e.*, they are *maximum distance separable MDS*). Indeed, the BCH bound gives $\delta \leq d \leq n - (n - (\delta - 1)) + 1 = \delta$, and the Singleton bound is then achieved with equality.

Remark. There exists another equivalent definition of Reed–Solomon codes; see the remark on page 45. RS codes are widely used in consumer electronics (CD, DVD, Blu-ray), data transmission technologies (DSL, WiMAX), broadcast systems, computer applications, and deep-space communications. □

Extended Reed–Solomon codes

A cyclic code C of length n being given, recall that the extended code of C is the set of vectors $(c_\infty, c_0, \ldots, c_{n-1})$, where $c_\infty = -(c_0 + \cdots + c_{n-1})$. It is a linear code of length $n+1$ and of the same dimension as C. When C is a Reed–Solomon code whose defining set has the form $\{1, 2, \ldots, \delta - 1\}$, its extended code is also MDS, because when $(c_0, \ldots, c_{n-1})$ is a codeword of C of minimal Hamming weight δ, we have $c_\infty \neq 0$ (again according to the BCH bound: if $c_\infty = 0$, then the polynomial $c_0 + c_1 X + \cdots + c_{n-1} X^{n-1}$ has also $\alpha^0 = 1$ for zero and has then Hamming weight at least $\delta + 1$, thanks to the BCH bound applied with the string $\{0, \ldots, \delta - 1\}$). Hence, either $(c_0, \ldots, c_{n-1})$ is a codeword of C of minimal Hamming weight δ and then $(c_\infty, c_0, \ldots, c_{n-1})$ has Hamming weight $\delta + 1$ or $(c_0, \ldots, c_{n-1})$ has Hamming weight at least $\delta + 1$ and $(c_\infty, c_0, \ldots, c_{n-1})$ has a fortiori Hamming weight at least $\delta + 1$. Hence the minimum distance of the extended code is $\delta + 1 = (n + 1) - (n - \delta + 1) + 1$. The extended code is MDS.

Cyclic codes and Boolean functions

Cyclic codes over $\mathbb{F}_2$ and of length $2^m - 1$ can be viewed as sets of m-variable Boolean functions. Indeed, any codeword in such cyclic code with defining set I can be represented in the form $\sum_{i=1}^{l} tr_n(a_i x^{-u_i}), a_i \in \mathbb{F}_{2^m}$, where $u_1, \ldots, u_l$ are representatives of the cyclotomic classes lying outside I (see Relation (2.20) in Subsection 2.2.2, page 45).

1.2.5 The MacWilliams identity and the notion of dual distance

Linear codes

A nice relationship, due to F. J. MacWilliams [809, page 127], exists between the Hamming weights in every binary linear code[13] and those in its dual: let C be any binary linear code of length n; consider the polynomial $W_C(X, Y) = \sum_{i=0}^{n} A_i X^{n-i} Y^i$, where A_i is the number of codewords of Hamming weight i. This polynomial is called the *weight enumerator* of C and describes[14] the *weight distribution* $(A_i)_{0 \leq i \leq n}$ of C. Then

$$W_C(X + Y, X - Y) = |C| \, W_{C^\perp}(X, Y). \tag{1.1}$$

---

[13] It exists for every linear code over a finite field and even for more general codes, but we shall need it only for binary codes.

[14] W_C is a homogeneous version of classical generating series for the weight distribution of C.

We give a sketch of proof[15] of this *MacWilliams' identity*: we observe first that $W_C(X, Y) = \sum_{x \in C} \prod_{i=1}^{n} X^{1-x_i} Y^{x_i}$; substituting X by $X + Y$ and Y by $X - Y$, we deduce that $W_C(X + Y, X - Y) = \sum_{x \in C} \prod_{i=1}^{n} (X + (-1)^{x_i} Y)$. We apply then the classical relation making possible to expand products of sums: for every $\lambda_1, \ldots, \lambda_n, \mu_1, \ldots, \mu_n$, we have $\prod_{i=1}^{n} (\lambda_i + \mu_i) = \sum_{b \in \mathbb{F}_2^n} \prod_{i=1}^{n} (\lambda_i^{1-b_i} \mu_i^{b_i})$ (indeed, choosing λ_i in the ith factor when $b_i = 0$ and μ_i when $b_i = 1$ provides when b ranges over $\mathbb{F}_2^n$ all the possible terms in the expansion). This gives here $W_C(X + Y, X - Y) = \sum_{x \in C} \sum_{b \in \mathbb{F}_2^n} \prod_{i=1}^{n} (X^{1-b_i} ((-1)^{x_i} Y)^{b_i})$. We obtain then $W_C(X + Y, X - Y) = \sum_{b \in \mathbb{F}_2^n} (X^{n-w_H(b)} Y^{w_H(b)} \sum_{x \in C} (-1)^{b \cdot x})$, where "$\cdot$" is the *usual inner product* in $\mathbb{F}_2^n$, and we conclude by observing that, if $b \notin C^{\perp}$, then the linear form $b \cdot x$ over the vector space C is nonzero, and takes then values 0 and 1 on two complementary hyperplanes, that is, the same number of times (we will find again this in Relation (2.38), page 58). This proves Relation (1.1). Of course, we deduce that $W_C(X, Y) = \frac{1}{|C^{\perp}|} W_{C^{\perp}}(X + Y, X - Y)$ and the same method shows, as observed in [37], that for every coset $a + C$, we have $W_{a+C}(X, Y) = \frac{1}{|C^{\perp}|} \left(2 W_{C^{\perp} \cap \{0_n, a\}^{\perp}}(X + Y, X - Y) - W_{C^{\perp}}(X + Y, X - Y)\right)$.

Remark. We have $|C| = \sum_{i=0}^{n} A_i = W_C(1, 1)$. The fact that the polynomial $\frac{1}{W_C(1,1)} W_C(X + Y, X - Y)$ has nonnegative integer coefficients is very specific (among all homogeneous polynomials $P(X, Y)$ whose coefficients are nonnegative integers). As far as we know, the characterization of all homogeneous polynomials $P(X, Y)$ over $\mathbb{N}$ such that $\frac{1}{P(1,1)} P(X + Y, X - Y)$ has nonnegative integer coefficients has never been investigated in a paper. $\square$

Remark. The average Hamming weight of the codewords of a linear binary code C equals $(W_C)'_Y(1, 1)$ (the value at $(1, 1)$ of the partial derivative of $W_C(X, Y)$ with respect to Y), divided by $|C|$. MacWilliams' identity writes $W_C(X, Y) = \frac{1}{|C^{\perp}|} W_{C^{\perp}}(X + Y, X - Y)$. Differentiating with respect to Y gives $(W_C)'_Y(X, Y) = \frac{1}{|C^{\perp}|}(W_{C^{\perp}})'_X(X + Y, X - Y) - \frac{1}{|C^{\perp}|}(W_{C^{\perp}})'_Y(X + Y, X - Y)$ and thus $(W_C)'_Y(1, 1) = \frac{1}{|C^{\perp}|}(W_{C^{\perp}})'_X(2, 0) - \frac{1}{|C^{\perp}|}(W_{C^{\perp}})'_Y(2, 0) = \frac{n2^{n-1}}{|C^{\perp}|} - \frac{1}{|C^{\perp}|}(W_{C^{\perp}})'_Y(2, 0)$, and the average Hamming weight of codewords equals $\frac{n}{2} - 2^{-n}(W_{C^{\perp}})'_Y(2, 0)$, which depends on the number of words of Hamming weight 1 in $C^{\perp}$ (see more in [809, page 131] on the moments of the weight distribution of codes) and is bounded above by $\frac{n}{2}$. In fact, it is easily seen directly that the average Hamming weight of codewords equals $\frac{n-r}{2}$, where r is the number of positions where all codewords are null, since if there is a codeword with 1 at position i, the average value of codewords at position i equals $\frac{1}{2}$. $\square$

Remark. Some authors call weight enumerator of C the univariate polynomial $A_C(Z) = \sum_{i=0}^{n} A_i Z^i$. MacWilliams' identity writes then $(1 + Z)^n A_C \left(\frac{1-Z}{1+Z}\right) = |C| W_{C^{\perp}}(Z)$, where n is the length of the binary code C. $\square$

---

[15] The classical proof uses Fourier–Hadamard transform; since this transform will be addressed later in this book, in Section 2.3, we give a proof more coding theory oriented.

The MacWilliams identity gives information on self-dual codes (*i.e.*, codes equal to their duals) through the *Gleason theorem*, which says that the weight enumerator of a self-dual code is in the ring generated by $X^2 + Y^2$ and $XY - Y^2$ (see [809, page 602]).

Unrestricted codes

The principle of MacWilliams' identity can also be applied to unrestricted codes. When C is not linear, the weight distribution of C has no great relevance. The distance distribution has more interest. We consider the *distance enumerator* of C:

$$D_C(X, Y) = \frac{1}{|C|} \sum_{i=0}^{n} B_i X^{n-i} Y^i,$$

where B_i is the size of the set $\{(x, y) \in C^2; d_H(x, y) = i\}$. Note that, if C is linear, then $D_C = W_C$. Similarly as above, we see the following:

$$D_C(X, Y) = \frac{1}{|C|} \sum_{(x,y)\in C^2} \prod_{i=1}^{n} X^{1-(x_i \oplus y_i)} Y^{x_i \oplus y_i};$$

we deduce as follows:

$$D_C(X + Y, X - Y) = \frac{1}{|C|} \sum_{(x,y)\in C^2} \prod_{i=1}^{n} (X + (-1)^{x_i \oplus y_i} Y).$$

Expanding these products by the same method as above, we obtain the following:

$$D_C(X + Y, X - Y) = \frac{1}{|C|} \sum_{(x,y)\in C^2} \sum_{b\in \mathbb{F}_2^n} \prod_{i=1}^{n} \left(X^{1-b_i} ((-1)^{x_i \oplus y_i} Y)^{b_i} \right);$$

that is,

$$D_C(X + Y, X - Y) = \frac{1}{|C|} \sum_{b\in \mathbb{F}_2^n} X^{n-w_H(b)} Y^{w_H(b)} \left(\sum_{x\in C} (-1)^{b\cdot x} \right)^2. \qquad (1.2)$$

Hence, $D_C(X+Y, X-Y)$ has nonnegative coefficients (but $D_C(X, Y)$ is not necessarily the weight enumerator of a code; note, however, that it is one in the case of distance-invariant codes, such as Kerdock codes; see Section 6.1.22).

Definition 4 *The smallest nonzero exponent of Y with nonzero coefficient in the polynomial $D_C(X + Y, X - Y)$, that is, the number*

$$\min \left\{ w_H(b); \ b \neq 0_n, \sum_{x\in C} (-1)^{b\cdot x} \neq 0 \right\},$$

often denoted by $d^{\perp}(C)$, is called the dual distance *of C.*

The dual distance of C is strictly larger than an integer t if and only if the restriction to C of any sum of at least one and at most t coordinate functions in $\mathbb{F}_2^n$ is *balanced* (*i.e.*, has uniform distribution), that is, any of the punctured codes of length t of C equals the whole vector space $\mathbb{F}_2^t$ and each vector in $\mathbb{F}_2^t$ is matched the same number of times.[16] Hence, as we shall see again at page 88, the size of a code of dual distance d is divisible by 2^{d-1}; note that for linear codes, this tells more than the Singleton bound applied to the dual.

This notion will play an important role with Boolean functions (see Definition 21, page 86; this is why we include Lemma 2 below) and with a recent kind of cryptanalysis that plays an important role nowadays: side channel attacks (see Section 12.1, page 425).

Lemma 2 *1. Any coset $a + C$ of a binary unrestricted code has the same dual distance as C. Any union of cosets of a linear code C has at least the same dual distance as C.*

2. *The dual distance of a punctured code is larger than or equal to the dual distance of the original code (assuming that the latter has minimum distance at least 2).*

3. *The dual distance of the Cartesian product of two binary unrestricted codes equals the minimum of their dual distances.*

4. *Let C_1 and C_2 be binary unrestricted codes of the same length n and*

$$C'' = \{(c_1, c_1 + c_2); c_1 \in C_1, c_2 \in C_2\},$$

then $d''^{\perp} = \min(d_1^{\perp}, 2\,d_2^{\perp})$.

The proof of this lemma is also an easy consequence of the properties of the Fourier–Hadamard transform that we shall see in Section 2.3.

Remark. When C is linear, $d^{\perp}$ equals the minimum distance of the *dual code $C^{\perp}$*. Hence, since the minimum distance of a linear code over $\mathbb{F}_q$ equals the minimum nonzero number of $\mathbb{F}_q$-linearly dependent columns in its parity check matrix, its dual distance equals the minimum nonzero number of $\mathbb{F}_q$-linearly dependent columns in its generator matrix. □

1.3 Boolean functions

We call *Boolean functions* (and sometimes we specify *n-variable* Boolean functions or *Boolean functions in dimension n*) the (single-output) functions from the n-dimensional vector space $\mathbb{F}_2^n$ over $\mathbb{F}_2$, to $\mathbb{F}_2$ itself. Their set is denoted by $\mathcal{BF}_n$. Number n will be named the number of variables, or of input bits. More generally,[17] we call n-variable *pseudo-Boolean* functions the functions from $\mathbb{F}_2^n$ to $\mathbb{R}$.

Boolean functions will also be viewed in some cases as taking their input in the field $\mathbb{F}_{2^n}$. Indeed, this field is an n-dimensional vector space over $\mathbb{F}_2$ and it can then be identified with the vector space $\mathbb{F}_2^n$ through the choice of a basis.

Boolean functions play roles in both cryptographic and error-correcting coding activities in *information protection*:

---

[16] This is a consequence of the properties of the Fourier–Hadamard transform that we shall see in Section 2.3, applied to the indicator of C; see Corollary 6, page 88, and Theorem 5.

[17] When we will consider Boolean functions as particular pseudo-Boolean functions, by viewing their output values 0 and 1 as elements of $\mathbb{Z}$ rather than $\mathbb{F}_2$ (for instance, when defining their numerical normal form in Subsection 2.2.4 or their Fourier–Hadamard transform in Section 2.3), adding their values will be made in $\mathbb{Z}$, with notation $+$; otherwise, it will be made modulo 2, with notation $\oplus$.

Table 1.1 Number of n-variable Boolean functions.

n	4	5	6	7	8
$\|\mathcal{BF}_n\|$	2^{16}	2^{32}	2^{64}	2^{128}	2^{256}
$\approx$	$6 \cdot 10^4$	$4 \cdot 10^9$	10^{19}	10^{38}	10^{77}

- Every binary unrestricted code of length 2^n, for some positive integer n, can be interpreted as a set of Boolean functions, since every n-variable Boolean function can be represented by its truth table (an ordering of the set of binary vectors of length n being first chosen) and thus associated with a binary word of length 2^n, and vice versa; important codes (Reed–Muller, Kerdock codes; see Sections 4.1 and 6.1.22) can be defined this way as sets of Boolean functions.
- The role of Boolean functions in conventional cryptography is even more important: cryptographic transformations can be designed by appropriate composition of Boolean functions.[18]

In both frameworks, n is rarely large, in practice:

- The error-correcting codes derived from n-variable Boolean functions have length 2^n; so, taking $n = 10$ already gives codes of length 1024.
- For reason of efficiency, the Boolean functions used in stream ciphers had about 10 variables until algebraic attacks were invented in 2003, and the number of variables is now most often limited to at most 20, except when the functions are particularly fast to compute.

Despite their low numbers of variables, the Boolean functions used in cryptography and satisfying the desired conditions (see Section 3.1 below) cannot be determined or studied by an exhaustive computer investigation: the number $|\mathcal{BF}_n| = 2^{2^n}$ of n-variable Boolean functions is too large when $n \geq 6$. We give in Table 1.1 below the values of this number for n ranging between 4 and 8.

Assume that visiting an n-variable Boolean function, and determining whether it has the desired properties, requires one nanosecond (10^{-9} seconds); then it would need millions of hours to visit all functions in six variables, and about 100 billions times the age of the universe to visit all those in seven variables. The number of eight-variable Boolean functions approximately equals the number of atoms in the whole universe! We see that trying to find functions satisfying the desired conditions by simply picking up functions at random is also impossible for these values of n, since visiting a nonnegligible part of all Boolean functions in seven or more variables is not feasible, even when parallelizing. The study of Boolean functions for constructing or studying codes or ciphers is essentially mathematical. But clever computer investigation is very useful to imagine or to test conjectures, and sometimes to generate interesting functions.

---

[18] Boolean functions play also a role in hash functions, but we shall not develop this aspect, for lack of space, and in the inner protection of some chips.

Figure 1.1 Vernam cipher.

Remark. Boolean functions play an important role in computational complexity theory, with the notion of NP-complete decisional problem (where "NP" stands for nondeterministic polynomial time), for which satisfiability problems (in particular, the 3-SAT problem) are central. These problems are related to representations of Boolean functions by disjunctive and conjunctive normal forms, which do not ensure uniqueness and are not much used in cryptography and error-correcting coding. We refer the reader interested in satisfiability problems and in the related complexity theory of Boolean functions to [31, 81, 1117]. □

A nice site under construction at the moment this book is written can be found at the URL http://boolean.h.uib.no/mediawiki.

1.3.1 Boolean functions and stream ciphers

Stream ciphers are based on the so-called *Vernam cipher* (see Figure 1.1) in which the plaintext (a binary string of some length) is bitwise added to a (binary) secret key of the same length, in order to produce the ciphertext. The Vernam cipher is also called the *one time pad* because a new random secret key must be used for every encryption. Indeed, the bitwise addition of two ciphertexts corresponding to the same key equals the addition of the corresponding plaintexts, which gives much information on these plaintexts when they code for instance natural language (it is often enough to recover both plaintexts, even when one of them is reversed; some secret services and spies learned this at their own expense).

The Vernam cipher, which is the only known cipher offering unconditional security (see [1034]) if the key is truly random and if it is changed for every new encryption, was used for the communication between the heads of the USA and the USSR during the cold war (the keys being carried by diplomats) and by some secret services.

In practice (except in the very sensitive situations indicated above), since in the Vernam cipher, the length of the private key must be equal to the length of the plaintext (which is impractical), a so-called *pseudorandom generator* (*PRG*) is used for producing a long *pseudorandom sequence* (the *keystream*, playing the role of the private key in the Vernam cipher) from the short random secret key. Only the latter is actually shared.[19] The unconditional security is then no longer ensured (this is the price to pay for making the cipher lighter). If the keystream only depends on the key (and not on the plaintext), the

---

[19] The PRG is supposed to be public since taking a part of the secret for describing it would reduce in practice the length of the key.

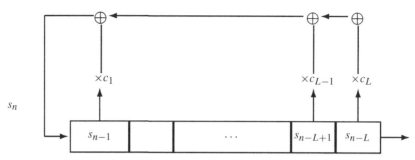

Figure 1.2 LFSR.

cipher is called *synchronous*.[20] Stream ciphers, because they operate on data units as small as a bit or a few bits, are suitable for fast telecommunication applications. Having also a very simple construction, they are easily implemented both in hardware and software. They need to resist all known attacks (see in Section 3.1 those that are known so far). The so-called *attacker model* for these attacks (that is, the description of the knowledge the attacker is supposed to have) is as follows: some knowledge on the plaintext may be unavoidable and it is then assumed that the attacker has access to a small part of it. Since the keystream equals the XOR of the plaintext and the ciphertext, the attacker is then assumed to have access to a part of the keystream, and he/she needs to reconstruct the whole sequence.

A first method for generating pseudorandom sequences from secret keys has used *linear feedback shift registers* (*LFSR*) [550]. In such an LFSR (see Figure 1.2, where $\times$ means multiplication), at every clock cycle, the bits $s_{n-1}, \ldots, s_{n-L}$ contained in the flip-flops of the LFSR move to the right. The right-most bit is the current output (a keystream of length N will then be produced after N clock cycles) and the leftmost flip-flop is fed with the linear combination $\bigoplus_{i=1}^{L} c_i s_{n-i}$, where the c_is are bits. Thus, such an LFSR outputs a recurrent sequence satisfying the relation

$$s_n = \bigoplus_{i=1}^{L} c_i s_{n-i}.$$

Such a sequence is always ultimately periodic[21] (if $c_L = 1$, then it is periodic; we shall assume that $c_L = 1$ in the sequel, because otherwise the same sequence can be output by an LFSR of a shorter length, except for its first bits, and this can be exploited in attacks) with period at most $2^L - 1$. The generating series $s(X) = \sum_{i \geq 0} s_i X^i$ of the sequence can be expressed in a nice way (see the chapter by Helleseth and Kumar in [959] and Section 10.2, "LFSR sequences and maximal period sequences", by Niederreiter in [890]): $s(X) = \frac{G(X)}{F(X)}$, where $G(X) = \sum_{i=0}^{L-1} X^i \left(\bigoplus_{j=0}^{i} c_{i-j} s_j \right)$ is a polynomial of degree smaller than L and $F(X) = 1 + c_1 X + \cdots + c_L X^L$ is the *feedback polynomial* (an equivalent representation

---

[20] There also exist self-synchronizing stream ciphers, in which each keystream bit depends on the n preceding ciphertext bits, which makes possible resynchronizing after n bits if an error of transmission occurs between Alice and Bob.

[21] Conversely, every ultimately periodic sequence can be generated by an LFSR.

uses the *characteristic polynomial*, which is the reciprocal of the feedback polynomial). The minimum length of the LFSR producing a sequence is called the *linear complexity* of the sequence (and sometimes its *linear span*). It equals L if and only if the polynomials F and G above are coprime and is equal in general to $N - deg\,(\gcd(X^N + 1, S(X)))$, where N is a period and $S(X)$ is the generating polynomial $S(X) = s_0 + s_1 X + \cdots + s_{N-1} X^{N-1}$. An *m-sequence* (or *maximum length sequence*) is a sequence of period $2^{\mathcal{L}} - 1$, where $\mathcal{L}$ is the linear complexity. Assuming that $L = \mathcal{L}$, this corresponds to taking a primitive feedback polynomial (see page 488). The sequence can then be represented in the form $s_i = tr_n(a\alpha^i)$, where α is a primitive element of $\mathbb{F}_{2^n}$ (see page 487) and tr_n is the trace function from $\mathbb{F}_{2^n}$ to $\mathbb{F}_2$ (see pages 42 and 489). The m-sequences have very strong properties; see the chapter by Helleseth and Kumar in [959].

The initialization $s_0, \ldots, s_{L-1}$ of the LFSR and the values of the *feedback coefficients* c_i must be kept secret (they are then computed from the secret key); if the feedback coefficients were public, the observation of L consecutive bits of the keystream would allow recovering all the subsequent sequence.

Berlekamp–Massey attack

The use of LFSRs as pseudorandom generators is cryptographically weak because of an attack found in the late 1970s called the *Berlekamp–Massey (BM) algorithm* [826]: let $\mathcal{L}$ be the linear complexity of the sequence, assumed to be unknown from the attacker; if he knows at least $2\mathcal{L}$ consecutive bits of the sequence, the BM algorithm allows him to recover the values of $\mathcal{L}$ and of the feedback coefficients of an LFSR of length $\mathcal{L}$ generating the sequence, as well as the initialization of this LFSR. The BM algorithm has quadratic complexity, that is, works in $\mathcal{O}(\mathcal{L}^2)$ elementary operations. Improvements of the algorithm exist, which have lower complexity: the main idea[22] is to use the extended Euclidean (EE) algorithm (or its variants). The way to use this algorithm is shown in the section "Linearly recurrent sequences" (Section 12.3) of the book *Modern Computer Algebra* by J. von zur Gathen and J. Gerhard [533] (Algorithm 12.9 in this book is essentially an EE algorithm). The complexity of an EE algorithm being $\mathcal{O}(M(\mathcal{L}) \log(\mathcal{L}))$, where $M(\mathcal{L})$ is the cost of the multiplication between two polynomials of degree $\mathcal{L}$, and this latter cost being quasilinear, the complexity of finding the retroaction polynomial of an LFSR is roughly $\mathcal{O}(\mathcal{L} \log(\mathcal{L}))$. The data complexity is still $2\mathcal{L}$, but these $2\mathcal{L}$ bits of the sequence do not need to be strictly consecutive: having k strings of $2\mathcal{L}/k$ consecutive bits is enough, thanks to a matrix version of the BM algorithm found by Coppersmith, coupled with an algorithm due to Beckerman and Labahn, or with a simpler (and implemented) one due to Thomé; see more in [1085].

The role of Boolean functions

Many keystream generators still use LFSRs, and to resist the Berlekamp–Massey attack, either combine several LFSRs (and possibly some additional memory) as in the case of E_0, the keystream generator that is part of the Bluetooth standard, or use Boolean functions; see [1006]. The first model that appeared in the literature for such use is the *combiner model* (see Figure 1.3).

---

[22] We thank Pierrick Gaudry for his kind explanations.

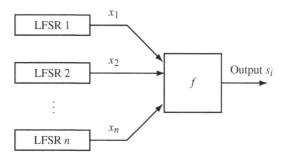

Figure 1.3 Combiner model.

Notice that the feedback coefficients of the n LFSRs used in such a generator can be public. The Boolean function is also public, in general, and the (short) secret key is necessary only for the initialization of the n LFSRs (also depending on an initial vector, which being public can be changed more often than the key): if we want to use for instance a 128-bit-long secret key, this makes possible using n LFSRs of lengths $L_1, \ldots, L_n$ such that $L_1 + \cdots + L_n = 128$.

Such system clearly outputs a periodic sequence whose period is at most the LCM of the periods of the sequences output by the n LFSRs (assuming that $c_L = 1$ in each LFSR; otherwise, the sequence is ultimately periodic and the period is shorter). So, this sequence satisfies a linear recurrence and can therefore be produced by a single LFSR. However, as we shall see, well-chosen Boolean functions allow the linear complexity of the sequence to be much larger than the sum of the lengths of the n LFSRs. Nevertheless, choosing LFSRs producing sequences of large periods, choosing these periods pairwise co-prime in order to have the largest possible global period, and choosing f such that the linear complexity is large enough too are not sufficient. As we shall see, the combining function should also not leak information about the individual LFSRs and behave as differently as possible from affine functions, in several different ways.

The combiner model is only a model, useful for studying attacks and related criteria. In practice, the systems are more complex (see for instance at URL www.ecrypt.eu.org/stream/ to see how the stream ciphers of the *eSTREAM Project* [495] are designed).

A more recent model is the *filter model*, which uses a single LFSR (of a longer length). A filtered LFSR outputs $f(x_1, \ldots, x_n)$, where f is some n-variable Boolean function, called a filtering function, and where $x_1, \ldots, x_n$ are the bits contained in some flip-flops of the LFSR; see Figure 1.4.

Such a system is equivalent to the combiner model using n copies of the LFSR. However, the attacks, even when they apply to both systems, do not work similarly (a first obvious difference is that the lengths of the LFSRs are different in the two models). Consequently, the criteria that the involved Boolean functions must satisfy to allow resistance to these attacks need to be studied for each model (we shall see that they are in practice not so different, except for one criterion that will be necessary for the combiner model but not for the filter model).

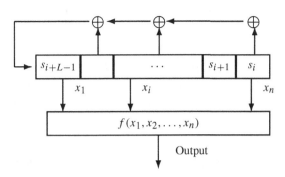

Figure 1.4 Filter model.

Note that in both models, the PRG is made of a *linear part* (constituted by the LFSRs), the linearity allowing speed, and a *nonlinear part* (made of the combiner/filter function) providing confusion (see the meaning of this term in Section 3.1). Generalizations of the two models have been proposed with the same structure "linear part, nonlinear part" [495, 901]. In practice, models will not be used as is; we shall add memory and/or few combinatoric stages and/or initialization registers; a high level security is ensured by the fact that the model, as is, is proved resistant to all known attacks, and the additional complexity will make the work of the attacker still more difficult.

Other kinds of pseudorandom generators exist that are not built on the same principle. A *feedback shift register* (FSR) has the same structure as an LFSR, but the leftmost flip-flop is feeded with $g(x_{i_1}, \ldots, x_{i_n})$, where $n \leq L$ and $x_{i_1}, \ldots, x_{i_n}$ are bits contained in the flip-flops of the FSR, and where g is some n-variable Boolean function called the feedback function (if g is not affine, then we speak of *NFSR*, where N stands for nonlinear). The linear complexity of the produced sequence can be near 2^L (see [640] for general FSRs and [344] for FSRs with a quadratic feedback function; see the definition of "quadratic" at page 36). Some finalists of the eSTREAM project [495] such as Grain and Trivium use NFSRs. But the theory of NFSRs is not completely understood. The linear complexity is difficult to study in general. Even the period is not easily determined, although some special cases have been investigated [630, 702, 1045, 1046]. Nice results similar to those on the m-sequences exist in the case of feedback with carry shift-registers (FCSRs); see [30, 559, 560, 703].

1.3.2 Boolean functions and error-correcting codes

As explained above, every binary *unrestricted code* whose length equals 2^n for some positive integer n can be interpreted as a set of Boolean functions. A particular class of codes has its very definition given by means of Boolean functions. This class is that of Reed–Muller codes. We shall see in Chapter 2 that an integer lying between 0 and n and called algebraic degree can be associated to every Boolean function over $\mathbb{F}_2^n$. The *Reed–Muller code* of order $k \in \{0, \ldots, n\}$ is made of all Boolean functions over $\mathbb{F}_2^n$ whose algebraic degree is bounded above by k; see Section 4.1. This linear code has length 2^n since each Boolean function is identified to the list of its values over $\mathbb{F}_2^n$, in some order. It is linear and has nice particularities, thanks to which Reed–Muller codes are still used nowadays, even if their parameters are not very good, except for the first-order Reed–Muller code. The second-order Reed–Muller code contains a nonlinear code, called the Kerdock code, which has minimum distance almost the same as that of the first-order Reed–Muller code of the same length and size roughly the square of its size. In fact, the parameters of the Kerdock code are so good that they are provably optimal among all unrestricted codes; see Section 6.1.22.

1.4 Vectorial functions

The functions from $\mathbb{F}_2^n$ to $\mathbb{F}_2^m$ are called (n, m)-*functions*. Such function F being given, the Boolean functions $f_1, \ldots, f_m$ defined at every $x \in \mathbb{F}_2^n$ by $F(x) = (f_1(x), \ldots, f_m(x))$, are called the *coordinate functions* of F. When the numbers m and n are not specified, (n, m)-functions are called *multioutput Boolean functions* or *vectorial Boolean functions*. Those vectorial functions whose role is to ensure confusion[23] in a cryptographic system are called *substitution boxes* (*S-boxes*).

Note that (n, m)-functions can also be viewed as taking their input in $\mathbb{F}_{2^n}$ as we have seen with Boolean functions, and if m divides n, then we shall see that the output can then be expressed as a polynomial function of the input. We shall be in particular interested in *power functions* $F(x) = x^d$, $x \in \mathbb{F}_{2^n}$.

1.4.1 Vectorial functions and stream ciphers

In the pseudorandom generators of stream ciphers, (n, m)-functions can be used to combine the outputs of n LFSRs or to filter the content of a single one, generating m bits at each clock cycle instead of only one, which increases the speed of the cipher (but risks decreasing its robustness). The attacks described about Boolean functions are obviously also efficient on these kinds of ciphers. They are in fact often more efficient – see Section 3.3, page 129 – since the attacker can combine in any way the m output bits of the function.

1.4.2 Vectorial functions and block ciphers

Vectorial functions play mainly a role with block ciphers. All known block ciphers are iterative, that is, are the iterations of a transformation depending on a key over each block of plaintext. The iterations are called *rounds* and the key used in an iteration is called a *round key*. The round keys are computed from the secret key (called the *master key*) by a *key scheduling algorithm*. The rounds consist of vectorial Boolean functions combined in different ways and involve the round key.

Remark. Boolean functions also play an important role in block ciphers, each of which admits as input a binary vector $(x_1, \ldots, x_n)$ (a block of plaintext) and outputs a binary vector $(y_1, \ldots, y_m)$; the coordinates $y_1, \ldots, y_m$ are the outputs of Boolean functions (depending on the key) over $(x_1, \ldots, x_n)$; see Figure 1.5.

But the number n of variables of these Boolean functions being large (often more than 100), they are hardly analyzed precisely.   □

---

[23] See Section 3.1 for the meaning of this term.

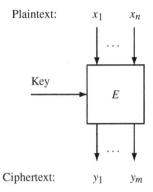

Figure 1.5 Block cipher.

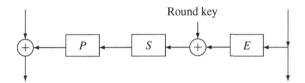

Figure 1.6 A DES round.

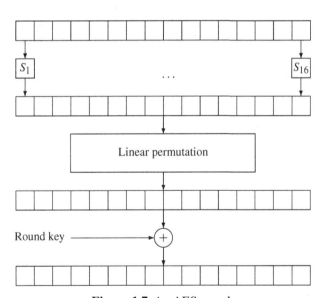

Figure 1.7 An AES round.

We give in Figures 1.6 and 1.7 a description of the rounds of the *Data Encryption Standard (DES)* [88] and of the *Advanced Encryption Standard (AES)* [404].

The input to a DES round is a binary string of length 64, divided into two strings of 32 bits each (in the figure, they enter the round, from above, on the left and on the right); confusion is achieved by the S-box, which is a nonlinear transformation of a binary string of 48 bits[24] into a 32-bit -long one. So, 32 Boolean functions on 48 variables are involved. But, in fact, this nonlinear transformation is the concatenation of eight sub-S-boxes, which transform binary strings of six bits into 4-bit-long ones. Before entering the next round, the two 32-bit-long halves of data are swapped. Such *Feistel cipher* structure does not need the involved vectorial functions (in particular the S-boxes) to be injective for the decryption to be possible. Indeed, any function of the form $(x, y) \mapsto (y, x + \phi(y))$ is a permutation. The number of output bits can be smaller than that of input bits like in the DES; it can also be larger, like in the CAST cipher [6], where input dimension is eight and output dimension is 32. However, if the S-boxes are not balanced (that is, if their output is not uniform), this represents a weakness against some attacks, and it obliges the designer to complexify the structure (for instance by including expansion boxes); see more in [957].

In the (standard) AES round, the input is a 128-bit-long string, divided into 16 strings of eight bits each; the S-box is the concatenation of 16 sub-S-boxes corresponding to 16×8 Boolean functions in eight variables. Such a *substitution permutation network* (SPN) needs the vectorial functions (in particular the S-boxes) to be bijective, so that decryption is possible. Then $n = m$. Another well-known example of such cipher is PRESENT [100]. A third general structure for block ciphers is ARX structure; see [708].

Remark.   Klimov and Shamir [705] have identified a particular kind of vectorial functions usable in stream and block ciphers (and in hash functions), called *T-functions*. These are mappings F from $\mathbb{F}_2^n$ to $\mathbb{F}_2^m$ such that each ith bit of $F(x)$ depends only on $x_1, \ldots, x_i$. For example, addition and multiplication in $\mathbb{Z}$, viewed in binary expansion, are T-functions; logical operations (XOR and AND, that is, addition and multiplication in $\mathbb{F}_2$) are T-functions too. Any composition of T-functions is a T-function as well. Their simplicity makes them appealing for lightweight cryptography. But they may be too simple to provide enough confusion; they have suffered attacks.   □

1.4.3 Vectorial functions and error-correcting codes

We shall see in Chapter 4 that interesting linear subcodes of the Reed–Muller codes and other (possibly nonlinear) codes can be built from vectorial functions.

---

[24] The E-box has expanded the 32-bit-long string into a 48-bit-long one.

2

Generalities on Boolean and vectorial functions

The set $\mathbb{F}_2^n$ of all binary vectors[1] of length n will be viewed as an $\mathbb{F}_2$-vector space (with null element 0_n). This vector space will sometimes be also endowed with the structure of the field $\mathbb{F}_{2^n}$ (denoted by $GF(2^n)$ by some authors), with null element 0; indeed, this field being an n-dimensional vector space over $\mathbb{F}_2$, each of its elements can be identified with the binary vector of length n of its coordinates relative to a fixed basis. The set of all Boolean functions $f : \mathbb{F}_2^n \to \mathbb{F}_2$ will be denoted by $\mathcal{BF}_n$. It is a vector space over $\mathbb{F}_2$. The *Hamming weight* $w_H(x)$ of a binary vector $x \in \mathbb{F}_2^n$ being the number of its nonzero coordinates (*i.e.*, the size of $supp(x) = \{i \in \{1, \dots, n\}; \; x_i \neq 0\}$, the *support of vector x*), the *Hamming weight* $w_H(f)$ of a Boolean function f on $\mathbb{F}_2^n$ is (also) the size of $supp(f) = \{x \in \mathbb{F}_2^n; \; f(x) \neq 0\}$, the *support of function f*. Note that if we denote by Δ the symmetric difference between two sets, we have $supp(f \oplus g) = supp(f) \, \Delta \, supp(g)$. The *Hamming distance* $d_H(f, g)$ between two functions f and g is the size of the set $\{x \in \mathbb{F}_2^n; \; f(x) \neq g(x)\}$. Thus it equals $w_H(f \oplus g)$.

Note. Some additions of bits will be considered in $\mathbb{Z}$ (in characteristic 0) and denoted then by $+$, and some will be computed in characteristic 2 and denoted by $\oplus$. These two different notations will be necessary for $\mathbb{F}_2$ because some representations of Boolean functions will live in characteristic 2 and some will live in characteristic 0. But the addition in the finite field $\mathbb{F}_{2^n}$ will be denoted by $+$, as usual in mathematics, as well as the addition in $\mathbb{F}_2^n$ when $n > 1$, since $\mathbb{F}_2^n$ will often be identified with $\mathbb{F}_{2^n}$, and because there will be no ambiguity.

2.1 A hierarchy of equivalence relations over Boolean and vectorial functions

Each notion that we shall study on Boolean or vectorial functions will be preserved by some equivalence relations that we need to define. It is important to determine precisely, for each notion, those equivalence relations that preserve it. Indeed, if we prove that some function has some property, say $\mathcal{P}$, preserved by a given equivalence relation, this implies automatically that all functions in the equivalence class containing this function share the same property $\mathcal{P}$; to *classify* the set of functions satisfying $\mathcal{P}$, we need to determine all equivalence classes of functions sharing $\mathcal{P}$. This is often a difficult task. Even determining the size of the union of these classes may be quite difficult. If classification is elusive, a possible contribution to the domain is to provide constructions of functions satisfying $\mathcal{P}$. For being able to say that some construction of functions satisfying $\mathcal{P}$ provides new functions, it

---

[1] Coders say "words."

27

is needed to prove that at least one function obtained through this construction is inequivalent (for every equivalence relation preserving $\mathcal{P}$) to all known functions satisfying $\mathcal{P}$. This may be a huge work.

There are five main notions of equivalence among vectorial functions and four in the subcase of Boolean functions (because the fifth notion is then equivalent to the fourth one). We give the definitions for vectorial functions; the corresponding definitions for Boolean functions are with $m = 1$ (then all the permutations composed with the functions on their left can be taken equal to identity).

Remark. In the next definition and in the sequel, we present linear functions over $\mathbb{F}_2^n$ in the form $L : (x_1, x_2, \ldots, x_n) \mapsto (x_1, x_2, \ldots, x_n) \times M$, with $(x_1, x_2, \ldots, x_n)$ a row vector, as it is usual in information protection, rather than dealing with a column vector, as it is usual in mathematics. Applying transposition to the expressions allows us to translate a representation into the other. $\qquad\square$

Definition 5 *The main notions of equivalence on Boolean and vectorial functions are as follows:*

1. *Two (n, m)-functions F and $\tau \circ F \circ \sigma$, where σ is a permutation of $\{1, \ldots, n\}$, extended to a permutation of $\mathbb{F}_2^n$ by*

$$\sigma : (x_1, x_2, \ldots, x_n) \in \mathbb{F}_2^n \mapsto (x_{\sigma(1)}, x_{\sigma(2)}, \ldots, x_{\sigma(n)}) \in \mathbb{F}_2^n$$

and τ is a permutation of $\{1, \ldots, m\}$, similarly extended to a permutation of $\mathbb{F}_2^m$, are called permutation equivalent.

2. *Two (n, m)-functions F and $L' \circ F \circ L$, where*

$$L : (x_1, x_2, \ldots, x_n) \in \mathbb{F}_2^n \mapsto (x_1, x_2, \ldots, x_n) \times M \in \mathbb{F}_2^n$$

is an $\mathbb{F}_2$-linear automorphism of $\mathbb{F}_2^n$, M being a nonsingular $n \times n$ matrix over $\mathbb{F}_2$, and L' is an $\mathbb{F}_2$-linear automorphism of $\mathbb{F}_2^m$, are called linearly equivalent.

3. *Two (n, m)-functions F and $L' \circ F \circ L$, where*

$$L : (x_1, x_2, \ldots, x_n) \in \mathbb{F}_2^n \mapsto (x_1, x_2, \ldots, x_n) \times M + (a_1, a_2, \ldots, a_n)$$

is an affine automorphism of $\mathbb{F}_2^n$ and L' is an affine automorphism of $\mathbb{F}_2^m$, are called affinely equivalent *or* affine equivalent *[907].*

4. *Two (n, m)-functions F and $L' \circ F \circ L + L''$, where L is an affine automorphism of $\mathbb{F}_2^n$, L' is an affine automorphism of $\mathbb{F}_2^m$, and $L'' : (x_1, x_2, \ldots, x_n) \in \mathbb{F}_2^n \mapsto (x_1, x_2, \ldots, x_n) \times M'' + (a_1, a_2, \ldots, a_m) \in \mathbb{F}_2^m$ is an affine (n, m)-function, M'' being an $n \times m$ binary matrix, are called (extended affine)* EA equivalent.

5. *Two (n, m)-functions F and G whose graphs $\mathcal{G}_F = \{(x, y) \in \mathbb{F}_2^n \times \mathbb{F}_2^m ; \ y = F(x)\}$ and $\mathcal{G}_G = \{(x, y) \in \mathbb{F}_2^n \times \mathbb{F}_2^m ; \ y = G(x)\}$ are affinely equivalent (i.e., such that $L(\mathcal{G}_F) = \mathcal{G}_G$ for some affine automorphism L on $\mathbb{F}_2^n \times \mathbb{F}_2^m$) are called Carlet–Charpin–Zinoviev (CCZ) equivalent[2] (the notion is from [257] and the term from [163]).*

---

[2] This notion was rediscovered by L. Breveglieri, A. Cherubini, and M. Macchetti at Asiacrypt 2004.

A property or a parameter will be called a permutation invariant *(resp. a* linear invariant, *an* affine invariant, *an* EA invariant, *or a* CCZ invariant*) if it is preserved by permutation (resp. linear, affine, extended affine, CCZ) equivalence.*

In [432], an asymptotic estimate is given for the number of EA equivalence classes of Boolean functions.

Note that if F and G are CCZ equivalent and if we write $L = (L_1, L_2)$, where L is the automorphism in Definition 5 (Item 5) with $L_1: \mathbb{F}_2^n \times \mathbb{F}_2^m \mapsto \mathbb{F}_2^n$ and $L_2: \mathbb{F}_2^n \times \mathbb{F}_2^m \mapsto \mathbb{F}_2^m$, and if, for every $x \in \mathbb{F}_2^n$, we define $F_1(x) = L_1(x, F(x))$ and $F_2(x) = L_2(x, F(x))$, then function F_1 is bijective because G is a function, and $G = F_2 \circ F_1^{-1}$. Note also that, given a function F, finding all functions CCZ equivalent to F consists in finding all affine automorphisms $L = (L_1, L_2)$ such that F_1 is bijective. Moreover, CCZ equivalent functions corresponding to a same F, a same L_1, and different L_2 are EA equivalent; see [163], which shows that an (n, n)-function G is EA equivalent to a function F or to F^{-1} (if it exists) if and only if there exists an affine permutation $L = (L_1, L_2)$ where L_1 depends only on x or y, and such that $L(\mathcal{G}_F) = \mathcal{G}_G$.

CCZ equivalence can be translated in terms of codes; see the remark on page 379.

Proposition 1 *For n and m ranging over $\mathbb{N}$, each equivalence relation in Definition 5 is a strict particular case of the next one.*

Proof The only nonobvious facts are that EA equivalence implies CCZ equivalence and that the converse is false. This can be seen as follows:

- If ϕ_1 and ϕ_2 are affine automorphisms of $\mathbb{F}_2^n$, $\mathbb{F}_2^m$, respectively, and if $G = \phi_2 \circ F \circ \phi_1$, then defining $L_1(x, y) = \phi_1^{-1}(x)$ and $L_2(x, y) = \phi_2(y)$, we have that $L = (L_1, L_2)$ is an affine automorphism of $\mathbb{F}_2^n \times \mathbb{F}_2^m$ that maps $\mathcal{G}_F$ onto $\mathcal{G}_G$, since $G(\phi_1^{-1}(x)) = \phi_2(F(x))$, and F and G are then CCZ equivalent.[3]
- If $\phi(x)$ is an affine function from $\mathbb{F}_2^n$ to $\mathbb{F}_2^m$ and $G(x) = F(x) + \phi(x)$, then $L(x, y) = (x, y + \phi(x))$ is an affine automorphism that maps $\mathcal{G}_F$ onto $\mathcal{G}_G$, and F and G are CCZ equivalent.
- EA equivalence preserves algebraic degree (see Definition 6, page 35) when it is larger than 1 and it is shown in [162, 163] that CCZ equivalence does not.   □

Note that if $m = n$ and $(L_1, L_2)(x, y) = (y, x)$, then $F_2 \circ F_1^{-1}$ is equal to F^{-1}.

2.1.1 Relations between these equivalences

For a lack of space, in this subsection, we shall refer to papers for the proofs.

It has been proved in [163] that CCZ equivalence between (n, n)-functions[4] is strictly more general than EA equivalence together with taking inverses of permutations, by exhibiting functions that are CCZ equivalent to the function $F(x) = x^3$ on $\mathbb{F}_{2^n}$, but that

---

[3] Conversely, if F and G are CCZ equivalent and $L_1(x, y)$ and $L_2(x, y)$ depend only on x and y, respectively, say $L_1(x, y) = \phi_1^{-1}(x)$ and $L_2(x, y) = \phi_2(y)$, then ϕ_1 and ϕ_2 are affine automorphisms of $\mathbb{F}_2^n$ and $\mathbb{F}_2^m$, respectively, and $G = \phi_2 \circ F \circ \phi_1$.
[4] For (n, m)-functions, see [149, 966].

cannot be obtained from F by any sequence of applications of EA equivalence and inverse transformation; see also [771].

However, CCZ equivalence coincides with EA equivalence when restricted to some classes of functions (whose definitions will be, in some cases, given after):

1. Boolean (*i.e.*, single-output) functions,[5] as shown in [149] (on the contrary, CCZ equivalence is shown to be strictly more general than EA equivalence in the case of (n, m)-*functions* when $n \geq 5$ and m is larger than or equal to the smallest divisor of n different from 1, *e.g.*, when n is even and $m \geq 2$).
2. Bent functions (see page 269) as proved in [148, 150] and more generally, functions having surjective derivatives (see page 38), as proved in [164].
3. Quadratic APN functions (see page 281), as shown in [1139] (extending [119]).

CCZ equivalence also coincides with EA equivalence (see page 281 as well):

• For n even, with plateaued APN functions, one of which is a power function.
• For a quadratic APN function and a power (APN) function (they are then EA equivalent to one of the Gold functions).

And the CCZ equivalence between two power functions coincides with their EA equivalence or with the EA equivalence between one function and the inverse of the other if it is bijective (see Proposition 113, page 281).

Remark.   It has been shown in [149] that the CCZ equivalence (*i.e.*, the EA equivalence, thanks to 1 above) between the indicators (*i.e.*, characteristic functions) of the graphs of two functions coincides with their CCZ equivalence.   □

Finding new EA inequivalent functions by using CCZ equivalence is not easy (this could be done in particular cases; see pages 396, 404). If (L_1, L_2) and (L_1, L_2') are linear permutations of $\mathbb{F}_2^n \times \mathbb{F}_2^m$ and $F_1 = L_1(x, F(x))$ is a permutation of $\mathbb{F}_2^n$, then since the functions F' and F'' obtained by CCZ equivalence from F by using (L_1, L_2) and (L_1, L_2') are EA equivalent, finding EA inequivalent functions by using CCZ equivalence requires finding new permutations F_1.

2.2 Representations of Boolean functions and vectorial functions

Among the classical representations of Boolean (resp. vectorial) functions, the most well known is the *truth table* (resp. the *lookup table*, or LUT), equal to the list of all pairs of an element of $\mathbb{F}_2^n$ and of the value of the function at this input (an ordering of $\mathbb{F}_2^n$ being chosen).

2.2.1 Algebraic normal form

The truth table is not much used for defining Boolean functions in the frameworks of cryptography and coding theory, because the features of Boolean functions that play a role in these two domains are not easily captured by such representation (except for the Hamming

---

[5]   If one function is Boolean (and viewed as multiouput thanks to $\mathbb{F}_2 \subset \mathbb{F}_{2^m}$), this suffices.

weight). The most used representation in cryptography and coding is the *algebraic normal form* (in brief the *ANF*).[6]

Algebraic normal form of Boolean functions

This is an n-variable polynomial representation over $\mathbb{F}_2$, of the form $f(x) =$

$$\bigoplus_{I\subseteq\{1,\dots,n\}} a_I \left(\prod_{i\in I} x_i\right) = \bigoplus_{I\subseteq\{1,\dots,n\}} a_I\, x^I \in \mathbb{F}_2[x_1,\dots,x_n]/(x_1^2 \oplus x_1,\dots,x_n^2 \oplus x_n). \quad (2.1)$$

Every coordinate x_i appears in this polynomial with exponents at most 1, because every bit in $\mathbb{F}_2$ equals its own square.

Example Let us consider the function f whose truth table is as follows:

x_1	x_2	x_3	x in hexa	$f(x)$
0	0	0	0	0
0	0	1	1	1
0	1	0	2	0
0	1	1	3	0
1	0	0	4	0
1	0	1	5	1
1	1	0	6	0
1	1	1	7	1

It is the sum (modulo 2 or not, no matter) of the *atomic functions* f_1, f_2, f_3:

x_1	x_2	x_3	x in hexa	$f_1(x)$	$f_2(x)$	$f_3(x)$
0	0	0	0	0	0	0
0	0	1	1	1	0	0
0	1	0	2	0	0	0
0	1	1	3	0	0	0
1	0	0	4	0	0	0
1	0	1	5	0	1	0
1	1	0	6	0	0	0
1	1	1	7	0	0	1

---

[6] It can have other names in circuit theory, such as Zhegalkin polynomial, modulo-2 sum-of-products, Reed–Muller-canonical expansion, and positive polarity Reed–Muller form.

The function $f_1(x)$ takes value 1 if and only if $1 \oplus x_1 = 1 \oplus x_2 = x_3 = 1$, that is, $(1 \oplus x_1)(1 \oplus x_2) x_3 = 1$. Thus the ANF of f_1 can be obtained by expanding the product $(1 \oplus x_1)(1 \oplus x_2) x_3$. After similar observations on f_2 and f_3, we see that the ANF of f equals $(1 \oplus x_1)(1 \oplus x_2) x_3 \oplus x_1(1 \oplus x_2) x_3 \oplus x_1 x_2 x_3 = x_1 x_2 x_3 \oplus x_2 x_3 \oplus x_3$. $\qquad \square$

Another possible representation of this same ANF uses an indexation by means of vectors of $\mathbb{F}_2^n$ instead of subsets of $\{1, \ldots, n\}$; if, for any such vector u, we denote by a_u what is denoted by $a_{supp(u)}$ in Relation (2.1) (where $supp(u)$ denotes the support of u), we have the following equivalent representation:

$$f(x) = \bigoplus_{u \in \mathbb{F}_2^n} a_u \left(\prod_{j=1}^{n} x_j^{u_j} \right).$$

The monomial $\prod_{j=1}^{n} x_j^{u_j}$ is often denoted[7] by x^u. We have $x^u x^v = x^{u \vee v}$, where $supp(u \vee v) = supp(u) \cup supp(v)$.

Existence and uniqueness of the ANF

By applying the method described in the example above, it is a simple matter to show the existence of the ANF of any Boolean function: we have

$$f(x) = \sum_{a \in \mathbb{F}_2^n} f(a)\delta_a(x) = \bigoplus_{a \in \mathbb{F}_2^n} f(a)\delta_a(x) \qquad (2.2)$$

where the function δ_a is the Dirac (or Kronecker) symbol at a and equals $\delta_a(x) = \prod_{i=1}^{n}(x_i \oplus a_i \oplus 1)$. Replacing in (2.2) each δ_a by this expression, expanding it, and simplifying (mod 2) gives an expression (2.1) for f, which shows the existence of an ANF of any Boolean function. This implies that the mapping from polynomials $P \in \mathbb{F}_2[x_1, \ldots, x_n]/(x_1^2 \oplus x_1, \ldots, x_n^2 \oplus x_n)$ to the corresponding functions $x \in \mathbb{F}_2^n \mapsto P(x)$, is onto $\mathcal{BF}_n$. Since the size of $\mathcal{BF}_n$ equals the size of $\mathbb{F}_2[x_1, \ldots, x_n]/(x_1^2 \oplus x_1, \ldots, x_n^2 \oplus x_n)$, this correspondence is one to one.[8] But more can be said.

Relationship between a Boolean function and its ANF

The product $x^I = \prod_{i \in I} x_i$ is nonzero if and only if x_i is nonzero (*i.e.*, equals 1) for every $i \in I$, that is, if I is included in the support of x; hence, the Boolean function $f(x) = \bigoplus_{I \subseteq \{1, \ldots, n\}} a_I x^I$ takes the value

$$f(x) = \bigoplus_{I \subseteq supp(x)} a_I, \qquad (2.3)$$

where $supp(x)$ denotes the support of x.

---

[7] The reader should not confuse this notation with a univariate monomial.
[8] Another argument is that this mapping is a linear mapping from a vector space over $\mathbb{F}_2$ of dimension 2^n to a vector space of the same dimension.

If we use the notation $f(x) = \bigoplus_{u \in \mathbb{F}_2^n} a_u x^u$, we obtain the relation $f(x) = \bigoplus_{u \preceq x} a_u$, where $u \preceq x$ means that $supp(u) \subseteq supp(x)$ (we say that u is *covered* by x). A Boolean function f° can be associated to the ANF of f: for every $x \in \mathbb{F}_2^n$, we set $f^\circ(x) = a_{supp(x)}$, that is, with the notation $f(x) = \bigoplus_{u \in \mathbb{F}_2^n} a_u x^u$: $f^\circ(u) = a_u$. Relation (2.3) shows that f is the image of f° by the so-called *binary Möbius transform*. The converse is also true:

Theorem 1 *Let f be a Boolean function on $\mathbb{F}_2^n$ and let $\bigoplus_{I \subseteq \{1,\ldots,n\}} a_I\, x^I$ be its ANF. We have:*

$$\forall I \subseteq \{1,\ldots,n\}, a_I = \bigoplus_{x \in \mathbb{F}_2^n;\, supp(x) \subseteq I} f(x). \tag{2.4}$$

Proof Let us denote $\bigoplus_{x \in \mathbb{F}_2^n;\, supp(x) \subseteq I} f(x)$ by b_I and consider the function $g(x) = \bigoplus_{I \subseteq \{1,\ldots,n\}} b_I\, x^I$. We have

$$g(x) = \bigoplus_{I \subseteq supp(x)} b_I = \bigoplus_{I \subseteq supp(x)} \left(\bigoplus_{y \in \mathbb{F}_2^n;\, supp(y) \subseteq I} f(y) \right)$$

$$= \bigoplus_{y \in \mathbb{F}_2^n} f(y) \left(\bigoplus_{I \subseteq \{1,\ldots,n\};\, supp(y) \subseteq I \subseteq supp(x)} 1 \right).$$

The sum $\bigoplus_{I \subseteq \{1,\ldots,n\};\, supp(y) \subseteq I \subseteq supp(x)} 1$ is null if $y \neq x$. Indeed, if $supp(y) \not\subseteq supp(x)$, then the sum is empty and if $supp(y) \subseteq supp(x)$, then the set $\{I \subseteq \{1,\ldots,n\}; supp(y) \subseteq I \subseteq supp(x)\}$ contains $2^{w_H(x)-w_H(y)}$ elements. Hence, $g = f$ and, by the uniqueness of the ANF of f, $b_I = a_I$ for every I. $\qquad\square$

Algorithm (Fast binary Möbius transform)

There exists a simple divide-and-conquer butterfly algorithm to compute the ANF from the truth table (or vice versa), called the *fast Möbius transform*. For every $u = (u_1,\ldots,u_n) \in \mathbb{F}_2^n$, the coefficient a_u of x^u in the ANF of f equals

$$\bigoplus_{(x_1,\ldots,x_{n-1}) \preceq (u_1,\ldots,u_{n-1})} \left[f(x_1,\ldots,x_{n-1},0) \right] \quad \text{if } u_n = 0 \text{ and}$$

$$\bigoplus_{(x_1,\ldots,x_{n-1}) \preceq (u_1,\ldots,u_{n-1})} \left[f(x_1,\ldots,x_{n-1},0) \oplus f(x_1,\ldots,x_{n-1},1) \right] \text{ if } u_n = 1.$$

Hence if, in the truth table of f, the binary vectors are ordered in lexicographic order, with the bit of higher weight on the right, the table of the ANF equals the concatenation of the ANFs of the $(n-1)$-variable functions $f(x_1,\ldots,x_{n-1},0)$ and $f(x_1,\ldots,x_{n-1},0) \oplus f(x_1,\ldots,x_{n-1},1)$. This gives the recursive algorithm below. Note that taking the lexicographic order with the bit of higher weight on the left (*i.e.*, the standard lexicographic order) would work as well (as would any other order corresponding to a permutation of $\{1,\ldots,n\}$).

1. Write the truth table of f, in which the binary vectors of length n are in lexicographic order with the bit of higher weight on the right.
2. Let f_0 and f_1 be the restrictions of f to $\mathbb{F}_2^{n-1} \times \{0\}$ and $\mathbb{F}_2^{n-1} \times \{1\}$, respectively;[9] replace the values of f_1 by those of $f_0 \oplus f_1$.
3. Apply recursively step 2, separately to the functions now obtained in the places of f_0 and f_1.

When the algorithm ends (*i.e.*, arrives to functions in one variable each), the global table gives the values of the ANF of f. The complexity of this algorithm is of $n\, 2^n$ XORs; it is then in $\mathcal{O}(N \log_2 N)$, where $N = 2^n$ is the size of its input f.

Algorithm 1: Computing the algebraic normal form.

Data: tt $\leftarrow$ truth table, n $\leftarrow$ number of variables
Result: anf $\leftarrow$ algebraic normal form
for $i = 0$ **to** $n - 1$ **do**
    for $j = 0$ **to** $2^{n-1} - 1$ **do**
        $t[j] = tt[2 * j]$;
        $u[j] = tt[2 * j] \oplus tt[2 * j + 1]$;
    end
    for $k = 0$ **to** $2^{n-1} - 1$ **do**
        $anf[k] = t[k]$;
        $anf[2^{n-1} + k] = u[k]$;
    end
end

We give in Table 2.1 an example of the computation of the ANF from the truth table using the algorithm of the fast binary Möbius transform, and of the computation of the truth table from the ANF, using this same algorithm.

Remark. The algorithm does not work if the order on $\mathbb{F}_{2^n}$ is not a permuted lexicographic order (for instance, an order by increasing weights of inputs). □

ANF of the graph indicator of a vectorial function

Denoting by $1_{\mathcal{G}_F}(x, y)$, the indicator (*i.e.*, the characteristic function) of the *graph* $\mathcal{G}_F = \{(x, F(x)); \ x \in \mathbb{F}_2^n\}$ of an (n, m)-function F (sometimes called its *codebook*), Relation (2.4) applied to $1_{\mathcal{G}_F}$ gives that, for every $I \subseteq \{1, \ldots, n\}, J \subseteq \{1, \ldots, m\}$, the coefficient of $x^I y^J$ in its ANF equals the following:

$$a_{I,J} = |\{x \in \mathbb{F}_2^n; \ supp(x) \subseteq I \text{ and } supp(F(x)) \subseteq J\}| \ [\text{mod } 2].$$

We have also the following:

---

[9] The truth table of f_0 (resp. f_1) corresponds to the upper (resp. lower) half of the table of f.

Table 2.1 ANF of a function from its truth table and recalculation of the truth table from ANF (for function $f(x) = x_2 \oplus x_1x_2x_3 \oplus x_1x_4$; $x = (x_1, x_2, x_3, x_4)$).

x_1	x_2	x_3	x_4	x in hexa	$f(x)$	$f^\circ(x)$							$f(x)$
0	0	0	0	0	0	0	0	0	0	0	0	0	0
1	0	0	0	1	0	0	0	0	0	0	0	0	0
0	1	0	0	2	1	1	1	1	1	1	1	1	1
1	1	0	0	3	1	1	1	1	0	0	0	0	1
0	0	1	0	4	0	0	0	0	0	0	0	0	0
1	0	1	0	5	0	0	0	0	0	0	0	0	0
0	1	1	0	6	1	1	0	0	0	0	1	1	1
1	1	1	0	7	0	0	1	1	1	1	1	1	0
0	0	0	1	8	0	0	0	0	0	0	0	0	0
1	0	0	1	9	1	1	1	1	1	1	1	1	1
0	1	0	1	a	1	0	0	0	0	1	1	1	1
1	1	0	1	b	0	1	1	0	0	0	0	1	0
0	0	1	1	c	0	0	0	0	0	0	0	0	0
1	0	1	1	d	1	1	0	0	0	0	1	1	1
0	1	1	1	e	1	0	0	0	0	0	1	1	1
1	1	1	1	f	1	1	0	0	0	1	1	0	1

Proposition 2 *[253, 254] Let F be any (n,m)-function, and let $f_1, \ldots, f_m$ be its coordinate functions. We have the following:*

$$1_{\mathcal{G}_F}(x, y) = \prod_{j=1}^{m}(y_j \oplus f_j(x) \oplus 1) = \bigoplus_{J\subseteq\{1,\ldots,m\}} y^J \prod_{j\in\{1,\ldots,m\}\setminus J} (f_j(x) \oplus 1).$$

Indeed, for every $y, y' \in \mathbb{F}_2^m$, we have $y = y'$ if and only if $\prod_{j=1}^{m}(y_j \oplus y'_j \oplus 1) = 1$. This, with $y' = F(x)$, proves the first assertion and the rest is straightforward.

Note that, if F is a permutation ($m = n$), then $1_{\mathcal{G}_F}(x, y) = 1_{\mathcal{G}_{F^{-1}}}(y, x)$, where F^{-1} is the compositional inverse of F, and thus

$$\bigoplus_{J\subseteq\{1,\ldots,n\}} y^J \prod_{j\in\{1,\ldots,n\}\setminus J} (f_j(x) \oplus 1) = \bigoplus_{I\subseteq\{1,\ldots,n\}} x^I \prod_{i\in\{1,\ldots,n\}\setminus I} (f'_i(y) \oplus 1), \qquad (2.5)$$

where the f'_i's are the coordinate functions of F^{-1}.

Algebraic degree of a Boolean function

Definition 6 *The degree of the ANF shall be denoted by $d_{alg}(f)$ and is called the* algebraic degree *of the function*[10]*: $d_{alg}(f) = \max\{|I|; a_I \neq 0\}$, where $|I|$ denotes the size of I (with the convention that the zero function has algebraic degree 0).*

This makes sense thanks to the existence and uniqueness of the ANF.

---

[10] Some authors also call it the nonlinear order of f, but this terminology is more or less obsolete.

Of course, given two n-variable Boolean functions f, g, we have $d_{alg}(f \oplus g) \leq$ $\max(d_{alg}(f), d_{alg}(g))$ and $d_{alg}(f\ g) \leq d_{alg}(f) + d_{alg}(g)$.

Note that a Boolean function is affine if and only if it has algebraic degree at most 1. We shall call *quadratic functions* the Boolean functions of algebraic degree at most 2 and *cubic functions* those of algebraic degree at most 3. Note that this means for instance that an affine function is a particular quadratic function (just as, by definition, a constant function is a particular affine function). This may be a little confusing for the reader, but we are obliged to adopt this terminology, since otherwise, we would have sentences like "all derivatives of a Boolean function are affine if and only if the function is quadratic or affine," "all second-order derivatives are affine if and only if the function is cubic or quadratic or affine," etc.

According to Relation (2.4), we have directly:

Proposition 3 *The algebraic degree $d_{alg}(f)$ of any n-variable Boolean function f equals the maximum dimension of the subspaces $\{x \in \mathbb{F}_2^n; supp(x) \subseteq I\}$ on which f takes value 1 an odd number of times. In particular:*

- *$d_{alg}(f) = n$ if and only if $w_H(f)$ is odd,*
- *$d_{alg}(f) = n - 1$ if and only if (1) $w_H(f)$ is even and (2) there exists i such that $|\{a \in supp(f); a_i = 0\}|$ is odd, or equivalently thanks to (1), $\sum_{a \in supp(f)} a \neq 0$.*

The index i is indeed characterized by $\bigoplus_{a \in supp(f)} a_i \neq 0$. The two latter properties above will be seen under another viewpoint in Corollary 2, page 46.

The algebraic degree is an affine invariant (*i.e.*, it is invariant under the action of the general affine group; see Section 2.1): for every affine automorphism $L : (x_1, x_2, \ldots, x_n) \in \mathbb{F}_2^n \mapsto (x_1, x_2, \ldots, x_n) \times M + (a_1, a_2, \ldots, a_n)$, where M is a nonsingular $n \times n$ matrix over $\mathbb{F}_2$, we have $d_{alg}(f \circ L) = d_{alg}(f)$. Indeed, the composition by L clearly cannot increase the algebraic degree, since the coordinates of $L(x)$ have degree 1. Hence we have $d_{alg}(f \circ L) \leq d_{alg}(f)$ (in fact, for every affine homomorphism). And applying this inequality to $f \circ L$ in the place of f and to L^{-1} in the place of L shows the inverse inequality.

Note in particular that, if F is an (n, n)-permutation, then we have $d_{alg}(1_{\mathcal{G}_F}) = d_{alg}(1_{\mathcal{G}_{F-1}})$: these two indicators correspond to each other by swapping x and y. For functions of algebraic degree strictly larger than 1, the algebraic degree is an *EA invariant* (but not a CCZ invariant; see [162, 163]).

The algebraic degree being an affine invariant, Proposition 3 implies that it also equals the maximum dimension of all the affine subspaces of $\mathbb{F}_2^n$ on which f takes value 1 an odd number of times. Equivalently:

Proposition 4 *A Boolean function has algebraic degree at most d if and only if its restriction to any $(d + 1)$-dimensional flat (i.e., affine subspace) has an even Hamming weight.*

This shows in particular that, given an n-variable Boolean function f and an affine subspace $A = a + E$ of $\mathbb{F}_2^n$ (where E is the vector space equal to the direction of A), the restriction of f to A, viewed as a k-variable function where k is the dimension of A (by identifying the elements of $a + E$ with the vectors of $\mathbb{F}_2^k$ through the choice of a basis of E), has algebraic degree at most $d_{alg}(f)$.

It is shown in [955] that, for every nonzero n-variable Boolean function f, denoting by g the *binary Möbius transform* of f, we have $d_{alg}(f) + d_{alg}(g) \geq n$. This same paper deduces characterizations and constructions of the functions that are equal to their binary Möbius transform, called *coincident functions*.

Remark. 1. Every atomic function has algebraic degree n, since its ANF equals $(x_1 \oplus \epsilon_1)$ $(x_2 \oplus \epsilon_2) \ldots (x_n \oplus \epsilon_n)$, where $\epsilon_i \in \mathbb{F}_2$. Thus, a Boolean function f has algebraic degree n if and only if, in its decomposition as a sum of atomic functions, the number of these atomic functions is odd, that is, if and only if $w_H(f)$ is odd. This property will have an important consequence on the *Reed–Muller codes*, and it will be also useful in Chapter 4.
2. If we know that the algebraic degree of an n-variable Boolean function f is bounded above by $d < n$, then the whole function can be recovered from some of its restrictions (*i.e.*, a unique function corresponds to this *partially defined* Boolean function). Precisely, according to the existence and uniqueness of the ANF, the knowledge of the restriction $f_{|E}$ of the Boolean function f (of algebraic degree at most d) to a set E implies the knowledge of the whole function if and only if the system of the equations $f(x)$ $= \bigoplus_{I \subseteq \{1,\ldots,n\}; |I| \leq d} a_I x^I$, with indeterminates $a_I \in \mathbb{F}_2$, and where x ranges over E (this makes $|E|$ equations), has a unique solution.[11]

This happens with the set E_d of all words of Hamming weights smaller than or equal to d (and then, by affine equivalence, it happens with every set E affinely equivalent to E_d), since Relation (2.4) gives the value of a_I for $|I| \leq d$ and the others are null by hypothesis. And since $|E_d| = |\{I \subseteq \{1,\ldots,n\}; |I| \leq d\}|$, any choice of $f_{|E_d}$ works.

Notice that Relation (2.3) makes it possible to express the value of $f(x)$ for every $x \in \mathbb{F}_2^n$ by means of the values taken by f on E. For instance, for $E = E_d$, we have the following (using the notation a_u instead of a_I, see above, and still using that $d_{alg}(f) \leq d$):

$$f(x) = \bigoplus_{\substack{u \preceq x}} a_u = \bigoplus_{\substack{u \preceq x \\ u \in E_d}} a_u = \bigoplus_{\substack{y \preceq x \\ y \in E_d}} f(y) \, |\{u \in E_d ; y \preceq u \preceq x|$$

$$= \bigoplus_{\substack{y \preceq x \\ y \in E_d}} f(y) \left[\left[\sum_{i=0}^{d - w_H(y)} \binom{w_H(x) - w_H(y)}{i} \right] [\text{mod } 2] \right].$$

These observations generalize to *pseudo-Boolean* (that is, real-valued) functions, if we consider the numerical degree (see below) instead of the algebraic degree, cf. [1090]. □

The simplest functions, from the viewpoint of the ANF, are those Boolean functions of algebraic degree at most 1, that is, *affine functions* (the sums of linear and constant functions, sometimes called parity functions; see, *e.g.*, [914]):

$$f(x) = a_0 \oplus a_1 x_1 \oplus \cdots \oplus a_n x_n; \quad a_i \in \mathbb{F}_2.$$

Denoting by $a \cdot x$, the *usual inner product* $a \cdot x = a_1 x_1 \oplus \cdots \oplus a_n x_n$ in $\mathbb{F}_2^n$ (already encountered in Section 1.2), or any other *inner product* (that is,[12] any symmetric bivariate

---

[11] Note that taking $f(x) = 0, \forall x \in E$, leads to another problem: determining the so-called annihilators f of the indicator 1_E of E (the characteristic function of E, defined by $1_E(x) = 1$ if $x \in E$ and $1_E(x) = 0$ otherwise). This is the core analysis of Boolean functions from the viewpoint of algebraic attacks; see Section 3.1.

[12] In nonzero characteristic, there is no possible notion of positivity.

function such that, for every $a \neq 0$, the function $x \to a \cdot x$ is a nonzero linear form[13] on $\mathbb{F}_2^n$), the general form of an n-variable affine function is $a \cdot x \oplus a_0 = \ell_a(x) \oplus a_0$ (with $a \in \mathbb{F}_2^n$; $a_0 \in \mathbb{F}_2$), since the nondegeneracy of the bilinear form implies that the mapping $a \mapsto \ell_a$ is injective and therefore bijective.

Affine functions play an important role in coding (they are involved in the definition of the Reed–Muller code of order 1; see Section 4.1) and in cryptography (the Boolean functions used as "nonlinear functions" in cryptosystems must behave as differently as possible from affine functions; see Section 3.1).

Algebraic degree and derivation

The derivation of Boolean functions must not be confused with the derivation of polynomials:

Definition 7 *Let f be an n-variable Boolean function and let a be any vector in $\mathbb{F}_2^n$. We call* derivative[14] *in the direction a (or with the input difference a) of f the Boolean function* $D_a f(x) = f(x) \oplus f(x + a)$.

For instance, the derivative of a function expressed in the form $g(x_1, \ldots, x_{n-1}) \oplus x_n h(x_1, \ldots, x_{n-1})$ in the direction $(0, \ldots, 0, 1)$ equals $h(x_1, \ldots, x_{n-1})$.

Proposition 5 *Any derivative of any nonconstant Boolean function f has an algebraic degree strictly smaller than the algebraic degree of f, and there exists at least one derivative of algebraic degree $d_{alg}(f) - 1$.*

Proof The first assertion can be checked easily for each monomial x^I, where $I \neq \emptyset$: we have $x^I \oplus (x + a)^I = \bigoplus_{J \subset I, J \neq I} \left(\prod_{j \in I \setminus J} a_j \right) x^J$. The second assertion is a direct consequence, by affine invariance of the algebraic degree, of the fact observed just above for direction $(0, \ldots, 0, 1)$. $\qquad\qquad\square$

Note that this implies that a function is affine if and only if all its derivatives are constant (this is more generally valid for every function defined over a vector space). And it is quadratic if and only if all its derivatives are affine. For a general function, the sets of those vectors a such that $D_a f$ is constant (resp. affine) are vector subspaces of $\mathbb{F}_2^n$; see page 99.

In [275], Boolean functions f whose restrictions to all affine hyperplanes have the same algebraic degree equal to $d_{alg}(f)$ and functions whose derivatives $D_a f(x)$, $a \neq 0_n$, have all the same algebraic degree $d_{alg}(f) - 1$ are studied. Three classes of Boolean functions are presented; the first class satisfies both conditions, the second class satisfies the first condition but not the second, and the third class satisfies the second condition but not the first. This same paper gives, for any fixed positive integer k and for all integers n, p, s such that $p \geq k + 1$, $s \geq k + 1$, and $n \geq ps$, a class $C_{n,p,s}$ of n-variable Boolean functions whose restrictions to all k-codimensional affine subspaces of $\mathbb{F}_2^n$ have the same algebraic degree as the function.

Higher-order derivatives have been introduced by Lai [735].

---

[13] That is, "$\cdot$" is a nondegenerate bilinear form.
[14] Some authors write "directional derivative".

Definition 8 *Let f be an n-variable Boolean function and let $a_1, \ldots, a_k$ be k vectors in $\mathbb{F}_2^n$. We call the k-th order derivative of f in the directions $a_1, \ldots, a_k$ the Boolean function $D_{a_1} D_{a_2} \cdots D_{a_k} f(x)$.*

It is easily seen by induction on k that if $a_1, \ldots, a_k$ are linearly independent, then $D_{a_1} D_{a_2} \cdots D_{a_k} f(x) = \bigoplus_{a \in E} f(x + a)$, where E is the $\mathbb{F}_2$-vector space spanned by $a_1, \ldots, a_k$, and otherwise $D_{a_1} D_{a_2} \cdots D_{a_k} f(x) = 0$.

Corollary 1 *Any k-th order derivative of any Boolean function f of an algebraic degree at least k has an algebraic degree at most $d_{alg}(f) - k$.*

The algebraic normal form of vectorial functions

The notion of the algebraic normal form of Boolean functions can easily be extended to (n, m)-functions. Given such function F, each coordinate function of F is uniquely represented by its ANF, which is an element of $\mathbb{F}_2[x_1, \ldots, x_n]/(x_1^2 \oplus x_1, \ldots, x_n^2 \oplus x_n)$. Function F is then represented in a unique way as an element of $\mathbb{F}_2^m[x_1, \ldots, x_n]/(x_1^2 \oplus x_1, \ldots, x_n^2 \oplus x_n)$:

$$F(x) = \sum_{I \subseteq \{1, \ldots, n\}} a_I \left(\prod_{i \in I} x_i \right) = \sum_{I \subseteq \{1, \ldots, n\}} a_I x^I, \tag{2.6}$$

where a_I belongs to $\mathbb{F}_2^m$ (maybe we should write

$$F(x) = \sum_{I \subseteq \{1, \ldots, n\}} \left(\prod_{i \in I} x_i \right) a_I = \sum_{I \subseteq \{1, \ldots, n\}} x^I a_I,$$

since $\prod_{i \in I} x_i$ is a scalar and a_I is a vector). According to our convention on the notation for additions, we used $\sum$ to denote the sum in $\mathbb{F}_2^m$, but recall that, coordinate by coordinate, this sum is a $\bigoplus$.

This polynomial is called the *algebraic normal form* (ANF) of F. According to Relation (2.3), we have $F(x) = \sum_{I \subseteq supp(x)} a_I$, and according to Relation (2.4), we have $a_I = \sum_{x \in \mathbb{F}_2^n; \, supp(x) \subseteq I} F(x)$ (these sums being calculated in $\mathbb{F}_2^m$).

Remark. An (n, m)-function $F(x)$ being given by its ANF and an (m, r)-function $G(y)$ being given by the ANF of the indicator $1_{\mathcal{G}_G}(y, z)$ of its *graph* $\mathcal{G}_G = \{(y, G(y)); \, y \in \mathbb{F}_2^m\}$, the ANF of the indicator $1_{\mathcal{G}_{G \circ F}}(x, z)$ of the graph of the *composite function* $G \circ F$ equals $1_{\mathcal{G}_G}(F(x), z)$, where we denote a function and its ANF the same way.

If we are given the ANF of $1_{\mathcal{G}_F}$ rather than that of $F(x)$, then as observed in [254], $1_{\mathcal{G}_{G \circ F}}(x, z)$ can be obtained by the elimination of y from the two equations $1_{\mathcal{G}_F}(x, y) = 1$ and $1_{\mathcal{G}_G}(y, z) = 1$. Since for every x, there is exactly one y such that $1_{\mathcal{G}_F}(x, y) = 1$, then $1_{\mathcal{G}_{G \circ F}}(x, z)$ equals $\sum_{y \in \mathbb{F}_2^m} 1_{\mathcal{G}_F}(x, y) 1_{\mathcal{G}_G}(y, z) = \bigoplus_{y \in \mathbb{F}_2^m} 1_{\mathcal{G}_F}(x, y) 1_{\mathcal{G}_G}(y, z)$. This formula can be easily iterated (with more than two functions), and we shall see that it gives information that is more exploitable than $1_{\mathcal{G}_{G \circ F}}(x, z) = 1_{\mathcal{G}_G}(F(x), z)$ because it deals with a multiplication instead of a composition. □

Algebraic degree of a vectorial function

The *algebraic degree* of an (n,m)-function is by definition the global degree of its ANF: $d_{alg}(F) = \max\{|I|; I \subseteq \{1,\ldots,n\}, a_I \neq 0_m\}$. It therefore equals the maximal algebraic degree of the coordinate functions of F. It also equals the maximal algebraic degree of the *component functions* (in brief, components) of F, that is, the nonzero linear combinations of the coordinate functions, *i.e.*, the functions of the form $v \cdot F$, where $v \in \mathbb{F}_2^m \setminus \{0_m\}$ and "$\cdot$" is an inner product in $\mathbb{F}_2^m$. The algebraic degree of vectorial functions is an affine invariant (that is, its value does not change when we compose F, on the right or on the left, by an affine automorphism). For functions of algebraic degree strictly larger than 1, it is an *EA invariant*, but it is not a CCZ invariant. In particular, the algebraic degrees of a permutation and its compositional inverse are in general not equal. It is, however, observed in [106] that if an (n,n)-permutation F has algebraic degree $n-1$ (the maximum for a permutation), then its inverse has also algebraic degree $n-1$. In fact, this is a direct consequence of Relation (2.5) by considering the terms $x^I y^J$ where $|I| = |J| = n-1$. Note that, according to Proposition 2 on the *graph*s of (n,m)-functions, writing $1_{\mathcal{G}_F}(x,y)$ in the form $\bigoplus_{J \subseteq \{1,\ldots,m\}} \varphi_J(x) y^J$, we have that $d_{alg}(F) = \max_{|J|=m-1} d_{alg}(\varphi_J(x))$ and

$$d_{alg}(1_{\mathcal{G}_F}) = \max_{J \subseteq \{1,\ldots,m\}} \left(d_{alg} \left(\prod_{j \in \{1,\ldots,m\} \setminus J} (f_j \oplus 1) \right) + |J| \right) \tag{2.7}$$

$$\geq \max(m, m-1+d_{alg}(F)). \tag{2.8}$$

If the algebraic degree of $1_{\mathcal{G}_F}$ is low (*i.e.*, close to m), then all the products of a few coordinate functions of F have low algebraic degree.

Proposition 2 and the relation $1_{\mathcal{G}_{G \circ F}}(x,z) = \bigoplus_{y \in \mathbb{F}_2^m} 1_{\mathcal{G}_F}(x,y) 1_{\mathcal{G}_G}(y,z)$ lead in [254] to the bounds

$$d_{alg}(G \circ F) \leq d_{alg}(1_{\mathcal{G}_F}) + d_{alg}(G) - m \quad \text{and} \tag{2.9}$$

$$d_{alg}(H \circ G \circ F) \leq d_{alg}\left(1_{\mathcal{G}_F}\right) + d_{alg}\left(1_{\mathcal{G}_G}\right) + d_{alg}(H) - m - r, \tag{2.10}$$

for every (n,m)-function F, (m,r)-function G and (r,s)-function H.

If F is a permutation, then, as observed in [253, 254], $1_{\mathcal{G}_{G \circ F}}(x,z)$ is equal to $\bigoplus_{y \in \mathbb{F}_2^m} 1_{\mathcal{G}_{F^{-1}}}(y,x) 1_{\mathcal{G}_G}(y,z)$, that is, according to Proposition 2, page 35, and Proposition 3, page 36:

$$1_{\mathcal{G}_{G \circ F}}(x,z) = \bigoplus_{\substack{I \subseteq \{1,\ldots,n\} \\ K \subseteq \{1,\ldots,r\}}} x^I z^K \left(\bigoplus_{y \in \mathbb{F}_2^m} \left[\prod_{i \in I^c} (f_i'(y) \oplus 1) \prod_{k \in K^c} (g_k(y) \oplus 1) \right] \right)$$

$$= \bigoplus_{\substack{I \subseteq \{1,\ldots,n\}, K \subseteq \{1,\ldots,r\}; \\ d_{alg}\left(\prod_{i \in I^c} (f_i' \oplus 1) \prod_{k \in K^c} (g_k \oplus 1)\right)=n}} x^I z^K, \tag{2.11}$$

where $I^c = \{1,\ldots,n\} \setminus I$, $K^c = \{1,\ldots,r\} \setminus K$ and the f_i's are the coordinate functions of F^{-1} and the g_ks are those of G. Then, still according to Proposition 2 and as proved in [254], we have directly from (2.11) that

$$d_{alg}(G \circ F) = \max_{k \in \{1,\ldots,r\}} \left(\max \left\{ |I|; d_{alg}\left((g_k \oplus 1) \prod_{i \in I^c} (f_i' \oplus 1) \right) = n \right\} \right). \quad (2.12)$$

Note that, according to Relation (2.5), page 35, and as observed by [106] (but in a more complex way), for every every integers k, l, the maximal algebraic degree of the product of at most k coordinate functions[15] of F, that we shall denote by $d_{alg}^{(k)}(F)$, satisfies: $d_{alg}^{(k)}(F) < n - l \Longleftrightarrow d_{alg}^{(l)}(F^{-1}) < n - k$.

The case of functions over $\mathbb{F}_{2^n}$ is also studied in [254].

Another notion of degree is also relevant to cryptography (and is also affine invariant): the minimum algebraic degree of all the component functions[16] of F, often called the *minimum degree*:

$$d_{min}(F) = \min\{d_{alg}(v \cdot F) : 0_m \neq v \in \mathbb{F}_2^m\} \leqslant d_{alg}(F).$$

2.2.2 Univariate and trace representations

A second kind of representation plays an important role in sequence theory, and is also used for defining and studying Boolean functions. For instance, it allows us to define the S-box of the AES and leads to the construction of the Kerdock codes (see Section 6.1.22). Recall that, for every n, there exists a (unique up to isomorphism) field $\mathbb{F}_{2^n}$ (also denoted by $GF(2^n)$ in some papers) of order 2^n; see [775, 890]. For making this book self-contained, we recall in Appendix (Chapter 14, page 480) the basics on finite fields, permutation polynomials and equations over finite fields. The vector space $\mathbb{F}_2^n$ can be endowed with the structure of this field $\mathbb{F}_{2^n}$ (by construction and because $\mathbb{F}_{2^n}$ has the structure of an n-dimensional $\mathbb{F}_2$-vector space; if we choose an $\mathbb{F}_2$-basis $(\alpha_1, \ldots, \alpha_n)$ of this vector space, then every element $x \in \mathbb{F}_2^n$ can be identified with $x_1 \alpha_1 + \cdots + x_n \alpha_n \in \mathbb{F}_{2^n}$). We shall still denote by x this element of the field.

Univariate representation of (n,n)-functions

Every mapping from $\mathbb{F}_{2^n}$ into $\mathbb{F}_{2^n}$ (and hence any (n, n)-function[17]) admits a (unique) representation as a polynomial over $\mathbb{F}_{2^n}$ in one variable and of (univariate) degree at most $2^n - 1$:

$$F(x) = \sum_{i=0}^{2^n-1} \delta_i x^i; \quad \delta_i \in \mathbb{F}_{2^n}. \quad (2.13)$$

Indeed, the function mapping every such polynomial to the corresponding polynomial function from $\mathbb{F}_{2^n}$ to $\mathbb{F}_{2^n}$ is $\mathbb{F}_{2^n}$-linear and has trivial kernel since a nonzero polynomial cannot have a number of distinct zeros larger than its degree. Since the dimensions of the $\mathbb{F}_{2^n}$-vector space of such polynomials and of the $\mathbb{F}_{2^n}$-vector space of all (n, n)-functions both equal 2^n, this function is a bijection.

---

[15] The algebraic degree of the product of k coordinate functions equals n if $k = n$ and is strictly smaller if $k < n$, as can be easily shown and is characteristic of permutations.

[16] Not just the coordinate functions; the notion would then not be affine invariant.

[17] Note that if m divides n, then any function from $\mathbb{F}_{2^n}$ into $\mathbb{F}_{2^m}$ is a function from $\mathbb{F}_{2^n}$ into $\mathbb{F}_{2^n}$; hence we also cover such (n, m)-functions here. When m does not divide n, we can view the elements of $\mathbb{F}_2^m$ as elements of $\mathbb{F}_2^m \times \{0_{n-m}\} \subset \mathbb{F}_2^n$ and represent them as elements of $\mathbb{F}_{2^n}$, but this is a little more artificial.

Definition 9 *We call* univariate representation *of an (n, n)-function F the unique polynomial $\sum_{i=0}^{2^n-1} \delta_i X^i$ satisfying (2.13).*

We shall also sometimes write that F is in *univariate form*.

Remark. $\mathbb{F}_{2^n}$ is the set of solutions of equation $x^{2^n} + x = 0$. We can then better view the univariate representation of (n, n)-functions as lying in the quotient ring $\mathbb{F}_{2^n}[X]/(X^{2^n} + X)$, each element of this ring being then represented as the remainder in the division by $X^{2^n} + X$. □

Note that the univariate representation of any (n, n)-function can be obtained by the Lagrange interpolation method or as follows: since every element x in $\mathbb{F}_{2^n}^*$ satisfies $x^{2^n-1} = 1$, the function $x^{2^n-1} + 1$ equals the Dirac (or Kronecker) symbol (*i.e.*, the indicator of $\{0\}$), the polynomial $\sum_{a \in \mathbb{F}_{2^n}} F(a)((X + a)^{2^n-1} + 1)$ is the univariate representation of F. Note in particular that the coefficient of x^{2^n-1} in this univariate representation equals the sum of all values $F(a)$. A way of obtaining more directly the univariate representation is by using the so-called Mattson–Solomon polynomial that we shall see at page 44.

Univariate representation of Boolean functions

Any Boolean function on $\mathbb{F}_{2^n}$ is a particular case of a vectorial function from $\mathbb{F}_{2^n}$ to $\mathbb{F}_{2^n}$ (since $\mathbb{F}_2$ is a subfield of $\mathbb{F}_{2^n}$) and has then a (unique) univariate representation. Recall that the mapping $x \mapsto x^2$ is a field automorphism called the *Frobenius automorphism*. The polynomial $\sum_{i=0}^{2^n-1} \delta_i X^i$, $\delta_i \in \mathbb{F}_{2^n}$, is the univariate representation of a Boolean function if and only if the functions $\left(\sum_{i=0}^{2^n-1} \delta_i x^i\right)^2$ and $\sum_{i=0}^{2^n-1} \delta_i x^i$ take the same value at every $x \in \mathbb{F}_{2^n}$, that is, if and only if $\sum_{i=0}^{2^n-1} \delta_i^2 X^{2i} \equiv \sum_{i=0}^{2^n-1} \delta_i X^i \, [\text{mod } X^{2^n} + X]$, that is, $\delta_0, \delta_{2^n-1} \in \mathbb{F}_2$ and, for every $i = 1, \ldots, 2^n - 2$, $\delta_{2i} = \delta_i^2$, where the index $2i$ is taken mod $2^n - 1$.

Absolute trace representation of Boolean functions and vectorial functions

The *absolute trace function* on $\mathbb{F}_{2^n}$, $tr_n(x) = x + x^2 + x^{2^2} + \cdots + x^{2^{n-1}}$, is addressed at page 489 (it is $\mathbb{F}_2$-linear, satisfies $(tr_n(x))^2 = tr_n(x^2) = tr_n(x)$, and is valued in $\mathbb{F}_2$). The function $(x, y) \mapsto tr_n(xy)$ is an inner product in $\mathbb{F}_{2^n}$ (recall that this means it is symmetric and, for every $y \neq 0$, the function $x \to tr_n(xy)$ is a nonzero linear form over $\mathbb{F}_{2^n}$). Every Boolean function can be written in the form $f(x) = tr_n(F(x))$, where F is a mapping from $\mathbb{F}_{2^n}$ into $\mathbb{F}_{2^n}$ (an example of such mapping F is defined by $F(x) = \lambda f(x)$, where $tr_n(\lambda) = 1$ and $f(x)$ is in univariate representation). Thus, every n-variable Boolean function f can be also represented in the form

$$f(x) = tr_n\left(\sum_{i=0}^{2^n-1} \beta_i x^i\right), \tag{2.14}$$

where $\beta_i \in \mathbb{F}_{2^n}$. Note that, thanks to the fact that tr_n is $\mathbb{F}_2$-linear and $tr_n(x^2) = tr_n(x)$ for every $x \in \mathbb{F}_{2^n}$, each term $\beta_i x^i$ in (2.14) can be replaced by its 2^jth power, for every j and without changing the value of the expression. We can then transform (2.14) into an expression $tr_n \left(\sum_{i \in I} \gamma_i x^i \right)$ where I contains at most one element of each *cyclotomic class* $\left\{ i \times 2^j \left[\bmod (2^n - 1) \right]; j \in \mathbb{N} \right\}$ of 2 modulo $2^n - 1$ (but this still does not make the representation unique).

More generally, if m is a divisor of n, then any (n, m)-function F admits a univariate polynomial representation in the form:

$$F(x) = tr_m^n \left(\sum_{j=0}^{2^n - 1} \delta_j x^j \right), \tag{2.15}$$

where $tr_m^n(x) = x + x^{2^m} + x^{2^{2m}} + x^{2^{3m}} + \cdots + x^{2^{n-m}}$ is the trace function from $\mathbb{F}_{2^n}$ to $\mathbb{F}_{2^m}$. Indeed, there exists a function G from $\mathbb{F}_{2^n}$ to $\mathbb{F}_{2^n}$ such that F equals $tr_m^n \circ G$ (for instance, $G(x) = \lambda F(x)$, where $tr_m^n(\lambda) = 1$, since tr_m^n is a $\mathbb{F}_{2^m}$-linear form). But there is no uniqueness of G in this representation as well.

Definition 10 *We shall call the representation (2.14), resp. (2.15), an* absolute trace representation *of Boolean function f (resp. of (n, m)-function F).*

Its use is convenient, with the drawback of nonuniqueness, which makes it more difficult to determine when two functions are equal.

Subfield trace representation of Boolean functions

We come back to the univariate representation $\sum_{i=0}^{2^n - 1} \delta_i X^i$. We have seen that for any Boolean function, we have $\delta_0, \delta_{2^n - 1} \in \mathbb{F}_2$, and for every $i = 1, \ldots, 2^n - 2$, $\delta_{2i} = \delta_i^2$, where the index $2i$ is taken modulo $2^n - 1$. Gathering all the elements of a same cyclotomic class of 2 modulo $2^n - 1$ allows the univariate representation of f in the following form:

$$f(x) = \sum_{j \in \Gamma(n)} tr_{n_j} (\beta_j x^j) + \beta_{2^n - 1} x^{2^n - 1}, \text{ with } \begin{cases} \forall j \in \Gamma(n), \beta_j \in \mathbb{F}_{2^{n_j}}, \\ \beta_{2^n - 1} \in \mathbb{F}_2 \end{cases} \tag{2.16}$$

where $\Gamma(n)$ is a set of representatives of the cyclotomic classes of 2 modulo $2^n - 1$ (the most usual choice of representative is the smallest element in the cyclotomic class, called the *coset leader* of the class) and n_j is the size of the cyclotomic class containing j. It is easily seen that n_j divides n and that $\beta_j \in \mathbb{F}_{2^{n_j}}$ because $\beta_j^{2^{n_j}} = \beta_j$. We also have that the jth power of every $x \in \mathbb{F}_{2^n}$ belongs to $\mathbb{F}_{2^{n_j}}$ because $j 2^{n_j} \equiv j \ [\bmod 2^n - 1]$ implies $(x^j)^{2^{n_j}} = x^j$. Hence, tr_{n_j} takes as an argument an element of $\mathbb{F}_{2^{n_j}}$, as it should. This representation allows uniqueness.

Definition 11 *We call (2.16) the* subfield trace representation *of function f.*

We shall also sometimes write more simply that f is in *trace form*.

Calculating the univariate and subfield trace representations of a Boolean function from its truth table

Denoting by α a *primitive element* of the field $\mathbb{F}_{2^n}$ (recall that this means that $\mathbb{F}_{2^n} = \{0, 1, \alpha, \alpha^2, \ldots, \alpha^{2^n-2}\}$), the *Mattson–Solomon polynomial*[18] of the vector $(f(1), f(\alpha), f(\alpha^2), \ldots, f(\alpha^{2^n-2}))$ is the polynomial [809, page 239]:

$$A(x) = \sum_{j=1}^{2^n-1} A_j x^{2^n-1-j} = \sum_{j=0}^{2^n-2} A_{2^n-1-j} x^j \tag{2.17}$$

with the following:

$$A_j = \sum_{k=0}^{2^n-2} f(\alpha^k) \alpha^{kj}. \tag{2.18}$$

Note that $A_j = a(\alpha^j)$, where $a(x) = \sum_{k=0}^{2^n-2} f(\alpha^k) x^k$.

We have, for every $0 \le i \le 2^n - 2$:

$$A(\alpha^i) = \sum_{j=1}^{2^n-1} A_j \alpha^{-ij} = \sum_{j=1}^{2^n-1} \sum_{k=0}^{2^n-2} f(\alpha^k) \alpha^{(k-i)j} = f(\alpha^i) \tag{2.19}$$

(since, if $1 \le k \ne i \le 2^n - 2$, then $\displaystyle\sum_{j=1}^{2^n-1} \alpha^{(k-i)j} = \sum_{j=0}^{2^n-2} \alpha^{(k-i)j} = \frac{\alpha^{(k-i)(2^n-1)} + 1}{\alpha^{k-i} + 1} = 0$,

and if $k - i = 0$, then $\sum_{j=1}^{2^n-1} \alpha^{(k-i)j} = 1$). Note that, with the usual convention $0^0 = 1$, we have $A(0) = A_{2^n-1}$. Hence, if $f(0) = A_{2^n-1} = \sum_{k=0}^{2^n-2} f(\alpha^k)$, that is, if f has even Hamming weight (*i.e.*, algebraic degree strictly less than n), the Mattson–Solomon polynomial $A(x)$ equals the univariate representation of $f(x)$. Otherwise, we have $f(x) = A(x) + 1 + x^{2^n-1}$, since $1 + x^{2^n-1}$ equals the Dirac (or Kronecker) function at 0 (*i.e.*, takes value 1 at 0 and 0 at every nonzero element of $\mathbb{F}_{2^n}$). This provides the following univariate representation:

$$f(x) = f(0) + \sum_{j=1}^{2^n-2} A_j x^{2^n-1-j} + (w_H(f) [\text{mod } 2]) x^{2^n-1}$$

and the subfield trace representation:

$$f(x) = \sum_{j \in \Gamma(n)} tr_{n_j} (A_{2^n-1-j} x^j) + (w_H(f) [\text{mod } 2])(1 + x^{2^n-1}).$$

Remark. For any Boolean function f, we have in (2.18) that $A_{2j} = A_j^2$ and this allows us to gather the terms corresponding to a same cyclotomic class. This provides the subfield trace representation of f. We can also, thanks to a change of the coefficients, write

---

[18] The Mattson–Solomon transform is a discrete Fourier transform (over $\mathbb{F}_{2^n}$); other discrete Fourier transforms exist (*e.g.*, over the complex field, as in [1110]).

$$f(\alpha^j) = \sum_{j=1}^{2^n-2} tr_n(a_j \alpha^{-ij}) \tag{2.20}$$

and obtain the absolute trace representation of f. This shows what was asserted at the end of Subsection 1.2.4. $\qquad\square$

Remark on RS codes. Relations (2.17), (2.18), and (2.19) are valid for every function f from $\mathbb{F}_{2^n}^*$ to $\mathbb{F}_{2^n}$. In this framework, $A(x)$, which according to Relation (2.17) is the polynomial representation (see page 12) of codeword $(A_{2^n-1}, A_{2^n-2}, \ldots, A_1)$, belongs to the *Reed–Solomon code* (see page 13) over $\mathbb{F}_{2^n}$ of length $2^n - 1$ and zeros $\alpha^{2^n-\delta}, \alpha^{2^n-\delta+1}, \ldots, \alpha^{2^n-2}$ (whose designed distance is δ) if and only if $a(x)$ has degree at most $2^n - 1 - \delta$ (according to Relation (2.19)), and the codeword $(A_{2^n-1}, A_{2^n-2}, \ldots, A_1)$ is an evaluation vector of this polynomial over $\mathbb{F}_{2^n}^*$, according to Relation (2.18). The BCH bound in this case corresponds to the fact that a nonzero polynomial of degree at most $2^n - 1 - \delta$ has at most $2^n - 1 - \delta$ zeros in $\mathbb{F}_{2^n}$ and therefore has at least δ nonzeros in $\mathbb{F}_{2^n}^*$. This generalizes to RS codes over $\mathbb{F}_q$. $\qquad\square$

Calculating the ANF of a Boolean function or a vectorial function from its univariate representation

We express x in the form $\sum_{i=1}^n x_i \alpha_i$, where $(\alpha_1, \ldots, \alpha_n)$ is a basis of the $\mathbb{F}_2$-vector space $\mathbb{F}_{2^n}$. Recall that, for every $j \in \mathbb{Z}/(2^n - 1)\mathbb{Z}$, the *binary expansion* of j has the form $\sum_{s \in E} 2^s$, where $E \subseteq \{0, 1, \ldots, n - 1\}$. The size of E is often called the *2-weight* of j and written $w_2(j)$. We write more conveniently the binary expansion of j in the form: $\sum_{s=0}^{n-1} j_s 2^s$, $j_s \in \{0, 1\}$. We have then the following:

$$F(x) = \sum_{j=0}^{2^n-1} \delta_j \left(\sum_{i=1}^n x_i \alpha_i \right)^j$$

$$= \sum_{j=0}^{2^n-1} \delta_j \left(\sum_{i=1}^n x_i \alpha_i \right)^{\sum_{s=0}^{n-1} j_s 2^s}$$

$$= \sum_{j=0}^{2^n-1} \delta_j \prod_{s=0}^{n-1} \left(\sum_{i=1}^n x_i \alpha_i^{2^s} \right)^{j_s}.$$

Expanding these last products and simplifying gives the ANF of F.

Proposition 6 *Any Boolean function (resp. any (n, n)-function) whose univariate representation equals (2.13) has algebraic degree $\max_{j=0,\ldots,2^n-1; \delta_j \neq 0} w_2(j)$.*

Proof According to the above equalities, the algebraic degree is bounded above by this number, and it cannot be strictly smaller, because the dimension of the $\mathbb{F}_2$-vector space (resp. the $\mathbb{F}_{2^n}$-vector space) of Boolean n-variable functions (resp. of (n, n)-functions) of algebraic degree at most d equals $\sum_{i=0}^d \binom{n}{i}$, which is also the dimension of the vector space of those polynomials $\sum_{j=0}^{2^n-1} \delta_j x^j$ such that $\delta_0, \delta_{2^n-1} \in \mathbb{F}_2$, $\delta_j \in \mathbb{F}_{2^n}$, $\delta_{2j} = \delta_j^2 \in \mathbb{F}_{2^n}$ for every $j = 1, \ldots, 2^n - 2$ and $\max_{j=0,\ldots,2^n-1; \delta_j \neq 0} w_2(j) \leq d$ (resp. of those polynomials $\sum_{j=0}^{2^n-1} \delta_j x^j$ such that $\delta_j \in \mathbb{F}_{2^n}$ for every $j = 0, \ldots, 2^n - 1$ and $\max_{j=0,\ldots,2^n-1; \delta_j \neq 0} w_2(j) \leq d$). $\qquad\square$

In particular, an (n, n)-function F is $\mathbb{F}_2$-linear (resp. affine) if and only if $F(x)$ is a *linearized polynomial* over $\mathbb{F}_{2^n}$: $F(x) = \sum_{j=0}^{n-1} \beta_j x^{2^j}; x, \beta_j \in \mathbb{F}_{2^n}$ (resp. a linearized polynomial plus a constant).

We have also the following proposition:

Proposition 7 *[209] Let a be any element of $\mathbb{F}_{2^n}$ and k any integer [mod $2^n - 1$]. If $f(x) = tr_n(ax^k)$ is not the null function, then it has algebraic degree $w_2(k)$.*

Proof Let n_k be again the size of the cyclotomic class containing k. Then the univariate representation of $f(x)$ equals

$$\left(a + a^{2^{n_k}} + a^{2^{2n_k}} + \cdots + a^{2^{n-n_k}} \right) x^k + \left(a + a^{2^{n_k}} + a^{2^{2n_k}} + \cdots + a^{2^{n-n_k}} \right)^2 x^{2k}$$

$$+ \cdots + \left(a + a^{2^{n_k}} + a^{2^{2n_k}} + \cdots + a^{2^{n-n_k}} \right)^{2^{n_k-1}} x^{2^{n_k-1}k}.$$

All the exponents of x have 2-weight $w_2(k)$ and their coefficients are nonzero if and only if f is not null. $\qquad\square$

Remark. An alternative (more complex but enlightening) way of showing Proposition 7 is also given in [209] as follows: let $r = w_2(k)$; we consider the r-linear function ϕ over the field $\mathbb{F}_{2^n}$ whose value at $(x_1, \ldots, x_r) \in (\mathbb{F}_{2^n})^r$ equals the sum of the images by f of all the 2^r possible linear combinations of the x_js. Then $\phi(x_1, \ldots, x_r)$ equals the sum, for all bijective mappings σ from $\{1, \ldots, r\}$ onto E (where $k = \sum_{s \in E} 2^s$) of $tr_n(a \prod_{j=1}^r x_j^{2^{\sigma(j)}})$. Proving that f has degree r is equivalent to proving that ϕ is not null, and it can be shown that if ϕ is null, then f is null. $\qquad\square$

Remark. For calculating the univariate representation from the ANF, we can only propose to calculate the truth table (resp. the LUT) by the fast Möbius transform and then to apply the method of page 44. Note, however, that the coefficient of $\prod_{i=1}^n x_i$ in the ANF of F is directly linked to the coefficient of x^{2^n-1} in its univariate representation since these two coefficients are equal to each other (up to the correspondence between $\mathbb{F}_2^n$ and $\mathbb{F}_{2^n}$) because they are both equal to the sum of all values $F(x)$. $\qquad\square$

To complete this subsection, we give a corollary of Proposition 6 (which for $d = n - 2$, $n - 1$ gives back the two last properties in Proposition 3, page 36):

Corollary 2 *A vectorial function $F : \mathbb{F}_{2^n} \mapsto \mathbb{F}_{2^n}$ has an algebraic degree at most d if and only if, for every nonnegative integer k of 2-weight at most $n - d - 1$, we have the following:*

$$\sum_{x \in \mathbb{F}_{2^n}} x^k F(x) = 0.$$

The condition is necessary by applying to function $x^k F(x)$ the fact that, for every (n, n)-function G of algebraic degree at most $n-1$, we have $\sum_{x \in \mathbb{F}_{2^n}} G(x) = 0$, and since, for every nonnegative integer i, we have $w_2(k + i) \leq w_2(k) + w_2(i)$. The condition is also sufficient since, for every (n, n)-function G of algebraic degree n, we have $\sum_{x \in \mathbb{F}_{2^n}} G(x) \neq 0$, and since, for every i of 2-weight strictly larger than d, there exists k of 2-weight at most $n-d-1$ such that $w_2(k + i) = n$; if i is taken with the highest possible 2-weight in the univariate representation of F, we can manage that $\sum_{x \in \mathbb{F}_{2^n}} x^{k+j} = 0$ for other $j \neq i$ such that x^j has nonzero coefficient in the univariate representation.

See more on the algebraic degree, in particular for composite functions, in ANF or univariate representations, in [253, 254].

2.2.3 Bivariate representation of functions with an even number of input bits

The *bivariate representation* of n-variable Boolean functions f and of (n, m)-functions F where n is even and $m = \frac{n}{2}$ is as follows: we identify $\mathbb{F}_2^n$ with $\mathbb{F}_{2^m} \times \mathbb{F}_{2^m}$ and we consider then the input to F as an ordered pair (x, y) of elements of $\mathbb{F}_{2^m}$. There exists a unique bivariate polynomial $\sum_{0 \leq i, j \leq 2^m - 1} a_{i,j} x^i y^j$ over $\mathbb{F}_{2^m}$ such that the given function is the bivariate polynomial function over $\mathbb{F}_{2^m}$ associated to it. Then the algebraic degree of the function equals $\max_{(i,j) \,|\, a_{i,j} \neq 0} (w_2(i) + w_2(j))$, and in the case of a Boolean function, the bivariate representation can be written in the form $f(x, y) = tr_m(P(x, y))$, where $P(x, y)$ is some polynomial in two variables over $\mathbb{F}_{2^m}$. This latter absolute trace representation is not unique. A unique representation uses relative traces; see [245, section 2.4.2].

Moving from bivariate to univariate representation and vice versa

Any bivariate Boolean or vectorial function $F(x, y)$ over $\mathbb{F}_{2^{n/2}}$ and valued in $\mathbb{F}_{2^{n/2}}$ can be represented as a function of $X \in \mathbb{F}_{2^n}$, which we can denote by $F(X)$ by abuse of notation, by posing $x = tr_{n/2}^n(aX) = aX + (aX)^{2^{n/2}}$ and $y = tr_{n/2}^n(bX) = bX + (bX)^{2^{n/2}}$ for some $\mathbb{F}_2^{n/2}$-linearly independent elements $a, b \in \mathbb{F}_{2^n}$ (constituting a basis of $\mathbb{F}_{2^n}$ over $\mathbb{F}_{2^{n/2}}$; choosing another basis would result in a linearly equivalent function). The obtained expression can be expressed by means of tr_n by using that, for every $\lambda \in \mathbb{F}_{2^{n/2}}$, we have $tr_{n/2}(\lambda) = tr_n(a\lambda)$ where $tr_{n/2}^n(a) = a + a^{2^{n/2}} = 1$. Conversely, given a Boolean or vectorial function $F(X)$ over $\mathbb{F}_{2^n}$ valued in $\mathbb{F}_{2^{n/2}}$ in univariate representation and a basis (u, v) of $\mathbb{F}_{2^n}$ over $\mathbb{F}_{2^{n/2}}$, we get its bivariate representation by decomposing X over this basis into $X = ux + vy$. The obtained expression can be expressed by means of $tr_{n/2}$ by using that, for every $u \in \mathbb{F}_{2^n}$, we have $tr_n(u) = tr_{n/2}(tr_{n/2}^n(u)) = tr_{n/2}(u + u^{2^{n/2}})$.

2.2.4 Representation over the reals (numerical normal form)

This version over $\mathbb{R}$ (in fact, over $\mathbb{Z}$, for Boolean and integer-valued functions over $\mathbb{F}_2^n$) of the algebraic normal form has proved itself useful for characterizing several cryptographic criteria [220, 292, 293] (see Chapters 6 and 7). When studied in these papers, it was already known in other domains of Boolean functions (see *e.g.*, [886, 905]), but rather informally studied.

Definition 12 *[292] We call* numerical normal form *(NNF) the representation of pseudo-Boolean functions (i.e., real-valued functions over $\mathbb{F}_2^n$) in the quotient ring*

$\mathbb{R}[x_1, \ldots, x_n]/(x_1^2 - x_1, \ldots, x_n^2 - x_n)$ *(or* $\mathbb{Z}[x_1, \ldots, x_n]/(x_1^2 - x_1, \ldots, x_n^2 - x_n)$ *for integer-valued functions).*

The existence of this representation for every pseudo-Boolean function can be shown with the same arguments as for the ANFs of Boolean functions (writing $1 - x_i$ instead of $1 \oplus x_i$). In the case of a Boolean function, it can also be directly deduced from the existence of the ANF, since, denoting $x^I = \prod_{i \in I} x_i$, we have the following:

$$f(x) = \bigoplus_{I \subseteq \{1, \ldots, n\}} a_I \, x^I \iff (-1)^{f(x)} = \prod_{I \subseteq \{1, \ldots, n\}} (-1)^{a_I \, x^I}$$

$$\iff 1 - 2 \, f(x) = \prod_{I \subseteq \{1, \ldots, n\}} (1 - 2 \, a_I \, x^I) \qquad (2.21)$$

and expanding (2.21) gives the NNF of $f(x)$.

The uniqueness of the NNF of any pseudo-Boolean function is deduced from its existence by the usual argument: the linear mapping from every element of the 2^n-dimensional $\mathbb{R}$-vector space $\mathbb{R}[x_1, \ldots, x_n]/(x_1^2 - x_1, \ldots, x_n^2 - x_n)$ to the corresponding pseudo-Boolean function on $\mathbb{F}_2^n$ being surjective, it is therefore one to one (the $\mathbb{R}$-vector space of pseudo-Boolean functions on $\mathbb{F}_2^n$ having also dimension 2^n).

Remark. The NNF does not contain properly speaking more information on a Boolean function than its ANF, since both are unique representations and contain then full information on the function. But the NNF contains more exploitable information in the sense that the coefficients of the ANF contain individually little information on the function, while we shall see that those of the NNF contain more.   □

Definition 13 *[292] We call the degree of the NNF of a Boolean or pseudo-Boolean function f its* numerical degree *and denote it by $d_{num}(f)$.*

Since the ANF of a Boolean function is the mod 2 version of its NNF, the numerical degree is always bounded below by the algebraic degree.

It is shown in [905] that, if a Boolean function f has no ineffective variable (*i.e.*, if it actually depends on each of its variables), then the numerical degree of f is larger than or equal to $\log_2 n - \mathcal{O}(\log_2 \log_2 n)$ (we shall give a proof of this bound – in fact, of a slightly more precise and stronger bound – in Proposition 15, page 67).

The numerical degree is *permutation invariant* but is not affine invariant. Nevertheless, the NNF leads to an affine invariant (see a proof of this fact in [293]) which is more discriminant than the algebraic degree:

Definition 14 *[293] Let f be a Boolean function on $\mathbb{F}_2^n$. We call the* generalized degree *of f the sequence $(d_i)_{i \geq 1}$ defined as follows:*
For every $i \geq 1$, d_i is the smallest integer $d > d_{i-1}$ (if $i > 1$) such that, for every multiindex I of a size strictly larger than d, the coefficient λ_I of x^I in the NNF of f is a multiple of 2^i.

Example The generalized degree of any nonzero affine function is the sequence of all positive integers.

Similarly to the case of the ANF, a (pseudo-) Boolean function $f(x) = \sum_{I \subseteq \{1,\ldots,n\}} \lambda_I x^I$ takes the following value:

$$f(x) = \sum_{I \subseteq supp(x)} \lambda_I. \tag{2.22}$$

But, contrary to what we observed for the ANF, the reverse formula is not identical to the direct formula:

Proposition 8 *[292] Let f be a pseudo-Boolean function on $\mathbb{F}_2^n$ and let its NNF be $\sum_{I \subseteq \{1,\ldots,n\}} \lambda_I x^I$. Then:*

$$\forall I \subseteq \{1,\ldots,n\}, \lambda_I = (-1)^{|I|} \sum_{x \in \mathbb{F}_2^n;\, supp(x) \subseteq I} (-1)^{w_H(x)} f(x). \tag{2.23}$$

In other words, function f and its NNF are related through the *Möbius transform* and its inverse (for which there exist algorithms similar to the fast binary Möbius transform).

Proof Let us denote the number $(-1)^{|I|} \sum_{x \in \mathbb{F}_2^n;\, supp(x) \subseteq I} (-1)^{w_H(x)} f(x)$ by μ_I and consider the function $g(x) = \sum_{I \subseteq \{1,\ldots,n\}} \mu_I x^I$. We have

$$g(x) = \sum_{I \subseteq supp(x)} \mu_I = \sum_{I \subseteq supp(x)} \left((-1)^{|I|} \sum_{y \in \mathbb{F}_2^n;\, supp(y) \subseteq I} (-1)^{w_H(y)} f(y) \right)$$

and thus

$$g(x) = \sum_{y \in \mathbb{F}_2^n} (-1)^{w_H(y)} f(y) \left(\sum_{I \subseteq \{1,\ldots,n\};\, supp(y) \subseteq I \subseteq supp(x)} (-1)^{|I|} \right).$$

The sum $\sum_{I \subseteq \{1,\ldots,n\};\, supp(y) \subseteq I \subseteq supp(x)} (-1)^{|I|}$ is null if $supp(y) \not\subseteq supp(x)$. It is also null if $supp(y)$ is included in $supp(x)$, but different. Indeed, denoting $|I| - w_H(y)$ by i, it equals $\pm \sum_{i=0}^{w_H(x)-w_H(y)} \binom{w_H(x)-w_H(y)}{i}(-1)^i = \pm(1-1)^{w_H(x)-w_H(y)} = 0$. Hence, $g = f$, and, by uniqueness of the NNF, we have $\mu_I = \lambda_I$ for every I. $\qquad\square$

Remark. According to Relation (2.4), page 33, the coefficient of x^I in the ANF of a Boolean function f is equal to zero if and only if $supp(f) \cap \{x \in \mathbb{F}_2^n; supp(x) \subseteq I\}$ has even size. According to Relation (2.23), the coefficient of x^I in the NNF of a Boolean function f is equal to zero if and only if $supp(f) \cap \{x \in \mathbb{F}_2^n; supp(x) \subseteq I\} \cap \{x \in \mathbb{F}_2^n; w_H(x) \text{ even}\}$ has same size as $supp(f) \cap \{x \in \mathbb{F}_2^n; supp(x) \subseteq I\} \cap \{x \in \mathbb{F}_2^n; w_H(x) \text{ odd}\}$. $\qquad\square$

Remark. Denoting function $\bigoplus_{i=1}^{n} x_i$ by $\ell(x)$ and taking $I \neq \emptyset$, Relation (2.23) can be interpreted as $\lambda_I = (-1)^{|I|} \sum_{x \in \mathbb{F}_2^n;\ supp(x) \subseteq I} \left(\frac{(-1)^{\ell(x)}}{2} - \frac{(-1)^{f(x) \oplus \ell(x)}}{2} \right)$, and, since I is not empty, ℓ is linear and nonconstant over the vector space $E_I = \{x \in \mathbb{F}_2^n;\ supp(x) \subseteq I\}$, and we have $\sum_{x \in \mathbb{F}_2^n;\ supp(x) \subseteq I} \frac{(-1)^{\ell(x)}}{2} = 0$. After replacing $(-1)^{f(x) \oplus \ell(x)}$ by $1 - 2(f \oplus \ell)(x)$, this gives

$$\lambda_I = (-1)^{|I|} \left(w_H((f \oplus \ell)_{|E_I}) - 2^{|I|-1} \right),$$

where $(f \oplus \ell)_{|E_I}$ is the restriction of the Boolean function $f \oplus \ell$ to E_I. Applying this to the function $f \oplus \ell$ instead of f, we can see that the coefficients in the NNF of $f \oplus \ell$ give the Hamming weights of the restrictions of f to all vector subspaces of $\mathbb{F}_2^n$ of the form $\{x \in \mathbb{F}_2^n;\ supp(x) \subseteq I\}$.   □

We have seen that the ANF $f(x) = \bigoplus_{I \subseteq \{1,\dots,n\}} a_I x^I$ of any Boolean function can be deduced from its NNF $f(x) = \sum_{I \subseteq \{1,\dots,n\}} \lambda_I x^I$ by reducing it modulo 2, and that, conversely, the NNF can be deduced from the ANF. The formula is obtained by expanding (2.21) (and has been first obtained in [292] by a slightly more complex way):

$$\lambda_I = \sum_{k=1}^{2^n} (-2)^{k-1} \sum_{\substack{\{I_1,\dots,I_k\}\ | \\ I_1 \cup \dots \cup I_k = I}} a_{I_1} \dots a_{I_k}, \tag{2.24}$$

where "$\{I_1,\dots,I_k\};\ I_1 \cup \dots \cup I_k = I$" means that the multiindices $I_1,\dots,I_k$ are all distinct, in indefinite order, and that their union equals I.

For instance, for the Boolean function $f(x) = \bigoplus_{i=1}^{n} x_i$, we have $\lambda_I = (-2)^{|I|-1}$. This, applied to f_i in the place of x_i, implies that, for every Boolean functions $f_1,\dots,f_k$, we have the following:

$$\bigoplus_{i=1}^{k} f_i = \sum_{\emptyset \neq I \subseteq \{1,\dots,k\}} (-2)^{|I|-1} \prod_{i \in I} f_i. \tag{2.25}$$

Applying then Relation (2.25) to each $J \subseteq \{1,\dots,k\}$ instead of $\{1,\dots,k\}$ provides the system of the relations $\bigoplus_{i \in J} f_i = \sum_{\emptyset \neq I \subseteq J} (-2)^{|I|-1} \prod_{i \in I} f_i$ which can be inverted and gives the expression of the product of the f_i's by means of their linear combinations over $\mathbb{R}$:

$$\prod_{i=1}^{l} f_i = \frac{1}{2^{l-1}} \sum_{\emptyset \neq J \subseteq \{1,\dots,l\}} (-1)^{|J|-1} \left(\bigoplus_{i \in J} f_i \right). \tag{2.26}$$

Indeed, $\sum_{J;\ I \subseteq J \subseteq \{1,\dots,l\}} (-1)^{|J|-1}$ equals $(-1)^{l-1}$ if $I = \{1,\dots,l\}$ and is null otherwise, and this shows that the matrices of the two systems of relations are inverses of each other.

A polynomial $P(x) = \sum_{J \subseteq \{1,\dots,n\}} \lambda_J x^J$, with real coefficients, is the NNF of some Boolean function if and only if we have $P^2(x) = P(x)$, for every $x \in \mathbb{F}_2^n$ (which is equivalent to $P = P^2$ in $\mathbb{R}[x_1,\ldots,x_n]/(x_1^2 - x_1,\ldots,x_n^2 - x_n))$, or equivalently, denoting $supp(x)$ by I:

$$\forall I \subseteq \{1,\ldots,n\}, \quad \left(\sum_{J \subseteq I} \lambda_J\right)^2 = \sum_{J \subseteq I} \lambda_J. \tag{2.27}$$

Remark. Imagine that we want to generate a random Boolean function through its NNF (this can be useful, since we will see below that the main cryptographic criteria, on Boolean functions, can be characterized, in simple ways, through their NNFs). Assume that we have already chosen the values λ_J for every $J \subseteq I$ (where $I \subseteq \{1,\ldots,n\}$ is some multiindex) except for I itself. Let us denote the sum $\sum_{J \subseteq I \,|\, J \neq I} \lambda_J$ by μ. Relation (2.27) gives $(\lambda_I + \mu)^2 = \lambda_I + \mu$. This equation of degree 2 has two solutions. One solution corresponds to the choice $P(x) = 0$ (where $I = supp(x)$) and the other one corresponds to the choice $P(x) = 1$. □

Thus, verifying that a polynomial $P(x) = \sum_{I \subseteq \{1,\ldots,n\}} \lambda_I\, x^I$ with real coefficients represents a Boolean function can be done by checking 2^n relations. But it can also be done by verifying a simple condition on P and checking a single equation.

Proposition 9 *[293] Any polynomial $P \in \mathbb{R}[x_1,\ldots,x_n]/(x_1^2 - x_1,\ldots,x_n^2 - x_n)$ is the NNF of an integer-valued function if and only if all of its coefficients are integers. Assuming that this condition is satisfied, then P is the NNF of a Boolean function if and only if:*
$\sum_{x \in \mathbb{F}_2^n} P^2(x) = \sum_{x \in \mathbb{F}_2^n} P(x)$.

Proof The first assertion is a direct consequence of Relations (2.22) and (2.23). If all the coefficients of P are integers, then we have $P^2(x) \geq P(x)$ for every x; this implies that the 2^n equalities (one for each x), expressing that the corresponding function is Boolean, can be reduced to the single one $\sum_{x \in \mathbb{F}_2^n} P^2(x) = \sum_{x \in \mathbb{F}_2^n} P(x)$. □

According to Relation (2.27), the translation of this characterization in terms of the coefficients λ_I of $P(x)$ is as follows:

$$\sum_{I \subseteq \{1,\ldots,n\}} 2^{n-|I|} \sum_{J,J' \subseteq \{1,\ldots,n\};\, I = J \cup J'} \lambda_J\, \lambda_{J'} = \sum_{I \subseteq \{1,\ldots,n\}} 2^{n-|I|}\lambda_I, \tag{2.28}$$

since the number of those $x \in \mathbb{F}_2^n$ such that $I \subseteq supp(x)$, equals $2^{n-|I|}$.

More results related to the NNF can be found in [292] and [293].

Case of vectorial functions

An extention of the NNF to (n,m)-*functions* is given in [484], but it seems simpler to consider the NNF of the *indicator* $1_{\mathcal{G}_F}$ of the *graph* $\mathcal{G}_F = \{(x, F(x));\ x \in \mathbb{F}_2^n\}$. We obtain a (unique) characterization of the following form:

$$\forall x \in \mathbb{F}_2^n, \forall y \in \mathbb{F}_2^m, (y = F(x)) \Leftrightarrow \left(\sum_{\substack{I \subseteq \{1,\ldots,n\} \\ J \subseteq \{1,\ldots,m\}}} \lambda_{I,J} x^I y^J = 1 \right).$$

Note that, if we have the NNF of each coordinate function f_j of F, for $j = 1, \ldots, m$, then the NNF of $1_{\mathcal{G}_F}$ can be deduced from the following:

$$1_{\mathcal{G}_F}(x, y) = \prod_{j=1}^m \left(1 - (f_j(x) - y_j)^2 \right)$$

$$= \prod_{j=1}^m \left(1 - f_j(x) + y_j(2 f_j(x) - 1) \right)$$

$$= \sum_{J \subseteq \{1,\ldots,m\}} \left(\prod_{j \in \{1,\ldots,m\} \setminus J} (1 - f_j(x)) \prod_{j \in J} (2 f_j(x) - 1) \right) y^J.$$

Note that in the case of a Boolean function f (*i.e.*, in the case of $m = 1$), we have then $1_{\mathcal{G}_F}(x, y) = 1 - f(x) + (2f(x) - 1) y$, for $x \in \mathbb{F}_2^n$ and $y \in \mathbb{F}_2$.

Remark. As we can see, some representations of Boolean functions (resp. of vectorial function) such as the ANF are such that any object having the form of an ANF is the ANF of some function. Some others such as the NNF do not have such property. The Fourier–Hadamard and Walsh transforms that we shall see below provide also representations of Boolean and vectorial functions, which are of the latter kind. Some other representations also exist; see, *e.g.*, [484], where their relationships are studied as well as their behavior with respect to composition, and their eigenanalysis in relation with graphs (see page 70), in the case of representations by square matrices. $\square$

2.3 The Fourier–Hadamard transform and the Walsh transform

2.3.1 Fourier–Hadamard transform of pseudo-Boolean functions

Almost all the characteristics needed for Boolean functions in cryptography and for sets of Boolean functions in coding can be expressed by means of the weights of two kinds of related Boolean functions: $f \oplus \ell$ where ℓ is linear,[19] and $D_a f(x) = f(x) \oplus f(x + a)$ (the derivatives of f). In this framework, the Fourier–Hadamard transform is an efficient tool: for a given Boolean function f, the Fourier–Hadamard transform of f provides the knowledge of the weights of all the functions $f \oplus \ell$, where ℓ is a linear (or an affine) form, and the weights of the *derivatives* $D_a f$ are also directly related to the Fourier–Hadamard transform.

---

[19] As far as we know, and as reported in [555, 1110], the weights of these functions have been originally considered by S. Golomb [549] to define what he called invariants: given a positive integer $t \leq n$, the tth invariant defined by Golomb is the unordered set of values $\max(w_H(f(x) \oplus u \cdot x), w_H(f(x) \oplus u \cdot x \oplus 1))$, where a ranges over $\mathbb{F}_2^n$.

Definition 15   *The* Fourier–Hadamard transform[20] *is the* $\mathbb{R}$*-linear mapping that maps any pseudo-Boolean function φ on $\mathbb{F}_2^n$ to the function $\widehat{\varphi}$ defined on $\mathbb{F}_2^n$ by*

$$\widehat{\varphi}(u) = \sum_{x \in \mathbb{F}_2^n} \varphi(x)\,(-1)^{u \cdot x}, \tag{2.29}$$

where "$\cdot$" is some chosen inner product in $\mathbb{F}_2^n$. We call the Fourier–Hadamard spectrum *of φ the multiset of all the values $\widehat{\varphi}(u)$, where $u \in \mathbb{F}_2^n$ and* Fourier–Hadamard support *of φ the set of those u such that $\widehat{\varphi}(u) \neq 0$.*

Remark.   The most used inner product in $\mathbb{F}_2^n$ is the *usual inner product* $u \cdot x = u_1 x_1 \oplus \cdots \oplus u_n x_n$. If $\mathbb{F}_2^n$ is identified to the finite field $\mathbb{F}_{2^n}$, then $u \cdot x = tr_n(ux)$; $u, x \in \mathbb{F}_{2^n}$, is better used; and if n is even, say $n = 2m$, and $\mathbb{F}_2^n$ is identified to $\mathbb{F}_{2^m}^2$, then it is $(u_1, u_2) \cdot (x_1, x_2) = tr_m(u_1 x_1 + u_2 x_2)$; $u_1, u_2, x_1, x_2 \in \mathbb{F}_{2^m}$. In all cases, the *Walsh functions* $(-1)^{u \cdot x}$ constitute an orthogonal basis of the vector space $\mathbb{R}^{\mathbb{F}_2^n}$ over $\mathbb{R}$, according to properties we shall see at page 58. $\square$

Recall that every linear form over $\mathbb{F}_2^n$ equals $\ell_u : x \mapsto u \cdot x$ for some unique u in $\mathbb{F}_2^n$. If φ is a Boolean function (viewed as an integer-valued function), then $\widehat{\varphi}(0)$ equals $w_H(\varphi)$ and, for $u \neq 0_n, \widehat{\varphi}(u) = \sum_{x \in \mathbb{F}_2^n} \varphi(x)\,(1 - 2\,u \cdot x)$ equals $w_H(\varphi) - 2 w_H(\varphi\,\ell_u) = w_H(\varphi \oplus \ell_u) - w_H(\ell_u) = w_H(\varphi \oplus \ell_u) - 2^{n-1}$. This proves what we asserted above. And we shall show a relation between $w_H(D_a f)$ and the Fourier–Hadamard transform.

Algorithm (Fast Fourier–Hadamard transform)

There exists a simple divide-and-conquer butterfly algorithm to compute $\widehat{\varphi}$, called the *fast Fourier–Hadamard transform* (FFT). Let us give it in the case where "$\cdot$" is the usual inner product. For every $a = (a_1, \ldots, a_{n-1}) \in \mathbb{F}_2^{n-1}$ and every $a_n \in \mathbb{F}_2$, the number $\widehat{\varphi}(a_1, \ldots, a_n)$ equals

$$\sum_{x = (x_1, \ldots, x_{n-1}) \in \mathbb{F}_2^{n-1}} (-1)^{a \cdot x}\left[\varphi(x_1, \ldots, x_{n-1}, 0) + (-1)^{a_n}\varphi(x_1, \ldots, x_{n-1}, 1)\right].$$

Hence, if in the tables of values of the functions the vectors are ordered, for instance, in lexicographic order with the bit of highest weight on the right, the table of $\widehat{\varphi}$ equals the concatenation of those of the Fourier–Hadamard transforms of the $(n-1)$-variable functions $\psi_0(x) = \varphi(x_1, \ldots, x_{n-1}, 0) + \varphi(x_1, \ldots, x_{n-1}, 1)$ and $\psi_1(x) = \varphi(x_1, \ldots, x_{n-1}, 0) - \varphi(x_1, \ldots, x_{n-1}, 1)$. We deduce the following algorithm:

1. Write the table of the values of φ (its truth table if φ is Boolean), in which the binary vectors of length n are in lexicographic order with the bit of highest weight on the right.

---

[20] We write "Fourier–Hadamard" because "Fourier" would be ambiguous (and for the reason that the matrix involved in the transform is the Hadamard matrix [609]; see page 191); even "discrete Fourier" would be ambiguous; see, *e.g.*, [1110].

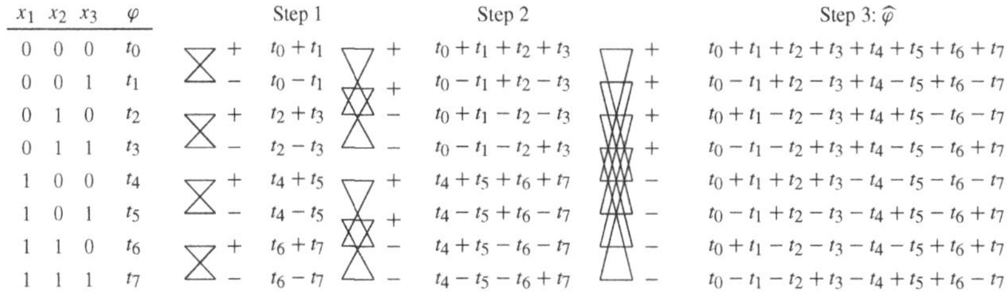

Figure 2.1 Fast Fourier–Hadamard transform.

2. Let φ_0 be the restriction of φ to $\mathbb{F}_2^{n-1} \times \{0\}$ and φ_1 the restriction of φ to $\mathbb{F}_2^{n-1} \times \{1\}$[21]; replace the values of φ_0 by those of $\varphi_0 + \varphi_1$ and those of φ_1 by those of $\varphi_0 - \varphi_1$.

3. Apply recursively step 2, separately from the functions now obtained in the places of φ_0 and φ_1.

When the algorithm ends (after arriving at functions in one variable each), the global table gives the values of $\widehat{\varphi}$. The complexity of this algorithm is of $n\, 2^n$ additions/substractions; it is then in $\mathcal{O}(N \log_2 N)$, where $N = 2^n$ is the size of its input f.

As for the fast binary Möbius transform, taking the lexicographic order with the bit of higher weight on the left (*i.e.*, the standard lexicographic order) works as well because, for every permutation σ of $\{1, \ldots, n\}$, we have $u \cdot x = \sigma(u) \cdot \sigma(x)$ for every u, x, and this implies that $\widehat{\varphi \circ \sigma}(u) = \sum_{x \in \mathbb{F}_2^n} \varphi(\sigma(x)) (-1)^{u \cdot x} = \sum_{x \in \mathbb{F}_2^n} \varphi(x) (-1)^{u \cdot \sigma^{-1}(x)} = \sum_{x \in \mathbb{F}_2^n} \varphi(x) (-1)^{\sigma(u) \cdot x} = \widehat{\varphi} \circ \sigma(u)$, and the final values are the same (but not the intermediate ones).

Remark. Here again, the algorithm may not work if the order on $\mathbb{F}_{2^n}$ is not a coordinate-wise permuted version of lexicographic order (for instance, if it is an order by increasing Hamming weights of inputs). $\square$

Figure 2.1 illustrates how this algorithm works (with a display of the rows in a different order, better adapted to apprehend the figure).

2.3.2 Fourier–Hadamard and Walsh transforms of Boolean functions

For a given Boolean function f, the Fourier–Hadamard transform can be applied to f itself, viewed as a function valued in $\{0, 1\} \subset \mathbb{Z}$ (we denote then by $\widehat{f}$ the corresponding Fourier–Hadamard transform of f). Notice that $\widehat{f}(0_n)$ equals the Hamming weight of f. Thus, the Hamming distance $d_H(f, g) = |\{x \in \mathbb{F}_2^n; f(x) \neq g(x)\}| = w_H(f \oplus g)$ between two functions f and g equals $\widehat{f \oplus g}(0_n)$.

Note that, by linearity of the Fourier–Hadamard transform, Relations (2.25), page 50, and (2.26) imply:

$$\widehat{\bigoplus_{i=1}^{k} f_i} = \sum_{\emptyset \neq I \subseteq \{1, \ldots, k\}} (-2)^{|I|-1} \widehat{\prod_{i \in I} f_i}, \tag{2.30}$$

---

[21] The table of values of φ_0 (resp. φ_1) corresponds to the upper (resp. lower) half of the table of φ.

$$\widehat{\prod_{i=1}^{l} f_i} = \frac{1}{2^{l-1}} \sum_{\emptyset \neq J \subseteq \{1,\dots,l\}} (-1)^{|J|-1} \widehat{\bigoplus_{i \in I} f_i}. \tag{2.31}$$

The Fourier–Hadamard transform can also be applied to the pseudo-Boolean function $f_\chi(x) = (-1)^{f(x)}$ (often called the *sign function*[22] of f) instead of f itself.

Definition 16 *We call the* Walsh transform[23] *of a Boolean function f the Fourier–Hadamard transform of the sign function f_χ, and we denote it[24] by W_f:*

$$W_f(u) = \sum_{x \in \mathbb{F}_2^n} (-1)^{f(x) \oplus u \cdot x}.$$

We call the Walsh spectrum *of f the multiset of all the values $W_f(u)$, where $u \in \mathbb{F}_2^n$. We call the* extended Walsh spectrum[25] *of f the multiset of their absolute values, and the* Walsh support *of f the set of those u such that $W_f(u) \neq 0$.*

We give in Table 2.2 an example of the computation of the Walsh transform, when the inner product chosen in $\mathbb{F}_2^n$ is the usual inner product, using the algorithm of the fast Fourier–Hadamard transform.[26]

Notice that f_χ being equal to $1 - 2f$, we have

$$W_f = 2^n \delta_0 - 2\widehat{f}, \tag{2.32}$$

where δ_0 denotes the *Dirac (or Kronecker) symbol, i.e.*, the indicator of the singleton $\{0_n\}$, defined by $\delta_0(u) = 1$ if u is the null vector and $\delta_0(u) = 0$ otherwise; see Proposition 10 for a proof of the relation $\widehat{1} = 2^n \delta_0$. Relations (2.30) and (2.31) give then the following:

$$W_{\bigoplus_{i=1}^{k} f_i}(a) = 2^{n-1}(1 + (-1)^k)\delta_0(a) + \sum_{\emptyset \neq I \subseteq \{1,\dots,k\}} (-2)^{|I|-1} W_{\prod_{i \in I} f_i}(a), \tag{2.33}$$

and $W_{\prod_{i=1}^{l} f_i}(a) =$

$$\left(2^n - 2^{n-l+1}\right)\delta_0(a) + \frac{1}{2^{l-1}} \sum_{\emptyset \neq J \subseteq \{1,\dots,l\}} (-1)^{|J|-1} W_{\bigoplus_{i \in I} f_i}(a), \tag{2.34}$$

since we have $1 - \sum_{\emptyset \neq I \subseteq \{1,\dots,k\}} (-2)^{|I|-1} = 1 - \frac{(1-2)^k - 1}{(-2)} = \frac{1+(-1)^k}{2}$ and $1 - \frac{1}{2^{l-1}} \sum_{\emptyset \neq I \subseteq \{1,\dots,l\}} (-1)^{|I|-1} = 1 + \frac{1}{2^{l-1}}((1-1)^l - 1) = 1 - \frac{1}{2^{l-1}}$.

---

[22] The symbol χ is used here because the sign function is the image of f by the nontrivial character over $\mathbb{F}_2$ (usually denoted by χ).

[23] Some authors specify "Walsh–Hadamard transform" like in signal processing, but most do not, since the risk of ambiguity is weaker than for the Fourier transform; note that a few authors use "Walsh" or "Hadamard–Walsh" for what we call "Fourier–Hadamard"; we shall use the term of "Walsh" only when dealing with the sign function.

[24] This notation is now widely used; a few years ago, diverse notations were used.

[25] "Extended" is in the sense of "extended by the addition of constant Boolean functions to f," since knowing $|W_f(u)|$ is equivalent to knowing the unordered pair $\{W_f(u), W_{f \oplus 1}(u)\}$, because $W_{f \oplus 1}$ and W_f take opposite values; we shall sometimes call the extended Walsh transform of f the function $|W_f|$.

[26] The truth table of the function is first directly calculated. We could also have applied the fast binary Möbius transform to obtain it; this has been done in Table 2.1 for the same function.

Algorithm 2: Computing the Walsh–Hadamard transform.

Data: tt $\leftarrow$ truth table, n $\leftarrow$ number of variables
Result: wt $\leftarrow$ Walsh–Hadamard spectrum
for $i = 0$ **to** $2^n - 1$ **do**
  $\mid$ $wt[i] = (-1)^{tt[i]}$;
end
for $i = 1$ **to** n **do**
  $\mid$ **for** $r = 0$ **to** $2^n - 1$ **by** 2^i **do**
  $\mid$ $\mid$ $t_1 = r$;
  $\mid$ $\mid$ $t_2 = r + 2^{i-1}$;
  $\mid$ $\mid$ **for** $j = 0$ **to** $2^{i-1} - 1$ **do**
  $\mid$ $\mid$ $\mid$ $a = wt[t_1]$;
  $\mid$ $\mid$ $\mid$ $b = wt[t_2]$;
  $\mid$ $\mid$ $\mid$ $wt[t_1] = a + b$;
  $\mid$ $\mid$ $\mid$ $wt[t_2] = a - b$;
  $\mid$ $\mid$ $\mid$ $t_1 = t_1 + 1$;
  $\mid$ $\mid$ $\mid$ $t_2 = t_2 + 1$;
  $\mid$ $\mid$ **end**
  $\mid$ **end**
end

Table 2.2 Truth table and Walsh spectrum of $f(x) = x_1 x_2 x_3 \oplus x_1 x_4 \oplus x_2$.

x_1	x_2	x_3	x_4	hexa	$x_1 x_2 x_3$	$x_1 x_4$	$f(x)$	$f_\chi(x)$				$W_f(x)$
0	0	0	0	0	0	0	0	1	2	4	0	0
1	0	0	0	1	0	0	0	1	0	0	0	0
0	1	0	0	2	0	0	1	−1	−2	−4	8	8
1	1	0	0	3	0	0	1	−1	0	0	0	8
0	0	1	0	4	0	0	0	1	2	0	0	0
1	0	1	0	5	0	0	0	1	0	0	0	0
0	1	1	0	6	0	0	1	−1	−2	0	0	0
1	1	1	0	7	1	0	0	1	0	0	0	0
0	0	0	1	8	0	0	0	1	0	0	0	4
1	0	0	1	9	0	1	1	−1	2	4	4	−4
0	1	0	1	a	0	0	1	−1	0	0	0	4
1	1	0	1	b	0	1	0	1	−2	0	4	−4
0	0	1	1	c	0	0	0	1	0	0	0	−4
1	0	1	1	d	0	1	1	−1	2	0	−4	4
0	1	1	1	e	0	0	1	−1	0	0	0	4
1	1	1	1	f	1	1	1	−1	2	−4	4	−4

Relation (2.33) has been originally obtained by induction and calculation in [204]. Relation (2.32) gives conversely $\widehat{f} = 2^{n-1}\delta_0 - \frac{W_f}{2}$ and in particular the following:

$$w_H(f) = 2^{n-1} - \frac{W_f(0_n)}{2}. \tag{2.35}$$

The mapping $f \mapsto W_f(0_n)$ playing an important role, and being applied in the sequel to various functions deduced from f, we shall also use the specific notation

$$\mathcal{F}(f) = W_f(0_n) = \sum_{x \in \mathbb{F}_2^n} (-1)^{f(x)}. \tag{2.36}$$

Relation (2.35) applied to $f \oplus \ell_a$, where $\ell_a(x) = a \cdot x$, gives the following:

$$d_H(f, \ell_a) = w_H(f \oplus \ell_a) = 2^{n-1} - \frac{W_f(a)}{2}. \tag{2.37}$$

Remark.   The Walsh transform represents the correlation between Boolean functions and affine functions and is related to attacks on stream ciphers using LFSR. The *best affine approximation*s of $f(x)$ are the functions $a \cdot x \oplus \epsilon$, where $|W_f(a)|$ is maximal and ϵ equals 0 if $W_f(a) > 0$ (since $f(x) \oplus a \cdot x$ has then low Hamming weight), and 1 otherwise.

In [302, 704], the *arithmetic Walsh transform* of Boolean functions is studied, which is based on modular arithmetic and is related to feedback with carry shift registers (FCSRs, having the operation of retroaction made with carry).   □

The supports of the Walsh transforms of Boolean functions have been studied in [308], among which we find all possible affine subspaces of $\mathbb{F}_2^n$ and the complements of singletons (for $n \geq 10$).

In [582] is proposed an algorithm, deduced from the formulae relating NNF and Walsh transform that we shall see in Subsection 2.3.4, page 66, for computing the Walsh transform (for a small set of points) from the ANF when the FFT is not efficient for computing it from the truth table (because the number of variables is too large, which happens when n is significantly larger than 30). For example, it is possible in certain cases to run their algorithm for 50 to 100 variable functions having a few hundreds of terms in their ANF.

In [373] are given concise representations of Walsh transform by binary decision diagrams (BDD) for functions with several hundred variables.

2.3.3 Properties of the Fourier–Hadamard and Walsh transforms of Boolean functions

The Fourier–Hadamard transform, as with other Fourier transforms, has very nice and useful properties. The number of these properties and the richness of their mutual relationship are impressive. All of these properties are very useful in practice for studying Boolean functions. We shall often refer to the relations below, by applying them to the Fourier–Hadamard transforms of pseudo-Boolean functions or to the Walsh transforms of Boolean functions (which are a particular case). Almost all properties can be deduced from the next two lemmas and proposition.

Lemma 3 *Let E be any vector space over $\mathbb{F}_2$ and ℓ any nonzero linear form on E. Then $\sum_{x \in E} (-1)^{\ell(x)}$ is null.*

Proof The linear form ℓ being nonzero, its support is an affine hyperplane of E and has $2^{\dim E - 1} = \frac{|E|}{2}$ elements.[27] Thus, $\sum_{x \in E} (-1)^{\ell(x)}$ being the sum of 1s and -1s in equal numbers, it is null.[28] $\qquad\square$

Proposition 10 *Let E be any vector subspace of $\mathbb{F}_2^n$. Denote by 1_E its indicator (i.e., the Boolean function defined by $1_E(x) = 1$ if $x \in E$ and $1_E(x) = 0$ otherwise). Then:*

$$\widehat{1_E} = |E| \, 1_{E^\perp}, \tag{2.38}$$

where $E^\perp = \{x \in \mathbb{F}_2^n; \; \forall y \in E, \; x \cdot y = 0\}$ is the orthogonal space of E with respect to the inner product "$\cdot$".

In particular, for $E = \mathbb{F}_2^n$, we have $\widehat{1} = 2^n \delta_0$.

Proof For every $u \in \mathbb{F}_2^n$, we have $\widehat{1_E}(u) = \sum_{x \in E} (-1)^{u \cdot x}$. If the linear form $x \in E \mapsto u \cdot x$ is not null on E (i.e., if $u \notin E^\perp$), then $\widehat{1_E}(u)$ is null, according to Lemma 3. And if $u \in E^\perp$, then $\widehat{1_E}(u)$ clearly equals $|E|$. $\qquad\square$

This proposition leads to the very important Poisson formula below. To be able to state this formula in its general form, we need the:

Lemma 4 *For every pseudo-Boolean function φ on $\mathbb{F}_2^n$ and every elements a, b, and u of $\mathbb{F}_2^n$, the value at u of the Fourier–Hadamard transform of the function $(-1)^{a \cdot x} \varphi(x + b)$ equals $(-1)^{b \cdot (a+u)} \widehat{\varphi}(a + u)$.*

Proof The value at u of the Fourier–Hadamard transform of the function $x \mapsto (-1)^{a \cdot x} \varphi(x + b)$ equals $\sum_{x \in \mathbb{F}_2^n} (-1)^{(a+u) \cdot x} \varphi(x + b) = \sum_{x \in \mathbb{F}_2^n} (-1)^{(a+u) \cdot (x+b)} \varphi(x)$ and thus equals $(-1)^{b \cdot (a+u)} \widehat{\varphi}(a + u)$. $\qquad\square$

We deduce from Proposition 10 and Lemma 4 the *Poisson summation formula*, which has been used to prove many cryptographic properties in [759], [797], [212] and later in [190, 191], and whose most general statement is:

Corollary 3 *For every pseudo-Boolean function φ on $\mathbb{F}_2^n$, for every vector subspace E of $\mathbb{F}_2^n$, and for every elements a and b of $\mathbb{F}_2^n$, we have:*

$$\sum_{u \in a+E} (-1)^{b \cdot u} \widehat{\varphi}(u) = |E| \, (-1)^{a \cdot b} \sum_{x \in b + E^\perp} (-1)^{a \cdot x} \varphi(x). \tag{2.39}$$

---

[27] Another way of seeing this is to choose $a \in E$ such that $\ell(a) = 1$ and observe that the mapping $x \mapsto x + a$ is a bijection between $\ker \ell$ and its complement.

[28] Alternatively, choosing again $a \in E$ such that $\ell(a) = 1$, we have
$\sum_{x \in E} (-1)^{\ell(x)} = \sum_{x \in E} (-1)^{\ell(x+a)} = (-1)^{\ell(a)} \sum_{x \in E} (-1)^{\ell(x)} = -\sum_{x \in E} (-1)^{\ell(x)}$.

Proof For $a = b = 0_n$, the sum $\sum_{u \in E} \widehat{\varphi}(u)$ equals $\sum_{u \in E} \sum_{x \in \mathbb{F}_2^n} \varphi(x)(-1)^{u \cdot x} = \sum_{x \in \mathbb{F}_2^n}$ $\varphi(x) \widehat{1_E}(x)$ by definition. Hence, according to Proposition 10:

$$\sum_{u \in E} \widehat{\varphi}(u) = |E| \sum_{x \in E^\perp} \varphi(x). \tag{2.40}$$

We apply this equality to function $(-1)^{a \cdot x} \varphi(x + b)$. Using Lemma 4, we deduce $\sum_{u \in E} (-1)^{b \cdot (a+u)} \widehat{\varphi}(a + u) = |E| \sum_{x \in E^\perp} (-1)^{a \cdot x} \varphi(x + b)$, that is, (2.39). $\qquad \square$

Relation (2.39) applied to $\varphi(x) = f_\chi$, the sign function of f, gives the following:

$$\sum_{u \in a+E} (-1)^{b \cdot u} W_f(u) = |E| (-1)^{a \cdot b} \sum_{x \in b+E^\perp} (-1)^{f(x) \oplus a \cdot x}. \tag{2.41}$$

Note that, according to this latter relation, for every Boolean function f, every vector subspace E of $\mathbb{F}_2^n$, and every $a, b \in \mathbb{F}_2^n$, we have $|\sum_{u \in a+E} (-1)^{b \cdot u} W_f(u)| \leq 2^n$ (with equality if and only if $f(x) \oplus a \cdot x$ is constant on $b + E^\perp$).

Relation (2.39) with $a = 0_n$ and $E = \mathbb{F}_2^n$ gives the following:

Corollary 4 *For every pseudo-Boolean function φ on $\mathbb{F}_2^n$:*

$$\widehat{\widehat{\varphi}} = 2^n \, \varphi. \tag{2.42}$$

Thus, the Fourier–Hadamard transform is a permutation on the set of pseudo-Boolean functions on $\mathbb{F}_2^n$ and is its own inverse, up to the division[29] by the constant 2^n. Relation (2.42) is called the *inverse Fourier–Hadamard transform formula* and writes $\sum_{u \in \mathbb{F}_2^n} \widehat{\varphi}(u) (-1)^{u \cdot x} = 2^n \varphi(x)$. It means that, viewing φ as a function of $x_\chi = ((-1)^{x_1}, \ldots, (-1)^{x_n})$, the number $2^{-n} \widehat{\varphi}(u)$ is the NNF coefficient indexed by u of the resulting function.[30] Applied to a sign function, Relation (2.42) is called the *inverse Walsh transform formula* and writes the following:

$$\sum_{u \in \mathbb{F}_2^n} W_f(u) (-1)^{u \cdot x} = 2^n (-1)^{f(x)}. \tag{2.43}$$

Corollary 4 shows easily that a given property observed on the Fourier–Hadamard transform of any pseudo-Boolean function φ having some specificity is in fact a necessary and sufficient condition for φ having this specificity. For instance, according to Proposition 10, the Fourier–Hadamard transform of any constant function φ takes the null value at every nonzero vector. Since the Fourier–Hadamard transform of a function null at every nonzero vector is constant, Corollary 4 implies that the Fourier–Hadamard transform is a bijection between the set of constant functions and the set of those functions null at every nonzero vector. Similarly, φ is constant on $\mathbb{F}_2^n \setminus \{0_n\}$ if and only if $\widehat{\varphi}$ is constant on $\mathbb{F}_2^n \setminus \{0_n\}$.

---

[29] In order to avoid this division, the Fourier–Hadamard transform is often normalized, that is, divided by $\sqrt{2^n} = 2^{\frac{n}{2}}$, so that it becomes its own inverse. We do not use this normalized transform here because the functions we consider are integer valued, and we want their Fourier–Hadamard transforms to be also integer valued.

[30] In [693, 779, 914], the authors call Fourier transform this representation of φ viewed as a polynomial in x_χ.

A classical property of the Fourier transform is to be an isomorphism from the set of functions endowed with the so-called convolutional product (denoted by $\otimes$) into this same set, endowed with the usual product (denoted by $\times$). We recall the definition[31] of the convolutional product between two functions φ and ψ:

$$(\varphi \otimes \psi)(x) = \sum_{y \in \mathbb{F}_2^n} \varphi(y)\psi(x+y).$$

Proposition 11 *Let φ and ψ be any pseudo-Boolean functions on $\mathbb{F}_2^n$. We have the following:*

$$\widehat{\varphi \otimes \psi} = \widehat{\varphi} \times \widehat{\psi}. \tag{2.44}$$

Consequently:

$$\widehat{\varphi} \otimes \widehat{\psi} = 2^n \widehat{\varphi \times \psi}. \tag{2.45}$$

Proof We have

$$\widehat{\varphi \otimes \psi}(u) = \sum_{x \in \mathbb{F}_2^n} (\varphi \otimes \psi)(x) (-1)^{u \cdot x} = \sum_{x \in \mathbb{F}_2^n} \sum_{y \in \mathbb{F}_2^n} \varphi(y)\psi(x+y) (-1)^{u \cdot y \oplus u \cdot (x+y)}.$$

Thus, by the change of variable $(x, y) \to (x+y, y)$, we have the following:

$$\widehat{\varphi \otimes \psi}(u) = \left(\sum_{y \in \mathbb{F}_2^n} \varphi(y)(-1)^{u \cdot y} \right) \left(\sum_{x \in \mathbb{F}_2^n} \psi(x) (-1)^{u \cdot x} \right) = \widehat{\varphi}(u) \widehat{\psi}(u).$$

This proves the first equality. Applying it to $\widehat{\varphi}$ and $\widehat{\psi}$ in the places of φ and ψ, we obtain $\widehat{\widehat{\varphi} \otimes \widehat{\psi}} = 2^{2n} \varphi \times \psi$, according to Corollary 4. Using again this same corollary, we deduce Relation (2.45). $\qquad\square$

Relation (2.45) applied at 0_n gives a relation sometimes called Plancherel's formula:

$$\sum_{x \in \mathbb{F}_2^n} \widehat{\varphi}(x)\widehat{\psi}(x) = 2^n \sum_{x \in \mathbb{F}_2^n} \varphi(x)\psi(x). \tag{2.46}$$

Taking $\psi = \varphi$ in (2.46), we obtain *Parseval's relation*:

Corollary 5 *For every pseudo-Boolean function φ, we have the following:*

$$\sum_{u \in \mathbb{F}_2^n} \widehat{\varphi}^2(u) = 2^n \sum_{x \in \mathbb{F}_2^n} \varphi^2(x).$$

If φ takes values ± 1 only, this becomes the following:

$$\sum_{u \in \mathbb{F}_2^n} \widehat{\varphi}^2(u) = 2^{2n}. \tag{2.47}$$

---

[31] Since the operations take place in $\mathbb{F}_2^n$, we have a $+$ in the formula, where for general groups we would have a $-$.

This is why, when dealing with Boolean functions, we most often prefer using the Walsh transform of f instead of the Fourier–Hadamard transform of f. Parseval's relation for Walsh transform writes the following:

$$\sum_{u \in \mathbb{F}_2^n} W_f^2(u) = 2^{2n}. \tag{2.48}$$

According to the inverse Walsh transform formula and to the Parseval formula, we have for every function f that $\left(\sum_{u \in \mathbb{F}_2^n} W_f(u) \right)^2 = \left(2^n (-1)^{f(0_n)} \right)^2 = \sum_{u \in \mathbb{F}_2^n} W_f^2(u)$, that is, $\sum_{u \neq v} W_f(u) W_f(v) = 0$. Note that this proves (as observed in [312]) that it is impossible, except when the function is affine, *i.e.*, when the Walsh transform is null except at one point, that all nonzero values of the Walsh transform have the same sign.

Relation (2.45) applied at $a \neq 0_n$ gives

$$\widehat{\varphi} \otimes \widehat{\psi}(a) = 2^n \, \widehat{\varphi \times \psi}(a) = 2^n \sum_{x \in \mathbb{F}_2^n} \varphi(x) \psi(x) (-1)^{a \cdot x}. \tag{2.49}$$

If φ takes values ± 1 only and $\psi = \varphi$, this becomes the following:

$$\sum_{u \in \mathbb{F}_2^n} \widehat{\varphi}(u) \widehat{\varphi}(u + a) = 0. \tag{2.50}$$

This provides the relation that some authors call the *Titsworth relation*:

$$\sum_{u \in \mathbb{F}_2^n} W_f(u) W_f(u + a) = 0, \quad \forall a \neq 0_n. \tag{2.51}$$

Note that in some cases (for instance, for designing correlation immune functions of low Hamming weights; see Section 7.1.9, page 303) using the Fourier–Hadamard transform of a Boolean function is more convenient.

When $\mathbb{F}_2^n$ is identified to $\mathbb{F}_{2^n}$, with *inner product $u \cdot x = tr_n(ux)$*, *Parseval's relation* is a particular case (corresponding to $a = 1$) of the following more general relation:

$$\sum_{u \in \mathbb{F}_{2^n}} W_f(u) W_f(au) = \sum_{u, x, y \in \mathbb{F}_{2^n}} (-1)^{f(y) \oplus f(x) \oplus tr_n(uy + aux)}$$

$$= 2^n \sum_{x \in \mathbb{F}_{2^n}} (-1)^{f(x) \oplus f(ax)}.$$

Relation (2.44) applied with $\psi = \varphi = f_\chi$ implies the *Wiener–Khintchine formula*:

$$\widehat{f_\chi \otimes f_\chi} = W_f^2, \tag{2.52}$$

which involves in fact the *derivatives* of the Boolean function, since for every $a \in \mathbb{F}_2^n$, we have $(f_\chi \otimes f_\chi)(a) = \sum_{x \in \mathbb{F}_2^n} (-1)^{D_a f(x)} = \mathcal{F}(D_a f)$ (the notation $\mathcal{F}$ was defined at Relation (2.36), page 57).

Definition 17 *The function $a \mapsto \mathcal{F}(D_a f)$ is called the* autocorrelation function *of f and denoted by Δ_f.*

Relation (2.52) means that W_f^2 is the Fourier–Hadamard transform of the autocorrelation function of f:

$$\forall u \in \mathbb{F}_2^n, \; \widehat{\Delta_f}(u) = \sum_{a \in \mathbb{F}_2^n} \Delta_f(a)(-1)^{u \cdot a} = W_f^2(u). \tag{2.53}$$

Equivalently, by applying the inverse Fourier transform formula, we have

$$\Delta_f(a) = 2^{-n} \sum_{u \in \mathbb{F}_2^n} W_f^2(u)(-1)^{u \cdot a}. \tag{2.54}$$

This property was first used (as far as we know) in the domain of cryptography in [211] to study the so-called partially-bent functions (see Section 6.2). It leads also to a lower bound on the numerical degree of Boolean functions by means of the Hamming weights of their derivatives (in directions of Hamming weight 1), first given in [905], that we shall give (and prove) as Relation (2.63), page 67.

Applied at vector 0_n, Relation (2.53) gives

$$\widehat{\Delta_f}(0_n) = \sum_{a \in \mathbb{F}_2^n} \mathcal{F}(D_a f) = \mathcal{F}^2(f). \tag{2.55}$$

Corollary 3 (the Poisson summation formula), page 58, and Relation (2.53) imply that, for every vector subspace E of $\mathbb{F}_2^n$ and every vectors a and b (cf. [191]):

$$\sum_{u \in a + E} (-1)^{b \cdot u} W_f^2(u) = |E|(-1)^{a \cdot b} \sum_{e \in b + E^\perp} (-1)^{a \cdot e} \mathcal{F}(D_e f). \tag{2.56}$$

This leads to an interesting relation, first shown in [191] for Boolean functions (but similar relations exist in other domains such as sequences and learning; see, *e.g.*, [779]), and that, because of its similarity with the Poisson summation formula, we shall call the *second-order Poisson summation formula*:[32]

Proposition 12 *Let E and E' be supplementary subspaces*[33] *of $\mathbb{F}_2^n$ (i.e., be two subspaces such that $E \cap E' = \{0_n\}$ and whose direct sum equals $\mathbb{F}_2^n$). For every $a \in E'$, let h_a be the restriction of f to the coset $a + E$ (h_a can be identified with a function on $\mathbb{F}_2^k$ where k is the dimension of E). Then*

$$\sum_{u \in E^\perp} W_f^2(u) = |E^\perp| \sum_{a \in E'} \mathcal{F}^2(h_a). \tag{2.57}$$

Proof Every element of $\mathbb{F}_2^n$ can be written in a unique way in the form $x + a$, where $x \in E$ and $a \in E'$.

---

[32] This formula is sometimes more convenient to use than the Poisson summation formula. An example where it helps proving more can be found in Section 10.4.

[33] Some authors say "complementary," but we prefer avoiding the confusion with complementary sets and use "supplementary."

For every $e \in E$, we have that $\mathcal{F}(D_e f) = \sum_{x \in E; a \in E'} (-1)^{f(x+a) \oplus f(x+e+a)} = \sum_{a \in E'} \mathcal{F}(D_e h_a)$. We deduce from Relation (2.56), applied with $E^\perp$ instead of E, and with $a = b = 0_n$, that

$$
\sum_{u \in E^\perp} W_f^2(u) = |E^\perp| \sum_{e \in E} \mathcal{F}(D_e f) = |E^\perp| \sum_{e \in E} \left(\sum_{a \in E'} \mathcal{F}(D_e h_a) \right)
$$

$$
= |E^\perp| \sum_{a \in E'} \left(\sum_{e \in E} \mathcal{F}(D_e h_a) \right).
$$

Thus, according to Relation (2.55) applied with E in the place of $\mathbb{F}_2^n$ (recall that E can be identified with $\mathbb{F}_2^k$ where k is the dimension of E): $\sum_{u \in E^\perp} W_f^2(u) = |E^\perp| \sum_{a \in E'} \mathcal{F}^2(h_a)$. $\quad\square$

Fourier–Hadamard transform and affine automorphisms

A last relation that must be mentioned shows what the composition with a linear isomorphism implies on the Fourier transform of a pseudo-Boolean function:

Proposition 13 *Let φ be any pseudo-Boolean function on $\mathbb{F}_2^n$. Let M be a nonsingular $n \times n$ binary matrix and L the linear automorphism $L : (x_1, x_2, \ldots, x_n) \mapsto (x_1, x_2, \ldots, x_n) \times M$. Let us denote by M' the transpose of M^{-1} and by L' the linear automorphism $L' : (x_1, x_2, \ldots, x_n) \mapsto (x_1, x_2, \ldots, x_n) \times M'$ (note that L' is the adjoint operator of L^{-1}, that is, it satisfies $u \cdot L^{-1}(x) = L'(u) \cdot x$ for every x and u, where $\cdot$ is the usual inner product). Then*

$$
\widehat{\varphi \circ L} = \widehat{\varphi} \circ L'. \tag{2.58}
$$

Proof By the change of variable $x \mapsto L^{-1}(x)$, we have that for every $u \in \mathbb{F}_2^n$, $\widehat{\varphi \circ L}(u) = \sum_{x \in \mathbb{F}_2^n} \varphi(L(x))(-1)^{u \cdot x}$ equals $\sum_{x \in \mathbb{F}_2^n} \varphi(x)(-1)^{u \cdot L^{-1}(x)}$ and, by the definition of L', equals then $\sum_{x \in \mathbb{F}_2^n} \varphi(x)(-1)^{L'(u) \cdot x}$. $\quad\square$

It is easily deduced from this Relation (2.58) and from Lemma 4, page 58, that the affine equivalence of Boolean functions translates into the affine equivalence of their extended Walsh transforms and in particular of their Walsh supports.

Given linear bijections L_1, L_2, a linear function L_3 and vectors a, b, c, the value of $W_{(L_1+a) \circ F \circ (L_2+b) + L_3 + c}(u, v) = \pm \sum_{x \in \mathbb{F}_2^n} (-1)^{v \cdot (L_1(F(L_2(x)+b))+L_3(x)) \oplus u \cdot x}$ equals $\pm W_F((L_3 \circ L_2^{-1})^*(v) + (L_2^{-1})^*(u), L_1^*(v))$, where $*$ is the adjoint operator.

Relationship between algebraic degree and Walsh transform

The following bound was shown in [737] (see also [212, Lemma 3]):

Theorem 2 *Let f be an n-variable Boolean function ($n \geq 2$), and let $1 \leq k \leq n$. Assume that the Walsh transform values of f are all divisible by 2^k (i.e., according to Relation (2.32), that its Fourier–Hadamard transform takes values divisible by 2^{k-1}, or equivalently, according to Relation (2.37), that all the Hamming distances between f and affine functions are divisible by 2^{k-1}). Then f has algebraic degree at most $n - k + 1$.*

Proof Let us suppose that f has algebraic degree $d > n - k + 1$ and consider a term x^I of degree d in its algebraic normal form. The Poisson summation formula (2.40) applied to $\varphi = f_\chi$ and to the vector space $E = \{u \in \mathbb{F}_2^n; \, \forall i \in I, \, u_i = 0\}$ gives $\sum_{u \in E} W_f(u) = 2^{n-d} \sum_{x \in E^\perp} f_\chi(x)$. The orthogonal $E^\perp$ of E equals $\{u \in \mathbb{F}_2^n; \, \forall i \notin I, \, u_i = 0\} = \{u \in \mathbb{F}_2^n; \, supp(u) \subseteq I\}$. According to Relation 2.4, we have that $\sum_{x \in E^\perp} f(x)$ is not even and therefore $\sum_{x \in E^\perp} f_\chi(x)$ is not divisible by 4. Hence, $\sum_{u \in E} W_f(u)$ is not divisible by 2^{n-d+2} and it is therefore not divisible by 2^k – a contradiction. $\quad\square$

Remark. The result is of course also valid for those vectorial (n, m)-functions whose Walsh transform values are divisible by 2^k. It is shown in [204] that for any (n, m)-function F having such a divisibility property and for every (m, r)-function G, we have $d_{alg}(G \circ F) \leq n - k + d_{alg}(G)$. This bound on the algebraic degree of *composite functions* is a direct consequence of Relation (2.34), page 55: all component functions of F having a Walsh transform values divisible by 2^k, then for every $l = 1, \ldots, k$, all products of l coordinate functions of F have a Walsh transform divisible by 2^{k-l+1}, and Theorem 2 completes the proof. As shown in [254], it is also a direct consequence of Relation (2.9), page 40. $\quad\square$

Remark.

1. The converse of Theorem 2 is valid if $k = 1$ (since the Walsh transform values of all Boolean functions are even by definition). It is also valid if $k = 2$, since the n-variable Boolean functions of degrees at most $n - 1$ are those Boolean functions of even Hamming weights, and $f(x) \oplus u \cdot x$ has degree at most $n - 1$ too for every u, since $n \geq 2$. It is finally also valid for $k = n$, since the affine functions are characterized by the fact that their Walsh transforms take values $\pm 2^n$ and 0 only (more precisely, their Walsh transforms take value $\pm 2^n$ once, and all their other values are null). The converse is false for any other value of k. Indeed, it is false for $k = n - 1$ ($n \geq 4$), since there exist *quadratic functions* f whose Walsh transforms take values $\pm 2^{\frac{n}{2}}$ for n even, ≥ 4, and $\pm 2^{(n+1)/2}$ for n odd, ≥ 5 (see Section 5.2, page 170). It is then an easy task to deduce that the converse of Theorem 2 is also false for any value of k such that $3 \leq k \leq n - 2$: we choose a quadratic function g in 4 variables, whose Walsh transform value at 0_n equals 2^2, that is, whose weight equals $2^3 - 2 = 6$, and we take $f(x) = g(x_1, x_2, x_3, x_4) x_5 \ldots x_l$ ($5 \leq l \leq n$). Such a function has the algebraic degree $l - 2$ and its weight equals 6; hence its Walsh transform value at 0_n equals $2^n - 12$ and is therefore not divisible by 2^k with $n - 2 \geq k = n - (l - 2) + 1 = n - l + 3 \geq 3$.

2. It is possible to characterize the functions whose Walsh transform values are all divisible by 2^{n-1} (*i.e.*, equal 0, $\pm 2^{n-1}$ and/or $\pm 2^n$): according to Theorem 2, they have algebraic degree at most 2, and the characterization follows from the results of Section 5.2 on

quadratic functions (see the last remark of page 173); these functions are the sums of an affine function and of the product of two affine functions (see, for instance, the observation after Theorem 10, page 172). Determining those Boolean functions (in the *Reed–Muller code* of order $n - k + 1$) whose Walsh transform is divisible by 2^k is an open problem for $3 \le k \le n - 2$. The *Poisson summation formula* provides some information; it shows by applying the proof of Theorem 2 to $W_f(a + u)$ that, for every supplementary subspaces E and E' of $\mathbb{F}_2^n$ (*i.e.*, such that $E \cap E' = \{0_n\}$ and whose direct sum equals $\mathbb{F}_2^n$), where E has dimension $d \ge n - k$, denoting for every $a \in E'$ by h_a the restriction of f to the coset $a + E$, the value of $\mathcal{F}(h_a)$ is divisible by 2^{k+d-n}; and we also have that the arithmetic mean (*i.e.*, average) of $\mathcal{F}(h_a)$ when a ranges over E' is divisible by 2^{k+d-n} (indeed, $\sum_{a \in E'} \mathcal{F}(h_a) = \mathcal{F}(f) = W_f(0_n)$ is divisible by 2^k). The *second-order Poisson summation formula* also provides complementary information on such functions: the quadratic mean (*i.e.*, the root mean square) of $\mathcal{F}(h_a)$ when a ranges over E' is also divisible by 2^{k+d-n}. Indeed, $\sum_{a \in E'} \mathcal{F}^2(h_a) = \frac{1}{|E^\perp|} \sum_{u \in E^\perp} W_f^2(u)$ is divisible by 2^{2k+d-n}; hence, the arithmetic mean of $\mathcal{F}^2(h_a)$ is divisible by $2^{2k+2d-2n}$. Summarizing, we have that the integer sequence $2^{-(k+d-n)} \mathcal{F}(h_a)$, of length 2^{n-d}, has integer arithmetic and quadratic means. Note that, according to *McEliece's theorem* (see page 13), given a monomial Boolean function $f(x) = tr_n(x^d)$ where $\gcd(d, 2^n - 1) = 1$, the largest possible exponent of a power of 2 dividing each Walsh transform value of f equals $\min\{w_2(t_0) + w_2(t_1); 1 \le t_0, t_1 < 2^n - 1, t_0 + t_1 d \equiv 0 \pmod{2^n - 1}$ (see the definition of w_2 at page 45). See bounds in [674, 676].

3. It is possible to characterize the fact that a Boolean function has algebraic degree at most d by means of its Fourier–Hadamard or Walsh transforms: since, as seen in Proposition 4, page 36, a Boolean function has an algebraic degree at most d if and only if its restriction to any $(d + 1)$-dimensional flat (*i.e.*, affine subspace) has even Hamming weight, we can apply Poisson summation formula (2.39). For instance, in terms of the Walsh transform, f has an algebraic degree at most d if and only if, for every $(n - d - 1)$-dimensional vector subspace E of $\mathbb{F}_2^n$ and every $b \in \mathbb{F}_2^n$, the sum $\sum_{u \in E} (-1)^{b \cdot u} W_f(u)$ is divisible by 2^{n-d+1}. But this characterization is not simple. $\quad\square$

Characterizing the Fourier–Hadamard transforms of pseudo-Boolean functions and the Walsh transforms of Boolean functions

According to the *inverse Fourier–Hadamard transform formula* (2.42), the Fourier–Hadamard transforms of integer-valued functions (resp. the Walsh transforms of Boolean functions) are those integer-valued functions over $\mathbb{F}_2^n$ whose Fourier–Hadamard transforms take values divisible by 2^n (resp. take values $\pm 2^n$). Also, according to the *inverse Walsh transform formula* (2.43), page 59, the Walsh transforms of Boolean functions are those integer-valued functions ψ over $\mathbb{F}_2^n$ such that $(\widehat{\psi})^2$ equals the constant function 2^{2n}; they are then those integer-valued functions ψ such that $\widehat{\psi \otimes \psi} = 2^{2n}$ (according to Relation (2.44) applied with $\varphi = \psi$), that is, $\psi \otimes \psi = 2^{2n} \delta_0$.

These characterizations need to check 2^n divisibilities by 2^n for the Fourier–Hadamard transforms of integer-valued functions, and 2^n equalities for the Walsh transforms of Boolean functions.

Case of monomial (or power) Boolean functions: So-called *monomial Boolean (univariate) functions* are those functions over $\mathbb{F}_{2^n}$ of the form $f(x) = tr_n(ax^d)$ (recall from page 42 that when $\mathbb{F}_2^n$ is identified with $\mathbb{F}_{2^n}$, an inner product is then $(x, y) \mapsto tr_n(x\,y)$). We shall give at page 72 the known results and a conjecture on the Walsh spectrum of such functions.

2.3.4 Fourier–Hadamard (and Walsh) transform and numerical normal form

Since the main cryptographic criteria on Boolean functions will be characterized as properties of their Fourier–Hadamard/Walsh transforms (see Section 3.1), it is useful to clarify the relationship between these and the NNF representation. Note that there is a similarity between the Fourier–Hadamard transform and the NNF of pseudo-Boolean functions:

- The functions $(-1)^{u \cdot x}$, $u \in \mathbb{F}_2^n$, constitute an orthogonal basis of the space of pseudo-Boolean functions, and the Fourier–Hadamard transform can be seen as a classical decomposition over an orthogonal basis.
- The NNF is defined similarly with respect to the basis of monomials, which is nonorthogonal but allows as well simple calculation of the coefficients in this decomposition.

Let us see now how each representation can be expressed by means of the other.

Let $\varphi(x)$ be any pseudo-Boolean function, and let $\sum_{I \subseteq \{1,\ldots,n\}} \lambda_I x^I$ be its NNF. For every vector $x \in \mathbb{F}_2^n$, we have: $\varphi(x) = \sum_{I \subseteq supp(x)} \lambda_I$. Setting $1_n = (1, \ldots, 1)$, we have $\varphi(x + 1_n) = \sum_{I \subseteq \{1,\ldots,n\}; \, supp(x) \cap I = \emptyset} \lambda_I$ (since the support of $x + 1_n$ equals $\mathbb{F}_2^n \setminus supp(x)$). Hence, $\varphi(x + 1_n) = \sum_{I \subseteq \{1,\ldots,n\}} \lambda_I \, 1_{E_I}$, where E_I is the $(n - |I|)$-dimensional vector subspace of $\mathbb{F}_2^n$ equal to $\{x \in \mathbb{F}_2^n; \, supp(x) \cap I = \emptyset\}$, whose orthogonal space equals $\{u \in \mathbb{F}_2^n; \, supp(u) \subseteq I\}$. Applying Lemma 4 with $a = 0_n$ and $b = 1_n$, and Proposition 10, we deduce (as proved in [292]) the following:

$$\widehat{\varphi}(u) = (-1)^{w_H(u)} \sum_{I \subseteq \{1,\ldots,n\}; \, supp(u) \subseteq I} 2^{n-|I|} \lambda_I. \qquad (2.59)$$

We deduce the following:

$$\lambda_I = 2^{-n}(-2)^{|I|} \sum_{u \in \mathbb{F}_2^n; \, I \subseteq supp(u)} \widehat{\varphi}(u). \qquad (2.60)$$

Indeed, according to Relation (2.59), we have $2^{-n}(-2)^{|I|} \sum_{u \in \mathbb{F}_2^n; \, I \subseteq supp(u)} \widehat{\varphi}(u) = 2^{-n}(-2)^{|I|} \sum_{J \subseteq \{1,\ldots,n\}} \left(\sum_{u \in \mathbb{F}_2^n; \, I \subseteq supp(u) \subseteq J} (-1)^{w_H(u)} \right) 2^{n-|J|} \lambda_J$, and the sum inside the parentheses equals 0 if $I \not\subseteq J$ and otherwise is also null if $J \neq I$ since it equals $(-1)^{|I|} \sum_{u \in \mathbb{F}_2^n; \, supp(u) \subseteq J \setminus I} (-1)^{w_H(u)} = (-1)^{|I|}(1 - 1)^{|J \setminus I|}$.

Relation (2.60) has been proved in [292] in a slightly more complex way. Applied when φ equals a Boolean function f and using that $W_f(u) = 2^n \delta_0(u) - 2\widehat{f}(u)$, we get the following:

$$W_f(u) = (-1)^{w_H(u)+1} \sum_{I \subseteq \{1,\ldots,n\}; \, supp(u) \subseteq I} 2^{n-|I|+1} \lambda_I \text{ if } u \neq 0_n, \qquad (2.61)$$

$$W_f(0_n) = 2^n - \sum_{I \subseteq \{1,\dots,n\}} 2^{n-|I|+1} \lambda_I,$$

and

$$\lambda_I = 2^{-n}(-2)^{|I|-1} \sum_{u \in \mathbb{F}_2^n;\ I \subseteq supp(u)} W_f(u) \text{ if } I \neq \emptyset, \tag{2.62}$$

$$\lambda_\emptyset = -2^{-(n+1)} \left(\sum_{u \in \mathbb{F}_2^n} W_f(u) - 2^n \right).$$

Remark. This provides a simpler proof of Theorem 2, page 63: according to Relations (2.61) and (2.62), the hypothesis of the theorem is equivalent to saying that, for every I such that $|I| \geq n - k + 1$, the coefficient λ_I of x^I in the NNF of f is divisible by $2^{|I|+k-n-1}$, and this implies that for $|I| \geq n - k + 2$, it is even. This gives also more information on those functions whose Walsh transform values are all divisible by 2^k. For instance, if $|I| \geq n - k + 3$, then since λ_I is divisible by 4, using Relation (2.24), page 50, we have that $\sum_{\substack{\{I_1,I_2\} \\ I_1 \cup I_2 = I}} a_{I_1} a_{I_2}$ is even, that is, $\bigoplus_{\substack{\{I_1,I_2\} \\ I_1 \cup I_2 = I}} a_{I_1} a_{I_2} = 0$. This is exploited in [301] for bounding numbers of functions (see pages 243 and 311). Other similar (but more complex) properties of the coefficients a_I can be obtained by considering the divisibility of λ_I by powers of 2 larger than 4. $\qquad\square$

We deduce the following from Relations (2.59) through (2.62):

Proposition 14 *Any pseudo-Boolean function φ has a numerical degree at most d if and only if $\widehat{\varphi}(u) = 0$ for every vector u of Hamming weight strictly larger than d. Any Boolean function f has a numerical degree at most d if and only if $W_f(u) = 0$ for every such vector.*

In other words, the numerical degree equals the maximal Hamming weight of those $u \in \mathbb{F}_2^n$ such that $W_f(u) \neq 0$.

This allows proving the fact mentioned at page 48 that, if a Boolean function f has no ineffective variable, then the numerical degree of f is larger than or equal to $\log_2 n - \mathcal{O}(\log_2 \log_2 n)$. In fact, we can prove a little more with the same method as in the sketch of proof given in [905]:

Proposition 15 *Let f be any n-variable Boolean function. Denoting by e_i the ith vector of the canonical basis of $\mathbb{F}_2^n$, the numerical degree of f satisfies the following:*

$$d_{num}(f) \geq 2^{-n} \sum_{i=1}^{n} w_H(D_{e_i} f). \tag{2.63}$$

If each variable x_i is effective in $f(x)$, that is, if each derivative $D_{e_i} f$ is nonzero, then we have

$$d_{num}(f) \geq n\, 2^{-d_{alg}(f)+1}. \tag{2.64}$$

and a fortiori

$$n \leq d_{num}(f) \, 2^{d_{num}(f)-1}. \tag{2.65}$$

Consequently:

$$d_{num}(f) \geq 1 + \log_2 n - \log_2(1 + \log_2 n). \tag{2.66}$$

Proof According to Relation (2.54), page 62, we have the following:

$$\sum_{i=1}^{n} \Delta_f(e_i) = 2^{-n} \sum_{u \in \mathbb{F}_2^n} W_f^2(u) \sum_{i=1}^{n} (-1)^{u \cdot e_i} = 2^{-n} \sum_{u \in \mathbb{F}_2^n} W_f^2(u)[n - 2w_H(u)],$$

and therefore, since $\Delta_f(e_i) = 2^n - 2w_H(D_{e_i} f)$:

$$\sum_{i=1}^{n} w_H(D_{e_i} f) = n2^{n-1} - 2^{-(n+1)} \sum_{u \in \mathbb{F}_2^n} W_f^2(u)[n - 2w_H(u)]. \tag{2.67}$$

Using *Parseval's relation*, we deduce that

$$\sum_{i=1}^{n} w_H(D_{e_i} f) = 2^{-n} \sum_{u \in \mathbb{F}_2^n} W_f^2(u) \, w_H(u) \leq 2^{-n} d_{num}(f) \sum_{u \in \mathbb{F}_2^n} W_f^2(u) = 2^n d_{num}(f).$$

This proves Relation (2.63).

If each derivative $D_{e_i} f$ is nonzero, then $w_H(D_{e_i} f)$ is at least $2^{n-d_{alg}(D_{e_i} f)} \geq 2^{n-d_{alg}(f)+1} \geq 2^{n-d_{num}(f)+1}$, since the minimum nonzero Hamming weight of n-variable Boolean functions of algebraic degree at most r equals 2^{n-r}, as we shall see in Theorem 7, page 152. According to Relation (2.63), we have then Relation (2.64) and that $d_{num}(f) \, 2^{d_{num}(f)} \geq 2n$, and this proves Relation (2.65).

Relation (2.66) is directly deduced, since for $x \geq 1$, function $x \, 2^x$ is increasing and we have $x \, 2^x = y \Rightarrow x + \log_2 x = \log_2 y \Rightarrow x \leq \log_2 y$, and therefore $x \, 2^x = y \Rightarrow x = \log_2 y - \log_2 x \geq \log_2 y - \log_2 \log_2 y$. $\qquad\square$

The value of $2^{-n} w_H(D_{e_i} f)$ is called in [905, 914] the *influence of variable* x_i and the sum of these values the total influence. See more in [652, 653].

Bound (2.66) is tight up to approximately the term in $\log_2 \log_2 n$. Indeed, the so-called *address function* $f(x, y) = x_{\varphi(y)}$, $x \in \mathbb{F}_2^{2^k}$, $y \in \mathbb{F}_2^k$, where $\varphi(y) = 1 + \sum_{i=1}^{k} y_i 2^{i-1}$, has for NNF: $\sum_{u \in \mathbb{F}_2^k} x_{\varphi(u)} \delta_u(y) = \sum_{u \in \mathbb{F}_2^k} x_{\varphi(u)} \prod_{i=1}^{k} (1 - y_i - u_i + 2y_i u_i)$. It has then $n = k + 2^k$ variables and numerical degree $1 + k$.

Remark. According to the calculations above, bound (2.63) is an equality if and only if the Walsh support of f is included in the set of vectors of Hamming weight $d_{num}(f)$ (*i.e.*, the Walsh transform of f is homogeneous; an example is affine functions). Under this condition, Bound (2.65) is an equality if and only if, for every $i = 1, \ldots, n$, we have that $d_{num}(D_{e_i} f) = d_{alg}(f) - 1$ and $D_{e_i} f$ is the indicator of an affine space (see Theorem 8). We do not know if such function exists. $\qquad\square$

Remark. Functions of very low numerical degree $d \approx \log_2 n$ (such as the address function) have a Walsh support of a size at most $D = \sum_{i=0}^{d} \binom{n}{i} \approx \frac{n^{\log_2 n}}{\lfloor \log_2 n \rfloor!}$, according to Proposition 14. It is interesting to see that the Walsh support's size can be that small, while the function depends on all its variables and can be rather complex. In fact, this size is still smaller when f is the address function above, since for every $a \in \mathbb{F}_2^{2^k}$ and $b \in \mathbb{F}_2^k$, we have then $W_f(a,b) = \sum_{y \in \mathbb{F}_2^k} (-1)^{b \cdot y} \sum_{x \in \mathbb{F}_2^{2^k}} (-1)^{x_{\varphi(y)} \oplus a \cdot x}$ and therefore $W_f(a,b) = 0$ if a has Hamming weight different from 1, and the Walsh support of f has size $2^{2k} < n^2$ (the size is exactly 2^{2k} since, if a is the jth vector of the canonical basis of $\mathbb{F}_2^{2^k}$, then for every $b \in \mathbb{F}_2^k$ we have $W_f(a,b) = 2^{2^k}(-1)^{b \cdot y} \neq 0$, where y is the unique element such that $\varphi(y) = j$). The Walsh support is the union of 2^k cosets of the k-dimensional linear subspace $\{0_{2^k}\} \times \mathbb{F}_2^k$ of $\mathbb{F}_2^{2^k} \times \mathbb{F}_2^k$.

The address function is a particular case of a general class of functions called Maiorana–McFarland, which we shall see at page 165, and which can provide more cases of small Walsh supports (see after Proposition 53, page 166). □

Determining, for all n, the exact minimum numerical degree of n-variable Boolean functions depending on all their variables is open.

Of course, if a function does not depend on all its n variables, we still have the bound $d_{num}(f) \geq 1 + \log_2 m - \log_2(1 + \log_2 m)$, where m is the number of effective variables in $f(x)$.

Remark. The NNF presents the interest of being a polynomial representation, but it can also be viewed as the transform that maps any pseudo-Boolean function $f(x) = \sum_{I \subseteq \{1,\dots,n\}} \lambda_I x^I$ to the pseudo-Boolean function g defined by $g(x) = \lambda_{supp(x)}$. Let us denote this mapping by Φ. Three other transforms have also been used for studying Boolean functions:

- The mapping Φ^{-1} (the formulae relating this mapping and the Walsh transform are slightly simpler than for Φ; see [985])
- A mapping defined by a formula similar to Relation (2.23), but in which $supp(x) \subseteq I$ is replaced by $I \subseteq supp(x)$; see [579]
- The inverse of this latter mapping □

Remark. An interesting question is, given a Boolean function f, what is the minimum *numerical degree* of all the Boolean functions affine equivalent to f (that is, thanks to the fact that the affine equivalence of functions implies the linear equivalence of their Walsh supports (see page 63), what is the minimum for all the sets S that are linearly equivalent to the Walsh support of f, of the maximum Hamming weight of the elements of S)? Note that there exist functions such that this minimum is strictly larger than the algebraic degree (this is the case of bent functions, for instance – see Definition 19, page 80 – since for these functions the minimum is n and the algebraic degree equals $n/2$). Note also that if we replace "minimum" with "maximum," the number is n for every nonconstant Boolean function, since for any element of $\mathbb{F}_2^n$, there exists a linear permutation that maps this element to the all-1 vector. □

2.3.5 *The size of the support of the Fourier–Hadamard transform and Cayley graphs*

In *graph theory*, an undirected graph is an ordered pair (V, E), where V is a set of points called *vertices* or *nodes*, and E is a set of pairs of vertices (that we shall assume distinct) called *edges* (more generally, in the case of *hypergraphs*, edges are subsets of more than two nodes). The degree of a vertex equals the number of edges it is in. Let f be a Boolean function, and let G_f be the *Cayley graph* associated to f: the vertices of this graph are the elements of $\mathbb{F}_2^n$ and there is an edge between two vertices u and v if and only if the vector $u + v$ belongs to the support of f. Then (see [68]), the values $\widehat{f}(a)$, $a \in \mathbb{F}_2^n$, of the Fourier–Hadamard transform of f are the eigenvalues of the graph G_f (that is, by definition, the eigenvalues of the adjacency matrix $(M_{u,v})_{u,v \in \mathbb{F}_2^n}$ of G_f, whose term $M_{u,v}$ equals 1 if $u + v$ belongs to the support of f, and equals 0 otherwise). Their product equals then the determinant of the adjacency matrix. Indeed, the matrix is $2^n \times 2^n$, and we have the 2^n linearly independent eigenvectors $((-1)^{a \cdot v})_{v \in \mathbb{F}_2^n}$, each one corresponding to an eigenvalue, since for every $a \in \mathbb{F}_2^n$, we have $\sum_{v \in \mathbb{F}_2^n; u + v \in supp(f)} (-1)^{a \cdot v} = \sum_{x \in supp(f)} (-1)^{a \cdot (u+x)}$ $= \widehat{f}(a)(-1)^{a \cdot u}, \forall u \in \mathbb{F}_2^n$.

As a consequence, the size $N_{\widehat{f}}$ of the support $\{a \in \mathbb{F}_2^n; \ \widehat{f}(a) \neq 0\}$ of the Fourier–Hadamard transform of any n-variable Boolean function f is larger than or equal to the size $N_{\widehat{g}}$ of the support of the Fourier–Hadamard transform of any restriction g of f, obtained by keeping constant some of its input bits. Indeed, the adjacency matrix M_g of the Cayley graph G_g is a submatrix of the adjacency matrix M_f of the Cayley graph G_f; the number $N_{\widehat{g}}$ equals the rank of M_g, and is then smaller than or equal to the rank $N_{\widehat{f}}$ of M_f.

This property can be generalized to any pseudo-Boolean function φ, with a simpler proof using the Poisson summation formula (2.39): let I be any subset of $\{1, \ldots, n\}$; let E be the vector subspace of $\mathbb{F}_2^n$ equal to $\{x \in \mathbb{F}_2^n; \ x_i = 0, \ \forall i \in I\}$; we have $E^\perp = \{x \in \mathbb{F}_2^n; \ x_i = 0, \ \forall i \in \{1, \ldots, n\} \setminus I\}$ and the sum of E and of $E^\perp$ is direct; then, for every $a \in E^\perp$ and every $b \in E$, the equality $\sum_{u \in a + E} (-1)^{b \cdot u} \widehat{\varphi}(u) = |E| (-1)^{a \cdot b} \widehat{\psi}(a)$, where ψ is the restriction of φ to $b + E^\perp$, implies that, if $N_{\widehat{\varphi}} = k$, that is, if $\widehat{\varphi}(u)$ is nonzero for exactly k vectors $u \in \mathbb{F}_2^n$, then clearly $\widehat{\psi}(a)$ is nonzero for at most k vectors $a \in E^\perp$.

Coming back to the case where φ is a Boolean function, say $\varphi = f$, where f has algebraic degree d, choosing for I a multiindex of size d such that x^I is part of the ANF of f, then the restriction $\psi = g$ has odd weight and its Fourier–Hadamard transform takes therefore nonzero values only. We deduce (as proved in [68]) that

$$N_{\widehat{f}} \geq 2^d.$$

Notice that $N_{\widehat{f}}$ equals 2^d if and only if at most one element (that is, exactly one) satisfying $\widehat{f}(u) \neq 0$ exists in each coset of E, that is, in each set obtained by keeping constant the coordinates x_i such that $i \in I$.

The number $N_{\widehat{\varphi}}$ is also bounded above by $\sum_{i=0}^{D} \binom{n}{i}$, where D is the *numerical degree* of φ. This is a direct consequence of Proposition 14.

The graph viewpoint gives insight on those Boolean functions whose Fourier–Hadamard spectra have at most three values, as can be seen in [68]. Bent functions (see Chapter 6) are those Boolean functions whose Cayley graphs are strongly regular of a particular type [68, 69]: those graphs such that, for all distinct vertices u, v, the number of those vertices that are adjacent to both u and v are the same.

A hypergraph (see page 70) can also be related to the ANF of a Boolean function f. A related (weak) upper bound on the nonlinearity of Boolean functions (see definition in Section 3.1) has been pointed out in [1179].

2.3.6 The Walsh transform of vectorial functions

Assuming that an inner product in $\mathbb{F}_2^n$ and an inner product in $\mathbb{F}_2^m$ have been chosen, both denoted by "·", we call the *Walsh transform* of an (n, m)-*function* F, and we denote by W_F, the function that maps any ordered pair $(u, v) \in \mathbb{F}_2^n \times \mathbb{F}_2^m$ to the value at u of the Walsh transform of the Boolean function $v \cdot F$:

$$W_F(u, v) = \sum_{x \in \mathbb{F}_2^n} (-1)^{v \cdot F(x) \oplus u \cdot x}; \ u \in \mathbb{F}_2^n, v \in \mathbb{F}_2^m.$$

We call the *Walsh spectrum* of F the multiset of all the values $W_F(u, v)$, where $u \in \mathbb{F}_2^n, v \in \mathbb{F}_2^m$. We call the *extended Walsh spectrum* of F the multiset of their absolute values, and *Walsh support* of F the set of those (u, v) such that $W_F(u, v) \neq 0$.

Remark. If we denote by $\mathcal{G}_F$ the *graph* $\{(x, y) \in \mathbb{F}_2^n \times \mathbb{F}_2^m; y = F(x)\}$ of F, and by $1_{\mathcal{G}_F}$ its *indicator* (taking value 1 on $\mathcal{G}_F$ and 0 outside), then we have $W_F(u, v) = \widehat{1_{\mathcal{G}_F}}(u, v)$. *The Walsh transform of any vectorial function is the Fourier–Hadamard transform of the indicator of its graph.*

The *autocorrelation function* $(a, v) \rightarrow \sum_{x \in \mathbb{F}_2^n} (-1)^{v \cdot (F(x) + F(x+a))}$ is directly connected to the Fourier transform of the function implementing the *difference table* $D_F(a, b) = |x; F(x) + F(x + a) = b|$ since we have $\sum_{x \in \mathbb{F}_2^n} (-1)^{v \cdot (F(x) + F(x+a))} = \sum_{b \in \mathbb{F}_2^m} D_F(a, b)(-1)^{v \cdot b}$, and $D_F(a, b)$ is then recovered from the autocorrelation function by the inverse Fourier transform formula for Boolean functions. □

The *inverse Walsh transform formula* (2.43) for vectorial functions writes the following:

$$\sum_{u \in \mathbb{F}_2^n} W_F(u, v) (-1)^{u \cdot x} = 2^n (-1)^{v \cdot F(x)}. \tag{2.68}$$

There is a simple way of expressing the value of the Walsh transform of the composition of two vectorial functions by means of those of the functions:

Proposition 16 *If we write the values of the function W_F in a $2^m \times 2^n$ matrix $(M_{v,u})_{v \in \mathbb{F}_2^m, u \in \mathbb{F}_2^n}$ where $M_{v,u} = W_F(u, v)$, then the matrix similarly corresponding to the composite function $F \circ H$, where H is an (r, n)-function, equals $2^{-n} M \times N$, where N is defined similarly with respect to H.*

Proof For every $w \in \mathbb{F}_2^r$ and every $v \in \mathbb{F}_2^m$, we have

$$\sum_{u \in \mathbb{F}_2^n} W_F(u, v) W_H(w, u) = \sum_{u \in \mathbb{F}_2^n; x \in \mathbb{F}_2^r; y \in \mathbb{F}_2^n} (-1)^{v \cdot F(y) \oplus u \cdot (y + H(x)) \oplus w \cdot x}$$

$$= 2^n \sum_{x \in \mathbb{F}_2^r; y \subset \mathbb{F}_2^n; y = H(x)} (-1)^{v \cdot F(y) \oplus w \cdot x}$$

$$= 2^n W_{F \circ H}(w, v),$$

since $\sum_{u \in \mathbb{F}_2^n} (-1)^{u \cdot (y + H(x))}$ equals 2^n if $y = H(x)$, and is null otherwise. □

Remark. Because of Proposition 16, it could seem more convenient to exchange the positions of u and v in $W_F(u, v)$. But we shall not do so because the common use is to respect the order (input, output). □

Remark. We have $W_F(u, v) = \sum_{b \in \mathbb{F}_2^m} \widehat{\varphi_b}(u)(-1)^{v \cdot b}$, where $\widehat{\varphi_b}$ is the Fourier–Hadamard transform of the indicator function φ_b of the preimage $F^{-1}(b) = \{x \in \mathbb{F}_2^n; \ F(x) = b\}$. □

In [201], it is shown that the possibility of building a function *CCZ equivalent* to a given (n, m)-function F depends on the structure of the set of zeros of its Walsh transform. Given an affine permutation $A = L + (a, b)$ of $\mathbb{F}_2^n \times \mathbb{F}_2^m$ (where $L = (L_1, L_2)$ is a linear permutation and (a, b) a point in $\mathbb{F}_2^n \times \mathbb{F}_2^m$), the image by A of the *graph* $\mathcal{G}_F$ of F is the graph of a function if and only if the image of $\mathbb{F}_2^n \times \{0_m\}$ by the adjoint operator L^* of L is included in the set $W_F^{-1}(0) \cup \{(0_n, 0_m)\}$. This is immediate: a necessary and sufficient condition is that $L_1(x, F(x))$ be a permutation and according to Proposition 35, page 112, this is equivalent to $\forall u \neq 0_n, \sum_{x \in \mathbb{F}_2^n} (-1)^{(u, 0_m) \cdot L(x, F(x))} = \sum_{x \in \mathbb{F}_2^n} (-1)^{L^*(u, 0_m) \cdot (x, F(x))} = 0$. A transformation called twisting allows then to move to another EA equivalence class within the same CCZ equivalence class: the output of F is viewed in the form $(T_y(x), U_x(y)) \in \mathbb{F}_2^t \times \mathbb{F}_2^{m-t}$, where $t \leq \min(n, m)$, $x \in \mathbb{F}_2^t, y \in \mathbb{F}_2^{n-t}$ and where T_y is assumed to be a permutation for every y. Then the t-twisting of F is the function $(T_y^{-1}(x), U_{T_y^{-1}(x)}(y))$, whose graph is obtained from that of F by swapping, in each vector of the graph, the subvector of indices $1, \ldots, t$ and the subvector of indices $n + 1, \ldots, n + t$. It is shown in [201] that every CCZ equivalent function to F can be obtained from F in three steps: applying EA equivalence, then twisting, then applying EA equivalence again. The number of EA equivalence classes in the CCZ equivalence class of F is bounded above by the number of n-dimensional vector spaces in $W_F^{-1}(0) \cup \{(0_n, 0_m)\}$ and below by this same number divided by the order of the *automorphism group of function F* (*i.e.*, the group of those affine automorphisms that preserve the graph of F).

The case of power functions

When $\mathbb{F}_2^n$ is identified with $\mathbb{F}_{2^n}$, we have seen at page 24 that *power functions* are those functions of the form $F(x) = x^d$. They usually have a lower implementation cost in hardware. Such F is a permutation of $\mathbb{F}_{2^n}$ if and only if d is coprime with $2^n - 1$. An inner product being for instance $(x, y) \mapsto tr_n(x\,y)$, for every $(u, v) \in (\mathbb{F}_{2^n}^*)^2$ and every d, we have (by the change of variable $x \mapsto \frac{x}{u}$) that $W_F(u, v) = W_F(1, \frac{v}{u^d})$, and if x^d is a permutation of $\mathbb{F}_{2^n}$, then we have $\left(\text{by the change of variable } x \mapsto \frac{x}{v^{\frac{1}{d}}}\right)$ that $W_F(u, v) = W_F\left(\frac{u}{v^{\frac{1}{d}}}, 1\right)$.

It has been conjectured in 1976 by Helleseth[34] in [592] that, for every $n \geq 2$ and every value of d coprime with $2^n - 1$, there exists $a \in \mathbb{F}_{2^n}^*$ such that $W_F(a, 1) = 0$. This conjecture is still open. It has been checked for $n \leq 25$ by Langevin and proved for $d = 2^n - 2$ (inverse function) in [733] (see more at page 215). We have the following propositions:

---

[34] The conjecture is stated for every characteristic p such that $d \equiv 1 \ [\mathrm{mod}\ p - 1]$.

Proposition 17 *[39] For every power permutation $F(x) = x^d$, there exists $a \in \mathbb{F}_{2^n}^*$ such that $W_F(a, 1) \equiv 0$ [mod 3].*

Proposition 18 *[673] If $\gcd(d, 2^n - 1) = 1$ and if the set $\{W_f(a); a \in \mathbb{F}_{2^n}^*\}$ has three distinct values exactly, then one of these values is 0.*

Proposition 19 *[673] If $\gcd(d, 2^n - 1) = 1$ and n is a power of 2, then the set $\{W_f(a); a \in \mathbb{F}_{2^n}^*\}$ cannot have three distinct values exactly.*

See more in [675]. Some results related to Gauss sums are also given in [38] and we have the following proposition:

Proposition 20 *[174] For every n equal to a power of 2 and every nonlinear power permutation $F(x) = x^d$ over $\mathbb{F}_{2^n}$, there exists $a \in \mathbb{F}_{2^n}^*$ such that $W_F(a, 1)$ is not divisible by $2^{\frac{n}{2}+1}$.*

It is observed in [38] that if n is even and $F(x) = x^d$ is constant over $\mathbb{F}_{2^{\frac{n}{2}}}^*$ and not over $\mathbb{F}_{2^n}^*$, then there exists $a \in \mathbb{F}_{2^n}^*$ such that $W_F(a, 1) = -2^{\frac{n}{2}}$. And using McEliece's theorem, it is proved that:

Proposition 21 *[194, 196] Let l and n be two positive integers. The Walsh values of a power function $F(x) = x^d$ over $\mathbb{F}_{2^n}$ are all divisible by 2^l if and only if, for all $u \in \mathbb{Z}/(2^n - 1)\mathbb{Z}$, $w_2(ud) \leq w_2(u) + n - l$.*

See also [746]. These results are complementary of Theorem 2, page 63 (recall that the algebraic degree of x^d equals $w_2(d)$). The latter will have consequences for the characterization of almost bent functions; see page 382.

Relation between the Walsh transform and NNF of the graph indicator

We know that $W_F(u, v) = \widehat{1_{\mathcal{G}_F}}(u, v)$. Relation (2.59), page 66, and Relation (2.60) show then that if the NNF of $1_{\mathcal{G}_F}(x, y)$ equals $\sum_{\substack{I \subseteq \{1,\dots,n\} \\ J \subseteq \{1,\dots,m\}}} \lambda_{I,J} \, x^I y^J$, then

$$W_F(u, v) = (-1)^{w_H(u)+w_H(v)} \sum_{\substack{I \subseteq \{1,\dots,n\}, J \subseteq \{1,\dots,m\} \\ \text{supp}(u) \subseteq I, \text{supp}(v) \subseteq J}} 2^{n+m-|I|-|J|} \lambda_{I,J},$$

$$\lambda_{I,J} = 2^{-(n+m)}(-2)^{|I|+|J|} \sum_{\substack{u \in \mathbb{F}_2^n, v \in \mathbb{F}_2^m \\ I \subseteq \text{supp}(u), J \subseteq \text{supp}(v)}} W_F(u, v).$$

2.3.7 The multidimensional Walsh transform

K. Nyberg defines in [911] a polynomial representation, called the *multidimensional Walsh transform*; let us define

$$\mathcal{W}(F)(z_1,\ldots,z_m) = \sum_{x\in\mathbb{F}_2^n} \prod_{j=1}^{m} z_j^{f_j(x)} \in \mathbb{Z}[z_1,\ldots,z_m]/(z_1^2 - 1,\ldots,z_m^2 - 1),$$

where $f_1,\ldots,f_m$ are the coordinate functions of F.

The multidimensional Walsh transform maps every linear (n,m)-function L to the polynomial $\mathcal{W}(F+L)(z_1,\ldots,z_m)$. This is a representation with uniqueness of F, since, for every L, the knowledge of $\mathcal{W}(F+L)$ is equivalent to that of the evaluation of $\mathcal{W}(F+L)$ at $(\xi_1,\ldots,\xi_m)$ for every choice of ξ_j, $j = 1,\ldots,m$, in the set $\{-1,1\}$ of roots of the polynomial $z_j^2 - 1$. For such a choice, let us define the vector $v \in \mathbb{F}_2^m$ by $v_j = 1$ if $\xi_j = -1$ and $v_j = 0$ otherwise. For every $j = 1,\ldots,m$, let us denote by a_j the vector of $\mathbb{F}_2^n$ such that the jth coordinate of $L(x)$ equals $a_j \cdot x$. We denote then by u the vector $\sum_{j=1}^{m} v_j a_j \in \mathbb{F}_2^n$. Then this evaluation equals $\sum_{x\in\mathbb{F}_2^n}(-1)^{v\cdot F(x)\oplus u\cdot x}$. We see that the correspondence between the multidimensional Walsh transform and the Walsh transform is the correspondence between a multivariate polynomial of $\mathbb{Z}[z_1,\ldots,z_m]/(z_1^2-1,\ldots,z_m^2-1)$ and its evaluation over $\{(z_1,\ldots,z_m) \in \mathbb{Z}^m / z_1^2 - 1 = \cdots = z_m^2 - 1 = 0\} = \{-1,1\}^m$. Consequently, the multidimensional Walsh transform satisfies a relation equivalent to the Parseval's relation (see [911]).

2.4 Fast computation of S-boxes

We shall see in Chapter 11 that substitution boxes are almost always expressed in univariate polynomial form $\sum_{j=0}^{2^n-1} b_j x^j$ (where $x, b_j \in \mathbb{F}_{2^n}$), because the structure of field is needed to generate them, although the multiplication plays no role in the criteria they must satisfy (only the addition playing a role). In such polynomial expression, the additions and scalar multiplications being linear mappings are fast to compute. Those multiplications whose two operands include variables (that we shall exceptionally represent explicitly by $\times$) are more complex to process fastly. Methods exist for multiplication processing (see more in [320]):

- The most efficient in terms of timing is *complete tabulation*, by reading the content of a table in ROM containing all the precomputed results. The size of the table is of $n2^{2n}$ bits, the timing is around five cycles.
- The most efficient in terms of memory is direct processing. The timing complexity is of order $\mathcal{O}(n^{\log_3(2)})$ with large constants, thanks to Karatsuba's method repeated recursively until getting low-cost multiplications:

$$m = \left\lceil \frac{n}{2} \right\rceil; \quad (a_h X^m + a_l) \times (b_h X^m + b_l) = c_h X^{2m} + c_{hl} X^m + c_l,$$

where $a_h, a_l, b_h, b_l, c_h, c_{hl}, c_l$ are polynomials of degree $\leq m$

$$c_h = a_h \times b_h, \quad c_l = a_l \times b_l,$$
$$c_{hl} = (a_h + a_l) \times (b_h + b_l) - c_h - c_l.$$

- A compromise is the so-called *log-alog* method, which assumes that the functions

$$log : x \in \mathbb{F}_{2^n} \mapsto i = \log_\alpha(x) \text{ and } alog : i \mapsto x = \alpha^i$$

have been tabulated in ROM for some primitive element α of the field. The processing of $a \times b$ then simply consists in processing:

$$c = alog[(log[a] + log[b]) \bmod 2^n - 1].$$

Its memory complexity is $n2^{n+1}$ bits, and its timing complexity is constant.

- Another compromise is obtained with the *tower field* approach. For $n = 2m$ even, the elements of $\mathbb{F}_{2^n}$ are viewed as elements of $\mathbb{F}_{2^m}[X]/(X^2 + X + \beta)$, where $X^2 + X + \beta$ is a degree-2 polynomial irreducible over $\mathbb{F}_{2^m}$. The field isomorphism mapping an element $a \in \mathbb{F}_{2^n}$ into the pair $(a_h, a_l) \in \mathbb{F}_{2^m}^2$ is denoted by L. The multiplication $a \times b$ is then executed as follows:

$$
\begin{aligned}
(a_h, a_l) &\leftarrow L(a); \quad (b_h, b_l) \leftarrow L(b); \quad c_l \leftarrow a_h \times b_h \times \beta + a_l \times b_l \\
c_h \quad &\leftarrow a_h \times (b_h + b_l) + a_l \times b_h; \quad c \leftarrow L^{-1}(c_h, c_l).
\end{aligned}
$$

This is recursively applied if n is a power of 2.

Methods also exist for evaluating whole polynomials (*e.g.*, the cyclotomic method and the Knuth–Eve method) that we shall present in Section 12.1.2 because they play a role with respect to countermeasures against side-channel attacks.

3

Boolean functions, vectorial functions, and cryptography

The design of conventional cryptographic systems relies on two fundamental principles introduced by Shannon [1034]: *confusion* and *diffusion*. Confusion aims at concealing any algebraic structure in the system. It is closely related to the complexity[1] of the involved (so-called nonlinear) functions. Diffusion consists in spreading out the influence of any minor modification of the input data or of the key over all outputs. These two principles were stated more than half a century ago. Since then, many attacks have been found against the diverse known cryptosystems, and the relevance of these two principles has always been confirmed. In this chapter, we describe the main attacks on symmetric cryptosystems and the related criteria on Boolean and vectorial functions. Two books exist on Boolean and vectorial functions for cryptography [401, 1125], which partly cover the state of the art. Several sections of the *Handbook of Finite Fields* [890] are also devoted to this same subject (in a reduced format). In the subsequent chapters, we shall develop as completely as possible the study of each criterion.

3.1 Cryptographic criteria (and related parameters) for Boolean functions

The known attacks on stream ciphers lead to criteria [842, 844, 970, 1041] that the implemented cryptographic functions must satisfy to resist attacks [388, 391, 826, 843, 1042]. More precisely, the resistance of the cryptosystems to the known attacks can be quantified through some fundamental characteristics (some, more related to confusion, and some, more related to diffusion) of the Boolean functions used in them; and the design of these cryptographic functions needs to consider various characteristics simultaneously. Some of these characteristics are affine invariants. Of course, all characteristics cannot be optimum at the same time, and trade-offs must be considered (see below).

3.1.1 Balancedness

Cryptographic Boolean functions must be *balanced* (their output must be uniformly, *i.e.*, equally, distributed over $\{0, 1\}$) for avoiding statistical dependence between the plaintext and the ciphertext. Indeed, we wish that it is not possible to distinguish the pair of a random plaintext and of the corresponding ciphertext from a random pair. Notice that f is balanced if and only if $W_f(0_n) = \mathcal{F}(f) = 0$.

---

[1] That is, the cryptographic complexity, which is different from circuit complexity, for instance.

3.1.2 Algebraic degree

Cryptographic functions must have high algebraic degrees (see Definition 6, page 35). Indeed, all cryptosystems using Boolean functions for confusion (combining or filtering functions in stream ciphers, functions involved in the S-boxes of block ciphers, etc.) can be attacked if the functions have low algebraic degrees. For instance, in the case of combining functions (see Figure 1.3, page 22), if n LFSRs having lengths $L_1, \ldots, L_n$ are combined by the function $f(x) = \bigoplus_{I \subseteq \{1,\ldots,n\}} a_I \left(\prod_{i \in I} x_i \right)$, then the sequence produced by f has *linear complexity*

$$\mathcal{L} \leq \sum_{I \subseteq \{1,\ldots,n\}} a_I \left(\prod_{i \in I} L_i \right)$$

(and $\mathcal{L}$ equals this number under the sufficient condition that the sequences output by the LFSRs are *m-sequences* of pairwise coprime periods), see [1007, 1183]. In the case of the filter model (see Figure 1.4, page 23), we have a less precise result [1006]: if L is the length of the LFSR and if the feedback polynomial is primitive, then the linear complexity of the sequence satisfies:

$$\mathcal{L} \leq \sum_{i=0}^{d_{alg}(f)} \binom{L}{i}.$$

Moreover, if L is a prime, then $\mathcal{L} \geq \binom{L}{d_{alg}(f)}$, and the fraction of functions f of a given algebraic degree that output a sequence of linear complexity equal to $\sum_{i=0}^{d_{alg}(f)} \binom{L}{i}$ is at least $e^{-1/L}$. In both models, the algebraic degree of f has to be high so that $\mathcal{L}$ can have high value (the number of those nonzero coefficients a_I, in the ANF of f, such that I has large size, can also play a role, but clearly a less important one).

When n tends to infinity, random Boolean functions have almost surely algebraic degrees at least $n - 1$ (the number $2^{\sum_{i=0}^{n-2} \binom{n}{i}} = 2^{2^n - n - 1}$ of Boolean functions of algebraic degree at most $n - 2$ is negligible with respect to the number 2^{2^n} of all Boolean functions). But we shall see that the functions of algebraic degree $n - 1$ or n do not allow achieving some other characteristics such as resiliency.

We have seen in Section 2.2 that the algebraic degree is an affine invariant.

3.1.3 Nonlinearity and higher-order nonlinearity

In order to provide confusion, cryptographic functions must lie at large Hamming distance from all affine functions. Let us explain why.

Correlations with linear functions and attacks

We shall say that there is a nonzero correlation between a Boolean function f and a linear function ℓ if $d_H(f, \ell)$ is different from 2^{n-1} (precisely, the correlation between f and $\ell_a(x) = a \cdot x$, where $a \in \mathbb{F}_2^n$, equals $\sum_{x \in \mathbb{F}_2^n} (-1)^{f(x) \oplus \ell_a(x)}$, that is $W_f(a)$). Because of Parseval's relation (2.48), page 61, and of Relation (2.37), page 57, any Boolean function has nonzero correlation with at least one linear function. But all correlations should be small (in magnitude). Indeed, a large positive correlation between a Boolean function f involved in a cryptosystem and a linear function ℓ means that $d_H(f, \ell)$ is small, and f is then efficiently approximated by ℓ; a large negative one means that it is approximated by $\ell \oplus 1$.

The existence of such affine approximations of f allows in various situations (block ciphers, stream ciphers) the building of attacks on this system.

In the case of stream ciphers, these attacks are the so-called *fast correlation attacks* [203, 369, 517, 645, 646, 647, 843]: let ℓ be a linear approximation of f (or of $f \oplus 1$, but then we shall study $f \oplus 1$), whose distance to f is smaller than 2^{n-1}, denoting by $\mathrm{Prob}\,[E]$ the probability of an event E, we have:

$$p = \mathrm{Prob}\,[f(x_1, \ldots, x_n) \neq \ell(x_1, \ldots, x_n)] = \frac{d_H(f, \ell)}{2^n} = \frac{1}{2} - \epsilon,$$

where $\epsilon > 0$. The pseudorandom sequence s corresponds then to the transmission with errors of the sequence σ that would be produced by the same model with the same LFSRs, but with ℓ instead of f. Attacking the cipher can be done by correcting the errors as in the transmission of the sequence σ over a noisy channel. Assume that we have N bits $s_u, \ldots, s_{u+N-1}$ of the pseudorandom sequence s, then $\mathrm{Prob}\,[s_i \neq \sigma_i] \approx p$. The set of possible sequences $\sigma_u, \ldots, \sigma_{u+N-1}$ is a vector space, that is, a linear code of length N and dimension at most L, where L is the size of the linear part of the PRG (the length of the LFSR in the case of the filter generator). We then use a decoding algorithm to recover $\sigma_u, \ldots, \sigma_{u+N-1}$ from $s_u, \ldots, s_{u+N-1}$, and since ℓ is linear, the linear complexity of the sequence σ is small and we obtain, for instance by the Berlekamp–Massey (BM) algorithm, the initialization of the LFSR. We can then compute the whole sequence s.

There are several ways for performing the decoding. The method exposed in [843] and improved by [369] is as follows. We call a *parity check polynomial* any polynomial $a(x) = 1 + \sum_{j=1}^{r} a_j x^j$ ($a_r \neq 0$), which is a multiple of the feedback polynomial of an LFSR generating the sequence σ_i. Denoting by $\sigma(x)$ the generating function $\sum_{i \geq 0} \sigma_i x^i$, the product $a(x)\sigma(x)$ is a polynomial of a degree less than r. We use for the decoding a set of parity check polynomials satisfying three conditions: their degrees are bounded by some integer m, the number of nonzero coefficients a_j in each of them is at most some number $t \geq 3$ (*i.e.*, each polynomial has Hamming weight at most $t+1$), and for every $j = 1, \ldots, m$, at most one polynomial has nonzero coefficient a_j. Each parity check polynomial $a(x) = 1 + \sum_{j=1}^{r} a_j x^j$ gives a linear relation $\sigma_i = \sum_{j=1}^{r} a_j \sigma_{i-j} = \sum_{j=1,\ldots,r\,;\,a_j \neq 0} \sigma_{i-j}$ for every $i \geq m$, and the relations corresponding to different polynomials involve different indices $i - j$. If we replace the (unknown) σ_is by the s_is, then some of these relations become false, but it is possible by using the method of Gallager [524] to compute a sequence z_i such that $\mathrm{Prob}\,(z_i = \sigma_i) > 1 - p$. Then it can be proved that iterating this process converges to the sequence σ (with a speed that depends on m, t, and p). The number of bits N needed to be known in the keystream, the offline time complexity P, and the online time complexity T are as follows (see [203]):

$$N = 2^{\frac{L}{t-1}} \left(\frac{1}{2\epsilon}\right)^{\frac{2(t-2)}{t-1}} \qquad P = \frac{N^{t-2}}{(t-2)!} \qquad T = 2^{\frac{L}{t-1}} \left(\frac{1}{2\epsilon}\right)^{\frac{2t(t-2)}{t-1}},$$

where L is the length of the LFSR and ϵ is the bias of the nonlinearity with respect to 2^{n-1}, that is, $\epsilon = \frac{2^{n-1} - nl(f)}{2^n}$, where $nl(f)$ is defined below. Note that the number of variables of the function does not play an explicit role.

In the case of block ciphers, we shall see in Section 3.4 that the Boolean functions involved in their S-boxes must also lie at large Hamming distances to *affine functions*, to allow resistance to the linear attacks [829].

The corresponding parameter and criterion for Boolean functions

Definition 18 *The* nonlinearity *of a Boolean function f is the minimum Hamming distance between f and affine functions. We shall denote it by $nl(f)$.*

The larger is the nonlinearity, the larger is p in the fast correlation attack and the less efficient is the attack. Hence, from the designer point of view, the nonlinearity must be large (in a sense that will be clarified below), and we shall see that this condition happens to be necessary against other attacks as well. A high nonlinearity is surely one of the most important cryptographic criteria.

By definition, the nonlinearity of any Boolean function is bounded above by its Hamming weight. The set of those Boolean functions that achieve this bound with equality (*i.e.*, of all possible *coset leaders* of the first-order Reed–Muller code) is unknown. Some functions belong obviously to it: n-variable Boolean functions of Hamming weight at most 2^{n-2} (since nonzero affine functions have at least twice the weight, and according to the triangular inequality); bent functions (see Definition 19 below) of Hamming weight $2^{n-1} - 2^{\frac{n}{2}-1}$; and more generally, plateaued functions (see Definition 63, page 258) of amplitude 2^r and Hamming weight $2^{n-1} - 2^{r-1}$. But the set is not completely determined. Note that each coset of the first-order Reed–Muller code contains at least one element of this set. In [1138], the Boolean functions of nonlinearities 2^{n-2} and $2^{n-2} + 1$ are studied.

The nonlinearity is an *EA invariant*, since $d_H(f \circ L \oplus \ell', \ell) = d_H(f, (\ell \oplus \ell') \circ L^{-1})$, for every function f, ℓ, and ℓ', and for every affine automorphism L, and since $(\ell \oplus \ell') \circ L^{-1}$ ranges over the whole set of affine functions when ℓ does.

The nonlinearity can be computed through the Walsh transform: let $\ell_a(x) = a_1 x_1 \oplus \cdots \oplus a_n x_n = a \cdot x$ be any linear function; according to Relation (2.37), we have $d_H(f, \ell_a) = 2^{n-1} - \frac{1}{2} W_f(a)$, and we deduce $d_H(f, \ell_a \oplus 1) = 2^{n-1} + \frac{1}{2} W_f(a)$; the nonlinearity of f is therefore equal to

$$nl(f) = 2^{n-1} - \frac{1}{2} \max_{a \in \mathbb{F}_2^n} |W_f(a)|. \tag{3.1}$$

Hence a function has high nonlinearity if and only if all of its Walsh values have low magnitudes. The value $\max_{a \in \mathbb{F}_2^n} |W_f(a)|$ is called the "linearity of f" by some authors and its "spectral amplitude" by some others.

Upper and lower bounds, bent functions

Parseval's relation $\sum_{a \in \mathbb{F}_2^n} W_f^2(a) = 2^{2n}$ implies that the arithmetic mean of $W_f^2(a)$ equals 2^n. The maximum of $W_f^2(a)$ being larger than or equal to its arithmetic mean, we deduce that $\max_{a \in \mathbb{F}_2^n} |W_f(a)| \geq 2^{\frac{n}{2}}$. This implies the following:

Theorem 3 *For every n-variable Boolean function f, we have*

$$nl(f) \leq 2^{n-1} - 2^{\frac{n}{2}-1}. \tag{3.2}$$

This bound, valid for every Boolean function and tight for every even n as we shall see, is called the *covering radius bound*[2]. It can be improved (*i.e.*, lowered) when we restrict ourselves to some subclasses of functions: resilient and correlation immune functions (see Chapter 7); functions $tr(ax^d)$ such that $a \in \mathbb{F}_{2^n}^*$ and $\gcd(d, 2^n - 1) = 1$, since their nonlinearity equals that of the vectorial function x^d and is then bounded above by $2^{n-1} - 2^{\frac{n-1}{2}}$, according to Theorem 6, page 118. A Boolean function will be considered as highly nonlinear if its nonlinearity lies near[3] the upper bound in its class. Note that, for general Boolean functions, there is no direct correlation between the nonlinearity and the algebraic degree: highly nonlinear n-variable functions can have an algebraic degree as low as 2 (see Section 5.2) and as large as n (but then the nonlinearity cannot be optimal; see Theorem 13, page 200), and functions with low nonlinearity (*e.g.*, functions of Hamming weight at most 2^{n-2}, whose nonlinearity equals the Hamming weight since the minimum distance of the Reed–Muller code of order 1 equals 2^{n-1} and because of the triangular inequality on Hamming distance) can have algebraic degree between 2 and n as well.

Olejár and Stanek [917] have shown that, when n tends to infinity, random Boolean functions on $\mathbb{F}_2^n$ have almost surely nonlinearity larger than $2^{n-1} - \sqrt{n} \, 2^{\frac{n-1}{2}}$ (this is easy to prove by counting – or more precisely by bounding from above – the number of functions whose nonlinearities are lower than or equal to a given number; see, *e.g.*, [224, 229], and using the so-called Shannon effect; see page 103). Rodier [1000] has shown later a more precise and strong result: asymptotically, almost all Boolean functions have nonlinearity between $2^{n-1} - 2^{\frac{n}{2}-1}\sqrt{n}\left(\sqrt{2\ln 2} + \frac{4\ln n}{n}\right)$ and $2^{n-1} - 2^{\frac{n}{2}-1}\sqrt{n}\left(\sqrt{2\ln 2} - \frac{5\ln n}{n}\right)$ and therefore located in the neighborhood of $2^{n-1} - 2^{\frac{n}{2}-1}\sqrt{2n\ln 2}$, where ln denotes the natural (*i.e.*, Neperian) logarithm.

The probability $\text{Prob}\,(\max_w |W_F(w)| \geq y)$ is equal to 1 when $y = 2^{n/2}$; it decreases slowly when y increases, decreases then suddenly to the neighborhood of 0 when y is approaching $2^{n/2}\sqrt{2n\ln 2}$, then it decreases slowly to 0 when y increases to 2^n. Further details can be given around $2^{n/2}\sqrt{2n\ln 2}$. The article [784] provides sharper results by a different method. For $n > 164$, we have $\text{Prob}\,(\max_w |W_F(w)| \geq 2^{n/2}\sqrt{2n\ln 2}) \leq (1 + o(1))/\sqrt{n\pi \ln 2}$.

Equality occurs in (3.2) if and only if $|W_f(a)| = 2^{\frac{n}{2}}$ for every vector a, since the maximum of $W_f^2(a)$ equals the arithmetic mean if and only if $W_f^2(a)$ is constant.

Definition 19 *An n variable Boolean function is called* bent *if its nonlinearity equals* $2^{n-1} - 2^{\frac{n}{2}-1}$, *or equivalently,* $W_f(a) = \pm 2^{\frac{n}{2}}$ *for every* $a \in \mathbb{F}_2^n$.

---

[2] The covering radius of the *Reed–Muller code* of order 1 equals by definition the maximum nonlinearity of Boolean functions; see Section 4.1.

[3] The meaning of "near" depends on the framework; see [650].

Table 3.1 Best-known nonlinearities nl of Boolean functions in small odd dimension [815].

n	5	7	9	11	13	15
$2^{n-1} - 2^{\frac{n-1}{2}}$	12	56	240	992	4,032	16,256
nl	12	56	242	996	4,040	16,276
$2\lfloor 2^{n-2} - 2^{\frac{n}{2}-2}\rfloor$	12	58	244	1,000	4,050	16,292

Such functions exist only for even values of n, because $2^{n-1} - 2^{\frac{n}{2}-1}$ must be an integer (in fact, they exist for every n even). Chapter 6 is devoted to them.

For n odd, Inequality (3.2) cannot be tight. The maximum nonlinearity of n-variable Boolean functions, that is, the *covering radius* of $RM(1,n)$, lies then between $2^{n-1} - 2^{\frac{n-1}{2}}$ (which can always be achieved, *e.g.*, by quadratic functions; see Section 5.2) and $2\lfloor 2^{n-2} - 2^{\frac{n}{2}-2}\rfloor$ [617]. It has been shown in [597, 894] that it equals $2^{n-1} - 2^{\frac{n-1}{2}}$ when $n = 1, 3, 5, 7$, and in [936, 937], by Patterson and Wiedemann[4] (with rotation symmetric functions, see Definitions 59 and 60 at page 248), that it is strictly larger than $2^{n-1} - 2^{\frac{n-1}{2}}$ if $n \geq 15$ (a review on what was known in 1999 on the best nonlinearities of functions on odd numbers of variables is given in [515]; see also [133, 747, 815]). This value $2^{n-1} - 2^{\frac{n-1}{2}}$ is called the *quadratic bound* because, as we already mentioned, such nonlinearity can be achieved by quadratic functions. It is also called the *bent concatenation bound* since it can also be achieved by the concatenation $x_n f(x_1, \ldots, x_{n-1}) \oplus (x_n \oplus 1)g(x_1, \ldots, x_{n-1})$ of two bent functions f, g in $n-1$ variables. It has been later proved by Kavut et al. in [684, 686] (see also [816], where balanced functions are obtained), thanks to rotation symmetric functions as well, that the best nonlinearity of Boolean functions in odd numbers of variables is strictly larger than the quadratic bound for any $n > 7$. See Table 3.1 for the best-known nonlinearities for n odd between 5 and 15 compared to the quadratic (or bent concatenation) lower bound and to the upper bound.

Bent functions being not balanced (since we have seen that f is bent if and only if $|W_f(a)|$ equals $2^{\frac{n}{2}}$ for every vector a and then $W_f(0_n) \neq 0$), and having too low algebraic degree (as we shall see with Theorem 13, page 200), they are improper for use in cryptosystems. For this reason, even when they exist (for n even), it is also necessary to study those functions that have large nonlinearities, say between $2^{n-1} - 2^{\frac{n-1}{2}}$ and $2^{n-1} - 2^{\frac{n}{2}-1}$, but are not bent, among which some balanced functions exist. The maximum nonlinearity of balanced functions is unknown for any $n \geq 8$. See Table 3.2 for the best-known nonlinearities for n between 4 and 15 compared to the upper bound $bnd = 2\lfloor 2^{n-2} - 2^{\frac{n}{2}-2}\rfloor$. Note that the 15-variable function can be made 1-resilient (see Definition 21, page 86).

As first observed in [1169, 1173], relations exist between the nonlinearity and the *derivatives* of Boolean functions. We give here simpler proofs of these facts. Applying Relation (2.56) to $E = \{0_n, e\}^\perp$, where $e \neq 0_n$, and to $b = 0_n$ and all $a \in \mathbb{F}_2^n$, and using that $\max_{u \in a+E} W_f^2(u) \geq \frac{1}{|E|} \sum_{u \in a+E} W_f^2(u)$, we have the following proposition:

---

[4] It has been later proved (see [466, 696, 820, 1016, 1027]) that balanced functions with nonlinearity strictly larger than $2^{n-1} - 2^{\frac{n-1}{2}}$, and with algebraic degree $n-1$, or satisfying $PC(1)$; see Definition 24, page 97, exist for every odd $n \geq 15$.

Table 3.2 Best-known nonlinearities nl of balanced Boolean functions in small dimension [685, 815, 816, 1016].

n	4	5	6	7	8	9	10	11	12	13	14	15
nl	4	12	26	56	116	240	492	992	2,010	4,036	8,120	16,272
bnd	6	12	28	58	120	244	496	1,000	2,016	4,050	8,128	16,292

Proposition 22 *For every $n \geq 1$ and every n-variable Boolean function f, we have*

$$nl(f) \leq 2^{n-1} - \frac{1}{2}\sqrt{2^n + \max_{e \neq 0_n} |\mathcal{F}(D_e f)|}.$$

This directly proves an important property of bent functions that we shall revisit in Chapter 6: f is bent if and only if all its derivatives $D_e f, e \neq 0_n$, are balanced.

The obvious relation $w_H(f) \geq \frac{1}{2} w_H(D_e f) = \frac{1}{2}\left(2^{n-1} - \frac{1}{2}\mathcal{F}(D_e f)\right)$, valid for every $e \in \mathbb{F}_2^n$, leads when applied to the functions $f(x) \oplus a \cdot x \oplus \epsilon$, where $a \in \mathbb{F}_2^n$ and $\epsilon \in \mathbb{F}_2$, to the inequality $d_H(f, a \cdot x \oplus \epsilon) \geq \frac{1}{2}\left(2^{n-1} - \frac{1}{2}(-1)^{a \cdot e}\mathcal{F}(D_e f)\right) \geq \frac{1}{2}\left(2^{n-1} - \frac{1}{2}|\mathcal{F}(D_e f)|\right)$. Hence, taking the maximum of this last expression when e ranges over $\mathbb{F}_2^n$, we deduce the lower bound:

Proposition 23 *For every positive integer n and every n-variable function f, we have*

$$nl(f) \geq 2^{n-2} - \frac{1}{4}\min_{e \in \mathbb{F}_2^n, e \neq 0_n} |\mathcal{F}(D_e f)|. \tag{3.3}$$

Another lower bound on the nonlinearity is given at the end of the remark located after Theorem 7, page 152, and a further one is given in [248, subsection 4.2]:

Proposition 24 *Let f be any n-variable Boolean function. Let $S = supp(f) = \{x \in \mathbb{F}_2^n;$ $f(x) = 1\}$ be the support of f and let $M_f =$*

$$\frac{\max_{z \in \mathbb{F}_2^n \setminus \{0_n\}} |\{(x, y) \in S^2; \ x + y = z\}| + \min_{z \in \mathbb{F}_2^n \setminus \{0_n\}} |\{(x, y) \in S^2; \ x + y = z\}|}{2}$$

and let $E_f =$

$$\frac{\max_{z \in \mathbb{F}_2^n \setminus \{0_n\}} |\{(x, y) \in S^2; \ x + y = z\}| - \min_{z \in \mathbb{F}_2^n \setminus \{0_n\}} |\{(x, y) \in S^2; \ x + y = z\}|}{2}.$$

Then:

$$nl(f) \geq 2^{n-1} - \max\left(|2^{n-1} - |S||, \sqrt{|S| - M_f + (2^n - 1)E_f}\right). \tag{3.4}$$

Any bent function achieves (3.4) with equality and it would be interesting to determine all functions f such that (3.4) is an equality.

Nonlinearity and codes

The nonlinearity of a Boolean function f equals the minimum distance of the linear code $RM(1,n) \cup (f \oplus RM(1,n))$. See more in Chapter 4. More generally, the minimum distance of an *unrestricted code* defined as the union of cosets $f \oplus RM(1,n)$ of the Reed–Muller code of order 1, where f ranges over a set $\mathcal{F}$ equals the minimum nonlinearity of the functions $f \oplus g$, where f and g are distinct and range over $\mathcal{F}$, since $d_H(f \oplus h, g \oplus h') = d_H(f \oplus g, h \oplus h')$ and $h \oplus h'$ ranges over $RM(1,n)$ when h, h' do. This observation allows constructing some optimal nonlinear codes such as Kerdock codes (see Section 6.1.22).

Higher-order nonlinearity

Changing one or a few bits in the output (in the truth table) of a low degree Boolean function gives a function with high degree and does not fundamentally modify the robustness of the system using it (explicit attacks using approximations by low-degree functions exist for block ciphers but not for all stream ciphers, however; see, *e.g.*, [707]). A relevant parameter is the *nonlinearity profile*:

Definition 20 *Let n and $r \leq n$ be positive integers. Let f be an n-variable Boolean function. We call the r-th order nonlinearity (and if r is not specified, the higher-order nonlinearity) of f and we denote by $nl_r(f)$, its Hamming distance to the Reed–Muller code of order r. The nonlinearity profile of f is the sequence of its r-th order nonlinearities, for all values of $r < n$.*

Several papers have shown the role played by this EA-invariant parameter against some cryptanalyses (but contrary to the first-order nonlinearity, it must have low value for allowing attacks) and studied it from an algorithmic viewpoint [387, 544, 638, 707, 831, 882]. It is related to the minimal distance to functions depending on a subset of variables (which plays a role with respect to the correlation attack, see below in Subsection 3.1.7, and is not EA invariant) since a function depending on k variables has algebraic degree at most k. Hence the r-th order nonlinearity is a lower bound for the distance to functions depending on at most r variables. The former is much more difficult to study than the latter. The best possible rth-order nonlinearity of Boolean functions equals the covering radius of the r-th order Reed–Muller code; see Subsection 4.1.6, page 157.

Upper and lower bounds and asymptotic behavior An upper bound on $nl_r(f)$ is given in [309] for $r \geq 2$, which we shall address in Section 4.1 (see page 158). Asymptotically, it gives

$$nl_r(f) \leq 2^{n-1} - \frac{\sqrt{15}}{2} \cdot (1 + \sqrt{2})^{r-2} \cdot 2^{\frac{n}{2}} + \mathcal{O}(n^{r-2}).$$

An asymptotic lower bound, given in [229], is as follows: let $c \in \mathbb{R}$, $c > 0$; for every $r \geq 0$, the density of the set of functions such that

$$nl_r(f) > 2^{n-1} - c \sqrt{\sum_{i=0}^{r} \binom{n}{i}} \; 2^{\frac{n-1}{2}}$$

(*i.e.*, the probability for a function to satisfy this inequality) is larger than $1 - 2^{(1-c^2 \log_2 e) \sum_{i=0}^{r} \binom{n}{i}}$ and, if $c^2 \log_2 e > 1$, it tends to 1 when n tends to ∞. This is easily proved: the number of functions of algebraic degree at most r equals $2^{\sum_{i=0}^{r} \binom{n}{i}}$. For every such function h, the number of Boolean functions f whose Hamming distance to h is bounded above by some number D equals $\sum_{0 \leq i \leq D} \binom{2^n}{i}$. Hence, the number of Boolean functions f such that $d_H(f,h) \leq 2^{n-1} - c \sqrt{\sum_{i=0}^{r} \binom{n}{i}} \, 2^{\frac{n-1}{2}}$

equals $\sum_{0 \leq i \leq 2^{n-1} - c\sqrt{\sum_{i=0}^{r}\binom{n}{i}} \, 2^{\frac{n-1}{2}}} \binom{2^n}{i}$. We know from [14] that, for every N, we have

$\sum_{0 \leq i \leq \lambda N} \binom{N}{i} < 2^N e^{-2N(1/2-\lambda)^2}$. We deduce that the number of Boolean functions f such that $d_H(f,h) \leq 2^{n-1} - c\sqrt{\sum_{i=0}^{r} \binom{n}{i}} \, 2^{\frac{n-1}{2}}$ is bounded above by $2^{2^n - c^2 \sum_{i=0}^{r} \binom{n}{i} \log_2 e}$. Thus, the number of those Boolean functions that have r-th order nonlinearity smaller than or equal to $2^{n-1} - c\sqrt{\sum_{i=0}^{r} \binom{n}{i}} \, 2^{\frac{n-1}{2}}$ is smaller than $2^{2^n + (1-c^2 \log_2 e) \sum_{i=0}^{r} \binom{n}{i}}$. The rest of the proof is straightforward.

A more precise and more recent result is given by K.-U. Schmidt in [1021], which generalizes the result on $r = 1$ by Rodier [1000] recalled at page 80, and a result from [435], which dealt with $r = 2$: for every $r \geq 1$, the ratio $\frac{2^{n-1} - nl_r(f)}{\sqrt{2^{n-1}\binom{n}{r} \ln 2}}$ tends to 1 almost surely when n tends to infinity (see more details in [1021]).

Unfortunately, this does not help obtaining explicit functions with nonweak r-th order nonlinearity.

Remark. We shall see in Section 4.1 that the minimum Hamming weight of nonzero n-variable Boolean functions of an algebraic degree at most r (*i.e.*, the minimum distance of the Reed–Muller code $RM(r,n)$) is equal to 2^{n-r} for every $r \leq n$. Hence, applying this property to $r+1$ instead of r, we have $nl_r(f) \geq 2^{n-r-1}$ for every function f of an algebraic degree exactly $r + 1 \leq n$. Moreover, we shall also see that the minimum weight n-variable Boolean functions of an algebraic degree $r+1$ are the characteristic functions of $(n-r-1)$-dimensional flats. Such functions have r-th order nonlinearity 2^{n-r-1} since the null function is the closest function of an algebraic degree at most r to such a function. $\square$

Computing the r-th order nonlinearity of a given function with an algebraic degree strictly larger than r is a hard task for $r > 1$ (for the first order, we have seen that much is known in theory and algorithmically thanks to the Walsh transform, which can be computed by the algorithm of the fast Fourier–Hadamard transform; but for $r > 1$, very little is known). Even the second-order nonlinearity is known only for a few peculiar functions and for functions in small numbers of variables. Some simple but useful facts are shown in [232]. A nice algorithm due to G. Kabatiansky and C. Tavernier and improved and implemented by Fourquet and Tavernier [518] works well for $r = 2$ and $n \leq 11$ (in some cases, $n \leq 13$) only. It can be applied for higher orders, but it is then efficient only for very small numbers of variables. Proving lower bounds on the r-th order nonlinearity of functions (and therefore proving their good behavior with respect to this criterion) is also a quite difficult task. Until 2008, there had been only one attempt, by Iwata and Kurosawa [638], to construct functions with r-th order nonlinearity bounded from below. But the obtained value, $2^{n-r-3}(r+5)$, of the lower bound was small. Also, lower bounds on the r-th order nonlinearity by means of the algebraic immunity of Boolean functions have been derived (see Chapter 9), but they are small too. In [232], a method is introduced for efficiently bounding from below the nonlinearity profile of a given function when lower bounds exist for the $(r-1)$-th order nonlinearities of the derivatives of f:

Theorem 4   *Let $f \in \mathcal{BF}_n$ and let $0 < r < n$ be an integer. We have:*

$$nl_r(f) \geq \frac{1}{2} \max_{a \in \mathbb{F}_2^n} nl_{r-1}(D_a f), \text{ and}$$

$$nl_r(f) \geq 2^{n-1} - \frac{1}{2}\sqrt{2^{2n} - 2\sum_{a \in \mathbb{F}_2^n} nl_{r-1}(D_a f)}.$$

The first bound is easily deduced from the inequality $w_H(f) \geq \frac{1}{2} w_H(D_a f)$ applied to $f \oplus h$, $d_{alg}(h) \leq r$, and the second one comes from the equalities $nl_r(f) = 2^{n-1} -$

$$\frac{1}{2} \max_{h \in \mathcal{BF}_n \,;\, d_{alg}(h) \leq r} \left| \sum_{x \in \mathbb{F}_2^n} (-1)^{f(x) \oplus h(x)} \right| \text{ and } \left(\sum_{x \in \mathbb{F}_2^n} (-1)^{f(x) \oplus h(x)} \right)^2 =$$

$$\sum_{a \in \mathbb{F}_2^n} \sum_{x \in \mathbb{F}_2^n} (-1)^{D_a f(x) \oplus D_a h(x)} = 2^{2n} - 2\sum_{a \in \mathbb{F}_2^n} d_H(D_a f, D_a h).$$

These bounds ease the determination of efficient lower bounds on the second-order nonlinearities of functions in some infinite classes, by reducing the problem to calculations and summations of first-order nonlinearities (often tricky, but feasible). This has been done in a series of papers (see, *e.g.*, in [714] the references and the table comparing the obtained second-order nonlinearities; see also [538]) that we shall not all cite. Such lower bounds were given as examples (about power functions, including the Welch function) in [232], but also bounds for the whole nonlinearity profile of the multiplicative *inverse function* $tr_n(x^{2^n-2})$: the r-th order nonlinearity of this function is approximately bounded below by $2^{n-1} - 2^{(1-2^{-r})n}$ and therefore asymptotically equivalent to 2^{n-1}, for every fixed r. Note that the extension of the Weil bound that we shall see in Section 5.6 is efficient for bounding below the r-th order nonlinearity of the inverse function only for $r = 1$. Indeed, already for $r = 2$, the univariate degree of a *quadratic function* in trace representation form can be bounded above by $2^{\lfloor \frac{n}{2} \rfloor} + 1$ only, and this gives a bound in 2^n on the maximum absolute value of the Walsh transform and therefore no information on the nonlinearity. In [240], the author similarly studied the (simplest) Dillon bent function $(x, y) \mapsto xy^{2^{n/2}-2}$, $x, y \in F_{2^{n/2}}$ (with an improvement in [1066]) and a univariate function. In [607], the authors asymptotically studied, for p an odd prime, the Boolean function taking value 0 over the binary expansions of the quadratic residues modulo p.

The relative positions of the two bounds of Theorem 4 with respect to each other have been studied in [872], where it is shown that for $r = 2$, there exist functions for which the first bound is stronger, and others where it is weaker.

3.1.4 Correlation immunity and resiliency

We have seen that the Boolean functions used in stream ciphers must be balanced. In both models of *pseudorandom generators*, there is a stronger condition related to balancedness to satisfy.

In the combiner model

Any combining function $f(x)$ must stay balanced when some number of coordinates x_i of x are kept constant.

Definition 21 *Let n be a positive integer and $t \leq n$ a nonnegative integer. A n-variable Boolean function f is called an t-th order* correlation immune *function if its output distribution probability is unaltered when at most t (or, equivalently, exactly t) of its input bits are kept constant. It is called a t-resilient function[5] if it is balanced and t-th order correlation immune, that is, if any of its restrictions obtained by fixing at most t (or exactly t) of its input coordinates x_i is balanced.*

Note that, by definition, 0-th order correlation immunity is an empty condition and 0-resiliency means balancedness.

Nota Bene. When we say that a function f is t-th order correlation immune (t-resilient if it is balanced), we do not mean that t is the maximum value of k such that f is k-th order correlation immune. We will call this maximum value the *correlation immunity order* of f (resp. its *resiliency order* if it is balanced).

The notion of correlation immune function has been introduced by Siegenthaler in [1041]. It has been observed later in [181] that the notion existed already in combinatorics and statistics. Indeed, saying that a function f is t-th order correlation immune is equivalent to saying that the array (*i.e.*, matrix) whose rows are the vectors of the support of f is a simple binary *orthogonal array*[6] of strength t.

Definition 22 *[988] An array (a matrix) over an alphabet A is an orthogonal array of strength t if, when we select any t columns in it, each vector of A^t appears the same number λ of times as a row in the array restricted to these columns. This orthogonal array is called simple if no two rows are equal. It is often called a $t - (|A|, n, \lambda)$ orthogonal array, where n is the number of columns in the array (in the case of correlation immune functions, the number of variables, with $|A| = 2$).*

---

[5] The term of resiliency was introduced in [370], in relationship with another cryptographic problem.
[6] This also relates then correlation immune functions to mutually orthogonal latin squares and threshold secret-sharing schemes.

Orthogonal arrays play a role in statistics, for the organization of experiments. Each row corresponds to the organization of an experiment and the n columns correspond to parameters. It is necessary to organize the experiments so that any combination of some number k of parameters will appear in the same number of experiments. This is achieved if all possible $|A|^n$ experiments are made, but this is not a solution since the number of rows needs to be minimized (exactly as in the case of countermeasures to side-channel attacks; see Subsection 12.1.1, page 431). There exist bounds: the number of rows in a binary orthogonal array of strength k is larger than or equal to $\sum_{i=0}^{\lfloor \frac{k}{2} \rfloor} \binom{n}{i}$ (Rao [988]) and to $2^n \left(1 - \frac{n}{2(k+1)} \right)$ (Friedman, [520]). There exists a monograph on orthogonal arrays [591].

Correlation immunity is a criterion for the resistance to an attack on the combiner model due to Siegenthaler, called *correlation attack* [1042]: if f is not t-th order correlation immune, then there exists a correlation between the output of the function and (at most) t coordinates of its input; if t is small, a divide-and-conquer attack uses this weakness for attacking a system using f as a combining function; in the original attack by Siegenthaler, all the possible initializations of the t LFSRs corresponding to these coordinates are tested (in other words, an exhaustive search of the initializations of these specific LFSRs is done); when we arrive to the correct initialization of these LFSRs, we observe a correlation (before that, the correlation is negligible, as for random pairs of sequences); now that the initializations of the t LFSRs are known, those of the remaining LFSRs can be found with an independent exhaustive search (or by applying again the Siegenthaler attack if possible).

An additional condition   It is shown in [187, 203] that, to make the correlation attack on the combiner model with a t-resilient combining function as inefficient as possible, the coefficient $W_f(u)$ of the function has to be small for every vector u of Hamming weight higher than but close to t. This condition is satisfied under the sufficient condition that the function is highly nonlinear (*i.e.*, has high nonlinearity). Hence we see that nonlinearity plays a role with respect to this attack as well.

Characterization of correlation immunity and resiliency by the Walsh transform
Resiliency and correlation immunity have been nicely characterized by means of the Fourier–Hadamard and Walsh transforms of f, first by S. Golomb in [549] (which is not widely known) and later by Xiao and Massey in [1128]. We propose to call this the *Golomb–Xiao–Massey characterization*:

Theorem 5   *[549] Any n-variable Boolean function f is t-th order correlation immune if and only if, for all $u \in \mathbb{F}_2^n$ such that $1 \leq w_H(u) \leq t$, we have $W_f(u) = 0$, i.e., $\widehat{f}(u) = 0$. And f is t-resilient if and only if $W_f(u) = 0$ for all $u \in \mathbb{F}_2^n$ such that $w_H(u) \leq t$.*

Proof   Let us prove the first assertion. The second is a direct consequence. By applying the *Poisson summation formula* (2.39), page 58, to $\varphi = f_\chi$, $a = 0_n$ and $E_I = \{x \in \mathbb{F}_2^n; \ x_i = 0, \ \forall i \notin I\}$, b ranging over $\mathbb{F}_2^n$, we obtain since $E_I^\perp = \{x \in \mathbb{F}_2^n; \ x_i = 0, \ \forall i \in I\}$ that f is t-th order correlation immune if and only if, for every I of size t, the value of the sum $\sum_{u \in E_I} (-1)^{b \cdot u} W_f(u)$ is independent of b. If, for every nonzero u of weight at most t, we have $W_f(u) = 0$ (that is, $\widehat{f}(u) = 0$ according to Relation (2.32)), then the sum $\sum_{u \in E_I} (-1)^{b \cdot u} W_f(u)$ is independent of b. Conversely, if this latter property is satisfied for every I of size t, then since $\sum_{u \in E_I} (-1)^{b \cdot u} W_f(u)$ is the Fourier–Hadamard transform of the function equal to $W_f(u)$ if $u \in E_I$ and to 0 otherwise, by the *inverse Fourier–Hadamard transform formula* (2.42), we have $W_f(u) = 0$ for every nonzero u of weight at most t.   □

Remark. For f balanced, there is another proof: we apply the second-order Poisson formula (2.57) to $E = \{x \in \mathbb{F}_2^n; \ x_i = 0, \ \forall i \in I\}$, where I is any set of indices of size t; the sum of E and $E^\perp = \{x \in \mathbb{F}_2^n; \ x_i = 0, \ \forall i \notin I\}$ is direct and equals $\mathbb{F}_2^n$; hence we can take $E' = E^\perp$ and we get $\sum_{u \in E^\perp} W_f^2(u) = |E^\perp| \sum_{a \in E^\perp} \mathcal{F}^2(h_a)$, where h_a is the restriction of f to $a + E$, that is, the restriction obtained by fixing the coordinates of x whose indices belong to I to the corresponding coordinates of a. The number $\mathcal{F}(h_a)$ is null if and only if h_a is balanced and clearly, all the numbers $\mathcal{F}(h_a)$, $a \in E^\perp$ are null if and only if all the numbers $W_f(u)$, $u \in E^\perp$ are null. Since this is valid for every multiindex I of size t, this completes the proof.   □

Another characterization of correlation immune and resilient functions exists, by the discrete Fourier transform: $j \in \{0, \ldots, 2^n - 1\} \mapsto \sum_{k=0}^{2^n-1} (-1)^{f(k)} \xi^{-kj}$, where j and k are identified respectively with their binary expansions and $\xi = e^{\frac{2\pi\sqrt{-1}}{2^n}}$; see [1110].

Theorem 5 directly implies the following corollary:

Corollary 6 *Let f be any n-variable Boolean function and $t \le n$. Then f is t-th order correlation immune if and only if its support, viewed as an unrestricted code, has dual distance at least $t + 1$.*

Proof Let C denote the support of f. The dual distance of C equals (by Definition 4, page 16) the number $\min\{w_H(u); \ u \ne 0_n, \ \sum_{x \in C} (-1)^{u \cdot x} = \widehat{f}(u) \ne 0\}$.   □

See more in [422, 423] (see also in [828] a generalization of this result to arrays over finite fields and other related nice results).

Hence, since the Hamming weight of a t-th order correlation immune function is by definition divisible by 2^t, the size of a code of dual distance d is divisible by 2^{d-1}, as we saw at page 17.

Automorphism group   Contrary to the algebraic degree, to the nonlinearity and to balancedness, the correlation immunity and resiliency orders are not *affine invariants* (they are *permutation invariants*), except for the null order (and for the order n, but the set of n-th order correlation immune functions is the set of constant functions and the set of n-resilient functions is empty, because of Parseval's relation (2.47), page 60). They are both invariant under any translation $x \mapsto x + b$, according to Lemma 4 and Theorem 5. The *automorphism group* of the set of t-resilient functions (that is, the group of all permutations σ of $\mathbb{F}_2^n$ that preserve resiliency) and the orbits under its action have been studied in [622]).

The whole Chapter 7 is devoted to correlation immune and resilient functions.

Remark. An interesting question is, given a Boolean function (resp. a balanced Boolean function) f, what is the best possible correlation immunity (resp. resiliency) order of the Boolean functions affine equivalent to f? Of course, the highest possible power of 2 dividing $w_H(f)$ plays a role, but the reply is not straightforward.   □

In the filter model

The divide-and-conquer method valid for the combiner model does not apply to the filter model, since there is only one LFSR in this model. The condition of high-order resiliency is then not needed. But a stronger condition than balancedness is also necessary in this model, in order to avoid so-called *distinguishing attacks*. These attacks are able to distinguish the pseudorandom sequence, say $(s_i)_{i \in \mathbb{N}}$, from a random sequence. A way of doing so is to observe that the distribution of the sequences $(s_{i+\gamma_1}, \ldots, s_{i+\gamma_n})$ is not uniform, where $\gamma_1, \ldots, \gamma_n$ are (for instance) the positions where the input bits to the filtering function are chosen [20]. Golić [545] has observed that if the feedback polynomial of the LFSR is primitive and if the filtering function has the form $g(x_1, \ldots, x_{n-1}) \oplus x_n$ (up to a permutation of variables), then the property of uniformity is satisfied whatever the tap positions are (where the input bits to the filter function are taken). Canteaut [189] has proved that this condition on the function is also necessary for having uniformity. For choosing a filtering function, we can choose a function g satisfying the cryptographic criteria listed in the present section, and use f defined by means of g in one of the two ways above. But better can be done (see Subsection 9.1.6, page 343). More is said in [567] on the requirements for the filter function.

3.1.5 Algebraic immunity and fast algebraic immunity

A new kind of attack, called *algebraic attacks*, was introduced in 2003 (see [388, 391, 497]) and has significantly changed the situation with Boolean functions in stream ciphers. These attacks recover the secret key, or at least the initialization of the system, by solving a system of multivariate algebraic equations.

Shannon's criterion

The idea that the key bits in a cryptosystem can be characterized as the solutions of a system of multivariate equations translating the specifications of the cryptosystem comes from C. Shannon [1034]. Until the invention of algebraic attacks, this bright observation led more to a design criterion (*i.e.*, the system should not be solvable in reasonable time with current means) than to an actual attack. Indeed, in practice, for cryptosystems that are robust against the usual attacks (*e.g.*, for stream ciphers resisting the Berlekamp–Massey attack), this system is too complex to be solved (its equations being highly nonlinear and the number of unknowns being too large for a nonlinear system of equations). However, in the case of stream ciphers, we can get a very overdefined system (*i.e.*, a system with a number of linearly independent equations much larger than the number of unknowns). Let us consider the combiner or the filter model, or any model with a linear part (the n LFSRs in the case of the combiner model, the single LFSR in the case of the filter model) of size N filtered by an n-variable Boolean function f. There exists a linear permutation $L : \mathbb{F}_2^N \mapsto \mathbb{F}_2^N$ updating the current state of the linear part into its next state[7], and a linear function $L' : \mathbb{F}_2^N \mapsto \mathbb{F}_2^n$ mapping the linear part to the n bits selected as input to f. Denoting by $(u_1, \ldots, u_N)$ the initialization of the linear part, the current state of the linear part at ith clock cycle equals $L^i(u_1, \ldots, u_N)$. Denoting by $(s_i)_{i \geq 0}$ the pseudorandom sequence output by the generator, we have for every $i \geq 0$,

$$s_i = f(L' \circ L^i(u_1, \ldots, u_N)). \tag{3.5}$$

These equations all have the same degree $d_{alg}(f)$. The number of those that are exploitable by the attacker equals the number of bits s_i known by him/her, and can then be much larger than the number of unknowns (but, of course, the larger the number of equations, the weaker the attack). The system of these equations can then be greatly overdefined if necessary[8]. This makes less complex the resolution of the system by using Gröbner bases (see [497]), and even allows linearizing the system[9] (*i.e.*, obtaining a system of linear equations by replacing every monomial of degree larger than 1 by a new unknown). The linear system obtained after linearization has, however, too many unknowns: this number is roughly $\sum_{j=0}^{d_{alg}(f)} \binom{N}{j}$.

Courtois' and Meier's improvement for stream ciphers

Courtois and Meier have had a simple but efficient idea. Assume that there exist functions $g \neq 0$ and h of low algebraic degrees (say, of algebraic degree at most d) such that $f\, g = h$ (where $f\, g$ denotes the Hadamard product of f and g, whose support is the intersection of the supports of f and g). For every $i \geq 0$, Relation (3.5) implies

$$s_i\, g(L' \circ L^i(u_1, \ldots, u_N)) = h(L' \circ L^i(u_1, \ldots, u_N)). \tag{3.6}$$

This equation in $u_1, \ldots, u_N$ has degree at most d, since L and L' are linear, and the system of equations obtained after linearization has then at most $\sum_{j=0}^{d} \binom{N}{j}$ unknowns and may be solved by Gaussian elimination (if d is small enough) in $O\left(\left(\sum_{i=0}^{d} \binom{N}{i}\right)^{\omega}\right)$ operations, where $\omega \approx 3$ is the exponent of the Gaussian reduction.[10] The attack needs about $\sum_{i=0}^{d} \binom{N}{i}$ bits of the keystream.

Low-degree relations have been shown to exist for several well-known constructions of stream ciphers, which were immune to all previously known attacks. This was the case, for instance, with functions whose *ANF*s had only few nonzero coefficients. Such functions had been used as combining/filter functions for reasons of efficiency in the design of some stream ciphers[11] (*e.g.*, LILI-128 and Toyocrypt stream ciphers; see the references in [842]).

---

[7] In the filter model, the matrix of L is simply a companion matrix; in the combiner model, it is a slightly more complex matrix having companion matrices around its diagonal and zeros elsewhere.

[8] The probability that N random equations in N variables have rank N equals roughly $1/2$ since the determinant of this system lives in $\mathbb{F}_2$.

[9] The known algorithms are, starting from the simplest one, linearization, XL, Buchberger, F4, and F5 (by Faugère); they have different complexities and do not need the same numbers of linearly independent equations.

[10] It can be taken equal to $\log_2 7 \approx 2.8$ and the coefficient in the O can be taken equal to 7, according to Strassen [1052]; a still better exponent is due to Coppersmith and Winograd, but the multiplicative constant is then inefficiently high for our framework.

[11] The designers of these stream ciphers had forgotten at their own expenses the basic rule of choosing, for cryptosystems, primitives behaving as randomly as possible.

Krause and Armknecht [28] extended algebraic attacks to combiners with memory. They studied the algebraic equations satisfied by such combiners and proved an upper bound on their possible degree by means of the input and memory sizes. Courtois [389] generalized their results to multioutput functions.

Algebraic immunity

As observed in [391], if we know the existence of a nonzero low *algebraic degree* multiple h of f, then the support of h being included in that of f, we have $(f \oplus 1)h = 0$, and taking $g = h$, we have the desired relation $fg = h$. But the existence of such multiple h of f is only a sufficient condition for having relation $fg = h$. A necessary and sufficient condition has been found in [842]:

Proposition 25 *Let f be any n-variable Boolean function. The existence of functions $g \neq 0$ and h, both of algebraic degree at most d, such that $fg = h$, is equivalent to the existence of a function $g \neq 0$ of algebraic degree at most d such that $fg = 0$ or $(f \oplus 1)g = 0$.*

Proof Equality $fg = h$ implies $f^2g = fh$, that is (since $f^2 = f$), $f(g \oplus h) = 0$, which gives the desired equality of the form $fg = 0$ (with $g \neq 0$) if $g \neq h$ by replacing $g \oplus h$ by g; and if $g = h$, then $fg = h$ is equivalent to $(f \oplus 1)g = 0$. This proves the implication from top to bottom. The converse is straightforward. $\square$

Note that Proposition 25 implies that the existence of a low algebraic degree nonzero multiple of f or of $f \oplus 1$ is a necessary and sufficient condition for the existence of low algebraic degree $g \neq 0$ and h such that $fg = h$ (since being a multiple of f, resp. of $f \oplus 1$, is equivalent to having null product with $f \oplus 1$, resp. with f).

Definition 23 *[842] Let f be any n-variable Boolean function. An n-variable Boolean function g such that $fg = 0$ is called an* annihilator *of f.*
The minimum algebraic degree of nonzero annihilators of f or $f \oplus 1$, i.e., the minimum algebraic degree of nonzero multiples of $f \oplus 1$ or f, or equivalently, the minimal value d such that there exist $g \neq 0$ and h, both of algebraic degree at most d, such that $fg = h$, is called the algebraic immunity *of f and is denoted by $AI(f)$.*

This notion has been generalized to functions over general finite fields in [52], with an upper bound on it.

Remark. The set of all annihilators of function f is equal to the ideal of all the multiples of $f \oplus 1$. $\square$

Remark. Algebraic immunity plays also a role in computational complexity; see [770], where a stronger notion is studied (for symmetric functions). $\square$

All of Chapter 9 is devoted to algebraic immunity.

Let g be a generic n-variable Boolean function of algebraic degree at most d. Let the ANF of g equal $\bigoplus_{I \subseteq \{1,\ldots,n\}; |I| \leq d} a_I x^I$, where the coefficients a_I can be any elements of $\mathbb{F}_2$. Then g is an annihilator of f if and only if $f(x) = 1$ implies $g(x) = 0$, that is, if and only if the coefficients a_I satisfy the system of homogeneous linear equations $\bigoplus_{I \subseteq \{1,\ldots,n\}; |I| \leq d} a_I u^I$, where u ranges over the support of f. In this system, we have $\sum_{i=0}^{d} \binom{n}{i}$ number of variables (the coefficients of the monomials of degrees at most d) and $w_H(f)$ many equations.[12] We shall denote by $M_{f,d}$ the matrix of this system.

Algebraic immunity is an *affine invariant* but not an EA invariant. More precisely, its automorphism group (that is, the group of all permutations σ of $\mathbb{F}_2^n$ such that $AI(f \circ \sigma) = AI(f)$ for every Boolean function f) equals the general affine group (as for Reed-Muller codes). Indeed, denoting by $An(f)$ the $\mathbb{F}_2$-vector space of annihilators of f, we have $An(f \circ \sigma) = An(f) \circ \sigma$.

A strength of algebraic attack comes from the fact that the algebraic degrees of g and h can always be made lower than or equal to the *Courtois–Meier bound* $\lceil \frac{n}{2} \rceil$:

Proposition 26   *[391] The algebraic immunity of any n-variable Boolean function is bounded above[13] by $\lceil \frac{n}{2} \rceil$ and by $d_{alg}(f)$.*

Proof   The number of monomials of algebraic degree at most $\lceil \frac{n}{2} \rceil$ is strictly larger than 2^{n-1}. The disjoint union of the family of these monomials and of the family of the products of f by these monomials has then size strictly larger than 2^n, which is the dimension of the $\mathbb{F}_2$-vector space $\mathcal{BF}_n$. The functions in this disjoint union are then necessarily $\mathbb{F}_2$-linearly dependent. Given a linear combination equal to function 0 and having not all-zero coefficients, let us gather separately the part dealing with the first family and the part dealing with the second. This gives two functions h and g, both of degree at most $\lceil \frac{n}{2} \rceil$, such that $h = f g$ and $(g,h) \neq (0,0)$, i.e., $g \neq 0$. This proves the first upper bound. The second comes from the fact that f and $f \oplus 1$ are annihilators of each other. $\square$

Remark.   For n odd, according to Proposition 26 and since $2 \sum_{i=0}^{\frac{n-1}{2}} \binom{n}{i} = 2^n$, we have $AI(f) = \frac{n+1}{2}$ if and only if the family $\{x^I f, |I| \leq \frac{n-1}{2}\} \cup \{x^J (f \oplus 1), |J| \leq \frac{n-1}{2}\}$ is a basis of the $\mathbb{F}_2$-vector space $\mathcal{BF}_n$. Note that this leads to new codes: for every $k \leq \frac{n-1}{2}$, the code $C_{f,k}$ of length 2^n and dimension $2 \sum_{i=0}^{k} \binom{n}{i}$ generated by $\{x^I f, |I| \leq k\} \cup \{x^J (f \oplus 1), |J| \leq k\}$. For $k = \frac{n-1}{2}$, it equals the whole space $\mathcal{BF}_n$. For $k = 1$, it equals the direct sum of the first-order Reed–Muller code punctured at the positions in the support of f and of the first-order Reed–Muller code punctured at the positions in the cosupport, and has minimum distance $\frac{1}{2} nl(f)$, since $w_H(fg)$ equals 2^{n-1} if $g = 1$ (because f is balanced according to Relation (9.5), page 330) and $w_H(fg) = \frac{w_H(f) + w_H(g) - w_H(f \oplus g)}{2} = \frac{2^n - w_H(f \oplus g)}{2} = \frac{w_H(f \oplus g \oplus 1)}{2}$ if g is affine nonconstant,

---

[12] Those corresponding to u of small weights may be used to simplify those corresponding to u of larger weights as shown in [27].

[13] Consequently, it is bounded above by $\lceil k/2 \rceil$ if, up to affine equivalence, it depends only on k variables, and by $\lceil k/2 + 1 \rceil$ if it has a linear kernel (see below) of dimension $n - k$, since it is then equivalent, according to Proposition 28, to a function in k variables plus an affine function.

and we have the same for $w_H((f \oplus 1)h)$. Note that the known functions f such that $AI(f) = \frac{n+1}{2}$ have diverse nonlinearities. □

Algebraic immunity of random functions

Random functions behave well with respect to algebraic immunity:[14] it has been proved in [437] (see a slightly more complete proof in [307] and its extension to vectorial functions) that, for all $a < 1$, when n tends to infinity, $AI(f)$ is almost surely larger than $\frac{n}{2} - \sqrt{\frac{n}{2} \ln \left(\frac{n}{2a \ln 2} \right)}$.

Consequences of the invention of algebraic attack on the design of stream ciphers

A difference by 1 in the algebraic immunity of a function f, used as combiner or filter in a stream cipher, makes a big difference in the efficiency of algebraic attack. The designer needs then to choose f with optimal or near-optimal algebraic immunity. Let then an n-variable function f, with algebraic immunity $\lceil \frac{n}{2} \rceil$, be used, for instance, as filter on an LFSR of length $N \geq 2k$, where k is the length of the key (otherwise, it is known that the system is not robust against an attack called time-memory-data trade-off attack). Then the complexity of an algebraic attack using one annihilator of degree $\lceil \frac{n}{2} \rceil$ is roughly $7 \left(\binom{N}{0} + \cdots + \binom{N}{\lceil \frac{n}{2} \rceil} \right)^{\log_2 7} \approx 7 \left(\binom{N}{0} + \cdots + \binom{N}{\lceil \frac{n}{2} \rceil} \right)^{2.8}$ (see [391]). Let us choose $k = 128$ (which is usual) and $N = 256$; then it is for $n \geq 13$ that the complexity of algebraic attack is at least 2^{80} (which is considered nowadays as just enough); and it is larger than the complexity of an exhaustive search, that is, 2^{128}, for $n \geq 15$. If the attacker knows several linearly independent annihilators of degree $\lceil \frac{n}{2} \rceil$, then the number of variables must be enhanced! In practice, the number of variables will have to be near 20 (but this poses then a problem of efficiency of the stream cipher). This has quite changed the situation with Boolean functions at the beginning of this century, since before algebraic attacks, the Boolean functions used had rarely more than 10 variables.

Fast algebraic attack

A high value of $AI(f)$ is even not a sufficient property for a resistance to algebraic attacks, because other algebraic attacks have been later invented. The *fast algebraic attack (FAA)* is an improvement to the standard algebraic attack. It can work even if the algebraic immunity of the function is large,[15] provided that there exist n-variable Boolean functions g nonzero of low algebraic degree, and h of reasonable algebraic degree (*i.e.*, of algebraic degree possibly larger than $\frac{n}{2}$ but significantly smaller than n) such that $fg = h$; see [388]. This attack is based on the observation that it is possible to obtain a low-degree equation from several ones of the form (3.6) by eliminating the large-degree terms in the right-hand sides of these equations, and that such elimination may be made offline by the attacker (that is, before that values of the s_is are known by him/her) and therefore benefit of a much longer time of computation. The efficiency of the precomputation and

---

[14] No result is known on the behavior of random functions against fast algebraic attacks.
[15] Fast algebraic attack has worked on the eSTREAM [495] proposal SFINKS [390], while the cipher was designed to withstand algebraic attack.

substitution steps has been improved by Hawkes and Rose [590] for the filter model (allowing a complexity of $\mathcal{O}\big(\big(\sum_{i=0}^{d_{alg}(h)}\binom{N}{i}\big)\log_2^3\big(\sum_{i=0}^{d_{alg}(h)}\binom{N}{i}\big)+\big(\sum_{i=0}^{d_{alg}(h)}\binom{N}{i}\big)N\log_2^2 N\big)$ operations, needing $2\big(\sum_{i=0}^{d_{alg}(g)}\binom{N}{i}\big)$ bits of stream for the former, and an online complexity of $O\big(\big(\sum_{i=0}^{d_{alg}(g)}\binom{N}{i}\big)^3+2\big(\sum_{i=0}^{d_{alg}(g)}\binom{N}{i}\big)\big(\sum_{i=0}^{d_{alg}(h)}\binom{N}{i}\big)\log_2\big(\big(\sum_{i=0}^{d_{alg}(h)}\binom{N}{i}\big)\big)\big)$ operations) and by Armknecht [25] for the combiner model, also when they are made more complex by the introduction of memory. Fast algebraic attacks need more data than standard ones (since several values s_i need to be known to obtain one equation), but may also be faster. Armknecht and Ars [26] introduced a variant of the FAA that reduced the data complexity (but not the time complexity).

On the existence of g and h   Given nonnegative integers d and e such that $e + d \geq n$, the number of monomials of degrees at most e and the number of monomials of degrees at most d have a sum strictly larger than 2^n, and there exist[16] then $g \neq 0$ of algebraic degree at most e and h of algebraic degree at most d such that $fg = h$. An n-variable Boolean function f is then optimal with respect to fast algebraic attacks if there do not exist two functions $g \neq 0$ and h such that $fg = h$, $d_{alg}(g) < \lceil\frac{n}{2}\rceil$ and $d_{alg}(g) + d_{alg}(h) < n$. Since $fg = h$ implies $fh = f^2 g = fg = h$, we see that h is then an annihilator of $f \oplus 1$, and if $h \neq 0$, its algebraic degree is then at least equal to the algebraic immunity of f.

Complexity of the attack and related parameters on Boolean functions   The complexity of FAA is roughly of the order (see [590])

$$O\left(\min\left\{N^{\max[d_{alg}(g)+d_{alg}(fg),3d_{alg}(g)]}, g \neq 0\right\}\right).$$

It can be seen that FAA with $g = 1$ is less efficient than the Rønjom–Helleseth attack (see below) and that FAA with $d_{alg}(g) \geq AI(f)$ is in fact the algebraic attack. This has led in [324] to studying the so-called *fast algebraic complexity*:

$$FAC(f) = \min\left\{\max\left[d_{alg}(g) + d_{alg}(fg), 3d_{alg}(g)\right]; 1 \leq d_{alg}(g) < AI(f)\right\},$$

whose value is invariant by changing f into $f \oplus 1$, and is bounded above by n and below by the so-called *fast algebraic immunity*:

$$FAI(f) = \min\left(2AI(f), \min\left\{d_{alg}(g) + d_{alg}(fg); 1 \leq d_{alg}(g) < AI(f)\right\}\right),$$

which had been informally introduced in a preliminary version of the paper [791] and used in [324, 870, 1106]. Note that FAI is also invariant by changing f into $f \oplus 1$, and is easier to study. If this latter parameter is close to n, then FAC is too, and the function provides then a good resistance to FAA.

Remark.   Since, for the resistance against FAA, there must not exist $g \neq 0$ such that $d_{alg}(g)$ is small and $d_{alg}(fg)$ is reasonably large, then if $d_{alg}(f)$ is not large, f does not resist FAA. Because of the Siegenthaler bound (see Proposition 117, page 285) and of the

---

[16] We do not require here that $fg \neq 0$; if such a requirement is imposed, the result is no more true, as observed by Gong [553].

fact that functions in the combiner model must be correlation immune, the combiner model cannot be used nowadays without extra protections.   □

Other algebraic attacks

Algebraic attack on the augmented function   Considering now f as a function in N variables, to simplify description, this attack due to [509] works with the vectorial function $F(x)$, whose output equals the vector $(f(x), f(L(x)), \ldots, f(L^{m-1}(x)))$, where L is the (linear) update function of the linear part of the generator. This attack can be more efficient than the standard algebraic attack. But the efficiency of the attack not only depends on the function f; it also depends on the update function (and naturally also on the choice of m), since for two different update functions L and L', the vectorial functions $F(x)$ and $F'(x) = (f(x), f(L'(x)), \ldots, f(L'^{m-1}(x))$ are not linearly equivalent; they are not even CCZ equivalent in general. The resistance to this attack is then more a matter with the pair (f, L) rather than with the single function f.

The Rønjom–Helleseth attack   This attack, introduced in [1003] and improved in [556, 600, 1001, 1002, 1004], also adapts the idea of algebraic attacks due to Shannon, but in a different way. An LFSR with a primitive retroaction polynomial (or equivalently a primitive characteristic polynomial) generates a sequence of the form $u_i = tr_N(\lambda \alpha^i)$, where α is a primitive element of $\mathbb{F}_{2^N}$. Essentially, an LFSR generates the field $\mathbb{F}_{2^N}^*$ and a classical filter generator keystream sequence is formed by applying a Boolean function in n variables to n of the N bits of the coefficient vector of the element u_i. Rønjom and Helleseth then observe that the coefficients in front of a particular monomial in the sequence of multivariate equations expressing the keystream bits form a so-called *coefficient sequence* that inherits highly structural finite field properties from the LFSR. In particular, from this observation they gain fine-grained control over the linear dependencies in the multivariate equation system, which enables very efficient reductions. They take advantage of this by proposing an attack whose computational complexity is in about $\sum_{i=0}^{d} \binom{N}{i}$ operations, where d is the algebraic degree of the filter function and N is the size of the LFSR (rather than $O\left(\left(\sum_{i=0}^{AI(f)} \binom{N}{i}\right)^{\omega}\right)$ in the case of standard algebraic attack, where $AI(f)$ is the algebraic immunity of the filter function and $\omega \approx 3$ is the exponent of the Gaussian reduction). It needs about $\sum_{i=0}^{d} \binom{N}{i}$ consecutive bits of the keystream output by the pseudorandom generator (rather than $\sum_{i=0}^{AI(f)} \binom{N}{i}$). Since d is supposed to be close to the number n of variables of the filter function, the number $\sum_{i=0}^{d} \binom{N}{i}$ is comparable to $\binom{N}{n}$. Since $AI(f)$ is supposed to be close to $\lceil \frac{n}{2} \rceil$, we can see that denoting by C the complexity of the Courtois–Meier attack and by C' the amount of data it needs, the complexity of the Rønjom–Helleseth attack roughly equals $C^{2/3}$ and the amount of data it needs is roughly C'^2. From the viewpoint of complexity, it is more efficient, and from the viewpoint of data it is less efficient.

It was later observed (see [556, 600, 1001]) that the multivariate representation essentially hides away more of the underlying finite field structure stemming from the LFSR, and that it follows straightforwardly from a univariate representation that the equation systems are cyclic Vandermonde type. In particular, in the univariate representation one has even more complete control over the dependencies of each coefficient and more freedom in comparison to the multivariate case. Here the keystream sequence is simply viewed as $a_i = P(u_i)$, where P is a univariate polynomial over $\mathbb{F}_{2^N}$. Then [556] introduced a parameter on sequences, called *spectral immunity*, an analogue to the algebraic immunity, but related to the approach of the Rønjom–Helleseth attack and to its improvements (in particular, the so-called selective discrete Fourier transform (DFT) attack, which multiplies the portion of known keystream by a sequence of smaller linear complexity, and which possibly results in a more efficient attack than FAA, or is able to work when the number of known consecutive bits of the keystream is too small for FAA). The spectral immunity $SI(s)$ of a binary sequence s is the lowest linear complexity of a nonzero binary annihilator s (*i.e.*, binary sequence a, satisfying $a\,s = 0$). In terms of univariate polynomials, the spectral immunity is equal to the minimal weight of a multiple of P or $P + 1$ in $\mathbb{F}_{2^N}$, thus linking security directly to the minimum distance of the associated algebraic codes defined by the univariate filter polynomials. Moving to a univariate representation over finite fields seems to be a more natural representation for this type of generator. For instance, it has been an open question in [188] whether the irregular equation systems resulting from an annihilator attack on the filter generator have full rank. As observed in [1001], from the univariate representation, this directly translates to a question about the singularity of generalized Vandermonde matrices over finite fields, which has already been solved by Shparlinski [1038] (most of such matrices have full rank). It has been shown that univariate cryptanalysis becomes particularly effective in practice in comparison to multivariate attacks when the LFSR is defined over larger fields (*i.e.*, word-based stream ciphers); see, for instance, [1001]. Although filter generators are usually building blocks in more complex designs, the technique has been used to practically break several ciphers, including a large part of the Welch–Gong family of generators and the recent Keccak/Farfalle-based pseudorandom function *Kravatte* [342]. It is an open problem how this change of representation can be used to also improve algebraic attacks on ciphers such as SNOW-3G, which use word-based LFSRs as components in more complex designs.

3.1.6 *Variants to these criteria in relationship with guess and determine attacks*

The *guess and determine* attacks make hypotheses on the values of some bits or some linear combinations of bits in the data processed by the stream cipher. Given the complexity, say C, of the attack when the hypothesis is satisfied, the global complexity of the attack is obtained by dividing C by the probability that the hypothesis is satisfied. There is then a trade-off to be found between this probability and C. In such framework, the input to the Boolean function at one moment in the process belongs, in the simplest case, to an affine subspace of $\mathbb{F}_2^n$ (which may be a different one at each moment). For a given Boolean function f to be used as combiner or filter function, all the criteria introduced in the previous subsections then also need to be studied for the restrictions of f to such affine spaces. It is difficult to say in general which affine spaces exactly are concerned and, as in the case of attacks on the augmented function, such study is hardly viewed as a study of the single Boolean function, except in particular cases. It depends on the whole cryptosystem. We shall see in Section 12.2 another case where functions need to be studied on subsets of $\mathbb{F}_2^n$ (which are no more affine spaces but sets of vectors of fixed Hamming weights).

3.1.7 *Avalanche criteria, nonexistence of nonzero linear structure, correlation with subsets of indices*

Strict avalanche criterion, propagation criterion, and global avalanche criteria

The *strict avalanche criterion* (*SAC*) has been introduced by Webster and Tavares [1116] and this concept was generalized into the *propagation criterion* (*PC*) by Preneel et al. [970] (see also [969]). The SAC and its generalizations are based on the properties of the derivatives of Boolean functions. These properties describe the behavior of a function whenever some coordinates of the input are complemented. Thus, they are related to the property of diffusion of the cryptosystems using the function. They concern more the Boolean functions involved in block ciphers.

Definition 24 *Let f be a Boolean function on $\mathbb{F}_2^n$ and E a subset of $\mathbb{F}_2^n$. Function f satisfies the PC with respect to E if, for all $a \in E$, the derivative $D_a f(x) = f(x) \oplus f(a + x)$ is balanced. It satisfies $PC(l)$ if it satisfies PC with respect to the set of all nonzero vectors of weight at most l. In other words, f satisfies $PC(l)$ if the autocorrelation coefficient $\mathcal{F}(D_a f)$ is null for every $a \in \mathbb{F}_2^n$ such that $1 \leq w_H(a) \leq l$. Criterion SAC corresponds to $PC(1)$.*

Some cryptographic applications require Boolean functions that still satisfy $PC(l)$ when a certain number k of coordinates of the input x are kept constant (whatever these coordinates are and whatever are the constant values chosen for them). We say that such functions satisfy the $PC(l)$ *of order* k. This notion, introduced in [970], is a generalization of the strict avalanche criterion of order k, $SAC(k)$ (which is equivalent to $PC(1)$ of order k), introduced in [516]. Obviously, if a function f satisfies $PC(l)$ of order $k \leq n - l$, then it satisfies $PC(l)$ of order k' for any $k' \leq k$.

There exists another notion, which is similar to $PC(l)$ of order k, but stronger [968, 970] (see also [219]): a Boolean function satisfies the *extended propagation criterion* $EPC(l)$ of order k if every derivative $D_a f$, with $a \neq 0_n$ of weight at most l, is k-resilient.

These parameters are not affine invariants.

A weakened version of the PC criterion has been studied in [721].

Global avalanche criteria: sum-of-squares and absolute indicators   The second moment of the autocorrelation coefficients

$$\mathcal{V}(f) = \sum_{b \in \mathbb{F}_2^n} \mathcal{F}^2(D_b f) \tag{3.7}$$

has been introduced by Zhang and Zheng [1167] for measuring the *global avalanche criterion* (GAC), and is also called the *sum-of-squares indicator*. The *absolute indicator* $\Delta_f = \max_{b \in \mathbb{F}_2^n, \, b \neq 0_n} | \mathcal{F}(D_b f) |$ is the other global avalanche criterion. Functions with high absolute indicator are weak against cube attacks [465]. Both indicators are clearly *affine invariants*. In order to achieve good diffusion, cryptographic functions should have low sum-of-squares indicators and absolute indicators. Obviously, we have $\mathcal{V}(f) \geq 2^{2n}$, since $\mathcal{F}^2(D_0 f) = 2^{2n}$. Note that every lower bound of the form $\mathcal{V}(f) \geq V$ straightforwardly implies that the absolute indicator is bounded below by $\sqrt{\frac{V - 2^{2n}}{2^n - 1}}$. The functions achieving

$\mathcal{V}(f) = 2^{2n}$ are those functions whose derivatives $D_b f(x)$, $b \neq 0_n$, are all balanced. We shall see in Chapter 6 that these are the bent functions, which are unbalanced. In [1180] and references therein are studied the balanced functions with minimal sum-of-square indicator $2^{2n} + 2^{n+3}$.

If f has a k-dimensional linear kernel $\{e \in \mathbb{F}_2^n; D_e f = cst\}$ (see the next subsection), then

$$\mathcal{V}(f) \geq 2^{2n+k} \tag{3.8}$$

(with equality if and only if f is partially-bent; see page 256).

Note that, according to Relation (2.55), page 62, applied to $D_b f$ for every b, we have

$$\mathcal{V}(f) = \sum_{a,b \in \mathbb{F}_2^n} \mathcal{F}(D_a D_b f), \tag{3.9}$$

where $D_a D_b f(x) = f(x) \oplus f(x+a) \oplus f(x+b) \oplus f(x+a+b)$ is the second-order *derivative* of f.

Note also that, according to Relation (2.45), page 60 (expressing the convolutional product of Fourier–Hadamard transforms), applied to $\varphi(b) = \psi(b) = \mathcal{F}(D_b f)$, and using that, according to Relation (2.53), the Fourier–Hadamard transform of φ equals W_f^2, we have for any n-variable Boolean function f

$$\forall a \in \mathbb{F}_2^n, \sum_{b \in \mathbb{F}_2^n} W_f^2(b) W_f^2(a+b) = 2^n \sum_{b \in \mathbb{F}_2^n} \mathcal{F}^2(D_b f)(-1)^{b \cdot a},$$

and thus, for $a = 0_n$:

$$\sum_{b \in \mathbb{F}_2^n} W_f^4(b) = 2^n \mathcal{V}(f), \tag{3.10}$$

as observed in [191].

We have: $\sum_{b \in \mathbb{F}_2^n} W_f^4(b) \leq \left(\sum_{b \in \mathbb{F}_2^n} W_f^2(b) \right) \left(\max_{b \in \mathbb{F}_2^n} W_f^2(b) \right) = 2^{2n} \max_{b \in \mathbb{F}_2^n} W_f^2(b)$ (according to Parseval's relation (2.47), page 60), and we deduce, using Relation (3.10) and inequality $\mathcal{V}(f) \geq 2^{2n}$: $\max_{b \in \mathbb{F}_2^n} W_f^2(b) \geq \frac{\mathcal{V}(f)}{2^n} \geq \sqrt{\mathcal{V}(f)}$; thus, according to Relation (3.1), page 79, relating the nonlinearity to the Walsh transform, we have (as first shown in [1169, 1173]):

Proposition 27 *For every n-variable Boolean function f, we have*

$$nl(f) \leq 2^{n-1} - 2^{-\frac{n}{2}-1} \sqrt{\mathcal{V}(f)} \leq 2^{n-1} - \frac{1}{2} \sqrt[4]{\mathcal{V}(f)},$$

with equality on the left-hand side if and only if f is plateaued (see Definition 63, page 258), in which case $\mathcal{V}(f) = 2^n \lambda^2$, where λ is the amplitude.

Denoting by N_{W_f} the cardinality of the support $\{a \in \mathbb{F}_2^n; W_f(a) \neq 0\}$ of the Walsh transform of f, Relation (3.10) also implies the following relation, first observed in [1173]: $\mathcal{V}(f) \times N_{W_f} \geq 2^{3n}$. Indeed, using for instance the Cauchy–Schwarz inequality, we see that $\left(\sum_{a \in \mathbb{F}_2^n} W_f^2(a) \right)^2 \leq \left(\sum_{a \in \mathbb{F}_2^n} W_f^4(a) \right) \times N_{W_f}$, and we have $\sum_{a \in \mathbb{F}_2^n} W_f^2(a) = 2^{2n}$, according to Parseval's relation.

According to the observations made above and below Proposition 27, the functions that satisfy $nl(f) = 2^{n-1} - 2^{\frac{n}{2}-1}\sqrt{\mathcal{V}(f)}$ (resp. $\mathcal{V}(f) \times N_{W_f} = 2^{3n}$) are the functions whose Walsh transforms take one nonzero absolute value (*i.e.*, are plateaued), and the functions satisfying $nl(f) = 2^{n-1} - \frac{1}{2}\sqrt[4]{\mathcal{V}(f)}$ are the bent functions.

Constructions of balanced Boolean functions with low absolute indicators and high nonlinearities have been studied in [813, 1072].

Remark. Zhang and Zheng conjectured that the absolute indicator of any balanced Boolean function of algebraic degree at least 3 is lower-bounded by $2^{\lfloor\frac{n+1}{2}\rfloor}$, but counterexamples were found by many people (Maitra-Sarkar, Burnett et al., Gangopadhyay-Keskar-Maitra, Kavut). $\qquad\square$

Remark. A related but different parameter is $\max\limits_{a\in\mathbb{F}_2^n, a\neq 0_n} \Delta_f(a)$ (recall that $\Delta_f(a) = \sum_{x\in\mathbb{F}_2^n}(-1)^{D_a f(x)}$ is the autocorrelation function), without absolute value. It has appeared recently in the framework of side-channel attacks (see Section 12.1). $\qquad\square$

Nonexistence of nonzero linear structure

The set of linear structures of a Boolean functions plays a role in its study, particularly when the function is a *quadratic function* (see Section 5.2).

Definition 25 *The* linear kernel *of an n-variable Boolean function f is the set of those vectors e such that $D_e f$ is a constant function. It is denoted by $\mathcal{E}_f$. Any element of the linear kernel is called a* linear structure[17] *of f.*

More generally, a linear structure e of a vectorial function F is such that $D_e F$ equals a constant function. Since for every n-variable Boolean function f (more generally, any vectorial function) and any $a, b \in \mathbb{F}_2^n$, we have $D_a f(x) \oplus D_b f(x) = f(x+a) \oplus f(x+b) = D_{a+b}f(x+a)$, the linear kernel of any Boolean function is an $\mathbb{F}_2$-subspace of $\mathbb{F}_2^n$. Moreover, the restriction of f to its linear kernel is affine since its derivatives are all constant. More generally, for every $r \leq n$, the set of those $e \in \mathbb{F}_2^n$ such that $D_e f$ has algebraic degree at most r is a vector space, and the restriction of f to this vector space has *algebraic degree* at most $r + 1$.

Nonlinear cryptographic functions used in block ciphers should have no nonzero linear structure (see [496]). The existence of nonzero linear structures, for the functions implemented in stream ciphers, is a potential risk and is better avoided.

Proposition 28 *Any n-variable Boolean function $f(x_1, \ldots, x_n)$ has a nonzero linear structure if and only if it is* linearly equivalent *to a function of the form*

$$g(x_1, \ldots, x_{n-1}) \oplus \epsilon\, x_n, \qquad (3.11)$$

---

[17] We also call linear structure a pair $(a, b) \in \mathbb{F}_2^n \times \mathbb{F}_2$ such that $D_a f$ equals constant function b.

where $\epsilon \in \mathbb{F}_2$. More generally, the linear kernel of f has dimension at least k if and only if f is linearly equivalent to a function of the form

$$g(x_1, \ldots, x_{n-k}) \oplus \epsilon_{n-k+1} x_{n-k+1} \oplus \cdots \oplus \epsilon_n x_n, \tag{3.12}$$

where $\epsilon_{n-k+1}, \ldots, \epsilon_n \in \mathbb{F}_2$.

Proof The conditions are clearly sufficient. Conversely, let f have a nonzero linear structure e, then by composing f on the right by a linear automorphism L on $\mathbb{F}_2^n$ such that $L(0, \ldots, 0, 1) = e$, we have $D_{(0,\ldots,0,1)}(f \circ L)(x) = f \circ L(x) \oplus f \circ L(x + (0, \ldots, 0, 1)) = f \circ L(x) \oplus f(L(x) + e) = D_e f(L(x))$. And it is easily seen that $D_{(0,\ldots,0,1)}(f \circ L)$ being then constant, $f \circ L$ has the form $g(x_1, \ldots, x_{n-1}) \oplus \epsilon x_n$. The case of dimension k is similar. □

Note that, according to Proposition 28, if f admits a nonzero linear structure, then since nonlinearity is an EA invariant, $nl(f)$ equals the nonlinearity of g given by (3.11) and viewed as an n-variable function, which equals $2nl(g)$, where g is now viewed as an $(n - 1)$-variable. Hence, according to the covering radius bound (3.2), page 80, applied to this $(n - 1)$-variable function, $nl(f)$ is bounded above by the bent concatenation bound $2^{n-1} - 2^{\frac{n-1}{2}}$. This implies that the functions achieving strictly larger nonlinearities (obtained by Patterson and Wiedemann and by Kavut et al.; see Section 3.1.3) cannot have any nonzero linear structure.

Similarly, if k is the dimension of the linear kernel of f, we have that $nl(f) \leq 2^{n-1} - 2^{\frac{n+k-2}{2}}$ as seen in [190], since $nl(f) = 2^k nl(g)$, where g is the $(n - k)$-variable function given in (3.12) and according to the covering radius bound applied on g with $n - k$ in the place of n.

Another characterization of linear structures is by the Walsh transform [486, 736] (see also [193]). In the next proposition, we separate the case where the linear structure e is such that $D_e f$ is the null function and the case where it is function 1.

Proposition 29 *Let f be any n-variable Boolean function. The derivative $D_e f$ equals the null function (resp. function 1) if and only if the support $supp(W_f) = \{u \in \mathbb{F}_2^n; W_f(u) \neq 0\}$ of W_f is included in $\{0_n, e\}^\perp$ (resp. in its complement).*

Proof Relation (2.56), page 62, with $b = 0_n$ and $E = \{0_n, e\}^\perp$, gives the equality

$$\sum_{u \in a+E} W_f^2(u) = 2^{n-1}(2^n + (-1)^{a \cdot e} \mathcal{F}(D_e f)). \tag{3.13}$$

If $D_e f$ is null, then let us fix a such that $a \cdot e = 1$ and if $D_e f = 1$, then let us fix it such that $a \cdot e = 0$. Then $W_f(u)$ is null for every $u \in a + E$, according to Relation (3.13). This proves the implication from top to bottom. The converse is straightforward. □

Notice that, if $D_e f$ is the constant function 1 for some $e \in \mathbb{F}_2^n$, then f is balanced (indeed, the relation $f(x + e) = f(x) \oplus 1$ implies that f takes the values 0 and 1 equally often). Thus, a nonbalanced function f has no nonzero linear structure if and only if there is no nonzero vector e such that $D_e f$ is null. According to Proposition 29, we deduce the following corollary:

Corollary 7 *Any nonbalanced function f has no nonzero linear structure if and only if the support of its Walsh transform has rank n.*

A similar characterization exists for balanced functions by replacing the function $f(x)$ by a nonbalanced function $f(x) \oplus b \cdot x$. It is deduced in [354] (see more in [1082]) that resilient functions of high orders must have linear structures.

Distance to linear structures The dimension of the linear kernel is an *affine invariant*. Hence, so is the criterion of nonexistence of nonzero linear structure. But, contrary to the criteria viewed before it, it is an all-or-nothing criterion. Meier and Staffelbach introduced in [844] a related criterion, leading to a characteristic (that is, a criterion that can be satisfied at levels quantified by numbers): a Boolean function on $\mathbb{F}_2^n$ being given, its *distance to linear structures* is its distance to the set of all Boolean functions admitting nonzero linear structures, among which we have all affine functions (hence, this distance is bounded above by the nonlinearity) but also other functions, such as all nonbent quadratic functions.

Proposition 30 *[844] The distance to linear structures of any n-variable Boolean function f equals* $2^{n-2} - \frac{1}{4} \max_{e \in \mathbb{F}_2^n \setminus \{0_n\}} |\mathcal{F}(D_e f)|.$

Proof Given e in $\mathbb{F}_2^n \setminus \{0_n\}$ and ϵ in $\mathbb{F}_2$, let $\mathcal{L}_{e,\epsilon}$ be the set of those n-variable Boolean functions g such that $D_e g = \epsilon$. Then a function g in $\mathcal{L}_{e,\epsilon}$ lies at minimum Hamming distance from f, among all elements of $\mathcal{L}_{e,\epsilon}$, if and only if, for every $x \in \mathbb{F}_2^n$ such that $D_e f(x) = \epsilon$, we have $g(x) = f(x)$ (and $g(x + e) = f(x + e)$), and for every $x \in \mathbb{F}_2^n$ such that $D_e f(x) = \epsilon \oplus 1$, we have $g(x) = f(x)$ or $g(x + e) = f(x + e)$ (and only one such equality can then happen). The Hamming distance between f and g equals then $\frac{1}{2} |\{x \in \mathbb{F}_2^n; D_e f(x) = \epsilon \oplus 1\}| = \frac{1}{2} \left(2^{n-1} - \frac{(-1)^\epsilon}{2} \mathcal{F}(D_e f) \right)$. This completes the proof since the set of functions admitting nonzero linear structures equals $\bigcup_{e \in \mathbb{F}_2^n \setminus \{0_n\}, \epsilon \in \mathbb{F}_2} \mathcal{L}_{e,\epsilon}$. $\square$

Note that Proposition 30 proves again Relation (3.3), page 82, and also proves, according to Theorem 12, page 192, that the distance of f to linear structures equals 2^{n-2} if and only if f is bent.

The maximum correlation with respect to a subset I of indices

This parameter has been introduced in [1155].

Definition 26 *Let f be any n-variable Boolean function and $I \subseteq \{1, \ldots, n\}$. The* maximum correlation *with respect to I equals* $C_f(I) = \max_{g \in \mathcal{BF}_{I,n}} \dfrac{\mathcal{F}(f \oplus g)}{2^n} = \max_{g \in \mathcal{BF}_{I,n}} \dfrac{|\mathcal{F}(f \oplus g)|}{2^n}$, *where $\mathcal{BF}_{I,n}$ is the set of n-variable Boolean functions depending on $\{x_i, i \in I\}$ only.*

According to Relation (2.35), page 57, the Hamming distance from f to $\mathcal{BF}_{I,n}$ is equal to $2^{n-1}(1 - C_f(I))$. As we saw already, denoting the size of I by r, this distance is bounded below by the r-th order nonlinearity of f (i.e., the minimum Hamming distance to functions of *algebraic degree* at most r). It can be much larger.

The maximum correlation of any combining function with respect to any subset I of small size should be small (i.e., its distance to $\mathcal{BF}_{I,n}$ should be large). It is straightforward to prove, by decomposing the sum $\mathcal{F}(f \oplus g)$ and using that an unrestricted Boolean function over $\mathbb{F}_2^I$ can take any binary value at any input $x \in \mathbb{F}_2^I$, that $C_f(I)$ equals $\sum_{j=1}^{2^{|I|}} \frac{|\mathcal{F}(h_j)|}{2^n}$, where $h_1, \ldots, h_{2^{|I|}}$ are the restrictions of f obtained by keeping constant the x_is for $i \in I$, and to see that the distance from f to $\mathcal{BF}_{I,n}$ is achieved by the functions g taking value 0 (resp. 1) when the corresponding value of $\mathcal{F}(h_j)$ is positive (resp. negative), and that we have $C_f(I) = 0$ if and only if all h_js are balanced (thus, f is m-resilient if and only if $C_f(I) = 0$ for every set I of size at most m).

The Cauchy–Schwarz inequality gives $\left(\sum_{j=1}^{2^{|I|}} |\mathcal{F}(h_j)| \right)^2 \le 2^{|I|} \sum_{j=1}^{2^{|I|}} \mathcal{F}^2(h_j)$, and the second-order Poisson formula (2.57), page 62, directly implies then the following inequality observed in [187]:

$$C_f(I) \le 2^{-n} \left(\sum_{\substack{u \in \mathbb{F}_2^n; \\ supp(u) \subseteq I}} W_f^2(u) \right)^{\frac{1}{2}} \le 2^{-n + \frac{|I|}{2}} \max_{u \in \mathbb{F}_2^n} |W_f(u)|$$

$$= 2^{-n + \frac{|I|}{2}} \left(2^n - 2\,nl(f) \right) \qquad (3.14)$$

or equivalently

$$d_H\left(f, \mathcal{BF}_{I,n} \right) \ge 2^{n-1} - \frac{1}{2} \left(\sum_{\substack{u \in \mathbb{F}_2^n; \\ supp(u) \subseteq I}} W_f^2(u) \right)^{\frac{1}{2}} \ge 2^{n-1} - 2^{\frac{|I|}{2} - 1} \max_{u \in \mathbb{F}_2^n} |W_f(u)|$$

$$= 2^{n-1} - 2^{n + \frac{|I|}{2} - 1} + 2^{\frac{|I|}{2}} nl(f).$$

This latter inequality shows that, contrary to the case of approximation by functions of algebraic degree at most r, for avoiding close approximations of f by functions of $\mathcal{BF}_{I,n}$ when I has small size, it is sufficient that the first-order nonlinearity of f be large.

Parameter $\max_{I \subseteq \{1,\ldots,n\}, |I| \le k} C_f(I)$ is *permutation invariant*. A related (but different) *affine invariant* parameter, also related to the distance to linear structures, is the minimum Hamming distance to those Boolean functions g whose linear kernel $\{e \in \mathbb{F}_2^n; D_e g = 0\}$ has dimension at least $n - k$. Indeed, the linear kernels of functions in $\mathcal{BF}_{I,n}$ contain $\mathbb{F}_2^{\{1,\ldots,n\} \setminus I}$. The results on the maximum correlation above generalize to this criterion [187].

Results in the domain of Boolean functions for circuit design and learning express that, if the total influence $2^{-n} \sum_{i=1}^n w_H(D_{e_i} f)$ of an n-variable Boolean function f is low, then the sum $\sum_{u \in \mathbb{F}_2^n; w_H(u) \ge k} W_f^2(u)$ is small for large k (and the function is "essentially determined by few coordinates"); see [519, 914]. This is related to Relation (2.67), page 68.

3.1.8 Complexity parameters

Among the criteria viewed above, the main cryptographic *complexity parameters* (related to Shannon's notion of confusion) are the algebraic degree, the nonlinearity and higher-order nonlinearity, the algebraic immunity, and the fast algebraic immunity. Other complexity parameters exist. Note that, as pointed out by Meier and Staffelbach in [843], they are supposed to be affine invariants, because the composition by affine automorphisms should not modify the complexity. And indeed, the attacks on cryptosystems using Boolean functions (stream or block ciphers) often work with similar complexities when using two *affinely equivalent* functions (maybe not exactly the same complexity, because diffusion plays also a role and may be different with both functions).

Algebraic thickness This parameter has been evoked in [844] and later studied in [222, 224, 229].

Definition 27 *Let f be any n-variable Boolean function. The minimum number of terms in the* algebraic normal forms *of all functions affinely equivalent to f is called the* algebraic thickness *of f. We shall denote it by $AT(f)$.*

As far as we know, this parameter is not directly related to an attack. Note, however, that if a function has very low algebraic thickness, then it has low algebraic immunity, since, for every set $\mathcal{I}$ of nonempty multiindices of $\{1,\dots,n\}$, an annihilator of the Boolean function of ANF $\bigoplus_{I\in\mathcal{I}} x^I$ equals $\prod_{I\in\mathcal{I}}(x_{i_I} \oplus 1)$, where, for every $I \in \mathcal{I}$, i_I is an index chosen in I (any one). We deduce that $AI(f) \le AT(f)$ for every Boolean function.

In the case of affine functions, and more generally of the *indicators* of flats (in particular, of function $\delta_0(x) = \prod_{i=1}^{n}(x_i \oplus 1) = \bigoplus_{I\subseteq\{1,\dots,n\}} x^I$, which has all monomials in its ANF), $AT(f)$ equals 1.

In the case of *quadratic functions*, thanks to the existence of the Dickson form of these functions that we shall see in Theorem 10, page 172, $AT(f)$ equals at most $\lceil\frac{n+1}{2}\rceil$, which is also rather small.

Boolean functions of algebraic degree not close to $n-1$ have also moderate algebraic thickness, since $AT(f) \le \sum_{i=0}^{d_{alg}(f)} \binom{n}{i}$.

But it has been shown that, asymptotically, almost all Boolean functions f (in the sense of probability theory) have large algebraic thickness. This property is related to the fact that the number 2^{2^n} of n-variable Boolean functions is strongly increasing when n grows, which allows proving in some cases the existence of functions possessing some complexity features, without being always able to exhibit any such function. This is possible by bounding above the number of functions that do not possess these features and showing that it is negligible when compared to 2^{2^n}. This phenomenon on Boolean functions, which is also valid with codes, is the so-called *Shannon effect* (this term has been introduced in [807]): Shannon in [1035] could prove this way the existence of Boolean functions with high circuit complexity.

Concerning algebraic thickness, it has been first proved in [222] that for every number $\lambda < 1/2$, the density in $\mathcal{BF}_n$ of the subset $\{f \in \mathcal{BF}_n \mid AT(f) \ge \lambda\, 2^n\}$ is larger than $1 - e^{-2^{n+1}(1/2-\lambda)^2 + (n^2+n)\log_2(e)}$ and tends to 1 when n tends to infinity. A more precise bound was proved shortly later:

Proposition 31 *[224] Let c be any strictly positive real number. The density in $\mathcal{BF}_n$ of the subset $\left\{ f \in \mathcal{BF}_n \mid AT(f) \geq 2^{n-1} - c\, n\, 2^{\frac{n-1}{2}} \right\}$ is larger than $1 - 2^{n^2+n}\, e^{-c^2 n^2}$ and, if $c^2 \log_2 e > 1$, then this density tends to 1 when n tends to infinity. For every $n \geq 3$, a Boolean function f such that $AT(f) \geq 2^{n-1} - n\, 2^{\frac{n-1}{2}}$ exists.*

Proof Let k be any positive integer. The number of n-variable Boolean functions whose ANF have at most k monomials equals $1 + \binom{2^n}{1} + \cdots + \binom{2^n}{k}$. The number of affine automorphisms on $\mathbb{F}_2^n$ equals $(2^n - 1)(2^n - 2)(2^n - 4) \ldots (2^n - 2^{n-1})\, 2^n < 2^{n^2+n}$. Thus, the number of Boolean functions f such that $AT(f) \leq k$ is smaller than $N(n,k) = \left(1 + \binom{2^n}{1} + \cdots + \binom{2^n}{k}\right) 2^{n^2+n}$. We have seen already at page 83 that, for every N, we have $\sum_{0 \leq i \leq \lambda N} \binom{N}{i} < 2^N e^{-2N(1/2-\lambda)^2}$. Hence, applying this with $N = 2^n$ and $\lambda = 1/2 - c\, n\, 2^{-(n+1)/2}$, we deduce that the density of the set $\{f \in \mathcal{BF}_n \mid AT(f) \geq 2^{n-1} - c\, n\, 2^{(n-1)/2}\}$ is larger than $1 - \frac{N(n,2^{n-1}-c\,n\,2^{(n-1)/2})}{2^{2^n}} > 1 - 2^{n^2+n}\, e^{-c^2 n^2} = 1 - 2^{n^2+n-c^2 n^2 \log_2 e}$, and tends to 1, if $c^2 \log_2 e > 1$. The last sentence is easy to check. $\qquad\square$

Proposition 31 implies that, for every $\lambda < 1/2$, there exists m such that, for every $n \geq m$, a Boolean function f such that $AT(f) \geq \lambda\, 2^n$ exists. But, unless λ is small, m is greater than 3. We can take $m = 9$ for $\lambda = \frac{1}{4}$ and $m = 12$ for $\lambda = \frac{3}{8}$.

Hence, almost all n-variable Boolean functions have algebraic thickness larger than half the whole number 2^n of monomials (see more in [956]). It may seem surprising that taking the minimum number of terms in the ANFs of all functions affinely equivalent to f does not affect significantly the number of terms in the ANF of a random function. This is due to the small number of affine automorphisms compared to the number of Boolean functions.

The lower bound of Proposition 31 is accompanied by an upper bound:

Proposition 32 *[222] For every $f \in \mathcal{BF}_n$, we have $AT(f) \leq \frac{2}{3}\, 2^n$.*

Proof The proof is by induction on n. The assertion is clearly valid for $n = 1$. Let n be any integer larger than 1 and assume that the assertion is valid for $n - 1$. Let f be any Boolean function in $\mathcal{BF}_n$ and let f_0 and f_1 be the Boolean functions on $\mathbb{F}_2^{n-1}$ such that $f(x_1, \ldots, x_n) = f_0(x_1, \ldots, x_{n-1}) \oplus x_n f_1(x_1, \ldots, x_{n-1})$. We shall denote by $|f|$ the number of terms in the ANF of f. We have $|f| = |f_0| + |f_1|$. By hypothesis, there exists an affine automorphism A of $\mathbb{F}_2^{n-1}$ such that $|f_1 \circ A| \leq 2/3\, 2^{n-1}$. Thus, we can assume without loss of generality that $|f_1| \leq 2/3\, 2^{n-1}$. Assume that $|f| = |f_0| + |f_1|$ is larger than $2/3\, 2^n$. Let r be the number of terms that are in both ANFs of f_0 and f_1. We have $|f_0| + |f_1| - r \leq 2^{n-1}$, since 2^{n-1} is the total number of monomials in $n - 1$ variables. Thus r is larger than or equal to $2/3\, 2^n - 2^{n-1} = 1/3\, 2^{n-1}$. Changing x_n into $x_n \oplus 1$ in the ANF of f keeps f_1 unchanged and replaces f_0 by $f_0 \oplus f_1$. We have $|f_0 \oplus f_1| + |f_1| = (|f_0| + |f_1| - r) - r + |f_1| \leq 2^{n-1} - 1/3\, 2^{n-1} + 2/3\, 2^{n-1} = 2/3\, 2^n$. $\qquad\square$

Given Propositions 31 and 32, we can consider that a function f has large thickness if $AT(f)$ equals $\lambda\, 2^n$, where λ is near $1/2$. Note that the algebraic degrees of such functions cannot be substantially smaller than $\frac{n}{2}$, since we have seen already that

$AT(f) \leq \sum_{i=0}^{d_{alg}(f)} \binom{n}{i}$. There exist functions with low algebraic thicknesses and with highest possible nonlinearity (*e.g.*, quadratic bent functions). There also exist functions with high algebraic thicknesses and low nonlinearities, since there exist functions with high algebraic thicknesses and low Hamming weights: take $\lambda < \lambda' < 1/2$; the number of functions of Hamming weights smaller than or equal to $2^n \lambda'$ equals $\sum_{i=0}^{2^n \lambda'} \binom{2^n}{i} \geq \frac{2^{2^n H_2(\lambda')}}{\sqrt{2^{n+3} \lambda' (1-\lambda')}}$ (cf. [809, page 310]), where $H_2(x) = -x \log_2(x) - (1-x) \log_2(1-x)$ is the entropy function. We have seen above that the number of functions f such that $AT(f) \leq 2^n \lambda$ is smaller than or equal to

$$\left(1 + \binom{2^n}{1} + \cdots + \binom{2^n}{k} \right) 2^{n^2+n} \leq 2^{2^n H_2(\lambda) + n^2 + n} ;$$

thus, the latter is asymptotically smaller than the former and there exist functions of weights smaller than or equal to $2^n \lambda'$ satisfying $AT(f) > 2^n \lambda$.

There also exist functions with algebraic degree at least $n - 1$, nonlinearity at least $2^{n-1} - 2^{\frac{n-1}{2}} \sqrt{n}$ and algebraic thickness at least $\lambda 2^n$, with $\lambda < 1/2$ as close to $1/2$ as we wish, since the probabilities that f has algebraic degree at most $n - 2$, resp. nonlinearity at most $2^{n-1} - 2^{\frac{n}{2}-1} \sqrt{n} \left(\sqrt{2 \ln 2} + \frac{4 \ln n}{n} \right)$, resp. algebraic thickness at most $\lambda 2^n$, tend all three to 0 (see Section 3.1).

Nonnormality Hans Dobbertin has introduced in [466] the following notion: for any n even, an n-variable Boolean function is a *normal function* (resp. a weakly normal function) if it is constant (resp. affine) on at least one $\frac{n}{2}$-dimensional flat. He used this notion for constructing balanced functions with high nonlinearities (see more at page 296). The notion has been generalized and extended (see, *e.g.*, [222, 224]):

Definition 28 *Let n and k $\leq$ n be positive integers. An n-variable Boolean function f is called a k-normal function (resp. a k-weakly normal function) if there exists a k-dimensional flat on which f is constant (resp. affine). For n even, $\frac{n}{2}$-normal functions are simply called normal.*

The notion of normality has been later related to an attack on stream ciphers [881]. The related parameter is studied in [276] as well as two other parameters that complete the information it gives. The notion of k-nonnormal function is a particular case of that of *affine disperser* of dimension k and is also related to that of affine extractor, a stronger notion needed for the extraction of randomness from few independent sources; see more precise definitions and constructions in [110, 1036]. It is also related to a similar notion coming from computational number theory: that of $k$wise independent random variables; see [12].

The complexity criterion we are interested in is k-nonnormality with small k. Even if almost all Boolean functions satisfy it, as we shall see, it is not satisfied by simple ones:

- Every quadratic Boolean function f on $\mathbb{F}_2^n$ is $\frac{n}{2}$-normal if n is even and $\frac{n+1}{2}$-weakly normal if n is odd, according to the properties of quadratic functions that we shall see in Section 5.2.
- Every symmetric Boolean function (*i.e.*, every function whose output is invariant under permutation of its input bits, and depends then only on the Hamming weight of the input; see Section 10.1) is $\left\lfloor\frac{n}{2}\right\rfloor$-normal and $\left\lceil\frac{n}{2}\right\rceil$-weakly-normal since its restriction to the $\left\lceil\frac{n}{2}\right\rceil$-dimensional flat

$$\left\{(x_1,\ldots x_n) \in \mathbb{F}_2^n \mid x_{i+\left\lfloor\frac{n}{2}\right\rfloor} = x_i \oplus 1, \forall i \leq \left\lfloor\frac{n}{2}\right\rfloor\right\}$$

  is constant if n is even and affine if n is odd. Indeed, if n is even, all the elements of this flat have same Hamming weight $\frac{n}{2}$ and $f(x)$ takes therefore a constant value; if n is odd, we have $f(x) = f(x_1,\ldots,x_{n-1},0) \oplus x_n[f(x_1,\ldots,x_{n-1},0) \oplus f(x_1,\ldots,x_{n-1},1)]$, where the functions $f(x_1,\ldots,x_{n-1},0)$ and $f(x_1,\ldots,x_{n-1},1)$ are constant on this flat.
- Every Boolean function on $\mathbb{F}_2^n$ with $n \leq 7$ is $\left\lfloor\frac{n}{2}\right\rfloor$-normal, as can be checked by computer investigation.

There is a mutual upper bound on k and on the nonlinearity of the function:

Proposition 33 *Let f be a k-weakly normal Boolean function on $\mathbb{F}_2^n$. Then*

$$nl(f) \leq 2^{n-1} - 2^{k-1},$$

or equivalently $k \leq \log_2[2^{n-1} - nl(f)] + 1$.

Proof Applying the *Poisson summation formula* (2.39), page 58, to the sign function f_χ, we see that if $f \oplus a \cdot x$ is constant on the flat $b \oplus E^\perp$, then the mean of $(-1)^{b \cdot u} W_f(u)$ when u ranges over $a \oplus E$ equals $\pm|E^\perp|$. And the maximum absolute value of a sequence of numbers is larger than or equal to the absolute value of its arithmetic mean. □

Hence, k-normality with large k implies low nonlinearity. Notice that, since every Boolean function has nonlinearity bounded above by $2^{n-1} - 2^{\frac{n}{2}-1}$, Proposition 33 gives no information if $k \leq \frac{n}{2}$. But the high nonlinearity $2^{n-1} - 2^{\frac{n}{2}-1}$ of bent functions implies that they cannot be $(\frac{n}{2} + 1)$-weakly normal.

Remark. A more general result due to Zheng et al., proved in a complex way in [1179], can be proved similarly: let A be any k-dimensional flat ($k \leq n$). Let f be a Boolean function on $\mathbb{F}_2^n$ and f' its restriction to A. Denote by $nl(f')$ the nonlinearity of f' (*i.e.*, the minimum Hamming distance between f' and any affine function on A). Then we have:[18]

$$nl(f) - nl(f') \leq 2^{n-1} - 2^{k-1}.$$

Indeed, according to the Poisson summation formula applied to f_χ with $A = b \oplus E^\perp$, we have $\max_{u \in \mathbb{F}_2^k} |W_{f'}(u)| \leq \max_{v \in \mathbb{F}_2^n} |W_f(v)|$, which completes the proof.

In fact, a little more can be said, as seen in [191]. Recall that, given two subspaces E of dimension k and E' of $\mathbb{F}_2^n$ such that $E \cap E' = \{0_n\}$ and whose direct sum equals $\mathbb{F}_2^n$, and

---

[18] Note that in Proposition 33, we have $nl(f') = 0$.

denoting for every $a \in E'$ by h_a the restriction of f to the coset $a + E$, the second-order Poisson formula (2.57) in Proposition 12 (page 62) implies

$$\max_{u \in \mathbb{F}_2^n} W_f^2(u) \geq \sum_{a \in E'} \mathcal{F}^2(h_a)$$

(indeed, the maximum of $W_f^2(u)$ is larger than or equal to its mean). Hence we have $\max_{u \in \mathbb{F}_2^n} W_f^2(u) \geq \mathcal{F}^2(h_a)$ for every a. Applying this property to $f \oplus \ell$, where ℓ is any linear function, and using Relation (3.1), page 79, between the nonlinearity and the maximum absolute value of the Walsh transform, we deduce

$$\forall a \in E', \ nl(f) \leq 2^{n-1} - 2^{k-1} + nl(h_a). \tag{3.15}$$

The approaches by the first and the second Poisson formulae lead to two different necessary conditions for the case of equality in (3.15); see [224], where the case of equality is studied. The proof above shows that, if equality occurs in the inequality $nl(f) \leq 2^{n-1} - 2^{k-1}$ for a given function f that coincides with an affine function ℓ on a k-dimensional flat, then $f \oplus \ell$ is balanced on every other coset of this flat. $\qquad\square$

As a consequence of Proposition 33, the maximum possible nonlinearity of *quadratic functions* (*i.e.*, the covering radius of the Reed-Muller code $RM(1, n)$ in the Reed–Muller code $RM(2, n)$) is bounded above by $2^{n-1} - 2^{\frac{n}{2}-1}$ if n is even, which tells nothing, and by $2^{n-1} - 2^{\frac{n-1}{2}}$ if n is odd (these values are in fact the exact ones).

For every $\alpha > 1$, when n tends to infinity, random Boolean functions are almost surely $[\alpha \log_2 n]$-nonnormal:

Proposition 34 *[222] Let c be larger than 1. Let $(k_n)_{n \in \mathbb{N}^*}$ be a sequence of positive integers such that $c \log_2 n \leq k_n \leq n$. The density in $\mathcal{BF}_n$ of the set of all Boolean functions on $\mathbb{F}_2^n$ that are not k_n-weakly normal is larger than $1 - 2^{n(k_n+1)-2^{k_n}}$. This density tends to 1 when n tends to infinity. Therefore, there exists a positive integer N such that, for every $n \geq N$, k_n-nonnormal functions exist. For $k_n = \lfloor \frac{n}{2} \rfloor$ we can take $N = 12$.*

Proof Let λ_n be the number of k_n-dimensional flats in $\mathbb{F}_2^n$. Fix such a flat A. Let μ_n be the number of Boolean functions whose restrictions to A are affine (clearly, this number does not depend on the choice of A). The number of k_n-weakly normal functions on $\mathbb{F}_2^n$ is smaller than or equal to $\lambda_n \mu_n$.

The number of k_n-dimensional vector subspaces of $\mathbb{F}_2^n$ equals (cf., *e.g.*, [809]):

$$\begin{bmatrix} n \\ k_n \end{bmatrix} = \frac{(2^n - 1)(2^n - 2)(2^n - 2^2) \cdots (2^n - 2^{k_n-1})}{(2^{k_n} - 1)(2^{k_n} - 2)(2^{k_n} - 2^2) \cdots (2^{k_n} - 2^{k_n-1})}$$

and the number of k_n-dimensional flats in $\mathbb{F}_2^n$ is: $\lambda_n = 2^{n-k_n} \begin{bmatrix} n \\ k_n \end{bmatrix}$.

We choose now as particular k_n-dimensional flat the set $\mathbb{F}_2^{k_n} \times \{0_{k_n}\}$. The restriction to $\mathbb{F}_2^{k_n} \times \{0_{k_n}\}$ of a Boolean function on $\mathbb{F}_2^n$ is affine if and only if the algebraic normal form of the function contains no monomial of degree at least 2 involving the coordinates $x_1, \ldots, x_{k_n}$ only. The number of such functions is $\mu_n = 2^{\nu_n}$, where $\nu_n = 2^n - 2^{k_n} + 1 + k_n$. The number of k_n-weakly normal functions on $\mathbb{F}_2^n$ is then smaller than or equal to $2^{n-k_n} \begin{bmatrix} n \\ k_n \end{bmatrix} 2^{\nu_n}$. The number of Boolean functions on $\mathbb{F}_2^n$ being equal to 2^{2^n}, the density of the subset $\mathcal{A}_n$ in $\mathcal{BF}_n$ of all Boolean functions on $\mathbb{F}_2^n$ that are not k_n-weakly normal is larger than or equal to $1 - 2^{n-k_n} \begin{bmatrix} n \\ k_n \end{bmatrix} 2^{\nu_n - 2^n}$.

We have $\begin{bmatrix} n \\ k_n \end{bmatrix} < 2^{nk_n - k_n^2 + k_n}$, since every factor in the numerator of $\begin{bmatrix} n \\ k_n \end{bmatrix}$ is smaller than 2^n and every factor in its denominator is larger than or equal to 2^{k_n-1}. Thus, the density of $\mathcal{A}_n$ is larger than or equal to

$$1 - 2^{n(k_n+1)+k_n+1-k_n^2-2^{k_n}} > 1 - 2^{n(k_n+1)-2^{k_n}}.$$

The exponent $n(k_n + 1) - 2^{k_n}$ is smaller than or equal to $2^{k_n/c}(k_n + 1) - 2^{k_n}$ and thus tends to $-\infty$ when n tends to $+\infty$. The last sentence of the proposition can be checked by computation (the sequences $1 - 2^{n-k_n} \begin{bmatrix} n \\ k_n \end{bmatrix} 2^{\nu_n - 2^n}$, n even, and n odd are increasing and positive respectively for $n \geq 12$ and $n \geq 13$). $\square$

Remark.   1. The result of Proposition 34 is easy to prove but pretty astonishing: the size of a k_n-dimensional flat is close to n.
2. Proposition 34 also remains essentially valid (except for the number "12") if, in the definition of k-weakly normal functions, we replace "there exists a k-dimensional flat on which the function is affine" with "there exists a k-dimensional flat such that the restriction of the function to this flat has degree $\leq l$," where l is some fixed positive integer: the value of ν_n has then to be changed into $2^n - 2^{k_n} + 1 + \binom{k_n}{1} + \cdots + \binom{k_n}{l}$. $\square$

The deterministic function with asymptotically lowest-known normality, due to Shaltiel [1036], has normality $2^{\log^{0.9} n}$. Other constructions are given in [47].

The behavior of normality for fixed algebraic degree functions is also interesting to determine. X.-D. Hou has shown in [616] that, for any odd $n \leq 13$, the maximum nonlinearity of all cubic functions is the same as for quadratic functions: $2^{n-1} - 2^{\frac{n-1}{2}}$. So we can wonder whether cubic Boolean functions behave for generic n as quadratic functions with respect to maximum nonlinearity or to normality. For nonlinearity, this is an open problem. But for normality, k_n-nonnormal Boolean functions of algebraic degree 3 exist, where k_n is negligible with respect to n (this confirms the feeling that cubic functions behave merely as general functions, considering their Hamming weights; see Section 5.3, page 180). Indeed, it has been shown in [222] that for every $\lambda > \frac{1}{2}$ and any sequence $(k_n)_{n \in \mathbb{N}^*}$ of positive integers such that $n^\lambda \leq k_n \leq n$, the density of the set of all Boolean functions of algebraic degree at most 3 on $\mathbb{F}_2^n$ that are not k_n-weakly normal in the set of all Boolean functions of algebraic degree at most 3 is larger than or equal to $1 - 2^{n(k_n+1)-k_n^2-\binom{k_n}{2}-\binom{k_n}{3}}$. This density tends to 1 when n tends to infinity.

As proved later in [377] (and recalled in [111]), for any constant d, a random algebraic degree d Boolean function has normality $\Omega(n^{1/(d-1)})$.

Remark.

1. All the results above are essentially valid if we restrict ourselves to balanced functions. Indeed, the number of balanced functions on $\mathbb{F}_2^n$ equals $\binom{2^n}{2^{n-1}} = \frac{(2^n)!}{((2^{n-1})!)^2} \sim \frac{\sqrt{2\pi 2^n}(2^n)^{2^n}e^{-2^n}}{\left(\sqrt{2\pi 2^{n-1}}(2^{n-1})^{2^{n-1}}e^{-2^{n-1}}\right)^2} = \sqrt{\frac{2}{\pi}}\, 2^{2^n - \frac{n}{2}}$, according to Stirling's formula, and all our arguments can be used, replacing the number of functions, 2^{2^n}, by $\binom{2^n}{2^{n-1}}$.

2. We can also deal with the distance to linear structures. Since the existence of a linear structure for a function f is equivalent to the existence of a Boolean function g on $\mathbb{F}_2^{n-1}$ and of a linear function l on $\mathbb{F}_2$ such that $f(x_1, \ldots, x_n)$ is affinely equivalent to the function $g(x_1, \ldots, x_{n-1}) \oplus l(x_n)$, the number of functions admitting linear structures is smaller than or equal to $2^{2^{n-1}}$, times the number of affine automorphisms, times 2. Thus, it is smaller than $2^{2^{n-1}+n^2+n+1}$. Moreover, let ρ be a positive number smaller than $1/2$. The number of Boolean functions on $\mathbb{F}_2^n$ that lie at distance smaller than or equal to $\rho\, 2^n$ from this set is smaller than or equal to $2^{2^{n-1}+n^2+n+1} \sum_{i=0}^{\rho 2^n} \binom{2^n}{i} \leq 2^{2^{n-1}+n^2+n+1+2^n H_2(\rho)}$. Thus, this number is negligible with respect to 2^{2^n} if $H_2(\rho) < 1/2$ and, asymptotically, almost all functions lie then at distance greater than $\rho\, 2^n$ from the set of all Boolean functions admitting linear structures. $\qquad\square$

We have seen that a low algebraic degree of Boolean functions does not imply their normality. Conversely, k-normality does not imply low algebraic degree: take a function of high algebraic degree on $\mathbb{F}_2^{n-1}$ (considered as a subspace of $\mathbb{F}_2^n$) and complete it by 0 to obtain a function on $\mathbb{F}_2^n$.

There exist functions f with low algebraic thicknesses (*e.g.*, functions of algebraic degree 3) which are k-nonnormal with small k; and there exist functions with high algebraic thicknesses that are k-normal with large k: take a function g on $\mathbb{F}_2^{n-1}$ with high $AT(g)$ and complete it by 0 to obtain a function f on $\mathbb{F}_2^n$; it is a simple matter to check that $AT(f) \geq AT(g)$. In [111, 377] (and references therein), the authors studied the relationship between algebraic thickness and nonnormality. The most interesting is that *almost all functions have high algebraic degrees, nonlinearities, and algebraic thicknesses and are non-k-normal with small k*.

Spectral complexity The size of the support of the Walsh transform of an n-variable function f, that is, 2^n minus the number of its zeros, is called the *spectral complexity* of f. We shall denote it by $SC(f)$. This criterion has been studied in [968, 1008]. Since, according to the *inverse Walsh transform formula* (2.43), page 59, the Walsh transform values $W_f(u)$ provide the decomposition of the sign function of f over the basis of the so-called *Walsh functions* $(-1)^{u \cdot x}$, and since these functions are realized by simple circuits, the spectral complexity is related to the circuit complexity of Boolean functions.

Note that, for every n-variable Boolean function f, an easy lower bound can be derived from the Cauchy–Schwarz inequality:

$$SC(f) \geq \frac{\left(\sum_{u \in \mathbb{F}_2^n} W_f^2(u)\right)^2}{\sum_{u \in \mathbb{F}_2^n} W_f^4(u)} = \frac{(2^{2n})^2}{2^n \sum_{\substack{(x,y,z,t) \in (\mathbb{F}_2^n)^4 \\ x+y+z+t=0_n}} (-1)^{f(x) \oplus f(y) \oplus f(z) \oplus f(t)}}$$

$$= \frac{2^{3n}}{\sum_{(x,y,z) \in (\mathbb{F}_2^n)^3} (-1)^{f(x) \oplus f(y) \oplus f(z) \oplus f(x+y+z)}}.$$

The average spectral complexity of n-variable Boolean functions, equal to $2^n - 2^{-2^n} \sum_{f \in \mathcal{BF}_n} |\{u \in \mathbb{F}_2^n; W_f(u) = 0\}|$, is also easily determined: for every $f \in \mathcal{BF}_n$ and $u \in \mathbb{F}_2^n$, we have $W_f(u) = 0$ if and only if function $f(x) \oplus u \cdot x$ is balanced. We have then $|\{f \in \mathcal{BF}_n; W_f(u) = 0\}| = \binom{2^n}{2^{n-1}}$ for every u. Hence, the average number of zeros of the Walsh transform equals $\frac{2^n \binom{2^n}{2^{n-1}}}{2^{2^n}} \sim \sqrt{\frac{2}{\pi}} \, 2^{\frac{n}{2}}$ and the average spectral complexity equals $2^n - \frac{2^n \binom{2^n}{2^{n-1}}}{2^{2^n}}$.

Ryazanov in [1008] shows the more precise result that the random variable equal to $\left(\frac{\pi}{2^{n+3}}\right)^{1/2}$ times the number of zeros of the Walsh transform tends in distribution to the constant function $\frac{1}{2}$ over $\{0, 1\}$. The proof is too long for being included here. He also studies the number of zeros of the Walsh transform of functions of even Hamming weights and shows then that the same random variable converges to 1 (in particular, functions of even Hamming weights have on average twice more zeros than general Boolean functions; this can be simply proved with the same method as previously described).

The evaluation can also be done for random (n, m)-functions. When F ranges over the set of (n, m)-functions and v ranges over $\mathbb{F}_2^m \setminus \{0_m\}$, the component function $v \cdot F$ ranges $2^m - 1$ times over the set of n-variable Boolean functions. Since for $v = 0_m$, we have $W_F(u, v) = 0$ for every $u \neq 0_n$ and $W_F(0_n, 0_m) = 2^n$, we deduce that the average number of zeros of the Walsh transform of (n, m)-functions equals $2^n - 1 + (2^m - 1) \frac{2^n \binom{2^n}{2^{n-1}}}{2^{2^n}}$.

And when restricting ourselves to (n, n)-permutations, we know that when $v \neq 0_n$, the component function $v \cdot F$ ranges uniformly over the set of balanced functions when F ranges over the set of permutations. Distinguishing the cases "$u = v = 0_n$," "$u = 0_n, v \neq 0_n$," "$u \neq 0_n, v = 0_n$" and "$u \neq 0_n, v \neq 0_n$," we obtain an average of $2(2^n - 1) + \frac{(2^n-1)^2 \binom{2^{n-1}}{2^{n-2}}^2}{\binom{2^n}{2^{n-1}}}$, since $|\{f \in \mathcal{BF}_n, f \text{ balanced}; W_f(u) = 0\}|$ equals $\binom{2^{n-1}}{2^{n-2}}^2$ for every $u \neq 0_n$, because $u \cdot x$ and $f(x) \oplus u \cdot x$ need to be both balanced, that is, we need $w_H(f(x)(u \cdot x)) = w_H(f(x)(u \cdot x \oplus 1)) = 2^{n-2}$, where $f(x)(u \cdot x)$ is the product of $f(x)$ and $u \cdot x$.

As in the case of Boolean functions above, by the Cauchy–Schwarz inequality, the spectral complexity of (n, m)-functions $SC(F) = |\{(u, v) \in \mathbb{F}_2^n \times \mathbb{F}_2^m; W_F(u, v) \neq 0\}|$ of F satisfies

$$SC(F) \geq \frac{\left(\sum_{u \in \mathbb{F}_2^n, v \in \mathbb{F}_2^m} W_F^2(u, v)\right)^2}{\sum_{u \in \mathbb{F}_2^n, v \in \mathbb{F}_2^m} W_f^4(u, v)}$$

$$= \frac{2^{3n+m}}{|\{(x, y, z, t) \in (\mathbb{F}_2^n)^4; \ x + y + z + t = 0_n, F(x) + F(y) + F(z) + F(t) = 0_m\}|}$$

$$= \frac{2^{3n+m}}{|\{(x, y, z) \in (\mathbb{F}_2^n)^3; \ F(x) + F(y) + F(z) + F(x + y + z) = 0_m\}|}.$$

In the case of an APN (n, n)-function (see Definition 41, page 137), this gives

$$SC(F) \geq \frac{2^{4n}}{3 \cdot 2^{2n} - 2^{n+1}} \approx \frac{2^{2n}}{3}.$$

A similar method with $v = 0_m$ apart gives $SC(F) \geq 1 + (2^n - 1) 2^{n-1} \approx 2^{2n-1}$.

Nonhomomorphicity For every even integer k such that $4 \leq k \leq 2^n$, the k-th order *nonhomomorphicity* [1171] of a Boolean function equals the number of k-tuples $(u_1, \ldots, u_k)$ of vectors of $\mathbb{F}_2^n$ such that $u_1 + \cdots + u_k = 0_n$ and $f(u_1) \oplus \cdots \oplus f(u_k) = 0$. It is a simple matter to show that it equals $2^{(k-1)n-1} + 2^{-n-1} \sum_{u \in \mathbb{F}_2^n} W_f^k(u)$. This parameter should be small (but no related attack exists on stream ciphers). It is maximum and equals $2^{(k-1)n}$ if and only if the function is affine. It is minimum and equals $2^{(k-1)n-1} + 2^{\frac{nk}{2}-1}$ if and only if the function is bent.

Conclusion of this section

As we can see, there are numerous cryptographic criteria for Boolean functions to be used in stream ciphers. The ones that must be necessarily satisfied are balancedness, a high algebraic degree, a high nonlinearity, a high algebraic immunity, and a good resistance to fast algebraic attacks. It is difficult but not impossible to find functions satisfying good trade-offs between all these criteria (see Chapter 9). Achieving additionally resiliency of a sufficient order, which is necessary for the combiner model, is impossible because of the Siegenthaler bound.[19] Hence, the filter model is more appropriate.

We saw that, asymptotically, almost all Boolean functions (in the sense of probability theory) have high algebraic degree, high nonlinearity, and high algebraic immunity. They have also high algebraic thickness and low normality. The related following randomness criteria for n-variable Boolean functions seem then appropriate:

- Algebraic degree close to $n - 1$ (since the number of functions of algebraic degree at most $n - 2$ is negligible compared to 2^{2^n})
- Nonlinearity lying within the interval

$$\left[2^{n-1} - 2^{\frac{n}{2}-1}\sqrt{n} \left(\sqrt{2 \ln 2} + \frac{4 \ln n}{n}\right); 2^{n-1} - 2^{\frac{n}{2}-1}\sqrt{n} \left(\sqrt{2 \ln 2} - \frac{5 \ln n}{n}\right)\right]$$

(according to Rodier's results; see Subsection 3.1.3)

---

[19] But to render f 1-resilient by composing it with a linear automorphism – which preserves the other features – we just need that there exist n linearly independent vectors at which the Walsh transform vanishes.

- Algebraic immunity at distance at most $\ln n$ from $\frac{n}{2}$ (according to Didier's results; see Subsection 3.1.5)
- Algebraic thickness equal to $\lambda 2^n$ with λ near $\frac{1}{2}$

Of course, these criteria make sense asymptotically.

3.2 Cryptographic criteria for vectorial functions in stream and block ciphers

Vectorial functions can be used (in the place of Boolean functions) as combiners or filters in stream ciphers (they then allow the PRG to generate several bits at each clock cycle, which increases the speed of the cipher) or as *S-box*es in block ciphers. These two situations are very different, but some criteria of resistance to attacks are the same. We study them in this section. We shall study in the two next sections those criteria and parameters that are specific to each use.

3.2.1 Balancedness of vectorial functions

Recall that an (n, m)-function is called *balanced* if its output distribution is uniformly distributed (with $m \leq n$), that is, if it takes every value of $\mathbb{F}_2^m$ the same number 2^{n-m} of times. By definition, F is then balanced if every Boolean function $\varphi_b = 1_{\{b\}} \circ F$ has *Hamming weight* 2^{n-m}. A vectorial function used as a combiner or as a filter needs to be balanced because any combination of its output bits can be made, and to avoid such a combination to give statistical information allowing one to distinguish when a pair of texts is a pair (plaintext, ciphertext), this needs the vectorial function to be balanced.

S-boxes in block ciphers are also better balanced. In every SPN (see Subsection 1.4.2), the S-boxes need to be permutations (with $m = n$) and are then balanced. In *Feistel ciphers*, we have seen that the S-boxes do not need to be balanced, but that it has been shown for instance in [957] that, when they are unbalanced, an attack may be possible; to withstand it, the designer needs to complexify the encryption algorithm, for instance with expansion boxes. Hence, balanced S-boxes are preferred.

Characterization through the component functions

The balanced S-boxes (and among them, the permutations) can be nicely characterized by the balancedness of their component functions:

Proposition 35 *[775] An (n, m)-function F is balanced if and only if its component functions $v \cdot F$, $v \neq 0_m$, are all balanced, that is, if and only if, for every nonzero $v \in \mathbb{F}_2^m$, we have $W_F(0_n, v) = 0$.*

Proof The relation

$$\sum_{v \in \mathbb{F}_2^m} (-1)^{v \cdot (F(x)+b)} = \begin{cases} 2^m \text{ if } F(x) = b \\ 0 \text{ otherwise} \end{cases} = 2^m \, \varphi_b(x), \qquad (3.16)$$

is valid for every (n, m)-function F, every $x \in \mathbb{F}_2^n$, and every $b \in \mathbb{F}_2^m$, since the function $v \mapsto v \cdot (F(x) + b)$, being linear, is either balanced or null. Thus, we have

$$\sum_{x \in \mathbb{F}_2^n; v \in \mathbb{F}_2^m} (-1)^{v \cdot (F(x)+b)} = 2^m |F^{-1}(b)| = 2^m \, w_H(\varphi_b), \tag{3.17}$$

where w_H denotes the Hamming weight. Hence, the Fourier–Hadamard transform of the function $v \mapsto \sum_{x \in \mathbb{F}_2^n} (-1)^{v \cdot F(x)}$ equals the function $b \mapsto 2^m \, |F^{-1}(b)|$. We know that a pseudo-Boolean function has constant Fourier–Hadamard transform if and only if it is null at every nonzero vector. We deduce that F is balanced if and only if the function $v \mapsto \sum_{x \in \mathbb{F}_2^n} (-1)^{v \cdot F(x)}$ is null on $\mathbb{F}_2^m \setminus \{0_m\}$. $\qquad\square$

Equivalently, F is balanced if and only if $\sum_{a \in \mathbb{F}_2^n} \mathcal{F}(D_a(v \cdot F)) = 0$ for every $v \neq 0_m$ (according to Wiener–Khintchine's formula (2.53), page 62). Note that, for $m = n$, F is a permutation if and only if $\sum_{v \in \mathbb{F}_2^n} \mathcal{F}(D_a(v \cdot F)) = 0$ for every $a \neq 0_n$ (since $\sum_{v \in \mathbb{F}_2^m} \mathcal{F}(v \cdot G) = 2^m |G^{-1}(0_m)|$ for every (n, m)-function G).

If F is balanced, then the f_i $(1 \leqslant i \leqslant m)$ being balanced, we have $d_{\text{alg}}(F) \leqslant n - 1$. Much more can be said, in particular for permutations: F is a permutation if and only if the product of strictly less than n coordinate functions of F has even Hamming weight, that is, algebraic degree strictly less than n, and the product of all n coordinate functions has algebraic degree n. The condition is clearly necessary, and it is easily seen that it is sufficient (since "$|F^{-1}(a)|$ is odd for every $a \in \mathbb{F}_2^n$" implies F bijective). Note that the relation between this characterization and Proposition 35 is given by Relations (2.25) and (2.26).

There is a nice property of the Walsh transform of permutations:

$$\forall v \neq w, \quad \sum_{u \in \mathbb{F}_2^n} W_F(u, v) W_F(u, w) = 0. \tag{3.18}$$

Indeed, we have $\sum_{u \in \mathbb{F}_2^n} W_F(u, v) W_F(u, w) = \sum_{u, x, y \in \mathbb{F}_2^n} (-1)^{u \cdot (x+y) \oplus v \cdot F(x) \oplus w \cdot F(y)} = 2^n \sum_{x \in \mathbb{F}_2^n} (-1)^{(v+w) \cdot F(x)}$. Note that for $v = w$, the sum in (3.18) equals 2^{2n} (this is Parseval's relation on the Boolean function $v \cdot F$). Of course, Relation (3.18) can be also applied to F^{-1} and since

$$W_{F^{-1}}(u, v) = W_F(v, u),$$

we obtain

$$\forall v \neq w, \quad \sum_{u \in \mathbb{F}_2^n} W_F(v, u) W_F(w, u) = 0.$$

Imbalance of an (n,m)-function

A natural way of quantifying the fact that some (n, m)-function F is unbalanced is by the variance of the random variable $b \to |F^{-1}(b)|$, where $|F^{-1}(b)|$ denotes the size of the preimage of b by F. In [267], the variance is multiplied by 2^m to give the following integer-valued parameter,[20] that we shall call the *imbalance* of F:

$$NbF = \sum_{b \in \mathbb{F}_2^m} \left(\left| F^{-1}(b) \right| - 2^{n-m} \right)^2 = \sum_{b \in \mathbb{F}_2^m} \left| F^{-1}(b) \right|^2 - 2^{2n-m}. \qquad (3.19)$$

It has the following properties:

- $NbF \geq 0$, for every vectorial function F, and $NbF = 0$ if and only if F is balanced.
- NbF is invariant under composition of F by permutations (on the right and on the left); in particular, it is *affine invariant*.
- $NbF = |\{(x, y) \in (\mathbb{F}_2^n)^2 ; F(x) = F(y)\}| - 2^{2n-m} \leq 2^{2n} - 2^{2n-m}$ and $NbF = 2^{2n} - 2^{2n-m}$ if and only if F is constant.
- $NbF = \sum_{a \in \mathbb{F}_2^n} |(D_a F)^{-1}(0_m)| - 2^{2n-m}$.

Parameter NbF can be expressed by means of the Walsh transform. We have

$$\sum_{v \in \mathbb{F}_2^m} W_F^2(0_n, v) = \sum_{x, y \in \mathbb{F}_2^n} \left(\sum_{v \in \mathbb{F}_2^m} (-1)^{v \cdot (F(x) + F(y))} \right)$$

$$= 2^m |\{(x, y) \in \mathbb{F}_2^n \mid F(x) = F(y)\}| = 2^m (NbF + 2^{2n-m}).$$

Hence:

$$NbF = 2^{-m} \sum_{v \in \mathbb{F}_2^m, v \neq 0_m} W_F^2(0_n, v). \qquad (3.20)$$

3.2.2 Algebraic degree of vectorial functions

The algebraic degree of vectorial functions has been defined at page 39. The output of the function used in a stream cipher being also the output of the PRG, the output bits can be combined and used in a Berlekamp–Massey attack. The algebraic degree is then an important parameter.

In block ciphers, the algebraic degree is a security parameter against structural attacks, such as integral [709], higher-order differential, cube [465], or, recently, attacks based on the division property[21] [1086] (see also the two first sections of [106] and the references therein). In particular, the *higher-order differential attack* [706, 735] (see also [204]) exploits the fact that the algebraic degree of the S-box F is low, or more generally that there exists a low-dimensional vector subspace V of $\mathbb{F}_2^n$ such that the function $D_V F(x) = \sum_{v \in V} F(x + v)$ (*i.e.*, $D_{a_1} \cdots D_{a_k} F(x)$ where $\{a_1, \ldots, a_k\}$ is a basis of V) is constant. A probabilistic version of this attack [638] allows the derivative not to be constant, and the S-box must then have high *higher-order nonlinearity* (a notion defined for Boolean functions in Definition 20,

---

[20] The framework of [267] is functions from Abelian groups to Abelian groups; we stick here to Boolean functions.

[21] A very elementary notion, from a viewpoint of Boolean functions, whose properties given in diverse papers are in fact well-known properties of Reed–Muller codes.

page 83; for vectorial functions, see page 349 in Subsection 9.2.4). *Stricto sensu*, the higher-order differential attack has been proved efficient for *quadratic functions* only. But since cryptographers like to have some security margin, even *cubic functions* may be viewed as weak (unless, as usual in cryptography, some precautions are taken with the global cipher). Quadratic S-boxes, if used, need care. It is observed in [204, 108, 106] (see page 64 and below) that the algebraic degree of the function resulting from the first rounds of the cipher may increase less than expected.

The algebraic degree of the computational inverse of a permutation plays also a role in the algebraic degree of the iterated rounds implementing it. This is shown in [106] by proving that $d_{alg}(G \circ F) \leq n - \left\lfloor \frac{n-1-d_{alg}(G)}{d_{alg}(F^{-1})} \right\rfloor$ for every (n,n)-permutation F and every (n,r)-function G. We do not recall the proof given in [106] for this bound, since as seen in [254] we have directly from Relation (2.12), page 41, the slightly stronger bound $d_{alg}(G \circ F) \leq n - \left\lceil \frac{n-d_{alg}(G)}{d_{alg}(F^{-1})} \right\rceil$, implied by $n = d_{alg}\left((g_k \oplus 1) \prod_{i \in I^c}(f_i' \oplus 1)\right) \leq d_{alg}(G) + (n-|I|) d_{alg}(F^{-1})$. And $d_{alg}(G \circ F)$ is bounded above by $\max\{t; d_{G,F^{-1}}(n-t) = n\}$, where $d_{G,F^{-1}}(n-t)$ equals the maximal numerical degree of the linear combinations in $\mathcal{BF}_n$ of at most one coordinate function of G and at most $n - t$ coordinate functions of F^{-1} (or more precisely of the parts of the NNFs of these functions that are not divisible by 2^{n-t}). Indeed, in the framework of Relation (2.12) again, we have $n = d_{alg}\left((g_k \oplus 1) \prod_{i \in I^c}(f_i' \oplus 1)\right) \leq d_{num}\left((g_k \oplus 1) \prod_{i \in I^c}(f_i' \oplus 1)\right) \leq d_{G,F^{-1}}(n-|I|)$, the latter inequality being due to Relation (2.26), page 50.

Remark. It is an open problem to know whether those high algebraic degree functions that are *CCZ equivalent* to low algebraic degree functions could be attacked by a modification of the higher-order differential attack. Thus, it is not clear whether the designer should also avoid functions CCZ equivalent to quadratic functions. □

3.2.3 Nonlinearity of vectorial functions

In stream ciphers, since the output bits can be combined by the attacker, the nonlinearity of all *component functions* must be large, and the minimum of these nonlinearities, called the nonlinearity of the vectorial function, is then a parameter related to the resistance to the fast correlation attack [843]. But nonlinear combinations of the output bits can also be used by the attacker, and this will lead in Subsection 3.3.2 to the introduction of a parameter more adapted to this framework.

In block ciphers, the *linear attack*, introduced by Matsui [829], is based on an idea from [1084]. It may have been unknown by the National Security Agency (NSA) at the time it was introduced; this could explain why it works better[22] than the differential attack on the DES. It seems that it was known or partly known from the USSR. It is, with the differential attack that we shall describe at page 134, one of the two most powerful general-purpose cryptographic attacks known to date. Its most common version is an attack on the *reduced cipher*, that is, the cipher obtained from the original one by removing its

---

[22] The differential attack needs 2^{47} pairs (plaintext, ciphertext) while the linear attack needs "only" 2^{13} pairs.

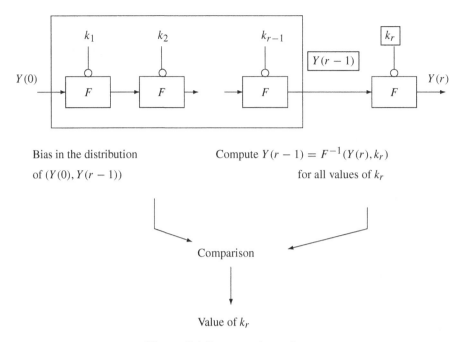

Figure 3.1 Last round attacks.

last round[23] (or more generally an attack on a round whose inputs and outputs can be computed from the plaintext and ciphertext and a number of key bits hopefully "small"). We describe the principle of the attack in the case it is applied to the reduced cipher. In Figure 3.1, $Y(r - 1)$ denotes the output of the reduced cipher corresponding to a plaintext $Y(0)$, and $Y(r)$ denotes the ciphertext. Assume that it is possible to distinguish the outputs of the reduced cipher from random outputs, by observing some statistical bias in their value distribution. The existence of such a *distinguisher* allows recovering the key used in the last round, either by an exhaustive search, which is efficient if this key is shorter than the master key, or by using specificities of the cipher allowing replacing the exhaustive search by, for instance, solving algebraic equations.

We describe now the attack in the case of exhaustive search, which is simpler to describe. The attacker, who knows a number of pairs (plaintext, ciphertext) of the (complete) cipher, visits all possible last round keys. For each try, he/she applies to all the ciphertexts in these pairs the inverse of what is the last round when the key corresponds to the try (this is possible since all except the key is supposed known to him/her; if not, say, if some parameter is unknown, the attacker will have to try all possibilities). He/she obtains in the case of the correct key guess the output of the reduced cipher and has then a number of pairs (plaintext, ciphertext) of the reduced cipher, on which he/she can observe the statistical bias. In all the other cases (incorrect guesses), the obtained pairs (plaintext, ciphertext) correspond to a

---

[23] The output of the reduced cipher is unknown if the last round key is unknown, but it is convenient to name this reduced cipher for describing the attack.

cipher equal to the original cipher with an additional round whose round key is random, and the pairs are then assumed random, with no observable bias. Such assumption is verified in practice. The number of pairs (m, c) that are known to the attacker needs then to be large enough to distinguish the bias (the smaller the bias, the larger the number of known pairs needed).

For distinguishing pairs (plaintext, ciphertext) of the reduced cipher, the linear attack uses triples (α, β, γ) of binary strings such that, a block m of plaintext and a key k being randomly chosen, the bit $\alpha \cdot m \oplus \beta \cdot c \oplus \gamma \cdot k$, where "·" denotes the *usual inner product* (between two strings of the same length) and c denotes the (reduced) ciphertext related to m, has a probability different from 1/2 of being null. The more distant from 1/2 the probability, the more efficient the attack. Note that when searching for triples (α, β, γ), both m and k are supposed ranging uniformly over their definition spaces (indeed, the plaintext can be any binary string of a given length, and the round key can be as well any string of a given length), while during the attack, m still ranges uniformly, but k is fixed.

The related criterion on any S-box F used in the cipher for allowing resistance to the attack is that the component functions $v \cdot F$, $v \neq 0_m$, be at Hamming distance to affine Boolean functions $u \cdot x \oplus \epsilon$ as close to 2^{n-1} as possible. In other words, the nonlinearities of all these component functions must be as large as possible. The generalization to vectorial functions of the notion of nonlinearity introduced by Nyberg [907] and studied by Chabaud and Vaudenay [341], is then as follows:

Definition 29 *The* nonlinearity *of an* (n, m)-*function is the minimum nonlinearity of its component functions:*

$$nl(F) = 2^{n-1} - \frac{1}{2} \max_{\substack{v \in \mathbb{F}_2^m \setminus \{0_m\} \\ u \in \mathbb{F}_2^n}} |W_F(u, v)| \; ; \; W_F(u, v) = \sum_{x \in \mathbb{F}_2^n} (-1)^{v \cdot F(x) \oplus u \cdot x}. \tag{3.21}$$

Note that "$\max_{v \in \mathbb{F}_2^m \setminus \{0_m\}; \, u \in \mathbb{F}_2^n}$" can be replaced by "$\max_{(u,v) \in \mathbb{F}_2^n \times \mathbb{F}_2^m ; (u,v) \neq (0_n, 0_m)}$", since we have $\sum_{x \in \mathbb{F}_2^n} (-1)^{u \cdot x} = 0$ for every nonzero u.

Nonlinearity is an EA invariant (see Definition 5, page 28), that is, it does not change when we compose the function by affine automorphisms nor when we add an affine function to it (this implies for instance that if A is a surjective affine function from $\mathbb{F}_2^r$ into $\mathbb{F}_2^n$, then $nl(F \circ A) = 2^{r-n} nl(F)$, since by affine invariance, we can assume without loss of generality that A is a projection and the equality is then easily shown). Nonlinearity is more strongly a *CCZ invariant*. Indeed, in Relation (3.21), $W_F(u, v)$ equals the *Fourier–Hadamard transform* of the graph $\{(x, F(x)), x \in \mathbb{F}_2^n\}$ of F, and $\max_{v \in \mathbb{F}_2^{m*}, u \in \mathbb{F}_2^n} |W_F(u, v)|$ is then invariant under affine transformation of this graph.

S. Dib has shown in [436] that for $0 < \beta < 1/4$ and $m \leq n$, when n tends to infinity, the nonlinearity of almost all (n, m)-functions (in terms of probability) is bounded above by $2^{n-1} - 2^{\frac{n-1}{2}} \sqrt{(n+m) \log 2} \, (1 - \beta)$, and that for $\beta > 0$, when $n + m$ tends to infinity, the nonlinearity of almost all (n, m)-functions is bounded below by $2^{n-1} - 2^{\frac{n-1}{2}} \sqrt{(n+m) \log 2} \, (1 + \beta)$.

The *covering radius bound* $2^{n-1} - 2^{\frac{n}{2}-1}$ (see page 80) on the nonlinearity of any n-variable Boolean function is obviously valid for (n, m)-functions. Naturally, this has led researchers to extend the notion of bentness to vectorial functions:

Definition 30 *Given two integers n and m (with n necessarily even), an (n, m)-function F is called bent if its nonlinearity $nl(F)$ achieves the optimum $2^{n-1} - 2^{n/2-1}$.*

We shall see with Proposition 104, page 269, that bent (n, m)-functions do not exist if $m > \frac{n}{2}$. This has led to asking whether better upper bounds than the covering radius bound could be proved in this case. Such bound has been found by Chabaud and Vaudenay in [341]. In fact, a bound on sequences due to Sidelnikov [1040] is equivalent for power functions to the bound obtained by Chabaud and Vaudenay, and its proof is valid for all functions. This is why the bound is now called the *Sidelnikov–Chabaud–Vaudenay (SCV) bound*:

Theorem 6 *Let n and m be any positive integers such that $m \geq n - 1$. Let F be any (n, m)-function. Then:*

$$nl(F) \leq 2^{n-1} - \frac{1}{2}\sqrt{3 \times 2^n - 2 - 2\frac{(2^n - 1)(2^{n-1} - 1)}{2^m - 1}}.$$

Proof   Recall that $nl(F) = 2^{n-1} - \frac{1}{2} \max\limits_{v \in \mathbb{F}_2^m \setminus \{0_m\}; \, u \in \mathbb{F}_2^n} |W_F(u, v)|$. We have

$$\max_{\substack{v \in \mathbb{F}_2^m \setminus \{0_m\} \\ u \in \mathbb{F}_2^n}} W_F^2(u, v) \geq \frac{\sum\limits_{\substack{v \in \mathbb{F}_2^m \setminus \{0_m\} \\ u \in \mathbb{F}_2^n}} W_F^4(u, v)}{\sum\limits_{\substack{v \in \mathbb{F}_2^m \setminus \{0_m\} \\ u \in \mathbb{F}_2^n}} W_F^2(u, v)}. \tag{3.22}$$

Parseval's relation states that, for every $v \in \mathbb{F}_2^m$:

$$\sum_{u \in \mathbb{F}_2^n} W_F^2(u, v) = 2^{2n}. \tag{3.23}$$

Using that any character sum $\sum_{x \in E} (-1)^{\ell(x)}$ associated to a linear function ℓ over any $\mathbb{F}_2$-vector space E is nonzero if and only if ℓ is null on E, we have

$$\sum_{v \in \mathbb{F}_2^m, \, u \in \mathbb{F}_2^n} W_F^4(u, v)$$

$$= \sum_{x,y,z,t \in \mathbb{F}_2^n} \left[\sum_{v \in \mathbb{F}_2^m} (-1)^{v \cdot (F(x)+F(y)+F(z)+F(t))} \right] \left[\sum_{u \in \mathbb{F}_2^n} (-1)^{u \cdot (x+y+z+t)} \right]$$

$$= 2^{n+m} \left| \left\{ (x, y, z, t) \in \mathbb{F}_2^{4n}; \begin{cases} x + y + z + t & = 0_n \\ F(x) + F(y) + F(z) + F(t) & = 0_m \end{cases} \right\} \right|$$

$$= 2^{n+m} |\{(x, y, z) \in \mathbb{F}_2^{3n}; \, F(x) + F(y) + F(z) + F(x + y + z) = 0_m\}| \tag{3.24}$$

$$\geq 2^{n+m} |\{(x, y, z) \in \mathbb{F}_2^{3n}; \, x = y \text{ or } x = z \text{ or } y = z\}|. \tag{3.25}$$

Clearly, $|\{(x, y, z); x = y \text{ or } x = z \text{ or } y = z\}|$ equals

$$3 \cdot |\{(x, x, y); x, y \in \mathbb{F}_2^n\}| - 2 \cdot |\{(x, x, x); x \in \mathbb{F}_2^n\}| = 3 \cdot 2^{2n} - 2 \cdot 2^n.$$

Hence, according to Relation (3.22),

$$\max_{v \in \mathbb{F}_2^m \setminus \{0_m\}; \, u \in \mathbb{F}_2^n} W_F^2(u, v) \geq \frac{2^{n+m}(3 \cdot 2^{2n} - 2 \cdot 2^n) - 2^{4n}}{(2^m - 1) \, 2^{2n}}$$

$$= 3 \times 2^n - 2 - 2 \frac{(2^n - 1)(2^{n-1} - 1)}{2^m - 1}$$

and this gives the desired bound, according to Relation (3.21), page 117. □

The condition $m \geq n - 1$ is assumed in Theorem 6 to make nonnegative the expression located under the square root. Note that for $m = n - 1$, this bound coincides with the covering radius bound. For $m \geq n$, it strictly improves upon it. For $m > n$, the square root in it cannot be an integer (see [341]). Hence, the SCV bound can be tight only if $n = m$ with n odd, in which case it states

$$nl(F) \leq 2^{n-1} - 2^{\frac{n-1}{2}}. \tag{3.26}$$

We shall see that, under this condition, it is actually tight.

Definition 31 *[341] The (n, n)-functions F that achieve (3.26) with equality are called almost bent (AB).*

Remark. The term of *almost* bent is a little misleading. It gives the feeling that these functions are not optimal. But they are, according to Theorem 6. Proposition 104, page 269, will give the values of n and m such that bent (n, m)-functions exist. □

According to Inequality (3.22), page 118, the AB functions are those (n, n)-functions such that, for every $u, v \in \mathbb{F}_2^n$, $v \neq 0_n$, the sum $\sum_{x \in \mathbb{F}_2^n} (-1)^{v \cdot F(x) \oplus u \cdot x} = W_F(u, v)$ equals 0 or $\pm 2^{\frac{n+1}{2}}$ (indeed, the maximum of a sequence of nonnegative and not all null integers equals the ratio of the sum of their squares over the sum of their values if and only if these integers take one nonzero value exactly). We shall see at page 262 that this is equivalent to saying that all component functions are *near-bent*. Note that this condition does not depend on the choice of the inner product.

We shall see that AB functions exist for every odd $n \geq 3$. Function $F(x) = x^3$, $x \in \mathbb{F}_{2^n}$, is the simplest one. Chapter 11 covers their topic.

Bounds on nonlinearity by means of imbalance

We follow [239] in this subsection. A bound is given on the nonlinearity of (n, m)-functions, by means of their imbalance (see the definition at page 114):

Proposition 36   *Let F be any (n, m)-function. The nonlinearity of F satisfies*

$$nl(F) \leq 2^{n-1} - \frac{1}{2}\sqrt{\frac{2^m}{2^m - 1}Nb_F}.$$

Proof   We have, using Relation (3.20), page 114:

$$\max_{\substack{v\in\mathbb{F}_2^m \,/\, v\neq 0_m \\ u\in\mathbb{F}_2^n}} W_F^2(u, v) \geq \max_{v\in\mathbb{F}_2^m \,/\, v\neq 0_m} W_F^2(0_n, v) \geq \frac{1}{2^m - 1} \sum_{v\in\mathbb{F}_2^m \,/\, v\neq 0_m} W_F^2(0_n, v)$$

$$= \frac{2^m}{2^m - 1}Nb_F.$$

Relation (3.21), page 117, completes the proof.   □

This bound shows that, to have a chance of having a high nonlinearity, a function must not differ too much from a balanced function.

The bound of Proposition 36 is tight (it is achieved with equality, for instance, by bent functions, since both inequalities above are equalities in that case). Moreover, it can be applied to $F + L$ (which has the same nonlinearity as F) for every linear (n, m)-function L. Note that we have in general $Nb_{F+L} \neq Nb_F$. Proposition 36 implies, denoting by $\mathcal{L}_{n,m}$ the set of linear (n, m)-functions,

$$nl(F) \leq 2^{n-1} - \frac{1}{2}\sqrt{\frac{2^m}{2^m - 1} \max_{L\in\mathcal{L}_{n,m}} Nb_{F+L}}, \tag{3.27}$$

which is obviously tight too.

Remark.   We have $v \cdot L(x) = L^*(v) \cdot x$ where L^* is the adjoint operator of L.
  Hence $\displaystyle\max_{\substack{v\in\mathbb{F}_2^m \,/\, v\neq 0_m \\ u\in\mathbb{F}_2^n}} W_F^2(u, v) = \max_{\substack{v\in\mathbb{F}_2^m \,/\, v\neq 0_m \\ L\in\mathcal{L}_{n,m}}} W_{F+L}^2(0_n, v).$ □

Relation (3.27) raises the question of determining the mean of Nb_{F+L}:

Proposition 37   *[239] Let F be any (n, m)-function. The mean of the random variable $L \in \mathcal{L}_{n,m} \rightarrow Nb_{F+L}$ equals $2^n - 2^{n-m}$. We have $\displaystyle\max_{L\in\mathcal{L}_{n,m}} Nb_{F+L} \geq 2^n - 2^{n-m}$, with equality if and only if F is bent.*

Proof   For every $L \in \mathcal{L}_{n,m}$, we have

$$Nb_{F+L} = \sum_{a\in\mathbb{F}_2^n} |(D_a(F + L))^{-1}(0_m)| - 2^{2n-m}$$

$$= \sum_{a\in\mathbb{F}_2^n} |(D_a F)^{-1}(L(a))| - 2^{2n-m}. \tag{3.28}$$

The size of $\mathcal{L}_{n,m}$ equals 2^{mn}. Given any nonzero element a of $\mathbb{F}_2^n$ and any element b of $\mathbb{F}_2^m$, the number of linear functions L such that $L(a) = b$ equals $2^{m(n-1)}$. We have then the following, distinguishing the case $a = 0_n$ from the others:

$$\sum_{L \in \mathcal{L}_{n,m}} \sum_{a \in \mathbb{F}_2^n} |(D_a F)^{-1}(L(a))| = 2^{mn} 2^n + 2^{m(n-1)} \sum_{\substack{a \in \mathbb{F}_2^n \\ a \neq 0_n}} \sum_{b \in \mathbb{F}_2^m} |(D_a F)^{-1}(b)|$$

$$= 2^{(m+1)n} + 2^{m(n-1)}(2^n - 1)2^n.$$

The mean $\frac{1}{|\mathcal{L}_{n,m}|} \sum_{L \in \mathcal{L}_{n,m}} \sum_{a \in \mathbb{F}_2^n} |(D_a F)^{-1}(L(a))|$ equals $2^n + 2^{n-m}(2^n - 1) = 2^{2n-m} + 2^n - 2^{n-m}$. This proves the first assertion. The second is then straightforward, and the case of equality is when the function $(a, b) \in (\mathbb{F}_2^n \setminus \{0_n\}) \times \mathbb{F}_2^m \mapsto |(D_a F)^{-1}(b)|$ is constant. We shall see in Section 6.4 that this is characteristic of bent functions. $\qquad \square$

Remark. The definition of nonlinearity given in Definition 29, page 117, is related to Matsui's linear attack [829], but the term of nonlinearity can also evoke the behavior of the functions $F + L$, where L is any linear (n, m)-function, which could lead to other "nonlinearity" notions. We see with Proposition 37 that bent functions, which are related to the classical notion of nonlinearity, are also related to the imbalance of functions $F + L$. $\quad \square$

Proposition 37 and Relation (3.27) give the covering radius bound, and show that the constancy of function $L \in \mathcal{L}_{n,m} \to Nb_{F+L}$ is characteristic of bent functions.

The fact that the average value of Nb_{F+L} is the same for all (n, m)-functions is not surprising: Relation (3.20) applied to the function $F + L$ gives

$$Nb_{F \oplus L} = 2^{-m} \sum_{v \in \mathbb{F}_2^m, v \neq 0_m} \left(\sum_{x \in \mathbb{F}_2^n} (-1)^{v \cdot F(x) \oplus L^*(v) \cdot x} \right)^2,$$

where L^* is the adjoint operator of L. Summing up this equality when L ranges over $\mathcal{L}_{n,m}$ allows, for every $v \neq 0_m$, the vector $L^*(v)$ to cover uniformly $\mathbb{F}_2^n$, and Parseval's relation leads then to the mean.

Remark. The number $\max_{L \in \mathcal{L}_{n,m}} Nb_{F+L}$ is, after $nl(F)$, a second parameter quantifying the nonaffineness of F (in a different way from $nl(F)$ but in a coherent one, according to Relation (3.27)). We shall see that it is also closely related to a third parameter NB_F that we shall introduce at page 138. Some easily proved properties of $\max_{L \in \mathcal{L}_{n,m}} Nb_{F+L}$ include the following:

- If F is affine, that is, if $F + L_0$ is constant for some linear function L_0, then we know that $\max_{L \in \mathcal{L}_{n,m}} Nb_{F+L} = Nb_{F+L_0} = 2^{2n} - 2^{2n-m}$ is maximal.
- If, on the opposite side, F is bent, then, for every L, we have $Nb_{F+L} = 2^n - 2^{n-m}$ and $\max_{L \in \mathcal{L}_{n,m}} Nb_{F+L} = 2^n - 2^{n-m}$ is minimal (according to Proposition 37); we can say that, for every L, the function $F + L$ is "almost balanced," which is the best that can be achieved for every linear function L.
- $F \mapsto \max_{L \in \mathcal{L}_{n,m}} Nb_{F+L}$ is EA-invariant since Nb is affine invariant.

For $m = n = 5$, $\max\limits_{L \in \mathcal{L}_{n,m}} Nb_{F+L} = 52 < 2\,(2^n - 1) = 62$ for every AB function.   □

Other bounds

Bounds have been obtained in relation with codes [267]:

$$nl(F) < 2^{n-1} - \frac{m}{2} \times \frac{2^{n-1}}{2^{n-1} - 1}; \; m < 2^n - 2 \tag{3.29}$$

and using the sphere packing bound:

$$\sum_{i=0}^{\left\lfloor \frac{nl(F)-1}{2} \right\rfloor} \binom{2^n}{i} \leq 2^{2^n - n - m - 1} \tag{3.30}$$

and the Griesmer bound:

$$\sum_{i=0}^{m+n} \left\lceil \frac{nl(F)}{2^i} \right\rceil \leq 2^n. \tag{3.31}$$

A construction using concatenated codes (see page 9) is given in [53], which allows approaching these bounds. Precisely, a $(2e - 1, (k - 2)e)$-function F is obtained for every $e \geq 2, k \geq 3$, such that $nl(F) = 2^{e-2}(2^e - k + 1)$.

A lower bound on the nonlinearity of vectorial functions is given in [234] and upper bounds in [1133] by means of parameter Nb_F of page 114, under particular conditions, in some cases. A table of the best-known nonlinearities is given in [53].

Another notion of nonlinearity of vectorial functions, sometimes denoted by nl_v, has been introduced in [266] and studied further in [788]: their minimum Hamming distance to affine vectorial functions.

Higher-order nonlinearity

This notion (see Definition 20, page 83) can be extended to vectorial functions by taking the minimum r-th order nonlinearity of *component functions*: $nl_r(F) = \min_{v \neq 0_m} nl_r(v \cdot F)$. We can more generally consider F composed by functions of higher degrees:

Definition 32 *For every (n, m)-function F, for every positive integers $s \leq m$ and $t \leq n + m$, and every nonnegative integer $r \leq n$, we define*

$$nl_{s,r}(F) = \min\{nl_r(f \circ F); \; f \in \mathcal{BF}_m, d_{alg}(f) \leq s, \; f \neq cst\},$$

$$and \quad NL_t(F) = \min\{w_H(h(x, F(x))); \; h \in \mathcal{BF}_{n+m}, d_{alg}(h) \leq t, \; h \neq cst\}.$$

Definition 32 excludes $f = cst$ and $h = cst$ for obvious reasons.

Clearly, for every function F and all integers $t \leq t'$, $s \leq s'$ and $r \leq r'$, we have $NL_t(F) \geq NL_{t'}(F)$ and $nl_{s,r}(F) \geq nl_{s',r'}(F)$. Note also that we have $NL_1(F) = nl_{1,1}(F) = nl(F)$.

As recalled in [233, section 3], which is devoted to these notions, T. Shimoyama and T. Kaneko have exhibited in [1037] several quadratic functions h and pairs (f, g) of quadratic functions showing that the nonlinearities NL_2 and $nl_{2,2}$ of some sub-S-boxes of the DES are null (and therefore that the global S-box of each round of the DES has the same property). They deduced a "higher-order nonlinear" attack (an attack using the principle of the linear attack by Matsui but with non-linear approximations), which needs 26% less data than Matsui's attack. This improvement is not very significant, practically, but the notions of NL_t and $nl_{s,r}$ may be related to potentially more powerful attacks. Note that we have $NL_{\max(s,r)}(F) \leq nl_{s,r}(F)$ by taking $h(x, y) = g(x) \oplus f(y)$ (since $f \neq cst$ implies then $h \neq cst$) and the inequality can be strict if $s > 1$ or $r > 1$ since it may happen that a function $h(x, y)$ of low algebraic degree and such that $w_H(h(x, F(x)))$ is small exists while no such function exists with separated variables x and y. This is the case, for instance, of the S-box of the AES for $s = 1$ and $r = 2$ (see below).

Proposition 38 *[233] For all positive integers n, m, r $\leq$ n, and s $\leq$ m and every (n, m)-function F, we have $NL_s(F) \leq 2^{n-s}$ and $nl_{s,r}(F) \leq 2^{n-s}$. These inequalities are strict if F is not balanced (that is, if its output is not uniformly distributed over $\mathbb{F}_2^m$).*

Indeed, there necessarily exists an $(m - s)$-dimensional affine subspace A of F_2^m (whose indicator 1_A has algebraic degree s) such that $|F^{-1}(A)| \leq 2^{n-s}$, and we can take $f(y) = h(x, y) = 1_A(y)$. See in [233] the rest of the proof.

The bound $nl_{s,r}(F) \leq 2^{n-s}$ is asymptotically almost tight (in a sense that will be made precisely in Proposition 40, page 124) for permutations when $r \leq s \leq .227\,n$.

Existence of permutations with higher-order nonlinearities bounded from below

The case of permutations is more interesting and useful than that of general functions when dealing with higher-order nonlinearity, but it is more delicate.

Proposition 39 *Let n and s be positive integers and let r be a nonnegative integer. Let D be the greatest integer such that*

$$\sum_{t=0}^{D} \binom{2^n}{t} \leq \frac{\binom{2^n}{2^{n-s}}}{2^{\sum_{i=0}^{s} \binom{n}{i} + \sum_{i=0}^{r} \binom{n}{i}}}.$$

There exist (n, n)-permutations F whose higher-order nonlinearity $nl_{s,r}(F)$ is strictly larger than D.

Proof   We recall the proof from [233]. Given a number D, a permutation F of $\mathbb{F}_2^n$ and two n-variable Boolean functions f and g, let us consider the support $E = supp((f \circ F) \oplus g)$, that is, $E = (F^{-1}(supp(f))) \, \Delta \, supp(g)$, where Δ is the symmetric difference operator. Then F^{-1} maps $supp(f)$ onto $supp(g) \, \Delta \, E$ (since the equality $1_E = f \circ F \oplus g$ implies $f \circ F = g \oplus 1_E$) and $\mathbb{F}_2^n \setminus supp(f)$ onto $(\mathbb{F}_2^n \setminus supp(g)) \, \Delta \, E$. If we have $d_H(f \circ F, g) \leq D$, then E has size at most D. For all integers $i \in [0, 2^n]$ and r, let us denote by $A_{r,i}$ the number of codewords of Hamming weight i in the Reed–Muller code of order r. If i is the size of $supp(f)$ (with $0 < i < 2^n$, since $f \neq cst$), then for every set E such that $|supp(g) \, \Delta \, E| = |supp(f)| = i$ and $|(\mathbb{F}_2^n \setminus supp(g)) \, \Delta \, E| = |\mathbb{F}_2^n \setminus supp(f)| = 2^n - i$, the number of permutations whose restriction to $supp(f)$ is a one-to-one function onto $supp(g) \, \Delta \, E$ and whose restriction to $\mathbb{F}_2^n \setminus supp(f)$ is a one-to-one function onto $(\mathbb{F}_2^n \setminus supp(g)) \, \Delta \, E$ equals $i! \, (2^n - i)!$. We deduce that the number of permutations F such that $nl_{s,r}(F) \leq D$ is bounded above by

$$\sum_{t=0}^{D} \binom{2^n}{t} \sum_{i=1}^{2^n-1} \sum_{j=0}^{2^n} A_{s,i} A_{r,j} \, i! \, (2^n - i)!$$

Since the nonconstant codewords of the Reed–Muller code of order s have Hamming weights between 2^{n-s} and $2^n - 2^{n-s}$, we deduce that the probability $P_{s,r,D}$ that a permutation F chosen at random (with uniform probability) satisfies $nl_{s,r}(F) \leq D$ is bounded above by

$$\sum_{t=0}^{D} \binom{2^n}{t} \sum_{j=0}^{2^n} A_{r,j} \sum_{2^{n-s} \leq i \leq 2^n - 2^{n-s}} A_{s,i} \frac{i! \, (2^n - i)!}{2^n!} = \sum_{t=0}^{D} \binom{2^n}{t} \sum_{j=0}^{2^n} A_{r,j} \sum_{2^{n-s} \leq i \leq 2^n - 2^{n-s}} \frac{A_{s,i}}{\binom{2^n}{i}}$$

$$< \frac{\left(\sum_{t=0}^{D} \binom{2^n}{t} \right) 2^{\sum_{i=0}^{s} \binom{n}{i} + \sum_{i=0}^{r} \binom{n}{i}}}{\binom{2^n}{2^{n-s}}}.$$
$$(3.32)$$

We deduce that, under the hypothesis of Proposition 39, we have $P_{s,r,D} < 1$, and there exist permutations F from $\mathbb{F}_2^n$ to itself, whose higher-order nonlinearity $nl_{s,r}(F)$ is strictly larger than D. This completes the proof. □

This lemma is translated into a table for small values of n in [233]. Let us see now what happens when n tends to ∞. Let $H_2(x) = -x \log_2(x) - (1 - x) \log_2(1 - x)$ be the binary entropy function.

Proposition 40 *Let $\frac{s_n}{n}$ tend to a limit ρ such that $1 - H_2(\rho) > \rho$ (which is approximately equivalent to $\rho \leq .227$) when n tends to ∞. If $r_n \leq \mu n$ for every n, where $1 - H_2(\mu) > \rho$ (e.g., if r_n/s_n tends to a limit strictly smaller than 1), then for every $\rho' > \rho$, almost all permutations F of $\mathbb{F}_2^n$ satisfy $nl_{s_n,r_n}(F) \geq 2^{(1-\rho')n}$.*

Proof We recall the proof from [233]. We know (see *e.g.*, [809, page 310]) that, for every integer n and every $\lambda \in [0, 1/2]$, we have $\sum_{i \leq \lambda n} \binom{n}{i} \leq 2^{nH_2(\lambda)}$. According to the Stirling formula, we have also, when i and j tend to ∞: $i! \sim i^i e^{-i} \sqrt{2\pi i}$ and $\binom{i+j}{i} \sim \frac{(\frac{i+j}{i})^i (\frac{i+j}{j})^j}{\sqrt{2\pi}} \sqrt{\frac{i+j}{ij}}$. For $i + j = 2^n$ and $i = 2^{n-s_n}$, this gives

$$\binom{2^n}{2^{n-s_n}} \sim \frac{(2^{s_n})^{2^{n-s_n}}}{\sqrt{2\pi}(1 - 2^{-s_n})^{2^n - 2^{n-s_n}}} \sqrt{\frac{2^{s_n}}{2^n - 2^{n-s_n}}}$$

$$= \frac{2^{s_n 2^{n-s_n}}}{\sqrt{2\pi} \, 2^{(2^n - 2^{n-s_n}) \ln(1-2^{-s_n}) \log_2 e}} \sqrt{\frac{2^{s_n}}{2^n - 2^{n-s_n}}}.$$

We deduce then from Inequality (3.32), page 124

$$\log_2 P_{s_n, r_n, D_n} = O\left(2^n \left[H_2\left(\frac{D_n}{2^n}\right) + 2^{-n(1-H_2(s_n/n))} + 2^{-n(1-H_2(r_n/n))}\right.\right.$$

$$\left.\left. -2^{-s_n + \log_2(s_n)} - 2^{-s_n}(1 - 2^{-s_n})\log_2 e\right]\right)$$

(we omit $-\frac{s_n}{2^{n+1}} + \frac{n}{2^{n+1}}\log_2(1 - 2^{-s_n})$ inside the brackets above; it is negligible).

If $\lim \frac{s_n}{n} = \rho$ where $1 - H_2(\rho) > \rho$, then there exists $\rho' > \rho$ such that $1 - H_2(\rho') > \rho'$ and such that asymptotically we have $s_n \le \rho' n$; hence $2^{-n(1-H_2(s_n/n))}$ is negligible with respect to 2^{-s_n}. And if $r_n \le \mu n$, where $1 - H_2(\mu) > \rho$, then we have $2^{-n(1-H_2(r_n/n))} = o(2^{-s_n})$, and for $D_n = 2^{(1-\rho')n}$, where ρ' is any number strictly larger than ρ, we have $H_2\left(\frac{D_n}{2^n}\right) = H_2\left(2^{-\rho' n}\right) = \rho' n 2^{-\rho' n} - (1 - 2^{-\rho' n})\log_2(1 - 2^{-\rho' n}) = o(2^{-\rho n}) = o(2^{-s_n})$. We obtain that, asymptotically, $nl_{s_n, r_n}(F) > 2^{(1-\rho')n}$ for every $\rho' > \rho$. $\qquad\square$

The inverse S-box

For $F_{inv}(x) = x^{2^n - 2}$ and $f_{inv}(x) = tr_n(F_{inv}(x))$, we have $nl_r(F_{inv}) = nl_r(f_{inv})$ as for any power permutation. Recall that, for $r = 1$, this parameter equals $2^{n-1} - 2^{\frac{n}{2}}$ when n is even and is close to this number when n is odd, and that for $r > 1$, it is approximately bounded below by $2^{n-1} - 2^{(1-2^{-r})n}$ (see more in [232]). We have $NL_2(F_{inv}) = 0$, since we have $w_H(h(x, F_{inv}(x))) = 0$ for the bilinear function $h(x, y) = tr_n(axy)$, where a is any nonzero element of null trace and xy denotes the product of x and y in $\mathbb{F}_{2^n}$. Indeed, we have $x F_{inv}(x) = 1$ for every nonzero x. As observed in [392], we have also $w_H(h(x, F_{inv}(x))) = 0$ for the bilinear functions $h(x, y) = tr_n(a(x + x^2 y))$ and $h(x, y) = tr_n(a(y + y^2 x))$, where a is now any nonzero element, and for the quadratic functions $h(x, y) = tr_n(a(x^3 + x^4 y))$ and $h(x, y) = tr_n(a(y^3 + y^4 x))$. These properties are the core properties used in the tentative algebraic attack on the AES by Courtois and Pieprzyk.

It is proved in [233] that, for every ordered pair (s, r) of strictly positive integers, we have

- $nl_{s,r}(F_{inv}) = 0$ if $r + s \ge n$;
- $nl_{s,r}(F_{inv}) > 0$ if $r + s < n$;

and that, in particular, for every ordered pair (s, r) of positive integers such that $r + s = n - 1$, we have $nl_{s,r}(F_{inv}) = 2$. The other values are unknown when $r + s < n$, except for small values of n.

3.2.4 Algebraic immunities of vectorial functions

Algebraic attacks can be performed on stream ciphers and on block ciphers; this is why we address the algebraic immunities of vectorial functions in the present section. But there are several definitions, and the relevant ones are not the same in both frameworks. Algebraic attacks can be applied to those stream ciphers that, for increasing the speed, use as combiners or filters vectorial (n, m)-functions F instead of single-output Boolean functions. Figures 3.2 and 3.3 below display how vectorial functions can be used in the pseudorandom generators of stream ciphers to speed up the ciphers.

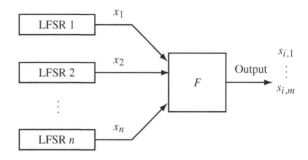

Figure 3.2 *combiner model.*

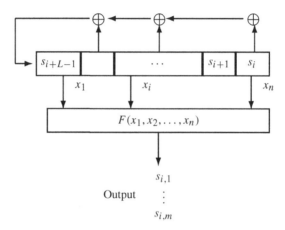

Figure 3.3 *filter model.*

The output bits of F can be combined in any way, that is, by applying any m-variable Boolean function h, and the algebraic attack can be performed on the combiner or filter model using the resulting Boolean function $h \circ F$. The minimum algebraic immunity of all these functions clearly equals the minimum algebraic immunity of the indicators of the preimages $F^{-1}(z)$ for $z \in \mathbb{F}_2^m$. This will lead to Definition 34.

Algebraic attacks also exist on block ciphers (see [392]), exploiting the existence of multivariate equations involving the input x to the S-box and its output y. In the case of the AES, whose S-box is the power function $x \in \mathbb{F}_{2^8} \to x^{2^8-2} \in \mathbb{F}_{2^8}$, an example of such an equation is $x^2 y = x$, where $x, y \in \mathbb{F}_{2^8}$. The main parameter playing a role in the complexity of algebraic attacks, to be studied for a given S-box F in a cipher, is the lowest algebraic degree d of Boolean relations between inputs and ouputs to F. If these are viewed in $\mathbb{F}_2^n$ and $\mathbb{F}_2^m$, the simplest relations to be considered are of the form $\sum_{I \subseteq \{1,\dots,n\}, J \subseteq \{1,\dots,m\}} a_{I,J}\, x^I (F(x))^J = 0$; $a_{I,J} \in \mathbb{F}_2$. Another parameter is the number of linearly independent relations of degree d. Since, for an (n,m)-function, the number of unknowns $a_{I,J}$ in the equations above equals $\sum_{i=0}^{d} \binom{n+m}{i}$ and the number of equations is 2^n, the number of linearly independent relations of degree d is at least $\sum_{i=0}^{d} \binom{n+m}{i} - 2^n$.

But the actual efficiency of algebraic attacks on block ciphers is difficult to study. The global number of variables in the large system of equations expressing the whole cipher, that is, the number of data bits and key bits in all the rounds of the cipher, is much larger than for stream ciphers, and the resulting systems of equations are not as overdefined as for stream ciphers; nobody is able to predict correctly the complexity of solving such polynomial systems. The AES allows bilinear relations between the input and the output bits of the S-boxes, and this may represent a threat, if an idea is found that would reduce the number of unknowns without increasing too much the degrees of the equations. In [392], the authors wrote that "it is not completely unreasonable to believe, that the structure of Rijndael and Serpent could allow attacks with complexity growing slowly with the number of rounds," and the authors added, "In this paper, it seems that we have found such an attack," but it is widely believed today that such an attack is not efficient on these two cryptosystems.

Several notions of *algebraic immunity* of vectorial functions have been studied in [29, 32]. We first need to recall the definition of *annihilator* and give the definition of the algebraic immunity of a set:

Definition 33 *We call* annihilator *of a subset E of $\mathbb{F}_2^n$ any n-variable Boolean function vanishing on E. We call algebraic immunity of E, and we denote by $AI(E)$ the minimum algebraic degree of all the nonzero annihilators of E.*

Note that the algebraic immunity of a Boolean function f equals by definition $\min(AI(f^{-1}(0)), AI(f^{-1}(1)))$.

The first generalization of algebraic immunity to *S-boxes* is its direct extension:

Definition 34 *The* basic algebraic immunity *of an (n,m)-function F is defined as follows:*

$$AI(F) = \min\{AI(F^{-1}(z)); \; z \in \mathbb{F}_2^m\}.$$

Note that $AI(F)$ also equals the minimum algebraic immunity of all the *indicators* φ_z of the preimages $F^{-1}(z)$ since, the algebraic immunity being a non-decreasing function over sets, we have $AI(\mathbb{F}_2^n \setminus F^{-1}(z)) \geq AI(F^{-1}(z'))$ for every distinct $z, z' \in \mathbb{F}_2^m$.

This version of algebraic immunity is relevant to stream ciphers. A second notion of algebraic immunity of S-boxes, more relevant to S-boxes in block ciphers, has been called the *graph algebraic immunity* and is defined as follows:

Definition 35 *The graph algebraic immunity of an (n,m)-function F is the algebraic immunity of the graph $\{(x, F(x)); \; x \in \mathbb{F}_2^n\}$ of the S-box, and is denoted by $AI_{gr}(F)$.*

Two other notions studied in [32] are essentially different expressions for the same $AI(F)$ and $AI_{gr}(F)$.

A third notion seems also natural:

Definition 36 *The* component algebraic immunity *of an (n,m)-function F is defined as follows:*

$$AI_{comp}(F) = \min\{AI(v \cdot F); \; v \in \mathbb{F}_2^m \setminus \{0_m\}\}.$$

Properties and relative bounds It has been observed in [29] that, for any (n, m)-function F, we have $AI(F) \leq AI_{gr}(F) \leq AI(F) + m$. The left-hand side inequality is straightforward (by restricting an annihilator of the graph to a value of y such that the annihilator does not vanish) and is shown tight in [235], and the right-hand side inequality comes from the fact that, since there exists z and a nonzero annihilator $g(x)$ of $F^{-1}(z)$ of algebraic degree $AI(F)$, the function $g(x) \prod_{i=1}^{m} (y_j \oplus z_j \oplus 1)$ is an annihilator of algebraic degree $AI(F) + m$ of the graph of F.

It has been also observed in [29] that, denoting by d the smallest integer such that $\sum_{i=0}^{d} \binom{n}{i} > 2^{n-m}$, we have $AI(F) \leq d$ (indeed, there is at least one z such that $|F^{-1}(z)| \leq 2^{n-m}$; the annihilators of $F^{-1}(z)$ are the solutions of $|F^{-1}(z)|$ linear equations in $\sum_{i=0}^{d} \binom{n}{i}$ unknowns – which are the coefficients in the *ANF* of an unknown annihilator of algebraic degree at most d – and the number of equations being strictly smaller than the number of unknowns, the system must have nontrivial solutions). It has been proved in [500] that this bound is tight. Note that it shows that for having a chance that $AI(F)$ be large, we need m small enough: we know (see [809, page 310]) that $\sum_{i=0}^{d} \binom{n}{i} \geq \frac{2^{nH_2(d/n)}}{\sqrt{8d(1-d/n)}}$, where $H_2(x) = -x \log_2(x) - (1-x) \log_2(1-x)$; for $AI(F)$ being possibly larger than a number k, we must have $\sum_{i=0}^{k} \binom{n}{i} \leq 2^{n-m}$, and therefore $\frac{2^{nH_2(k/n)}}{\sqrt{8k(1-k/n)}} \leq 2^{n-m}$, that is, $m \leq n(1 - H_2(k/n)) + \frac{1}{2}(3 + \log_2(k(1-k/n)))$. It also implies that $AI(F) \leq n - m$; see more in [235].

Finally, it has also been proved in [29] that, denoting by D the smallest integer such that $\sum_{i=0}^{D} \binom{n+m}{i} > 2^n$, we have $AI_{gr}(F) \leq D$ (the proof is similar, considering annihilators in $n + m$ variables of the graph), but it is not known whether this bound is tight (it is shown in [29] that it is tight for $n \leq 14$). This implies that $AI_{gr}(F) \leq n$; see more in [235].

Since the algebraic immunity of any Boolean function is bounded above by its algebraic degree, the component algebraic immunity of any vectorial function is bounded above by its minimum degree and therefore by its algebraic degree:

$$AI_{comp}(F) \leq d_{alg}(F).$$

We have also

$$AI_{comp}(F) \geq AI(F)$$

since $AI_{comp}(F)$ equals $AI(F^{-1}(H))$ for some affine hyperplane H of $\mathbb{F}_2^m$ because AIcomp(F) equals the algebraic immunity of the Boolean function $v \cdot F$ for some $v \neq 0_m$, and since AI is a nondecreasing function over sets. We have

$$AI_{comp}(F) \geq AI_{gr}(F) - 1$$

since:

- If g is a nonzero annihilator of $v \cdot F$, $v \neq 0_m$, then the product $h(x, y) = g(x)(v \cdot y)$ is a nonzero annihilator of the graph of F.

- If g is a nonzero annihilator of $v \cdot F \oplus 1$, then $h(x, y) = g(x)(v \cdot y) \oplus g(x)$ is a nonzero annihilator of the graph of F. More bounds on these three parameters are given in [235].

Remark. As in the case of Boolean functions (see Subsection 3.1.6, page 96), the variants of these parameters (and of the ones to come in the next sections) in relationship with guess and determine attacks should be studied as well. $\square$

3.3 Cryptographic criteria and parameters for vectorial functions in stream ciphers

3.3.1 Correlation immunity and resiliency of vectorial functions

The notion of resilient Boolean function, when extended to vectorial functions, is relevant in cryptology to quantum cryptographic key distribution (see [58]) and to stream ciphers with multioutput combiners or filters.

Recall that an (n, m)-function is called balanced if the distribution of $F(x)$ when x ranges over $\mathbb{F}_2^n$ is uniform over $\mathbb{F}_2^m$.

Definition 37 *Let n and m be two positive integers. Let t be an integer such that $0 \leq t \leq n$. An (n, m)-function $F(x)$ is called t-th order* correlation immune *if its output distribution does not change when at most t coordinates x_i of x are kept constant. It is called t-resilient if it is balanced and t-th order correlation immune, that is if it stays balanced when at most t coordinates x_i of x are kept constant.*

This notion has a relationship with another notion that also plays a role in cryptography: an (n, m)-function F is called a *multipermutation* (see [1095]) if any two ordered pairs $(x, F(x))$ and $(x', F(x'))$ such that $x, x' \in \mathbb{F}_2^n$ are distinct, differ in at least $m + 1$ distinct positions (that is, collide in at most $n - 1$ positions); such a (n, m)-function ensures then a perfect diffusion; an (n, m)-function is a multipermutation if and only if the indicator of its graph $\{(x, F(x)); x \in \mathbb{F}_2^n\}$ is an n-th order correlation immune Boolean function (see [179]).

Since *S-box*es must be balanced, we shall focus on resilient functions, but most of the results below can also be stated for correlation immune functions.

We call an (n, m) function that is t-resilient an (n, m, t)-function. Clearly, if such a function exists, then $m \leq n - t$, since balanced (n, m)-functions can exist only if $m \leq n$. This bound is weak (it is tight if and only if $m = 1$ or $t = 1$). It is shown in [370] (see also [79]) that, if an (n, m, t)-function exists, then $m \leq n - \log_2 \left[\sum_{i=0}^{t/2} \binom{n}{i} \right]$ if t is even and $m \leq n - \log_2 \left[\binom{n-1}{(t-1)/2} + \sum_{i=0}^{(t-1)/2} \binom{n}{i} \right]$ if t is odd. This can be deduced from the bound on orthogonal arrays due to Rao [988]; see page 87. But, as shown in [79] (see also [760]), potentially better bounds can be deduced from the linear programming bound due to Delsarte [421]: if an (n, m, t)-function exists, then $t \leq \left\lfloor \frac{2^{m-1} n}{2^m - 1} \right\rfloor - 1$ and $t \leq 2 \left\lfloor \frac{2^{m-2}(n+1)}{2^m - 1} \right\rfloor - 1$.

Note that composing a t-resilient (n, m)-function by a permutation on $\mathbb{F}_2^m$ does not change its resiliency order (this obvious result was first observed in [1168]). Also, the t-resiliency of

S-boxes can be expressed by means of the t-resiliency and t-th order correlation immunity of Boolean functions:

Proposition 41 *Let n and m be two positive integers and $0 \leq t \leq n$. Let F be an (n,m) function. Then F is t-resilient if and only if one of the following conditions is satisfied:*

1. *For every nonzero vector $v \in \mathbb{F}_2^m$, the Boolean function $v \cdot F(x)$ is t-resilient, that is, $W_F(u,v) = 0$, for every $u \in \mathbb{F}_2^n$ such that $w_H(u) \leq t$.*
2. *For every balanced m-variable Boolean function g, the n-variable Boolean function $g \circ F$ is t-resilient, that is, $\sum_{x \in \mathbb{F}_2^n} (-1)^{g(F(x)) \oplus u \cdot x} = 0$, for every $u \in \mathbb{F}_2^n$ such that $w_H(u) \leq t$.*
3. *For every vector $b \in \mathbb{F}_2^m$, the Boolean function $\varphi_b = \delta_{\{b\}} \circ F$ is t-th order correlation immune and has Hamming weight 2^{n-m}.*

Proof   We prove that the t-resiliency of F implies Condition 2, which implies Condition 1, which implies Condition 3, which implies that F is t-resilient.

- If F is t-resilient, then, for every balanced m-variable Boolean function g, the function $g \circ F$ is t-resilient, by definition; hence Condition 2 is satisfied.
- Condition 2 clearly implies Condition 1, since the function $g(x) = v \cdot x$ is balanced for every nonzero vector v.
- If Condition 1 is satisfied, then Relation (3.16), page 112, implies that, for every nonzero vector $u \in \mathbb{F}_2^n$ such that $w_H(u) \leq t$ and for every $b \in \mathbb{F}_2^m$, we have $\widehat{\varphi_b}(u) = 2^{-m} \sum_{x \in \mathbb{F}_2^n, v \in \mathbb{F}_2^m} (-1)^{v \cdot (F(x)+b) \oplus u \cdot x} = 0$, and φ_b is t-th order correlation immune for every b. Also, according to Proposition 35, page 112, Condition 1 implies that F is balanced, i.e. φ_b has Hamming weight 2^{n-m}, for every b. These two conditions obviously imply, by definition, that F is t-resilient. $\square$

Consequently, the t-resiliency of vectorial functions is invariant under the same transformations as for Boolean functions.

3.3.2 *Unrestricted nonlinearity of vectorial functions*

The classical notions of nonlinearity of vectorial functions (Definition 29, page 117) and higher-order nonlinearity (Definition 32, page 122), have been introduced in the framework of block ciphers: due to the iterative structure of these ciphers, the knowledge of a function f such that $nl(f \circ F)$ or $nl_r(f \circ F)$ is low does not necessarily lead to an attack, unless the algebraic degree of f is low, and r is low too in the latter case. This is why, in Definition 32, the algebraic degree of f is also specified.

On the contrary, the structure of pseudorandom generators in stream ciphers is not iterative, and all of the m output bits of the (n,m)-function used as combiner or filter can be combined by a linear or nonlinear (but nonconstant) m-variable Boolean function f to perform (fast) correlation attacks. Consequently, a second generalization to (n,m)-functions of the notion of nonlinearity has been introduced (in [318], directly related to the Zhang–Chan attack [1156]).

Definition 38 *Let F be an (n, m)-function. The* unrestricted nonlinearity *of F, denoted by $unl(F)$, is the minimum Hamming distance between all nonconstant affine functions and all Boolean functions $g \circ F$, where g is a nonconstant Boolean function in m variables.*

If $unl(F)$ is small, then one of the linear or nonlinear (nonconstant) combinations of the output bits of F has high correlation to a nonconstant affine function of the input, and a (fast) correlation attack is feasible.

Remark.

1. In Definition 38, the considered affine functions are nonconstant, because the minimum distance between all Boolean functions $g \circ F$ (g nonconstant) and all constant functions equals $\min_{b \in \mathbb{F}_2^m} |F^{-1}(b)|$ (each number $|F^{-1}(b)|$ is indeed equal to the distance between the null function and $g \circ F$, where g equals the indicator of the singleton $\{b\}$); it is therefore an indicator of the balancedness of F. It is bounded above by 2^{n-m} (and it equals 2^{n-m} if and only if F is balanced).
2. We can replace "nonconstant affine functions" with "nonzero linear functions" in the statement of Definition 38 (replacing g with $g \oplus 1$, if necessary).
3. Thanks to the fact that the affine functions considered in Definition 38 are nonconstant, we can relax the condition that g is nonconstant: the distance between a constant function and a nonconstant affine function equals 2^{n-1}, and $unl(F)$ is clearly always smaller than 2^{n-1}. □

The unrestricted nonlinearity of any (n, m)-function F is obviously unchanged when F is right-composed with an affine invertible mapping. Moreover, if A is a surjective linear (or affine) function from $\mathbb{F}_2^p$ (where p is some positive integer) into $\mathbb{F}_2^n$, then it is easily shown that $unl(F \circ A) = 2^{p-n} unl(F)$. Also, for every (m, p)-function ϕ, we have $unl(\phi \circ F) \geq unl(F)$ (indeed, the set $\{g \circ \phi, g \in \mathcal{BF}_p\}$, where $\mathcal{BF}_p$ is the set of p-variable Boolean functions, is included in $\mathcal{BF}_m$), and if ϕ is a permutation on $\mathbb{F}_2^m$, then we have $unl(\phi \circ F) = unl(F)$ (by applying the inequality above to $\phi^{-1} \circ F$).

A further generalization of the Zhang-Chan attack, called the *generalized correlation attack*, has been introduced in [299]: considering implicit equations that are linear in the input variable x and of any degree in the output variable $z = F(x)$, the following probability is considered, for any nonconstant function g and all functions $w_i : \mathbb{F}_2^m \to \mathbb{F}_2$:

$$\text{Prob}\,[g(z) + w_1(z)\,x_1 + w_2(z)\,x_2 + \cdots + w_n(z)\,x_n = 0], \qquad (3.33)$$

where $z = F(x)$, and where x uniformly ranges over $\mathbb{F}_2^n$.

The knowledge of such approximation g with a probability significantly higher than 1/2 leads to an attack, because $z = F(x)$ corresponding to the output keystream is known, and therefore $g(z)$ and $w_i(z)$ are known for all $i = 1, \ldots, n$.

This led to a new notion of generalized nonlinearity:

Definition 39 *Let $F : \mathbb{F}_2^n \to \mathbb{F}_2^m$. The* generalized Hadamard transform $\hat{F} : (\mathbb{F}_2^{2^m})^{n+1} \to \mathbb{R}$ *is defined as follows:*

$$\hat{F}(g(\cdot), w_1(\cdot), \ldots, w_n(\cdot)) = \sum_{x \in \mathbb{F}_2^n} (-1)^{g(F(x)) + w_1(F(x)) x_1 + \cdots + w_n(F(x)) x_n},$$

where the input is in $\mathcal{BF}_m^{n+1}$.

Let $\mathcal{W}$ be the set of all n-tuple functions $w(\cdot) = (w_1(\cdot), \ldots, w_n(\cdot)) \in \mathcal{BF}_m^n$, where $w(z) \neq 0_n$ for all $z \in \mathbb{F}_2^m$.

The generalized nonlinearity *is defined as follows:*

$$gnl(F) = \min \left\{ \min_{0 \neq u \in \mathbb{F}_2^m} \left(w_H(u \cdot F), 2^n - w_H(u \cdot F) \right), nl_{gen} F \right\},$$

where

$$nl_{gen} F = 2^{n-1} - \frac{1}{2} \max_{g \in \mathcal{BF}_m, w \in \mathcal{W}} \hat{F}(g(\cdot), w_1(\cdot), \ldots, w_n(\cdot)). \tag{3.34}$$

The generalized nonlinearity can be much smaller than the other nonlinearity measures and provides linear approximations with better bias for (fast) correlation attacks.

Relations to the Walsh transforms and lower bounds

The unrestricted nonlinearity of F can be related to the values of the *Fourier–Hadamard transforms* of the functions $\varphi_b = 1_{\{b\}} \circ F$ (see page 112), and a lower bound (observed in [1156]) depending on $nl(F)$ can be directly deduced:

Proposition 42 *For every (n, m)-function, we have*

$$unl(F) = 2^{n-1} - \frac{1}{2} \max_{u \in \mathbb{F}_2^n \setminus \{0_n\}} \sum_{b \in \mathbb{F}_2^m} |\widehat{\varphi_b}(u)| \geq 2^{n-1} - 2^{m/2} \left(2^{n-1} - nl(F) \right). \tag{3.35}$$

This bound does not give an idea of the best possible unrestricted nonlinearities: even if $nl(F)$ is close to the nonlinearity of bent functions $2^{n-1} - 2^{\frac{n}{2}-1}$, it implies that $unl(F)$ is approximately larger than $2^{n-1} - 2^{\frac{n+m}{2}-1}$, whereas there exist balanced $(n, \frac{n}{2})$-functions F such that $unl(F) = 2^{n-1} - 2^{\frac{n}{2}}$ (see below).

Proposition 43 *[299] Let $F : \mathbb{F}_2^n \to \mathbb{F}_2^m$ and let $w(\cdot)$ denote the n-tuple of m-bit Boolean functions $(w_1(\cdot), \ldots, w_n(\cdot))$. Then*

$$nl_{gen} F = 2^{n-1} - 1/2 \sum_{z \in \mathbb{F}_2^m} \max_{w(z) \in \mathbb{F}_2^n \setminus \{0_n\}} |\widehat{\varphi_b}(w(z))|$$

$$= 2^{n-1} - \frac{1}{2^{m+1}} \sum_{z \in \mathbb{F}_2^m} \max_{\substack{0 \neq w(z) \in \\ \mathbb{F}_2^n}} \left| \sum_{v \in \mathbb{F}_2^m} (-1)^{v \cdot z} W_F(w(z), v) \right|,$$

where W_F denotes the Walsh transform. Hence

$$gnl(F) \geq 2^{n-1} - (2^m - 1)\left(2^{n-1} - nl(F)\right).$$

Upper bounds

If F is balanced, the minimum distance between the component functions $v \cdot F$ and the affine functions cannot be achieved by constant affine functions, because $v \cdot F$, which is balanced, has distance 2^{n-1} to constant functions. Hence:

Proposition 44 (*covering radius bound*) *For every balanced S-box F:*

$$unl(F) \leq nl(F) \leq 2^{n-1} - 2^{\frac{n}{2}-1}. \tag{3.36}$$

Another upper bound:

$$unl(F) \leq 2^{n-1} - \frac{1}{2}\left(\frac{2^{2m} - 2^m}{2^n - 1} + \sqrt{\frac{2^{2n} - 2^{2n-m}}{2^n - 1} + \left(\frac{2^{2m} - 2^m}{2^n - 1} - 1\right)^2} - 1\right)$$

has been obtained in [318]. It improves upon (*i.e.*, is lower than) the covering radius bound only for $m \geq \frac{n}{2} + 1$, and the question of knowing whether it is possible to improve upon the covering radius bound for $m \leq \frac{n}{2}$ is open. In any case, this improvement will not be dramatic, at least for $m = \frac{n}{2}$, since it is shown (by using Relation (3.35)) in this same paper that the balanced function $F(x, y) = \begin{cases} \frac{x}{y} & \text{if } y \neq 0 \\ x & \text{if } y = 0 \end{cases}$ satisfies $unl(F) = 2^{n-1} - 2^{\frac{n}{2}}$ (see other examples of S-boxes in [698], whose unrestricted nonlinearities seem low, however). It is pretty astonishing that an S-box with such high unrestricted nonlinearity exists; but it can be shown that this balanced function does not contribute to a good resistance to algebraic attacks and has null generalized nonlinearity (see below).

Proposition 45 *Let $F : \mathbb{F}_2^n \rightarrow \mathbb{F}_2^m$. Then the following inequality holds:*

$$nl_{gen} F \leq 2^{n-1} - \frac{1}{4}\sum_{z \in \mathbb{F}_2^m} \sqrt{\frac{2^{n+2}|F^{-1}(z)| - 4|F^{-1}(z)|^2}{2^n - 1}}.$$

Furthermore if $F(x)$ is balanced, then we have

$$gnl(F) \leq 2^{n-1} - 2^{n-1}\sqrt{\frac{2^m - 1}{2^n - 1}}.$$

It is proved in [300] that the balanced function $F(x, y) = \begin{cases} \frac{x}{y} & \text{if } y \neq 0 \\ x & \text{if } y = 0 \end{cases}$ has null generalized nonlinearity. Hence, a vectorial function may have very high unrestricted nonlinearity and have zero generalized nonlinearity. Some functions with good generalized nonlinearity are given in [300]:

1. $F(x) = tr_m^n(x^k)$, where $k = 2^i + 1$, $\gcd(i, n) = 1$, is a Gold exponent.
2. $F(x) = tr_m^n(x^k)$, where $k = 2^{2i} - 2^i + 1$ is a Kasami exponent, $3i \equiv 1 \ [\text{mod}] \ n$,

where m divides n and n is odd, and where tr_m^n is the trace function from $\mathbb{F}_{2^n}$ to $\mathbb{F}_{2^m}$, have generalized nonlinearity satisfying $gnl(F) \geq 2^{n-1} - 2^{(n-1)/2+m-1}$.

Power functions and sums of *power functions* represent for the designer of the cryptosystem using them the interest of being more easily computable than general functions (which makes it possible to use them with more variables while maintaining good efficiency). Power functions have the peculiarity that, denoting the set $\{x^d; x \in \mathbb{F}_{2^n}^*\}$ by U, two functions $tr_n(ax^d)$ and $tr_n(bx^d)$ such that $a/b \in U$ are *linearly equivalent*. It is not clear whether this is more an advantage for the designer or for the attacker of a system using such function.

3.4 Cryptographic criteria and parameters for vectorial functions in block ciphers

We have seen in Subsection 3.2.3 a first example of the role played by *S-box*es in the robustness of the block ciphers in which they are involved, and of how the main attacks on block ciphers result in design criteria for the S-boxes they implement. We shall see now a second example, whose importance is comparable.

3.4.1 Differential uniformity

The *differential attack*, introduced by Biham and Shamir [82] (but which was already known by the NSA and kept secret), is anterior to the linear attack. It assumes the existence of ordered pairs (α, β), $\alpha \neq 0$, of binary strings of the same length as the blocks (which are binary strings too), such that, a block m of plaintext being randomly chosen and c and c' being the ciphertexts related to m and $m + \alpha$, the bitwise difference $c + c'$ (recall that $+$ denotes the bitwise addition/difference in $\mathbb{F}_2^n$) has a larger probability to equal β than if c and c' were randomly chosen binary strings. Such an ordered pair (α, β) corresponding to a *bias in the output distribution* is called a *differential* and can be exploited in differential attacks; the larger the probability of the differential, the more efficient the attack. As for the linear attack, there are several ways to mount such *differential cryptanalysis*. The most common (and most efficient) is to use differentials for the *reduced cipher* (see Figure 3.1, page 116). The existence of a differential allows one to distinguish, in a *last round attack*, the reduced cipher output from a random permutation. The existence of such *distinguisher* allows recovering the key used in the last round, by an exhaustive search, which is efficient if this key is shorter than the master key, or by using specificities of the cipher allowing replacing the exhaustive search by, for instance, solving algebraic equations.

Here also, we describe the attack in the case of exhaustive search, which is simpler to describe. Similar to what we have seen at page 116, the attacker, who knows a number of pairs (plaintext, ciphertext) corresponding to the original cipher and of the form (m, c) and $(m + \alpha, c')$, where (α, β) is a differential for the reduced cipher, visits all possible last round keys. For each try of such a candidate as last round key, he/she inverts the last round and obtains in the case of the correct key guess the output of the reduced cipher; the attacker observes then the statistical bias of the differential. In all the other cases (incorrect guesses), the obtained binary string is considered as random, with no observable bias. The number of pairs (m, c) and $(m + \alpha, c')$, which are known to him/her, needs then to be large enough to distinguish the bias. This number depends on how the probability of the differential is larger than for a random pair. In the case of DES, the number was 2^{47} (which is huge and made the attack impractical).

The existence of differential attacks leads to a criterion on (n, m)-functions F, when used as S-boxes in the round functions of the cipher, which corresponds to minimizing the possibilities for the attacker to find differentials whose probability is large. Since the differentials cannot be determined by direct computer investigation and must then be approximately evaluated by "chaining" differentials inside each round, the criterion is that the output of the derivatives $D_a F(x) = F(x) + F(x + a); x, a \in \mathbb{F}_2^n, a \neq 0_n$, be as uniformly distributed as possible. This leads to the following parameter.

Definition 40 *[906, 907, 912] Let n, m, δ be positive integers. An (n, m)-function F is called* differentially δ-uniform *if, for every nonzero $a \in \mathbb{F}_2^n$ and every $b \in \mathbb{F}_2^m$, the equation $F(x) + F(x + a) = b$ has at most δ solutions. The minimum of those values δ having such property, that is, the maximum number of solutions of such equations, is denoted by δ_F and called the* differential uniformity *of F.*

The differential uniformity δ_F is necessarily even since the solutions of equation $D_a F(x) = b$ go by pairs: if x is a solution of $F(x) + F(x + a) = b$, then $x + a$ is also a solution. The lower is δ_F, the better is the contribution of the S-box to the resistance to the differential attack, as shown in [908, 912]. The differential uniformity δ_F of any (n, m)-function F is bounded below by 2^{n-m} (as observed by Nyberg) since $D_a F$ being an (n, m)-function, at least one element of $\mathbb{F}_2^m$ has at least 2^{n-m} preimages by $D_a F$. The differential uniformity equals 2^{n-m} if and only if every derivative $D_a F, a \neq 0_n$, is balanced. We say then that F is *perfect nonlinear*, and we shall see in Chapter 6 that this is equivalent to saying that F is bent. According to a result from Nyberg that we shall see in Proposition 104, page 269, (n, m)-functions have differential uniformity strictly larger than 2^{n-m} when n is odd or $m > n/2$.

The differential uniformity of an S-box being determined, its differential spectrum also affects the security of the corresponding cipher. The *differential spectrum* is the multiset of the values:

$$\delta_F(a, b) = |\{x \in \mathbb{F}_2^n; \ D_a F(x) = F(x) + F(x + a) = b\}| = (1_{\mathcal{G}_F} \otimes 1_{\mathcal{G}_F})(a, b), \quad (3.37)$$

(where $1_{\mathcal{G}_F}$ is the graph indicator of F; see page 35) and the *difference distribution table* (DDT) is the table that displays them (note that, given a permutation F, all these data are the same for F and F^{-1}, up to exchanging a and b, since $1_{\mathcal{G}_F}(x, y) = 1_{\mathcal{G}_{F^{-1}}}(y, x)$).

For every $u \in \mathbb{F}_2^n$ and $v \in \mathbb{F}_2^m$, we have $\sum_{a \in \mathbb{F}_2^n, b \in \mathbb{F}_2^m} \delta_F(a, b)(-1)^{u \cdot a \oplus v \cdot b} = \sum_{a, x \in \mathbb{F}_2^n} (-1)^{u \cdot a \oplus v \cdot D_a F(x)} = \sum_{a \in \mathbb{F}_2^n} \Delta_{v \cdot F}(a)(-1)^{u \cdot a}$, by the change of variable $b = D_a F(x)$, and since $v \cdot D_a F = D_a(v \cdot F)$, and the Wiener–Khintchine formula (2.53), page 62 (or Property (2.44), page 60, applied to expression (3.37)), shows that the Fourier transform of function δ_F equals W_F^2.

Differential uniformity is in fact a notion on the graph $\mathcal{G}_F = \{(x, y) \in \mathbb{F}_2^n \times \mathbb{F}_2^m;$ $y = F(x)\}$ of the function: it is the maximum number of solutions $(X, Y) \in \mathcal{G}_F^2$ of the equation $X + Y = (a, b)$ when $(a, b) \in (\mathbb{F}_2^n \setminus \{0_n\}) \times \mathbb{F}_2^m$. For this reason, differential uniformity is a *CCZ invariant* (see Definition 5, page 28). The necessary and sufficient condition, recalled from [201] and that we reported at page 72, ensuring that the image by an affine permutation $A = L + (a, b)$ of the *graph* $\mathcal{G}_F$ of F is the graph of a function, is equivalent to the fact that the image of $\{0_n\} \times \mathbb{F}_2^m$ by L^{-1} is included in the set $\delta_F^{-1}(0) \cup \{(0_n, 0_m)\}$.

It is observed in [910, 1060] that, because of the truncated differential attack [706], the differential uniformity of the (so-called chopped) functions obtained by withdrawing a few coordinate functions should also be considered and can be low for some vectorial functions having good differential uniformity.

Note that if a function has good nonlinearity, then it does not have necessarily a good differential uniformity too: take an (n, m)-function F and consider the $(n + 1, m)$-function F' such that $F'(x, x_{n+1}) = F(x)$ for every $x \in \mathbb{F}_2^n, x_{n+1} \in \mathbb{F}_2$; the nonlinearity of F' is twice that of F and can then be rather good, while the differential uniformity of F' equals 2^n and is then bad. The converse is not true either: take any (n, m)-function F and consider the $(n, m + 1)$-function F' obtained by adding a null coordinate function; the nonlinearity of F' is null while the differential uniformity equals that of F and can then be good.

The asymptotic behavior of δ_F for general (n, n)-functions F has been studied in [1098], after being studied in [643] for power functions over $\mathbb{F}_{2^n}$:

Proposition 46   *[1098] For any $d > 4$ with $d \equiv 0, 3$ [mod 4], the limit when n to infinity of the ratio*

$$\frac{\left| \left\{ F \in \mathbb{F}_{2^n}[x];\ deg(F) = d \text{ and } \delta_F = \begin{array}{l} d - 1 \text{ for } d \text{ odd} \\ d - 2 \text{ for } d \text{ even} \end{array} \right\} \right|}{|\{F \in \mathbb{F}_{2^n}[x];\ deg(F) = d\}|},$$

where $deg(F)$ denotes the polynomial degree, equals 1.

For more general (n, m)-functions, see [405, 589, 913]; the average differential uniformity of (n, m)-functions is much larger than 2^{n-m}.

Almost perfect nonlinear functions   The smaller the differential uniformity, the better the contribution to the resistance against differential cryptanalysis. When $m \geq n$, the smallest possible value of δ_F (which is always even) is 2, and differentially 2-uniform functions can exist only when $m \geq n$ (indeed, we need $m \geq n - 1$, and $m = n - 1$ is impossible except if $n \leq 2$ since differentially 2-uniform $(n, n - 1)$-functions are perfect nonlinear, and we would then need to have $n - 1 \leq n/2$, as we shall see in Proposition 104, page 269). We use the term of APN function only when $m = n$. Note that the notion of APN function and the differential property of the multiplicative *inverse function* had been investigated starting from 1968 by V. Bashev and B. Egorov in the USSR.

Definition 41   *[71, 908, 912] An (n, n)-function F is called* almost perfect nonlinear *(APN) if it is differentially 2-uniform, that is, if for every $a \in \mathbb{F}_2^n \setminus \{0_n\}$ and every $b \in \mathbb{F}_2^n$, the equation $F(x) + F(x + a) = b$ has 0 or 2 solutions (i.e., $|\{D_a F(x), x \in \mathbb{F}_2^n\}| = 2^{n-1}$). Equivalently, for distinct elements x, y, z, t of $\mathbb{F}_2^n$, the equality $x + y + z + t = 0_n$ implies $F(x) + F(y) + F(z) + F(t) \neq 0_n$, that is, the restriction of F to any 2-dimensional flat (i.e., affine plane) of $\mathbb{F}_2^n$ is nonaffine.*

We have already encountered APN functions when proving the SCV bound, and the equivalence between these three properties is easily seen: Inequality (3.25), page 118, is an equality if and only if $F(x) + F(y) + F(z) + F(x + y + z) = 0_n$ can be achieved only when $x = y$ or $x = z$ or $y = z$, and this is equivalent to any of the following properties:

-   The restriction of F to any two-dimensional flat (*i.e.,* affine plane) of $\mathbb{F}_2^n$ is non-affine, that is, does not sum up to 0_n, (indeed, the set $\{x, y, z, x + y + z\}$ is a flat and it is two-dimensional if and only if $x \neq y$ and $x \neq z$ and $y \neq z$; and $F(x) + F(y) + F(z) + F(x + y + z) = 0_n$ is equivalent to saying that the restriction of F to this flat is affine, since we know that a function F is affine on a flat A if and only if, for every x, y, z in A we have $F(x + y + z) = F(x) + F(y) + F(z)$).
-   For every distinct nonzero (that is, $\mathbb{F}_2$-linearly independent) vectors a and a', the second-order derivative $D_a D_{a'} F(x) = F(x) + F(x + a) + F(x + a') + F(x + a + a')$ takes only nonzero values.
-   The equality $F(x) + F(x + a) = F(y) + F(y + a)$ (obtained from $F(x) + F(y) + F(z) + F(x + y + z) = 0_n$ by denoting $x + z$ by a) can be achieved only for $a = 0_n$ or $x = y$ or $x = y + a$.
-   For every $a \in \mathbb{F}_2^n \setminus \{0_n\}$ and every $b \in \mathbb{F}_2^n$, the equation $D_a F(x) = F(x) + F(x + a) = b$ has at most two solutions (that is, zero or two solutions, since if it has one solution x, then it has $x + a$ for a second solution).

Remark.   As in the case of AB functions, the term of *almost* perfect nonlinear gives the feeling that these functions are almost optimal while they are optimal.   □

Chapter 11 covers the whole topic of APN functions.

Related nonlinearity parameters

– We have seen at page 121 the nonlinearity parameter alternative to the classical nonlinearity, equal to the maximum imbalance of the sums of F and linear functions: $\max_{L \in \mathcal{L}_{n,m}} Nb_{F+L}$.

If $m = n$ and F is APN, then according to the properties seen at page 114, $Nb_{F+L} = \sum_{a \subset \mathbb{F}_2^n} |(D_a F)^{-1}(L(a))| - 2^n = \sum_{a \in \mathbb{F}_2^n \setminus \{0_n\}} |(D_a F)^{-1}(L(a))|$ is bounded above by

$2(2^n - 1)$, for every L, which implies that $\max_{L \in \mathcal{L}_{n,m}} Nb_{F+L}$ lies in the interval $]2^n - 1; 2(2^n - 1)]$ (since we know from Proposition 37, page 120, that it is larger than or equal to $2^n - 2^{n-m}$, and we know that it cannot equal $2^n - 2^{n-m}$ since F would be bent). Moreover, when n is even, the maximum $2(2^n - 1)$ is achieved by all APN power functions; indeed, Dobbertin proved (and we shall see in Proposition 165, page 385) that for any APN power function F, there are $\frac{2^n - 1}{3}$ elements of $\mathbb{F}_{2^n}^*$ having three preimages each by F, and all the other elements of $\mathbb{F}_{2^n}^*$ have no preimage (see, e.g., [237]), which implies, using (3.19), that $Nb_F = 1 + 9 \cdot \frac{2^n - 1}{3} - 2^n = 2(2^n - 1)$.

APN functions in five variables have been classified under EA equivalence and CCZ equivalence in [134]. When F is the inverse function, $\max_{L \in \mathcal{L}_{n,m}} Nb_{F+L}$ equals 56. There is no other APN and non-AB function for $n = 5$.

For $m = n = 6$ and $m = n = 8$, the functions CCZ equivalent to x^3, found in [162, 163], match the maximum $2(2^n - 1)$, as do the APN power functions. We do not know if some APN functions can have a smaller value of $\max_{L \in \mathcal{L}_{n,m}} Nb_{F+L}$ for n even. And it is not clear to us whether $\max_{L \in \mathcal{L}_{n,m}} Nb_{F+L}$ can take diverse values when F is AB for n odd and whether it is CCZ invariant.

– The bentness/perfect nonlinearity of a function being characterized by the balancedness of its derivatives, the following nonlinearity indicator has been introduced in [267]:

$$NB_F = \sum_{a \in \mathbb{F}_2^n \setminus \{0_n\}} Nb_{D_a F} = \sum_{a \in \mathbb{F}_2^n \setminus \{0_n\}} \sum_{b \in \mathbb{F}_2^m} |(D_a F)^{-1}(b)|^2 - (2^n - 1)2^{2n-m}. \quad (3.38)$$

This indicator is directly related to Nyberg's and Chabaud–Vaudenay's results and proofs; it allows clarifying some properties found by them (see, *e.g.*, Relation (3.40) below) and saying a bit more. We shall call it the *derivative imbalance* of F. It has the following properties, as mentioned in [239, 267]:

- $NB_F \geq 0$, for every function F, and $NB_F = 0$ if and only if F is bent/perfect nonlinear.
- NB is *CCZ invariant* since NB_F equals $\sum_{a \in \mathbb{F}_2^n \setminus \{0_n\}} |\{(x, y) \in (\mathbb{F}_2^n)^2 / D_a F(x) = D_a F(y)\}| - (2^n - 1)2^{2n-m}$ and equals therefore

$$\left| \left\{ (x, x', y, y') \in (\mathbb{F}_2^n)^4 / \begin{array}{c} x + x' = y + y' \neq 0_n \\ F(x) + F(x') = F(y) + F(y') \end{array} \right\} \right| - (2^n - 1)2^{2n-m}$$

$$= \left| \left\{ (X, X', Y, Y') \in \mathcal{G}_F^4 / X + X' = Y + Y' \neq 0_{n+m} \right\} \right| - (2^n - 1)2^{2n-m},$$

where $\mathcal{G}_F = \{(x, F(x)) \in \mathbb{F}_2^n \times \mathbb{F}_2^m\}$ is the graph of F.

- $NB_F \geq (2^n - 1)(2^{n+1} - 2^{2n-m})$ (this inequality comes from the Cauchy–Schwarz inequality $\sum_{b \in \mathbb{F}_2^m} |F^{-1}(b)|^2 \geq \frac{\left(\sum_{b \in \mathbb{F}_2^m} |F^{-1}(b)| \right)^2}{|Im(F)|} = \frac{2^{2n}}{|Im(F)|}$ applied to $D_a F$ and from $|Im(D_a F)| \leq 2^{n-1}$; see an improvement in [522, proposition 3]); note that this proves again that (n, n)-functions cannot be perfect nonlinear; there is equality if and only if, for every $a \neq 0_n$, $|Im(D_a F)|$ equals 2^{n-1} and $|(D_a F)^{-1}(b)|$ is constant for $b \in Im(D_a F)$. For $n = m$, there is then equality if and only if F is APN;

- $NB_F = \displaystyle\sum_{\substack{a,a' \in \mathbb{F}_2^n \\ \text{linearly indept}}} \left| (D_a D_{a'} F)^{-1}(0_m) \right| - (2^n - 1)(2^{2n-m} - 2^{n+1}).$

- $NB_F \le (2^n - 1)(2^{2n} - 2^{2n-m})$, for every function $F : \mathbb{F}_2^n \to \mathbb{F}_2^m$ (see a refinement in [522, proposition 4]) and $NB_F = (2^n - 1)(2^{2n} - 2^{2n-m})$ if and only if F is affine.

Remark. A parameter[24] has been introduced afterward in [922, 925] and studied further[25] in [921, 923, 924], without comparing it to NB_F. We give here its definition for (n, m)-functions but, as NB_F, it can be defined for any function from an Abelian group to an Abelian group: the *ambiguity* $\mathcal{A}(F)$ equals

$$\sum_{i \ge 0} \binom{i}{2} |\{(a,b) \in (\mathbb{F}_2^n \setminus \{0_n\}) \times \mathbb{F}_2^m ; |(D_a F)^{-1}(b)| = i\}|.$$

$\mathcal{A}(F)$ is the same as NB_F, up to a constant and to the multiplication by $\frac{1}{2}$:

$$\begin{aligned}
\mathcal{A}(F) &= \frac{1}{2} \sum_{(a,b) \in (\mathbb{F}_2^n \setminus \{0_n\}) \times \mathbb{F}_2^m} |(D_a F)^{-1}(b)|^2 - \frac{1}{2} \sum_{(a,b) \in (\mathbb{F}_2^n \setminus \{0_n\}) \times \mathbb{F}_2^m} |(D_a F)^{-1}(b)| \\
&= \frac{1}{2}(NB_F + (2^n - 1)2^{2n-m}) - \frac{(2^n - 1)2^n}{2} \\
&= \frac{1}{2} NB_F + (2^n - 1)(2^{2n-m-1} - 2^{n-1}).
\end{aligned}$$

In [522], the necessary work of unification of the results on NB_F and on ambiguity is made. The known bounds on NB_F and those on ambiguity are compared, and all the results are translated from one definition to the other. More results are also given.   □

Parameter NB_F can be expressed by means of the Walsh transform. Thanks to Relation (3.20), page 114, we have

$$NB_F = 2^{-m} \sum_{a \in \mathbb{F}_2^n, a \neq 0_n} \sum_{v \in \mathbb{F}_2^m, v \neq 0_m} W_{D_a F}^2(0_n, v). \tag{3.39}$$

Chabaud–Vaudenay's calculations recalled in the proof of Theorem 6, more precisely at page 118, show that $\sum_{\substack{v \in \mathbb{F}_2^m, v \neq 0_m \\ u \in \mathbb{F}_2^n}} W_F^4(u, v) =$

$$2^{n+m} |\{(x, y, a) \in \mathbb{F}_2^{3n} / F(x) + F(x + a) = F(y) + F(y + a)\}| - 2^{4n}$$

$$= 2^{3n+m} + 2^{n+m} \sum_{a \in \mathbb{F}_2^n, a \neq 0_n} |\{(x, y) \in \mathbb{F}_2^{3n} / D_a F(x) = D_a F(y)\}| - 2^{4n}$$

---

[24] A second parameter called deficiency is also introduced and studied in the same papers: $\mathcal{D}(F) = |\{(a, b) \in (\mathbb{F}_2^n \setminus \{0_n\}) \times \mathbb{F}_2^m ; |(D_a F)^{-1}(b)| = 0\}|$. It plays a less important role.

[25] In particular for functions from $\mathbb{Z}/n\mathbb{Z}$ (resp. from the additive/multiplicative group of a finite field) to itself, and for some specific functions over finite fields, including all permutation polynomials over finite fields up to degree 6 and reversed Dickson polynomials (which we shall see more in detail at page 389).

$$= 2^{3n+m} - 2^{4n} + 2^{n+m} \sum_{a \in \mathbb{F}_2^n, a \neq 0_n} \sum_{b \in \mathbb{F}_2^m} |D_a F^{-1}(b)|^2$$

$$= 2^{3n}(2^m - 1) + 2^{n+m} N B_F. \tag{3.40}$$

The Sidelnikov–Chabaud–Vaudenay bound can then be specified as follows:

$$nl(F) \leq 2^{n-1} - \frac{1}{2}\sqrt{2^n + \frac{2^{m-n}}{2^m - 1} N B_F}. \tag{3.41}$$

(This obviously implies the covering radius bound since $N B_F \geq 0$, and the SCV bound, because of the inequality $N B_F \geq (2^n - 1)(2^{n+1} - 2^{2n-m})$ recalled above). We can immediately see that the bound in (3.41) is tight for $m \leq n/2$, n even (since the covering radius bound is then tight) and for $m = n$, n odd (since the Sidelnikov–Chabaud–Vaudenay bound is then tight). In fact, it is tight for all values of n and m: the proof in [267] shows that it is an equality for a given F if and only if F is *plateaued with single amplitude* (see Definition 67, page 274). It would be interesting to determine for which triples $(n, m, N B_F)$, or equivalently for which triples $(n, m, nl(F))$, the bound is tight (which would be determined if we know all possible amplitudes for plateaued (n, m)-functions with single amplitude).

Two other bounds on the nonlinearity involving the imbalance are given in [1133]. We have seen with Proposition 37, page 120, that the mean of the random variable $L \to N b_{F+L}$ is the same for every function. We shall see now that its variance equals $N B_F$, up to a multiplicative factor.

Proposition 47 *[239, 267] Let F be any (n, m)-function. The variance of the random variable $L \in \mathcal{L}_{n,m} \to N b_{F+L}$ equals $2^{-m} N B_F$.*

Proof Let us denote by V_F the variance of the random variable $L \in \mathcal{L}_{n,m} \to N b_{F+L}$, equal to that of the random variable $L \to \sum_{a \in \mathbb{F}_2^n \setminus \{0_n\}} |(D_a F)^{-1}(L(a))|$ according to Relation (3.28), page 120, whose mean equals $2^{2n-m} - 2^{n-m}$, according to Proposition 37. Hence V_F equals

$$\frac{1}{|\mathcal{L}_{n,m}|} \sum_{\substack{L \in \mathcal{L}_{n,m} \\ a,a' \in \mathbb{F}_2^n \setminus \{0_n\}}} |(D_a F)^{-1}(L(a))| \, |(D_{a'} F)^{-1}(L(a'))| - \left(2^{2n-m} - 2^{n-m}\right)^2.$$

Let us distinguish the case where $a = a' \neq 0_n$ and the case where a and a' are linearly independent. We have seen that, when a is a fixed nonzero vector, the number of linear functions L such that $L(a) = b$ equals $2^{m(n-1)} = 2^{-m}|\mathcal{L}_{n,m}|$, for every vector b; similarly, when a, a' are fixed linearly independent vectors, the number of linear functions L such that $L(a) = b$ and $L(a') = b'$ equals $2^{m(n-2)} = 2^{-2m}|\mathcal{L}_{n,m}|$, for all vectors b, b'. We obtain

$$V_F = 2^{-m} \sum_{a \in \mathbb{F}_2^n \setminus \{0_n\}} \sum_{b \in \mathbb{F}_2^m} |(D_a F)^{-1}(b)|^2 + 2^{-2m} \mu_F - \left(2^{2n-m} - 2^{n-m}\right)^2, \text{ where}$$

$$\mu_F = \sum_{\substack{a,a' \in \mathbb{F}_2^n \setminus \{0_n\} \\ a \neq a'}} \sum_{b,b' \in \mathbb{F}_2^m} |(D_a F)^{-1}(b)| \, |(D_{a'} F)^{-1}(b')|$$

$$= \sum_{\substack{a,a' \in \mathbb{F}_2^n \setminus \{0_n\} \\ a \neq a'}} \left(\sum_{b \in \mathbb{F}_2^m} |(D_a F)^{-1}(b)| \right) \left(\sum_{b \in \mathbb{F}_2^m} |(D_{a'} F)^{-1}(b)| \right)$$

$$= (2^n - 1)(2^n - 2) \, 2^{2n}.$$

Then by the definition of NB_F, $V_F = 2^{-m}(NB_F + (2^n - 1)2^{2n-m}) + 2^{4n-2m} - 3 \cdot 2^{3n-2m} + 2 \cdot 2^{2n-2m} - (2^{4n-2m} - 2 \cdot 2^{3n-2m} + 2^{2n-2m}) = 2^{-m} NB_F.$ □

Remark. In [239], it is shown that the mean of Nb_{F+L} when L ranges over the subset of balanced linear (n, m)-functions is the highest when F is balanced, but that its value is then not much larger than the mean in Proposition 37. □

A recent stronger criterion for permutations

Boomerang attacks [1101] (and their variants, called sandwich attacks) are a possible alternative to differential attacks when differentials (see Subsection 3.4.1, page 134) having sufficiently large probability are not known. The parameter that quantifies the contribution of an (n, n)-permutation F to the resistance to these attacks (the smaller the parameter, the better the resistance) (see [371]) is the so-called *boomerang uniformity* (see [107]):

$$\max_{(a,b) \in (\mathbb{F}_2^n \setminus \{0_n\})^2} |\{x \in \mathbb{F}_2^n; F(F^{-1}(x) + a) + F(F^{-1}(x + b) + a) = b\}| = \quad (3.42)$$

$$\max_{(a,b) \in (\mathbb{F}_2^n \setminus \{0_n\})^2} |\{y \in \mathbb{F}_2^n; F^{-1}(F(y) + b) + F^{-1}(F(y + a) + b) = a\}| =$$

$$\max_{(a,b) \in (\mathbb{F}_2^n \setminus \{0_n\})^2} |\{(x, y) \in \mathbb{F}_2^{n2}; F(x + a) + F(y + a) = b \text{ and } F(x) + F(y) = b\}|$$

(the first equality being shown by using that $F(F^{-1}(x) + a) + F(F^{-1}(x + b) + a) = b$ is equivalent to $F^{-1}(x + b) + a = F^{-1}(F(F^{-1}(x) + a) + b)$ and setting $y = F^{-1}(x) + a$). It is easily shown that the boomerang uniformity is affine invariant, and as we can see, it is also invariant when changing F into F^{-1}, but it is not EA invariant (see [107]) and therefore not CCZ invariant. We have that, denoting $y = F^{-1}(x) + a$ and $z = F^{-1}(x + b) + a$, the boomerang uniformity equals $\max_{(a,b) \in (\mathbb{F}_2^n \setminus \{0_n\})^2} |\{(x, y) \in (\mathbb{F}_2^n)^2; F(y) + F(z) = F(y + a) + F(z + a) = b\}|$. The necessary condition $F(y) + F(z) = F(y + a) + F(z + a)$ being equivalent to $D_a F(y) = D_a F(z)$, if F is APN then, since this latter equality implies $y = z$ or $y = z + a$ and since $y = z$ is impossible because $b \neq 0_n$, the boomerang uniformity equals

2. But APN permutations are known only for n odd and $n = 6$. For general permutations, we can see by considering the particular case $z = y + a$ that the boomerang uniformity is larger than or equal to the differential uniformity δ_F (see Definition 40, page 135). In [107], is shown that the boomerang uniformity of the multiplicative inverse (n, n)-function for n even equals 6 if 4 divides n and 4 otherwise. Its value is characterized when $n = 4$ for all differentially 4-uniform permutations (showing that it is at least 6). It is shown that if F is differentially 4-uniform and quadratic, then its boomerang uniformity is at most 12.

Quadratic permutations whose Boomerang Connectivity Table (BCT) is optimal (in the sense that the maximal value in the BCT equals the lowest known differential uniformity) have been derived in [875]. Moreover, boomerang uniformities of some specific permutations (mainly the ones with low differential uniformity) as well as a characterization by means of the Walsh transform of those functions F from $\mathbb{F}_{2^n}$ to itself with boomerang uniformity δ_F have been considered in [762].

3.4.2 Other features also related to attacks

Univariate degree

The *interpolation attack* [639] is efficient when the degree of the univariate polynomial representation of the S-box over $\mathbb{F}_{2^n}$ is low or when the distance of the S-box to the set of low univariate degree functions is small. A vectorial function should then not have low-degree *univariate representation* nor be approximated by such a function.

Attacks without related criteria on Boolean functions

The *slide attack* [89], when it can be mounted, has a complexity independent of the number of rounds in the block cipher, contrary to the attacks previously described. It analyzes the weaknesses of the key schedule (the most common case of weakness being when round keys repeat in a cyclic way) to break the cipher. The slide attack is efficient when the cipher can be decomposed into multiple rounds of an identical F function vulnerable to a known plaintext attack.

3.5 Search for functions achieving the desired features

3.5.1 The difficulty of designing good S-boxes

Substitution boxes in block ciphers need to satisfy many criteria:

- The S-boxes for SPN networks must be bijective. The S-boxes for Feistel cryptosystems are better surjective and in fact balanced; see [957, 995].
- The S-boxes are better APN or differentially 4-uniform, or at least differentially 6-uniform.
- They have better high nonlinearity, say near $2^{n-1} - 2^{n/2}$.
- They have better not too low algebraic degree; degree 2 is often too small because of the higher-order differential attack [706, 735].

- For reason of efficiency (see page 401), in software, n is better even, $n/2$ too ... that is, n is better a power of 2. In hardware, n can be any number. But general-purpose cryptosystems must be implementable in both hardware and software. Then $n = 4, 8$ are preferred ($n = 4$ for lightweight ciphers).
- The S-box should be easy to protect against physical (side-channel and fault injection) attacks; see Section 12.1.1, page 431. Hence, the number of nonlinear multiplications in $\mathbb{F}_{2^n}$ to compute the output (when the S-box is expressed over this field) should be small.

Examples of S-boxes used in practice:

- $(4, 4)$-S-boxes: Serpent, PRESENT, CLEFIA, NOEKEON, LED, RECTANGLE
- $(6, 4)$-S-boxes: DES
- $(8, 8)$-S-boxes (inverse function): AES, CLEFIA, CAMELLIA
- $(9, 9)$ and $(7, 7)$-S-boxes, combined (AB functions Gold x^5 and Kasami $x^{13} \sim x^{81}$): MISTY, KASUMI
- $(8, 32)$-S-boxes: CAST

Other examples:

- Key-dependent S-boxes: CAST, Twofish
- Pseudorandomly generated $(4, 4)$-S-boxes: KHAZAD
- Round function based on x^3 in $\mathbb{F}_{2^{37}}$ or $\mathbb{F}_{2^{33}}$ according to the versions: KN
- Mixing operations from different groups: IDEA, CAST, RC6

3.5.2 Constructions versus computer investigations of Boolean and vectorial functions

We shall give in Chapters 5 through 11 constructions of Boolean and vectorial functions satisfying the criteria we have seen in the present chapter. We shall study how these constructions can allow obtaining functions providing good trade-offs between several criteria. Such constructions provide in general infinite classes of functions (in any numbers of variables ranging over some infinite sets). These functions are rather well structured, compared with random functions satisfying the same criteria. This is a quality (it simplifies the study of criteria) but also a drawback (the structure may be usable by attackers).

It is then also useful to search by computer investigation for functions, in numbers of variables small enough for search to be feasible, meeting one or several criteria, and if possible to classify as in [124] these functions under proper notions of equivalence (which needs mathematical tools as well). Of course, such searches are also useful to guess infinite classes and constructions. They often show that the functions built by algebraic constructions have peculiarities.

General classification

The classification of Boolean functions dates back to the 1950s [549] and 1960s [588]. It has been realized in [66] under affine equivalence for all Boolean functions up to five variables (with 48 equivalence classes), for all six-variable Boolean functions in [812] (see also Fuller's thesis, "Analysis of affine equivalent Boolean functions for cryptography," Queensland University of Technology, 2003), for those seven-variable Boolean functions of algebraic degree at most 3 modulo those of degree 1 in [613, 102], for those eight-variable Boolean functions of algebraic degree 4 modulo those of degree 3 in [739]; and under CCZ, EA, affine and permutation equivalences for (4, 4)-functions in [756, 183, 1009, 1158]. Note that Burnside's lemma [171] states that, if G is a group of permutations acting on a set X, then the number of orbits induced on X is given by $\frac{1}{|G|} \sum_{\sigma \in G} |\{x \in X \,;\, \sigma(x) = x\}|$.

More targeted computer investigations

Many papers report computer searches of specific functions (made after mathematical work). A few first examples are [1005] for six-variable bent Boolean functions, [741] for eight-variable bent Boolean functions, [134] for APN (5, 5)-functions (with a classification), and [135] for APN (n, n)-functions with $n = 6, 7, 8$.

The survey of the recent literature shows that many results using heuristics (providing specific instances of Boolean functions, not general ones that algebraic constructions can give, but allowing the creation of many different solutions satisfying certain properties) are now obtained with evolutionary algorithms and to a lesser extent with other methods used for diverse kinds of searches. For instance, [694] implements hill-climbing algorithms, which are a different type of heuristic than evolutionary algorithms (even if evolutionary algorithms can work as hill-climbing algorithms). Other examples are [1051], which uses satisfiability (SAT) solvers, and [74], which uses similarly a satisfiability modulo theory tool.

Usually, there is no guarantee that the solutions are not equivalent to each others, and a hard part of the work (when it is done) is to check inequivalence.

A list of recent papers making computer investigations can be found in [952].

As far as we know, the first application of genetic algorithms (GA) to the evolution of cryptographically suitable Boolean functions has been done in [884], where the aim was to reach high nonlinearity. The authors worked up to 16 variables and concluded that GA combined with hill climbing is much faster than random search.

In [945, 946], several types of evolutionary algorithms to find correlation immune Boolean functions with minimal Hamming weight are used, and [951] is the first attempt (as far as we are aware) to mathematically show why finding balanced Boolean functions with high nonlinearity is hard for evolutionary algorithms.

In [947], the authors evolved *secondary constructions* of bent Boolean functions (*i.e.*, of bent functions from bent functions), the goal being to reach many dimensions; there is no further analysis of whether such obtained constructions are valid for an infinite number of dimensions or whether they are new, up to equivalence.

These results show that techniques with heuristics can compete with algebraic constructions of Boolean functions when the numbers of inputs are not too big (for larger n, it becomes a computationally intensive process to examine a large number of functions generated by heuristics).

For vectorial Boolean functions, the situation is less positive. In [883], genetic algorithms to evolve S-boxes with high nonlinearity and low autocorrelation value are used. The selection of the appropriate genetic algorithm parameters is discussed. In [372], the authors use simulated annealing and hill-climbing algorithms to evolve bijective S-boxes of sizes up to 8×8 with high nonlinearity values. In [170], a heuristic method to generate MARS-like S-boxes is used, generating a number of S-boxes of appropriate size that satisfy all the requirements placed on the MARS S-box and even managing to find S-boxes with improved nonlinearity values. Bent (n, m)-functions are obtained in [948] with evolutionary computation. Picek et al. use several types of evolutionary algorithms to find differentially-6 uniform $(n, n - 2)$ functions but are not able to report success for any previously unknown size [949]. In [682], functions with particular symmetries are searched.

The results for vectorial Boolean functions obtained with heuristics cannot really compete with algebraic constructions even when considering the nonlinearity property. While algebraic constructions reach nonlinearity of 112 for 8×8 S-box size, the best result for heuristics is currently 104. Optimal values of nonlinearity and differential uniformity have been obtained with heuristics only recently for sizes larger than 4×4 (see [950], where proper cellular automata rules are found and used to construct S-boxes). The biggest advantage of using heuristics in the design of S-boxes lies in the fact that such techniques can account for properties, such as resistance against side-channel attacks, that algebraic constructions cannot (see, *e.g.*, [297]). Finally, if we consider not only cryptographic properties of S-boxes but also their implementation cost (such as area and power), then the heuristics could have an advantage over algebraic constructions. As an example of such a direction, Picek et al. use evolutionary algorithms to construct S-boxes that are either area or power efficient [953].

3.6 Boolean and vectorial functions for diffusion, secret sharing, and authentication

Designing diffusion layers for block ciphers is related to codes and to Boolean vectorial functions. It is addressed in Subsection 4.2.3, page 161. The motivation for secret sharing is cryptographic and that is why we cover it in this chapter, but it could have also been covered in the next one.

3.6.1 Secret sharing, access structures, and minimal codes

In [1030], Shamir introduced a simple and elegant way to (probabilistically) split a secret $a \in \mathbb{F}_q$ into a number n of shares so that no set of shares with cardinality (strictly) less than m gives any information on a, where m is some positive integer smaller than or equal to n, and at least m shares allow reconstructing (deterministically) the secret. Such scheme is called an (n, m) threshold *secret sharing scheme*. Blakeley in [90] presented independently an idea for realizing the same; we shall not describe his slightly less efficient scheme. Shamir's scheme associates the secret a with a polynomial $P_a(X)$ over $\mathbb{F}_q$ defined as $P_a(X) = a + \sum_{i=1}^{m-1} u_i X^i$, where the u_i denote random coefficients. Then, $n \geq m$ distinct nonzero elements $\alpha_0, \ldots, \alpha_{n-1}$ are publicly chosen in $\mathbb{F}_q^*$ and the polynomial $P_a(X)$ is evaluated in the α_i to construct a so-called *n-sharing* $(a_0, a_1, \ldots, a_{n-1})$ of a such that $a_i = P_a(\alpha_i)$ for every $i \in [0, \dots, n-1]$. To reconstruct a from at least m shares $(\alpha_i, a_i); i \in I$, Lagrange's polynomial interpolation is first applied to reconstruct $P_a(X) = \sum_{i \in I} a_i \prod_{k \in I, k \neq i} \frac{X - \alpha_k}{\alpha_i - \alpha_k}$. Then the polynomial is evaluated in 0. This allows a *dealer* to distribute the shares to n *players* so that at least m of them are able to reconstruct the secret, while less have no information on it. We have

$$a = \sum_{i \in I} a_i \cdot \beta_i, \tag{3.43}$$

where the constants β_i are defined as follows: $\beta_i = \prod_{k \in I, k \neq i} \frac{\alpha_k}{\alpha_k - \alpha_i}$. The constants can be precomputed once for all and be public.

Shamir's scheme is related to a problem in distributed storage systems, the *exact repair problem*, described in [583]: a file (cut into blocks) to be stored is interpreted as a degree d polynomial F over a field $\mathbb{F}$, each block being a coefficient of the polynomial; to distribute the file over n nodes, n elements $\alpha_1, \dots, \alpha_n$ of $\mathbb{F}$ are chosen, and $F(\alpha_i)$ is sent to node i; if a node fails, we may recover it by polynomial interpolation from the information on any m other nodes. It is possible to organize the distribution by breaking symbols into subsymbols belonging to subfields, so that to repair a failed node, one needs only a part of the information from other nodes (more than m nodes, but with a smaller amount of information needed globally). A lower bound is given in [583] on the amount of information needed (the repair bandwidth), and empirical constructions are proposed that make it possible to approach it.

Secret sharing schemes play also a central role in *multiparty computation* protocols, first introduced in [1136], in which n participants (also called players) are supposed to compute the image of a given function by making computations on the shares of the input provided by a secret sharing scheme, each player having one share. Such protocol is supposed to enable the coalition of players to securely evaluate the function, while some of the players are corrupted by an adversary. The protocol is called t-private if any t players cannot get from the protocol execution more information than their own shares; this is possible for any function when the number of players is at least $2t + 1$. This happens to be closely related to the problematics of masking functions (S-boxes) and of probing security that we shall see in Chapter 12, and is also connected with threshold implementation (see the same chapter).

Shamir's scheme is a *linear secret sharing scheme* in the sense that the set $\{(a, a_0, a_1, \dots, a_{n-1}) \in \mathbb{F}_q^{n+1}\}$ of those vectors of all possible $a \in \mathbb{F}_q$ concatenated with all possible sharings of a is a vector subspace of $\mathbb{F}_q^{n+1}$ (a linear code) and a is a linear function of the vector of its shares. As observed by Massey[26] in [827], given any linear $[n+1, k, d]_q$-code with (in the framework of the present book) $q = 2^n$ (and assuming in practice that $d \geq 2$ and that the corresponding *dual code* has a minimum distance $d^\perp \geq 2$, even if this is not specified by Massey), one can define a (linear) n-sharing over $\mathbb{F}_q$. Indeed, let G denote a generator matrix of the code; we assume that its first column is nonzero (this

----

[26] We shall borrow much from his paper in the present subsection.

can be ensured by permuting the codeword coordinates if necessary, thanks to the fact that
$d^\perp \geq 2$). Then the sharing $(a_0, a_1, \ldots, a_{n-1})$ of a is built from a k-tuple $(r_1, \ldots, r_k)$ such
that a equals the (usual) inner product between $(r_1, \ldots, r_k)$ and the first column of G, and
chosen with a uniform probability under this constraint, and the sharing $(a_0, a_1, \ldots, a_{n-1})$
is defined by $(a, a_0, a_1, \ldots, a_{n-1}) = (r_1, \ldots, r_k) \times G$. For simplicity, up to a permutation
of codeword coordinates again, and to a change of generator matrix, we can assume that
the first column of G equals the first vector $(1, 0, \ldots, 0)$ of the canonical basis of $\mathbb{F}_q^k$ (we
can even assume that G is in *systematic form* $G = [I_k \mid M]$, where I_k is the k-dimensional
identity matrix over $\mathbb{F}_q$), and we have then $r_1 = a$ (and the other r_i are random). The
reconstruction of a from its sharing $(a_0, \ldots, a_{n-1})$ is obtained by choosing a row of a parity
check matrix whose first coordinate is nonzero (which exists because we have $d \geq 2$;
otherwise the vector $(1, 0, \ldots, 0)$ would belong to the code; note that it is not the only
nonzero one since $d^\perp \geq 2$) and writing that the (usual) inner product between this row and
$(a, a_0, a_1, \ldots, a_{n-1})$ equals 0. The next proposition is from [991].

Proposition 48 *Given a linear $[n + 1, k, d]_q$-code used for secret sharing as described
above, with $d, d^\perp \geq 2$, the knowledge of any $d^\perp - 2$ shares gives no information on the
secret, and $n - d + 2$ shares allow reconstructing the secret.*

Indeed, those vectors of length $d^\perp - 1$ whose first term equals a generic secret and the
other ones are the shares of this secret at $d^\perp - 2$ positions cover uniformly the whole vector
space $\mathbb{F}_q^{d^\perp - 1}$, by definition of the dual distance (see the observations and footnote after
Definition 4, page 16), and the code of length $n - d + 1$ built the same way with $n - d + 2$
shares instead of $d^\perp - 2$ has straightforwardly minimum distance at least 2 and has dual
distance at least 2 as well (since the dual distance of this punctured code is larger than or
equal to the dual distance of the original code; see Lemma 2, page 17).

Some of such known secret sharing schemes use Boolean or vectorial functions, as
initiated in [269] and developed in other papers; see [456, 867, 874] and the references
therein. And as already observed in 1996 in [461, page 148 and figure 7.1], correlation
immune and resilient Boolean functions (see Definition 21, page 86) being related to the
dual distance of codes by Corollary 6, page 88, they can, in accordance with Proposition 48,
be employed for secret sharing.

But the determination of the so-called *qualified coalitions* of players, which are able
to (uniquely) reconstruct the secret, is more difficult to do in general than for Shamir's
construction (which is equivalent to using as code a possibly punctured Reed–Solomon code,
and is simple because such code being *MDS*, any set of k positions is an information set [see
pages 9 and 161], and any k positions of a codeword determine then the full codeword
uniquely). As also observed in [461] (see theorem 2.5), MDS codes lead then to so-called
threshold secret sharing schemes (in which qualified sets are exactly those of sufficient
sizes), and conversely. For general codes, the set of all qualified coalitions satisfies the
monotone property. An important notion is then the *access structure* of a secret sharing
scheme, that is, the class of minimal qualified coalitions (for which, if any share is removed,
the remaining shares give no information about the secret).

Let us recall how the access structure of a code can be determined.[27] Recall that we say that a vector u over a finite field $\mathbb{F}_q$ covers a vector v, and we write $v \preceq u$ if $supp(v) \subseteq supp(u)$. A nonzero codeword u of a code $\mathcal{C}$ is called a *minimal codeword* of $\mathcal{C}$ if it covers no codeword of $\mathcal{C}$ different from au, with $a \in \mathbb{F}_q$ (*i.e.*, no $\mathbb{F}_q$-linearly independent codeword) [103, 104]. Minimum weight codewords are minimal, but the converse is in general not true, except for MDS codes, in which the minimal codewords are the codewords of weight $n - k + 1$.

As observed by Massey, no two $\mathbb{F}_q$-linearly independent minimal codewords of a linear code can have the same support, since otherwise any linear combination would be a codeword that both of the former codewords would cover. This means that each support of a minimal codeword corresponds uniquely to this minimal codeword, up to linear dependency. In fact, as shown in [33], a set I of indices is the support of a minimal codeword if and only if a parity check matrix H restricted to the columns indexed by I has rank $|I| - 1$. The fact that it has rank less than $|I|$ is equivalent to the existence of a codeword whose support is included in I, and the fact that it has rank $|I| - 1$, say that the columns indexed in $I' \subset I$ with $|I'| = |I| - 1$ are linearly independent, is then equivalent to the fact that this codeword has support I and is minimal, since otherwise we could find by linear combination a codeword whose support would be I', a contradiction. This is a condition on I that does not require to know the minimal codeword of support I. This also proves that any minimal codeword has Hamming weight at most $n - k + 1$.

Every codeword is a linear combination of minimal codewords, since if a codeword u is not minimal, it covers a minimal codeword v, and there exists a linear combination $u + cv$, $c \in \mathbb{F}_q$, which has Hamming weight strictly smaller than $w_H(u)$; the process can continue (with $u + cv$) a finite number of steps and, when it ends, it provides a linear decomposition of u over minimal codewords it covers. Hence, for every nonzero position in a codeword, this codeword covers a minimal codeword that is nonzero at this position.

As shown by Massey [827] (and recalled in [33]), the access structure of the secret sharing scheme corresponding to a linear code is specified by those minimal codewords in the dual code, whose first component is nonzero (the set of shares corresponding then to the locations where this minimal codeword is nonzero, except the first). Indeed, as we saw, the secret is a linear combination of the shares and the vector of the coefficients of the resulting null linear combination belongs to the dual. Note that this property also proves that codewords of Hamming weight at most $2d - 1$ in a binary $[n, k, d]$ code are minimal. More generally, it is shown in [33] for every $[n, k, d]_q$ code that the codewords of Hamming weight at most $\frac{qd}{q-1} - 1$ are all minimal, since given such codeword u, and supposing the existence of a nonzero codeword $v \preceq u$ linearly independent of u, we have $\sum_{c \in \mathbb{F}_q^*} w_H(u - cv) = (q - 1)w_H(u) - w_H(v) \leq (q - 1)w_H(u) - d$ and the average of $w_H(u - cv)$ when $c \in \mathbb{F}_q^*$ is then at most $w_H(u) - \frac{d}{q-1} \leq \frac{qd}{q-1} - 1 - \frac{d}{q-1} = d - 1$; one of these codewords has then Hamming weight at most this value, a contradiction since none can be the zero codeword by hypothesis.

The minimal codewords have been determined in [33] for the (not necessarily binary) Hamming codes and for the binary Reed–Muller codes of order at most 2 (all nonzero

---

[27] In practice, this is often a very hard task.

codewords in $RM(1,n)$ are minimal except the all-1 codeword, and all codewords in $RM(2,n)$ are minimal except those of Hamming weight $2^{n-1} + 2^{n-1-h}$ for $h = 0, 1, 2$ and for some of those of Hamming weight 2^{n-1}; the proof, too technical to be included here, is based on the facts that $2d = 2^{n-1}$ and that any nonminimal codeword in a binary code equals the sum of two codewords with disjoint supports).

The codes whose nonzero codewords are all minimal are particularly interesting (this makes the code easily decodable and simplifies the access structures of the secret sharing scheme; it plays also a role in multiparty computation; see *e.g.*, [339]). A code having such property is called a *minimal code*. We have the following proposition:

Proposition 49 *[33] Let C be a linear code over $\mathbb{F}_q$. If $\frac{w_{min}}{w_{max}} > \frac{q-1}{q}$, where w_{min} and w_{max} denote respectively the minimum and maximum nonzero weights in C; then C is minimal.*

We do not give the proof. The hypothesis of Proposition 49 seems very strong as soon as q is large, but many examples of codes satisfying it exist and no example of a nonbinary minimal code not satisfying it is known in characteristic 2. Infinite families of minimal binary linear codes (related to Boolean functions) not meeting this condition have been recently found in [345, 456].

A recent necessary and sufficient condition for linear codes to be minimal is:

Proposition 50 *[456, 602] A linear code C over $\mathbb{F}_q$ is minimal if and only if, for each pair of $\mathbb{F}_q$-linearly independent codewords u and v in C, we have*

$$\sum_{c \in \mathbb{F}_q^*} w_H(u + cv) \neq (q-1)w_H(u) - w_H(v). \tag{3.44}$$

Hence, the minimality of C is completely determined by the weights of its codewords, and it is more easily handled if the numbers of these weights is small. Minimal codes derived from finite geometry (hyperovals; see page 219) are given in [862] in relation with bent vectorial functions.

A code is called a *two-weight code* if its nonzero elements have two possible weights only. Examples related to Boolean functions will be seen with Proposition 68, page 195. It is shown in [602] that if C is a two-weight linear code with length N and weights w_1 and w_2, such that $0 < w_1 < w_2 < N$ and $j w_1 \neq (j-1)w_2$ for every integer j such that $2 \leq j \leq q$, then C is minimal.

Binary three weight minimal codes are also investigated in [456].

3.6.2 Authentication schemes

The framework is as follows: Alice wishes to transmit to Bob a message m (a vector over the field $\mathbb{F}_{2^n}$) in the form (m, t), where t is a tag corresponding to m and depending on a secret key k shared between Alice and Bob, in order that Bob can verify the validity of the signature and nobody other than Alice and Bob can forge a valid message.

A *systematic authentication scheme* is a tuple $(M, T, K, \{E_k : k \in K\})$, where $E_k : M \mapsto T$ is the encoding rule related to k. To transmit an information $m \in M$ to Bob,

Alice calculates $t = E_k(m)$ and sends the tuple (m, t) to Bob over the public channel. Bob verifies that the relation $t = E_k(m)$ is satisfied. There exist two kinds of attacks: the attacker can try to forge (m, t) from scratch, hoping that it is accepted by Bob – this is called the "impersonation attack" – or he can observe a valid tuple (m, t) and try to modify it – this is called the "substitution attack." The maximal success probabilities of these attacks are denoted by P_I and P_S, respectively.

$$P_I = \max_{m \in M, t \in T} \frac{|\{k \in K; E_k(m) = t\}|}{|K|};$$

$$P_S = \max_{m \neq m' \in M, t, t' \in T} \frac{|\{k \in K; E_k(m) = t \text{ and } E_k(m') = t'\}|}{|\{k \in K; E_k(m) = t\}|}.$$

An example

Let $\mathbb{F}_{2^h}$ be a subfield of $\mathbb{F}_{2^n}$ and F a vectorial function from $\mathbb{F}_{2^n}$ to $\mathbb{F}_{2^n}$. We define the following scheme from [268]: $M = \mathbb{F}_{2^n} \times \mathbb{F}_{2^n}$, $T = \mathbb{F}_{2^h}$, $K = \mathbb{F}_{2^n} \times \mathbb{F}_{2^h}$, $E = \{E_k : k \in K\}$, where for every $k = (k_1, k_2) \in K$ and $m = (a, b) \in M$, we have $E_k(m) = tr_h^n(aF(k_1) + bk_1) + k_2$, where tr_h^n is the trace function from $\mathbb{F}_{2^n}$ into $\mathbb{F}_{2^h}$: $tr_h^n(a) = \sum_{j=0}^{\frac{n}{h}-1} a^{2^{hj}}$.

Function $k \mapsto E_k$ is a bijection from K to E and

$$P_I = \frac{1}{2^h}, \quad P_S \leq \frac{1}{2^h} + \left(1 - \frac{1}{2^h}\right)\left(1 - \frac{nl(F)}{2^{n-1}}\right),$$

where $nl(F)$ denotes the nonlinearity of F and $|M| = 2^{2n}$, $|T| = 2^h$, $|K| = |E| = 2^{n+h}$. Other examples can be found, for instance, in [268, 303, 460].

Boolean functions, vectorial functions, and error-correcting codes

Nota bene: Symbol n being traditionally used to denote the number of variables of Boolean functions, what was denoted by m in Section 1.2 is changed in this chapter into n. The codes have then length 2^n, and not n as it is usual in coding.

4.1 Reed–Muller codes

Reed–Muller codes have been introduced by David Muller in [891], and their decoding algorithm has been given by Irving Reed in [989]. They have played an important role in the history of error-correcting codes. For instance, they were used in the 1960s and early 1970s for the transmission of the first photographs of Mars by the Mariner series of spacecrafts. A Reed–Muller code of length 32, dimension 6, and minimum distance 16 was used (precisely, the first-order Reed–Muller code $RM(1,5)$). Each codeword corresponded to a level of darkness, this made 64 different levels and up to $\left\lfloor \frac{16-1}{2} \right\rfloor = 7$ errors could be corrected in the transmission of each codeword. Reed–Muller codes were also used in the third generation (3G) of mobile phones (developed in the late 1990s for release in the early 2000s), in the so-called Transport Format Combination Indicator (TFCI, part of the initial "handshake" between the mobile device and the base station, designed to inform the receiver of what type of communication will come next), for which it is extremely important to get information correct. The same code as for Mariner spacecrafts was first used and it was later replaced by a punctured subcode of the second-order Reed–Muller code $RM(2,5)$, which had dimension 10 and minimum distance 12.

Reed–Muller codes still play an important role thanks to their specific properties (see, *e.g.*, [1, 457]) and their roles with respect to new problematics (such as Locally Correctable Codes [778]), despite the fact that their parameters are not good,[1] except for the lowest and largest orders. They also constitute a useful framework for the study of Boolean functions.

Definition 42 *For every nonnegative integer r and every positive integer $n \geq r$, the Reed–Muller code $RM(r,n)$ of order r and length 2^n is the binary linear code of all words of length 2^n corresponding to the evaluations over $\mathbb{F}_2^n$ (on which some order has been chosen) of all n-variable Boolean functions of* algebraic degree *at most r.*

---

[1] In the late 1970s, for transmitting color photographs of Mars, the Voyager spacecrafts used the extended binary Golay code and later *Reed–Solomon codes*.

In other words, codewords are the last columns in the *truth tables* of these functions. *By abuse of language, we shall say that $RM(r,n)$ is the $\mathbb{F}_2$-vector space of all n-variable Boolean functions of algebraic degree at most r.*

For $r = 0$, $RM(0,n)$ equals the pair of constant functions.

For $r = 1$, $RM(1,n)$ equals the vector space of all *affine functions*. Note that we have seen in Section 1.2 that the codewords of the simplex code are the lists of values taken on $\mathbb{F}_2^n \setminus \{0_n\}$ by all linear functions. Hence $RM(1,n)$ is the $\mathbb{F}_2$-vector space generated by the extended simplex code and the constant function 1.

For $r = n$, $RM(n,n)$ equals the whole space of n-variable Boolean functions, since every n-variable Boolean functions has an ANF and then algebraic degree at most n.

The dimension of $RM(r,n)$ equals $1 + n + \binom{n}{2} + \cdots + \binom{n}{r}$ since this is the number of monomials of degrees at most r, which constitute a basis of $RM(r,n)$.

Remark. Let $\mathcal{G} = \mathbb{F}_2[\mathbb{F}_2^n]$ be the so-called *group algebra* of $\mathbb{F}_2^n$ over $\mathbb{F}_2$, consisting of the formal sums $\sum_{g \in \mathbb{F}_2^n} a_g\, g$, where $a_g \in \mathbb{F}_2$. The algebra $\mathcal{G}$ has only one maximal ideal, called its *radical*:

$$\mathcal{R} = \left\{ \sum_{g \in \mathbb{F}_2^n} x_g X^g; \sum_{g \in \mathbb{F}_2^n} x_g = 0 \right\},$$

whose elements correspond to the words of even Hamming weight. The ideals $\mathcal{R}^j$, $j \geq 1$, generated by the products of j elements of $\mathcal{R}$, provide the decreasing sequence

$$\mathcal{G} \supset \mathcal{R} \supset \cdots \supset \mathcal{R}^n = \{0_{2^n}, 1_{2^n}\},$$

with $\mathcal{R}^i \mathcal{R}^j = \mathcal{R}^{i+j}$. Berman [67] observed that, for any r, $RM(r,n) = \mathcal{R}^{n-r}$.   □

$RM(r,n)$, being a linear code, can be described by a generator matrix G. For instance, a generator matrix of the Reed–Muller code $RM(1,4)$ can be as follows:

$$G = \begin{bmatrix} 1 & 1 & 1 & 1 & 1 & 1 & 1 & 1 & 1 & 1 & 1 & 1 & 1 & 1 & 1 & 1 \\ 0 & 1 & 0 & 0 & 0 & 1 & 1 & 1 & 0 & 0 & 0 & 1 & 1 & 1 & 0 & 1 \\ 0 & 0 & 1 & 0 & 0 & 1 & 0 & 0 & 1 & 1 & 0 & 1 & 1 & 0 & 1 & 1 \\ 0 & 0 & 0 & 1 & 0 & 0 & 1 & 0 & 1 & 0 & 1 & 1 & 0 & 1 & 1 & 1 \\ 0 & 0 & 0 & 0 & 1 & 0 & 0 & 1 & 0 & 1 & 1 & 0 & 1 & 1 & 1 & 1 \end{bmatrix}.$$

The first row corresponds to the monomial of degree 0 (the constant function 1) and the other rows correspond to the monomials of degree 1 (the coordinate functions $x_1, \ldots, x_4$), when ordering the words of length 4 by increasing Hamming weights (we could choose other orderings; we have seen that this would lead to so-called equivalent codes, as shown at page 8).

4.1.1 Minimum distance and minimum weight codewords

Theorem 7 *The minimum distance of $RM(r,n)$ equals 2^{n-r}.*

This was historically proved by double induction over r and n (see [809, page 375]), but there exists a simpler proof.

Proof Code $RM(r,n)$ being linear, its minimum distance d equals the minimum nonzero Hamming weight of codewords. Let us first prove that $d \geq 2^{n-r}$. Since 2^{n-r} is a decreasing function of r, it is sufficient to show the bound for functions of algebraic degree r. Let $\prod_{i \in I} x_i$ be a monomial of degree r in the ANF of a Boolean function f of algebraic degree r; consider the 2^{n-r} restrictions of f obtained by keeping fixed the $n - r$ coordinates of x, whose indices lie outside I. Each of these restrictions, viewed as a function on $\mathbb{F}_2^r$, has an ANF of degree r because, when fixing these $n - r$ coordinates, the monomial $\prod_{i \in I} x_i$ is unchanged and all the monomials different from $\prod_{i \in I} x_i$ in the ANF of f give either 0 or monomials of degrees strictly less than r. Thus, any such restriction has an odd (and hence a nonzero) Hamming weight (see Section 2.2). The Hamming weight of f being equal to the sum of the Hamming weights of its restrictions, f has Hamming weight at least 2^{n-r}.

To complete the proof, we just need to exhibit a codeword of Hamming weight 2^{n-r}. The simplest example is the Boolean function $f(x) = \prod_{i=1}^{r} x_i$, that is, the indicator of the affine space $\{(1, \ldots, 1)\} \times \mathbb{F}_2^{n-r}$. □

Remark.

1. The proof of Theorem 7 shows in fact that, if a monomial $\prod_{i \in I} x_i$ has coefficient 1 in the ANF of f, and if every other monomial $\prod_{i \in J} x_i$ such that $I \subset J$ has coefficient 0 (*i.e.*, if I is maximal), then the function has Hamming weight at least $2^{n-|I|}$. Applying this observation to the Möbius transform $f°$ of f – whose definition has been given after Relation (2.3), page 32 – shows that, if there exists a vector $x \in \mathbb{F}_2^n$ such that $f(x) = 1$ and $f(y) = 0$ for every vector $y \neq x$ whose support contains $supp(x)$ (*i.e.*, if x is maximal in the support of f), then the ANF of f has at least $2^{n-w_H(x)}$ terms; this has been first observed in [1179]. Indeed, the Möbius transform of $f°$ is f.

2. The d-dimensional subspace $E = \{x \in \mathbb{F}_2^n ; x_i = 0, \forall i \notin I\}$, in the proof of Theorem 7, is a *maximal odd weighting* subspace: the restriction of f to E has odd Hamming weight (*i.e.*, has algebraic degree equal to the dimension d when viewed as a d-variable function), and the restriction of f to any of its proper superspaces has even Hamming weight (*i.e.*, the restriction of f to any coset of E has odd Hamming weight). Similarly as above, it can be proved, as in [1179], that any Boolean function admitting a d-dimensional maximal odd weighting subspace E has Hamming weight at least 2^{n-d}, and if $d \geq 2$, applying this observation to $f \oplus \ell$, where ℓ is affine, we have that f has nonlinearity at least 2^{n-d}. Indeed, the restriction of f to a d-dimensional affine space has algebraic degree d if and only if the restriction of $f \oplus \ell$ does. See more in [191], where the proofs are given in terms of group rings/algebras (see page 152; see [283, 323] for other examples where these are used). □

Notice that all nonconstant affine functions have Hamming weight 2^{n-1}, their supports being affine hyperplanes. Thus, nonconstant affine functions are the codewords of minimum Hamming weight in $RM(1,n)$. More generally, the codewords of minimum Hamming weight in $RM(r,n)$ have been characterized (see, *e.g.*, [809]). We give below another proof, more Boolean function oriented, of this characterization.

Theorem 8 *The Boolean functions of algebraic degree r and of Hamming weight 2^{n-r} are the* indicators *of $(n-r)$-dimensional flats (i.e., the functions whose supports are $(n-r)$-dimensional affine subspaces of $\mathbb{F}_2^n$).*

Proof The indicators of $(n-r)$-dimensional flats have clearly Hamming weight 2^{n-r} and they have algebraic degree r, since they are affinely equivalent to the function $\prod_{i=1}^{r} x_i$, because two affine subspaces of $\mathbb{F}_2^n$ of the same dimension are affinely equivalent (and recall from page 36 that the algebraic degree is an affine invariant). Conversely, let f be a function of algebraic degree r and of Hamming weight 2^{n-r}. Let $\prod_{i \in I} x_i$ be a monomial of degree r in the ANF of f and let $I^c = \{1, \ldots, n\} \setminus I$. For every vector $\alpha \in \mathbb{F}_2^{I^c}$, let us denote by f_α the restriction of f to the flat $\{x \in \mathbb{F}_2^n; \forall j \in I^c, x_j = \alpha_j\}$, viewed as a function over $\mathbb{F}_2^I$. According to the proof of Theorem 7, and since f has Hamming weight 2^{n-r}, each function f_α is the indicator δ_{a_α} of a singleton $\{a_\alpha\}$ of $\mathbb{F}_2^I$. Moreover, the mapping $\alpha \in \mathbb{F}_2^{I^c} \to a_\alpha \in \mathbb{F}_2^I$ is affine, i.e., for every $\alpha, \beta, \gamma \in \mathbb{F}_2^{I^c}$, we have $a_{\alpha+\beta+\gamma} = a_\alpha + a_\beta + a_\gamma$. Indeed, the r-variable function $f_\alpha \oplus f_\beta \oplus f_\gamma \oplus f_{\alpha+\beta+\gamma}$ being the restriction to $\mathbb{F}_2^I$ of $D_{\alpha+\beta} D_{\alpha+\gamma} f(x+\alpha)$, where $D_{\alpha+\beta} D_{\alpha+\gamma} f$ is a second-order derivative of f, it has algebraic degree at most $r - 2$, according to Corollary 1, page 39. And it is easily seen by using that $\delta_a(x) = \prod_{i=1}^{n}(x_i \oplus a_i \oplus 1)$ or by using Relation (2.3), page 32, that, for every $i \in \{1, \ldots, n\}$, the coefficient of the degree $r-1$ monomial $\prod_{j \neq i} x_j$ in $(f_\alpha \oplus f_\beta \oplus f_\gamma \oplus f_{\alpha+\beta+\gamma})(x)$ (which is null) equals the ith coordinate of $a_\alpha + a_\beta + a_\gamma + a_{\alpha+\beta+\gamma}$. This completes the proof since, denoting by x_I (resp. x_{I^c}) the restriction of x to I (resp. to I^c), the support of f equals the set $\{x \in \mathbb{F}_2^n; x_I = a_{x_{I^c}}\}$ and that the equality $x_I = a_{x_{I^c}}$ is equivalent to r linearly independent linear equations. □

See more in [34], from a design viewpoint. The minimum weight codewords of $RM(r, n)$ generate the code over $\mathbb{F}_2$; see [420].

4.1.2 Dual

The dual of a *Reed–Muller code* is a Reed–Muller code:

Theorem 9 *For every positive n and every nonnegative $r < n$, the dual*

$$RM(r, n)^\perp = \{f \in \mathcal{BF}_n; \forall g \in RM(r, n), f \cdot g = \bigoplus_{x \in \mathbb{F}_2^n} f(x) g(x) = 0\}$$

equals $RM(n - r - 1, n)$.

Proof We have seen in Section 2.2 that the n-variable Boolean functions of even Hamming weights are the elements of $RM(n - 1, n)$ (which equals then the parity code of length 2^n). Thus, $RM(r, n)^\perp$ is the set of those functions f such that, for every function g of algebraic degree at most r, the product function fg (whose value at any $x \in \mathbb{F}_2^n$ equals $f(x)g(x)$) has algebraic degree at most $n - 1$. This is clearly equivalent to the fact that f has algebraic degree at most $n - r - 1$. □

Note that, since $RM(1, n)$ is the $\mathbb{F}_2$-vector space generated by the extended *simplex code* and the constant function 1, its dual $RM(n - 2, n)$ is the intersection of the dual of the extended simplex code and the parity code. It also equals the extended *Hamming code*, according to Lemma 1, page 9, applied to $RM(1, n)$.

Characterization in the field $\mathbb{F}_{2^n}$

If the vector-space $\mathbb{F}_2^n$ is identified with the field $\mathbb{F}_{2^n}$, then the family of those functions $tr_n(ax^j)$ such that $a \in \mathbb{F}_{2^n} \setminus \{0\}$ and $w_2(j) \leq n - r - 1$ generates $RM(n - r - 1, n)$ (according to what we have seen on the trace representation of Boolean functions). We have then that a Boolean function f belongs to $RM(r, n)$ if and only if, for every nonzero j such that $w_2(j) \leq n - r - 1$, we have $\sum_{x \in \mathbb{F}_{2^n}} f(x) \, tr_n(ax^j) = tr_n(a \sum_{x \in \mathbb{F}_{2^n}} f(x)x^j) = 0$ for every $a \in \mathbb{F}_{2^n}$, as expressed in the following corollary:

Corollary 8 *For every positive n and every nonnegative $r < n$, a Boolean function f over $\mathbb{F}_{2^n}$ belongs to $RM(r, n)$ if and only if, for every nonzero j such that $w_2(j) \leq n - r - 1$, we have $\sum_{x \in \mathbb{F}_{2^n}} f(x) \, x^j = 0$.*

4.1.3 Automorphism group

The Reed–Muller codes are invariant under the action of the *general affine group* (*i.e.*, the group of affine permutations over $\mathbb{F}_2^n$). More precisely, it is a simple matter to show the following:

Proposition 51 *For any $1 \leq r \leq n - 1$, the automorphism group of $RM(r, n)$ (that is, the group of all permutations σ of $\mathbb{F}_2^n$ such that $f \circ \sigma \in RM(r, n)$ for every $f \in RM(r, n)$) equals the general affine group.*

The sets $RM(r, n)$ or $RM(r, n)/RM(r', n)$ have been classified under this action for some values of r, of $r' < r$ and of n; see [130, 611, 613, 615, 812, 1053, 1057].

4.1.4 Cyclicity of the punctured code $R^*(r, n)$

Let us identify $\mathbb{F}_2^n$ with the finite field $\mathbb{F}_{2^n}$. The *punctured code* $R^*(r, n)$ obtained from $RM(r, n)$ by erasing in each codeword f the coordinate at zero input, and ordering the resulting vector as $(f(1), f(\alpha), f(\alpha^2), \ldots, f(\alpha^{2^n - 2}))$, where α is a *primitive element* of $\mathbb{F}_{2^n}$, is a *cyclic code*. Indeed, the cyclic shift $(f(1), f(\alpha), f(\alpha^2), \ldots, f(\alpha^{2^n - 2})) \mapsto (f(\alpha^{2^n - 2}), f(1), f(\alpha), \ldots, f(\alpha^{2^n - 3}))$ is equivalent to changing function $f(x)$ into $f(\frac{x}{\alpha})$, and such transformation on Boolean functions does not change the algebraic degree since it is linear bijective. For any $r < n$, the Reed–Muller code $RM(r, n)$ is then an extended cyclic code [809, page 383].

Proposition 52 *For every $r < n$, the zeros of the punctured Reed–Muller code $R^*(r, n)$ of order r and length $2^n - 1$ are the elements α^i such that $1 \leq i \leq 2^n - 2$ and such that the 2-weight of i is at most $n - r - 1$.*

Proof   We have seen that any Boolean function f of algebraic degree at most r has a univariate polynomial representation of the form $\sum_{\substack{0 \le j \le 2^n - 2 \\ w_2(j) \le r}} f_j \, x^j$. The codeword $(f(1), f(\alpha), f(\alpha^2), \ldots, f(\alpha^{2^n - 2}))$ of the cyclic code $R^*(r, n)$ is represented by the polynomial $\sum_{0 \le l \le 2^n - 2} f(\alpha^l) X^l$ (see Section 1.2), whose value at α^i equals

$$\sum_{0 \le l \le 2^n - 2} f(\alpha^l) \alpha^{li} = \sum_{\substack{0 \le j \le 2^n - 2 \\ w_2(j) \le r}} f_j \left(\sum_{0 \le l \le 2^n - 2} \alpha^{l(i+j)} \right).$$

The sum $\sum_{0 \le l \le 2^n - 2} \alpha^{l(i+j)}$ equals 0 when $w_2(i) \le n - r - 1$ and $w_2(j) \le r$ since $i + j \ge i \ge 1$ cannot equal $2^n - 1$ since $w_2(i + j) \le w_2(i) + w_2(j)$, and then, α^{i+j} cannot equal 1, and then $\sum_{0 \le l \le 2^n - 2} \alpha^{l(i+j)} = \frac{1 + \alpha^{(2^n - 1)(i+j)}}{1 + \alpha^{i+j}} = 0$. Hence, the α^i such that $1 \le i \le 2^n - 2$ and $w_2(i) \le n - r - 1$ are zeros of the code. Since their number equals the codimension of the code, they are the only zeros of the code.   □

4.1.5   The problem of determining the weight distributions of Reed–Muller codes

What are in $RM(r, n)$ the possible Hamming distances between codewords, or equivalently the possible Hamming weights (or better, the weight distribution)? The answer, useful for improving the efficiency of the decoding algorithms, for evaluating their complexities, and for many other issues, is known for every n if $r \le 2$: see Section 5.2. For $r \ge n - 3$, it can also be deduced from the MacWilliams' identity (1.1), which theoretically allows us to deduce the weight distribution of $RM(n - r - 1, n)$ from the weight distribution of $RM(r, n)$. Practically, it is necessary to be able to explicitly expand the factors $(X + Y)^{2^n - i}(X - Y)^i$ and to simplify the obtained expression for $W_C(X + Y, X - Y)$; this is possible up to some value of n (around 35) by running a computer.

The cases $3 \le r \le n - 4$ remain unsolved (except for small values of n, see [66], and for $n = 2r$, because the code is then self-dual, see [809, 959]). Asymptotically tight bounds exist [679].

McEliece's theorem [833] or *Ax's theorem* [41] (see also the *Stickelberger theorem*, e.g., in [740, 746]) shows that the Hamming weights (and thus the distances) in $RM(r, n)$ are all divisible by $2^{\lceil \frac{n}{r} \rceil - 1} = 2^{\lfloor \frac{n-1}{r} \rfloor}$, where $\lceil u \rceil$ denotes the ceiling (the smallest integer larger than or equal to u) and $\lfloor u \rfloor$ denotes the integer part. For instance, it is shown in [677] (see also [623]) that if $d_{alg}(g) \le d_{alg}(f)$, then $d_H(f, g) \equiv w_H(f) \left[\mod 2^{\left\lceil \frac{n - d_{alg}(g)}{d_{alg}(f)} \right\rceil} \right]$ and this proves the McEliece's divisibility property by taking $g = f$.

McEliece's divisibility bound is tight and can also be shown by using the properties of the *NNF*; it is deduced in [292] from the fact that, if s is the number of monomials of degree $d_{alg}(f) > 0$ in the ANF of f, then the coefficient λ_u of x^u in its NNF is a multiple of $2^{\left\lfloor \frac{w_H(u) - 1}{d_{alg}(f)} \right\rfloor}$ if $w_H(u) > 0$ and of $2^{\left\lfloor \frac{w_H(u) - s - 1}{d_{alg}(f) - 1} \right\rfloor}$ if $w_H(u) > s$ and $d_{alg}(f) > 1$. Moreover, it is also shown in [292] that if $s < \frac{n}{d_{alg}(f)}$, then the Hamming weight of f is a multiple of $2^{\left\lceil \frac{n-s}{d_{alg}(f)-1} \right\rceil - 1}$ (larger than what gives McEliece's theorem).

Further properties of Hamming weights are given in [185] within the coset $f \oplus RM(1, n)$.

Kasami and Tokura [670] have shown that, for $r \geq 2$, the only Hamming weights in $RM(r, n)$ occurring in the range $[2^{n-r}; 2^{n-r+1}[$ are of the form $2^{n-r+1} - 2^i$ for some i; and they have completely characterized the codewords: the corresponding functions are affinely equivalent either to $x_1 \cdots x_{r-2}(x_{r-1}x_r \oplus x_{r+1}x_{r+2} \oplus \cdots \oplus x_{r+2l-3}x_{r+2l-2})$, $2 \leq 2l \leq n - r + 2$, or to $x_1 \cdots x_{r-l}(x_{r-l+1} \cdots x_r \oplus x_{r+1} \cdots x_{r+l})$, $3 \leq l \leq \min(r, n - r)$. The functions whose Hamming weights are strictly less than 2.5 times the minimum distance 2^{n-r} have later been studied in [671].

It is shown in [210] (and reported in Section 5.3 below, page 180) that for every Boolean function f on $\mathbb{F}_2^n$, there exists an integer m and a Boolean function g of algebraic degree at most 3 on $\mathbb{F}_2^{n+2m}$ whose Walsh transform satisfies: $W_g(0_{n+2m}) = 2^m W_f(0_n)$. Hence, the Hamming weight of f is related in a simple way to the Hamming weight of a cubic function (in a number of variables that can be exponentially larger). This shows that the distances in $RM(3, n)$ can be very diverse, contrary to those in $RM(2, n)$. See also [65].

4.1.6 Covering radius

The *covering radius* of $RM(r, n)$, which we shall denote by $\rho(r, n)$, equals by definition (see Section 1.2) the maximum, when f ranges over $\mathcal{BF}_n$, of the minimum Hamming distance between f and all n-variable Boolean functions of algebraic degree at most r (*i.e.*, of the distance between f and $RM(r, n)$); this distance is called the r-th order nonlinearity of f, and more simply its nonlinearity when $r = 1$; see Section 3.1).

- We have $\rho(1, n) = 2^{n-1} - 2^{\frac{n}{2}-1}$ when $n \geq 2$ is even (see Chapter 6). When n is odd, as we already saw in Section 3.1, $\rho(1, n)$ is unknown, except for $n \leq 7$, in which case it equals $2^{n-1} - 2^{\frac{n-1}{2}}$ [894]. For $n \geq 9$ odd, $\rho(1, n)$ lies strictly between $2^{n-1} - 2^{\frac{n-1}{2}}$ and $2\lfloor 2^{n-2} - 2^{\frac{n}{2}-2} \rfloor$ [617, 684, 686, 936, 937].

- We have $\lim_{n \to \infty} \left(2^{n/2} - \frac{\rho(1,n)}{2^{n/2-1}} \right) = 1$ (this fact, conjectured by Patterson and Wiedemann in 1983 [936], has been proved by Schmidt [1022] in 2019, who also proved the same limit when restricting to balanced functions).

- $\rho(2, n)$ is known for $n \leq 7$ (see [1102]). In [715], the authors calculated the second-order nonlinearity of all Boolean functions in the infinite class of those cubic functions[2] whose degree 3 part, up to affine equivalence, has the form $\bigoplus_{i=1}^s x_i q_i(x)$, $s \leq n$, where s is minimal and the q_i are quadratic on separate sets of variables, and where each q_i does not depend on $x_1, \ldots, x_i$. This is done by translating in a systematic way what is known on the best affine approximations of quadratic functions, and deducing formulae allowing a direct computation of the second-order nonlinearity of the cubic functions above, without needing the Walsh transform. This provides a lower bound on $\rho(2, n)$

---

[2] These functions are closely related to Maiorana–McFarland's (MM) functions; see page 165. In the case of the so called separable functions, they are MM (up to quadratic functions).

Table 4.1 Lower and upper bounds on the covering radii of Reed–Muller codes for small n.

$r\backslash n$	1	2	3	4	5	6	7	8	9
1	0	1	2	6	12	28	56	120	242–244[686]
2		0	1	2	6	18[1020]	40[1102]	84–100	171–220
3			0	1	2	8	20–23[610]	43–67	111–167
4				0	1	2	8	22–31	58–98
5					0	1	2	10	23–41
6						0	1	2	10
7							0	1	2
8								0	1
9									0

(more precisely, on the covering radius of $RM(2, n)$ in $RM(3, n)$). This lower bound is compared with the upper bound from [309] that we shall recall as Relation (4.1) below; for $n \leq 20$, the lower and upper bounds are not that far from each other, and the lower bound performs also well asymptotically. These results are extended to more general Maiorana–McFarland functions in [714], with a focus on functions $f(x, y) = x \cdot \phi(y)$, where ϕ is perfect nonlinear, showing that some of these functions have best quadratic approximation achieved by affine functions and that the lower bound of [715] on $\rho(2, n)$ can be improved. See also [1109].

- $\rho(n, n)$, $\rho(n-1, n)$ and $\rho(n-2, n)$ equal respectively 0, 1, and 2.
- $\rho(n-3, n)$, $n \geq 3$, has been determined in [837]: it equals $n + 1$ if n is odd and $n + 2$ if n is even.
- More results can be found in [610, 612, 614, 616].

We summarize what is known for small numbers of variables in Table 4.1.

General lower and upper bounds and more results are given in [375, 378, 379]. A first lower bound is simply the translation of the sphere covering bound: $2^{1+n+\binom{n}{2}+\cdots+\binom{n}{r}}$ $\sum_{i=0}^{\rho(r,n)} \binom{n}{i} \geq 2^{2^n}$, and two other lower bounds are due to [378]: $\rho(r, n) \geq$
$\begin{cases} 2^{n-r-3}(r+4), r \text{ even} \\ 2^{n-r-3}(r+5), r \text{ odd} \end{cases}$ for $r \leq n - 3$ and $\rho(r, n) \geq 2^{n-r}$ for $2 \leq r \leq n - 3$ and $n \geq 6$. The best-known upper bound, from [309], is as follows:

- A bound is first obtained for $r = 2$:

$$\rho(2, n) \leq \left\lfloor 2^{n-1} - \frac{\sqrt{15}}{2} \cdot 2^{\frac{n}{2}} \cdot \left(1 - \frac{122929}{21 \cdot 2^n} - \frac{155582504573}{4410 \cdot 2^{2n}}\right) \right\rfloor. \quad (4.1)$$

- This bound is generalized to every r by using the inequality $\rho(r, n) \leq \rho(r-1, n-1) + \rho(r, n-1)$, which is easily proved.
- This implies that, asymptotically, $\rho(r, n)$ is bounded above by

$$2^{n-1} - \frac{\sqrt{15}}{2} \cdot (1 + \sqrt{2})^{r-2} \cdot 2^{\frac{n}{2}} + \mathcal{O}(n^{r-2}).$$

The principle of the proof of (4.1) is to use that, for any two n-variable Boolean functions f and g, we have $\sum_{x \in \mathbb{F}_2^n} (-1)^{f(x) \oplus g(x)} = 2^n - 2\, d_H(f, g)$, which shows

$$\rho(2, n) = 2^{n-1} - \frac{1}{2} \min_{f \in B\mathcal{F}_n} \max_{g \in RM(2,n)} \left| \sum_{x \in \mathbb{F}_2^n} (-1)^{f(x) \oplus g(x)} \right|$$

and to use that:

$$\max_{g \in RM(2,n)} \left| \sum_{x \in \mathbb{F}_{2^n}} (-1)^{f(x) \oplus g(x)} \right| \geq \sqrt{\frac{\sum_{g \in RM(2,n)} \left(\sum_{x \in \mathbb{F}_2^n} (-1)^{f(x) \oplus g(x)} \right)^{2k+2}}{\sum_{g \in RM(2,n)} \left(\sum_{x \in \mathbb{F}_2^n} (-1)^{f(x) \oplus g(x)} \right)^{2k}}}.$$

We have

$$\sum_{g \in RM(2,n)} \left(\sum_{x \in \mathbb{F}_2^n} (-1)^{f(x) \oplus g(x)} \right)^{2k} = \sum_{x_1, \ldots, x_{2k} \in \mathbb{F}_2^n} (-1)^{\oplus_{i=1}^{2k} f(x_i)} \left(\sum_{g \in RM(2,n)} (-1)^{\oplus_{i=1}^{2k} g(x_i)} \right),$$

and the mapping $g \in RM(2, n) \mapsto \oplus_{i=1}^{2k} g(x_i)$ being an $\mathbb{F}_2$-linear form over $RM(2, n)$, the sum $\sum_{g \in RM(2,n)} (-1)^{\oplus_{i=1}^{2k} g(x_i)}$ equals the size of $RM(2, n)$ when $\oplus_{i=1}^{2k} g(x_i)$ is the null function, and otherwise, this sum equals 0. We refer to [309] for the rest of the proof, which is more technical.

We have seen at page 84 that the suitably normalised r-th order nonlinearity of a random Boolean function converges strongly for all $r \geq 1$ as shown in [1021], but no limit on $\rho(r, n)$ similar to the one recalled above for $\rho(1, n)$ is known yet.

Remark. The so-called Gowers norm (whose definition involves *k-th order derivatives* of Boolean functions) is related to the *covering radius* of Reed–Muller codes. We devote Section 12.4 to it. □

A notion on cosets of the first-order Reed–Muller code called *orphan* or *urcoset* is related to the notion of *plateauedness* of Boolean functions; see page 262.

4.2 Other codes related to Boolean functions

4.2.1 Linear codes

There exist mainly two principles of constructions of linear codes (which are binary[3]) from Boolean functions and vectorial functions (surveys can be found in [454] and [455]):

- *Codes from Boolean functions*: Let f be an n-variable Boolean function. Recall that we denote its support by $supp(f)$. We choose an order on it and assume that it has rank n. We define the linear code $C_{supp(f)}$, whose codewords are the lists of values of the restrictions to $supp(f)$ of the linear functions $v \cdot x$, where $v \in \mathbb{F}_2^n$ and "·" is an *inner*

---

[3] There also exist constructions of nonbinary codes from so-called *p-ary functions*, that is, Boolean-like functions in characteristic p.

product in $\mathbb{F}_2^n$. In other words, $C_{supp(f)}$ equals the code of all linear functions punctured at all the positions that are not in $supp(f)$. Any linear code whose generator matrix G has its columns all different[4] can be obtained by this construction, introduced in the early 1970's and called nowadays the defining-set construction. Indeed, the codewords of such code are obtained as $(v \times G)_{v \in \mathbb{F}_2^k}$. The support of f having rank n, the parameters of this code are $[w_H(f), n, d]$, where d needs to be determined for each function f. A generator matrix is made of the elements of $supp(f)$ put in columns. When f is a bent function in $n \geq 4$ variables (n even), the code has two weights (this property is characteristic) and d is their minimum (see [1120] and other papers by Wolfmann written in French, whose results have been rediscovered in [453] among many other results); we recall why in Chapter 6 at page 195 and give more characterizations. More generally, we can consider the code obtained from any Reed–Muller code by puncturing it at all positions outside $supp(f)$. Note that $\mathbb{F}_2^n$ can be identified with $\mathbb{F}_{2^n}$, and the inner product can then be $v \cdot x = tr_n(vx)$.

Cyclic codes are also related to algebraic immunity; see page 326.

- *Codes from vectorial functions*:

    – Given inner products in $\mathbb{F}_2^n$ and $\mathbb{F}_2^m$ (which we shall both denote by "·" for simplicity) the subcodes C'_F and C''_F of $RM(r, n)$, where $r \geq 2$ is the algebraic degree of F, whose codewords are the Boolean functions $v \cdot F(x) \oplus u \cdot x$, respectively $v \cdot F(x) \oplus u \cdot x \oplus \epsilon$, where u ranges over $\mathbb{F}_2^n$, v over $\mathbb{F}_2^m$, and ϵ over $\mathbb{F}_2$ can be associated to each vectorial function $F : \mathbb{F}_2^n \mapsto \mathbb{F}_2^m$ having no affine component (*i.e.*, having strictly positive nonlinearity). More precisely, the codewords are the lists of values of these functions, some order being chosen on $\mathbb{F}_2^n$. The Hamming weight of codeword $v \cdot F(x) \oplus u \cdot x$ (resp. $v \cdot F(x) \oplus u \cdot x \oplus \epsilon$) equals $2^{n-1} - \frac{1}{2}W_F(u, v)$ (resp. $2^{n-1} - \frac{(-1)^\epsilon}{2}W_F(u, v)$). Code C''_F equals the union of the cosets $v \cdot F + RM(1, n)$, where v ranges over $\mathbb{F}_2^m$. The parameters of C''_F are $[2^n, n + m + 1, d]$, where d is the nonlinearity of F; see more in [257, 1099, 269, 1147, 53]. A generator matrix of

    $$C'_F \text{ is } \begin{bmatrix} \cdots & x & \cdots \\ \cdots & F(x) & \cdots \end{bmatrix}, \text{ and a generator matrix of } C''_F \text{ is } \begin{bmatrix} \cdots & 1 & \cdots \\ \cdots & x & \cdots \\ \cdots & F(x) & \cdots \end{bmatrix},$$

    where x and $F(x)$ are column vectors and x ranges over $\mathbb{F}_2^n$. Conversely, let C be a linear $[2^n, k, d]$ binary code such that $k > n + 1$ and including the Reed–Muller code $RM(1, n)$ as a subcode. Let $(b_1, \ldots, b_k)$ be a basis of C completing a basis $(b_1, \ldots, b_{n+1})$ of $RM(1, n)$. The n-variable Boolean functions corresponding to the vectors $b_{n+2}, \ldots, b_k$ are the coordinate functions of an $(n, k - n - 1)$-function whose nonlinearity is d.

    The CCZ equivalence between (n, m)-functions can be expressed in terms of these codes (see the remark at page 379).

    Often, we have $m = n$ and $\mathbb{F}_2^n$ is identified with $\mathbb{F}_{2^n}$, the inner product being then $u \cdot x = tr_n(ux)$.

    – When $m = n$, the dual of the code $C'_F{}^*$, equal to C'_F punctured at the zero position, plays an important role with respect to APN functions F (defined in Definition 41,

---

[4] Such codes are sometimes called projective.

page 137) such that $F(0_n) = 0_m$; see Proposition 160, page 378. The dual of C_F'' plays a similar role with respect to general APN functions (see the remark at page 379). When F is a *power function*, $C_F'^*$ is cyclic; we find among such codes related to APN functions in particular the dual of the historical 2-error-correcting BCH code of length $2^n - 1$.

- Codes (which are constant-weight) are deduced in [862] from o-polynomials in relation with vectorial bent functions (see Definition 30, page 118).

- The other notion of nonlinearity of vectorial functions nl_v introduced at page 122 has been studied in [788] in relation with codes.

A hybrid construction is proposed in [1071], and other constructions of cyclic codes from vectorial (possibly APN) functions are given in [452, 464].

We have seen (in the remark at page 92) connections between algebraic immunity and linear codes. Connections exist with cyclic codes; see page 326.

4.2.2 Unrestricted codes

Boolean functions play an important role with nonlinear codes, as we shall see in Section 6.1.22 about Kerdock codes.

Vectorial functions also play a role. Given any (n, m)-function F, we can consider the code $\mathcal{G}_F = \{(x, F(x)); x \in \mathbb{F}_2^n\}$ (the graph of F viewed as a code). When F is linear, $\mathcal{G}_F$ is a linear code, but it happens that nonlinear functions F provide better parameters, as in the case of Kerdock and Preparata codes.

Codes of the form $\mathcal{G}_F$ are *systematic*: the set of n first indices has the property that every possible n-tuple occurs in exactly one codeword within the coordinates of indices $1, \ldots, n$. We call $\{1, \ldots, n\}$ an *information set* of C. Conversely, if a subset I of $\{1, \ldots, N\}$, where N is the length C, is an information set, then, up to permutation of the coordinates, it has the form $\mathcal{G}_F$. It is easily shown that all linear codes have such property: the generator matrix having rank k, it has k linearly independent columns, and placing them in the k first positions, we can multiply the resulting permuted generator matrix on the left by the inverse of the invertible square matrix made of its first k columns; this provides a systematic permuted generator matrix.

Such codes play a role in relation with countermeasures to side channel attacks, see Section 12.1.1, page 431. They need then to be complementary information set codes (CIS) (see the same page) in the sense that they admit two complementary information sets. This is a necessary and sufficient condition so that F can be a permutation.

4.2.3 Codes and diffusion layers in block ciphers

The diffusion (see the definition at page 76) ensured by a mapping F can be studied by analyzing the pairs $(x - y, F(x) - F(y))$. In practice, q will be a power of 2 and $-$ will be the same as $+$.

These pairs play also a role with respect to the differential attack.

Definition 43 *Let q be a power of a prime. The differential branch number of a function F :*
$\mathbb{F}_q^n \mapsto \mathbb{F}_q^m$ is defined as $\beta(F) = \min_{x,y \in \mathbb{F}_q^n, x \neq y} \{d_H(x, y) + d_H(F(x), F(y))\}$, the minimum
distance of code $\mathcal{G}_F$. The differential branch number of a linear function $F : \mathbb{F}_q^n \mapsto \mathbb{F}_q^m$ (or
of its matrix) is then defined as $\beta(F) = \min_{x \in \mathbb{F}_q^n, x \neq 0_n} \{w_H(x) + w_H(F(x))\}$.

$\beta(F)$ quantifies the level of diffusion induced by F when it is used as a diffusion layer in
a block cipher. When $q = 2^n$ and F diffuses the outputs of (n, n)-S-boxes, $\beta(F)$ indicates
the minimum number of *active* S-boxes.

Also, the larger $\beta(F)$, the more difficult the research of *characteristics* needed for
mounting differential attacks (see page 134). An r-round characteristic constitutes an $(r+1)$-
tuple of difference patterns: $(\Delta X_0, \Delta X_1, \ldots, \Delta X_r)$. The probability of this characteristic
is the probability that an initial difference pattern ΔX_0 propagates to difference patterns
$\Delta X_1, \ldots, \Delta X_r$ after $1, 2, \ldots, r$ rounds.

If F is linear[5], then $\mathcal{G}_F$ is linear and the diffusion is studied by analyzing the pairs
$(a, F(a))$.

It is easily shown that the differential branch number of a linear permutation equals that
of its inverse and that, for every $F : \mathbb{F}_q^n \mapsto \mathbb{F}_q^m$, we have $\beta(F) \leq m + 1$, with equality if and
only if the code $\mathcal{G}_F = \{(x, F(x)); x \in \mathbb{F}_q^n\}$ is *MDS*.

If $\mathcal{G}_F$ is an MDS $[N, k, d]$-code such that $N > k$ then any *punctured code* obtained, for
instance, by erasing the last coordinate of each codeword is an MDS $[N - 1, k, d - 1]$ code.
For every prime power q, every $N < q$ and every $k \leq N$, we know that there exist MDS
codes over $\mathbb{F}_q$ of parameters $[N, k, N - k + 1]$ (Reed–Solomon codes, for instance). This
allows us to build optimal diffusion layers.

Definition 44 *The linear branch number of a linear function $F : \mathbb{F}_q^n \mapsto \mathbb{F}_q^m$ is defined as*
follows:

$$\beta'(F) = \min_{\substack{a,b \in \mathbb{F}_q^n, (a,b) \neq (0_n, 0_n) \\ a \cdot x \oplus b \cdot F(x) \text{ unbalanced}}} \{w_H(a) + w_H(b)\}.$$

The linear branch number of a function $F : \mathbb{F}_q^n \mapsto \mathbb{F}_q^m$ is the *dual distance* of the code
$\{(x, F(x)), x \in \mathbb{F}_q^n\}$. Then if F is linear and F' is the linear mapping whose matrix is the
transpose of that of F, we have $\beta'(F) = \beta(F')$.

In [795], the authors propose a nonlinear diffusion layer based on Kerdock codes.

4.2.4 Codes and association schemes

Association schemes, originated in statistics, have been used in coding theory and combinatorics in the 1970s by Delsarte, McEliece, and others to obtain strong upper bounds on
the size of codes and other combinatorial objects, and to characterize those objects (such as
perfect codes) that meet these bounds. They have also been studied in relation to Boolean
functions. They are related to graphs (which we encountered at page 70). For more details,
the reader is referred to [411, 424].

---

[5] Contrary to a substitution layer, a diffusion layer does not need to be nonlinear; for reasons of speed, it is then
better to choose it to be linear.

Definition 45 *Let V be a finite set of vertices and $\{G_0, G_1, \ldots, G_d\}$ be binary relations on V with $G_0 = \{(x, x) : x \in V\}$. Then the decomposition $(V; G_0, G_1, \ldots, G_d)$ (represented in short as $(V, \{G_i\}_{0 \leq i \leq d})$) is called an association scheme of class d on V provided that the following properties hold:*

- *$V \times V = G_0 \cup G_1 \cup \cdots \cup G_d$ and $G_i \cap G_j = \emptyset$ for $i \neq j$.*
- *${}^t G_i = G_{i'}$ for some $i' \in \{0, 1, \ldots, d\}$, where ${}^t G_i = \{(x, y) : (y, x) \in G_i\}$. (If $i' = i$, then we call G_i symmetric)*
- *For $i, j, k \in \{0, 1, \ldots, d\}$ and $x, y \in V$ with $(x, y) \in G_k$, the number $p_{ij}^k := \#\{z \in V : (x, z) \in G_i, (z, y) \in G_j\}$ is a constant.*

An association scheme is said to be symmetric if each G_i is symmetric.

One of the well-known construction methods of association schemes is to use Schur rings. Constuctions of association schemes from bent functions (in odd characteristic) have been considered in the literature (see, *e.g.*, [964]). In [506], the authors studied Boolean functions arising in some popular association schemes.

4.2.5 Codes and secret sharing

We have seen in Subsection 3.6.1, page 145, how codes play a role with respect to secret sharing and that Boolean functions can play a role in this domain.

5

Functions with weights, Walsh spectra, and nonlinearities easier to study

In this chapter, we visit diverse types of Boolean and vectorial functions, whose study is simpler than for general functions. We will encounter them again in almost all subsequent chapters.

5.1 Affine functions and their combinations

Affine functions are weak cryptographically (see Sections 3.1 and 3.4), and many criteria seen in Chapter 3 quantify the difference between cryptographic functions and affine functions. However, good functions can be obtained by combining affine functions in different ways. Before presenting them, we briefly address affine functions themselves.

Affine Boolean functions

The Hamming weights and the Walsh spectra of affine Boolean functions (*i.e.*, of the codewords of $RM(1, n)$) are peculiar.

The Hamming weight of any non-constant affine function is 2^{n-1} since this is the size of any affine hyperplane. The Hamming weights of the two constant functions are of course 0 and 2^n.

Recall from page 38 that, given any *inner product* "$\cdot$", any affine Boolean function can be written in the form $\ell(x) = a \cdot x \oplus \epsilon$, where $a \in \mathbb{F}_2^n$ and $\epsilon \in \mathbb{F}_2$. The Walsh transform of such a function takes null value at every vector $u \neq a$ and takes value $2^n (-1)^\epsilon$ at a. The Walsh support is then a singleton.

Conversely, every Boolean function whose Walsh support is a singleton is an affine function, according to the inverse Walsh transform formula (2.43), page 59, and to Parseval's relation (2.47), page 60.

Of course, the nonlinearity of any affine Boolean function is null, and this is characteristic of affine functions.

Affine vectorial functions

The component functions of affine (n, m)-functions are affine Boolean functions (this property is characteristic of affine vectorial functions). If $F(x) = L(x) + a$ where L is a linear (n, m)-function and $a \in \mathbb{F}_2^m$, then, for every $(u, v) \in \mathbb{F}_2^n \times \mathbb{F}_2^m$, $W_F(u, v) = \sum_{x \in \mathbb{F}_2^n} (-1)^{v \cdot L(x) \oplus u \cdot x \oplus v \cdot a} = \sum_{x \in \mathbb{F}_2^n} (-1)^{(L^*(v)+u) \cdot x \oplus v \cdot a}$ equals $2^n (-1)^{v \cdot a}$ if $u = L^*(v)$ and is null otherwise, where L^* is the adjoint operator of L, that is, where $v \cdot L(x) = L^*(v) \cdot x$

for every v and x (in the case where "·" is the *usual inner product*, the matrix of L^* is simply the transpose of that of L). Of course, the nonlinearity of any affine vectorial function is null, but this is not characteristic of affine vectorial functions (it is characteristic of the fact that at least one component function of F is affine).

5.1.1 Maiorana–McFarland functions

Since the Walsh transform of affine functions behaves so simply, it is natural to try building more robust functions by using them as building blocks in constructions. A first way is based on the additive structure of $\mathbb{F}_2^n$ as an $\mathbb{F}_2$-vector space. This leads to considering those functions whose restrictions to each coset $a + E$ of some $\mathbb{F}_2$-vector subspace E of $\mathbb{F}_2^n$ are affine. Up to affine equivalence, we can take $E = \mathbb{F}_2^r \times \{0_{n-r}\}$. Then the corresponding functions are called *Maiorana–McFarland* (MM) functions, since originally, the idea of such functions comes from Maiorana and McFarland [834], as reported in [441]. The general class, obtained by considering all *affinely equivalent* functions to Maiorana–McFarland functions, is called the *completed Maiorana–McFarland class*.

Maiorana–McFarland Boolean functions

They have been first investigated for building bent functions (see Section 6.1.15, page 209), and later been considered in [181] for constructing correlation immune and resilient functions (see Subsection 7.1.8, page 291). Recall that every affine Boolean function has the form $a \cdot x \oplus \epsilon$. The idea of Maiorana–McFarland's construction corresponds to making a and ϵ vary. For convenience, instead of denoting the input to the global function by $x = (x_1, \ldots, x_n)$, we denote it then by (x, y), where $x = (x_1, \ldots, x_r)$ and $y = (x_{r+1}, \ldots, x_n)$.

Definition 46 *Let n and r be any positive integers such that $r \leq n$. We call Maiorana–McFarland's function any n-variable Boolean function of the form:*

$$f(x, y) = x \cdot \phi(y) \oplus g(y); \quad x \in \mathbb{F}_2^r, \ y \in \mathbb{F}_2^{n-r}, \tag{5.1}$$

where ϕ is a function from $\mathbb{F}_2^{n-r}$ to $\mathbb{F}_2^r$ and g is an $(n - r)$-variable Boolean function. We denote by MM_r the corresponding class.

The size of this class roughly equals $2^{(r+1)2^{n-r}}$.

An example already seen of a Maiorana–McFarland Boolean function is the address function (see page 68), with $r \approx n - \log_2(n)$. Note that, for every $r < n$, we have $MM_{r+1} \subseteq MM_r$ (this can be seen directly with Relation (5.1) or by the fact that the restriction of an affine function to an affine subspace is affine) and that $MM_1 = \mathcal{BF}_n$ (since every function in one variable is necessarily affine).

The algebraic degree of f in (5.1) is at most $n-r+1$ (and at most $n-r$ if $\sum_{y\in\mathbb{F}_2^{n-r}} \phi(y) = 0_r$) since the algebraic degree of ϕ is at most $n - r$ (and at most $n - r - 1$ if $\sum_{y\in\mathbb{F}_2^{n-r}} \phi(y) = 0_r$). We shall see in Section 5.2 that all *quadratic functions* belong to the completed $MM_{\lceil \frac{n}{2} \rceil}$ class.

Remark.   Maiorana–McFarland functions can be viewed as the concatenations of *affine functions*. Indeed, let us order all the binary words of length n in lexicographic order, with the bit of higher weight on the right-hand side. Then, the *truth table* of f is the concatenation of the truth tables of its restrictions obtained by fixing the values of the $n - r$ last bits of the input and letting the r first input bits freely range over $\mathbb{F}_2$. And f is an MM$_r$ function if and only if all these restrictions are affine.   □

The calculation of Hamming weight, Walsh spectrum, and nonlinearity are easier for functions in MM$_r$, $r \geq 2$, than for general Boolean functions, and in some cases can be completely determined. Note that since the input to f is written in the form (x, y), where $x \in \mathbb{F}_2^r$, $y \in \mathbb{F}_2^{n-r}$, the input to W_f is better written (u, v), where $u \in \mathbb{F}_2^r$, $v \in \mathbb{F}_2^{n-r}$.

Proposition 53   *Let f be the function given by Relation (5.1). Then, assuming that the inner product in $\mathbb{F}_2^r \times \mathbb{F}_2^{n-r}$ writes $(u, v) \cdot (x, y) = u \cdot x \oplus v \cdot y$ (where we use the same notation "$\cdot$" for denoting inner products in $\mathbb{F}_2^r$ and $\mathbb{F}_2^{n-r}$), we have*

$$W_f(u, v) = 2^r \sum_{y \in \phi^{-1}(u)} (-1)^{g(y) \oplus v \cdot y}; \quad u \in \mathbb{F}_2^r, \ v \in \mathbb{F}_2^{n-r},$$

where $\phi^{-1}(u)$ denotes the preimage of u by ϕ. Hence

$$w_H(f) = 2^{n-1} - 2^{r-1} \sum_{y \in \phi^{-1}(0_r)} (-1)^{g(y)}$$

and

$$nl(f) = 2^{n-1} - 2^{r-1} \max_{u \in \mathbb{F}_2^r, \ v \in \mathbb{F}_2^{n-r}} \left| \sum_{y \in \phi^{-1}(u)} (-1)^{g(y) \oplus v \cdot y} \right|.$$

Proof   We have

$$W_f(u, v) = \sum_{x \in \mathbb{F}_2^r, y \in \mathbb{F}_2^{n-r}} (-1)^{f(x,y) \oplus u \cdot x \oplus v \cdot y}$$

$$= \sum_{y \in \mathbb{F}_2^{n-r}} \left((-1)^{g(y) \oplus v \cdot y} \sum_{x \in \mathbb{F}_2^r} (-1)^{(\phi(y)+u) \cdot x} \right)$$

$$= 2^r \sum_{y \in \phi^{-1}(u)} (-1)^{g(y) \oplus v \cdot y},$$

since $\sum_{x \in \mathbb{F}_2^r} (-1)^{(\phi(y)+u) \cdot x}$ is null when $\phi(y) \neq u$.   □

Proposition 53 shows that the Walsh support of f is included in $Im(\phi) \times \mathbb{F}_2^{n-r}$. Note that this Walsh support can be made very small (minimizing the size of $Im(\phi)$ and the value of $n - r$), even while ensuring some properties such as the nonexistence of linear structure.

We shall see that MM$_r$ class provides easy constructions of bent (or highly nonlinear) functions, correlation immune functions, and resilient functions. It will then be important to be able to say if a given Boolean function is in the completed MM$_r$ class or not. The following proposition is an easy extension of an observation from [441]:

Proposition 54 *An n-variable Boolean function f belongs to the completed MM$_r$ class if and only if there exists an r-dimensional vector space E such that $D_a D_b f$ is the null function for every $a, b \in E$.*

Proof The condition is clearly necessary. It is also sufficient since it means that each restriction of f to a coset of E is affine. □

Note that for such function, E is in general not the linear kernel of f (see Definition 25, page 99); it can be a superset of the linear kernel.

Maiorana–McFarland vectorial functions

It is easily seen that an r-variable vectorial function is linear if and only if all its component functions are linear. Let n, r and m be positive integers such that $r \leq n$. Let F be any function of the form

$$F : (x, y) \in \mathbb{F}_2^r \times \mathbb{F}_2^{n-r} \mapsto \psi(x, y) + G(y) \in \mathbb{F}_2^m, \qquad (5.2)$$

where G is any function from $\mathbb{F}_2^{n-r}$ to $\mathbb{F}_2^m$ and $\psi : \mathbb{F}_2^r \times \mathbb{F}_2^{n-r} \mapsto \mathbb{F}_2^m$ is such that, for every $y \in \mathbb{F}_2^{n-r}$, the function $x \mapsto \psi(x, y)$ is linear. Then, for every $y \in \mathbb{F}_2^{n-r}$ and $w \in \mathbb{F}_2^m$, there exists $\phi(y, w) \in \mathbb{F}_2^r$ such that $w \cdot \psi(x, y) = \phi(y, w) \cdot x$, and this property is characteristic of the functions of the form (5.2). For every $(u, v, w) \in \mathbb{F}_2^r \times \mathbb{F}_2^{n-r} \times \mathbb{F}_2^m$, we have

$$W_F((u, v), w) = \sum_{(x,y) \in \mathbb{F}_2^r \times \mathbb{F}_2^{n-r}} (-1)^{(\phi(y,w)+u) \cdot x \oplus w \cdot G(y) \oplus v \cdot y}$$

$$= 2^r \sum_{y \in \mathbb{F}_2^{n-r}; \, \phi(y,w)=u} (-1)^{w \cdot G(y) \oplus v \cdot y}.$$

Remark. If r divides n, then we can endow $\mathbb{F}_2^n$ with the structure of the field $\mathbb{F}_{2^n}$ and $\mathbb{F}_2^r$ with the structure of subfield $\mathbb{F}_{2^r}$ of $\mathbb{F}_{2^n}$. In particular, if $r = \frac{n}{2}$ (which will be well suited for designing bent functions), we can identify $\mathbb{F}_2^n$ with $\mathbb{F}_{2^{\frac{n}{2}}} \times \mathbb{F}_{2^{\frac{n}{2}}}$ and we consider the functions of the form

$$F(x, y) = L(x \, \phi(y)) + G(y), \qquad (5.3)$$

where the product $x \, \phi(y)$ is calculated in $\mathbb{F}_{2^{\frac{n}{2}}}$ and L is any linear or affine function from $\mathbb{F}_{2^{\frac{n}{2}}}$ to $\mathbb{F}_2^m$, ϕ is any function from $\mathbb{F}_{2^{\frac{n}{2}}}$ to itself, and G is any $(\frac{n}{2}, m)$-function. □

5.1.2 Niho and $\mathcal{PS}_{ap}$-like functions

When $\mathbb{F}_2^n$ is identified with $\mathbb{F}_{2^n}$, we can also use the multiplicative structure of $\mathbb{F}_{2^n}^*$ to build Boolean functions from affine functions. Similarly to the case of Maiorana–McFarland functions, in which we considered additive subgroups of $\mathbb{F}_2^n$ and their cosets, we can consider multiplicative subgroups of $\mathbb{F}_{2^n}^*$ and their cosets. A natural choice[1] as a subgroup is the multiplicative group of a subfield $\mathbb{F}_{2^m}$ of $\mathbb{F}_{2^n}$ (where m is a divisor of n). We can view $\mathbb{F}_{2^n}^*$ as the union of the cosets $\mu \mathbb{F}_{2^m}^*$ of $\mathbb{F}_{2^m}^*$, where μ ranges over a subset U of $\mathbb{F}_{2^n}^*$ containing one representative of each coset of $\mathbb{F}_{2^m}^*$ and one only (U has then $\frac{2^n-1}{2^m-1}$ elements). Under some condition, it is possible to take U equal to the multiplicative subgroup of $\mathbb{F}_{2^n}^*$ of order $\frac{2^n-1}{2^m-1}$. This is possible when $2^m - 1$ and $\frac{2^n-1}{2^m-1}$ are coprime (which is always the case if n is even and $m = \frac{n}{2}$, in which case the representation of the elements of $\mathbb{F}_{2^n}^*$ in the form μx, $x \in \mathbb{F}_{2^m}^*$, is often called *polar representation*[2]), since there exist then relative integers i, j such that $i(2^m - 1) + j\frac{2^n-1}{2^m-1} = 1$, and given a *primitive element* α of $\mathbb{F}_{2^n}$, we have then

$$\alpha = (\alpha^{2^m-1})^i \left(\alpha^{\frac{2^n-1}{2^m-1}} \right)^j \text{ and } \alpha^{2^m-1} \in U, \alpha^{\frac{2^n-1}{2^m-1}} \in \mathbb{F}_{2^m}^*.$$ It is observed in [804] that, if[3] $n = 2m$, any (n, n)-function F (and therefore any n-variable Boolean function) can then be uniquely represented by a polynomial in the form $F(\mu x) = \sum_{s=0}^{2^m-2} \sum_{t=0}^{2^m} a_{s,t} \mu^t x^s$, where $a_{s,t} \in \mathbb{F}_{2^n}$, $\mu \in U$, $x \in \mathbb{F}_{2^m}^*$ (with additionally the indication of the value of $F(0)$), and that if $F(0) = \sum_{\mu \in U, x \in \mathbb{F}_{2^m}^*} F(\mu x)$, its algebraic degree equals the maximal 2-weight of $s(2^m + 1)u + t(2^m - 1)v \pmod{2^n - 1}$ such that $a_{s,t} \neq 0$, where $(2^m + 1)u + (2^m - 1)v = 1$.

We consider then those n-variable Boolean functions whose restrictions to the cosets $\mu \mathbb{F}_{2^m}^*$, where m divides n, coincide with affine functions:

$$f(\mu x) = tr_m(x\, \phi(\mu)) + g(\mu); \quad \mu \in U, \ x \in \mathbb{F}_{2^m}^*, \tag{5.4}$$

where ϕ is a function from U to $\mathbb{F}_{2^m}$ and g is a Boolean function over U. And a value must still be chosen for $f(0)$. Note that if each restriction to $\mu\mathbb{F}_{2^m}^*$ has algebraic degree less than m (in particular if $d_{alg}(f) < m$), then the univariate representation $f(z) = \sum_{i=0}^{2^n-2} a_i z^i$ of f satisfies "$(i \neq 0$ and $a_i \neq 0) \Rightarrow (i \pmod{2^m - 1} \in I)$", where $I = \{2^j; j = 0, \dots, m - 1\}$: this sufficient condition is indeed necessary since, assuming without loss of generality that $a_0 = 0$, for every $\omega \in \mathbb{F}_{2^n}^*$, the function $x \in \mathbb{F}_{2^m} \mapsto f(\omega x) = \sum_{i=0}^{2^n-2} a_i \omega^i x^{i \pmod{2^m-1}}$ being linear, we have that $k \notin I \Rightarrow \sum_{\substack{0 \leq i \leq 2^n-2 \\ i \equiv k \pmod{2^m-1}}} a_i \omega^i = 0$, and by uniqueness of the univariate representation of the functions of $\omega \in \mathbb{F}_{2^n}$, this completes the proof [311].

Recall that functions tr_n, tr_m, and tr_m^n (see page 43) satisfy that, for every $a \in \mathbb{F}_{2^n}$, we have $tr_n(a) = tr_m(tr_m^n(a))$, and that, for every $u \in \mathbb{F}_{2^n}$ and $x \in \mathbb{F}_{2^m}$, we have $tr_m^n(ux) = x\, tr_m^n(u)$. Therefore, for $\mu \in U$, $x \in \mathbb{F}_{2^m}$, we have $tr_n(u\mu x) = tr_m(x\, tr_m^n(u\mu))$. We have then, for every $u \in \mathbb{F}_{2^n}$:

$$W_f(u) = (-1)^{f(0)} + \sum_{\mu \in U, x \in \mathbb{F}_{2^m}^*} (-1)^{tr_m(x\, [\phi(\mu) + tr_m^n(u\mu)]) \oplus g(\mu)}$$

$$= (-1)^{f(0)} - \sum_{\mu \in U} (-1)^{g(\mu)} + 2^m \sum_{\mu \in U; \phi(\mu) + tr_m^n(u\mu) = 0} (-1)^{g(\mu)}, \tag{5.5}$$

---

[1] But not the only one; investigations could be made on other subgroups, such as those of order $\frac{2^n-1}{2^m-1}$, where m divides n (for which affinity would no more be the property on which the functions would be built).

[2] A slightly different representation is the trace 0/trace 1 representation; see [547].

[3] More general cases are studied there.

$$w_H(f) = 2^{n-1} - \frac{1}{2}\left((-1)^{f(0)} - \sum_{\mu \in U}(-1)^{g(\mu)} + 2^m \sum_{\mu \in \phi^{-1}(0)}(-1)^{g(\mu)}\right)$$

and

$$nl(f) = 2^{n-1} - \frac{1}{2}\max_{u \in \mathbb{F}_{2^n}}\left|(-1)^{f(0)} - \sum_{\mu \in U}(-1)^{g(\mu)} + 2^m \sum_{\mu \in U; \phi(\mu)+tr_m^n(u\mu)=0}(-1)^{g(\mu)}\right|.$$

A subcase is when function g is null in (5.4) (*i.e.*, when the restrictions to the cosets $\mu\,\mathbb{F}_{2^m}^*$ coincide with linear functions), which leads (when $n = 2m$) to the so-called Niho Boolean functions (the name comes from a theorem by Niho [902] dealing with power functions; see a survey on their applications in [769]):

$$f(\mu x) = tr_m(x\,\phi(\mu)); \quad \mu \in U, x \in \mathbb{F}_{2^m}^*, \tag{5.6}$$

among which are bent functions; see Subsection 6.1.15. Another subcase is (also when $n = 2m$) when function ϕ is null in (5.4) (*i.e.*, when the restrictions to the cosets $\mu\,\mathbb{F}_{2^m}^*$ coincide with constant functions), which leads to the so-called $\mathcal{PS}_{ap}$-like class of Boolean functions:

$$f(\mu x) = g(\mu); \quad \mu \in U, x \in \mathbb{F}_{2^m}^*, \tag{5.7}$$

among which are also bent functions; see Subsection 6.1.15 as well. Niho power functions with few Walsh values are studied in [769].

Niho and $\mathcal{PS}_{ap}$-like classes in bivariate form

The last sum in (5.5) is not always easily simplified further since it deals with U, which has no additive structure in general. This can be circumvented when $n = 2m$ (this case can be generalized) by representing the elements of $\mathbb{F}_{2^n}$ by ordered pairs of elements of $\mathbb{F}_{2^m}$ (which is possible since $\mathbb{F}_{2^n}$ is a plane over $\mathbb{F}_{2^m}$). It is then easily seen that the subset U introduced at the beginning of the present subsection can be taken equal to $\{(0, 1)\} \cup \{(1, \lambda), \lambda \in \mathbb{F}_{2^m}\}$ and one of the cosets of $\mathbb{F}_{2^m}^*$ becomes then $\{(0, y), y \in \mathbb{F}_{2^m}^*\}$ and the others become the sets $\{x, \lambda x\}, x \in \mathbb{F}_{2^m}^*\}$ where $\lambda \in \mathbb{F}_{2^m}$. We have then

$$f(x, y) = \begin{cases} tr_m\left(x\,\phi\left(\frac{y}{x}\right)\right) + g\left(\frac{y}{x}\right); & x \in \mathbb{F}_{2^m}^*, y \in \mathbb{F}_{2^m} \\ tr_m(a\,y) + \epsilon; & x = 0, y \in \mathbb{F}_{2^m}^* \\ f(0, 0); & x = y = 0, \end{cases} \tag{5.8}$$

where $a \in \mathbb{F}_{2^m}, \epsilon \in \mathbb{F}_2$, ϕ is a function from $\mathbb{F}_{2^m}$ to $\mathbb{F}_{2^m}$, g is a Boolean function over $\mathbb{F}_{2^m}$, and where the products $x\,\phi(\frac{y}{x})$ and $a\,y$ are calculated in $\mathbb{F}_{2^m}$.

We have then, for every $u, v \in \mathbb{F}_{2^m}$, that $W_f(u, v)$ equals

$$(-1)^{f(0)} + \sum_{y \in \mathbb{F}_{2^m}^*} (-1)^{tr_m(y(a+v))+\epsilon} + \sum_{x \in \mathbb{F}_{2^m}^*, y \in \mathbb{F}_{2^m}} (-1)^{tr_m(x[\phi(\frac{y}{x})+u+v\frac{y}{x}])+g(\frac{y}{x})}$$

$$= (-1)^{f(0)} - (-1)^{\epsilon} + \sum_{y \in \mathbb{F}_{2^m}} (-1)^{tr_m(y(a+v))+\epsilon} + \sum_{\substack{x \in \mathbb{F}_{2^m}^* \\ z \in \mathbb{F}_{2^m}}} (-1)^{tr_m(x[\phi(z)+u+vz])+g(z)}$$

$$= (-1)^{f(0)} + (2^m \delta_a(v) - 1)(-1)^{\epsilon} + 2^m \sum_{\substack{z \in \mathbb{F}_{2^m}; \\ \phi(z)+u+vz=0}} (-1)^{g(z)} - \sum_{z \in \mathbb{F}_{2^m}} (-1)^{g(z)}. \quad (5.9)$$

We have then $w_H(f) =$

$$2^{n-1} - \frac{1}{2} \left((-1)^{f(0)} + (2^m \delta_0(a) - 1)(-1)^{\epsilon} + 2^m \sum_{z \in \phi^{-1}(0)} (-1)^{g(z)} - \sum_{z \in \mathbb{F}_{2^m}} (-1)^{g(z)} \right)$$

and

$$nl(f) = 2^{n-1} - \frac{1}{2} A,$$

where A equals

$$\max_{u, v \in \mathbb{F}_{2^m}} \left| (-1)^{f(0)} + (2^m \delta_a(v) - 1)(-1)^{\epsilon} + 2^m \sum_{\substack{z \in \mathbb{F}_{2^m}; \\ \phi(z)+u+vz=0}} (-1)^{g(z)} - \sum_{z \in \mathbb{F}_{2^m}} (-1)^{g(z)} \right|.$$

5.2 Quadratic functions and their combinations

The next functions to be naturally considered after affine ones are quadratic ones. We shall see that they offer a compromise between robustness and simplicity. They will play roles in almost all domains addressed in the subsequent chapters.

5.2.1 *Quadratic Boolean functions*

The behavior of quadratic Boolean functions (*i.e.*, of the codewords of $RM(2, n)$) is rather simple (less, though, than that of affine functions). There are many results on their Walsh transform, that we shall try to present completely, but without being able to give all proofs, since this would take too much space.

Absolute value of the Walsh transform

Recall that Relation (2.55), page 62, states that, for every Boolean function f, we have $\mathcal{F}^2(f) = \sum_{b \in \mathbb{F}_2^n} \mathcal{F}(D_b f)$, where $\mathcal{F}(f) = \sum_{x \in \mathbb{F}_2^n} (-1)^{f(x)}$. If f is quadratic, then $D_b f$ is affine for every $b \in \mathbb{F}_2^n$, and is therefore either balanced or constant. Since $\mathcal{F}(g) = 0$ for every balanced function g, we deduce

$$\mathcal{F}^2(f) = 2^n \sum_{b \in \mathcal{E}_f} (-1)^{D_b f(0_n)}, \quad (5.10)$$

where $\mathcal{E}_f$ is the linear kernel (*i.e.*, the set of all $b \in \mathbb{F}_2^n$ such that $D_b f$ is constant; see Section 3.1). Since f is quadratic, $\mathcal{E}_f$ is also the kernel $\{x \in \mathbb{F}_2^n; \; \forall y \in \mathbb{F}_2^n, \; \beta_f(x, y) = 0\}$ of the symplectic[4] form associated to f:

$$\beta_f(x, y) = f(0_n) \oplus f(x) \oplus f(y) \oplus f(x + y).$$

In other words, $\mathcal{E}_f$ is the *radical* of the quadratic form.

The restriction of the function $b \mapsto D_b f(0_n) = f(b) \oplus f(0_n)$ to $\mathcal{E}_f$ being linear, since we have already seen after Definition 25, page 99, that the restriction of f to $\mathcal{E}_f$ is affine, we deduce from (5.10) that $\mathcal{F}^2(f)$ equals $2^n |\mathcal{E}_f|$ if $f(b) \oplus f(0_n)$ is null on $\mathcal{E}_f$ (*i.e.*, if f is constant on $\mathcal{E}_f$) and is null otherwise. Note that in the former case, f is constant on any coset $a + \mathcal{E}_f$ of $\mathcal{E}_f$, since f and $D_a f$ are constant on $\mathcal{E}_f$. According to Relation (2.35), page 57 (and since the linear kernel of $f(x) \oplus a \cdot x$ equals that of f), this proves the following proposition, which shows in particular that the absolute value of the Walsh transform of every quadratic Boolean function takes only two values, one of which is 0 (such functions will be called plateaued in Section 6.2).

Proposition 55 *[209] Let n be any positive integer. Any n-variable quadratic function f is unbalanced if and only if its restriction to its linear kernel $\mathcal{E}_f$ (i.e., the kernel of its associated symplectic form) is constant, or equivalently, if every constant derivative of f is null. Then, f is constant on any coset of $\mathcal{E}_f$ and the Hamming weight of f equals $2^{n-1} \pm 2^{\frac{n+k}{2}-1}$, where k is the dimension of $\mathcal{E}_f$.*

For every $a \in \mathbb{F}_2^n$ and every n-variable quadratic function f, $W_f(a)$ is nonzero if and only if the restriction of $f(x) \oplus a \cdot x$ to $\mathcal{E}_f$ is constant. Then, $W_f(a)$ equals $\pm 2^{\frac{n+k}{2}}$.

Note that Proposition 55 implies that f is balanced if and only if there exists $b \in \mathbb{F}_2^n$ such that the derivative $D_b f(x) = f(x) \oplus f(x + b)$ equals the constant function 1. For nonquadratic Boolean functions, this condition for f to be balanced is sufficient but not necessary.

Note that, according to Parseval's relation, there exists a such that $W_f(a) \neq 0$.

Proposition 55 implies that $\frac{n+k}{2}$ is an integer (because the Hamming weight is an integer), and then that the codimension of $\mathcal{E}_f$ must be even. This co-dimension is the *rank of β_f*, also called by abuse of language the rank of f. Note that, given two quadratic functions f and g, we have $|rank(f \oplus g) - rank(f)| \leq rank(g)$ because the rank of matrices is subadditive: $rank(A + B) \leq rank(A) + rank(B)$.

We also deduce

Corollary 9 *Let n be any positive integer and f any n-variable quadratic function. The nonlinearity of f equals $2^{n-1} - 2^{\frac{n+k}{2}-1} = 2^{n-1} - 2^{n-\frac{r_k(f)}{2}-1}$, where k is the dimension of the linear kernel of f and $r_k(f)$ is the rank of β_f.*

The Hamming weight of an n-variable quadratic Boolean function belongs then to the set $\{2^{n-1}\} \cup \{2^{n-1} \pm 2^i; i = \lceil \frac{n}{2} \rceil - 1, \ldots, n - 1\}$ and can be any element of this set, since

---

[4] Bilinear, symmetric, and null for $x = y$; the associated matrix is called a *symplectic matrix*.

it is easily seen that the dimension of the linear kernel in the case of function $x_1 x_2 \oplus x_3 x_4 \oplus \cdots \oplus x_{2r-1} x_{2r}$ equals $n - 2r$. The nonlinearity of an n-variable quadratic Boolean function can be any element of the set $\{2^{n-1} - 2^i; i = \lceil \frac{n}{2} \rceil - 1, \ldots, n - 1\}$, and if f has Hamming weight $2^{n-1} \pm 2^i$, then for every affine function l, the Hamming weight of the function $f \oplus l$ belongs to the set $\{2^{n-1} - 2^i, 2^{n-1}, 2^{n-1} + 2^i\}$.

The method seen above is particularly simple,[5] but it does not allow determining whether the Hamming weight is $2^{n-1} - 2^i$ or $2^{n-1} + 2^i$ when the function is not balanced, nor determining the sign of the Walsh transform. It may be much more difficult to calculate this sign than the absolute value. Such calculation is sometimes necessary. This is the case for instance when trying to determine the absolute value of the Walsh transform of a cubic function by applying Relation (2.55), page 62, or when we calculate the size of the preimage of an element $u \in \mathbb{F}_2^m$ by a quadratic function $F : \mathbb{F}_2^n \mapsto \mathbb{F}_2^m$, thanks to the formula $|\{x \in \mathbb{F}_2^n; F(x) = u\}| = 2^{-m} \sum_{x \in \mathbb{F}_2^n, v \in \mathbb{F}_2^m} (-1)^{v \cdot (F(x) + u)}$.

Dickson form of a quadratic function

A first important step, anterior to the method above, has been made by Dickson for calculating explicitly the Hamming weight of *quadratic functions*, by showing as described in [809, page 438] that any nonaffine quadratic Boolean function f over $\mathbb{F}_2^n$ is affinely equivalent to

$$x_1 x_2 \oplus \cdots \oplus x_{2r-1} x_{2r} \oplus \ell, \tag{5.11}$$

where $2r$ is the rank of the quadratic function and ℓ is an affine function (which can be taken equal, up to affine equivalence, to 0, 1 or x_{2r+1}). This is easily shown: by hypothesis, f has a monomial of degree 2 in its ANF, and we can assume without loss of generality that this monomial is $x_1 x_2$. The function has then the form $x_1 x_2 \oplus x_1 f_1(x_3, \ldots, x_n) \oplus x_2 f_2(x_3, \ldots, x_n) \oplus f_3(x_3, \ldots, x_n)$, where f_1, f_2 are affine functions and f_3 is quadratic. Then, $f(x) = (x_1 \oplus f_2(x_3, \ldots, x_n))(x_2 \oplus f_1(x_3, \ldots, x_n)) \oplus f_1(x_3, \ldots, x_n) f_2(x_3, \ldots, x_n) \oplus f_3(x_3, \ldots, x_n)$ is affinely equivalent to the function $x_1 x_2 \oplus f_1(x_3, \ldots, x_n) f_2(x_3, \ldots, x_n) \oplus f_3(x_3, \ldots, x_n)$. Applying this method recursively shows

Theorem 10 *Every quadratic nonaffine function is affinely equivalent to*

$$x_1 x_2 \oplus \cdots \oplus x_{2r-1} x_{2r} \oplus x_{2r+1} \tag{5.12}$$

(where $r \leq \frac{n-1}{2}$) if it is balanced, to

$$x_1 x_2 \oplus \cdots \oplus x_{2r-1} x_{2r} \tag{5.13}$$

(where $r \leq \frac{n}{2}$) if it has Hamming weight smaller than 2^{n-1} and to

$$x_1 x_2 \oplus \cdots \oplus x_{2r-1} x_{2r} \oplus 1 \tag{5.14}$$

(where $r \leq \frac{n}{2}$) if it has Hamming weight larger than 2^{n-1}.

---

[5] Theoretically; in practice, calculating the dimension of the linear kernel is not always an easy task.

The unique expressions (5.12), (5.13), and (5.14) are called the *Dickson form* of the quadratic function. They allow describing precisely the weight distribution of $RM(2, n)$ [809, page 441].

Walsh transform when the function is given by its ANF

We have seen how a quadratic Boolean function can be put in the form $g(L(x)+b)$, where L is a linear automorphism and g is in Dickson form. Thanks to Relation (2.58), page 63, and to Lemma 4, page 58, it is then enough to be able to calculate $\sum_{x \in \mathbb{F}_2^n} (-1)^{x_1 x_2 \oplus \cdots \oplus x_{2r-1} x_{2r} \oplus u \cdot x}$, for every $u \in \mathbb{F}_2^n$ and every $r \in \{1, \ldots, \lfloor \frac{n}{2} \rfloor\}$. This sum equals

$$\sum_{x \in \mathbb{F}_2^n} (-1)^{\bigoplus_{i=1}^r [(x_{2i-1} \oplus u_{2i})(x_{2i} \oplus u_{2i-1}) \oplus u_{2i-1} u_{2i}] \oplus u_{2r+1} x_{2r+1} \oplus \cdots \oplus u_n x_n}$$

and equals then $2^{n-r}(-1)^{\bigoplus_{i=1}^r u_{2i-1} u_{2i}}$ if $u_{2r+1} = \cdots = u_n = 0$ and 0 otherwise. Since the dimension k of the kernel $\mathcal{E}_f$ of the symplectic form $\beta_f(x, y)$ equals $n - 2r$, this shows again that the Walsh transform $W_f(u)$ lies in $\{0, \pm 2^{(n+k)/2}\} = \{0, \pm 2^{n-r}\}$ for every u. But we have also the sign of $W_f(u)$.

Remark. Any quadratic function belongs to the *completed Maiorana–McFarland class*; this can be easily seen from its Dickson form. Note, however, that given a quadratic function in Maiorana–McFarland form $f(x, y) = x \cdot (L(y) + b) \oplus g(y)$, where $x \in \mathbb{F}_2^k$, $y \in \mathbb{F}_2^{n-k}$ and L is linear, the linear kernel of f is not $E = \mathbb{F}_2^k \times \{0_k\}$, in general, despite the fact that $D_a D_{a'} f$ is null for $a, a' \in E$. Indeed, writing $a = (a_1, a_2)$, we have $D_a f(x, y) = x \cdot L(a_2) \oplus a_1 \cdot L(y + a_2) \oplus a_1 \cdot b \oplus D_{a_2} g(y)$, and we do not have necessarily that $D_a f$ is contant for $a \in E$. □

Remark. According to Theorem 2, page 63, the functions whose Walsh transform values are all divisible by 2^{n-1} are quadratic. According to Theorem 10, they are the sums of an affine function and of the product of two affine functions. This proves one of the points that we asserted at page 65. □

More general approach on the Walsh transform

Calculating the Dickson form of a quadratic Boolean function in generic number n of variables is most often impossible when the function is given by its trace representation. As originally shown by Dillon and Dobbertin in [448, appendix A] for the case of functions $tr_n(x^{2^i+1})$ and generalized by Hou to all quadratic functions, there is a possibility of relating all the values of the Walsh transform to one of them (which needs of course to be nonzero; we know by the Parseval relation that such nonzero value necessarily exists). If the sign of one of these nonzero Walsh values is known, then all will be deduced.

X. Hou in [625] calculates the product of two nonzero Walsh values, instead of calculating the square of one value as we did in Proposition 55. This has the interest of providing the sign of every value $W_f(u)$, knowing one of them. Hou works with quadratic functions in trace form. This does not reduce theoretically the generality of his results since any function admits a trace form. However, in practice, if a Boolean function is given by its

ANF, it is nonnegligible work to first determine its trace representation; and if, instead of working with a particular function in a particular number of variables, we work with all functions with an ANF of some form in arbitrary number of variables, it is most often impossible. We shall then revisit Hou's result in a way that will not depend on a particular representation of the functions. Subsequently, we shall see what this result gives in trace representation.

Hou needs to assume that $W_f(0_n) \neq 0$ (*i.e.*, that f is unbalanced). This does not reduce the generality since, if f is balanced, we can apply the result to one of the unbalanced functions $f(x) \oplus b \cdot x$. We assume then that $W_f(0_n) \neq 0$. This means according to Proposition 55 that any constant derivative of f is null on $\mathbb{F}_2^n$, *i.e.*, for every $x \in \mathcal{E}_f$, we have $f(x) = f(0_n)$.

We have $W_f(0_n)W_f(a) = \displaystyle\sum_{x,y\in\mathbb{F}_2^n} (-1)^{f(x)\oplus f(y)\oplus a\cdot y} = \sum_{x,y\in\mathbb{F}_2^n} (-1)^{f(x+y)\oplus f(y)\oplus a\cdot y}$. For every $x \in \mathbb{F}_2^n$, function $y \mapsto f(x+y)\oplus f(y)\oplus a\cdot y$ is affine. We are then in the same situation as in Proposition 55, but with the advantage that we shall know the product of the signs of $W_f(0_n)$ and $W_f(a)$ when $W_f(a)$ will be nonzero. The sum $\sum_{y\in\mathbb{F}_2^n}(-1)^{f(x+y)\oplus f(y)\oplus a\cdot y}$ is nonzero if and only if function $y \mapsto f(x+y) \oplus f(y) \oplus a \cdot y$ is constant over $\mathbb{F}_2^n$. The set of those $x \in \mathbb{F}_2^n$ having such property either is empty or is a coset of the linear kernel $\mathcal{E}_f$, since $f(x+y)\oplus f(y)\oplus a\cdot y\oplus f(x'+y)\oplus f(y)\oplus a\cdot y = D_{x+x'}f(x+y)$. Moreover, the constant values of $f(x+y) \oplus f(y) \oplus a \cdot y$ are the same for all those x that belong to this coset, since $W_f(0_n)$ being nonzero, D_xf is the zero function for every $x \in \mathcal{E}_f$ (according to Proposition 55). The next proposition is a version made as general as possible of the main result from [625].

Proposition 56 *Let n be any positive integer and f any unbalanced quadratic n-variable function. Let W_f be the Walsh transform associated to some inner product ".". Then, for every $a \in \mathbb{F}_2^n$, the value of $W_f(a)$ is nonzero if and only if there exists x in $\mathbb{F}_2^n$ such that the function $y \mapsto f(x+y) \oplus f(y) \oplus a \cdot y$ is constant on $\mathbb{F}_2^n$. The set of such x is then a coset of $\mathcal{E}_f$ and we have $W_f(0_n)W_f(a) = 2^{n+dim\,\mathcal{E}_f}(-1)^{f(x)\oplus f(0_n)}$.*

The determination, for given a, of the set of those x such that $a \cdot y$ coincides with function $D_xf(y)$ or with function $D_xf(y)\oplus 1$ leads in Hou's method to the resolution of an equation, which is over $\mathbb{F}_{2^n}$ in his paper since f is taken in trace representation, and that we shall see below. This determination is necessary for calculating $W_f(a)$ explicitly and is the difficult part of this method in practice.

We now introduce a slightly different viewpoint (which has never been addressed as is, as far as we know). We start with the vector space $\{a \in \mathbb{F}_2^n; \exists x \in \mathbb{F}_2^n; \forall y \in \mathbb{F}_2^n, a \cdot y = \beta_f(x,y)\}$, which we denote by $\mathcal{E}'_f$, for reasons that will appear below. After identification between $\mathbb{F}_2^n$ and the vector space of its linear forms[6] through the correspondence $a \longleftrightarrow (y \to a \cdot y)$, we can view $\mathcal{E}'_f$ as the image of $\mathbb{F}_2^n$ by the linear function $x \to (y \to \beta_f(x,y))$. This linear function having kernel $\mathcal{E}_f$, the dimension of $\mathcal{E}'_f$ equals $n - dim\,\mathcal{E}_f$. Moreover,

---

[6] This vector space is called in mathematics the dual space (here of $\mathbb{F}_2^n$), but we shall avoid using this denomination, for obvious reasons.

if $a \in \mathcal{E}'_f$ then $a \cdot y$ is null over $\mathcal{E}_f$, and since the dimension of the vector space $\mathcal{E}_f^{\perp} = \{a \in \mathbb{F}_2^n ; \forall y \in \mathcal{E}_f, a \cdot y = 0\}$ is equal to $n - dim\, \mathcal{E}_f$ as well, we have

$$\mathcal{E}'_f = \mathcal{E}_f^{\perp}.$$

According to Proposition 55, for every $b \in \mathbb{F}_2^n$, $W_f(b)$ is nonzero if and only if the function $x \mapsto f(x) \oplus f(0_n) \oplus b \cdot x$ is null on $\mathcal{E}_f$, and the Walsh support of f equals then $b + \mathcal{E}_f^{\perp} = b + \mathcal{E}'_f$. For every $a \in \mathcal{E}'_f$, choosing $x \in \mathbb{F}_2^n$ such that $a \cdot y = \beta_f(x, y)$, we have

$$\begin{aligned}
W_f(a + b) &= \sum_{y \in \mathbb{F}_2^n} (-1)^{f(y) \oplus (a+b) \cdot y} = \sum_{y \in \mathbb{F}_2^n} (-1)^{f(y) \oplus \beta_f(x,y) \oplus b \cdot y} \\
&= \sum_{y \in \mathbb{F}_2^n} (-1)^{f(x+y) \oplus f(x) \oplus f(0_n) \oplus b \cdot y} = \sum_{y \in \mathbb{F}_2^n} (-1)^{f(y) \oplus f(x) \oplus f(0_n) \oplus b \cdot (x+y)} \\
&= (-1)^{f(x) \oplus f(0_n) \oplus b \cdot x} \sum_{y \in \mathbb{F}_2^n} (-1)^{f(y) \oplus b \cdot y} = (-1)^{f(x) \oplus f(0_n) \oplus b \cdot x} \, W_f(b).
\end{aligned}$$

Proposition 57 *Let f be any quadratic n-variable Boolean function and let W_f be its Walsh transform associated to some inner product "$\cdot$". Let $\beta_f(x, y) = f(x + y) \oplus f(x) \oplus f(y) \oplus f(0_n)$ be the symplectic form associated to f. Let b be any element of $\mathbb{F}_2^n$ such that $W_f(b) \neq 0$. Then, for every $a \in \mathbb{F}_2^n$, we have $W_f(a + b) \neq 0$ if and only if $a \in \mathcal{E}_f^{\perp} = \{u \in \mathbb{F}_2^n; u \cdot y = 0, \forall y \in \mathcal{E}_f\}$, which is equivalent to saying that there exists $x \in \mathbb{F}_2^n$ such that the functions $y \mapsto a \cdot y$ and $y \mapsto \beta_f(x, y)$ coincide over $\mathbb{F}_2^n$, and we have then*

$$W_f(a + b) = (-1)^{f(x) \oplus f(0_n) \oplus b \cdot x} \, W_f(b).$$

Quadratic functions in trace form

We know (see Subsection 2.2.2, page 41) that any quadratic function $f(x)$ over $\mathbb{F}_{2^n}$ can be written in a unique way under the form

$$f(x) = tr_n \left(\sum_{k=1}^{\lfloor (n-1)/2 \rfloor} a_k x^{2^k+1} \right) \oplus q(x); \quad a_k \in \mathbb{F}_{2^n}, \tag{5.15}$$

where

$$\begin{cases} \text{if } n \text{ is even, } q(x) = tr_{n/2} \left(a_{n/2} x^{2^{n/2}+1} \right) + \ell(x); \; a_{n/2} \in \mathbb{F}_{2^{n/2}}, \; \ell \text{ affine,} \\ \text{if } n \text{ is odd, } q(x) = \ell(x); \; \ell \text{ affine.} \end{cases} \tag{5.16}$$

We have then, using that, for every $u \in \mathbb{F}_2^n$ and $j \in \mathbb{N}$, we can replace $tr_n(u)$ by $tr_n(u^{2^j})$ and u^{2^n} by u:

$$\beta_f(x, y) = tr_n \left(y \left[\sum_{k=1}^{\lfloor (n-1)/2 \rfloor} \left(a_k x^{2^k} + a_k^{2^{n-k}} x^{2^{n-k}} \right) \right] \right) + \beta_q(x, y),$$

where $\beta_q(x, y) = tr_{n/2}(a_{n/2}(x^{2^{n/2}}y + xy^{2^{n/2}})) = tr_{n/2}(a_{n/2}tr^n_{n/2}(x^{2^{n/2}}y)) = tr_n(a_{n/2}yx^{2^{n/2}})$
for n even and $\beta_q(x, y) = 0$ for n odd. We have then

$$
\mathcal{E}_f = \begin{cases} \left\{ x \in \mathbb{F}_{2^n}; \sum_{k=1}^{\frac{n}{2}-1} \left(a_k x^{2^k} + a_k^{2^{n-k}} x^{2^{n-k}} \right) + a_{n/2} x^{2^{n/2}} = 0 \right\}, & \text{for } n \text{ even,} \\ \left\{ x \in \mathbb{F}_{2^n}; \sum_{k=1}^{\frac{n-1}{2}} \left(a_k x^{2^k} + a_k^{2^{n-k}} x^{2^{n-k}} \right) = 0 \right\}, & \text{for } n \text{ odd.} \end{cases}
$$

Hou has observed a useful property for evaluating the size of $\mathcal{E}_f$, and therefore the nonlinearity, of any quadratic Boolean function in trace form:

Proposition 58 *[625] Let f be any quadratic n-variable function in the form (5.15), with $q = 0$. Denoting by K the maximal value of k such that $a_k \neq 0$, $|\mathcal{E}_f|$ equals the degree of the following polynomial:*

$$
gcd\left(\left(\sum_{k=1}^{\lfloor(n-1)/2\rfloor} \left(a_k x^{2^k} + a_k^{2^{n-k}} x^{2^{n-k}} \right) \right)^{2^K}, x^{2^n} + x \right).
$$

Indeed, $x^{2^n} + x$ splits completely over $\mathbb{F}_{2^n}$ and $|\mathcal{E}_f|$ equals the number of solutions in $\mathbb{F}_{2^n}$ of the equation $\sum_{k=1}^{\lfloor(n-1)/2\rfloor} \left(a_k x^{2^k} + a_k^{2^{n-k}} x^{2^{n-k}} \right) = 0$, which has no repeated root, because its derivative (as a polynomial) has no common zero with the equation.

Let us see now how the method we introduced works in univariate representation. According to Proposition 57, and taking for inner product $a \cdot x = tr_n(ax)$, we have the following:

Proposition 59 *Let $f(x)$ be any quadratic function. Let*

$$
tr_n\left(\sum_{k=1}^{\lfloor(n-1)/2\rfloor} a_k x^{2^k+1} \right) + q(x)
$$

be its trace form, where $q(x)$ is defined in Relation (5.16). Let

$$
P_f(x) = \sum_{k=1}^{\lfloor(n-1)/2\rfloor} \left(a_k x^{2^k} + a_k^{2^{n-k}} x^{2^{n-k}} \right) \text{ if } n \text{ is odd,} \tag{5.17}
$$

and

$$
P_f(x) = \sum_{k=1}^{\lfloor(n-1)/2\rfloor} \left(a_k x^{2^k} + a_k^{2^{n-k}} x^{2^{n-k}} \right) + a_{n/2} x^{2^{n/2}} \text{ if } n \text{ is even.} \tag{5.18}
$$

Let b be any element of $\mathbb{F}_{2^n}$ such that $W_f(b)$ is nonzero. For every $a \in \mathbb{F}_{2^n}$, $W_f(a + b)$ is nonzero if and only if there exists $x \in \mathbb{F}_{2^n}$ such that $a = P_f(x)$ and we have then

$$
W_f(a + b) = (-1)^{f(x) \oplus f(0) \oplus b \cdot x} W_f(b).
$$

Remark. The observation that $\mathcal{E}_f^{\perp}$ is at the same time equal to $\{a \in \mathbb{F}_{2^n}; \exists x \in \mathbb{F}_{2^n}; \forall y \in \mathbb{F}_{2^n}, a \cdot y = \beta_f(x, y)\}$ and to $\{a \in \mathbb{F}_{2^n}; \forall y \in \mathcal{E}_f, a \cdot y = 0\}$ gives, when applied to function

f in (5.15), that $P_f(a) = 0$ if and only if there exists $x \in \mathbb{F}_{2^n}$ such that $a = P_f(x)$, where P_f is defined by (5.17) (resp. (5.18)). This gives a parameterized form of the set of solutions. □

Particular classes of *quadratic functions* Particular quadratic Boolean functions have been successfully investigated in the 1970s. For some of them, the explicit Walsh transform could be given in a rather simple statement. This begun with Kerdock [689] when he constructed the so-called Kerdock codes (but the question of the sign was not posed, because his code is a union of cosets of the first-order Reed–Muller code, and two complementary functions f and $f \oplus 1$ have opposite Walsh transforms). Then Carlitz showed in [332] the following equalities on so-called *cubic sums* $\sum_{x \in \mathbb{F}_{2^n}} (-1)^{tr_n(wx^3 + ux)}$, $w \neq 0$ (this name being a reference to the polynomial degree of the functions, not to their algebraic degree, which is 2):

- Let n be an odd integer and $u \in \mathbb{F}_{2^n}$. For $tr_n(u) = 1$, we denote by $\gamma \in \mathbb{F}_{2^n}$ any element in $\mathbb{F}_{2^n}$ such that $u = \gamma^4 + \gamma + 1$. We have

$$
\sum_{x \in \mathbb{F}_{2^n}} (-1)^{tr_n(x^3 + ux)} = \begin{cases} (-1)^{tr_n(\gamma^3 + \gamma)} (\frac{2}{n}) 2^{\frac{n+1}{2}} & \text{when } tr_n(u) = 1 \\ 0 & \text{when } tr_n(u) = 0, \end{cases}
$$

where $(\frac{2}{n})$ denotes the *Jacobi symbol* that equals $(-1)^{\frac{n^2-1}{8}}$ when n is odd. If we know the sign of the Walsh transform at 1, this can be deduced from Propositions 55 and 59, after observing that the linear kernel of function $tr_n(x^3)$ equals $\{x \in \mathbb{F}_{2^n}; x^2 + x^{2^{n-1}} = 0\} = \{0\} \cup \{x \in \mathbb{F}_{2^n}; x^3 = 1\}$, which equals $\mathbb{F}_2$ since n is odd. The additional information we have thanks to Carlitz is the sign of the Walsh transform at 1.

The value of $\sum_{x \in \mathbb{F}_{2^n}} (-1)^{tr_n(wx^3 + ux)}$ equals $\sum_{x \in \mathbb{F}_{2^n}} (-1)^{tr_n\left(x^3 + \frac{u}{w^{1/3}} x\right)}$ (by the change of variable $x \mapsto \frac{x}{w^{\frac{1}{3}}}$; note that since n is odd, function x^3 is a permutation of $\mathbb{F}_{2^n}$; we denote the inverse function by $x^{\frac{1}{3}}$; the value of $\frac{1}{3}$ can be found in [731, 907]).
- Let n be an even integer. Then we have two cases according to whether w is a cube or not:

  - If $w \neq 0$ is a cube, say $w = v^3$, then for $tr_2^n(uv^{-1}) = 0$, we denote by γ_0 any element in $\mathbb{F}_{2^n}$ such that $\gamma_0^4 + \gamma_0 = u^2 v^{-2}$. We have

$$
\sum_{x \in \mathbb{F}_{2^n}} (-1)^{tr_n(wx^3 + ux)} = \begin{cases} (-1)^{\frac{n}{2}+1+tr_n(\gamma_0^3)} 2^{\frac{n}{2}+1} & \text{when } tr_2^n(uv^{-1}) = 0 \\ 0 & \text{when } tr_2^n(uv^{-1}) \neq 0. \end{cases}
$$

    If we know the sign of the Walsh transform at 0, this is deduced from Propositions 55 and 59 after observing that the linear kernel of function $tr_n(wx^3)$ equals $\{x \in \mathbb{F}_{2^n}; wx^2 + (wx)^{2^{n-1}} = 0\} = \{0\} \cup \{x \in \mathbb{F}_{2^n}; wx^3 = 1\} = v\mathbb{F}_4$.
  - If w is not a cube, then let γ_1 be the unique element in $\mathbb{F}_{2^n}$ such that $w^2 \gamma_1^4 + w\gamma_1 = u^2$. Such γ_1 exists and is unique because the linear function $\gamma \mapsto w^2 \gamma^4 + w\gamma$ has a

trivial kernel (the linear kernel of function $tr_n(wx^3)$ equals $\{0\}$ since w is not a cube) and is then bijective. Then we have

$$\sum_{x\in\mathbb{F}_{2^n}} (-1)^{tr_n(wx^3+ux)} = (-1)^{\frac{n}{2}+tr_n(w\gamma_1^3)}2^{\frac{n}{2}}.$$

Coulter [384, 385] and Dillon–Dobbertin [448] generalized Carlitz's results to exponents of the form 2^k+1 instead of 3. Their results can be deduced from Proposition 59 as well. To illustrate how, let us assume that n is odd and $\gcd(k,n)=1$. Then x^{2^k+1} is a permutation. We can then reduce ourselves to the sums $\sum_{x\in\mathbb{F}_{2^n}} (-1)^{tr_n(x^{2^k+1}+ux)}$. The linear kernel of quadratic function $tr_n(x^{2^k+1})$ has equation $x^{2^k} + x^{2^{-k}} = 0$, that is, $x^{2^{2k}} + x = 0$, which has for solutions in $\mathbb{F}_{2^n}$ the elements of $\mathbb{F}_{2^{\gcd(2k,n)}} = \mathbb{F}_2$, and $tr_n(x^{2^k+1} + ux)$ is then balanced if and only if $tr_n(u) = 0$. We assume then $tr_n(u) = 1$, and there exists a such that $u = 1 + a^{2^k} + a^{2^{-k}}$. Then since $tr_n((x+a)^{2^k+1}) = tr_n(x^{2^k+1} + (a^{2^k} + a^{2^{-k}})x + a^{2^k+1})$, we have $\sum_{x\in\mathbb{F}_{2^n}} (-1)^{tr_n(x^{2^k+1}+ux)} = (-1)^{tr_n(a^{2^k+1})} \sum_{x\in\mathbb{F}_{2^n}} (-1)^{tr_n(x^{2^k+1}+x)}$.

As we wrote, much work has been done on the Walsh transform of quadratic functions in univariate form. We shall give the next ones without giving clues on their proofs.

For n odd, the quadratic functions of nonlinearity $2^{n-1} - 2^{\frac{n-1}{2}}$ (called *semi-bent functions* or *near-bent* functions; their extended Walsh spectra only contain values 0 and $2^{\frac{n+1}{2}}$; see Section 6.2) of the form $tr_n(\sum_{i=1}^{(n-1)/2} c_i x^{2^i+1})$ have been studied by Khoo et al. [697, 699]. The study of such functions is simplified when all coefficients c_i belong to $\mathbb{F}_2$ since the linearized polynomial $\sum_{i=1}^{(n-1)/2}(c_i x^{2^i} + (c_i x)^{2^{n-i}}) = \sum_{i=1}^{(n-1)/2} c_i(x^{2^i} + x^{2^{n-i}})$ is then a 2-polynomial over $\mathbb{F}_2$ (see page 490), and its study can be done through its 2-associate polynomial $c(x) = \sum_{i=1}^{(n-1)/2} c_i(x^i + x^{n-i})$, more precisely, its gcd with $x^n + 1$ (e.g., near-bentness is equivalent to $\gcd(c(x), x^n + 1) = x + 1$), and the factorization of $x^n + 1$ (see [697, 699], and see more in [19, 510, 672, 840, 841]). If n and $2n + 1$ are primes, the function is near-bent for all non-all-zero c_i. This study has been generalized to n even by Charpin et al. in [355] ($\gcd(c(x), x^n + 1) = x + 1$ is then replaced by $\gcd(c(x), x^n + 1) = x^2 + 1$) and nonquadratic bent functions have been deduced by concatenation of such near-bent functions. Further functions of this kind have been given and studied in [629, 672, 699, 840, 841].

The sign of the values of the Walsh transform of AB Gold and Kasami functions (see pages 206 and 230) is studied in [734]. The former are quadratic (the latter are not, but they are related to quadratic functions). In [548], the result of [734] is generalized: for every AB power function x^d over $\mathbb{F}_{2^n}$ whose restriction to any subfield of $\mathbb{F}_{2^n}$ is also AB, the value $\sum_{x\in\mathbb{F}_{2^n}} (-1)^{tr_n(x^d+x)}$ equals $2^{\frac{n+1}{2}}$ if $n \equiv \pm 1$ [mod 8] and $-2^{\frac{n+1}{2}}$ if $n \equiv \pm 3$ [mod 8]. In [383], the authors studied the Walsh transform values of the functions $tr_n(x^{2^a+1} + x^{2^b+1})$, $\gcd(b - a, n) = \gcd(b + a, n) = 1$.

X. Hou in [625] has been able to address whole subclasses of quadratic functions (and even more since he could view such functions over every field extension of $\mathbb{F}_{2^n}$). With the method of calculating $W_f(0)W_f(a)$, he determined the Walsh transform of any quadratic function whose trace form involves exponents of the form $2^k + 1$, where k has fixed 2-valuation.

X. Zhang et al. in [1165] use that, given a linear function $L(x) = \sum_{k=0}^{n-1} a_k x^{2^k} \in \mathbb{F}_{2^n}[x]$, and denoting $\widetilde{L}(x) = \sum_{k=0}^{n-1} a_k^{2^{n-k}} x^{2^{n-k}}$, we have $tr_n(x L(y)) = tr_n(y \widetilde{L}(x))$ for every $x, y \in \mathbb{F}_{2^n}$. For every linear permutation L and linear function L', we have $tr_n\big(x\,(\widetilde{L} \circ L' \circ L(x))\big) = tr_n\big(L(x)\,(L' \circ L(x))\big)$, and then

$$\sum_{x \in \mathbb{F}_{2^n}} (-1)^{tr_n(x(\widetilde{L} \circ L' \circ L(x)))} = \sum_{x \in \mathbb{F}_{2^n}} (-1)^{tr_n(L(x)\,(L' \circ L(x)))} = \sum_{x \in \mathbb{F}_{2^n}} (-1)^{tr_n(xL'(x))}.$$

The functions $f(x) = tr_n\big(x\,(\widetilde{L} \circ L' \circ L(x))\big)$ and $g(x) = tr_n\big(x\,L'(x)\big)$ satisfy then $\mathcal{F}(f) = \mathcal{F}(g)$. This provides in fact an equivalence relation between quadratic functions, which preserves the mapping $f \mapsto \mathcal{F}(f)$.

5.2.2 Concatenations of quadratic functions

Concatenated quadratic functions (instead of affine functions) generalize the Maiorana–McFarland construction. These functions are a little harder to study than Maiorana–McFarland's functions, but they are more numerous and they avoid the property of null second-order derivatives seen in Proposition 54, page 167, which may be a cryptographic weakness. There are at least two classes:

- A first class [221] is built on the Dickson form of quadratic functions:

$$f_{\psi,\phi,g}(x, y) = \bigoplus_{i=1}^{t} x_{2i-1} x_{2i}\, \psi_i(y) \oplus x \cdot \phi(y) \oplus g(y), \tag{5.19}$$

with $x \in \mathbb{F}_2^r$, $y \in \mathbb{F}_2^s$, where $n = r + s$, $t = \lfloor \frac{r}{2} \rfloor$, and where $\psi : \mathbb{F}_2^s \to \mathbb{F}_2^t$, $\phi : \mathbb{F}_2^s \to \mathbb{F}_2^r$ and $g : \mathbb{F}_2^s \to \mathbb{F}_2$ can be chosen arbitrarily.

The size of this class roughly equals $2^{(t+r+1)2^s}$. The Walsh transform is easily deduced from the observation that, for every quadratic Boolean function of the form $f(x) = \bigoplus_{i=1}^{t} u_i x_{2i-1} x_{2i} \oplus \sum_{j=1}^{2t} v_j x_j \oplus c$, where $u_i, v_j, c \in \mathbb{F}_2, x \in \mathbb{F}_2^{2t}$, and for every element a of $\mathbb{F}_2^{2t}$, if there exists $i = 1, \ldots, t$ such that $u_i = 0$ and $v_{2i-1} \neq a_{2i-1}$ or $v_{2i} \neq a_{2i}$, then we have $W_f(a) = 0$, and otherwise, $W_f(a)$ is equal to $2^{2t - w_H(u)}(-1)^{\sum_{i=1}^{t}(v_{2i-1} \oplus a_{2i-1})(v_{2i} \oplus a_{2i}) \oplus c}$, where $u = (u_1, \ldots, u_t)$. This implies that, for every function f of the form (5.19), for every $a \in \mathbb{F}_2^r$ and every $b \in \mathbb{F}_2^s$, we have

$$W_{f_{\psi,\phi,g}}(a, b) = \sum_{y \in E_a} 2^{r - w_H(\psi(y))}(-1)^{\sum_{i=1}^{t}(\phi_{2i-1}(y) \oplus a_{2i-1})(\phi_{2i}(y) \oplus a_{2i}) \oplus g(y) \oplus y \cdot b},$$

where E_a is the superset of $\phi^{-1}(a)$ equal if r is even to

$$\big\{ y \in \mathbb{F}_2^s / \ \forall i \leq t, \ \psi_i(y) = 0 \Rightarrow (\phi_{2i-1}(y) = a_{2i-1} \text{ and } \phi_{2i}(y) = a_{2i}) \big\},$$

and if r is odd to

$$\left\{ y \in \mathbb{F}_2^s / \ \left\{ \begin{array}{l} \forall i \leq t, \ \psi_i(y) = 0 \Rightarrow (\phi_{2i-1}(y) = a_{2i-1} \text{ and } \phi_{2i}(y) = a_{2i}) \\ \phi_r(y) = a_r \end{array} \right. \right\}.$$

- A second class [317] has for elements the concatenations of quadratic functions of rank at most 2, of the form

$$f_{\phi_1,\phi_2,\phi_3,g}(x,y) = (x \cdot \phi_1(y))(x \cdot \phi_2(y)) \oplus x \cdot \phi_3(y) \oplus g(y), \qquad (5.20)$$

with $x \in \mathbb{F}_2^r$, $y \in \mathbb{F}_2^s$, where ϕ_1, ϕ_2 and ϕ_3 are three functions from $\mathbb{F}_2^s$ into $\mathbb{F}_2^r$ and g is any Boolean function on $\mathbb{F}_2^s$. The size of this class roughly equals $2^{(3r+1)2^s}$ (the exact number, which is unknown, is smaller since a function can be represented in this form in several ways) and is larger than for the first class.

The Walsh transform is deduced from the fact that, for every positive integer r and every Boolean function f on $\mathbb{F}_2^r$ of the form $(u \cdot x)(v \cdot x) \oplus w \cdot x$; $u,v,w \in \mathbb{F}_2^r$:

- If u and v are $\mathbb{F}_2$-linearly independent (*i.e.*, $u \neq 0_r, v \neq 0_r$ and $u \neq v$), then f is balanced if and only if w is outside the vectorspace $< u,v > = \{0_r, u, v, u+v\}$ spanned by u and v, and otherwise, if $w \in \{0_r, u, v\}$, then $\sum_{x \in \mathbb{F}_2^r}(-1)^{f(x)}$ equals 2^{r-1}, and if $w = u+v$, then it equals -2^{r-1}.
- If u and v are $\mathbb{F}_2$-linearly dependent, then if we have $w = 0_r$ and $u = 0_r$ or $v = 0_r$, or if we have $u = v = w$, then $\sum_{x \in \mathbb{F}_2^r}(-1)^{f(x)}$ equals 2^r; otherwise, $\sum_{x \in \mathbb{F}_2^r}(-1)^{f(x)}$ is null.

We deduce that for any function $f_{\phi_1,\phi_2,\phi_3,g}$ of the form (5.20) with $\phi_2(y) \neq 0_r$ for every $y \in \mathbb{F}_2^s$, denoting by E the set of all $y \in \mathbb{F}_2^s$ such that the vectors $\phi_1(y)$ and $\phi_2(y)$ are $\mathbb{F}_2$-linearly independent, for every $a \in \mathbb{F}_2^r$ and every $b \in \mathbb{F}_2^s$, $W_{f_{\phi_1,\phi_2,\phi_3,g}}(a,b)$ equals

$$2^{r-1} \sum_{\substack{y \in E; \\ \phi_3(y)+a \in \{0_r,\phi_1(y),\phi_2(y)\}}} (-1)^{g(y) \oplus b \cdot y} - 2^{r-1} \sum_{\substack{y \in E; \\ \phi_3(y)+a=\phi_1(y)+\phi_2(y)}} (-1)^{g(y) \oplus b \cdot y}$$

$$+ 2^r \sum_{\substack{y \in \mathbb{F}_2^s \setminus E; \\ \phi_3(y)+a=\phi_1(y)}} (-1)^{g(y) \oplus b \cdot y}.$$

5.3 Cubic functions

The *Hamming weight*s and the Walsh spectra of nonquadratic cubic Boolean functions (*i.e.*, of the codewords in $RM(3,n) \setminus RM(2,n))$ behave in a much less peculiar way than quadratic functions.[7] This has been shown in [210] as follows. Let f_1, f_2 and f_3 be any Boolean functions on $\mathbb{F}_2^n$. Define the function on $\mathbb{F}_2^{n+2}$: $f(x,y_1,y_2) = y_1 y_2 \oplus y_1 f_1(x) \oplus y_2 f_2(x) \oplus f_3(x)$. Then we have

$$\mathcal{F}(f) = \sum_{x \in \mathbb{F}_2^n; y_1,y_2 \in \mathbb{F}_2} (-1)^{(y_1 \oplus f_2(x))(y_2 \oplus f_1(x)) \oplus f_1(x) f_2(x) \oplus f_3(x)}$$

$$= \sum_{x \in \mathbb{F}_2^n; y_1,y_2 \in \mathbb{F}_2} (-1)^{y_1 y_2 \oplus f_1(x) f_2(x) \oplus f_3(x)} = 2 \sum_{x \in \mathbb{F}_2^n} (-1)^{f_1(x) f_2(x) \oplus f_3(x)}.$$

---

[7] Except that, according to McEliece's theorem, the Hamming weights are divisible by $2^{\lceil \frac{n}{3} \rceil - 1}$ and the Walsh transform values are divisible by $2^{\lceil \frac{n}{3} \rceil}$).

So, starting with a function $g = f_1 f_2 \oplus f_3$, we can relate $\mathcal{F}(g)$ to $\mathcal{F}(f)$, in two more variables, in which the term $f_1 f_2$ has been replaced by $y_1 y_2 \oplus y_1 f_1(x) \oplus y_2 f_2(x)$. Applying this repeatedly ("breaking" this way all the monomials of degrees at least 4), this shows that, for every Boolean function g on $\mathbb{F}_2^n$, there exists an integer m and a Boolean function f of algebraic degree at most 3 on $\mathbb{F}_2^{n+2m}$ whose Walsh transform takes the value $W_f(0_{n+2m}) = 2^m W_g(0_n)$ at zero. This proves that the functions of algebraic degree 3 can have Hamming weights much more diverse than functions of degrees at most 2, since function g from which we started can have for Hamming weight any integer between 0 and 2^n, and then $W_g(0_n)$ can take any even value between -2^n and 2^n.

Note, however, that the weights of some cubic functions (and even some quartic ones) are easily determined. The weight of the product fg of two quadratic functions and of its sum with any affine function can be deduced from $fg = \frac{f+g-(f\oplus g)}{2}$. And the Fourier–Hadamard transform being $\mathbb{R}$-linear, we have $\widehat{fg} = \frac{\hat{f}+\hat{g}-\widehat{f\oplus g}}{2}$. This works, for instance, for $\sigma_3 = \sigma_1 \sigma_2$, where σ_i is the ith elementary symmetric Boolean function. See also [745].

5.4 Indicators of flats

As we have already seen, a Boolean function f is the *indicator* of a flat A of codimension r if and only if it has the form $f(x) = \prod_{i=1}^r (a_i \cdot x \oplus \epsilon_i)$, where $a_1, \ldots, a_r \in \mathbb{F}_2^n$ are $\mathbb{F}_2$-linearly independent and $\epsilon_1, \ldots, \epsilon_r \in \mathbb{F}_2$. Then f has Hamming weight 2^{n-r}. Moreover, for any $a \in \mathbb{F}_2^n$, if a is $\mathbb{F}_2$-linearly independent of $a_1, \ldots, a_r$, then the function $f(x) \oplus a \cdot x$ is balanced (and hence $W_f(a) = 0$), since it is linearly equivalent to a function of the form $g(x_1, \ldots, x_r) \oplus x_{r+1}$. If a is $\mathbb{F}_2$-linearly dependent of $a_1, \ldots, a_r$, say $a = \sum_{i=1}^r \eta_i a_i$ with $\eta_i \in \mathbb{F}_2$, then $a \cdot x$ takes constant value $\bigoplus_{i=1}^r \eta_i (a_i \cdot x) = \bigoplus_{i=1}^r \eta_i (\epsilon_i \oplus 1)$ on the flat; hence, $\hat{f}(a) = \sum_{x \in A}(-1)^{a \cdot x}$ equals $2^{n-r}(-1)^{\bigoplus_{i=1}^r \eta_i (\epsilon_i \oplus 1)}$. Thus, if $a = \sum_{i=1}^r \eta_i a_i \neq 0_n$, then we have $W_f(a) = -2^{n-r+1}(-1)^{\bigoplus_{i=1}^r \eta_i (\epsilon_i \oplus 1)}$; and we have $W_f(0_n) = 2^n - 2|A| = 2^n - 2^{n-r+1}$.

Note that the nonlinearity of f equals 2^{n-r} and is bad as soon as $r \geq 2$. But indicators of flats can be used to design Boolean functions with good nonlinearities, by concatenating sums of indicators of flats and of affine functions; see below.

Remark. As recalled in Section 4.1, the functions of $RM(r, n)$ whose weights occur in the range $[2^{n-r}; 2^{n-r+1}[$ have been characterized by Kasami and Tokura [670]; any such function is the product of the indicator of a flat and of a quadratic function or is the sum (modulo 2) of two indicators of flats. The Walsh spectra of such functions can also be precisely computed. $\qquad\square$

5.4.1 Concatenations of sums of indicators of flats and affine functions

Concatenating sums of indicators of flats and of affine functions gives another superclass, studied in [226], of Maiorana–McFarland's class. The functions of this generalized class are of the form

$$f(x, y) = \prod_{i=1}^{t(y)} (x \cdot \phi_i(y) \oplus g_i(y) \oplus 1) \oplus x \cdot \phi(y) \oplus g(y); \quad (x, y) \in \mathbb{F}_2^r \times \mathbb{F}_2^s, \quad (5.21)$$

where t is a function from $\mathbb{F}_2^s$ into $\{0, 1, \ldots, r\}$, and where $\phi_1, \ldots, \phi_r, \phi$ are functions from $\mathbb{F}_2^s$ into $\mathbb{F}_2^r$ such that, for every $y \in \mathbb{F}_2^s$, the vectors $\phi_1(y), \ldots, \phi_{t(y)}(y)$ are linearly independent; $g_1, \ldots, g_r$ and g are Boolean functions on $\mathbb{F}_2^s$.

Let f be defined by (5.21). For every $a \in F_2^r$ and every $b \in F_2^s$, we have

$$W_f(a, b) = 2^r \sum_{y \in \phi^{-1}(a)} (-1)^{g(y) \oplus b \cdot y} - \sum_{y \in F_a} 2^{r-t(y)+1} (-1)^{g(y) \oplus b \cdot y \oplus \bigoplus_{i=1}^{t(y)} \eta_i(a,y) \, g_i(y)},$$

where F_a is the set of all the vectors y of the space $\mathbb{F}_2^s$ such that a belongs to the flat $\phi(y) + \langle \phi_1(y), \ldots, \phi_{t(y)}(y) \rangle$ (by convention equal to $\{\phi(y)\}$ if $t(y) = 0$), and where $\eta_i(a, y)$ is defined (with uniqueness) for every $i \leq t(y)$ by the relation $a + \phi(y) = \sum_{i=1}^{t(y)} \eta_i(a, y) \, \phi_i(y)$.

The cryptographic parameters of such functions are studied in [226, section 5].

5.5 Functions admitting (partial) covering sequences

5.5.1 The case of Boolean functions

The notion of covering sequence of a Boolean function has been introduced in [326].

Definition 47 *Let f be an n-variable Boolean function. An integer-valued[8] sequence $(\lambda_a)_{a \in \mathbb{F}_2^n}$ is called a* covering sequence *of f if the integer-valued function $\sum_{a \in \mathbb{F}_2^n} \lambda_a D_a f(x)$ takes a constant value. This constant value is called the* level *of the covering sequence. If the level is nonzero, we say that the covering sequence is a* nontrivial covering sequence.

For instance, any balanced quadratic function admits a nontrivial atomic covering sequence (see page 171). Note that the sum $\sum_{a \in \mathbb{F}_2^n} \lambda_a D_a f(x)$ involves both kinds of additions: the addition $\sum$ in $\mathbb{Z}$ and the addition $\oplus$ in $\mathbb{F}_2$ (which is concealed inside $D_a f$). It has been shown in [326] that any function admitting a nontrivial covering sequence is balanced (see Proposition 61 below for a proof) and that any balanced function admits the constant sequence 1 as covering sequence (the level of this sequence is 2^{n-1}).

A characterization of covering sequences by means of the Walsh transform was also given in [326]: denote again by $supp(W_f)$ the support $\{u \in \mathbb{F}_2^n \mid W_f(u) \neq 0\}$ of W_f; then:

Proposition 60 *Let f be any n-variable Boolean function and $\lambda = (\lambda_a)_{a \in \mathbb{F}_2^n}$ an integer-valued sequence. Then f admits λ as covering sequence if and only if the Fourier–Hadamard transform $\widehat{\lambda}$ of the function $a \mapsto \lambda_a$ takes a constant value on $supp(W_f)$. This constant value is $\left(\sum_{a \in \mathbb{F}_2^n} \lambda_a - 2\rho \right)$, where ρ is the level of the covering sequence.*

Proof Replacing $D_a f(x)$ by $\frac{1}{2} - \frac{1}{2}(-1)^{D_a f(x)} = \frac{1}{2} - \frac{1}{2}(-1)^{f(x)}(-1)^{f(x+a)}$ in the equality $\sum_{a \in \mathbb{F}_2^n} \lambda_a D_a f(x) = \rho$, we see that f admits the covering sequence λ with level ρ if and only if, for every $x \in \mathbb{F}_2^n$, we have $\sum_{a \in \mathbb{F}_2^n} \lambda_a (-1)^{f(x+a)} = \left(\sum_{a \in \mathbb{F}_2^n} \lambda_a - 2\rho \right)(-1)^{f(x)}$. These two integer-valued functions are equal if and only

---

[8] or real-valued, or complex-valued; but taking real or complex sequences instead of integer-valued ones has no practical sense.

if their Fourier–Hadamard transforms are equal to each other, that is, if for every $b \in \mathbb{F}_2^n$, the sum $\sum_{a,x \in \mathbb{F}_2^n} \lambda_a (-1)^{f(x+a) \oplus x \cdot b}$, which by changing x into $x + a$ equals $\left(\sum_{a \in \mathbb{F}_2^n} \lambda_a (-1)^{a \cdot b} \right) W_f(b) = \widehat{\lambda}(b) W_f(b)$, equals $\left(\sum_{a \in \mathbb{F}_2^n} \lambda_a - 2\rho \right) W_f(b)$. The characterization follows. $\square$

Any Boolean function f on $\mathbb{F}_2^n$ is balanced (*i.e.*, satisfies $0_n \notin supp(W_f)$) if and only if it admits at least one nontrivial covering sequence: the condition is clearly sufficient according to Proposition 60 (since $\widehat{\lambda}(0_n) = \sum_{a \in \mathbb{F}_2^n} \lambda_a$ and $\rho \neq 0$), and it is also necessary since the constant sequence 1 is a covering sequence for all balanced functions. See more in [308].

We shall see in Chapter 7 that covering sequences play a role with respect to correlation immunity and resiliency. But knowing a covering sequence for f gives no information on the nonlinearity of f, since it gives only information on the support of the Walsh transform, not on the nonzero values it takes. In [231], the author weakens the definition of covering sequence, so that it can help computing the (nonzero) values of the Walsh transform.

Definition 48 *Let f be a Boolean function on $\mathbb{F}_2^n$. A partial covering sequence for f is a sequence $(\lambda_a)_{a \in \mathbb{F}_2^n}$ such that $\sum_{a \in \mathbb{F}_2^n} \lambda_a D_a f(x)$ takes two values ρ and ρ' (distinct or not) called the* levels *of the sequence. The partial covering sequence is called* nontrivial *if one of the constants is nonzero.*

The interest of nontrivial partial covering sequences is that they give information on the Hamming weight and the Walsh transform.

Proposition 61 *Let $(\lambda_a)_{a \in \mathbb{F}_2^n}$ be a partial covering sequence of a Boolean function f, of levels ρ and ρ'.*

Let $A = \{x \in \mathbb{F}_2^n \, ; \, \sum_{a \in \mathbb{F}_2^n} \lambda_a D_a f(x) = \rho'\}$ (assuming that $\rho' \neq \rho$; otherwise, when λ is in fact a covering sequence of level ρ, we set $A = \emptyset$).

Then, for every vector $b \in \mathbb{F}_2^n$, we have

$$\left(\widehat{\lambda}(b) - \widehat{\lambda}(0_n) + 2\rho \right) W_f(b) = 2 \, (\rho - \rho') \sum_{x \in A} (-1)^{f(x) \oplus b \cdot x}.$$

Hence, if $\rho \neq 0$, we have

$$2^n - 2w_H(f) = W_f(0_n) = \left(1 - \frac{\rho'}{\rho} \right) \sum_{x \in A} (-1)^{f(x)}.$$

Proof By definition, we have, for every $x \in \mathbb{F}_2^n$:

$$\sum_{a \in \mathbb{F}_2^n} \lambda_a D_a f(x) = \rho' \, 1_A(x) + \rho \, 1_{A^c}(x)$$

and therefore

$$\sum_{a \in \mathbb{F}_2^n} \lambda_a (-1)^{D_a f(x)} = \sum_{a \in \mathbb{F}_2^n} \lambda_a (1 - 2 D_a f(x)) = \sum_{a \in \mathbb{F}_2^n} \lambda_a - 2\rho' \, 1_A(x) - 2\rho \, 1_{A^c}(x).$$

We deduce:

$$\sum_{a\in\mathbb{F}_2^n}\lambda_a(-1)^{f(x+a)}=(-1)^{f(x)}\left(\sum_{a\in\mathbb{F}_2^n}\lambda_a-2\,\rho'\,1_A(x)-2\,\rho\,1_{A^c}(x)\right). \qquad (5.22)$$

We have already seen that the Fourier–Hadamard transform of the function $(-1)^{f(x+a)}$ maps every vector $b\in\mathbb{F}_2^n$ to the value $(-1)^{a\cdot b}\,W_f(b)$. Hence, taking the Fourier–Hadamard transform of both terms of equality (5.22), we get

$$\left(\sum_{a\in\mathbb{F}_2^n}\lambda_a(-1)^{a\cdot b}\right)W_f(b)$$

$$=\left(\sum_{a\in\mathbb{F}_2^n}\lambda_a\right)W_f(b)-2\,\rho'\sum_{x\in A}(-1)^{f(x)\oplus b\cdot x}-2\,\rho\sum_{x\in A^c}(-1)^{f(x)\oplus b\cdot x},$$

that is,

$$\widehat{\lambda}(b)\,W_f(b)=\widehat{\lambda}(0_n)\,W_f(b)-2\,\rho\,W_f(b)+2\,(\rho-\rho')\sum_{x\in A}(-1)^{f(x)\oplus b\cdot x}.$$

Hence

$$\left(\widehat{\lambda}(b)-\widehat{\lambda}(0_n)+2\,\rho\right)W_f(b)=2\,(\rho-\rho')\sum_{x\in A}(-1)^{f(x)\oplus b\cdot x}. \qquad \square$$

A simple example of nontrivial partial covering sequence is as follows: let $\mathcal{E}$ be any set of derivatives of f. Assume that $\mathcal{E}$ contains a nonzero function and is stable under addition (*i.e.*, is a nontrivial $\mathbb{F}_2$-vector space). Then $\sum_{g\in\mathcal{E}}g$ takes on values 0 and $\frac{|\mathcal{E}|}{2}$. Thus, if $\mathcal{E}=\{D_af;\ a\in E\}$ (where we choose E minimum, so that any two different vectors of the set E give different functions of $\mathcal{E}$), then 1_E is a nontrivial partial covering sequence.

Corollary 10   *Let $\mathcal{E}$ be any set of derivatives of an n-variable Boolean function f. Assume that $\mathcal{E}$ contains a nonzero function and is stable under addition (i.e., is a nontrivial $\mathbb{F}_2$-vector space). Then*

$$2^n-2w_H(f)=W_f(0_n)=\sum_{x\in A}(-1)^{f(x)}.$$

See more in [231], with the notion of *linear set of derivatives* (which are sets of derivatives stable under addition and provide partial covering sequences), combined with Proposition 61, and applied to the computation of the Hamming weights and Walsh spectra of quadratic and Maiorana–McFarland functions and of other examples of functions.

5.5.2 *The case of vectorial functions*

The generalization of the notion of covering sequence to vectorial functions has been studied in [319]. A covering sequence for a Boolean function can be seen as a function φ from $\mathbb{F}_2^n$

into $\mathbb{R}$ such that $\sum_{a \in \mathbb{F}_2^n; \ D_a F(x)=1} \varphi(a) = \rho$, for every $x \in \mathbb{F}_2^n$. This generalizes to vectorial functions:

Definition 49 *We call covering sequence of an (n,m)-function F, a pair of functions (φ, ψ) from, respectively, $\mathbb{F}_2^n$ and $\mathbb{F}_2^m$ into $\mathbb{R}$, such that*

$$\forall x \in \mathbb{F}_2^n, \forall b \in \mathbb{F}_2^m, \quad \sum_{a \in \mathbb{F}_2^n; \ D_a F(x)=b} \varphi(a) = \psi(b). \tag{5.23}$$

Note that this equality between functions $b \mapsto \sum_{a \in \mathbb{F}_2^n; \ D_a F(x)=b} \varphi(a)$ and $b \mapsto \psi(b)$ is equivalent to the equality between their Fourier transforms, that is,

$$\forall v \in \mathbb{F}_2^m, \ \forall x \in \mathbb{F}_2^n, \ \sum_{a \in \mathbb{F}_2^n} \varphi(a)(-1)^{v \cdot D_a F(x)} = \sum_{b \in \mathbb{F}_2^m} \psi(b)(-1)^{v \cdot b},$$

which is equivalent to

$$\sum_{a \in \mathbb{F}_2^n} \varphi(a)(-1)^{v \cdot F(x+a)} = (-1)^{v \cdot F(x)} \widehat{\psi}(v),$$

that is,

$$\varphi \otimes \chi_F(\cdot, v) = \widehat{\psi}(v) \chi_F(\cdot, v), \tag{5.24}$$

where $\chi_F(\cdot, v)$ denotes function $x \mapsto \chi_F(x, v) = (-1)^{v \cdot F(x)}$ and $\otimes$ is the convolutional product.

Proposition 62 *An (n,m)-function F is balanced if and only if it admits at least one covering sequence (φ, ψ) satisfying $\widehat{\psi}(v) \neq \widehat{\varphi}(0_n)$ for every nonzero vector v of $\mathbb{F}_2^m$. Any balanced (n,m)-function F admits the pair of constant functions $(1, 2^{n-m})$ for covering sequence.*

Proof Assume that (φ, ψ) is a covering sequence of F, then Equation (5.24) is satisfied and by applying the Fourier transform at 0_n to both sides of this functional equality, we obtain

$$\forall v \in \mathbb{F}_2^m, \ \widehat{\varphi}(0_n) W_F(0_n, v) = \widehat{\psi}(v) W_F(0_n, v),$$

that is, $(\widehat{\varphi}(0_n) - \widehat{\psi}(v)) W_F(0_n, v) = 0$ for every $v \in \mathbb{F}_2^m$. This gives $\widehat{\varphi}(0_n) = \widehat{\psi}(0_m)$. If $\widehat{\varphi}(0_n) - \widehat{\psi}(v)$ is nonzero for every nonzero $v \in \mathbb{F}_2^m$, then the function $v \mapsto W_F(0_n, v)$ is null on $\mathbb{F}_2^m \setminus \{0_m\}$, which implies that F is balanced, according to Proposition 35.

Conversely, if F is balanced, then, for every pair $(b, x) \in \mathbb{F}_2^m \times \mathbb{F}_2^n$, the cardinality of the set $\{a \in \mathbb{F}_2^n; D_a F(x) = b\}$ is constant equaling 2^{n-m} since the equation $D_a F(x) = b$ is equivalent to $F(x + a) = b + F(x)$. Let $\varphi : \mathbb{F}_2^n \mapsto \mathbb{R}$ and $\psi : \mathbb{F}_2^m \mapsto \mathbb{R}$ be respectively the constant function $x \mapsto 1$ and the constant function $y \mapsto 2^{n-m}$, then the pair (φ, ψ) is a covering sequence of F satisfying the relation $\widehat{\psi}(v) = 0 \neq \widehat{\psi}(0_m) = \widehat{\varphi}(0_n) = 2^{n-m}$ for every element v of $\mathbb{F}_2^m \setminus \{0_m\}$. $\qquad\square$

Remark.   Finding a second covering sequence is often a difficult problem. It is shown in [319] that the Maiorana–McFarland functions that satisfy the hypothesis of Proposition 128, page 315, admit several covering sequences.   □

Definition 50   *A covering sequence* (φ, ψ) *of an* (n, m)-*function* F *is said to be* nontrivial *if* $\widehat{\psi}(v)$ *never equals* $\widehat{\varphi}(0_n)$ *(that is,* $\widehat{\psi}(0_m)$*) when* v *ranges over* $\mathbb{F}_2^m \setminus \{0_m\}$.

Thus, according to Proposition 62, an (n, m)-function F is balanced if and only if it admits a nontrivial covering sequence. This definition and this observation generalize what was known for Boolean functions.

Remark.   If ψ is a function from $\mathbb{F}_2^m$ into $\mathbb{R}_+$, then we have $\widehat{\psi}(v) \neq \widehat{\psi}(0_m)$ for every element v of $\mathbb{F}_2^m \setminus \{0_m\}$ if and only if the support of ψ has rank m (*i.e.*, spans the whole vector space $\mathbb{F}_2^m$). Indeed, we have

$$\forall v \in \mathbb{F}_2^m \setminus \{0_m\}, \ \widehat{\psi}(v) \neq \widehat{\psi}(0_m) \iff \forall v \in \mathbb{F}_2^m \setminus \{0_m\}, \ \sum_{b \in \mathbb{F}_2^m, b \in (v^\perp)^c} \psi(b) \neq 0$$

and, since $\psi(b) \geq 0, \forall b \in \mathbb{F}_2^m$, this relation is equivalent to saying that the support of ψ is not included in a linear hyperplane of $\mathbb{F}_2^m$.   □

Let us now generalize to vectorial functions the characterization of covering sequences of Boolean functions by means of their Fourier transforms and of the Walsh support of F.

Proposition 63   *Let* F *be an* (n, m)-*function, and let* (φ, ψ) *be any pair of real-valued functions respectively defined on* $\mathbb{F}_2^n$ *and on* $\mathbb{F}_2^m$. *Then* F *admits* (φ, ψ) *for covering sequence if and only if, for every pair* (u, v) *belonging to Supp* W_F, *we have* $\widehat{\varphi}(u) = \widehat{\psi}(v)$.

Proof   Thanks to the bijectivity of the Fourier transform, for every nonzero vector $v \in \mathbb{F}_2^m$, the functions $\widehat{\psi}(v) \chi_F(\cdot, v)$ and $\varphi \otimes \chi_F(\cdot, v)$ of Relation (5.24) are equal if and only if their Fourier transforms on $\mathbb{F}_2^n$ are equal, that is:

$$\forall v \in \mathbb{F}_2^m, \ \forall u \in \mathbb{F}_2^n, \ \widehat{\varphi}(u) W_F(u, v) = \widehat{\psi}(v) \, W_F(u, v),$$

that is, if and only if

$$((u, v) \in Supp \ W_F) \Longrightarrow \left(\widehat{\varphi}(u) = \widehat{\psi}(v) \right).$$ □

Corollary 11   *Let* F *be an* (n, m)-*function admitting* (φ, ψ) *for covering sequence. If the sets* $\widehat{\varphi}\left(\{ u \in \mathbb{F}_2^n / \ w_H(u) \leq t \} \right)$ *and* $\widehat{\psi}(\mathbb{F}_2^m \setminus \{0_m\})$ *are disjoint, then* F *is* t-*resilient*.

It is deduced in [319] from Proposition 63 that if an (n, m)-function F admits a covering sequence (φ, ψ) such that the functions φ and ψ are, respectively, different from the zero function on $\mathbb{F}_2^n$ and different from the zero function on $\mathbb{F}_2^m \setminus \{0_m\}$, then, for every vector $u \in \mathbb{F}_2^n$, there exists $v \in \mathbb{F}_2^m \setminus \{0_m\}$ such that $W_F(u, v) = 0$, and for every vector $v \in \mathbb{F}_2^m$, there exists a vector $u \in \mathbb{F}_2^n$ such that $W_F(u, v) = 0$.

We show now that the notion of covering sequence behaves well with respect to composition.

Proposition 64 *[319] Let $F : \mathbb{F}_2^n \mapsto \mathbb{F}_2^m$ and $G : \mathbb{F}_2^m \mapsto \mathbb{F}_2^k$ be two functions admitting respectively (φ, ψ) and (ψ, θ) for covering sequences. Then, (φ, θ) is a covering sequence of $G \circ F$.*

Proof For every pair $(x, a) \in \mathbb{F}_2^n \times \mathbb{F}_2^n$, we have, denoting $D_a F(x)$ by b:

$$D_a[G \circ F](x) = G(F(x)) + G(F(x + a)) = G(F(x)) + G(F(x) + b) = (D_b G)(F(x)).$$

Thus, for every pair $(x, c) \in \mathbb{F}_2^n \times \mathbb{F}_2^k$, we have

$$\sum_{a \in \mathbb{F}_2^n, D_a[G \circ F](x) = c} \varphi(a) = \sum_{b \in \mathbb{F}_2^m, (D_b G)(F(x)) = c} \left(\sum_{a \in \mathbb{F}_2^n, D_a F(x) = b} \varphi(a) \right).$$

For every pair $(x, b) \in \mathbb{F}_2^n \times \mathbb{F}_2^m$, we have $\sum_{a \in \mathbb{F}_2^n, D_a F(x) = b} \varphi(a) = \psi(b)$ and thus

$$\sum_{a \in \mathbb{F}_2^n, D_a[G \circ F](x) = c} \varphi(a) = \sum_{b \in \mathbb{F}_2^m, (D_b G)(F(x)) = c} \psi(b).$$

Let y denote $F(x)$, then

$$\sum_{a \in \mathbb{F}_2^n, D_a[G \circ F](x) = c} \varphi(a) = \sum_{b \in \mathbb{F}_2^m, D_b G(y) = c} \psi(b). \tag{5.25}$$

Since (ψ, θ) is a covering sequence of G, the sum $\sum_{b \in \mathbb{F}_2^m, D_b G(y) = c} \psi(b)$ takes constant value $\theta(c)$ for every pair $(y, c) \in \mathbb{F}_2^m \times \mathbb{F}_2^k$ and we deduce

$$\forall x \in \mathbb{F}_2^n, \ \forall c \in \mathbb{F}_2^k, \qquad \sum_{a \in \mathbb{F}_2^n, D_a G \circ F(x) = c} \varphi(a) = \theta(c). \qquad \square$$

In [319], the authors give a similar (more technical) result on the concatenation of functions, with consequences on Maiorana–McFarland functions. An attack on ciphers using functions admitting covering sequences is also presented.

5.6 Functions with low univariate degree and related functions

The following Weil's theorem is very well known in finite field theory (cf. [775, theorem 5.38]):

Theorem 11 *Let q be a prime power and $F(x) \in \mathbb{F}_q[x]$ a univariate polynomial of degree $d \geq 1$ with $\gcd(d, q) = 1$. Let χ be a nontrivial character of $\mathbb{F}_q$. Then*

$$\left| \sum_{x \in \mathbb{F}_q} \chi(F(x)) \right| \leq (d - 1) q^{1/2}.$$

For $q = 2^n$, this *Weil's bound* means that, for every nonzero $a \in \mathbb{F}_{2^n}$, we have $\left| \sum_{x \in \mathbb{F}_{2^n}} (-1)^{tr_n(aF(x))} \right| \leq (d-1) \, 2^{\frac{n}{2}}$. And since adding a linear function $tr_n(bx)$ to the function $tr_n(aF(x))$ corresponds to adding $(b/a)\, x$ to $F(x)$ and does not change its univariate degree, we deduce that, if $d > 1$ is odd and $a \neq 0$, then

$$nl(tr_n(aF)) \geq 2^{n-1} - (d-1) \, 2^{\frac{n}{2}-1}.$$

An extension of the Weil bound to the character sums of functions of the form $F(x) + G(1/x)$ (where $1/x = x^{2^n - 2}$ takes value 0 at 0), among which are the so-called *Kloosterman sums* $\sum_{x \in \mathbb{F}_{2^n}} (-1)^{tr_n(1/x + ax)}$, has been first obtained by Carlitz and Uchiyama [333] and extended by Shanbhag et al. [1032]: if F and G have odd univariate degrees, then

$$\sum_{x \in \mathbb{F}_{2^n}} (-1)^{tr_n(F(x^{-1}) + G(x))} \leq (d_{alg}(F) + d_{alg}(G)) \, 2^{\frac{n}{2}}.$$

More can also be found in [678] for the case where a function with sparse univariate representation is added to F.

6

Bent functions and plateaued functions

Bent functions are fascinating extremal mathematical objects. Bent Boolean functions play a role in coding theory, with Kerdock codes (see Subsection 6.1.22, page 254), and in other domains of communications (for instance, they are used to build the so-called bent function sequences for telecommunications [919] and are related to Golay Complementary Sequences [416]). Bent vectorial functions allow constructing good codes [453, 865, 866] and pose interesting problems related to coding theory [278, 854].

The role of bent Boolean functions in cryptography is less obvious nowadays since, because of fast *algebraic attacks* and Theorem 22, page 332 (which shows that Boolean functions obtained from bent functions by modifying a few values cannot allow resisting them), we do not know an efficient construction using bent functions that would provide Boolean functions having all the necessary features for being used in stream ciphers. Concerning block ciphers, since bent vectorial functions are not balanced and do not exist when $m > \frac{n}{2}$, they are rarely used as substitution boxes in block ciphers.[1] Bijectivity is mandatory in the kind of ciphers called substitution permutation networks, and unbalancedness can represent a weakness in the other kind of ciphers called Feistel (see, *e.g.*, [957]). But vectorial bent functions can, however, be used in block ciphers at the cost of additional diffusion/compression/expansion layers, or as building blocks for constructions of substitution boxes. Moreover, constructions of bent Boolean functions are often transposable into constructions of Boolean functions for stream ciphers, and bent vectorial functions are used to construct algebraic manipulation detection codes (see Section 12.1.6), which play an important role in cryptography. Hence, even from a cryptographic viewpoint, it seems important to devote a chapter to them. This is all the more true that bent (Boolean or vectorial) functions possess properties that are cryptographically very interesting: they have optimal nonlinearity, by definition, and their derivatives are balanced (in other words, changing the input to a bent function by the addition of a nonzero vector induces a uniform change among the 2^n outputs; this has of course relationship with the differential attack on block ciphers). And it often happens that the cryptographic interest of notions on Boolean functions be renewed with the apparition of new ways of using them (see Section 12.1).

The notion of bent function has been generalized to functions over $\mathbb{Z}_4$ and to the wider domain of generalized bent functions. The page limit of this book does not allow us to address them.

---

[1] But the S-boxes in the block ciphers CAST-128 and CAST-256 are modified from bent functions, as well as the round functions in the cryptographic hash algorithms MD4, MD5, and HAVAL, and the nonlinear-feedback shift registers (NLFSR) in the stream cipher Grain.

Plateaued functions are a generalization of bent functions that free themselves from some cryptographic weaknesses inherent to bent functions (in particular, their unbalancedness, the fact that their numbers of variables are necessarily even, and for vectorial functions the nonexistence of bent (n,m)-functions when $m > n/2$) but not all of them (for instance, they also have *limited algebraic degree*, which represents a weakness with respect to *fast algebraic attack*s).

The history of bent functions begins in the 1960s.[2] The first paper in English on bent Boolean functions was written by O. Rothaus in 1966 and published ten years later [1005]. It seems that, already in 1962, bent functions had been studied in the Soviet Union under the name of minimal functions, as mentioned by Tokareva in [1089]. V. A. Eliseev and O. P. Stepchenkov had proved that their algebraic degree is bounded above by half the number of variables (except in the case of two variables); they had also proposed an analogue of the Maiorana–McFarland construction. Their technical reports have never been declassified. The extension of the notion to vectorial (n,m)-functions is due to Kaisa Nyberg [906]. A book by S. Mesnager [865] that we recommend and a slightly more recent survey [313] exist on bent functions.

The introduction of plateaued Boolean functions is due to Zheng and Zhang [1173] as a generalization of partially-bent functions [211]. Recently it has been shown in [247] that plateaued vectorial functions share with quadratic vectorial functions most of their nice properties, which considerably simplify in particular the study of their APNness; see Chapter 11 (but the property of plateauedness is not easy to prove in general).

6.1 Bent Boolean functions

We first recall for the convenience of the reader what we have seen on bent functions in Section 3.1, and we add some observations:

- A Boolean function f on $\mathbb{F}_2^n$ (n even) is called bent if its Hamming distance to the code $RM(1,n)$ of n-variable *affine function*s (the nonlinearity of f) equals $2^{n-1} - 2^{\frac{n}{2}-1}$ (*i.e.*, is optimal).
- f is bent if and only if its Walsh transform W_f (with respect to some inner product) takes values $\pm 2^{\frac{n}{2}}$ only.[3] This characterization is independent of the choice of the inner product on $\mathbb{F}_2^n$, since any other inner product has the form $\langle x,s \rangle = x \cdot L(s)$, where L is an autoadjoint linear automorphism, *i.e.*, when "$\cdot$" is the *usual inner product*, an automorphism whose associated matrix is symmetric. The condition in this characterization can be slightly weakened, without losing the property of being necessary and sufficient:

---

[2] In fact, bent functions had been studied before the adjective "bent" was invented, since the supports of bent Boolean functions are difference sets [651] in elementary Abelian 2-groups. Nevertheless, mathematicians were not much interested in such groups at that time.

[3] In [1093], the authors show that Boolean functions with two Walsh values are affine functions and bent functions, possibly modified at 0_n.

Lemma 5 *Let $n \geq 2$ be even. Any n-variable Boolean function f is bent if and only if, for every $a \in \mathbb{F}_2^n$, we have $W_f(a) \equiv 2^{\frac{n}{2}}[\bmod\ 2^{\frac{n}{2}+1}]$, or equivalently $\widehat{f}(a) \equiv 2^{\frac{n}{2}-1}[\bmod\ 2^{\frac{n}{2}}]$.*

Proof This necessary condition is also sufficient, since, if it is satisfied, then writing $W_f(a) = 2^{\frac{n}{2}}\lambda_a$, where λ_a is odd for every a, Parseval's relation (2.47) implies $\sum_{a \in \mathbb{F}_2^n} \lambda_a^2 = 2^n$, and hence $\lambda_a^2 = 1$ for every a. $\qquad\qquad\square$

A slightly different viewpoint on bent functions is that of bent sequences: for each vector X in $\{-1, 1\}^{2^n}$, define: $\hat{X} = \frac{1}{\sqrt{2^n}} H_n X$, where H_n is the Walsh–Hadamard matrix, recursively defined by

$$H_n = \begin{bmatrix} H_{n-1} & H_{n-1} \\ H_{n-1} & -H_{n-1} \end{bmatrix}, H_0 = [1].$$

The vectors X such that $\hat{X}$ belongs to $\{-1, 1\}^{2^n}$ are called bent sequences. They are the images by character $\chi = (-1)^{\cdot}$ of the bent functions on $\mathbb{F}_2^n$. In [993], the authors consider some generalized bent notions (among which the *nega-bent* notion) from the domain of quantum error-correcting codes, corresponding to flat spectra with respect to some unitary transforms (whose matrices U are such that $UU^\dagger$ equals the identity matrix, where "$\dagger$" means transpose-conjugate, and generalize Walsh–Hadamard matrices).

- An n-variable Boolean function f is bent if and only if its Hamming distance to any affine function equals $2^{n-1} \pm 2^{\frac{n}{2}-1}$; then half of the elements of the Reed–Muller code of order 1 lie at distance $2^{n-1} + 2^{\frac{n}{2}-1}$ from f and half lie at distance $2^{n-1} - 2^{\frac{n}{2}-1}$ (since if ℓ lies at distance $2^{n-1} + 2^{\frac{n}{2}-1}$ from f, then $\ell \oplus 1$ lies at distance $2^{n-1} - 2^{\frac{n}{2}-1}$ and vice versa). Conversely, a Boolean function is affine if and only if it lies at maximal distance from the set of bent functions (this is shown in [1088] but was probably known earlier by Dillon, Dobbertin, and others, although maybe not explicitly written). In other words, the set of affine functions and the set of bent functions are *metric complements* of each other and constitute a so-called *pair of metrically regular sets* in the Boolean hypercube. It is shown by Tokareva after observing that for any nonaffine Boolean function f in even dimension, there exists a bent function g such that $f \oplus g$ is not bent.
- Bent Boolean functions are not balanced. As soon as n is large enough (say $n \geq 20$), the difference $2^{\frac{n}{2}-1}$ between their Hamming weights and the weight 2^{n-1} of balanced functions is very small with respect to this weight. However, according to [42, theorem 6], 2^n bits of the pseudorandom sequence output by f in a combiner or a filter model are enough to distinguish it from a random sequence. Nevertheless, we shall see that highly nonlinear balanced functions can be built from bent functions.

Remark. Given a bent Boolean function f, the functions $f \oplus \ell$ where ℓ is affine are not balanced, but their weights are globally as close to 2^{n-1} as possible: according to Parseval's relation, there do not exist functions f such that the functions $f \oplus \ell$ have all weights closer to 2^{n-1}. $\qquad\qquad\square$

6.1.1 Extended affine invariance of bentness and automorphism group of a function

The nonlinearity being an *EA invariant*, so is the notion of bent function. A class of bent functions shall be called a *complete class* if it is preserved by EA equivalence.

The *automorphism group* of the set of bent functions is the general affine group. It indeed contains the general affine group, and the reverse inclusion is a direct consequence of the property that, given a Boolean function g, if for every bent function f, function $f \oplus g$ is also bent, then g is affine (which shows that the automorphism group of the set of all bent functions is included in that of all affine functions; Proposition 51, page 155, completes then the proof).

Other notions of equivalence between bent functions come from design theory; see Subsection 6.1.9.

Given a (Boolean or vectorial) function f, recall that the group (already seen at page 72) of those affine automorphisms A that preserve f (alternatively,[4] those that preserve its graph) is called the *automorphism group of function f* and is denoted by $Aut(f)$. The determination of $Aut(f)$ for f bent is often a difficult problem; see [56, 426, 659]. In [1162], the authors only studied the so-called symmetric group (the subgroup of those input coordinate permutations that preserve the function).

6.1.2 Characterization of bentness by the derivatives

Characterization by first-order derivatives

Thanks to Relation (2.53), page 62, and to the fact that the Fourier–Hadamard transform of a pseudo-Boolean function is constant if and only if the function equals δ_0 times some constant, we have

Theorem 12 *Any n-variable Boolean function (n even[5]) is bent if and only if, for any nonzero vector a, the Boolean function $D_a f(x) = f(x) \oplus f(x + a)$ is balanced, that is, if and only if f satisfies $PC(n)$.*

In [190, 191] (see also [353]), the authors observed that, for every linear hyperplane H of $\mathbb{F}_2^n$, the condition of Theorem 12 can be weakened into "for any nonzero a in H, function $D_a f$ is balanced." Indeed, for $H = \{0_n, \alpha\}^{\perp}$, we have $W_f^2(\alpha) = \sum_{a \in \mathbb{F}_2^n} (-1)^{a \cdot \alpha} \mathcal{F}(D_a f)$, $W_f^2(0_n) + W_f^2(\alpha) = 2 \sum_{a \in H} \mathcal{F}(D_a f)$, and this necessary condition is also sufficient since n being even, the sum of these two squares equals 2^{n+1} if and only if each square equals 2^n (see, *e.g.*, [191]). The functions whose derivatives $D_a f$, $a \in H$, $a \neq 0_n$ are all balanced for n odd are also characterized in [190, 191] as well as, for every n, the functions whose derivatives $D_a f$, $a \in E$, $a \neq 0_n$ are all balanced, where E is a vector subspace of $\mathbb{F}_2^n$ of dimension $n - 2$.

---

[4] In the cases of Boolean functions and of bent functions, it makes less difference [149, 150].
[5] In fact, according to the observations above, "n even" is implied by "f satisfies $PC(n)$"; functions satisfying $PC(n)$ do not exist for odd n.

Because of Theorem 12, bent (Boolean) functions are also called *perfect nonlinear* functions.[6] Equivalently, as noted by Rothaus and Welch, f is bent if and only if the $2^n \times 2^n$ matrix $H = [(-1)^{f(x+y)}]_{x,y \in \mathbb{F}_2^n}$ is a Hadamard matrix (*i.e.*, satisfies $H \times H^t = 2^n I$, where I is the identity matrix). This implies that the Cayley graph G_f (see Subsection 2.3.5, page 70) is strongly regular (see [68] for more precision and for a characterization).

Characterization by second-order derivatives and second-order covering sequences

Proposition 65 *[317] An n-variable Boolean function f is bent if and only if*

$$\forall x \in \mathbb{F}_2^n, \sum_{a,b \in \mathbb{F}_2^n} (-1)^{D_a D_b f(x)} = 2^n. \tag{6.1}$$

Proof If we multiply both terms of Relation (6.1) by $f_\chi(x) = (-1)^{f(x)}$, we obtain the (equivalent) relation: $\forall x \in \mathbb{F}_2^n, f_\chi \otimes f_\chi \otimes f_\chi(x) = 2^n f_\chi(x)$; indeed, we have $f_\chi \otimes f_\chi \otimes f_\chi(x) = \sum_{b \in \mathbb{F}_2^n} \left(\sum_{a \in \mathbb{F}_2^n} (-1)^{f(a) \oplus f(a+b)} \right) (-1)^{f(b+x)} = \sum_{a,b \in \mathbb{F}_2^n} (-1)^{f(a+x) \oplus f(a+b+x) \oplus f(b+x)}$. According to the bijectivity of the Fourier–Hadamard transform and to Relation (2.44), page 60, this is equivalent to

$$\forall u \in \mathbb{F}_2^n, W_f^3(u) = 2^n W_f(u).$$

Thus, we have $\sum_{a,b \in \mathbb{F}_2^n} (-1)^{D_a D_b f(x)} = 2^n$ if and only if, for every $u \in \mathbb{F}_2^n$, $W_f(u)$ equals $\pm \sqrt{2^n}$ or 0. According to Parseval's relation, the value 0 cannot be achieved by W_f and this is therefore equivalent to the bentness of f. □

Relation (6.1) is equivalent to the relation $\sum_{a,b \in \mathbb{F}_2^n} (1 - 2D_a D_b f(x)) = 2^n$, that is, $\sum_{a,b \in \mathbb{F}_2^n} D_a D_b f(x) = 2^{2n-1} - 2^{n-1}$, and hence to the fact that f admits the *second-order covering sequence* with all-1 coefficients and with level $2^{2n-1} - 2^{n-1}$.

6.1.3 Characterization of bentness by power moments of the Walsh transform

For every even integer $w \geq 4$, bent functions are characterized by the property that the sum $\sum_{a \in \mathbb{F}_2^n} W_f^w(a)$ is minimum:

Proposition 66 *Let n be any positive integer and f be any n-variable Boolean function. Then, for every even integer $w \geq 4$, we have*

$$\sum_{u \in \mathbb{F}_2^n} W_f^w(u) \geq 2^{(\frac{w}{2}+1)n},$$

with equality if and only if f is bent.

---

[6] The characterization of Theorem 12 leads to a generalization of the notion of bent function to nonbinary functions. In fact, several generalizations exist [16, 718, 802] (see [266] for a survey); the equivalence between being bent and being perfect nonlinear is no more valid it we consider functions defined over residue class rings (see, *e.g.*, [271]).

This is straightforward for $w = 4$ by using for instance the Cauchy–Schwarz inequality and its case of equality, and for $w \geq 6$, it is a direct consequence of the well-known inequality on the L^w norm: if $w' \geq w$ and $\lambda_i \geq 0, \forall i \in I$, then $(\sum_{i \in I} \lambda_i^{w'})^{\frac{1}{w'}} \geq |I|^{\frac{1}{w'} - \frac{1}{w}} (\sum_{i \in I} \lambda_i^w)^{\frac{1}{w}}$.

Such sums (for even or odd w) play a role with respect to *fast correlation attacks* [189, 203] (when these sums have small magnitude for low values of w, this contributes to a good resistance to fast correlation attacks).

Note that for $w = 4$, we have, according to (3.9) and (3.10), page 98:

$$\sum_{u \in \mathbb{F}_2^n} W_f^4(u) = 2^n \mathcal{V}(f) = 2^n \sum_{x,a,b \in \mathbb{F}_2^n} (-1)^{D_a D_b f(x)}.$$

Hence:

Corollary 12 *Let n be any positive integer and f any n-variable Boolean function. Then*

$$\sum_{x,a,b \in \mathbb{F}_2^n} (-1)^{D_a D_b f(x)} \geq 2^{2n},$$

with equality if and only if f is bent.

Remark. There is no such characterization for w odd, except in particular cases, such as Niho functions; see Proposition 82, at page 222.   ☐

Corollary 13 *Let n be any positive integer, w any even integer larger than or equal to 4, and E an $\mathbb{F}_2$-vector space of n-variable Boolean functions. There exists an (n, m)-function F such that $E \setminus \{0\}$ is the set of component functions of F. All functions except the null one in E are bent if and only if F is bent, and this happens if and only if*

$$|\{(x_1, \ldots, x_w) \in (\mathbb{F}_2^n)^w; \sum_{i=1}^w F(x_i) = 0_m \text{ and } \sum_{i=1}^w x_i = 0_n\}| =$$
$$2^{(w-1)n-m} + (2^m - 1) \cdot 2^{\frac{wn}{2} - m}.$$

Proof The first assertion is by definition, and, according to Proposition 66, the component functions $v \cdot F, v \in \mathbb{F}_2^m \setminus \{0_m\}$, are all bent if and only if we have $\sum_{u \in \mathbb{F}_2^n, v \in \mathbb{F}_2^m} W_F^w(u, v) = 2^{wn} + (2^m - 1) \cdot 2^{(\frac{w}{2}+1)n}$ (distinguishing the case $v = 0_m$ from the cases $v \neq 0_m$), that is, if and only if we have

$$\sum_{u, x_1, \ldots, x_w \in \mathbb{F}_2^n, v \in \mathbb{F}_2^m} (-1)^{v \cdot \sum_{i=1}^w F(x_i) \oplus u \cdot \sum_{i=1}^w x_i} =$$

$$2^{n+m} |\{(x_1, \ldots, x_w) \in (\mathbb{F}_2^n)^w; \sum_{i=1}^w F(x_i) = 0_m \text{ and } \sum_{i=1}^w x_i = 0_n\}| =$$

$$2^{wn} + (2^m - 1) \cdot 2^{(\frac{w}{2}+1)n}.$$ ☐

6.1.4 Characterization of bentness by the NNF

The *ANF* does not allow directly characterizing bent functions, but the *NNF* does, and this provides then a possible characterization through the ANF by using Relation (2.24), page 50 (however, this characterization is complex, and we then do not state it explicitly).

The direct relationship between the Walsh transform values and the coefficients of the NNF gives

Proposition 67 *[292] Let $f(x) = \sum_{I \subseteq \{1,\dots,n\}} \lambda_I x^I$ be the NNF of a Boolean function f on $\mathbb{F}_2^n$. Then f is bent if and only if*

1. *For every I such that $\frac{n}{2} < |I| < n$, the coefficient λ_I is divisible by $2^{|I|-\frac{n}{2}}$;*
2. *$\lambda_{\{1,\dots,n\}} \equiv 2^{\frac{n}{2}-1}$ [mod $2^{\frac{n}{2}}$].*

Proof According to Lemma 5, page 190, f is bent if and only if, for every $a \in \mathbb{F}_2^n$, $\widehat{f}(a) \equiv 2^{\frac{n}{2}-1} \left[\mathrm{mod}\ 2^{\frac{n}{2}} \right]$. We deduce that, according to Relation (2.59), page 66, applied with $\varphi = f$, Conditions *1.* and *2.* are sufficient for f to be bent.

Conversely, Condition *1.* is necessary, according to Relation (2.60). Condition *2.* is also necessary since $\widehat{f}(1_n) = (-1)^n \lambda_{\{1,\dots,n\}}$, from Relation (2.59) or (2.60). □

The related characterization of bent functions by the ANF mentioned above implies conditions on the coefficients of the ANFs of bent functions, which have been observed and used in [301] (see more at page 243) and also partially observed by Hou and Langevin in [627].

Point 1 in Proposition 67 can be expressed by a single equation; see [293]. It is proved in this same reference that bentness can also be characterized by the generalized degree introduced at page 48.

6.1.5 Characterization of bentness by codes

A way of looking at bent functions deals with linear codes (as we mentioned in Section 4.1, at page 159): let f be any n-variable Boolean function (n even); we write its support $supp(f) = \{x \in \mathbb{F}_2^n;\ f(x) = 1\}$ as $\{u_1, \dots, u_{w_H(f)}\}$; we consider the matrix G whose columns are all the vectors of $supp(f)$, without repetition, and call C the linear code generated by the rows of this matrix. Then C is the set of all the vectors $U_v = (v \cdot u_1, \dots, v \cdot u_{w_H(f)})$, where v ranges over $\mathbb{F}_2^n$, and:

Proposition 68 *[1120] Let $n \geq 4$ be an even integer. Any n-variable Boolean function f is bent if and only if the linear code C whose generator matrix is the matrix whose columns are all the vectors of $supp(f)$ has dimension n, and has exactly two nonzero Hamming weights: 2^{n-2} and $w_H(f) - 2^{n-2}$.*

Indeed, for every nonzero v in $\mathbb{F}_2^n$, the Hamming weight of codeword U_v equals $\sum_{x \in \mathbb{F}_2^n} f(x) \times v \cdot x = \sum_{x \in \mathbb{F}_2^n} f(x) \frac{1-(-1)^{v \cdot x}}{2} = \frac{\widehat{f}(0_n) - \widehat{f}(v)}{2}$. Hence, according to Relation (2.32), page 55, relating Fourier–Hadamard and Walsh transforms, $w_H(U_v)$ equals

Table 6.1 Weight distribution of C_f for f bent.

Hamming weight	Multiplicity
0	1
2^{n-1}	$2^n - 1$
$2^{n-1} - 2^{\frac{n}{2}-1}$	$2^{n-1} + (-1)^{f(0_n)} 2^{\frac{n}{2}-1}$
$2^{n-1} + 2^{\frac{n}{2}-1}$	$2^{n-1} - (-1)^{f(0_n)} 2^{\frac{n}{2}-1}$

$2^{n-2} + \frac{W_f(v) - W_f(0_n)}{4}$. Thus, if f is bent, this weight is never null and C has then dimension n; moreover, either $W_f(v) = W_f(0_n)$ and $w_H(U_v) = 2^{n-2}$, or $W_f(v) = -W_f(0_n)$ and $w_H(U_v) = 2^{n-2} - \frac{W_f(0_n)}{2} = 2^{n-2} - \frac{2^n - 2w_H(f)}{2} = w_H(f) - 2^{n-2}$. Conversely, if C has dimension n and has exactly the two nonzero Hamming weights 2^{n-2} and $w_H(f) - 2^{n-2}$, then according to the relation $w_H(U_v) = 2^{n-2} + \frac{W_f(v) - W_f(0_n)}{4}$, for every v we have either $W_f(v) = W_f(0_n)$ or $W_f(v) = W_f(0_n) + 4w_H(f) - 2^{n+1} = -W_f(0_n)$ and, according to Parseval's relation (2.48), page 61, $W_f(v)$ equals then $\pm 2^{\frac{n}{2}}$ for every v, *i.e.*, f is bent.

C being linear, the minimum distance of C equals the minimum of these two nonzero weights: 2^{n-2} if $w_H(f) = 2^{n-1} + 2^{\frac{n}{2}-1}$ and $2^{n-2} - 2^{\frac{n}{2}-1}$ if $w_H(f) = 2^{n-1} - 2^{\frac{n}{2}-1}$.

There exist two other characterizations by Wolfmann [1120] dealing with C:

1. C has dimension n and C has exactly two weights, whose sum equals $w_H(f)$.
2. The length $w_H(f)$ of C is even, C has exactly two weights, and one of these weights is 2^{n-2}.

Of course, any bent Boolean function f can also be viewed as a (vectorial) $(n, 1)$-function and be related to the code C'_f seen at page 160, which has then weight distribution given by Table 6.1 (deduced from the Parseval and inverse Walsh transform formulae).

In [633, 634], the authors introduce the so-called near weight enumerator of a bent function f, equal to $W_{C_f}(X, Y) + 2^{\frac{n}{2}-1} X^n$, where W_{C_f} is the weight enumerator (see page 14) of the code $C_f = supp(f)$. A related Mac-Williams-like identity is shown between dual bent functions (see Definition 51, page 197), leading to a notion of formally self-dual bent function and a Gleason-type theorem (see Gleason's theorem at page 16). As an application is proved in [634], the non-existence of bent functions in $2n$ variables with lowest degree of nonconstant terms in their ANF equal to $n - k$, for any nonnegative integer k and $n \geq N$, where N is the smallest integer satisfying $\binom{N+k+1}{k+1} < 2^{N-1} - 1$.

6.1.6 Characterization of bentness by difference sets, relative difference sets, and structures of finite geometries

A subset D of a finite additive group G is called a $(|G|, |D|, \lambda)$-difference set in G if every nonzero element in G can be written in exactly λ ways as the difference between two elements of D (which implies $\lambda(|G| - 1) = |D|(|D| - 1)$). Equivalently, the incidence matrix $[D]$ defined by $[D]_{u,v} = 1$ if $u + v \in D$ and $[D]_{u,v} = 0$ otherwise satisfies $[D]^2 = (|D| - \lambda)I + \lambda J$, where I is the identity matrix and J the all-1 matrix [440]. Then $G \setminus D$ is also a difference set. Moreover, for any $g \in G$, $g + D$ is a difference set, called translate of D (we shall see in the next subsection that the set of all translates forms a symmetric block design).

It is observed in [441, 1005] that a Boolean function $f : \mathbb{F}_2^n \mapsto \mathbb{F}_2$ is bent if and only if its support $supp(f)$ is a nontrivial *difference set* in the elementary Abelian 2-group $\mathbb{F}_2^n$. It is known from Mann [824] that the parameters of such a difference set must then be $(|G|, |D|, \lambda) = (2^n, 2^{n-1} \pm 2^{\frac{n}{2}-1}, 2^{n-2} \pm 2^{\frac{n}{2}-1})$. Such a difference set is called a *Hadamard difference set*.

Note that the EA equivalence of two bent functions does not necessarily imply the equivalence of the related difference sets (see, *e.g.*, [695, page 265]).

A subset R of a finite additive group G is called a $(\frac{|G|}{|N|}, |N|, |R|, \lambda)$ *relative difference set* in G relative to a subgroup N of G if every element in $G \setminus N$ can be written in exactly λ ways as the difference between two elements of R and no nonzero element of N can be written this way. An n-variable Boolean function is bent if and only if its graph is a relative difference set relative to $\{0_n\} \times \mathbb{F}_2$. This property extends to vectorial functions. See more in [965] on the connections between Boolean or vectorial functions and such structures.

In [428], the author also characterized some bent functions by means of the notion of dimensional doubly dual hyperoval, in finite geometry.

6.1.7 The dual of a bent Boolean function

As linear codes, bent functions go by pairs:

Definition 51 *For every n even and every bent n-variable Boolean function f, the* dual *function $\widetilde{f}$ of f, is defined by*

$$\forall u \in \mathbb{F}_2^n, \ W_f(u) = 2^{\frac{n}{2}}(-1)^{\widetilde{f}(u)}.$$

Proposition 69 *[441, 1005] The dual of any bent function is also bent, and its own dual is f itself.*

Indeed, the inverse Walsh transform property (2.43), page 59, gives, for every $a \in \mathbb{F}_2^n$: $\sum_{u \in \mathbb{F}_2^n} (-1)^{\widetilde{f}(u) \oplus a \cdot u} = 2^{\frac{n}{2}}(-1)^{f(a)}$.

Let f and g be two bent functions, then Relation (2.46), page 60, applied with $\varphi(x) = f_\chi(x) = (-1)^{f(x)}$ and $\psi = g_\chi$, shows that

$$\mathcal{F}(\widetilde{f} \oplus \widetilde{g}) = \mathcal{F}(f \oplus g). \tag{6.2}$$

Thus, $f \oplus g$ and $\widetilde{f} \oplus \widetilde{g}$ have the same Hamming weight and:

Proposition 70 *[209, 212] The mapping $f \mapsto \widetilde{f}$ is an isometry of the class of bent n-variable Boolean functions.*

Remark. This isometry clearly cannot be extended into an isometry of the whole space $\mathcal{BF}_n$. Indeed, there would exist then a permutation π of $\mathbb{F}_2^n$ and an n-variable Boolean function g such that $\widetilde{f} = f \circ \pi \oplus g$ for every bent function f, and the examples of duals of bent functions we know (with Maiorana–McFarland functions, for instance) show that such π, g do not exist. $\square$

The mapping $f \mapsto \widetilde{f}$ also preserves EA equivalence, as originally observed in [441] in different terms. Indeed, for every linear automorphism L, we have according to Relation (2.58), page 63, that $\widetilde{f \circ L} = \widetilde{f} \circ L'$, where L' is the adjoint operator of L^{-1}, and, for every $a, b \in \mathbb{F}_2^n$, we have according to Lemma 4, page 58, that $\widetilde{f \circ t_b \oplus \ell_a} = \widetilde{f} \circ t_a \oplus \ell_b \oplus a \cdot b$, where t_a is the translation by a.

Denoting $b \cdot x$ by $\ell_b(x)$, Relation (6.2), applied with $g(x) = f(x + b) \oplus a \cdot x$, gives

$$\mathcal{F}(D_a \widetilde{f} \oplus \ell_b) = (-1)^{a \cdot b} \mathcal{F}(D_b f \oplus \ell_a), \tag{6.3}$$

and applied with $g(x) = f(x) \oplus \ell_a(x)$ and with $f(x + b)$ in the place of $f(x)$, it gives the following property, first observed in [219] (and rediscovered in [193]):

$$\mathcal{F}(D_a \widetilde{f} \oplus \ell_b) = \mathcal{F}(D_b f \oplus \ell_a). \tag{6.4}$$

This implies in particular the following relation that we shall need in the sequel:

$$\sum_{a,b \in \mathbb{F}_2^n} \mathcal{F}(D_a \widetilde{f} \oplus \ell_b) = \sum_{a,b \in \mathbb{F}_2^n} \mathcal{F}(D_b f \oplus \ell_a). \tag{6.5}$$

Moreover, from Relations (6.3) and (6.4), we deduce

Proposition 71 *[236] Let f be any n-variable bent function. For every $a, b \in \mathbb{F}_2^n$, let us denote $\ell_b(x) = b \cdot x$ and $\ell_a(x) = a \cdot x$. Then $D_a \widetilde{f}$ and $D_b f$ satisfy Relation (6.4). Moreover, if $a \cdot b = 1$, then $\mathcal{F}(D_a \widetilde{f} \oplus \ell_b) = \mathcal{F}(D_b f \oplus \ell_a) = 0$.*

In fact, Relation (6.4) is in a way characteristic of bent functions:

Proposition 72 *[236] If a pair of n-variable Boolean functions f and f' satisfies the relation $\mathcal{F}(D_a f' \oplus \ell_b) = \mathcal{F}(D_b f \oplus \ell_a)$ for every $a, b \in \mathbb{F}_2^n$, then these functions are bent and are the dual of each other, up to the addition of a constant function.*

Proof Taking $a = 0_n$ in the equality $\mathcal{F}(D_a f' \oplus \ell_b) = \mathcal{F}(D_b f \oplus \ell_a)$ shows that $D_b f$ is balanced for every $b \neq 0_n$ and taking $b = 0_n$ shows that $D_a f'$ is balanced for every $a \neq 0_n$. This proves the first assertion. Let us sum up the relations $\mathcal{F}(D_a f' \oplus \ell_b) = \mathcal{F}(D_b f \oplus \ell_a)$ for b ranging over $\mathbb{F}_2^n$. We obtain the equalities $\sum_{x,b \in \mathbb{F}_2^n} (-1)^{f'(x) \oplus f'(x+a) \oplus b \cdot x} = \sum_{x,b \in \mathbb{F}_2^n} (-1)^{f(x) \oplus f(x+b) \oplus a \cdot x} = \sum_{x,y \in \mathbb{F}_2^n} (-1)^{f(x) \oplus f(y) \oplus a \cdot x} = W_f(0_n) \times W_f(a)$, and this gives $2^n (-1)^{f'(0_n) \oplus f'(a)} = 2^n (-1)^{\widetilde{f}(0_n) \oplus \widetilde{f}(a)}$, that is, $f'(0_n) \oplus f'(a) = \widetilde{f}(0_n) \oplus \widetilde{f}(a)$, for every a. $\square$

Notice that, for every a and b, we have $D_b f = \ell_a \oplus \epsilon$ if and only if $D_a \widetilde{f} = \ell_b \oplus \epsilon$.

Rothaus already observed that "many" bent functions are equal to their duals, *i.e.*, are *self-dual bent functions*. The characterization of self-dual bent functions is an open problem, partially addressed in [265, 502, 626] (the latter reference classifies self-dual bent quadratic functions under the action of the orthogonal group, *i.e.*, the group of $n \times n$ matrices M

such that $MM^t = I$). See also [806]. It is observed in [265] that a Boolean n-variable function is self-dual bent or anti-self-dual bent (*i.e.*, bent such that $\tilde{f} = f \oplus 1$) if and only if its so-called *Rayleigh quotient* $\sum_{x,y \in \mathbb{F}_2^n} (-1)^{f(x) \oplus f(y) \oplus x \cdot y} = \sum_{x \in \mathbb{F}_2^n} (-1)^{f(x)} W_f(x)$ has maximal modulus (that is, has modulus $2^{\frac{3n}{2}}$), which is easier to handle in the case of quadratic functions: [626] uses that the associate *symplectic matrix* (see the footnote at page 171) is then involutive.

Remark. Since Boolean functions can be expressed in different forms, the question of moving from one form to another is important. For general functions, we have addressed this question at page 47. Regarding the duals, we have the easily proved following lemma (see, *e.g.*, [311]), in which an autodual basis is a pair (u, v) such that $tr_{n/2}^n(u) = tr_{n/2}^n(v) = 1$ and $tr_{n/2}^n(uv) = 0$. ☐

Lemma 6 *Let n be even and $m = \frac{n}{2}$. Let (u, v) be an autodual basis of $\mathbb{F}_{2^n}$ over $\mathbb{F}_{2^m}$. Let f be bent over $\mathbb{F}_{2^n}$ and $g(x, y) = f(ux + vy)$, $x, y \in \mathbb{F}_{2^m}$.*
Then

$$W_f(au + bv) = W_g(a, b),$$

where W_f is calculated with respect to the inner product $X \cdot Y = tr_n(XY)$ and W_g is calculated with respect to the inner product $(x, y) \cdot (x', y') = tr_m(xx' + yy')$. Hence, if f is bent, then $\tilde{f}(au + bv) = \tilde{g}(a, b)$.

Numerical normal form of the dual

The *numerical normal form* of $\tilde{f}$ can be deduced from that of f. Indeed, using equality $\tilde{f} = \frac{1 - (-1)^{\tilde{f}}}{2}$, we have $\tilde{f} = \frac{1}{2} - 2^{-\frac{n}{2}-1} W_f = \frac{1}{2} - 2^{\frac{n}{2}-1} \delta_0 + 2^{-\frac{n}{2}} \hat{f}$. Applying now to $\varphi = f$ Relation (2.59), page 66, expressing the value of the Fourier–Hadamard transform by means of the coefficients of the NNF, we deduce that if $\sum_{I \subseteq \{1,...,n\}} \lambda_I x^I$ is the NNF of f, then

$$\tilde{f}(x) = \frac{1}{2} - 2^{\frac{n}{2}-1} \delta_0(x) + (-1)^{w_H(x)} \sum_{I \subseteq \{1,...,n\}; \, supp(x) \subseteq I} 2^{\frac{n}{2}-|I|} \lambda_I.$$

Changing I into $\{1, \ldots, n\} \setminus I$ in this relation, and observing that $supp(x)$ is included in $\{1, \ldots, n\} \setminus I$ if and only if $x_i = 0, \forall i \in I$, we obtain the NNF of $\tilde{f}$ by expanding the following relation: $\tilde{f}(x) =$

$$\frac{1}{2} - 2^{\frac{n}{2}-1} \prod_{i=1}^n (1 - x_i) + (-1)^{w_H(x)} \sum_{I \subseteq \{1,...,n\}} 2^{|I|-\frac{n}{2}} \lambda_{\{1,...,n\} \setminus I} \prod_{i \in I} (1 - x_i). \qquad (6.6)$$

We deduce again that, for every $I \neq \{1, \ldots, n\}$ such that $|I| > \frac{n}{2}$, the coefficient of x^I in the NNF of $\tilde{f}$ (resp. of f) is divisible by $2^{|I|-\frac{n}{2}}$.

Reducing Relation (6.6) modulo 2 proves Rothaus' bound (see Theorem 13 below) and the following fact:

Proposition 73 *[1005] Let $n \geq 4$ be even and f be any n-variable bent Boolean function. For every $I \subset \{1, \ldots, n\}$ such that $|I| = \frac{n}{2}$, the coefficient of x^I in the ANF of $\tilde{f}$ equals the coefficient of $x^{\{1, \ldots, n\} \setminus I}$ in the ANF of f.*

Using Relation (2.24), page 50, expressing the NNF by means of the ANF, Equality (6.6) can be related to the main result of [619] (but this result by Hou is stated in a complex way).

The *Poisson summation formula* (2.39), page 58, applied to $\varphi = f_\chi = (-1)^f$ gives (see [212]) that for every vector subspace E of $\mathbb{F}_2^n$, and for every elements a and b of $\mathbb{F}_2^n$, we have

$$\sum_{x \in a + E} (-1)^{\tilde{f}(x) \oplus b \cdot x} = 2^{-\frac{n}{2}} |E| (-1)^{a \cdot b} \sum_{x \in b + E^\perp} (-1)^{f(x) \oplus a \cdot x}. \tag{6.7}$$

In particular, $f(x) \oplus a \cdot x$ is constant on $b + E^\perp$ if and only if $\sum_{x \in a + E} (-1)^{\tilde{f}(x) \oplus b \cdot x} = \pm 2^{\frac{n}{2}}$, and if E has dimension $\frac{n}{2}$, this is equivalent to the fact that $\tilde{f}(x) \oplus b \cdot x$ is constant (with the same value on $a + E$ as $f(x) \oplus a \cdot x$ on $b + E^\perp$ if $a \cdot b = 0$). Note that if $f(0_n) = 0$ and $b = 0_n$, this means that the constant value of $\tilde{f}(x)$ on $a + E$ is zero. This is particularly interesting when f is self-dual.

6.1.8 Bound on algebraic degree and related properties

The algebraic degree of any Boolean function f being equal to the maximum size of the multi-index I such that x^I has an odd coefficient in the NNF of f, Proposition 67, page 195, gives:

Theorem 13 *[441, 1005] Let $n \geq 4$ be an even integer. The algebraic degree of any bent function on $\mathbb{F}_2^n$ is at most $\frac{n}{2}$.*

In the case that $n = 2$, the bent functions have degree 2, since they have odd Hamming weight (in fact, they are the functions of odd weights).

The minimal possible Hamming distance between two bent n-variable functions is $2^{\frac{n}{2}}$, since this is the minimum distance of $RM(\frac{n}{2}, n)$ (see Theorem 7), and since such distance is achieved by bent functions.

The bound of Theorem 13 is called *Rothaus' bound*. It shows, as observed by Dillon and Rothaus, that n-variable bent functions of algebraic degree $n/2$ can not be the direct sums (see page 232) of (necessarily bent) functions in less variables. Theorem 13 can also be proved with the same method as for proving Theorem 2, page 63, which also allows obtaining a bound, shown in [620], relating the gaps between $\frac{n}{2}$ and the algebraic degrees of f and $\tilde{f}$:

Proposition 74 *The algebraic degrees of any n-variable bent function and of its dual satisfy*

$$\frac{n}{2} - d_{alg}(f) \geq \frac{\frac{n}{2} - d_{alg}(\tilde{f})}{d_{alg}(\tilde{f}) - 1}. \tag{6.8}$$

Proof of Proposition 74 and alternative proof of Theorem 13: Let us denote by d (resp. by $\tilde{d}$) the algebraic degree of f (resp. of $\tilde{f}$) and consider a term x^I of degree d in the ANF of f. The Poisson summation formula (2.40), page 59, applied to $\varphi = f_\chi$ and to the vector space $E = \{u \in \mathbb{F}_2^n; \forall i \in I, u_i = 0\}$ gives $\sum_{u \in E}(-1)^{\widetilde{f}(u)} = 2^{\frac{n}{2}-d} \sum_{x \in E^\perp} f_\chi(x)$. The orthogonal $E^\perp$ of E equals $\{u \in \mathbb{F}_2^n; \forall i \notin I, u_i = 0\}$. According to Relation (2.4), page 33, the restriction of f to $E^\perp$ has odd Hamming weight w, thus $\sum_{x \in E^\perp} f_\chi(x) = 2^d - 2w$ is not divisible by 4. Hence, $\sum_{u \in E}(-1)^{\widetilde{f}(u)}$ is not divisible by $2^{\frac{n}{2}-d+2}$.

We deduce first Theorem 13: suppose that $d > \frac{n}{2}$, then $\sum_{u \in E}(-1)^{\widetilde{f}(u)}$ is not even, a contradiction since E has an even size (indeed, we have $I \neq \{1, \dots, n\}$, because f has algebraic degree smaller than n, since it has even Hamming weight).

We prove now Proposition 74: according to McEliece's theorem (or Ax's theorem), page 156, $\sum_{u \in E}(-1)^{\widetilde{f}(u)}$ is divisible by $2^{\left\lceil \frac{n-d}{d} \right\rceil}$. We deduce the inequality $\frac{n}{2} - d + 2 > \left\lceil \frac{n-d}{d} \right\rceil$, that is, $\frac{n}{2} - d + 1 \geq \frac{n-d}{d}$, which is equivalent to (6.8). $\qquad\square$

Using Relation (2.22), page 49, instead of Relation (2.4) gives a more precise result than Theorem 13, shown in [292], which will be given in Section 6.1.18.

Proposition 74 can also be deduced from Proposition 67 and from some divisibility properties, shown in [292], of the coefficients of the NNFs of Boolean functions of algebraic degree d.

More on the algebraic degree of bent functions can be said for *homogeneous functions* (see page 248).

Remark. The *numerical degree* of a bent function equals n since the Walsh transform does not vanish. $\qquad\square$

6.1.9 Bent Boolean functions and designs

A *balanced incomplete block design* (BIBD), or *2-design*, is a collection of subsets (called blocks) of the same size in some finite set, such that each pair of distinct elements is included in the same number λ of blocks (then any element is contained in the same number of blocks as well). A BIBD is symmetric if the number of block equals the number of elements.[7] As recalled in [313], at least two designs are associated with any bent function f (cf. [441, 450, 656]):

1. The *difference set design* $D(f)$, in which the blocks are the translates $c + D$, $c \in \mathbb{F}_2^n$, of the support $D = supp(f) = f^{-1}(1)$ (or of the *co-support@cosupport* $f^{-1}(0_n)$). Suppose for instance that f has Hamming weight $2^{n-1} + 2^{n/2-1}$ and that $D = f^{-1}(0_n)$; given a pair $\{x, y\}$ of distinct elements, the number of c such that $\{x, y\} \subset c + D$ equals $|\{c \in \mathbb{F}_2^n; f(x+c) = f(y+c) = 0\}|$, that is, $w_H(f \oplus 1) - \frac{w_H(D_{x+y} f \oplus 1)}{2} = 2^{n-2} - 2^{n/2-1}$ (since we have $|(x + D) \cap (y + D)| = |D| - \frac{(x+D) \Delta (y+D)}{2}$).

2. The *code design* $C(f)$, in which the blocks are the supports D'_c of the functions $f(x) \oplus c \cdot x \oplus \epsilon$, where ϵ is chosen such that $w_H(f(x) \oplus c \cdot x \oplus \epsilon) = 2^{n-1} - 2^{n/2-1}$. That is, $\epsilon = \widetilde{f}(c)$; hence $D'_c = \{x; f(x) \oplus c \cdot x \oplus \widetilde{f}(c) = 1\}$; this design has the same parameters as the difference set design (designs with such parameters are called *Menon designs*): denoting $l_x(c) = c \cdot x$, the number of those c such that a pair $\{x, y\}$

---

[7] When $\lambda = 1$, we have a projective plane; the blocks are the lines.

of distinct elements is included in D'_c equals $w_H((\widetilde{f} \oplus l_x \oplus f(x))(\widetilde{f} \oplus l_y \oplus f(y))) =$
$\frac{w_H(\widetilde{f}\oplus l_x\oplus f(x))+w_H(\widetilde{f}\oplus l_y\oplus f(y))-w_H(l_{x+y}\oplus f(x)\oplus f(y))}{2} = \frac{2^{n-1}-2^{n/2-1}+2^{n-1}-2^{n/2-1}-2^{n-1}}{2} =$
$2^{n-2} - 2^{n/2-1}$.

$D(f)$ admits all translations as automorphisms, but $C(f)$ has no obvious automorphism.

Related notions of equivalence can then be studied: two bent functions f and g could be called "difference set design equivalent" if $D(f)$ and $D(g)$ are isomorphic designs, and "code design equivalent" if $C(f)$ and $C(g)$ are isomorphic designs.

Note that the designs $D(f)$ and $C(f)$ are equal if and only if f is quadratic. Indeed, the quadratic bent functions have the property that for every linear function $l(x)$, the function $f(x) \oplus l(x)$ equals $f(x+a) \oplus \epsilon$, for some $a \in \mathbb{F}_2^n$ and some $\epsilon \in \mathbb{F}_2$. The set $\{D_a f, a \in \mathbb{F}_2^n\} + \mathbb{F}_2$ equals then the Reed–Muller code of order 1; this allows proving that $D(f) = C(f)$. Conversely, $D(f) = C(f)$ for a bent Boolean function implies that all derivatives have algebraic degree at most 1, which is equivalent to "f is quadratic."

6.1.10 Bent Boolean functions and affine subspaces

The Poisson summation formula (2.39), page 58, applied on f or on f_χ with $a = 0_n$, shows that the intersection between the support D of an n-variable bent function and a k-dimensional affine subspace $b + E$ of $\mathbb{F}_2^n$, where $k \geq n/2$, equals $2^{k-n}(2^{n-1} - 2^{n/2-1} \sum_{u \in E^\perp}(-1)^{\widetilde{f}(u)\oplus b\cdot u})$ and lies then between $2^{k-1} - 2^{n/2-1}$ and $2^{k-1} + 2^{n/2-1}$, as observed by Dillon. This implies that D can contain $b + E$ or be disjoint from $b + E$ only if $k = n/2$, and that if D contains $b + E$ (resp. is disjoint from $b + E$), then D has balanced intersection with any proper coset, and $D \setminus (b + E)$ (resp. $D \cup (b + E)$) is also a difference set. Studying the intersection of the supports of bent functions and affine spaces results in studying the sums of bent functions and indicators of flats:

Theorem 14 *[212] Let $b + E$ be any flat in $\mathbb{F}_2^n$ (E being a linear subspace of $\mathbb{F}_2^n$). Let f be any bent function on $\mathbb{F}_2^n$ (n even). The function $f^* = f \oplus 1_{b+E}$ is bent if and only if one of the following equivalent conditions is satisfied:*

1. *For any a in $\mathbb{F}_2^n \setminus E$, the function $D_a f$ is balanced on $b + E$.*
2. *The restriction of the function $\widetilde{f}(x) \oplus b \cdot x$ to any coset of $E^\perp$ is either constant or balanced.*

If f and f^* are bent, then E has dimension larger than or equal to $n/2$ and the algebraic degree of the restriction of f to $b + E$ is at most $\dim(E) - \frac{n}{2} + 1$.

  If f is bent, E has dimension $\frac{n}{2}$, and the restriction of f to $b + E$ has algebraic degree at most $\dim(E) - \frac{n}{2} + 1 = 1$, i.e., is affine, then conversely f^* is bent too.

Proof The equivalence between Condition 1 and the bentness of f^* is directly deduced from the fact that $\mathcal{F}(D_a f^*)$ equals $\mathcal{F}(D_a f)$ if $a \in E$, and equals $\mathcal{F}(D_a f) - 4 \sum_{x \in b+E}(-1)^{D_a f(x)}$ otherwise (since when $a \notin E$, the cosets $b + E$ and $b + a + E$ are disjoint, and $D_a f$ takes the same values on both of them).

Condition 2 is also necessary and sufficient, since we have $W_f(a) - W_{f^*}(a) = 2\sum_{x \in b+E}(-1)^{f(x) \oplus a \cdot x}$, and using Relation (6.7), page 200, applied with $E^\perp$ in the place of E, we have then, for every $a \in \mathbb{F}_2^n$:

$$\sum_{u \in a+E^\perp} (-1)^{\widetilde{f}(u) \oplus b \cdot u} = 2^{\dim(E^\perp) - \frac{n}{2} - 1}(-1)^{a \cdot b}\left(W_f(a) - W_{f^*}(a)\right).$$

Then $W_f(a) - W_f^*(a)$ takes value 0 or $\pm 2^{\frac{n}{2}+1}$ for every a (which is necessary, and is sufficient according to Lemma 5, page 190) if and only if Condition 2 is satisfied.

Let us now assume that f and f^* are bent. Then $1_{b+E} = f^* \oplus f$ has algebraic degree at most $\frac{n}{2}$, according to Rothaus' bound, and thus $\dim(E) \geq \frac{n}{2}$.

The values of the Walsh transform of the restriction of f to $b + E$ being equal to those of $\frac{1}{2}\left(W_f - W_{f^*}\right)$, they are divisible by $2^{\frac{n}{2}}$ and thus the restriction of f to $b+E$ has algebraic degree at most $\dim(E) - \frac{n}{2} + 1$, according to Theorem 2.

If f is bent, E has dimension $\frac{n}{2}$, and the restriction of f to $b + E$ is affine, then the relation $W_f(a) - W_f^*(a) = 2\sum_{x \in b+E}(-1)^{f(x) \oplus a \cdot x}$ shows that f^* is bent too, according to Lemma 5.   □

Remark. Relation (6.7) applied to $E^\perp$ in the place of E, where E is some $\frac{n}{2}$-dimensional subspace, shows that, if f is a bent function on $\mathbb{F}_2^n$, then $f(x) \oplus a \cdot x$ is constant on $b + E$ if and only if $\widetilde{f}(x) \oplus b \cdot x$ is constant on $a + E^\perp$. The same relation shows that $f(x) \oplus a \cdot x$ is then balanced on every other coset of E and $\widetilde{f}(x) \oplus b \cdot x$ is balanced on every other coset of $E^\perp$. Notice that Relation (6.7) shows also that $f(x) \oplus a \cdot x$ cannot be constant on a flat of dimension strictly larger than $\frac{n}{2}$ (*i.e.*, that f cannot be k-weakly normal with $k > \frac{n}{2}$).   □

Remark. Let f be bent on $\mathbb{F}_2^n$. Let a and a' be two linearly independent elements of $\mathbb{F}_2^n$. Let us denote by E the orthogonal of the subspace spanned by a and a'. According to Condition 2 in Theorem 14, the function $f \oplus 1_E$ is bent if and only if $D_a D_{a'} \widetilde{f}$ is null (indeed, a 2-variable function is constant or balanced if and only if it has even Hamming weight, and $\widetilde{f}$ has even weight on any coset of the vector subspace spanned by a and a' if and only if, for every vector x, we have $f(x) \oplus f(x + a) \oplus f(x + a') \oplus f(x + a + a') = 0$). This result, stated in [193] and used in [198, Corollary 15] to design a new class of bent functions, is then a direct consequence of Theorem 14.   □

6.1.11 Affine spaces of bent Boolean functions

It is observed in [210] that k-dimensional affine spaces of bent Boolean n-variable functions with k even correspond to bent functions in $n + k$ variables of a particular form. We shall denote these affine spaces in the form $f+ < f_1, \ldots, f_k >$, where $< f_1, \ldots, f_k >$ denotes the vector space over $\mathbb{F}_2$ spanned by $\mathbb{F}_2$-linearly independent functions $f_1, \ldots, f_k$.

Proposition 75 *[210] For every positive even integers n, k, a k-dimensional affine space of Boolean n-variable functions $f+ < f_1, \ldots, f_k >$ contains only bent functions if and only if the Boolean function*

$$h : (x, y) \in \mathbb{F}_2^n \times \mathbb{F}_2^k \mapsto \bigoplus_{i=1}^{\frac{k}{2}} (y_{2i-1} \oplus f_{2i-1}(x))(y_{2i} \oplus f_{2i}(x)) \oplus f(x)$$

is bent.

The proof is a generalization of the calculations made in Section 5.3, page 180.

Proof   For every $(a, b) \in \mathbb{F}_2^n \times \mathbb{F}_2^k$, we have $W_h(a, b) =$

$$\sum_{(x,y) \in \mathbb{F}_2^n \times \mathbb{F}_2^k} (-1)^{\bigoplus_{i=1}^{\frac{k}{2}} (y_{2i-1} \oplus f_{2i-1}(x) \oplus b_{2i})(y_{2i} \oplus f_{2i}(x) \oplus b_{2i-1}) \oplus f(x) \oplus a \cdot x}$$

$$\cdot (-1)^{\bigoplus_{i=1}^{\frac{k}{2}} [b_{2i} b_{2i-1} \oplus b_{2i} f_{2i}(x) \oplus b_{2i-1} f_{2i-1}(x)]} =$$

$$\sum_{(x,y) \in \mathbb{F}_2^n \times \mathbb{F}_2^k} (-1)^{\bigoplus_{i=1}^{\frac{k}{2}} y_{2i-1} y_{2i} \oplus f(x) \oplus a \cdot x \oplus \bigoplus_{i=1}^{\frac{k}{2}} [b_{2i} b_{2i-1} \oplus b_{2i} f_{2i}(x) \oplus b_{2i-1} f_{2i-1}(x)]} =$$

$$2^{\frac{k}{2}} \sum_{x \in \mathbb{F}_2^n} (-1)^{\bigoplus_{i=1}^{\frac{k}{2}} [b_{2i} b_{2i-1} \oplus b_{2i} f_{2i}(x) \oplus b_{2i-1} f_{2i-1}(x)] \oplus f(x) \oplus a \cdot x} =$$

$$\pm 2^{\frac{k}{2}} W_{\bigoplus_{j=1}^k b_j f_j(x) \oplus f(x)}(a)$$

(by making the changes of variables $y_{2i-1} \mapsto y_{2i-1} \oplus f_{2i-1}(x) \oplus b_{2i}$ and $y_{2i} \mapsto y_{2i} \oplus f_{2i}(x) \oplus b_{2i-1}$ and using that $\sum_{y \in \mathbb{F}_2^k} (-1)^{\bigoplus_{i=1}^{\frac{k}{2}} y_{2i-1} y_{2i}} = 2^{\frac{k}{2}}$). Hence h is bent if and only if each function $\bigoplus_{j=1}^k b_j f_j(x) \oplus f(x)$ is bent. $\square$

Remark.   The situation with k-dimensional affine spaces of bent functions is quite different from what we have with k-dimensional vector spaces of Boolean functions whose nonzero elements are all bent: these latter vector spaces are in correspondence with bent (n, k)-functions: their nonzero elements are the component functions of these bent vectorial functions (see Section 6.4, page 268) and can then exist only if $k \leq \frac{n}{2}$ (see Proposition 104, page 269). $\square$

An example of application of Proposition 75 is given in [210], providing a large number of $(m - 2)$-variable bent functions of algebraic degree 4 from any m-variable cubic bent function: let h be any such function, and we have that each derivative $D_u h(x)$ is quadratic and balanced for every $u \neq 0_m$, since h is bent. According to Proposition 55, page 171 (see also the few lines following the proposition), for each $u \neq 0_m$, there exists v such that $D_v D_u h$ equals the constant function 1, that is, $D_u h(x + v) = D_u h(x) \oplus 1$, that is, $h(x + u + v) = h(x) \oplus h(x + u) \oplus h(x + v)] \oplus 1$, and hence:

$$\forall x \in \mathbb{F}_2^m, \forall y_1, y_2 \in \mathbb{F}_2, h(y_1 u + y_2 v + x) = h(x) \oplus y_1 D_u h(x) \oplus y_2 D_v h(x) \oplus y_1 y_2.$$

(This can be checked for each value of (y_1, y_2).) We can then see that Proposition 75 can be applied with $n = m - 2, k = 2$, by taking for f the restriction of $h(x) + D_u h(x) D_v h(x)$ to an $(m - 2)$-dimensional vector space E not containing u, v nor $u + v$ (identifying then this vector space with $\mathbb{F}_2^n$), for f_1 the restriction of $D_u h$ to E and for f_2 the restriction of $D_v h$ to E. We deduce that the two-dimensional affine space $(h \oplus D_u h D_v h)_{|E} + < D_u h_{|E}, D_v h_{|E} >$ contains only bent functions. These bent functions have algebraic degree 4 in general.

6.1.12 A graph related to bent functions

In [716], the author studies the graph G whose vertices are the bent functions and whose edges connect vertices at Hamming distance $2^{\frac{n}{2}}$ of each other. It is shown that the degree of any vertex is not more than $2^{\frac{n}{2}} \prod_{i=1}^{n/2}(2^i + 1)$, and that this bound is achieved with equality by quadratic bent functions, and only by them.

The minimal codewords of Reed–Muller codes being indicators of affine spaces (see Theorem 8, page 154), if two bent functions lie at distance $2^{\frac{n}{2}}$ from each other, then according to Rothaus' bound and to Theorem 14, page 202, they are weakly normal and they differ by the indicator of the $\frac{n}{2}$-dimensional space on which they are affine. Hence, if a bent function is not weakly normal, there is no bent function at Hamming distance $2^{\frac{n}{2}}$ from it. According to the existence of bent functions for $n \geq 14$, which are not weakly normal, G is disconnected if $n \geq 14$ (it is connected if $n \leq 6$; the question whether it is disconnected for $8 \leq n \leq 12$ seems open). Does it remain disconnected when we take off all vertices corresponding to functions being not weakly normal ? See more in [716].

6.1.13 Bent Boolean functions of low algebraic degrees

Quadratic bent functions

All the quadratic bent functions are known. According to the properties recalled in Section 5.2, any quadratic function

$$f(x) = \bigoplus_{1 \leq i < j \leq n} a_{i,j} \, x_i \, x_j \oplus h(x) \; (h \text{ affine}, a_{i,j} \in \mathbb{F}_2)$$

is bent if and only if one of the following equivalent properties is satisfied:

1. Its Hamming weight is equal to $2^{n-1} \pm 2^{\frac{n}{2}-1}$.
2. Its associated symplectic form $\beta_f : (x, y) \mapsto f(0_n) \oplus f(x) \oplus f(y) \oplus f(x + y)$ is nondegenerate (*i.e.*, has kernel $\{0_n\}$).
3. The matrix of this symplectic form, that is, the skew-symmetric matrix $M = (m_{i,j})_{i,j \in \{1,\dots,n\}}$ over $\mathbb{F}_2$, defined by $m_{i,j} = a_{i,j}$ if $i < j$, $m_{i,j} = 0$ if $i = j$, and $m_{i,j} = a_{j,i}$ if $i > j$, is nonsingular (*i.e.*, has determinant 1).
4. $f(x)$ is equivalent, up to an affine nonsingular transformation, to the function. $x_1 x_2 \oplus x_3 x_4 \oplus \cdots \oplus x_{n-1} x_n \oplus \epsilon \; (\epsilon \in \mathbb{F}_2)$.

Hence, there is a unique EA equivalence class of bent functions, as Rothaus and Dillon already observed in different terms.

Remark. According to these characterizations, there exist (quadratic) bent functions for every even positive n (we can take the simplest one $x_1 x_2 \oplus \cdots \oplus x_{n-1} x_n$). Thus, the *covering radius* of the Reed–Muller code of order 1 equals $2^{n-1} - 2^{\frac{n}{2}-1}$ when n is even. $\qquad\square$

Note that when f is bent in Proposition 57, page 175, that is, when $\mathcal{E}_f$ is the trivial vector space, $\mathcal{E}_f^\perp$ equals the whole space $\mathbb{F}_2^n$ and the linear functions $y \mapsto \beta_f(x, y)$ cover then all linear forms on $\mathbb{F}_2^n$ (once each) when x ranges over $\mathbb{F}_2^n$. Examples of quadratic bent functions over $\mathbb{F}_2^n$ are

- The so-called Maiorana–McFarland (see below) quadratic bent functions $f(x, y) = x \cdot \pi(y) \oplus h(y)$, where $x, y \in \mathbb{F}_2^{n/2}$ and π is an affine permutation of $\mathbb{F}_2^{n/2}$.
- The elementary quadratic *symmetric Boolean function* $\sigma_2(x) = \binom{w_H(x)}{2}$ [mod 2] $= \bigoplus_{1 \le i < j \le n} x_i x_j$ (which is, up to the addition of an affine symmetric function, the only symmetric bent function; see Section 10.1). This function is bent because the kernel of it associated symplectic form $\varphi(x, y) = \bigoplus_{1 \le i \ne j \le n} x_i y_j$, equal to $\{(x_1, \ldots, x_n) \in \mathbb{F}_2^n;\ \forall i = 1, \ldots, n, \bigoplus_{j \ne i} x_j = 0\}$ is reduced to $\{0_n\}$, since n is even.

Quadratic bent functions in trace representation We have seen at page 176 how the Hamming weight and Walsh transform values of quadratic Boolean functions in trace form can be calculated.

A generic quadratic function $tr_n \left(\sum_{k=1}^{\frac{n}{2}-1} a_k x^{2^k+1} \right) + tr_{n/2} \left(a_{n/2} x^{2^{n/2}+1} \right) + \ell(x)$, where $a_1, \ldots, a_{\frac{n}{2}-1} \in \mathbb{F}_{2^n}$, $a_{n/2} \in \mathbb{F}_{2^{n/2}}$ and ℓ is affine, is bent if and only if the equation $\sum_{k=1}^{\frac{n}{2}-1} \left(a_k x^{2^k} + a_k^{2^{n-k}} x^{2^{n-k}} \right) + a_{n/2} x^{2^{n/2}} = 0$ has 0 for the only solution, that is, the linearized polynomial on the left-hand side is a permutation polynomial.

In the case of *Gold Boolean functions* $f(x) = tr_n(ax^{2^i+1})$; $a \in \mathbb{F}_{2^n}^*$, Carlitz' result shows that, for $i = 1$, f is bent if and only if a is not a cube (see page 177). For general i, raising the equation $ax^{2^i} + (ax)^{2^{n-i}} = 0$ to the 2^ith power gives $a^{2^i} x^{2^{2i}} + ax = 0$. Hence, $x \ne 0$ is a solution if and only if $(ax^{2^i+1})^{2^i-1} = 1$, that is, $ax^{2^i+1} \in \mathbb{F}_{2^n} \cap \mathbb{F}_{2^i} = \mathbb{F}_{2^{\gcd(i,n)}}$ and since $2^i + 1$ and $2^i - 1$ are coprime and $x \mapsto x^{2^i+1}$ is then a permutation in $\mathbb{F}_{2^{\gcd(i,n)}}$, the existence of such x is equivalent to that of x such that $x^{2^i+1} = \frac{1}{a}$; function $tr_n(ax^{2^i+1})$ is then bent if and only if $a \notin \{x^{2^i+1}, x \in \mathbb{F}_{2^n}\}$. Such a exists if and only if function x^{2^i+1} is not a permutation on $\mathbb{F}_{2^n}$, that is, $\gcd(2^i+1, 2^n-1) \ne 1$, and since $2^{2i} - 1 = (2^i-1)(2^i+1)$ and $2^i - 1$ and $2^i + 1$ are coprime, we have $\gcd(2^i + 1, 2^n - 1) = \frac{\gcd(2^{2i}-1, 2^n-1)}{\gcd(2^i-1, 2^n-1)} = \frac{2^{\gcd(2i,n)}-1}{2^{\gcd(i,n)}-1}$; the condition is then that $\frac{n}{\gcd(i,n)}$ is even. Being quadratic, these functions belong to the completed Maiorana–McFarland class.

Another classical example of quadratic bent function is

$$f(x) = tr_n \left(\sum_{i=1}^{\frac{n}{2}-1} x^{2^i+1} \right) + tr_{\frac{n}{2}} \left(x^{2^{\frac{n}{2}}+1} \right).$$

The equation $\sum_{i=1}^{\frac{n}{2}-1} (x^{2^i} + x^{2^{n-i}}) + x^{2^{n/2}} = 0$, that is, $x + tr_n(x) = 0$ has indeed clearly 0 as the only solution, since $tr_n(x) \in \mathbb{F}_2$ and $tr_n(1) = 0$.

Quadratic bent functions are studied in [355, 629, 632, 699, 1144] (with the viewpoint of linearized permutation polynomials in the latter reference) and deduced in [768] from generalized bent functions.

An example of bivariate bent function over $\mathbb{F}_{2^n}$ for every n is from [236]. Function

$$f(x, y) = tr_n(x^{2^i+1} + y^{2^i+1} + xy); \quad x, y \in \mathbb{F}_{2^n}, \quad \gcd(n, 3) = \gcd(n, i) = 1,$$

is bent. Its associated symplectic form equals $\beta_f : ((x, y), (x', y')) \to f(0, 0) \oplus f(x, y) \oplus$
$f(x', y') \oplus f(x+x', y+y') = tr_n(x^{2^i}x' + xx'^{2^i} + y^{2^i}y' + yy'^{2^i} + xy' + x'y)$. The kernel of β_f

equals $\left\{ (x, y) \in \mathbb{F}_{2^n}^2 ; \begin{array}{c} x^{2^i} + x^{2^{n-i}} + y = 0 \\ y^{2^i} + y^{2^{n-i}} + x = 0 \end{array} \right\}$, equal to $\{(0, 0)\}$ since denoting $z = x+y$

we have $z^{2^i} + z^{2^{n-i}} + z = 0$, which implies $z^{2^{2i}} = z^{2^i} + z$ and therefore $z^{2^{3i}} = z$, that is, $z \in$
$\mathbb{F}_{2^{3i}}$, and therefore $z \in \mathbb{F}_2$ and $z = 1$ being not a solution of the equation $z^{2^i} + z^{2^{n-i}} + z = 0$,
we have $x = y$ and $x^{2^i} + x^{2^{n-i}} + x = 0$, that is, $x = 0$.

Remark. Another representation of Boolean functions, in which, instead of identifying
$x = (x_1, \ldots, x_n)$ with a field element (by the use of a basis of the vector space $\mathbb{F}_{2^n}$ over
$\mathbb{F}_2$), we identify $(x_1, \ldots, x_{n-1})$ with a field element in $\mathbb{F}_{2^{n-1}}$, and keep x_n in $\mathbb{F}_2$, leads to the
Kerdock code; see Section 6.1.22, where the bent functions leading to this code are given.
The so-called *cyclic bent functions*, such that, for any $a \neq b \in \mathbb{F}_{2^{n-1}}$ and any $\epsilon \in \mathbb{F}_2$,
$f(ax_1, x_2) + f(bx_1, x_2 + \epsilon)$ is bent (as well as f itself), are proposed in [458], with applications in codes, codebooks, designs, mutually unbiased bases (MUBs), and sequences. $\quad\square$

The unique EA equivalence class of quadratic bent functions has simplest representative
$tr_n(x^{2^m+1})$ in univariate representation and $tr_m(xy)$ in *bivariate representation*.

Cubic bent functions

Any Boolean function f being bent if and only if every derivative of f in a nonzero direction
is balanced, and every quadratic Boolean function being balanced if and only if one of its
derivatives is the constant function 1, we have:

Proposition 76 *Let n be any positive integer and f any cubic n-variable Boolean function.
Then f is bent if and only if, for every nonzero $a \in \mathbb{F}_2^n$, there exists $b \in \mathbb{F}_2^n$ such that the
second-order derivative $D_a D_b f$ equals constant function 1.*

Up to an affine transformation, we may assume in Proposition 76 that $a = (1, 0, \ldots, 0)$
and $b = (0, 1, 0, \ldots, 0)$ and any cubic bent function is then affinely equivalent to a function
of the form $x_1 x_2 \oplus x_1 f_1(x_3, \ldots, x_n) \oplus x_2 f_2(x_3, \ldots, x_n) \oplus f_3(x_3, \ldots, x_n)$, but it seems difficult
to go further in the determination of cubic bent functions.

The characterization given by Corollary 12, page 194, simplifies itself in the case
of a cubic function: denoting the set $\{(a, b) \in \mathbb{F}_2^n; \ D_a D_b f = cst\}$ by $\mathcal{E}_f^{(2)}$, we
have $\sum_{x, a, b \in \mathbb{F}_2^n} (-1)^{D_a D_b f(x)} = 2^n \sum_{(a, b) \in \mathcal{E}_f^{(2)}} (-1)^{D_a D_b f(0_n)}$, since the second-order derivatives of f, which are affine, are constant or balanced. Then f is bent if and only if
$\sum_{a, b \in \mathcal{E}_f^{(2)}} (-1)^{D_a D_b f(0_n)} = 2^n$. Note that, for every $a \in \mathbb{F}_2^n$, the section $\{b \in \mathbb{F}_2^n; \ (a, b) \in$
$\mathcal{E}_f^{(2)}\}$ of $\mathcal{E}_f^{(2)}$ at a equals $\mathcal{E}_{D_a f}$ and is then a linear subspace of $\mathbb{F}_2^n$. Hence, $\mathcal{E}_f^{(2)}$ is a bilinear
space. Moreover, according to the property observed for quadratic functions at page 171,

and since $D_a f$ is quadratic, function $b \mapsto D_a D_b f(0_n)$ is linear over $\mathcal{E}_{D_a f}$ for every a, that is, function $(a, b) \mapsto D_a D_b f(0_n)$ is bilinear over $\mathcal{E}_f^{(2)}$.

We deduce that $\displaystyle\sum_{a,b \in \mathcal{E}_f^{(2)}} (-1)^{D_a D_b f(0_n)} = \sum_{\substack{a \in \mathbb{F}_2^n \\ \forall b \in \mathcal{E}_{D_a f}, D_a D_b f(0_n) = 0}} |\mathcal{E}_{D_a f}|$ and that f is bent if

and only if $\displaystyle\sum_{\substack{a \in \mathbb{F}_2^n \\ \forall b \in \mathcal{E}_{D_a f}, D_a D_b f(0_n) = 0}} |\mathcal{E}_{D_a f}| = 2^n$, and since for $a = 0_n$ we have $\mathcal{E}_{D_a f} = \mathbb{F}_2^n$ and

$\forall b \in \mathcal{E}_{D_a f}, D_a D_b f(0_n) = 0$, this proves again Proposition 76.

But it is still an open problem to characterize the bent functions of algebraic degree 3 (that is, classify them under the action of the general affine group). This has been done for $n \leq 6$ in [1005] (see also [968], where the number of bent functions is computed for these values of n). For $n = 8$, it has been done in [618] (and completed in [9]); all of these functions have at least one affine derivative $D_a f, a \neq 0_n$ (it has been proved in [193] that this happens for $n \leq 8$ only).

6.1.14 Bent Boolean functions in few variables

Bent functions in two variables are the Boolean functions of odd Hamming weight, *i.e.*, of algebraic degree 2.

Bent functions in four variables are quadratic and therefore known.

Bent Boolean functions in six variables

The determination of all bent 6-variable functions has been done in [1005], where a search for all cubic bent functions in six variables was made, *i.e.*, of all 6-variable bent functions of maximal algebraic degree. Rothaus determined, up to affine equivalence, four possible degree 3 parts of cubic Boolean functions in six variables. Determining all 6-variable bent functions was then possible by visiting all $2^{\binom{6}{2}} = 2^{15}$ quadratic parts for each of these four cases. Bart Preneel in his thesis [968] made this work again and found a fifth class of degree 3 parts, but this fifth class did not give any bent function. It was also proved by R. E. Kibler (as mentioned by Dillon in [440]) and rediscovered 30 years later in [124] (while classifying EA equivalence classes of 6-variable Boolean functions according to some cryptographic properties) that every bent function in six variables is affinely equivalent to a function of the Maiorana–McFarland class (see below). It was later observed in [212] that any bent function of algebraic degree 3 in six variables is affine equivalent to a function of the form $x_1 x_2 x_3 \oplus x_1 h_1(x_4, x_5, x_6) \oplus x_2 h_2(x_4, x_5, x_6) \oplus x_3 h_3(x_4, x_5, x_6) \oplus g(x_4, x_5, x_6)$, where the mapping $(x_1, x_2, x_3) \mapsto (h_1(x_4, x_5, x_6), h_2(x_4, x_5, x_6), h_3(x_4, x_5, x_6))$ is a permutation and where $h_1 \oplus h_2 \oplus h_3$ is affine (for any function of this form, this double condition is necessary and sufficient). This implies in particular that any bent function in at most six variables is affinely equivalent to its dual.

Bent Boolean functions in eight variables

The (impressive) determination of all bent 8-variable functions has been completed in [743], after that Langevin and Leander enumerated them in [741] (Hou had previously classified cubic bent functions in [618].)

In [347], the authors constructed bent *homogeneous functions* (*i.e.*, bent functions whose ANFs are the sums of monomials of the same degree) on 12 (and less) variables by using the invariant theory (which makes feasible the computer searchs).

6.1.15 Primary constructions of bent Boolean functions

Except for small values of n, there does not exist a classification of bent functions under the action of the general affine group, and the structure of the set of bent functions is not clear. In order to understand better this structure, and also to have bent functions for applications, researchers have designed constructions. We describe them below. It is not clear whether these constructions give some insight on general bent functions or if on the contrary they draw our attention to peculiar bent functions. Nevertheless, they represent some important knowledge and have practical interest. Some of the known constructions are *ex nihilo* (from scratch). We call them *primary constructions* and address them in the present subsection. The others, which use as building blocks previously constructed bent functions (often called *initial functions*), and sometimes lead to recursive constructions, are called *secondary constructions*. We shall address them in the next subsection.

1. The *Maiorana–McFarland original class* $\mathcal{M}$ (see [441, 834]) is the set of all the Boolean functions on $\mathbb{F}_2^n = \{(x, y); x, y \in \mathbb{F}_2^{n/2}\}$, of the form

$$f(x, y) = x \cdot \pi(y) \oplus g(y), \tag{6.9}$$

where "$\cdot$" is an *inner product* in $\mathbb{F}_2^{n/2}$, π is any permutation on $\mathbb{F}_2^{n/2}$, and g any Boolean function on $\mathbb{F}_2^{n/2}$.

In *bivariate representation*, this gives $(x, y) = tr_{n/2}(x \, \pi(y)) + g(y)$, where π is any permutation polynomial over $\mathbb{F}_{2^{n/2}}$ and g any Boolean function on $\mathbb{F}_{2^{n/2}}$.

Proposition 77 *Any function of the form* (6.9) *is bent if and only if π is a permutation. The dual of this bent function equals then $\widetilde{f}(a, b) = b \cdot \pi^{-1}(a) \oplus g(\pi^{-1}(a))$, where π^{-1} is the inverse permutation of π.*

This is a direct consequence[8] of Proposition 53, page 166, which writes here

$$W_f(a, b) = 2^{\frac{n}{2}} \sum_{y \in \pi^{-1}(a)} (-1)^{g(y) \oplus b \cdot y}, \tag{6.10}$$

where $\pi^{-1}(a)$ denotes the preimage of a by π^{-1}. We see that the dual function of f also belongs to Maiorana–McFarland class but with its two inputs swapped.

As we saw already in Section 5.1, the fundamental idea of Maiorana–McFarland's construction consists in concatenating affine functions. If we order all the binary words of length n in lexicographic order, with the bit of higher weight on the right, then the truth table of f is the concatenation of the restrictions of f obtained by setting the value of y and letting x freely range over $\mathbb{F}_2^{n/2}$. These restrictions are affine.

---

[8] The input is here cut in two pieces x and y of the same length; cutting it in pieces of different lengths is addressed in Proposition 79 below; bentness is then obviously not characterized by the bijectivity of π.

Of course, $\mathcal{M}$ is a particular case of the general Maiorana–McFarland construction of Boolean functions seen in Subsection 5.1.1, which has been a generalization of $\mathcal{M}$ first investigated in [181].

Note that function f above is such that, for every function $h(y)$, function $f(x, y) \oplus h(y)$ is bent. This property is characteristic of the functions of the form (6.9):

Proposition 78 *A Boolean function $f(x, y)$, $x, y \in \mathbb{F}_2^{n/2}$, belongs to class $\mathcal{M}$ if and only if, for every function $h(y)$, the function $f(x, y) \oplus h(y)$ is bent.*

Proof The condition is necessary, according to Proposition 77. For proving that it is also sufficient, let us take $h = \delta_a$ (the indicator of $\{a\}$). For every $a, u, v \in \mathbb{F}_2^{\frac{n}{2}}$, we have that $\sum_{x,y \in \mathbb{F}_2^{\frac{n}{2}}} (-1)^{f(x,y) \oplus u \cdot x \oplus v \cdot y \oplus \delta_a(y)} = \sum_{x,y \in \mathbb{F}_2^{\frac{n}{2}}} (-1)^{f(x,y) \oplus u \cdot x \oplus v \cdot y} - 2 \sum_{x \in \mathbb{F}_2^{\frac{n}{2}}} (-1)^{f(x,a) \oplus u \cdot x \oplus v \cdot a}$, and if $f(x, y)$ and $f(x, y) \oplus \delta_a(y)$ are both bent, then we have $\pm 2^{\frac{n}{2}} = \pm 2^{\frac{n}{2}} \pm 2 \sum_{x \in \mathbb{F}_2^{\frac{n}{2}}} (-1)^{f(x,a) \oplus u \cdot x}$. Hence for every $a, u \in \mathbb{F}_2^{\frac{n}{2}}$, we have $\sum_{x \in \mathbb{F}_2^{\frac{n}{2}}} (-1)^{f(x,a) \oplus u \cdot x} \in \{0, \pm 2^{\frac{n}{2}}\}$. Clearly, having, for some a, that $\sum_{x \in \mathbb{F}_2^{\frac{n}{2}}} (-1)^{f(x,a) \oplus u \cdot x} = 0$ for every u is impossible because of Parseval's relation. Then, for every $a \in \mathbb{F}_2^{\frac{n}{2}}$, there exists $u \in \mathbb{F}_2^{\frac{n}{2}}$ such that $\sum_{x \in \mathbb{F}_2^{\frac{n}{2}}} (-1)^{f(x,a) \oplus u \cdot x} = \pm 2^{\frac{n}{2}}$ that is $f(x, a) = u \cdot x$ or $f(x, a) = u \cdot x \oplus 1$. $\square$

When a new method of construction of bent functions is found, it is necessary (for showing that it does not only provide functions that could be obtained with already known methods) to prove that some constructed functions are affinely inequivalent to Maiorana–McFarland functions.[9] We know thanks to Proposition 54, page 167, that an n-variable Boolean function with n even belongs to the completed Maiorana–McFarland class (the smallest possible complete class including $\mathcal{M}$) if and only if there exists an $\frac{n}{2}$-dimensional linear subspace E of $\mathbb{F}_2^n$ such that function $D_a D_b f$ is identically null for every $a, b \in E$. According to Proposition 78, this is also equivalent to the fact that there exists an $\frac{n}{2}$-dimensional affine subspace A and an $\frac{n}{2}$-dimensional linear subspace E of $\mathbb{F}_2^n$ such that every element of $\mathbb{F}_2^n$ can be expressed in a unique way in the form $x + y$, where $x \in E$, $y \in A$, and such that $f \oplus h$ is bent for every function $h(x + y)$ depending only on y.

The completed class of $\mathcal{M}$ contains all bent functions in at most six variables [440] and all quadratic bent functions (according to point 4 in the characterization of quadratic bent functions of page 205, taking $\pi = id$ and g constant in (6.9)).

Derived classes $\mathcal{C}$ and $\mathcal{D}$ Two classes of bent functions have been obtained in [212] by adding to functions of Maiorana–McFarland's class the indicators of vector subspaces:

---

[9] This should ideally be checked for all known classes of bent functions; this represents much (hard) work; checking this with class $\mathcal{M}$ is usually considered as mandatory because $\mathcal{M}$ is simpler and provides the widest class of bent functions.

– The class, denoted by $\mathcal{D}$, whose elements are the functions of the form $f(x, y) = x \cdot \pi(y) \oplus 1_{E_1}(x) 1_{E_2}(y)$, where π is any permutation on $\mathbb{F}_2^{n/2}$ and E_1, E_2 are two linear subspaces of $\mathbb{F}_2^{\frac{n}{2}}$ such that $\pi(E_2) = E_1^{\perp}$ (1_{E_1} and 1_{E_2} denote their indicators). The dual of f belongs to the completed class of $\mathcal{D}$.

A subclass $\mathcal{D}_0$ of $\mathcal{D}$ has for elements the functions of the form $f(x, y) = x \cdot \pi(y) \oplus \delta_0(x)$ (recall that δ_0 is the Dirac symbol). The dual of such f is the function $y \cdot \pi^{-1}(x) \oplus \delta_0(y)$. It is proved in [212] that $\mathcal{D}_0$ is not included[10] in the completed versions of classes $\mathcal{M}$ and $\mathcal{PS}$ and that every bent function in six variables is affinely equivalent to a function of this class, up to the addition of an affine function.

– The class $\mathcal{C}$ of all the functions of the form $f(x, y) = x \cdot \pi(y) \oplus 1_L(x)$, where L is any linear subspace of $\mathbb{F}_2^{n/2}$ and π any permutation on $\mathbb{F}_2^{n/2}$ such that, for any element a of $\mathbb{F}_2^{n/2}$, the set $\pi^{-1}(a + L^{\perp})$ is a flat. It is a simple matter to see, as shown in [198], that, under the same hypothesis on π, if g is a Boolean function whose restriction to every flat $\pi^{-1}(a + L^{\perp})$ is affine, then the function $x \cdot \pi(y) \oplus 1_L(x) \oplus g(y)$ is also bent.

The fact that any function in class $\mathcal{D}$ or class $\mathcal{C}$ is bent comes from Theorem 14, page 202. In [822], existence and nonexistence results of such π and L are given for many of the known classes of permutations, inducing generic methods of constructions. In [1154], sufficient conditions on π and L so that f is provably outside the completed Maiorana–McFarland class are found. In particular, it is shown that the $\mathcal{C}$ functions described in [822] do not belong to the completed Maiorana–McFarland class. The more difficult question whether these functions are also outside the completed $\mathcal{PS}$ class remains open.

Maiorana–McFarland construction as a secondary construction The original Maiorana–McFarland's construction is a particular case of a more general construction of bent functions, which is a *secondary construction* for $r < \frac{n}{2}$ and a primary one for $r = \frac{n}{2}$:

Proposition 79 *[223] Let $n = r + s$ ($r \leq s$) be even. Let ϕ be any mapping from $\mathbb{F}_2^s$ to $\mathbb{F}_2^r$ such that, for every $a \in \mathbb{F}_2^r$, the set $\phi^{-1}(a)$ is an $(n - 2r)$-dimensional affine subspace of $\mathbb{F}_2^s$. Let g be any Boolean function on $\mathbb{F}_2^s$ whose restriction to $\phi^{-1}(a)$ (viewed as a Boolean function on $\mathbb{F}_2^{n-2r}$ via an affine isomorphism between $\phi^{-1}(a)$ and this vector space) is bent for every $a \in \mathbb{F}_2^r$, if $n > 2r$ (no condition on g being imposed if $n = 2r$). Then the function $f_{\phi,g}(x, y) = x \cdot \phi(y) \oplus g(y)$ is bent on $\mathbb{F}_2^n$.*

Proof This is a direct consequence of Proposition 53, page 166, which writes

$$W_{f_{\phi,g}}(a, b) = 2^r \sum_{y \in \phi^{-1}(a)} (-1)^{g(y) \oplus b \cdot y}. \tag{6.11}$$

According to Relation (6.11), the function $f_{\phi,g}$ is bent if and only if $r \leq \frac{n}{2}$ and $\sum_{y \in \phi^{-1}(a)} (-1)^{g(y) \oplus b \cdot y} = \pm 2^{\frac{n}{2}-r}$ for every $a \in \mathbb{F}_2^r$ and every $b \in \mathbb{F}_2^s$. The hypothesis in Proposition 79 is a sufficient condition for that (but it is not a necessary one). $\square$

---

[10] We have seen in Proposition 54 that there is a rather simple way to show that a function f does not belong to the completed class of $\mathcal{M}$; it is more difficult to show that it does not belong to the completed class of $\mathcal{PS}$.

This construction is pretty general: the choice of any partition of $\mathbb{F}_2^s$ in 2^r flats of dimension $s - r = n - 2r$ and of an $(n - 2r)$-variable bent function on each of these flats leads to an n-variable bent function. Note that ϕ, defined so that the elements of this partition are the preimages of the elements of $\mathbb{F}_2^r$ by ϕ, is balanced (*i.e.*, has output uniformly distributed over $\mathbb{F}_2^r$). In fact, it is observed in [802] that, if a bent function has the form $f_{\phi,g}$, then ϕ is balanced. This is a direct consequence of the characterization of balanced vectorial functions by Proposition 35, page 112, and of the fact that, for every nonzero $a \in \mathbb{F}_2^r$, the Boolean function $a \cdot \phi$ is balanced, since it equals the derivative $D_{(a,0_s)} f_{\phi,g}$.

Obviously, every Boolean function can be represented (in several ways) in the form $f_{\phi,g}$ for some values of $r \geq 1$ and s and for some mapping $\phi : \mathbb{F}_2^s \mapsto \mathbb{F}_2^r$ and Boolean function g on $\mathbb{F}_2^s$.

Remark. There exist $\frac{n}{2}$-dimensional vector spaces of n-variable Boolean functions whose nonzero elements are all bent. This is equivalent to the existence of bent $(n, \frac{n}{2})$-functions. Maiorana–McFarland's construction allows constructing such functions, as we shall see at page 270. Dimension $\frac{n}{2}$ is maximal, since a result by K. Nyberg shows that bent (n, m)-functions cannot exist for $m > \frac{n}{2}$. □

2. The *partial spread class* $\mathcal{PS}$, introduced in [441] by J. Dillon, is the set of all the sums (modulo 2) of the indicators of $2^{\frac{n}{2}-1}$ or $2^{\frac{n}{2}-1} + 1$ pairwise *supplementary subspaces* of dimension $\frac{n}{2}$ of $\mathbb{F}_2^n$ (*i.e.*, such that the intersection of any two of them equals $\{0_n\}$, and given their dimension, whose sum is direct and equals $\mathbb{F}_2^n$). A set of pairwise supplementary subspaces is called a *partial spread*, and a (full) *spread* if it covers $\mathbb{F}_2^n$. Some $\mathcal{PS}$ functions are built with partial spreads that are parts of full spreads, and some are built with partial spreads that cannot be extended into full spreads (we shall see a quadratic example below).

Proposition 80 *Any sum (modulo 2) of the indicators of $2^{\frac{n}{2}-1}$ or $2^{\frac{n}{2}-1} + 1$ pairwise supplementary subspaces of dimension $\frac{n}{2}$ of $\mathbb{F}_2^n$ is a bent function. The dual of such function has the same form, all the $\frac{n}{2}$-dimensional spaces involved in the definition being replaced by their orthogonals.*

Definition 52 *Class $\mathcal{PS}$ is the set of bent functions defined in Proposition 80. The sums of $2^{\frac{n}{2}-1}$ such indicators constitute subclass $\mathcal{PS}^-$ (whose elements have Hamming weight $2^{\frac{n}{2}-1}(2^{\frac{n}{2}-1} - 1) = 2^{n-1} - 2^{\frac{n}{2}-1}$) and the sums of $2^{\frac{n}{2}-1} + 1$ of them constitute subclass $\mathcal{PS}^+$ (whose elements have Hamming weight $(2^{\frac{n}{2}-1} + 1) 2^{\frac{n}{2}} - 2^{\frac{n}{2}-1} = 2^{n-1} + 2^{\frac{n}{2}-1}$).*

We shall see that Proposition 80 is a particular case of a theorem (Theorem 17) that we shall state at page 241. The bentness of the functions in $\mathcal{PS}$ can also be alternatively shown: for each pair of supplementary subspaces E_i and E_j and every $a \in \mathbb{F}_2^n$, the set $E_i \cap (a + E_j)$ is a singleton; this allows proving that, for every nonzero a, the product of any function $f(x)$ in $\mathcal{PS}^-$ (resp. in $\mathcal{PS}^+$) with its shifted function $f_a(x) = f(x + a)$ has Hamming weight $2^{\frac{n}{2}-1}(2^{\frac{n}{2}-1} - 1) = 2^{n-2} - 2^{\frac{n}{2}-1}$ if $f(a) = 0$ and $(2^{\frac{n}{2}-1} - 1)(2^{\frac{n}{2}-1} - 2) + 2^{\frac{n}{2}} - 2 = 2^{n-2} - 2^{\frac{n}{2}-1}$ if $f(a) = 1$ (resp. $(2^{\frac{n}{2}-1} + 1)2^{\frac{n}{2}-1} = 2^{n-2} + 2^{\frac{n}{2}-1}$ if $f(a) = 0$ and $2^{\frac{n}{2}-1}(2^{\frac{n}{2}-1} - 1) + 2^{\frac{n}{2}} = 2^{n-2} + 2^{\frac{n}{2}-1}$ if $f(a) = 1$), which implies in all cases that the derivative $D_a f$ (whose Hamming weight equals $2(w_H(f) - w_H(ff_a)))$ is balanced, and thus that f is bent, according to Theorem 12, page 192.

The $\mathcal{PS}^-$ functions built with a full spread are the complements of the elements of $\mathcal{PS}^+$ built with the same full spread and vice versa, but the complement of a general $\mathcal{PS}$ bent function is not necessarily in $\mathcal{PS}$.

Remark. The Boolean functions equal to the sums of some number of indicators of pairwise supplementary $\frac{n}{2}$-dimensional subspaces of $\mathbb{F}_2^n$ share with quadratic functions the nice and convenient property of being bent if and only if they have the Hamming weight of a bent function (which is $2^{n-1} \pm 2^{\frac{n}{2}-1}$). $\qquad\square$

All the elements of $\mathcal{PS}^-$ have *algebraic degree* $\frac{n}{2}$ exactly (indeed, by applying a linear isomorphism of $\mathbb{F}_2^n$, we may assume that $\mathbb{F}_2^{n/2} \times \{0_{n/2}\}$ is among the $2^{\frac{n}{2}-1}$ pairwise supplementary spaces defining the function, and since the function vanishes at 0_n, Relation (2.4), page 33, shows that the monomial $x_1 \ldots x_{\frac{n}{2}}$ appears in its ANF).

On the contrary, the elements of $\mathcal{PS}^+$ do not all have algebraic degree $\frac{n}{2}$: Dillon observed in [441] that, when $\frac{n}{2}$ is even, all quadratic bent functions are $\mathcal{PS}^+$ functions or their complements. Indeed, by affine equivalence, we can restrict ourselves to the function $(x, \epsilon, y, \eta) \in \mathbb{F}_{2^{n/2-1}} \times \mathbb{F}_2 \times \mathbb{F}_{2^{n/2-1}} \times \mathbb{F}_2 \to tr_{n/2-1}(xy) \oplus \epsilon\eta \oplus 1$, where $tr_{n/2-1}$ is the trace function from $\mathbb{F}_{2^{n/2-1}}$ to $\mathbb{F}_2$; the support of this function equals the union of the $2^{n/2-1} + 1$ vector spaces of dimension $n/2$ (and very much related to the Kerdock code) $S_\emptyset = \{0\} \times \{0\} \times \mathbb{F}_{2^{n/2-1}} \times \mathbb{F}_2$ and $S_a = \{(x, \epsilon, a^2x + atr_{n/2-1}(ax) + a\epsilon, tr_{n/2-1}(ax)); (x, \epsilon) \in \mathbb{F}_{2^{n/2-1}} \times \mathbb{F}_2\}$ for $a \in \mathbb{F}_{2^{n/2-1}}$. Indeed, we have $tr_{n/2-1}(xy) \oplus \epsilon\eta = 0$ if and only if $x = \epsilon = 0$ or there exists a such that $y = a^2x + atr_{n/2-1}(ax) + a\epsilon$ and $\eta = tr_{n/2-1}(ax)$. Note that since f has algebraic degree strictly less than $\frac{n}{2}$ for $n \geq 8$, this partial spread is not extendable to a full spread.

It is an open problem to characterize the *algebraic normal form*s of the elements of class $\mathcal{PS}$ or their trace representations. It is then necessary to identify within the $\mathcal{PS}$ construction, classes of explicit bent functions.[11]

Class $\mathcal{PS}_{ap}$ in *bivariate representation*   J. Dillon exhibits in [441] a subclass of $\mathcal{PS}^-$, denoted by $\mathcal{PS}_{ap}$ (where *ap* stands for "affine plane"), whose elements (that we shall call *Dillon's functions*) are defined in an explicit form, that we already addressed in Subsection 5.1.2 (more precisely at page 169).

The vector space $\mathbb{F}_2^n$ is identified with the affine plane $\mathbb{F}_{2^{n/2}} \times \mathbb{F}_{2^{n/2}}$ (an *inner product* being $(x, y) \cdot (x', y') = tr_{\frac{n}{2}}(xx' + yy')$; we know that the notion of bent function is independent of the choice of the inner product). The affine plane $\mathbb{F}_{2^{n/2}} \times \mathbb{F}_{2^{n/2}}$ is equal to the union of its $2^{n/2} + 1$ lines through the origin $E_\emptyset = \{0\} \times \mathbb{F}_{2^{n/2}}$ and $E_a = \{(x, ax); x \in \mathbb{F}_{2^{n/2}}\}$, $a \in \mathbb{F}_{2^{n/2}}$; these lines are $n/2$-dimensional $\mathbb{F}_2$-subspaces of $\mathbb{F}_2^n$ and constitute the so-called *Desarguesian spread*. Choosing any $2^{n/2-1}$ of the lines, and taking them different from E_0

---

[11] The situation with $\mathcal{PS}$ is then similar to the situation with general bent functions: we have a nice and simple definition, but no systematic way of determining all the elements that satisfy it.

and $E_\emptyset$ (of equations $x = 0$ and $y = 0$), leads, by definition, to an element of $\mathcal{PS}_{ap}$, of the form $f(x, y) = g\left(x\, y^{2^{n/2}-2}\right)$, i.e., $g\left(\frac{x}{y}\right)$ with $\frac{x}{y} = 0$ if $y = 0$, where g is a balanced Boolean function on $\mathbb{F}_2^{n/2}$ which vanishes at 0. *In the sequel, we shall always take this convention that $\frac{1}{0} = 0$ and write $\frac{x}{y}$ instead of $x\, y^{2^{n/2}-2}$.* The bentness of the resulting function is a consequence of Relation (5.9), page 170, with $\phi = f(0) = \epsilon = a = 0$.

The complements $g\left(\frac{x}{y}\right) \oplus 1$ of these functions are the functions $h(\frac{x}{y})$ where h is balanced and does not vanish at 0; they belong to class $\mathcal{PS}^+$.

For every balanced function g, the dual of the bent function $g(\frac{x}{y})$ is $g(\frac{y}{x})$ (this will be a direct consequence of Theorem 17, page 241).

Class $\mathcal{PS}_{ap}$ in *univariate representation* We have already seen at pages 167 and 169, the notion of $\mathcal{PS}_{ap}$ Boolean function in univariate representation (but without studying the condition under which such a function is bent). A univariate representation of the elements of Desarguesian spread is $\{u\, \mathbb{F}_{2^{n/2}}, u \in U\}$, where $U = \{u \in \mathbb{F}_2^n; u^{2^{n/2}+1} = 1\}$ is the cyclic group of $(2^{n/2} + 1)$th roots of unity in $\mathbb{F}_2^n$ (*i.e.*, the multiplicative subgroup of $\mathbb{F}_{2^n}^*$ of order $2^{n/2} + 1$). Each line through the origin of the plane $\mathbb{F}_{2^n}$ over $\mathbb{F}_{2^{n/2}}$, instead of being identified by the constant value x/y of its nonzero elements $(x, y) \in \mathbb{F}_{2^{n/2}}^2$ (which makes with the convention $1/0 = 0$ that the two lines of equations $x = 0$ and $y = 0$ provide necessarily the same output by the $\mathcal{PS}_{ap}$ function) is identified by the unique element of U its contains. Then g is viewed as a Boolean function over U such that $g(\alpha_1) = g(\alpha_2) = 0 = f(0)$, where (α_1, α_2) is the basis chosen for the plane $\mathbb{F}_{2^n}$ over $\mathbb{F}_{2^{n/2}}$, assuming without loss of generality that α_1, α_2 both belong to U. Relation (5.5), page 168, with $m = n/2$, and $(-1)^{f(0)} - \sum_{\mu \in U}(-1)^{g(\mu)} = 0$ (since g is taken balanced on $U \setminus \{\alpha_i\}$, $i = 1, 2$), and $\phi = 0$ gives an alternative proof of the bentness of the $\mathcal{PS}_{ap}$ functions defined by Dillon, since $tr_m^n(z) = 0$ if and only if $z \in \mathbb{F}_{2^m}$. Moreover, for every $x \in \mathbb{F}_{2^{n/2}}^*$ and every $u \in U$, we have $(ux)^{2^{n/2}-1} = u^{-2}$ and $u \mapsto u^{-2}$ is a permutation of U; this leads to an expression of $\mathcal{PS}_{ap}$ bent functions of the form $h\left(z^{2^{n/2}-1}\right)$, $z \in \mathbb{F}_{2^n}$, where h is a Boolean function over $\mathbb{F}_{2^n}$ such that $h(0) = 0$ and whose restriction to U has Hamming weight $2^{\frac{n}{2}-1}$.

Dillon shows in [442] that all bent functions of the form $tr_n\left(az^{2^{n/2}-1}\right)$, $z \in \mathbb{F}_{2^n}$, are affinely inequivalent to the Maiorana–McFarland functions.

It is possible to deduce the univariate representation of $\mathcal{PS}_{ap}$ functions from their bivariate representation. We have seen at page 47 that any bivariate function $f(x, y)$ over $\mathbb{F}_{2^{n/2}}$ can be represented as a function of $z \in \mathbb{F}_{2^n}$, which we shall also denote by $f(z)$ (by abuse of notation), by posing $x = tr_{n/2}^n(az) = az + (az)^{2^{n/2}}$ and $y = tr_{n/2}^n(bz) = bz + (bz)^{2^{n/2}}$ for some elements $a, b \in \mathbb{F}_{2^n}$ that need to be $\mathbb{F}_2^{n/2}$-linearly independent (for instance, we can choose $\omega \in \mathbb{F}_{2^n} \setminus \mathbb{F}_{2^{n/2}}$, and the pair $(1, \omega)$ is then a basis of the $\mathbb{F}_{2^{n/2}}$-vector space $\mathbb{F}_{2^n}$; we then take for (a, b) a basis orthonormal with $(1, \omega)$). For $f(x, y) = g\left(\frac{x}{y}\right)$, we have then the following expression valid for $z \neq 0$:

$$f(z) = g\left(\left(a + a^{2^{n/2}} z^{2^{n/2}-1}\right)\left(b + b^{2^{n/2}} z^{2^{n/2}-1}\right)^{2^{n/2}-2}\right).$$

Given a primitive element α of $\mathbb{F}_{2^n}$, we have for $i = 0, \ldots, 2^{n/2}$ and $j = 0, \ldots, 2^{n/2} - 2$:

$$f\left(\alpha^{i+j(2^{n/2}+1)}\right) = g\left((a + a^{2^{n/2}}\beta^i)(b + b^{2^{n/2}}\beta^i)^{2^{n/2}-2}\right),$$

where $\beta = \alpha^{2^{n/2}-1}$.

Dillon [442], observing that function $tr_n(az^{2^{n/2}-1})$, $z \in \mathbb{F}_{2^n}$, $a \in \mathbb{F}_{2^n}^*$, is bent if and only if (see above) the restriction of $tr_n(az)$ to U has *Hamming weight* $2^{n/2-1}$, conjectures that such a exists for every even n. He gives the translation of this conjecture in terms of cyclic codes: let θ be a primitive element of U (*i.e.*, a primitive $(2^{n/2} + 1)$th root of unity in $\mathbb{F}_{2^n}$), then the condition is that the *cyclic code* $C = \{(tr_n(a), tr_n(a\theta), tr_n(a\theta^2), tr_n(a\theta^3), \ldots, tr_n(a\theta^{2^{n/2}}); a \in \mathbb{F}_{2^n}\}$ contains codewords of Hamming weight $2^{n/2-1}$. Since multiplying a by an element of U corresponds to a cyclic shift, he can restrict himself to $a \in \mathbb{F}_{2^{n/2}}$. Then $tr_n(a\theta^j) = tr_{n/2}(a\,tr_{n/2}^n(\theta^j)) = tr_{n/2}(a\,(\theta^j + \theta^{-j}))$. We know (see Appendix, page 491 and foll.) that when $j = 1, \ldots, 2^{n/2}$, $\theta^j + \theta^{-j}$ (*i.e.*, when $z \in U \setminus \{1\}$, $z + z^{-1}$) takes twice each value in $\{x \in \mathbb{F}_{2^{n/2}}^*; tr_{n/2}(x^{-1}) = 1\}$. The condition on a is then that $\displaystyle\sum_{x \in \mathbb{F}_{2^{n/2}}^*; tr_{n/2}(x^{-1})=1} (-1)^{tr_{n/2}(ax)} = 2^{n/2-1} - 2 \cdot 2^{n/2-2} = 0$, which is equivalent to $\displaystyle\sum_{x \in \mathbb{F}_{2^{n/2}}^*} \left(1 - (-1)^{tr_{n/2}(x^{-1})}\right)(-1)^{tr_{n/2}(ax)} = 0$. The conjecture is then that a exists in $\mathbb{F}_{2^{n/2}}^*$ such that $\displaystyle\sum_{x \in \mathbb{F}_{2^{n/2}}^*} (-1)^{tr_{n/2}(x^{-1}+ax)} = -1$. We have already seen at page 188 that such sum added with 1 is called a Kloosterman sum. Lachaud and Wolfmann proved this conjecture in [733]; they proved that the values of such Kloosterman sums are all the numbers divisible by 4 in the range $[-2^{n/4+1} + 1; 2^{n/4+1} + 1]$, by relating such sums to elliptic curves (and this relation was exploited later in [781] for deriving an algorithm checking bentness more efficiently in such a context).

It has been later observed that all these results remain valid with exponents of the form $j \cdot (2^{\frac{n}{2}} - 1)$, where $\gcd(j, 2^{\frac{n}{2}} + 1) = 1$, with the same arguments (the mapping $x \mapsto x^j$ by which function $x \mapsto x^{2^{\frac{n}{2}}-1}$ is composed being a permutation of U). These exponents are now widely called *Dillon exponents*. Leander [750] has found another proof that gives more insight; a small error in his proof has been corrected in [350].

Dillon checked that one of the functions in $\mathcal{PS}_{ap}$ does not belong to the completed $\mathcal{M}$ (Maiorana–McFarland) class: function $tr_8(x^{15})$ over $\mathbb{F}_{2^8}$, is affinely inequivalent to $\mathcal{M}$ functions because (we omit the proof) there cannot exist an $n/2$-dimensional subspace W of $\mathbb{F}_2^n$ such that $D_a D_b f$ is null for every a and b both in W.

It may be more difficult to prove that a given function is not affinely equivalent to $\mathcal{PS}$ functions than to $\mathcal{M}$ functions; see an example in [212].

Extended $\mathcal{PS}_{ap}$ class Class $\mathcal{PS}_{ap}$ is slightly extended into the subclass of $\mathcal{PS}^-$ denoted by $\mathcal{PS}_{ap}^\#$, of those Boolean functions over $\mathbb{F}_{2^n}$ that can be obtained from those of $\mathcal{PS}_{ap}$ by composition by the transformations $x \in \mathbb{F}_{2^n} \mapsto \delta x$, $\delta \neq 0$, and by addition of a constant.[12] The elements of $\mathcal{PS}_{ap}^\#$ arc thc Boolcan functions f of Hamming weight $2^{n-1} \pm 2^{n/2} \,{}^1$

---

[12] The functions of $\mathcal{PS}_{ap}$ are among them those satisfying $f(0) = f(1) = 0$.

on $\mathbb{F}_{2^n}$ such that, denoting by α a primitive element of this field, $f(\alpha^{2^{n/2}+1}x) = f(x)$ for every $x \in \mathbb{F}_{2^n}$. We shall see in Subsection 6.1.20 that the functions in $\mathcal{PS}_{ap}^{\#}$ have a stronger property than bentness, called hyper-bentness. It is proved in [278] (by extension of the results of [441]) that they are the functions of Hamming weight $2^{n-1} \pm 2^{n/2-1}$, which can be written as $\sum_{i=1}^{r} tr_n(a_i x^{j_i})$ for $a_i \in \mathbb{F}_{2^n}$ and j_i a multiple of $2^{n/2} - 1$ with $j_i \le 2^n - 1$.

Other classes of $\mathcal{PS}$ functions in explicit form   The functions in $\mathcal{PS}_{ap}$ are not the only $\mathcal{PS}$ bent functions that can be given with explicit trace representation (useful for applications, *e.g.*, in telecommunications).

For instance, the $\mathcal{PS}$ bent functions related to André's spreads[13] have been studied in [246]. These spreads introduced by J. André in the 1950s and independently by Bruck later are defined as follows: let k and m be positive integers such that k divides m, say $m = kl$. Let N_k^m be the norm map from $\mathbb{F}_{2^m}$ to $\mathbb{F}_{2^k}$:

$$N_k^m(x) = x^{\frac{2^m-1}{2^k-1}}.$$

Let ϕ be any function from $\mathbb{F}_{2^k}$ to $\mathbb{Z}/l\mathbb{Z}$. Then, denoting $\phi \circ N_k^m$ by φ (it can be any function from $\mathbb{F}_{2^m}$ to $\mathbb{Z}/l\mathbb{Z}$ that is constant on any coset of the subgroup U of order $\frac{2^m-1}{2^k-1}$ of $\mathbb{F}_{2^m}^*$), the $\mathbb{F}_2$-vector subspaces:

$$\{(0, y), y \in \mathbb{F}_{2^m}\} \text{ and } \{(x, x^{2^{k\varphi(z)}}z), x \in \mathbb{F}_{2^m}\},$$

where $z \in \mathbb{F}_{2^m}$ form together a spread of $\mathbb{F}_{2^m}^2$. Indeed, these subspaces have trivial pairwise intersection: suppose that $x^{2^{k\varphi(y)}}y = x^{2^{k\varphi(z)}}z$ for some nonzero elements x, y, z of $\mathbb{F}_{2^m}$ (the other cases of trivial intersection are obvious), then we have $N_k^m(x^{2^{k\varphi(y)}}y) = N_k^m(x^{2^{k\varphi(z)}}z)$, that is, $N_k^m(x^{2^{k\varphi(y)}})N_k^m(y) = N_k^m(x^{2^{k\varphi(z)}})N_k^m(z)$. Equivalently, since $x \mapsto x^{2^{k\varphi(z)}}$ is in the Galois group of $\mathbb{F}_{2^m}^2$ over $\mathbb{F}_{2^k}$, $N_k^m(x)N_k^m(y) = N_k^m(x)N_k^m(z)$, hence $N_k^m(y) = N_k^m(z)$ and $\varphi(y) = \varphi(z)$, which together with $x^{2^{k\varphi(y)}}y = x^{2^{k\varphi(z)}}z$ implies then $y = z$.

Those spreads provide asymptotically the largest part of the known examples, due to the large number of choices for the map ϕ.

The trace representation of the $\mathcal{PS}$ bent functions associated to André's spreads is easily obtained. A pair $(x, y) \in \mathbb{F}_{2^m}^* \times \mathbb{F}_{2^m}$ belongs to $\{(x, x^{2^{k\varphi(z)}}z), x \in \mathbb{F}_{2^m}\}$ if and only if

$$y = x^{2^{k\varphi(z)}}z = x^{2^{k\phi(N_k^m(z))}}z = x^{2^{k\phi\left(\frac{N_k^m(y)}{N_k^m(x)}\right)}}z = x^{2^{k\varphi(y/x)}}z. \tag{6.12}$$

Then a Boolean function in this class has the form

$$f(x, y) = g\left(\frac{y}{x^{2^{k\varphi(y/x)}}}\right) \tag{6.13}$$

(with the usual convention $\frac{y}{0} = 0$) where g is balanced on $\mathbb{F}_{2^m}$ and vanishes at 0. Such a bent function is in $\mathcal{PS}$ and is potentially inequivalent to $\mathcal{PS}_{ap}$ functions (this needs to be further studied, though).

Let us study now the dual of f. If S is the support of g, then since $0 \notin S$, the support of f is equal to the union $\bigcup_{z \in S}\{(x, x^{2^{k\varphi(z)}}z), x \in \mathbb{F}_{2^m}\}$, less $\{0\}$. The support of the dual

---

[13] We thank W. Kantor for mentioning these spreads, which lead to numerous bent functions.

of f is the union of the orthogonals of these subspaces, less $\{0\}$ as well (see Proposition 80). A pair $(x', y') \in \mathbb{F}_{2^m}^2$ belongs to the orthogonal of $\{(x, x^{2^{k\varphi(z)}} z), x \in \mathbb{F}_{2^m}\}$ if and only if $tr_m(xx' + x^{2^{k\varphi(z)}} zy') = tr_m((x' + (zy')^{2^{m-k\varphi(z)}})x)$ equals 0 for all $x \in \mathbb{F}_{2^m}$, that is, if $x' + (zy')^{2^{m-k\varphi(z)}} = 0$, that is, if $x' = y' = 0$ or $z = \frac{x'^{2^{k\varphi(z)}}}{y'}$. Hence we have

$$\widetilde{f}(x, y) = g\left(\frac{x^{2^{k\varphi(x/y)}}}{y}\right). \tag{6.14}$$

Of course, if g does not vanish at 0, the function defined by (6.13) is bent as well. We can see this by changing g into its complement $g \oplus 1$ (which changes f and its dual into their complements as well).

Note that class $\mathcal{PS}_{ap}$ corresponds to the case where φ is the null function. It also corresponds to the case $k = m$, since we have then $f(x, y) = g\left(\frac{y}{x}\right)$, because $x^{2^m} = x$. Note finally that if $k = 1$, then $N_k^m(x) = 1$ for every $x \neq 0$, and the groups of the spread are $\{(0, y), y \in \mathbb{F}_{2^m}\}$, $\{(x, 0), x \in \mathbb{F}_{2^m}\}$, and $\{(x, x^{2^j} z), x \in \mathbb{F}_{2^m}\}, z \in \mathbb{F}_{2^m}^*$ for some j and $f(x, y) = g\left(\frac{y}{x^{2^j}}\right)$; the functions are in the $\mathcal{PS}_{ap}$ class up to linear equivalence.

Finite prequasifield spreads from finite geometry (see [963]) have also been investigated by Wu [1123] to give explicit forms of the related functions in $\mathcal{PS}$ and of their duals, thanks to the determination of the compositional inverses of certain parametric permutation polynomials. In particular, Wu has considered the Dempwolff–Muller prequasifields and the Knuth presemifields to obtain the expressions of the corresponding $\mathcal{PS}$ bent functions. The constructed functions and their dual functions are in a similar shape as the $\mathcal{PS}_{ap}$ functions, but are more complex. See more in [663].

Explicit constructions of bent functions derived from symplectic presemifields associated to pseudoplanar functions (see page 269) $\sum_{i<j} a_{i,j} x^{2^i + 2^j}$ (whose multiplicative operation is $x \circ y = xy + \sum_{i<j} a_{i,j}^{2^{m-j}} x^{2^{m+i-j}} y^{2^{m-j}} + \sum_{i<j} a_{i,j}^{2^{m-i}} x^{2^{j-i}} y^{2^{m-i}}$) have been obtained in [4]; see also [660].

Class $\mathcal{PS}$ has been generalized into the generalized partial spread class $\mathcal{GPS}$; see Definition 56, page 242.

3. Class $\mathcal{H}$ and Niho functions: We have already seen in Subsection 5.1.2, at pages 167 and 169, the principle of Niho Boolean functions, among which we shall characterize (in Corollary 14) those that are bent. It is proved in [311, proposition 5] that all bent functions affine on each coset of $\mathbb{F}_{2^{n/2}}^*$ are EA equivalent to $\mathcal{PS}_{ap}$ or Niho functions possibly added with the indicator of one coset of $\{0\} \cup \mathbb{F}_{2^{n/2}}^*$. As observed in [311], Niho bent functions happen to be the univariate version of bivariate bent Boolean functions that we shall introduce with class $\mathcal{H}$ below in Definition 53, and that are closely related to the functions introduced by Dillon in [441] as the elements of a family that he denoted by H. The functions of this family were defined as $f(x, y) = tr_{n/2}\left(y + x G\left(yx^{2^{n/2}-2}\right)\right)$; $x, y \in \mathbb{F}_{2^{n/2}}$, where G is a permutation[14] of $\mathbb{F}_{2^{n/2}}$ such that, for every $b \in \mathbb{F}_{2^{n/2}}^*$, the function $G(x) + bx$ is two-to-one (that is, the preimage of any element of $\mathbb{F}_{2^{n/2}}$ by this function contains zero or

---

[14] Dillon also assumed that $G(x) + x$ does not vanish, but this condition is not necessary for bentness.

two elements). We shall see below why these conditions characterize bentness. New bent functions were found recently within this framework. The linear term $tr_{n/2}(y)$ being not useful in the function above, we take it off and consider those functions of the form

$$f(x,y) = \begin{cases} tr_{n/2}\left(x\, G\left(\frac{y}{x}\right)\right) & \text{if } x \neq 0 \\ 0 & \text{if } x = 0, \end{cases} \tag{6.15}$$

where G is any function from $\mathbb{F}_{2^{n/2}}$ to itself. As seen at page 170, we have

$$\begin{aligned} W_f(a,b) &= \sum_{x \in \mathbb{F}^*_{2^{n/2}}, y \in \mathbb{F}_{2^{n/2}}} (-1)^{tr_{n/2}\left(x\, G\left(\frac{y}{x}\right)+ax+by\right)} + \sum_{y \in \mathbb{F}_{2^{n/2}}} (-1)^{tr_{n/2}(by)} \\ &= \sum_{x \in \mathbb{F}^*_{2^{n/2}}, z \in \mathbb{F}_{2^{n/2}}} (-1)^{tr_{n/2}(x(G(z)+a+bz))} + 2^{n/2}\delta_0(b) \\ &= 2^{n/2}\left(|\{z \in \mathbb{F}_{2^{n/2}}; \, G(z)+a+bz = 0\}| + \delta_0(b) - 1\right). \end{aligned} \tag{6.16}$$

Proposition 81 *[311, 441] Any Boolean function of the form (6.15) is bent if and only if G is a permutation of $\mathbb{F}_{2^{n/2}}$ and*

$$\textit{for every } b \in \mathbb{F}^*_{2^{n/2}}, \textit{ the function } z \mapsto G(z) + bz \textit{ is 2-to-1 on } \mathbb{F}_{2^{n/2}}. \tag{6.17}$$

The dual function of f in (6.15) is

$$\widetilde{f}(a,b) = \begin{cases} 1 & \text{if the equation } G(z)+bz = a \text{ has no solution in } \mathbb{F}_{2^{n/2}} \\ 0 & \text{otherwise.} \end{cases}$$

Note that an n-variable function (6.15), or a Niho function (see below), is then bent if and only if $\sum_{u \in \mathbb{F}_2^n} W_f^3(u) = 2^{2n}$, that is, $\sum_{x,y \in \mathbb{F}_2^n} (-1)^{f(x)\oplus f(y)\oplus f(x+y)} = 2^n$ (the same characterization is valid for quadratic functions vanishing at 0_n, but for general functions, we have only a necessary condition). Indeed, $|\{z \in \mathbb{F}_{2^{n/2}}; \, G(z)+a+bz = 0\}| + \delta_0(b) - 1 \geq -1$ implies $(|\{z \in \mathbb{F}_{2^{n/2}}; \, G(z)+a+bz = 0\}| + \delta_0(b) - 1)^3 \geq |\{z \in \mathbb{F}_{2^{n/2}}; \, G(z)+a+bz = 0\}| + \delta_0(b) - 1$ and then $\sum_{u \in \mathbb{F}_2^n} W_f^3(u) \geq 2^n \sum_{u \in \mathbb{F}_2^n} W_f(u) = 2^{2n}$, with equality if and only if $W_f(u) \in \{\pm 2^{n/2}, 0\}$ for all u, and therefore $W_f(u) \in \{\pm 2^{n/2}\}$ because of Parseval's relation.

Class $\mathcal{H}$ The restrictions of f to the lines through the origin of the *affine plane* are linear. More generally, any function whose restriction to each subspace in the Desarguesian spread is linear has the form

$$g(x,y) = \begin{cases} tr_{n/2}\left(x\psi\left(\frac{y}{x}\right)\right) & \text{if } x \neq 0 \\ tr_{n/2}(\mu y) & \text{if } x = 0, \end{cases} \tag{6.18}$$

where $\mu \in \mathbb{F}_{2^{n/2}}$ and ψ is a mapping from $\mathbb{F}_{2^{n/2}}$ to itself; this is a particular case of (5.8).

Definition 53   *The set of those bent functions of the form (6.18) (i.e., which are linear over each element of the Desarguesian spread) is denoted by $\mathcal{H}$.*

All the functions in class $\mathcal{H}$ being clearly *EA equivalent* to functions of the form (6.15), Proposition 81 settles the case of all Niho bent functions ([311] also settled the more general case where the restrictions are affine).

As seen in [311] (see Lemma 7 below for a proof), Condition (6.17) implies the bijectivity of G and is then necessary and sufficient for f to be bent. The set of those functions G that satisfy (6.17) is stable under some transformations, among which $G \mapsto G^{-1}$, and [311] observed that the functions corresponding to G and G^{-1} are in general EA inequivalent. Three other transformations, leading to bent functions that are in general EA inequivalent as well, have been investigated in [154].

$\mathcal{H}$ functions and o-polynomials   A connection between functions in class $\mathcal{H}$ and oval polynomials has been shown in [311]; *oval polynomials* (also called *o-polynomials*) are a notion in finite geometry related to hyperovals in the *projective plane* $PG(2, 2^{n/2})$. Recall that, for a given power q of 2, $PG(2, q)$ has for points all the one-dimensional subspaces in $\mathbb{F}_q^3$ and for lines all the two-dimensional subspaces of $\mathbb{F}_q^3$. In other words, the points of this projective plane are the equivalence classes of $\mathbb{F}_q^3 \setminus \{(0, 0, 0)\}$ modulo the equivalence relation of proportionality.[15] Then two distinct lines always intersect in one point. More precisely, the projective plane can be obtained from the affine plane by adding points at infinity in the following way: each set of parallel lines in the affine plane defines a point at infinity, and this gives one point at infinity corresponding to the parallel lines $x = a$, and q others corresponding to the parallel lines $y = bx + a$. The lines of the projective plane are the lines of the affine plane completed with their corresponding points at infinity and the line at infinity (made of all points at infinity). A *hyperoval* of the projective plane $PG(2, q)$ is a set of $q + 2$ points no three of which are on a same line; any hyperoval is equivalent to a hyperoval containing the following four points: $(1 : 0 : 0), (0 : 1 : 0), (0 : 0 : 1), (1 : 1 : 1)$; it can then be represented as $\{(1 : t : G(t)); t \in \mathbb{F}_q\} \cup \{(0 : 1 : 0), (0 : 0 : 1)\}$, where $G(0) = 0, G(1) = 1$ and G is equivalently an o-polynomial on $\mathbb{F}_q$:

Definition 54   *Let m be any positive integer. A permutation polynomial G over $\mathbb{F}_{2^m}$ is called an o-polynomial (an oval polynomial) if, for every $c \in \mathbb{F}_{2^m}$, the function*

$$z \in \mathbb{F}_{2^m} \mapsto \begin{cases} \frac{G(z+c)+G(c)}{z} & \text{if } z \neq 0 \\ 0 & \text{if } z = 0 \end{cases}$$

is a permutation of $\mathbb{F}_{2^m}$.

As observed in [311]:

Lemma 7   *Condition (6.17) is equivalent to the fact that G is an o-polynomial on $\mathbb{F}_{2^{n/2}}$.*

---

[15] The coordinates $(x : y : z)$ of a point in $PG(2, q)$, which are defined up to multiplication by a nonzero element of $\mathbb{F}_q$, are called homogeneous coordinates; we can consider that $PG(2, q)$ contains one special affine plane whose points have the form $(1 : x : y)$ while points at infinity are of the form $(0 : x : y)$, among which is the so-called nucleus $(0 : 1 : 0)$.

Proof For every $b, c \in \mathbb{F}_{2^m}$, $m = n/2$, the equation $G(z) + bz = G(c) + bc$ is satisfied by c. Thus, if Condition 6.17 is satisfied, then for every $b \in \mathbb{F}_{2^m}^*$ and every $c \in \mathbb{F}_{2^m}$, there exists exactly one $z \in \mathbb{F}_{2^m}^*$ such that $G(z+c) + b(z+c) = G(c) + bc$, that is, $\frac{G(z+c)+G(c)}{z} = b$. Then, for every $c \in \mathbb{F}_{2^m}$, the function $z \in \mathbb{F}_{2^m}^* \mapsto \frac{G(z+c)+G(c)}{z} \in \mathbb{F}_{2^m}^*$ is bijective, that is, G and the function $z \in \mathbb{F}_{2^m} \mapsto \begin{cases} \frac{G(z+c)+G(c)}{z} & \text{if } z \neq 0 \\ 0 \text{ if } z = 0 \end{cases}$ are permutations. Hence, G is an o-polynomial. Conversely, if G is an o-polynomial, then for every $c \in \mathbb{F}_{2^m}$, we have $\frac{G(z+c)+G(c)}{z} \neq 0$ for every $z \neq 0$, and for every $b \neq 0$ there exists exactly one nonzero z such that $G(z+c) + G(c) = bz$. Then for every $u \in \mathbb{F}_{2^m}$, either the equation $G(z) + bz = u$ has no solution, or it has at least a solution c and then exactly one second solution $z + c$ ($z \neq 0$). This completes the proof. □

Remark. We have already observed with Lemma 5, page 190, that any Boolean function is bent if and only if its Walsh transform takes values congruent with $2^{n/2}$ modulo $2^{n/2+1}$. This property and Relation (6.16) show that a permutation polynomial is an o-polynomial if and only if any equation $G(z) + bz = c$ with $b \neq 0$ has an even number of solutions. □

The known classes of inequivalent o-polynomials are[16] (see [168, 311] and their references):

1. $G(z) = z^{2^i}$, where i is co-prime with m.
2. $G(z) = z^6$, where m is odd.
3. $G(z) = z^{3 \cdot 2^k + 4}$, where $m = 2k - 1$.
4. $G(z) = z^{2^k + 2^{2k}}$, where $m = 4k - 1$.
5. $G(z) = z^{2^{2k+1} + 2^{3k+1}}$, where $m = 4k + 1$.
6. $G(z) = z^{2^k} + z^{2^k + 2} + z^{3 \cdot 2^k + 4}$, where $m = 2k - 1$.
7. $G(z) = z^{\frac{1}{6}} + z^{\frac{1}{2}} + z^{\frac{5}{6}}$ where m is odd; note that $G(z) = D_5\left(z^{\frac{1}{6}}\right)$, where D_5 is the Dickson polynomial of index 5 (see the definition of Dickson polynomials at page 389).
8. $G(z) = \frac{\delta^2(z^4+z)+\delta^2(1+\delta+\delta^2)(z^3+z^2)}{z^4+\delta^2 z^2+1} + z^{1/2}$, where $tr_m(1/\delta) = 1$ and, if $m \equiv 2 \; [\mathrm{mod}\; 4]$, then $\delta \notin \mathbb{F}_4$.
9. $G(z) = \frac{1}{tr_m^n(v)}\left[tr_m^n(v^r)(z+1) + tr_m^n\left[(vz + v^{2^m})^r\right]\left(z + tr_m^n(v)z^{1/2} + 1\right)^{1-r}\right] + z^{1/2}$, where m is even, $r = \pm\frac{2^m-1}{3}$, $v \in \mathbb{F}_{2^{2m}}$, $v^{2^m+1} = 1$ and $v \neq 1$.

The two last classes are related to Subiaco and Adelaide hyperovals, whose description has been simplified in [3] thanks to a new type of homogeneous coordinates. The known o-polynomials provided a number of potentially new bent functions detailed in [311], since each class of o-polynomials gives rise to several EA inequivalent classes of bent functions; see more in [154, 942]. Continuing the work of the author and Mesnager, [2] gives geometrical characterization of Niho bent functions; it shows that they are in one-to-one correspondence with the so-called *line ovals* in the *affine plane* (which are sets of $q + 1$ nonparallel lines no three of which are concurrent, where q is the order of the base field)

---

[16] Two more, given in [168], are equivalent to z^{2^i}; another in the list of [769] has a typo.

and that their dual functions are the complements of the characteristic functions of these line ovals; it extends this to arbitrary spreads.

Remark. A new notion of equivalence between bent functions in class $\mathcal{H}$ is deduced from Lemma 7. Hyperovals being called equivalent if they are mapped to each other by *collineations* (*i.e.*, permutations mapping lines to lines), it provides a notion of equivalence between o-polynomials, and between the related bent functions, called *projective equivalence*. In particular, as recalled in [414], the group $P\Gamma L(2, 2^m)$ of all $\mathbb{F}_2$-linear automorphisms of $\mathbb{F}_{2^m}$ of the form $L(x^{2^j})$, where L is an element of $GL(2, 2^m)$ (associated with a 2×2 matrix over $\mathbb{F}_{2^m}$) acts on $PG(2, 2^m)$, and then acts on o-polynomials; see more in [414]. EA equivalence classes of Niho bent functions are in one-to-one correspondence with projective equivalence classes of ovals in the projective plane $PG(2, q)$ [2, 942]. Notions of duality for bent functions and duality for projective planes are consistent for Niho bent functions (a duality of $PG(2, q)$ is a bijection from the set of points of PG(2,q) to the set of lines, which preserves incidence of points and lines). □

Niho bent functions In *univariate representation*, functions in class $\mathcal{H}$ are those functions whose restrictions to the multiplicative cosets $\mu \mathbb{F}_{2^{n/2}}$ of $\mathbb{F}_{2^{n/2}}^*$ are linear, *i.e.*, are Niho functions (5.6). Niho bent functions have been investigated in [479] and [749, 752] without that the authors notice their relationship with class H. Relation (5.5), page 168 (in which we can take for U the multiplicative subgroup of $\mathbb{F}_{2^n}^*$ of order $2^m + 1$ since $n = 2m$) gives for $g = 0$ and $f(0) = 0$

$$\forall u \in \mathbb{F}_{2^n}, \quad W_f(u) = 2^m \left(|\{\mu \in U; \phi(\mu) + tr_m^n(u\mu) = 0\}| - 1 \right).$$

We deduce, denoting by U the multiplicative subgroup of $\mathbb{F}_{2^n}^*$ of order $2^m + 1$:

Corollary 14 *Let f be any Niho function (5.6) in n variables (n even). Then f is bent if and only if, for every $u \in \mathbb{F}_{2^n}$, we have $|\{\mu \in U; \phi(\mu) + tr_{n/2}^n(u\mu) = 0\}| \in \{0, 2\}$.*

A few examples of infinite classes of Niho bent functions are known up to affine equivalence. The simplest one is quadratic and has been already encountered in Section 5.2: $tr_{n/2}\left(ax^{2^{n/2}+1}\right)$, where $a \in \mathbb{F}_{2^{n/2}}^*$, $x \in \mathbb{F}_{2^n}$. The other examples, from [479], are binomials of the form $f(x) = tr_n(\alpha_1 x^{d_1} + \alpha_2 x^{d_2})$, $x \in \mathbb{F}_{2^n}$, $d_1, d_2 \in \mathbb{Z}/(2^n - 1)\mathbb{Z}$, where $2d_1 = 2^{n/2} + 1$ and $\alpha_1, \alpha_2 \in \mathbb{F}_{2^n}^*$ are such that $(\alpha_1 + \alpha_1^{2^{n/2}})^2 = \alpha_2^{2^{n/2}+1}$. Equivalently, denoting $a = (\alpha_1 + \alpha_1^{2^{n/2}})^2$ and $b = \alpha_2$, we have $a = b^{2^{n/2}+1} \in \mathbb{F}_{2^{n/2}}^*$ and $f(x) = tr_{n/2}(ax^{2^{n/2}+1}) + tr_n(bx^{d_2})$ (note that if $b = 0$ and $a \neq 0$, then f is also bent, but it belongs then to the class of quadratic Niho bent functions seen above). The values of d_2 are (see [479] for the proofs):

1. $d_2 = (2^{n/2} - 1)3 + 1$ (originally in [479] was included the condition that, if $n \equiv 4$ [mod 8], then $b = \alpha_2$ is the fifth power of an element in $\mathbb{F}_{2^n}$, but as observed in [596], the value of b can be taken arbitrarily under the condition that $a = b^{2^{n/2}+1}$).
2. $4d_2 = (2^{n/2} - 1) + 4$ (with the condition that $n/2$ is odd), This example has been extended by Leander and Kholosha [749, 752] into the functions: $tr_n\left(\alpha x^{2^{n/2}+1} + \sum_{i=1}^{2^{r-1}-1} x^{s_i}\right)$,

$r > 1$ such that $gcd(r, n/2) = 1$, $\alpha \in \mathbb{F}_{2^n}$ such that $\alpha + \alpha^{2^{n/2}} = 1$, $s_i = (2^{n/2} - 1)\frac{i}{2^r} + 1 \pmod{2^{n/2} + 1}$, $i \in \{1, \ldots, 2^{r-1} - 1\}$. It is shown in [763] that the functions $\sum_{i=1}^{2^r-1} tr_n(\alpha x^{(i 2^{n/2-r}+1)(2^{n/2}-1)+1})$; $\alpha \in \mathbb{F}_{2^n}$, $\alpha + \alpha^{2^{n/2}} \neq 0$, enter in this class up to EA equivalence while they cover it for $\alpha + \alpha^{2^{n/2}} = 1$, with a nice original proof of their bentness.

3. $6d_2 = (2^{n/2} - 1) + 6$ (with the condition that $n/2$ is even).

As observed in [479] and in [155], these functions have respectively *algebraic degree* $n/2$, 3 and $n/2$. In [475], the value distribution of the Walsh spectrum of the monomial function corresponding to the first exponent d_2 above was determined for $n/2$ odd, in terms of Kloosterman sums.

After [311], several works investigated the properties of the known Niho bent functions and their relation with o-polynomials (when transformed from univariate form to bivariate form); we follow here the survey [313] on bent functions:

– The dual function of the second example above (with $4d_2 = (2^{n/2} - 1) + 4$) has been calculated (in [311]) as well as that of the Niho bent function consisting of 2^r exponents (see [155, 296]); it has been shown in [155, 311] that the dual bent functions are not of the Niho type; this replied negatively to an open question stated in [479].

– The quadratic monomial and (as shown in [311]) the second example above belong to the completed $\mathcal{M}$ class, but (as proved in [155]), when $m = n/2 > 2$, the two others and the generalization of the second example do not; this gives a positive answer to an open question (since 1974) whether completed class H differs from completed class $\mathcal{M}$.

– It is shown in [296] that the o-polynomials associated with the Leander–Kholosha bent functions are equivalent to *Frobenius automorphisms*; the relation between the binomial Niho bent functions with $d_2 = (2^m - 1)3 + 1$ and $6d_2 = (2^m - 1) + 6$ and the Subiaco and Adelaide classes of hyperovals (related to the two last o-polynomials above) was found in [596]; this allowed when $m \equiv 2 \pmod 4$ to expand the class of bent functions corresponding to Subiaco hyperovals. Later, in [168], the o-polynomials associated to all known Niho bent functions have been identified and the class of Niho bent functions consisting of 2^r terms has been extended by inserting coefficients of the power terms in the original function; it can then give any Niho bent function. Several classes of explicit Niho bent functions have been deduced (as also detailed in [769, section 3]).

Remark. We have seen in Proposition 66, page 193, a characterization of bent functions by power moments of even exponents of the Walsh transform. In the case of Niho functions, we have a characterization with odd exponents as well:

Proposition 82 *Let $n = 2m$ be any even positive integer, w any odd integer such that $w \geq 3$, and f any Niho n-variable Boolean function. Then we have*

$$\sum_{u \in \mathbb{F}_{2^n}} W_f^w(u) \geq 2^{(w+1)m}, \; i.e. \; \sum_{x_1, \ldots, x_{w-1} \in \mathbb{F}_{2^n}} (-1)^{\bigoplus_{i=1}^{w-1} f(x_i) \oplus f(\sum_{i=1}^{w-1} x_i)} \geq 2^{(w-1)m}$$

with equality if and only if f is bent.

Proof We still denote by U the multiplicative subgroup of $\mathbb{F}_{2^n}^*$ of order $2^m + 1$, where $n = 2m$. Let $f(\mu x) = tr_m(x \phi(\mu))$, $\mu \in U$, $x \in \mathbb{F}_{2^m}$, where ϕ is some function from U to $\mathbb{F}_{2^m}$. We have $W_f(0) = \mathcal{F}(0) = \sum_{x \in \mathbb{F}_{2^m}, \mu \in U}(-1)^{tr_m(x\phi(\mu))} - 2^m = 2^m(|\phi^{-1}(0)| - 1)$.

For every $u \in \mathbb{F}_{2^n}$, the function $f(z) + tr_n(uz)$ is Niho too since its value at $z = \mu x$ equals $tr_m(x \phi_u(\mu))$, where $\phi_u(\mu) = \phi(\mu) + tr_m^n(u\mu)$. We have then $W_f(u) = 2^m(|\phi_u^{-1}(0)| - 1)$ and $\sum_{u \in \mathbb{F}_{2^n}} W_f^w(u) = 2^{wm} \sum_{u \in \mathbb{F}_{2^n}} (|\{\mu \in U; \phi(\mu) = tr_m^n(u\mu)\}| - 1)^w$.

For all $u \in \mathbb{F}_{2^n}$, we have $|\{\mu \in U; \phi(\mu) = tr_m^n(u\mu)\}| - 1 \geq -1$ and therefore

$$(|\{\mu \in U; \phi(\mu) = tr_m^n(u\mu)\}| - 1)^w \geq |\{\mu \in U; \phi(\mu) = tr_m^n(u\mu)\}| - 1. \tag{6.19}$$

We deduce that $\sum_{u \in \mathbb{F}_{2^n}} (|\{\mu \in U; \phi(\mu) = tr_m^n(u\mu)\}| - 1)^w \geq \sum_{u \in \mathbb{F}_{2^n}} (|\{\mu \in U; \phi(\mu) = tr_m^n(u\mu)\}| - 1) = \sum_{\mu \in U} |\{u \in \mathbb{F}_{2^n}; \phi(\mu) = tr_m^n(u\mu)\}| - 2^n$. For each μ, since $u\mu$ ranges over $\mathbb{F}_{2^n}$ when u ranges over $\mathbb{F}_{2^n}$, and since $tr_m^n(z)$ ranges uniformly over $\mathbb{F}_{2^m}$ when z ranges over $\mathbb{F}_{2^n}$, we have $|\{u \in \mathbb{F}_{2^n}; \phi(\mu) = tr_m^n(u\mu)\}| = 2^m$. Hence $\sum_{u \in \mathbb{F}_{2^n}} W_f^w(u) \geq 2^{wm}((2^m + 1)2^m - 2^n) = 2^{(w+1)m}$ with equality if and only if, for every $u \in \mathbb{F}_{2^n}$, we have equality in (6.19), that is, $|\{\mu \in U; \phi(\mu) = tr_m^n(u\mu)\}| \in \{0, 1, 2\}$, that is,[17] $W_f(u) \in \{-2^m, 0, 2^m\}$. Moreover, this last condition is equivalent to $W_f(u) \in \{-2^m, 2^m\}$ for every u, that is, f is bent, because of the Parseval identity $\sum_{u \in \mathbb{F}_{2^n}} W_f^2(u) = 2^{2n}$. And we have $\sum_{u \in \mathbb{F}_2^n} W_f^w(u) = 2^n \sum_{x_1, \ldots, x_{w-1} \in \mathbb{F}_{2^n}} (-1)^{\bigoplus_{i=1}^{w-1} f(x_i) \oplus f(\sum_{i=1}^{w-1} x_i)}$. $\qquad \square$

Proposition 82 allows proving the bentness of classes of Niho functions: a set E of Niho functions is made of bent functions if and only if $\sum_{f \in E} \sum_{a \in \mathbb{F}_{2^n}} W_f^w(a) = 2^{(w+1)m}|E|$. And handling $w = 3$ is easier than $w = 4$. Corollary 13, page 194, and the remark that follows it generalize to odd exponents.

Note that this characterization is not valid for all Boolean functions, even if their algebraic degree is bounded above by $\frac{n}{2}$ (like bent functions). For instance, it is easily seen that the function, which is null when $x_1 = x_2 = \cdots = x_{\frac{n}{2}} = 0$ and has value 1 everywhere else, has a value of $\sum_{a \in \mathbb{F}_{2^n}} W_f^3(a)$ negative and has algebraic degree bounded above by $\frac{n}{2}$ (since the value of the function depends in half its variables only).

However, it is interesting to see that this characterization is also valid for those *quadratic functions* that are null at 0, since for any quadratic function f, we have $\sum_{a \in \mathbb{F}_{2^n}} W_f^3(a) = (-1)^{f(0)} 2^n \sum_{x,y \in \mathbb{F}_{2^n}} (-1)^{\beta_f(x,y)} = (-1)^{f(0)} 2^{2n}|\mathcal{E}_f|$, where β_f is the symplectic form $\beta_f(x, y) = f(x + y) \oplus f(x) \oplus f(y) \oplus f(0)$ and $\mathcal{E}_f$ is its kernel, and we know that f is bent if and only if $\mathcal{E}_f = \{0\}$.

It has been shown in [861] that the only bent functions of the form (5.4), page 168, equivalently (5.8), are, up to translation, those corresponding to Niho-bent and $\mathcal{PS}_{ap}^{\#}$ classes.

Niho-like and $\mathcal{H}$-like bent functions It is possible to extend to other spreads (than the Desarguesian spread) the principle of $\mathcal{H}$ and Niho functions (*i.e.*, considering Boolean functions whose restrictions to the elements of a spread are linear). This has been done with André's spreads in [246] and with three spreads from prequasifields and presemifields

---

[17] Recall that w is odd; for $w \geq 4$ even, there cannot be equality, and we know it already from Proposition 66.

in [335] and in [246], independently.[18] Probably many other spreads could be investigated, since many more exist; see [425, 649, 661]. But we wish to find explicit examples of such bent functions (and the associated o-likepolynomials).

Let us first study the general framework into which these four examples of spreads will fit. Consider a spread whose elements are the subspace $\{(0, y), y \in \mathbb{F}_{2^{n/2}}\}$ and the $2^{n/2}$ subspaces of the form $\{(x, L_z(x)), x \in \mathbb{F}_{2^{n/2}}\}$, where, for every $z \in \mathbb{F}_{2^{n/2}}$, function L_z is linear. The property of being a spread corresponds to the fact that, for every nonzero $x \in \mathbb{F}_{2^{n/2}}$, the mapping $z \mapsto L_z(x)$ is a permutation of $\mathbb{F}_{2^{n/2}}$. Let us denote by Γ_x the compositional inverse of this bijection.

A Boolean function over $\mathbb{F}_{2^{n/2}}^2$ is linear over each element of the spread if and only if there exists a mapping $G : \mathbb{F}_{2^{n/2}} \mapsto \mathbb{F}_{2^{n/2}}$ and an element v of $\mathbb{F}_{2^{n/2}}$ such that, for every $y \in \mathbb{F}_{2^{n/2}}$, $f(0, y) = tr_{n/2}(vy)$ and for every $x, z \in \mathbb{F}_{2^{n/2}}$, $x \neq 0$,

$$f(x, L_z(x)) = tr_{n/2}(G(z)x). \tag{6.20}$$

Note that, up to EA equivalence, we can assume that $v = 0$. Indeed, we can add the linear n-variable function $(x, y) \mapsto tr_{n/2}(vy)$ to f; this changes v into 0 and $G(z)$ into $G(z) + L_z^*(v)$, where L_z^* is the adjoint operator of L_z, since for $y = L_z(x)$, we have $tr_{n/2}(vy) = tr_{n/2}(xL_z^*(v))$. We take $v = 0$ and define $\Gamma_0(y) = 0$. By definition of Γ_x, Relation (6.20) is equivalent to

$$\forall x, y \in \mathbb{F}_{2^{n/2}}, \ f(x, y) = tr_{n/2}\left(G\left(\Gamma_x(y)\right)x\right). \tag{6.21}$$

The value of the Walsh transform $W_f(a, b) = \sum_{x,y \in \mathbb{F}_{2^{n/2}}} (-1)^{f(x,y)+tr_{n/2}(ax+by)}$ equals then, for every $(a, b) \in \mathbb{F}_{2^{n/2}}^2$,

$$\sum_{(x,y) \in \mathbb{F}_{2^{n/2}}^2} (-1)^{tr_{n/2}(G(\Gamma_x(y))x+ax+by)}$$

$$= 2^{n/2} \delta_0(b) + \sum_{x \in \mathbb{F}_{2^{n/2}}^*, z \in \mathbb{F}_{2^{n/2}}} (-1)^{tr_{n/2}(G(z)x+ax+bL_z(x))}$$

$$= 2^{n/2}(\delta_0(b) - 1) + \sum_{z \in \mathbb{F}_{2^{n/2}}} \sum_{x \in \mathbb{F}_{2^{n/2}}} (-1)^{tr_{n/2}((G(z)+a+L_z^*(b))x)}$$

$$= 2^{n/2}\left(\delta_0(b) - 1 + |\{z \in \mathbb{F}_{2^{n/2}}; \ G(z) + a + L_z^*(b) = 0\}|\right).$$

Hence f is bent if and only if G is a permutation and

$$|\{z \in \mathbb{F}_{2^{n/2}}; \ G(z) + a + L_z^*(b) = 0\}| \in \{0, 2\}, \forall a, b \in \mathbb{F}_{2^{n/2}}, b \neq 0. \tag{6.22}$$

This condition on $G(z)$ is similar to the definition of o-polynomials. In the case of André's spreads, it is a generalization of the notion of o-polynomial.

---

[18] Reference [335] is a little more general: it deals with functions affine on each spread and also addresses odd characteristics. It shows that bent functions from $\mathbb{F}_p^m \times \mathbb{F}_p^m$ to $\mathbb{F}_p$, which are affine on the elements of a given spread of $\mathbb{F}_p^m \times \mathbb{F}_p^m$, either arise from partial spread bent functions, or are a generalization in characteristic 2 of class $\mathcal{H}$. Reference [246] is slightly more general as well since it also addresses spreads not related to prequasifields.

Remark. As explained for instance in the nice survey by W. Kantor [661], every spread has a dual in the space of linear forms. Viewing this in $\mathbb{F}_{2^{n/2}}^2$ the subspaces belonging to this spread are the orthogonals of those corresponding to the original spread. In other words, the fact that for every $x \neq 0$ and every $b \neq 0$, the function $z \mapsto tr_{n/2}(bL_z(x)) = tr_{n/2}(xL_z^*(b))$ is balanced implies that function $z \mapsto L_z^*(b)$ is also a permutation and the elements of the dual spread are the subspace $\{(x, 0), x \in \mathbb{F}_{2^{n/2}}\}$ and the $2^{n/2}$ subspaces $\{(L_z^*(y), y), y \in \mathbb{F}_{2^{n/2}}\}$. $\qquad\square$

It is shown in [246] that, as in the case of o-polynomials, the condition that G is a permutation is implied by Relation (6.22).

The question that can lead to new bent functions when addressed positively is: can we build efficiently permutations G of $\mathbb{F}_{2^{n/2}}$ and linear mappings $L_z : \mathbb{F}_{2^{n/2}} \mapsto \mathbb{F}_{2^{n/2}}$, with $z \in \mathbb{F}_{2^{n/2}}$, such that function $z \mapsto L_z(x)$ is bijective for every $x \neq 0$ and that the equation $G(z) + L_z(b) = a$ has zero or two solutions for every $a \in \mathbb{F}_{2^{n/2}}$ and every $b \in \mathbb{F}_{2^{n/2}}^*$? Equivalently, by denoting by H_x the permutation $z \mapsto L_z(x)$, can we find a permutation G and a set of permutations $H_x, x \in \mathbb{F}_{2^{n/2}}^*$, such that, denoting $H_0 = 0$, the set $\{H_x, x \in \mathbb{F}_{2^{n/2}}\}$ is a vector space and every function $G + H_x, x \in \mathbb{F}_{2^{n/2}}^*$, is two-to-one? Note that finding nine classes of o-polynomials has been a hard 40-year-long mathematical work and we can expect that finding such o-like-polynomials will be also difficult, except maybe for a few simple cases like with o-polynomials.

In the case of André's spreads, we have $L_z(x) = x^{2^{k\varphi(z)}} z$. According to (6.12), we have then $\Gamma_x(y) = \frac{y}{x^{2^{k\varphi(y/x)}}}$ and $L_z^*(b) = (bz)^{2^{m-k\varphi(z)}}$. Relation (6.21) becomes

$$\forall x, y \in \mathbb{F}_{2^{n/2}}, \; f(x, y) = tr_{n/2}\left(G\left(\frac{y}{x^{2^{k\varphi(y/x)}}} \right) x \right). \tag{6.23}$$

The condition for such f to be bent is that, for every $b \in \mathbb{F}_{2^{n/2}}^*$ and every $a \in \mathbb{F}_{2^{n/2}}$, there exist two values of z or none such that $G(z) + (bz)^{2^{m-k\varphi(z)}} = a$.

As shown for instance in [425, 649] (and recalled by Kantor in [662]), a spread can be derived from any prequasifield, that is, any Abelian finite group having a second law $*$ that is left-distributive with respect to the first law and is such that the right and left multiplications by a nonzero element are bijective, and that the multiplications by 0 are absorbent. The elements of this spread are the $\mathbb{F}_2$-vector subspaces $\{(0, y), y \in \mathbb{F}_{2^{n/2}}\}$ and $\{(x, z * x), x \in \mathbb{F}_{2^{n/2}}\}$, $z \in \mathbb{F}_{2^{n/2}}$. Wu [1123] has studied three particular examples for designing $\mathcal{PS}$ functions (many others could have been studied), and he determined explicitly the related functions Γ_x. Let us see what we obtain with them in the framework of Niho-like functions.

The Dempwolff–Müller prequasifield is defined as follows. Let k and m be co-prime odd integers. Let $e = 2^{m-1} - 2^{k-1} - 1$, $L(x) = \sum_{i=0}^{k-1} x^{2^i}$, and define $x * y = x^e L(xy)$. Then $(\mathbb{F}_{2^m}, +, *)$ is a prequasifield [431], leading to the spread of the $\mathbb{F}_2$-vector subspaces $\{(0, y), y \in \mathbb{F}_{2^m}\}$ and $\{(x, z * x), x \in \mathbb{F}_{2^m}\} = \{(x, z^e L(xz)), x \in \mathbb{F}_{2^m}\}, z \in \mathbb{F}_{2^m}$. Then $\Gamma_x(y) = \dfrac{1}{x D_d\left(\frac{y^2}{x^{2^k+1}} \right)}$, where D_d is the Dickson polynomial (see the definition at page 389) of index the inverse d of $2^k - 1$ modulo $2^m - 1$, and $L_z^*(b) = \sum_{i=0}^{k-1}(bz^e)^{2^i} z$. Relation (6.21) becomes

$$\forall x, y \in \mathbb{F}_{2^m}, \; f(x, y) = tr_m \left(G \left(\frac{1}{x D_d \left(\frac{y^2}{x^{2^k+1}} \right)} \right) x \right), \tag{6.24}$$

and such f is bent if and only if the equation $G(z) + \sum_{i=0}^{k-1} (bz^e)^{2^{-i}} z = a$ has 0 or 2 solutions for every $b \neq 0$ and every a.

The Knuth commutative presemifield is defined as follows. Let m be an odd integer and $b \in \mathbb{F}_{2^m}^*$. Then $x * y = xy + x^2 tr_m(by) + y^2 tr_m(bx)$ defines a presemifield (a prequasifield that remains one when $a * b$ is replaced by $b * a$), leading to the spread of the $\mathbb{F}_2$-vector subspaces $\{(0, y), \; y \in \mathbb{F}_{2^m}\}$ and $\{(x, z * x), x \in \mathbb{F}_{2^m}\} = \{(x, zx + x^2 tr_m(bz) + z^2 tr_m(bx)), x \in \mathbb{F}_{2^m}\}, z \in \mathbb{F}_{2^m}$.

Then $\Gamma_x(y) = (1 + tr_m(bx))\frac{y}{x} + x tr_m \left(b\frac{y}{x} \right) + x tr_m(bx) C_{\frac{1}{bx}} \left(\frac{y}{x^2} \right)$, where $C_a(x) = \sum_{i=0}^{m-1} c_i x^{2^i}$, where $c_0 = \frac{1}{a^{2^i}} + \frac{1}{a^{3 \cdot 2^i}} + \cdots + \frac{1}{a^{(m-3) \cdot 2^i}}$, $c_i = 1 + \frac{1}{a^{2^i}} + \frac{1}{a^{3 \cdot 2^i}} + \cdots + \frac{1}{a^{(i-2) \cdot 2^i}} + \frac{1}{a^{(i+1) \cdot 2^i}} + \cdots + \frac{1}{a^{(m-1) \cdot 2^i}}$ if i is odd and $c_i = 1 + \frac{1}{a^{2 \cdot 2^i}} + \frac{1}{a^{4 \cdot 2^i}} + \cdots + \frac{1}{a^{(i-2) \cdot 2^i}} + \frac{1}{a^{(i+1) \cdot 2^i}} + \cdots + \frac{1}{a^{(m-2) \cdot 2^i}}$ if i is even. We have $L_z^*(b) = bz + b^{2^{m-1}} tr_m(bz) + b tr_m(b^{2^{m-1}} z)$. Relation (6.21) becomes

$$tr_m \left(G \left((1 + tr_m(bx))\frac{y}{x} + x tr_m \left(b\frac{y}{x} \right) + x tr_m(bx) C_{\frac{1}{bx}} \left(\frac{y}{x^2} \right) \right) x \right), \tag{6.25}$$

and such f is bent if and only if the equation $G(z) + bz + b^{2^{m-1}} tr_m(bz) + b tr_m(b^{2^{m-1}} z) = a$ has zero or two solutions for every $b \neq 0$ and every a.

There are more examples of semifields due to Knuth [710] that could be studied.

A third example is the dual of the symplectic version of the Knuth commutative presemifield. Assume m is an odd integer. Then $x * y = x^2 y + tr_m(xy) + x tr_m(y)$ defines a presemifield [659], leading to two spreads:

- The spread of the $\mathbb{F}_2$-vector subspaces $\{(0, y), \; y \in \mathbb{F}_{2^m}\}$ and $\{(x, z * x), x \in \mathbb{F}_{2^m}\} = \{(x, z^2 x + tr_m(zx) + z tr_m(x)), x \in \mathbb{F}_{2^m}\}$
- The spread of the $\mathbb{F}_2$-vector subspaces $\{(0, y), \; y \in \mathbb{F}_{2^m}\}$ and $\{(x, x * z), x \in \mathbb{F}_{2^m}\} = \{(x, x^2 z + tr_m(xz) + x tr_m(z)), x \in \mathbb{F}_{2^m}\}$, where $z \in \mathbb{F}_{2^m}$ (two such spreads are sometimes called *opposite* of each other)

In the first case, the corresponding function Γ_x has been determined in [1123] and $L_z^*(b) = bz^2 + z tr_m(b) + tr_m(bz)$. Then $f(x, y)$ equals

$$tr_m \left(G \left(\left[(xy)^{2^{m-1}} + \sum_{i=0}^{\frac{m-1}{2}} (xy)^{2^{2i}-1} + \sum_{i=0}^{\frac{m-3}{2}} x^{2^{2i}} tr_m(xy) \right] \frac{tr_m(x)}{x} \right.\right.$$
$$\left.\left. + x^{2^{m-1}-1} y^{2^{m-1}} + x^{2^{m-1}-1} tr_m(xy) \right) x \right), \tag{6.26}$$

and such f is bent if and only if the equation $G(z) + bz^2 + z tr_m(b) + tr_m(bz) = a$ has zero or two solutions for every $b \neq 0$ and every a.

In the second case, the relation $y = x^2 z + tr_m(xz) + x tr_m(z)$ implies for $x \neq 0$ that

$$
\begin{cases}
z = \frac{y}{x^2} + \frac{tr_m(xz)}{x^2} + \frac{tr_m(z)}{x} \\
tr_m(xz) = tr_m\left(\frac{y}{x}\right) + tr_m(xz) tr_m\left(\frac{1}{x}\right) + tr_m(z) \\
tr_m(z) = tr_m\left(\frac{y}{x^2}\right) + (tr_m(xz) + tr_m(z)) \, tr_m\left(\frac{1}{x}\right)
\end{cases}
\quad \text{and is equivalent to}
$$

$$
z = \frac{y}{x^2} + tr_m\left(\frac{1}{x}\right) \left(\frac{tr_m\left(\frac{y}{x^2}\right)}{x^2} + \frac{tr_m\left(\frac{y}{x}\right)}{x} \right)
$$

$$
+ \left(tr_m\left(\frac{1}{x}\right) + 1 \right) \left(\frac{tr_m\left(\frac{y}{x^2}\right) + tr_m\left(\frac{y}{x}\right)}{x^2} + \frac{tr_m\left(\frac{y}{x^2}\right)}{x} \right),
$$

which gives $\Gamma_x(y)$. We have $L_z^*(b) = (bz)^{2^{m-1}} + z tr_m(b) + b tr_m(z)$. Then $f(x, y)$ equals

$$
tr_m \left(G \left(\frac{y}{x^2} + tr_m\left(\frac{1}{x}\right) \left(\frac{tr_m\left(\frac{y}{x^2}\right)}{x^2} + \frac{tr_m\left(\frac{y}{x}\right)}{x} \right) + \left(tr_m\left(\frac{1}{x}\right) + 1 \right) \right. \right.
$$

$$
\left. \left. \left(\frac{tr_m\left(\frac{y}{x^2}\right) + tr_m\left(\frac{y}{x}\right)}{x^2} + \frac{tr_m\left(\frac{y}{x^2}\right)}{x} \right) \right) x \right),
$$

(6.27)

and such f is bent if and only if the equation $G(z) + (bz)^{2^{m-1}} + z tr_m(b) + b tr_m(z) = a$ has zero or two solutions for every $b \neq 0$ and every a.

See in [5] more constructions of bent functions linear on elements of presemifield spreads and a survey on this topic, with explicit descriptions of such functions for known commutative presemifields and related (new types of) oval polynomials.

4. Class C^+ has been introduced by Dillon [441]. Since $\mathcal{PS}_{ap}$ functions have for supports the unions of multiplicative cosets of the subgroup $\mathbb{F}_{2^{n/2}}^*$ of $\mathbb{F}_{2^n}^*$ (i.e., the subgroup of all $(2^{n/2}+1)$th powers), plus possibly the 0 element, he addressed the other possible subgroup U of $(2^{n/2} - 1)$th powers in $\mathbb{F}_{2^n}^*$, and studied then the functions of the form $f(z) = g(z^{2^{n/2}+1})$, where $z \in \mathbb{F}_{2^n}$ and g is balanced over $\mathbb{F}_{2^{n/2}}$ (note that $z^{2^{n/2}+1} \in \mathbb{F}_{2^{n/2}}$) and vanishes at 0 (if not, we can apply the result to $g \oplus 1$). He showed that such function is bent if and only if the mapping $a \in \mathbb{F}_{2^{n/2}} \mapsto W_g(a^{-1}) = \sum_{x \in \mathbb{F}_{2^{n/2}}} (-1)^{g(x) + tr_{n/2}(a^{-1}x)}$, with the convention $0^{-1} = 0$, equals the Walsh transform of some Boolean function over $\mathbb{F}_{2^{n/2}}$.

Dillon refers to the Singer difference set in his proof. An elementary proof is as follows: using polar representation ux (with $x \in \mathbb{F}_{2^{n/2}}^*$, $u \in U$) in $\mathbb{F}_{2^n}^*$, we have for every $\lambda \in \mathbb{F}_{2^n}$ that

$$
W_f(\lambda) = \sum_{z \in \mathbb{F}_{2^n}} (-1)^{g(z^{2^{n/2}+1}) + tr_n(\lambda z)} = 1 + \sum_{u \in U} \sum_{x \in \mathbb{F}_{2^{n/2}}^*} (-1)^{g(x^2) + tr_{n/2}((\lambda u + \lambda^{2^{n/2}} u^{2^{n/2}})x)} =
$$

$$
-2^{n/2} + \sum_{u \in U} W_g((\lambda u + \lambda^{2^{n/2}} u^{2^{n/2}})^2). \text{ If } \lambda = 0, \text{ then } W_f(\lambda) = -2^{n/2} + (2^{n/2} + 1) W_g(0) =
$$

$-2^{n/2}$. Otherwise, we can assume without loss of generality that λ belongs to $\mathbb{F}_{2^{n/2}}^*$ (since

$W_f(\lambda)$ is clearly invariant when multiplying λ by an element of U), and we have then $W_f(\lambda) = -2^{n/2} + \sum_{u \in U} W_g \left(\lambda^2 \left(u + u^{2^{n/2}}\right)^2\right)$. It is well known that, when u ranges over $U \setminus \{1\}$, $u + u^{2^{n/2}}$ ranges twice over the set $\{z \in \mathbb{F}_{2^{n/2}}^*, tr_{n/2}\left(z^{-1}\right) = 1\}$ (indeed, we have $u^{2^{n/2}} = u^{-1}$ and the equation $u + u^{-1} = z$, i.e., $\left(\frac{u}{z}\right)^2 + \frac{u}{z} = z^{-2}$, has solutions in $U \setminus \{1\}$ if and only if $tr_{n/2}\left(z^{-1}\right) = 1$). Then, since g is balanced, $W_f(\lambda)$ equals

$$-2^{n/2} + 2 \sum_{z \in \mathbb{F}_{2^{n/2}}^*; \, tr_{n/2}(z^{-1})=1} W_g\left((\lambda z)^2\right) = -2^{n/2} + \sum_{z \in \mathbb{F}_{2^{n/2}}} W_g\left((\lambda z)^2\right)\left(1 - (-1)^{tr_{n/2}(z^{-2})}\right)$$

and $W_f(\lambda)$ is equal to $-2^{n/2} + 2^{n/2}(-1)^{g(0)} - \sum_{z \in \mathbb{F}_{2^{n/2}}} W_g\left(\lambda^2 z\right)(-1)^{tr_{n/2}(z^{-1})} = -\sum_{z \in \mathbb{F}_{2^{n/2}}} W_g\left(z^{-1}\right)(-1)^{tr_{n/2}(\mu z)}$, where $\mu = \lambda^2 \neq 0$.

Hence, f is bent if and only if $\sum_{z \in \mathbb{F}_{2^{n/2}}} W_g\left(z^{-1}\right)(-1)^{tr_{n/2}(\mu z)} \in \{2^{n/2}, -2^{n/2}\}$ for every $\mu \neq 0$, which is then equivalent to the condition stated by Dillon, according to the inverse Fourier transform formula, since it is always verified for $\mu = 0$.

Dillon mentions the example where g is the absolute trace function $tr_{n/2}(x)$ over $\mathbb{F}_{2^{n/2}}$; the resulting function is quadratic and so belongs to class $\mathcal{M}$ completed, and it also belongs to class $\mathcal{H}$, up to EA equivalence. No example is known yet lying outside known completed classes.

5. Dobbertin's class, introduced in [466], is a class of bent functions that contains both $\mathcal{PS}_{ap}$ and $\mathcal{M}$ and is based on the so-called *triple construction*. The elements of this class are the functions f defined by $f(x, \phi(y)) = g\left(\frac{x + \psi(y)}{y}\right)$, where g is a balanced Boolean function on $\mathbb{F}_{2^{\frac{n}{2}}}$ and ϕ, ψ are two mappings from $\mathbb{F}_{2^{\frac{n}{2}}}$ to itself such that, if T denotes the affine subspace of $\mathbb{F}_{2^{\frac{n}{2}}}$ spanned by the support of function W_g, then, for any a in $\mathbb{F}_{2^{\frac{n}{2}}}$, the functions ϕ and ψ are affine on $aT = \{ax, x \in T\}$. The mapping ϕ must additionally be one-to-one. Dobbertin gives two explicit examples of bent functions constructed this way. In both, ϕ is a power function.

6. The class of functions γ related to almost bent functions exists when $n \equiv 2$ [mod 4]. Recall that a vectorial Boolean function $F : \mathbb{F}_{2^{n/2}} \to \mathbb{F}_{2^{n/2}}$ is called almost bent (see Definition 31, page 119) if the Walsh transforms of all component functions $v \cdot F$, $v \neq 0$ in $\mathbb{F}_{2^{n/2}}$ take values in $\{-2^{\frac{n/2+1}{2}}, 0, 2^{\frac{n/2+1}{2}}\}$. The function $\gamma_F(a, b)$, $a, b \in \mathbb{F}_{2^{n/2}}$, equal to 1 if the equation $F(x) + F(x + a) = b$ admits solutions, with $a \neq 0$ in $\mathbb{F}_{2^{n/2}}$, and equal to 0 otherwise, is then bent (see Proposition 158, page 375), and the dual of γ_F is the indicator of the Walsh support of F, deprived of $(0, 0)$. Several classes of AB functions are known (see Section 11.4, page 394). The bent functions γ_F associated to known AB functions have been investigated in [152]. We give them below:

- *Gold:* $F(x) = x^{2^i+1}$, $\gcd(i, n/2) = 1$, $\gamma_F(a, b) = tr_{n/2}(\frac{b}{a^{2^i+1}})$ with $\frac{1}{0} = 0$
- *Inverse:* $F(x) = x^{2^n-2}$, $\gamma_F(a, b) = tr_n(\frac{1}{ab}) + 1 + \delta_0(a) + \delta_0(b) + \delta_0(a)\delta_0(b) + \delta_0(ab+1)$, where $\delta_0(x)$ is the Dirac (or Kronecker) function
- *Kasami–Welch* $F(x) = x^{2^{2i}-2^i+1}$, $\gcd(i, n/2) = 1$, *Welch* $F(x) = x^{2^{\frac{n/2-1}{2}}+3}$, *Niho*
  $F(x) = x^{2^{\frac{n/2-1}{2}}+2^{\frac{n/2-1}{4}}-1}$ *if* $n \equiv 1$ *[mod 4]*, $F(x) = x^{2^{\frac{n/2-1}{2}}+2^{3\frac{n/2-1}{2}+1}-1}$ *if* $n \equiv 3$ *[mod 4]*

We have $F(x+1) + F(x) = q(x^{2^s} + x)$, where $\gcd(s, n/2) = 1$ and q is in each case a permutation determined by Dobbertin (see [470]):

1. Kasami–Welch: $s = i$, $q(x) = \dfrac{x^{2^i+1}}{\sum_{j=1}^{i'} x^{2^{ji}} + \alpha tr_{n/2}(x)} + 1$, where $i' \equiv 1/i$ [mod $n/2$],
   $$\alpha = \begin{cases} 0 & \text{if } i' \text{ is odd} \\ 1 & \text{otherwise.} \end{cases}$$

2. Welch: $s = \frac{n/2-1}{2}$, $q(x) = x^{2^{\frac{n/2-1}{2}+1}+1} + x^3 + x + 1$.

3. Niho: $s = \frac{n/2-1}{4}$ if $n \equiv 1$ [mod 4] and $s = \frac{3\frac{n/2-1}{2}+1}{2}$ if $n \equiv 3$ [mod 4], $q(x) =$
   $$\begin{cases} \frac{1}{g(x^{2^s-1})+1} + 1 & \text{if } x \notin \mathbb{F}_2 \\ 1 & \text{otherwise,} \end{cases} \quad \text{where}$$
   $$g(x) = x^{2^{2s+1}+2^{s+1}+1} + x^{2^{2s+1}+2^{s+1}-1} + x^{2^{2s+1}+1} + x^{2^{2s+1}-1} + x.$$

and $F(x+1) + F(x) = b$ has solutions if and only if $tr_{n/2}(q^{-1}(b)) = 0$. Then
$$\gamma_F(a, b) = \begin{cases} tr_{n/2}(q^{-1}(b/a^d)) + 1 & \text{if } a \neq 0, \\ 0 & \text{otherwise.} \end{cases}$$

The functions γ_F associated to Kasami–Welch, Welch, and Niho functions with $n/2 = 7, 9$, are neither in the completed $\mathcal{M}$ class nor in the completed $\mathcal{PS}_{ap}$ class.

The other known infinite classes of AB functions are quadratic; their associated γ_F belong to the completed $\mathcal{M}$ class.

7. Classes of *bent monomial Boolean univariate functions* (which can more simply be called *monomial bent* functions and are sometimes called *power bent* functions), that is, functions of the form $f(x) = tr_n(ax^d)$, where $x \in \mathbb{F}_{2^n}$ and a belongs to some subset[19] of $\mathbb{F}_{2^n}^*$.

Obviously, $tr_n(ax^d)$ can be bent only if the mapping $x \to x^d$ is not a permutation (otherwise, the function would be balanced, a contradiction), that is, if d is not coprime with $2^n - 1$.

---

[19] It is impossible that $tr_n(ax^d)$ be bent for every $a \neq 0$ since this would mean that the (n, n)-function x^d is bent, and we shall see in Proposition 104, page 269, that this is impossible.

It has been proved in [750] that d must be coprime either with $2^{\frac{n}{2}} - 1$ or with $2^{\frac{n}{2}} + 1$. Indeed, since $f(x)$ is invariant under multiplication of x by $\beta = \alpha^{\frac{2^n-1}{\gcd(d,2^n-1)}}$ where α is a primitive element of $\mathbb{F}_{2^n}$, and is then invariant under multiplication by any element of the multiplicative group of order $\gcd(d, 2^n - 1)$, we have $W_f(0) \equiv 1 \pmod{\gcd(d, 2^n - 1)}$. Hence, $\gcd(d, 2^n - 1)$, which equals $\gcd(d, 2^{n/2} - 1)\gcd(d, 2^{n/2} + 1)$, since $2^{\frac{n}{2}} - 1$ and $2^{\frac{n}{2}} + 1$ are coprime, divides $W_f(0) - 1$. If $W_f(0) = 2^{\frac{n}{2}}$ then $\gcd(d, 2^{\frac{n}{2}} + 1) = 1$ and if $W_f(0) = -2^{\frac{n}{2}}$, then $\gcd(d, 2^{\frac{n}{2}} - 1) = 1$.

Apart from the particular case of quadratic bent function $f(x) = tr_{\frac{n}{2}}(x^{2^{n/2}+1})$, already encountered, the known values of d for which there exists at least one a such that $tr_n(ax^d)$ is bent (such values are called *bent exponents*) are the following (up to conjugacy $d \to 2^j d$ [mod $2^n - 1$]):

- The *Gold exponents* (already seen at page 206) $d = 2^j + 1$, where $\frac{n}{\gcd(j,n)}$ is even and $a \notin \{x^d, x \in \mathbb{F}_{2^n}\} = \{x^{\gcd(d,2^n-1)}, x \in \mathbb{F}_{2^n}\}$; being quadratic, function $tr_n(ax^{2^j+1})$ belongs to the completed Maiorana–McFarland class; these functions have been generalized in [355, 629, 669, 699, 701, 808, 1144] to functions of the form $tr_n(\sum_{i=1}^{n/2-1} a_i x^{2^i+1}) + tr_{n/2}(a_{n/2}x^{2^{n/2}+1})$, $a_i \in \mathbb{F}_2$. Being quadratic, these functions all belong to completed class $\mathcal{M}$.

  A particular case of Gold exponents is when $\gcd(j,n) = 1$, function $tr_n(ax^{2^j+1})$ is then bent if and only if a is not the $(2^j + 1)$th power of an element of $\mathbb{F}_{2^n}$, that is (since $\gcd(2^j + 1, 2^n - 1) = 3$), a is not a cube in $\mathbb{F}_{2^n}$. The same result exists with

- The *Kasami exponents*: $2^{2i} - 2^i + 1$ with $\gcd(i,n) = 1$: function $tr_n(ax^{2^{2i}-2^i+1})$ is bent if and only if a is not a cube (this is proved in [448, Theorem 11] for n not divisible by 3 and is true also for n divisible by 3 as seen by Leander [750]). Note that since the functions in Maiorana–McFarland's and $\mathcal{PS}^+$ classes are normal and functions in the $\mathcal{PS}^-$ class have algebraic degree $\frac{n}{2}$, the Kasami bent functions, which have algebraic degree $w_2(4^k - 2^k + 1) = k + 1$, do not belong, in general, to these classes (see page 253).

- The *Dillon exponents* [440] (already seen at page 215): $d = j \cdot (2^{\frac{n}{2}} - 1)$, where $\gcd(j, 2^{\frac{n}{2}} + 1) = 1$; function $tr_n(ax^d)$, with $a \in \mathbb{F}_{2^{\frac{n}{2}}}$ without loss of generality, is bent if and only if the Kloosterman sum $\sum_{x \in \mathbb{F}_{2^{\frac{n}{2}}}} (-1)^{tr_{\frac{n}{2}}(x^{-1}+ax)}$ is null, where $1/0 = 0$ (it belongs then to the PS$_{ap}$ class); see also [750].

- Two exponents that we give without proof:

  - The *Leander exponent* $d = (2^{n/4} + 1)^2$, where n is divisible by 4 but not by 8; see [750]; see also [352], where the set of all a such that the corresponding function $tr_n(ax^d)$ is bent is determined: $a = a'b^i$, $a' \in w\mathbb{F}_{2^{n/4}}$, $w \in \mathbb{F}_4 \setminus \mathbb{F}_2$, $b \in \mathbb{F}_{2^n}$; the function belongs to the Maiorana–McFarland class.

  - The *Canteaut–Charpin–Kyureghyan exponent* [197] $d = 2^{n/3} + 2^{n/6} + 1$, where n is divisible by 6 (the corresponding function $tr_n(ax^d)$ is bent if and only if $a = a'b^i$, $a' \in \mathbb{F}_{2^{\frac{n}{2}}}$ such that $tr_{\frac{n}{2}}^{n/6}(a') = a' + a'^{2^{n/6}} + a'^{2^{2n/6}} = 0$, $b \in \mathbb{F}_{2^n}$; it belongs to the Maiorana–McFarland class).

It has been checked by Canteaut that all bent functions $tr_n(ax^i)$ are covered by these classes for $n \leq 20$ and shown in [352] that there is no other cubic exponent giving infinite classes of bent functions in the Maiorana–McFarland class.

Remark. The bent sequences given in [1137] are particular cases of the constructions given above (using also some of the secondary constructions given below). □

8. Classes of bent polynomial functions in *univariate representation*. We also give them without proof. See more in [227]:

- Quadratic bent functions; see page 206.
- $f(x) = tr_n\left(a[x^{2^i+1} + (x^{2^i} + x + 1)tr_n(x^{2^i+1})]\right)$, where $n \geq 6$, $\frac{n}{2}$ does not divide i, $\frac{n}{\gcd(i,n)}$ even, $a \in \mathbb{F}_{2^n} \setminus \mathbb{F}_{2^i}$, $\{a, a+1\} \cap \{x^{2^i+1}; x \in \mathbb{F}_{2^n}\} = \emptyset$; these functions found in [150] by applying CCZ equivalence to nonbent vectorial functions belong to completed $\mathcal{M}$ when $a \in \mathbb{F}_{2^{n/2}}$
- $f(x) = tr_n\left(a\left[\left(x + tr_3^n\left(x^{2(2^i+1)} + x^{4(2^i+1)}\right) + tr_n(x)tr_3^n\left(x^{2^i+1} + x^{2^{2i}(2^i+1)}\right)\right)^{2^i+1}\right]\right)$,

    where $6 \mid n$, $\frac{n}{2}$ does not divide i, $\frac{n}{\gcd(i,n)}$ even, $b + d + d^2 \notin \{x^{2^i+1}; x \in \mathbb{F}_{2^n}\}$ for every $d \in \mathbb{F}_{2^3}$; these functions found in [150]) belong to completed $\mathcal{M}$
- The four known classes of Niho bent functions studied above;
- Classes of bent functions via Dillon exponents and their generalizations [350, 441, 448, 478, 479, 629, 749, 752, 764, 851, 852, 853, 871, 1144] (we develop some of them in other subsections of this book and do not have the room for detailing each)
- The trace function of the *multinomial APN functions* that we shall describe at page 406 [116].
- Sums of some known bent functions and products of linear functions [1131].

9. Classes of bent polynomial functions in *bivariate representation*. Except for Maiorana–McFarland functions, $\mathcal{PS}_{ap}$ functions, and functions in class $\mathcal{H}$ in bivariate form, there is the isolated class seen at page 207, $f(x, y) = tr_m(x^{2^i+1} + y^{2^i+1} + xy)$, $x, y \in \mathbb{F}_{2^m}$, where $\gcd(3, n) = \gcd(i, n) = 1$.

10. Bent functions obtained as restrictions and extensions. In [734], the authors studied if the restrictions to hyperplanes of Gold functions $tr_n(x^{2^i+1})$ (see page 206) on $\mathbb{F}_{2^n}$, for n odd, $\gcd(i, n) = 1$, could be bent. It is shown that this happens with any linear hyperplane not containing element 1. It was already known[20] from [57] that, for any (n, n)-function F satisfying $F(0) = 0$ and such that, for every $a \in \mathbb{F}_{2^n}^*$, the set $H_a = \{D_a F(x); x \in \mathbb{F}_2^n\}$ is the complement of a linear hyperplane,[21] the restriction of the Boolean function $1_{H_a} \circ F$ to any linear hyperplane not containing a is bent. Note that the restriction to its complement

---

[20] But [734] also determines the dual function.
[21] Reference [57] calls these functions *crooked*, but we shall use this term at page 278 for a slightly more general notion.

$a + H_a$ is bent too, since $1_{H_a} \circ F(x) + 1_{H_a} \circ F(x + a)$ equals constant function 1, because $F(x) + F(x + a) \in H_a$ implies that $F(x) \in H_a$ is equivalent to $F(x + a) \notin H_a$.

For $F(x) = x^{2^i+1}$, we have $H_a = \{a^{2^i+1}(x^{2^i} + x + 1); x \in \mathbb{F}_{2^n}\}$ and $1_{H_a} \circ F(x) = tr_n\left(\left(\frac{x}{a}\right)^{2^i+1}\right)$. In [548], the authors prove that the restriction of any Gold AB function to any linear hyperplane is bent.

Dillon and McGuire studied in [449] the more difficult case of Kasami functions $tr_n(x^{4^i-2^i+1})$ (see page 230) on $\mathbb{F}_{2^n}$, for n odd, $gcd(i, n) = 1$. They showed that for n not divisible by 3, there is one Kasami exponent with $n = 3k \pm 1$ for which the function is bent when restricted to one particular hyperplane (of equation $tr_n(x) = 0$). This function is not bent when restricted to any other hyperplane. They also presented a criterion for the restriction of a near-bent function (see Subsection 6.2.4) to a hyperplane to be bent. More investigations between bent restrictions and near-bent extensions were made in [754]; see also some results in [191]. In [755], Leander and McGuire have considered, in the other sense, the problem of going from a near-bent n-variable function to a bent $(n + 1)$-variable function; using the construction of bent functions by the concatenation (f, g) of two near-bent functions f, g whose Walsh spectra are complementary (this condition is straightforwardly necessary and sufficient), that is, disjoint, and consequently that function $(f, f \oplus tr_n)$ is bent if and only if the indicator h of the support of W_f satisfies $D_1 h = 1$, where $1 \in \mathbb{F}_{2^n}$ (which is also easily seen and is equivalent to the bentness of the restrictions of f to $\{x \in \mathbb{F}_{2^n}; tr_n(x) = 0\}$ and its complement), they deduced from the Kasami near-bent functions, the first examples of non-weakly normal bent functions in dimensions 10 and 12.

6.1.16 Secondary constructions of bent Boolean functions

Since very few bent functions are known from primary constructions, it seems useful to derive secondary constructions.[22] We have already seen in Proposition 79, page 211, a *secondary construction* based on the Maiorana–McFarland construction. We describe now the others (which have been found so far).

1. The *direct sum* is the first secondary construction given by J. Dillon and O. Rothaus in [441, 1005]: let f be a bent function on $\mathbb{F}_2^n$ (n even) and g a bent function on $\mathbb{F}_2^m$ (m even), then the function h defined on $\mathbb{F}_2^{n+m}$ by $h(x, y) = f(x) \oplus g(y)$ is bent. Indeed, a straightforward calculation gives

$$W_h(a, b) = W_f(a) \times W_g(b). \tag{6.28}$$

This construction provides *decomposable functions* only (a Boolean function is called decomposable if it is equivalent to the sum of two functions that depend on two disjoint subsets of coordinates). Such peculiarity is easy to detect and can be used for designing divide-and-conquer attacks, as pointed out by J. Dillon in [442]. However, in some cases (see an example in [839]), this construction provides nice solutions to specific problems. Anyway, if the direct sum provides weak functions in a given framework, the indirect sum (see below) is an alternative, since it has almost the same property with respect to the Walsh transform and does not have the drawback of direct sum.

---

[22] However, as Dobbertin and Leander write in [477], "most bent functions appear without any roots to bent functions in lower dimensions which could explain their existence."

2. The *Rothaus construction* was introduced by the same authors: if g, h, k, and $g \oplus h \oplus k$ are bent on $\mathbb{F}_2^n$ (n even), then the function defined at every element (x, y_1, y_2) of $\mathbb{F}_2^{n+2}$ ($x \in \mathbb{F}_2^n$, $y_1, y_2 \in \mathbb{F}_2$) by $f(x, y_1, y_2) =$

$$g(x)h(x) \oplus g(x)k(x) \oplus h(x)k(x) \oplus [g(x) \oplus h(x)]y_1 \oplus [g(x) \oplus k(x)]y_2 \oplus y_1 y_2$$

is bent. We do not give a proof since this construction will be a particular case of Theorem 15 below (see also [876]). A method is proposed in [329] to construct three bent functions that can be used as initial functions in the Rothaus construction.

3. The *indirect sum* generalizes the direct sum. It has first been found as a construction of resilient functions, which generalized and unified several previous constructions; see Theorem 21, page 300. The same principle allows constructing bent functions:

Proposition 83 *[225] Let f_1 and f_2 be two n-variable bent functions (n even) and let g_1 and g_2 be two m-variable bent functions (m even). Define[23]*

$$h(x, y) = f_1(x) \oplus g_1(y) \oplus (f_1 \oplus f_2)(x) (g_1 \oplus g_2)(y); \ x \in \mathbb{F}_2^n, \ y \in \mathbb{F}_2^m.$$

Then h is bent and its dual is obtained from $\widetilde{f_1}, \widetilde{f_2}, \widetilde{g_1}$ and $\widetilde{g_2}$ by the same formula as h is obtained from $f_1, f_2, g_1,$ and g_2.

We do not give a proof of this result either, since we shall see that it is also a particular case of Theorem 15 below.

Similarly to the direct sum and contrary to the Rothaus construction above and to the bent concatenation construction below, the indirect sum requires no condition on the bent functions $f_1, f_2, g_1,$ and g_2 used.

An interest of this construction, compared to the direct sum, is that it allows designing functions h, which are more complex (in particular, which may have larger algebraic degree and algebraic immunity) than the functions $f_1, f_2, g_1,$ and g_2 used.

The indirect sum has been modified and generalized in several ways. These generalizations often require conditions on the functions used. In [329], the authors introduced the constructions

1. $f(x, y) = f_1(x) \oplus g_1(y) \oplus (f_1 \oplus f_2)(x)(g_1 \oplus g_2)(y) \oplus (f_2 \oplus f_3)(x)(g_2 \oplus g_3)(y),$

where $f_1, f_2,$ and f_3 are bent functions in n variables such that $f_1 \oplus f_2 \oplus f_3$ is bent and has $\widetilde{f_1} \oplus \widetilde{f_2} \oplus \widetilde{f_3}$ for dual, and $g_1, g_2,$ and g_3 are bent functions in m variables such that $g_1 \oplus g_2 \oplus g_3$ is bent.

2. $f(x, y) = f_0(x) \oplus g_0(y) \oplus (f_0 \oplus f_1)(x)(g_0 \oplus g_1)(y) \oplus (f_1 \oplus f_2)(x)(g_1 \oplus g_2)(y) \oplus$

$$(f_2 \oplus f_3)(x)(g_2 \oplus g_3)(y),$$

with a slightly more complex condition on functions $f_0, \ldots, f_3, g_0, \ldots, g_3$.

---

[23] h can be seen as the concatenation of the four functions $f_1, f_1 \oplus 1, f_2,$ and $f_2 \oplus 1$, in an order controlled by $g_1(y)$ and $g_2(y)$.

A modified indirect sum is also introduced in [1153], in which functions f_1 and f_2 (resp. g_1 and g_2) are the restrictions of a bent function f (resp. g) to two hyperplanes, complementary of each other.

4. The *semidirect sum* [336] $f(x) \oplus g(y + H(x))$, where f and g are bent and H is such that $f \oplus u \cdot H$ is bent for every u.

5. The *bent concatenation construction* generalizes the direct sum, the Rothaus construction, the indirect sum, and the semidirect sum (but as with the semidirect sum, it needs to find initial bent functions satisfying additional conditions):

Theorem 15 *[215] Let n and m be two even positive integers. Let f be a Boolean function on $\mathbb{F}_2^{n+m} = \mathbb{F}_2^n \times \mathbb{F}_2^m$ such that, for any element y of $\mathbb{F}_2^m$, the function $f_y : x \in \mathbb{F}_2^n \mapsto f(x, y)$ is bent. Then f is bent if and only if, for any element s of $\mathbb{F}_2^n$, the function*

$$\varphi_s : y \mapsto \widetilde{f_y}(s)$$

is bent on $\mathbb{F}_2^m$. If this condition is satisfied, then the dual of f is the function $\widetilde{f}(s,t) = \widetilde{\varphi_s}(t)$ (taking as inner product in $\mathbb{F}_2^n \times \mathbb{F}_2^m : (x, y) \cdot (s, t) = x \cdot s \oplus y \cdot t$).

This very general result is easy to prove, using that, for every $s \in \mathbb{F}_2^n$,

$$\sum_{x \in \mathbb{F}_2^n} (-1)^{f(x,y) \oplus x \cdot s} = 2^{\frac{n}{2}} (-1)^{\widetilde{f_y}(s)} = 2^{\frac{n}{2}} (-1)^{\varphi_s(y)},$$

and thus that $W_f(s,t) = 2^{\frac{n}{2}} \sum_{y \in \mathbb{F}_2^m} (-1)^{\varphi_s(y) \oplus y \cdot t}$.

A very particular case of this construction had been previously considered by Adams and Tavares [7] under the name of bent-based functions, and later studied by J. Seberry and X.-M. Zhang in [1025]. The direct sum and Rothaus' constructions are particular cases of Theorem 15 (the latter covers the case $m = 2$). Several classes of bent functions have been deduced in [215], and later in [620]. It is also deduced in [245] (where more details on secondary constructions can be found) that if f, g are n-variable Boolean functions, g being bent, and if ϕ is a mapping from $\mathbb{F}_2^n$ to itself, then the $2n$-variable function $f(x) \oplus \widetilde{g}(y) \oplus \phi(x) \cdot y$ is bent if and only if $f(x) \oplus g(\phi(x) + b)$ is bent for every b. Three cases of application are exhibited; all three use two bent functions g and h, and we have

- If g and h differ by a quadratic function, then the $2n$-variable function $(g \oplus h)(x) \oplus \widetilde{g}(y) \oplus x \cdot y$ is bent,
- If g is quadratic and ϕ is an affine permutation, then the $2n$-variable function $g(\phi(x)) \oplus h(x) \oplus \widetilde{g}(y) \oplus \phi(x) \cdot y$ is bent.
- If $Im(\phi) = \{\phi(x); \; x \in \mathbb{F}_2^n\}$ is either included in or disjoint from any translate of $supp(g)$, then the $2n$-variable function $f(x) \oplus \widetilde{g}(y) \oplus \phi(x) \cdot y$ is bent.

The *indirect sum* is a particular case of the bent concatenation construction of Theorem 15: let h be defined as in Proposition 83, then for every y, the function $h_y(x)$ of Theorem 15 (with h instead of f) equals $f_1(x)$ plus the constant $g_1(y)$ if $g_1(y) = g_2(y)$ and $f_2(x)$ plus the constant $g_1(y)$ if $g_1(y) \neq g_2(y)$; thus it is bent and function $\varphi_s(y)$ equals $\widetilde{f_1}(s) \oplus g_1(y)$ if $g_1(y) = g_2(y)$ and $\widetilde{f_2}(s) \oplus g_1(y)$ if $g_1(y) \neq g_2(y)$, that is, equals $\widetilde{f_1}(s) \oplus g_1(y) \oplus (\widetilde{f_1} \oplus \widetilde{f_2})(s)(g_1 \oplus g_2)(y)$; hence, $\varphi_s(y)$ is bent too since it equals $\widetilde{f_1}(s) \oplus g_1(y)$ or $\widetilde{f_1}(s) \oplus g_2(y)$ according to whether $(\widetilde{f_1} \oplus \widetilde{f_2})(s)$ vanishes or not, and according to Theorem 15, h is then bent and its dual equals

$$\widetilde{h}(s,t) = \widetilde{f_1}(s) \oplus \widetilde{g_1}(t) \oplus (\widetilde{f_1} \oplus \widetilde{f_2})(s)(\widetilde{g_1} \oplus \widetilde{g_2})(t).$$

The semidirect sum is also a direct consequence thanks to $\widetilde{g \circ t_a} = \widetilde{g} \oplus \ell_a, t_a(y) = y + a, \ell_a(s) = a \cdot s$.

Another simple application of Theorem 15, called *extension of Maiorana–McFarland type*, is given in [270]: let m be even and π be a permutation of $\mathbb{F}_2^{m/2}$ and g an $m/2$-variable Boolean function, and let $f_{\pi,g}(z, y) = z \cdot \pi(y) \oplus g(y)$ be the related Maiorana–McFarland bent function; let $(h_y)_{y \in \mathbb{F}_2^{m/2}}$ be a collection of bent functions on $\mathbb{F}_2^n$ for some even integer n, then the function

$$(x, y, z) \in \mathbb{F}_2^n \times \mathbb{F}_2^{m/2} \times \mathbb{F}_2^{m/2} \to h_y(x) \oplus f_{\pi,g}(z, y) \qquad (6.29)$$

is bent. Indeed, Theorem 15 with (z, y) in the place of y applies with $x \mapsto h_y(x) \oplus f_{\pi,g}(z, y)$ in the place of f_y, and with $\varphi_s(z, y) = \widetilde{h_y}(s) \oplus f_{\pi,g}(z, y)$, which is a bent Maiorana–McFarland function.

This generalizes a construction due to Davis and Jedwab [415] that was slightly posterior to [215] but anterior to [270]: let n and m be two positive even integers; let $h_y(x)$ be a collection of bent functions on $\mathbb{F}_2^n$ for $y \in \mathbb{F}_2^{m/2}$, then the function $(x, y, z) \in \mathbb{F}_2^n \times \mathbb{F}_2^{m/2} \times \mathbb{F}_2^{m/2} \mapsto h_y(x) \oplus y \cdot z$ is bent.

Note that in (6.29), no term involves both x and z, so the structure of the bent function is peculiar (to a lesser extent than for a direct sum, though); instead can be tried $(x, y) \in \mathbb{F}_2^n \times \mathbb{F}_2^n \to h_y(x) \oplus f_{\pi,g}(x, y)$. The restriction of such function when fixing y is bent since that of $f_{\pi,g}(x, y)$ is affine. Then for the global function to be bent, it is necessary and sufficient that $\varphi_s(y) = \widetilde{h_y}(s + \pi(y)) \oplus g(y)$ be bent for all s. Note that the semidirect sum is a particular case of its dual.

Of course, if $f(x, y)$ is an $(n + s)$-variable function such that, for any $y \in \mathbb{F}_2^s$, the n-variable function $f_y : x \mapsto f(x, y)$ is s-plateaued (see the definition at page 258) and the supports of the Walsh transforms of these functions f_y are pairwise disjoint, then these supports constitute a partition of $\mathbb{F}_2^n$ and f is bent.

6. A permutation-based construction due to X.-D. Hou and P. Langevin is built on a very simple observation that leads to potentially new bent functions:

Proposition 84 *[627] Let f be a Boolean function on $\mathbb{F}_2^n$, n even. Let σ be a permutation of $\mathbb{F}_2^n$. We denote its coordinate functions by $\sigma_1, \ldots, \sigma_n$ and we assume that, for every $a \in \mathbb{F}_2^n$, we have*

$$d_H\left(f,\bigoplus_{i=1}^{n}a_i\,\sigma_i\right)=2^{n-1}\pm 2^{\frac{n}{2}-1}.$$

Then $f\circ\sigma^{-1}$ is bent.

Indeed, the Hamming distance between $f\circ\sigma^{-1}$ and the linear function $\ell_a(x)=a\cdot x$ equals $d_H(f,\bigoplus_{i=1}^{n}a_i\,\sigma_i)$.

Hou and Langevin proposed two frameworks for applying Proposition 84:

- If h is an affine function on $\mathbb{F}_2^n$ and f_1, f_2, and g are Boolean functions on $\mathbb{F}_2^n$ such that the following function is bent

$$f(x_1,x_2,x)=x_1\,x_2\,h(x)\oplus x_1\,f_1(x)\oplus x_2\,f_2(x)\oplus g(x);\ x\in\mathbb{F}_2^n,\ x_1,x_2\in\mathbb{F}_2,$$

then the function

$$f(x_1,x_2,x)\oplus(h(x)\oplus 1)\,f_1(x)f_2(x)\oplus f_1(x)\oplus(x_1\oplus h(x)\oplus 1)\,f_2(x)\oplus x_2\,h(x)$$

is bent; in [932] are given cases of application by taking f as the indirect sum of bent functions and using semi-bent 4-decomposition of bent functions.
- If f is a bent function on $\mathbb{F}_2^n$ whose algebraic degree is at most 3, and if σ is a permutation of $\mathbb{F}_2^n$ such that, for every $i=1,\dots,n$, there exists a subset U_i of $\mathbb{F}_2^n$ and an affine function h_i such that

$$\sigma_i(x)=\bigoplus_{u\in U_i}(f(x)\oplus f(x+u))\oplus h_i(x),$$

then $f\circ\sigma^{-1}$ is bent.

X.-D. Hou in [620] deduced that if $f(x,y)$ $(x,y\in\mathbb{F}_2^{n/2})$ is a Maiorana–McFarland function of the particular form $x\cdot y\oplus g(y)$ and if $\sigma_1,\dots,\sigma_n$ are all of the form $\bigoplus_{1\le i<j\le\frac{n}{2}}a_{i,j}x_i\,y_j\oplus b\cdot x\oplus c\cdot y\oplus h(y)$, then $f\circ\sigma^{-1}$ is bent. He gave several examples of application of this result.

7. A construction without extension of the number of variables[24] has been introduced in [227] and is based on the following result:

Proposition 85 *Let f_1, f_2 and f_3 be three Boolean functions on $\mathbb{F}_2^n$. Denote by s_1 the Boolean function equal to $f_1\oplus f_2\oplus f_3$ and by s_2 the Boolean function equal to $f_1f_2\oplus f_1f_3\oplus f_2f_3$. Then we have $f_1+f_2+f_3=s_1+2s_2$. This implies the following equality between the Fourier–Hadamard transforms $\widehat{f_1}+\widehat{f_2}+\widehat{f_3}=\widehat{s_1}+2\widehat{s_2}$ and the similar equality between the Walsh transforms*

$$W_{f_1}+W_{f_2}+W_{f_3}=W_{s_1}+2\,W_{s_2}.\tag{6.30}$$

Proof The fact that $f_1+f_2+f_3=s_1+2s_2$ (the sums being computed in $\mathbb{Z}$ and not modulo 2) can be checked easily. The $\mathbb{R}$-linearity of the Fourier–Hadamard transform implies then

---

[24] Note that Hou–Langevin's permutation-based construction above does not increase either the number of variables, contrary to most other secondary constructions.

$\widehat{f_1} + \widehat{f_2} + \widehat{f_3} = \widehat{s_1} + 2\widehat{s_2}$. The equality $f_1 + f_2 + f_3 = s_1 + 2s_2$ also directly implies $f_{1_\chi} + f_{2_\chi} + f_{3_\chi} = s_{1_\chi} + 2s_{2_\chi}$, thanks to the equality $f_\chi = 1 - 2f$ valid for every Boolean function, which implies Relation (6.30). □

Remark. It is observed in [8, lemma 1] that, given four Boolean functions f_1, f_2, f_3, f_4, the pseudo-Boolean function $1/2(W_{f_1} + W_{f_2} + W_{f_3} + W_{f_4})$ is the Walsh transform of a Boolean function, say g, if and only if $f_1 \oplus f_2 \oplus f_3 \oplus f_4$ equals constant function 1 (this is easily deduced from the fact that, by the $\mathbb{R}$-linearity of the Fourier–Hadamard transform on pseudo-Boolean functions and its bijectivity, we have equivalently $(-1)^g = \frac{1}{2}((-1)^{f_1} + (-1)^{f_2} + (-1)^{f_3} + (-1)^{f_4})$. This means that $f_4 = s_1 \oplus 1$ and then according to (6.30), we have $g = f_1 f_2 \oplus f_1 f_3 \oplus f_2 f_3$, as also observed in [8]. □

Proposition 85 leads then to a double construction of bent functions:

Corollary 15 *[227] Let f_1, f_2, and f_3 be three n-variable bent functions, n even. Let $s_1 = f_1 \oplus f_2 \oplus f_3$ and $s_2 = f_1 f_2 \oplus f_1 f_3 \oplus f_2 f_3$. Then:*

– *If s_1 is bent and if $\tilde{s}_1 = \tilde{f}_1 \oplus \tilde{f}_2 \oplus \tilde{f}_3$, then s_2 is bent, and $\tilde{s}_2 = \tilde{f}_1 \tilde{f}_2 \oplus \tilde{f}_1 \tilde{f}_3 \oplus \tilde{f}_2 \tilde{f}_3$.*
– *If $W_{s_2}(a)$ is divisible by $2^{\frac{n}{2}}$ for every a (e.g., if s_2 is bent, or quadratic, or more generally if it is plateaued; see the definition in Section 6.2), then s_1 is bent.*

Proof

– If s_1 is bent and if $\tilde{s}_1 = \tilde{f}_1 \oplus \tilde{f}_2 \oplus \tilde{f}_3$, then, for every a, Relation (6.30) implies

$$W_{s_2}(a) = \left[(-1)^{\tilde{f}_1(a)} + (-1)^{\tilde{f}_2(a)} + (-1)^{\tilde{f}_3(a)} - (-1)^{\tilde{f}_1(a) \oplus \tilde{f}_2(a) \oplus \tilde{f}_3(a)}\right] 2^{\frac{n-2}{2}}$$

$$= (-1)^{\tilde{f}_1(a)\tilde{f}_2(a) \oplus \tilde{f}_1(a)\tilde{f}_3(a) \oplus \tilde{f}_2(a)\tilde{f}_3(a)} 2^{\frac{n}{2}}.$$

Indeed, as we already saw above with the relation $f_{1_\chi} + f_{2_\chi} + f_{3_\chi} = s_{1_\chi} + 2s_{2_\chi}$, for every bits ϵ, η, and τ, we have $(-1)^\epsilon + (-1)^\eta + (-1)^\tau - (-1)^{\epsilon \oplus \eta \oplus \tau} = 2(-1)^{\epsilon \eta \oplus \epsilon \tau \oplus \eta \tau}$.
– If $W_{s_2}(a)$ is divisible by $2^{\frac{n}{2}}$ for every a, then the number $W_{s_1}(a)$, which is equal to $\left[(-1)^{\tilde{f}_1(a)} + (-1)^{\tilde{f}_2(a)} + (-1)^{\tilde{f}_3(a)}\right] 2^{\frac{n}{2}} - 2 W_{s_2}(a)$, according to Relation (6.30), is congruent with $2^{\frac{n}{2}}$ modulo $2^{\frac{n}{2}+1}$ for every a. This is sufficient to imply that s_1 is bent, according to Lemma 5, page 190. □

Corollaries are deduced in [227] that revisit results from [327] (this latter reference also includes constructions of plateaued functions).

This construction has been used in [860, 864] (where it is observed that, conversely, if f_1, f_2, f_3, s_1, and s_2 are bent, then $\tilde{s}_1 = \tilde{f}_1 \oplus \tilde{f}_2 \oplus \tilde{f}_3$) and is called Carlet's secondary construction in [386, 873]. It is used in [711, 873] with linear structures. In the continuation of [863], it is shown in [386] that using Corollary 15, three involutions whose sum is an involution give rise through the Maiorana–McFarland construction to bent functions in bivariate representation.

The construction of Corollary 15 was extended to more than three functions:

Proposition 86 *[227] Let $f_1, \ldots, f_m$ be Boolean functions on $\mathbb{F}_2^n$. For every positive integer l, let s_l be the Boolean function defined by*

$$s_l = \bigoplus_{1 \leq i_1 < \ldots < i_l \leq m} \prod_{j=1}^{l} f_{i_j} \quad \text{if } l \leq m \text{ and } s_l = 0 \text{ otherwise.}$$

Then we have $f_1 + \ldots + f_m = \sum_{i \geq 0} 2^i \, s_{2^i}$ (sums in $\mathbb{Z}$). This implies $\widehat{f_1} + \cdots + \widehat{f_m} = \sum_{i \geq 0} 2^i \, \widehat{s_{2^i}}$. Moreover, if m is primitive, say $m = 2^r - 1$, then

$$W_{f_1} + \cdots + W_{f_m} = \sum_{i=0}^{r-1} 2^i \, W_{s_{2^i}}. \tag{6.31}$$

Proof Let $x \in \mathbb{F}_2^n$ and $j_x = \sum_{k=1}^{m} f_k(x)$. According to Lucas' theorem (see page 487), the binary expansion of j_x is $\sum_{i \geq 0} \left[2^i \left(\binom{j_x}{2^i} [\text{mod } 2] \right) \right]$. It is a simple matter to check that $\binom{j_x}{2^i} [\text{mod } 2] = s_{2^i}(x)$. Thus, $f_1 + \ldots + f_m = \sum_{i \geq 0} 2^i \, s_{2^i}$. The linearity of the Walsh transform with respect to the addition in $\mathbb{R}$ implies then directly $\widehat{f_1} + \cdots + \widehat{f_m} = \sum_{i \geq 0} 2^i \, \widehat{s_{2^i}}$.

If $m = 2^r - 1$ (recall that in coding theory, such number is called *primitive*), then we have $m = \sum_{i=0}^{r-1} 2^i$. Thus, we deduce $(-1)^{f_1} + \ldots + (-1)^{f_m} = \sum_{i=0}^{r-1} 2^i (-1)^{s_{2^i}}$ from $f_1 + \ldots + f_m = \sum_{i=0}^{r-1} 2^i \, s_{2^i}$. The linearity of the Walsh transform implies then Relation (6.31). $\qquad\square$

Corollary 16 *[227] Let n be any positive even integer and $f_1, \ldots, f_m$ ($m \leq 7$) be bent functions on $\mathbb{F}_2^n$.*

- *Assume that s_1 is bent, and that, for every $a \in \mathbb{F}_2^n$, the number $W_{s_4}(a)$ is divisible by $2^{n/2}$. Then:*

  - *If $m = 5$ and $\widetilde{s_1} = \widetilde{f_1} \oplus \ldots \oplus \widetilde{f_5} \oplus 1$, then s_2 is bent.*
  - *If $m = 7$ and $\widetilde{s_1} = \widetilde{f_1} \oplus \ldots \oplus \widetilde{f_7}$, then s_2 is bent.*

- *Assume that $m \in \{5, 7\}$ and, for every $a \in \mathbb{F}_2^n$, the number $W_{s_4}(a)$ is divisible by $2^{n/2-1}$ and the number $W_{s_2}(a)$ is divisible by $2^{n/2}$, then s_1 is bent.*

Proof We have for $i = 1, \ldots, m$ and for every vector $a \neq 0$: $W_{f_i}(a) = -2\widehat{f_i}(a) = (-1)^{\widetilde{f_i}(a)} 2^{n/2}$ and $\widehat{f_1}(a) + \cdots + \widehat{f_m}(a) = \sum_{i \geq 0} 2^i \, \widehat{s_{2^i}}(a)$.

- If s_1 is bent and, for every $a \in \mathbb{F}_2^n$, the number $W_{s_4}(a)$ is divisible by $2^{n/2}$, then $W_{s_2}(a)$ is congruent with $\left[(-1)^{\widetilde{f_1}(a)} + \cdots + (-1)^{\widetilde{f_m}(a)} - (-1)^{\widetilde{s_1}(a)} \right] 2^{n/2-1}$ modulo $2^{n/2+1}$, for every $a \neq 0_n$.

  If $m = 5$ and $\widetilde{s_1} = \widetilde{f_1} \oplus \ldots \oplus \widetilde{f_5} \oplus 1$ then, denoting by k the Hamming weight of the word $(\widetilde{f_1}(a), \ldots, \widetilde{f_5}(a))$, the number $W_{s_2}(a)$ is congruent with $[5 - 2k + (-1)^k] 2^{n/2-1}$ modulo $2^{n/2+1}$.

  If $m = 7$ and $\widetilde{s_1} = \widetilde{f_1} \oplus \ldots \oplus \widetilde{f_7}$, then, denoting by k the Hamming weight of the word $(\widetilde{f_1}(a), \ldots, \widetilde{f_7}(a))$, the number $W_{s_2}(a)$ is congruent with $[7 - 2k - (-1)^k] 2^{n/2-1}$

modulo $2^{n/2+1}$. So, in both cases, we have $W_{s_2}(a) \equiv 2^{n/2}$ [mod $2^{n/2+1}$], and s_2 is bent, according to Lemma 5, page 190.

- If, for every $a \in \mathbb{F}_2^n$, the number $W_{s_4}(a)$ is divisible by $2^{n/2-1}$ and the number $W_{s_2}(a)$ is divisible by $2^{n/2}$, then, for every $a \neq 0_n$, the number $W_{s_1}(a)$ is congruent with $\left[(-1)^{\widetilde{f_1}(a)} + \cdots + (-1)^{\widetilde{f_m}(a)}\right] 2^{n/2} \mod 2^{n/2+1}$. Since $m \in \{5,7\}$, it is then congruent with $2^{n/2} \mod 2^{n/2+1}$ and s_1 is bent, according to Lemma 5 again. □

8. A construction related to the notion of normal extension of bent function can be found in Proposition 93, page 253.

9. A construction related to bent rectangles. In [8, 10] are represented n-variable Boolean functions f by matrices called *rectangles* (among which squares, when n is even). The rows of such matrices are the Walsh transforms of the restrictions of f obtained by fixing m coordinates at fixed positions (say, at the first m positions), where $1 \leq m \leq n - 1$: denoting by f_u the restriction of f obtained by fixing $x_i = u_i$ for $i = 1, \ldots, m$, the term at the row indexed by $u \in \mathbb{F}_2^m$ and column indexed by $v \in \mathbb{F}^{n-m}$ equals[25] $W_{f_u}(v) = \sum_{y \in \mathbb{F}_2^{n-m}} (-1)^{f(u,y) \oplus v \cdot y}$ (i.e. the row is the Walsh transform vector of f_u). It is proved in [10] that f is bent if and only if the columns, when multiplied by $2^{m-\frac{n}{2}}$, are also the Walsh transforms of Boolean functions. This is, in a way, a generalization of Theorem 15, page 234, since m does not need to be even and the restrictions do not need to be bent. The condition is necessary since, for every $a \in \mathbb{F}_2^m$ and $v \in \mathbb{F}_2^{n-m}$, we have $\sum_{u \in \mathbb{F}_2^m} W_{f_u}(v)(-1)^{u \cdot a} = \sum_{u \in \mathbb{F}_2^m, y \in \mathbb{F}_2^{n-m}} (-1)^{f(u,y) \oplus v \cdot y \oplus u \cdot a} = W_f(a,v) = 2^{\frac{n}{2}}(-1)^{\widetilde{f}(a,v)}$, and denoting by $\widetilde{f}_v$ the restriction of $\widetilde{f}$ obtained by fixing its $n - m$ last input coordinates to the corresponding values of v, and by applying the inverse Walsh transform formula to $\widetilde{f}_v$, we see that the column indexed by v and multiplied by $2^{m-\frac{n}{2}}$ equals the Walsh transform of $\widetilde{f}_v$. It is also easily seen that the condition is sufficient. Constructions of bent squares are deduced in [10] by using so-called biaffine transformations and partitions of $\mathbb{F}_2^n$ into affine planes of equal dimension (but it is not checked whether such constructions can provide new bent functions nor whether the constructions themselves fall within known ones or not).

10. A general construction in the framework of the so-called $\mathbb{Z}$-*bent functions*. Most constructions above build bent functions from bent functions. The idea of $\mathbb{Z}$-bent functions is to extend the corpus in order to embed bent functions into a recursive context. This has been initiated by Dobbertin in 2005, and G. Leander has presented the results and given guidelines for further research in a paper posthumously coauthored by Hans Dobbertin [477] (see also [476]).

$\mathbb{Z}$-bent functions are integer-valued functions φ on $\mathbb{F}_2^n$ whose normalized Fourier transform $\widehat{\varphi}_{norm} = 2^{-n/2}\widehat{\varphi}$, is also integer valued. Bent Boolean functions (or more precisely their sign functions) will be among $\mathbb{Z}$-bent functions those which are ± 1 valued.

---

[25] There seems to be a slight confusion between rows and columns in the description given at the bottom of page 5 in [10].

The following nested subsets of $\mathbb{Z}$ are defined: $W_0 = \{\pm 1\}$ and for $r \neq 0$, $W_r = \{w \in \mathbb{Z} \mid -2^{r-1} \leq w \leq 2^{r-1}\}$. They satisfy $W_r \pm W_r = W_{r+1}$ for $r > 0$ and lead to a hierarchy on $\mathbb{Z}$-bent functions:

Definition 55 *[477] A function $\varphi : \mathbb{F}_2^n \rightarrow W_r$ is called a $\mathbb{Z}$-bent function of size $\frac{n}{2}$ and level r if $\widehat{\varphi}_{norm}$ is also valued in W_r.*

In this hierarchy, the (sign functions of) usual bent functions are the zero level $\mathbb{Z}$-bent functions. Since the normalized Fourier transform is self-inverse, $\widehat{\varphi}_{norm}$ is then also a $\mathbb{Z}$-bent function of size $n/2$ and level r, which is called the dual of φ.

$\mathbb{Z}$-bent functions of level r on n variables can be used to construct all $\mathbb{Z}$-bent functions of level $r - 1$ on $(n + 2)$ variables. This is referred to as "gluing" technique. All bent functions in $(n + 2r)$ variables (*i.e.*, all $\mathbb{Z}$-bent functions of level 0 in $(n + 2r)$ variables) are eventually reached this way.

The construction of partial spread ($\mathcal{PS}$) bent functions has been generalized to partial spread $\mathbb{Z}$-bent functions of arbitrary level in [526]. This led to a new construction of bent Boolean functions. A bent function in eight variables outside the completed $\mathcal{M}$ and $\mathcal{PS}_{ap}$ classes was deduced; all bent functions in six variables can be obtained, up to equivalence, by this construction.

Secondary construction of bent functions from near-bent functions have been also proposed, for instance in [1122].

6.1.17 Decompositions of bent functions

The following theorem is a direct consequence of the second-order Poisson formula (2.57), page 62, applied to $f \oplus \ell$ where ℓ is linear, and to a linear hyperplane E of $\mathbb{F}_2^n$, and of the well-known (easy to prove) fact that, for every even integer n, the sum of the squares of two integers equals 2^n (resp. 2^{n+1}) if and only if one of these squares is null and the other one equals 2^n (resp. both squares equal 2^n):

Theorem 16 *[191] Let $n \geq 4$ be an even integer and let f be an n-variable Boolean function. Then the following properties are equivalent.*

1. *f is bent.*
2. *For every (or some) hyperplane E of $\mathbb{F}_2^n$, the restrictions of f to E and $\mathbb{F}_2^n \setminus E$ (viewed as Boolean functions on $\mathbb{F}_2^{n-1}$) are plateaued with amplitude $2^{\frac{n}{2}}$ (i.e., are near-bent), and their Walsh supports partition the whole space $\mathbb{F}_2^{n-1}$.*
3. *For every (or some) linear hyperplane E of $\mathbb{F}_2^n$, every derivative $D_e f$, $e \in E \setminus \{0_n\}$ is balanced.*

The fact that Property 3 is enough comes from Relation (2.56), page 62. Note that we have also (see [191]) that, if a function in an odd number of variables is such that, for some nonzero $a \in \mathbb{F}_2^n$, every derivative $D_u f$, $u \neq 0_n$, $u \in a^\perp$, is balanced, then its restriction to the linear hyperplane $a^\perp$ or to its complement is bent.

It is also proved in [191] that the Walsh transforms of the four restrictions of a bent function to an $(n - 2)$-dimensional vector subspace E of $\mathbb{F}_2^n$ and its cosets have the same sets of absolute values. It is a simple matter to see that, denoting by a and b two vectors such that $E^\perp$ is the linear space spanned by a and b, these four restrictions are bent if and only if $D_a D_b \widetilde{f}$ takes on constant value 1, and as observed in [193] that[26] $f \oplus 1_E$ is bent if and only if $D_a D_b \widetilde{f}$ takes on constant value 0 (see examples in [198, corollary 15]). More on decomposing bent functions can be found in [191, 193, 349].

6.1.18 Class $\mathcal{GPS}$ and a geometric characterization of bent Boolean functions

Class $\mathcal{PS}$ generalizes to a class introduced in [213] and called $\mathcal{GPS}$ (for generalized partial spreads), which led to a characterization of bent functions that we call geometric characterization. This characterization, given below in Theorem 17, can be proved rather simply by using Proposition 67, page 195, which is posterior to the introduction of $\mathcal{GPS}$ and to Theorem 17:

Theorem 17 *[290] Let f be a Boolean function on $\mathbb{F}_2^n$. Then f is bent if and only if there exist $n/2$-dimensional subspaces $E_1, \ldots, E_k$ of $\mathbb{F}_2^n$ (with no constraint on number k) and integers $m_1, \ldots, m_k$ (positive or negative) such that, for any element x of $\mathbb{F}_2^n$:*

$$f(x) \equiv \sum_{i=1}^{k} m_i 1_{E_i}(x) - 2^{\frac{n}{2}-1} \delta_0(x) \quad \left[mod \ 2^{\frac{n}{2}} \right]. \tag{6.32}$$

If we have $f(x) = \sum_{i=1}^{k} m_i 1_{E_i}(x) - 2^{\frac{n}{2}-1} \delta_0(x)$, then the dual of f equals $\widetilde{f}(x) = \sum_{i=1}^{k} m_i 1_{E_i^\perp}(x) - 2^{\frac{n}{2}-1} \delta_0(x)$.

Proof (sketch of): Relation (6.32) is a sufficient condition for f being bent, according to Lemma 5 and to Relation (2.38), page 58. This same Relation (2.38) also implies the last sentence of Theorem 17. Conversely, if f is bent, then Proposition 67 allows to deduce Relation (6.32), by expressing all the monomials x^I by means of the indicators of subspaces of dimension at least $n - |I|$ (indeed, the NNF of the indicator of the subspace $\{x \in \mathbb{F}_2^n; x_i = 0, \forall i \in I\}$ being equal to $\prod_{i \in I}(1 - x_i) = \sum_{J \subseteq I}(-1)^{|J|} x^J$, the monomial x^I can be expressed by means of this indicator and of the monomials x^J, where J is strictly included in I) and by using Lemma 8 below. $\square$

Lemma 8 *Let F be any d-dimensional subspace of $\mathbb{F}_2^n$. There exist $n/2$-dimensional subspaces $E_1, \ldots, E_k$ of $\mathbb{F}_2^n$ and integers $m, m_1, \ldots, m_k$ such that, for any element x of $\mathbb{F}_2^n$:*

$$2^{\frac{n}{2}-d} 1_F(x) \equiv m + \sum_{i=1}^{k} m_i 1_{E_i}(x) \left[mod \ 2^{\frac{n}{2}} \right] \ if \ d < \frac{n}{2}, \ and$$

$$1_F(x) \equiv \sum_{i=1}^{k} m_i 1_{E_i}(x) \left[mod \ 2^{\frac{n}{2}} \right] \ if \ d > \frac{n}{2}.$$

This lemma completes the proof of Theorem 17 since $d \geq n - |I|$ implies $|I| - n/2 \geq n/2 - d$.

---

[26] We have seen in the second remark of page 203 that this is a direct consequence of Theorem 14.

Definition 56 *The class of those functions f that satisfy the relation obtained from (6.32) by withdrawing "[mod $2^{\frac{n}{2}}$]" is called* generalized partial spread *class and denoted by $\mathcal{GPS}$.*

Class $\mathcal{GPS}$ includes $\mathcal{PS}$, see [213]. The dual $\widetilde{f}$ of such function f of $\mathcal{GPS}$ equaling $\widetilde{f}(x) = \sum_{i=1}^{k} m_i 1_{E_i^{\perp}}(x) - 2^{\frac{n}{2}-1}\delta_0(x)$, it belongs to $\mathcal{GPS}$ too.

There is no uniqueness of the representation of a given bent function in the form (6.32). There exists another characterization, shown in [291], in the form $f(x) = \sum_{i=1}^{k} m_i 1_{E_i}(x) \pm 2^{\frac{n}{2}-1}\delta_0(x)$, where $E_1, \ldots, E_k$ are vector subspaces of $\mathbb{F}_2^n$ of dimensions $n/2$ or $n/2 + 1$ and where $m_1, \ldots, m_k$ are integers (positive or negative). There is not a unique way, either, to choose these spaces E_i. But it is possible to define some subclass of $n/2$-dimensional and $(n/2 + 1)$-dimensional spaces such that there is uniqueness, if the spaces E_i are chosen in this subclass.

P. Guillot has proved subsequently in [579] that, *up to the composition by a translation $x \mapsto x + a$, every bent function belongs to $\mathcal{GPS}$.* The proof is a little too technical for being included here.

6.1.19 On the number of bent Boolean functions

Nonexistence of efficient lower bounds

The original Maiorana–McFarland class is one of the the the widest classes. The number of bent functions of the form (6.9), page 209, equals $(2^{\frac{n}{2}})! \times 2^{2^{\frac{n}{2}}}$, which is asymptotically equivalent to $\left(\frac{2^{\frac{n}{2}+1}}{e}\right)^{2^{\frac{n}{2}}} \sqrt{2^{\frac{n}{2}+1}\pi}$ (according to Stirling's formula) while the other important straightforward construction of bent functions, $\mathcal{PS}_{ap}$, leads only to $\binom{2^{\frac{n}{2}}}{2^{\frac{n}{2}-1}} \approx \frac{2^{2^{\frac{n}{2}}+\frac{1}{2}}}{\sqrt{\pi 2^{\frac{n}{2}}}}$ functions.[27]

However, the number of bent Maiorana–McFarland functions seems negligible with respect to the total number of bent functions. The size of the completed Maiorana–McFarland's class is unknown; it is at most equal to the number of Maiorana–McFarland's functions times the number of affine automorphisms, which equals $2^n(2^n - 1)(2^n - 2) \ldots (2^n - 2^{n-1})$. It seems also negligible with respect to the total number of bent functions. In fact, the lower bounds that can be deduced from all known constructions of bent functions seem very far from the actual number. For instance, in eight variables, there are approximately 2^{106} different bent functions,[28] see below, and about 2^{77} correspond to the known constructions. The problem of determining an efficient lower bound on the number of n-variable bent functions is then open.

There exists a related open question by N. Tokareva in [1087] (that she calls the bent sum decomposition problem) whether all Boolean functions of *algebraic degree* at most $n/2$ are equal to the sums of two n-variable bent functions (which is equivalent to asking whether the set of such sums is stable under addition [977]). The reply to this question seems probably negative, but there is no proof that it is, and it is shown in [977] that the reply is positive when restricting ourselves to a number of subclasses (Boolean functions in at most six variables,

---

[27] Its extension with André's spreads, see page 216, has nevertheless more elements.
[28] Among which probably many could lead to new infinite classes; this shows how limited is our knowledge.

quadratic Boolean functions, Maiorana–McFarland bent functions, partial spread functions). And the usual parameters and properties of Boolean functions (ANF, NNF and numerical degree, generalized degree, divisibility of the Fourier transform or of the coefficients of the NNF, other properties of the Fourier or Walsh transform values) do not seem to allow discriminating sums of two bent functions from other Boolean functions of degrees at most $n/2$. If the reply to Tokareva's question was finally positive, this would give a straightforward lower bound on the number of bent functions that would be much better than what is known.

Upper bounds

Rothaus' inequality recalled in Section 6.1.8 (Theorem 13, page 200) states that any bent function has algebraic degree at most $n/2$. Thus, the number of bent functions is at most

$$2^{1+n+\cdots+\binom{n}{n/2}} = 2^{2^{n-1}+\frac{1}{2}\binom{n}{n/2}}.$$

We shall call this upper bound the *naive bound*. For $n = 6$, the number of bent functions is known and is approximately equal to $2^{32.3}$ (see [968]), which is much less than the naive bound gives: 2^{42}. For $n = 8$, the number is also known: it has been first shown in [744] that it is inferior to $2^{129.2}$; it has been later calculated by Langevin et al. [743] and equals approximately $2^{106.3}$ (the naive bound gives 2^{163}). Hence picking at random an 8-variable Boolean function of algebraic degree bounded above by 4 does not allow obtaining bent functions (but more clever methods exist; see [278, 413]). An upper bound improving upon the naive bound has been found in [301]. It is exponentially better than the naive bound since it divides it by approximately $2^{2^{\frac{n}{2}}-\frac{n}{2}-1}$. But it seems to be still far from the exact number of bent functions: for $n = 6$, it gives roughly 2^{38} (to be compared with $2^{32.3}$), and for $n = 8$ it gives roughly 2^{152} (to be compared with $2^{106.3}$). But the bound of [301] could not be improved since it was obtained.

Number of bent components of a vectorial function

It is shown in [962] that the number of bent components of any (n, n)-function is at most $2^n - 2^{\frac{n}{2}}$ and that this upper bound is achieved with equality by the Niho power function $x^{2^{\frac{n}{2}}+1}$, and the function $x^{2^i}(x + x^{2^{\frac{n}{2}}})$ for all $i = 0, \ldots, n - 1$ (these latter functions are pairwise EA/CCZ inequivalent for $i \neq 0, n/2$). In [877], it is shown that the set of those (n, n)-functions having maximum number of bent components is preserved by CCZ equivalence and does not contain any APN plateaued function.

6.1.20 Hyper-bent, homogeneous, symmetric/rotation symmetric bent Boolean functions

Hyper-bent Boolean functions

Hyper-bent functions were initially proposed by Golomb and Gong [554] in relation with the security of symmetric cryptosystems, for the reason that when $\gcd(i, 2^n - 1) = 1$, both functions $tr_n(ax)$ and $tr(ax^i)$ provide m-sequences. But no explicit attack was proposed. In [202], Canteaut and Rotella showed that, in the context of filtered LFSR, a relevant criterion is the minimum distance between the function and the Boolean functions of the form $tr_n(ax^i) \oplus \epsilon$, where $\gcd(i, 2^n - 1) = 1$, $a \in \mathbb{F}_{2^n}$ and $\epsilon \in \mathbb{F}_2$: they showed that if $f(x) \oplus tr_n(ax^i)$ is biased, then a *fast correlation attack* can be performed to recover the initial state. Even the case when i is not coprime with $2^n - 1$ leads to an attack, and this provides a new criterion to evaluate the security of filtered LFSR. Nevertheless, these new considerations confirm the interest of the definition introduced by Golomb and Gong.

Definition 57 *Let n be any even positive integer. An n-variable Boolean function f on the field $\mathbb{F}_{2^n}$ is a* hyper-bent *function if, for every positive integer i coprime with $2^n - 1$, function $f(x^i)$ is bent (or equivalently, since the compositional inverse of a generic power permutation x^i is a generic power permutation, if for any such i, we have $\sum_{x \in \mathbb{F}_{2^n}} (-1)^{f(x) + tr_n(a x^i)} = \pm 2^{n/2}$ for every $a \in \mathbb{F}_{2^n}$).*

Remark. In [214], the author determined those Boolean functions on $\mathbb{F}_2^n$ such that, for a given even integer k ($2 \le k \le n - 2$), any of the Boolean functions on $\mathbb{F}_2^{n-k}$, obtained by keeping constant k coordinates among $x_1, \ldots, x_n$, is bent (*i.e.*, those functions that satisfy the propagation criterion of degree $n - k$ and order k). These are the four bent *symmetric Boolean functions* (see Section 10.1). They were called hyper-bent in [214], but we keep this term for the notion introduced by Golomb and Gong. □

Hyper-bent functions can be characterized in terms of the *extended Walsh transform* [554]:

$$W_f(a, i) = \sum_{x \in \mathbb{F}_{2^n}} (-1)^{f(x) + tr_n(ax^i)}, \forall a \in \mathbb{F}_{2^n}, \text{ with } \gcd(i, 2^n - 1) = 1,$$

as those functions whose extended Walsh transform takes only the values $\pm 2^{\frac{n}{2}}$.

The condition seems difficult to satisfy. However, A. Youssef and G. Gong, who introduced the term in [1143], showed that hyper-bent functions exist. Recall that class $\mathcal{PS}_{ap}^{\#}$, defined at page 215, is the set of those bent functions over $\mathbb{F}_{2^n}$ that can be obtained from those of $\mathcal{PS}_{ap}$ by composition by the transformations $x \in \mathbb{F}_{2^n} \mapsto \delta x$, $\delta \neq 0$, and by addition of a constant. We have:

Proposition 87 *[278] All the functions of class $\mathcal{PS}_{ap}^{\#}$ are hyper-bent.*

Let us give here a direct proof of this fact.

Proof We can restrict ourselves without loss of generality to the functions of class $\mathcal{PS}_{ap}$. Let ω be any element in $\mathbb{F}_{2^n} \setminus \mathbb{F}_{2^{n/2}}$. The pair $(1, \omega)$ is a basis of the $\mathbb{F}_{2^{n/2}}$-vector space $\mathbb{F}_{2^n}$. Hence, we have $\mathbb{F}_{2^n} = \mathbb{F}_{2^{n/2}} + \omega \mathbb{F}_{2^{n/2}}$, and the elements of class $\mathcal{PS}_{ap}$ are the functions $f(y' + \omega y) = g\left(\frac{y'}{y}\right)$, with $\frac{y'}{y} = 0$ if $y = 0$, where g is balanced on $\mathbb{F}_2^{n/2}$ and vanishes at 0. Note that every element y of $\mathbb{F}_{2^{n/2}}$ satisfies $y^{2^{n/2}} = y$ and therefore $tr_n(y) = y + y^2 + \cdots + y^{2^{n/2-1}} + y + y^2 + \cdots + y^{2^{n/2-1}} = 0$. Consider the inner product in $\mathbb{F}_{2^n}$ defined by $y \cdot y' = tr_n(y y')$; the subspace $\mathbb{F}_{2^{n/2}}$ is then its own orthogonal; hence, according to

Relation (2.38), page 58, any sum of the form $\sum_{y\in\mathbb{F}_{2^{n/2}}}(-1)^{tr_n(\lambda y)}$ is null if $\lambda\notin\mathbb{F}_{2^{n/2}}$ and equals $2^{n/2}$ if $\lambda\in\mathbb{F}_{2^{n/2}}$. For every $a\in\mathbb{F}_{2^n}$, we have

$$\sum_{x\in\mathbb{F}_{2^n}}(-1)^{f(x)+tr_n(a\,x^i)} = \sum_{y,y'\in\mathbb{F}_{2^{n/2}}}(-1)^{g\left(\frac{y'}{y}\right)+tr_n(a\,(y'+\omega y)^i)}.$$

Denoting $\frac{y'}{y}$ by z, we see that

$$\sum_{y\in\mathbb{F}^*_{2^{n/2}},y'\in\mathbb{F}_{2^{n/2}}}(-1)^{g\left(\frac{y'}{y}\right)+tr_n(a\,(y'+\omega y)^i)} = \sum_{z\in\mathbb{F}_{2^{n/2}},y\in\mathbb{F}^*_{2^{n/2}}}(-1)^{g(z)+tr_n(a\,y^i(z+\omega)^i)}.$$

The remaining sum $\sum_{y'\in\mathbb{F}_{2^{n/2}}}(-1)^{g(0)+tr_n(a\,y'^i)} = \sum_{y'\in\mathbb{F}_{2^{n/2}}}(-1)^{tr_n(a\,y')}$ equals $2^{n/2}$ if $a\in\mathbb{F}_{2^{n/2}}$ and is null otherwise.

Thus, $\sum_{x\in\mathbb{F}_{2^n}}(-1)^{f(x)+tr_n(a\,x^i)}$ equals

$$\sum_{z\in\mathbb{F}_{2^{n/2}}}\left((-1)^{g(z)}\sum_{y\in\mathbb{F}_{2^{n/2}}}(-1)^{tr_n(a(z+\omega)^i\,y)}\right) - \sum_{z\in\mathbb{F}_{2^{n/2}}}(-1)^{g(z)} + 2^{n/2}1_{\mathbb{F}_{2^{n/2}}}(a).$$

The sum $\sum_{z\in\mathbb{F}_{2^{n/2}}}(-1)^{g(z)}$ is null since g is balanced.

The sum $\sum_{z\in\mathbb{F}_{2^{n/2}}}\left((-1)^{g(z)}\sum_{y\in\mathbb{F}_{2^{n/2}}}(-1)^{tr_n(a(z+\omega)^i\,y)}\right)$ equals $\pm 2^{n/2}$ if $a\notin\mathbb{F}_{2^{n/2}}$, since we prove in the next lemma that there exists then exactly one $z\in\mathbb{F}_{2^{n/2}}$ such that $a(z+\omega)^i\in\mathbb{F}_{2^{n/2}}$; and this sum is null if $a\in\mathbb{F}_{2^{n/2}}$ (this can be checked, if $a=0$ thanks to the balancedness of g, and if $a\neq 0$ because y ranges over $\mathbb{F}_{2^{n/2}}$ and $a(z+\omega)^i\notin\mathbb{F}_{2^{n/2}}$). This completes the proof. $\square$

Lemma 9 *Let n be any positive integer. Let a and ω be two elements of the set $\mathbb{F}_{2^n}\setminus\mathbb{F}_{2^{n/2}}$, and let i be coprime with 2^n-1. There exists a unique element $z\in\mathbb{F}_2^{n/2}$ such that $a(z+\omega)^i\in\mathbb{F}_2^{n/2}$.*

Proof Let j be the inverse of i modulo 2^n-1. We have $a(z+\omega)^i\in\mathbb{F}_2^{n/2}$ if and only if $z\in\omega+a^{-j}\times\mathbb{F}_2^{n/2}$. The sets $\omega+a^{-j}\times\mathbb{F}_2^{n/2}$ and $\mathbb{F}_2^{n/2}$ are two flats whose directions $a^{-j}\times\mathbb{F}_2^{n/2}$ and $\mathbb{F}_2^{n/2}$ are subspaces whose sum is direct and equals $\mathbb{F}_{2^n}$. Hence, they have a unique vector in their intersection. $\square$

The duals of hyper-bent functions in $\mathcal{PS}^{\#}_{ap}$ are also in $\mathcal{PS}^{\#}_{ap}$ and then are hyper-bent.

Relationships between the notion of hyper-bent function and *cyclic codes* are studied in [278], and it is deduced that:

Proposition 88 *[278] Every hyper-bent function $f:\mathbb{F}_{2^n}\to\mathbb{F}_2$ can be represented as: $f(x)=\sum_{i=1}^r tr_n(a_i x^{t_i})+\epsilon$, where $a_i\in\mathbb{F}_{2^n},\epsilon\in\mathbb{F}_2$ and $w_2(t_i)=n/2$, where w_2 denotes the 2-weight (see page 45). Consequently, all hyper-bent functions have algebraic degree $n/2$.*

It is also shown in [278] that the elements in $\mathcal{PS}_{ap}^{\#}$ are the functions of Hamming weight $2^{n-1} \pm 2^{n/2-1}$, which can be written in the form $\sum_{i=1}^{r} tr_n(a_i x^{j_i})$, where $a_i \in \mathbb{F}_{2^n}$ and j_i is a multiple of $2^{n/2} - 1$. Hence, $\mathcal{PS}_{ap}^{\#}$ coincides with the set of bent functions whose trace form involves Dillon-like exponents $r(2^{n/2} - 1)$ only.

In [350], it is proved that, for every n even, $\lambda \in \mathbb{F}_{2^{n/2}}^{*}$ and $r \in]0; \frac{n}{2}[$ such that the cyclotomic cosets of 2 modulo $2^{n/2} + 1$ containing respectively $2^r - 1$ and $2^r + 1$ have size n and such that the function $tr_{\frac{n}{2}}\left(\lambda x^{2^r+1}\right)$ is balanced on $\mathbb{F}_{2^{n/2}}$, the function $tr_n\left(\lambda \left(x^{(2^r-1)(2^{n/2}-1)} + x^{(2^r+1)(2^{n/2}-1)}\right)\right)$ is bent (*i.e.*, hyper-bent) if and only if the function $tr_{\frac{n}{2}}\left(x^{-1} + \lambda x^{2^r+1}\right)$ is also balanced on $\mathbb{F}_{2^{n/2}}$.

Computer experiments have been reported in [278]. For $n = 4$, there exist hyper-bent functions that are not in $\mathcal{PS}_{ap}^{\#}$. Hence, *stricto sensu*, the set of hyper-bent functions contains strictly $\mathcal{PS}_{ap}^{\#}$, but no other example was found for $n > 4$. See more in [725].

Constructions of hyper-bent functions in univariate trace form and characterizations

The simplest examples of hyper-bent functions (belonging to $\mathcal{PS}_{ap}^{\#}$) in trace form are the (generalized) Dillon monomial functions $tr_n(ax^{r(2^{n/2}-1)})$, $x \in \mathbb{F}_{2^n}$, $a \in \mathbb{F}_{2^n}^{*}$, $\gcd(r, 2^{n/2} + 1) = 1$, where the restriction of $tr_n(ax)$ to U has Hamming weight $2^{n/2-1}$ (see page 215). The bentness (hyper-bentness) of such functions has been studied by several authors: in the case $r = 1$ by Dillon [441], next by Leander [750], and when r is coprime with $2^{n/2} + 1$, by Charpin and Gong [350]:

1. The bentness of $tr_n(ax^{r(2^{n/2}-1)})$ does not depend on the choice of r.

2. It is bent if and only if the Kloosterman sum $\sum_{x \in \mathbb{F}_{2^{n/2}}} (-1)^{tr_{n/2}(a^{2^{n/2}+1}x+\frac{1}{x})}$ equals 0.

3. When bent, $tr_n(ax^{r(2^{n/2}-1)})$ is self-dual.

The other known examples are

– *Binomial hyper-bent functions*, mainly due to S. Mesnager [851, 853] who made deep work on this subject; these functions are the sums of a Dillon monomial function and of a function expressed by means of the trace function over the subfield $\mathbb{F}_4$ of $\mathbb{F}_{2^n}$:

- $tr_n\left(ax^{r(2^{n/2}-1)}\right) + tr_2\left(bx^{\frac{2^n-1}{3}}\right)$, where $a \in \mathbb{F}_{2^n}^{*}$, $b \in \mathbb{F}_4^{*}$, $\gcd(r, 2^{n/2} + 1) = 1$. When $n/2$ is odd larger than 3, such function is hyperbent if and only if $\sum_{x \in \mathbb{F}_{2^{n/2}}} (-1)^{tr_{n/2}(a^{2^{n/2}+1}x+\frac{1}{x})} = 4$ (and this implies $tr_{n/2}(a^{\frac{2^{n/2}+1}{3}}) = 0$); the function belongs then to class $\mathcal{PS}_{ap}^{\#}$ (it belongs to $\mathcal{PS}_{ap}$ if $b \in \mathbb{F}_2$). The dual has the same form. When $n/2$ is even, the characterization of the bentness of this function is an open problem (but we know that $\sum_{x \in \mathbb{F}_{2^{n/2}}} (-1)^{tr_{n/2}(a^{2^{n/2}+1}x+\frac{1}{x})} = 4$ is necessary), and it is not known whether the function, when bent, belongs to the class $\mathcal{PS}^{-}$ or not.

- $tr_n\left(a\zeta^i x^{3(2^{n/2}-1)}\right) + tr_2\left(\beta^j x^{\frac{2^n-1}{3}}\right)$, where $a \in \mathbb{F}_{2^{n/2}}^{*}$, β is a primitive element of $\mathbb{F}_4$, ζ a generator of the cyclic group of $(2^m + 1)$th of unity, and with $n/2$ odd and not congruent with 3 mod 6, is a *hyper-bent function* if and only if we are in one of the following cases:

- $tr_{n/2}(a^{1/3}) = 0$ and $\sum_{x \in \mathbb{F}_{2^{n/2}}} (-1)^{tr_{n/2}(ax+\frac{1}{x})} = 4$,

- $tr_{n/2}(a^{1/3})=1, i \in \{1,2\}$, and $\sum_{x \in \mathbb{F}_{2^{n/2}}} (-1)^{tr_{n/2}(ax+\frac{1}{x})} + \sum_{x \in \mathbb{F}_{2^{n/2}}} (-1)^{tr_{n/2}(a(x+x^3))} = 4$.

When these functions are bent, they belong to class $\mathcal{PS}^\#$ (and to $\mathcal{PS}_{ap}$ if $b \in \mathbb{F}_2$) and the dual function has the same form.

Note that $n/2$ being odd, $3(2^{n/2} - 1)$ is not a Dillon exponent because 3 divides $2^{n/2} + 1$, contrary to when $n/2$ is even; hence this second class is not included in the first class.

In [871], the authors study the hyper-bentness of more general binomial functions and obtain a long list of (potentially new) hyper-bent functions.

- Polynomial hyper-bent functions:

- In [350] in the form $\sum_{r \in R} tr_n(\beta_r x^{r(2^{n/2}-1)})$, $\beta_r \in \mathbb{F}_{2^n}$, where R is a set of representatives of full size[29] cyclotomic cosets modulo $2^{n/2} + 1$, with a characterization of hyper-bentness by means of Dickson polynomials (see also [475, 782]). When r is coprime with $2^{n/2} + 1$, the functions are the sums of several Dillon monomial functions.

- In [546] in the form:

  - $\sum_{i=1}^{2^{n/2-1}-1} tr_n\left(\beta x^{i(2^{n/2}-1)}\right)$; $\beta \in \mathbb{F}_{2^{n/2}} \setminus \mathbb{F}_2$,

  - $\sum_{i=1}^{2^{n/2-2}-1} tr_n\left(\beta x^{i(2^{n/2}-1)}\right)$; $n/2$ odd and $\beta^{(2^{n/2}-4)^{-1}} \in \{x \in \mathbb{F}_{2^{n/2}}^* ; tr_{n/2}(x) = 0\}$.

- In [852] (in [350] for $b = 0$) in the form $\sum_{r \in R} tr_n(a_r x^{r(2^{n/2}-1)}) + tr_2(bx^{\frac{2^n-1}{3}})$, $x \in \mathbb{F}_{2^n}$, $b \in \mathbb{F}_4$.

  Hyper-bentness can be characterized by means of exponential sums involving Dickson polynomials (see also [511]).

  When b is a primitive element of $\mathbb{F}_4$, the condition reduces to the evaluation of the Hamming weight of some Boolean functions.

- In [871] in the form $\sum_{r \in R} tr_n(a_r x^{r(2^{n/2}-1)}) + tr_t(bx^{s(2^{n/2}-1)})$, where

  - R is a set of representatives of the cyclotomic classes modulo $2^{n/2}+1$ (not necessarily of maximal size).
  - The coefficients a_r are in $\mathbb{F}_{2^{n/2}}$.
  - s divides $2^{n/2} + 1$, *i.e.*, $s(2^{n/2} - 1)$ is a Dillon-like exponent; we set $\tau = \frac{2^{n/2}+1}{s}$.
  - t is the size of the cyclotomic coset of s modulo $2^{n/2} + 1$.
  - $b \in \mathbb{F}_{2^t}$.

  But the characterization of hyper-bentness in terms of exponential sums is so complex that no new hyper-bent function could be deduced except in some particular cases.

- In [1062], more Dillon exponent hyper-bent functions (see also [764]), with coefficients in $\mathbb{F}_{2^n}$ (with a general result unifying results from the references above), and generalized exponents in [1063].

See also [512].

---

[29] It has been shown later in [871] that it is enough to assume that the size does not divide $n/2$.

Homogeneous bent functions

Definition 58 *[975] A Boolean function is called a* homogeneous function *if all the monomials of its* algebraic normal form *have the same degree.*

In [347], Charnes et al. showed how to use invariant theory to construct homogeneous bent functions. They showed connections between homogeneous *cubic functions* and 1-designs and certain graphs and proved that there exist cubic homogeneous bent functions in each even number of variables $n \geq 6$. They studied the equivalence between the constructed bent functions and the properties of the associated elementary Abelian difference sets. It is proved in [1126] that no homogeneous bent function of degree $n/2$ exists in n variables for $n > 6$, and in [848] that, for any nonnegative integer k, if n is large enough, there exists no homogeneous bent function in n variables having degree $n/2 - k$ at least. Partial results toward a conjectured nonexistence of homogeneous rotation symmetric bent functions (see below) having algebraic degree larger than 2 have been obtained in [847].

Rotation symmetric bent functions and idempotent bent functions

Symmetry, that is, invariance under any permutation of input variables, simplifies the study of Boolean functions, but all symmetric Boolean bent functions (see Section 10.1, page 352) are quadratic and belong then to one EA equivalence class of Boolean functions. The superclass of *rotation symmetric* Boolean functions has then been introduced by Pieprzyk and Qu in [954].

Definition 59 *Let n be any positive integer. A Boolean function over $\mathbb{F}_2^n$ is called* rotation symmetric (RS) *if it is invariant under any cyclic shift of input coordinates, which is equivalent to saying that it is invariant under a primitive cyclic shift, for instance: $(x_0, x_1, \ldots, x_{n-1}) \rightarrow (x_{n-1}, x_0, x_1, \ldots, x_{n-2})$.*

RS functions are in fact linked to a notion that had been anteriorly introduced by Filiol and Fontaine in [503, 515] as observed by them:

Definition 60 *Let n be any positive integer. A Boolean function f on $\mathbb{F}_{2^n}$ is called an* idempotent function *(or briefly an idempotent) if it satisfies $f(x) = f(x^2)$, for all $x \in \mathbb{F}_{2^n}$.*

Note that a Boolean function given in univariate form $f(x) = \sum_{j=0}^{2^n-1} \delta_j \, x^j$ (or in subfield trace representation; see page 43) is an idempotent if and only if every coefficient δ_j belongs to $\mathbb{F}_2$. The link between RS functions and idempotents is through normal bases. Recall that for every n, there exists a primitive element α in $\mathbb{F}_{2^n}$ such that $(\alpha, \alpha^2, \alpha^{2^2}, \ldots, \alpha^{2^{n/2-1}})$ is a basis of the vector space $\mathbb{F}_{2^n}$ (see [775, 890]). Such basis is called a *normal basis*.

Proposition 89 *For any Boolean function $f(x)$ over $\mathbb{F}_{2^n}$, and every normal basis $(\alpha, \alpha^2, \ldots, \alpha^{2^{n-1}})$ of $\mathbb{F}_{2^n}$, the function*

$$(x_0, \ldots, x_{n-1}) \in \mathbb{F}_2^n \mapsto f\left(\sum_{i=0}^{n-1} x_i \alpha^{2^i}\right)$$

is RS if and only if f is an idempotent.

This is easily proved. Hence the two notions are theoretically equivalent (but knowing infinite classes for each notion is not equivalent). Proposition 89 leads to a notion of circulant equivalence of RS functions; see, *e.g.*, [245].

The *bivariate representation* and more general k-variate representation of RS functions and of idempotent functions is studied in [281], where the link between these notions is studied further; see Section 10.2, page 360.

Quadratic RS functions and idempotents The quadratic part of any quadratic RS Boolean function has the form

$$\bigoplus_{i=1}^{n/2-1} c_i \left(\bigoplus_{j=0}^{n-1} x_j x_{i+j}\right) \oplus c_{n/2} \left(\bigoplus_{j=0}^{n/2-1} x_j x_{n/2+j}\right), \tag{6.33}$$

where $c_1, \ldots, c_{n/2} \in \mathbb{F}_2$ and where the indices of x are modulo n. We have:

Proposition 90 *[531] Let n be any even integer. Any RS quadratic function (6.33) is bent if and only if the polynomial $P(X) = \sum_{i=1}^{n/2-1} c_i(X^i + X^{n-i}) + c_{n/2}X^{n/2}$ is coprime with $X^n + 1$, that is, the linearized polynomial $L(X) = \sum_{i=1}^{n/2-1} c_i(X^{2^i} + X^{2^{n-i}}) + c_{n/2}X^{2^{n/2}}$ is a permutation polynomial.*

Indeed, according to the characterization of quadratic bent functions recalled at page 205, the function is bent if and only if the matrix of its associated symplectic form is nonsingular, that is, the *cyclic code* generated by the rows of this matrix equals $\mathbb{F}_2^n$, and the generator polynomial of this code equals $\gcd(\sum_{i=1}^{n/2-1} c_i(X^i + X^{n-i}) + c_{n/2}X^{n/2}, X^n + 1)$.

Infinite classes of bent quadratic RS functions have been deduced:

- $\bigoplus_{j=0}^{n/2-1} x_j x_{n/2+j}$ (and we can add $h(x_0 \oplus x_{n/2}, \ldots, x_{n/2-1} \oplus x_{n-1})$ to this Maiorana-McFarland function, where h is any RS function, as observed in [1065]).
- $\bigoplus_{i=1}^{n/2-1}(\bigoplus_{j=0}^{n-1} x_j x_{i+j}) \oplus (\bigoplus_{j=0}^{n/2-1} x_j x_{n/2+j})$.

These two examples correspond to $c_{n/2} = 1$ and $c_i = 0$ for $i \neq n/2$ in the former case and $c_i = 1$ for $i = 1, \ldots, n/2 - 1$ in the latter case. Note that $L(X)$ equals $X^{2^{n/2}}$ in the former case and $X + tr_n(X)$ in the latter case, and these are permutation polynomials since n is even; equivalently $P(X)$ equals $X^{n/2}$ in the former case and $\sum_{i=1}^{n-1} X^i$ in the latter case, and these are coprime with $X^n + 1$. More examples can be found, as observed in [245]. For instance, let k be such that $2^k - 2$ divides n (and $2^k - 1$ is coprime with n). Then we have that the function $\left(\frac{X^{2^k-1}+1}{X+1}\right)^{\frac{n}{2^k-2}} + X^n + 1$ has the form $\sum_{i=1}^{n/2-1} c_i(X^i + X^{n-i}) + c_{n/2}X^{n/2}$

(indeed, $\left(\frac{X^{2^k-1}+1}{X+1}\right)^{\frac{n}{2^k-2}}$ is self-reciprocal, has degree n, and is normalized) and is coprime

with $X^n + 1$ (indeed, the zeros of $\left(\frac{X^{2^k-1}+1}{X+1}\right)^{\frac{n}{2^k-2}}$ in the algebraic closure of $\mathbb{F}_2$ are the

elements of $\mathbb{F}_{2^k} \setminus \mathbb{F}_2$ and for any $\xi \in \mathbb{F}_{2^k} \setminus \mathbb{F}_2$ we have $\xi^n + 1 \neq 0$, since $\xi \mapsto \xi^n$ is a

permutation of $\mathbb{F}_{2^k}^*$). Taking for example $k = 2$, we have $\left(X^2 + X + 1\right)^{n/2} + X^n + 1 =$

$$\sum_{\substack{0 \leq u,v,w \leq n/2 \\ u+v+w=n/2, 2u+v \notin \{0,n\}}} \frac{(n/2)!}{u!\,v!\,w!} X^{2u+v},$$ and for n not divisible by 3, the following function is RS

bent:

$$\bigoplus_{\substack{0 \leq u,v,w \leq n/2 \\ u+v+w=n/2, 2u+v \in \{1,\dots,n/2-1\}}} \frac{(n/2)!}{u!\,v!\,w!} \left(\bigoplus_{j=0}^{n-1} x_j x_{2u+v+j}\right) \oplus \left(\bigoplus_{j=0}^{n/2-1} x_j x_{n/2+j}\right),$$

where the coefficients are taken modulo 2.

Another example is as follows. If n is a power of 2, then according to [1043, proposition 3.1], the function $\bigoplus_{i=1}^{n/2-1} c_i(\bigoplus_{j=0}^{n-1} x_j x_{i+j}) \oplus c_{n/2}(\bigoplus_{j=0}^{n/2-1} x_j x_{n/2+j})$ is bent if and only if $\bigoplus_{i=0}^{n-1} c_i = 1$ (with $c_{n-i} = c_i$), that is, $c_{n/2} = 1$. See more in [245].

Quadratic bent idempotents have been also characterized: as shown in [808], for $c_1, \dots, c_{n/2} \in \mathbb{F}_2$, the function equal to $\sum_{i=1}^{n/2-1} c_i tr_n(x^{2^i+1}) + c_{n/2} tr_{n/2}(x^{2^{n/2}+1})$ is bent if and only if $gcd(\sum_{i=1}^{n/2-1} c_i(X^i + X^{n-i}) + c_{n/2}X^{n/2}, X^n + 1) = 1$ (and necessarily, $c_{n/2} = 1$). This condition is the same as that obtained for quadratic RS bent functions above. The infinite classes of RS bent functions seen above provide the following bent idempotents:

- The bent quadratic monomial idempotent $f'(x) = tr_{n/2}(x^{2^{n/2}+1})$.
- Functions $f'(x) = \sum_{i=1}^{n/2-1} tr_n(x^{2^i+1}) + tr_{n/2}(x^{2^{n/2}+1})$.
- For n a power of 2, all nonzero quadratic idempotents.
- For n not divisible by 3, functions

$$tr_{n/2}(z^{2^{n/2}+1}) + \sum_{\substack{0 \leq u,v,w \leq n/2 \\ u+v+w=n/2, 2u+v \in \{1,\dots,n/2-1\}}} \frac{(n/2)!}{u!\,v!\,w!} tr_n(z^{2^{2u+v}+1}),$$

  where the coefficients are taken modulo 2 [245]. Of course, what is written above for RS functions when n is a power of 2 is valid here.
- More results can be found in [1144].

The similarities between the quadratic RS bent functions and the quadratic bent idempotents seen above leads to considering below a transformation of RS functions into idempotents. Before that, let us recall what is known for nonquadratic functions.

Nonquadratic RS functions and idempotents   Two infinite classes of cubic RS bent functions (belonging to the completed Maiorana–McFarland class) are

- $\bigoplus_{i=0}^{n-1} (x_i x_{t+i} x_{n/2+i} \oplus x_i x_{t+i}) \oplus \bigoplus_{i=0}^{n/2-1} x_i x_{n/2+i}$, where $\frac{n/2}{\gcd(n/2,t)}$ is odd [531] (and here also we can of course add $h(x_0 \oplus x_{n/2}, \ldots, x_{n/2-1} \oplus x_{n-1})$ to this MM function, where h is any RS function, [1065]).

- $\bigoplus_{i=0}^{n-1} x_i x_{i+r} x_{i+2r} \oplus \bigoplus_{i=0}^{2r-1} x_i x_{i+2r} x_{i+4r} \oplus \bigoplus_{i=0}^{n/2-1} x_i x_{i+n/2}$, where $n/2 = 3r$ [282].

The Dillon and Kasami power functions with coefficient 1, and the Niho bent functions $tr_{n/2}(z^{2^{n/2}+1}) + tr_n(z^{d_2})$ (see page 221) are bent idempotents. The extension of the second class of Niho bent functions by Leander and Kholosha gives also a bent idempotent.

For $n = 6r$, $r \geq 1$, $tr_n(z^{1+2^r+2^{2r}}) + tr_{2r}(z^{1+2^{2r}+2^{4r}}) + tr_{3r}(z^{1+2^t}) = tr_r((z + z^{2^{3r}})^{1+2^r+2^{2r}}) + tr_{3r}(z^{1+2^t})$ is a bent idempotent [282].

More bent idempotents of any algebraic degrees between 2 and $n/2$ are given in [1075] in the form $g(x) \oplus h(tr_n(\alpha x), tr_n(\alpha^2 x), \ldots, tr_n(\alpha^{2^{n/2-1}} x))$, where g is an n-variable bent function satisfying a strong condition and h is an $n/2$-variable rotation symmetric function.

Remark. The generalized Dillon and Mesnager functions could be viewed as bent idempotent candidates, but the conditions happen not to be satisfiable: it is known that

- For every $m = n/2$ such that $K_m(1)$ is null, $g_1(x) = tr_n(x^{r(2^m-1)})$ is bent when $\gcd(r, 2^m + 1) = 1$.
- For every $m = n/2$ odd such that $K_m(1) = 4$, $g_2(x) = tr_n(x^{r(2^m-1)}) + tr_2(x^{\frac{2^n-1}{3}})$ is bent when $\gcd(r, 2^m + 1) = 1$.

But the condition $K_m(1) = 0$ never happens as shown in [783, theorem 2.2], and it can be checked by computer that the condition $K_m(1) = 4$ never happens as well for $5 \leq m \leq 20$. $\square$

Other nonquadratic functions A *secondary construction* of rotation symmetric functions (and equivalently of idempotent bent functions) from near-bent RS functions (the definition of near-bent functions is given in Subsection 6.2.4, page 262) based on the indirect sum (see page 233) is given in [281] (see also [245]): let f_1 and f_2 be two m-variable RS near-bent functions (m odd); if the Walsh supports of f_1 and f_2 are complementary, then function

$$h(x_0, y_1, x_2, y_3, \ldots, x_{n-2}, y_{n-1}) = f_1(x_0, x_1, \ldots, x_{m-1}) \oplus f_1(y_0, y_1, \ldots, y_{m-1}) \oplus$$
$$(f_1 \oplus f_2)(x_0, x_1, \ldots, x_{m-1})(f_1 \oplus f_2)(y_0, y_1, \ldots, y_{m-1})$$

is bent RS. This provides constructions of RS functions and idempotent bent functions of *algebraic degree* 4, for m odd: given the two RS functions $f_1(x) = \bigoplus_{i=0}^{m-1}(x_i \oplus x_i x_{(m-1)/2+i})$ and $f_2(x) = \bigoplus_{i=0}^{m-1} x_i x_{1+i}$, where the subscripts are taken modulo m, function $h(x_0, y_1, x_2, y_3, \ldots, x_{n-2}, y_{n-1}) = f_1(x_0, \ldots, x_{m-1}) \oplus f_1(y_0, \ldots, y_{m-1}) \oplus (f_1 \oplus f_2)(x_0, \ldots, x_{m-1})(f_1 \oplus f_2)(y_0, \ldots, y_{m-1})$ is an RS bent function. Similarly, given the m-variable idempotent functions $f_1(x) = tr_m(x) + tr_m(x^{2^{(m-1)/?}+1})$ and $f_2(x) = tr_m(x^3)$, function $h(x, y) = f_1(x) \oplus f_1(y) \oplus (f_1 \oplus f_2)(x)(f_1 \oplus f_2)(y)$ is a bent idempotent.

Su and Tang [1054] have proposed, for any even n, constructions of rotation symmetric bent functions with any possible algebraic degree ranging from 2 to $n/2$, obtained by the modification of quadratic symmetric bent functions, and of bent idempotent functions of algebraic degree $n/2$, obtained by the modification of the bent quadratic monomial idempotent (see page 250).

A transformation   As observed with quadratic RS functions and idempotents, there is a natural way of transforming an RS function into an idempotent: let $f(x_0, \cdots, x_{n-1}) = \sum_{u \in \mathbb{F}_2^n} a_u \prod_{i=0}^{n-1} x_i^{u_i}$, $a_u \in \mathbb{F}_2$, be any Boolean RS function over $\mathbb{F}_2^n$, then $f'(x) = f(x, x^2, \ldots, x^{2^{n-1}}) = \sum_{u \in \mathbb{F}_2^n} a_u x^{\sum_{i=0}^{n-1} u_i 2^i}$ is a Boolean idempotent, and any idempotent Boolean function can be obtained this way. We have seen that if f is a quadratic RS function, then f is bent if and only if f' is bent.[30] But for nonquadratic functions, it is shown in [281, 282] that all cases can happen: examples are given of an infinite class of cubic bent RS functions f such that f' is not bent, of an infinite class of cubic bent idempotents f' such that f is not bent, and of infinite classes of bent RS functions f such that f' is bent.

6.1.21 Normal and nonnormal bent Boolean functions

We have seen the definition of normal functions in Definition 28, page 105.

As observed in [212] (see Theorem 14, page 202), if a bent function f is normal (resp. weakly normal), that is, constant (resp. affine) on an $n/2$-dimensional flat $b + E$, where E is a subspace of $\mathbb{F}_2^n$, then its dual $\widetilde{f}$ is such that $\widetilde{f}(u) \oplus b \cdot u$ is constant on $E^\perp$ (resp. on $a + E^\perp$, where a is a vector such that $f(x) \oplus a \cdot x$ is constant on E). Thus, $\widetilde{f}$ is weakly normal. Moreover, we have already seen that f (resp. $f(x) \oplus a \cdot x$) is balanced on each of the other cosets of the flat.

H. Dobbertin used normal bent functions to construct *balanced* functions with high nonlinearities: take a bent function f in n variables that is constant on an $n/2$-dimensional flat A of $\mathbb{F}_2^n$; replace the values of f on A by the values of a highly nonlinear balanced function on A (identified to a function g on $\mathbb{F}_2^{n/2}$); note that this process is recursive since such $n/2$-variable Boolean function g can be obtained by the same process (as long as $n/2$ is even) with n replaced by $n/2$; when n becomes odd (say $n = 2k + 1$), replace the constant value by a balanced function of best-known nonlinearity nl_{2k+1} (larger than or equal to $2^{2k} - 2^k$); this provides a balanced function (as we shall see in Proposition 121, page 296) whose nonlinearity equals $2^{n-1} - 2^{n/2-1} - \cdots - 2^{2k} + (nl_{2k+1} - 2^{2k}) \geq 2^{n-1} - 2^{n/2-1} - \cdots - 2^{2k} - 2^k$.

The existence of nonnormal (and even non-weakly normal) bent functions, *i.e.*, bent functions that are nonconstant (resp. nonaffine) on every $n/2$-dimensional flat, has been shown, contradicting a conjecture made by several authors that such bent function did not exist. It is proved in [448] that the so-called Kasami function defined over $\mathbb{F}_{2^n}$ by $f(x) = tr_n\left(ax^{2^{2k}-2^k+1}\right)$, with $\gcd(k, n) = 1$, is bent if n is not divisible by 3 and if $a \in \mathbb{F}_{2^n}$ is not a cube. As shown in [198] (thanks to [412]), if $a \in \mathbb{F}_4 \setminus \mathbb{F}_2$ and $k = 3$,

---

[30] Note that if $n \equiv 2 \pmod 4$, then there exists a self-dual normal basis of $\mathbb{F}_{2^n}$ and that f' expressed over $\mathbb{F}_2^n$ by means of such basis is then the same function as f; this is also the case if n is odd.

then for $n = 10$, the function $f(x) \oplus tr_n(bx)$ is nonnormal for some b, and for $n = 14$, the function $f(x)$ is not weakly normal (while the Kasami function is normal for n divisible by 4 or $k = 1$). A nonnormal bent function in 12 variables is given in [278]. Cubic bent functions on eight variables are all normal, as shown in [349].

The direct sum (see the definition in Subsection 6.1.16) of two normal functions is obviously a normal function, while the direct sum of two nonnormal functions can be normal. What about the sum of a normal bent function and of a nonnormal bent function? This question has been studied in [270]. To this aim, a notion more general than normality has been introduced as follows:

Definition 61 *Let $U \subseteq V$ be two vector spaces over $\mathbb{F}_2$. Let $\beta : U \to \mathbb{F}_2$ and $f : V \to \mathbb{F}_2$ be bent functions. Then we say that f is a* normal extension *of β, in symbols $\beta \preceq f$, if there is a direct decomposition $V = U \oplus W_1 \oplus W_2$ such that (i) $\beta(u) = f(u + w_1)$ for all $u \in U$, $w_1 \in W_1$, and (ii) $\dim W_1 = \dim W_2$.*

Obviously, we get a normal extension of any β by taking any normal bent function g and making its direct sum with β. The relation $\preceq$ is transitive and if $\beta \preceq f$ then the same relation exists between the duals: $\widetilde{\beta} \preceq \widetilde{f}$.

A bent function is normal if and only if $\epsilon \preceq f$, where $\epsilon \in \mathbb{F}_2$ is viewed as a Boolean function over the vector space $\mathbb{F}_2^0 = \{0\}$.

Examples of normal extensions are given in [270] (some by the construction of Theorem 15, page 234, and its particular cases, the indirect sum and the extension of Maiorana–McFarland type).

The clarification about the sum of a normal bent function and of a nonnormal bent function comes from the two following propositions (see the proofs in [270]):

Proposition 91 *Let $f_i : V_i \to \mathbb{F}_2$, $i = 1, 2$, be bent functions. The direct sum $f_1 \oplus f_2$ is normal if and only if bent functions β_1 and β_2 exist such that f_i is a normal extension of β_i ($i = 1, 2$) and either β_1 and β_2 or β_1 and $\beta_2 \oplus 1$ are linearly equivalent.*

Proposition 92 *Suppose that $\beta \preceq f$ for bent functions β and f. If f is normal, then also β is normal.*

Hence, since the direct sum of a bent function β and of a normal bent function g is a normal extension of β, the direct sum of a normal and a nonnormal bent function is always nonnormal.

Normal extension leads to a secondary construction of bent functions:

Proposition 93 *Let β be a bent function on U and f a bent function on $V = U \times W \times W$. Assume that $\beta \preceq f$. Let*

$$\beta' : U \to \mathbb{F}_2$$

be any bent function. Modify f by setting for all $x \in U$, $y \in W$

$$f'(x, y, 0) = \beta'(x),$$

while $f'(x, y, z) = f(x, y, z)$ for all $x \in U$, $y, z \in W$, $z \neq 0$. Then f' is bent and we have $\beta' \preceq f'$.

Hence, we can replace β by any other bent function on U and get again a normal extension.

6.1.22 Kerdock codes

For every even n, the *Kerdock code* $\mathcal{K}_n$ [689] is a supercode of $RM(1, n)$ (i.e., contains $RM(1, n)$ as a subset) and is a subcode of $RM(2, n)$. More precisely $\mathcal{K}_n$ is a union of cosets $f_u \oplus RM(1, n)$ of $RM(1, n)$, where the functions f_u are quadratic (one of them is null and all the others have algebraic degree 2). The difference $f_u \oplus f_v$ between two distinct functions f_u and f_v being bent, $\mathcal{K}_n$ has minimum distance $2^{n-1} - 2^{\frac{n}{2}-1}$ (n even), which is the best possible minimum distance for a code equal to a union of cosets of $RM(1, n)$, according to the covering radius bound. The size of $\mathcal{K}_n$ equals 2^{2n}. This is the best possible size for such length and minimum distance (see [177, 422]). The Kerdock code of length 16 is called the *Nordstrom–Robinson code*. We describe now how the construction of Kerdock codes can be simply presented.

Construction of the Kerdock code

We revisit Kerdock's construction, which was presented by means of idempotents, that we shall not need here. The function, already seen at page 206,

$$f(x) = \sigma_2(x) = \binom{w_H(x)}{2} \, [\text{mod } 2] = \bigoplus_{1 \leq i < j \leq n} x_i x_j \tag{6.34}$$

is bent. Thus, the linear code $RM(1, n) \cup (f \oplus RM(1, n))$ has minimum distance $2^{n-1} - 2^{\frac{n}{2}-1}$.

We have recalled at page 41 and foll. and at page 248 some properties of the field $\mathbb{F}_{2^m}$ (where m is any positive integer). In particular, we have seen that $\mathbb{F}_{2^m}$ admits normal bases $(\alpha, \alpha^2, \ldots, \alpha^{2^{m-1}})$. If m is odd, there exists a self-dual normal basis, that is, a normal basis such that $tr_m(\alpha^{2^i+2^j}) = 1$ if $i = j$ (that is, $tr_m(\alpha) = 1$) and $tr_m(\alpha^{2^i+2^j}) = 0$ otherwise (see [775, 890]). As a consequence, for all $x = x_1\alpha + \cdots + x_m\alpha^{2^{m-1}}$ in $\mathbb{F}_{2^m}$, we have

$$tr_m(x) = \bigoplus_{i=1}^m x_i \qquad tr_m(x^{2^j+1}) = \bigoplus_{i=1}^m x_i x_{i+j},$$

(where $i + j$ is taken mod m).

The function f of Relation (6.34), viewed as a function $f(x, x_n)$ on $\mathbb{F}_{2^m} \times \mathbb{F}_2$, where $m = n - 1$ is odd – say $m = 2t + 1$ – can now be written as

$$f(x, x_n) = tr_m \left(\sum_{j=1}^t x^{2^j+1} \right) + x_n tr_m(x),$$

and this expression can be taken as the definition of f. Notice that the associated symplectic form $\beta_f((x, x_n), (y, y_n))$ associated to f equals $tr_m(x)tr_m(y) + tr_m(xy) + x_n tr_m(y) + y_n tr_m(x)$.

Let us denote $f(ux, x_n)$ by $f_u(x, x_n)$ ($u \in \mathbb{F}_{2^m}$), then $\mathcal{K}_n$ is defined as the union, when u ranges over $\mathbb{F}_{2^m}$, of the cosets $f_u + RM(1, n)$.

$\mathcal{K}_n$ contains all 2^{n+1} affine functions (since for $u = 0$, we have $f_u = 0$) and $2^{2n} - 2^{n+1}$ quadratic bent functions. Its minimum distance equals $2^{n-1} - 2^{\frac{n}{2}-1}$ since the sum of two distinct functions f_u and f_v is bent. Indeed, the kernel of the associated symplectic form equals the set of all ordered pairs (x, x_n) such that $tr_m(ux)tr_m(uy) + tr_m(u^2 xy) + x_n tr_m(uy) + y_n tr_m(ux) = tr_m(vx)tr_m(vy) + tr_m(v^2 xy) + x_n tr_m(vy) + y_n tr_m(vx)$ for every $(y, y_n) \in \mathbb{F}_{2^m} \times \mathbb{F}_2$, which is equivalent to $u tr_m(ux) + u^2 x + x_n u = v tr_m(vx) + v^2 x + x_n v$ and $tr_m(ux) = tr_m(vx)$; it is a simple matter to show that it equals $\{(0, 0)\}$.

A more general approach to the construction of Kerdock codes is developed in [327].

Open problem: Other examples of codes having the same parameters exist; see [657] (see also [658] and observations in [72, 208, 217]). All are equal to subcodes of the Reed–Muller code of order 2, up to affine equivalence. We do not know how to obtain the same parameters with nonquadratic functions (up to code equivalence). This would be useful for cryptographic purposes and for the design of sequences for code division multiple access (CDMA) in telecommunications.

Remark. The Kerdock codes are not linear. However, they share some nice properties with linear codes: the distance distribution between any codeword and all the other codewords does not depend on the choice of the codeword (we say that the Kerdock codes are *distance invariant*; this results in the fact that their *distance enumerator*s are equal to their weight enumerators); and, as proved by Semakov and Zinoviev [1029], the weight enumerators of the Kerdock codes satisfy a MacWilliams-like relation, similar to Relation (1.1), page 14, in which C is replaced by $\mathcal{K}_n$ and $C^{\perp}$ is replaced by the so-called Preparata code [43] of the same length (we say that the Kerdock codes and the Preparata codes are formally dual). An explanation of this astonishing property has been given in [586]: the Kerdock code is stable under an addition inherited of the addition in $\mathbb{Z}_4 = \mathbb{Z}/4\mathbb{Z}$ (we say it is $\mathbb{Z}_4$-linear), and the MacWilliams identity still holds in this different framework. Such an explanation had been an open problem for two decades. $\qquad\square$

6.2 Partially-bent and plateaued Boolean functions

We have seen that bent Boolean functions can never be balanced, which makes them improper for a direct cryptographic use. This has led to a research on superclasses of the class of bent functions, whose elements can have high nonlinearities, but can also be balanced[31] (and possibly be resilient).

---

[31] The functions found will, however, still have bounded algebraic degree, which is cryptographically crippling in many situations.

6.2.1 Partially-bent functions

A first superclass of possibly balanced functions with high nonlinearity has been obtained as the set of those functions that achieve a bound conjectured by B. Preneel in [969] and expressing some trade-off between the number of unbalanced derivatives (*i.e.*, of nonzero autocorrelation coefficients) of a Boolean function and the number of nonzero values of its Walsh transform.

Proposition 94 *[211] Let n be any positive integer. Let f be any Boolean function on $\mathbb{F}_2^n$. Let us denote the cardinalities of the sets $\{b \in \mathbb{F}_2^n \mid \mathcal{F}(D_b f) \neq 0\}$ and $\{a \in \mathbb{F}_2^n \mid W_f(a) \neq 0\}$ by N_{Δ_f} and N_{W_f}, respectively. Then:*

$$N_{\Delta_f} \times N_{W_f} \geq 2^n. \tag{6.35}$$

Moreover, $N_{\Delta_f} \times N_{W_f} = 2^n$ if and only if, for every $b \in \mathbb{F}_2^n$, the derivative $D_b f$ is either balanced or constant. This property is also equivalent to the fact that there exist two linear subspaces E (of even dimension) and E' of $\mathbb{F}_2^n$, whose direct sum equals $\mathbb{F}_2^n$, and Boolean functions g, bent on E, and h, affine on E', such that

$$\forall x \in E, \forall y \in E', f(x + y) = g(x) \oplus h(y). \tag{6.36}$$

Inequality (6.35) comes directly from the Wiener–Khintchine relation (2.53), page 62: since the value of the autocorrelation coefficient $\mathcal{F}(D_b f)$ lies between -2^n and 2^n for every $b \in \mathbb{F}_2^n$, the arithmetic mean of $(-1)^{u \cdot b} \mathcal{F}(D_b f)$ when b ranges over the set $\{b \in \mathbb{F}_2^n \mid \mathcal{F}(D_b f) \neq 0\}$ is at most 2^n, for every $u \in \mathbb{F}_2^n$, and we have then $N_{\Delta_f} \geq 2^{-n} \sum_{b \in \mathbb{F}_2^n} (-1)^{u \cdot b} \mathcal{F}(D_b f) = 2^{-n} W_f^2(u)$ and thus $N_{\Delta_f} \geq 2^{-n} \max_{u \in \mathbb{F}_2^n} W_f^2(u)$. Moreover, we have $N_{W_f} \geq \frac{\sum_{u \in \mathbb{F}_2^n} W_f^2(u)}{\max_{u \in \mathbb{F}_2^n} W_f^2(u)} = \frac{2^{2n}}{\max_{u \in \mathbb{F}_2^n} W_f^2(u)}$. This proves Inequality (6.35).

This inequality is an equality if and only if both inequalities above are equalities, that is, for every $b \in \mathbb{F}_2^n$, the autocorrelation coefficient $\mathcal{F}(D_b f)$ equals 0 or $2^n(-1)^{u_0 \cdot b}$, where $\max_{u \in \mathbb{F}_2^n} W_f^2(u) = W_f^2(u_0)$ (and this implies that, for every $b \in \mathbb{F}_2^n$, $D_b f$ is either balanced or constant) and f is plateaued (see page 258).

The single condition that $D_b f$ is either balanced or constant for every b implies that f has the form (6.36). Indeed, let E be any supplementary space of the linear kernel $\mathcal{E}_f$, then E having trivial intersection with $\mathcal{E}_f$, the restriction of f to E has balanced derivatives (their balancedness over E being equivalent to their balancedness over $\mathbb{F}_2^n$) and is then bent, and f has the form (6.36) with $E' = \mathcal{E}_f$. Then it is easily seen that (6.35) is an equality. This completes the proof. $\qquad\square$

See some more properties in [338].

A generalization of Relation (6.35) to *pseudo-Boolean* functions has been obtained in [986].

Definition 62 *The n-variable Boolean functions such that (6.35) is an equality, that is, whose derivatives are all either balanced or constant, that is, the functions of the form (6.36), are called* partially-bent functions.

Bounds similar to Relation (6.35) but different are obtained in [1178] and lead to other characterizations of partially-bent functions.

Every quadratic function is partially-bent. Partially-bent functions share with *quadratic functions* almost all of their nice properties (the Walsh spectrum is easier to calculate, they have potential good nonlinearity, and good resiliency order); see [211], where the cryptographic properties of partially-bent functions are characterized. In particular, the values of the Walsh transform equal 0 or $\pm 2^{dim(E')+dim(E)/2}$. The support of such plateaued function is a coset (*i.e.*, a translate) of E. Note that, viewing a function of the form (6.36) as a bivariate function, its Walsh transform equals $W_f(u,v) = W_g(u)W_h(v)$.

Instead of using Relation (2.53), we can use Relations (3.7), page 97, and (3.10), page 98. We have then $N_{\Delta_f} \geq 2^{-2n}\sum_{b\in\mathbb{F}_2^n}\mathcal{F}^2(D_bf) = 2^{-2n}\mathcal{V}(f)$ and $N_{W_f} \leq$

$$\frac{\sum_{u\in\mathbb{F}_2^n}W_f^4(u)}{\min\{W_f^4(u);u\in\mathbb{F}_2^n,W_f(u)\neq 0\}} = \frac{2^n\,\mathcal{V}(f)}{\min\{W_f^4(u);u\in\mathbb{F}_2^n,W_f(u)\neq 0\}}, \text{ and therefore:}$$

Proposition 95 *Let n be any positive integer. Let f be any Boolean function on $\mathbb{F}_2^n$. With the same notation as in Proposition 94, we have*

$$\frac{N_{\Delta_f}}{N_{W_f}} \geq 2^{-3n}\min\{W_f^4(u);\ u\in\mathbb{F}_2^n,\ W_f(u)\neq 0\},$$

with equality if and only if f is partially-bent.

We can also use Relations (3.9) and (3.10). Denoting by $N_{\Delta_f^{(2)}}$ the size of the set $\{(a,b)\in(\mathbb{F}_2^n)^2\mid\mathcal{F}(D_aD_bf)\neq 0\}$, we have then $N_{\Delta_f^{(2)}} \geq 2^{-n}\sum_{a,b\in\mathbb{F}_2^n}\mathcal{F}(D_aD_bf) = 2^{-n}\mathcal{V}(f)$ and $N_{W_f} \leq \frac{2^n\,\mathcal{V}(f)}{\min\{W_f^4(u);u\in\mathbb{F}_2^n,W_f(u)\neq 0\}}$, and therefore

$$\frac{N_{\Delta_f^{(2)}}}{N_{W_f}} \geq 2^{-2n}\min\{W_f^4(u);\ u\in\mathbb{F}_2^n,\ W_f(u)\neq 0\}, \tag{6.37}$$

with equality if and only if both inequalities are equalities, which is equivalent to the fact that all second-order derivatives of f are either balanced or equal to the constant function 0 and that f is plateaued. We leave open the determination of such functions.

The functions achieving (6.37) with equality seem somewhat related to the so-called *second–order bent functions* introduced in [275], which are by definition those Boolean functions such that, for every $\mathbb{F}_2$-linearly independent elements $a,b\in\mathbb{F}_2^n$ (*i.e.*, $a\neq 0_n,b\neq 0_n,a\neq b$), D_aD_bf is balanced (which is a more demanding condition on the second-order derivatives but does not require that f be plateaued). In fact, there is no intersection between the two sets of functions, because no second-order bent function can be plateaued. Indeed, it is shown in [275] that f is second-order bent if and only if, for all $b,c\in\mathbb{F}_2^n$, we have

$$\sum_{u\in\mathbb{F}_2^n}W_f(u+b+c)W_f(u+b)W_f(u+c)W_f(u) = \begin{cases} -2^{2n+1} \text{ if } b\neq 0_n,c\neq 0_n,b\neq c, \\ 3\cdot 2^{3n}-2^{2n+1} \text{ if } b-c-0_n, \\ 2^{3n}-2^{2n+1} \text{ otherwise .} \end{cases}$$

Then taking $b = c = 0_n$, we see that if f is plateaued, its amplitude (see Definition 63) must divide $2^{\lfloor \frac{2n+1}{4} \rfloor}$ and therefore must divide $2^{\frac{n-1}{2}}$ (since n is odd; see below) and the size of the support of the Walsh transform of f is then a multiple of $3 \cdot 2^{n+2} - 2^3$, which is impossible since it cannot be larger than 2^n.

The only known second-order bent functions are the 3-variable functions equal to $x_1 x_2 x_3$ plus a quadratic function. It is shown in [275] that second-order bent n-variable functions can exist only if $n \equiv 3$ [mod 4], and the existence of such functions in more than three variables is an open question.

Remark. Partially-bent functions must not be mistaken for *partial bent functions*, studied by P. Guillot in [578]. By definition, the Fourier–Hadamard transforms of partial bent functions take exactly two values[32] λ and $\lambda + 2^{\frac{n}{2}}$ on $\mathbb{F}_2^n \setminus \{0_n\}$ (n even). Rothaus' bound on the degree generalizes to partial bent functions. The dual $\widetilde{f}$ of f, defined by $\widetilde{f}(u) = 0$ if $\widehat{f}(u) = \lambda$ and $\widetilde{f}(u) = 1$ if $\widehat{f}(u) = \lambda + 2^{\frac{n}{2}}$, is also partial bent; and its dual is f. Two kinds of partial bent functions f exist: those such that $\widehat{f}(0_n) - f(0_n) = -\lambda(2^{\frac{n}{2}} - 1)$, and those such that $\widehat{f}(0_n) - f(0_n) = (2^{\frac{n}{2}} - \lambda)(2^{\frac{n}{2}} + 1)$. This can be deduced from Parseval's relation (2.47). The sum of two partial bent functions of the same kind, whose supports share at most the zero vector, is partial bent. An interest of partial bent functions is in the possibility of using them as building blocks for constructing bent functions. $\qquad\square$

6.2.2 Plateaued Boolean functions

In spite of their good properties, partially-bent functions, when they are not bent, have by definition nonzero linear structures and so do not give full satisfaction. The class of plateaued functions, already encountered above in Section 3.1 (and sometimes called *three-valued functions*), is a natural extension of that of partially-bent functions. They have been first studied by Zheng and Zhang in [1173, 1174, 1176] and more recently in [247, 317, 858, 1178].

Definition 63 *A function is called* plateaued *if its Walsh transform takes at most one nonzero absolute value* λ, *that is, takes at most three values* 0 *and* $\pm\lambda$ *(where* λ *is some positive integer, which we call the* amplitude *of the plateaued function).*

Because of Parseval's relation (2.47), the amplitude λ of any plateaued function must be of the form 2^j, where $j \geq \frac{n}{2}$ (since $N_{W_f} \leq 2^n$). Then some authors call f a $(2j - n)$-plateaued function (*i.e.*, call r-plateaued the plateaued functions of amplitude $2^{\frac{n+r}{2}}$), and bent functions are 0-plateaued, near-bent functions are 1-plateaued, and semi-bent functions in even dimension are 2-plateaued. According to *Parseval's relation* (2.47), a plateaued function is bent if and only if its Walsh transform never takes the value 0. The Walsh spectrum of a plateaued function of amplitude λ is (thanks to Parseval's and inverse Walsh transform formulae)

---

[32] Partial bent functions are the indicators of partial difference sets.

Walsh transform value	Frequency
0	$2^n - 2^{2n-2j}$
2^j	$2^{2n-2j-1} + (-1)^{f(0_n)} 2^{n-j-1}$
-2^j	$2^{2n-2j-1} - (-1)^{f(0_n)} 2^{n-j-1}$

and we have $\sum_{a \in \mathbb{F}_{2^n}} W_f^3(a) = (-1)^{f(0_n)} 2^{n+2j}$ and $\sum_{a \in \mathbb{F}_{2^n}} W_f^4(a) = 2^{2n+2j}$.

The characterization of bent functions by difference sets has been extended in [918] to a characterization of plateaued functions by so-called one-and-half difference sets.

Of course, an n-variable Boolean function f is plateaued with amplitude λ if and only if its Walsh transform satisfies $W_f^2 = \lambda^2 \, 1_{supp(W_f)}$, where $supp(W_f)$ is the Walsh support of f and $1_{supp(W_f)}$ is its indicator. Since the autocorrelation function Δ_f has W_f^2 for Fourier transform, partially-bent functions are then those plateaued functions whose Walsh support is an affine subspace of $\mathbb{F}_2^n$. Indeed, this condition is necessary and it is also sufficient since Relation (6.35) is then an equality because N_{Δ_f} equals then the size of the dual of the vector space equal to the direction of $supp(W_f)$, and it equals then $\frac{2^n}{N_{W_f}}$.

Note that, according to Parseval's relation, for every n-variable Boolean function f, we have $N_{W_f} \times \max_{a \in \mathbb{F}_2^n} W_f^2(a) \geq 2^{2n}$ and therefore, according to Relation (3.1), page 79,

$nl(f) \leq 2^{n-1} \left(1 - \frac{1}{\sqrt{N_{W_f}}}\right)$. Equality is achieved if and only if f is *plateaued*.

According to Theorem 2, page 63, we have:

Proposition 96 *The algebraic degree of any n-variable plateaued function is bounded above by $n - j + 1$, where $\lambda = 2^j$ is the amplitude of f, and therefore by $n/2 + 1$ if n is even (and by $n/2$ in the particular case of bent functions), and by $\frac{n+1}{2}$ if n is odd.*

Note that the second part of the remark at page 67 gives additional information on the ANF of plateaued functions.

Proposition 96 makes all plateaued functions weak against fast algebraic and Rønjom–Helleseth attacks on stream ciphers. The class of plateaued functions contains those functions that achieve the best possible trade-offs among resiliency, nonlinearity, and algebraic degree: the order of resiliency and the nonlinearity of any Boolean function are bounded by Sarkar et al.'s bound (see Chapter 7 below), and the best compromise between those two criteria is achieved by plateaued functions only; the third criterion – the algebraic degree – is then also optimal. Other properties of plateaued functions can be found in [191, 692].

6.2.3 Characterizations of plateaued Boolean functions

A few characterizations of plateaued functions are given in [1173] for Boolean functions, which are direct consequences of the definition. Plateaued functions have been more recently characterized by their derivatives, their autocorrelation functions, and power moments of their Walsh transforms.

Characterization by means of the derivatives

Proposition 97   *[317] A Boolean function f on $\mathbb{F}_2^n$ is plateaued if and only if there exists $\lambda \in \mathbb{N}$ such that, for every $x \in \mathbb{F}_2^n$*

$$\sum_{a,b\in\mathbb{F}_2^n} (-1)^{D_a D_b f(x)} = \lambda^2. \tag{6.38}$$

λ is then the amplitude of the plateaued function.

The proof is very similar to that of Proposition 6.1, page 193. A function f is plateaued with amplitude λ if and only if, for every $u \in \mathbb{F}_2^n$, we have $W_f(u)\big(W_f^2(u) - \lambda^2\big) = 0$, that is, $W_f^3(u) - \lambda^2 W_f(u) = 0$. Applying the Fourier–Hadamard transform to both terms of this equality and using Relations (2.42), page 59, and (2.44) iterated (with three functions), page 60, we see that this is equivalent to the fact that, for every $a \in \mathbb{F}_2^n$, we have

$$\sum_{x,y\in\mathbb{F}_2^n} (-1)^{f(x)\oplus f(y)\oplus f(x+y+a)} = \lambda^2 (-1)^{f(a)},$$

and this completes the proof (after moving $(-1)^{f(a)}$ to the other hand side and changing x, y, a into $x + a, x + b, x$).

The fact that quadratic functions are *plateaued* is a direct consequence of Proposition 97, since their second-order derivatives are constant; and Proposition 97 gives more insight on the relationship between the nonlinearity of a quadratic function and the number of its nonzero second-order derivatives.

Characterization by means of the autocorrelation function

A Boolean function f being plateaued of amplitude λ if and only if the functions $W_f^2 \times W_f^2$ and $\lambda^2 W_f^2$ are equal, applying the Fourier transform to both functions, and using the formula $\widehat{\varphi \times \psi} = 2^{-n} \widehat{\varphi} \otimes \widehat{\psi}$ with $\varphi = \psi = W_f^2$, where $\otimes$ denotes the convolutional product, gives

Proposition 98   *[247] Let n be any positive integer and f any Boolean function. Let $\Delta_f(a) = \sum_{x\in\mathbb{F}_2^n}(-1)^{f(x)\oplus f(x+a)}$ be the autocorrelation function of f. Then f is plateaued of amplitude λ if and only, for every $x \in \mathbb{F}_2^n$:*

$$\sum_{a\in\mathbb{F}_2^n} \Delta_f(a)\Delta_f(a+x) = \lambda^2 \Delta_f(x).$$

Characterization by means of power moments of the Walsh transform

The sum $\sum_{a,b\in\mathbb{F}_2^n}(-1)^{D_a D_b f(x)}$ in Proposition 97, equals

$$2^{-n} \cdot \sum_{a,b,c,w\in\mathbb{F}_2^n} (-1)^{f(x)\oplus f(a)\oplus f(b)\oplus f(c)\oplus w\cdot(x+a+b+c)}.$$

Let us apply the Fourier transform to this real-valued function of x and use that any function of x is constant if and only if its Fourier transform is null at every nonzero vector

α. We deduce that f is plateaued if and only if, for every nonzero $\alpha \in \mathbb{F}_2^n$, the sum $\sum_{x,a,b,c,w \in \mathbb{F}_2^n} (-1)^{f(x) \oplus f(a) \oplus f(b) \oplus f(c) \oplus w \cdot (x+a+b+c) \oplus \alpha \cdot x}$ is null. This latter sum equals:

$$\sum_{w \in \mathbb{F}_2^n} \sum_{x \in \mathbb{F}_2^n} (-1)^{f(x) \oplus (w+\alpha) \cdot x} \sum_{a \in \mathbb{F}_2^n} (-1)^{f(a) \oplus w \cdot a} \sum_{b \in \mathbb{F}_2^n} (-1)^{f(b) \oplus w \cdot b} \sum_{c \in \mathbb{F}_2^n} (-1)^{f(c) \oplus w \cdot c}.$$

We deduce:

Proposition 99 *[247] Any n-variable Boolean function f is* plateaued *if and only if, for every nonzero $\alpha \in \mathbb{F}_2^n$, we have*

$$\sum_{w \in \mathbb{F}_2^n} W_f(w + \alpha) \, W_f^3(w) = 0.$$

Another characterization of plateaued functions by means of the Walsh transform exists. For a plateaued Boolean function of amplitude λ, we have, using Parseval's relation, that $\sum_{a \in \mathbb{F}_2^n} W_f^4(a) = 2^{2n} \lambda^2$. We also have, for every $b \in \mathbb{F}_2^n$, that $\sum_{a \in \mathbb{F}_2^n} (-1)^{a \cdot b} W_f^3(a) = \lambda^2 \sum_{a \in \mathbb{F}_2^n} (-1)^{a \cdot b} W_f(a) = \lambda^2 2^n (-1)^{f(b)}$. A necessary condition for f to be plateaued is then that, for every $b \in \mathbb{F}_2^n$, $\sum_{a \in \mathbb{F}_2^n} W_f^4(a) = 2^n (-1)^{f(b)} \sum_{a \in \mathbb{F}_2^n} (-1)^{a \cdot b} W_f^3(a)$. Conversely, if this property is satisfied by f, then the function $b \in \mathbb{F}_2^n \mapsto (-1)^{f(b)} \sum_{a \in \mathbb{F}_2^n} (-1)^{a \cdot b} W_f^3(a)$ is constant. Then the Fourier transform of this function, that is, the function that maps every $\alpha \in \mathbb{F}_2^n$ to the sum $\sum_{b \in \mathbb{F}_2^n} \sum_{a \in \mathbb{F}_2^n} (-1)^{(a+\alpha) \cdot b \oplus f(b)} W_f^3(a) = \sum_{a \in \mathbb{F}_2^n} W_f(a + \alpha) W_f^3(a)$ is null at every nonzero α, and f is plateaued, according to Proposition 99:

Corollary 17 *[247] Any n-variable Boolean function f is* plateaued *if and only if, for every $b \in \mathbb{F}_2^n$:*

$$\sum_{a \in \mathbb{F}_2^n} W_f^4(a) = 2^n (-1)^{f(b)} \sum_{a \in \mathbb{F}_2^n} (-1)^{a \cdot b} W_f^3(a).$$

More characterizations exist. An obvious one is that, for every positive integer k, an n-variable Boolean function f is plateaued if and only if there exists $v \in \mathbb{Z}$ such that we have $\sum_{a \in \mathbb{F}_2^n} W_f^{2k}(a) \left(W_f^2(a) - v \right)^2 = 0$ (v equals then the square of the amplitude of the plateaued function). This nonnegative expression of degree 2 in v writes $\sum_{a \in \mathbb{F}_2^n} W_f^{2k+4}(a) - 2v \sum_{a \in \mathbb{F}_2^n} W_f^{2k+2}(a) + v^2 \sum_{a \in \mathbb{F}_2^n} W_f^{2k}(a)$; hence, the reduced discriminant $\left(\sum_{a \in \mathbb{F}_2^n} W_f^{2k+2}(a) \right)^2 - \left(\sum_{a \in \mathbb{F}_2^n} W_f^{2k+4}(a) \right) \left(\sum_{a \in \mathbb{F}_2^n} W_f^{2k}(a) \right)$ is nonpositive and is null if and only if f is plateaued. We deduce (see more in [247]):

Proposition 100 *[247, 858] For every n-variable Boolean function f and every $k \in \mathbb{N}^*$, we have*

$$\left(\sum_{a \in \mathbb{F}_2^n} W_f^{2k+2}(a) \right)^2 \leq \left(\sum_{a \in \mathbb{F}_2^n} W_f^{2k}(a) \right) \left(\sum_{a \in \mathbb{F}_2^n} W_f^{2k+4}(a) \right),$$

with equality if and only if f is plateaued.

Table 6.2 Weight distribution of C'_f for f plateaued of amplitude λ.

Hamming weight w	Multiplicity A_w
0	1
2^{n-1}	$2^{n+1} - \frac{2^{2n}}{\lambda^2} - 1$
$2^{n-1} - \frac{\lambda}{2}$	$\frac{2^{2n-1}}{\lambda^2} + (-1)^{f(0_n)} \frac{2^{n-1}}{\lambda}$
$2^{n-1} + \frac{\lambda}{2}$	$\frac{2^{2n-1}}{\lambda^2} - (-1)^{f(0_n)} \frac{2^{n-1}}{\lambda}$

Characterization by means of codes

Any plateaued Boolean function f, viewed as a (vectorial) $(n, 1)$-function, can be related to the code C'_f seen at page 160, which has then the weight distribution given by Table 6.2.

See in [874] examples of such codes.

Langevin proved in [738] that, if f is a plateaued function, then the coset $f \oplus RM(1,n)$ of the Reed–Muller code of order 1 is an *orphan of $RM(1,n)$*. The notion of orphan has been introduced in [599] (with the term "urcoset" instead of orphan) and studied in [137]. A coset of $RM(1,n)$ is an orphan if it is maximum with respect to the following partial order relation: $g \oplus RM(1,n)$ is smaller than $f \oplus RM(1,n)$ if there exists in $g \oplus RM(1,n)$ an element g_1 of Hamming weight $nl(g)$ (that is, of minimum Hamming weight in $g \oplus RM(1,n)$), and in $f \oplus RM(1,n)$ an element f_1 of Hamming weight $nl(f)$, such that $supp(g_1) \subseteq supp(f_1)$. Clearly, if f is a function of maximum nonlinearity, then $f \oplus RM(1,n)$ is an orphan of $RM(1,n)$ (the converse is false, since plateaued functions with nonoptimal nonlinearity exist). The notion of orphan can be used in algorithms searching for functions with high nonlinearities.

6.2.4 *The subclasses of semi-bent and near-bent functions*

– Recall that for n odd, *near-bent* functions (also called *semi-bent functions*) are those plateaued functions of amplitude $2^{\frac{n+1}{2}}$. In [191], the authors observed that the class of so-called *three-valued almost optimal* functions, such that the coset $f \oplus RM(1,n)$ takes exactly three weights and whose nonlinearity is at least $2^{n-1} - 2^{\frac{n-1}{2}}$, coincides with that of near-bent functions (such functions are plateaued because there are three weights and because the coset is stable under complementation, and the amplitude of such plateaued functions is minimal). Parseval's identity shows that the support of their Walsh transform has cardinality 2^{n-1}. Other properties have been shown in [1121] in connection with the theory of *cyclic codes* and in [427] in connection with that of designs.

According to the properties seen in Section 5.2, page 170, quadratic Boolean functions are near-bent if and only if their linear kernel has dimension 1, that is, their rank equals $n - 1$.

Several constructions of quadratic near-bent functions exist; see a survey in [859]. All the component functions of almost bent (n,n)-functions (see Subsection 11.3, page 371) are near-bent, by definition, and the restriction of any bent Boolean function to an affine hyperplane is near-bent (the restrictions to an affine hyperplane and to its complement

Table 6.3 Weight distribution of the code $C_{supp(f)}$ for f near-bent such that $f(0_n) = 0$.

Hamming weight	Multiplicity
0	1
$\frac{w_H(f)-2^{(n-1)/2}}{2}$	$w_H(f)[1 - 2^{-n}w_H(f) - 2^{-(n+1)/2}]$
$\frac{w_H(f)}{2}$	$2^n - 1 - w_H(f)(2^n - w_H(f))2^{-(n-1)}$
$\frac{w_H(f)+2^{(n-1)/2}}{2}$	$w_H(f)[1 - 2^{-n}w_H(f) + 2^{-(n+1)/2}]$

have complementary Walsh supports and conversely such a pair of near-bent functions arises from a bent function).

In [453], Ding extended Proposition 68, page 195, to near-bent functions: any n-variable Boolean function f such that $f(0_n) = 0$ is near-bent if and only if the dimension of the linear code $C_{supp(f)}$, whose generator matrix has for columns the vectors of $supp(f)$, equals n, and has weight distribution given by Table 6.3.

This provides codes with three weights.

- For n even, as also seen at page 178, *semi-bent functions* are those plateaued functions of amplitude $2^{\frac{n+2}{2}}$. The term of semi-bent has been introduced in [357], but as for n odd, these functions had been anteriorly studied under the name of three-valued almost optimal Boolean functions in [191], where it is observed that the class of such functions whose nonlinearity is at least $2^{n-1} - 2^{\frac{n}{2}}$ coincides with that of semi-bent functions. In [312], the authors show that the sum of a Boolean function g equal to the linear combination of the indicators of the elements of a spread and of a Boolean function h whose restrictions to these elements are linear is semi-bent if and only if g and h are both bent; related infinite classes are specified and a version with partial spreads is also given. Other recent works on semi-bent functions are [206, 282, 711, 855, 856, 857, 868, 876, 1131]. Up to recently, the known semi-bent functions were often quadratic or the component functions of *power functions* (see, *e.g.*, [355]). More constructions have been proposed in [376] to derive semi-bent functions from bent functions. See a survey in [859].

6.2.5 Primary constructions of plateaued Boolean functions

All quadratic Boolean functions and all bent and semi-bent Boolean functions are plateaued. We recall from [247] the other *primary constructions*. Most of them have been already presented above for constructing bent functions; they are extended here to more general plateaued functions.

Maiorana–McFarland *(MM) functions*

Any function $f_{\phi,h}(x, y) = x \cdot \phi(y) \oplus h(y)$; $\quad x \in \mathbb{F}_2^r, y \in \mathbb{F}_2^s$, is plateaued if and only if $|\sum_{y \in \phi^{-1}(a)} (-1)^{b \cdot y \oplus h(y)}|$ can take two values, one of which is 0, when $(a, b) \in \mathbb{F}_2^r \times \mathbb{F}_2^s$, since $W_{f_{\phi,h}}(a,b) = 2^r \displaystyle\sum_{y \in \phi^{-1}(a)} (-1)^{b \cdot y \oplus h(y)}$. If ϕ is injective (resp. takes exactly two times each value of $Im\,(\phi)$), then $f_{\phi,h}$ is plateaued of amplitude 2^r (resp. 2^{r+1}). Note that the *address function* (see page 68) is plateaued as observed in [692] and easily checked.

Zheng–Zhang's functions In [1173], Zheng and Zhang introduce a class of *plateaued* functions and prove that some of them are not partially-bent. These functions are defined as follows: let t and k be two integers such that $k < 2^t < 2^k$ and let $E \subseteq \mathbb{F}_2^k$ be a subset of 2^t elements such that any linear nonnull function on $\mathbb{F}_2^k$ is not constant on E. For every element e_i of E, let ξ_i denote the truth table of the linear function $x \mapsto x \cdot e_i$ on $\mathbb{F}_2^k$. Then, the Boolean function f on $\mathbb{F}_2^{k+t}$ having for the truth table the concatenation $\xi_0\xi_1 \cdots \xi_{2^t-1}$ of these truth tables is plateaued on $\mathbb{F}_2^{k+t}$ and its amplitude equals 2^k. Such a function is the concatenation of distinct linear functions. Then, as already observed in [317], it belongs to the Maiorana–McFarland class and satisfies the first hypothesis above.

Generalizations of Maiorana–McFarland functions

Concatenations of quadratic functions in Dickson form Let n and r be positive integers such that $r \le n$. As proved in [223] and recalled at page 179, the function

$$f_{\psi,\phi,g}(x,y) = \bigoplus_{i=1}^{t} x_{2i-1}x_{2i}\psi_i(y) \oplus x \cdot \phi(y) \oplus g(y)$$

$$= \bigoplus_{i=1}^{t} x_{2i-1}x_{2i}\psi_i(y) \oplus \bigoplus_{j=1}^{r} x_i\phi_i(y) \oplus g(y); \quad x \in \mathbb{F}_2^r, \ y \in \mathbb{F}_2^s,$$

where $t = \lfloor \frac{r}{2} \rfloor$, satisfies $W_{f_{\psi,\phi,g}}(a,b) =$

$$\sum_{y \in E_a} 2^{r-w(\psi(y))}(-1)^{\bigoplus_{i=1}^{t}(\phi_{2i-1}(y)\oplus a_{2i-1})(\phi_{2i}(y)\oplus a_{2i})\oplus g(y)\oplus y \cdot b},$$

where $w(\psi(y))$ denotes the Hamming weight and E_a is the superset of $\phi^{-1}(a)$ equal if r is even to

$$\left\{ y \in \mathbb{F}_2^s; \ \forall i \le t, \ \begin{array}{l} \psi_i(y) = 0 \Rightarrow \\ (\phi_{2i-1}(y) = a_{2i-1} \text{ and } \phi_{2i}(y) = a_{2i}) \end{array} \right\},$$

and if r is odd to

$$\left\{ y \in \mathbb{F}_2^s; \ \begin{array}{l} \forall i \le t, \ \psi_i(y) = 0 \Rightarrow \\ \quad (\phi_{2i-1}(y) = a_{2i-1} \text{ and } \phi_{2i}(y) = a_{2i}) \\ \phi_r(y) = a_r \end{array} \right\}.$$

As observed in [317], if E_a has size 0 or 1 (respectively 0 or 2) for every a and if ψ has constant weight, then $f_{\psi,\phi,g}$ is plateaued.

Concatenations of quadratic functions of rank 2 As seen at page 180, assuming that $\phi_2(y) \ne 0_r$ for every $y \in \mathbb{F}_2^s$ and denoting by E the set of $y \in \mathbb{F}_2^s$ such that $\phi_1(y)$ and $\phi_2(y)$

are linearly independent, function $f_{\phi_1,\phi_2,\phi_3,g}(x,y) = (x \cdot \phi_1(y))(x \cdot \phi_2(y)) \oplus x \cdot \phi_3(y) \oplus g(y)$
satisfies $W_{f_{\phi_1,\phi_2,\phi_3,g}}(a,b) =$

$$
2^{r-1} \sum_{\substack{y \in E; \\ \phi_3(y)+a \in \{0_r,\phi_1(y),\phi_2(y)\}}} (-1)^{g(y) \oplus b \cdot y} - 2^{r-1} \sum_{\substack{y \in E; \\ \phi_3(y)+a=\phi_1(y)+\phi_2(y)}} (-1)^{g(y) \oplus b \cdot y}
$$

$$
+ 2^r \sum_{\substack{y \in \mathbb{F}_2^s \setminus E; \\ \phi_3(y)+a=\phi_1(y)}} (-1)^{g(y) \oplus b \cdot y},
$$

for every $a \in \mathbb{F}_2^r$ and $b \in \mathbb{F}_2^s$. As shown in [317], if $E = \mathbb{F}_2^s$ and the two-dimensional
flats $\phi_3(y) + \langle \phi_1(y), \phi_2(y) \rangle$; $y \in \mathbb{F}_2^s$, are pairwise disjoint, then $f_{\phi_1,\phi_2,\phi_3,g}$ is plateaued of
amplitude 2^{r-1}. And assuming that $\phi_2(y)$ is nonzero for every $y \in \mathbb{F}_2^s$ and denoting by
F'_a (resp. F''_a), the set of all $y \in \mathbb{F}_2^s$ such that $\phi_1(y)$ and $\phi_2(y)$ are linearly independent
(resp. dependent) and such that a belongs to the flat $\phi_3(y) + \langle \phi_1(y), \phi_2(y) \rangle$ (resp. $a =
\phi_3(y) + \phi_1(y)$), we have that if, for every $a \in \mathbb{F}_2^r$, the number $|F'_a| + 2|F''_a|$ equals 0 or 2,
then $f_{\phi_1,\phi_2,\phi_3,g}$ is plateaued of amplitude 2^r. See a little more in [1058].

6.2.6 Secondary constructions of plateaued Boolean functions

The *direct sum* preserves plateauedness since $h(x,y) = f(x) \oplus g(y)$, $x \in \mathbb{F}_2^r, y \in \mathbb{F}_2^s$
satisfies $W_h(a,b) = W_f(a)W_g(b)$ (and we have then $nl(h) = 2^s nl(f) + 2^r nl(g) -
2nl(f)nl(g)$). The *indirect sum* does too, under some conditions:

Proposition 101 *[247] Let $h(x,y) = f_1(x) \oplus g_1(y) \oplus (f_1 \oplus f_2)(x)(g_1 \oplus g_2)(y)$, then
if f_1 and f_2 are plateaued with the same amplitude, g_1 and g_2 are plateaued with the same
amplitude, and*

- *f_1 and f_2 have the same Walsh support (i.e., the same extended Walsh spectrum),*
- *or g_1 and g_2 have the same Walsh support (idem)*
- *or f_1 and f_2 have disjoint Walsh supports and g_1 and g_2 have disjoint Walsh supports,*

then h is plateaued.

Proof We have seen already that

$$
W_h(a,b) = \frac{1}{2} W_{f_1}(a) \left[W_{g_1}(b) + W_{g_2}(b) \right] + \frac{1}{2} W_{f_2}(a) \left[W_{g_1}(b) - W_{g_2}(b) \right]. \tag{6.39}
$$

Moreover, if f_1 and f_2 have both amplitude λ, and if g_1 and g_2 have both amplitude μ, then
according to Relation (6.39), we have the following:

- If g_1 and g_2 have the same Walsh support, then $W_h(a,b) \in \{0, \pm\lambda\mu\}$ (indeed, at most
  one of the two values $W_{g_1}(b) + W_{g_2}(b)$ and $W_{g_1}(b) - W_{g_2}(b)$ is then nonzero, and this
  value equals $\pm 2\mu$).
- If f_1 and f_2 have the same Walsh support, then $W_h(a,b) \in \{0, \pm\lambda\mu\}$ (same argument,
  after exchanging the roles of the f_i's and the g_i's in (6.39)).
- If f_1 and f_2 have disjoint Walsh supports and g_1 and g_2 have disjoint Walsh supports,
  then $W_h(a,b) \in \{0, \pm\frac{\lambda\mu}{2}\}$.

Hence, h is plateaued. $\qquad \square$

In [1152], a *secondary construction* of plateaued functions (with disjoint supports) is given from three bent functions and three plateaued functions, under some conditions.

The *construction without extension of the number of variables* viewed at page 236 can be easily adapted to plateaued functions:

Proposition 102   *[247] Let f_1, f_2 and f_3 be three n-variable Boolean functions. Denote by s_1 the Boolean function $f_1 + f_2 + f_3$ and by s_2 the Boolean function $f_1 f_2 + f_1 f_3 + f_2 f_3$. We have*

$$W_{f_1} + W_{f_2} + W_{f_3} = W_{s_1} + 2 W_{s_2}.$$

Moreover,

- *If f_1, f_2, f_3, and s_1 are plateaued with the same amplitude λ and with disjoint Walsh supports, then s_2 is plateaued with amplitude $\frac{\lambda}{2}$.*
- *If f_1, f_2, f_3, and s_1 are plateaued with the same amplitude λ and with Walsh supports whose multiset equals twice some subset of $\mathbb{F}_2^n$, then s_2 is plateaued with amplitude λ.*
- *If f_1, f_2, f_3 are plateaued with the same amplitude λ and with disjoint Walsh supports, and s_2 is plateaued with amplitude $\lambda/2$ and Walsh support disjoint from those of f_1, f_2, f_3, then s_1 is plateaued with amplitude λ.*
- *If f_1, f_2, f_3 are plateaued with the same amplitude λ, s_2 is plateaued with amplitude $\lambda/2$ and the Walsh supports of f_1, f_2, f_3 and s_2 make a multiset equal to twice some subset of $\mathbb{F}_2^n$, then s_1 is plateaued with amplitude 2λ.*

6.3 Bent$_4$ and partially-bent$_4$ functions

There exist several generalizations of the notion of bent function; see, *e.g.*, [313]. We shall not address them here since we focus on Boolean functions. But bent$_4$ functions [17, 18, 529, 927, 993] are Boolean functions (whose definition is a modification of that of bent function); we need then to give the main definitions and results on them, even if their use in cryptography and coding is not so clear.[33] In even dimension, bent$_4$ functions are defined as bent functions, but with respect to a transformation called *unitary transformation* that we recall below, and which generalizes the Walsh transform. They can also be defined by the balancedness of so-called *modified derivatives*. In odd dimension, there is a one-to-one correspondence between the set of bent$_4$ functions and the set of semi-bent functions satisfying additional properties that we shall describe as well.

Definition 64   *[993, 18] Let n be any positive integer and f a Boolean function over $\mathbb{F}_{2^n}$. For any element $c \in \mathbb{F}_{2^n}$, the unitary transformation $\mathcal{V}_f^c : \mathbb{F}_{2^n} \to \mathbb{C}$ is defined as*

$$\mathcal{V}_f^c(u) = \sum_{x \in \mathbb{F}_{2^n}} (-1)^{f(x) + \sigma^c(x)} i^{tr_n(cx)} (-1)^{tr_n(ux)},$$

---

[33] The motivation given in [993] comes from the quantum domain; another motivation comes from the relation to the notion of modified planar functions; see [18], where it is proved that bent$_4$ functions describe the components of modified planar functions.

where $\sigma^c(x)$ is the Boolean function whose univariate representation equals

$$\sigma^c(x) = \sum_{0 \le i < j \le n-1} (cx)^{2^i} (cx)^{2^j}.$$

For $c = 0$, the transformation $\mathcal{V}_f^c$ is simply the well-known Walsh transform. For $c = 1$, $\mathcal{V}_f^c$ is the nega-Hadamard transform (see [927]).

In even dimension, the class of *bent$_4$* functions can be defined as follows in terms of the unitary transformation:

Definition 65 *Let n be an even integer. A Boolean function f is called a c-bent$_4$ function, for some $c \in \mathbb{F}_{2^n}$, if the unitary transformation $\mathcal{V}_f^c$ satisfies $|\mathcal{V}_f^c(u)| = 2^{n/2}$ for all $u \in \mathbb{F}_{2^n}$. A function is bent$_4$ if it is c-bent$_4$ for some $c \in \mathbb{F}_{2^n}$.*

In other words, a Boolean function is c-bent$_4$ if it has a flat spectrum with respect to at least one of the transforms $\mathcal{V}_f^c$. Note that when $c = 0$, a c-bent$_4$ function is a classical bent, and when $c = 1$, a c-bent is so-called *nega-bent*.

Proposition 103 *[18] Let n be an even integer. A Boolean function $f : \mathbb{F}_{2^n} \to \mathbb{F}_2$ is c-bent$_4$ if and only if $f \oplus \sigma^c$ is bent.*

Proof We will employ Jacobi's two-square theorem stating that for an even integer n, the integer solutions of the Diophantine equation $R^2 + I^2 = 2^n$ are $(R, I) = (0, \pm 2^{n/2})$ or $(\pm 2^{n/2}, 0)$. One has

$$\mathcal{V}_f^c(u) = \sum_{x \in \mathbb{F}_{2^n}} (-1)^{f(x) + \sigma^c(x)} i^{tr_n(cx)} (-1)^{tr_n(ux)}$$

$$= \sum_{x \in \mathbb{F}_{2^n}} (-1)^{f(x) + \sigma^c(x) + tr_n(ux)} \left(\frac{1 + (-1)^{tr_n(cx)}}{2} + i \frac{1 - (-1)^{tr_n(cx)}}{2} \right)$$

$$= \frac{W_{f \oplus \sigma^c}(u) + W_{f \oplus \sigma^c}(u + c)}{2} + i \frac{W_{f \oplus \sigma^c}(u) - W_{f \oplus \sigma^c}(u + c)}{2}$$

If f is c-bent$_4$ then $|\mathcal{V}_f^{(c)}(u)| = 2^{n/2}$, that is,

$$\left(W_{f \oplus \sigma^c}(u) + W_{f \oplus \sigma^c}(u + c) \right)^2 + \left(W_{f \oplus \sigma^c}(u) - W_{f \oplus \sigma^c}(u + c) \right)^2 = 2^{n+2}. \tag{6.40}$$

Now, by Jacobi's two-square theorem, one has $|W_{f \oplus \sigma^c}(u)| = |W_{f \oplus \sigma^c}(u + c)| = 2^{n/2}$, which proves that $f \oplus \sigma^c$ is bent. The converse of the statement comes immediately from Equation (6.40). □

Some authors call such f a *shifted bent* function (*i.e.*, f is the shifted version of the bent function $f \oplus \sigma^c$).

Remark. $\frac{W_{f \oplus \sigma^c}(u) + W_{f \oplus \sigma^c}(u+c)}{2}$ (resp. $\frac{W_{f \oplus \sigma^c}(u) - W_{f \oplus \sigma^c}(u+c)}{2}$) ranges (twice, when u ranges over $\mathbb{F}_{2^n}$) over the Walsh spectrum of the restriction of $f \oplus \sigma^c$ to the linear hyperplane of equation $tr_n(cx) = 0$ (resp. its complement) and we know from Theorem 16, page 240, that $f \oplus \sigma^c$ is bent if and only if these two restrictions are semi-bent (*i.e.*, near-bent) with complementary Walsh supports.   □

An alternative definition of a c-bent$_4$ function f can be given in relation to the so-called *modified derivative* of f. More specifically, it has been proved in [18] that f is c-bent$_4$ if and only if the modified derivative $f(x + a) \oplus f(x) \oplus tr_n(c^2ax)$ is balanced for all nonzero $a \in \mathbb{F}_{2^n}$. This corresponds to the characterization of bent functions via derivatives when $c = 0$.

Bent$_4$ functions exist also in odd dimension. More precisely, let n be an odd integer. Then a function $f : \mathbb{F}_{2^n} \to \mathbb{F}_2$ is c-bent$_4$ if and only if $f \oplus \sigma^c(x)$ is a *semi-bent function* and $|W_{f \oplus \sigma^c}(u)| \neq |W_{f \oplus \sigma^c}(u + c)|$ for all $u \in \mathbb{F}_{2^n}$.

In [17], the authors have introduced the notion of partially-bent$_4$ functions, which are functions whose modified derivative is either constant or balanced for every element of the input set. It is known that every quadratic function is partially c-bent$_4$.

6.4 Bent vectorial functions

Definition 66 *An (n, m) function is called bent if all its* component functions $v \cdot F$, $v \in \mathbb{F}_2^m \setminus \{0_m\}$ *(where "$\cdot$" is an inner product in $\mathbb{F}_2^m$), are bent Boolean functions, that is, if* $W_F^2(u, v) = 2^n$ *for every $v \in \mathbb{F}_2^m \setminus \{0_m\}$ and every $u \in \mathbb{F}_2^n$. Equivalently, all the derivatives* $D_a F$, $a \in \mathbb{F}_2^n \setminus \{0_n\}$, *are balanced.*

The equivalence between these two characteristic properties, called respectively bentness and perfect nonlinearity,[34] is a direct consequence of Theorem 12, page 192, which implies that F is bent if and only if, for every $v \in \mathbb{F}_2^m \setminus \{0_m\}$ and every $a \in \mathbb{F}_2^n \setminus \{0_n\}$, the function $v \cdot D_a F$ is balanced, and of Proposition 35, page 112, applied to $D_a F$.

Up to linear equivalence (precisely, up to the composition on the left by a linear automorphism), the knowledge of a bent (n, m)-*function* is equivalent to that of an m-dimensional $\mathbb{F}_2$-vector space of Boolean functions, all being bent except the zero one (the vector space is made of all component functions and of the zero function); from such an m-dimensional space E, we can build a bent (n, m)-function by choosing its coordinate functions as m linearly independent functions in E.

Bent vectorial functions are never balanced since their component functions are not balanced. More precisely, we saw at page 113 that their *imbalance* $Nb_F = \sum_{b \in \mathbb{F}_2^m} \left(|F^{-1}(b)| - 2^{n-m} \right)^2$ satisfies $Nb_F = \sum_{a \in \mathbb{F}_2^n} |(D_a F)^{-1}(0_m)| - 2^{2n-m} = 2^n - 2^{n-m}$ (and that $Nb_{F+L} = 2^n - 2^{n-m}$ for every linear function L). We have also seen that $NB_F = \sum_{a \in \mathbb{F}_2^n \setminus \{0_n\}} Nb_{D_a F}$ equals 0 if and only if F is bent.

The algebraic degree of any bent (n, m)-function is at most $n/2$, since this bound is true for any component function.

Remark. We have seen with Proposition 37, page 120, that it is possible, as for Boolean functions, to characterize the bentness of (n, m)-functions F by a property of the functions

---

[34] There are then (over $\mathbb{F}_2^n$) two different terminologies for the same class of functions.

$F + L$, where L is a linear (n, m)-function expressing that $F + L$ is not far from a balanced function. □

Bent vectorial functions have been initially considered by Nyberg who proved:

Proposition 104 *[906] Bent (n, m)-functions exist if and only if n is even and $m \leq \frac{n}{2}$.*

Proof It is easily seen that the condition is sufficient, thanks to the constructions of bent functions that we shall see in Subsection 6.4.1, page 270. Let us prove that it is necessary. We have seen in Relation (3.17), page 113, that, for every (n, m)-function F and any element $b \in \mathbb{F}_2^m$, the size of $F^{-1}(b)$ is equal to $2^{-m} \sum_{x \in \mathbb{F}_2^n; v \in \mathbb{F}_2^m} (-1)^{v \cdot (F(x)+b)}$. Assuming that F is bent and denoting, for every $v \in \mathbb{F}_2^n \setminus \{0_n\}$, by $\widetilde{v \cdot F}$ the dual of the bent Boolean function $x \mapsto v \cdot F(x)$, we have, by definition, $\sum_{x \in \mathbb{F}_2^n} (-1)^{v \cdot F(x)} = 2^{\frac{n}{2}} (-1)^{\widetilde{v \cdot F}(0_n)}$. The size of $F^{-1}(b)$ equals then $2^{n-m} + 2^{\frac{n}{2}-m} \sum_{v \in \mathbb{F}_2^n \setminus \{0_n\}} (-1)^{\widetilde{v \cdot F}(0_n) \oplus v \cdot b}$. Since the sum $\sum_{v \in \mathbb{F}_2^n \setminus \{0_n\}} (-1)^{\widetilde{v \cdot F}(0_n) \oplus v \cdot b}$ has an odd value ($\mathbb{F}_2^n \setminus \{0_n\}$ having an odd size), we deduce that, if $m \leq n$, then $2^{\frac{n}{2}-m}$ must be an integer. And it is also easily shown that $m > n$ is impossible. □

Remark. The situation with PN functions is different for odd characteristic, in which PN (n, n)-functions (defined similarly) do exist for every n (they are also called *planar*). A notion of planar function in characteristic 2 (stating that $x \in \mathbb{F}_{2^n} \mapsto D_a F(x) + ax$ is bijective for every $a \neq 0$) sometimes called *pseudoplanar* or *modified planar* has been proposed in [1023] (see also [963]). Such functions share many of the properties of planar functions in odd characteristic, in relation with relative difference sets and finite geometries. □

A survey on bent vectorial functions can be found in [310].

In [337] are called *dual-bent vectorial functions* the bent (n, m)-functions having the property that the duals of their component functions form, together with the zero function, a vector space of dimension m, and are then the component functions of some vectorial bent function, called a vectorial dual of F; classical classes are then studied from this viewpoint.

CCZ equivalence and EA equivalence coincide for bent functions [148, 150]: let F be a bent (n, m)-function (n even, $m \leq n/2$) and let (without loss of generality) L_1 and L_2 be two linear functions from $\mathbb{F}_2^n \times \mathbb{F}_2^m$ to (respectively) $\mathbb{F}_2^n$ and $\mathbb{F}_2^m$, such that (L_1, L_2) is a permutation of $\mathbb{F}_2^n \times \mathbb{F}_2^m$ and $F_1(x) = L_1(x, F(x))$ is a permutation of $\mathbb{F}_2^n$. For every vector v in $\mathbb{F}_2^n$, the function $v \cdot F_1$ is necessarily non-bent since, if $v = 0_m$, then it is null, and if $v \neq 0_m$, then it is balanced. Let us denote $L_1(x, y) = L'(x) + L''(y)$. We have then $F_1(x) = L'(x) + L'' \circ F(x)$. The adjoint operator L''' of L'' (satisfying by definition $v \cdot L''(y) = L'''(v) \cdot y$) is then the null function, since if $L'''(v) \neq 0_m$, then $v \cdot F_1(x) = v \cdot L'(x) \oplus L'''(v) \cdot F(x)$ is bent. This means that L'' is null and L_1 depends then only on x, which corresponds to EA equivalence.

We have seen in Proposition 104 that bent (n, m)-functions exist if and only if n is even and $m \leq n/2$. Better bounds than the *covering radius bound* are open problems for:

- n odd and $m < n$ (for $m \geq n$, the Sidelnikov–Chabaud–Vaudenay bound, and other bounds if m is large enough, are better)
- n even and $n/2 < m < n$

In [459], the authors provided a coding-theoretic characterization of bent vectorial functions and used them for the construction of a two-parameter family of binary linear codes that do not satisfy the conditions of the Assmus–Mattson theorem [36], but nevertheless hold 2-designs.

6.4.1 *Primary constructions of bent vectorial functions*

Recall that bent (n, m)-functions can exist only for n even and $m \leq n/2$, that we shall assume satisfied. The main classes of bent Boolean functions lead to classes of bent (n, m)-functions (this was first observed in [906] by Nyberg, who proposed constructions within the Maiorana–McFarland and $\mathcal{PS}_{ap}$ constructions).

Constructions in bivariate representation

The three first *primary constructions* below are by increasing order of generality. We follow [310, 313] for the description. When necessary (*i.e.*, when we need to make multiplications or divisions), we endow $\mathbb{F}_2^{\frac{n}{2}}$ with the structure of the field $\mathbb{F}_{2^{\frac{n}{2}}}$ and we identify $\mathbb{F}_2^n$ with $\mathbb{F}_{2^{\frac{n}{2}}} \times \mathbb{F}_{2^{\frac{n}{2}}}$.

- Bent (n, m)-functions in the strict class of Maiorana–McFarland are defined as $F(x, y) = L(x\,\pi(y)) + G(y)$, $x, y \in \mathbb{F}_{2^{n/2}}$, where π is a permutation of $\mathbb{F}_{2^{n/2}}$, $L : \mathbb{F}_{2^{n/2}} \mapsto \mathbb{F}_2^m$ is linear surjective, and G is any $(n/2, m)$-function. An example is given in [1018] (which achieves optimal algebraic degree $n/2$): the i-th coordinate of this function is defined as $f_i(x, y) = tr_{\frac{n}{2}}(x\,\phi_i(y)) \oplus g_i(y)$, $x, y \in \mathbb{F}_{2^{\frac{n}{2}}}$, where g_i is any Boolean function on $\mathbb{F}_{2^{\frac{n}{2}}}$ and where $\phi_i(y) = \begin{cases} 0 \text{ if } y = 0 \\ \alpha^{dec(y)+i-1} \text{ otherwise} \end{cases}$, where α is a primitive element of $\mathbb{F}_{2^{\frac{n}{2}}}$ and $dec(y) = 2^{\frac{n}{2}-1}y_1 + 2^{\frac{n}{2}-2}y_2 + \cdots + y_{\frac{n}{2}}$. This function belongs to the strict Maiorana–McFarland class because the mapping $y \to \begin{cases} 0 \text{ if } y = 0 \\ \alpha^{dec(y)} \text{ otherwise} \end{cases}$ is a permutation from $\mathbb{F}_2^{\frac{n}{2}}$ to $\mathbb{F}_{2^{\frac{n}{2}}}$, and the function $L : x \in \mathbb{F}_{2^{\frac{n}{2}}} \to (tr_{\frac{n}{2}}(x), tr_{\frac{n}{2}}(\alpha x), \ldots, tr_{\frac{n}{2}}(\alpha^{\frac{n}{2}-1}x)) \in \mathbb{F}_2^{\frac{n}{2}}$ is an isomorphism.
- Bent (n, m)-functions in the extended class of Maiorana–McFarland are defined as $F(x, y) = \psi(x, y) + G(y)$, where G is any $(n/2, m)$-function and ψ is such that, for all $y \in \mathbb{F}_{2^{n/2}}$, the function $x \mapsto \psi(x, y)$ is linear and for all $x \in \mathbb{F}_{2^{n/2}} \setminus \{0\}$, the function $y \mapsto \psi(x, y)$ is balanced.
- Bent (n, m)-functions in the general class of Maiorana–McFarland are defined such that, for all $v \in \mathbb{F}_{2^m}^*$, function $v \cdot F$ belongs, up to affine equivalence, to the Maiorana–McFarland class of Boolean bent functions. Some bent quadratic functions, elements of the general class, may not belong to the strict class are open problems.
- Modifications of the Maiorana–McFarland bent functions have been proposed in [909], using the classes $\mathcal{C}$ and $\mathcal{D}$ of bent Boolean functions.

- Bent (n,m)-functions in the $\mathcal{PS}_{ap}$ class of vectorial functions are defined as $F(x,y) = G(xy^{2^n-2}) = G\left(\frac{x}{y}\right)$, with the convention $1/0 = 0$, where G is a balanced $(n/2,m)$-function. These functions are hyper-bent in the sense that their component functions are hyper-bent. In [804], the authors give their expression in the *polar representation* that we saw at page 168.

- Bent $(n+n',m)$-functions (where n' is also even) can be defined in the form $F(x,y) = K(\frac{x}{y},\frac{z}{t})$, where K is a $(\frac{n+n'}{2},m)$-function such that, for all $x \in \mathbb{F}_{2^{n/2}}$, the function $y \in \mathbb{F}_{2^{n'/2}} \mapsto K(x,y)$ is balanced and for all $y \in \mathbb{F}_{2^{n'/2}}$, the function $x \in \mathbb{F}_{2^{n/2}} \mapsto K(x,y)$ is balanced.

- Bent $(n,n/2)$-functions from class $\mathcal{H}$ of bent Boolean functions (see page 218) are defined as: $F(x,y) = xG(yx^{2^{n/2}-2})$, where G is an o-polynomial on $\mathbb{F}_{2^{n/2}}$; see [862]. A version in univariate form can be found in [479]; see also [310].

- Bent (n,m)-functions are built from m-dimensional vector spaces of functions whose nonzero elements are all bent. Examples are $(n,2)$-functions derived from the Kerdock codes; see [310]. Another example (found by the author in common with G. Leander) takes $n \equiv 2 \pmod 4$; then $\mathbb{F}_{2^{\frac{n}{2}}}$ consists of cubes only (since $\gcd(3, 2^{\frac{n}{2}} - 1) = 1$). If $w \in \mathbb{F}_{2^n}$ is not a cube, then all the nonzero elements of the vector space $E = w\mathbb{F}_{2^{\frac{n}{2}}}$ are noncubes. Then if $F(z) = z^d$, where $d = 2^i + 1$ (Gold exponent) or $2^{2i} - 2^i + 1$ (Kasami exponent) and $\gcd(n,i) = 1$, all the functions $tr_n(vF(z))$, where $v \in E^*$, are bent. This leads to the bent $(n,\frac{n}{2})$-functions $z \in \mathbb{F}_{2^n} \to (tr_n(\beta_1 wz^d), \ldots, tr_n(\beta_{\frac{n}{2}} wz^d)) \in \mathbb{F}_2^{\frac{n}{2}}$, where $(\beta_1, \ldots, \beta_{\frac{n}{2}})$ is a basis of $\mathbb{F}_{2^{\frac{n}{2}}}$ over $\mathbb{F}_2$. To make such function valued in $\mathbb{F}_{2^{\frac{n}{2}}}$, we choose a basis $(\alpha_1, \ldots, \alpha_{\frac{n}{2}})$ of $\mathbb{F}_{2^{\frac{n}{2}}}$ orthogonal to $(\beta_1, \ldots, \beta_{\frac{n}{2}})$, that is, such that $tr_{\frac{n}{2}}(\alpha_i \beta_j) = \delta_{i,j}$ (the Kronecker symbol). For every $y \in \mathbb{F}_{2^{\frac{n}{2}}}$, we have then $y = \sum_{j=1}^{\frac{n}{2}} \alpha_j tr_{\frac{n}{2}}(\beta_j y)$. The image of every $z \in \mathbb{F}_{2^n}$ by the function equals $\sum_{j=1}^{\frac{n}{2}} \alpha_j tr_n(\beta_j wz^d) = \sum_{j=1}^{\frac{n}{2}} \alpha_j tr_{\frac{n}{2}}(\beta_j(wz^d + (wz^d)^{2^{\frac{n}{2}}})) = wz^d + (wz^d)^{2^{\frac{n}{2}}}$. In the case of the Gold exponent, it can be made a function from $\mathbb{F}_{2^{\frac{n}{2}}} \times \mathbb{F}_{2^{\frac{n}{2}}}$ to $\mathbb{F}_{2^{\frac{n}{2}}}$: we express z in the form $x + wy$, where $x,y \in \mathbb{F}_{2^{\frac{n}{2}}}$ and if n is not a multiple of 3, we can take w primitive in $\mathbb{F}_4$ (otherwise, all elements of $\mathbb{F}_4$ are cubes and we have then to take w outside $\mathbb{F}_4$), for which we have then $w^2 = w + 1$, $w^{2^i} = w^2$ (since i is necessarily odd) and $w^{2^i+1} = w^3 = 1$. We have then $z^d = x^{2^i+1} + wx^{2^i}y + w^2xy^{2^i} + y^{2^i+1}$ and $wz^d + (wz^d)^{2^{\frac{n}{2}}} = (w+w^2)x^{2^i+1} + (w^2+w)x^{2^i}y + (w^3+w^3)xy^{2^i} + (w+w^2)y^{2^i+1} = x^{2^i+1} + x^{2^i}y + y^{2^i+1}$. We can extend the construction to $\gcd(i,n) \neq 1$; the exact condition is that $\frac{n}{\gcd(i,n)}$ is even and $v \notin \{x^d, x \in \mathbb{F}_{2^n}\}$.

Constructions of bent vectorial functions in univariate representation

The bent (n,m)-functions built from m-dimensional vector spaces of functions above provide first examples, like $tr_{n/2}^n(wx^d)$, where w is not a cube and $d = 2^i + 1$ or $4^i - 2^i + 1$, $\gcd(i,n) = 1$. The other functions above, which are defined in bivariate representation (over $\mathbb{F}_{2^{\frac{n}{2}}} \times \mathbb{F}_{2^{\frac{n}{2}}}$ and valued in $\mathbb{F}_{2^{\frac{n}{2}}}$), can be seen in univariate representation, from $\mathbb{F}_{2^n}$ to itself. If $n/2$ is odd, this is quite easy: we have then $\mathbb{F}_{2^{\frac{n}{2}}} \cap \mathbb{F}_4 = \mathbb{F}_2$ and we can choose the basis $(1,w)$ of the two-dimensional vector space $\mathbb{F}_{2^n}$ over $\mathbb{F}_{2^{\frac{n}{2}}}$, where w is a primitive element of $\mathbb{F}_4$. Then $w^2 = w + 1$ and $w^{2^{\frac{n}{2}}} = w^2$ since $n/2$ is odd. A general element of $\mathbb{F}_{2^n}$

has the form $z = x + wy$, where $x, y \in \mathbb{F}_{2^{\frac{n}{2}}}$ and we have $z^{2^{\frac{n}{2}}} = x + w^2 y = z + y$ and therefore $y = z + z^{2^{\frac{n}{2}}}$, and $x = z^{2^{\frac{n}{2}}} + w^2 y = w^2 z + w z^{2^{\frac{n}{2}}}$. For instance, the univariate representation of the simplest Maiorana–McFarland function, that is, the function $(x, y) \to xy$, is $(z + z^{2^{\frac{n}{2}}})(w^2 z + w z^{2^{\frac{n}{2}}})$, that is, up to linear terms: $z^{1+2^{\frac{n}{2}}}$.

We describe now the constructions that are given directly in univariate form.

In [935], the authors observed that if $tr_n(ax^d)$ is a bent Boolean function and x^d permutes $\mathbb{F}_{2^m}$ for some divisor m of $n \geq 4$, then $tr_m^n(ax^d)$ is bent (the double condition is necessary if $m = n/2$; see [1133]); more is obtained in [892] for multiple trace term functions with Dillon-like exponents. In [483, 935, 1064], the authors studied (further) bent vectorial functions of the form $tr_{n/2}^n(ax^d)$. All functions $tr_m^n(ax^d)$ where m divides n are addressed in the recent paper [1133], where it is proved that if $m \mid n$ and $\gcd\left(2^m - 1, \frac{2^n-1}{2^m-1}\right) = 1$, and if the (n, m)-function $tr_m^n(ax^d)$ is bent, then $\gcd\left(d, \frac{2^n-1}{2^m-1}\right) \neq 1$. Characterizations are given when d is a Gold $2^i + 1$ (with any i), a Kasami $2^{2i} - 2^i + 1$ (idem), a Leander $(2^{n/4} + 1)^2$, a Canteaut–Charpin–Khyureghyan $2^{n/3} + 2^{n/6} + 1$, and a Dillon $j \cdot (2^{\frac{n}{2}} - 1)$ exponent (with precisions and corrections of errors from previous papers) as well as functions with multiple terms with Niho and Dillon exponents. The authors of [483] also propose a method to construct bent vectorial functions based on $\mathcal{PS}^-$ and $\mathcal{PS}^+$ bent functions. In [892], the authors derive three necessary and sufficient conditions for a function of the form $F(x) = tr_{n/2}^n(\sum_{i=1}^r a_i x^{r_i(2^{n/2}-1)})$ to be bent. The first characterization is a direct consequence of a result in [854]. The second characterization provides an interesting link between the bentness of F and its evaluation on the cyclic group U. The third characterization is stated in terms of the evaluation of certain elementary symmetric polynomials, and can be transformed into some explicit conditions regarding the choice of some coefficients. In [961], the authors studied the quadratic vectorial functions of the form $F(x) = tr_{n/2}^n(ax^{2^i}(x^{2^j} + (x^{2^j})^{2^{n/2}}))$, where $n \geq 4$ is even and $a \notin \mathbb{F}_{2^{n/2}}$, which are all bent.

The existence, and the constructions in case of existence, of bent vectorial functions of the form $tr_{n/2}^n(P(x))$ where $P(x) \in \mathbb{F}_{2^n}[x]$ has been studied on the basis of known Boolean bent functions of the form $tr_n(P(x))$. For instance, the nonexistence of some bent vectorial functions with binomial trace representation in $\mathcal{PS}^-$ has been proved in [930, 931]: for $n \equiv 0 \pmod 4$, there is no bent vectorial function of the form $F(x) = tr_{n/2}^n(x^{2^{n/2}-1} + ax^{r(2^{n/2}-1)})$, where $1 \leq r \leq 2^{n/2}$ and $a \in \mathbb{F}_{2^n}$.

We have seen at pages 30 and 269 that CCZ equivalence on bent functions coincides with EA equivalence and then does not provide new (bent) functions. However, applied to nonbent functions, it can give functions having some bent components and lead to bent vectorial functions with less output bits (but possibly larger algebraic degree). Examples like $F(x) = x^{2^i+1} + (x^{2^i} + x + 1)tr_n(x^{2^i+1})$, for $n \geq 6$ even, and $F(x) = \left(x + tr_3^n(x^{2(2^i+1)} + x^{4(2^i+1)}) + tr_n(x)tr_3^n(x^{2^i+1} + x^{2^{2i}(2^i+1)})\right)^{2^i+1}$, where $6 \mid n$ and in both cases $\frac{n}{\gcd(i,n)}$ even, are given in [150] (deduced from functions in [163]). Ideas for deriving bent vectorial functions from AB functions are given in [248, Subsection 4.3].

In [1143], Youssef and Gong have extended the notion of *hyper-bent function* to vectorial functions: such F is called hyper-bent if all its *component functions* are hyper-bent. Muratović-Ribić et al. [893] have characterized a class of vectorial hyper-bent functions of the form $F(x) = tr_{n/2}^n(\sum_{i=0}^{2^{n/2}} a_i x^{i(2^{n/2}-1)})$ from the class $\mathcal{PS}_{ap}$, and determined the number of such hyper-bent functions.

6.4.2 Secondary constructions of bent vectorial functions

Given any bent (n,m)-function F, any chopped function obtained by deleting some coordinates of F (or more generally by composing it on the left with any surjective affine mapping) is obviously still bent. But there exist other more useful *secondary constructions* (that is, constructions of new bent functions from known ones). The secondary construction of Boolean bent functions of Proposition 79, page 211, generalizes directly to vectorial functions [234]:

Proposition 105 *Let r and s be two positive integers with the same parity and such that $r \leq s/3$. Let ψ be any (balanced) mapping from $\mathbb{F}_2^s$ to $\mathbb{F}_{2^r}$ such that, for every $a \in \mathbb{F}_{2^r}$, the set $\psi^{-1}(a)$ is an $(s-r)$-dimensional affine subspace of $\mathbb{F}_2^s$. Let H be any (s,r)-function whose restriction to $\psi^{-1}(a)$ (viewed as an $(s-r,r)$-function via an affine isomorphism between $\psi^{-1}(a)$ and $\mathbb{F}_2^{s-r}$) is bent for every $a \in \mathbb{F}_{2^r}$. Then the function $F_{\psi,H}(x,y) = x\psi(y) + H(y)$, $x \in \mathbb{F}_{2^r}$, $y \in \mathbb{F}_2^s$, is a bent function from $\mathbb{F}_2^{r+s}$ to $\mathbb{F}_{2^r}$.*

Indeed, taking $x \cdot y = tr_r(xy)$ for inner product in $\mathbb{F}_{2^r}$, for every $v \in \mathbb{F}_{2^r}^*$, the function $tr_r(v F_{\psi,H}(x,y))$ is bent, according to Proposition 79, with $\phi(y) = v\psi(y)$ and $g(y) = tr_r(v H(y))$ (the more restrictive condition $r \leq s/3$ is meant so that $r \leq \frac{s-r}{2}$, which is necessary, according to Proposition 104, for allowing the restrictions of H to be bent). The condition on ψ being easily satisfied,[35] it is then a simple matter to choose H. Hence, this construction is quite effective (but only for designing bent (n,m)-functions such that $m \leq n/4$, since $r \leq s/3$ is equivalent to $r \leq \frac{r+s}{4}$).

The construction of Theorem 15, page 234, can also be adapted to vectorial functions as follows [234]:

Proposition 106 *Let r and s be two positive even integers and m a positive integer such that $m \leq r/2$. Let H be a function from $\mathbb{F}_2^n = \mathbb{F}_2^r \times \mathbb{F}_2^s$ to $\mathbb{F}_2^m$. Assume that, for every $y \in \mathbb{F}_2^s$, the function $H_y : x \in \mathbb{F}_2^r \to H(x,y)$ is a bent (r,m)-function. For every nonzero $v \in \mathbb{F}_2^m$ and every $a \in \mathbb{F}_2^r$ and $y \in \mathbb{F}_2^s$, let us denote by $f_{a,v}(y)$ the value at a of the dual of the Boolean function $v \cdot H_y$, defined by $\sum_{x\in\mathbb{F}_2^r}(-1)^{v\cdot H(x,y)\oplus a\cdot x} = 2^{r/2}(-1)^{f_{a,v}(y)}$. Then H is bent if and only if, for every nonzero $v \in \mathbb{F}_2^m$ and every $a \in \mathbb{F}_2^r$, the Boolean function $f_{a,v}$ is bent.*

Indeed, we have, for every nonzero $v \in \mathbb{F}_2^m$ and every $a \in \mathbb{F}_2^r$ and $b \in \mathbb{F}_2^s$:

$$\sum_{\substack{x\in\mathbb{F}_2^r \\ y\in\mathbb{F}_2^s}}(-1)^{v\cdot H(x,y)\oplus a\cdot x\oplus b\cdot y} = 2^{r/2}\sum_{y\in\mathbb{F}_2^s}(-1)^{f_{a,v}(y)\oplus b\cdot y}.$$

---

[35] Note that it does not make ψ necessarily affine.

An example of application of Proposition 106 is when we choose every H_y in the Maiorana–McFarland's class: $H_y(x, x') = x \pi_y(x') + G_y(x')$, $x, x' \in \mathbb{F}_{2^{r/2}}$, where π_y is bijective for every $y \in \mathbb{F}_2^s$. According to the results on the duals of Maiorana–McFarland's functions, for every $v \in \mathbb{F}_{2^{r/2}}^*$ and every $a, a' \in \mathbb{F}_{2^{r/2}}$, we have then $f_{(a,a'),v}(y) = tr_{\frac{r}{2}}\left(a' \pi_y^{-1}\left(\frac{a}{v}\right) + v G_y\left(\pi_y^{-1}\left(\frac{a}{v}\right)\right)\right)$, where $tr_{\frac{r}{2}}$ is the trace function from $\mathbb{F}_{2^{r/2}}$ to $\mathbb{F}_2$. Then H is bent if and only if, for every $v \in \mathbb{F}_{2^{r/2}}^*$ and every $a, a' \in \mathbb{F}_{2^{r/2}}$, the function $y \to tr_{\frac{r}{2}}\left(a' \pi_y^{-1}(a) + v G_y(\pi_y^{-1}(a))\right)$ is bent on $\mathbb{F}_2^s$. A simple possibility for achieving this is for $s = r/2$ to choose π_y^{-1} such that, for every a, the mapping $y \to \pi_y^{-1}(a)$ is an affine automorphism of $\mathbb{F}_{2^{r/2}}$ (e.g., $\pi_y^{-1}(a) = \pi_y(a) = a + y$) and to choose G_y such that, for every a, the function $y \to G_y(a)$ is bent.

An obvious corollary of Proposition 106 is that the so-called *direct sum of bent functions* gives bent functions: we define $H(x, y) = F(x) + G(y)$, where F is any bent (r, m)-function and G any bent (s, m)-function, and we have then $f_{a,v}(y) = \widetilde{v \cdot F}(a) \oplus v \cdot G(y)$, which is a bent Boolean function for every a and every $v \neq 0_m$. Hence, H is bent.

Remark. Identifying $\mathbb{F}_2^m$ with $\mathbb{F}_{2^m}$ and defining $H(x, y) = F_1(x) + G_1(y) + (F_1(x) + F_2(x))(G_1(y) + G_2(y))$, a component function $v \cdot H_y(x) = tr_m(v F_1(x)) + tr_m(v G_1(y)) + tr_m(v (F_1(x) + F_2(x))(G_1(y) + G_2(y)))$ does not enter, in general, in the framework of Proposition 83 nor of Proposition 106. Note that the function $f_{a,v}$ exists under the sufficient condition that, for every nonzero ordered pair $(v, w) \in \mathbb{F}_{2^m} \times \mathbb{F}_{2^m}$, the function $tr_m(v F_1(x)) + tr_m(w F_2(x))$ is bent (which is equivalent to saying that the $(r, 2m)$-function (F_1, F_2) is bent).

There are particular cases where the construction works, as shown in [310]: let F_1 and F_2 be two bent (n, r)-functions and $G = (g_1, \dots, g_{r+1})$ an $(m, r + 1)$-function such that for every nonzero v in $\mathbb{F}_2^{r+1}$ different from $(1, 0, \dots, 0)$, the component function $v \cdot G$ is bent, then the function $H(x, y) = F_1(x) + G_1(y) + g_1(y)(F_1(x) + F_2(x))$, where G_1 is the (m, r)-function $(g_2, \dots, g_{r+1})$, is a bent $(n + m, r)$-function. This indirect sum has been generalized in [310]. □

Remark. In [18], bent$_4$ functions have been extended to *vectorial bent$_4$ functions* (over finite fields), which correspond to relative difference sets in certain groups. The authors have provided conditions under which Maiorana–McFarland functions are bent$_4$. □

6.5 Plateaued vectorial functions

There exist three notions of plateauedness for vectorial functions:

Definition 67   *An (n, m)-function is called* strongly plateaued *if all its component functions $v \cdot F$; $v \in \mathbb{F}_2^m$, $v \neq 0_m$, where "·" is an inner product in $\mathbb{F}_2^m$, are partially-bent (see Definition 62, page 256).*

An (n, m)-function is called plateaued with single amplitude *if all its component functions are plateaued with the same amplitude (see Definition 63, page 258).*

An (n, m)-function is called plateaued *if all its component functions are plateaued, with possibly different amplitudes.*

The reason why the first notion is called strongly plateaued will be made clear with Corollary 18 below. The two first notions are independent in the sense that none is a particular case of the other (there exist indeed strongly plateaued vectorial functions with different amplitudes and plateaued functions with single amplitude that are not strongly plateaued). Both are a particular case of the third. Quadratic functions (which are all strongly plateaued) can have components with different amplitudes (this is the case for instance of the Gold functions x^{2^i+1}, $gcd(i, n) = 1$, for n even). They can also have single amplitude (this is the case of Gold functions for n odd). Of course, the two definitions of plateaued functions and of plateaued with single amplitude functions coincide for Boolean functions.

Note that, since the Walsh transform values of plateaued (n, m)-functions are divisible by $2^{\lceil \frac{n}{2} \rceil}$ and the Walsh transform of F equals the Fourier transform of the *indicator* $1_{\mathcal{G}_F}$ of its graph $\mathcal{G}_F$, the algebraic degree of $1_{\mathcal{G}_F}$ is at most $n + m - \lceil \frac{n}{2} \rceil = \lfloor \frac{n}{2} \rfloor + m$, according to Theorem 2, page 63. Applying Relation (2.7), page 40, we have then that, for every subset J of $\{1, \ldots, m\}$, we have $d_{alg}\left(\prod_{j \in \{1,\ldots,m\} \setminus J}(f_j \oplus 1) \right) \leq \lfloor \frac{n}{2} \rfloor + m - |J|$, where the f_j are the coordinate functions of F. And if F is plateaued with single amplitude 2^r, then we have $d_{alg}\left(\prod_{j \in \{1,\ldots,m\} \setminus J}(f_j \oplus 1) \right) \leq n + m - r - |J|$. This gives much more information than the single inequality $d_{alg}(F) \leq \lfloor \frac{n}{2} \rfloor + 1$ (resp. $\leq n - r + 1$) provided by Proposition 96, page 259.

It has been proved in [174] that, when n is a power of 2, no power plateaued (n, n)-permutation exists[36] and in [835] that, when n is divisible by 4, no such function exists with the Walsh spectrum $\{0, \pm 2^{\frac{n}{2}+1}\}$.

The set of plateaued vectorial functions with single amplitude is *CCZ invariant*: if the graphs $\{(x, F(x)); \; x \in \mathbb{F}_2^n\}$ and $\{(x, G(x)); \; x \in \mathbb{F}_2^n\}$ of two (n, m)-functions F, G correspond to each other by an affine permutation of $\mathbb{F}_2^n \times \mathbb{F}_2^m$, then one is plateaued with single amplitude if and only if the other is. The larger set of plateaued vectorial functions is (only) *EA invariant*: it is indeed invariant under composition on the right by affine automorphisms and under addition of an affine function, and it is also invariant under composition on the left by a linear automorphism L since $W_{L \circ F}(u, v) = W_F(L^*(v), u)$, where L^* is the adjoint operator of L.

6.5.1 Characterizations of plateaued vectorial functions

The characterization of plateaued Boolean functions by Proposition 97, page 260, has been generalized to vectorial functions for each notion, by means of the value distributions of their *derivatives*. This allowed one to derive several characterizations of APN functions in this framework. Characterizations of plateaued vectorial functions have been also obtained by means of their autocorrelation functions and of the power moments of their Walsh transforms. We survey below all these results from [247].

---

[36] A conjecture by T. Helleseth states that there is no power permutation having three Walsh transform values when n is a power of 2.

Characterization by means of the derivatives

Applying Proposition 97, page 260, an (n, m)-function F is plateaued if and only if, for every $v \in \mathbb{F}_2^m$, the expression $\sum_{a,b \in \mathbb{F}_2^n} (-1)^{v \cdot D_a D_b F(x)}$ does not depend on $x \in \mathbb{F}_2^n$ and F is plateaued with single amplitude if and only if this sum does not depend on x nor on $v \neq 0_m$.

Theorem 18 *[247] Let F be an (n, m)-function. Then:*

- *F is plateaued if and only if, for every $w \in \mathbb{F}_2^m$, the size of the set*

$$\{(a, b) \in (\mathbb{F}_2^n)^2 \, ; \, D_a D_b F(x) = w\} \tag{6.41}$$

 does not depend on $x \in \mathbb{F}_2^n$ (in other words, the value distribution of $D_a D_b F(x)$ when (a, b) ranges over $(\mathbb{F}_2^n)^2$ is independent of $x \in \mathbb{F}_2^n$).
- *F is plateaued with single amplitude if and only if the size of the set in (6.41) does not depend on $x \in \mathbb{F}_2^n$, nor on $w \in \mathbb{F}_2^m$ when $w \neq 0_m$.*

Moreover:

- *For every (n, m)-function F, the value distribution of $D_a D_b F(x)$ when (a, b) ranges over $(\mathbb{F}_2^n)^2$ equals the value distribution of $D_a F(b) + D_a F(x)$.*
- *If two plateaued functions F, G have the same such distribution, then for every v, their component functions $v \cdot F$ and $v \cdot G$ have the same amplitude.*

Proof Recall that any two integer-valued functions over $\mathbb{F}_2^n$ are equal if and only if their Fourier transforms are equal, and that any integer-valued function is constant except at 0_n if and only if its Fourier transform is constant except at 0_n as well. Applying this to the functions $v \mapsto \sum_{a,b \in \mathbb{F}_2^n} (-1)^{v \cdot D_a D_b F(x)}$ for different values of x, we deduce that F is plateaued if and only if, for every $w \in \mathbb{F}_2^m$, the sum $\displaystyle\sum_{v \in \mathbb{F}_2^m} \sum_{a,b \in \mathbb{F}_2^n} (-1)^{v \cdot D_a D_b F(x) \oplus v \cdot w}$, which is equal to $\displaystyle\sum_{a,b \in \mathbb{F}_2^n} \sum_{v \in \mathbb{F}_2^m} (-1)^{v \cdot (D_a D_b F(x) + w)} = 2^m |\{(a, b) \in (\mathbb{F}_2^n)^2 \, ; \, D_a D_b F(x) = w\}|$, does not depend on $x \in \mathbb{F}_2^n$, and F is plateaued with single amplitude if and only if this size does not depend on x nor on $w \neq 0_m$. This proves the first part.

By the change of variable $b \mapsto b + x$, we have that $|\{(a, b) \in (\mathbb{F}_2^n)^2 \, ; \, D_a D_b F(x) = w\}|$ equals $|\{(a, b) \in (\mathbb{F}_2^n)^2 \, ; \, D_a D_{b+x} F(x) = w\}|$, that is, $|\{(a, b) \in (\mathbb{F}_2^n)^2 \, ; \, F(x) + F(x + a) + F(b) + F(b + a) = w\}|$. This proves the first item of the second part.

The last item is a direct consequence of the fact that, for a plateaued function F, the sum $\sum_{a,b \in \mathbb{F}_2^n} (-1)^{v \cdot D_a D_b F(x)}$ equals the square of the amplitude of $v \cdot F$. $\square$

It is observed in [194, 196] that $|\{(a, b, x) \in (\mathbb{F}_2^n)^3 \, ; \, D_a D_b F(x) = 0_n, a \neq 0_n, b \neq 0_n, a \neq b\}| \leq (2^n - 1)(\max_{u, v \in \mathbb{F}_2^n, v \neq 0_n} W_F(u, v)^2 - 2^{n+1})$, for every (n, n)-function F, with equality if and only if F is plateaued with single amplitude.

Note that the algebraic degree $d = 2$ (for which the first item of Theorem 18 is straightforwardly satisfied since the second-order derivatives are then constant) is the only one for which all functions of algebraic degree at most d are plateaued, since we know that cubic Boolean functions can have values of the Walsh transform at 0_n different from 0 and from powers of 2 (see Section 5.3, page 180), and therefore be nonplateaued.

Examples

1. Almost bent (AB) functions (see Definition 31, page 119), are an example of plateaued functions with single amplitude. The distribution of values of the second-order derivatives in Relation (6.41) is as follows: the equation $D_a D_b F(x) = w$ has $3 \cdot 2^n - 2$ solutions (a, b) for any x if $w = 0_n$ and $2^n - 2$ solutions if $w = 0_n$ (see Corollary 27, page 377). Conversely, any function having this property is AB.

2. Let n now be even and $F(x) = x^{2^i+1}$ be a Gold APN function, $(i, n) = 1$. We have $D_a D_b F(x) = a^{2^i} b + a b^{2^i}$. The number of solutions (a, b) of $D_a D_b F(x) = 0$ equals again $3 \cdot 2^n - 2$ (as for any APN function), and for $w \neq 0$ the number of solutions (a, b) of $D_a D_b F(x) = w$ is constant when w ranges over a coset of the multiplicative group of all cubes in $\mathbb{F}_{2^n}^*$, since for every $\lambda \in \mathbb{F}_{2^n}^*$, $(\lambda a)^{2^i} (\lambda b) + (\lambda a)(\lambda b)^{2^i} = \lambda^{2^i+1} (a^{2^i} b + a b^{2^i})$ and $\lambda \mapsto \lambda^{2^i+1}$ is three-to-one over $\mathbb{F}_{2^n}^*$ and has the group of cubes for range. This allows taking $w = 1$ without loss of generality when w is a cube, and $a^{2^i} b + a b^{2^i} = 1$ is equivalent when $b \neq 0$ to $\left(\frac{a}{b}\right)^{2^i} + \frac{a}{b} = \frac{1}{b^{2^i+1}}$ and has two solutions a for every b such that $\frac{1}{b^{2^i+1}}$ has null trace (and none otherwise). The number of such nonzero b equals $2^{n-1} \pm 2^{\frac{n}{2}} - 1$ since $f(x) = tr_n(x^{2^i+1})$ has the same Hamming weight as $tr_n(x^3)$, which is $2^{n-1} \pm 2^{\frac{n}{2}}$ according to Carlitz' result recalled at page 177. When w is not a cube, $a^{2^i} b + a b^{2^i} = w$ is equivalent when $b \neq 0$ to $\left(\frac{a}{b}\right)^{2^i} + \frac{a}{b} = \frac{w}{b^{2^i+1}}$ and has two solutions a for every b such that $\frac{w}{b^{2^i+1}}$ has null trace. The number of such nonzero b equals $2^{n-1} \pm 2^{\frac{n}{2}-1} - 1$ since $tr_n(w b^{2^i+1})$ is bent (see page 206). Hence the number of solutions (a, b) of $D_a D_b F(x) = w$ equals

$$\begin{cases} 3 \cdot 2^n - 2 & \text{for } w = 0, \\ 2^n \pm 2^{\frac{n}{2}+1} - 2 & \text{for } w \text{ a nonzero cube } (\frac{2^n-1}{3} \text{ cases}) \\ 2^n \pm 2^{\frac{n}{2}} - 2 & \text{for } w \text{ a non-cube } (2 \cdot \frac{2^n-1}{3} \text{ cases}), \end{cases}$$

where, among the two "$\pm$" above, one is a "+" and one is a "−." We shall see below that the Kasami APN functions (see page 400) have the same distribution.

3. The case of functions $F(x, y) = (x\pi(y) + \phi(y), x(\pi(y))^{2^i} + \psi(y))$ (which are plateaued (n, n)-functions when π is a permutation, as we shall see in Proposition 115, page 282) is studied in [247]. $\square$

A particular case where the condition of Theorem 18 is satisfied is when, for each fixed value of a, the value distribution of the function $b \mapsto D_a D_b F(x)$ is independent of x. It is easily seen, as in the proof of Theorem 18, that an (n, m)-function F has this property if and only if all of its component functions have it, and that, for every Boolean function f, the size, for every $a \in \mathbb{F}_2^n, w \in \mathbb{F}_2$, of the set $\{b \in \mathbb{F}_2^n ; D_a f(b) = D_a f(x) + w\}$ does not depend on x if and only if the derivatives of f are either constant or balanced, that is, f is partially-bent. The condition is indeed sufficient, and it is necessary because if $D_a f$ is not constant, then it means that $\{b \in \mathbb{F}_2^n ; D_a f(b) = 0\}| = \{b \in \mathbb{F}_2^n ; D_a f(b) = 1\}$. Hence:

Corollary 18   *[247] A vectorial function F is strongly plateaued if and only if, for every a in $\mathbb{F}_2^n$ and every w, the size of the set $\{b \in \mathbb{F}_2^n \,;\, D_a D_b F(x) = w\}$ does not depend on $x \in \mathbb{F}_2^n$, or equivalently the size of the set $\{b \in \mathbb{F}_2^n \,;\, D_a F(b) = D_a F(x) + w\}$ does not depend on $x \in \mathbb{F}_2^n$.*

Proposition 107   *[247] For every strongly plateaued (n, m)-function F, the image set $Im(D_a F) = (D_a F)(\mathbb{F}_2^n)$ of any derivative $D_a F$ is an affine space.*

Proof   By hypothesis, every derivative $D_a F$ of F matches the same number of times any two values $D_a F(x) + w$ and $D_a F(y) + w$. Hence, it matches at least once $D_a F(x) + w$ (i.e., we have $w \in D_a F(x) + Im(D_a F)$) if and only if it matches at least once $D_a F(y) + w$ (i.e., we have $w \in D_a F(y) + Im(D_a F)$). Hence, the set $Im(D_a F)$ is invariant under translation by any element of $Im(D_a F) + Im(D_a F)$ and is then an affine space.   □

Crooked functions   According to Proposition 107, if F is a *strongly plateaued* APN (n, n)-function, then it is a so-called *crooked* function, in the sense[37] of [80, 727, 729]:

Definition 68   *An (n, n)-function F is called crooked if, for every nonzero a, the set $\{D_a F(x); x \in \mathbb{F}_2^n\}$ is an affine hyperplane (i.e., a linear hyperplane or its complement).*

Conversely, crooked functions are strongly plateaued (and APN), *i.e.*, their component functions are partially-bent [247, 252, 730], because the affine hyperplane $\{D_a F(x), x \in F_2^n\}$ is matched twice and the function $y \rightarrow v \cdot y$ restricted to an affine hyperplane is either constant or balanced for every v. This allows us to show more directly some results that were first obtained in [729, 730]): crooked functions are plateaued, and for n odd, they are then AB (since we know that "plateaued APN" implies AB for n odd; see Proposition 163, page 382). Their *component functions* being partially-bent, they all satisfy $N_{\Delta_{v \cdot F}} \times N_{W_{v \cdot F}} = 2^n$ (see page 256); therefore, in the case of n odd, we have $N_{\Delta_{v \cdot F}} = 2$ for every $v \neq 0_n$, that is, there exists a unique $a \neq 0_n$ such that $\Delta_{v \cdot F}(a) \neq 0$, i.e., $\{D_a F(x), x \in \mathbb{F}_2^n\} = \{0_n, v\}^\perp$ or $\{D_a F(x), x \in \mathbb{F}_2^n\} = \mathbb{F}_2^n \setminus \{0_n, v\}^\perp$. And for every n, a function F is crooked if and only if, for every $a \neq 0_n$, there exists a unique $v \neq 0_n$ such that $W_{D_a F}(0_n, v) \neq 0$ and then $W_{D_a F}(0_n, v) = 2^n$ and $\{D_a F(x), x \in \mathbb{F}_2^n\} = \{0_n, v\}^\perp$ or $W_{D_a F}(0_n, v) = -2^n$ and $\{D_a F(x), x \in \mathbb{F}_2^n\} = \mathbb{F}_2^n \setminus \{0_n, v\}^\perp$. Indeed, a set E is an affine hyperplane if and only if there exists a unique $v \neq 0_n$ such that $\sum_{y \in E} (-1)^{v \cdot y}$ equals $\pm|E|$ and that such sum is null for any other v. This characterization can be expressed by means of the Walsh transform of F since $W_{D_a F}(0_n, v) = \Delta_{v \cdot F}(a) = 2^{-n} \sum_{u \in \mathbb{F}_2^n} W_F^2(u, v)(-1)^{u \cdot a}$.

Of course, all quadratic APN functions are crooked; the question of knowing whether nonquadratic crooked functions exist is open. It is proved in [728, 729] that the reply is no for *power functions* (monomials) and in [80] that it is no for binomials.

---

[37] This is nowadays the most used definition of crooked functions, but originally in [57], they were defined such that, for every nonzero a, the set $\{D_a F(x); x \in \mathbb{F}_2^n\}$ is the complement of a linear hyperplane; this restricted definition required that crooked functions be bijective; they were also AB. Some authors call "generalized crooked" the functions we call crooked here.

Assuming that $F(0_n) = 0_n$, it is proved in [57] that the set $H_a = \{D_a F(x); x \in \mathbb{F}_2^n\}$ is the complement of a linear hyperplane for every nonzero a (*i.e.*, F is crooked in the original restricted sense of [57]) if and only if F is APN and for every nonzero a, we have $D_a F(x) + D_a F(y) + D_a F(z) \neq 0_n$ for every x, y, z; n is then necessarily odd. Then, F is bijective (take $x = y = z$) and AB, and we have seen that all the sets H_a, for $a \neq 0_n$, are distinct (and therefore every complement of a linear hyperplane equals H_a for some unique $a \neq 0_n$). More characterizations are given in [539], in relation with nonlinear codes. Note that crookedness may represent a weakness; see [200].

The case of power functions It is often simpler to consider power functions than general functions. In the case of plateaued functions, we have:

Corollary 19 *[247] Let $F(x) = x^d$ be any power function. Then, for every $w \in \mathbb{F}_{2^n}$, every $x \in \mathbb{F}_{2^n}$, and every $\lambda \in \mathbb{F}_{2^n}^*$, $|\{(a, b) \in \mathbb{F}_{2^n}^2 ; D_a F(b) + D_a F(x) = w\}|$ equals $|\{(a, b) \in \mathbb{F}_{2^n}^2 ; D_a F(b) + D_a F(x/\lambda) = w/\lambda^d\}|$ and $|\{(a, b) \in \mathbb{F}_{2^n}^2 ; D_a F(b) + D_a F(0) = w\}|$ is invariant when w is multiplied by any dth power in $\mathbb{F}_{2^n}^*$. Then:*

- *F is plateaued if and only if, for every $w \in \mathbb{F}_{2^n}$*

$$|\{(a, b) \in \mathbb{F}_{2^n}^2 ; D_a F(b) + D_a F(1) = w\}| = |\{(a, b) \in \mathbb{F}_{2^n}^2 ; D_a F(b) + D_a F(0) = w\}|.$$

- *F is plateaued with single amplitude if and only if additionally this common size does not depend on $w \neq 0$.*

If d is co-prime with $2^n - 1$, then F is plateaued if and only if it is plateaued with single amplitude.

This is a more or less direct consequence of the fact that, for every $\lambda \neq 0$, we have $D_{\lambda a} F(\lambda x) = \lambda^d D_a F(x)$.

The case of unbalanced components In the particular case where all the *component functions* of a function are unbalanced (we shall see that this is for instance the case of all APN power functions x^d when n is even, since they satisfy, as proved by Dobbertin, see Proposition 165, page 385, that $\gcd(d, 2^n - 1) = 3$), plateauedness is simpler to study because, for each v, the value of $|W_F(0_n, v)|$ being nonzero, equals the amplitude of the component function $v \cdot F$. Hence, according to Proposition 97, page 260, if F is plateaued with unbalanced components then, for every v, x, the sum $\sum_{a,b \in \mathbb{F}_2^n} (-1)^{v \cdot D_a D_b F(x)}$ equals $W_F^2(0_n, v) = \sum_{a,b \in \mathbb{F}_2^n} (-1)^{v \cdot (F(a) + F(b))}$. The converse is straightforward too since, when constant, $\sum_{a,b \in \mathbb{F}_2^n} (-1)^{v \cdot D_a D_b F(x)}$ is equal to the squared amplitude and cannot then be null, and this gives by the same method as in the proof of Theorem 18:

Theorem 19 *[247] Let F be any (n, m)-function. Then F is plateaued with component functions all unbalanced if and only if, for every $w, x \in \mathbb{F}_2^n$, we have*

$$\left| \{(a, b) \in (\mathbb{F}_2^n)^2 ; D_a D_b F(x) = w\} \right| = \left| \{(a, b) \in (\mathbb{F}_2^n)^2 ; F(a) + F(b) = w\} \right|.$$

Moreover, F is then plateaued with single amplitude if and only if, additionally, this common value does not depend on w for $w \neq 0_n$.

This theorem will have interesting consequences in Subsection 11.3, page 371.

Characterization by means of the autocorrelation functions and related value distributions

We have seen in Proposition 98, page 260, that a Boolean function f is plateaued of amplitude λ if and only if $\sum_{a \in \mathbb{F}_2^n} \Delta_f(a) \Delta_f(a + x) = \lambda^2 \Delta_f(x)$. To be able to deduce a characterization of plateaued vectorial functions, we need to eliminate λ^2 from this relation. The value of λ can be obtained from this same relation, with $x = 0_n$: $\sum_{a \in \mathbb{F}_2^n} \Delta_f^2(a) = \lambda^2 \Delta_f(0_n) = \lambda^2 2^n$. Hence, if f is plateaued, then $2^n \Delta_f \otimes \Delta_f = [\sum_{a \in \mathbb{F}_2^n} \Delta_f^2(a)] \Delta_f$. Conversely, if $2^n \Delta_f \otimes \Delta_f = (\sum_{a \in \mathbb{F}_2^n} \Delta_f^2(a)) \Delta_f$ then $\Delta_f \otimes \Delta_f = \lambda^2 \Delta_f$, where $\sum_{a \in \mathbb{F}_2^n} \Delta_f^2(a) = \lambda^2 2^n$ and f is plateaued of amplitude λ. We deduce:

Proposition 108 *Any (n, m)-function F is plateaued if and only if, for every $x \in \mathbb{F}_2^n$ and every $v \in \mathbb{F}_2^m$, we have*

$$2^n \sum_{a \in \mathbb{F}_2^n} \Delta_{v \cdot F}(a) \Delta_{v \cdot F}(a + x) = [\sum_{a \in \mathbb{F}_2^n} \Delta_{v \cdot F}^2(a)] \Delta_{v \cdot F}(x).$$

It is plateaued with single amplitude λ if and only if, for every $x \in \mathbb{F}_2^n$ and every $v \in \mathbb{F}_2^m$, we have

$$\sum_{a \in \mathbb{F}_2^n} \Delta_{v \cdot F}(a) \Delta_{v \cdot F}(a + x) = \lambda^2 \Delta_{v \cdot F}(x).$$

Characterization by means of power moments of the Walsh transform

We have seen in Proposition 99, page 261, that any n-variable Boolean function f is plateaued if and only if, for every nonzero $\alpha \in \mathbb{F}_2^n$, we have $\sum_{u \in \mathbb{F}_2^n} W_f(u + \alpha) W_f^3(u) = 0$. We deduce:

Proposition 109 *[247] Any (n, m)-function F is plateaued if and only if*

$$\forall v \in \mathbb{F}_2^m, \forall \alpha \in \mathbb{F}_2^n, \alpha \neq 0_n, \sum_{u \in \mathbb{F}_2^n} W_F(u + \alpha, v) W_F^3(u, v) = 0.$$

F is plateaued with single amplitude if and only if, additionally, $\sum_{u \in \mathbb{F}_2^n} W_F^4(u, v)$ does not depend on v for $v \neq 0_m$.

We deduce also from Corollary 17, page 261:

Corollary 20 *[247] Any (n, m)-function F is plateaued if and only if, for every $b \in \mathbb{F}_2^n$ and every $v \in \mathbb{F}_2^m$,*

$$\sum_{a \in \mathbb{F}_2^n} W_F^4(a, v) = 2^n (-1)^{v \cdot F(b)} \sum_{a \in \mathbb{F}_2^n} (-1)^{a \cdot b} W_F^3(a, v).$$

And F is plateaued with single amplitude if and only if, additionally, these sums do not depend on v, for v $\neq 0_m$.

We have seen that plateaued functions can be characterized by the constance of the ratio of two consecutive Walsh power moments of even orders [858].

We deduce from Proposition 100, page 261:

Proposition 110   *[247, 858] For every (n, m)-function F, and every k $\in \mathbb{N}^*$, we have*

$$\sum_{v \in \mathbb{F}_2^m} \left(\sum_{a \in \mathbb{F}_2^n} W_F^{2k+2}(a, v) \right)^2 \leq \sum_{v \in \mathbb{F}_2^m} \left(\sum_{a \in \mathbb{F}_2^n} W_F^{2k}(a, v) \right) \left(\sum_{a \in \mathbb{F}_2^n} W_F^{2k+4}(a, v) \right),$$

with equality if and only if F is plateaued.

See more in [247, 858].

6.5.2 CCZ and EA equivalence of plateaued functions

In [247], the author deduced from Theorem 18, page 276, the following:

Corollary 21   *Let n be any even integer, n ≥ 4. Let F be an (n, n)-function CCZ equivalent to a Gold APN function $G(x) = x^{2^i+1}$ or to a Kasami APN function $G(x) = x^{4^i - 2^i + 1}$, (i, n) = 1. Then F is plateaued if and only if it is EA equivalent to G(x).*

This result has been later generalized in [1141] by S. Yoshiara:

Proposition 111   *Let F and G be plateaued APN functions on $\mathbb{F}_{2^n}$ with n even. Assume that F is a power function, then it is CCZ equivalent to G if and only if F is EA equivalent to G.*

This same author had proved in [1139]:

Proposition 112   *Two quadratic APN functions are CCZ equivalent if and only if they are EA equivalent.*

and in [1140]:

Proposition 113   *For any n ≥ 3, two power APN functions x^d and x^e over $\mathbb{F}_{2^n}$ are CCZ equivalent if and only if there is an integer a such that $0 \leq a \leq n - 1$ and either $e = 2^a d$ [mod $2^n - 1$] or $de = 2^a$ [mod $2^n - 1$], where the latter case occurs only when n is odd.*

Proposition 114   *Any quadratic APN function is CCZ equivalent to a power APN function if and only if it is EA equivalent to one of the Gold APN functions.*

From Proposition 113 are deduced all cases of CCZ equivalence/inequivalence between the known APN functions; see Proposition 177.

6.5.3 Constructions of plateaued vectorial functions

Primary constructions

All quadratic functions are plateaued. The Maiorana–McFarland construction $F(x, y) = x\pi(y) + \phi(y)$; $x, y \in \mathbb{F}_{2^m}$, allows constructing nonquadratic ones; it gives a plateaued $(2m, m)$-function when π is a permutation (F is then bent) and when π is 2-to-1, ϕ being any (m, m)-function in both cases. Erasing some coordinates from their output provides plateaued (n, m)-functions with $m \le n/2$.

We recall from [247] an example of *primary construction* of plateaued (n, n)-functions also based on the Maiorana–McFarland construction. Let π be a permutation of $\mathbb{F}_{2^m}$ and ϕ, ψ two functions from $\mathbb{F}_{2^m}$ to $\mathbb{F}_{2^m}$. Let i be an integer coprime with m. We define the $(2m, 2m)$-function $F(x, y) = (x\pi(y) + \phi(y), x(\pi(y))^{2^i} + \psi(y)) \in \mathbb{F}_{2^m} \times \mathbb{F}_{2^m}$. For every element $(a, b) \in \mathbb{F}_{2^m} \times \mathbb{F}_{2^m}$, the Walsh transform at (a, b) of $(u, v) \cdot F(x, y)$ equals

$$\sum_{x, y \in \mathbb{F}_{2^m}} (-1)^{tr_m(ux\pi(y) + vx(\pi(y))^{2^i} + u\phi(y) + v\psi(y) + ax + by)} =$$

$$\sum_{y \in \mathbb{F}_{2^m}} (-1)^{tr_m(u\phi(y) + v\psi(y) + by)} \left(\sum_{x \in \mathbb{F}_{2^m}} (-1)^{tr_m((u\pi(y) + v(\pi(y))^{2^i} + a)x)} \right) =$$

$$2^m \sum_{\substack{y \in \mathbb{F}_{2^m} \\ u\pi(y) + v(\pi(y))^{2^i} = a}} (-1)^{tr_m(u\phi(y) + v\psi(y) + by)}.$$

The number of solutions of the equation $u\pi(y) + v(\pi(y))^{2^i} = a$ equals the number of solutions of the linear equation $uy + vy^{2^i} = a$. If $u = 0$ and $v \ne 0$, or if $u \ne 0$ and $v = 0$, the number of solutions of this equation equals 1; hence, $(u, v) \cdot F$ is plateaued of amplitude 2^m (*i.e.*, is bent). If $u \ne 0$ and $v \ne 0$, this number either equals 0 or equals the number of solutions of the associated homogeneous equation $uy + vy^{2^i} = 0$, that is, 2 (indeed, $uy + vy^{2^i} = 0$ is equivalent to $y = 0$ or $y^{2^i - 1} = u/v \ne 0$ and i being coprime with m, $2^i - 1$ is coprime with $2^m - 1$); hence, $(u, v) \cdot F(x, y)$ is plateaued of amplitude 2^{m+1} (*i.e.*, is semi-bent). Then:

Proposition 115   *[247] Let m be a positive integer, π a permutation of $\mathbb{F}_{2^m}$, and ϕ, ψ two functions from $\mathbb{F}_{2^m}$ to $\mathbb{F}_{2^m}$. Let i be an integer coprime with m. Then function $F(x, y) = (x\pi(y) + \phi(y), x(\pi(y))^{2^i} + \psi(y))$ is plateaued (but does not have single amplitude).*

Of course, this observation more generally applies when $(\pi(y))^{2^i}$ is replaced by any other permutation $\pi'(y)$ such that, for every $u \ne 0$, $v \ne 0$, the equation $u\pi(y) + v\pi'(y) = a$ has 0 or a fixed number (depending on u and v only) of solutions.

There exist other examples of nonquadratic plateaued (n, n)-functions, such as AB functions (see page 395) and Kasami APN functions in even dimension (see page 400); erasing some coordinates gives plateaued (n, m)-functions with $n/2 < m \leq n$.

Secondary constructions

Let r, s, t, p be positive integers. Let F be a *plateaued* (r, t)-function and G a plateaued (s, p)-function, then function $H(x, y) = (F(x), G(y))$; $x \in \mathbb{F}_2^r, y \in \mathbb{F}_2^s$ is a plateaued $(r + s, t + p)$-function. Indeed, for every $(a, b) \in \mathbb{F}_2^r \times \mathbb{F}_2^s$ and every $(u, v) \in \mathbb{F}_2^t \times \mathbb{F}_2^p$, we have: $W_H((a, b), (u, v)) = W_F(a, u) W_G(b, v)$. Note that this works even if u or v is null, but such a function is never with single amplitude, except when F and G are affine.

7

Correlation immune and resilient functions

The notion of correlation immune Boolean function is due to Siegenthaler [1041] as a criterion for resistance to his correlation attack on the *combiner model* of stream cipher, as we saw at page 86. Balanced correlation immune functions have soon been called resilient after [370], which dealt with another cryptographic issue: the bit extraction problem. It has been later observed in [181] that the notion of correlation immune Boolean function already existed in combinatorics (in a wider framework) under another name, since the support of a correlation immune function is an orthogonal array (see Definition 22, page 86). Resilient functions have been extensively studied in the 1990s in relation with nonlinearity. But in 2003 were invented the *fast algebraic attack* [388] and the Rønjom–Helleseth attack [1003], which are very efficient against stream ciphers using nonlinear functions whose algebraic degrees are not large. Since correlation immune and resilient functions have algebraic degree bounded from above, this made them weak. But, as we already recalled at page 147, correlation immune and resilient Boolean functions can be employed for secret sharing, as shown in [461]. Recently, the interest of correlation immune functions has been also renewed in the framework of side-channel attacks (see [286] and Section 12.1). The functions need then to have low Hamming weight (and this excludes resilient functions).

7.1 Correlation immune and resilient Boolean functions

For the convenience of the reader, we recall in the next definition what we have seen in Section 3.1, page 86, on correlation immune and resilient functions.

Definition 69 *Let n be a positive integer and $t \leq n$ a nonnegative integer. An n-variable Boolean function f is called a t-th order correlation immune (t-CI) function if its output distribution probability (i.e., the density of the support) is unaltered when at most t (or, equivalently, exactly t) of its input bits are kept constant, that is, if the code equal to its support has* dual distance *(see Definition 4, page 16) at least $t + 1$. It is called a t-resilient function if it is balanced and t-th order correlation immune. Equivalently, f is t-th order correlation immune if $W_f(u) = 0$, i.e. $\widehat{f}(u) = 0$, for all $u \in \mathbb{F}_2^n$ such that $1 \leq w_H(u) \leq t$, and it is t-resilient if $W_f(u) = 0$ for all $u \in \mathbb{F}_2^n$ such that $w_H(u) \leq t$.*

This generalizes to other alphabets [178]. Note that thanks to the $\mathbb{R}$-linearity of the Fourier–Hadamard transform, the sum of t-th order correlation immune functions with disjoint supports is a t-th order correlation immune function.

The combining functions in stream ciphers must be t-resilient with large t. As with any cryptographic functions, they must also have high algebraic degrees (which is partially contradictory with correlation immunity, but trade-offs can be found), high nonlinearities (idem), and since 2003 high resistance to algebraic attacks and fast algebraic attacks (which is problematic).

Notation: By an $(n, t, d, \mathcal{N})$- function, we mean an n-variable, t-resilient function having algebraic degree at least d and nonlinearity at least $\mathcal{N}$.

7.1.1 Bound on the correlation immunity order

The correlation immunity order of n-variable functions (*i.e.*, the maximum d such that they are d-CI) is unbounded (that is, it can be as high as n, since constant functions are n-th order correlation immune), and their resiliency order is only bounded above by $n - 1$, since the Boolean function $\bigoplus_{i=1}^{n} x_i$ is $(n-1)$-resilient. In the case of unbalanced and nonconstant correlation immune functions, the situation is different:

Proposition 116 *[514] Let f be an unbalanced nonconstant t-th order correlation immune Boolean function. Then $t \le \frac{2n}{3} - 1$.*

Proof Let f be an unbalanced nonconstant t-CI Boolean function. Since f is unbalanced, we have $W_f(0_n) \ne 0$, and since f is nonconstant, there exists $a \in \mathbb{F}_2^n$ nonzero such that $W_f(a) \ne 0$. The Golomb–Xiao–Massey characterization (Theorem 5, page 87) gives that $w_H(a) \ge t + 1$.

Suppose that $t > \frac{2n}{3} - 1$. By the Titsworth relation (2.51), page 61, we have:

$$\sum_{u \in \mathbb{F}_2^n} W_f(u) W_f(u + a) = 0. \tag{7.1}$$

For $u = 0_n$, the summand in the left part of (7.1) equals 2^{2n}, according to Parseval's identity. If $1 \le w_H(u) \le \frac{2}{3}n < t + 1$, then $W_f(u) = 0$. If $w_H(u) > \frac{2}{3}n$, then the vectors u and a have more than $\frac{n}{3}$ common 1s, therefore $w_H(u + a) < \frac{2}{3}n$. Thus the left-hand side of Equation (7.1) has exactly two equal nonzero summands (for $u = 0_n$ and $u = a$), therefore the equality in Equation (7.1) cannot be achieved. $\square$

7.1.2 Bounds on algebraic degree

The *Siegenthaler bound* states:

Proposition 117 *[1041] Let n be any positive integer and let $0 \le t \le n$. Any t-th order correlation immune n-variable Boolean function has* Hamming weight *divisible by 2^t and algebraic degree smaller than or equal to $n - t$. Any t-resilient function has algebraic degree smaller than or equal to $n - t - 1$ if $t \le n - 2$ and to 1 (i.e., is affine) if $t = n - 1$. Moreover, if a t-th order correlation immune function has* Hamming weight *divisible by 2^{t+1}, then it satisfies the same bound as t-resilient functions.*

Siegenthaler's bound gives an example of the trade-offs that must be accepted in the design of combiner generators.[1]

The first assertion in Proposition 117 comes directly from the fact that all the restrictions obtained by fixing t coordinates of the input have the same Hamming weight. The other results can be proved directly by using Relation (2.4), page 33, since the bit $\bigoplus_{x \in \mathbb{F}_2^n;\, supp(x) \subseteq I} f(x)$ equals the parity of the Hamming weight of the restriction of f obtained by setting to 0 the coordinates of x that lie outside I. It is then null if $|I| > n - t$. In the case that the restriction by fixing t input coordinates has even Hamming weight, that is, when $w_H(f)$ is divisible by 2^{t+1}, this bit is null if $|I| \geq n - t$. Note that we can also use the *Golomb–Xiao–Massey characterization* (Theorem 5, page 87, resulting in Definition 69, page 284) together with the *Poisson summation formula* (2.40), page 59, applied to $\varphi = f$ and with $E^\perp = \{x \in \mathbb{F}_2^n;\, supp(x) \subseteq I\}$, where I has size strictly larger than $n - t - 1$. But this gives a less simple proof.

7.1.3 Characterization by the NNF

Siegenthaler's bound is also a direct consequence of a characterization of correlation immune and of resilient functions through their NNFs and of the facts that the ANF equals the NNF mod 2 and that the Hamming weight of a t-th order correlation immune function with $t \geq 1$ is even (the Walsh transform at 0_n is then divisible by 4).

Proposition 118 *[220, 293] Let n be any positive integer and $t < n$ a non-negative integer. A Boolean function f on $\mathbb{F}_2^n$ is t-th order correlation immune if and only if the numerical normal form $\sum_{I \subseteq \{1,\dots,n\}} \lambda_I\, x^I$ of the function $g(x) = f(x) \oplus x_1 \oplus \cdots \oplus x_n$ satisfies that, for every I of size larger than or equal to $n - t$, $(-2)^{n-|I|}\lambda_I$ is independent of the choice of I. And f is t-resilient if and only if the numerical normal form $\sum_{I \subseteq \{1,\dots,n\}} \lambda_I\, x^I$ of g has degree at most $n - t - 1$.*

Proof For each vector $a \in \mathbb{F}_2^n$, we denote by $\overline{a}$ the componentwise complement of a equal to $a + 1_n$. We have $W_f(a) = W_g(\overline{a})$. Thus, f is t-th order correlation immune (resp. t-resilient) if and only if, for every vector $u \neq (1, \dots, 1)$ of Hamming weight larger than or equal to $n - t$ (resp. for every vector u of Hamming weight larger than or equal to $n - t$), the number $W_g(u)$ is null. According to Relations (2.61), (2.62), page 67, and (2.32), page 55, applied to g, we have for nonzero u

$$W_g(u) = (-1)^{w_H(u)+1} \sum_{I \subseteq \{1,\dots,n\};\, supp(u) \subseteq I} 2^{n-|I|+1} \lambda_I,$$

and for nonempty I

$$\lambda_I = 2^{-n}(-2)^{|I|-1} \sum_{u \in \mathbb{F}_2^n;\, I \subseteq supp(u)} W_g(u).$$

This completes the proof.   □

---

[1] One approach to avoid such a trade-off is to allow memory in the nonlinear combination generator, that is, to replace the combining function by a finite state machine; see [845].

Proposition 118 proves, by applying Relation (2.64), page 67, to $g(x) = f(x) \oplus x_1 \oplus \cdots \oplus x_n$, that if t is the resiliency order of an n-variable function f of algebraic degree at least 2, and each variable x_i is effective in $g(x)$, then $n - t - 1 \geq n \, 2^{-d_{alg}(f)+1}$, that is,

$$d_{alg}(f) \geq \log_2 \left(\frac{2n}{n - t - 1} \right).$$

Remark. According to Proposition 118, a nonaffine balanced n-variable Boolean function g has its *algebraic degree* and *numerical degree* equal to each other if and only if, given Boolean function $f(x) = g(x) \oplus x_1 \oplus \cdots \oplus x_n$ and its resiliency order, Siegenthaler's bound is an equality. $\qquad\qquad\Box$

Proposition 118 has been used by X.-D. Hou in [621] for constructing resilient functions.

7.1.4 Bounds on the nonlinearity

Sarkar and Maitra showed that:

Proposition 119 *[1012] The values of the Walsh transform of an n-variable, t-resilient (resp. t-th order correlation immune) function are divisible by 2^{t+2} (resp. 2^{t+1}) if $0 \leq t \leq n - 3$ (resp. $1 \leq t \leq n - 2$).*

A more precise result being given in Proposition 120 below, we skip the proof of Proposition 119. More is proved in [220, 322]; in particular: if the Hamming weight of a t-th order correlation immune function is divisible by 2^{t+1}, then the values of its Walsh transform are divisible by 2^{t+2}. This *Sarkar–Maitra's divisibility bound* and its extension have provided nontrivial upper bounds on the nonlinearity of resilient functions, independently obtained by Tarannikov [1080] and by Zheng and Zhang [1177]:

Theorem 20 *[1012, 1080, 1177] For every n and $t \leq n - 2$, the nonlinearity of any tth-order correlation immune (resp. t-resilient) function is bounded above by $2^{n-1} - 2^t$ (resp. $2^{n-1} - 2^{t+1}$).*

Of course, this brings information only if $2^{n-1} - 2^t$ (resp. $2^{n-1} - 2^{t+1}$) is smaller than $2^{n-1} - 2^{\frac{n}{2}-1}$. Zheng and Zhang [1177] showed that correlation immune functions of high orders satisfy the same upper bound on the nonlinearity as resilient functions of the same orders. In [1083] (where the authors also obtained a bound on Δ_f for f resilient and studied the resiliency order of all quadratic functions), Tarannikov et al. showed for each $i \in \{1, 2\}$ that if t is larger than some rather complex expression of i and n, then for every unbalanced nonconstant t-CI function, we have $nl(f) \leq 2^{n-1} - 2^{t+i}$. The maximal higher-order nonlinearity of resilient functions has also been studied in [101, 719] and determined for low order (≤ 2) or low number of variables (≤ 7).

The bound of Theorem 20 for resilient functions is tight when $t \geq 0.6 \, n$, see [1080, 1081]. We shall call it *Sarkar et al.'s bound*. Notice that, if a t-resilient function f achieves nonlinearity $2^{n-1} - 2^{t+1}$, then f is plateaued. Indeed, the distances between f and affine functions lie then between $2^{n-1} - 2^{t+1}$ and $2^{n-1} + 2^{t+1}$ and must be therefore equal to

$2^{n-1} - 2^{t+1}$, 2^{n-1} and $2^{n-1} + 2^{t+1}$ because of the divisibility result of Sarkar and Maitra. Thus, the Walsh transform of f takes three values 0 and $\pm 2^{t+2}$. Moreover, it is proved in [1080] (and is a direct consequence of Proposition 120 below) that such function f also achieves Siegenthaler's bound (and as proved in [814], achieves minimum *sum-of-squares indicator*).

If $2^{n-1} - 2^{t+1}$ is larger than the best possible nonlinearity of all balanced functions (and in particular if it is larger than the covering radius bound), then, obviously, a better bound than in Theorem 20 exists. In the case of n even, the best possible nonlinearity of all balanced functions being strictly smaller than $2^{n-1} - 2^{\frac{n}{2}-1}$, Sarkar and Maitra deduce that $nl(f) \leq 2^{n-1} - 2^{\frac{n}{2}-1} - 2^{t+1}$ for every t-resilient function f with $t \leq \frac{n}{2} - 2$. In the case of n odd, they state that $nl(f)$ is smaller than or equal to the highest multiple of 2^{t+1}, which is less than or equal to the best possible nonlinearity of all Boolean functions. But a potentially better upper bound can be given, whatever is the parity of n. Indeed, Sarkar–Maitra's divisibility bound shows that $W_f(a) = \omega(a) \times 2^{t+2}$, where $\omega(a)$ is integer-valued. Parseval's relation (2.48), page 61, and the fact that $W_f(a)$ is null for every vector a of Hamming weight $\leq t$ imply

$$\sum_{a \in \mathbb{F}_2^n;\ w_H(a)>t} \omega^2(a) = 2^{2n-2t-4}$$

and, thus,

$$\max_{a \in \mathbb{F}_2^n} |\omega(a)| \geq \sqrt{\frac{2^{2n-2t-4}}{2^n - \sum_{i=0}^{t}\binom{n}{i}}} = \frac{2^{n-t-2}}{\sqrt{2^n - \sum_{i=0}^{t}\binom{n}{i}}}.$$

Hence, we have $\max_{a \in \mathbb{F}_2^n} |\omega(a)| \geq \left\lceil \frac{2^{n-t-2}}{\sqrt{2^n - \sum_{i=0}^{t}\binom{n}{i}}} \right\rceil$, and this implies

$$nl(f) \leq 2^{n-1} - 2^{t+1} \left\lceil \frac{2^{n-t-2}}{\sqrt{2^n - \sum_{i=0}^{t}\binom{n}{i}}} \right\rceil. \tag{7.2}$$

When n is even and $t \leq \frac{n}{2} - 2$, this number is always less than or equal to the number $2^{n-1} - 2^{\frac{n}{2}-1} - 2^{t+1}$ (given by Sarkar and Maitra), because $\frac{2^{n-t-2}}{\sqrt{2^n - \sum_{i=0}^{t}\binom{n}{i}}}$ is strictly larger than $2^{\frac{n}{2}-t-2}$ and $2^{\frac{n}{2}-t-2}$ is an integer, and, thus, $\left\lceil \frac{2^{n-t-2}}{\sqrt{2^n - \sum_{i=0}^{t}\binom{n}{i}}} \right\rceil$ is at least $2^{\frac{n}{2}-t-2}+1$. And when n increases, the right-hand side of Relation (7.2) is strictly smaller than $2^{n-1} - 2^{\frac{n}{2}-1} - 2^{t+1}$ for an increasing number of values of $t \leq \frac{n}{2} - 2$ (but this improvement does not appear when we compare the values we obtain with this bound to the values indicated in the table given by Sarkar and Maitra in [1012], because the values of n they consider in this table are small).

When n is odd, it is difficult to say if Inequality (7.2) is better than the bound given by Sarkar and Maitra, because their bound involves a value that is unknown for $n \geq 9$ (the best possible nonlinearity of all balanced Boolean functions). In any case, this makes (7.2) better usable.

We know (see [809, page 310]) that $\sum_{i=0}^{t} \binom{n}{i} \geq \frac{2^{nH_2(t/n)}}{\sqrt{8t(1-t/n)}}$, where $H_2(x) = -x \log_2(x) - (1-x) \log_2(1-x)$, the so-called *binary entropy function*, satisfies $H_2(\frac{1}{2} - x) = 1 - 2x^2 \log_2 e + o(x^2)$. Thus, we have

$$nl(f) \leq 2^{n-1} - 2^{t+1} \left\lceil \frac{2^{n-t-2}}{\sqrt{2^n - \frac{2^{nH_2(t/n)}}{\sqrt{8t(1-t/n)}}}} \right\rceil. \tag{7.3}$$

Remark. If a Boolean function f is t-th order correlation immune (resp. t-resilient), then for every $1 \leq e \leq t$ and every set $\{i_1, \ldots, i_e\}$ of size e, its restriction obtained by fixing coordinates $x_{i_1}, \ldots, x_{i_e}$ is a $(t-e)$-th order correlation immune (resp. $(t-e)$-resilient) $(n-e)$-variable function. But the n-variable function equal to the product of f with the monomial function $m(x) = \prod_{j=1}^{e} x_{i_j}$ of degree e is not $(t-e)$-th order correlation immune, although the support of fm equals the intersection of the support of f with the set $\{i_1, \ldots, i_e\}$: fixing $(t-e)$ coordinates of x preserves the output distribution probability only if these coordinates are outside $\{i_1, \ldots, i_e\}$. Nevertheless, it is possible to prove that such fm has same Walsh divisibility property as a $(t-e)$-th order correlation immune (resp. $(t-e)$-resilient) function. $\square$

Proposition 119 has been improved:

Proposition 120 *[220, 322] Let n be any positive integer and let $t \leq n-2$ be a nonnegative integer. Let f be any n-variable t-th order correlation immune function (resp. any t-resilient function or any t-th order correlation immune function whose Hamming weight is divisible by $2^{t+1+\lfloor \frac{n-t-2}{d} \rfloor}$) and let d be its algebraic degree. The values of the Walsh transform of f are divisible by $2^{t+1+\lfloor \frac{n-t-1}{d} \rfloor}$ (resp. by $2^{t+2+\lfloor \frac{n-t-2}{d} \rfloor}$). Hence the nonlinearity of f is divisible by $2^{t+\lfloor \frac{n-t-1}{d} \rfloor}$ (resp. by $2^{t+1+\lfloor \frac{n-t-2}{d} \rfloor}$).*

A little more can be said in the former case; see [322].

The approach for proving this tight bound was first to use the numerical normal form (we refer the reader to [220] for this proof, for the tightness, and for an improvement when the number of terms of highest degree in the ANF is small enough). Later, a second proof using only the properties of the Fourier–Hadamard transform was given in [322]:

Proof The Poisson summation formula (2.40), page 59, applied to $\varphi = f_\chi$ and to the vector space $E = \{u \in \mathbb{F}_2^n; \ \forall i \in \{1, \ldots, n\}, u_i \leq v_i\}$, where v is some vector of $\mathbb{F}_2^n$, whose orthogonal equals $E^\perp = \{u \in \mathbb{F}_2^n; \ \forall i \in \{1, \ldots, n\}, u_i \leq v_i \oplus 1\}$, gives $\sum_{u \in E} W_f(u) = 2^{w_H(v)} \sum_{x \in E^\perp} f_\chi(x)$. It is then a simple matter to prove the result by induction on the Hamming weight of v, starting with the vectors of weight t (resp. $t+1$), and using McEliece's divisibility property (see Subsection 4.1.5, page 156). $\square$

Proposition 120 gives directly more precise upper bounds on the nonlinearity of any t-resilient function of degree d: for instance, this nonlinearity is bounded above by $2^{n-1} - 2^{t+1+\lfloor \frac{n-t-2}{d} \rfloor}$. This gives a simpler proof that it can be equal to $2^{n-1} - 2^{t+1}$ only if $d = n - t - 1$, i.e., if Siegenthaler's bound is achieved with equality. Moreover, the proof above also shows that the nonlinearity of any t-resilient n-variable Boolean function is bounded above by $2^{n-1} - 2^{t+1+\lfloor \frac{n-t-2}{d} \rfloor}$, where d is the minimum algebraic degree of the restrictions of f to the subspaces $\{u \in \mathbb{F}_2^n;\ \forall i \in \{1, \ldots, n\},\ u_i \leq v_i \oplus 1\}$ such that v has Hamming weight $t + 1$ and $W_f(v) \neq 0$. See more in [322].

7.1.5 Bound on the maximum correlation with index subsets

An upper bound on the maximum correlation of t-resilient functions with respect to subsets I of $\{1, \ldots, n\}$ can be directly deduced from Relation (3.14), page 102, and from Sarkar et al.'s bound. Note that we get an improvement by using that the support of W_f, restricted to the set of vectors $u \in \mathbb{F}_2^n$ such that $u_i = 0,\ \forall i \notin I$, contains at most $\sum_{i=t+1}^{|I|} \binom{|I|}{i}$ vectors. In particular, if $|I| = t+1$, the maximum correlation of f with respect to I equals $2^{-n}|W_f(u)|$, where u is the vector of support I, see [187, 203, 1155]. The optimal number of LFSRs that should be considered together in a correlation attack on a cryptosystem using a t-resilient combining function is $t + 1$; see [187].

7.1.6 Relationship with other criteria

The relationships between resiliency and other criteria have been studied in [354, 814, 1083, 1175]. For instance, t-resilient $PC(l)$ functions can exist only if $t + l \leq n - 1$. This is a direct consequence of Relation (2.56), page 62, applied with $a = b = 0_n$, $E = \{x \in \mathbb{F}_2^n;\ x_i = 0, \forall i \in I\}$ and $E^\perp = \{x \in \mathbb{F}_2^n;\ x_i = 0,\ \forall i \notin I\}$, where I has size $n - t$: if $l \geq n - t$, then the right-hand side term of Relation (2.56) is nonzero while the left-hand side term is null. Equality $t + l = n - 1$ is possible only if $l = n - 1$, n is odd and $t = 0$ [354, 1175]. The known upper bounds on the nonlinearity can then be improved for such functions.

The definition of resiliency has been weakened in [126, 294, 720, 721] in order to relax some of the trade-offs recalled above, without weakening the cryptosystem against the correlation attack.

Resiliency is related to the notion of corrector (useful for the generation of random sequences having good statistical properties) introduced by Lacharme in [732].

7.1.7 Relationship with covering sequences

According to Proposition 60, page 182, knowing a covering sequence $\lambda = (\lambda_a)_{a \in \mathbb{F}_2^n}$ (trivial or not) of a function f allows knowing that $supp(W_f) \subseteq \widehat{\lambda}^{-1}(\widehat{\lambda}(0_n) - 2\rho)$, where ρ is the level of the sequence. Hence, as observed in [326], f is t-th order correlation immune where $t + 1$ is the minimum Hamming weight of nonzero $b \in \mathbb{F}_2^n$ such that $\widehat{\lambda}(b) = \widehat{\lambda}(0_n) - 2\rho$, and if $\rho \neq 0$, it is then t-resilient. Conversely, if f is t-th order correlation immune (resp. t-resilient) and if it is not $(t + 1)$-th order correlation immune (resp. $(t + 1)$-resilient), then there exists at least one (nontrivial) covering sequence $\lambda = (\lambda_a)_{a \in \mathbb{F}_2^n}$ with level ρ such that $t + 1$ is the minimum Hamming weight of $b \in \mathbb{F}_2^n$ satisfying $\widehat{\lambda}(b) = \widehat{\lambda}(0_n) - 2\rho$.

A particularly simple covering sequence is the indicator of the set of vectors of Hamming weight 1. The functions that admit this covering sequence are called regular; they are $(\rho - 1)$-resilient, where ρ is the level. More generally, any function admitting as covering sequence the indicator of a set of vectors of weight 1 has this same property (this generalizes to any vectors with disjoint supports). We speak then of a simple covering sequence; see [326], where the algebraic degree and the nonlinearity of regular functions are studied, and where constructions are given as well as bounds on the number of variables.

7.1.8 Primary constructions of correlation immune and resilient functions

In the 1990s, high-order resilient functions with the best possible algebraic degree and nonlinearity were needed for applications in stream ciphers using the combiner model. But *fast algebraic attacks (FAA)* have changed the situation. The combiner model is now considered problematic, because of Siegenthaler's bound and the fact that combiner or filter functions need to have very high algebraic degree for resisting FAA. For the sake of completeness and also because building correlation immune functions means building orthogonal arrays (see Definition 22, page 86), which are of interest in combinatorics and statistics, and because a new way of using low-weight correlation immune functions exists (see Section 12.1), and new ways of using resilient functions may be found in the future, we report the state of the art for constructing highly nonlinear correlation immune and resilient functions. As we shall see, most constructions build in fact resilient functions, and these constructions unfortunately do not allow us to construct low-weight correlation immune functions. More work is then needed to build such functions. Such work, which we shall report at the end of this subsection, has been initiated in [258] and continued in [1104].

The *primary constructions* (which allow designing resilient functions without using known ones) are supposed to lead potentially to wider classes of functions than secondary constructions (recall that the number of Boolean functions on $n - 1$ variables is only equal to the square root of the number of n-variable Boolean functions). But the known primary constructions of resilient Boolean functions do not lead to very large classes of functions. In fact, only one reasonably large class of Boolean functions is known, whose elements can be analyzed with respect to the cryptographic criteria recalled in Section 3.1. So we observe some imbalance in the knowledge on cryptographic functions for stream ciphers: much is known on the properties of resilient functions, but little is known on how to construct them. Examples of t-resilient functions achieving the best possible nonlinearity $2^{n-1} - 2^{t+1}$ (and thus the best algebraic degree) have been obtained for $n \leq 10$ in [934, 1011, 1012] and for every $t \geq 0.6\, n$ [1080, 1081] (n being then not limited). But $n \leq 10$ is too small for applications and $t \geq 0.6\, n$ is too large (because of Siegenthaler's bound).[2] Moreover, these examples give very limited numbers of functions (they are often defined recursively

---

[2] And almost nothing is known on the immunity of these functions to algebraic attacks; anyway, their resistance to FAA is bad.

or obtained after a computer search), and many of these functions have cryptographic weaknesses such as linear structures (see [354, 814]). Balanced Boolean functions with high nonlinearities have been obtained by Fontaine in [515] and by Filiol and Fontaine in [503], who made a computer investigation – but for $n = 7, 9$, which is too small – on the corpus of idempotent functions (see the definition at page 248). These functions, whose *ANF*s are invariant under the cyclic shifts of the coordinates x_i, have been called later *rotation symmetric* (see Section 10.2, page 360). Other ad hoc constructions can be found in [819, 1011].

A construction derived from the characterization of correlation immunity by the dual distance

It has been observed in [417] that the characterization of Corollary 6, page 88, can be straightforwardly applied to build correlation immune functions from linear codes. In fact, this was already known from [58].

Corollary 22   *Let C be any (linear) $[n, k, d]$-code and G a generator matrix of C. Then for every k-variable function g, the n-variable function $f(x) = g(x \times G^t)$ is $(d-1)$-th order correlation immune (and it is $(d-1)$-resilient if g is balanced).*

Proof   If g is the indicator δ_0 of the singleton $\{0_k\}$, the result is a direct consequence of Corollary 6, page 88, since we have $f(x) = 0$ if and only if $x \times G^t = 0_k$, that is, $x \in C^\perp$. It is easily seen that if $g = \delta_a$, we have then that $f(x) = 0$ if and only if x belongs either to the empty set or to a coset of $C^\perp$. Then f is $(d-1)$-th order correlation immune according to Corollary 6, since the dual distance is invariant by translation. And if g is any sum of such atomic functions, that is, any Boolean function, we have the same result since the sum of t-th order correlation immune functions with disjoint supports is a t-th order correlation immune function. Finally, G being a generator matrix, function $x \in \mathbb{F}_2^n \mapsto x \times G^t \in \mathbb{F}_2^k$ is balanced and then f is balanced if and only if g is balanced.   □

Such a correlation immune function can have at most algebraic degree $d_{alg}(g) \leq k$ (and $\leq k - 1$ if it is resilient).

Remark.   Given $k < n$, a k-variable function g, a surjective linear mapping $L : \mathbb{F}_2^n \to \mathbb{F}_2^k$, and an element u of $\mathbb{F}_2^n$, the function $f(x) = g \circ L(x) \oplus u \cdot x$ is $(d-1)$-resilient, where d is the Hamming distance between u and the linear code C whose generator matrix equals the matrix of L. Indeed, for any vector $a \in \mathbb{F}_2^n$ of Hamming weight at most $d - 1$, the vector $u + a$ does not belong to C. This implies that the Boolean function $f(x) \oplus a \cdot x$ is linearly equivalent to the function $g(x_1, \ldots, x_k) \oplus x_{k+1}$, since we may assume without loss of generality that L is systematic (*i.e.*, has the form $[Id_k|N]$). Boolean function $f(x) \oplus a \cdot x$ is therefore balanced. This construction is similar to that of Corollary 22 but different (note that g does not need to be balanced for f to be balanced).

In both constructions, f has nonzero linear structures since it is EA equivalent to $g(x_1, \ldots, x_k)$; then it does not give full satisfaction.   □

Maiorana–McFarland's construction

An extension of the class of bent functions that we called above the *Maiorana–McFarland* original class has been given in [181] (where are also characterized the quadratic *n*-variable correlation immune functions of order $n - 3$), based on the same principle of concatenating affine functions[3] (we have already met in Section 5.1 this generalization): let r be a positive integer smaller than n; we denote $n - r$ by s; let g be any Boolean function on $\mathbb{F}_2^s$ and let ϕ be a mapping from $\mathbb{F}_2^s$ to $\mathbb{F}_2^r$. Then we define the function

$$f_{\phi,g}(x, y) = x \cdot \phi(y) \oplus g(y) = \bigoplus_{i=1}^{r} x_i \phi_i(y) \oplus g(y), \ x \in \mathbb{F}_2^r, \ y \in \mathbb{F}_2^s \qquad (7.4)$$

where $\phi_i(y)$ is the *i*th coordinate function of $\phi(y)$.

For every $a \in \mathbb{F}_2^r$ and every $b \in \mathbb{F}_2^s$, we have seen in Section 6.1.15 that

$$W_{f_{\phi,g}}(a, b) = 2^r \sum_{y \in \phi^{-1}(a)} (-1)^{g(y) \oplus b \cdot y}. \qquad (7.5)$$

This can be used to design resilient functions: if every element in $\phi(\mathbb{F}_2^s)$ has Hamming weight strictly larger than t, then $f_{\phi,g}$ is t-resilient (in particular, if $\phi(\mathbb{F}_2^s)$ does not contain the null vector, then $f_{\phi,g}$ is balanced). Indeed, if $w_H(a) \le t$ then $\phi^{-1}(a)$ is empty in Relation (7.5); hence, if $w_H(a) + w_H(b) \le t$, then $W_{f_{\phi,g}}(a, b)$ is null. The t-resiliency of $f_{\phi,g}$ under this hypothesis can also be deduced from the facts that any affine function $x \in \mathbb{F}_2^r \mapsto c \cdot x \oplus \epsilon$ ($c \in \mathbb{F}_2^r$ nonzero, $\epsilon \in \mathbb{F}_2$) is $(w_H(c) - 1)$-resilient, and that any Boolean function equal to the concatenation of t-resilient functions is a t-resilient function (see secondary construction 3 below).

It is possible (see [221, 223, 398]) to obtain a t-resilient function with (7.4) when every element in $\phi(\mathbb{F}_2^s)$ has Hamming weight larger than or equal to t (instead of strictly larger): we know that such function is $(t - 1)$-resilient by the observation above, and it is moreover t-resilient if, for every $a \in \mathbb{F}_2^r$ of Hamming weight t, we have $\sum_{y \in \phi^{-1}(a)} (-1)^{g(y)} = 0$. We just need then that, for every $a \in \mathbb{F}_2^r$ of Hamming weight t, if $\phi^{-1}(a) \ne \emptyset$, then $\phi^{-1}(a)$ has even size and the restriction of g to $\phi^{-1}(a)$ is balanced.

It is more difficult to construct unbalanced correlation immune functions with this method: in practice, we need that every nonzero element in $\phi(\mathbb{F}_2^s)$ has Hamming weight strictly larger than t and that, for every $b \in \mathbb{F}_2^s$ such that $1 \le w_H(b) \le t$, we have $\sum_{y \in \phi^{-1}(0_r)} (-1)^{g(y) \oplus b \cdot y} = 0$. If $\phi^{-1}(0_r)$ is an affine space, then this results in a condition on the restriction of g to $\phi^{-1}(0_r)$, which is similar to t-th order correlation immunity (this gives a construction that is more secondary than primary) and if $\phi^{-1}(0_r)$ has no such structure, then g needs to be built from scratch (very little work has been done on that).

Degree: The algebraic degree of $f_{\phi,g}$ is at most $s + 1 = n - r + 1$. It equals $s + 1$ if and only if ϕ has algebraic degree s (i.e., if at least one of its coordinate functions has algebraic degree s, that is, has odd Hamming weight, which is equivalent to $\sum_{y \in \mathbb{F}_2^s} \phi(y) \ne 0_r$). If we assume that every element in $\phi(\mathbb{F}_2^s)$ has Hamming weight strictly larger than t, then ϕ can have algebraic degree s only if $t \le r - 2$, since if $t = r - 1$, then ϕ is constant. Thus,

---

[3] These functions have also been studied under the name of linear-based functions in [7, 1137].

the algebraic degree of $f_{\phi,g}$ reaches Siegenthaler's bound $n - t - 1$ if and only if either $t = r - 2$ and ϕ has algebraic degree $s = n - t - 2$ or $t = r - 1$ and g has algebraic degree $s = n - t - 1$.

Nonlinearity: Relations (3.1), page 79, relating the nonlinearity to the Walsh transform, and (7.5) above lead straightforwardly to a general lower bound on the nonlinearity of Maiorana–McFarland's functions (first observed in [1026]):

$$nl(f_{\phi,g}) \geq 2^{n-1} - 2^{r-1} \max_{a \in \mathbb{F}_2^r} |\phi^{-1}(a)| \tag{7.6}$$

(where $|\phi^{-1}(a)|$ denotes the size of $\phi^{-1}(a)$). An upper bound obtained in [221] strengthens a bound previously obtained in [358, 359], which stated $nl(f_{\phi,g}) \leq 2^{n-1} - 2^{r-1}$:

$$nl(f_{\phi,g}) \leq 2^{n-1} - 2^{r-1} \left\lceil \sqrt{\max_{a \in \mathbb{F}_2^r} |\phi^{-1}(a)|} \right\rceil. \tag{7.7}$$

Proof of (7.7): The sum

$$\sum_{b \in \mathbb{F}_2^s} \left(\sum_{y \in \phi^{-1}(a)} (-1)^{g(y) \oplus b \cdot y} \right)^2 = \sum_{y,z \in \phi^{-1}(a); b \in \mathbb{F}_2^s} (-1)^{g(y) \oplus g(z) \oplus b \cdot (y+z)}$$

equals $2^s |\phi^{-1}(a)|$ (since the sum $\sum_{b \in \mathbb{F}_2^s} (-1)^{b \cdot (y+z)}$ is null if $y \neq z$). The maximum of a set of values being always larger than or equal to its arithmetic mean, we deduce

$$\max_{b \in \mathbb{F}_2^s} \left| \sum_{y \in \phi^{-1}(a)} (-1)^{g(y) \oplus b \cdot y} \right| \geq \sqrt{|\phi^{-1}(a)|}$$

and thus, according to Relation (7.5):

$$\max_{a \in \mathbb{F}_2^r; b \in \mathbb{F}_2^s} |W_{f_{\phi,g}}(a,b)| \geq 2^r \left\lceil \sqrt{\max_{a \in \mathbb{F}_2^r} |\phi^{-1}(a)|} \right\rceil.$$

Relation (3.1) completes the proof. □

This bound allowed characterizing the Maiorana–McFarland's functions $f_{\phi,g}$ such that $w_H(\phi(y)) > k$ for every y and achieving nonlinearity $2^{n-1} - 2^{k+1}$: Relation (7.7) implies $\sqrt{\max_{a \in F_2^r} |\phi^{-1}(a)|} \leq 2^{k-r+2}$ and thus $k + 1 \leq r \leq k + 2$ since $\max_{a \in F_2^r} |\phi^{-1}(a)| \geq 1$ and it also implies the inequality $nl(f_{\phi,g}) \leq 2^{n-1} - \frac{2^{r+\frac{s}{2}-1}}{\sqrt{\sum_{i=k+1}^r \binom{r}{i}}}$.

If $r = k+1$, then ϕ is the constant 1_s and $\max_{a \in F_2^r} |\phi^{-1}(a)| = 2^s$, thus $s \leq 2(k-r+2) = 2$ and $n \leq k + 3$. Either $s = 1$ and $g(y)$ is then any function in one variable, or $s = 2$ and g (which is then bent) is any function of the form $y_1 y_2 \oplus \ell(y)$ where ℓ is affine.

If $r = k + 2$, then ϕ is injective, therefore $2^s \leq \binom{r}{r-1} + \binom{r}{r} = r + 1$ and thus $n \leq k + 2 + \log_2(k+3)$, g is any function on $n - k - 2$ variables and $d_{alg}(f_{\phi,g}) \leq 1 + \log_2(k+3)$. See more in [221] on how to optimize the nonlinearity.

A simple example of k-resilient Maiorana–McFarland's functions such that $nl(f_{\phi,g}) = 2^{n-1} - 2^{k+1}$ (and thus achieving Sarkar et al.'s bound) can be given for any $r \geq 2^s - 1$ and for $k = r-2$ (see [221]). And, for every even $n \leq 10$, Sarkar et al.'s bound with $t = \frac{n}{2}-2$ can be achieved by Maiorana–McFarland's functions. Also, functions with high nonlinearities but not achieving Sarkar et al.'s bound with equality exist in Maiorana–McFarland's class (for every $n \equiv 1 \,[\bmod\, 4]$, there exist such $\frac{n-1}{4}$-resilient functions on $\mathbb{F}_2^n$ with nonlinearity $2^{n-1} - 2^{\frac{n-1}{2}}$).

Generalizations of Maiorana–McFarland's construction

Such generalizations, whose general frameworks have been seen in the present book in Subsections 5.2.2 and 5.4.1, have been introduced in [221] and [317]; the latter generalization has been further generalized into a class introduced in [226]. A motivation for introducing such generalizations is that Maiorana–McFarland's functions have the weakness that $x \mapsto f_{\phi,g}(x, y)$ is affine for every $y \in \mathbb{F}_2^s$ and have high divisibilities of their Fourier–Hadamard spectra (indeed, if we want to ensure that f is t-resilient with a large value of t, then we need to choose r large; then the Walsh spectrum of f is divisible by 2^r according to Relation (7.5); there is a risk that this property can be used in attacks, as it is used in [204] to attack block ciphers). The functions constructed in [221, 317] are concatenations of quadratic functions and those of [226] concatenations of indicators of flats. We have seen already in Subsections 5.2.2 and 5.4.1 the two classes:

1.
$$f_{\psi,\phi,g}(x, y) = \bigoplus_{i=1}^{k} x_{2i-1} x_{2i}\, \psi_i(y) \oplus x \cdot \phi(y) \oplus g(y),$$

with $x \in \mathbb{F}_2^r$, $y \in \mathbb{F}_2^s$, where $n = r + s$, $k = \lfloor \frac{r}{2} \rfloor$, and where $\psi : \mathbb{F}_2^s \to \mathbb{F}_2^k$, $\phi : \mathbb{F}_2^s \to \mathbb{F}_2^r$ and $g : \mathbb{F}_2^s \to \mathbb{F}_2$ can be chosen arbitrarily.

2. $\forall (x, y) \in \mathbb{F}_2^r \times \mathbb{F}_2^s,\ f(x, y) = \displaystyle\prod_{i=1}^{\varphi(y)} (x \cdot \phi_i(y) \oplus g_i(y) \oplus 1) \oplus x \cdot \phi(y) \oplus g(y),$

where φ is a function from $\mathbb{F}_2^s$ into $\{0, 1, \ldots, r\}$, $\phi_1, \ldots, \phi_r$ and ϕ are functions from $\mathbb{F}_2^s$ into $\mathbb{F}_2^r$ such that, for every $y \in \mathbb{F}_2^s$, the vectors $\phi_1(y), \ldots, \phi_{\varphi(y)}(y)$ are linearly independent, and $g_1, \ldots, g_r$ and g are Boolean functions on $\mathbb{F}_2^s$.

We have seen at pages 179 and 181 the formulae for the Walsh transforms of the functions of these classes, which result in sufficient conditions for their resiliency and in bounds on their nonlinearities; see [221, 226], where the author also studied how to optimize these parameters.

More complex ways of adapting the Maiorana–McFarland construction and other constructions can be found in [817, 928, 934, 1013, 1163, 1164], where some better parameters can be found but trade-offs are less clear.

Other constructions

A *construction derived from* $\mathcal{PS}_{ap}$ *construction* is introduced in [216] to obtain resilient functions: let k and r be positive integers and $n \geq r$; we denote $n - r$ by s; the vector space $\mathbb{F}_2^r$ is identified to the Galois field $\mathbb{F}_{2^r}$. Let g be any Boolean function on $\mathbb{F}_{2^r}$ and ϕ an $\mathbb{F}_2$-linear mapping from $\mathbb{F}_2^s$ to $\mathbb{F}_{2^r}$; set $a \in \mathbb{F}_{2^r}$ and $b \in \mathbb{F}_2^s$ such that, for every y in $\mathbb{F}_2^s$ and every z in $\mathbb{F}_{2^r}$, $a + \phi(y)$ is nonzero and $\phi^*(z) + b$ has Hamming weight larger than k, where ϕ^* is the adjoint of ϕ (satisfying $u \cdot \phi(x) = \phi^*(u) \cdot x$ for every x and u). Then, the function

$$f(x, y) = g\left(\frac{x}{a + \phi(y)}\right) \oplus b \cdot y, \text{ where } x \in \mathbb{F}_{2^r}, y \in \mathbb{F}_2^s, \tag{7.8}$$

is t-resilient with $t \geq k$. There exist bounds on the nonlinearities of these functions (see [223]), similar to those existing for Maiorana–McFarland's functions. But this class has much fewer elements than Maiorana–McFarland's class, because ϕ is linear.

Dobbertin's construction: We have seen at page 252 this method for modifying bent functions into balanced functions with high nonlinearities. Up to affine equivalence, we can assume that the bent function that starts the method, say $f(x, y)$, $x \in \mathbb{F}_2^{n/2}$, $y \in \mathbb{F}_2^{n/2}$, is such that $f(x, 0_{n/2}) = \epsilon$ ($\epsilon \in \mathbb{F}_2$) for every $x \in \mathbb{F}_2^{n/2}$ and that $\epsilon = 0$ (otherwise, consider $f \oplus 1$).

Proposition 121 *Let $f(x, y)$, $x \in \mathbb{F}_2^{n/2}$, $y \in \mathbb{F}_2^{n/2}$ be any bent function such that $f(x, 0_{n/2}) = 0$ for every $x \in \mathbb{F}_2^{n/2}$ and let g be any balanced function on $\mathbb{F}_2^{n/2}$. Then the Walsh transform of the function $h(x, y) = f(x, y) \oplus \delta_0(y) g(x)$, where δ_0 is the Dirac (or Kronecker) symbol, satisfies*

$$W_h(u, v) = 0 \text{ if } u = 0_{n/2} \text{ and } W_h(u, v) = W_f(u, v) + W_g(u) \text{ otherwise.} \tag{7.9}$$

Proof We have $W_h(u, v) = W_f(u, v) - \sum_{x \in \mathbb{F}_2^{n/2}} (-1)^{u \cdot x} + \sum_{x \in \mathbb{F}_2^{n/2}} (-1)^{g(x) \oplus u \cdot x} = W_f(u, v) - 2^{\frac{n}{2}} \delta_0(u) + W_g(u)$. Function g being balanced, we have $W_g(0_{n/2}) = 0$. And $W_f(0_{n/2}, v)$ equals $2^{\frac{n}{2}}$ for every v, since f is null on $\mathbb{F}_2^{n/2} \times \{0_{n/2}\}$ and according to Relation (6.7), page 200, applied to $E = \{0_{n/2}\} \times \mathbb{F}_2^{n/2}$ and $a = b = 0_{n/2}$ (or see the remark after Theorem 14, page 203). □

We deduce that

$$\max_{u, v \in \mathbb{F}_2^{n/2}} |W_h(u, v)| \leq \max_{u, v \in \mathbb{F}_2^{n/2}} |W_f(u, v)| + \max_{u \in \mathbb{F}_2^{n/2}} |W_g(u)|,$$

i.e., that $2^n - 2nl(h) \leq 2^n - 2nl(f) + 2^{\frac{n}{2}} - 2nl(g)$, that is,

$$nl(h) \geq nl(f) + nl(g) - 2^{\frac{n}{2}-1} = 2^{n-1} - 2^{\frac{n}{2}} + nl(g).$$

Applying recursively this principle (if $\frac{n}{2}$ is even, g can be constructed in the same way), we see that if $n = 2^k n'$ (n' odd), Dobbertin's method allows reaching the nonlinearity $2^{n-1} - 2^{\frac{n}{2}-1} - 2^{\frac{n}{4}-1} - \cdots - 2^{n'-1} - 2^{\frac{n'-1}{2}}$ since we know that, for every odd n', the nonlinearity of functions on $\mathbb{F}_2^{n'}$ can be as high as $2^{n'-1} - 2^{\frac{n'-1}{2}}$, and that balanced (quadratic) functions can achieve this value. If $n' \leq 7$, then this value is the best possible and $2^{n-1} - 2^{\frac{n}{2}-1} - 2^{\frac{n}{4}-1} - \cdots - 2^{n'-1} - 2^{\frac{n'-1}{2}}$ is therefore the best-known nonlinearity of balanced functions in general. For $n' > 7$, the best nonlinearity of balanced n'-variable functions is larger than $2^{n'-1} - 2^{\frac{n'-1}{2}}$ (see the paragraph devoted to nonlinearity in Section 3.1) and

$2^{n-1} - 2^{\frac{n}{2}-1} - 2^{\frac{n}{4}-1} - \cdots - 2^{2n'-1} - 2^{n'} + nl(g)$, where g is an n'-variable balanced function, can therefore reach higher values.

Dobbertin's conjecture on balanced functions is that his construction allows reaching the best nonlinearities of balanced functions in even numbers of variables. This question is still open, and it is, in particular, an open problem to find an 8-variable balanced Boolean function with nonlinearity 118.

Unfortunately, according to Relation (7.9), Dobbertin's construction cannot produce t-resilient functions with $t > 0$ since, g being a function defined on $\mathbb{F}_2^{n/2}$, there cannot exist more than one vector a such that $W_g(a)$ equals $\pm 2^{\frac{n}{2}}$. Modifying bent functions into resilient functions has been studied in [821].

7.1.9 Secondary constructions of correlation immune and resilient functions

There exist several simple *secondary constructions*, which can be combined to obtain resilient functions achieving the bounds of Sarkar et al. and Siegenthaler. We list them below in chronological order.

I. The *direct sum* of functions

A. *Adding a variable*

Let f be an r-variable t-resilient function. The Boolean function on $\mathbb{F}_2^{r+1}$:

$$h(x_1, \ldots, x_r, x_{r+1}) = f(x_1, \ldots, x_r) \oplus x_{r+1}$$

is $(t+1)$-resilient [1041], since, for $a \in \mathbb{F}_2^r$ and $a_{r+1} \in \mathbb{F}_2$, we have $W_h(a, a_{r+1}) = 2 W_f(a) \delta_1(a_{r+1})$. If f is an $(r, t, r - t - 1, 2^{r-1} - 2^{t+1})$ function[4], then h is an $(r+1, t+1, r-t-1, 2^r - 2^{t+2})$ function, and thus achieves Siegenthaler's and Sarkar et al.'s bounds. But h has the linear structure $(0, \ldots, 0, 1)$.

B. *Generalization*

If f is an r-variable t-resilient function ($t \geq 0$) and if g is an s-variable m-resilient function ($m \geq 0$), then the function

$$h(x_1, \ldots, x_r, x_{r+1}, \ldots, x_{r+s}) = f(x_1, \ldots, x_r) \oplus g(x_{r+1}, \ldots, x_{r+s})$$

is $(t + m + 1)$-resilient, since

$$W_h(a, b) = W_f(a) \times W_g(b), \quad a \in \mathbb{F}_2^r, \ b \in \mathbb{F}_2^s. \tag{7.10}$$

We have also $d_{alg}(h) = \max(d_{alg}(f), d_{alg}(g))$ and, thanks to Relation (3.1), page 79, relating the nonlinearity to the Walsh transform, $nl(h) = 2^{r+s-1} - \frac{1}{2}(2^r - 2nl(f))(2^s - 2nl(g)) = 2^r nl(g) + 2^s nl(f) - 2nl(f)nl(g)$. Such a function, called decomposable, does not give full satisfaction since such particular structure may be used in attacks. Moreover, h has a low algebraic degree, in general. And if $nl(f) = 2^{r-1} - 2^{t+1}$ ($t \leq r - 2$) and $nl(g) = 2^{s-1} - 2^{m+1}$ ($m \leq s - 2$, which is not the case when adding one variable), *i.e.*, if $nl(f)$ and $nl(g)$ have maximum possible values, then $nl(h) = 2^{r+s-1} - 2^{t+m+3}$ and h does not achieve Sarkar's and Maitra's bound. Function h has no nonzero linear structure if

---

[4] Recall that, by an $(n, m, d, \mathcal{N})$- function, we mean an n-variable, t-resilient function having algebraic degree at least d and nonlinearity at least $\mathcal{N}$.

and only if f and g both have no nonzero linear structure (we see then that having no linear structure is not a sufficient criterion).

Note that the result does not work with unbalanced functions.

II. Siegenthaler's construction

Let f and g be two Boolean functions on $\mathbb{F}_2^r$. Let us consider the function

$$h(x_1, \ldots, x_r, x_{r+1}) = (x_{r+1} \oplus 1) f(x_1, \ldots, x_r) \oplus x_{r+1} g(x_1, \ldots, x_r)$$

on $\mathbb{F}_2^{r+1}$. Note that the *truth table* of h can be obtained by concatenating the truth tables of f and g. Then:

$$W_h(a_1, \ldots, a_r, a_{r+1}) = W_f(a_1, \ldots, a_r) + (-1)^{a_{r+1}} W_g(a_1, \ldots, a_r). \tag{7.11}$$

Thus:

1. If f and g are t-resilient, then h is t-resilient [1041]; moreover, if for every $a \in \mathbb{F}_2^r$ of Hamming weight $t + 1$, we have $W_f(a) + W_g(a) = 0$, then h is $(t + 1)$-resilient. Note that the construction recalled in **I.A** corresponds to $g = f \oplus 1$ and satisfies this condition. Another possible choice of a function g satisfying this condition (first pointed out in [181]) is $g(x) = f(x_1 \oplus 1, \ldots, x_r \oplus 1) \oplus \epsilon$, where $\epsilon = t \, [\mathrm{mod} \, 2]$, since $W_g(a) = \sum_{x \in \mathbb{F}_2^r} (-1)^{f(x) \oplus \epsilon \oplus (x \oplus 1_r) \cdot a} = (-1)^{\epsilon + w_H(a)} W_f(a)$. It leads to a function h having also a nonzero linear structure. $-$

2. The value $\max_{a_1, \ldots, a_{r+1} \in \mathbb{F}_2} |W_h(a_1, \ldots, a_r, a_{r+1})|$ is bounded above by the number $\max_{a_1, \ldots, a_r \in \mathbb{F}_2} |W_f(a_1, \ldots, a_r)| + \max_{a_1, \ldots, a_r \in \mathbb{F}_2} |W_g(a_1, \ldots, a_r)|$; this implies $2^{r+1} - 2nl(h) \leq 2^{r+1} - 2nl(f) - 2nl(g)$, that is $nl(h) \geq nl(f) + nl(g)$.

   a. If f and g achieve maximum possible nonlinearity $2^{r-1} - 2^{t+1}$ and if h is $(t + 1)$-resilient, then the nonlinearity $2^r - 2^{t+2}$ of h is the best possible.

   b. If f and g are such that, for every vector a, at least one of the numbers $W_f(a)$, $W_g(a)$ is null (in other words, if the supports of the Walsh transforms of f and g are disjoint), then we have $\max_{a_1, \ldots, a_{r+1} \in \mathbb{F}_2} |W_h(a_1, \ldots, a_r, a_{r+1})| = \max \left(\max_{a_1, \ldots, a_r \in \mathbb{F}_2} |W_f(a_1, \ldots, a_r)|; \max_{a_1, \ldots, a_r \in \mathbb{F}_2} |W_g(a_1, \ldots, a_r)| \right)$. Hence we have $2^{r+1} - 2nl(h) = 2^r - 2 \min(nl(f), nl(g))$ and $nl(h)$ equals therefore $2^{r-1} + \min(nl(f), nl(g))$; thus, if f and g achieve best possible nonlinearity $2^{r-1} - 2^{t+1}$, then h achieves best possible nonlinearity $2^r - 2^{t+1}$.

3. If the monomials of highest degree in the algebraic normal forms of f and g are not all the same, then $d_{alg}(h) = 1 + \max(d_{alg}(f), d_{alg}(g))$. Note that this condition is not satisfied in the two cases indicated above in **1**, for which h is $(t + 1)$-resilient.

4. For every $a = (a_1, \ldots, a_r) \in \mathbb{F}_2^r$ and every $a_{r+1} \in \mathbb{F}_2$, we have, denoting $(x_1, \ldots, x_r)$ by x: $D_{(a, a_{r+1})} h(x, x_{r+1}) = D_a f(x) \oplus a_{r+1}(f \oplus g)(x) \oplus x_{r+1} D_a(f \oplus g)(x) \oplus a_{r+1} D_a(f \oplus g)(x)$. If $d_{alg}(f \oplus g) \geq d_{alg}(f)$, then $D_{(a,1)} h$ is nonconstant, for every a. And if, additionally, there does not exist $a \neq 0_r$ such that $D_a f$ and $D_a g$ are constant and equal to each other, then h admits no nonzero linear structure.

This construction allows obtaining from any two t-resilient functions f and g having disjoint Walsh spectra, achieving nonlinearity $2^{r-1} - 2^{t+1}$ and such that $d_{alg}(f \oplus g) =$

$r - t - 1$, a t-resilient function h having algebraic degree $r - t$ and having nonlinearity $2^r - 2^{t+1}$, that is, achieving Siegenthaler's and Sarkar et al.'s bounds; note that this construction increases (by 1) the algebraic degrees of f and g. And since, from any t-resilient function f having algebraic degree $r - t - 1$ and nonlinearity $2^{r-1} - 2^{t+1}$, we can deduce a function h having resiliency order $t + 1$ and nonlinearity $2^r - 2^{t+2}$, that is, achieving Siegenthaler's and Sarkar et al.'s bounds and having same algebraic degree as f (but having nonzero linear structures), we can by combining these two methods keep best trade-offs among resiliency order, algebraic degree, and nonlinearity, and increase by 1 the degree and the resiliency order.

Generalization: Let $(f_y)_{y \in \mathbb{F}_2^s}$ be a family of r-variable t-resilient functions; then the function on $\mathbb{F}_2^{r+s}$ defined by $f(x, y) = f_y(x)$ ($x \in \mathbb{F}_2^r$, $y \in \mathbb{F}_2^s$) is t-resilient. Indeed, we have $W_f(a, b) = \sum_{y \in \mathbb{F}_2^s} (-1)^{b \cdot y} W_{f_y}(a)$. Function f corresponds to the concatenation of the functions f_y; hence, this secondary construction can be viewed as a generalization of Maiorana–McFarland's construction (in which the functions f_y are t-resilient affine functions).

More on the resilient functions achieving high nonlinearities and constructed by using, among others, the secondary constructions above (as well as algorithmic methods) can be found in [696].

III. Tarannikov's elementary construction

Let g be any Boolean function on $\mathbb{F}_2^r$. We define the Boolean function h on $\mathbb{F}_2^{r+1}$ by $h(x_1, \ldots, x_r, x_{r+1}) = x_{r+1} \oplus g(x_1, \ldots, x_{r-1}, x_r \oplus x_{r+1})$. By the change of variable $x_r \leftarrow x_r \oplus x_{r+1}$, we see that the Walsh transform $W_h(a_1, \ldots, a_{r+1})$ is equal to

$$\sum_{x_1, \ldots, x_{r+1} \in \mathbb{F}_2} (-1)^{a \cdot x \oplus g(x_1, \ldots, x_r) \oplus (a_r \oplus a_{r+1} \oplus 1) x_{r+1}}, \text{ where } a = (a_1, \ldots, a_r) \text{ and } x = (x_1, \ldots, x_r);$$

if $a_r \oplus a_{r+1} = 0$, then this value is null, and if $a_r \oplus a_{r+1} = 1$, then it equals $2 W_g(a_1, \ldots, a_{r-1}, a_r)$. Thus:

1. $nl(h) = 2 \, nl(g)$.
2. If g is t-resilient, then h is t-resilient, since $w_H(a_1, \ldots, a_r) \leq w_H(a_1, \ldots, a_{r+1})$. And h is $(t+1)$-resilient if and only if, for every vector $(a_1, \ldots, a_{r+1})$ of Hamming weight $t + 1$ such that $a_r \oplus a_{r+1} = 1$, we have $W_g(a_1, \ldots, a_r) = 0$, and the only case not implied by the t-resiliency of g is when $a_r = 1$ and $a_{r+1} = 0$; hence, h is $(t+1)$-resilient if and only if $W_g(a_1, \ldots, a_{r-1}, 1)$ is null for every vector $(a_1, \ldots, a_{r-1})$ of Hamming weight t; note that, in such a case, if g has nonlinearity $2^{r-1} - 2^{t+1}$ then the nonlinearity of h, which equals $2^r - 2^{t+2}$, achieves then Sarkar et al.'s bound too. The condition that $W_g(a_1, \ldots, a_{r-1}, 1)$ is null for every vector $(a_1, \ldots, a_{r-1})$ of Hamming weight at most t is achieved if g does not actually depend on its last input bit; but the construction is then a particular case of the construction recalled in **I.A**. The condition is also achieved if g is obtained from two t-resilient functions, by using Siegenthaler's construction (recalled in **II**), according to Relation (7.11).
3. $d_{alg}(h) = d_{alg}(g)$ if $d_{alg}(g) \geq 1$.
4. h has the nonzero linear structure $(0, \ldots, 0, 1, 1)$.

Tarannikov combined in [1080] this construction with the direct sum and Siegenthaler constructions recalled in **I** and **II**, to build a more complex secondary construction, which allows increasing at the same time the resiliency order and the algebraic degree of the functions and which leads to an infinite sequence of functions achieving Siegenthaler's and Sarkar et al.'s bounds. Increasing then, by using the construction recalled in **I.A**, the set of ordered pairs (r, m) for which such functions can be constructed, he deduced the existence of r-variable t-resilient functions achieving Siegenthaler's and Sarkar et al.'s bounds for any number of variables r and any resiliency order t such that $t \geq \frac{2r-7}{3}$ and $t > \frac{r}{2} - 2$ (but these functions have nonzero linear structures). In [934], Pasalic et al. slightly modified this more complex Tarannikov's construction into a construction that we shall call *Tarannikov et al.'s construction*, which allowed, when iterating it together with the construction recalled in **I.A**, to relax slightly the condition on t into $t \geq \frac{2r-10}{3}$ and $t > \frac{r}{2} - 2$.

IV. Indirect sum of functions
Tarannikov et al.'s construction has been in its turn generalized into a construction that has been named *indirect sum* a few years after it was introduced, and that we already encountered at page 233 as a construction of bent functions. Indirect sum builds a function h from four functions, while the previous constructions used at most two functions. All the secondary constructions listed above are particular cases of it: they correspond to fixing two or three of the four functions.

Theorem 21 *[225] Let r and s be positive integers and let t and m be non-negative integers such that $t < r$ and $m < s$. Let f_1 and f_2 be two r-variable functions. Let g_1 and g_2 be two s-variable functions. We define the $(r + s)$-variable function:*

$$h(x, y) = f_1(x) \oplus g_1(y) \oplus (f_1 \oplus f_2)(x)(g_1 \oplus g_2)(y); \quad x \in \mathbb{F}_2^r, y \in \mathbb{F}_2^s.$$

If f_1 and f_2 are distinct and if g_1 and g_2 are distinct, then the algebraic degree of h equals $\max(d_{alg}(f_1), d_{alg}(g_1), d_{alg}(f_1 \oplus f_2) + d_{alg}(g_1 \oplus g_2))$; otherwise, it equals $\max(d_{alg}(f_1), d_{alg}(g_1))$. The Walsh transform of h takes value at (a, b), where $a \in \mathbb{F}_2^r, b \in \mathbb{F}_2^s$:

$$W_h(a, b) = \frac{1}{2} W_{f_1}(a) \left[W_{g_1}(b) + W_{g_2}(b) \right] + \frac{1}{2} W_{f_2}(a) \left[W_{g_1}(b) - W_{g_2}(b) \right]. \quad (7.12)$$

If f_1 and f_2 are t-resilient and g_1 and g_2 are m-resilient, then h is $(t + m + 1)$-resilient.

If the Walsh transforms of f_1 and f_2 have disjoint supports and if the Walsh transforms of g_1 and g_2 have disjoint supports, then

$$nl(h) = \min_{i,j \in \{1,2\}} \left(2^{r+s-2} + 2^{r-1} nl(g_j) + 2^{s-1} nl(f_i) - nl(f_i) nl(g_j) \right). \quad (7.13)$$

In particular, if f_1 and f_2 are two $(r, t, -, 2^{r-1} - 2^{t+1})$ functions with disjoint Walsh supports, if g_1 and g_2 are two $(s, m, -, 2^{s-1} - 2^{m+1})$ functions with disjoint Walsh supports, and if $f_1 \oplus f_2$ has degree $r - t - 1$ and $g_1 \oplus g_2$ has algebraic degree $s - m - 1$, then h is a $(r + s, t + m + 1, r + s - t - m - 2, 2^{r+s-1} - 2^{t+m+2})$ function, and thus achieves Siegenthaler's and Sarkar et al.'s bounds.

Proof For every $a \in \mathbb{F}_2^r, b \in \mathbb{F}_2^s$, we have:

$$
W_h(a,b) = \sum_{y \in \mathbb{F}_2^s; g_1 \oplus g_2(y)=0} \left(\sum_{x \in \mathbb{F}_2^r} (-1)^{f_1(x) \oplus a \cdot x} \right) (-1)^{g_1(y) \oplus b \cdot y}
$$

$$
+ \sum_{y \in \mathbb{F}_2^s; g_1 \oplus g_2(y)=1} \left(\sum_{x \in \mathbb{F}_2^r} (-1)^{f_2(x) \oplus a \cdot x} \right) (-1)^{g_1(y) \oplus b \cdot y}
$$

$$
= W_{f_1}(a) \sum_{\substack{y \in \mathbb{F}_2^s; \\ g_1 \oplus g_2(y)=0}} (-1)^{g_1(y) \oplus b \cdot y} + W_{f_2}(a) \sum_{\substack{y \in \mathbb{F}_2^s; \\ g_1 \oplus g_2(y)=1}} (-1)^{g_1(y) \oplus b \cdot y}
$$

$$
= W_{f_1}(a) \sum_{y \in \mathbb{F}_2^s} (-1)^{g_1(y) \oplus b \cdot y} \left(\frac{1 + (-1)^{(g_1 \oplus g_2)(y)}}{2} \right)
$$

$$
+ W_{f_2}(a) \sum_{y \in \mathbb{F}_2^s} (-1)^{g_1(y) \oplus b \cdot y} \left(\frac{1 - (-1)^{(g_1 \oplus g_2)(y)}}{2} \right).
$$

We deduce Relation (7.12). If (a,b) has Hamming weight at most $t + m + 1$, then a has Hamming weight at most t or b has Hamming weight at most t; hence we have $W_h(a,b) = 0$. Thus, h is $t + m + 1$-resilient.

If $f_1 \oplus f_2$ and $g_1 \oplus g_2$ are nonconstant, then the algebraic degree of h equals $\max(d_{alg}(f_1), d_{alg}(g_1), d_{alg}(f_1 \oplus f_2) + d_{alg}(g_1 \oplus g_2))$ because the terms of highest degrees in $(g_1 \oplus g_2)(y)(f_1 \oplus f_2)(x)$, in $f_1(x)$ and in $g_1(y)$ cannot cancel each other. We deduce from Relation (7.12) that if the supports of the Walsh transforms of f_1 and f_2 are disjoint, as well as those of g_1 and g_2, then

$$
\max_{(a,b) \in \mathbb{F}_2^r \times \mathbb{F}_2^s} |W_h(a,b)| = \frac{1}{2} \max_{i,j \in \{1,2\}} \left(\max_{a \in \mathbb{F}_2^r} |W_{f_i}(a)| \max_{b \in \mathbb{F}_2^s} |W_{g_j}(b)| \right)
$$

and according to Relation (3.1) relating the nonlinearity to the Walsh transform, this implies

$$
2^{r+s} - 2nl(h) = \frac{1}{2} \max_{i,j \in \{1,2\}} \left((2^r - 2nl(f_i))(2^s - 2nl(g_j)) \right),
$$

which is equivalent to Relation (7.13). □

Note that function h, defined this way, is the concatenation of the four functions $f_1, f_1 \oplus 1, f_2$ and $f_2 \oplus 1$, in an order controlled by $g_1(y)$ and $g_2(y)$.

This construction is nicely general and does not need the initial functions f_1, f_2 and g_1, g_2 to satisfy complex conditions, contrary to other constructions that have been derived later for building bent functions (see pages 233 and foll.) and could be adapted for designing resilient functions.

Examples of pairs (f_1, f_2) (or (g_1, g_2)) satisfying the hypotheses of Theorem 21 can be found in [225]. The interest of the indirect sum compared to the direct sum is that it allows designing functions h that are more complex (have larger algebraic degree and possibly larger algebraic immunity and fast algebraic immunity).

Remark. The indirect sum (as well as all its particular cases viewed above) is less well adapted to constructing correlation immune functions: Relation (7.12) shows that if $W_{f_1}(a) = W_{f_2}(a) = W_{g_1}(b) = W_{g_2}(b) = 0$, then $W_h(a,b) = 0$, but when for instance $a = 0_r$ and $b \neq 0_s$, we have $W_h(a,b) = \frac{1}{2}W_{f_1}(0_r)\left[W_{g_1}(b) + W_{g_2}(b)\right] + \frac{1}{2}W_{f_2}(0_r)\left[W_{g_1}(b) - W_{g_2}(b)\right]$, and there are additional conditions on the values of $W_{f_1}(0_r)$, $W_{f_2}(0_r)$, $W_{g_1}(b)$, and $W_{g_2}(b)$ when $w_H(b) \geq m + 1$ (and on the values of $W_{g_1}(0_s)$, $W_{g_2}(0_s)$, $W_{f_1}(a)$, and $W_{f_2}(a)$ when $w_H(a) \geq t + 1$) for allowing h to be more than $(\min(t,m))$-th order correlation immune. □

V. Constructions without extension of the number of variables
Proposition 85, page 236, leads to the following construction:

Proposition 122 *[227] Let n be any positive integer and t any nonnegative integer such that $t \leq n$. Let f_1, f_2, and f_3 be three t-th order correlation immune (resp. t-resilient) functions. Then the function $s_1 = f_1 \oplus f_2 \oplus f_3$ is t-th order correlation immune (resp. t-resilient) if and only if the function $s_2 = f_1 f_2 \oplus f_1 f_3 \oplus f_2 f_3$ is t-th order correlation immune (resp. t-resilient). Moreover,*

$$nl(s_2) \geq \frac{1}{2}\left(nl(s_1) + \sum_{i=1}^{3} nl(f_i)\right) - 2^{n-1} \tag{7.14}$$

and if the Walsh supports of f_1, f_2, and f_3 are pairwise disjoint (that is, if at most one value $W_{f_i}(s)$, $i = 1,2,3$ is nonzero, for every vector s), then

$$nl(s_2) \geq \frac{1}{2}\left(nl(s_1) + \min_{1 \leq i \leq 3} nl(f_i)\right). \tag{7.15}$$

Proof Relation (6.30), page 236, and the fact that, for every nonzero vector (resp. any vector) a of Hamming weight at most t, we have $W_{f_i}(a) = 0$ for $i = 1,2,3$ imply that $W_{s_1}(a) = 0$ if and only if $W_{s_2}(a) = 0$. Relations (7.14) and (7.15) are also direct consequences of Relation (6.30) and of Relation (3.1), page 79, relating the nonlinearity to the Walsh transform. □

Note that this secondary construction is proper to allow achieving high algebraic immunity with s_2, given functions with lower algebraic immunities f_1, f_2, f_3, and s_1, since the support of s_2 can be made more complex than those of these functions. This is done without changing the number of variables and keeping similar resiliency order and nonlinearity.

Remark. Let g and h be two Boolean functions on $\mathbb{F}_2^n$ with disjoint supports and let f be equal to $g \oplus h = g + h$. Then f is balanced if and only if $w_H(g) + w_H(h) = 2^{n-1}$. By linearity of the Fourier–Hadamard transform, we have $\widehat{f} = \widehat{g} + \widehat{h}$. Thus, if g and h are t-th order correlation immune, then f is t-resilient. For every nonzero $a \in \mathbb{F}_2^n$, we have $|W_f(a)| = 2|\widehat{f}(a)| \leq 2|\widehat{g}(a)| + 2|\widehat{h}(a)| = |W_g(a)| + |W_h(a)|$. Thus, assuming that f is balanced, we have $nl(f) \geq nl(g) + nl(h) - 2^{n-1}$. The algebraic degree of f is bounded above by (and can be equal to) the maximum of the algebraic degrees of g and h. □

The largest part of the secondary constructions of bent functions described in Subsection 6.1.16 can be altered into constructions of correlation immune and resilient functions; see [216].

The generalization of Proposition 85 given by Proposition 86, page 237, leads to:

Proposition 123 *[227] Let n be any positive integer and k any nonnegative integer such that $k \leq n$. Let $f_1, \ldots, f_7$ be k-th order correlation immune (resp. k-resilient) functions. If two among the functions $s_1 = f_1 \oplus \ldots \oplus f_7$, $s_2 = f_1 f_2 \oplus f_1 f_3 \oplus \ldots \oplus f_6 f_7$ and*

$$s_4 = \bigoplus_{1 \leq i_1 < \ldots < i_4 \leq 7} \prod_{j=1}^{l} f_{i_j} \text{ is } k\text{-th order correlation immune (resp. } k\text{-resilient), then the}$$

third one is k-th order correlation immune (resp. k-resilient).

Low Hamming weight *correlation immune functions*

Except for the secondary construction without extension of the number of variables, the primary and secondary constructions of resilient functions recalled above do not work well for building unbalanced correlation immune functions, as we observed for the indirect sum in the remark at the head of page 302. We shall see in Section 12.1, page 425, that low Hamming weight correlation immune functions are useful for countermeasures to side-channel attacks. More constructions are then needed.

We denote by $CI_{n,t}$ the set of n-variable t-th order correlation immune Boolean functions and by $\omega_{n,t}$ the minimal Hamming weight of nonzero functions in $CI_{n,t}$.

According to Proposition 120, page 289, the Hamming weight of a t-th order correlation immune function is divisible by $2^{t + \left\lfloor \frac{n-t-1}{d_{alg}(f)} \right\rfloor}$.

The only n-variable n-th order correlation immune Boolean functions are the two constant functions. The only $(n-1)$-th order correlation immune nonconstant Boolean functions are the $(n-1)$-resilient functions $\bigoplus_{i=1}^{n} x_i$ and $\bigoplus_{i=1}^{n} x_i \oplus 1$. Then $\omega_{n,n} = 2^n$ and $\omega_{n,n-1} = 2^{n-1}$.

We have of course $\omega_{n,t} \leq \omega_{n,t+1}$ and more precisely:

Lemma 10 *Let $1 \leq t \leq n$ be integers. Then*

$$\omega_{n+1,t} \leq 2\omega_{n,t} \leq \omega_{n+1,t+1}.$$

Proof For every $f \in CI_{n,t}$, the $(n+1)$-variable function $g(x, x_{n+1}) = f(x)$ belongs to $CI_{n+1,t}$, since, for every a, we have $\widehat{g}(a, 0) = 2\widehat{f}(a)$ and $\widehat{g}(a, 1) = 0$. Moreover, g has Hamming weight $2w_H(f)$. This proves the left-hand side inequality. For every $f \in CI_{n+1,t+1}$, the restriction of f to the hyperplane of equation $x_{n+1} = 0$ is a tth-order correlation immune Boolean function with half weight. This proves the right-hand side inequality. □

As observed in [591], the largest dimension $k_{\max}(n, t+1)$ of a binary linear code $[n, k, t+1]$ provides the upper bound $\omega_{n,t} \leq 2^{n-k_{\max}(n,t+1)}$, according to Corollary 6, page 88, and to the fact that the dual of a linear code of dimension k has dimension $n - k$. Since a binary MDS code of parameters $[n, n-1, 2]$ exists, we have then $\omega_{n,1} = 2$ for every n.

Table 7.1 Lower bound on $\omega_{n,t}$ from Delsarte's linear programming bound [74].

n \ t	1	2	3	4	5	6	7	8	9	10	11	12	13
1	2												
2	2	4											
3	2	4	8										
4	2	6	8	16									
5	2	8	12	16	32								
6	2	8	16	32	32	64							
7	2	8	16	48	64	64	128						
8	2	10	16	64	88	112	128	256					
9	2	12	20	96	128	192	224	256	512				
10	2	12	24	96	192	320	384	512	512	1,024			
11	2	12	24	96	192	512	640	1,024	1,024	1,024	2,048		
12	2	14	24	112	176	768	1,024	1,536	1,792	2,048	2,048	4,096	
13	2	16	28	128	224	1,024	1,536	2,560	3,072	3,584	4,096	4,096	8,192

Table 7.2 Minimum weight of t-th order correlation immune nonzero n-variable functions.

n \ t	1	2	3	4	5	6	7	8	9	10	11	12	13
1	2												
2	2	4											
3	2	4	8										
4	2	8	8	16									
5	2	8	16	16	32								
6	2	8	16	32	32	64							
7	2	8	16	64	64	64	128						
8	2	12	16	64	128	128	128	256					
9	2	12	24	128	128	256	256	256	512				
10	2	12	24	128	256	512	512	512	512	1,024			
11	2	12	24	128	256	512	1,024	1,024	1,024	1,024	2,048		
12	2	16	24	???	256	512	1,024	2,048	2,048	2,048	2,048	4,096	
13	2	16	32	???	???	???	1,024	4,096	4,096	4,096	4,096	4,096	8,192

As also observed in [591], $\omega_{n,t}$ being equal to the minimal number of rows in a simple binary orthogonal array of strength t, Delsarte's linear programming bound [422] provides a lower bound on $\omega_{n,t}$ that we give in Table 7.1.

The Satisfiability Modulo Theory (SMT) tool has been used to search for correlation immune Boolean functions in [74] together with the upper bound deduced from known constructions of binary codes, the lower bound of Table 7.1, and the divisibility of $\omega_{n,t}$ by 2^t.

Table 7.2, displaying the known values of $\omega_{n,t}$ for $n \le 13$, is taken from [74, 258, 287, 1104]. The entries in light gray follow from $\omega_{n,1} = 2$ and $\omega_{n,n} = 2^n$. The entries in dark gray follow from $\omega_{n,n-1} = 2^{n-1}$ and from Lemma 10 above, which imply $\omega_{n,t} \le \omega_{n,n-1} = 2^{n-1}$, and from Theorem 116, page 285, which implies that $\omega_{n,t} = 2^{n-1}$ for $\lceil \frac{2n-2}{3} \rceil \le t \le n-1$. The entry $n = 11, t = 4$ is obtained in [74, 1104] and the entries $n = 11, t = 5$; $n = 12, t = 5$; and $n = 12, t = 7$ follow from Proposition 124 below. The entries in bold have been obtained by the SMT tool. A triple question mark in this table indicates that the value is unknown. Note, however, that upper bounds are known for these entries: [946] makes a detailed exploration of several evolutionary algorithms for finding Boolean functions that have various orders of correlation immunity and minimal Hamming weight. These investigations show that $\omega_{11,4} \leq 128$, $\omega_{11,5} \leq 256$, $\omega_{12,5} \leq 256$, $\omega_{12,6} \leq 1,024$, $\omega_{13,7} \leq 2,048$.

It is an open question to determine whether the columns in this table (and more generally for every value of n and t) are nondecreasing, that is, $\omega_{n,t} \leq \omega_{n+1,t}$ for every n and t. If the reply to this question is positive, then these values are optimal. It is also shown in [946] that $\omega_{12,4} \leq 256$, $\omega_{13,4} \leq 256$, $\omega_{13,5} \leq 512$, $\omega_{13,6} \leq 1024$. See also [112], where nonexistence results are proved.

It is shown in [1104] that $\omega_{n,2} \geq 4 \left\lceil \frac{n+1}{4} \right\rceil$ for $n \geq 2$ (and the proof can be slightly simplified): the Golomb–Xiao–Massey characterization of correlation immune functions (Theorem 5, page 87) directly gives that a Boolean function f is in $CI_{n,2}$ if and only if the matrix $H = ((-1)^{e_i \cdot x})_{\substack{x \in supp(f) \\ i=0,1,\ldots,n}}$, where $e_0 = 0_n$ and $(e_1, \ldots, e_n)$ is the canonical basis of $\mathbb{F}_2^n$ over $\mathbb{F}_2$, satisfies $H^t \times H = w_H(f) I_{n+1}$, where I_{n+1} is the identity matrix (*i.e.*, H is a Hadamard matrix); this shows that $\omega_{n,2} \geq 4 \left\lceil \frac{n+1}{4} \right\rceil$ since we know that 4 divides $\omega_{n,2}$ and that matrix I_{n+1} has rank $n + 1$, while matrix H has rank at most $w_H(f)$ and $H^t \times H$ has necessarily rank smaller than or equal to that of H.

It is deduced in [1104] that for each known Hadamard $4k \times 4k$ matrix, a function in $CI_{4k-1,2}$ of (minimum) Hamming weight $4k$ (and functions in $CI_{4k+i,2}$ of Hamming weight $4k$ for every $i = 0, 1, 2$) can be deduced. It has been conjectured by J. Hadamard that there exists a $4k \times 4k$ Hadamard matrix for every k. According to the observations above, this conjecture is equivalent to conjecturing that $\omega_{n,2} = 4 \left\lceil \frac{n+1}{4} \right\rceil$ for every n.

Proposition 124 *[258] Let t be any even integer such that $2 \leq t \leq n$. Then*

$$\omega_{n+1,t+1} = 2\,\omega_{n,t}.$$

Proof For every $f \in CI_{n,t}$, the $(n + 1)$-variable function

$$g(x, x_{n+1}) = \begin{cases} f(x), & \text{when } x_{n+1} = 0 \\ f(x + 1_n), & \text{when } x_{n+1} = 1, \end{cases}$$

has Hamming weight $2\,w_H(f)$ and is a $(t + 1)$-th order correlation immune Boolean function. Indeed, for any $u \in \mathbb{F}_2^n$ and any $u_{n+1} \in \mathbb{F}_2$, we have:

$$\widehat{g}(u, u_{n+1}) = \sum_{(x,x_{n+1}) \in \mathbb{F}_2^{n+1}} g(x, x_{n+1})(-1)^{(u,u_{n+1}) \cdot (x,x_{n+1})}$$

$$= \sum_{x \in \mathbb{F}_2^n} f(x)(-1)^{u \cdot x} + \sum_{x \in \mathbb{F}_2^n} f(x + 1_n)(-1)^{(u,u_{n+1}) \cdot (x,1)}$$

$$= \widehat{f}(u) + \sum_{x \in \mathbb{F}_2^n} f(x)(-1)^{(u,u_{n+1})\cdot(x+1_n,1)}$$

$$= (1 + (-1)^{w_H(u,u_{n+1})})\, \widehat{f}(u).$$

If $w_H(u, u_{n+1}) = t + 1$, then since t is an even integer, we have $1 + (-1)^{w_H(u,u_{n+1})} = 1 + (-1)^{t+1} = 0$, thus $\widehat{g}(u, u_{n+1}) = 0$.

If $u = 0_n$ and $u_{n+1} = 1$, then $1 + (-1)^{w_H(u,u_{n+1})} = 0$, and $\widehat{g}(u, u_{n+1}) = 0$.

If $1 \leq w_H(u, u_{n+1}) \leq t$ and $u \neq 0_n$, we have that $1 \leq w_H(u) \leq t$, and since $f(x) \in CI_{n,t}$, we have $\widehat{f}(u) = 0$, then $\widehat{g}(u, u_{n+1}) = 0$.

Hence, if $1 \leq w_H(u, u_{n+1}) \leq t + 1$, then $\widehat{g}(u, u_{n+1}) = 0$ and $g(x, x_{n+1})$ is a $(t + 1)$th-order correlation immune Boolean function. Thus, $\omega_{n+1,t+1} \leq 2\omega_{n,t}$ when t is even, and since $2\omega_{n,t} \leq \omega_{n+1,t+1}$ for any $1 \leq t \leq n$ according to Lemma 10, this completes the proof. $\qquad\qquad\square$

This leads to the bound $\omega_{n,3} \geq 8\lceil \frac{n}{4} \rceil$ for $n \geq 3$. It is conjectured in [258] that for $n \geq 3$, we have $\omega_{n,3} = 8\lceil \frac{n}{4} \rceil$. Using the characterization of functions in $CI_{n,2}$ given above Proposition 124 by means of Hadamard matrices and the known existence of infinitely many $4k \times 4k$ Hadamard matrices, Wang deduced in [1104] that infinitely many values $n \equiv i \pmod 4$ satisfy the conjecture for each $i = -1, 0, 1, 2$. He observed that the conjecture (which is still open) is equivalent to that of Hadamard, which is more than 100 years old.

A construction of functions of weight 2^m in $CI_{n,t}$ has been given in [1104], which defines their support as made of the 2^m vectors of the form $(v \cdot u_1, \ldots, v \cdot u_n)$, where v ranges over $\mathbb{F}_2^m$ and the u_j are such that none of them depends linearly on at most $t - 1$ others. This construction is nothing more than Corollary 6, page 88, with a linear code whose generator matrix is made of the u_j by columns (recall that the dual distance of such code is the minimum number of linearly dependent columns), or Corollary 22, page 292. The construction, however, allowed completing some entries in the table that was given in [74, 287] (Table 7.2 is the completed table).

Using the Fourier–Hadamard transform *instead of the Walsh transform to construct correlation immune functions*

We have seen that correlation immune functions are characterized by both the Fourier–Hadamard transform and the Walsh transform. We have also seen that most known constructions of correlation immune functions were based on the properties of the Walsh transform and that they built in fact resilient functions, mostly. The Fourier–Hadamard transform and the Walsh transform are closely related through Relation (2.32), page 55. However, they behave differently with respect to the operations in $\mathcal{BF}_n$: while the Walsh transform behaves well with respect to the addition of Boolean functions (for instance, the Walsh transform of a direct sum equals the product of the Walsh transforms; see Relation (7.10), page 297), the Fourier–Hadamard transform behaves well with respect to the multiplication of functions; in particular, the Fourier–Hadamard transform of a direct product equals the product of the Fourier–Hadamard transforms, since

$$\sum_{x\in\mathbb{F}_2^n, y\in\mathbb{F}_2^m} f(x)g(y)(-1)^{a\cdot x\oplus b\cdot y} = \left(\sum_{x\in\mathbb{F}_2^n} f(x)(-1)^{a\cdot x}\right)\left(\sum_{y\in\mathbb{F}_2^m} g(y)(-1)^{b\cdot y}\right).$$

Multiplying Boolean functions produces unbalanced functions, and if the functions have low Hamming weights, the product has low Hamming weight as well. A related general construction of correlation immune functions by multiplication is deduced in [258] that we report now. In the next proposition, given a matrix $M \in \mathbb{F}_2^{ns \times ns}$ and given $i, j = 1, \ldots, s$, we denote by $M^{(i,j)}$ the $n \times n$ matrix (called a block of M) obtained from M by selecting its rows of indices between $n(i-1)+1$ and ni and its columns of indices between $n(j-1)+1$ and nj. Assuming that M is nonsingular, denoting the inverse matrix of M by M^{-1} and the transposed matrix of M^{-1} by M', we denote by $M^{-1(i,j)}$ and $M'^{(i,j)}$ the matrices obtained similarly from M^{-1} and M'. Since $M'^{(j,i)}$ is the transposed matrix of $M^{-1(i,j)}$, we have, for any $x, y \in \mathbb{F}_2^n$

$$x \cdot (y \times M^{-1(i,j)}) = y \cdot (x \times M'^{(j,i)}), \tag{7.16}$$

where "$\cdot$" is the *usual inner product*.

Proposition 125 *[258] Let s be a positive integer and M be an $ns \times ns$ nonsingular matrix over $\mathbb{F}_2$. Let $f_j \in CI_{n,t_j}$ for some nonnegative integers t_j, $1 \leq j \leq s$. Define the following ns-variable function h, whose input is written in the form $(x^{(1)}, x^{(2)}, \ldots, x^{(s)})$, where $x^{(1)}, x^{(2)}, \ldots, x^{(s)} \in \mathbb{F}_2^n$:*

$$h(x^{(1)}, x^{(2)}, \ldots, x^{(s)}) = \prod_{j=1}^{s} f_j\left(\sum_{i=1}^{s} x^{(i)} \times M^{(i,j)}\right).$$

Assume that if $1 \leq w_H(u^{(1)}, u^{(2)}, \ldots, u^{(s)}) \leq t$, then $1 \leq j \leq s$, exists such that

$$1 \leq w_H\left(\sum_{i=1}^{s} u^{(i)} \times M'^{(i,j)}\right) \leq t_j.$$

Then h belongs to $CI_{ns,t}$ and has Hamming weight $\prod_{j=1}^{s} w_H(f_j)$.

Proof For any $(u^{(1)}, u^{(2)}, \ldots, u^{(s)}) \in (\mathbb{F}_2^n)^s$, we have $\widehat{h}(u^{(1)}, u^{(2)}, \ldots, u^{(s)})$

$$= \sum_{x^{(1)}, \ldots, x^{(s)} \in \mathbb{F}_2^n} \left(\prod_{j=1}^{s} f_j\left(\sum_{i=1}^{s} x^{(i)} \times M^{(i,j)}\right)\right)(-1)^{\oplus_{j=1}^{s} u^{(j)} \cdot x^{(j)}}.$$

Replace $\sum_{i=1}^{s} x^{(i)} \times M^{(i,j)}$ by $y^{(j)}$ for $1 \leq j \leq s$, then $(y^{(1)}, y^{(2)}, \ldots, y^{(s)}) = (x^{(1)}, x^{(2)}, \ldots, x^{(s)}) \times M$, according to the well-known method of multiplication of matrices by blocks. Thus

$$(x^{(1)}, x^{(2)}, \ldots, x^{(s)}) = (y^{(1)}, y^{(2)}, \ldots, y^{(s)}) \times M^{-1},$$

which means $x^{(j)} = \sum_{i=1}^{s} y^{(i)} \times M^{-1(i,j)}$ for $1 \le j \le s$. Using (7.16), we have

$$\widehat{h}(u^{(1)}, u^{(2)}, \ldots, u^{(s)})$$

$$= \sum_{y^{(1)}, \ldots, y^{(s)} \in \mathbb{F}_2^n} \left(\prod_{j=1}^{s} f_j(y^{(j)}) \right) (-1)^{\bigoplus_{j=1}^{s} u^{(j)} \cdot \left(\sum_{i=1}^{s} y^{(i)} \times M^{-1(i,j)} \right)}$$

$$= \sum_{y^{(1)}, \ldots, y^{(s)} \in \mathbb{F}_2^n} \left(\prod_{j=1}^{s} f_j(y^{(j)}) \right) (-1)^{\bigoplus_{i=1}^{s} y^{(i)} \cdot \left(\sum_{j=1}^{s} u^{(j)} \times M'^{(j,i)} \right)}$$

$$= \sum_{y^{(1)}, \ldots, y^{(s)} \in \mathbb{F}_2^n} \left(\prod_{j=1}^{s} f_j(y^{(j)}) \right) (-1)^{\bigoplus_{j=1}^{s} y^{(j)} \cdot \left(\sum_{i=1}^{s} u^{(i)} \times M'^{(i,j)} \right)}$$

$$= \prod_{j=1}^{s} \left(\sum_{y^{(j)} \in \mathbb{F}_2^n} f_j(y^{(j)}) (-1)^{y^{(j)} \cdot \left(\sum_{i=1}^{s} u^{(i)} \times M'^{(i,j)} \right)} \right)$$

$$= \prod_{j=1}^{s} \widehat{f}_j \left(\sum_{i=1}^{s} u^{(i)} \times M'^{(i,j)} \right).$$

According to the hypothesis, for any $(u^{(1)}, u^{(2)}, \ldots, u^{(s)}) \in (\mathbb{F}_2^n)^s$ satisfying $1 \le w_H(u^{(1)}, u^{(2)}, \ldots, u^{(s)}) \le t$, there exists $1 \le j \le s$ such that

$$1 \le w_H \left(\sum_{i=1}^{s} u^{(i)} \times M'^{(i,j)} \right) \le t_j.$$

Since f_j is a t_j-th order correlation immune Boolean function for any $1 \le j \le s$, h is a t-th order correlation immune Boolean function. And h being affine equivalent to the direct product of f_j, we have $w_H(h) = \prod_{j=1}^{s} w_H(f_j)$.   □

Corollary 23 *[258] Let n, t, s be positive integers satisfying $t \le n$ and $s \ge 2$. Assume that $f_1 \in CI_{n,t}$ and $f_j \in CI_{n, \lfloor \frac{t}{2} \rfloor}$ for any $2 \le j \le s$. Define*

$$h(x^{(1)}, x^{(2)}, \ldots, x^{(s)}) = f_1(x^{(1)}) \prod_{j=2}^{s} f_j(x^{(1)} + x^{(j)}),$$

where $x^{(1)}, x^{(2)}, \ldots, x^{(s)} \in \mathbb{F}_2^n$. Then h belongs to $CI_{ns,t}$ and has Hamming weight $\prod_{j=1}^{s} w_H(f_j)$.

Proof Let M be the $ns \times ns$ nonsingular matrix whose representation by $n \times n$ blocks equals

$$
M = \begin{bmatrix}
I & I & I & \cdots & I \\
0 & I & 0 & \cdots & 0 \\
0 & 0 & I & \cdots & 0 \\
\vdots & \vdots & \vdots & \cdots & \vdots \\
0 & 0 & 0 & \cdots & I
\end{bmatrix},
$$

where I is the identity $n \times n$ matrix and 0 is the all-0 $n \times n$ matrix. Then:

$$
M' = \begin{bmatrix}
I & 0 & 0 & \cdots & 0 \\
I & I & 0 & \cdots & 0 \\
I & 0 & I & \cdots & 0 \\
\vdots & \vdots & \vdots & \cdots & \vdots \\
I & 0 & 0 & \cdots & I
\end{bmatrix}.
$$

We have:

$$
h(x^{(1)}, x^{(2)}, \ldots, x^{(s)}) = \prod_{j=1}^{s} f_j \left(\sum_{i=1}^{s} x^{(i)} \times M^{(i,j)} \right).
$$

For any $(u^{(1)}, u^{(2)}, \ldots, u^{(s)}) \in (\mathbb{F}_2^n)^s$ satisfying $1 \leq w_H(u^{(1)}, u^{(2)}, \ldots, u^{(s)}) \leq t$, we have either

$$
1 \leq w_H \left(\sum_{i=1}^{s} u^{(i)} \times M'^{(i,1)} \right) = w_H \left(\sum_{i=1}^{s} u^{(i)} \right) \leq t,
$$

or $\sum_{i=1}^{s} u^{(i)} = 0_n$, in which case there exists $2 \leq j \leq s$ such that $u^{(j)} \neq 0_n$ and

$$
w_H(u^{(j)}) = w_H \left(\sum_{i=1, i \neq j}^{s} u^{(i)} \right) = \frac{w_H(u^{(j)}) + w_H \left(\sum_{i=1, i \neq j}^{s} u^{(i)} \right)}{2} \leq \frac{\sum_{i=1}^{s} w_H(u^{(i)})}{2} \leq \frac{t}{2}.
$$ Proposition 125 completes the proof. $\qquad\square$

Corollary 24 *[258] Let n, s, t be positive integers satisfying $t \leq n$ and $s \geq 2$. We have the following:*

$$
\omega_{ns,t} \leq \left(\omega_{n, \lfloor \frac{t}{2} \rfloor} \right)^{s-1} \omega_{n,t}.
$$

A construction of low-weight t-th order correlation immune Boolean functions through Kronecker sum

The *Kronecker sum* of two vectors

$$
(x^{(1)}, x^{(2)}) = ((x_1^{(1)}, \ldots, x_{n_2}^{(1)}), (x_1^{(2)}, \ldots, x_{n_1}^{(2)})) \in \mathbb{F}_2^{n_2} \times \mathbb{F}_2^{n_1} \to
$$

$$
x^{(1)} \boxplus x^{(2)} = (x_{i_2}^{(1)} \oplus x_{i_1}^{(2)})_{\substack{1 \leq i_1 \leq n_1 \\ 1 \leq i_2 \leq n_2}} \in \mathbb{F}_2^{n_1 n_2}
$$

generalizes to s variables as follows: let $n_1, \ldots, n_s$ be positive integers and $\mathcal{I} = \{1, \ldots, n_1\} \times \cdots \times \{1, \ldots, n_s\}$, then for every $I = (i_1, \ldots, i_s) \in \mathcal{I}$ and every $1 \leq r \leq s$, we denote by $I^{(r)}$ the vector $(i_1, \ldots, i_{r-1}, i_{r+1}, \ldots, i_s)$. Writing

$$x^{(r)} = (x^{(r)}_{i_1, \ldots, i_{r-1}, i_{r+1}, \ldots, i_s})_{\substack{i_1 \in \{1, \ldots, n_1\} \\ \cdots \\ i_s \in \{1, \ldots, n_s\}}} \in \mathbb{F}_2^{n_1 \cdots n_{r-1} n_{r+1} \cdots n_s},$$

the *s-th order Kronecker sum* is defined as

$$(x^{(1)}, x^{(2)}, \ldots, x^{(s)}) \to x^{(1)} \boxplus \cdots \boxplus x^{(s)} = \left(\bigoplus_{r=1}^{s} x^{(r)}_{I^{(r)}} \right)_{I \in \mathcal{I}} \in \mathbb{F}_2^{n_1 \cdots n_s}.$$

Proposition 126 *[258] Let s, t be positive integers such that $2^s > t$. Let $f_1(x^{(1)})$ be an $(n_2 \cdots n_s)$-variable t-th order correlation immune Boolean function and $f_2(x^{(2)})$ an $(n_1 n_3 \cdots n_s)$-variable $2\lfloor \frac{t}{2} \rfloor$-th order correlation immune Boolean function. For every $r = 3, 4, \ldots, s$, let $f_r(x^{(r)})$ be an $(n_1 \cdots n_{r-1} n_{r+1} \cdots n_s)$-variable Boolean function such that, for every $w \in \mathbb{F}_2^{n_r}$ satisfying $1 \leq w_H(w) \leq t$ with $w_H(w)$ even, we have $\widehat{f_r}(w) = 0$. We define the $\big((n_1 + 1) n_2 n_3 \cdots n_s\big)$-variable function h by its support as follows: $\mathrm{Supp}(h) =$*

$$\left\{ \left(x^{(1)} \boxplus \cdots \boxplus x^{(s)}, x^{(1)} \right); \; x^{(1)} \in \mathrm{Supp}(f_1), x^{(2)} \in \mathrm{Supp}(f_2), \ldots, x^{(s)} \in \mathrm{Supp}(f_s) \right\},$$

then h is t-th order correlation immune of Hamming weight $\prod_{r=1}^{s} w_H(f_r)$.

In particular, if f_1 is a t-th order correlation immune Boolean function and if each function f_r is $2\lfloor \frac{t}{2} \rfloor$-th order correlation immune for $r = 2, \ldots, s$, then h is a t-th order correlation immune Boolean function of Hamming weight $\prod_{r=1}^{s} w_H(f_r)$.

Proof Let us calculate the Fourier–Hadamard transform of h. Its input is any pair (u, v), where u is a binary vector of the same length as $x^{(1)} \boxplus \cdots \boxplus x^{(s)}$ and v is a binary vector of the same length as $x^{(1)}$, that is, $u = (u_I)_{I \in \mathcal{I}} \in \mathbb{F}_2^{n_1 n_2 \cdots n_s}$ and $v = (v_J)_{J \in \mathcal{J}} \in \mathbb{F}_2^{n_2 \cdots n_s}$, $\mathcal{J} = \{1, \ldots, n_2\} \times \cdots \times \{1, \ldots, n_s\}$. We have

$$\widehat{h}(u, v) = \sum_{\substack{x^{(1)} \in \mathrm{Supp}(f_1), \\ \ldots, x^{(s)} \in \mathrm{Supp}(f_s)}} (-1)^{\bigoplus_{I \in \mathcal{I}} u_I \left(\bigoplus_{r=1}^{s} x^{(r)}_{I^{(r)}} \right) \oplus v \cdot x^{(1)}}.$$

Let us write $u_{0, i_2, \ldots, i_s} = v_{i_2, \ldots, i_s}$; $\overrightarrow{u_1} = \left(\bigoplus_{i_1=0}^{n_1} u_{i_1, 1, \ldots, 1}, \ldots, \bigoplus_{i_1=0}^{n_1} u_{i_1, n_2, \ldots, n_s} \right)$ and $\overrightarrow{u_r} = \left(\bigoplus_{i_r=1}^{n_r} u_{1, \ldots, 1, i_r, 1, \ldots, 1}, \ldots, \bigoplus_{i_r=1}^{n_r} u_{n_1, \ldots, n_{r-1}, i_r, n_{r+1}, \ldots, n_s} \right)$, for every $r = 2, \ldots s$. We have then

$$\widehat{h}(u, v) = \left(\sum_{x^{(1)} \in \mathrm{Supp}(f_1)} (-1)^{\bigoplus_{I \in \mathcal{I}} u_I x^{(1)}_{I^{(1)}} \oplus v \cdot x^{(1)}} \right)$$

$$\times \prod_{r=2}^{s} \left(\sum_{x^{(r)} \in \mathrm{Supp}(f_r)} (-1)^{\bigoplus_{I \in \mathcal{I}} u_I x^{(r)}_{I^{(r)}}} \right) = \widehat{f_1}(\overrightarrow{u_1}) \times \prod_{r=2}^{s} \widehat{f_r}(\overrightarrow{u_r}).$$

For $1 \leq w_H(u, v) \leq t$, we have $w_H(\overrightarrow{u_1}) \leq w_H(u, v) \leq t$.

- If $w_H(\overrightarrow{u_1}) \neq 0$, then since f_1 is t-th order correlation immune, we have $\widehat{h}(u, v) = 0$.
- If $w_H(\overrightarrow{u_1}) = 0$, then $w_H(u, v)$ is even since $w_H(u, v)$ (mod 2) $= w_H(\overrightarrow{u_1})$ (mod 2), and then $w_H(u, v) \leq 2\lfloor \frac{t}{2} \rfloor$. We have then that:
- If $w_H(\overrightarrow{u_2}) \neq 0$, then we have $1 \leq w_H(\overrightarrow{u_2}) \leq w_H(u) \leq w_H(u, v) \leq 2\lfloor \frac{t}{2} \rfloor$, and since f_2 is $2\lfloor \frac{t}{2} \rfloor$-th order correlation immune, we deduce $\widehat{h}(u, v) = 0$.
- If $w_H(\overrightarrow{u_2}) = \ldots = w_H(\overrightarrow{u_{j-1}}) = 0$ and $w_H(\overrightarrow{u_j}) \neq 0$, where $3 \leq j \leq s$, then $w_H(u)$ and $w_H(\overrightarrow{u_j})$ are even since $w_H(u)$ (mod 2) $= w_H(\overrightarrow{u_2})$ (mod 2) $= w_H(\overrightarrow{u_j})$ (mod 2) and we have $2 \leq w_H(\overrightarrow{u_j}) \leq 2\lfloor \frac{t}{2} \rfloor$, and the hypothesis on f_j implies $\widehat{h}(u, v) = 0$.
- If $w_H(\overrightarrow{u_2}) = \ldots = w_H(\overrightarrow{u_s}) = 0$, then since $w_H(u, v) \neq 0$ and $w_H(\overrightarrow{u_1}) = 0$, there exist $0 \leq i_1'' < i_1' \leq n_1, 1 \leq i_2 \leq n_2, \ldots, 1 \leq i_s \leq n_s$ such that $u_{i_1', i_2, \ldots, i_s} = u_{i_1'', i_2, \ldots, i_s} = 1$. Since $w_H(\overrightarrow{u_s}) = 0$, there exist in fact two values of i_s such that $u_{i_1', i_2, \ldots, i_s} = 1$. Since $w_H(\overrightarrow{u_{s-1}}) = 0$, there exist then four values of (i_{s-1}, i_s) such that $u_{i_1', i_2, \ldots, i_s} = 1$. By induction, we have then $w_H(u, v) \geq 2^s$. But we have $1 \leq w_H(u, v) \leq t < 2^s$ by hypothesis, a contradiction. Hence, $w_H(\overrightarrow{u_1}) = w_H(\overrightarrow{u_2}) = \ldots = w_H(\overrightarrow{u_s}) = 0$ cannot happen. This completes the proof. $\qquad \square$

A corollary can be found in [258], as well as variants of the construction of Proposition 126, one of which needs weaker hypotheses but does not include the term in $x^{(1)}$ in the support of h (and provides then functions in fewer variables) and the other deals with third-order correlation immune functions.

7.1.10 On the number of correlation immune and resilient functions

It is important to ensure that the selected criteria for the Boolean functions, supposed to be used in some cryptosystems, do not restrict the choice of the functions too severely. Hence, the set of functions should be enumerated. But this enumeration is unknown for most criteria, and the cases of correlation immune and resilient functions make no exception. We recall below what is known. More than for bent functions, the class of resilient functions produced by Maiorana–McFarland's construction[5] is by far the widest class, compared to the classes obtained from the other usual constructions, and the number of provably resilient Maiorana–McFarland functions seems negligible with respect to the total number of functions with the same properties. For balanced (*i.e.*, 0-resilient) functions, this can be checked: for every positive r, the number of balanced Maiorana–McFarland functions (7.4) obtained by choosing ϕ such that $\phi(y) \neq 0_r$, for every y, equals $(2^r - 1)^{2^s} 2^{2^s}$, and is smaller than or equal to $2^{2^{n-1}}$ (since $r \geq 1, s = n - r$). It is negligible with respect to the number $\binom{2^n}{2^{n-1}} \approx \frac{2^{2^n + \frac{1}{2}}}{\sqrt{\pi 2^n}}$ of all balanced functions on $\mathbb{F}_2^n$. The number of t-resilient Maiorana–McFarland functions obtained by choosing ϕ such that $w_H(\phi(y)) > t$ for every y equals $\left[2 \sum_{i=t+1}^{r} \binom{r}{i} \right]^{2^{n-r}}$, and is probably also very small compared to the number of all t-resilient functions. But this number is unknown.

---

[5] We have seen that this construction hardly allows building unbalanced correlation immune functions.

The exact number of t-resilient functions is known for $t \geq n - 3$ (see [181], where $(n-3)$-resilient functions are characterized) and $(n-4)$-resilient functions have been characterized [256, 125].

As for bent function, upper bounds on the numbers of correlation immune and resilient functions come directly from the Siegenthaler bound on the algebraic degree: the number of t-th order correlation immune (resp. t-resilient) n-variable functions is bounded above by $2^{\sum_{i=0}^{n-m} \binom{n}{i}}$ (resp. $2^{\sum_{i=0}^{n-m-1} \binom{n}{i}}$). These bounds are the so-called naive bounds. In 1990, Yang and Guo published an upper bound on the number of first-order correlation immune functions. At the same time, Denisov obtained a rather strong result (see below), but his result being published in Russian, it was not known internationally. His paper was translated into English two years later [433] but was not widely known either. This explains why several papers appeared, some of which with weaker results, that we describe first. Park et al. [926] improved upon Yang–Guo's bound. Schneider [1024] proved that the number of t-resilient n-variable Boolean functions is less than

$$\prod_{i=1}^{n-m} \binom{2^i}{2^{i-1}}^{\binom{n-i-1}{m-1}} ,$$

but this result was known; see [520]. A general upper bound on the number of Boolean functions whose distances to affine functions are all divisible by 2^t has been obtained in [301]. It implies an upper bound on the number of t-resilient functions, which improves upon previous bounds for about half the values of (n, m) (it is better for t large). This bound divides the naive bound by approximately $2^{\sum_{i=0}^{n-m-1} \binom{m-1}{i} - 1}$ if $m \geq \frac{n}{2}$ and by approximately $2^{2^{2m+1}-1}$ if $m < \frac{n}{2}$.

An upper bound on t-resilient functions ($m \geq \frac{n}{2} - 1$) partially improving upon this latter bound thanks to a refinement of its method was obtained for $\frac{n}{2} - 1 \leq m < n - 2$ in [285]: the number of n-variable t-resilient functions is lower than

$$2^{\sum_{i=0}^{n-m-2} \binom{n}{i}} + \frac{\binom{n}{n-m-1}}{2^{\binom{m+1}{n-m-1}+1}} \prod_{i=1}^{n-m} \binom{2^i}{2^{i-1}}^{\binom{n-i-1}{m-1}} .$$

The expressions of these bounds seem difficult to compare mathematically. Tables have been computed in [285].

The problem of counting resilient functions is related to counting integer solutions of a system of linear equations; see [850].

The main result given by Denisov in [433] is an asymptotic formula for the number of t-th order correlation immune functions, where t is negligible compared to n. This formula was later believed incorrect by the author, and a correction was given by him in [434], but it has been shown later in [182] that the correct expression was the original one, at least under the condition $1 \leq t \leq (\frac{\ln 2}{6} - \epsilon)\frac{n}{\ln n}$ where $\epsilon > 0$: this number is then equivalent to

$$2^{2^n - t + \sum_{j=0}^{t} j\binom{n}{j}} (2^{n-1}\pi)^{-\frac{\sum_{j=1}^{t} \binom{n}{j}}{2}} ,$$

and the number of t-resilient functions is equivalent to

$$2^{2^n + \sum_{j=0}^t j \binom{n}{j}} (2^{n-1} \pi)^{-\frac{\sum_{j=0}^t \binom{n}{j}}{2}}.$$

For large resiliency orders, Tarannikov and Kirienko showed in [1082] that, for every positive integer t, there exists a number $p(m)$ such that for $n > p(m)$, any $(n - m)$-resilient function $f(x_1, \ldots, x_n)$ is equivalent, up to permutation of its input coordinates, to a function of the form $g(x_1, \ldots, x_{p(m)}) \oplus x_{p(m)+1} \oplus \cdots \oplus x_n$. It is then a simple matter to deduce that the number of $(n - m)$-resilient functions equals $\sum_{i=0}^{p(m)} A(m, i) \binom{n}{i}$, where $A(m, i)$ is the number of i-variable $(i - m)$-resilient functions that depend on all inputs x_1, $x_2, \ldots, x_i$ nonlinearly. Hence, it is equivalent to $\frac{A(m, p(m))}{p(m)!} n^{p(m)}$ for t constant when n tends to infinity, and it is at most $A_m \, n^{p(m)}$, where A_m depends on t only. It is proved in [1083] that $3 \cdot 2^{t-2} \leq p(m) \leq (m - 1)2^{t-2}$ and in [1082] that $p(4) = 10$; hence the number of $(n - 4)$-resilient functions equals $(1/2)n^{10} + \mathcal{O}(n^9)$. It is also shown in [1082] that for $n \geq 10$, there does not exist an unbalanced nonconstant $(n - 4)$-th order correlation immune function and that for $n \geq 11$, there does not exist an $(n - 4)$-resilient function depending nonlinearly on all its variables.

The classification of first-order correlation immune functions and of 1-resilient functions has been studied in [758], with an exact enumeration for $n = 7$ and a precise estimation for $n = 8$.

7.2 Resilient vectorial Boolean functions

For the convenience of the reader, we recall what we have seen in Section 3.3.1, page 129: an (n, m)-*function* $F(x)$ is t-th order *correlation immune* if its output distribution does not change when at most t coordinates x_i of x are kept constant.

S-boxes being better balanced, F is called t-*resilient* if it is balanced and t-th order correlation immune. If such an (n, m, t)-*function* F exists, then we have the bounds $t \leq \left\lfloor \frac{2^{m-1} n}{2^m - 1} \right\rfloor$, $t \leq 2 \left\lfloor \frac{2^{m-2}(n+1)}{2^m - 1} \right\rfloor - 1$, $m \leq n - t$ in general, $m \leq n - \log_2 \left[\sum_{i=0}^{t/2} \binom{n}{i} \right]$ if t is even and $m \leq n - \log_2 \left[\binom{n-1}{(t-1)/2} + \sum_{i=0}^{(t-1)/2} \binom{n}{i} \right]$ if t is odd, and more complex bounds based on linear programming [78, 520].

Composing a t-resilient (n, m)-function by a permutation of $\mathbb{F}_2^m$ does not change its resiliency order. Function F is t-resilient if and only if one of the following conditions is satisfied (see Proposition 41, page 130):

(i) $\sum_{x \in \mathbb{F}_2^n} (-1)^{v \cdot F(x) \oplus u \cdot x} = 0$, for every $u \in \mathbb{F}_2^n$ such that $w_H(u) \leq t$ and every $v \in \mathbb{F}_2^m \setminus \{0_m\}$.

(ii) $\sum_{x \in \mathbb{F}_2^n} (-1)^{g(F(x)) \oplus u \cdot x} = 0$, for every $u \in \mathbb{F}_2^n$ such that $w_H(u) \leq t$ and every balanced t-variable Boolean function g.

Finally, F is t-resilient if and only if:

(iii) for every vector $b \in \mathbb{F}_2^m$, the Boolean function $\varphi_b = \delta_{\{b\}} \circ F$ is t-th order correlation immune and has Hamming weight 2^{n-m}.

7.2.1 Constructions of resilient vectorial Boolean functions

Linear or affine resilient functions

The construction of t-resilient linear functions is easy: Bennett et al. [58] and Chor et al. [370] give the connection between linear resilient functions and linear codes (correlation immune functions being related to orthogonal arrays; see [181, 180], this relationship is in fact due to Delsarte [422]). There exists a linear (n, m, t)-function if and only if there exists a binary linear $[n, m, t + 1]$ code.

Proposition 127 *[58] Let G be a generating matrix for an $[n, m, d]$ binary linear code. We define $L : \mathbb{F}_2^n \mapsto \mathbb{F}_2^m$ by the rule $L(x) = x \times G^T$, where G^T is the transpose of G. Then L is an $(n, m, d - 1)$-function.*

This is a direct consequence of Corollary 22, page 292, and of Proposition 41. It can also be seen directly: for every nonzero $v \in \mathbb{F}_2^m$, the vector $v \cdot L(x) = v \cdot (x \times G^t)$ has the form $u \cdot x$, where $u = v \times G$ is a nonzero codeword. Hence, u has Hamming weight at least d and the linear function $v \cdot L$ is $(d - 1)$-resilient, since it has at least d independent terms of degree 1 in its ANF.

The converse of Proposition 127 is clearly also true.

Proposition 127 is still straightforwardly true if L is affine instead of linear, that is, $L(x) = x \times G^t + a$, where a is a vector of $\mathbb{F}_2^k$.

Stinson [1049] considered the equivalence between resilient functions and what he called large sets of orthogonal arrays. According to Proposition 41, an (n, m)-function is t-resilient if and only if there exists a set of 2^m disjoint binary arrays of dimensions $2^{n-m} \times n$, such that, in any t columns of each array, each of the 2^t elements of $\mathbb{F}_2^t$ occurs in exactly 2^{n-m-t} rows and no two rows are identical. The construction of (n, m, t)-functions by Proposition 127 can be generalized by considering nonlinear codes of length n (that is, subsets of $\mathbb{F}_2^n$) and of size 2^{n-m}, whose *dual distance* (see Definition 4, page 16) is at least $t + 1$ (see [1050]). In the case of Proposition 127, C is the dual of the code of generating matrix G. The nonlinear code needs also to be *systematic* (that is, there must exist a subset I of $\{1, \ldots, n\}$ called an *information set* of C, necessarily of size $n - m$ since the code has size 2^{n-m}, such that every possible tuple occurs in exactly one codeword within the specified coordinates x_i; $i \in I$; we have seen this notion at page 161) to allow the construction of an $(n, m, d^\perp - 1)$-function: the image of a vector $x \in \mathbb{F}_2^n$ is the unique vector y of $\mathbb{F}_2^n$ such that $y_i = 0$ for every $i \in I$ and such that $x \in y + C$ (in other words, to calculate y, we first determine the unique codeword c of C, which matches with x on the information set and we have $y = x + c$). It is deduced in [1050] that, for every $r \geq 3$, a $(2^{r+1}, 2^{r+1} - 2r - 2, 5)$-resilient function exists (the construction is based on the Kerdock code), and that no affine resilient function with such good parameters exists.

Maiorana–McFarland resilient functions

The idea of designing resilient vectorial functions by generalizing the Maiorana–MacFarland construction is natural. One can find a first reference of such construction in a paper by Nyberg [906], but for generating perfect nonlinear functions. This technique has been used by Kurosawa et al. [723], Johansson and Pasalic [648], Pasalic and Maitra

[933], and Gupta and Sarkar [580] to produce functions having high resiliency and high nonlinearity.[6]

Definition 70 *The class of Maiorana–McFarland* (n, m)-*functions is the set of those functions F that can be written in the form*

$$F(x, y) = x \times \begin{pmatrix} \varphi_{11}(y) & \cdots & \varphi_{1m}(y) \\ \vdots & \ddots & \vdots \\ \varphi_{r1}(y) & \cdots & \varphi_{rm}(y) \end{pmatrix} + H(y), \ (x, y) \in \mathbb{F}_2^r \times \mathbb{F}_2^s \qquad (7.17)$$

where r and s are two integers satisfying $r + s = n$, *H is any* (s, m)-*function and, for every* $i \leq r$ *and every* $j \leq m$, φ_{ij} *is a Boolean function on* $\mathbb{F}_2^s$.

The concatenation of t-resilient functions being still t-resilient, if the transpose matrix of the matrix involved in Equation (7.17) is the generator matrix of a linear $[r, m, d]$-code for every vector y ranging over $\mathbb{F}_2^s$, then the (n, m)-function F is $(d - 1)$-resilient.

After denoting, for every $i \leq m$, by ϕ_i the (s, r)-function that admits for coordinate functions the Boolean functions $\varphi_{1i}, \ldots, \varphi_{ri}$ (in ith column of the matrix above), we can rewrite Relation (7.17) as

$$F(x, y) = (x \cdot \phi_1(y) \oplus h_1(y), \ldots, x \cdot \phi_m(y) \oplus h_m(y)). \qquad (7.18)$$

Resiliency   Equivalently to what is written above in terms of codes, we have:

Proposition 128 *Let n, m, r, and s be integers such that* $n = r + s$. *Let F be a Maiorana–McFarland* (n, m)-*function defined as in (7.18) and such that, for every* $y \in \mathbb{F}_2^s$, *the family* $(\phi_i(y))_{i \leq m}$ *is a basis of an m-dimensional subspace of* $\mathbb{F}_2^r$ *having* $t + 1$ *for minimum Hamming weight, then F is at least t-resilient.*

Nonlinearity   According to Proposition 53, page 166, the nonlinearity $nl(F)$ of any Maiorana–McFarland (n, m)-function defined as in Relation (7.18) satisfies

$$nl(F) = 2^{n-1} - 2^{r-1} \max_{(u, u') \in \mathbb{F}_2^r \times \mathbb{F}_2^s, v \in \mathbb{F}_2^m \setminus \{0_m\}} \left| \sum_{y \in E_{u,v}} (-1)^{v \cdot H(y) \oplus u' \cdot y} \right|, \qquad (7.19)$$

where $E_{u,v}$ denotes the set $\{y \in \mathbb{F}_2^s; \ \sum_{i=1}^m v_i \phi_i(y) = u\}$.

The bounds given by Relations (7.6) and (7.7), page 294, imply the following:

$$2^{n-1} - 2^{r-1} \max_{u \in \mathbb{F}_2^r, v \in \mathbb{F}_2^m \setminus \{0_m\}} |E_{u,v}| \leq nl(F) \leq 2^{n-1} - 2^{r-1} \left\lceil \sqrt{\max_{u \in \mathbb{F}_2^r, v \in \mathbb{F}_2^m \setminus \{0_m\}} |E_{u,v}|} \right\rceil.$$

If, for every element y, the vector space spanned by the vectors $\phi_1(y), \ldots, \phi_m(y)$ admits m for dimension and has a minimum Hamming weight strictly larger than k (so that F is

---

[6] But, as seen in Subsection 3.3.2, this notion of nonlinearity is not relevant to S-boxes for stream ciphers. The generalized nonlinearity, which is the correct notion, needs to be further studied for resilient functions and for MM functions.

t-resilient with $t \geq k$), then we have

$$nl(F) \leq 2^{n-1} - 2^{r-1} \left\lceil \frac{2^{s/2}}{\sqrt{\sum_{i=k+1}^{r} \binom{r}{i}}} \right\rceil. \tag{7.20}$$

The nonlinearity can be exactly calculated in two situations (at least): if, for every vector $v \in \mathbb{F}_2^m \setminus \{0_m\}$, the (s,r)-function $y \mapsto \sum_{i \leq m} v_i \phi_i(y)$ is injective (resp. takes exactly two times each value of its range), then F admits $2^{n-1} - 2^{r-1}$ (resp. $2^{n-1} - 2^r$) for nonlinearity.

Johansson and Pasalic described in [648] a way to specify the vectorial functions $\phi_1, \ldots, \phi_m$ so that this kind of condition is satisfied. Their result can be generalized in the following form:

Lemma 11 *Let C be a binary linear $[r, m, t + 1]$ code. Let $\beta_1, \ldots, \beta_m$ be a basis of the $\mathbb{F}_2$-vector space $\mathbb{F}_{2^m}$, and L_0 a linear isomorphism between $\mathbb{F}_{2^m}$ and C. Then the functions $L_i(z) = L_0(\beta_i z)$, $i = 1, \ldots, m$, are such that, for every $v \in \mathbb{F}_2^m \setminus \{0_m\}$, the function $z \in \mathbb{F}_{2^m} \mapsto \sum_{i=1}^{m} v_i L_i(z)$ is a bijection from $\mathbb{F}_{2^m}$ into C.*

Proof For every vector v in $\mathbb{F}_2^m$ and every element z of $\mathbb{F}_{2^m}$, we have $\sum_{i=1}^{m} v_i L_i(z) = L_0\left((\sum_{i=1}^{m} v_i \beta_i) z \right)$. If the vector v is nonzero, then the element $\sum_{i=1}^{m} v_i \beta_i$ is nonzero. Hence, the function $z \in \mathbb{F}_{2^m} \mapsto \sum_{i=1}^{m} v_i L_i(z)$ is a bijection. $\square$

Since the functions $L_1, L_2, \ldots, L_m$ vanish at zero input, they do not satisfy the hypothesis of Proposition 128. A solution to derive a family of vectorial functions also satisfying the hypothesis of Proposition 128 is then to right-compose the functions L_i with a same injective (or two-to-one) function π from $\mathbb{F}_2^s$ into $\mathbb{F}_{2^m}^*$. Then, for every nonzero vector $v \in \mathbb{F}_2^m \setminus \{0_m\}$, the function $y \in \mathbb{F}_2^s \mapsto \sum_{i=1}^{m} v_i L_i[\pi(y)]$ is injective (or two-to-one) from $\mathbb{F}_2^s$ into C^*. This gives the following construction:[7]

Given integers $m < r$, let C be an $[r, m, t + 1]$-code such that t is as large as possible (Grassl gives in [570] a precise overview of the best-known parameters of codes). Then define m linear functions $L_1, \ldots, L_m$ from $\mathbb{F}_{2^m}$ into C as in Lemma 11. Choose an integer s strictly lower than m (resp. lower than or equal to m) and define an injective (resp. two-to-one) function π from $\mathbb{F}_2^s$ into $\mathbb{F}_{2^m}^*$. Choose any (s, m)-function $H = (h_1, \ldots, h_m)$ and denote $r + s$ by n. Then the (n, m)-function F whose coordinate functions are defined by $f_i(x, y) = x \cdot [L_i \circ \pi](y) \oplus h_i(y)$ is t-resilient and admits $2^{n-1} - 2^{r-1}$ (resp. $2^{n-1} - 2^r$) for nonlinearity.

All the primary constructions presented in [648, 723, 907, 933] are based on this principle. The construction of (n, m, t)-functions defined in [580] is also a particular application of this construction, as shown in [319].

---

[7] Another construction based on Lemma 11 involves a family of *nonintersecting codes* (*i.e.*, of codes with trivial pairwise intersection) having the same length, dimension, and minimum distance; however, this construction is often worse for large resiliency orders, as shown in [319].

Other constructions

Constructions of highly nonlinear resilient vectorial functions, based on elliptic curves theory and on the trace of some power functions $x \mapsto x^d$ on finite fields, have been designed respectively by Cheon [367] and by Khoo and Gong [696]. However, it is still an open problem to design highly nonlinear functions with high algebraic degrees and high resiliency orders with Cheon's method. Besides, the number of functions that can be designed by these methods is very small. In [1157, 1159, 1161] are designed resilient functions whose nonlinearity exceeds the bent concatenation bound.

Zhang and Zheng proposed in [1168, 1170] a secondary construction consisting in the composition $F = G \circ L$ of a linear resilient (n, m, t)-function L with a highly nonlinear (m, k)-function. The resulting function F is obviously t-resilient, admits $2^{n-m} nl(G)$ for nonlinearity, where $nl(G)$ denotes the nonlinearity of G, and its degree is the same as that of G. Taking for function G the *inverse function* $x \mapsto x^{-1}$ on the finite field $\mathbb{F}_{2^m}$, Zhang and Zheng obtained t-resilient functions having a nonlinearity larger than or equal to $2^{n-1} - 2^{n-m/2}$ and having $m-1$ for algebraic degree. But the linear (n, m)-functions involved in the construction of Zhang and Zheng introduce a weakness: their unrestricted nonlinearity (see Definition 38, page 131) being null, this kind of function cannot be used as a multioutput combination function in stream ciphers. Nevertheless, this drawback can be avoided by concatenating such functions (recall that the concatenation of t-resilient functions gives t-resilient functions, and a good nonlinearity can be obtained by concatenating functions with disjoint Walsh supports). We obtain this way a modified Maiorana–McFarland construction, which could be investigated further.

More *secondary constructions* of resilient vectorial functions can be derived from the secondary constructions of resilient Boolean functions (see, *e.g.*, [180, 225]).

8

Functions satisfying SAC, PC, and EPC, or having good GAC

The research on Boolean functions achieving the propagation criterion $PC(l)$ of order $1 \leq l < n$ was active in the 1990s. The class of $PC(l)$ functions is a super-class of that of bent functions (bent functions achieve $PC(n)$). For $l \leq n - 3$ when n is even and for $l \leq n - 1$ when n is odd, its elements can be balanced and highly nonlinear. Strict avalanche property (corresponding to $l = 1$) and propagation properties give more features to Boolean functions in the framework of stream ciphers (see an example with [60]), even if it is more related to block ciphers (and to the differential attack). In the framework of stream ciphers, the invention of algebraic attacks and the difficulty of designing then Boolean functions satisfying all the mandatory criteria have more or less refocused research on Boolean functions meeting mandatory criteria only (including algebraic immunity and fast algebraic immunity). In the framework of block ciphers, studying individually the coordinate or component functions of S-boxes is not the most relevant approach. Nevertheless, to be complete,[1] we devote a short chapter to such avalanche criteria.

8.1 $PC(l)$ criterion

For the convenience of the reader, we summarize Definition 24, page 97:

Definition 71 *For $1 \leq l \leq n$, an n-variable Boolean function f satisfies the propagation criterion of order l (in brief, $PC(l)$) if $\mathcal{F}(D_e f) = 0$ for every $e \in \mathbb{F}_2^n$ such that $1 \leq w_H(e) \leq l$. Strict avalanche criterion (SAC) corresponds to $PC(1)$ [516, 581].*

It is shown in [605, 218, 219]that, if n is even, then $PC(n-2)$ implies $PC(n)$; so for n even we can find balanced n-variable $PC(l)$ functions only if $l \leq n - 3$. For odd $n \geq 3$, it is also known that the functions that satisfy $PC(n-1)$ are those functions of the form $g(x_1 \oplus x_n, \ldots, x_{n-1} \oplus x_n) \oplus \ell(x)$, where g is bent and ℓ is affine, and that the $PC(n-2)$ functions are those functions of a similar form, but where, for at most one index i, the term $x_i \oplus x_n$ may be replaced by x_i or by x_n (other equivalent characterizations exist [219]).

The *algebraic degree* of $PC(l)$ functions is bounded above by $n - 1$. A lower bound on their nonlinearity is easily shown [1169]: if there exists an l-dimensional subspace F such that, for every nonzero $e \in F$, the derivative $D_e f$ is balanced, then $nl(f) \geq 2^{n-1} - 2^{n-\frac{l}{2}-1}$. Indeed, Relation (2.56), page 62, applied with $b = 0_n$ and $E = F^\perp$, shows that every value $W_f^2(u)$ is then bounded above by 2^{2n-l}; this implies, taking $F = \{e \in \mathbb{F}_2^n; e \preceq u\}$ for

---

[1] Note that the avalanche and propagation criteria also play a role with hash functions.

$w_H(u) = l$, that $PC(l)$ functions have nonlinearities bounded below by $2^{n-1} - 2^{n-\frac{l}{2}-1}$. Equality can occur only if $l = n - 1$ (n odd) and $l = n$ (n even).

The maximum correlation of Boolean functions satisfying $PC(l)$ (and in particular, of bent functions) with respect to subsets of indices can be deduced from Relations (3.14), page 102, and (2.56); see [187].

There exist characterizations of the propagation criterion. A first obvious one is that, according to Relation (2.54), page 62, f satisfies $PC(l)$ if and only if $\sum_{u \in \mathbb{F}_2^n} (-1)^{a \cdot u} W_f^2(u) = 0$ for every nonzero vector a of Hamming weight at most l. A second one (direct consequence of Relation (2.56), page 62) is:

Proposition 129 *[219] Any n-variable Boolean function f satisfies $PC(l)$ if and only if, for every vector u of Hamming weight at least $n-l$, and every vector v, $\sum_{w \preceq u} W_f^2(w+v) = 2^{n+w_H(u)}$.*

Maiorana–McFarland's construction can be used to produce functions satisfying the propagation criterion: the derivative $D_{(a,b)}(x, y)$ of a function of the form (5.1), page 165, being equal to $x \cdot D_b \phi(y) \oplus a \cdot \phi(y + b) \oplus D_b g(y)$, the function satisfies $PC(l)$ under the sufficient condition that

1. For every nonzero $b \in \mathbb{F}_2^s$ of Hamming weight smaller than or equal to l, and every vector $y \in \mathbb{F}_2^s$, the vector $D_b \phi(y)$ is nonzero (or equivalently every set $\phi^{-1}(u)$, $u \in \mathbb{F}_2^r$, either is empty or is a singleton or has minimum distance strictly larger than l).
2. Every linear combination of at least one and at most l coordinate functions of ϕ is balanced (this condition corresponds to the case $b = 0_s$).

Constructions of such functions have been given in [218, 219, 722].

According to Proposition 129 above, Dobbertin's construction cannot produce functions satisfying $PC(l)$ with $l \geq \frac{n}{2}$. Indeed, if u is for instance the vector with $\frac{n}{2}$ first coordinates equal to 0, and with $\frac{n}{2}$ last coordinates equal to 1, we have, according to Relation (7.9), page 296, $W_h^2(w) = 0$ for every $w \preceq u$.

8.2 PC(l) of order k and EPC(l) of order k criteria

Definition 72 *An n-variable Boolean function satisfies the propagation criterion $PC(l)$ of order k (resp. the extended propagation criterion $EPC(l)$ of order k) if it satisfies $PC(l)$ when k coordinates of the input x are kept constant (resp. if every derivative $D_e f$, with $e \neq 0_n$ of weight at most l, is k-resilient).*

According to the characterization of resilient functions and its proof, we have:

Proposition 130 *[968] A function f satisfies $EPC(l)$ (resp. $PC(l)$) of order k if and only if, for any vector e of Hamming weight smaller than or equal to l and any vector c of Hamming weight smaller than or equal to k, if $(e, c) \neq (0_n, 0_n)$ (resp. if $(e, c) \neq (0_n, 0_n)$ and if e and c have disjoint supports) then*

$$W_{D_e f}(c) = \sum_{x \in \mathbb{F}_2^n} (-1)^{f(x) \oplus f(x+e) \oplus c \cdot x} = 0.$$

A characterization by the Walsh transform of f has been deduced in [987].

It has been shown in [970] that $SAC(k)$ (*i.e.* $PC(1)$ of order k) functions have algebraic degrees at most $n - k - 1$. In [797], the criterion $SAC(n - 3)$ was characterized through the *ANF* of the function, and its properties were further studied. A construction of $PC(l)$ of order k functions based on Maiorana–McFarland's method is given in [722] (the mapping ϕ being linear and constructed from linear codes) and generalized in [218, 219] (the mapping ϕ being not linear and constructed from nonlinear codes). A construction of n-variable balanced functions satisfying $SAC(k)$ and having algebraic degree $n - k - 1$ is given, for $n-k-1$ odd, in [722] and, for $n-k-1$ even, in [1011] (where balancedness and nonlinearity are also considered).

It is shown in [219] that, for every positive even $l \leq n - 4$ (with $n \geq 6$) and every odd l such that $5 \leq l \leq n - 5$ (with $n \geq 10$), the functions that satisfy $PC(l)$ of order $n - l - 2$ are the functions of the form $\bigoplus_{1 \leq i < j \leq n} x_i x_j \oplus h(x_1, \ldots, x_n)$, where h is affine.

8.3 Absolute indicator

In [1167], the authors state the conjecture that any balanced function on an odd number n of variables satisfies $\Delta_f \geq 2^{(n+1)/2}$. In [527, 820], for $n = 15$ and 21 the authors give balanced functions with $\Delta_f < 2^{(n+1)/2}$ (an error on the 21-variable functions found by computer investigation has been corrected in [681]). In [684], the first construction giving $\Delta_f < 2^{n/2}$ for even n (a balanced 10-variable function with $\Delta_f = 24$) is found. In [1074] a construction is given of n-variable balanced functions with $\Delta_f < 2^{n/2}$, where $n > 44$ and $n \equiv 2$ [mod 4], with specific examples for $n = 18, 22, 26$. In [683], results for $n = 12, 14, \ldots, 26$ are obtained (the journal version to appear also provides n-variable balanced functions with $\Delta_f < 2^{n/2}$, where $n > 50$ and $n \equiv 0$ [mod 4]).

Bounds between the absolute indicator and the nonlinearity are given in [1178].

Remark. The block sensitivity $bs(f)$ of an n-variable Boolean function f equals the maximum number of vectors $a^{(1)}, \ldots, a^{(k)} \in \mathbb{F}_2^n$ with disjoint supports and such that $D_{a^{(i)}} f(x) = 1, \forall i = 1, \ldots, k$. Its (basic) sensitivity $s(f)$ is defined similarly with all vectors $a^{(i)}$ of Hamming weight 1. The 30-year-old *sensitivity conjecture* states that there exists a constant C independent of n such that $bs(f) \leq (s(f))^C$ for every f [905]. This conjecture has been proved in [631]. $\square$

9

Algebraic immune functions

The invention of *algebraic attacks* and of *fast algebraic attacks* has deeply modified the research on Boolean functions for stream ciphers. Before 2003, functions had about ten variables (to be fastly computable) and were mainly supposed to be balanced, have large algebraic degree and nonlinearity and in the case of the combiner generator, ensure good trade-off between algebraic degree, nonlinearity, and resiliency order. Since 2003, the designer needs also to ensure resistance to the algebraic attack (which needs in practice optimal or almost optimal algebraic immunity) and good resistance to fast algebraic attacks and to the Rønjom–Helleseth attack and its improvements. This implies a larger number of variables (say, between 16 and 20; it can be more if the function is particularly quickly computable) and an algebraic degree close to n (this is a necessary but not sufficient condition for the resistance against fast algebraic attacks). For this reason, the combiner generator seems less adapted nowadays; it needs to be made more complex, for instance with memory. Even the filter generator has posed a problem: during five years, no function usable in it could be found (the known functions with optimal algebraic immunity had bad nonlinearity and bad resistance to fast algebraic attacks; see [27]). In 2008, an infinite class of functions possessing all mandatory features was found in [273]. The functions in this class are rather fastly computable, but since stream ciphers need to be faster than block ciphers (which can be used as *pseudorandom generators*), there is still a need of functions satisfying all mandatory criteria and being very fast to compute, like the hidden weight bit function (HWBF), which has been more recently investigated; see below. To be complete in this introduction, we need to mention that a new way of using Boolean functions came recently with the so-called filter permutator, like in the FLIP cryptosystem [839], which posed new problems on Boolean functions (see [306]); see more in Section 12.2.

9.1 Algebraic immune Boolean functions

For the convenience of the reader, we summarize the definitions seen in Section 3.1 on algebraic immune functions.

Definition 73 *Let f be any n-variable Boolean function. The minimum algebraic degree of nonzero annihilators of f or of $f \oplus 1$ (i.e., of nonzero multiples of $f \oplus 1$ or of f), is called the* algebraic immunity *of f and is denoted by $AI(f)$.*

The fast algebraic immunity *of f is the integer:*

$$FAI(f) = \min \left(2AI(f), \min \left\{ d_{alg}(g) + d_{alg}(fg); \ 1 \le d_{alg}(g) < AI(f) \right\} \right).$$

The fast algebraic complexity *of f is the integer:*

$$FAC(f) := \min\{\max\left[d_{alg}(g) + d_{alg}(fg), 3d_{alg}(g)\right]; 1 \leq d_{alg}(g) < AI(f)\}.$$

All three parameters are stable under complementation $f \mapsto f \oplus 1$; see more in [324]. We have $AI(f) \leq \min(d_{alg}(f), \lceil \frac{n}{2} \rceil)$ and $FAI(f) \leq FAC(f) \leq n$ for any n-variable function f.

A standard algebraic attack on a stream cipher using some Boolean function f in the combiner model or the filter model is all the more efficient as $AI(f)$ is smaller and many linearly independent lowest degree annihilators of f or $f \oplus 1$ exist. Parameter $FAC(f)$ and its simplified version $FAI(f)$ play a similar role with respect to fast algebraic attacks. In [793], the authors call *perfect algebraic immune* (PAI) the n-variable Boolean functions f such that, for any pair of strictly positive[1] integers (e, d) such that $e+d < n$ and $e < \frac{n}{2}$, there is no nonzero function g of algebraic degree at most e such that fg has algebraic degree at most d (while we have seen at page 94 that for every n-variable function f and every (e, d) such that $e + d \geq n$, such function g exists). Such functions have perfect immunity against the standard and fast algebraic attacks (indeed, as shown in [793, 789], a PAI function and an almost PAI function with an even number of variables have optimal algebraic immunity, where almost PAI is defined similarly with $e + d < n - 1$ and $e < \frac{n-1}{2}$ instead of $e + d < n$ and $e < \frac{n}{2}$). It is shown in [485, 793] that perfect algebraic immune functions, when balanced, can exist only if n equals 1 plus a power of 2, and when unbalanced, can exist only if n is a power of 2. Indeed, it is easily seen that, for any perfect algebraic immune function f, we have $d_{alg}(f) \geq n - 1$ and it is proved in [793] that if $d_{alg}(f) = n - 1$ (resp. $d_{alg}(f) = n$), then for $e < \frac{n}{2}$ such that $\binom{n-1}{e} \equiv 1 \pmod 2$ (resp. $\binom{n-1}{e} \equiv 0 \pmod 2$), there exists a nonzero function g such that $d_{alg}(g) \leq e$ and $d_{alg}(fg) \leq n - e - 1$, and such e exists unless $n = 2^s + 1$ (resp. 2^s). It is shown in [791] that no *symmetric Boolean function* can be perfect algebraic immune for $n \geq 5$.

In [929], Pasalic introduced a slightly different notion of optimal resistance to FAA: an n-variable Boolean function f is said to satisfy the high-degree product property (HDP) of order n if, for every n-variable Boolean function g of algebraic degree e such that $1 \leq e < \lceil \frac{n}{2} \rceil$ and that is not an annihilator of f, we have $d_{alg}(fg) \geq n - e$. Then [929] proves that $f \oplus 1$ has the same property and $AI(f) = \lceil \frac{n}{2} \rceil$; such a function is then called algebraic attack resistant (AAR).

As we already saw at page 92, since a Boolean function g is an annihilator of f if and only if $g(x) = 0$ for every element x in the support of f, to determine whether f (resp. $f \oplus 1$) admits nonzero annihilators of algebraic degree at most d, we consider a general Boolean function $g(x)$ by its ANF $g(x) = \bigoplus\limits_{\substack{I \subseteq \{1,\ldots,n\} \\ |I| \leq d}} a_I \left(\prod\limits_{i \in I} x_i\right)$ and consider the system (see page 92) of the $w_H(f)$ (resp. $2^n - w_H(f)$) equations in the $\sum_{i=0}^{d} \binom{n}{i}$ unknowns $a_I \in \mathbb{F}_2$ expressing that $g(x) = 0$ for $x \in supp(f)$ (resp. $x \notin supp(f)$). The matrix $M_{f,d}$ (resp. $M_{f \oplus 1, d}$) of this system has term $\prod_{i \in I} x_i$ at a row indexed by x and a column indexed by I, where $x \in supp(f)$ (resp. $x \notin supp(f)$). Calculating the algebraic immunity of a function

---

[1] Assuming that e can be null would oblige f to have algebraic degree n and it could then not be balanced.

f by applying the definition consists then in determining the minimum value of d such that the ranks $rk(M_{f,d})$ and $rk(M_{f\oplus1,d})$ of the matrices of these two systems do not both equal $\sum_{i=0}^{d}\binom{n}{i}$, and the dimension $\dim(An_d(f))$ of the vector space of annihilators of algebraic degree at most d of f equals $\sum_{i=0}^{d}\binom{n}{i} - rk(M_{f,d})$.

The dimension of $An_d(f)$ has been determined for all d in [228] for some classes of functions: minimum weight elements f of the Reed–Muller codes (*i.e.*, indicators of affine subspaces of $\mathbb{F}_2^n$), their complements $f \oplus 1$, their sums with affine functions when these are balanced, and complements of threshold functions (see more on these latter functions in Subsection 10.1.7).

Remark. Given an n-variable Boolean function f, denoting by $LDA_n(f)$ the $\mathbb{F}_2$-vector space made of the annihilators of f of algebraic degree $AI(f)$ (assuming that some exist; otherwise, we change f into $f \oplus 1$) and the zero function, we have, as observed in [261]:

1. $\dim LDA_n(f) \leq \binom{n}{AI(f)}$, since two distinct annihilators of algebraic degree $AI(f)$ cannot have the same degree $AI(f)$ part in their algebraic normal forms (otherwise, their sum would be a nonzero annihilator of algebraic degree strictly smaller than $AI(f)$).
2. If f is balanced and $AI(f) = \frac{n}{2}$, n even, then $\dim LDA_n(f) \geq \frac{1}{2}\binom{n}{\frac{n}{2}}$, since matrix $M_{f,\frac{n}{2}}$ has 2^{n-1} rows and $\sum_{i=0}^{\frac{n}{2}}\binom{n}{i} = 2^{n-1} + \frac{1}{2}\binom{n}{\frac{n}{2}}$ columns.
3. If f is such that $AI(f) = \frac{n+1}{2}$, n odd, then $\dim LDA_n(f) = \binom{n}{\frac{n+1}{2}}$, since we know that $w_H(f) = 2^{n-1}$, and $M_{f,\frac{n-1}{2}}$ is then a $2^{n-1} \times 2^{n-1}$ square matrix whose rank equals 2^{n-1}; matrix $M_{f,\frac{n+1}{2}}$ has then rank 2^{n-1}. $\qquad\square$

9.1.1 General properties of the algebraic immunity and its relationship with some other criteria

We have seen that the algebraic immunity of any n-variable Boolean function is an affine invariant and is bounded above by $\lceil\frac{n}{2}\rceil$. The functions used in stream ciphers must have an algebraic immunity close to this maximum. In the next paragraphs, we give properties and characterizations, some of which are new.

Algebraic immunity of monomial functions

It has been shown in [899, 900] that if the number $r(d)$ of runs of 1s in the binary expansion of the exponent d of a power function $tr_n(ax^d)$ (that is, the number of full subsequences of consecutive 1s) is smaller than $\sqrt{n}/2$, then the algebraic immunity is bounded above by

$$r(d)\lfloor\sqrt{n}\rfloor + \left\lceil\frac{n}{\lfloor\sqrt{n}\rfloor}\right\rceil - 1. \tag{9.1}$$

This comes from the fact that there exists g of algebraic degree $\left\lceil\frac{n}{\lfloor\sqrt{n}\rfloor}\right\rceil$ such that fg has algebraic degree at most (9.1). This property also allows us to prove that $FAI(f) \leq r(d)\lfloor\sqrt{n}\rfloor + 2\left\lceil\frac{n}{\lfloor\sqrt{n}\rfloor}\right\rceil - 1$, as observed in [870].

Note that (9.1) is better than the general bound $\lceil \frac{n}{2} \rceil$ for only a negligible part of power mappings, but it addresses all those whose exponents have a constant *2-weight* or a constant number of runs – the *power function*s studied as potential S-boxes in block ciphers enter in this framework. Moreover, the bound is further improved when n is odd and the function is almost bent: the algebraic immunity of such functions is bad since bounded above by $2 \lfloor \sqrt{n} \rfloor$. The exact value of the algebraic immunity of the multiplicative *inverse function* $tr_n(ax^{2^n-2})$, $a \neq 0$, has been given in [498]; it equals $\lceil 2\sqrt{n} \rceil - 2$, which is not good either.

Algebraic immunity of a restriction

If the restriction of a function f to an affine space, for instance obtained by fixing x_i to a_i for any $i \in I \subseteq \{1, \ldots, n\}$, has a nonzero annihilator g of some algebraic degree d, then f has for nonzero annihilator the function $g(x) 1_A(x)$, equal to $g(x) \left(1 \oplus \prod_{i \in I} (x_i \oplus a_i \oplus 1)\right)$ in the latter example, in which case the algebraic degree equals $d + n - dim(A) = d + |I|$. By applying this to f and to $f \oplus 1$, whose restrictions cannot be both null, the algebraic immunity of the restriction is at least $AI(f) - n + dim(A) = AI(f) - |I|$, as observed in [407]. Moreover, the annihilators of the restriction of f are the restrictions of the annihilators of f.

To have a chance of having large algebraic immunity, a function needs then not only to have large enough algebraic degree but also that each restriction to an affine space of large dimension, for instance the restriction obtained by fixing a few input coordinates, has large enough algebraic degree. This implies that Maiorana–McFarland functions defined by Relation (5.1), page 165, with r large have bad algebraic immunity. It is observed in [279] that a Maiorana–McFarland function $x \cdot \phi(y) \oplus g(y)$, where $x \in \mathbb{F}_2^r, y \in \mathbb{F}_2^{n-r}$, can have algebraic immunity $n - r + 1$ (which is its maximal possible algebraic degree) only if, for every affine subspace A of $\mathbb{F}_2^{n-r}$, we have $\sum_{y \in A} \phi(y) \neq 0_r$. Indeed, the products of f and $f \oplus 1$ by the indicator function of $\mathbb{F}_2^r \times A$ are annihilators of $f \oplus 1$ and f and are not both null; they equal the products of the restrictions of f and $f \oplus 1$ to $\mathbb{F}_2^r \times A$ (which have algebraic degree $1 + \dim A$ if this nonnullity condition is satisfied and at most $\dim A$ otherwise) and of the function of y equal to the indicator function of A (which has algebraic degree $n - r - \dim A$).

Characterization of annihilators by the Walsh transform

For every $x \in \mathbb{F}_2^n$, we have $(fg)(x) = (\frac{1}{2} - \frac{(-1)^{f(x)}}{2})(\frac{1}{2} - \frac{(-1)^{g(x)}}{2}) = \frac{1}{4}(1 - (-1)^{f(x)} - (-1)^{g(x)} + (-1)^{f(x) \oplus g(x)})$. Recall that the Fourier transform is its own inverse up to a multiplicative factor and that this implies that any integer-valued function φ over $\mathbb{F}_2^n$ is

1. Equal to the zero function if and only if its Fourier transform $\widehat{\varphi}$ is null
2. Constant if and only if $\widehat{\varphi}(a)$ is null at any input $a \neq 0_n$

We deduce a characterization first observed in [128], that we slightly complete:

Proposition 131 *Let n be any positive integer and f, g any n-variable Boolean functions. Then*

$$g \in An(f) \iff \forall a \in \mathbb{F}_2^n, \quad W_{f \oplus g}(a) + 2^n \delta_0(a) = W_f(a) + W_g(a),$$

where δ_0 is the Dirac (or Kronecker) symbol. Moreover, if f is different from the constant function 1, we have:

$$g \in An(f) \Longleftrightarrow \forall a \neq 0, \quad W_{f \oplus g}(a) = W_f(a) + W_g(a).$$

Indeed, the first equivalence is a consequence of observation 1 above applied to the two members of the equality above or to $\varphi = f + g - f \oplus g = 2fg$, using the linearity of the Fourier transform and Relation (2.32), page 55. The second equivalence is then a straightforward consequence of observation 2, since fg constant means $fg = 0$ because $fg = 1$ is impossible, f being not constant function 1.

Note that the bound $AI(f) \leq \lceil \frac{n}{2} \rceil$ shows then that, for every nonconstant n-variable Boolean function f, there exists a nonzero n-variable Boolean function g of algebraic degree at most $\lceil \frac{n}{2} \rceil$, such that either $W_{f \oplus g}(a) = W_f(a) + W_g(a)$ for all $a \neq 0_n$ (g being an annihilator of $f \neq 1$) or $W_{f \oplus g}(a) = W_f(a) - W_g(a)$ for all $a \neq 0_n$ (g being an annihilator of $f \oplus 1 \neq 1$).

Moreover, since $(-1)^{(f \oplus g)(x)} = (-1)^{f(x)}(-1)^{g(x)}$, we have by applying Relation (2.45), page 60,

$$2^n W_{f \oplus g} = W_f \otimes W_g,$$

where $W_f \otimes W_g(a) = \sum_{u \in \mathbb{F}_2^n} W_f(a + u) W_g(u)$. We deduce:

Corollary 25 *Let n be any positive integer and f any n-variable Boolean function. We have $g \in An(f)$ if and only if*

$$\forall a \in \mathbb{F}_2^n, \quad W_f \otimes W_g(a) - 2^n W_g(a) = 2^n W_f(a) - 2^{2n} \delta_0(a) \tag{9.2}$$

and if f is not constant function 1, this condition with $a \neq 0_n$ suffices.

The Walsh transforms of the annihilators of f are then the solutions of the system of the 2^n linear equations (9.2) indexed by a, in the 2^n unknowns $W_g(a)$, $a \in \mathbb{F}_2^n$, whose matrix equals $M - 2^n I$, where I is the identity matrix and M is the matrix whose coefficient at a row indexed by a and a column indexed by u equals $W_f(a + u)$. Note that we have $M \times M^t = M \times M = 2^{2n} I$, where M^t is the transpose of M, since, for every $a, b \in \mathbb{F}_2^n$, we have $\sum_{u \in \mathbb{F}_2^n} W_f(a + u) W_f(b + u) = \sum_{u \in \mathbb{F}_2^n} W_f(u) W_f(a + b + u) = 2^{2n} \delta_0(a + b)$, according to the Parseval and Titsworth relations (2.48) and (2.51), page 61.

It is interesting to see that the annihilators of any Boolean function f combine two linear algebraic properties over different fields:

- The set of annihilators of f is an $\mathbb{F}_2$-vector space.
- The set of their Walsh transforms is the intersection between an $\mathbb{R}$-vector space (the set of solutions of the system given above) and the set of integer-valued functions $W : \mathbb{F}_2^n \mapsto \mathbb{Z}$ satisfying the equation $\sum_{u \in \mathbb{F}_2^n} W(a + u) W(u) = 2^{2n} \delta_0(a)$ for every $a \in \mathbb{F}_2^n$ (we know indeed that these 2^n quadratic equations are characteristic of the Walsh transforms of Boolean functions).

Characterization of annihilators by the NNF

The determination of annihilators can be handled in a simple way (with two equations over $\mathbb{Z}$, one quadratic and one linear, instead of $w_H(f)$ linear ones over $\mathbb{F}_2$ as we saw with the ANF) through the NNF representation (see Subsection 2.2.4, page 47): let $\sum_{I \subseteq \{1,...,n\}} \lambda_I x^I$, $\lambda_I \in \mathbb{Z}$, be the NNF of a Boolean function $f(x)$; we know from (2.28), page 51, that an integer-valued function $g(x) = \sum_{I \subseteq \{1,...,n\}} \mu_I x^I$, $\mu_I \in \mathbb{Z}$, is Boolean if and only if the single quadratic equation

$$\sum_{I \subseteq \{1,...,n\}} 2^{n-|I|} \sum_{J,J' \subseteq \{1,...,n\};\, I=J\cup J'} \mu_J \mu_{J'} = \sum_{I \subseteq \{1,...,n\}} 2^{n-|I|} \mu_I \qquad (9.3)$$

is satisfied. We have that g is an annihilator of f if and only if[2] $\sum_{x \in \mathbb{F}_2^n} f(x)g(x) = 0$. Hence, since $\sum_{x \in \mathbb{F}_2^n} x^I = |\{x \in \mathbb{F}_2^n; I \subseteq supp(x)\}| = 2^{n-|I|}$:

Proposition 132 *Let f be any n-variable Boolean function and let its NNF equal $\sum_{I \subseteq \{1,...,n\}} \lambda_I x^I$, $\lambda_I \in \mathbb{Z}$. Then the annihilators of f are the functions $g(x) = \sum_{I \subseteq \{1,...,n\}} \mu_I x^I$, $\mu_I \in \mathbb{Z}$, which satisfy (9.3) and*

$$\sum_{I \subseteq \{1,...,n\}} 2^{n-|I|} \sum_{J,J' \subseteq \{1,...,n\};\, I=J\cup J'} \lambda_J \mu_{J'} = 0.$$

Algebraic immunity and codes

It is observed in [600, theorem 1 and corollary 1] that the problem of estimating the algebraic immunity of Boolean functions over $\mathbb{F}_{2^n}$ is connected to cyclic codes. We modify the statement of this result (and give a slightly different proof) so as to complete [600] by taking into account the facts that if $f(0) = 1$, then the annihilators g of f must satisfy $g(0) = 0$ and that annihilators of algebraic degree n may exist.

Proposition 133 *Let $f(x)$ be an n-variable Boolean function in univariate form. Then the annihilators of $f(x)$ in univariate representation are those multiples $g(x)$ of $\gcd(f(x)+1, x^{2^n}+x)$ in $\mathbb{F}_{2^n}[x]/(x^{2^n}+x)$ that satisfy $(g(x))^2 = g(x)$.*

If $f(0) = 0$, then the annihilators of algebraic degree at most $n-1$ are the codewords of the cyclic code *of length $2^n - 1$ over $\mathbb{F}_{2^n}$ and of generator polynomial $\gcd(f(x)+1, x^{2^n-1}+1)$ that satisfy $(g(x))^2 = g(x)$.*

Proof We know that the annihilators of $f \in \mathcal{BF}_n$ are those Boolean functions that are multiples of $f \oplus 1$ in $\mathcal{BF}_n$. These annihilators in univariate representation are then the multiples of $f(x)+1$ in $\mathbb{F}_{2^n}[x]/(x^{2^n}+x)$ that satisfy $(g(x))^2 = g(x)$, and since being such a multiple is equivalent to being a multiple of $\gcd(f(x)+1, x^{2^n}+x)$ [mod $x^{2^n}+x$], this proves the first part. The rest is straightforward since, if $f(0) = 0$, then $\gcd(f(x) + 1, x^{2^n} + x) = \gcd(f(x)+1, x^{2^n-1}+1)$, and since reducing mod $x^{2^n} + x$ or mod $x^{2^n-1}+1$ a polynomial of algebraic degree at most $n-1$, that is, of degree at most $2^n - 2$, is the same. □

---

[2] Recall that $\sum$ denotes sums in $\mathbb{Z}$.

Corollary 26   *Let $f(x)$ be an n-variable Boolean function in univariate form. Then $AI(f)$ equals the minimum, among all those nonzero elements $g(x)$ of $\mathbb{F}_{2^n}[x]/(x^{2^n}+x)$ that satisfy $(g(x))^2 = g(x)$ and are multiples either of $\gcd(f(x)+1, x^{2^n}+x)$ or of $\gcd(f(x), x^{2^n}+x)$, of the maximum 2-weight of the exponents in the terms of these polynomials.*

It is also shown in [600] that the *spectral immunity* (defined at page 96) of a Boolean function $f(x)$ (in univariate form) is equal to the minimal weight of the nonzero codewords of the cyclic codes over $\mathbb{F}_{2^n}$ of generator polynomials $\gcd(f(x) + 1, x^{2^n-1} + 1)$ and $\gcd(f(x), x^{2^n-1} + 1)$.

In [869], it is shown that, given an n-variable Boolean function f, if the minimum distance of the linear code $\{(a_0, \ldots, a_{2^n-1}) \in \mathbb{F}_{2^n}^{2^n}; \sum_{i=0}^{2^n-1} a_i x^i = 0, \forall x \in supp(f)\}$ (*i.e.*, the vector space of univariate representations of $\mathbb{F}_{2^n}$-valued annihilators of f), which we shall denote by C_f, is strictly larger than $\sum_{i=0}^{d} \binom{n}{i}$ for a given d, then the minimum algebraic degree of nonzero annihilators of f is strictly larger than d. Indeed, if a nonzero annihilator of f has algebraic degree at most d, then its Hamming weight as a codeword of C_f is at most $\sum_{i=0}^{d} \binom{n}{i}$, a contradiction.

There is, however, an issue with this result when $f(0) = 0$, since C_f has then minimum distance 2, because it includes the codeword $(1, 0, \ldots, 0, 1)$; the result gives then no information in that case. This difficulty can be easily addressed since the codeword $(1, 0, \ldots, 0, 1)$ corresponds to an annihilator of algebraic degree n (the indicator of $\{0\}$, *i.e.*, function δ_0) and presents then no interest from the viewpoint of algebraic immunity. We can slightly modify the result of [869] by considering, instead of C_f, the code $C'_f = \{(a_0, \ldots, a_{2^n-2}) \in \mathbb{F}_{2^n}^{2^n-1}; \sum_{i=0}^{2^n-2} a_i x^i = 0, \forall x \in supp(f)\}$ (*i.e.*, the vector space of univariate representations of $\mathbb{F}_{2^n}$-valued annihilators of f of algebraic degree at most $n-1$); the result also works for C'_f, unless all nonzero annihilators of f have algebraic degree n, that is, unless $f = 1 \oplus \delta_a$ for some $a \in \mathbb{F}_{2^n}$.

We consider now the cyclic code (also introduced in [869]) $\overline{C}_f = \{(a_1, \ldots, a_{2^n-1}) \in \mathbb{F}_{2^n}^{2^n-1}; \sum_{i=1}^{2^n-1} a_i x^i = 0, \forall x \in supp(f)\}$ (*i.e.*, the subcode of C_f whose elements are the univariate representations of $\mathbb{F}_{2^n}$-valued annihilators of f null at position 0), punctured at 0. The minimum distance (*i.e.*, nonzero weight) of C'_f equals at least the minimum distance of $\overline{C}_f$. Indeed, if $f(0) = 1$, then the minimum distances of C_f and $\overline{C}_f$ are equal to each other, and if $f(0) = 0$, then $C_f = \{(0, 0, \ldots, 0, 0), (1, 0, \ldots, 0, 1)\} + \{0\} \times \overline{C}_f$ and the minimum distance of C'_f is then larger than or equal to that of $\overline{C}_f$.

The interest of this observation is that $\overline{C}_f$ is cyclic and we can apply the BCH bound to this cyclic code. This gives a direct lower bound on the minimum algebraic degree of nonzero annihilators of f.

Relationship between normality and algebraic immunity

Normality of order larger than $\frac{n}{2}$ represents a weakness with respect to algebraic immunity:

Proposition 134   *For any positive n and $k \le n$, if an n-variable function f is k-normal, then its algebraic immunity is at most $n - k$.*

Indeed, the fact that $f(x) = \epsilon \in \mathbb{F}_2$ for every $x \in A$, where A is a k-dimensional flat, implies that the indicator of A is an annihilator of $f + \epsilon$. This bound is tight since, being a *symmetric Boolean function*, the majority function (see page 335) is $\lfloor \frac{n}{2} \rfloor$-normal for every n and has algebraic immunity $\lceil \frac{n}{2} \rceil$. Obviously, $AI(f) \leq \ell$ does not imply conversely that f is $(n - \ell)$-normal, since when n tends to infinity, for every $a > 1$, n-variable Boolean functions are almost surely non-$(a \log_2 n)$-normal [222, 224] and the algebraic immunity is always bounded above by $\frac{n}{2}$.

Functions in odd numbers of variables with optimal algebraic immunity

In [188], A. Canteaut has observed the following property:

Proposition 135 *If an n-variable balanced function f, with n odd, admits no nonzero annihilator of algebraic degree at most $\frac{n-1}{2}$, then it has optimal algebraic immunity $\frac{n+1}{2}$.*

This result is a direct consequence of Proposition 136 below, which has been proved later. It means that we do not need to check also that $f \oplus 1$ has no nonzero annihilator of algebraic degree at most $\frac{n-1}{2}$ for showing that f has optimal algebraic immunity.[3]

The original proof (simplified in the end) of Proposition 135 is as follows: consider the *Reed–Muller code* of length 2^n and of order $\frac{n-1}{2}$. This code is self-dual (*i.e.*, is its own dual), according to Theorem 9, page 154. Let G be a generator matrix of this code. Each column of G is labeled by the vector of $\mathbb{F}_2^n$ obtained by keeping its coordinates of indices $2, \ldots, n + 1$ (assuming that the first row of G is the all-1 vector, corresponding to constant function 1, and that the next n rows correspond to the coordinate functions). Saying that f has no nonzero annihilator of algebraic degree at most $\frac{n-1}{2}$ is equivalent to saying that the matrix obtained by selecting those columns of G corresponding to the elements of the support of f has full rank $\sum_{i=0}^{\frac{n-1}{2}} \binom{n}{i} = 2^{n-1}$. By hypothesis, f has Hamming weight 2^{n-1}. In terms of coding theory, the support of the function is an *information set*. Then the complement of the support of f being an information set of the dual (recall that if $G = [I_k : M]$ is a systematic generator matrix of a linear code, then $[-M^t : I_{n-k}]$ is a parity check matrix of the code) and the code being self-dual, this complement is also an information set of the code (*i.e.*, the code is complementary information set CIS; see page 459).

More relationship between the existence of low degree annihilators of f and of $f \oplus 1$

We have, from [800] (we slightly modify the proof):

Proposition 136 *If, for some $k < \lceil \frac{n}{2} \rceil$, we have $rk(M_{f,k}) = w_H(f)$ (i.e., all the rows of $M_{f,k}$ are $\mathbb{F}_2$-linearly independent), then $rk(M_{f\oplus 1,k}) = \sum_{i=0}^k \binom{n}{i}$ (i.e., $f \oplus 1$ has no nonzero annihilator of algebraic degree at most k).*

Proof Suppose there exists a nonzero annihilator g of algebraic degree at most k of $f \oplus 1$. We have then $supp(g) \subseteq supp(f)$. Since all the rows of $M_{f,k}$ are $\mathbb{F}_2$-linearly independent,

---

[3] The same has been shown for n even but for (less interesting) unbalanced functions.

all those of $M_{g,k}$ are $\mathbb{F}_2$-linearly independent, and for every choice of $(b_x)_{x \in supp(g)} \in \mathbb{F}_2^{w_H(g)}$, the system of linear equations whose matrix is $M_{g,k}$ and whose constants are these b_x has a solution. In particular, for every $x \in supp(g)$, there exists g' of algebraic degree at most k such that $gg' = \delta_x$ (the Dirac symbol at x, *i.e.*, the indicator function of the singleton $\{x\}$), a contradiction with $d_{alg}(gg') \leq d_{alg}(g) + d_{alg}(g') < n$. $\qquad\square$

Minimum Hamming distance to functions of large algebraic immunity bounded below by means of the dimensions of vector spaces of functions

Lobanov has made in two papers [800, 801] the following observations (that we gather in a single proposition):

Proposition 137 *For any n-variable Boolean functions f, h and any integers $0 \leq k, l \leq n$, we have*

$$d_H(f, h) \geq \dim(An_k(h)) - \dim(An_k(f)) + \dim(An_l(h \oplus 1)) - \dim(An_l(f \oplus 1)).$$

Moreover, if $d \leq AI(f)$, then we have

$$d_H(f, h) \geq \dim(An_{d-1}(h)) + \dim(An_{d-1}(h \oplus 1)). \tag{9.4}$$

Proof Among the $rk(M_{f,k})$ linearly $\mathbb{F}_2$-independent rows of $M_{f,k}$ that can be selected, there exist at least $rk(M_{f,k}) - rk(M_{h,k}) = \dim(An_k(h)) - \dim(An_k(f))$ ones that are not rows of $M_{h,k}$, and there are then at least the same number of distinct elements of $\mathbb{F}_2^n$ in the support of f that are not in the support of h. We can apply this to $f \oplus 1$ and $h \oplus 1$ as well, with l in the place of k. This gives the first inequality. Moreover, if $d \leq AI(f)$, then $\dim(An_{d-1}(f)) = \dim(An_{d-1}(f \oplus 1)) = 0$. This completes the proof. $\qquad\square$

Lobanov notes that, if $k \geq l$, then the mapping $(g_1, g_2) \mapsto g_1 \oplus g_2$ is an $\mathbb{F}_2$-linear isomorphism between the vector spaces $An_k(h) \times An_l(h \oplus 1)$ and

$$B_{k,l}(h) = \{g \in \mathcal{BF}_n; d_{alg}(g) \leq k \text{ and } d_{alg}(hg) \leq l\}.$$

Indeed, the image set of this mapping is included in $B_{k,l}(h)$, since we have $(g_1 \oplus g_2)h = g_2$, and composing it with the mapping $g \in B_{k,l}(h) \mapsto (g \oplus hg, hg) \in An_k(h) \times An_l(h \oplus 1)$ gives identity. Hence, we have

- $\dim(An_k(h)) + \dim(An_l(h \oplus 1)) = \dim B_{k,l}(h)$
- $\dim(An_k(f)) + \dim(An_l(f \oplus 1)) = \dim B_{k,l}(f)$
- $\dim(An_{d-1}(h)) + \dim(An_{d-1}(h \oplus 1)) = \dim B_{d-1,d-1}(h)$.

In [800], it is shown[4] that, for every $d \leq \lceil \frac{n}{2} \rceil$ and every function h such that $\dim(An_{d-1}(h)) + \dim(An_{d-1}(h \oplus 1)) > 0$, there exists f for which Bound (9.4) is an equality and such that $AI(f) \geq d$. Let us give a proof of this astonishingly general result. Let C_1 (resp. C_0) be a maximal subset of $supp(h)$ (resp. $supp(h \oplus 1)$) such that the corresponding rows of $M_{h,d-1}$ (resp. $M_{h \oplus 1,d-1}$) are $\mathbb{F}_2$-linearly independent. We have

---

[4] Originally it was assumed the condition that the algebraic degree of h is at most $\lceil \frac{n}{2} \rceil$, but after clarifying the proof with M. Lobanov, we could see that this is not necessary.

$|C_1| = \sum_{i=0}^{d-1} \binom{n}{i} - \dim(An_{d-1}(h))$ and $|C_0| = \sum_{i=0}^{d-1} \binom{n}{i} - \dim(An_{d-1}(h \oplus 1))$. According to Proposition 136 applied to the indicator function 1_{C_1} (resp. 1_{C_0}) and with $k = d - 1$, the ranks of $M_{1_{C_1} \oplus 1, d-1}$ and $M_{1_{C_0} \oplus 1, d-1}$ both equal $\sum_{i=0}^{d-1} \binom{n}{i}$. Since $C_0 \subseteq supp(1_{C_1} \oplus 1)$ (resp. $C_1 \subseteq supp(1_{C_0} \oplus 1)$), there exists outside $C_1 \cup C_0$, a subset C_0' of size $\sum_{i=0}^{d-1} \binom{n}{i} - |C_0| = \dim(An_{d-1}(h \oplus 1))$ (resp. C_1' of size $\sum_{i=0}^{d-1} \binom{n}{i} - |C_1| = \dim(An_{d-1}(h)))$ such that the rows of $M_{1_{C_1} \oplus 1, d-1}$ (resp. $M_{1_{C_0} \oplus 1, d-1}$) corresponding to the elements of $C_0 \cup C_0'$ (resp. $C_1 \cup C_1'$) are $\mathbb{F}_2$-linearly independent. Since C_0 and C_1 were taken maximal, we have $C_1' \subseteq supp(h \oplus 1)$ and $C_0' \subseteq supp(h)$. The function $f = h \oplus 1_{C_0'} \oplus 1_{C_1'}$ satisfies $d_H(f, h) = \dim(An_{d-1}(h)) + \dim(An_{d-1}(h \oplus 1))$. And we have $AI(f) \geq d$, since $rk(M_{f, d-1}) \geq |C_1| + |C_1'| = \sum_{i=0}^{d-1} \binom{n}{i}$ and similarly $rk(M_{f \oplus 1, d-1}) \sum_{i=0}^{d-1} \binom{n}{i}$.

Relationship between algebraic immunity, Hamming weight, algebraic degree, nonlinearity, and higher-order nonlinearity

We have seen that nonlinearity and algebraic degree are rather uncorrelated: there are Boolean functions with high nonlinearity and low algebraic degree (since there exist quadratic bent functions), with low nonlinearity and low algebraic degree, with high nonlinearity and high algebraic degree,[5] and with low nonlinearity and high algebraic degree. Interestingly, if we replace the algebraic degree by the algebraic immunity, the latter case cannot happen. We need preliminary results that have their own interest.

Proposition 138   *[261] For every n-variable Boolean function, we have:*

$$\sum_{i=0}^{AI(f)-1} \binom{n}{i} \leq w_H(f) \leq \sum_{i=0}^{n-AI(f)} \binom{n}{i}. \tag{9.5}$$

Indeed, if the left-hand side inequality is not satisfied, then $M_{f, AI(f)-1}$ has rank at most $w_H(f) < \sum_{i=0}^{AI(f)-1} \binom{n}{i}$, a contradiction. The right-hand side inequality is obtained from the other one by replacing f by $f \oplus 1$.

This implies again that $AI(f) \leq \lceil \frac{n}{2} \rceil$ (since applied with $AI(f) \geq \lceil \frac{n}{2} \rceil + 1$, it leads to a contradiction, because the lower bound is then strictly larger than the upper bound), and it also implies that a function f such that $AI(f) = \frac{n+1}{2}$ (n odd) must be balanced.

In [261, Lemma 1] has been stated:

Proposition 139   *For any two n-variable Boolean functions f and h, we have*

$$AI(f) - d_{alg}(h) \leq AI(f \oplus h) \leq AI(f) + d_{alg}(h). \tag{9.6}$$

The proof was incomplete: let $g \neq 0$ be such that $fg = 0$ (resp. $(f \oplus 1)g = 0$) and have algebraic degree $AI(f)$, then we have $(f \oplus h)((h \oplus 1)g) = 0$ (resp. $(f \oplus 1 \oplus h)((h \oplus 1)g) = 0$); it was written that this proves the inequality on the right since $d_{alg}((h \oplus 1)g) \leq AI(f) + d_{alg}(h)$, but this conclusion is correct only if $(h \oplus 1)g \neq 0$. Let us address the case $(h \oplus 1)g = 0$: we have then $(f \oplus h \oplus 1)g = 0$ (resp. $(f \oplus h)g = 0$), and g being a nonzero

---

[5] But not with maximal nonlinearity and high algebraic degree because of the Rothaus bound.

annihilator of $f \oplus h \oplus 1$ (resp. $f \oplus h$), we have $AI(f \oplus h) \leq AI(f) \leq AI(f) + d_{alg}(h)$. This completes the proof of the inequality on the right. Applying it to $f \oplus h$ instead of f gives then the inequality on the left.

Note that these relations are valid if f and h are defined on different (maybe intersecting) sets of variables and n is the global number of variables (indeed, algebraic immunity does not change if we consider a function with more variables, the additional variables being fictitious). Moreover, if these sets of variables are disjoint, then we have $AI(f) \leq AI(f \oplus h) \leq AI(f) + d_{alg}(h)$, since it is then possible to obtain a nonzero annihilator of algebraic degree $AI(f \oplus h)$ of f or of $f \oplus 1$ as the restriction of a nonzero annihilator of $f \oplus h$ or of $f \oplus h \oplus 1$.

It is deduced in [261] that low nonlinearity implies low algebraic immunity (but high algebraic immunity does not imply high nonlinearity, as well as high nonlinearity does not imply high algebraic immunity): Relation (9.5) applied to $f \oplus h$ with h affine and Relation (9.6) show that

$$nl(f) \geq \sum_{i=0}^{AI(f)-2} \binom{n}{i}$$

and more generally (by applying Relation (9.5) to $f \oplus h$ with $d_{alg}(h) \leq r$)

$$nl_r(f) \geq \sum_{i=0}^{AI(f)-r-1} \binom{n}{i}. \tag{9.7}$$

These lower bounds, which play a role with respect to probabilistic algebraic attacks, (see [792, 793]), have been improved in all cases for the first-order nonlinearity into

$$nl(f) \geq 2 \sum_{i=0}^{AI(f)-2} \binom{n-1}{i}$$

by Lobanov [798, 799] and in most cases for the r-th order nonlinearity into

$$nl_r(f) \geq 2 \sum_{i=0}^{AI(f)-r-1} \binom{n-r}{i} \tag{9.8}$$

in [228] (in fact, the improvement was slightly stronger than this, but more complex). Another improvement

$$nl_r(f) \geq \sum_{i=0}^{AI(f)-r-1} \binom{n}{i} + \sum_{i=AI(f)-2r}^{AI(f)-r-1} \binom{n-r}{i} \tag{9.9}$$

(which always improves upon (9.7) and improves upon (9.8) for low values of r) has been subsequently obtained by Mesnager in [849] and slightly later by Lobanov in [800], who gives a general proof for all these bounds, which we recall below. Precisions on the bounds, involving the maximum between the minimal algebraic degree of the nonzero annihilators of f and the minimal algebraic degree of the nonzero annihilators of $f \oplus 1$, have been also given in [998].

Here is Lobanov's general proof: Bound (9.4), page 329, and the observations that follow it imply that, for every n-variable Boolean function f and every positive integer $r \leq n$, we have[6]

$$nl_r(f) \geq \min_{h \in \mathcal{BF}_n, d_{alg}(h) \leq r} \dim(B_{AI(f)-1, AI(f)-1}(h)). \tag{9.10}$$

Then, if $d_{alg}(h) = r$:

- $\dim(B_{k,k}(h)) \geq \sum_{i=0}^{k-r} \binom{n}{i}$, because all n-variable functions of algebraic degree at most $k - r$ belong to $B_{k,k}(h)$; then (9.10) implies (9.7),
- $\dim(B_{k,k}(h)) \geq 2 \sum_{i=0}^{k-r} \binom{n-r}{i}$, because, if $\prod_{i \in I} x_i$ is a monomial of degree r in the ANF of h, then all n-variable functions of the form $h g_1 \oplus (h \oplus 1) g_2$ where g_1, g_2 have algebraic degree at most $k - r$ and depend only on variables $x_i, i \notin I$, belong to $B_{k,k}(h)$ and are distinct since the linear mapping $(g_1, g_2) \mapsto h g_1 \oplus (h \oplus 1) g_2$ has trivial kernel, because $h g_1 \oplus (h \oplus 1) g_2 = 0$ if and only if $h g_1 = (h \oplus 1) g_2 = 0$; then, (9.10) implies (9.8).
- $\dim(B_{k,k}(h)) \geq \sum_{i=0}^{k-r} \binom{n}{i} + \sum_{i=k-2r+1}^{k-r} \binom{n-r}{i}$, because, if $\prod_{i \in I} x_i$ is a monomial of degree r in the ANF of h, then all n-variable functions of the form $g_1 \oplus h g_2$, where g_1, g_2 have algebraic degree at most $k - r$ and g_2 depends only on variables $x_i, i \notin I$, and has only monomials of degree at least $k - 2r + 1$, belong to $B_{k,k}(h)$ and are distinct since the linear mapping $(g_1, g_2) \mapsto g_1 \oplus h g_2$ has trivial kernel; then (9.10) implies (9.9).

An obvious upper bound on the higher-order nonlinearity exists that also involves the algebraic immunity, as observed in [227]: if $AI(f) \leq r$ and if f is balanced, then we have $nl_r(f) \leq 2^{n-1} - 2^{n-r}$, since by hypothesis, there exists a nonzero function g of algebraic degree at most r such that $g \preceq f$ or $g \preceq f \oplus 1$, and g being nonzero and belonging to the Reed–Muller code of order r, it has Hamming weight at least the minimum distance of this code, that is, 2^{n-r}. If $g \preceq f$, for instance, then $d_H(f, g) = w_H(f \oplus g) = w_H(f) - w_H(g) \leq 2^{n-1} - 2^{n-r}$ and $nl_r(f) \leq 2^{n-1} - 2^{n-r}$.

A bound between $nl_r(f)$ and $FAI(f)$ has been also given in [1106]: $nl_r(f) \geq \sum_{i=0}^{\lfloor \frac{FAI(f)-r}{2} \rfloor} \binom{n}{i}$, but the proof has several shortcomings and the result seems false. For instance, with the help of a computer, we can check that the unbalanced function in [1067] with $n = 6$ has FAI 6 and the result above would imply that there exists a function with second-order nonlinearity at least 22, but it is known that the covering radius of RM(2,6) is 18. In fact, $FAI(f) - r$ should be $FAI(f) - r - 1$ in this bound, but even if such correction is made, the proof does not address all issues. Such a result is important to show that some functions cannot have good behavior against fast algebraic attacks, like functions obtained by modifying bent functions (e.g., those of [1091]). We give in the next theorem a corrected result (the first bound in Theorem 22 is more or less the only interesting one; we include also the second to give a correct alternative to a bound given in [1106] and to show what were the difficulties missed by its proof).

---

[6] A slightly more complex bound is deduced in [801] from the first bound in Proposition 137, which allows one to improve upon lower bounds (9.8) and (9.9) in some subcases.

Theorem 22 *For any positive integer n and any nonnegative integer $r \leq n$, let f be any n-variable function and $k = \min \{d_{alg}(g) + d_{alg}(fg); \ g \neq 0\}$. We have then*

$$nl_r(f) \geq \sum_{i=0}^{\left\lfloor \frac{k-r-1}{2} \right\rfloor} \binom{n}{i}.$$

Moreover, if $nl_r(f) \neq 0$ and if $AI(f) > AI(f \oplus h)$ for at least one function h of algebraic degree at most r such that $d_H(f, h) = nl_r(f)$, then

$$nl_r(f) \geq \sum_{i=0}^{\left\lfloor \frac{FAI(f)-r-1}{2} \right\rfloor} \binom{n}{i}.$$

Proof Suppose first that $nl_r(f) < \sum_{i=0}^{\left\lfloor \frac{k-r-1}{2} \right\rfloor} \binom{n}{i}$. Let h be a Boolean function of algebraic degree at most r whose Hamming distance $w_H(f \oplus h)$ to f equals $nl_r(f)$. Since $f \oplus h$ has Hamming weight strictly smaller than $\sum_{i=0}^{\left\lfloor \frac{k-r-1}{2} \right\rfloor} \binom{n}{i}$, the rank of matrix $M_{f \oplus h, \left\lfloor \frac{k-r-1}{2} \right\rfloor}$ is also strictly smaller and there exists a nonzero annihilator g of $f \oplus h$ whose algebraic degree is at most $\left\lfloor \frac{k-r-1}{2} \right\rfloor$. We have then $fg = hg$ with $g \neq 0$ and $d_{alg}(g) + d_{alg}(fg) = d_{alg}(g) + d_{alg}(hg) \leq 2 \left\lfloor \frac{k-r-1}{2} \right\rfloor + r < k$, a contradiction.

We address now the second bound. Suppose that $nl_r(f) < \sum_{i=0}^{\left\lfloor \frac{FAI(f)-r-1}{2} \right\rfloor} \binom{n}{i}$ and let us fix h of algebraic degree at most r such that $AI(f) > AI(f \oplus h)$. For such h, similarly to above, there exist annihilators $g \neq 0$ of $f \oplus h$ such that $d_{alg}(g) \leq \left\lfloor \frac{FAI(f)-r-1}{2} \right\rfloor$ and one of these annihilators at least has algebraic degree $AI(f \oplus h) < AI(f)$. Then:

- If one of these annihilators equals constant function 1, then $f = h$ and therefore $nl_r(f) = 0$, a contradiction.
- In the other case, we arrive to a contradiction as above. $\qquad \square$

For instance, if k is near from n and $r = n/2$, we have $nl_{n/2}(f) \geq \sum_{i=0}^{\lambda n} \binom{n}{i} \geq \frac{2^n H_2(\lambda)}{\sqrt{8n\lambda(1-\lambda)}}$, where $\lambda \approx \frac{1}{4}$ (cf. [809, page 310]), and where $H_2(x) = -x \log_2(x) - (1-x) \log_2(1-x)$ is the entropy function, whose value at $\frac{1}{4}$ equals $\frac{1}{2} + \frac{3}{4}(2 - \log_2(3)) = 2 - \frac{3}{4} \log_2(3) \approx 0.8$. Note that $2^{\frac{n}{2}-1}$ is then negligible with respect to $\frac{2^n H_2(\lambda)}{\sqrt{8n\lambda(1-\lambda)}}$ (this will play a role at page 339).

Remark. If $nl_r(f) \neq 0$, the condition $g \neq 0$ in the definition of k can be replaced by $d_{alg}(g) \geq 1$. Indeed, if there is no other nonzero annihilator of $f \oplus h$ of algebraic degree at most $\left\lfloor \frac{k-r-1}{2} \right\rfloor$ than $g = 1$, this means that $k \leq r + 1$. If $k \leq r$, then $\left\lfloor \frac{k-r-1}{2} \right\rfloor < 0$ and the result holds, and if $k = r + 1$, then the only case where the bound would not hold is if $nl_r(f) = 0$, which is excluded. $\qquad \square$

9.1.2 The problem of finding functions achieving high algebraic immunity and high nonlinearity

Recall that, in the framework of stream ciphers, we do not have security proofs but we need functions allowing resistance to all known attacks and having enough randomness for hoping they will not be too weak against new attacks. These functions must be as quickly computable as possible.

No known primary construction viewed in Chapters 5, 6, and 7 allows obtaining classes of functions satisfying all important criteria, and no secondary construction is known for designing new functions satisfying all the criteria from already defined functions satisfying them. We know, however, that functions achieving optimal or suboptimal algebraic immunity and at the same time high algebraic degree and high nonlinearity must exist thanks to the results of [437, 1000]. But knowing that almost all functions have high algebraic immunity does not mean that constructing such functions is easy.

Lobanov's bound seen at page 331 does not ensure high enough nonlinearity:

- For n even and $AI(f) = \frac{n}{2}$, it gives $nl(f) \geq 2^{n-1} - 2\binom{n-1}{\frac{n}{2}-1} = 2^{n-1} - \binom{n}{\frac{n}{2}}$, which is much smaller than the best possible nonlinearity $2^{n-1} - 2^{\frac{n}{2}-1}$ and, more problematically, much smaller than the asymptotic almost sure nonlinearity of Boolean functions, which is, when n tends to ∞, located in the neighborhood of $2^{n-1} - 2^{\frac{n}{2}-1}\sqrt{2n \ln 2}$ as we saw. Until 2008, the best nonlinearity reached by the known functions with optimal AI was that of the majority function and of the iterative construction (see more details below on these functions): $2^{n-1} - \binom{n-1}{\frac{n}{2}} = 2^{n-1} - \frac{1}{2}\binom{n}{\frac{n}{2}}$ [409]. This was a little better than what gives Lobanov's bound, but insufficient.
- For n odd and $AI(f) = \frac{n+1}{2}$, Lobanov's bound gives $nl(f) \geq 2^{n-1} - \binom{n-1}{(n-1)/2} \simeq 2^{n-1} - \frac{1}{2}\binom{n}{(n-1)/2}$, which is a little better than in the n even case, but still far from the average nonlinearity of Boolean functions. Until 2008, the best-known nonlinearity was that of the majority function and matched this bound.

Efficient algorithms have been given in [27, 438, 439] for computing the algebraic immunity, with respective complexities $\mathcal{O}\left(2^n\binom{n}{AI(f)}\right)$ and $\mathcal{O}\left(n2^n\binom{n}{AI(f)}\right)$ (the latter being slightly worse but on the other hand the amount of memory needed being smaller). Algorithms for evaluating the immunity to fast algebraic attacks are also given in these references with complexity $\mathcal{O}\left(e\binom{d+1}{e}\binom{n}{e}\sqrt{\binom{n}{d}} + \binom{n}{e}^3\right)$, where e is significantly smaller than $AI(f)$ and d is comparable to $AI(f)$, and $\mathcal{O}\left(n2^n\binom{n}{k}\right)$, where k is the degree of the algebraic system to be solved in the last step of the attacks. They showed the poor resistance of the majority function to FAA. In [997, 999], Rizomiliotis introduced three matrices to evaluate the behavior of Boolean functions against fast algebraic attacks using univariate polynomial representation. Later was shown in [794] that one matrix is enough.

9.1.3 The functions with high algebraic immunity found so far and their parameters

Sporadic functions

In [407], 7-variable rotation symmetric (RS) functions with nonlinearity 56, resiliency order 2, algebraic immunity 4, and a large number of 8-variable RS functions with nonlinearity

116, resiliency order 1, and algebraic immunity 4 are exhibited. These authors claimed there exist such functions having good resistance against fast algebraic attacks, but Siegenthaler's bound shows that this resistance is limited and eight variables is small; rotation symmetry presents also a risk that the attacker can use such a strong structure in specific attacks.

Balanced highly nonlinear functions in up to 20 variables (derived from power functions) with high algebraic immunities have been exhibited in [279] and [27]. Some other interesting ideas of constructions have been proposed, either using simulated annealing [836] (but the number of variables is limited, the gain in terms of nonlinearity is not large, and, of course, this cannot produce infinite classes) or using the genetic hill climbing algorithm, starting from the function of Theorem 23 that we shall see at page 337 and applying a few swaps on its truth table [694] (this can increase a little its nonlinearity, but it could not lead to infinite classes either).

In [1031] are calculated the algebraic immunity and nonlinearity of the 20-variable function used as nonlinear filter in the lightweight stream cipher Hitag2. The algebraic immunity is no more than 6.

Note that the construction of Proposition 85, page 236, allows increasing the complexity of Boolean functions while keeping their high nonlinearities and may allow increasing their algebraic immunity as well.

Primary constructions of infinite classes of functions, with insufficient nonlinearity

- The *majority function*, considered by Key et al. [691] in the context (equivalent to that of algebraic immune functions) of the erasure channel, and rediscovered in the context of algebraic immunity [127, 409]), defined as $f(x) = 1$ if $w_H(x) \geq \frac{n}{2}$ and $f(x) = 0$ otherwise,[7] has optimal algebraic immunity. Note that, for n odd, Proposition 135 materializes, in the case of this function, in a rather simple way, since $(f \oplus 1)(x) = f(x + 1_n)$ and f and $f \oplus 1$ are then affine equivalent. The proof of its optimal algebraic immunity is easy. We give it for n odd (the case n even is slightly more technical): an annihilator of $f \oplus 1$ being equal to 0 at every input of Hamming weight at most $\frac{n-1}{2}$, Relation (2.4), page 33, makes that its *ANF* has no term of degree at most $\frac{n-1}{2}$; a nonzero anihilator must then have algebraic degree at least $\frac{n+1}{2}$. The majority function is balanced when n is odd. It is a *symmetric Boolean function* (which can represent a weakness but also allows using it with more variables while ensuring the same or even a better speed), and when n is odd it is the only one with optimal AI, up to the addition of function 1; see more at page 357. It has two main weaknesses: its nonlinearity is weak[8] and its resistance to *fast algebraic attack* is bad too (as shown in [27], there exist Boolean functions $g \neq 0$ and h such that $fg = h$, where $d_{alg}(h) = \lfloor n/2 \rfloor + 1$ and $d_{alg}(g) = d_{alg}(h) - 2^j$, where j is maximum so that this number is strictly positive). The nonlinearity has been determined in [409]; the proof using Krawtchouk polynomials is very technical and cannot be included here. A simpler proof has been given by Cusick (and not published). There is a way of showing that the nonlinearity of the majority function (which is adaptable to many other functions similar to it) cannot be good: let us take for instance n odd and apply the second-order Poisson formula (2.57), page 62, with

---

[7] Changing $w_H(x) \geq \frac{n}{2}$ into $w_H(x) > \frac{n}{2}$ or $w_H(x) \leq \frac{n}{2}$ or $w_H(x) < \frac{n}{2}$ changes the function into an *affinely equivalent* one, up to addition of the constant 1, and therefore does not change the AI.

[8] This crippling drawback is shared by all the classes of rotation symmetric functions (see definition in Section 10.2, page 360) with optimal AI presented in numerous papers, which are not mentioned in this book.

$E = \{x \in \mathbb{F}_2^n; \ x \preceq b\}$, where b is a vector of Hamming weight $\frac{n-1}{2}$, and $E' = E^\perp = \{x \in \mathbb{F}_2^n; \ x \preceq b + 1_n\}$. For every $a \in E'$, when x ranges over E, the Hamming weight of $a + x$ equals $w_H(a) + w_H(x)$ (since the two vectors have disjoint supports) and is larger than or equal to $\frac{n+1}{2}$ if and only if $w_H(x) \geq \frac{n+1}{2} - w_H(a)$. Hence, we have $\mathcal{F}(h_a) = \sum_{i=0}^{\frac{n-1}{2}-w_H(a)} \binom{\frac{n-1}{2}}{i} - \sum_{i=\frac{n+1}{2}-w_H(a)}^{\frac{n-1}{2}} \binom{\frac{n-1}{2}}{i} = \sum_{i=0}^{\frac{n-1}{2}-w_H(a)} \binom{\frac{n-1}{2}}{i} - \sum_{i=0}^{w_H(a)-1} \binom{\frac{n-1}{2}}{i} =$

$$\begin{cases} \sum_{i=w_H(a)}^{\frac{n-1}{2}-w_H(a)} \binom{\frac{n-1}{2}}{i} & \text{if } w_H(a) \leq \frac{n-1}{4} \\ -\sum_{i=\frac{n+1}{2}-w_H(a)}^{w_H(a)-1} \binom{\frac{n-1}{2}}{i} & \text{if } w_H(a) \geq \frac{n+3}{4} \end{cases}.$$

The absolute value of $\mathcal{F}(h_a)$ is then larger than or equal to $\binom{\frac{n-1}{2}}{\lfloor \frac{n-1}{4} \rfloor}$, unless it is null, that is, unless $\frac{n-1}{2} - w_H(a) = w_H(a) - 1$, which happens only if $n \equiv 3 \ [\text{mod } 4]$ and $w_H(a) = \frac{n+1}{4}$. Since $b + 1_n$ has Hamming weight $\frac{n+1}{2}$, the size of E' equals $2^{\frac{n+1}{2}}$. According to (2.57), the arithmetic mean of $W_f^2(u)$ when $u \in E^\perp$ is then at least $(2^{\frac{n+1}{2}} - 1)\left(\binom{\frac{n-1}{2}}{\lfloor \frac{n-1}{4} \rfloor}\right)^2 \approx 2^{\frac{3n-1}{2}}$ (recall that the Stirling formula implies that $\binom{n}{n/2} \sim 2^n \sqrt{\frac{2}{\pi n}}$) and therefore $nl(f)$ is smaller than or equal to approximately $2^{n-1} - 2^{\frac{3n-3}{4}}$.

Some variants of the majority function have also optimal algebraic immunity and are balanced for n even, but they have more or less the same drawbacks.

It is proved in [127] that, for n even, changing the value at 1_n of the majority function preserves its optimal algebraic immunity, as well as, for $n \geq 8$, changing its values at the inputs of Hamming weights $\frac{n}{2} \pm 4$ and, for $n \geq 10$, making these two changes simultaneously. All such functions happen to be weak against FAA as shown in [27].

- An iterative construction of an infinite class of functions with optimal algebraic immunity has been given in [408] and further studied in [261]; however, the functions it produces are neither balanced (which can be fixed) nor highly nonlinear (which cannot, unless many variables are added), and it is weak against fast algebraic attacks, as also shown in [27].

- More numerous functions with optimal algebraic immunity were given in [230]. Among them are functions with better nonlinearities, but the method did not allow reaching high nonlinearities (see [328]) and some functions constructed in [766, 767] seem still worse from this viewpoint. In [929], Pasalic introduced an iterative concatenation method for constructing maximum AI functions with suboptimal FAI, but the nonlinearity of the resulting functions was insufficient. Hence, the question of designing infinite classes of functions achieving all the necessary criteria remained open after these papers.

A first primary construction of an infinite class of functions satisfying all criteria

A function with optimal algebraic immunity, good immunity to fast algebraic attacks, provably much better nonlinearity than the functions mentioned above, and, in fact, according to computer investigations, quite sufficient nonlinearity has been exhibited in 2008 (five years after the invention of algebraic attacks) in [273]. This *primary construction* is defined over the field $\mathbb{F}_{2^n}$. It has been originally defined as the Boolean function whose support equals $\{0, 1, \alpha, \dots, \alpha^{2^{n-1}-2}\}$, where α is any *primitive element* of $\mathbb{F}_{2^n}$. This original function is the Boolean (single-output) case of a class of vectorial functions studied in [500], where the optimal algebraic immunity was proved. The contribution of [273] (which resulted in the authors of the subsequent papers giving these functions the name of *Carlet–Feng functions*) was to observe that all the cryptographic parameters of this function were good (not only the algebraic immunity) and to provide a simpler proof of the optimal algebraic immunity, which gave a better view of why it happens. The proof has been later slightly simplified further in [242]. The authors of the papers that soon after 2008 have modified this function in order to find more functions [1091, 1148] preferred using the function of support $\{\alpha^s, \ldots, \alpha^{2^{n-1}+s-1}\}$, where s is some integer. The two definitions coinciding for $s = 2^{n-1} - 1$ up to addition of constant function 1, and two different values of s giving *linearly equivalent* functions, the two definitions deal with essentially the same function. In the next theorem, we take the modified definition.[9]

Theorem 23 *[273, 500] For every positive integer n, every integer s, and every primitive element α of $\mathbb{F}_{2^n}$, the balanced Boolean function over $\mathbb{F}_{2^n}$ whose support is $\{\alpha^s, \ldots, \alpha^{2^{n-1}+s-1}\}$ has optimal algebraic degree $n - 1$ and optimal algebraic immunity $\lceil \frac{n}{2} \rceil$.*

Proof It is shown in [273] that the univariate representation of the original function equals $1 + \sum_{i=1}^{2^n-2} \frac{\alpha^i}{(1+\alpha^i)^{1/2}} x^i$, where $u^{1/2} = u^{2^{n-1}}$, which shows that the algebraic degree of f equals $n - 1$ (optimal for a balanced function). This proves the first property. Up to linear equivalence, s can be taken equal to 0. Let g be any Boolean function of algebraic degree strictly less than n and $g(x) = \sum_{i=0}^{2^n-2} g_i x^i$, $g_i \in \mathbb{F}_{2^n}$, its univariate representation in the field $\mathbb{F}_{2^n}$ (since g has algebraic degree less than n, we have $g_{2^n-1} = 0$). Then:

$$
\begin{pmatrix} g(1) \\ g(\alpha) \\ g(\alpha^2) \\ \vdots \\ g(\alpha^{2^n-2}) \end{pmatrix} = \begin{pmatrix} 1 & 1 & 1 & \cdots & 1 \\ 1 & \alpha & \alpha^2 & \cdots & \alpha^{2^n-2} \\ 1 & \alpha^2 & \alpha^4 & \cdots & \alpha^{2(2^n-2)} \\ \vdots & \vdots & \vdots & \cdots & \vdots \\ 1 & \alpha^{2^n-2} & \alpha^{2(2^n-2)} & \cdots & \alpha^{(2^n-2)(2^n-2)} \end{pmatrix} \times \begin{pmatrix} g_0 \\ g_1 \\ g_2 \\ \vdots \\ g_{2^n-2} \end{pmatrix}.
$$

If g is an annihilator of f, then $g(1) = g(\alpha) = \cdots = g(\alpha^{2^{n-1}-1}) = 0$ and the coefficients $g_0, \ldots, g_{2^n-2}$ satisfy then

$$
\begin{pmatrix} 1 & 1 & 1 & \cdots & 1 \\ 1 & \alpha & \alpha^2 & \cdots & \alpha^{2^n-2} \\ 1 & \alpha^2 & \alpha^4 & \cdots & \alpha^{2(2^n-2)} \\ \vdots & \vdots & \vdots & \cdots & \vdots \\ 1 & \alpha^{2^{n-1}-1} & \alpha^{2(2^{n-1}-1)} & \cdots & \alpha^{(2^{n-1}-1)(2^n-2)} \end{pmatrix} \times \begin{pmatrix} g_0 \\ g_1 \\ g_2 \\ \vdots \\ g_{2^n-2} \end{pmatrix} = \begin{pmatrix} 0 \\ 0 \\ 0 \\ \vdots \\ 0 \end{pmatrix}.
$$

If at most 2^{n-1} of the g_i are nonzero, then erasing $2^{n-1} - 1$ null coefficients (and the corresponding matrix columns) from the system above leads to a homogeneous system of

---

[9] This same function has been later rediscovered with another presentation by Q. Wang, J. Peng, H. Kan and X. Xue in IEEE Transactions on Inf. Th., as shown in [238] (and in another paper published later by H. Chen, T. Tian and W. Qi in DCC).

linear equations whose matrix is a $2^{n-1} \times 2^{n-1}$ Vandermonde matrix and is then nonsingular. We have then proved that the vector $(g_0, \ldots, g_{2^n-2})$ is either null or has Hamming weight at least $2^{n-1} + 1$ (in the framework of coding theory, this result is called the *BCH bound*). This implies that any nonzero annihilator of f has algebraic degree at least $\lceil \frac{n}{2} \rceil$ (since otherwise, the number of its nonzero coefficients would be at most 2^{n-1}, because $\sum_{i=0}^{\lceil n/2 \rceil - 1} \binom{n}{i} \leq 2^{n-1}$).

If g is an annihilator of $f \oplus 1$, then we have $g(\alpha^i) = 0$ for every $i = 2^{n-1}, \ldots, 2^n - 2$, and for the same reasons as above, the vector $(g_0, \ldots, g_{2^n-2})$ has Hamming weight at least 2^{n-1}. Moreover, suppose that function g has algebraic degree at most $\frac{n-1}{2}$ and that the vector $(g_0, \ldots, g_{2^n-2})$ has Hamming weight 2^{n-1} exactly. Then n is odd and all the coefficients $g_i; 0 \leq i \leq 2^n - 2, w_2(i) \leq (n-1)/2$, are nonzero[10], but $g_0 \neq 0$ contradicts then $g(0) = 0$. This completes the proof. $\qquad\qquad\qquad\qquad\qquad\qquad\qquad\qquad\qquad\qquad\qquad\qquad\qquad\qquad\quad\square$

The nonlinearity of the function is also good, at least for values of n for which the function can be used in stream ciphers. In fact, this nonlinearity had been previously studied in [129] (but the algebraic immunity was not considered there) and a lower bound on the nonlinearity was shown, similar to the one later given in [273]:

$$nl(f) \geq 2^{n-1} - n \cdot \ln 2 \cdot 2^{\frac{n}{2}} - 1. \qquad (9.11)$$

Bound (9.11) is not sufficient for showing that f has good nonlinearity. It has been improved several times, but the improvements are marginal and insufficient for asserting that the function allows resisting the fast correlation attack. The actual values of the nonlinearity have been computed up to $n = 26$ and happen to be very good and quite sufficient for such a resistance. Note that the nonlinearity depends on the choice of the primitive element α and the bounds mentioned above are in fact bounds on the minimum Hamming distance between f and all functions of the form $tr(ax^j + b)$ where j is coprime with $2^n - 1$, which we can call the *hyper-nonlinearity* (in relation to the notion of *hyper-bent function* seen in Definition 57, page 244). It is an open question to determine whether a significantly better lower bound on the hyper-nonlinearity of f can be proved (some ideas are given in [248, subsection 4.2]) or if the gap between the bound and the actual hyper-nonlinearity reduces when n takes values larger than 26.

The good resistance to *fast algebraic attacks* has first been checked by computer for $n \leq 12$, using an algorithm from [27], and later shown mathematically in [793] for all n:

Proposition 140 *Let e be a positive integer less than $\frac{n}{2}$ and f be the function of Theorem 23. Then, if $\binom{n-1}{e}$ is even, there exists no nonzero function g with algebraic degree at most e such that fg has algebraic degree at most $n - e - 1$, and if $\binom{n-1}{e}$ is odd, there exists no nonzero function g with degree at most e such that fg has degree at most $n - e - 2$.*

In particular, f is PAI (see page 322) when n is a power of 2, plus 1 (this was known before only for $n = 3, 5, 9$).

---

[10] There is a small inaccuracy in what is written in the proofs provided in [236, 242, 273] since the g_i are not necessarily in $\mathbb{F}_2$.

The computation of the function of Theorem 23 is reasonably fast, at least for some values of $n \leq 20$. This may seem surprising, because the complexity of its computation is clearly the same as that of the discrete logarithm, which is known to be asymptotically high (this has led to a whole branch of public-key cryptography), but for small values of n (like $n \leq 20$), the function is fast to be computed, all the more if $2^n - 1$ is the product of small factors (this is the case of 18 and 20, for instance), because this allows using the Pohlig–Hellman algorithm; in the case of these two values of n, computing one output bit per cycle is possible with 40,000 transistors, as observed in [238]. This allows avoiding needing using a look-up table (of about one megabits, which is too heavy for some devices) for computing the output of the function.

Hence, the functions of this class gather all the properties needed for allowing the stream ciphers, using them as filtering functions to resist all the main attacks (the Berlekamp–Massey [BM] algorithm, fast correlation attacks, standard and fast algebraic attacks, and Rønjom–Helleseth attacks).

Modifications of the functions of Theorem 23

- Classes of functions have been proposed, obtained by replacing a part of the support of the function by another part of the same size. In [997], Rizomiliotis proposed a matrix approach (instead of the BCH bound) for proving optimal AI, and the (balanced) function of support $\{1, \alpha, \ldots, \alpha^{\sum_{i=1}^{\lceil \frac{n}{2} \rceil - 1} \binom{n}{i}}\} \cup U$, where $U \subset \{\alpha^{\sum_{i=0}^{\lceil \frac{n}{2} \rceil - 1} \binom{n}{i}}, \ldots, \alpha^{1 + \sum_{i=0}^{\lceil \frac{n}{2} \rceil} \binom{n}{i}}\}$ has size $2^{n-1} - \sum_{i=0}^{\lceil \frac{n}{2} \rceil - 1} \binom{n}{i}$, is proved to have optimal AI. In [1148], three classes based on the same method are proposed; for some values of n, better nonlinearity than with the function of Theorem 23 could be reached, and for other values of n, the nonlinearity is worse. The good resistance to FAA has been checked by computer for small values of n.

- Another kind of modification of this same function has been proposed in [1091]. It is based on the $\mathcal{PS}_{ap}$ construction. The so-called *Tu–Deng function* is the $2n$-variable function defined over $\mathbb{F}_{2^n}^2$ mapping (x, y) to $f(xy^{2^n - 2})$, where f is the function of Theorem 23. Note that $xy^{2^n - 2}$ equals $\frac{x}{y}$ when $y \neq 0$ and is null when $y = 0$. Since f is balanced, the Tu–Deng function is bent (and therefore has optimal nonlinearity $2^{2n-1} - 2^{n-1}$) as we saw at page 213. Moreover, its AI has optimal value n, up to a combinatorial conjecture, which was still an open problem (studied in [513] and other papers but not solved yet) as this book was written, but which has been checked up to $n = 29$; this is quite enough in cryptographic context, since $n = 29$ makes 58 variables. We know that bent functions are not balanced, but it is shown in [1091] that modifying 2^{n-1} output values of the Tu–Deng function can give a balanced function with optimal AI and very large nonlinearity.

  Unfortunately, the resulting balanced function lies then at Hamming distance at most 2^{n-1} from the Reed–Muller code of order n and length 2^{2n} (the set of Boolean functions in $2n$ variables of algebraic degree at most n), since because of Theorem 13, page 200, any $2n$-variable bent function has algebraic degree at most n. According to Theorem 22, page 332, and to the observation that follows it, applied with $2n$ instead of n and with $r = n$, the balanced function is weak against fast algebraic attacks (see more precise calculations in [1106, lemmas 1–2]), as are the 1-resilient functions obtained from it in some papers by modifying a few terms.

The Tu–Deng construction has been generalized to vectorial functions in [501].

- The Tu–Deng function has been modified in [1067] into a class of $2n$-variable functions having the same nice properties as the function of Theorem 23. As recalled in the survey [242]:

Proposition 141 *[1067] Let $n = 2^r m \geq 2$, where $r \geq 0$ and $m > 0$ is odd, and let f be the function of Theorem 23. We consider the functions*

$$f_1(x, y) = f(xy); x, y \in \mathbb{F}_{2^n}, \tag{9.12}$$

$$f_2(x, y) = \begin{cases} f_1(x, y), & x \neq 0 \\ u(y), & x = 0 \end{cases} \tag{9.13}$$

where u is a balanced Boolean function on $\mathbb{F}_{2^n}$ satisfying $u(0) = 0$, $deg(u) = n - 1$, and $\max_{a \in \mathbb{F}_{2^n}} |W_u(a)| \leq 2^{\frac{m+1}{2}}$ if $r = 0$ and $\max_{a \in \mathbb{F}_{2^n}} |W_u(a)| \leq \sum_{i=1}^{r} 2^{\frac{n}{2^i}} + 2^{\frac{m+1}{2}}$ if $r \geq 1$. Then f_2 is balanced, f_1 and f_2 have optimal AI (equal to n), f_1 has algebraic degree $2n - 2$, f_2 has algebraic degree $2n - 1$, $nl(f_1) > 2^{2n-1} - \left(\frac{\ln 2}{\pi} n + 0.42\right) 2^n - 1$.

There is a little more complex lower bound on $nl(f_2)$, first given in [1067] and later improved in [1108]; it is slightly smaller than for $nl(f_1)$. Function u does exist; see [1076, 1149].

The proof of optimal AI is obtained up to a conjecture similar to that of Tu–Deng, but slightly different, which has been finally proved in [374]. The same gap between the bound on the nonlinearity of f_2 and its actual values is observed when computing them up to $n = 19$; see [1067]. The nonlinearities of f_2 and f are similar when they are taken with the same numbers of variables; in some cases, $nl(f)$ is better, and in some cases, $nl(f_2)$ is better. The good behavior of f_2 with respect to FAA has been shown mathematically in [794].

In [789, 790], the authors introduced a larger class of functions achieving optimal algebraic immunity and almost perfect immunity to fast algebraic attacks. The exact nonlinearity of some functions of this larger class is good (slightly smaller than that of Carlet–Feng functions), and some functions of this family have a slightly larger nonlinearity than those of [1067] with the same numbers of variables. The class of [789, 790] also contains a class presented in [644], whose resistance to fast algebraic attacks is also studied in [789, 790, 794] without that a positive answer be clearly obtained. The class of [1067] is modified in [1068] to ensure first-order resiliency.

Other constructions

Constructions that we shall not detail are given in [761, 777, 997] and other papers, as well as constructions in [587, 796, 1124, 1172] based on the decomposition of the multiplicative group of $\mathbb{F}_{2^n}^*$ corresponding to what we called *polar representation* at page 168 or more general multiplicative decompositions.

In [776] is proposed a new method, based on deriving new properties of minimal codewords of the punctured *Reed–Muller code* $RM^*(\lfloor \frac{n-1}{2} \rfloor, n)$. Recall that we say that a vector $(a_0, \ldots, a_{N-1}) \in \mathbb{F}_2^N$ is *covered* by a vector $(c_0, \ldots, c_{N-1}) \in \mathbb{F}_2^N$ if for every $i = 0, \ldots, N-1$, we have $c_i = 0 \Rightarrow a_i = 0$, and that the codewords of *cyclic codes* are represented by polynomials (see page 12).

Proposition 142 *[776] Let n be an integer, $\alpha \in \mathbb{F}_{2^n}$ be a primitive element, and f be the n-variable Boolean function with $supp(f) = \{\alpha^{m_0}, \ldots, \alpha^{m_s}\}$, where $m_0 = 0$ and $m_0 < \cdots < m_s < 2^n - 1$. Then $f \oplus 1$ has no annihilator with algebraic degree less than $\lceil \frac{n}{2} \rceil$ if and only if there is no nonzero even weight codeword of the cyclic code $RM^*(\lfloor \frac{n-1}{2} \rfloor, n)$ covered by $c(x) = 1 + x^{m_1} + \cdots + x^{m_s}$.*

This result allows generalizing the function of Theorem 23 for any n, and leads for n odd, thanks to Proposition 135, to large classes of new functions with optimal algebraic immunity and good behavior against fast algebraic attacks, and high nonlinearity.

9.1.4 Secondary constructions of algebraic immune functions

Algebraic immunity and direct sum

For any positive integers n, m, any n-variable function f, and any m-variable function g depending on disjoint sets of variables, denoting $r = \max(d_{alg}(f), d_{alg}(g))$, we have

$$\max(AI(f), AI(g)) \leq AI(f \oplus g) \leq \min(AI(f) + AI(g), r). \tag{9.14}$$

Indeed, for some $\epsilon, \eta \in \mathbb{F}_2$, let h be a nonzero annihilator of algebraic degree $AI(f)$ of $f \oplus \epsilon$ and k a nonzero annihilator of algebraic degree $AI(g)$ of $g \oplus \eta$, then the product of h and k is a nonzero[11] annihilator of algebraic degree at most $AI(f) + AI(g)$ of $f \oplus g \oplus \epsilon \oplus \eta$, and we know also that $AI(f \oplus g) \leq d_{alg}(f \oplus g)$. This proves the right-hand side inequality. And if h is a nonzero annihilator of the $(n + m)$-variable function $f \oplus g$, then at least one of its restrictions obtained by fixing x (resp. y) in $f(x) \oplus g(y)$ is nonzero; this proves the left-hand side inequality.

Remark. When the sum is not direct, the inequality $AI(f \oplus g) \leq AI(f) + AI(g)$ can be false [227]: let h be an n-variable Boolean function and let l be an n-variable nonzero linear function, then the functions $f = hl$ and $g = h(l \oplus 1)$ have algebraic immunities at most 1, since $f(l \oplus 1) = gl = 0$, and their sum equals h. If $AI(h) > 2$, we obtain a counter example. □

Of course, the double inequality of (9.14) generalizes to the direct sum of more than two functions. We have also $FAI(f \oplus g) \geq \max(FAI(f), FAI(g))$ and $FAC(f \oplus g) \geq \max(FAC(f), FAC(g))$. These inequalities are not valid if the sum of f and g is not direct.

The algebraic immunity of direct sums of monomials is studied in Section 10.3; see Relation (10.6) at page 363. The upper bound in (9.14) is tight. It is shown in [305] that the upper bound is achieved with equality when the function with the lower algebraic immunity

---

[11] Thanks to the fact that h and k depend on disjoint sets of variables.

(in a broad sense) is nonconstant and the other function f and its complement $f \oplus 1$ have different nonzero annihilator minimum degrees (this is applied in particular to determine the algebraic immunity of the direct sum of a threshold function, see page 358, and affine functions). Another example where the upper bound is achieved with equality is with the direct sum g of an n-variable function f and of a monomial m of degree $AI(f) + 1$; as shown in [279], this gives indeed a function of algebraic immunity $AI(f) + 1$ because the restriction h_1 to $\mathbb{F}_2^n \times \{0_{AI(f)+1}\}$ of a nonzero degree at most $AI(f)$ annihilator h of g is an annihilator of f, which then either has algebraic degree $AI(f)$ or is null, and in the former case, $gh = 0$ is impossible because mh_1 has degree $2AI(f) + 1$ while $m(h_1 \oplus h)$ has degree at most $2AI(f)$ (since each monomial of $h + h_1$ has at least one coordinate in common with m), and in the latter case, fh cannot contain multiples of m and then cannot equal mh since $d_{alg}(h) \leq AI(f) < d_{alg}(m)$. We shall see at page 363 with triangular functions an example of application.

Note that the upper bound in (9.14) shows that the direct sum of two functions can have optimal algebraic immunity only if each has optimal algebraic immunity, except when both are in odd dimension (an example of a direct sum with maximal algebraic immunity of two functions not both having optimal algebraic immunity is function $x_1 \oplus x_2x_3 \oplus x_4x_5x_6$, of algebraic immunity 3 in six variables, which is the direct sum of $x_1 \oplus x_2x_3$, of algebraic immunity 2 in three variables, and of $x_4x_5x_6$, of algebraic immunity 1 in three variables).

The lower bound of (9.14) is also tight. An example where the lower bound is an equality is with two functions $f(x)$ and $g(y)$ whose algebraic immunities equal their algebraic degrees, since we have then $\max(d_{alg}(f), d_{alg}(g)) = \max(AI(f), AI(g)) \leq AI(f \oplus g) \leq d_{alg}(f \oplus g) = \max(d_{alg}(f), d_{alg}(g))$. In [305], it is observed that if $d_{alg}(g) > 0$, and if (say) $\max(AI(f), AI(g)) = AI(f)$, and if $f \oplus 1$ has no nonzero annihilator of algebraic degree $AI(f)$, then the lower bound cannot be an equality.

Algebraic immunity and Siegenthaler's construction

Proposition 143 *[261] Let f, g be two n-variable Boolean functions with $AI(f) = d_1$ and $AI(g) = d_2$. Let $h = (1 \oplus x_{n+1})f \oplus x_{n+1}g \in \mathcal{BF}_{n+1}$. Then:*

1. *If $d_1 \neq d_2$ then $AI(h) = \min\{d_1, d_2\} + 1$.*
2. *If $d_1 = d_2 = d$, then $d \leq AI(h) \leq d + 1$, and $AI(h) = d$ if and only if there exists $f_1, g_1 \in \mathcal{BF}_n$ of algebraic degree d such that $\{ff_1 = 0, gg_1 = 0\}$ or $\{(1 \oplus f)f_1 = 0, (1 \oplus g)g_1 = 0\}$ and $d_{alg}(f_1 \oplus g_1) \leq d - 1$.*

Proof 1. If f has an algebraic degree d_1 nonzero annihilator f_1, and g has an algebraic degree d_2 nonzero annihilator g_1, then we have $(1 \oplus x_{n+1})f_1 h = 0$ and $x_{n+1}g_1 h = 0$, which proves, after addressing similarly the cases where f_1 is an annihilator of $f \oplus 1$ and/or g_1 is an annihilator of $g \oplus 1$, that $AI(h) \leq \min\{AI(f), AI(g)\} + 1$.

Let $p = (1 \oplus x_{n+1})p_1 \oplus x_{n+1}p_2$ be a lowest algebraic degree nonzero annihilator of h. We have $hp = (1 \oplus x_{n+1})fp_1 \oplus x_{n+1}gp_2 = 0$. So $fp_1 = 0$ and $gp_2 = 0$. Similarly, if p is an annihilator of $h \oplus 1$, then $(1 \oplus f)p_1 = 0$ and $(1 \oplus g)p_2 = 0$. Now there can be three cases in both scenarios:

(i) p_1 is zero and p_2 is nonzero, then $d_{alg}(p_2) \geq d_2$, which gives $d_{alg}(p) \geq d_2 + 1$.

(ii) p_2 is zero and p_1 is nonzero, then $d_{alg}(p_1) \geq d_1$, which gives $d_{alg}(p) \geq d_1 + 1$.

(iii) Both p_1, p_2 are nonzero, then $d_{alg}(p_1) \geq d_1$ and $d_{alg}(p_2) \geq d_2$, which gives $d_{alg}(p) \geq \max\{d_1, d_2\} + 1$, when $d_1 \neq d_2$ and $d_{alg}(p) \geq d$, when $d_1 = d_2 = d$. So for $d_1 \neq d_2$ we get $AI(h) \geq \min\{d_1, d_2\} + 1$.

2. According to the observations above, we have $d \leq AI(h) \leq d + 1$. And $AI(h)$ equals d if and only if we are in case (iii) and the degree d terms of p_1 and p_2 are the same. □

Corollaries are given in [261], and more complex constructions are studied in [407].

9.1.5 Another direction of research of Boolean functions suitable for stream ciphers

All the functions described in Subsection 9.1.3 are of optimal algebraic immunity, and the best ones have good other parameters, given their number of variables. They should be taken with a number of variables large enough for ensuring sufficient resistance to all attacks but also small enough for ensuring good speed. An alternative method is to find functions with good but not optimal parameters, which would be quickly enough computable for being used with larger numbers of variables, so as to ensure same (and possibly better) resistance to attacks and also same and possibly better speed. The main example of this kind is with the Boolean function (mentioned by Knuth in Vol. 4 of "The Art of Computer Programming") called *hidden weight bit function* (*HWBF*). The principle of this function is as follows: we compute from the input $x = (x_1, \ldots, x_n) \in \mathbb{F}_2^n$ a value, say $\phi(x)$ belonging to $\{1, \ldots, n\}$, and the output of the function is the value of the coordinate of index $\phi(x)$:

$$f(x_1, \ldots, x_n) = x_{\phi(x)}, \text{ where } \phi : \mathbb{F}_2^n \mapsto \{1, \ldots, n\}.$$

If the computation of $\phi(x)$ is fast, then that of the Boolean function is fast. In the case of HWBF, $\phi(x)$ equals $w_H(x)$ if $x \neq 0_n$ and $\phi(0_n)$ equals any integer between 1 and n (the value of $f(0_n)$ being 0 for any choice). It is proved in [1105] that the function is then balanced and has algebraic degree $n - 1$ (optimal) for $n \geq 3$ and that its algebraic immunity is at least $\lfloor \frac{n}{3} \rfloor + 1$, which is quite good since the function can be taken in many more variables than the function of Theorem 23, for instance. But the nonlinearity equals $2^{n-1} - 2\binom{n-2}{\lceil \frac{n-2}{2} \rceil}$, which is not quite good, since this gives a too large bias of the nonlinearity with respect to 2^{n-1}, that is, $\epsilon = \frac{2^{n-1} - nl(f)}{2^n}$, and the complexity of the fast correlation attack is then too small; see page 78. The too large value of ϵ is here not compensated by the number of variables, but as shown in [1105], it can be reduced by making a direct sum with a function with large nonlinearity (however, the direct sum represents some risk of attacks). Nevertheless, more functions of this kind need to be investigated. Some attempts have been made but with no significant gain.

9.1.6 An additional condition modifying the study of Boolean functions for stream ciphers

As recalled in [324], a stronger condition than balancedness is necessary in the filter model, if we wish to avoid additionally those attacks which are able, for some choice of the tapping sequence (*i.e.*, of the positions inside the LFSR where the inputs to the filter function are taken), to distinguish the *keystream* $(s_i)_{i \in \mathbb{N}}$ output by the pseudorandom generator from a random sequence, by the observation of the distribution of a vectorial sequence of the form $(s_{i+j_1}, \ldots, s_{i+j_n})$; see page 89. We have seen that, for avoiding such attacks, the filter function must have one of the two equivalent forms $x_1 \oplus f(x_2, \ldots, x_n)$ and $f(x_1, \ldots, x_{n-1}) \oplus x_n$ [189, 545, 1044]. Studying if a function of the desired form $f(x_1, \ldots, x_{n-1}) \oplus x_n$ (say) satisfies the criteria listed above is not equivalent to the same study for f (taking a function in $n - 1$ variables providing the best trade-off between all criteria and adding the extra variable x_n in order to obtain the desired form gives an algebraic immunity that can be either equal to that of the original function or larger by 1, and it results in functions that no longer ensure the best possible algebraic degree). The constructions in Subsection 9.1.3 have been modified in [324] in order to achieve inside this desired form the best possible values.

Constructions of 1-resilient algebraic immune functions have also been found, but only in even dimension;[12] see, *e.g.*, [261, 1055, 1070, 1076, 1092, 1111, 1115], but many lack good nonlinearity and/or have bad resistance to *FAA* (some because their $\frac{n}{2}$-th order nonlinearity is low) and the behavior of the others may not be optimal.

9.2 Algebraic immune vectorial functions

We have seen at page 125 that algebraic attacks concern also vectorial functions used in stream ciphers and in block ciphers. As far as we know, only standard algebraic attacks have been considered in the literature for stream ciphers using vectorial functions (whose PRG output several bits at each clock cycle), and fast algebraic attacks do not have reality for block ciphers. Different related notions of *algebraic immunity* exist for vectorial Boolean functions, according to whether these functions are used as multioutput filters in stream ciphers or as S-boxes in block ciphers. They have been studied in [29, 32, 235]. We first give the definition of the algebraic immunity of a set:

Definition 74 *We call annihilator of a subset E of $\mathbb{F}_2^n$ any n-variable Boolean function vanishing on E. We call algebraic immunity of E, and we denote by $AI(E)$, the minimum algebraic degree of all nonzero annihilators of E.*

The algebraic immunity of an n-variable Boolean function f is then equal to $\min(AI(f^{-1}(0)), AI(f^{-1}(1)))$, according to Definition 23, page 91.

The first generalization of algebraic immunity to S-boxes, introduced in [29], is its direct extension:

Definition 75 *The basic algebraic immunity $AI(F)$ of any (n, m)-function F is the minimum algebraic immunity of all the preimages $F^{-1}(z)$ of the elements z of $\mathbb{F}_2^m$ by F.*

---

[12] One class of functions in odd dimension has first-order correlation immunity: the concatenation of the majority function f in n even variables and of $f(x + 1_n)$.

The basic algebraic immunity is invariant under affine equivalence. Note that $AI(F)$ also equals the minimum algebraic immunity of the *indicators* of these preimages $F^{-1}(z)$ since, the algebraic immunity being a nondecreasing function over sets, we have for every $z \in \mathbb{F}_2^m$

$$AI(\mathbb{F}_2^n \setminus F^{-1}(z)) \geq AI(F^{-1}(z')), \; \forall z \neq z'.$$

$AI(F)$ quantifies the resistance to standard algebraic attacks of the stream ciphers using F as a combiner or as a filter function. Indeed, the attacker can combine the output bits of the generator in any way; in other words, the attacker can try a standard algebraic attacks on any stream cipher using Boolean function $h \circ F$ as filter or combiner, where h is any nonconstant m-variable Boolean function, and such an attack is the most efficient when h has Hamming weight 1 (again because the algebraic immunity is a nondecreasing function over sets).

A second notion of algebraic immunity of vectorial functions [29, 235, 368, 392], more relevant for S-boxes in block ciphers, has been called the graph algebraic immunity.

Definition 76 *The graph algebraic immunity $AI_{gr}(F)$ of any (n, m)-function F is the algebraic immunity of the graph $\{(x, F(x)); \; x \in \mathbb{F}_2^n\}$ of the S-box.*

By definition, the graph algebraic immunity is invariant under *CCZ equivalence*.

A third notion, introduced in [235] and called the component algebraic immunity, seems also natural:

Definition 77 *The component algebraic immunity $AI_{comp}(F)$ of any (n, m)-function F is the minimal algebraic immunity of the component functions $v \cdot F$ ($v \neq 0_m$ in $\mathbb{F}_2^m$) of the S-box.*

The interest of AI_{comp} is that it has a sense for both cases of stream ciphers and block ciphers, and it helps studying the two other notions.

9.2.1 Known bounds on algebraic immunities

Note that we have $AI(F) \leq AI_{comp}(F)$, since $AI_{comp}(F)$ equals $AI(F^{-1}(H))$ for some affine hyperplane H of $\mathbb{F}_2^m$, and since AI is nondecreasing; we also have $AI_{gr}(F) \leq AI_{comp}(F) + 1$, since if g is a nonzero annihilator of $v \cdot F$, $v \neq 0_m$, then the product $h(x, y) = g(x)(v \cdot y)$ is a nonzero annihilator of the graph of F, and if g is a nonzero annihilator of $v \cdot F \oplus 1$, then $h(x, y) = g(x)(v \cdot y) \oplus g(x)$ is a nonzero annihilator of the graph of F. A few observations are deduced in [235].

It has been observed in [29] that, for any (n, m)-function F, we have

$$AI(F) \leq AI_{gr}(F) \leq AI(F) + m.$$

Indeed, given any minimum degree nonzero annihilator $g(x, y)$ of the graph of F, there exists y such that the function $x \mapsto g(x, y)$ is not the zero function, and this function is a nonzero annihilator of $F^{-1}(y)$, which proves the left-hand side inequality. And given a minimum degree nonzero annihilator g of $F^{-1}(z)$, where z is such that $AI(F^{-1}(z)) =$

Table 9.1 The values of $d_{n,m}$.

$n \backslash m$	1	2	3	4	5	6	7	8	9	10	11	12	13	14	15	16	17
5	3	2	1	1	1	0											
6	3	2	2	1	1	1	0										
7	4	3	2	2	1	1	1	0									
8	4	3	2	2	1	1	1	1	0								
9	5	3	3	2	2	1	1	1	1	0							
10	5	4	3	3	2	2	1	1	1	1	0						
11	6	4	4	3	2	2	2	1	1	1	1	0					
12	6	5	4	3	3	2	2	2	1	1	1	1	0				
13	7	5	4	4	3	3	2	2	2	1	1	1	1	0			
14	7	6	5	4	4	3	3	2	2	2	1	1	1	1	0		
15	8	6	5	5	4	3	3	3	2	2	2	1	1	1	1	0	
16	8	7	6	5	4	4	3	3	2	2	2	1	1	1	1	1	0
17	9	7	6	5	5	4	4	3	3	2	2	2	1	1	1	1	1
18	9	8	7	6	5	5	4	4	3	3	2	2	2	1	1	1	1
19	10	8	7	6	5	5	4	4	3	3	3	2	2	2	1	1	1
20	10	8	7	7	6	5	5	4	4	3	3	3	2	2	2	1	1

$AI(F)$, the function $g(x) \prod_{j=1}^{m}(y_j \oplus z_j \oplus 1)$ is an annihilator of algebraic degree $AI(F)+m$ of the graph of F; this proves the right-hand side inequality.

Denoting by $d_{n,m}$ the smallest integer such that $\sum_{i=0}^{d_{n,m}} \binom{n}{i} > 2^{n-m}$, we have

$$AI(F) \leq d_{n,m} \leq d_{n,m-1} \leq \cdots \leq d_{n,1} = \left\lceil \frac{n}{2} \right\rceil.$$

Indeed, there is at least one z such that $|F^{-1}(z)| \leq 2^{n-m}$ and according to Relation (9.5), page 330, with $f = 1_{|F^{-1}(z)|}$, we have $\sum_{i=0}^{AI(f)-1} \binom{n}{i} \leq 2^{n-m}$ and therefore $AI(f) - 1 < d_{n,m}$. Since $AI(F) \leq AI(f)$, this proves the first inequality, originally observed in [29], and proved tight in [500] thanks to the function that we shall introduce at page 350; the other inequalities are straightforward.

We give in Table 9.1 taken from [235] the values of $d_{n,m}$, for n ranging from 5 to 20 and for m ranging from 1 to 17.

Similarly, as also proved in [29], denoting by $D_{n,m}$ the smallest integer such that $\sum_{i=0}^{D_{n,m}} \binom{n+m}{i} > 2^n$, we have

$$AI_{gr}(F) \leq D_{n,m} \leq D_{n,m-1} \leq \cdots \leq D_{n,1} = \left\lceil \frac{n+1}{2} \right\rceil.$$

Note that we have $D_{n,m} = d_{n+m,m}$. In [235] is given the table of the values of $D_{n,m}$, for n ranging from 5 to 20 and for m ranging from 1 to 17.

9.2.2 Bounds on the numbers $d_{n,m}$ and $D_{n,m}$

We have $d_{n,m} \leq n - m$ and $D_{n,m} \leq n$, since $\sum_{i=0}^{n-m} \binom{n}{i} > \sum_{i=0}^{n-m} \binom{n-m}{i} = 2^{n-m}$. The bound $d_{n,m} \leq \left\lceil \frac{n}{2} \right\rceil$ is stronger than $d_{n,m} \leq n - m$ if and only if $m < \frac{n-1}{2}$, and the bound $D_{n,m} \leq \left\lceil \frac{n+1}{2} \right\rceil$ is stronger than $D_{n,m} \leq n$ if and only if $n \geq 3$. The inequality $D_{n,m} \leq \left\lceil \frac{n+1}{2} \right\rceil$

Table 9.2 The values of $1 - H_2(\lambda)$.

λ	0.1	0.2	0.3	0.4
$1 - H_2(\lambda)$	0.53	0.28	0.19	0.03

gives $d_{n+m,m} \leq \left\lceil \frac{n+1}{2} \right\rceil$ and therefore, for $n > m$: $d_{n,m} \leq \left\lceil \frac{n-m+1}{2} \right\rceil$, which is stronger than $d_{n,m} \leq \left\lceil \frac{n}{2} \right\rceil$ and than $d_{n,m} \leq n - m$. We know from [809, page 310] that, for any positive number $\lambda \leq 1/2$ and every positive integer n, we have $\sum_{i=0}^{\lceil \lambda n \rceil} \binom{n}{i} \geq \frac{2^{nH_2(\lambda)}}{\sqrt{8\lambda n(1-\lambda)}}$. This bound implies, for every m

$$d_{n,m} \leq \min\left\{ \lceil \lambda n \rceil \mathbin{/} n\, H_2(\lambda) - \frac{1}{2}\left(3 + \log_2 n + \log_2 \lambda + \log_2(1 - \lambda)\right) > n - m \right\}$$

(note that the term in $\frac{1}{2}\left(3 + \log_2 n + \log_2 \lambda + \log_2(1 - \lambda)\right)$ is asymptotically negligeable with respect to n). Hence:

Proposition 144 *[235] Let $\lambda \leq 1/2$ be a positive real number. For all positive integers n and m such that*

$$m > n\,(1 - H_2(\lambda)) + \frac{1}{2}\left(3 + \log_2 n + \log_2 \lambda + \log_2(1 - \lambda)\right),$$

where $H_2(x) = -x \log_2(x) - (1 - x) \log_2(1 - x)$, we have $d_{n,m} \leq \lceil \lambda n \rceil$.

For any two positive integers n and m such that

$$m\, H_2(\lambda) > n\,(1 - H_2(\lambda)) + \frac{1}{2}\left(3 + \log_2(n + m) + \log_2 \lambda + \log_2(1 - \lambda)\right),$$

we have $D_{n,m} \leq \lceil \lambda(n + m) \rceil$.

We give in Table 9.2 the values of $1 - H_2(\lambda)$ for λ ranging in $\{.1, .2, .3, .4\}$.
These general bounds can be improved for specific values of m.

9.2.3 Consequences on the number of output bits and on the tightness of the bounds

$AI(F)$ can be larger than a number k, only if $m \leq n\,(1 - H_2(k/n)) + \frac{1}{2}\,(3 + \log_2(k(1 - k/n)))$, according to Proposition 144. Hence, vectorial (n, m)-functions can be used as combiners or filters only if m is small enough compared to n.

The bound $AI(F) \leq AI_{gr}(F)$ is tight. Indeed:

Proposition 145 *[235] Let F be an (n, m)-function such that, for every $b \in \mathbb{F}_2^m$, there exists $a \in \mathbb{F}_2^n$ such that the ordered pair (a, b) is a linear structure of F (i.e., $D_a F$ equals constant function b). Then $AI(F) = AI_{gr}(F)$.*

Proof Let $(e_1, \ldots, e_m)$ be the canonical basis of $\mathbb{F}_2^m$ and for every $i \leq m$, let (α_i, e_i) be a linear structure of F. Let z be such that $AI(F) = AI(F^{-1}(z))$. We can assume, without loss of generality up to translation, that $z = 0_m$. Let $g(x)$ be a nonzero annihilator of algebraic degree $AI(F)$ of $F^{-1}(0_m)$. Then, let $h(x, y) =$

$\sum_{b \in \mathbb{F}_2^m} \left(\prod_{i=1}^m (y_i \oplus b_i \oplus 1) \right) g \left(x + \sum_{i=1}^m b_i \alpha_i \right)$. Note that $\prod_{i=1}^m (y_i \oplus b_i \oplus 1)$ equals 1 if and only if $y = b$; hence, for every $x \in \mathbb{F}_2^n$, denoting by I the support of the vector $F(x)$, we have $h(x, F(x)) = g(x + \sum_{i \in I} \alpha_i)$. Since $F(x + \sum_{i \in I} \alpha_i) = F(x) + \sum_{i \in I} e_i = 0_m$, we have $x + \sum_{i \in I} \alpha_i \in F^{-1}(0_m)$ and therefore $h(x, F(x)) = 0$ and h is an annihilator of the graph of F.

Moreover, expanding $h(x, y)$ in the form $\sum_{J \subseteq \{1, \dots, m\}} \left(\prod_{i \in J} y_i \right) \phi_J(x)$, for every vector $b \in \mathbb{F}_2^m$, denoting by I the support of b, we have $\prod_{i=1}^m (y_i \oplus b_i \oplus 1) = \sum_{\substack{J \subseteq \{1, \dots, m\} / \\ I \subseteq J}} \left(\prod_{i \in J} y_i \right)$,

and then, $\phi_J(x) = \sum_{b \in \mathbb{F}_2^m / supp(b) \subseteq J} g(x + \sum_{i=1}^m b_i \alpha_i)$ is a derivative of g of order $|J|$ and has an algebraic degree that is at most $d^\circ g - |J|$. Hence, we have $d^\circ h \leq d^\circ g$ (and in fact $d^\circ h = d^\circ g$, since the part $\phi_\emptyset$ independent of y in $h(x, y)$ equals g(x)). This implies $AI_{gr}(F) \leq AI(F)$, and since we know that $AI(F) \leq AI_{gr}(F)$, then $AI(F) = AI_{gr}(F)$. $\qquad \square$

As seen above, we have two upper bounds on the graph algebraic immunity: $AI_{gr}(F) \leq AI(F) + m$ and $AI_{gr}(F) \leq D_{n,m}$. It is shown in [235] that the latter implies that the former cannot be tight when $AI(F) > 0$, $m \geq n/2$ and $n \geq 3$, nor when $AI(F) > 0$, $m \geq n/3$ and $n \geq 25$, and it is deduced that for $n \geq 2$ and $m \geq n/3$ we have $d_{n,m} \leq m$ and for $n \geq 20$ and $m \geq n/4$, we have also $d_{n,m} \leq m$.

The vectorial functions studied in [273, 500] achieve the bound $AI(F) \leq d_{n,m}$ with equality, which shows that this bound is tight for every n, m such that $1 \leq m < n$. It is not known whether the bound $AI_{gr}(F) \leq D_{n,m}$ is tight too. It is shown in [29] that it is tight for $n \leq 14$.

9.2.4 Nonlinearity and higher-order nonlinearity

Lower bounds on the nonlinearity

As proved in [233], the lower bound $nl(f) \geq 2 \sum_{i=0}^{AI(f)-2} \binom{n-1}{i}$ due to Lobanov on the nonlinearity of Boolean functions generalizes to (n, m)-*functions* as follows:

$$nl(F) \geq 2^m \sum_{i=0}^{AI(F)-2} \binom{n-1}{i},$$

where $AI(F)$ is the basic algebraic immunity of F. But we have seen that for large m, $AI(F) - 2$ is negative. So a bound involving $AI_{gr}(F)$ is also needed. Applying Lobanov's bound to the component functions of F, we obtain

$$nl(F) \geq 2 \sum_{i=0}^{AI_{comp}(F)-2} \binom{n-1}{i}.$$

The inequality $AI_{comp}(F) \geq AI_{gr}(F) - 1$ implies then

$$nl(F) \geq 2 \sum_{i=0}^{AI_{gr}(F)-3} \binom{n-1}{i}.$$

Lower bounds on the higher-order nonlinearities

For every positive integer r, the r-th order nonlinearity of a vectorial function F is the minimum r-th order nonlinearity of its component functions (recall that the r-th order nonlinearity of a Boolean function equals its minimum Hamming distance to functions of algebraic degree at most r). As proved in [233], the bounds known for Boolean functions generalize to (n, m)-functions as follows:

$$nl_r(F) \geq 2^m \sum_{i=0}^{AI(F)-r-1} \binom{n-r}{i}$$

and

$$nl_r(F) \geq 2^{m-1} \sum_{i=0}^{AI(F)-r-1} \binom{n}{i} + 2^{m-1} \sum_{i=AI(F)-2r}^{AI(F)-r-1} \binom{n-r}{i}$$

(the first of these two bounds can be slightly improved as for Boolean functions).

Applying the bounds valid for Boolean functions to the component functions of F, we have also

$$nl_r(F) \geq 2 \sum_{i=0}^{AI_{comp}(F)-r-1} \binom{n-r}{i}$$

and

$$nl_r(F) \geq \sum_{i=0}^{AI_{comp}(F)-r-1} \binom{n}{i} + \sum_{i=AI_{comp}(F)-2r}^{AI_{comp}(F)-r-1} \binom{n-r}{i}.$$

The inequality $AI_{comp}(F) \geq AI_{gr}(F) - 1$ implies then

$$nl_r(F) \geq 2 \sum_{i=0}^{AI_{gr}(F)-r-2} \binom{n-r}{i}$$

and

$$nl_r(F) \geq \sum_{i=0}^{AI_{gr}(F)-r-2} \binom{n}{i} + \sum_{i=AI_{gr}(F)-2r-1}^{AI_{gr}(F)-r-2} \binom{n-r}{i}.$$

9.2.5 Constructions of algebraic immune vectorial functions

Feng et al.'s class

In [274], the class introduced in [500] is studied further. We assume that $n \geq 2$ and $1 \leq m \leq n$. For any fixed integer s, $0 \leq s \leq 2^n - 2$, $\mathbb{F}_{2^n}$ is a disjoint union of the following 2^m subsets:

$$S_0 = \{\alpha^l \mid s \leq l \leq s + 2^{n-m} - 2\} \cup \{0\}$$
$$S_j = \{\alpha^l \mid s + 2^{n-m} j - 1 \leq l \leq s + 2^{n-m}(j+1) - 2\}; \ 1 \leq j \leq 2^m - 1, \tag{9.15}$$

where α is a primitive element. Each integer j, $0 \leq j \leq 2^m - 1$, has a 2-adic expansion

$$j = j_0 + j_1 2 + \cdots + j_{m-1} 2^{m-1} \qquad (j_0, \ldots, j_{m-1} \in \{0, 1\})$$

and corresponds to the vector $\overline{j} = (j_0, \ldots, j_{m-1}) \in \mathbb{F}_2^m$. For each integer i, $0 \leq i \leq m - 1$, we define the Boolean function $f_i : \mathbb{F}_{2^n} \to \mathbb{F}_2$ by

$$f_i(x) = \begin{cases} 1, & \text{if } x \in \displaystyle\bigcup_{\substack{0 \leq j \leq 2^m - 1 \\ j_i = 1}} S_j \\ 0, & \text{otherwise.} \end{cases} \tag{9.16}$$

Then for the (n, m)-function

$$F = (f_0, \ldots, f_{m-1}) : \mathbb{F}_{2^n} \to \mathbb{F}_2^m,$$

we have, for each $\overline{j} = (j_0, \ldots, j_{m-1}) \in \mathbb{F}_2^m$ and $j = \displaystyle\sum_{i=0}^{m-1} j_i 2^i$,

$$\begin{aligned} x \in F^{-1}(\overline{j}) \ &\Leftrightarrow \ f_i(x) = j_i \qquad (0 \leq i \leq m - 1) \\ &\Leftrightarrow \ x \in \bigcap \{S_k \mid 0 \leq k \leq 2^m - 1, k_i = j_i\} \qquad (0 \leq i \leq m - 1) \\ &\Leftrightarrow \ x \in S_j. \end{aligned}$$

Therefore the (n, m)-function F can be characterized by

$$F^{-1}(\overline{j}) = S_j \qquad (\text{for each } j, 0 \leq j \leq 2^m - 1) \tag{9.17}$$

It is proved in [274] by observation and calculation of the coefficients of x^{2^n-1} and x^{2^n-2} in the univariate representations of the coordinate functions that:

Proposition 146 *(1) For every $1 \leq m \leq n$, function F is balanced.*
(2) We have $d_{\text{alg}}(F) = n - 1$.
(3) We have $d_{min}(F) = n - 1$ if and only if $\frac{\alpha}{1+\alpha}, (\frac{\alpha}{1+\alpha})^2, \ldots, (\frac{\alpha}{1+\alpha})^{2^{m-1}}$ are linearly independent over $\mathbb{F}_2$.

It is also proved in this same paper that the basic algebraic immunity of F is optimal:

Proposition 147 *For every n, m such that $1 \leq m \leq n$, we have $AI(F) = d_{n,m}$.*

The proof is very similar to the Boolean case, by application of the BCH bound.

A lower bound on the (hyper-)nonlinearity of F is also proved in [274] by the use of Gauss sums, which allow transforming the expression of the Walsh transform, and by bounding from above some trigonometric sums with integrals:

Proposition 148 $nl(F) \geq 2^{n-1} - \frac{2^{\frac{n}{2}+m}}{\pi} \ln(\frac{4(2^n-1)}{\pi}) - 1 \sim 2^{n-1} - \frac{\ln 2}{\pi} 2^{\frac{n}{2}+m} \cdot n.$

A class obtained through group decomposition

In [804], the authors constructed a class of balanced (n, m)-functions over $\mathbb{F}_{2^n}$ (n even), with $m \leq n/2$, and with high basic algebraic immunity and optimal algebraic degree, based on the decomposition of the multiplicative group of $\mathbb{F}_{2^n}^*$ corresponding to what we called *polar representation* at page 168.

10

Particular classes of Boolean functions

10.1 Symmetric functions

A function is called a *symmetric Boolean function* if it is invariant under the action of the symmetric group (*i.e.*, if its output is invariant under permutation of its input bits). Its output depends then only on the Hamming weight of the input (and can be implemented with a number of gates linear in the number of input variables [1117], with a reduced amount of memory required for storing the function). So a Boolean function f is symmetric if and only if there exists a function f from $\{0, 1, \ldots, n\}$ to $\mathbb{F}_2$ such that

$$f(x) = f(w_H(x)).$$

The vector $(f(0), \ldots, f(n))$ is sometimes called the *simplified value vector* of f.

Such functions are of some interest for cryptography, as they allow us to implement in an efficient way nonlinear functions on large numbers of variables. Let us consider, for example, an LFSR filtered by a 63-variable symmetric function f, whose input is the content of an interval of 63 consecutive flip-flops of the LFSR. This device may be implemented with a cost similar to that of a 6-variable Boolean function, thanks to a 6 bit counter calculating the Hamming weight of the input to f (this counter is incremented if a 1 is shifted in the interval and decremented if a 1 is shifted out). However, the pseudorandom sequence obtained this way has a correlation with transitions (sums of consecutive bits), and a symmetric function should not take all its inputs in a full interval. In fact, it is not yet completely clarified whether the advantage of allowing many more variables and the cryptographic weaknesses these symmetric functions may introduce result in an advantage for the designer or for the attacker.

10.1.1 Representation

Let $r = 0, \ldots, n$ and let $1_{E_{n,r}}$ be the Boolean function whose support is the set $E_{n,r}$ of all vectors of Hamming weight r in $\mathbb{F}_2^n$. Then, according to Relation (2.23), page 49, relating the values of the coefficients of the NNF to the values of the function, the coefficient of x^I in the *NNF* of $1_{E_{n,r}}$ equals $(-1)^{|I|} \sum_{\substack{x \in \mathbb{F}_2^n; \, w_H(x)=r \\ supp(x) \subseteq I}} (-1)^{w_H(x)} = (-1)^{|I|-r} \binom{|I|}{r}$, and we have

then:

$$1_{E_{n,r}}(x) = \sum_{I \subseteq \{1, \ldots, n\}} (-1)^{|I|-r} \binom{|I|}{r} x^I. \tag{10.1}$$

Any symmetric function f being equal to $\bigoplus_{r=0}^{n} f(r) \, 1_{E_{n,r}}$, it equals $\sum_{r=0}^{n} f(r) \, 1_{E_{n,r}}$, since the functions $1_{E_{n,r}}$ have disjoint supports. The coefficient of x^I in its NNF equals then

$$\sum_{r=0}^{n} f(r)(-1)^{|I|-r} \binom{|I|}{r}$$

and depends only on the size of I. Denoting

$$S_i(x) = \sum_{\substack{I \subseteq \{1,\ldots,n\} \\ |I|=i}} x^I = \binom{w_H(x)}{i} = \begin{cases} \frac{w_H(x)\,(w_H(x)-1)\ldots(w_H(x)-i+1)}{i!} & \text{if } w_H(x) \geq i \\ 0 & \text{otherwise,} \end{cases}$$

the NNF of f equals then

$$f(x) = \sum_{i=0}^{n} c_i \, S_i(x), \text{ where } c_i = \sum_{r=0}^{n} f(r)(-1)^{i-r} \binom{i}{r}. \tag{10.2}$$

According to Relation (10.2), we see by definition of f that this function coincides on $\{0, \ldots, n\}$ with the polynomial

$$f(z) = \sum_{i=0}^{n} c_i \binom{z}{i} = \sum_{i=0}^{n} c_i \frac{z\,(z-1)\ldots(z-i+1)}{i!},$$

of degree $\max\{i; \, c_i \neq 0\}$ (which is also the degree of the NNF of f). Note that since this degree is at most n, and the values taken by this polynomial at $n+1$ points are determined by the values of f, this polynomial representation is unique and can be obtained by the Lagrange interpolation formula.

Function $\sigma_i(x) = S_i(x) \, [\bmod \, 2]$ is the ith elementary symmetric function:

$$\sigma_i(x) = \bigoplus_{1 \leq j_1 < \cdots < j_i \leq n} \prod_{k=1}^{i} x_{j_k}.$$

According to Lucas' theorem (see page 487 or [809, page 404]), $\sigma_i(x)$ equals 1 if and only if the binary expansion $\sum_{l=1}^{\lfloor \log_2 n \rfloor} i_l \, 2^{l-1}$ of i is covered by that of $w_H(x)$ (i.e., writing $w_H(x) = \sum_{l=1}^{\lfloor \log_2 n \rfloor} j_l \, 2^{l-1}$, we have $i_l \leq j_l, \forall l = 1, \ldots, \lfloor \log_2 n \rfloor$; we write $i \preceq w_H(x)$). Note that this implies that $\sigma_i = \prod_{\substack{l \in \{1, \ldots, \lfloor \log_2 n \rfloor\} \\ i_l = 1}} \sigma_{2^l}$. Reducing Relation (10.2) modulo 2, we deduce from Lucas' theorem again that the *ANF* of f equals:

$$[ANF] \quad f(x) = \bigoplus_{i=0}^{n} \epsilon_i \, \sigma_i(x), \text{ where } \epsilon_i = c_i \, [\bmod \, 2] = \sum_{r \preceq i} f(r) \, [\bmod \, 2]. \tag{10.3}$$

The algebraic degree of f equals $\max\{i; \, \epsilon_i = 1\}$ (in particular, in the case of $f = 1_{E_{n,r}}$, we have that ϵ_i equals 1 if and only if $r \preceq i$ and the algebraic degree equals $\max\{i \in \{r, \ldots, n\}; r \preceq i\}$).

Using that the *binary Möbius transform* is involutive, or using that $\sigma_i(x) = 1$ if and only if $\binom{w_H(x)}{i}$ is odd and Lucas' theorem again, we deduce from (10.3) that $f(j) = \bigoplus_{i \preceq j} \epsilon_i$. The vector $(\epsilon_0, \ldots, \epsilon_n)$ is sometimes called the *simplified ANF vector*. Relation (10.3) gives the expression of the simplified ANF vector by means of the simplified value vector, and this relation gives the reverse expression.

According to the observations above, nonzero symmetric Boolean functions are, up to the addition of constant function 1, the component functions of the (n, n)-function $\Sigma(x)$ whose ith coordinate function is the elementary symmetric function $\sigma_i(x)$. Note that, for every $x, y \in \mathbb{F}_2^n$, we have $w_H(x) = w_H(y)$ if and only if $\Sigma(x) = \Sigma(y)$, since the σ_i generate by linear combinations all those symmetric Boolean functions null at input 0_n, and two vectors x, y have the same nonzero Hamming weight if and only if every symmetric Boolean function null at 0_n takes the same value at inputs x and y. This translation of an equality between the Hamming weights of two vectors x and y into the equality between the images of x and y by a vectorial function is nicely simple. We have then $w_H(x) = k$ for some nonnegative k if and only if, for every $i = 1, \ldots, n$, we have $\sigma_i(x) \equiv \binom{k}{i}$ [mod 2]. We have also $w_H(x) \leq k$ if and only if $\sigma_i(x) = 0$ for all $i > k$ (this necessary condition is sufficient because $\sigma_{w_H(x)}(x) = 1$).

Note that a symmetric Boolean function f has algebraic degree 1 if and only if it equals $\bigoplus_{i=1}^n x_i$ or $\bigoplus_{i=1}^n x_i \oplus 1$, that is, if the binary function f(r) equals r [mod 2] or $r + 1$ [mod 2], and that it is quadratic if and only if it equals $\bigoplus_{1 \leq i < j \leq n} x_i x_j$ plus a symmetric function of algebraic degree at most 1, that is, if the function f(r) equals $\binom{r}{2}$ [mod 2] or $\binom{r}{2} + r$ [mod 2] or $\binom{r}{2} + 1$ [mod 2] or $\binom{r}{2} + r + 1$ [mod 2]. Hence, f has algebraic degree 1 if and only if f satisfies f$(r + 1) = $ f$(r) \oplus 1$ and it has degree 2 if and only if f satisfies f$(r + 2) = $ f$(r) \oplus 1$.

As observed in [205], the algebraic degree of a symmetric function f is at most $2^t - 1$, for some positive integer t such that $2^t < n$, if and only if the sequence $(f(r))_{r \geq 0}$ is periodic with period 2^t (sufficiency is a direct consequence of (10.3) and necessity of the reverse relation). Here again, it is not clear whether this is more an advantage for the designer of a cryptosystem using such symmetric function f (since, to compute the image of a vector x by f, it is enough to compute the number of nonzero coordinates $x_1, \ldots, x_t$) or for the attacker.

10.1.2 Hamming weight

In [173] is given a closed formula for the correlation between any two symmetric Boolean functions (and in particular the weight of a symmetric function). In [532], von zur Gathen and Roche determined all balanced symmetric Boolean functions up to 128 variables. More recently, it has been proved in [530] that balanced symmetric Boolean functions of fixed algebraic degree $d > 1$ and sufficiently large number of variables are *trivial*. This term means that n is odd and the simplified value vector f is antisymmetric with respect to the middle of $[0, \ldots, n]$, that is, f$(n - i) = $ f$(i) \oplus 1, \forall i$. This same paper also shows (proving a conjecture by Cusick) the nonexistence of trivial balanced elementary symmetric Boolean functions except for $n = 2^{t+1}l - 1$ and $d = 2^t$, where t and l are any nonnegative integers.

10.1.3 Fourier–Hadamard and Walsh transforms

For every $a \in \mathbb{F}_2^n$ and $r \in \{0, \ldots, n\}$, denoting by ℓ the Hamming weight of a, we have $\widehat{1_{E_{n,r}}}(a) = \sum_{x \in \mathbb{F}_2^n;\ w_H(x)=r} (-1)^{a \cdot x} = \sum_{j=0}^n (-1)^j \binom{\ell}{j} \binom{n - \ell}{r - j}$, denoting by j the size of $supp(a) \cap supp(x)$. The polynomials $K_{n,r}(X) = \sum_{j=0}^{n}(-1)^j\binom{X}{j}\binom{n-X}{r-j}$ are called *Krawtchouk polynomials*. They are characterized by their generating series:

$$\sum_{r=0}^{n} K_{n,r}(\ell)z^r = (1-z)^\ell(1+z)^{n-\ell}$$

and have nice resulting properties (see, *e.g.*, [328, 809]). By $\mathbb{R}$-linearity, we deduce that the value at a of the Fourier–Hadamard transform of any symmetric function $\sum_{r=0}^{n} f(r) 1_{E_{n,r}}$

equals $\sum_{r=0}^{n} f(r) K_{n,r}(w_H(a))$.

From the Fourier–Hadamard transform, we can deduce the Walsh transform thanks to Relation (2.32), page 55.

In [334], the exponential sums of symmetric Boolean functions and their asymptotic behavior are studied further.

10.1.4 Nonlinearity

If n is even, then the restriction of every symmetric function f on $\mathbb{F}_2^n$ to the $\frac{n}{2}$-dimensional flat $A = \{(x_1, \ldots, x_n) \in \mathbb{F}_2^n ; x_{i+n/2} = x_i \oplus 1, \forall i \leq \frac{n}{2}\}$ is constant, since all the elements of A have the same Hamming weight $n/2$. Thus, f is $\frac{n}{2}$-normal (see Definition 28, page 105). But Relation (3.15), page 107, does not improve upon the covering radius bound (3.2), page 80. The symmetric functions that achieve this bound, *i.e.*, that are bent, have been first characterized by Savicky in [1019]: the bent symmetric functions are the four symmetric functions of algebraic degree 2 already described above: $f_1(x) = \bigoplus_{1 \leq i < j \leq n} x_i x_j$, $f_2(x) = f_1(x) \oplus 1$, $f_3(x) = f_1(x) \oplus x_1 \oplus \cdots \oplus x_n$ and $f_4(x) = f_3(x) \oplus 1$. A stronger result can be proved in a very simple way:

Proposition 149 *[566] For every positive even n, the $PC(2)$ n-variable symmetric functions are the functions f_1, f_2, f_3, and f_4 above.*

Proof Let f be any $PC(2)$ n-variable symmetric function and let $1 \leq i < j \leq n$. Let us denote by x' the vector: $x' = (x_1, \ldots, x_{i-1}, x_{i+1}, \ldots, x_{j-1}, x_{j+1}, \ldots, x_n)$. Since $f(x)$ is symmetric, it has the form $x_i x_j g(x') \oplus (x_i \oplus x_j) h(x') \oplus k(x')$. Let us denote by $e_{i,j}$ the vector of Hamming weight 2 whose nonzero coordinates stand at positions i and j. The derivative $D_{e_{i,j}} f$ equals $(x_i \oplus x_j \oplus 1)g(x')$ and is balanced, by hypothesis. Then g must be equal to the constant function 1 (indeed, if $g(x') = 1$ for some x', then $(x_i \oplus x_j \oplus 1)g(x')$ equals 1 for half of the inputs (x_i, x_j), and otherwise it equals 1 for none). Hence, the degree at least 2 part of the ANF of f equals $\bigoplus_{1 \leq i < j \leq n} x_i x_j$. □

Results on the propagation criterion for symmetric functions are in [205].

If n is odd, then the restriction of any symmetric function f to the $\frac{n+1}{2}$-dimensional flat $A = \{(x_1, \ldots, x_n) \in \mathbb{F}_2^n ; x_{i+\frac{n-1}{2}} = x_i \oplus 1, \forall i \leq \frac{n}{2}\}$ is affine, since the Hamming weight function w_H is constant on the hyperplane of A of equation $x_n = 0$ and on its complement. Thus, f is $\frac{n+1}{2}$-weakly normal. According to Relation (3.15), page 107, this implies that its nonlinearity is upper bounded by $2^{n-1} - 2^{\frac{n-1}{2}}$. It also allows showing that the only symmetric functions achieving this bound with equality are the same as the four functions f_1, f_2, f_3, and f_4 above, but with n odd (this has been first proved by Maitra and Sarkar [818], in a more complex way). Indeed:

Proposition 150 *[224] Let n be any positive integer and let f be any symmetric function on $\mathbb{F}_2^n$. Let l be any integer satisfying $0 < l \leq \frac{n}{2}$. Denote by h_l the symmetric Boolean function on $n - 2l$ variables defined by $h_l(y_1, \ldots, y_{n-2l}) = f(x_1, \ldots, x_l, x_1 \oplus 1, \ldots, x_l \oplus 1, y_1, \ldots, y_{n-2l})$, where the values of $x_1, \ldots, x_l$ are arbitrary (equivalently, h_l can be defined by $h_l(r) = f(r + l)$, for every $0 \leq r \leq n - 2l$). Then $nl(f) \leq 2^{n-1} - 2^{n-l-1} + 2^l nl(h_l)$.*

Proof Let $A = \{(x_1, \ldots, x_n) \in \mathbb{F}_2^n \mid x_{i+l} = x_i \oplus 1, \forall i \leq l\}$. For every element x of A, we have $f(x) = h_l(x_{2l+1}, \ldots, x_n)$. Let us consider the restriction g of f to A as a Boolean function on $\mathbb{F}_2^{n-l}$, say $g(x_1, \ldots, x_l, x_{2l+1}, \ldots, x_n)$. Then, since $g(x_1, \ldots, x_l, x_{2l+1}, \ldots, x_n) = h_l(x_{2l+1}, \ldots, x_n)$, g has nonlinearity $2^l nl(h_l)$. According to Relation (3.15) applied with $h_a = g$ and $k = n - l$, we have $nl(f) \leq 2^{n-1} - 2^{n-l-1} + 2^l nl(h_l)$. □

The characterizations recalled above of those symmetric functions achieving best possible nonlinearity can be straightforwardly deduced. Moreover, if for some $0 \leq l < \left\lfloor \frac{n-1}{2} \right\rfloor$, the nonlinearity of an n-variable symmetric function f is strictly larger than $2^{n-1} - 2^{n-l-1} + 2^l \left(2^{n-2l-1} - 2^{\left\lfloor \frac{n-2l-1}{2} \right\rfloor} - 1 \right) = 2^{n-1} - 2^{\left\lfloor \frac{n-1}{2} \right\rfloor} - 2^l$, then, thanks to these characterizations and to Proposition 150, the function h_l must be quadratic, and f satisfies $f(r+2) = f(r) \oplus 1$, for all $l \leq r \leq n - 2 - l$ (this property has been observed in [205, theorem 6] a little after that [224] was published, and proved slightly differently).

Further properties of the nonlinearities of symmetric functions can be found in [205, 224].

10.1.5 Correlation immunity and resiliency

The correlation immunity of symmetric functions has been studied in [138, 887, 1135] and their resiliency in [370, 557].

There exists a conjecture on symmetric Boolean functions and, equivalently, on functions defined over $\{0, 1, \ldots, n\}$ and valued in $\mathbb{F}_2$: if f is a nonconstant symmetric Boolean function, then the *numerical degree* of f (hence, the degree of the univariate polynomial representation of f) is larger than or equal to number $n - 3$. It is easily shown that this numerical degree is more than $\frac{n}{2}$ (otherwise, the polynomial $f^2 - f$ would have degree at most n, and being null at $n + 1$ points, it would equal the null polynomial, a contradiction with the fact that f is assumed not to be constant). But the gap between $\lfloor \frac{n}{2} \rfloor + 1$ and $n - 3$ is open. According to Proposition 118, page 286, the conjecture is equivalent to saying that there does not exist any nonaffine symmetric 3-*resilient* function. And proving this conjecture is also a problem on binomial coefficients since the numerical degree of f is bounded above by d if and only if, for every k such that $d < k \leq n$:

$$\sum_{r=0}^{k}(-1)^r \binom{k}{r} f(r) = 0. \tag{10.4}$$

The conjecture is equivalent to saying that this Relation (10.4), with $d = n-4$, has no binary solution $f(0), \ldots, f(n)$. Von zur Gathen and Roche [532] have observed that all symmetric n-variable Boolean functions have numerical degrees larger than or equal to $n - 3$, for any $n \leq 128$ (they exhibited Boolean functions with numerical degree $n - 3$; see also [557]).

The same authors also observed that, if the number $m = n + 1$ is a prime, then all nonconstant n-variable symmetric Boolean functions have numerical degree n (and therefore, considering the function $g(x) = f(x) \oplus x_1 \oplus \cdots \oplus x_n$ and applying Proposition 118, all nonaffine n-variable symmetric Boolean functions are unbalanced): indeed, m being a prime, the binomial coefficient $\binom{n}{r}$ is congruent with $\frac{(-1)(-2)\ldots(-r)}{1 \cdot 2 \ldots r} = (-1)^r$, modulo m, and the sum $\sum_{r=0}^{n}(-1)^r \binom{n}{r} f(r)$ is then congruent with $\sum_{r=0}^{n} f(r)$, modulo m, and Relation (10.4) with $k = n$ implies then that f must be constant.

Notice that, applying Relation (10.4) with $k = p-1$, where p is the largest prime less than or equal to $n + 1$, shows that the numerical degree of any symmetric nonconstant Boolean function is larger than or equal to $p-1$ (or equivalently that no symmetric nonaffine Boolean function is $(n - p + 1)$-resilient): otherwise, reducing (10.4) modulo p, we would have that the string $f(0), \ldots, f(k)$ is constant, and f having univariate degree less than or equal to k, the function f, and thus f itself, would be constant.

More results on the balancedness and resiliency/correlation immunity of symmetric functions can be found in [78, 205, 887, 1014, 1135]. The resiliency order of a symmetric function of algebraic degree d cannot exceed $2^{\lfloor \log_2 d \rfloor + 1} - 2$ [205].

10.1.6 Algebraic immunity and fast algebraic immunity

We have seen in Section 3.1 that, for every n-variable Boolean function f, there exist $g \neq 0$ and h, both of algebraic degree at most $\lceil \frac{n}{2} \rceil$ and such that $f g = h$ (equivalently, there exist nonzero annihilators of f or of $f \oplus 1$ of algebraic degree at most $\lceil \frac{n}{2} \rceil$). The same property can be proven when dealing with symmetric functions only: the elementary symmetric functions of degrees at most $\lceil \frac{n}{2} \rceil$ and their products with f give a family of $2(\lceil \frac{n}{2} \rceil + 1) > n + 1$ symmetric functions, which must be linearly dependent since they live in a vector space of dimension $n + 1$. There exist then $g \neq 0$ and h of degree at most $\lceil \frac{n}{2} \rceil$ such that $f g = h$ and the conclusion follows (using also the proof of Proposition 25, page 91). However, given an n-variable symmetric function f, there do not necessarily exist symmetric functions $g \neq 0$ and h of algebraic degree as small as $AI(f)$ such that $f g = h$.

We have seen that the majority function, which is symmetric, has optimal algebraic immunity. In the case n is odd, it is the only symmetric function having such property, up to the addition of a constant (see [979], which completed a partial result of [765]). In the case n is even, other symmetric functions exist (up to the addition of a constant and to the transformation $x \rightarrow \bar{x} = (x_1 \oplus 1, \ldots, x_n \oplus 1)$) with this property and all are known; more precisions and more results on the algebraic immunity of symmetric functions can be found in [127, 364, 774, 785, 941, 976, 978, 979, 1103] and the references therein. In particular, all symmetric functions of optimal algebraic immunity in numbers of variables that are powers of 2 are determined in [785], and it is shown in [127] that for $n = 2^j, 2^j - 1$ and $2^j - 2$, the elementary symmetric function $\sigma_{2^{j-1}}$ has optimal algebraic immunity, and that these are the only cases where an elementary symmetric function can have optimal AI. In [941] the authors show, thanks to a result of [786], that the corpus of potential annihilators of f or $f \oplus 1$ that needs to be investigated to prove the optimal algebraic immunity of a given function can be reduced in the case it is symmetric (and some necessary conditions on the simplified value vector for symmetric functions to achieve high AI are given), and this allows a description of optimal AI symmetric functions (and also of the suboptimal ones), whose other parameters are also studied (none is balanced and the nonlinearity is bad).

We have seen at page 322 that, as shown in [791], no symmetric Boolean function can be perfect algebraic immune. Large classes of symmetric functions are very vulnerable to fast algebraic attacks despite their proven resistance against standard algebraic attacks: for $2^m \leq n \leq 2^m + 2^{m-1} - 1$, for every symmetric n-variable function f of algebraic immunity at least 2^{m-1}, there exists g such that $1 \leq d_{alg}(f) \leq n - 2^m + 1$ and $d_{alg}(fg) \leq n - 2^{m-1} + 1$. Even the other cases often pose a problem, since if $d_{alg}(f) > 2^k$, where 2^k does not divide $d_{alg}(f)$, then there exists g such that $d_{alg}(g) \leq e = d_{alg}(f)$ [mod 2^k] and $d_{alg}(fg) \leq d_{alg}(f) - e - 1$, and the FAI of a symmetric function f whose algebraic degree $d_{alg}(f)$ is not a power of 2 is smaller than $d_{alg}(f)$.

10.1.7 The subclass of threshold functions

For every $d \leq n$, we call[1] *threshold function*[2] of index d, and we denote by $t_{n,d}$ the n-variable Boolean function whose support equals the set of vectors of Hamming weights at least d. The majority functions are examples. The reservations we made about symmetric functions are of course valid for threshold functions. Moreover, we shall see that threshold functions (as many symmetric functions and as all monotone functions; see page 363) have bad nonlinearity. They may then be improper for use in most cryptographic frameworks. But their output is very fast to compute. They can then be used in many more variables than more complex functions (this is the case for all symmetric functions, but still more for threshold functions). They deserve then some attention since they may present interest in some settings like the FLIP cryptosystem (see page 453).

The class of threshold functions has the interest of being preserved by the action of fixing the values of some variables (fixing one variable to 0 in $t_{n,d}$ gives the function $t_{n-1,d}$, and fixing one variable to 1 gives $t_{n-1,d-1}$). The results on them allow then not only to study their contributions to the resistance against classical attacks, but also against guess and determine attacks (see page 96). This is also true more generally with symmetric functions, but less is known on this wider class.

---

[1] Our use of the term of threshold function is a little more restrictive than in [914]; more investigation is then needed.

[2] Not to be confused with the threshold implementation of vectorial functions, which we shall address in Subsection 12.1.4, page 436.

Note that, for each value of d, functions $t_{n,d}$ and $t_{n,n-d+1}$ are *EA equivalent*:

$$\forall x \in \mathbb{F}_2^n, \quad t_{n,n-d+1}(x) = 1 \oplus t_{n,d}(x + 1_n).$$

The majority function for n odd is balanced, but all other threshold functions are unbalanced.

We have $t_{n,d}(x) = \sum_{I \subseteq \{1,\dots,n\}} \lambda_I \, x^I$, where, for $d > 0$, $\lambda_\emptyset = t_{n,d}(0) = 0$ and according to Relation (2.23), page 49, for $I \neq \emptyset$:

$$\lambda_I = (-1)^{|I|} \sum_{\substack{x \in \mathbb{F}_2^n; \, supp(x) \subseteq I}} (-1)^{w_H(x)} t_{n,d}(x) = (-1)^{|I|} \sum_{\substack{x \in \mathbb{F}_2^n; \, supp(x) \subseteq I \\ w_H(x) \geq d}} (-1)^{w_H(x)}$$

$$= (-1)^{|I|} \sum_{k=d}^{|I|} (-1)^k \binom{|I|}{k} = (-1)^{|I|-1} \sum_{k=0}^{d-1} (-1)^k \binom{|I|}{k} = (-1)^{|I|-d} \binom{|I|-1}{d-1}$$

(using $\sum_{k=0}^{|I|} (-1)^k \binom{|I|}{k} = 0$, and the last equality being easily checked by induction on d). According to Lucas' theorem (see page 487 or [809, page 404]), the coefficient of x^I in the ANF of $t_{n,d}$ equals 1 (*i.e.*, λ_I is odd) if and only if the binary expansion of $d-1$ is covered by (*i.e.*, has support included in) that of $|I|-1$, and the algebraic degree of $t_{n,d}$ equals then $k+1$, where k is the largest number smaller than n whose binary expansion covers that of $d-1$, that is, where $k-d+1$ is the largest number smaller than $n-d+1$, whose binary expansion is disjoint from that of $d-1$.

Moreover, according to Relation (2.61), page 66, if $u \neq 0_n$, then $W_{t_{n,d}}(u)$ equals $2(-1)^{w_H(u)+1} \sum_{\substack{I \subseteq \{1,\dots,n\} \\ supp(u) \subseteq I}} 2^{n-|I|} \lambda_I$, that is:

$$W_{t_{n,d}}(u) = 2(-1)^{w_H(u)+1} \sum_{\substack{I \subseteq \{1,\dots,n\} \\ supp(u) \subseteq I}} 2^{n-|I|} (-1)^{|I|-d} \binom{|I|-1}{d-1}.$$

Recall from Relation (10.1), page 352, that the NNF of the indicator of the set $E_{n,r}$ of vectors of Hamming weight r has $(-1)^{|I|-r} \binom{|I|}{r}$ for coefficient of x^I. We deduce that $W_{1_{E_{n,r}}}(u) = 2(-1)^{w_H(u)+1} \sum_{\substack{I \subseteq \{1,\dots,n\} \\ supp(u) \subseteq I}} 2^{n-|I|} (-1)^{|I|-r} \binom{|I|}{r}$. Therefore, for every u, the Walsh transform of function $1_{E_{n,d}}$ at $u \in \mathbb{F}_2^n$ equals the opposite of the Walsh transform of function $t_{n+1,d+1}$ at $(u, 1)$ (where "," symbolizes concatenation). And since these two functions are symmetric, this implies that the maximum absolute value of the Walsh transform of $1_{E_{n,d}}$ equals the maximum absolute value of the Walsh transform of $t_{n+1,d+1}$ at nonzero inputs. But the nonlinearities of the two functions are different because the nonlinearity of $1_{E_{n,r}}$ equals its Hamming weight (since this weight is small), and hence, $|W_{1_{E_{n,r}}}|$ takes its maximum at the zero entry. It is easily deduced that

$$nl(t_{n,d}) = \begin{cases} 2^{n-1} - \binom{n-1}{(n-1)/2} & \text{if } d = \frac{n+1}{2}, \\[2mm] \sum_{k=d}^{n} \binom{n}{k} = w_H(t_{n,d}) & \text{if } d > \frac{n+1}{2}, \\[2mm] \sum_{k=0}^{d-1} \binom{n}{k} = 2^n - w_H(t_{n,d}) & \text{if } d < \frac{n+1}{2}, \end{cases}$$

since this is known from [409] in the case $d = \frac{n+1}{2}$, and for $d > \frac{n+1}{2}$, we have

$$|W_{1_{E_{n-1,d-1}}}(u)| = 2\Big| \sum_{x \in E_{n-1,d-1}} (-1)^{u \cdot x} \Big| \le 2\, w_H(1_{E_{n-1,d-1}}) = 2\binom{n-1}{d-1},$$

for every $u \ne 0_n$, and since $[|W_{t_{n,d}}(0_n)| = 2^n - 2\sum_{i=d}^{n} \binom{n}{i} = \sum_{i=n-d+1}^{d-1} \binom{n}{i}$, and using Pascal's identity $\binom{n}{i} = \binom{n-1}{i} + \binom{n-1}{i-1}$, we deduce that $|W_{t_{n,d}}|$ takes its maximum at the 0_n input, and this completes the proof in this case, and also in the last case according to the identity $t_{n,n-d+1}(x) = 1 \oplus t_{n,d}(x + 1_n)$.

It is also known from [305] that $AI(t_{n,d}) = \min(d, n - d + 1)$, and the vector space of minimum algebraic degree annihilators can be determined. Indeed, applying the transformation $x \mapsto x + 1_n$ changes $t_{n,d}$ into the indicator of the set of vectors of Hamming weight at most $n - d$; the linear combinations over $\mathbb{F}_2$ of the monomials of degrees at least $n - d + 1$ vanish over the words of Hamming weight at most $n - d$ and are then annihilators of this indicator; the dimension $\sum_{i=n-d+1}^{n} \binom{n}{i}$ of this vector space of annihilators being equal to the dimension of the vector space of all annihilators, that is, $2^n - w_H(t_{n,d})$, these linear combinations are all the annihilators of the indicator; the annihilators of $t_{n,d}$ are obtained from these linear combinations by the transformation $x \mapsto x + 1_n$. They can have every algebraic degree at least $n - d + 1$. And the annihilators of $1 \oplus t_{n,d}$ are the linear combinations over $\mathbb{F}_2$ of the monomials of degrees at least d. They can have every algebraic degree at least d. Hence $AI(t_{n,d}) = \min(d, n - d + 1)$.

10.2 Rotation symmetric, idempotent, and other similar functions

We have already encountered *rotation symmetric* (RS) and *idempotent functions* in Chapters 6 and 7 (see Definitions 59 and 60, page 248). We have seen how, through the choice of a normal basis, the latter are related to the former (see Proposition 89, page 248). RS functions constitute a superclass of symmetric functions, which has been investigated from the viewpoints of bentness and correlation immunity (see, *e.g.*, [503, 1048]). These functions, which represent an interesting (reasonably small) corpus for computer investigation, have also played a role in the study of nonlinearity. It could be shown in [684, 686], thanks to such computer investigation, that the best nonlinearity of Boolean functions in odd number n of variables is strictly larger than the quadratic bound if and only if $n > 7$. Indeed, a 9-variable function of nonlinearity 241 could be found (while the quadratic bound gives 240, and the covering radius bound 244), and using direct sum with quadratic functions, it gave then 11-variable functions of nonlinearity 994 (while the quadratic bound gives 992 and the covering radius bound 1,000), and 13-variable functions of nonlinearity 4,036 (while the quadratic bound gives 4,032 and the covering radius bound 4,050). Later it was checked that 241 is the best nonlinearity of 9-variable rotation symmetric functions, but that 9-variable functions whose *truth tables* (or equivalently ANFs) are invariant under cyclic shifts by three steps and under inversion of the order of the input bits can reach nonlinearity 242, which led to 11-variable functions of nonlinearity 996 and 13-variable functions of nonlinearity 4,040. Balanced functions in 13 variables beating the quadratic bound could also be found. The construction with RS functions does not beat the nonlinearity of the Patterson–Wiedemann functions for 15 variables.

Hence rotation symmetry is an interesting notion for investigating the parameters of Boolean functions. Cryptographically speaking, the strong structure it provides may represent a risk with respect to attacks, while rotation symmetric functions are more difficult to use with large numbers of variables than symmetric functions (because they are slower to compute in general).

For $n = 2m$ even, we can consider the *bivariate representation* alongside the univariate representation of idempotent functions. We can see how obtaining the univariate (resp. multivariate) form from the bivariate form and vice versa, and exploit this correspondence to construct more functions; this has been done in [281], and we follow below this reference. For m odd, the situation is simplified and we place then ourselves in such case: choosing $w \in \mathbb{F}_4 \setminus \mathbb{F}_2$, we have $w^2 = w + 1$, $w^4 = w$, and since $\frac{w^2}{w} \notin \mathbb{F}_{2^m}$, we can take (w, w^2) for a basis of $\mathbb{F}_{2^n}$ over $\mathbb{F}_{2^m}$. Any element of $\mathbb{F}_{2^n}$ is then written in the form $xw + yw^2$, where $x, y \in \mathbb{F}_{2^m}$. Given a normal basis $(\alpha, \alpha^2, \ldots, \alpha^{2^{m-1}})$ of $\mathbb{F}_{2^m}$, a natural normal basis of $\mathbb{F}_{2^n}$ is

$$\left(\alpha w, \alpha^2 w^2, \alpha^4 w, \ldots, \alpha^{2^{m-2}} w^2, \alpha^{2^{m-1}} w, \alpha w^2, \ldots, \alpha^{2^{m-2}} w, \alpha^{2^{m-1}} w^2\right). \tag{10.5}$$

Since $(xw + yw^2)^2 = y^2 w + x^2 w^2$, the mapping $z \in \mathbb{F}_{2^n} \mapsto z^2 \in \mathbb{F}_{2^n}$ corresponds to the mapping $(x, y) \in \mathbb{F}_{2^m}^2 \mapsto (y^2, x^2) \in \mathbb{F}_{2^m}^2$. Given a function $f(x, y)$ in bivariate form, the related Boolean function over $\mathbb{F}_2^n$ obtained by decomposing the input $xw + yw^2$ over the normal basis (10.5) is then RS if and only if $f(x, y) = f(y^2, x^2)$. Note that applying this identity m times gives $f(x, y) = f(y, x)$, and applying it $m + 1$ times gives $f(x, y) = f(x^2, y^2)$; the double condition "$f(x, y) = f(y, x)$, and $f(x, y) = f(x^2, y^2)$" is necessary and sufficient for f being idempotent.

Definition 78 *A polynomial $f(z)$ over $\mathbb{F}_{2^n}$, $n = 2m \equiv 2 \pmod{4}$, is called a weak idempotent if its associate bivariate expression $f(x, y) = f(xw + yw^2)$, $w \in \mathbb{F}_4 \setminus \mathbb{F}_2$, $x, y \in \mathbb{F}_{2^m}$, satisfies $f(x, y) = f(x^2, y^2)$.*

Proposition 151 *For $n \equiv 2 \pmod{4}$, idempotents are those polynomials $f(z)$ over $\mathbb{F}_{2^n}$ whose associate bivariate expression $f(x, y) = f(xw + yw^2)$, $w \in \mathbb{F}_4 \setminus \mathbb{F}_2$, satisfies $f(x, y) = f(y^2, x^2)$. Their set is included in that of weak idempotents. An idempotent is a weak idempotent invariant under the swap $x \leftrightarrow y$.*

See more in [245, subsection 5.3]. The corresponding definition at the bit level is obtained by decomposing the univariate representation over the basis (10.5) and the *bivariate representation* over the basis $(\alpha, \alpha^2, \ldots, \alpha^{2^{m-1}})$:

Definition 79 *Let $n = 2m \equiv 2$ (mod 4). A Boolean function*

$$f(x_0, y_1, x_2, y_3, \ldots, x_{n-2}, y_{n-1})$$

(where each index is reduced modulo m) over $\mathbb{F}_2^n$ is weak RS if it is invariant under the transformation $(x_j, y_j) \mapsto (x_{j+1}, y_{j+1})$.

Note the particular disposition of the indices in $f(x_0, y_1, x_2, y_3, \ldots, x_{n-2}, y_{n-1})$: the index 0 for y does not come at the second position (where we have y_1) but at the mth position. Since m is odd, the invariance of f under the transformation $(x_j, y_j) \mapsto (x_{j+1}, y_{j+1})$ over (x, y) is equivalent to its invariance under $(x_j, y_j) \mapsto (x_{j+2}, y_{j+2})$. Hence:

Proposition 152 *The Boolean function $f(x_0, y_1, x_2, y_3, \ldots, x_{n-2}, y_{n-1})$ is weak RS if and only if it is invariant under the square of the shift ρ_n.*

Such weak RS function (that some authors call 2-RS function; see, e.g., [685]) is RS if and only if it is invariant under the swap of x and y. A simple example of a weak RS function is the *direct sum* $f(x) \oplus g(y)$, which is RS when $f = g$, where f and g are RS functions with m variables. More generally, the indirect sum is studied in [281] (see also [245]), with explicit examples of resulting bent idempotents. There exist also examples of bent and semibent weak idempotents [311, 312, 699, 871].

The *secondary constructions* recalled above have led to the construction of RS functions and idempotent bent functions from near-bent RS functions seen at page 251.

The k-variate representation can be studied similarly to the bivariate representation; see [245].

The weights of rotation symmetric functions are studied in [399]. RS functions with optimal algebraic immunity have been constructed (see, e.g., [1015]), but these functions never reached good nonlinearity.

In [748], the class of Matriochka symmetric functions is introduced, which are the sums of symmetric functions whose sets of variables are different and nested.

The notion of rotation symmetry has been generalized to vectorial functions in [994]. An (n, n)-function is RS if it commutes with the cyclic shift: $F \circ s = s \circ F$. This is equivalent to saying that each coordinate function equals (cyclically) the previous one composed by the cyclic shift. Identifying $\mathbb{F}_2^n$ with $\mathbb{F}_{2^n}$ thanks to a normal basis, this is equivalent to $(F(x))^2 = F(x^2)$ and therefore to the fact that the univariate representation of F has all its coefficients in $\mathbb{F}_2$ (using the uniqueness of such representation). Kavut [680] enumerated all bijective rotation symmetric $(6, 6)$-functions with maximum nonlinearity 24, showing that, up to affine equivalence, there are only four functions with differential uniformity 4 and algebraic degree 5.

10.3 Direct sums of monomials

Functions $f(x) = \bigoplus_{I \subseteq \{1, \ldots, n\}} a_I x^I$, where $(a_I = a_J = 1$ and $I \neq J) \Rightarrow (I \cap J = \emptyset)$, are well adapted to situations where Boolean functions must be particularly simple, for instance, when they are used with large numbers of variables and when addition and/or multiplication are costly, like in the FLIP cryptosystem (see page 453). As for threshold functions, the class of direct sums of monomials is preserved by the action of fixing the values of some variables and their study addresses then also their behavior against guess and determine attacks resulting in fixing some input values to the functions.

It is convenient to identify a direct sum of monomials whose value at 0_n is 0 by its *direct sum vector* $[m_1, m_2, \ldots, m_k]$, of length $k = d_{alg}(f)$, in which each m_i is the number of monomials of degree i (this allows us to determine uniquely the function up to permutation of variables). We shall assume that all variables are effective, *i.e.*, that the number of variables equals $\sum_{i=1}^{k} i \, m_i$. The property seen in Relation (6.28), page 232, that the Walsh transform of a direct sum equals the product of the Walsh transforms of the ingredient functions, the *Golomb–Xiao–Massey characterization* of resiliency by the Walsh transform (Theorem 5, page 87), and Relation (3.1), page 79, imply that the resiliency order of f equals $m_1 - 1$ (with the convention that an unbalanced function has resiliency order -1) and that its nonlinearity equals $2^{n-1} - 2^{m_1-1} \prod_{i=2}^{k} \left(2^i - 2\right)^{m_i}$. The algebraic immunity is more complex to determine but it is shown in [306] that if $f(x_1, x_2, x_3, \ldots, x_n)$ is a Boolean function in n variables such that

$$\forall x \in \mathbb{F}_2^{n-2} \; f(x, 0, 0) = f(x, 0, 1) = f(x, 1, 0),$$

then the Boolean function $f'(x_1, \ldots, x_{n-1})$ defined by

$$\forall x \in \mathbb{F}_2^{n-2} \; f'(x, 1) = f(x, 1, 1) \text{ and } f'(x, 0) = f(x, 0, 0)$$

satisfies that $AI(f') \leq AI(f)$. Using this property and the algebraic immunity of triangular functions (see below), the algebraic immunity of sums of monomials has been determined in [305]:

$$AI(f) = \min_{0 \leq d \leq k} \left(d + \sum_{i=d+1}^{k} m_i \right). \tag{10.6}$$

It is also shown in this same reference that, in some cases, the fast algebraic immunity of such functions can be close to their algebraic immunity.

10.3.1 Triangular functions

Direct sums of monomials are called *triangular functions* when their direct sum vector is the all-1 vector (that is, when they have one monomial of each degree). We assume here also that all variables are effective. The kth triangular function equals $\bigoplus_{i=1}^{k} \prod_{j=1}^{i} x_{j+i(i-1)/2}$. Its nonlinearity equals $2^{n-1} - \prod_{i=2}^{k} \left(2^i - 2\right)$, according to what we have seen with direct sums of monomials, and its algebraic immunity equals k, as first observed in [279] (and used in [839]). This property is easily shown by induction on k since we have seen at page 342 that making the direct sum of a function f and of a monomial of degree $AI(f) + 1$ gives a function of algebraic immunity $AI(f) + 1$.

10.4 Monotone functions

An n-variable Boolean function f is (increasing) *monotone* if, for every $x, y \in \mathbb{F}_2^n$ such that $x \preceq y$ (*i.e.*, such that $supp(x) \subseteq supp(y)$; see page 32), we have $f(x) \leq f(y)$. Any *monomial Boolean (multivariate) function* $\prod_{i \in I} x_i$ is monotone. Other examples are threshold functions; see above.

As mentioned in [298, 249], monotone Boolean functions play a role in voting theory (a voting scheme should be monotone), reliability theory (a system currently working should not fail when we replace a defective component by an operative one), hypergraphs (the stability function of a hypergraph, which takes value 1 at x when supp(x) contains at least one edge, is monotone Boolean), and learning (monotone Boolean functions are easier to learn). The question addressed here is whether they can also play a role with stream ciphers (as filter functions), and our conclusion at the end of this section will be essentially negative.

The balancedness and the algebraic immunity of monotone Boolean functions are addressed in [298], which also recalls what their ANF is and how they can be constructed. This reference studies their Walsh spectrum and their nonlinearity, showing that no monotone bent n-variable function exists for $n \geq 4$, and that every monotone n-variable function f has nonlinearity at most $2^{n-1} - 2^{\frac{n-1}{2}}$ for $n \geq 5$ odd. Let us show how these results are obtained. For every $y \in \mathbb{F}_2^n$ such that $f(y) = 0$, we have, according to the *Poisson summation formula* (2.41), page 59, applied with $a = b = 0_n$ and $E^{\perp} = \{x \in \mathbb{F}_2^n; x \preceq y\}$, $E = \{u \in \mathbb{F}_2^n; u \preceq y + 1_n\}$:

$$\sum_{u \in \mathbb{F}_2^n; u \preceq y+1_n} W_f(u) = 2^n,$$

and this implies that $\max_{u \in \mathbb{F}_2^n; u \preceq y+1_n} |W_f(u)| \geq 2^{w_H(y)}$, since the maximum of a sequence cannot be smaller than its arithmetic mean. And when $f(y) = 1$:

$$\sum_{u \in \mathbb{F}_2^n; u \preceq y} (-1)^{1_n \cdot u} W_f(u) = -2^n,$$

and this implies that $\max_{u \in \mathbb{F}_2^n; u \preceq y} |W_f(u)| \geq 2^{n - w_H(y)}$. Then:

Proposition 153 *[298] For every odd $n \geq 5$ and every monotone n-variable function f, we have $nl(f) \leq 2^{n-1} - 2^{(n-1)/2}$.*

Indeed, the observations above and Relation (3.1), page 79, imply this bound when there exists y of Hamming weight at least $\frac{n+1}{2}$ such that $f(y) = 0$, or of Hamming weight at most $\frac{n-1}{2}$ such that $f(y) = 1$, and the only case left is when f is the majority function, which has nonlinearity $2^{n-1} - \binom{n-1}{(n-1)/2}$.

But no general upper bound for n even could be shown. Indeed, only the case where $f(x)$ differs from the majority function for at least one input x of Hamming weight different from $n/2$ can be easily handled similarly. The case where $f(x)$ coincides with the majority function for every input x of Hamming weight different from $n/2$ must be handled by other means. Then [298] only conjectured the upper bound $nl(f) \leq 2^{n-1} - 2^{\frac{n}{2}}$ for n even large enough.

This conjecture was proved in [249]. We give its proof (and this will also prove the nonexistence of monotone bent functions). According to the observations above, we can restrict ourselves to the case where n is even and f equals the majority function at every input x of Hamming weight different from $n/2$. We can assume f different from the strict and large majority functions, since the nonlinearity of these two functions, equal to

$2^{n-1} - \binom{n-1}{n/2}$, is larger than $2^{n-1} - 2^{n/2}$ for n large enough. What makes the proof work is the *second-order Poisson summation formula* (see Relation (2.57), page 62):

$$\sum_{u \in E^\perp} W_f^2(u) = |E^\perp| \sum_{a \in E'} \left(\sum_{x \in E} (-1)^{f(a+x)} \right)^2, \tag{10.7}$$

valid for any Boolean function f and supplementary subspaces E and E' of $\mathbb{F}_2^n$.

For a given y of Hamming weight $n/2$ and such that $f(y) = 0$, let us take $E = \{x \in \mathbb{F}_2^n; x \preceq y\}$. Then $E^\perp = \{u \in \mathbb{F}_2^n; u \preceq y + 1_n\}$ is supplementary of E, and we can then take $E' = E^\perp$; we obtain, f being null on E since it is monotone

$$\sum_{u \in \mathbb{F}_2^n; u \preceq y+1_n} W_f^2(u) = 2^{n/2} \sum_{a \in \mathbb{F}_2^n; a \preceq y+1_n} \left(\sum_{x \in \mathbb{F}_2^n; x \preceq y} (-1)^{f(a+x)} \right)^2$$

$$= 2^{3n/2} + 2^{n/2} \sum_{a \in \mathbb{F}_2^n; a \preceq y+1_n; a \neq 0_n} \left(\sum_{x \in \mathbb{F}_2^n; x \preceq y} (-1)^{f(a+x)} \right)^2.$$

Using again that the maximum is bounded below by the mean, we deduce the inequality

$\max_{u \in \mathbb{F}_2^n; u \preceq y+1_n} W_f^2(u) \geq 2^n + \sum_{a \preceq y+1_n; a \neq 0_n} \left(\sum_{x \in \mathbb{F}_2^n; x \preceq y} (-1)^{f(a+x)} \right)^2$.

For $a \preceq y + 1_n$, denoting $w_H(a)$ by j, if $x \preceq y$ has Hamming weight strictly less than $n/2 - j$, then $a + x$ has Hamming weight strictly less than $n/2$ and $f(a + x)$ equals 0, and if $x \preceq y$ has Hamming weight strictly larger than $n/2 - j$, then $a + x$ has Hamming weight strictly larger than $n/2$ and $f(a + x)$ equals 1. If $x \preceq y$ has Hamming weight $n/2 - j$, then $a + x$ has weight $n/2$ and the value of $f(a + x)$ is unknown. The value of $\sum_{x \in \mathbb{F}_2^n; x \preceq y} (-1)^{f(a+x)}$ lies then between $\sum_{i=0}^{n/2-1-j} \binom{n/2}{i} - \sum_{i=n/2+1-j}^{n/2} \binom{n/2}{i} - \binom{n/2}{n/2-j}$ and $\sum_{i=0}^{n/2-1-j} \binom{n/2}{i} - \sum_{i=n/2+1-j}^{n/2} \binom{n/2}{i} + \binom{n/2}{n/2-j}$.

Replacing $\binom{n/2}{i}$ by $\binom{n/2}{n/2-i}$ in the sum $\sum_{i=n/2+1-j}^{n/2} \binom{n/2}{i}$, we obtain $\sum_{i=0}^{j-1} \binom{n/2}{i}$. Then for $j < n/4$, we have $n/2 - 1 - j \geq j$ and $\left(\sum_{x \in \mathbb{F}_2^n; x \preceq y} (-1)^{f(a+x)} \right)^2 \geq \left(\sum_{i=j}^{n/2-1-j} \binom{n/2}{i} - \binom{n/2}{n/2-j} \right)^2 = \left(\sum_{i=j+1}^{n/2-1-j} \binom{n/2}{i} \right)^2$, and for $j > n/4$, we have $j - 1 \geq n/2 - j$ and $\left(\sum_{x \in \mathbb{F}_2^n; x \preceq y} (-1)^{f(a+x)} \right)^2 \geq \left(\sum_{i=n/2-j}^{j-1} \binom{n/2}{i} - \binom{n/2}{n/2-j} \right)^2 = \left(\sum_{i=n/2-j+1}^{j-1} \binom{n/2}{i} \right)^2$. We then deduce that $\max_{u \in \mathbb{F}_2^n; u \preceq y+1_n} W_f^2(u) \geq 2^n +$

$$\sum_{1 \leq j < n/4} \binom{n/2}{j} \left(\sum_{i=j+1}^{n/2-1-j} \binom{n/2}{i} \right)^2 + \sum_{n/4 < j \leq n/2} \binom{n/2}{j} \left(\sum_{i=n/2-j+1}^{j-1} \binom{n/2}{i} \right)^2$$

$$= 2^n + 2 \sum_{1 \leq j < n/4} \binom{n/2}{j} \left(\sum_{i=j+1}^{n/2-1-j} \binom{n/2}{i} \right)^2 + \left(\sum_{i=1}^{n/2-1} \binom{n/2}{i} \right)^2$$

$$= 2^n + 2 \sum_{1 \leq j < n/4} \binom{n/2}{j} \left(2^{n/2} - 2 \sum_{i=0}^{j} \binom{n/2}{i} \right)^2 + \left(2^{n/2} - 2 \right)^2.$$

And we have $2\sum_{1\leq j<n/4}\binom{n/2}{j}\left(2^{n/2}-2\sum_{i=0}^{j}\binom{n/2}{i}\right)^2+\left(2^{n/2}-2\right)^2\geq 3\cdot 2^n$ for every $n\geq 10$, since the expression of n equal to

$$2^{-n}\left[2\sum_{1\leq j<n/4}\binom{n/2}{j}\left(2^{n/2}-2\sum_{i=0}^{j}\binom{n/2}{i}\right)^2+\left(2^{n/2}-2\right)^2\right]$$

is nondecreasing and is larger than 3 for $n=10$. We deduce then

Proposition 154   *[249] For every even $n\geq 10$ and every monotone n-variable function f, we have $nl(f)\leq 2^{n-1}-2^{n/2}$.*

Since $2^{n-1}-2^{(n-1)/2}$ (n odd) and $2^{n-1}-2^{n/2}$ (n even) are good nonlinearities for Boolean functions in n variables, the bounds above do not tell us if monotone Boolean functions can have good nonlinearity. But a stronger bound, valid for every n, can be proved as also shown in [249]. Indeed, the inequalities $\max_{u\in\mathbb{F}_2^n}|W_f(u)|\geq 2^{w_H(y)}$ for $f(y)=0$ and $\max_{u\in\mathbb{F}_2^n}|W_f(u)|\geq 2^{n-w_H(y)}$ for $f(y)=1$ can be refined by using the second-order Poisson summation formula (10.7) again.

-   If there exist vectors of Hamming weight strictly larger than $n/2$ whose image by f is 0, let then y have maximal Hamming weight (say, w) among all vectors satisfying $f(y)=0$. We have with the same arguments as above:

$$\max_{u\in\mathbb{F}_2^n;\,u\preceq y+1_n}W_f^2(u)\geq 2^{2w}+\sum_{a\in\mathbb{F}_2^n;\,a\preceq y+1_n;\,a\neq 0_n}\left(\sum_{x\in\mathbb{F}_2^n;\,x\preceq y}(-1)^{f(a+x)}\right)^2.\qquad(10.8)$$

For every $a\preceq y+1_n$ (of Hamming weight $j\leq n-w$), we have $f(a+x)=1$ for every $x\preceq y$ such that $a+x$ has Hamming weight at least $w+1$ (that is, for every $x\preceq y$ of Hamming weight at least $w-j+1$), and we deduce $\sum_{x\in\mathbb{F}_2^n;\,x\preceq y}(-1)^{f(a+x)}\leq 2^w-2\sum_{i=w-j+1}^{w}\binom{w}{i}$. Note that we have $2^w-2\sum_{i=w-j+1}^{w}\binom{w}{i}\leq 0$ if and only if $w-j+1\leq\frac{w}{2}$, that is, $j\geq\frac{w}{2}+1$. We have $\sum_{\substack{a\in\mathbb{F}_2^n;\,a\neq 0_n\\a\preceq y+1_n}}\left(\sum_{x\in\mathbb{F}_2^n;\,x\preceq y}(-1)^{f(a+x)}\right)^2\geq\sum_{j=\lceil\frac{w}{2}\rceil+1}^{n-w}\binom{n-w}{j}\left(2\sum_{i=w-j+1}^{w}\binom{w}{i}-2^w\right)^2$. We deduce then from (10.8) that

$$\max_{u\in\mathbb{F}_2^n;\,u\preceq y+1_n}W_f^2(u)\geq 2^{2w}+\sum_{j=\lceil\frac{w}{2}\rceil+1}^{n-w}\binom{n-w}{j}\left(2^w-2\sum_{i=0}^{w-j}\binom{w}{i}\right)^2.$$

Denoting $2w=n+k$ (where $k>0$ has the same partity as n), we have then

$$\max_{u \in \mathbb{F}_2^n; u \preceq y + 1_n} W_f^2(u) \geq 2^{n+k} + \sum_{j=\lceil \frac{n+k}{4} \rceil + 1}^{\frac{n-k}{2}} \binom{\frac{n-k}{2}}{j} \left(2^{\frac{n+k}{2}} - 2 \sum_{i=0}^{\frac{n+k}{2}-j} \binom{\frac{n+k}{2}}{i} \right)^2 .$$

Hence, we have

$$nl(f) \leq 2^{n-1} - \frac{1}{2} \sqrt{2^{n+k} + \sum_{j=\lceil \frac{n+k}{4} \rceil + 1}^{\frac{n-k}{2}} \binom{\frac{n-k}{2}}{j} \left(2^{\frac{n+k}{2}} - 2 \sum_{i=0}^{\frac{n+k}{2}-j} \binom{\frac{n+k}{2}}{i} \right)^2 } .$$

- If there exist vectors of Hamming weight smaller than $n/2$ and whose image by f equals 1, let y have minimal Hamming weight w such that $f(y) = 1$ ($w < n/2$). Applying the upper bound above to the monotone function $f(x + 1_n) \oplus 1$, whose nonlinearity equals that of f, and denoting $w' = n - w = \frac{n+k'}{2}$, where $k' > 0$ has the same partity as n, we have

$$nl(f) \leq 2^{n-1} - \frac{1}{2} \sqrt{2^{n+k'} + \sum_{j=\lceil \frac{n+k'}{4} \rceil + 1}^{\frac{n-k'}{2}} \binom{\frac{n-k'}{2}}{j} \left(2^{\frac{n+k'}{2}} - 2 \sum_{i=0}^{\frac{n+k'}{2}-j} \binom{\frac{n+k'}{2}}{i} \right)^2 } .$$

- If none of the two cases above happens, then f coincides with the majority function at every input x of Hamming weight different from $n/2$ and either (i) f is a majority function and $nl(f)$ equals then $2^{n-1} - \binom{n-1}{n/2}$ if n is even and $2^{n-1} - \binom{n-1}{(n-1)/2}$ if n is odd, or (ii) n is even and $nl(f) \leq 2^{n-1} - \frac{1}{2}\sqrt{A}$ where A equals $2^n +$

$$2 \sum_{1 \leq j < n/4} \binom{n/2}{j} \left(2^{n/2} - 2 \sum_{i=0}^{j} \binom{n/2}{i} \right)^2 + \left(2^{n/2} - 2 \right)^2 . \text{ We deduce:}$$

Theorem 24 *[249] For every n and every monotone n-variable function f, we have $nl(f) \leq 2^{n-1} - \frac{1}{2}\sqrt{M}$, where $M = \min(A, B, C)$ if n is even and $M = \min(B, C)$ if n is odd, with*

$$A = 2^n + 2 \sum_{1 \leq j < n/4} \binom{n/2}{j} \left(2^{n/2} - 2 \sum_{i=0}^{j} \binom{n/2}{i} \right)^2 + \left(2^{n/2} - 2 \right)^2 ,$$

$$B = \min_{\substack{1 \leq k \leq n/2 \\ n+k \, even}} \left(2^{n+k} + \sum_{j=\lceil \frac{n+k}{4} \rceil + 1}^{\frac{n-k}{2}} \binom{\frac{n-k}{2}}{j} \left(2^{\frac{n+k}{2}} - 2 \sum_{i=0}^{\frac{n+k}{2}-j} \binom{\frac{n+k}{2}}{i} \right)^2 \right) ,$$

and $C = \left[2 \binom{n-1}{\lfloor \frac{n}{2} \rfloor} \right]^2 .$

The behavior of A, B, and C when n tends to infinity is studied in [249] and shows that $\min(A, B, C)$ is asymptotically equivalent to an expression of n at least equal to $2^{\frac{3n\lambda_n}{2}}$ for some λ_n tending to 1. Tables are given, indicating for each value of n between 4 and 31 the value given by the upper bound of Theorem 24. These tables confirm that the nonlinearity of monotone Boolean functions is bad (much worse than what was suggested by the upper bounds obtained, resp. conjectured, in [298]). This shows that the rather large class of monotone Boolean functions contains no element that could be used as a nonlinear function in a cryptosystem.

Highly nonlinear vectorial functions with low differential uniformity

A large nonlinearity is one of the most important criteria for vectorial functions, valid for all uses in stream and block ciphers. Nonlinearity is not the only parameter quantifying the difference in behavior between a vectorial function and *affine functions*, but it is the most important. According to Dib's results [436], the average nonlinearity of vectorial functions is not bad.

Differential uniformity has the same importance as nonlinearity but is specific to *S-boxes* in block ciphers. According to Voloch's results [1098], the average differential uniformity of (n, n)-functions is bad, and this is probably also the case for (n, m)-*functions*. The relationship between nonlinearity and differential uniformity is not completely clarified. For instance, as seen at page 136, there exist vectorial functions with good nonlinearity and bad differential uniformity and vice versa, but most known functions with optimal differential uniformity have good nonlinearity. Further work is needed to understand better this relationship. But the work done in general on the study of S-boxes (see a survey in [94]) is significant and has had important practical applications. The design of the AES has taken advantage of the studies (in particular by K. Nyberg) on the notions of nonlinearity and differential uniformity. This has made it possible in the AES to use S-boxes working on bytes (at the time, it would not have been possible to find a good 8-bit-to-8-bit S-box by a computer search as this had been done for the 6-bit-to-4-bit S-boxes of the DES). We recommend the book [141].

We briefly recall the main information given in Subsection 3.2.3, page 115. The *nonlinearity* $nl(F)$ of an (n, m)-function F is the minimum Hamming distance between all *component functions* of F and all affine functions in n variables:

$$nl(F) = 2^{n-1} - \frac{1}{2} \max_{v \in \mathbb{F}_2^m \setminus \{0_m\}; \, u \in \mathbb{F}_2^n} |W_F(u, v)|.$$

Nonlinearity quantifies the contribution of functions to the resistance against linear attacks, when they are used as S-boxes in block ciphers, and partly against fast correlation attacks, when they are used as filters or combiners in stream ciphers.

We have seen that the nonlinearity is a CCZ invariant. In particular, if $n = m$ and if F is a permutation, then F and its inverse F^{-1} have the same nonlinearity.

We have also seen at page 160 the relationship between the maximal possible nonlinearity of (n, m)-functions and the possible parameters of the linear supercodes of the Reed–Muller code of order 1. Existence and nonexistence results[1] on highly nonlinear vectorial functions are deduced in [1099].

11.1 The covering radius bound; bent/perfect nonlinear functions

As seen at page 117, the covering radius bound is valid for every (n, m)-function:

$$nl(F) \leq 2^{n-1} - 2^{\frac{n}{2}-1}, \tag{11.1}$$

and an (n, m) function is called *bent* if it achieves the covering radius bound (11.1) with equality.

The notion of bent vectorial function is invariant under *CCZ equivalence*[2] (since the nonlinearity is), but we have seen at Subsection 6.4, page 269, that CCZ equivalence coincides with EA equivalence for bent vectorial functions. We have also seen that an (n, m)-function is bent if and only if all the component functions $v \cdot F$, $v \neq 0_m$ of F are bent and that bent (n, m)-functions exist if and only if n is even and $m \leq \frac{n}{2}$. Recall also that an (n, m)-function is bent if and only if all its derivatives $D_a F(x) = F(x) + F(x + a)$, $a \in \mathbb{F}_2^n \setminus \{0_n\}$, are balanced, that is, "bent" and "perfect nonlinear (PN)" are equivalent. Bent vectorial functions contribute then also to an optimal resistance to the differential attack of those cryptosystems in which they are involved (but they are not balanced). They can be used to design *authentication schemes* (or codes); see [346].

Thanks to the observations made in Subsection 2.3.7 (where we saw that the evaluation of the multidimensional Walsh transform corresponds in fact to the evaluation of the Walsh transform), it is a simple matter to characterize bent functions as those functions whose squared expression of the multidimensional Walsh transform at L is the same for every L.

Note that if a bent (n, m)-function F is normal in the sense that it is null on (say) an $\frac{n}{2}$-dimensional vector space E, then F is balanced on any translate of E. Indeed, for every $v \neq 0_m$ in $\mathbb{F}_2^m$ and every $u \in \mathbb{F}_2^n \setminus E$, the function $v \cdot F$ is balanced on $u + E$.

We have recalled at Subsections 6.1.15 and 6.1.16 what are the known primary and secondary constructions of bent functions.

11.2 The Sidelnikov–Chabaud–Vaudenay bound

We have seen with Theorem 6, page 118, that a better upper bound than the covering radius bound exists for (n, n)-functions:

$$nl(F) \leq 2^{n-1} - 2^{\frac{n-1}{2}},$$

and that the functions that achieve it with equality (for n necessarily odd) are called *almost bent (AB)*. There exists a bound on the algebraic degree of AB functions, similar to the bound for bent functions:

Proposition 155 *[257] Let F be any (n, n)-function ($n \geq 3$, odd). If F is AB, then the algebraic degree of F is less than or equal to $(n + 1)/2$.*

---

[1] Using the linear programming bound due to Delsarte.
[2] But the number of bent components of general (n, m)-functions is not.

This is a direct consequence of the fact that the Walsh transform of any function $v \cdot F$ is divisible by $2^{\frac{n+1}{2}}$ and of Theorem 2, page 63. The bound is tight; it is achieved with equality for instance by the inverse of x^3.

Note that the divisibility plays also a role with respect to the algebraic degree of the composition of two vectorial functions: in [204] has been proved (as we recalled in a remark at page 64) that, if the Walsh transform values of a vectorial function $F : \mathbb{F}_2^n \rightarrow \mathbb{F}_2^m$ are divisible by 2^k then, for every vectorial function $G : \mathbb{F}_2^n \rightarrow \mathbb{F}_2^l$, the algebraic degree of *composite function* $G \circ F$ is at most equal to the algebraic degree of G plus $n - k$. This means that using AB functions as S-boxes in block ciphers may not be a good idea (suboptimal functions as the multiplicative inverse function, see Chapter 11, may be better, as often in cryptography).

Remark. There is a big gap between the best possible nonlinearity $2^{n-1} - 2^{\frac{n-1}{2}}$ of (n, n)-functions for n odd, achieved by AB functions (see examples below), and the best-known nonlinearity $2^{n-1} - 2^{n/2}$ of (n, n)-functions for n even, which is achieved (see below) by the Gold APN functions, the Kasami APN functions, and the multiplicative inverse function $x^{2^n - 2}$ (n odd). The gap could seem not so important, but it is, since what matters for the complexity of attacks by linear approximation is not the value of $nl(F)$ but the value of $\frac{2^{n-1} - nl(F)}{2^{n-1}}$. Finding functions with better nonlinearity (and still more relevantly to cryptography, with better nonlinearity and good differential uniformity) or proving that such function does not exist is an open question. □

We recall now the definition of the *differential uniformity* of an (n, m)-function F (see Definition 40, page 135)

$$\delta_F = \max_{\substack{a \in \mathbb{F}_2^n, b \in \mathbb{F}_2^m \\ a \neq 0_n}} |\{x \in \mathbb{F}_2^n; \ D_a F(x) = b\}|$$

is the maximum number of ordered pairs of distinct elements of the graph $\mathcal{G}_F = \{(x, y) \in \mathbb{F}_2^n \times \mathbb{F}_2^m; \ y = F(x)\}$ of F whose sum equals some value $(a, b) \in (\mathbb{F}_2^n \setminus \{0_n\}) \times \mathbb{F}_2^m$. The smaller δ_F, the better the contribution of F to the resistance to differential cryptanalysis. For every (n, m)-function F, we have $\delta_F \geq 2^{n-m}$ (as observed by Nyberg) with equality if and only if F is perfect nonlinear (which can exist if and only if n is even and $m \leq n/2$), and when $m \geq n$, the smallest possible value of δ_F is 2, since δ_F is always even.

We have seen that the differential uniformity is a CCZ invariant (and here also, if $n = m$ and if F is a permutation, then F and its inverse F^{-1} have the same differential uniformity).

11.3 Almost perfect nonlinear and almost bent functions

We have seen in Definition 41, page 137, that differentially 2-uniform (n, n)-functions are called *almost perfect nonlinear* (in brief, *APN*) and contribute to a maximal resistance to differential cryptanalysis.

AB functions contribute to a maximal resistance to both linear and differential cryptanalyses; indeed, according to the proof of the SCV bound and as observed by Chabaud and Vaudenay:

Proposition 156 *For every n odd, AB (n, n)-functions are APN.*

The converse of Proposition 156 is false in general; it is true for quadratic functions in odd dimension [257] and in more general cases that we shall see at page 382. The implication of Proposition 156 can be more precisely changed into a characterization of AB functions:

Proposition 157 *Any vectorial function $F : \mathbb{F}_2^n \to \mathbb{F}_2^n$ is AB if and only if F is APN and plateaued with single amplitude (see Definition 67, page 274).*

This comes directly from Relations (3.22) and (3.25), page 118. *We shall see in Proposition 163, page 382, that if n is odd, the condition "with the same amplitude" is in fact not necessary.*

AB functions exist for every odd $n \geq 3$. APN functions exist for every $n \geq 2$. Function $F(x) = x^3$, $x \in \mathbb{F}_{2^n}$, is an example; others will be given below.

According to Relations (3.24) and (3.25), and to the two lines following them, APN (n, n)-functions F are characterized[3] by the fact that the power sum of degree 4 of the values of their Walsh transform is minimal:

$$\sum_{v \in \mathbb{F}_2^n, u \in \mathbb{F}_2^n} W_F^4(u, v) = 3 \cdot 2^{4n} - 2 \cdot 2^{3n} \tag{11.2}$$

or equivalently, replacing $\sum_{u \in \mathbb{F}_2^n} W_F^4(u, 0_n)$ by its value 2^{4n}:

Theorem 25 *[341] Any (n, n)-function F is APN if and only if*

$$\sum_{v \in \mathbb{F}_2^n \setminus \{0_n\}, u \in \mathbb{F}_2^n} W_F^4(u, v) = 2^{3n+1}(2^n - 1), \tag{11.3}$$

which is the minimal possible value of this sum for all (n, n)-functions.

We have seen at page 111 that this implies that the Walsh support of APN (n, n)-functions has size at least $1 + (2^n - 1) \, 2^{n-1}$.

Using Relation (3.10), page 98, F is then APN if and only if $\sum_{v \in \mathbb{F}_2^n \setminus \{0_n\}} \mathcal{V}(v \cdot F) = 2^{2n+1}(2^n - 1)$. In fact, as observed in [910], F is APN if and only if, for every $a \in \mathbb{F}_2^n \setminus \{0_n\}$, $\sum_{v \in \mathbb{F}_2^n} \mathcal{F}^2(D_a(v \cdot F)) = 2^n |\{(x, y) \in (\mathbb{F}_2^n)^2; \ D_a F(x) = D_a F(y)\}|$ equals 2^{2n+1} (*i.e.*, is minimal), and Theorem 25 can also be referred to [910].

Using Parseval's relation (3.23) and Relation (11.3), any (n, n)-function F is APN if and only if

$$\sum_{\substack{v \in \mathbb{F}_2^n \setminus \{0_n\} \\ u \in \mathbb{F}_2^n}} W_F^2(u, v) \left(W_F^2(u, v) - 2^{n+1} \right) = 0. \tag{11.4}$$

This characterization will have nice consequences in the sequel.

It is easily shown as in the proof of the SCV bound, that for every (n, n)-function, the power sum of degree 3: $\sum_{v \in \mathbb{F}_2^n, u \in \mathbb{F}_2^n} \left(\sum_{x \in \mathbb{F}_2^n} (-1)^{v \cdot F(x) \oplus u \cdot x} \right)^3$ equals

---

[3] This characterization is equivalent to a characterization due to Helleseth [592] in the framework of sequences.

$$2^{2n} \left| \left\{ (x, y) \in \mathbb{F}_2^{2n}; \ F(x) + F(y) + F(x + y) = 0_n \right\} \right|.$$

Applying (with $z = 0_n$) the property that, for every APN function F, the relation $F(x) + F(y) + F(z) + F(x + y + z) = 0_n$ can be achieved only when $x = y$ or $x = z$ or $y = z$, we have then, for every APN function such that $F(0_n) = 0_n$:

$$\sum_{v \in \mathbb{F}_2^n, u \in \mathbb{F}_2^n} W_F^3(u, v) = 3 \cdot 2^{3n} - 2 \cdot 2^{2n}. \tag{11.5}$$

But this property is not characteristic (except for plateaued functions; see below) of APN functions among those (n, n)-functions such that $F(0_n) = 0_n$, since it is only characteristic of the fact that $\sum_{x \in E} F(x) \neq 0_n$ for every two-dimensional vector subspace E of $\mathbb{F}_2^n$ (which is more restrictive than for every two-dimensional flat).

As already seen at page 111, the spectral complexity of an APN function satisfies $|\{(u, v) \in \mathbb{F}_2^n \times \mathbb{F}_2^m; \ W_F(u, v) \neq 0\}| \geq \frac{2^{4n}}{3 \cdot 2^{2n} - 2^{n+1}} \approx \frac{2^{2n}}{3}$.

Note that for every APN function F, we have

$$\left| \{ (a, b) \in (\mathbb{F}_2^n)^2, a \neq b; \ F(a) = F(b) \} \right| \leq 2 \cdot (2^n - 1)$$

since $F(a) = F(b)$ is equivalent to $D_{a+b} F(a) = 0_n$.

Hence, we have $|\{(a, b) \in (\mathbb{F}_2^n)^2; \ F(a) = F(b)\}| = \sum_{z \in \mathbb{F}_2^n} |F^{-1}(z)|^2 \leq 3 \cdot 2^n - 2$ and therefore $|F^{-1}(z)| \leq \lfloor \sqrt{3 \cdot 2^n - 2} \rfloor \leq 2^{n/2+1}$, for every $z \in \mathbb{F}_2^n$.

We have seen at page 137 the different ways of expressing that a function is APN. It is observed in [71, theorem 3] (recalled in [94] and slightly modified in [353]) that, given any linear hyperplane H in $\mathbb{F}_2^n$ and any (n, n)-function F, the necessary property (for F to be APN) that $D_a F$ is 2-to-1 when a is nonzero and belongs to H is also sufficient. Let us give a simple proof: suppose that F is not APN, then there exists an affine plane P in $\mathbb{F}_2^n$, say $P = u + E$, where E is a linear plane, on which F is affine (see page 137). The direction E of P contains at least one nonzero element a of H, because $\dim E + \dim H > n$; then $D_a F$ is not 2-to-1, a contradiction.

We have seen at page 278 that a subclass of APN functions (and superclass of AB quadratic permutations), called crooked functions, has been considered in [57], further studied in [172, 410, 726], and generalized in [80, 727, 729]. There are only two known cases of crooked functions corresponding to the original definition: Gold power AB functions and the class of quadratic AB binomials constructed in [151, 158]. All known crooked functions in the larger sense are quadratic APN, and we have several constructions of them. Among the known 487 quadratic AB functions over $\mathbb{F}_{2^7}$, only Gold functions are CCZ equivalent to permutations (among AB functions, permutations are rare). It can be proved [728] that every power crooked function is a Gold function (see the definition below).

The maximal algebraic degree of APN functions is unknown: for n odd, it is probably $n - 1$ (achieved by $x^{2^n - 2}$), but it is unproven that it is not n, and for n even, it is still more undetermined. All known APN functions (see pages 395 and 400) have algebraic degree at most $n - 1$. It has been proved in [156], thanks to characterizations by means of derivatives and power moments of the Walsh transform, that APN functions of algebraic degree n do not exist for $n \geq 3$ within the classes of power functions modified at input 0 (and the nonexistence for power functions modified in one point was checked by computer for $n \leq 13$) and of plateaued functions modified in one point. See more in [153, 654], and in [167], where the notion of APNness is weakened (differently from [24]).

11.3.1 Other characterizations of AB and APN functions

We have seen above the main characterizations, but others exist:

Characterization by the degrees of univariate polynomials

An (n, n)-function F, given in univariate form, is APN if and only if, for every $a \in \mathbb{F}_{2^n}^*$ and every $b \in \mathbb{F}_{2^n}$, the polynomial $\gcd(x^{2^n} + x, F(x) + F(x+a) + b)$ has degree at most 2 (that is, has degree 0 or 2). Indeed, $x^{2^n} + x$ splits completely over $\mathbb{F}_{2^n}$ and its roots, all simple, are all the elements of $\mathbb{F}_{2^n}$. The polynomial $P(x) = F(x) + F(x + a) + b$ has then a number of zeros in $\mathbb{F}_{2^n}$ equal to the degree of $Q(x) = \gcd(P(x), x^{2^n} + x)$. The degree of $Q(x)$ is 2, that is, the equation $F(x) + F(x + a) = b$ has solutions, if and only if $\gamma_F(a, b) = 1$, where γ_F has been defined at page 229 and will be studied more in detail in Proposition 158 below.

Remark.   If F is a quadratic (n, n)-function, the equation $F(x) + F(x+a) = b$ is a linear equation. It admits then at most two solutions for every nonzero a and every b if and only if the related homogeneous equation $F(x) + F(x+a) + F(0_n) + F(a) = 0_n$ admits at most two solutions for every nonzero a. We shall see that this generalizes to plateaued functions. In the case of a quadratic function, F is APN if and only if the associated bilinear symmetric $(2n, n)$-function $\beta_F(x, y) = F(0_n) + F(x) + F(y) + F(x + y)$ never vanishes when x and y are $\mathbb{F}_2$-linearly independent vectors of $\mathbb{F}_2^n$. For functions of higher degrees, the fact that $\beta_F(x, y)$ (which is no longer bilinear) never vanishes when x and y are linearly independent is only necessary for APNness (sufficient for plateaued functions).   □

Characterization by the ANF

By definition, an (n, n)-function is APN if and only if, for every nonzero $a \in \mathbb{F}_2^n$,

$$\delta_0\Big(F(x) + F(x + a) + F(y) + F(y + a) \Big) \oplus \delta_0\Big(x + y \Big) \oplus \delta_0\Big(x + y + a \Big) \equiv 0$$

(where $\equiv 0$ means "equals the zero function"), where $\delta_0(z) = \prod_{i=1}^n (z_i \oplus 1)$ is the Dirac (or Kronecker) symbol. Indeed, this equation expresses that $F(x) + F(x+a) = F(y) + F(y+a)$ if and only if $x = y$ or $x = y + a$. Equivalently, denoting by H_a any linear hyperplane excluding a, function $D_a F$ is injective on H_a, that is:

$$1_{H_a}(x) \, 1_{H_a}(y) \, \big[\delta_0(F(x) + F(x + a) + F(y) + F(y + a)) \oplus \delta_0(x + y) \big] \equiv 0.$$

These identities, when considered as multivariate polynomial equalities, need to be viewed in $\mathbb{F}_2[x, y]/(x_i^2 + x_i, y_i^2 + y_i; i = 1, \ldots, n)$.

They can also be considered as univariate identities over $\mathbb{F}_{2^n}$, where $\delta_0(z) = 1 + z^{2^n - 1}$, and they need then to be reduced modulo $x^{2^n} + x$ and modulo $y^{2^n} + y$ before being checked as identically zero.

Characterization by the ANFs of affine equivalent functions

A necessary condition dealing with *quadratic terms in the ANF of any APN function* has been observed in [71]. Given any APN function F (quadratic or not), every quadratic term

$x_i x_j$ $(1 \leq i < j \leq n)$ must appear with a nonnull coefficient in the *algebraic normal form* of F. Indeed, we know that the coefficient of any monomial $\prod_{i \in I} x^i$ in the ANF of F equals $a_I = \sum_{x \in \mathbb{F}_2^n; \, supp(x) \subseteq I} F(x)$ (this sum being calculated in $\mathbb{F}_2^n$). Applied for instance to $I = \{n-1, n\}$, this gives $a_I = F(0, \ldots, 0, 0, 0) + F(0, \ldots, 0, 0, 1) + F(0, \ldots, 0, 1, 0) + F(0, \ldots, 0, 1, 1)$, and F being APN, this vector cannot be null. Note that, since the notion of almost perfect nonlinearity is affine invariant (see below), this condition must be satisfied by all of the functions $L' \circ F \circ L$, where L' and L are affine automorphisms of $\mathbb{F}_2^n$. Extended this way (*i.e.*, writing that all degree 2 terms have nonnull coefficients in the ANF of every affinely equivalent function), the condition becomes necessary and sufficient (indeed, for every distinct x, y, z in $\mathbb{F}_2^n$, there exists an affine automorphism L of $\mathbb{F}_2^n$ such that $L(0, \ldots, 0, 0, 0) = x$, $L(0, \ldots, 0, 1, 0) = y$ and $L(0, \ldots, 0, 0, 1) = z$; so the condition tells that $\sum_{x \in P} F(x)$ is nonzero for every two-dimensional affine space P).

Characterizations by the Hamming weight and the bentness of associated Boolean functions

The properties of APNness and ABness can be translated in terms of Boolean functions, as observed in [257] and already encountered at page 229:

Proposition 158 *Let F be any (n, n)-function. For every $a, b \in \mathbb{F}_2^n$, let $\gamma_F(a, b)$ equal 1 if the equation $F(x) + F(x + a) = b$ admits solutions, with $a \neq 0_n$. Otherwise, let $\gamma_F(a, b)$ be null. Then:*

1. *F is APN if and only if γ_F has Hamming weight $2^{2n-1} - 2^{n-1}$, and we have then, for every $u, v \in \mathbb{F}_2^n$:* $W_{\gamma_F}(u, v) = \begin{cases} 2^n \text{ if } (u, v) = (0_n, 0_n) \\ 2^n - W_F^2(u, v) \text{ otherwise.} \end{cases}$
2. *F is AB if and only if γ_F is bent. The dual of γ_F is then the indicator of the Walsh support of F, deprived of $(0_n, 0_n)$.*

Proof

1. If F is APN, then for every $a \neq 0_n$, the mapping $x \mapsto F(x) + F(x + a)$ is 2-to-1 (that is, the size of the preimage of any vector equals 0 or 2). Hence, γ_F has Hamming weight $2^{2n-1} - 2^{n-1}$. The converse is also straightforward.

    We assume now that F is APN. We have $W_{\gamma_F}(0_n, 0_n) = 2^{2n} - 2w_H(\gamma_F) = 2^n$. For $(u, v) \neq (0_n, 0_n)$, we have

$$W_{\gamma_F}(u, v) = -2\widehat{\gamma_F}(u, v) = -\sum_{a \neq 0_n, x \in \mathbb{F}_2^n} (-1)^{u \cdot a \oplus v \cdot (F(x) + F(x+a))}$$

$$= 2^n - \sum_{a, x \in \mathbb{F}_2^n} (-1)^{u \cdot a \oplus v \cdot (F(x) + F(x+a))}$$

$$= 2^n - \sum_{x, y \in \mathbb{F}_2^n} (-1)^{u \cdot (x+y) \oplus v \cdot (F(x) + F(y))} = 2^n - W_F^2(u, v).$$

2. We deduce that F is AB if and only if $W_{\gamma_F}(u, v) = \pm 2^n$ for every $(u, v) \in \mathbb{F}_2^n \times \mathbb{F}_2^n$, *i.e.*, γ_F is bent. Then for every $(u, v) \neq (0_n, 0_n)$, we have $\widetilde{\gamma_F}(u, v) = 0$, that is,

$W_{\gamma_F}(u,v) = 2^n$ if and only if $W_F(u,v) = 0$. Hence, the dual of γ_F is the indicator of the Walsh support of F, deprived of $(0_n, 0_n)$. $\qquad\square$

Denoting by $L = (L_1, L_2)$ an affine automorphism mapping the graph of F to the graph of G, we have $\gamma_F = \gamma_G \circ \mathcal{L}$, where $\mathcal{L}$ is the linear automorphism such that $L = \mathcal{L} + cst$. Indeed, we have $G = F_2 \circ F_1^{-1}$, where $F_1(x) = L_1(x, F(x))$ and $F_2(x) = L_2(x, F(x))$; the value $\gamma_G(a,b)$ equals 1 if and only if $a \neq 0_n$ and there exists (x, y) in $\mathbb{F}_2^n \times \mathbb{F}_2^n$ such that $F_1(x) + F_1(y) = a$ and $F_2(x) + F_2(y) = b$, that is, $\mathcal{L}(x, F(x)) + \mathcal{L}(y, F(y)) = \mathcal{L}(x + y, F(x) + F(y)) = (a, b)$. Hence, $\gamma_G \circ \mathcal{L}(a, b) = 1$ if and only if $\gamma_F(a, b) = 1$. Note that different functions may have the same γ_F; see in [561] a study when the function γ_F is the one associated to Gold functions. The linear equivalence between functions γ_F could potentially lead to an equivalence notion strictly more general than CCZ equivalence; this needs to be studied. It is observed in this same reference that if two functions F, F' are such that $\gamma_F = \gamma_{F'}$, then for any function G taken EA equivalent to F, there exists G', which is EA equivalent to F' and such that $\gamma_G = \gamma_{G'}$. In [109], it is observed that if two functions F, F' have the same DDT, then for any function G taken CCZ equivalent to F, there exists G', which is CCZ equivalent to F' and such that G and G' have the same DDT (and the same is true with EA instead of CCZ); it is also shown that, for any APN permutation F and any pair $\{a, a'\}$ of distinct nonzero elements, the functions $\gamma_F(a, x)$ and $\gamma_F(a', x)$ are different. It is conjectured in this same reference that two permutations F and G having such property and such that $\gamma_F = \gamma_G$ (*i.e.*, with the same DDT) are such that $G(x) = F(x + a) + b$. A guess-and-determine algorithm for reconstructing an S-box from its DDT is given, which is outperformed by an algorithm from [489].

The γ_F functions associated to some AB functions are addressed at page 229 and those associated to some of the known APN functions are determined in [152, 257], (for some other cases, it is an open problem).

Remark. Let F be APN. According to Relation (3.3), page 82, we have $nl(F) = \min_{v \in \mathbb{F}_2^n, v \neq 0_n} nl(v \cdot F) \geq 2^{n-2} - \frac{1}{4} \max_{v \in \mathbb{F}_2^n, v \neq 0_n} \min_{e \in \mathbb{F}_2^n, e \neq 0_n} |\mathcal{F}(v \cdot D_e F)| = 2^{n-2} - \frac{1}{2} \max_{v \neq 0_n} \min_{e \neq 0_n} |\sum_{b \in \mathbb{F}_2^n} \gamma_F(e, b)(-1)^{v \cdot b}|$. We obtain then $nl(F) \geq 2^{n-2} - \frac{1}{2} \max_{v \neq 0_n} \min_{e \neq 0_n} |\widehat{\gamma_{F,e}}(v)| \geq 2^{n-2} - \frac{1}{2} \min_{e \neq 0_n} \max_{v \neq 0_n} |\widehat{\gamma_{F,e}}(v)| = \max_{e \neq 0_n} nl(\gamma_{F,e}) - 2^{n-2}$, where $\gamma_{F,e}(b) = \gamma_F(e, b)$. These lower bounds are not efficient for highly nonlinear functions like AB functions, since they are below 2^{n-2} which is much smaller than $2^{n-1} - 2^{\frac{n-1}{2}}$, but since little is known on the nonlinearity of APN non-AB functions, they are worth mentioning. $\qquad\square$

Characterizations by the numbers of solutions of systems of equations

There exists a characterization of AB functions by van Dam and Fon-Der-Flaass in [410] similar to the characterization of APN functions by the fact that, for every $(a, b) \neq (0_n, 0_n)$,

the system $\begin{cases} x + y &= a \\ F(x) + F(y) &= b \end{cases}$ admits zero or two solutions:

Proposition 159 *Any (n,n)-function F is AB if and only if the system*

$$\begin{cases} x + y + z & = & a \\ F(x) + F(y) + F(z) & = & b \end{cases} \tag{11.6}$$

admits $3 \cdot 2^n - 2$ solutions if $b = F(a)$ and $2^n - 2$ solutions otherwise.

Indeed, F is AB if and only if, for every $v \in \mathbb{F}_2^n \setminus \{0_n\}$ and every $u \in \mathbb{F}_2^n$, we have $\left(\sum_{x \in \mathbb{F}_2^n}(-1)^{v \cdot F(x) \oplus u \cdot x}\right)^3 = 2^{n+1} \sum_{x \in \mathbb{F}_2^n}(-1)^{v \cdot F(x) \oplus u \cdot x}$, and we know that two *pseudo-Boolean* functions are equal to each other if and only if their Fourier–Hadamard transforms are equal. The value at (a, b) of the Fourier–Hadamard transform of the function of (u, v) equal to $\left(\sum_{x \in \mathbb{F}_2^n}(-1)^{v \cdot F(x) \oplus u \cdot x}\right)^3$ if $v \neq 0_n$, and to 0 otherwise equals

$$\sum_{\substack{u \in \mathbb{F}_2^n \\ v \in \mathbb{F}_2^n}} \left(\sum_{x \in \mathbb{F}_2^n}(-1)^{v \cdot F(x) \oplus u \cdot x}\right)^3 (-1)^{a \cdot u \oplus b \cdot v} - 2^{3n} =$$

$$2^{2n} \left| \left\{ (x, y, z) \in \mathbb{F}_2^{3n} ; \begin{cases} x + y + z = a \\ F(x) + F(y) + F(z) = b \end{cases} \right\} \right| - 2^{3n},$$

and the value of the Fourier–Hadamard transform of the function that is equal to $2^{n+1} \sum_{x \in \mathbb{F}_2^n}(-1)^{v \cdot F(x) \oplus u \cdot x}$ if $v \neq 0_n$, and to 0 otherwise equals

$$2^{3n+1} \left| \left\{ x \in \mathbb{F}_2^n ; \begin{cases} x = a \\ F(x) = b \end{cases} \right\} \right| - 2^{2n+1}.$$

This proves the result. Note that $3 \cdot 2^n - 2$ is the number of triples (x, x, a), (x, a, x) and (a, x, x), where x ranges over $\mathbb{F}_2^n$. Hence the condition when $F(a) = b$ means that these particular triples are the only solutions of the system (11.6). This is equivalent to saying that F is APN, and we can replace the first condition of van Dam and Fon-Der-Flaass by "F is APN." Denoting $c = F(a) + b$, we have then

Corollary 27 *Let n be any positive integer and F any APN (n,n)-function. Then F is AB if and only if, for every $c \neq 0_n$ and every a in $\mathbb{F}_2^n$, the equation $F(x) + F(y) + F(a) + F(x + y + a) = c$ has $2^n - 2$ solutions.*

Let us denote by $\mathcal{A}_2$ the set of two-dimensional flats of $\mathbb{F}_2^n$ and by Φ_F the mapping $A \in \mathcal{A}_2 \to \sum_{x \in A} F(x) \in \mathbb{F}_2^n$. Corollary 27 is equivalent to saying that an APN function is AB if and only if, for every $a \in \mathbb{F}_2^n$, the restriction of Φ_F to those flats that contain a is a $\frac{2^{n-1}-1}{3}$-to-1 function (indeed, there are six different ways of ordering the three elements other than a in such flat). Note that the number of two-dimensional flats of $\mathbb{F}_2^n$ containing a equals $\frac{(2^n-1)(2^n-2)}{(2^2-1)(2^2-2)} = (2^n - 1)\frac{2^{n-1}-1}{3}$ and the size of $\mathbb{F}_2^n \setminus \{0_n\}$ equals $2^n - 1$. We have then:

Corollary 28 *Any (n, n)-function F is APN if and only if Φ_F is valued in $\mathbb{F}_2^n \setminus \{0_n\}$, and F is AB if and only if, additionally, for every $a \in \mathbb{F}_2^n$, the restriction of $\Phi_F : \mathcal{A}_2 \to \mathbb{F}_2^n \setminus \{0_n\}$ to those flats that contain a is balanced (that is, has uniform output).*

Note that, for every APN function F and any two distinct vectors a and a', the restriction of Φ_F to those flats that contain a and a' is injective, since for two such distinct flats $A = \{a, a', x, x + a + a'\}$ and $A' = \{a, a', x', x' + a + a'\}$, we have $\Phi_F(A) + \Phi_F(A') = F(x) + F(x + a + a') + F(x') + F(x' + a + a') = \Phi_F(\{x, x + a + a', x', x' + a + a'\}) \neq 0_n$. But this restriction of Φ_F cannot be surjective since the number of flats containing a and a' equals $2^{n-1} - 1$, which is less than $2^n - 1$.

Remark. Other characterizations can be derived with the same method as in Proposition 159's proof. For instance, F is AB if and only if, for every $v \in \mathbb{F}_2^n \setminus \{0_n\}$, $u \in \mathbb{F}_2^n$, we have

$$\left(\sum_{x \in \mathbb{F}_2^n} (-1)^{v \cdot F(x) \oplus u \cdot x} \right)^4 = 2^{n+1} \left(\sum_{x \in \mathbb{F}_2^n} (-1)^{v \cdot F(x) \oplus u \cdot x} \right)^2.$$ By applying again the Fourier–

Hadamard transform and dividing by 2^{2n}, we deduce that F is AB if and only if, for every (a, b) in $(\mathbb{F}_2^n)^2$, we have

$$\left| \left\{ (x, y, z, t) \in \mathbb{F}_2^{4n}; \begin{cases} x + y + z + t = a \\ F(x) + F(y) + F(z) + F(t) = b \end{cases} \right\} \right| - 2^{2n} =$$

$$2^{n+1} \left| \left\{ (x, y) \in \mathbb{F}_2^{2n}; \begin{cases} x + y = a \\ F(x) + F(y) = b \end{cases} \right\} \right| - 2^{n+1}.$$

Hence, F is AB if and only if the system $\begin{cases} x + y + z + t = a \\ F(x) + F(y) + F(z) + F(t) = b \end{cases}$ admits $3 \cdot 2^{2n} - 2^{n+1}$ solutions if $a = b = 0_n$ (this is equivalent to saying that F is APN), $2^{2n} - 2^{n+1}$ solutions if $a = 0_n$ and $b \neq 0_n$ (note that this condition corresponds to adding all the conditions of Corollary 27 with c fixed to b and with a ranging over $\mathbb{F}_2^n$), and $2^{2n} + 2^{n+2} \gamma_F(a, b) - 2^{n+1}$ solutions if $a \neq 0_n$ (indeed, F is APN; note that this gives a new property of AB functions). $\qquad \square$

Characterization of APN functions by the minimum distance of related codes, and of AB functions by the weight distribution of these codes

A relationship has been observed in [641] (not exactly in terms of APNness since this notion was not known by the authors) and developed further in [257]) (see also [642, 1099]) between the properties, for an (n, n)-function, of being APN or AB and properties of related codes. This is the reason that APN functions are generalizations of the cube (n, n)-function x^3, whose related code is the 2-error correcting BCH code (see page 10):

Proposition 160 *[257] Let F be any function from $\mathbb{F}_{2^n}$ to $\mathbb{F}_{2^n}$ such that $F(0) = 0$. Let H be the matrix* $\begin{bmatrix} 1 & \alpha & \alpha^2 & \cdots & \alpha^{2^n-2} \\ F(1) & F(\alpha) & F(\alpha^2) & \cdots & F(\alpha^{2^n-2}) \end{bmatrix}$*, where α is a primitive element* *of* $\mathbb{F}_{2^n}$, *where each symbol stands for the column of its coordinates with respect to a basis of the* $\mathbb{F}_2$-*vector space* $\mathbb{F}_{2^n}$, *and where only linearly independent rows are kept. Let* C_F *be the linear code admitting* H *for parity check matrix. Then* F *is APN if and only if* C_F *has minimum distance 5, and* F *is AB if and only if* $C_F^\perp$ (*admitting* H *for generator matrix*) *has Hamming weights* $0, 2^{n-1} - 2^{\frac{n-1}{2}}, 2^{n-1},$ *and* $2^{n-1} + 2^{\frac{n-1}{2}}$ (*equivalently, has nonzero Hamming weights between* $2^{n-1} - 2^{\frac{n-1}{2}}$ *and* $2^{n-1} + 2^{\frac{n-1}{2}}$).

Proof Since H contains no zero column, C_F has no codeword of Hamming weight 1, and since all columns of H are distinct vectors, C_F has no codeword of Hamming weight 2. Hence[4], C_F has minimum distance at least 3. This minimum distance is also at most 5, since otherwise, a $[2^n - 2, k, d \geq 5]$ code with $k \geq 2^n - 1 - 2n$ would exist by puncturing, and we know from [482] that this is impossible. The fact that C_F has no codeword of weight 3 or 4 is by definition equivalent to the APNness of F, since a vector $(c_0, c_1, \ldots, c_{2^n-2}) \in \mathbb{F}_2^{2^n-1}$ is a codeword if and only if $\begin{cases} \sum_{i=0}^{2^n-2} c_i \alpha^i = 0 \\ \sum_{i=0}^{2^n-2} c_i F(\alpha^i) = 0 \end{cases}$. The nonexistence of codewords of Hamming weight 3 is then equivalent to the fact that $\sum_{x \in E} F(x) \neq 0$ for every two-dimensional vector subspace E of $\mathbb{F}_{2^n}$ and the nonexistence of codewords of Hamming weight 4 is equivalent to the fact that $\sum_{x \in A} F(x) \neq 0$ for every two-dimensional flat A not containing 0. The characterization of ABness through the weights of $C_F^\perp$ comes directly from the characterization of AB functions by their Walsh transform values, respectively by their nonlinearity, and from the fact that the Hamming weight of the Boolean function $v \cdot F(x) \oplus u \cdot x$ equals $2^{n-1} - \frac{1}{2} W_F(u, v)$. $\qquad\square$

Remark.

1. If F is APN and $n > 2$, then C_F has dimension $2^n - 1 - 2n$ exactly (*i.e.*, all the rows in the matrix $H = \begin{bmatrix} 1 & \alpha & \alpha^2 & \cdots & \alpha^{2^n-2} \\ F(1) & F(\alpha) & F(\alpha^2) & \cdots & F(\alpha^{2^n-2}) \end{bmatrix}$ are linearly independent), since according to [482] again, $[2^n - 1, 2^n - 2n, 5]$ codes do not exist. A direct proof of the fact that $C_F^\perp$ has indeed dimension $2n$ is given by Dillon in [447]. This property of $C_F^\perp$ is equivalent to the fact that F has nonzero nonlinearity. Dillon uses Relation (11.2), page 372, and observes that if $v_0 \cdot F$ is affine for some $v_0 \neq 0$, then $\sum_{\substack{u,v \in \mathbb{F}_{2^n} \\ v \notin \{0,v_0\}}} W_F^4(u, v) =$

   $(2^n - 2) \cdot 2^{3n}$, which means that all component functions of F except $v_0 \cdot F$ are bent. This allows building a bent $(n, n - 1)$-function, a contradiction with Nyberg's result (Proposition 104, page 269). A slightly different proof (also using Nyberg's result) was known earlier; see Proposition 161 below.
2. Any subcode of dimension $2^n - 1 - 2n$ of the $[2^n - 1, n, 3]$ Hamming code is a code C_F for some function F.
3. Proposition 160 assumes that $F(0) = 0$. If we want to express the APNness of any (n, n)-function, another matrix can be considered as in [135]: the $(2n + 1) \times (2^n - 1)$

---

[4] We can also say that C_F is a subcode of the *Hamming code* (see page 8).

matrix $\begin{bmatrix} 1 & 1 & 1 & 1 & \cdots & 1 \\ 0 & 1 & \alpha & \alpha^2 & \cdots & \alpha^{2^n-2} \\ F(0) & F(1) & F(\alpha) & F(\alpha^2) & \cdots & F(\alpha^{2^n-2}) \end{bmatrix}$. Then F is APN if and only

if the code $\widetilde{C}_F$ admitting this parity check matrix has parameters $[2^n, 2^n - 1 - 2n, 6]$. To prove this, note first that this code does not change if we add a constant to F (contrary to C_F). Hence, by adding the constant $F(0)$, we can assume that $F(0) = 0$. Then the code $\widetilde{C}_F$ is the *extended code* of C_F (obtained by adding to each codeword of C_F a first coordinate equal to the sum modulo 2 of its coordinates). Since $F(0) = 0$, we can apply Proposition 160, and it is clear that C_F is a $[2^n - 1, 2^n - 1 - 2n, 5]$ code if and only if $\widetilde{C}_F$ is a $[2^n, 2^n - 1 - 2n, 6]$ code, since we know from [482] that C_F cannot have minimum distance larger than 5.

Note that Proposition 156, page 371, means that if $\widetilde{C}_F^{\perp}$ has the highest possible minimum distance $2^{n-1} - 2^{\frac{n-1}{2}}$, then $\widetilde{C}_F$ has minimum distance at least 6.

4. As observed in [135], given two (n, n)-functions F and G such that $F(0) = G(0) = 0$, there exists a linear automorphism[5] that maps $\mathcal{G}_F$ to $\mathcal{G}_G$ if and only if the codes C_F and C_G are equivalent (that is, are equal up to some permutation of the coordinates of their codewords). Indeed, the graph $\mathcal{G}_F$ of F equals the (unordered) set of columns in the parity check matrix of the code C_F, plus an additional point equal to the all-zero vector. Hence, the existence of a linear automorphism that maps $\mathcal{G}_F$ onto $\mathcal{G}_G$ is equivalent to the fact that the parity check matrices[6] of the codes C_F and C_G are equal up to multiplication (on the left) by an invertible matrix and to permutation of the columns. Since two codes with given parity check matrices are equal if and only if these matrices are equal up to multiplication on the left by an invertible matrix, this completes the proof.

Similarly, two functions F and G taking any values at 0 are *CCZ equivalent* if and only if the codes $\widetilde{C}_F$ and $\widetilde{C}_G$ are equivalent.

5. For every (n, n)-function F such that $F(0) = 0$, the two first power moments of W_F are known: we have $\sum_{u,v \in \mathbb{F}_{2^n}} W_F(u, v) = 2^n \sum_{v \in \mathbb{F}_{2^n}} (-1)^{v \cdot F(0)} = 2^{2n}$, and $\sum_{u,v \in \mathbb{F}_{2^n}} W_F^2(u, v) = 2^{3n}$ (the former equality is given by the *inverse Walsh transform formula* (2.43), page 59, and the latter is given by the Parseval relation (2.48), page 61). If F is APN, then we have also the two next power moments: Relations (11.2) and (11.5), page 373. In the case F is AB, this makes possible to determine the value distribution of W_F and therefore the weight distribution of $C_F^{\perp}$ uniquely.[7] Indeed, there are only three nonzero weights, which are known, and we need then only to determine the three numbers of codewords of each weight; the four equations obtained, which are linear in these numbers, make this possible. There are one codeword of null Hamming weight, $(2^n - 1)(2^{n-2} + 2^{\frac{n-3}{2}})$ codewords of Hamming weight $2^{n-1} - 2^{\frac{n-1}{2}}$, $(2^n - 1)(2^{n-2} - 2^{\frac{n-3}{2}})$ codewords of Hamming weight $2^{n-1} + 2^{\frac{n-1}{2}}$, and $(2^n - 1)(2^{n-1} + 1)$ codewords of Hamming weight 2^{n-1}. See more details in [257] (the calculations are made there equivalently with the

---

[5] Note that this is a subcase of CCZ equivalence – in fact, a strict subcase as shown in [135].
[6] This is true also for the generator matrices of the codes.
[7] The determination of such weight distribution is not known so often (when the code does not contain the all-one vector) since determining the Walsh value distribution of the function is much more difficult in general than determining the absolute value distribution, which for an AB function is easily deduced from the single Parseval's relation.

Pless power moment equalities of [958]). We shall see that function x^3 over $\mathbb{F}_{2^n}$ is an AB function (for n odd). The code $C_F^{\perp}$ corresponding to this function is an important code: the dual of the 2-error-correcting BCH code of length $2^n - 1$. $\square$

We have seen that if F is APN on $\mathbb{F}_{2^n}$, $n > 2$, and $F(0) = 0$, the code $C_F^{\perp}$ has dimension $2n$. Equivalently, the code whose generator matrix equals $\left[F(1)\ F(\alpha)\ F(\alpha^2)\ \cdots\ F(\alpha^{2^n-2}) \right]$, and which can therefore be seen as the code $\{tr_n(vF(x)); v \in \mathbb{F}_{2^n}\}$, has dimension n and intersects the *simplex code* $\{tr_n(ux); u \in \mathbb{F}_{2^n}\}$ of generator matrix $\left[1\ \alpha\ \alpha^2\ \cdots\ \alpha^{2^n-2} \right]$ only in the null vector. This can be proved directly:

Proposition 161 *[237] Let F be APN over $\mathbb{F}_2^n$ with $n > 2$. Then $nl(F)$ cannot be null and, assuming that $F(0_n) = 0_n$, the code $C_F^{\perp}$ has dimension $2n$.*

Proof Suppose there exists $v \neq 0_n$ such that $v \cdot F$ is affine. Without loss of generality (by composing F with an appropriate linear automorphism and adding an affine function to F), we can assume that $v = (0, \ldots, 0, 1)$ and that $v \cdot F$ is null. Then, every derivative of F is 2-to-1 and has null last coordinate. Hence, for every $a \neq 0_n$ and every b, the equation $D_a F(x) = b$ has no solution if $b_n = 1$ and it has two solutions if $b_n = 0$. The $(n, n-1)$ function obtained by erasing the last coordinate of $F(x)$ has therefore balanced derivatives; hence it is a bent $(n, n-1)$-function, a contradiction with Nyberg's result (Proposition 104, page 269), since $n - 1 > \frac{n}{2}$. The last sentence in the statement is straight forward. $\square$

For $n = 2$, the nonlinearity can be null; example: function $(x_1, x_2) \rightarrow (x_1 x_2, 0)$.

Remark. As observed at page 136, the nonlinearity and the differential uniformity of general functions do not seem correlated. However, Proposition 161 shows that, for APN functions, a null nonlinearity is impossible. Moreover, all known APN functions have a rather good nonlinearity (probably at least $2^{n-1} - 2^{\frac{3n}{5}-1} - 2^{\frac{2n}{5}-1}$, but this has to be confirmed since the nonlinearity of the Dobbertin function is unknown except for small values of n). The question of knowing whether it is because we know too few APN functions or because there is some correlation in the case of such optimal functions seems wide open. $\square$

J. Dillon (private communication) observed that the property of Proposition 161 implies that, for every nonzero $c \in \mathbb{F}_{2^n}$, the equation $F(x) + F(y) + F(z) + F(x + y + z) = c$ must have a solution (that is, the function Φ_F introduced after Corollary 27 is onto $\mathbb{F}_2^n \setminus \{0_n\}$; we have seen this for AB functions since we saw that this function is balanced, but it is new for APN functions). Indeed, otherwise, for every Boolean function $g(x)$, the function $F(x) + c\, g(x)$ would be APN. But this is contradictory with Proposition 161 if we take $g(x) = v_0 \cdot F(x)$ (that is, $g(x) = tr_n(v_0 F(x))$ if we have identified $\mathbb{F}_2^n$ with the field $\mathbb{F}_{2^n}$) with $v_0 \notin c^{\perp}$, since we have then $v_0 \cdot [F(x) + c\, g(x)] = v_0 \cdot F(x) \oplus g(x)\, (v_0 \cdot c) = 0$.

Characterization of AB functions by uniformly packed codes

Proposition 162 *[257] Let F be any (n, n)-function, n odd. Then F is AB if and only if C_F is a uniformly packed code (see Definition 2, page 10) of length $N = 2^n - 1$ with minimum distance 5 and covering radius 3.*

It is deduced in [257, Corollary 3] that an APN function is AB if and only if $\{W_F(u, v); u, v \in \mathbb{F}_2^n, v \neq 0_n\}$ has three values.

Characterization of AB functions, among APN functions, by the divisibility of their Walsh transform values (n odd); consequence for plateaued functions

We have seen that all AB functions are APN. The converse is false, in general. But if n is odd and if F is APN, then, as shown in [186, 195], there exists a nice necessary and sufficient condition, for F being AB: the weights of $C_F^\perp$ are all divisible by $2^{\frac{n-1}{2}}$ (see also [196], where the divisibilities for several types of such codes are calculated, where tables of exact divisibilities are computed, and where proofs are given that a great deal of power functions are not AB). In other words and slightly more generally:

Proposition 163 *Let F be an APN (n, n)-function. Then F is AB if and only if all the values $W_F(u, v)$ of the Walsh spectrum of F are divisible by $2^{\lceil \frac{n+1}{2} \rceil}$.*

Proof The condition is clearly necessary (with n necessarily odd). Conversely, assume that F is APN and that all the values $W_F(u, v) = \sum_{x \in \mathbb{F}_2^n} (-1)^{v \cdot F(x) \oplus u \cdot x}$ are divisible by $2^{\lceil \frac{n+1}{2} \rceil}$. Writing $W_F^2(u, v) = 2^{n+1} \lambda_{u,v}$, where all $\lambda_{u,v}$'s are integers, Relation (11.4), page 372, implies then

$$\sum_{v \in \mathbb{F}_2^{n*}, u \in \mathbb{F}_2^n} (\lambda_{u,v}^2 - \lambda_{u,v}) = 0, \tag{11.7}$$

and since all the integers $\lambda_{u,v}^2 - \lambda_{u,v}$ are nonnegative ($\lambda_{u,v}$ being an integer), we deduce that $\lambda_{u,v}^2 = \lambda_{u,v}$ for every $v \in \mathbb{F}_2^{n*}, u \in \mathbb{F}_2^n$, i.e. $\lambda_{u,v} \in \{0, 1\}$. $\square$

Proposition 163 shows that if n is odd and an APN (n, n)-function F is plateaued, or more generally if $F = F_1 \circ F_2^{-1}$, where F_2 is a permutation and the linear combinations of the coordinate functions of F_1 and F_2 are plateaued, then F is AB, since $\sum_{x \in \mathbb{F}_2^n} (-1)^{v \cdot F(x) \oplus u \cdot x} = \sum_{x \in \mathbb{F}_2^n} (-1)^{v \cdot F_1(x) \oplus u \cdot F_2(x)}$ is divisible by $2^{\frac{n+1}{2}}$.

This makes it possible to deduce easily the AB property of Gold and Kasami functions (see their definitions below) from their APN property, since the Gold AB functions are quadratic and the Kasami AB functions are equal, when n is odd, to $F_1 \circ F_2^{-1}$ where $F_1(x) = x^{2^{3i}+1}$ and $F_2(x) = x^{2^i+1}$ are quadratic.[8]

Proposition 163 also allows us to characterize AB functions among APN power functions, thanks to Proposition 21, page 73. Sufficient conditions for power functions not to be AB are given in [194].

Complementary observation on APN functions for n even

If F is APN, then there must exist $v \in \mathbb{F}_2^n \setminus \{0_n\}, u \in \mathbb{F}_2^n$ such that $W_F(u, v)$ is not divisible by $2^{\frac{n}{2}+1}$. Indeed, suppose that all the Walsh values of F have such divisibility,

---

[8] The component functions of Kasami APN functions are plateaued for every n even too. This has been proved in [448, theorem 11] when n is not divisible by 6 and for every n even in [1142].

then writing again $W_F^2(u, v) = 2^{n+1}\lambda_{u,v}$, we have Relation (11.7), in which each nonzero $\lambda_{u,v}$ being now even satisfies $\lambda_{u,v}^2 - \lambda_{u,v} > 0$. All the values $\lambda_{u,v}^2 - \lambda_{u,v}$ are then nonnegative integers and (for each $v \neq 0_n$) at least one value is strictly positive, a contradiction.

If all the Walsh values of F are divisible by $2^{\frac{n}{2}}$ (e.g., if F is plateaued), then we deduce that there must exist $v \in \mathbb{F}_2^n \setminus \{0_n\}, u \in \mathbb{F}_2^n$ such that $W_F(u, v) \equiv 2^{\frac{n}{2}} \pmod{2^{\frac{n}{2}+1}}$. It is also shown in [24] that for every APN, or more generally *weakly APN*, permutation F (whose derivatives at nonzero directions take strictly more than 2^{n-2} distinct values), at most $\frac{2^n-1}{3}$ component functions of F can be partially-bent (and, in particular, F cannot then be strongly plateaued); indeed, each partially-bent component function of a permutation has a *linear kernel* of dimension at least 2 (bent functions being not balanced), and has then at least three constant derivatives at nonzero directions, and if there was $t > \frac{2^n-1}{3}$ partially-bent component functions of F, since $3t > |\mathbb{F}_2^n \setminus \{0_n\}|$, there would exist $a \neq 0_n$ and two distinct nonzero elements v_1, v_2 of $\mathbb{F}_2^n$ such that $v_1 \cdot D_a F$ and $v_2 \cdot D_a F$ are constant, a contradiction since $\{D_a F(x); x \in \mathbb{F}_2^n\}$ would then have at most 2^{n-2} elements.

More can be said in the case of APN plateaued functions; see page 391.

APN functions and finite geometry

We refer the reader to [430] and the references therein for the relations between APN functions and dimensional dual hyperovals or bilinear dimensional dual hyperovals. Other relations with finite geometry are shown in [895].

11.3.2 The particular case of power functions

Identifying $\mathbb{F}_2^n$ with the field $\mathbb{F}_{2^n}$ (in which we can take $x \cdot y = tr_n(xy)$ for inner product) allows considering those (n, n)-functions of the form $F(x) = x^d, d \in \mathbb{Z}/(2^n - 1)\mathbb{Z}$, called power (n, n)-functions (and sometimes, *monomial vectorial functions*). If such F is APN, then d is called an *APN exponent* over $\mathbb{F}_{2^n}$.

Note that if d is an APN exponent over $\mathbb{F}_{2^n}$ and r divides n, then $d \pmod{(2^r - 1)}$ is an APN exponent over $\mathbb{F}_{2^r}$ (in particular, it cannot be a power of 2 if $r \geq 2$); more generally, if r divides n and $F(x)$ is an APN polynomial function over $\mathbb{F}_{2^n}$ with coefficients in $\mathbb{F}_{2^r}$, then F is APN over $\mathbb{F}_{2^r}$).

Relation between AB power functions and sequences

There is a close relationship between the nonlinearity of power functions and *sequences* used for radars and for spread-spectrum communications. Recall that a binary sequence that can be generated by an LFSR, or equivalently that satisfies a linear recurrence relation $s_i = a_1 s_{i-1} \oplus \cdots \oplus a_n s_{i-n}$, is called an *m-sequence* or a *maximum length sequence* if its period equals $2^n - 1$, which is a maximum. Such a sequence has the form $tr_n(\lambda\alpha^i)$, where $\lambda \in \mathbb{F}_{2^n}$ and α is some primitive element of $\mathbb{F}_{2^n}$. Consequently, its autocorrelation values $\sum_{i=0}^{2^n-2}(-1)^{s_i \oplus s_{i+t}}$ ($1 \leq t \leq 2^n - 2$) are all equal to -1, that is, are optimal. This is useful for radars and for code division multiple access (CDMA) in telecommunications, since it allows sending a signal easily distinguished from any time-shifted version of itself. Finding a highly nonlinear power function (in particular, an AB power function)

x^d on the field $\mathbb{F}_{2^n}$ makes it possible to have a d-decimation[9] $s_i' = tr_n(\lambda\alpha^{di})$ of the sequence, whose cross-correlation values $\sum_{i=0}^{2^n-2}(-1)^{s_i \oplus s_{i+t}'} = \sum_{x\in\mathbb{F}_{2^n}^*}(-1)^{tr_n(\lambda(x^d+\alpha^{-t}x))}$ ($0 \leq t \leq 2^n - 2$) with the sequence s_i have small (minimum) overall magnitude[10] [551, 552, 598]. In the case of an AB function, we speak of a *preferred cross-correlation*; see, e.g., [174, 598]. The exponents of AB power functions have then been investigated as the decimations with preferred cross-correlation by the researchers on sequences (those whose names have been given to special classes of sequences and will be used for naming the corresponding classes of AB functions, and also S. Golomb [550] who has been one of the main initiators of the theory of sequences; see [555]). They proved the preferred cross-correlation in some cases and made conjectures for others. Hence, when the notion of AB function was invented by Chabaud and Vaudenay, some work had been already done for searching such functions. A survey on cross-correlation distributions is given in [593]. See also [1127].

Simplification of the checking of APNness

When F is a power function, it is enough to check the APN property for $a = 1 \in \mathbb{F}_{2^n}$, since for $a \neq 0$, changing x into ax in the equation $F(x)+F(x+a) = b$ gives $F(x)+F(x+1) = \frac{b}{F(a)}$. Hence, according to what we saw on the characterization by the ANF at page 374, $F(x) = x^d$ is APN if and only if

$$\delta_0\left(x^d + (x + 1)^d + y^d + (y + 1)^d\right) + \delta_0\left(x + y\right) + \delta_0\left(x + y + 1\right) \left[\text{mod } x^{2^n} + x, y^{2^n} + y\right]$$

equals the zero function, where $\delta_0(z) = 1 + z^{2^n-1}$, or equivalently

$$1_H(x)1_H(y)\left(\left(x^d + (x + 1)^d + y^d + (y + 1)^d\right)^{2^n-1} + \left(x + y\right)^{2^n-1}\right),$$

similarly reduced, equals the zero function, where H is a linear hyperplane excluding 1. Moreover, checking the AB property $\sum_{x\in\mathbb{F}_{2^n}}(-1)^{tr_n(vF(x)+ux)} \in \{0, \pm2^{\frac{n+1}{2}}\}$, for every $u, v \in \mathbb{F}_{2^n}$, $v \neq 0$, is enough for $u = 0$ and $u = 1$ (and every $v \neq 0$), since changing x into $\frac{x}{u}$ (if $u \neq 0$) in this sum gives $\sum_{x\in\mathbb{F}_{2^n}}(-1)^{tr_n(v'F(x)+x)}$, for some $v' \neq 0$. If F is a permutation, then checking the AB property is also enough for $v = 1$ and every u, since changing x into $\frac{x}{F^{-1}(v)}$ in this sum gives $\sum_{x\in\mathbb{F}_{2^n}}(-1)^{tr_n\left(F(x)+\frac{u}{F^{-1}(v)}x\right)}$. And in the characterization of Proposition 159, page 376, if $a \neq 0$, then it can be reduced similarly to $a = 1$, and if $a = 0$, we can assume that $z \neq 0$ and replace x by xz and y by yz, we get $(x^d + y^d + 1)z^d = b$, which has the same number of solutions for every nonzero b since F is a permutation; the characterization of ABness reduces then to: the equation $x^d + y^d + (x + y + 1)^d = b$ has $2^n - 2$ solutions for every $b \neq 1$. Then a power permutation F in odd dimension is AB if and only if the function $(x, y) \rightarrow x^d + y^d + (x + y + 1)^d$ is $(2^n - 2) - to - 1$ from $\{(x, y) \in (\mathbb{F}_{2^n} \setminus \{1\})^2; x \neq y\}$ to $\mathbb{F}_{2^n} \setminus \{1\}$ (the fact that this never takes value 1 is equivalent to F APN).

---

[9] Another m-sequence if d is coprime with $2^n - 1$.
[10] This makes possible, in code division multiple access, to give different signals to different users.

Additional information on bijectivity

It was proved in [257] that, when n is even, no APN function exists in a class of permutations including power permutations, which we describe now. Let $k = \frac{2^n - 1}{3}$ (which is an integer, since n is even) and let α be a primitive element of the field $\mathbb{F}_{2^n}$. Then $\beta = \alpha^k$ is a primitive element of $\mathbb{F}_4$. Hence, $\beta^2 + \beta + 1 = 0$. For every j, the element $(\beta + 1)^j + \beta^j = \beta^{2j} + \beta^j$ equals 1 if j is coprime with 3 (since β^j is then also a primitive element of $\mathbb{F}_4$), and is null otherwise. Let $F(x) = \sum_{j=0}^{2^n-1} \delta_j x^j$, ($\delta_j \in \mathbb{F}_{2^n}$) be an (n, n)-function. According to the observations above, β and $\beta + 1$ are the solutions of the equation $F(x) + F(x + 1) = \sum_{\gcd(j,3)=1} \delta_j$. Also, the equation $F(x) + F(x+1) = \sum_{j=1}^{2^n-1} \delta_j$ admits 0 and 1 for solutions. Thus:

Proposition 164 *Let n be even and let $F(x) = \sum_{j=0}^{2^n-1} \delta_j x^j$ be any APN (n, n)-function, then $\sum_{j=1}^{\frac{2^n-1}{3}} \delta_{3j} \neq 0$. If F is a power function, $F(x) = x^d$, then 3 divides d and F cannot be a permutation.*

H. Dobbertin gives in [469] a result valid only for power functions but slightly more precise, and he completes it in the case that n is odd:

Proposition 165 *If a power function $F(x) = x^d$ over $\mathbb{F}_{2^n}$ is APN, then for every $x \in \mathbb{F}_{2^n}$, we have $x^d = 1$ if and only if $x^3 = 1$, that is, $F^{-1}(1) = \mathbb{F}_4 \cap \mathbb{F}_{2^n}^*$. If n is odd, then $\gcd(d, 2^n - 1)$ equals 1 and, if n is even, then $\gcd(d, 2^n - 1)$ equals 3. Consequently, APN power functions are permutations if n is odd, and are three-to-one over $\mathbb{F}_{2^n}^*$ if n is even.*

Proof Let $x \neq 1$ be such that $x^d = 1$. There is a (unique) y in $\mathbb{F}_{2^n}$, $y \neq 0, 1$, such that $x = (y+1)/y$. The equality $x^d = 1$ implies $(y+1)^d + y^d = 0 = (y^2+1)^d + (y^2)^d$. By the APN property and since $y^2 \neq y$ because $x \neq 1$, we conclude $y^2 + y + 1 = 0$. Thus, y, and therefore x, are in $\mathbb{F}_4$ and $x^3 = 1$. Conversely, if $x \in \mathbb{F}_{2^n} \setminus \mathbb{F}_2$ is such that $x^3 = 1$, then 3 divides $2^n - 1$ and n must be even. Moreover, d must also be divisible by 3 (indeed, otherwise, the restriction of x^d to $\mathbb{F}_4$ would coincide with the function $x^{\gcd(d,3)} = x$ and would be therefore linear, a contradiction). Hence, we have $x^d = 1$. The rest is straightforward. $\square$

Note that for n even, $3 | d$ can be proved directly: if $3 \nmid d$, then x^d being APN on $\mathbb{F}_{2^n}$, $x^{d \pmod 3}$ is APN on $\mathbb{F}_4$, a contradiction since $d \pmod 3 \in \{1, 2\}$.

In [62], it is similarly observed that, if all the coefficients in the univariate representation of an APN function $F(x)$ belong to a subfield $\mathbb{F}_{2^r}$ of $\mathbb{F}_{2^n}$, then the equality $D_a F(x) = b$ for some $a, b \in \mathbb{F}_{2^r}$ and $x \in \mathbb{F}_{2^n} \setminus \mathbb{F}_{2^r}$ implies $x^{2^r} = x + a$.

In [406], it is shown that, for any n, if an (n, n)-function F fixes 0_n and is such that, for every nonzero $u \in \mathbb{F}_2^n$, the preimage $F^{-1}(u)$ either is empty or equals a set of three distinct nonzero elements of the form $\{a, b, a + b\}$ (i.e., is a two-dimensional $\mathbb{F}_2$-linear space less 0_n),[11] then F is APN if and only if

$$\begin{cases} F(x) \neq F(y) \\ F(z) \notin \{F(x), F(y), F(x + y)\} \end{cases} \implies F(x) + F(y) + F(z) + F(x + y + z) \neq 0_n.$$

---

[11] This needs that n be even, and it happens then with any APN power function, and also with other functions like $x^3 + tr_n(x^9)$.

Indeed, this condition is necessary since $\begin{cases} F(x) \neq F(y) \\ F(z) \notin \{F(x), F(y), F(x+y)\} \end{cases}$ implies that $\{x, y, z, x+y+z\}$ is a two-dimensional flat and the restriction of an APN function to any two-dimensional flat must not sum up to 0_n; this condition is also sufficient since, if four distinct elements of $\mathbb{F}_2^n$ have null sum as well as their images, then the condition being assumed satisfied, either these four elements come by pairs with the same image in each pair, and this is impossible since if for instance, $F(x) = F(y)$ and $F(z) = F(x+y+z)$, then because of the assumption on the preimages, we have $F(z) = F(x+y) = F(x) = F(y) = F(x+y+z)$, which is impossible since $F^{-1}(F(z))$ has only three elements, or they are such that $F(z) = F(x+y)$ and the same happens since we have then $F(z) = F(x+y) = F(x+y+z) = F(x) = F(y)$. Note that a sufficient condition for F to be APN is that $F(\mathbb{F}_2^n)$ is a *Sidon set* (see Definition 80, page 388), but it is shown in [406] that such sets of size $\frac{2^n-1}{3} + 1$ do not exist for $n \geq 6$ even.

Nonlinearity

An upper bound valid not only for APN functions but restricted to power functions is proved in [189]:

Proposition 166 *For every n even, if a power function $F(x) = x^d$ on $\mathbb{F}_{2^n}$ is not a permutation (i.e., if $\gcd(d, 2^n - 1) > 1$), then the nonlinearity of F is bounded above by $2^{n-1} - 2^{\frac{n}{2}}$.*

Proof Let $d_0 = \gcd(d, 2^n - 1)$; for every $v \in \mathbb{F}_{2^n}$, the sum $\sum_{x \in \mathbb{F}_{2^n}} (-1)^{tr_n(vx^d)}$ equals $\sum_{x \in \mathbb{F}_{2^n}} (-1)^{tr_n(vx^{d_0})}$; hence, $\sum_{v \in \mathbb{F}_{2^n}} \left(\sum_{x \in \mathbb{F}_{2^n}} (-1)^{tr_n(vx^d)} \right)^2$ is equal to $2^n |\{(x, y), x, y \in \mathbb{F}_{2^n}, x^{d_0} = y^{d_0}\}|$. The number of elements in the image of $\mathbb{F}_{2^n}^*$ by the mapping $x \to x^{d_0}$ is $(2^n - 1)/d_0$ and every element of this image has d_0 preimages. Hence, $\sum_{v \in \mathbb{F}_{2^n}^*} \left(\sum_{x \in \mathbb{F}_{2^n}} (-1)^{tr_n(vx^d)} \right)^2$ equals $2^n[(2^n - 1)d_0 + 1] - 2^{2n} = 2^n(2^n - 1)(d_0 - 1)$ and $\max_{v \in \mathbb{F}_{2^n}^*} \left(\sum_{x \in \mathbb{F}_{2^n}} (-1)^{tr_n(vx^d)} \right)^2 \geq 2^n(d_0 - 1)$. The proof is completed by using that the values of $\sum_{x \in \mathbb{F}_{2^n}} (-1)^{tr_n(vx^3)}$ are known. $\square$

Reference [189] also studies the case of equality. The possible values of the sum $\sum_{x \in \mathbb{F}_{2^n}} (-1)^{tr_n(vx^d)}$ are determined in [62] for APN power functions for n even.

It happens that all known APN power functions have rather good nonlinearity. To clarify the situation for general power APN functions, we need to show lower bounds on their nonlinearity and/or to find such functions with lower nonlinearity. The next bound is shown in [250] (the proof below is from this reference):

Proposition 167 *Let F be any APN power function. Then, if n is odd, we have $nl(F) \geq 2^{n-1} - 2^{\frac{3n-3}{4}}$ and if n is even, we have $nl(F) \geq 2^{n-1} - 2^{\frac{3n-2}{4}}$.*

Proof If n is odd then, for every $v \neq 0$, the sum $\sum_{u \in \mathbb{F}_{2^n}} W_F^4(u, v)$ is independent[12] of the choice of v and, according to the characterization of APN functions by the fourth moment of Walsh transform, equals then 2^{3n+1}. Hence, we have $W_F^4(u, v) \leq 2^{3n+1}$ for every u and the result follows from (3.21), page 117. If n is even, then, since according to Proposition 165, the value of $\sum_{u \in \mathbb{F}_{2^n}} W_F^4(u, v)$ does not change when v is multiplied by a nonzero cube, it takes, when v ranges over $\mathbb{F}_{2^n}^*$, $\frac{2^n - 1}{3}$ times the value $\sum_{u \in \mathbb{F}_{2^n}} W_F^4(u, 1)$, $\frac{2^n - 1}{3}$ times the value $\sum_{u \in \mathbb{F}_{2^n}} W_F^4(u, \alpha)$, and $\frac{2^n - 1}{3}$ times the value $\sum_{u \in \mathbb{F}_{2^n}} W_F^4(u, \alpha^2)$ (α primitive in $\mathbb{F}_{2^n}$). Hence we have $\sum_{u \in \mathbb{F}_{2^n}} W_F^4(u, 1) + \sum_{u \in \mathbb{F}_{2^n}} W_F^4(u, \alpha) + \sum_{u \in \mathbb{F}_{2^n}} W_F^4(u, \alpha^2) = 3 \cdot 2^{3n+1}$. We have, by the Cauchy–Schwarz inequality, that $\sum_{u \in \mathbb{F}_2^n} W_F^4(u, v) \geq \frac{\left(\sum_{u \in \mathbb{F}_2^n} W_F^2(u, v) \right)^2}{2^n} = 2^{3n}$ for $v \neq 0$. Hence, we have by complementation that each of the sums $\sum_{u \in \mathbb{F}_{2^n}} W_F^4(u, 1), \sum_{u \in \mathbb{F}_{2^n}} W_F^4(u, \alpha)$ and $\sum_{u \in \mathbb{F}_{2^n}} W_F^4(u, \alpha^2)$ is bounded above by $3 \cdot 2^{3n+1} - 2 \cdot 2^{3n} = 2^{3n+2}$. We have then $W_F^4(u, v) \leq 2^{3n+2}$ for every u, v such that $v \neq 0$ and Relation (3.21) completes the proof. $\square$

The bound of Proposition 167 has been extended in [356] to differential uniform power functions but only for permutations. For explaining the good nonlinearity of known APN functions, there remains to tackle that of quadratic functions. Less is known for them; see observations in [250].

Relation with cyclic codes

If F is a power function, then the linear codes C_F and $C_F^\perp$ viewed in Proposition 160, page 378, are *cyclic codes* (see [257], where several results are given in this framework). Indeed, $(c_0, \ldots, c_{2^n-2})$ belongs to C_F if and only if $c_0 + c_1 \alpha + \cdots + c_{2^n-2} \alpha^{2^n-2} = 0$ and $c_0 + c_1 \alpha^d + \cdots + c_{2^n-2} \alpha^{(2^n-2)d} = 0$; this implies (by multiplying these equations by α and α^d, respectively) $c_{2^n-2} + c_0 \alpha + \cdots + c_{2^n-3} \alpha^{2^n-2} = 0$ and $c_{2^n-2} + c_0 \alpha^d + \cdots + c_{2^n-3} \alpha^{(2^n-2)d} = 0$. The *BCH bound* (see page 13) shows in the case $F(x) = x^3$ that C_F has minimum distance (at least) 5 (*i.e.*, that F is APN) and (in an original but rather complex way) that the function $x^{2^{\frac{n-1}{2}}+1}$, n odd, is AB: by definition, the *defining set* I of C_F (see page 12) equals the union of the cyclotomic classes of 1 and $2^{\frac{n-1}{2}} + 1$, that is, $I = \{1, 2, \ldots, 2^{n-1}\} \cup \{2^{\frac{n-1}{2}} + 1, 2^{\frac{n+1}{2}} + 2, \ldots, 2^{n-1} + 2^{\frac{n-1}{2}}, 2^{\frac{n+1}{2}} + 1, 2^{\frac{n+3}{2}} + 2, \ldots, 2^{n-1} + 2^{\frac{n-3}{2}}\}$. Since there is no element equal to $2^{n-1} + 2^{\frac{n-1}{2}} + 1, \ldots, 2^n - 1$ in I, the defining set $\mathbb{Z}/(2^n - 1)\mathbb{Z} \setminus \{-i; i \notin I\}$ of $C_F^\perp$ contains a string of length $2^{n-1} - 2^{\frac{n-1}{2}} - 1$. Hence the nonzero codewords of this code have Hamming weights larger than or equal to $2^{n-1} - 2^{\frac{n-1}{2}}$. This is not sufficient for concluding that the function is AB, but we can apply the previous reasoning to the *cyclic code* $C_F^\perp \cup (1_{2^n-1} + C_F^\perp)$: the defining set of the dual of this code being equal to that of C_F, plus 0, the defining set of the code equals that of $C_F^\perp$ less 0, which gives a string of length $2^{n-1} - 2^{\frac{n-1}{2}} - 2$ instead of $2^{n-1} - 2^{\frac{n-1}{2}} - 1$. Hence the complements of the codewords of

---

[12] Such a property will be called CAPNness at page 390 and implies the former inequality.

$C_F^\perp$ have Hamming weights at least $2^{n-1} - 2^{\frac{n-1}{2}} - 1$ and the codewords of $C_{\bar{F}}^\perp$ have then Hamming weights at most $2^{n-1} + 2^{\frac{n-1}{2}}$.

The powerful McEliece theorem (see, *e.g.*, [809]) that we recalled at Section 4.1 (page 151) gives the exact divisibility of the codewords of cyclic codes. Translated in terms of vectorial functions, it says that if d is relatively prime to $2^n - 1$, the exponent e_d of the greatest power of 2 dividing all the Walsh coefficients of the power function x^d is given by $e_d = \min\{w_2(t_0) + w_2(t_1), \ 1 \leq t_0, t_1 < 2^n - 1; \ t_0 + t_1 d \equiv 0 \ [\mathrm{mod} \ 2^n - 1]\}$. It can be used in relationship with Proposition 163. This has led in [195] to the proof, by Canteaut et al., of a several decade old conjecture due to Welch.

Note finally that, if F is a power function, then Boolean function γ_F seen in Proposition 158 is within the framework of Dobbertin's *triple construction* [466].

Relation with the notions of Sidon sets and sum-free sets

In [316], is observed that APN exponents have a property involving two well-known notions in additive combinatorics. We refer the reader to this paper and to the references therein for complements.

Definition 80   *A subset of $\mathbb{F}_2^n$ is a* Sidon set *if it does not contain four distinct elements whose sum is null.*

This notion due to Sidon is preserved by affine equivalence and by decreasing inclusion. Denoting by P_S the set of pairs in S, it is equivalent to saying that $\{x, y\} \in P_S \mapsto x + y$ is one-to-one. The size $|S|$ is then such that $\binom{|S|}{2} \leq 2^n - 1$.

Note that an (n, n)-function F is APN if and only if its *graph* $\mathcal{G}_F = \{(x, F(x)); x \in \mathbb{F}_2^n\}$ is a Sidon set in $((\mathbb{F}_2^n)^2, +)$, since saying that, given four distinct elements x, y, z, t of $\mathbb{F}_2^n$, if $x + y + z + t = 0_n$ then $F(x) + F(y) + F(z) + F(t) \neq 0_n$, is equivalent to saying that, given four distinct elements x, y, z, t, we have $x+y+z+t \neq 0_n$ or $F(x)+F(y)+F(z)+F(t) \neq 0_n$.

Definition 81   *A subset S of $\mathbb{F}_2^n$ is called a* sum-free set *if it does not contain elements x, y, z such that $x + y = z$ (i.e., if $S \cap (S + S) = \emptyset$).*

This notion due to Erdös is preserved by linear equivalence and by decreasing inclusion. The size $|S|$ is then smaller than or equal to 2^{n-1}, because $|S + S| \geq |S|$, and if $|S| > 2^{n-1}$, then the two sets $S + S$ and S have intersection. Note that S cannot contain 0_n. A basic example of a sum-free set (with minimum size) is the complement of a linear hyperplane. The size $|S|$ of a sum-free Sidon set satisfies $\frac{|S|(|S|+1)}{2} \leq 2^n - 1$, since $S \cup \{0_n\}$ is then a Sidon set.

Proposition 168   *[316] For every positive integers n and d and for every $j \in \mathbb{Z}/n\mathbb{Z}$, let $e_j = \gcd(d - 2^j, 2^n - 1) \in \mathbb{Z}/(2^n - 1)\mathbb{Z}$, and let G_{e_j} be the multiplicative subgroup $\{x \in \mathbb{F}_{2^n}^* ; x^{d-2^j} = 1\} = \{x \in \mathbb{F}_{2^n}^* ; x^{e_j} = 1\}$ of order e_j. If d is an APN exponent over $\mathbb{F}_{2^n}$, then, for every $j \in \mathbb{Z}/n\mathbb{Z}$, G_{e_j} is a Sidon sum-free set in $\mathbb{F}_{2^n}$.*

Proof For every $x \in G_{e_j} \setminus \{1\}$, let $s = \frac{x}{x+1}$. Then $x = \frac{s}{s+1}$, and $x^{d-2^j} = 1$ implies $s^{d-2^j} + (s+1)^{d-2^j} = 0$, which implies after multiplication by $s^{2^j} + 1 = (s+1)^{2^j}$ that $s^d + (s+1)^d = s^{d-2^j} = \frac{1}{(x+1)^{d-2^j}}$. Note that if $s = \frac{x}{x+1}$ and $s' = \frac{x'}{x'+1}$, with $x \neq 1$ and $x' \neq 1$, then we have $s = s'$ if and only if $x = x'$ and $s = s' + 1$ if and only if $x' = x^{-1}$.

Suppose that G_{e_j} is not a Sidon set, then let x, y, z, t be distinct elements of G_{e_j} such that $x + y = z + t$. Making the changes of variables $x \to xt, y \to yt, z \to zt$ and dividing the equality by t, we obtain distinct elements x, y, z of $G_{e_j} \setminus \{1\}$ such that $x + y + z = 1$. Making now the change of variable $y \to zy$, we obtain elements x, y, z in $G_{e_j} \setminus \{1\}$ such that $x + 1 = z(y + 1)$, $x \neq y$ and $x \neq y^{-1}$. We have then $\frac{1}{(x+1)^{d-2^j}} = \frac{1}{(y+1)^{d-2^j}}$ and $\frac{x}{x+1} \neq \frac{y}{y+1}$, $\frac{x}{x+1} \neq \frac{y}{y+1} + 1$, a contradiction with the APNness of F.

Suppose that G_{e_j} is not sum-free, then $G_{e_j} \cap (G_{e_j} + 1) \neq \emptyset$. Let $x \in G_{e_j} \cap (G_{e_j} + 1)$ and $s = \frac{x}{x+1}$; we have then $\frac{1}{(x+1)^{d-2^j}} = 1$ and $s^d + (s+1)^d = 1$ and the equation $z^d + (z+1)^d = 1$ has four solutions $0, 1, s$, and $s + 1$ in $\mathbb{F}_{2^n}$, a contradiction. $\square$

Remark. Denoting $e = gcd(d, 2^n - 1)$, we have that G_e itself is a Sidon set since, as recalled above, we have $e = 1$ if n is odd and $e = 3$ if n is even, and $G_1 = \{1\}$, $G_3 = \mathbb{F}_4^*$ are Sidon sets (since they do not contain four distinct elements). But G_e is a sum-free set only for n odd, since $\mathbb{F}_4^*$ is not sum-free. $\square$

A geometric characterization of the fact that some integer d coprime with $2^n - 1$ is an APN exponent over $\mathbb{F}_{2^n}$ for n odd by means of the *Singer set* $S_d = \{x \in \mathbb{F}_{2^n}; tr_n(x^d) = 1\}$ is also given in [252].

Alternative characterization of APN exponents, relation with the Dickson polynomials

When x ranges over $\mathbb{F}_{2^n} \setminus \{1\}$, $s = \frac{x}{x+1}$ ranges over $\mathbb{F}_{2^n} \setminus \{1\}$ and $s^d + (s+1)^d = \frac{x^d+1}{(x+1)^d}$. Then, considering separately the equation $s^d + (s+1)^d = 1$ and the equations $s^d + (s+1)^d = b \neq 1$, we have directly:

Proposition 169 *[316] Let n be any positive integer, then a power function $F(x) = x^d$ over $\mathbb{F}_{2^n}$ is APN if and only if the function $x \mapsto \frac{x^d+1}{(x+1)^d}$ is 2-to-1 from $\mathbb{F}_{2^n} \setminus \mathbb{F}_2$ to $\mathbb{F}_{2^n} \setminus \{1\}$.*

By definition, we have $x^d + (x+1)^d = \phi_d(x^2 + x)$ where ϕ_d is the *reversed Dickson polynomial*, that is, $\phi_d(X) = D_d(1, X)$, where D_d is classically defined by $D_d(X + Y, XY) = X^d + Y^d$; see [628] and [890, page 227]. Then $F(x) = x^d$ is APN if and only if function ϕ_d is injective over the hyperplane $H = \{x^2 + x; x \in \mathbb{F}_{2^n}\} = \{y \in \mathbb{F}_{2^n}; tr_n(y) = 0\}$. Moreover, if x^d is APN over $\mathbb{F}_{2^n}$ for n even, then ϕ_d is a permutation polynomial of $\mathbb{F}_{2^{n/2}}$, which in turn implies that x^d is APN over $\mathbb{F}_{2^{n/2}}$, see [890, theorem 8.1.97, page 227]. We also have $\frac{x^d+1}{(x+1)^d} = \psi_d(x + x^{-1})$, where $(\psi_d(X))^2 = \frac{D_d(X,1)}{X^d}$, where $D_d(X, 1)$ is the *Dickson polynomial* [890] since $\left(\frac{x^d+1}{(x+1)^d}\right)^2 = \frac{x^d + x^{-d}}{(x + x^{-1})^d}$. According to Proposition 169, function F is then APN if and only if ψ_d is injective from $\{x + x^{-1}; x \in \mathbb{F}_{2^n} \setminus \mathbb{F}_2\} = \{y \in \mathbb{F}_{2^n}^*; tr_n(y^{-1}) = 0\}$ to $\mathbb{F}_{2^n} \setminus \{1\}$. Note that $\frac{D_d(y^{-1},1)}{(y^{-1})^d} = y^d D_d(y^{-1}, 1)$ is the value at y of the reciprocal polynomial of $D_d(X, 1)$. Hence:

Proposition 170   *[316] For every positive integer n and d, function $F(x) = x^d$ is APN if and only if the reciprocal polynomial $\widetilde{D_d(X, 1)} = X^d D_d(X^{-1}, 1)$ of the Dickson polynomial $D_d(X, 1)$ is injective and does not take value 1 over $H^* = \{y \in \mathbb{F}_{2^n}^*; tr_n(y) = 0\}$.*

And it has been proved in [316] that for every positive integer d, the reversed Dickson polynomial of index $2d$ and the reciprocal of Dickson polynomial of index d are equal. In fact, as observed with X.-D. Hou, for any characteristic, we have $X^d D_d(\frac{1}{X} - 2, 1) = D_{2d}(1, X)$.

Search for APN exponents

Dobbertin and Canteaut have independently determined all APN exponents for $n \leq 26$, and Leander–Langevin did the same up to $n = 33$ for AB exponents in [753]; all belong to the classical classes of APN exponents that we shall list in Subsection 11.4, page 394. Edel checked the same for $n \leq 34$ and $n = 36, 38, 40, 42$. The main idea for his computer investigation was to consider all the elements in $\mathbb{Z}/(2^n - 1)\mathbb{Z}$, discard all those which are not coprime with $2^n - 1$ for n odd and do not have gcd equal to 3 with $2^n - 1$ for n even, and all the remaining exponents whose reduction mod $2^r - 1$ is not an APN exponent in $\mathbb{F}_{2^r}$ for some divisor r of n. Then, checking APNness was made for one member of each remaining cyclotomic class of 2 modulo $2^n - 1$ only since x^d and x^{2d} are linearly equivalent. No unclassified APN exponent could be found. A new search has been made in [316] in which were also discarded all those exponents d that were known not to satisfy Proposition 168, thanks to a work on the Sidon and sum-free multiplicative subgroups of $\mathbb{F}_{2^n}^*$ made in [315], which shows in particular that $G_e = \{x \in \mathbb{F}_{2^n}^* \mid x^e = 1\}$ is a Sidon set (resp. a sum-free set) if and only if, for every $u \in \mathbb{F}_{2^n}^*$ (resp. for $u = 1$), the polynomial $\gcd(X^e + 1, (X + 1)^e + u)$ has at most two zeros in $\mathbb{F}_{2^n}$ (resp. has no zero[13]). The condition for sum-free case is equivalent to saying that $\gcd(X^e + 1, (X + 1)^e + 1, X^{2^n} + X)$, that is, $\gcd(X^e + 1, (X + 1)^e + 1)$ since $X^e + 1$ divides $X^{2^n - 1} + 1$, equals 1, and this can be handled without computing in the field $\mathbb{F}_{2^n}$ (which needs huge computational power for large values of n) since all the coefficients playing a role in the Euclidean algorithm belong to $\mathbb{F}_2$. Unfortunately, this did not discard enough additional APN candidates to allow us to find new APN exponents.

11.3.3 Componentwise APNness (CAPNness)

Chabaud–Vaudenay's characterization of APN functions by the fourth moment of the Walsh transform (see Relation (11.2), page 372) leads to a notion called componentwise APNness (CAPNness) in [251], stronger than APNness, in which the value on the left-hand side of (11.2) is the same for every component function:

---

[13] This condition can be compared to the condition that $X^d + (X + 1)^d + 1$ has no zero in $\mathbb{F}_{2^n} \setminus \mathbb{F}_2$, which expresses (as it can be easily checked) that the cyclic code C_F (see Proposition 160, page 378, and see page 387) has no codeword of Hamming weight 3.

Definition 82 *Let n be any positive integer and F any (n, n)-function. We call F componentwise APN (CAPN) if, given any nonzero v in $\mathbb{F}_2^n$, its Walsh transform satisfies the equality:*

$$\sum_{u \in \mathbb{F}_2^n} W_F^4(u, v) = 2^{3n+1}. \tag{11.8}$$

Using Relation 3.10, page 98, F is CAPN if and only if $\mathcal{V}(v \cdot F) = 2^{2n+1}$ for every $v \neq 0_n$. This EA-invariant notion had been first studied by Berger et al. in [62] without this specific name being introduced by these authors. They had observed that AB functions and power APN permutations have this property (for straightforward reasons); in particular, all known APN functions in odd dimension are CAPN. They had stated an open question on the existence or nonexistence of such functions for n even. The nonexistence has been proved in [251], by showing that F is CAPN if and only if, for every $w \neq 0_n$, the set $\{(x, y, z) \in \mathbb{F}_2^n;\ F(x) + F(y) + F(z) + F(x + y + z) = w\}$ has size $2^{2n} - 2^{n+1}$ and observing that this size is divisible by 3.

11.3.4 Plateaued APN functions

In the case n odd, we have seen in Proposition 163, page 382, that *plateaued* APN n-variable functions are almost bent.

In the case n even, we have seen at page 382 that for any plateaued APN n-variable function F, there must exist $v \in \mathbb{F}_2^{n*}$ such that the Boolean function $v \cdot F$ is bent. *Note that this implies that F cannot be a permutation*, according to Proposition 35, page 112, and since a bent Boolean function is never balanced. This was first observed in [62].

When F is plateaued and APN, the numbers $\lambda_{u,v}$ involved in Relation (11.7), page 382, can be divided into two categories (since we know that the amplitude of a plateaued Boolean function equals 2^j with $j \geq \frac{n}{2}$): those such that the function $v \cdot F$ is bent (for each such v, we have $\lambda_{u,v} = 2^{2j-n-1} = 1/2$ for every u and therefore $\sum_{u \in \mathbb{F}_2^n} (\lambda_{u,v}^2 - \lambda_{u,v}) = -2^{n-2}$); and those such that $v \cdot F$ is not bent (then $\lambda_{u,v} \in \{0, 2^i\}$ for some $i \geq 1$ depending on v, and therefore $\lambda_{u,v}^2 = 2^i \lambda_{u,v}$, and we have, thanks to Parseval's relation applied to the Boolean function $v \cdot F$, $\sum_{u \in \mathbb{F}_2^n} (\lambda_{u,v}^2 - \lambda_{u,v}) = (2^i - 1) \sum_{u \in \mathbb{F}_2^n} \lambda_{u,v} = (2^i - 1) \frac{2^{2n}}{2^{n+1}} = (2^i - 1) 2^{n-1} \geq 2^{n-1}$). Equation (11.7) implies then that the number B of those v such that $v \cdot F$ is bent satisfies $-B\, 2^{n-2} + (2^n - 1 - B)\, 2^{n-1} \leq 0$, which implies that *the number of bent functions among the functions $v \cdot F$ is at least $\frac{2}{3}(2^n - 1)$* (this has been first observed in [910] for APN functions with partially-bent components, Nyberg generalizing a result given without a complete proof in [1028] for quadratic functions, and in [62] for plateaued APN functions).

This bound is achieved with equality by the Gold APN functions $F(x) = x^{2^i+1}$, $\gcd(i, n) = 1$ (see page 399). Indeed, we saw at page 206 that the function $tr_n(vF(x))$ is bent if and only if v is not the third power of an element of $\mathbb{F}_{2^n}$.

Note that, given an APN plateaued function F, saying that the number of bent functions among the functions $tr_n(vF(x))$ equals $\frac{2}{3}(2^n - 1)$ is equivalent to saying, according to the observations above, that there is no v such that $\lambda_{u,v} = \pm 2^i$ with $i > 1$, that is, F has nonlinearity $2^{n-1} - 2^{\frac{n}{2}}$ and it is also equivalent to saying that F has the same extended Walsh spectrum as the Gold functions.

The fact that an APN function F has same extended Walsh spectrum as the Gold functions can be characterized by using a similar method as for proving Corollary 27, page 377: this situation happens if and only if, for every $v \in \mathbb{F}_2^n \setminus \{0_n\}$ and every $u \in \mathbb{F}_2^n$, we have $W_F(u,v) \in \{0, \pm 2^{\frac{n}{2}}, \pm 2^{\frac{n+2}{2}}\}$ (where $W_F(u,v) = \sum_{x \in \mathbb{F}_2^n} (-1)^{v \cdot F(x) \oplus u \cdot x}$), that is,

$$W_F(u,v)\left(W_F^2(u,v) - 2^{n+2}\right)\left(W_F^2(u,v) - 2^n\right) = 0,$$

or equivalently $W_F^5(u,v) - 5 \cdot 2^n W_F^3(u,v) + 2^{2n+2} W_F(u,v) = 0$. Applying the Fourier–Hadamard transform and dividing by 2^{2n}, this is equivalent to the fact that

$$\left| \left\{ (x_1, \ldots, x_5) \in \mathbb{F}_2^{5n}; \begin{cases} \sum_{i=0}^5 x_i = a \\ \sum_{i=0}^5 F(x_i) = b \end{cases} \right\} \right| - 2^{3n} -$$

$$5 \cdot 2^n \left(\left| \left\{ (x_1, \ldots, x_3) \in \mathbb{F}_2^{3n}; \begin{cases} \sum_{i=0}^3 x_i = a \\ \sum_{i=0}^3 F(x_i) = b \end{cases} \right\} \right| - 2^n \right) +$$

$$2^{2n+2} \left(\left| \left\{ x \in \mathbb{F}_2^n; \begin{cases} x = a \\ F(x) = b \end{cases} \right\} \right| - 2^{-n} \right) = 0$$

for every $a, b \in \mathbb{F}_2^n$. A necessary condition is (taking $b = F(a)$ and using that F is APN) that, for every $a, b \in \mathbb{F}_2^n$, we have

$$\left| \left\{ (x_1, \ldots, x_5) \in \mathbb{F}_2^{5n}; \begin{cases} \sum_{i=0}^5 x_i = a \\ \sum_{i=0}^5 F(x_i) = b \end{cases} \right\} \right| =$$

$$2^{3n} + 5 \cdot 2^n (3 \cdot 2^n - 2 - 2^n) - 2^{2n+2}(1 - 2^{-n}) = 2^{3n} + 3 \cdot 2^{2n+1} - 3 \cdot 2^{n+1}.$$

There exist APN quadratic functions whose Walsh spectra are different from the Gold functions. K. Browning et al. [135] exhibit such function in six variables: $F(x) = x^3 + \alpha^{11}x^5 + \alpha^{13}x^9 + x^{17} + \alpha^{11}x^{33} + x^{48}$ (α primitive), for which 46 functions $tr_6(vF(x))$ are bent, 16 are plateaued with amplitude 16, and one is plateaued with amplitude 32. For $n = 8$, among the 8,179 quadratic APN functions identified in [1145], there are 487 functions with the spectrum $\{*-64^6, -32^{2240}, -16^{20880}, 0^{15600}, 16^{23664}, 32^{2880}, 64^{10}*\}$ and 12 functions with the spectrum $\{*-64^{12}, -32^{2100}, -16^{21360}, 0^{14880}, 16^{24208}, 32^{2700}, 64^{20}*\}$, and the rest have a Gold-like Walsh spectrum [655]. $\qquad \square$

For all n, characterizations of APN functions among plateaued vectorial functions

Thanks to the characterizations of plateaued functions recalled in Subsection 6.5, page 274, we shall see that all the main results known for quadratic APN functions generalize to plateaued APN functions, simplifying the study of the APNness of (n, n)-functions when they are known to be plateaued.[14]

---

[14] In [247], characterizations of plateaued functions among APN functions are also given.

In particular, it is much used in papers on APN functions that, if a function F is quadratic, then given $a \neq 0_n$, the property that all equations $F(x) + F(x+a) = v$ (which are then linear equations) have at most two solutions is equivalent (as we saw already) to the fact that the single homogeneous equation $F(x) + F(x+a) = F(0_n) + F(a)$ has exactly two solutions. Proving APNness results then in proving that, for every $a \neq 0_n$, this equation has 0_n and a for only solutions. This is probably the main reason why many results on APN functions [80, 147, 151, 157, 158, 160, 239, 283, 1118, 1145] were found for quadratic functions. The property above generalizes to all plateaued functions:

Proposition 171 *[247] Any plateaued (n, n)-function F is APN if and only if, for every $a \neq 0_n$ in $\mathbb{F}_2^n$, the equation $F(x) + F(x+a) = F(0_n) + F(a)$ has the two solutions 0_n and a only.*

Indeed, for every $v \in \mathbb{F}_2^n$, the size $|\{(a, b) \in (\mathbb{F}_2^n)^2 \, ; \, F(x) + F(x+a) + F(x+b) + F(x+a+b) = v\}|$ does not depend on $x \in \mathbb{F}_2^n$, according to Theorem 18, page 276, and we can reduce ourselves in this characterization to a and b linearly independent. Function F is then APN if and only if, for such a, b, this size is null for $v = 0_n$. This completes the proof by taking $x = 0_n$, and fixing $a \neq 0_n$.

Another particularity of plateaued functions, extending that of *quadratic functions*, is the sufficiency for APNness of the necessary condition (11.5), page 373:

Proposition 172 *[247] Let F be any plateaued (n, n)-function. Assume that $F(0_n) = 0_n$. Then F is APN if and only if the set $\{(x, a) \in (\mathbb{F}_2^n)^2 \mid F(x) + F(x+a) + F(a) = 0_n\}$ has size $3 \cdot 2^n - 2$. Equivalently:*

$$\sum_{u, v \in \mathbb{F}_2^n, v \neq 0_n} W_F^3(u, v) = 2^{2n+1}(2^n - 1).$$

Indeed, each equation $F(x) + F(x+a) = F(a), a \neq 0_n$ has at least a and 0_n for solutions; Proposition 171 shows then the first assertion; and we have $\sum_{(u,v) \in (\mathbb{F}_2^n)^2} W_F^3(u, v) = 2^{2n} |\{(x, a) \in (\mathbb{F}_2^n)^2 \mid F(x) + F(x+a) + F(a) = 0_n\}|$.

See in [247] several inequalities by means of power moments of the Walsh transform, valid for all vectorial functions, and achieved with equality by APN functions only.

The case of unbalanced component functions: Theorem 19, page 279, implies:

Proposition 173 *[247] Let F be any plateaued (n, n)-function having all its component functions unbalanced, then*

$$\left| \{(a, b) \in (\mathbb{F}_2^n)^2, a \neq b \, ; \, F(a) = F(b)\} \right| \geq 2 \cdot (2^n - 1), \tag{11.9}$$

with equality if and only if F is APN.

Hence, the APNness of plateaued (n, n)-functions with unbalanced component functions depends only on their value distribution (for instance, any plateaued (n, n)-function, n even, having similar value distribution as APN power functions, is APN and, since $\sum_{a,b \in \mathbb{F}_2^n}(-1)^{v \cdot D_a D_b F(x)} = W_F^2(0_n, v)$, has the same extended Walsh spectrum as the APN Gold functions). The case of power functions simplifies further [247].

We have $\left|\{(a, b) \in (\mathbb{F}_2^n)^2, a \neq b; F(a) = F(b)\}\right| = \sum_{a \in \mathbb{F}_2^n; a \neq 0_n}\left|(D_a F)^{-1}(0_n)\right|$ and this is the parameter Nb_F of page 114. Each set $(D_a F)^{-1}(0_n)$ has then size exactly 2. Any function F having this latter property is called *zero-difference 2-balanced*;[15] see [451, 462]. The zero-difference 2-balancedness of some classes of quadratic APN functions seen in [283] is a corollary of Proposition 173 since the functions in these classes have unbalanced components. Note, as observed in [283], that for every δ, all quadratic zero-difference δ-balanced functions are differentially δ-uniform.

11.4 The known infinite classes of AB functions

We begin with AB functions, because when dealing subsequently with APN functions, we shall just complete the list, and also for historical reasons, since AB functions were considered first (under different names in the domain of sequences, as seen at page 383). All the functions in this subsection and the next one are viewed within the structure of the finite field $\mathbb{F}_{2^n}$, n odd; that of semifield has been used in [77, 896]; we refer the reader to these papers for more details.

11.4.1 Power AB functions

The first known examples of AB functions have been power functions $x \mapsto x^d$ on the field $\mathbb{F}_{2^n}$ (n odd) for reasons also explained at page 383. The exponents d of these power functions are (1) those given below (and summarized in Table 11.1), whose largest classes are the two first and (2) the inverses modulo $2^n - 1$ of these values. These inverses have been studied in [731, 908].

- $d = 2^i + 1$ with $\gcd(i, n) = 1$ and $1 \leq i \leq \frac{n-1}{2}$ (proved by Gold, see [540, 908]). The condition $1 \leq i \leq \frac{n-1}{2}$ (here and below) is not necessary but we mention it because the other values of i give *EA equivalent* functions. These power functions are called *Gold AB functions*.

- $d = 2^{2i} - 2^i + 1 = \frac{2^{3i}+1}{2^i+1}$ with $\gcd(i, n) = 1$ and $2 \leq i \leq \frac{n-1}{2}$ (we exclude $i = 1$ since then the function is the cube function, that is a Gold function). The AB property of this function is equivalent to a result historically due to Welch, but never published by him, and is a particular case of a result of Kasami [669]; see other proofs in [470] and [443]. These power functions are called *Kasami AB functions* (some authors call them *Kasami–Welch functions*). Note that, denoting by $G_i(x)$ the Gold AB function x^{2^i+1} over $\mathbb{F}_{2^n}$, and by $L(x)$ the linear function $x^{2^{2i}} + x$, Kasami function $K_i(x)$ not only equals $G_{3i} \circ G_i^{-1}$ but also equals $G_i \circ L \circ G_i^{-1}(x) + x^{2^{2i}} + x^{2^i} + x$ (and is therefore EA equivalent to $G_i \circ L \circ G_i^{-1}$); more generally, for every nonzero $\mu \in \mathbb{F}_{2^n}$, denoting $L_\mu(x) = x^{2^{2i}} + \mu x$, function $\mu K_i(x)$ equals $G_i \circ L_\mu \circ G_i^{-1}(x) + x^{2^{2i}} + \mu^{2^i} x^{2^i} + \mu^{2^i+1} x$;

---

[15] Such ZDB functions have, however, more applications when they are over cyclic groups.

Table 11.1 Known AB exponents on $\mathbb{F}_{2^n}$ (n odd) up to equivalence and to inversion.

Functions	Exponents d	Conditions
Gold	$2^i + 1$	$\gcd(i, n) = 1$
Kasami	$2^{2i} - 2^i + 1$	$\gcd(i, n) = 1$
Welch	$2^t + 3$	$n = 2t + 1$
Niho	$2^t + 2^{\frac{t}{2}} - 1, t$ even	$n = 2t + 1$
	$2^t + 2^{\frac{3t+1}{2}} - 1, t$ odd	

indeed, $G_i \circ L_\mu \circ G_i^{-1}(x) = \left(x^{\frac{2^{2i}}{2^i+1}} + \mu \, x^{\frac{1}{2^i+1}} \right)^{2^i+1} = x^{2^{2i}} + \mu \, x^{\frac{2^{3i}+1}{2^i+1}} + \mu^{2^i} x^{\frac{2^{2i}+2^i}{2^i+1}} +$

$\mu^{2^i+1} x = x^{2^{2i}} + \mu \, K_i(x) + \mu^{2^i} x^{2^i} + \mu^{2^i+1} x$. More is observed in [144].

- $d = 2^{(n-1)/2} + 3$ (conjectured by Welch and proved by Canteaut, Charpin, and Dobbertin see [195, 196, 471]). These functions are called *Welch functions*.
- $d = 2^{(n-1)/2} + 2^{(n-1)/4} - 1$ if $n \equiv 1 \pmod 4$, $d = 2^{(n-1)/2} + 2^{(3n-1)/4} - 1$ if $n \equiv 3 \pmod 4$ (conjectured by Niho, proved by Hollmann and Xiang, after the work by Dobbertin; see [472, 608]). These functions are called *Niho functions*.

The almost bentness can be proved in two steps: (1) prove the almost perfect nonlinearity; the noneasy cases (Kasami, Welch, and Niho) can be treated by Dobbertin's general method introduced in [472] and further developed in [474], called the multivariate method (see the end of the Appendix for an example of this method); (2) prove then ABness by using Proposition 163, page 382, and McEliece's theorem, page 156, in the cases of the Welch and Niho functions. The global proofs of ABness are not easy except in the case of Gold functions, and too long to be included here.

The direct proof that the Gold function above is AB is easy by using the properties of quadratic functions. Since it is a power permutation, we can restrict the study of the Walsh transform to the component function $tr_n(x^{2^i+1})$. The linear kernel of this component function $\{x \in \mathbb{F}_{2^n}; tr_n(x^{2^i}y + xy^{2^i}) = tr_n((x^{2^i} + x^{2^{n-i}})y) = 0, \forall y \in \mathbb{F}_{2^n}\}$ has the equation $x^{2^{2i}} + x = 0$, and equals then $\mathbb{F}_2$, since $\gcd(2^{2i} - 1, 2^n - 1) = 1$. Function $tr_n(x^{2^i+1} + ax)$ is constant on $\mathbb{F}_2$ if and only if $tr_n(a) = 1$. The value at a of the Walsh transform equals then $\pm 2^{\frac{n+1}{2}}$ if $tr_n(a) = 1$ and is null otherwise. This proves ABness. The support of $W_F(u, v)$ has equation $tr_n\left(\frac{u}{v^{\frac{1}{2^i+1}}}\right) = 1$. The Walsh transform sign is studied in [734].

The inverse of x^{2^i+1} is x^d, where $d = \sum_{k=0}^{\frac{n-1}{2}} 2^{2ik}$, and x^d has therefore the algebraic degree $\frac{n+1}{2}$ [908] (hence, the bound of Proposition 155, page 370, is tight).

It has been proved in [443, theorem 7] and [448, theorem 15] that, if $3i$ is congruent with 1 mod n, then the Walsh support of the Kasami Boolean function $tr_n(x^{2^{2i}-2^i+1})$ equals[16] the

---

[16] For n even, it equals the set $\{x \in \mathbb{F}_{2^n}; tr_2^n(x^{2^i+1}) = 0\}$, where tr_2^n is the trace function from $\mathbb{F}_{2^n}$ to the field $\mathbb{F}_{2^2}$: $tr_2^n(x) = x + x^4 + x^{4^2} + \cdots + x^{4^{\frac{n}{2}-1}}$.

support of the Gold Boolean function $tr_n(x^{2^i+1})$ (*i.e.*, the set $\{x \in \mathbb{F}_{2^n}; tr_n(x^{2^i+1}) = 1\}$). The Walsh support of the Kasami functions is also determined in [742] when $5i \equiv 1 \,[\text{mod } n]$ (it is more complex). The knowledge of the Walsh support gives the absolute value (but not the sign) of the Walsh transform of the Kasami function, this function being a permutation. It has been shown in [548, 734] that, for every AB power function x^d over $\mathbb{F}_{2^n}$ whose restriction to any subfield of $\mathbb{F}_{2^n}$ is also AB, the value $\sum_{x \in \mathbb{F}_{2^n}} (-1)^{tr_n(x^d+x)}$ equals $2^{\frac{n+1}{2}}$ if $n \equiv \pm 1 \,[\text{mod } 8]$ and $-2^{\frac{n+1}{2}}$ if $n \equiv \pm 3 \,[\text{mod } 8]$.

Note that the knowledge of the support of the Walsh transform gives also an information on autocorrelation: according to the Wiener–Khintchine formula, the Fourier–Hadamard transform of function $a \rightarrow \mathcal{F}(D_a f) = \sum_{x \in \mathbb{F}_2^n} (-1)^{D_a f(x)}$ equals the square of the Walsh transform of f. In the case that $3i$ is congruent with 1 mod n for instance, since the value at b of the square of the Walsh transform of f equals $2^{n+1} tr_n(x^{2^i+1})$, then by applying the inverse Fourier–Hadamard transform (that is, by applying the Fourier–Hadamard transform again and dividing by 2^n), $\mathcal{F}(D_a f)$ equals twice the Fourier–Hadamard transform of the function $tr_n(x^{2^i+1})$. We deduce that, except at the zero vector, $\mathcal{F}(D_a f)$ equals the opposite of the Walsh transform of the function $tr_n(x^{2^i+1})$.

It is proved in [429] (see also [159, 1140]) that power functions are CCZ equivalent if and only if their exponents or their inverses are in the same cyclotomic coset. The algebraic degrees of functions in Table 11.1 show their pairwise CCZ inequivalence in general.

It was conjectured by Hans Dobbertin that the list of power AB functions is complete. No counterexample to this conjecture has been found (see page 390).

11.4.2 Nonpower AB functions

It had been conjectured in [257] that all AB functions are equivalent to power functions (and then to permutations). This conjecture has been disproved, in a first step by exhibiting in [163] AB functions that are EA inequivalent to any power function and to any permutation, but that are by construction CCZ equivalent to the Gold function $x \rightarrow x^3$, and in a second step by finding AB functions that are CCZ inequivalent to power functions (at least for some values of n) [158]. Note that an easy case where a function is provably EA inequivalent to power functions is when a component function $tr_n(vF)$ has algebraic degree larger than 1 and different from the algebraic degree of F [163].

AB functions CCZ equivalent to power functions

To construct APN (n, n)-functions, and AB functions from known ones by using CCZ equivalence, is needed, given such a function F, to find an affine permutation $\mathcal{L}$ of $\mathbb{F}_2^n \times \mathbb{F}_2^n$ such that, denoting $\mathcal{L}(x, y) = (L_1(x, y), L_2(x, y))$, where $L_1(x, y), L_2(x, y) \in \mathbb{F}_2^n$, the function $F_1(x) = L_1(x, F(x))$ is a permutation. This is a necessary and sufficient condition for the image of the graph of F by $\mathcal{L}$ to be the graph of a function. Two cases of such $\mathcal{L}$ were found in [162, 163] for the function $F(x) = x^{2^i+1}$, where $(i, n) = 1$, giving new classes of AB functions:

- The function $F(x) = x^{2^i+1} + (x^{2^i} + x)\, tr_n(x^{2^i+1} + x)$, where $n > 3$ is odd and $\gcd(n, i) = 1$, is AB. It is provably EA inequivalent to any power function [162, 163] and it is EA inequivalent to any permutation [163, 771], which disproved the conjecture above.

- For n odd, $m \mid n$, $m \neq n$ and $\gcd(n, i) = 1$, the (n, n)-function

$$x^{2^i+1} + tr_m^n(x^{2^i+1}) + x^{2^i} tr_m^n(x) + x \, tr_m^n(x)^{2^i} +$$

$$[tr_m^n(x)^{2^i+1} + tr_m^n(x^{2^i+1}) + tr_m^n(x)]^{\frac{1}{2^i+1}} (x^{2^i} + tr_m^n(x)^{2^i} + 1) +$$

$$[tr_m^n(x)^{2^i+1} + tr_m^n(x^{2^i+1}) + tr_m^n(x)]^{\frac{2^i}{2^i+1}} (x + tr_m^n(x)),$$

where tr_m^n denotes the trace function $tr_m^n(x) = \sum_{i=0}^{n/m-1} x^{2^{mi}}$ from $\mathbb{F}_{2^n}$ to $\mathbb{F}_{2^m}$, is an AB function of algebraic degree $m + 2$, which is provably EA inequivalent to any power function; the question of knowing whether it is EA inequivalent to any permutation is open.

  It would be good to find similarly classes of AB functions by using CCZ equivalence with Kasami (resp. Welch, Niho) functions. For n odd, the Kasami $x^{4^k-2^k+1}$ function equals $F_2 \circ F_1^{-1}(x)$, where $F_1(x)$ and $F_2(x)$ are respectively the Gold functions x^{2^k+1} and $x^{2^{3k}+1}$. Hence, the first step would be to investigate permutations of the form $L_1(x^{2^k+1}) + L_2(x^{2^{3k}+1})$, that is, to find L_1^1 and L_1^2 linear such that for every $u \neq 0$ and every x, we have $L_1^1(x^{2^k}u + xu^{2^k} + u^{2^k+1}) + L_1^2(x^{2^{3k}}u + xu^{2^{3k}} + u^{2^{3k}+1}) \neq 0$. However, it is conjectured in [145] that for a non-Gold power APN (or AB) function, CCZ equivalence coincides with EA equivalence together with inverse transformation, and it is proven (with the help of a check by computer) that this conjecture is true for $n \leq 8$.

- The AB functions constructed in [162, 163] cannot be obtained from power functions by applying only EA equivalence and inverse transformation, but Budaghyan shows in [140] that some AB functions EA inequivalent to power functions can be constructed by only applying EA equivalence and inverse transformation to power AB functions, for instance the function $\left(x^{\frac{1}{2^i+1}} + tr_3^n(x + x^{2^{2i}}) \right)^{-1}$.

AB functions CCZ inequivalent to power functions

The problems of (in)existence of AB functions CCZ inequivalent to power functions and of quadratic APN functions EA inequivalent to Gold functions remained open after finding the two classes above. A paper by Edel et al. [493] introduced two quadratic APN functions from $\mathbb{F}_{2^{10}}$ (resp. $\mathbb{F}_{2^{12}}$) to itself. The first one, $x^3 + \alpha x^{36}$, was proved CCZ inequivalent to power functions.

These two (quadratic) APN functions were sporadic, and this left open the question of knowing whether a whole infinite class of APN functions being not CCZ equivalent to power functions could be exhibited. Moreover, the question of existence of such AB functions was still open.

- The new following class of *binomial AB functions* for n divisible by 3 was found in [151, 158] by Budaghyan, the author, Felke, and Leander:

Proposition 174 *Let s and k be positive integers with* $\gcd(s, 3k) = 1$ *and* $t \in \{1, 2\}$, $i = 3 - t$. *Let* $d = 2^{ik} + 2^{tk+s} - (2^s + 1)$, $g_1 = \gcd(2^{3k} - 1, d/(2^k - 1))$ *and* $g_2 = \gcd(2^k - 1, d/(2^k - 1))$. *If* $g_1 \neq g_2$, *then the function*

$$F : \mathbb{F}_{2^{3k}} \to \mathbb{F}_{2^{3k}}$$

$$x \mapsto x^{2^s+1} + \alpha^{2^k-1} x^{2^{ik}+2^{tk+s}},$$

where α *is primitive in* $\mathbb{F}_{2^{3k}}$ *is AB when k is odd and APN when k is even.*

It could be proved (mathematically) in [151, 158] that some of these functions are EA inequivalent to power functions and CCZ inequivalent to some AB power functions, deducing that they are CCZ inequivalent to all power functions for some values of n:

Proposition 175 *Let s and* $k \geq 4$ *be positive integers such that* $s \leq 3k - 1$, $\gcd(k, 3) = \gcd(s, 3k) = 1$, *and* $i = sk$ *[mod 3],* $t = 2i$ *[mod 3],* $n = 3k$. *If* $a \in \mathbb{F}_{2^n}$ *has the order* $2^{2k} + 2^k + 1$, *then the function* $F(x) = x^{2^s+1} + ax^{2^{ik}+2^{tk+s}}$ *is an AB permutation on* $\mathbb{F}_{2^n}$ *when n is odd and is APN when n is even. It is EA inequivalent to power functions and CCZ inequivalent to Gold and Kasami mappings as shown by a computer-free proof.*

This class was the first infinite family of APN and AB functions CCZ inequivalent to power functions, disproving a conjecture from [257] on the nonexistence of quadratic AB functions inequivalent to Gold functions. This class has been generalized in [116, 118] (see page 405), with Walsh spectra determined in [117].

- It has been shown by Budaghyan et al. in [160] that:

Proposition 176 *For every odd positive integer, the function* $x^3 + tr_n(x^9)$ *is AB on* $\mathbb{F}_{2^n}$ *(and that it is APN for n even).*

This function is one of the only examples[17] with x^3 of a function AB for any n odd. It is CCZ inequivalent to any Gold, inverse and Dobbertin functions on $\mathbb{F}_{2^n}$ if $n \geq 7$ and EA inequivalent to power functions [160]. It has been extended in the same reference into the AB function $x^3 + a^{-1}tr_n(a^3 x^9)$ (which is CCZ inequivalent to all power functions according to [1140], since it has been proved that it is not equivalent to Gold), and in [161] for n divisible by 3 and odd into $x^3 + a^{-1}tr_n^3(a^3 x^9 + a^6 x^{18})$ and $x^3 + a^{-1}tr_n^3(a^6 x^{18} + a^{12} x^{36})$. Coefficient a for all three functions can be reduced to $a = 1$ up to equivalence.[18] The principle of adding a Boolean function to an APN function has been generalized into the so-called *switching method* (see page 407).

- The eighth entry of Table 11.4, page 407 (displaying the known classes of quadratic APN polynomials CCZ inequivalent to power functions) is potentially an infinite class, and has been found in [142] by applying to the cube function x^3 the so-called *isotopic*

---

[17] If we do not take into account that n is present in the definition of tr_n.
[18] The situation is different for n even, with two different functions for $a = 1$ and a primitive.

shift $F \mapsto F_L(x) = F(x + L(x)) - F(x) - F(L(x))$ (where L is linear), adapted from an equivalence notion originally defined by Albert in the study of presemifields in odd characteristic.[19]

An open question is to find infinite classes of AB functions CCZ inequivalent to power functions and to quadratic functions. Actually, the very existence of such functions is an open problem too. A former question on the existence of AB functions CCZ inequivalent to permutations has been solved: for $n = 7$, all 484 quadratic AB functions found in [1145] are CCZ inequivalent to permutations (Yuyin Yu, private communication, 2018). At the moment, the only known AB functions CCZ equivalent to permutations are the power AB functions and the binomials of Proposition 174.

11.5 The known infinite classes of APN functions

We list below the known infinite classes of APN functions (those which are not already seen as AB functions).

11.5.1 Sporadic APN (and AB) functions

In four and five variables, all APN functions are known (they are classified under EA and CCZ equivalences by Brinkmann and Leander in [134]; for $n = 4$, there are two EA equivalence classes, one of which is not EA equivalent to a power function, and there is one CCZ equivalence class; for $n = 5$, there are seven EA equivalence classes, two of which are not EA equivalent to any power function, and all APN functions are CCZ equivalent to one of three power functions). In six to eight variables, known APN functions lying outside the known infinite classes are listed by Browning et al. and by Yu et al. in [135, 1145] (see a few more, some of which in more variables, in [493, 494, 1118]). We refer the reader to these papers for the tables they contain, which are useful when trying to state conjectures on APN functions and for having precise knowledge of all known APN functions. For $n = 6$, the classification of quadratic APN functions is complete: 13 quadratic APN functions are given in [135] and, as proven in [492], up to CCZ equivalence these are the only quadratic APN functions. Only one nonquadratic APN function is known outside the infinite classes up to CCZ equivalence (it is, for $n = 6$, the Brinkmann–Leander–Edel–Pott function [494], see page 407). In [1145], by establishing a correspondence between quadratic APN functions and those $n \times n$ matrices over $\mathbb{F}_{2^n}$ which are symmetric with only zeros on the main diagonal and such that every nonzero linear combination of the rows has rank $n - 1$, it is shown that there are at least 490 CCZ inequivalent APN $(7, 7)$-functions (487 of which are quadratic) and at least 8,180 for $n = 8$ (8,179 quadratic). For n odd, all power APN functions and the known APN binomials (see Proposition 174) are permutations. For n even, the only known APN permutation is constructed in [136] for $n = 6$. The existence of APN permutations for even $n \geq 8$ is an open problem.

---

[19] All quadratic APN (6,6)-functions can be obtained from x^3 by isotopic shift; an extension in [143], where instead of $xL(x)^{2^i} + x^{2^i}L(x)$, given by the isotopic shift of x^{2^i+1}, is taken $xL_1(x)^{2^i} + x^{2^i}L_2(x)$, with L_1 and L_2 linear, leads to 15 new APN (9,9)-functions.

11.5.2 Power APN functions

As in the case of AB functions, the first known APN functions have been power functions $x \mapsto x^d$ over $\mathbb{F}_{2^n}$; the exponents d of these power functions are those given below (and summarized in Table 11.2) and their inverses (when n is odd); we do not repeat below the exponents of AB functions, but we do in Table 11.2:

- $d = 2^i + 1$ with $\gcd(i, n) = 1$, n even and $1 \leq i \leq \frac{n-2}{2}$ (*Gold APN functions*; see [540, 908]). The proof that these functions are APN (whatever is the parity of n) is easy: the equality $F(x) + F(x+1) = F(y) + F(y+1)$ is equivalent to $(x+y)^{2^i} = (x+y)$, and thus implies that $x + y = 0$ or $x + y = 1$, since i and n are coprime. Hence, any equation $F(x) + F(x + 1) = b$ admits at most two solutions. Gold functions being quadratic are plateaued.
- $d = 2^{2i} - 2^i + 1$ with $\gcd(i, n) = 1$, n even and $2 \leq i \leq \frac{n-2}{2}$ (*Kasami APN functions*; see [641], see also [468]). The proof that such a function is APN is difficult. It comes down to showing that the restriction to the hyperplane of equation $tr_n(x) = 0$ of a function ϕ such that $F(x) + F(x + 1) = \phi(x^2 + x)$ (which exists since $F(x) + F(x + 1)$ is invariant by translation by 1) is injective; Dobbertin shows a close connection between ϕ and the polynomial $P(x) = \frac{(tr_i(x))^{2^i+1}}{x^{2^i}}$, called *Müller–Cohen–Matthews polynomial* (*MCM polynomial*) [380] and proves that ϕ is a bijection in [468, 474]. Kasami APN functions are plateaued as proved when 3 does not divide n in [448] and for every even n in [1142].
- $d = 2^n - 2$, n odd. The corresponding so-called *multiplicative inverse permutation* (or simply *inverse function*) $x \mapsto F(x) = x^{2^n-2}$ (which equals $\frac{1}{x}$ if $x \neq 0$, and 0 otherwise) is APN [71, 908]. Indeed, the equation $x^{2^n-2} + (x + 1)^{2^n-2} = b$ (that we can take with $b \neq 0$, since the inverse function is a permutation) admits 0 and 1 for solutions if and only if $b = 1$; and it (also) admits (two) solutions different from 0 and 1 if and only if there exists $x \neq 0, 1$ such that $\frac{1}{x} + \frac{1}{x+1} = b$, that is, $x^2 + x = \frac{1}{b}$. It is well known that such existence is equivalent to the fact that $tr_n\left(\frac{1}{b}\right) = 0$ (since 0 and 1 do not satisfy this latter equation). Hence, F is APN if and only if $tr_n(1) = 1$, that is, if n is odd.

  Consequently, the functions $x \mapsto x^{2^n-2^i-1}$, which are *linearly equivalent* to F (through the linear isomorphism $x \mapsto x^{2^i}$), are also APN, if n is odd.

Table 11.2 Known APN exponents up to equivalence (any n) and up to inversion (n odd).

Functions	Exponents d	Conditions
Gold	$2^i + 1$	$\gcd(i, n) = 1$
Kasami	$2^{2i} - 2^i + 1$	$\gcd(i, n) = 1$
Welch	$2^t + 3$	$n = 2t + 1$
Niho	$2^t + 2^{\frac{t}{2}} - 1, t$ even	$n = 2t + 1$
	$2^t + 2^{\frac{3t+1}{2}} - 1, t$ odd	
Inverse	$2^{2t} - 1$	$n = 2t + 1$
Dobbertin	$2^{4t} + 2^{3t} + 2^{2t} + 2^t - 1$	$n = 5t$

If n is even, then the equation $x^{2^n-2} + (x+1)^{2^n-2} = b$ admits at most two solutions if $b \neq 1$ and admits four solutions (the elements of $\mathbb{F}_4$) if $b = 1$, which means that F opposes a good (but not optimal) resistance against differential cryptanalysis.

The inverse function is not plateaued, since we have seen that the set of values of its Walsh spectrum equals the set of all integers $s \equiv 0 \pmod 4$ in the range $[-2^{\frac{n}{2}+1} + 1; 2^{\frac{n}{2}+1} + 1]$. The values of $\mathcal{V}(v \cdot F)$ are calculated in [351]. A connection between the differential properties of function x^3 and of the multiplicative inverse function (and more generally between functions x^{2^t-1} and $x^{2^{n-t+1}-1}$, using that $x^{2^t-1} + (x+1)^{2^t-1} + 1 = \frac{(x^{2^{t-1}}+x)^2}{x^2+x}$) is shown in [93], with a focus on $t = 3$.

In [757], it is proved that any function $F(x) = x^{-1} + G(x)$, where G is any non-affine polynomial, is APN on at most a finite number of fields $\mathbb{F}_{2^n}$.

- $d = 2^{\frac{4n}{5}} + 2^{\frac{3n}{5}} + 2^{\frac{2n}{5}} + 2^{\frac{n}{5}} - 1$, with n divisible by 5 (*Dobbertin function*; see [473]). It has been shown by Canteaut et al. [196] that this function cannot be AB: they showed that $C_F^{\perp}$ contains words whose Hamming weights are not divisible by $2^{\frac{n-1}{2}}$ (the Walsh spectrum values of F are divisible by $2^{\frac{n}{5}}$ but not all by $2^{\frac{2n}{5}+1}$). The proof that the Dobbertin function is APN is also difficult and comes down as well to showing that some mapping is a permutation. Neither the nonlinearity nor the Walsh spectrum of the Dobbertin function is known. The Dobbertin function is not plateaued as seen in [473].

Nonlinearity

For n even, the Gold, Kasami, and inverse functions have the best-known nonlinearity $2^{n-1} - 2^{\frac{n}{2}}$ [540, 669] (knowing whether there exist (n, n)-functions with nonlinearity strictly larger than this value when n is even is an open question). This is easily shown in the former case by using the properties of quadratic functions; it has been proved by Kasami in the second case, and it was first shown in [333] in the latter case. Dobbertin functions have worse nonlinearity.

The *inverse function* $x \mapsto x^{2^n-2} = x^{-1}$ has been chosen for the S-boxes of the AES with $n = 8$ because of its bijectivity, good nonlinearity, good differential uniformity (which is suboptimal:[20] equal to 4), highest possible algebraic degree $n - 1$, nonplateauedness, simplicity, etc. The computation of its output can be adapted to the device on which it is done thanks to the fact that 8 is a power of 2 and x^{-1} can then be computed by decomposition over subfields. An example of such decomposition is as follows: we can write $x^{-1} = x^{2^{n/2}}(x^{2^{n/2}+1})^{-1}$; we have then a product between $x^{2^{n/2}}$, which is a linear function over $\mathbb{F}_{2^n}$, and the inverse of $x^{2^{n/2}+1}$, which lives in the subfield $\mathbb{F}_{2^{n/2}}$. This method can be iterated; note that over $\mathbb{F}_{2^2}$, the inverse function equals x^2 and is then linear. This allows minimizing the number of nonlinear multiplications needed for computing x^{-1}, which plays a role with respect to countermeasures against side-channel attacks (see page 433).

For n odd, Gold and Kasami functions are AB. The nonlinearity of inverse function equals the highest even number bounded above by $2^{n-1} - 2^{\frac{n}{2}}$, as also shown in [333] (this result has drawn K. Nyberg to focus on the inverse function in [908], which contributed to the

---

[20] We speak here of the sub-S-boxes; the global AES S-box is the concatenation of 16 differentially 4-uniform functions and has then differential uniformity $4 \cdot 2^{15 \cdot 8} = 2^{122}$.

invention of AES). Lachaud and Wolfmann proved (as we already mentioned at page 215) in [733] that the set of values of its Walsh spectrum equals the set of all integers $s \equiv 0$ [mod 4] in the range $[-2^{\frac{n}{2}+1} + 1; 2^{\frac{n}{2}+1} + 1]$, whatever is the parity of n; see more in [601]. See [196] for a list of all known *permutations* with best-known nonlinearity. See also [467].

Inequivalence between functions

It is shown in [159] that distinct Gold functions are CCZ inequivalent. We have seen at page 281 that two power functions are CCZ equivalent if and only if they are EA equivalent or one of them is EA equivalent to the inverse of the other. Hence, given the algebraic degrees of Kasami functions, any two distinct functions taken among Gold and Kasami functions[21] are CCZ inequivalent (which was already shown in [159] when one function is Gold and the other is Kasami). And in [1140] is shown the CCZ inequivalence between any n-variable Gold function and any Niho function for $n \geq 9$. It is also shown in [247] that any plateaued function in even dimension that is CCZ equivalent to a Gold or Kasami APN function is necessarily EA equivalent to it. This result is revisited in [1141, corollary 1] after a study of the more general framework of plateaued APN functions.

Inverse and Dobbertin functions are CCZ inequivalent to all other known APN functions and between them because of their peculiar Walsh spectra, as also first observed in [159]. The situation is summarized:

Proposition 177   *[1140, proposition 2]*

(i)   *The Gold functions x^{2^s+1} and x^{2^t+1} on $\mathbb{F}_{2^n}$; $s, t < n/2$, are CCZ equivalent if and only if $s = t$.*

(ii) *The Gold function x^{2^s+1} and the Kasami function $x^{4^r-2^r+1}$ on $\mathbb{F}_{2^n}$; $s, r < n/2$, are CCZ equivalent if and only if either $s = r = 1$ or $(n, s, r) = (5, 1, 2)$.*

(iii) *On $\mathbb{F}_{2^n}$ with n odd and $n \geq 9$, the Gold function x^{2^s+1} and the Welch function are always CCZ inequivalent.*

(iv) *On $\mathbb{F}_{2^n}$ with n odd and $n \geq 9$, the Gold function x^{2^s+1} and the Niho function are always CCZ inequivalent.*

(v)   *The Kasami functions $x^{4^r-2^r+1}$ and $x^{4^s-2^s+1}$ on $\mathbb{F}_{2^n}$; $r, s < n/2$, are CCZ equivalent if and only if $r = s$.*

(vi) *On $\mathbb{F}_{2^n}$ with n odd and $n \geq 9$, the Kasami function $x^{4^r-2^r+1}$ and the Welch function are always CCZ inequivalent.*

(vii) *On $\mathbb{F}_{2^n}$ with n odd and $n \geq 9$, the Kasami function $x^{4^r-2^r+1}$ and the Niho function are always CCZ inequivalent.*

(viii)*On $\mathbb{F}_{2^n}$ with n odd and $n \geq 11$, the Welch function and the Niho function are always CCZ inequivalent.*

It is proven in [134] that there exists no APN function CCZ inequivalent to power mappings on $\mathbb{F}_{2^n}$ for $n \leq 5$. See also [494, table 3], where the so-called switching classes related to the *switching* construction described at page 407 are investigated for $n = 5$; there are three classes with representatives x^3, x^5 and x^{-1}; in general, a switching class containing an APN function F is not included in the CCZ equivalence class containing F, but in the

---

[21] A Gold function with $i = 1$ and a Kasami function with $i = 1$ as well are not distinct.

case of $\mathbb{F}_{2^5}$, they are the same. This fact is given as a comment in the second paragraph after remark 2 in this same paper [494], where it is also indicated that, in the case $n = 8$, the EA switching class of the Gold function x^3 contains 17 CCZ inequivalent functions.

Remark. Proving the CCZ inequivalence between two functions is mathematically (and also computationally) difficult, unless some CCZ invariant parameters can be proved different for the two functions. Examples of direct proofs of CCZ inequivalence using only the definition can be found in [158, 159, 160]. □

Examples[22] of *CCZ invariant* parameters are the following (see [135] and [494] where they are introduced and used, as well as *group algebra* interpretations):

- The extended Walsh spectrum.
- The equivalence class of the code $\widetilde{C}_F$ defined at page 379 (under the relation of equivalence of codes), and all the invariants related to this code (the weight enumerator of $\widetilde{C}_F$, the weight enumerator of its dual–but it corresponds to the extended Walsh spectrum of the function–the automorphism group etc., which coincide with some of the invariants below).
- The Γ-rank: let $\mathcal{G} = \mathbb{F}_2[\mathbb{F}_2^n \times \mathbb{F}_2^n]$ be the *group algebra* of $\mathbb{F}_2^n \times \mathbb{F}_2^n$ over $\mathbb{F}_2$, consisting of the formal sums $\sum_{g \in \mathbb{F}_2^n \times \mathbb{F}_2^n} a_g \, g$, where $a_g \in \mathbb{F}_2$. If S is a subset of $\mathbb{F}_2^n \times \mathbb{F}_2^n$, then it can be identified with the element $\sum_{s \in S} s$ of $\mathcal{G}$. The dimension of the ideal of $\mathcal{G}$ generated by the graph $\mathcal{G}_F = \{(x, F(x)); x \in \mathbb{F}_2^n\}$ of F is called the Γ-*rank* of F. The Γ-rank equals (see [494]) the rank of the matrix $M_{\mathcal{G}_F}$ whose term indexed by $(x, y) \in \mathbb{F}_2^n \times \mathbb{F}_2^n$ and by $(a, b) \in \mathbb{F}_2^n \times \mathbb{F}_2^n$ equals 1 if $(x, y) \in (a, b) + \mathcal{G}_F$ and equals 0 otherwise.
- The Δ-rank, that is, the dimension of the ideal of $\mathcal{G}$ generated by the set $D_F = \{(a, F(x) + F(x + a)); a, x \in \mathbb{F}_2^n; a \neq 0\}$ (according to Proposition 158, this set has size $2^{2n-1} - 2^{n-1}$ and is a difference set when F is AB). The Δ-rank equals the rank of the matrix M_{D_F} whose term indexed by (x, y) and by (a, b) equals 1 if $(x, y) \in (a, b) + D_F$ and equals 0 otherwise.
- The order of the automorphism group of the design $dev(\mathcal{G}_F)$, whose points are the elements of $\mathbb{F}_2^n \times \mathbb{F}_2^n$ and whose blocks are the sets $(a, b) + \mathcal{G}_F$ (and whose incidence matrix is $M_{\mathcal{G}_F}$); this is the group of all those permutations on $\mathbb{F}_2^n \times \mathbb{F}_2^n$ that map every such block to a block.
- The order of the automorphism group of the design $dev(D_F)$, whose points are the elements of $\mathbb{F}_2^n \times \mathbb{F}_2^n$ and whose blocks are the sets $(a, b) + D_F$ (and whose incidence matrix is M_{D_F}).
- The order of the automorphism group $\mathcal{M}(\mathcal{G}_F)$ of the so-called multipliers of $\mathcal{G}_F$, that is, the permutations π of $\mathbb{F}_2^n \times \mathbb{F}_2^n$ such that $\pi(\mathcal{G}_F)$ is a translate $(a, b) + \mathcal{G}_F$ of $\mathcal{G}_F$. This order is easier to compute, and it makes it possible in some cases to prove CCZ inequivalence easily. As observed in [135], $\mathcal{M}(\mathcal{G}_F)$ is the automorphism group of the code $\widetilde{C}_F$.
- The order of the automorphism group $\mathcal{M}(D_F)$.
- A CCZ-invariant lower bound on the minimum distance to other APN functions [153].

CCZ equivalence does not preserve crookedness nor the algebraic degree.

---

[22] There are other CCZ invariants known; we describe all those efficient for APN functions.

Exceptional exponents

The exponents d such that the function x^d is APN on infinitely many extensions $\mathbb{F}_{2^n}$ of $\mathbb{F}_2$ are called *exceptional* (see [135, 444, 642]). We have seen above that a power function x^d is APN if and only if the function $x^d + (x + 1)^d + 1$ (we write "+1" so that 0 is a root, which simplifies presentation) is 2-to-1 and that, for every (n, n)-function F over $\mathbb{F}_{2^n}$, there exists a polynomial P such that $F(x) + F(x + 1) + F(1) = P(x + x^2)$. In each case of the Gold and Kasami functions, one of these polynomials P is an exceptional polynomial (*i.e.*, is a permutation over infinitely many fields $\mathbb{F}_{2^n}$); from there comes the term. In the case of the Gold function x^{2^i+1}, we have $P(x) = x + x^2 + x^{2^2} + \cdots + x^{2^{i-1}}$, which is a linear function over the algebraic closure of $\mathbb{F}_2$ having kernel $\{x \in \mathbb{F}_{2^i} ; tr_i(x) = 0\}$ and is therefore a permutation over $\mathbb{F}_{2^n}$ for every n coprime with i. In the case of Kasami exponents, the polynomial is related to the MCM polynomials; see page 400. It had been conjectured in [642] that Gold and Kasami exponents are the only exceptional exponents. This conjecture has been shown in [603]. It has been shown in [40] that if the degree of a function given in univariate representation is not divisible by 4, and if this degree is not a Gold or a Kasami exponent, and if the polynomial contains a term of odd degree, then the function cannot be APN over infinitely many extensions of $\mathbb{F}_2$. See more on *exceptional* APN functions in [418, 419] and the references therein.

11.5.3 Nonpower APN functions

As for AB functions, it had been wrongly conjectured that all APN functions were *EA equivalent* to power functions.

APN functions CCZ equivalent to power functions

Using also the notion of CCZ equivalence, two more infinite classes of APN functions have been introduced by Budaghyan, the author, and Pott in [162, 163], which disprove the conjecture above:

- The function $F(x) = x^{2^i+1} + (x^{2^i} + x + 1) tr_n(x^{2^i+1})$, where $n \geq 4$ is even and $\gcd(n, i) = 1$, which is EA inequivalent to any power function.
- For n even and divisible by 3, the function $F(x)$ equal to

$$[x + tr_{n/3}(x^{2(2^i+1)} + x^{4(2^i+1)}) + tr_n(x) tr_{n/3}(x^{2^i+1} + x^{2^{2i}(2^i+1)})]^{2^i+1},$$

where $\gcd(n, i) = 1$, is APN and is EA inequivalent to any known APN function.

We display in Table 11.3 the APN functions found this way. Finding classes of APN functions by using CCZ equivalence with Kasami (resp. Welch, Niho, Dobbertin, inverse) functions is an open problem.

In [1166], some observations about the fact that, starting from a quadratic APN function, it is possible to obtain a CCZ-equivalent function that is EA inequivalent to any quadratic function are made.

Table 11.3 Some APN functions CCZ equivalent to Gold functions and EA inequivalent to power functions on $\mathbb{F}_{2^n}$ (constructed in [162, 163]).

Functions	Conditions	d_{alg}
$x^{2^i+1} + (x^{2^i} + x + tr_n(1) + 1)tr_n(x^{2^i+1} + x\, tr_n(1))$	$n \geq 4$ $\gcd(i,n) = 1$	3
$[x + tr_{n/3}(x^{2(2^i+1)} + x^{4(2^i+1)}) + tr_n(x)tr_{n/3}(x^{2^i+1} + x^{2^{2i}(2^i+1)})]^{2^i+1}$	$6\|n$ $\gcd(i,n) = 1$	4
$x^{2^i+1} + tr_m^n(x^{2^i+1}) + x^{2^i}tr_m^n(x) + xtr_m^n(x)^{2^i}$ $+ [tr_m^n(x)^{2^i+1} + tr_m^n(x^{2^i+1}) + tr_m^n(x)]^{\frac{1}{2^i+1}}(x^{2^i} + tr_m^n(x)^{2^i} + 1)$ $+ [tr_m^n(x)^{2^i+1} + tr_m^n(x^{2^i+1}) + tr_m^n(x)]^{\frac{2^i}{2^i+1}}(x + tr_m^n(x))$	$m \neq n$ n odd $m\|n$ $\gcd(i,n) = 1$	$m+2$

APN functions CCZ inequivalent to power functions

- As recalled at page 397, two quadratic APN functions from $\mathbb{F}_{2^{10}}$ (resp. $\mathbb{F}_{2^{12}}$) to itself have been introduced in [493]. The first one, $F(x) = x^3 + ux^{36}$, where $u \in \mathbb{F}_4 \backslash \mathbb{F}_2$, was proved to be CCZ inequivalent to any power function by computing its Δ-rank. Proposition 174, page 397, which gives binomial AB functions when n is odd, gives *binomial APN functions* when n is even, which generalize the second function: $F(x) = x^3 + \alpha^{15}x^{528}$, where α is a *primitive element* of $\mathbb{F}_{2^{12}}$. Some of them can be proven CCZ inequivalent to Gold and Kasami mappings, as seen in Proposition 175, and therefore, they are CCZ inequivalent to all power mappings due to a result of [1140] (that if a quadratic function is CCZ equivalent to a power function, then it is EA equivalent to a Gold map). A similar class but with n divisible by 4 was later given in [157]. A common framework exists for the class of Proposition 175 and this new class:

Proposition 178 *Let $n = tk$ be a positive integer, with $t \in \{3, 4\}$, and s be such that t, s, k are pairwise coprime and such that t is a divisor of $k + s$. Let α be a primitive element of $\mathbb{F}_{2^n}$ and $w = \alpha^e$, where e is a multiple of $2^k - 1$, coprime with $2^t - 1$. Then the following function is APN:*

$$F(x) = x^{2^s+1} + wx^{2^{k+s}+2^{k(t-1)}}.$$

For $n \geq 12$, these functions are EA inequivalent to power functions and CCZ inequivalent to Gold and Kasami mappings as shown by a computer-free proof [158]. This implies that they are CCZ inequivalent to all power mappings [1140].

- Proposition 175, page 398, has been generalized[23] in [118] for n divisible by 3 by Bracken et al. into *quadrinomial APN functions*:

$$F(x) = u^{2^k}x^{2^{2k}+2^{k+s}} + ux^{2^s+1} + vx^{2^{2k}+1} + wu^{2^k+1}x^{2^{k+s}+2^s} \qquad (11.10)$$

---

[23] Note that Proposition 174 covers a larger class of APN functions than Proposition 175.

is APN on $\mathbb{F}_{2^{3k}}$, when $3 \mid k + s$, $(s, 3k) = (3, k) = 1$ and u is primitive in $\mathbb{F}_{2^{3k}}$, $v \neq w^{-1} \in \mathbb{F}_{2^k}$. It contains the trinomials introduced in [116]. The Walsh spectrum has been determined in [123]. The general class of Proposition 178 is not generalized for the n divisible by 4 case.

- The same paper [118] obtained *multinomial APN functions* for $n \equiv 2 \pmod 4$:

$$F(x) = bx^{2^s+1} + b^{2^k} x^{2^{k+s}+2^k} + cx^{2^k+1} + \sum_{i=1}^{k-1} r_i x^{2^{i+k}+2^i}, \qquad (11.11)$$

where k, s are odd and coprime, $b \in \mathbb{F}_{2^{2k}}$ is not a cube, and $c \in \mathbb{F}_{2^{2k}} \setminus \mathbb{F}_{2^k}$, $r_i \in \mathbb{F}_{2^k}$, is APN on $\mathbb{F}_{2^{2k}}$. Recently, in [146], it has been proved that these functions (11.11) are EA equivalent to the functions of Proposition 181 below, which is itself generalized by the class in [239]; see below.

- The construction of AB functions of Proposition 176, page 398, works for APN functions: *for any positive integer n, function $x^3 + tr_n(x^9)$ is APN on $\mathbb{F}_{2^n}$*. It is shown in [160] that, if F is an APN quadratic (n, n)-function and f is quadratic Boolean such that, for every $a \in \mathbb{F}_{2^n}^*$, there exists a linear Boolean function ℓ_a satisfying $\beta_f(x, a) = f(x + a) + f(x) + f(a) + f(0) = \ell_a(\beta_F(x, a))$, then $F(x) + f(x)$ is APN provided that, if $\beta_F(x, a) = 1$ for some $x \in \mathbb{F}_{2^n}$, then $\ell_a(1) = 0$.

  Function $x^3 + tr_n(x^9)$ is CCZ inequivalent to any Gold function on $\mathbb{F}_{2^n}$ if $n \geq 7$, as proved in [160], and therefore it is CCZ inequivalent to any power function [1140]. The extended Walsh spectrum of this function is the same as for the Gold functions as shown in [114].

  The approach that has led to function $x^3 + tr_n(x^9)$ has been generalized (as for AB functions) and new functions have been deduced: $x^3 + a^{-1} tr_n(a^3 x^9)$ in [160], and for n divisible by 3, $x^3 + a^{-1} tr_n^3(a^3 x^9 + a^6 x^{18})$ and $x^3 + a^{-1} tr_n^3(a^6 x^{18} + a^{12} x^{36})$ in [161] (for n even, each such function defines two CCZ inequivalent functions, one for $a = 1$ and one for any $a \neq 1$). Their APNness is proved in this latter reference by showing for n even that if L is linear and $F(x) = x + L(x^3)$ is a permutation[24] over $\mathbb{F}_{2^n}$, then $F(x^3)$ is APN, and by showing a more complex result for n odd. The Walsh spectra of the functions above are determined in [114, 166] (they are Gold-like Walsh spectra). When F is a Gold function, all possible APN mappings $F(x) + f(x)$, where f is a Boolean function have been computed until dimension 15. The only possibilities different from $x^3 + tr_n(x^9)$, are for $n = 5$ the function $x^5 + tr_n(x^3)$ (CCZ equivalent to Gold functions) and for $n = 8$ the function $x^9 + tr_n(x^3)$ (CCZ inequivalent to power functions); see more in [1096]. In Table 11.4 are displayed all the known classes of APN functions CCZ inequivalent to power functions. It is shown in [161]:

Proposition 179 *Let n be any positive integer and K some field extension of $\mathbb{F}_{2^n}$. Let L be an $\mathbb{F}_2$-linear mapping from $\mathbb{F}_{2^n}$ to $\mathbb{F}_{2^n}$ extended to an $\mathbb{F}_2$-linear mapping from K to K. Let E be a coset in K of a vector space containing $L(\mathbb{F}_{2^n})$. Assume that $F(x) = x + L(x^3)$ is injective on E and that the set $\{x^2 + x + 1; x \in E\}$ contains the set of elements y of $\mathbb{F}_{2^n}$ such that $tr_n(y) = 0$. Then $F(x^3)$ is APN over $\mathbb{F}_{2^n}$.*

---

[24] Sufficient conditions are given in [161] for that.

Table 11.4 Known classes of quadratic APN polynomials CCZ inequivalent to power functions on $\mathbb{F}_{2^n}$.

Functions	Conditions	Proven
$x^{2^s+1} + \alpha^{2^k-1} x^{2^{ik}+2^{tk+s}}$	$n = pk,\ \gcd(k,p)=\gcd((s,pk))=1$, $p \in \{3,4\},\ i = sk \bmod p,\ t = p - i$, $n \geq 12,\ \alpha$ primitive in $\mathbb{F}_{2^n}^*$	Prop. 174, 175 178; [158]
$ax^{2^i(q+1)} + x^{2^i+1} + x^{q(2^i+1)}$ $+x^{q+1} + cx^{2^iq+1} + c^q x^{2^i+q}$	$q = 2^m, n = 2m,\ \gcd(i,m)=1$, $c \in \mathbb{F}_{2^n}, a \in \mathbb{F}_{2^n} \setminus \mathbb{F}_q$, $X^{2^i+1} + cX^{2^i} + c^q X + 1$ has no zero in $\mathbb{F}_{2^n}$ s.t. $x^{q+1} = 1$	Prop. 181 [147]
$x^3 + a^{-1} tr_n(a^3 x^9)$	$a \neq 0$	[160]
$x^3 + a^{-1} tr_3^n(a^3 x^9 + a^6 x^{18})$	$3\|n, a \neq 0$	[161]
$x^3 + a^{-1} tr_3^n(a^6 x^{18} + a^{12} x^{36})$	$3\|n, a \neq 0$	[161]
$\alpha x^{2^s+1} + \alpha^{2^k} x^{2^{2k}+2^{k+s}} +$ $vx^{2^{2k}+1} + w\alpha^{2^k+1} x^{2^s+2^{k+s}}$	$n = 3k,\ \gcd(k,3)=\gcd(s,3k)=1$, $v, w \in \mathbb{F}_{2^k}, vw \neq 1$, $3\|(k+s)\ \alpha$ primitive in $\mathbb{F}_{2^n}^*$	see page 405 [116]
$(x+x^{2^m})^{2^k+1} +$ $\beta(\alpha x + \alpha^{2^m} x^{2^m})^{(2^k+1)2^i} +$ $\alpha(x+x^{2^m})(\alpha x + \alpha^{2^m} x^{2^m})$	$n = 2m, m \geq 2$ even, $\gcd(k,m) = 1$ and $i \geq 2$ even α primitive in $\mathbb{F}_{2^n}^*, \beta \in \mathbb{F}_{2^m}$ not cube	[1182]
$a^2 x^{2^{2m+1}+1} + b^2 x^{2^{m+1}+1} +$ $ax^{2^{2m}+2} + bx^{2^m+2} +$ $(c^2 + c)x^3$	$n = 3m, m$ odd; U subgroup of $\mathbb{F}_{2^n}^*$ of order $2^{2m} + 2^m + 1$, $L(x) =$ $ax^{2^{2m}} + bx^{2^m} + cx \in \mathbb{F}_{2^n}[x]$, s.t. $\forall v,t \in U, L(v) \notin \{0,v\}$ and $v^2 L(t)$ $+tL(v)^2 \neq 0 \Rightarrow \frac{t^2L(v)+vL(t)^2}{v^2L(t)+tL(v)^2} \notin \mathbb{F}_{2^m}$	[142]
$\alpha(\alpha^q x + \alpha x^q)(x^q + x)+$ $(\alpha^q x + \alpha x^q)^{2^{2i}+2^{3i}} +$ $a(\alpha^q x + \alpha x^q)^{2^{2i}}(x^q + x)^{2^i} +$ $b(x^q + x)^{2^i+1}$	$q = 2^m, n = 2m, \gcd(i,m) = 1$ $X^{2^i+1} + aX + b$ has no zero in $\mathbb{F}_{2^m}$	[1077]
$x^3 + \beta(x^{2^i+1})^{2^k} + \beta^2 x^{3 \cdot 2^m} +$ $(x^{2^{i+m}+2^m})^{2^k}$	$n = 2m; m$ odd; $3 \nmid m$ $i = m - 2$ or $i = (m - 2)^{-1} \pmod n$ β primitive in $\mathbb{F}_4$	[165]

Note that if the output of $x^3 + tr_n(x^9)$ is decomposed over an $\mathbb{F}_2$-basis of $\mathbb{F}_{2^n}$ that contains element 1, function $x^3 + tr_n(x^9)$ differs from x^3 for only one coordinate function. This is an example of the idea originally due to Dillon (after [160]) and developed in [494] of the *switching* construction: starting with a known APN function, one of the coordinate functions is changed; this gives a function which is differentially 4-uniform and, in some rare cases, APN. In general, each change of a coordinate function in an S-box can at most multiply its differential uniformity δ by 2. Indeed, changing, for instance, the last coordinate function and denoting by F' the function obtained from F by erasing the last coordinate, the equation $F'(x) + F'(x + a) = b'$ corresponds to $F(x) + F(x + a) = (b', 0)$ or $F(x) + F(x + a) = (b', 1)$, and the differential uniformity of any function obtained by changing the last coordinate function is then at most 2δ (but this change can lower the nonlinearity to 0). This has led in [494] to an APN (6,6)-function CCZ inequivalent to power functions and to quadratic functions (the only known, currently), which had been already found in [134] but missed as a non quadratic function; we shall call it the *Brinkmann–Leander–Edel–Pott function*; it equals, given α primitive:

$$x^3 + \alpha^{17}(x^{17} + x^{18} + x^{20} + x^{24}) + tr_2(x^{21}) + tr_3(\alpha^{18}x^9)$$
$$+ \alpha^{14} tr_6 (\alpha^{52}x^3 + \alpha^6 x^5 + \alpha^{19}x^7 + \alpha^{28}x^{11} + \alpha^2 x^{13}).$$

On the basis of a generalized switching construction, Göloğlu has proposed in [547] the function $x^{2^k+1} + (tr_m^n(x))^{2^k+1}$, where $\gcd(k,n) = 1$ and $n = 2m$, m even, but this function was proved affine equivalent to the Gold function in [166].

- An idea of J. Dillon [445] was that (n,n)-functions (over $\mathbb{F}_{2^n}$) of the form

$$F(x) = x(Ax^2 + Bx^q + Cx^{2q}) + x^2(Dx^q + Ex^{2q}) + Gx^{3q},$$

where $q = 2^{\frac{n}{2}}$, n even, have good chances to be differentially 4-uniform. Such F is quadratic. For $a \in \mathbb{F}_{2^n}^*$, we consider then the equation $G_1 := F(x+a) + F(x) + F(a) = a_1 x + a_2 x^2 + a_3 x^q + a_4 x^{2q} = 0$, where $a_1, \ldots, a_4 \in \mathbb{F}_{2^n}$. We deduce $G_2 := a_2^q G_1 + a_4 G_1^q = b_1 x + b_2 x^2 + b_3 x^q = 0$, $G_3 := b_3^2 G_1 + a_3 b_3 G_2 + a_4 G_2^2 = c_1 x + c_2 x^2 + c_3 x^4 = 0$. If either c_1, c_2, or c_3 is nonzero, then F is differentially 4-uniform and possibly APN. This idea was applied to more general functions by Budaghyan and the author in [147]; this resulted in *trinomial APN functions*:

Proposition 180 *Let n be even and let $\gcd(i, \frac{n}{2}) = 1$. Set $q = 2^{\frac{n}{2}}$ and let $c, b \in \mathbb{F}_{2^n}$ be such that $c^{q+1} = 1$, $c \notin \{\lambda^{(2^i+1)(q-1)}, \lambda \in \mathbb{F}_{2^n}\}$, $cb^q + b \neq 0$. Then*

$$F(x) = x^{2^{2i}+2^i} + bx^{q+1} + cx^{q(2^{2i}+2^i)}$$

is APN on $\mathbb{F}_{2^n}$. Such vectors b, c do exist if and only if $\gcd(2^i + 1, q + 1) \neq 1$. For $\frac{n}{2}$ odd, this is equivalent to saying that i is odd.

The extended Walsh spectrum of these functions is the same as that of the Gold functions [1181]. But it has been recently proved in [146] that these functions are EA equivalent to the functions of the next proposition.

- The method also resulted in a class of *hexanomial APN functions*:

Proposition 181 *[147] Let n be even and i be coprime with $\frac{n}{2}$. Set $q = 2^{\frac{n}{2}}$ and let $c \in \mathbb{F}_{2^n}$ and $a \in \mathbb{F}_{2^n} \setminus \mathbb{F}_q$. If the polynomial $X^{2^i+1} + cX^{2^i} + c^q X + 1$ has no zero $x \in \mathbb{F}_{2^n}$ such that $x^{q+1} = 1$ (in particular if it is irreducible over $\mathbb{F}_{2^n}$), then the following function is APN on $\mathbb{F}_{2^n}$:*

$$F(x) = x(x^{2^i} + x^q + cx^{2^i q}) + x^{2^i}(c^q x^q + ax^{2^i q}) + x^{(2^i+1)q}.$$

The condition was shown achievable by computer investigation, then mathematically in [122] and [97]; finally in [547], all the polynomials satisfying it have been characterized, constructed, and counted. This class was generalized (up to CCZ equivalence) in [239]; see below (the question whether this generalizing bivariate construction gives new functions up to CCZ equivalence is open). It was checked with a computer that some of the APN functions provided by Proposition 181 are CCZ inequivalent to power functions for $n = 6, 8, 10$. It remains open to prove the same property for every even $n \geq 12$.

Cases where the hypothesis of Proposition 181 is satisfied were exhibited in [97, 122, 980]. The polynomials $X^{2^i+1} + cX^{2^i} + c^q X + 1$ are directly related to the polynomials $X^{2^i+1} + X + a$. In [122], the coefficients $a \in \mathbb{F}_{2^n}^*$, such that this latter polynomial has no zero in $\mathbb{F}_{2^n}$ when $\gcd(i,n) = 1$ and n is even, are characterized. In particular, for $i = 1$, the polynomial $X^3 + X + a$ has no zero (*i.e.*, is irreducible) if and only if $a = u + u^{-1}$ where u is not a cube in $\mathbb{F}_{2^n}$. Note that $X^3 + X$ is the *Dickson polynomial D_3* (seen at page 389).

As shown in [146], this hexanomial construction is more general than those constructions of Proposition 180 and those of (11.11) (strictly more general, because it is also defined for n even divisible by 4 while these are not).

- A method has been introduced by the author in [239] for constructing APN functions from bent functions. Let B be a bent $(n, \frac{n}{2})$-function and let G be a function from $\mathbb{F}_2^n$ to $\mathbb{F}_2^{\frac{n}{2}}$. Let $F : x \in \mathbb{F}_2^n \to (B(x), G(x)) \in \mathbb{F}_2^{\frac{n}{2}} \times \mathbb{F}_2^{\frac{n}{2}}$. Then F is APN if and only if, for every nonzero $a \in \mathbb{F}_2^n$, and for every $c, d \in \mathbb{F}_2^{\frac{n}{2}}$, the system of equations
$$\begin{cases} B(x) + B(x+a) &= c \\ G(x) + G(x+a) &= d \end{cases}$$ has zero or two solutions. Since B is bent, the number of solutions of the first equation always equals $2^{\frac{n}{2}}$ and such regularity can help. Functions EA equivalent to the Brinkmann–Leander–Edel–Pott function can be obtained in the form $(B(x,y), G(x,y))$ with $B(x,y) = sx^3 + ty^3 + ux^2y + vx\,y^2$.

Taking B equal to the Maiorana–McFarland function $B(x,y) = xy$ on $\mathbb{F}_{2^{\frac{n}{2}}} \times \mathbb{F}_{2^{\frac{n}{2}}}$, where xy is the product of x and y in the field $\mathbb{F}_{2^{\frac{n}{2}}}$, and writing then (a,b) with $a, b \in \mathbb{F}_{2^{\frac{n}{2}}}$ instead of $a \in \mathbb{F}_2^n$, the system of equations above becomes, after changing c into $c + ab$: $\begin{cases} bx + ay &= c \\ G(x,y) + G(x+a, y+b) &= d \end{cases}$. Then, by considering separately the cases $a = 0, b \neq 0$ and $a \neq 0$, F is APN if and only if:

1. For every $c \in \mathbb{F}_{2^{\frac{n}{2}}}$, the function $y \in \mathbb{F}_{2^{\frac{n}{2}}} \to G(c, y)$ is APN.
2. For every $b, c \in \mathbb{F}_{2^{\frac{n}{2}}}$, the function $x \in \mathbb{F}_{2^{\frac{n}{2}}} \to G(x, bx + c)$ is APN (this is easily seen by replacing b and c respectively by ab and ac in the latter system).

This leads to the following *bivariate APN functions*:

Proposition 182 *[239] Let n be any even integer; let i, j be integers such that $\gcd(n/2, i - j) = 1$, and let $s \neq 0$, $t \neq 0$, u and v be elements of $\mathbb{F}_{2^{n/2}}$. Set $G(x,y) = sx^{2^i+2^j} + ux^{2^i}y^{2^j} + vx^{2^j}y^{2^i} + ty^{2^i+2^j}$. Then the function*

$$F : (x, y) \in \mathbb{F}_{2^{n/2}} \times \mathbb{F}_{2^{n/2}} \to (x\,y, G(x,y)) \in \mathbb{F}_{2^{n/2}} \times \mathbb{F}_{2^{n/2}}$$

is APN if and only if $G(x, 1) = sx^{2^i+2^j} + ux^{2^i} + vx^{2^j} + t$ has no zero in $\mathbb{F}_{2^{n/2}}$.

For $j = 0$ and $s = 1$ (as in Proposition 181), such polynomials are called "projective" by some authors. In [239], examples where the condition of Proposition 182 is satisfied are investigated and it is shown that Propositions 180 and 181 and the APN functions of Bracken et al. recalled above are cases of application of Proposition 182 (note that the bivariate function $(x, y) \in \mathbb{F}_{2^{n/2}}^2 \mapsto xy$ is EA equivalent to the univariate function $x \in \mathbb{F}_{2^n} \mapsto x^{2^{n/2}+1}$); see more in [243], where the univariate representation of these functions is investigated and generalized in several ways. Note that it was mentioned (but unpublished) by Göloğlu, Krasnayova, and Lisoněk at the conference Fq13, in 2017, that any APN function of the particular form $x^3 + ax^{3 \cdot 2^{\frac{n}{2}}} + bx^{2 \cdot 2^{\frac{n}{2}}+1} + cx^{2+2^{\frac{n}{2}}}$, $a, b, c \in \mathbb{F}_{2^{\frac{n}{2}}}$, is equivalent to x^3 or to $x^{2^{\frac{n}{2}-1}+1}$ or when $n = 6$ to the so-called Kim function (see the definition of this function at page 411).

The construction of function $(x, y) \mapsto (xy, x^{2^i+1} + ay^{2^j(2^i+1)})$, where $a \neq 0$ is assumed impossible to be written in the form $b^{2^i+1}(c + c^{2^i})^{1-2^j}$, has been proposed by Zhou and Pott in [1182]. It is similar to the one of Proposition 182 but different. It has been generalized in [243]:

Proposition 183 *Let n be any even integer; let i be any integer coprime with $m = n/2$, and let $P, Q, R,$ and S be linear homomorphisms of $\mathbb{F}_{2^m}$. Set $G(x, y) = P(x^{2^i+1}) + Q(x^{2^i}y) + R(xy^{2^i}) + S(y^{2^i+1})$. Then the function*

$$F : (x, y) \in \mathbb{F}_{2^m} \times \mathbb{F}_{2^m} \rightarrow (x\,y, G(x, y) \in \mathbb{F}_{2^m} \times \mathbb{F}_{2^m}$$

is APN if and only if, for every a and b in $\mathbb{F}_{2^m}$ such that $(a, b) \neq (0, 0)$, the linear function $T_{a,b}(y) := P(a^{2^i+1}y) + Q(a^{2^i}by) + R(ab^{2^i}y) + S(b^{2^i+1}y)$ satisfies

- *If m is odd, then $T_{a,b} : \mathbb{F}_{2^m} \mapsto \mathbb{F}_{2^m}$ is bijective.*
- *If m is even, then $(\ker T_{a,b}) \cap \{u^{2^i+1}(t^{2^i} + t); u \in \mathbb{F}_{2^m}^*, t \in \mathbb{F}_{2^m}\} = \{0\}$.*

- A new class has been found by Zhou and Pott in [1182]; see Table 11.4.
- Very recently has been found in [1077] the penultimate entry in Table 11.4, which enters in the framework of the proposition above.
- Still more recently has been found in [165] the last entry in the table.
  Note that each class of functions can be described in many different ways due to equivalences. The reader must then not be surprised if there are small differences between the representations given in Table 11.4 and in the body of the section. The descriptions in the table are in some cases for subclasses, for which inequivalences between the different entries could be shown. This table as well as other tables with data on APN functions is periodically renewed at https://boolean.h.uib.no/mediawiki/index.php/Tables.

An APN permutation and the big open APN problem

The APN functions listed above for n even are not permutations. This is problematic since for implementation reasons (see, *e.g.*, page 401), n even is preferred. Block ciphers using bijective APN $(7, 7)$-functions and $(9, 9)$-functions as S-boxes exist, such as the MISTY block cipher [830] and its variant KASUMI [687], but have drawbacks. Most block ciphers use then differentially 4-uniform permutations in even dimension. The question (called the big open APN problem by Dillon) of knowing whether there exist APN permutations when n is even (which would allow simplifying the structure) was wide open (as first mentioned in [910] and answered negatively for $n = 4$ in [624] thanks to a computer investigation and in [176] mathematically) until Browning et al. exhibited in [136] an APN permutation (of algebraic degree $n - 2$ and nonlinearity $2^{n-1} - 2^{\frac{n}{2}}$) in $n = 6$ variables (used later in the cryptosystem Fides [84], which has been subsequently broken due to its weaknesses in the linear component). This permutation is CCZ equivalent to the so-called Kim function $x^3 + x^{10} + \alpha x^{24}$ (given in [135]), whose associated code C_F (see Proposition 160) is therefore a double simplex code (see page 10). It is EA equivalent to an involution and is studied further in [199, 944] where the *butterfly construction* is introduced. This construction works with concatenations of bivariate functions $R(x, y)$ over $\mathbb{F}_{2^{n/2}}$ ($n/2$ odd), which are viewed as $R_y(x)$ and are such that R_y is bijective for every y. The resulting butterflies have two CCZ equivalent representations, one of which, called closed butterfly, can be taken quadratic (and may not be bijective) and has the form $(R_y(x), R_x(y))$, while the other, called open butterfly, is the involution of the form $(R_{R_y^{-1}(x)}(y), R_y^{-1}(x))$. This construction includes the APN permutation of [136], but unfortunately it is shown in [199, 943] that it does not allow obtaining APN permutations in more than six variables. The butterfly construction gives differentially 4-uniform involutions; see page 421.

The question of existence of APN permutations in even dimension n remains open for $n \geq 8$. There exist nonexistence results within the following classes:

- Plateaued functions (when APN, they have bent components; see page 391).
- A class of functions including power functions (see page 383).
- Functions whose univariate representation coefficients lie in $\mathbb{F}_{2^{\frac{n}{2}}}$, or in $\mathbb{F}_{2^4}$ for n divisible by 4 [624].
- Functions whose univariate representation coefficients satisfy $\sum_{i=0}^{\frac{2^n-1}{3}} a_{3i} = 0$ [184].
- Functions having at least one partially-bent component; it is indeed proved in [176] (starting from the same idea as in [24], see page 383) that no component function of an APN permutation can be partially-bent (this improves upon several previous results on the components of APN permutations): n being even, the linear kernel of such balanced partially-bent component function $v \cdot F$ would have dimension at least 2, and since for every a, b, we have $D_a(v \cdot F)(x) \oplus D_b(v \cdot F)(x) = D_{a+b}(v \cdot F)(x + a)$, there would exist $a \neq 0$ such that $D_a(v \cdot F) = 0$, and since $Im(D_a F)$ has 2^{n-1} elements because F is APN, $Im(D_a F)$ would include 0, a contradiction with the bijectivity of F.

Finding infinite classes of APN functions CCZ inequivalent to power functions and to quadratic functions is an open problem too.

11.5.4 The extended Walsh spectra of known APN functions

For n odd, the known APN functions have three possible spectra (all satisfying $\mathcal{V}(v \cdot F) = 2^{2n+1}$ for every $v \neq 0$); see, *e.g.,* [62]:

- The spectrum of the AB functions, which gives a nonlinearity of $2^{n-1} - 2^{\frac{n-1}{2}}$.
- The spectrum of the inverse function, which takes any value divisible by 4 in $\lfloor -2^{\frac{n}{2}+1} + 1; 2^{\frac{n}{2}+1} + 1 \rfloor$ and gives a nonlinearity close to $2^{n-1} - 2^{\frac{n}{2}}$.

- The spectrum of the *Dobbertin function* which is more complex (it is divisible by $2^{n/5}$ and not divisible by $2^{2n/5+1}$ [196]); its nonlinearity seems to be bounded below by approximately $2^{n-1} - 2^{3n/5-1} - 2^{2n/5-1}$ – maybe equal – but this has to be proven (or disproven).

For *n* even, the spectra may be more diverse:

- The Gold functions (and all known infinite classes of quadratic APN functions [117, 123, 1061]), whose component functions are bent for a third of them and have nonlinearity $2^{n-1} - 2^{\frac{n}{2}}$ for the rest of them; the Kasami functions, which have the same extended spectra.
- The Dobbertin function (same observation as above).
- As soon as $n \geq 6$, we find (quadratic) APN functions with different spectra (*e.g.,* $x^3 + \alpha^{11} x^5 + \alpha^{13} x^9 + x^{17} + \alpha^{11} x^{33} + x^{48}$, for $n = 6$, with a seven-valued Walsh spectrum found by Dillon).

The nonlinearities seem also bounded below by approximately $2^{n-1} - 2^{3n/5-1} - 2^{2n/5-1}$ (but this has to be proven ... or disproven too). Note that the question of classifying APN functions is open even when restricting ourselves to quadratic APN functions in more than six variables (even classifying their Walsh spectra is open for even numbers of variables). There is only one known example of quadratic APN function (with $n = 6$) having non-Gold-like nonlinearity; see [445].

11.5.5 Conclusion on known APN functions

As we can see, very few functions usable as S-boxes have emerged so far. The only known APN permutations are in odd dimension or in dimension 6, which is not convenient for implementation. Besides, Gold functions, all the other found quadratic functions, and the Welch functions have too low algebraic degrees for being widely chosen for the design of new S-boxes. The Kasami functions themselves seem too closely related to quadratic functions. The *inverse function* has many very nice properties: large Walsh spectrum and good nonlinearity, differential uniformity of order at most 4, and fast implementation. But differential uniformity 2 in a dimension equal to a power of 2 would be better, and the inverse function has a potential weakness against algebraic attacks, which did not lead yet to efficient attacks, but may in the future. So further studies on APN permutations seem essential for the future designs of SP networks.

11.6 Differentially uniform functions

11.6.1 Characterizations by the Walsh transform

We have seen that APN functions are nicely characterized by their Walsh transform through Relation (11.2), page 372. It is shown in [250] that other characterizations by the Walsh transform exist for APN functions and that more generally, for each value of δ, several (in fact, an infinity of) characterizations by the Walsh transform of differentially δ-uniform functions exist. We follow here the presentation of [252]. Denoting for every $a, b \in \mathbb{F}_2^n$ and every (n, m)-function F by $N_F(b, a)$ the size of the set $\{x \in \mathbb{F}_2^n; D_a F(x) = D_a F(b)\}$, we have that F is differentially δ-uniform if and only if, for every $a \neq 0_n$ in $\mathbb{F}_2^n$ and every $b \in \mathbb{F}_2^n$, we have $N_F(b, a) \in \{2, 4, \ldots, \delta\}$. For every polynomial $\phi_\delta(X) = \sum_{j \geq 0} A_j X^j \in \mathbb{R}[X]$ such that $\phi_\delta(u) = 0$ for $u = 2, 4, \ldots, \delta$ and $\phi_\delta(u) > 0$ for every even $u \in \{\delta + 2, \ldots, 2^n\}$, we have then for every (n, m)-function F that

$$\sum_{j \geq 0} A_j \sum_{\substack{a, b \in \mathbb{F}_2^n \\ a \neq 0_n}} (N_F(b, a))^j = \sum_{\substack{a, b \in \mathbb{F}_2^n \\ a \neq 0_n}} \sum_{j \geq 0} A_j (N_F(b, a))^j \geq 0,$$

and that F is differentially δ-uniform if and only if this inequality is an equality.

The sum $\sum_{a, b \in \mathbb{F}_2^n} (N_F(b, a))^j$ is easily expressed by means of the Walsh transform of F:

Lemma 12 *Let F be any (n, m)-function. We have for $j \geq 1$:*

$$\sum_{a, b \in \mathbb{F}_2^n} (N_F(b, a))^j = \sum_{a, b \in \mathbb{F}_2^n, a \neq 0_n} (N_F(b, a))^j + 2^{n(j+1)} =$$

$$2^{-j(m+n)} \sum_{\substack{u_1, \ldots, u_j \in \mathbb{F}_2^n \\ v_1, \ldots, v_j \in \mathbb{F}_2^m}} W_F^2 \left(\sum_{i=1}^j u_i, \sum_{i=1}^j v_i \right) \prod_{i=1}^j W_F^2(u_i, v_i). \tag{11.12}$$

This technical lemma is proved in [250] by raising at the jth power the equality $N_F(b, a) = 2^{-m} \sum_{x \in \mathbb{F}_2^n, v \in \mathbb{F}_2^m} (-1)^{v \cdot (D_a F(x) + D_a F(b))}$, obtaining $(N_F(b, a))^j = 2^{-jm} \sum_{\substack{x_i \in \mathbb{F}_2^n, v_i \in \mathbb{F}_2^m \\ i=1, \ldots, j}} (-1)^{\bigoplus_{i=1}^j v_i \cdot (F(x_i) + F(x_i + a) + F(b) + F(b+a))}$, and using that $y_i = x_i + a$ if and only if $\sum_{u_i \in \mathbb{F}_2^n} (-1)^{u_i \cdot (x_i + y_i + a)} = 2^n$ (idem for $c = b + a$). We deduce from Lemma 12:

Theorem 26 *[250] Let n, m, and δ be positive integers, with δ even, and let F be any (n, m)-function. Let*

$$\phi_\delta(X) = \sum_{j \geq 0} A_j X^j \in \mathbb{R}[X]$$

be any polynomial such that $\phi_\delta(u) = 0$ for $u = 2, 4, \ldots, \delta$ and $\phi_\delta(u) > 0$ for every even $u \in \{\delta + 2, \ldots, 2^n\}$. Then we have

$$2^n(2^n - 1)A_0 + \sum_{j \geq 1} 2^{-j(n+m)} A_j \left((W_F^2)^{\otimes(j+1)}(0_n, 0_m) - 2^{(2j+1)n+jm} \right) \geq 0, \tag{11.13}$$

where $(W_F^2)^{\otimes(j+1)}$ is the $(j + 1)$-th order convolutional product of W_F:

$$(W_F^2)^{\otimes(j+1)}(0_n, 0_m) = \sum_{\substack{u_1, \ldots, u_j \in \mathbb{F}_2^n \\ v_1, \ldots, v_j \in \mathbb{F}_2^m}} W_F^2 \left(\sum_{i=1}^j u_i, \sum_{i=1}^j v_i \right) \prod_{i=1}^j W_F^2(u_i, v_i).$$

Moreover, this inequality is an equality if and only if F is differentially δ-uniform.

Relation (11.2), page 372, can then be deduced from Theorem 26 by choosing $\phi_2(X) = X - 2$. Theorem 26 gives other interesting characterizations. We shall give one for each case $\delta = 2$ and $\delta = 4$, but more can be found in [250]. Taking $\phi_2(X) = (X - 2)(X - 4)$, we obtain:

Corollary 29   *[250] Every (n, n)-function F is APN if and only if*

$$\sum_{\substack{u_1, u_2 \in \mathbb{F}_2^n; v_1, v_2 \in \mathbb{F}_2^n \\ v_1 \neq 0_n, v_2 \neq 0_n, v_1 \neq v_2}} W_F^2(u_1, v_1) W_F^2(u_2, v_2) W_F^2(u_1 + u_2, v_1 + v_2) =$$

$$2^{5n}(2^n - 1)(2^n - 2). \tag{11.14}$$

Moreover, every (n, n)-function satisfies a version of (11.14) with "$\geq$" in the place of "$=$," but to show this, Theorem 26 must be applied with $\phi_4(X) = (X - 2)(X - 4)$ and also with $\phi_2(X) = X - 2$ (see [250]).

Applying Theorem 26 with $\phi_4(X) = (X - 2)(X - 4)$ when $m = n - 1$ gives:

Corollary 30   *[250] Every $(n, n - 1)$-function F is differentially 4-uniform if and only if*

$$\sum_{\substack{u_1, u_2 \in \mathbb{F}_2^n; v_1, v_2 \in \mathbb{F}_2^{n-1} \\ v_1 \neq 0_{n-1}, v_2 \neq 0_{n-1}, v_1 \neq v_2}} W_F^2(u_1, v_1) W_F^2(u_2, v_2) W_F^2(u_1 + u_2, v_1 + v_2) =$$

$$2^{5n}(2^{n-1} - 1)(2^{n-1} - 2). \tag{11.15}$$

And every $(n, n - 1)$-functions satisfies a version of (11.15) with "$\geq$" in the place of "$=$."

Note the similarity between these two corollaries, which shows that the two optimal notions of APN (n, n)-function and differentially 4-uniform $(n, n - 1)$-function are close.

In [252], Theorem 26 is generalized into a characterization of all the criteria on vectorial functions dealing with the numbers of solutions of equations of the form $\sum_{i \in I} F(x + u_{i,a}) + L_a(x) + u_a = 0_m$, with L_a linear. In particular, injective functions are characterized this way. A characterization of o-polynomials originally given in [314] can also be obtained by this generalization. And a generalization to differentially δ-uniform functions of a characterization by Nyberg of APN functions by means of the Walsh transforms of their *derivatives* is also derived.

11.6.2 Componentwise Walsh uniformity (CWU)

We have seen at page 390 that the characterization of APNness by Relation (11.2) leads to a stronger notion called CAPNness, in which the relation is satisfied by each component function. The characterizations of APN (n, n)-functions and differentially 4-uniform $(n, n - 1)$-functions by Relations (11.14) and (11.15) in Corollaries 29 and 30 lead similarly to the following EA invariant notion introduced in [251]: we call *componentwise Walsh uniform* (*CWU*) those functions $F : \mathbb{F}_2^n \mapsto \mathbb{F}_2^m$, with $m \in \{n - 1, n\}$, which satisfy (11.14), respectively (11.15), for each pair of *component functions*.

Definition 83 *[251] An (n, m)-function F with $m \in \{n - 1, n\}$ is called CWU if, for all distinct nonzero $v_1, v_2 \in \mathbb{F}_2^m$, we have*

$$\sum_{u_1, u_2 \in \mathbb{F}_2^n} W_F^2(u_1, v_1) W_F^2(u_2, v_2) W_F^2(u_1 + u_2, v_1 + v_2) = 2^{5n}.$$

If $m = n$, then CWUness implies APNness. The converse is not true in general, but we have the following result (we refer the reader to [251] for the proof):

Proposition 184 *Any crooked function (in particular, any quadratic APN (n, n)-function) is CWU.*

An investigation of CWU functions among all known nonquadratic APN power functions was made in [251] for $n \leq 11$. Two potential infinite classes of nonquadratic CWU power functions arised:

- All Kasami APN functions (n odd or even)
- The inverse of the Gold APN permutation $x^{2^{\frac{n-1}{2}}+1}$ (n odd)

None of the other known classes of nonquadratic APN power functions is made of CWU functions only. We have:

Proposition 185 *[251] The compositional inverse of the Gold APN permutation $x^{2^{\frac{n-1}{2}}+1}$ is CWU for every odd n.*

The proof is rather long, so we refer to [251] for it. Finding a proof (after confirmation of the investigation results) of the same property for Kasami functions is an open problem (see some observations in [251] and more in [252]).

11.6.3 Cyclic difference sets, cyclic-additive difference sets, and the CWU property

We have seen the notion of additive difference set in $\mathbb{F}_2^n$ when dealing with bent functions at page 196: every nonzero element can be written in the same number of ways as the difference $x - y$ (that is, $x + y$) between two elements of the set. This notion exists for every group structure. When this group structure is that of $\mathbb{F}_{2^n}^*$, we speak of cyclic difference set, since $\mathbb{F}_{2^n}^*$ is cyclic (and $x - y$ has to be replaced by $\frac{x}{y}$). A particular case that plays a role with APN functions (see [448]) is the following:

Definition 84 *A subset Δ of size 2^{n-1} of the multiplicative group $\mathbb{F}_{2^n}^*$ is called a cyclic difference set with Singer parameters if, for all distinct v_1, v_2 in $\mathbb{F}_{2^n}^*$, we have $|\{(x, y) \in \Delta^2; v_1 x + v_2 y = 0\}| = 2^{n-2}$.*

Equivalently, the symmetric difference between Δ and $a\Delta$ equals 2^{n-1} for every $a \in \mathbb{F}_{2^n}^* \setminus \{1\}$, that is, $\sum_{x \in \mathbb{F}_{2^n}^*} (-1)^{1_\Delta(x) \oplus 1_\Delta(ax)} = -1$ (*i.e.*, the sequence $s_i = 1_\Delta(\alpha^i)$, where

α is primitive, has *ideal autocorrelation*). Any *Singer set* (already seen at page 389) $S_d = \{x \in \mathbb{F}_{2^n}; tr_n(x^d) = 1\}$, $\gcd(d, 2^n - 1) = 1$, has such a property since $x \mapsto x^d$ is a (multiplicative) group automorphism and the intersection between two distinct affine hyperplanes has dimension $n - 2$. Maschietti [825] (see also [443]) proves that, for every d coprime with $2^n - 1$ and such that the mapping $x \mapsto x + x^d$ is 2-to-1 over $\mathbb{F}_{2^n}$, the complement of the image of this mapping is a cyclic difference set with Singer parameters. It is proved in [443, 448] that, for every APN Kasami function $F(x) = x^{4^k - 2^k + 1}$ over $\mathbb{F}_{2^n}$, $n = 3k \pm 1$, the set $\{F(x) + F(x + 1); x \in \mathbb{F}_{2^n}\}$ (or its complement if it contains 0) is a cyclic difference set with Singer parameters (note that $x \mapsto F(x) + F(x + 1)$ is also 2-to-1) and in [448] that the complement of its translation by 1, that is, of $\Delta_F = \{F(x) + F(x + 1) + 1; x \in \mathbb{F}_{2^n}\}$, is a cyclic difference set with Singer parameters (the proof is deduced from an elegant calculation of the Fourier transform of the indicator of the set $D_F = \{x^{\frac{1}{2^i + 1}}; x \in \Delta_F\}$), under the weaker condition that $\gcd(k, n) = 1$[25]. Known facts are summarized with their proofs, and a few new observations are made in [252].

A relationship is shown in [251] between CWU power permutations and a new notion similar to the cyclic difference set property.

Definition 85   *A set $\Delta \subseteq \mathbb{F}_{2^n}$ is called a* cyclic-additive difference set *if, for every distinct nonzero v_1, v_2 in $\mathbb{F}_{2^n}$, we have:*

$$|\{(x, y, z) \in \Delta^3; v_1 x + v_2 y + (v_1 + v_2)z = 0\}| = 2^{2n-3}.$$

Every power function F is APN if and only if the set $\{F(x) + F(x + 1) + 1; x \in \mathbb{F}_{2^n}\}$ has size 2^{n-1}.

Proposition 186   *Let F be any power APN permutation. Then, F is CWU if and only if the set $\{F(x) + F(x + 1) + 1; x \in \mathbb{F}_{2^n}\}$ (or equivalently its complement) is a cyclic-additive difference set.*

There are differences between cyclic and cyclic-additive difference sets:

- The notion of cyclic difference set is invariant under raising the elements to a power coprime with $2^n - 1$, and if two sets Δ and Δ' are such that $W_{1_\Delta}(a) = W_{1_{\Delta'}}(a^k)$, where k is coprime with $2^n - 1$, then Δ is a cyclic difference set if and only if Δ' is one, while these properties are not true for cyclic-additive difference sets.
- The notion of cyclic-additive difference set is invariant under translation $x \mapsto x + a$ while that of cyclic difference set is not (see [448]).

It seems impossible to deduce the cyclic-additive property of Δ_F in the case of Kasami APN permutations from the fact proved by Dillon and Dobbertin in [448] that the Fourier transform of the *indicator* of the set $D_F = \{x^{\frac{1}{2^i + 1}}; x \in \Delta_F\}$ takes at any input $a \in \mathbb{F}_{2^n}$ the same value as the Walsh transform of the Boolean function $tr_n(x^3)$ at $a^{\frac{2^i + 1}{3}}$.

---

[25] For Gold APN functions, we have the same, but the set is the *classical Singer set* S_1.

11.6.4 The known differentially 4-uniform (n, n)-permutations, n even

For computational reasons (explained at page 401 for the inverse function but valid in a more general context), (n, n)-functions are better used as S-boxes when n is even, the best being when n is a power of 2. In practice, we have most often $n = 4$ (for lightweight cryptosystems, to be implemented, for instance, on cheaper smart cards) and $n = 8$ (for cryptosystems implemented on more powerful devices), since $n = 16$ seems still too large for current computational means. We have seen that only one APN permutation, in six variables, is known. It is then important to find as many differentially 4-uniform permutations as possible in even dimension.

Note that if these permutations are involutions, this allows reducing further the complexity of the algorithm, since the same implemented function can then be used for encryption and decryption. Several block ciphers such as AES, Khazad, Anubis, or PRINCE use involutive functions (up to affine equivalence) in their S-boxes. Note that, as already mentioned at page 411 and shown in [136], the 6-variable permutation exhibited in this reference is EA equivalent to an involution.

The smallest differential uniformity and largest nonlinearity achievable by a $(4, 4)$-permutation are respectively 4 and 4 [183, 756]. Up to affine equivalence, there are 16 classes of such permutations. All have algebraic degree 3 and are also optimal against algebraic attacks. Half have a component function of algebraic degree 2, which should be avoided, and half have all their component functions cubic. There are six CCZ equivalence classes.

The smallest differential uniformity and largest nonlinearity achievable by an $(8, 8)$-permutation are respectively 4 and 112 (achieved by Gold, Kasami, and inverse functions).

We describe now the known infinite classes of differentially 4-uniform (n, n)-functions. We begin with the functions obtained by *primary constructions*, starting with power functions:

- The *inverse function* $x^{2^n - 2}$ (the only known involutive differentially 4-uniform (n, n)-permutation; see [521]) for n even first proposed in [908] is used (composed by an affine permutation) for the *S-box of the AES*[26] with $n = 8$. This class of functions has best-known nonlinearity $2^{n-1} - 2^{n/2}$ and has maximum algebraic degree $n - 1$. It is the worst possible against algebraic attacks (which are not efficient on the AES, but some risk exists that they will be improved as they were for stream ciphers) since if we denote $y = x^{-1}$, then we have the bilinear relation $x^2 y = x$.

- The *Gold functions* $x^{2^i + 1}$, where $\gcd(i, n) = 2$ are differentially 4-uniform and they are bijective (*i.e.* $\gcd(2^i + 1, 2^n - 1) = 1$) if and only if $n \equiv 2 \pmod 4$ since, $2^i - 1$ and $2^i + 1$ being coprime, we have $\gcd(2^i + 1, 2^n - 1) = \frac{\gcd(2^{2i} - 1, 2^n - 1)}{\gcd(2^i - 1, 2^n - 1)} = \frac{2^{\gcd(2i,n)} - 1}{2^{\gcd(i,n)} - 1}$ (but n is then not a power of 2 and these functions are quadratic). They have best-known nonlinearity. Gold functions are never involutive.

---

[26] Often represented by a double-entry look-up table with 16 rows and 16 columns, whose indices belong to $\mathbb{F}_2^4$ (and can be written in *hexadecimal* from 0 to f), which provides the $16^2 = 256$ entries (which, when represented in hexadecimal, belong to $\{00, \dots, ff\}$).

- The *Kasami functions* $x^{2^{2i}-2^i+1}$ such that $n \equiv 2$ [mod 4] and $\gcd(i,n) = 2$ are differentially 4-uniform as proved in [669] (see also [604]) and bijective as well, since $\gcd(2^i+1, 2^n-1) = 1$ and since $2^{2i} - 2^i + 1 = \frac{2^{3i}+1}{2^i+1}$ implies $\gcd(2^{2i} - 2^i + 1, 2^n - 1) = \gcd(2^{3i} + 1, 2^n - 1) = \frac{\gcd(2^{6i}-1, 2^n-1)}{\gcd(2^{3i}-1, 2^n-1)} = \frac{2^{\gcd(6i,n)}-1}{2^{\gcd(3i,n)}-1} = 1$ since $2^{3i} - 1$ and $2^{3i} + 1$ are coprime. They are not quadratic but they have the same Walsh spectrum as the Gold functions (thus, with best known nonlinearity). They are in fact rather closely related to quadratic functions, since they have the form $F = R_1 \circ R_2^{-1}$, where R_1 and R_2 are quadratic permutations, which has some similarity with a function CCZ equivalent to a quadratic function. There is a threat that this could be used in a modified version of the higher-order differential attack (but adapting the attack to such kind of function is an open problem). This class of functions never reaches the maximum algebraic degree $n-1$ (but this is not really a problem). Kasami functions are never involutive.

Remark. While all APN permutations have, by definition of APNness, the same differential spectrum, this is different for differentially 4-uniform permutations. For instance, the inverse function and the Gold and Kasami functions have different differential spectra (the inverse function has a better differential spectrum, in which value 4 is obtained less often). More on power functions can be found in [92]. □

- The function $x^{2^{n/2+n/4+1}}$ introduced by Dobbertin [467] and shown by Bracken and Leander to be differentially 4-uniform [120] has best-known nonlinearity $2^{n-1} - 2^{n/2}$ as well. It is bijective (but not involutive) if n is divisible by 4 but not by 8; in this case, n is not a power of 2; the function has algebraic degree 3, which is rather low.
- The APN binomials of Proposition 175 share many properties of Gold power functions. In particular, relaxing conditions on involved parameters leads to differentially 2^t-uniform permutations [121]. Let $n = 3k$ and t be a divisor of k, where $3 \nmid k$ and $\frac{k}{t}$ is odd. Let s be an integer such that $\gcd(3k, s) = t$ and $3|(k + s)$. Then the functions $\alpha x^{2^s+1} + \alpha^{2^k} x^{2^{-k}+2^{k+s}}$, where α is a primitive element of $\mathbb{F}_{2^n}$, are differentially 2^t-uniform and bijective. This class of functions has nonlinearity $2^{n-1} - 2^{(n+t-2)/2}$ if $n+t$ is even and $2^{n-1} - 2^{(n+t-3)/2}$ if $n + t$ is odd. A conjecture of [121] that quadratic quadrinomial APN functions (11.10) allow similar generalization to differentially 2^t-uniform permutations is disproved in [983].
  It is shown in [356], among other results, that for n even, any quadratic differentially 4-uniform permutation has all its $\delta_F(a, b)$ values in $\{0, 4\}$ for $a \neq 0$, has nonlinearity $2^{n-1} - 2^{n/2}$, and is plateaued with single amplitude.
- The author proposed in [241], for constructing differentially 4-uniform permutations, to use the structure of the field $\mathbb{F}_{2^{n+1}}$ instead of that of $\mathbb{F}_{2^n}$ (of course, $\mathbb{F}_{2^{n+r}}$ could be also tried with $r \geq 2$). The idea consists in finding an (N, N)-function, where $N = n + 1$, whose restriction to an affine hyperplane of $\mathbb{F}_{2^N}$ has for image set an affine hyperplane. This restriction provides then an (n, n)-permutation since any affine hyperplane of $\mathbb{F}_{2^N}$ is affinely equivalent to $\mathbb{F}_2^n$. Let the affine hyperplane be $A = u + E$, where E is a linear hyperplane, the restriction to A is differentially 4-uniform if the restriction to A of any derivative in a nonzero direction belonging to E is 2-to-1. An example given in [241] is with the Dickson polynomials D_k, seen at page 389. Recall that every element

of $\mathbb{F}_{2^N}^*$ can be expressed uniquely in the form $h + \frac{1}{h}$ where $h \in \mathbb{F}_{2^{2N}}^*$ – more precisely, $h \in \mathbb{F}_{2^N}^* \cup U$, where $U = \{x^{2^N-1}; x \in \mathbb{F}_{2^{2N}}^*\}$ is the multiplicative subgroup of $\mathbb{F}_{2^{2N}}^*$ of order $2^N + 1$. Then $D_k(h + \frac{1}{h}, 1) = h^k + \frac{1}{h^k}$ by definition. Moreover, the image of $\mathbb{F}_{2^N}$ by this function equals $\{\frac{1}{x}; x \in \mathbb{F}_{2^N}, tr_N(x) = 0\}$ (with the usual convention $\frac{1}{0} = 0$) and the image of $U \setminus \{1\}$ equals $\{\frac{1}{x}; x \in \mathbb{F}_{2^N}, tr_N(x) = 1\}$. If k is coprime with $2^N + 1$, then the mapping $h \mapsto h^k$ is a permutation of $U \setminus \{1\}$ and induces then a permutation of $\{\frac{1}{x}; x \in \mathbb{F}_{2^N}, tr_N(x) = 1\}$, whose expression coincides with $D_k(x, 1)$ on this set. The function $\frac{1}{D_k(\frac{1}{x}, 1)}$ is then a permutation of the hyperplane H of $\mathbb{F}_{2^N}$ of equation $tr_N(x) = 1$. For $k = 3$, N must be even, and we have $D_3(x, 1) = x^3 + x$ and $\frac{1}{\frac{1}{x^3} + \frac{1}{x}} = \frac{x^3}{x^2+1} = x + \frac{1}{x+1} + \frac{1}{x^2+1}$, which is EA equivalent to $\frac{1}{x} + \frac{1}{x^2}$ and is differentially 4-uniform over H. But the argument given in [241] for this last property is not correct: it is written that the function $x \to x + x^2$ is 2-to-1 which is true, and that the inverse function is APN, which is false since N is even. The correct argument is that H excluding 0, the equation $x^{2^n-2} + (x + a)^{2^n-2} = b$ (where $a \neq 0$ and therefore $b \neq 0$ since the inverse function is a permutation) is equivalent to $\frac{1}{x} + \frac{1}{x+a} = b$, that is, $x^2 + ax = \frac{a}{b}$ and has then at most two solutions.

This differentially 4-uniform permutation is in odd dimension. We complete here the study by addressing the case n even: if k is coprime with $2^N - 1$, then the mapping $h \mapsto h^k$ is a permutation of $\mathbb{F}_{2^N}$ and induces then a permutation of $\{\frac{1}{x}; x \in \mathbb{F}_{2^N}, tr_N(x) = 0\}$, whose expression coincides with $D_k(x, 1)$ on this set. The function $\frac{1}{\frac{1}{x^3} + \frac{1}{x}} = x + \frac{1}{x+1} + \frac{1}{x^2+1}$ restricted now to the hyperplane of equation $tr_N(x) = 0$ is bijective. It is differentially 4-uniform since N being odd, the inverse function is APN. And it is shown in [241] that the nonlinearity is at least $2^{n-1} - 2^{\frac{n}{2}+1}$ (not optimal) and the algebraic degree equals $n - 1$. A similar proposal in even dimension is given in [1107].

In [772], Li and Wang have used again the idea of working with functions F over $\mathbb{F}_{2^N}$ with $N = n + 1$, and of taking their restrictions to hyperplanes. They need F to be a quadratic APN permutation over $\mathbb{F}_{2^N}$, and they take N odd so that n is even (then this permutation is AB, but this is not used). They consider for every nonzero $u \in \mathbb{F}_{2^N}$ the linear function $L_u(x) = F(x + u) + F(x) + F(u) + F(0)$, whose range H_u is a linear hyperplane (since F is APN) such that $F(u) + F(0) \notin H_u$ (since F is bijective). Then the restriction of $L_u \circ F^{-1}$ to H_u is injective because $L_u \circ F^{-1}(x_1) = L_u \circ F^{-1}(x_2)$ and $x_1 \neq x_2$ imply $F^{-1}(x_1) + F^{-1}(x_2) = u$, since F is APN, and therefore, $L_u \circ F^{-1}(x_2) = F(F^{-1}(x_2) + u) + F(F^{-1}(x_2)) + F(u) + F(0) = x_1 + x_2 + F(u) + F(0)$, and the relation $x_1 + x_2 = F(u) + F(0) + L_u(F^{-1}(x_2)) \in (F(u) + F(0) + H_u) \cap H_u = \emptyset$ is impossible. This permutation is differentially 4-uniform by construction since L_u is 2-to-1 and F^{-1} is APN; it is then a differentially 4-uniform permutation of H_u. They obtained with F equal to Gold functions three classes of differentially 4-uniform bijections in even dimension with best-known nonlinearity $2^{n-1} - 2^{n/2}$ and algebraic degree $\frac{n}{2} + 1$.

It seems difficult to prove that any of the functions presented in this paragraph is CCZ inequivalent to power functions and to quadratic functions (but we see no reason why such equivalence could happen since the field structures of $\mathbb{F}_{2^n}$ and $\mathbb{F}_{2^N}$ are independent of each other).

We continue now with permutations obtained by modifications of known differentially 4-uniform bijections.

- Qu et al. [982] proposed two classes of differentially 4-uniform bijections in even dimension. These functions were obtained through the switching construction, by adding Boolean functions to the inverse function. The first class has the form $x^{2^n-2} + tr_n(x^2(x+1)^{2^n-2})$. It has optimal algebraic degree $n-1$ and nonlinearity larger than $2^{n-1} - 2^{n/2+1} - 2$. The second class has the form $x^{2^n-2} + tr_n(x^{(2^n-2)d} + (x^{2^n-2} + 1)^d)$, where $d = 3(2^t + 1)$, $2 \leq t \leq n/2 - 1$. It has algebraic degree $n-1$ as well and nonlinearity at least $2^{n-2} - 2^{n/2-1} - 1$. The authors did not study whether their functions are CCZ inequivalent to the inverse function, but this can be checked for even $n = 6, \ldots, 12$ with a computer. A generalized method for constructing differentially 4-uniform permutations in even dimension is presented in the same reference (by determining conditions for their differential uniformity), which includes the former two classes of functions, and produces many CCZ inequivalent differentially 4-uniform bijections in even dimension (the authors could show that the number of CCZ inequivalent differentially 4-uniform permutations over $\mathbb{F}_{2^{2k}}$ grows exponentially when k increases). Zha et al. in [1151], Qu et al. in [981] (who made more systematic the approach of [982] and obtained more functions), Peng and Tan in [938], and Chen et al. in [362] proposed more functions of the form $x^{2^n-2} + g(x)$, where g is a Boolean function (thanks to more precise conditions in the latter reference). In [1146], the authors also built differentially 4-uniform permutations by swapping two values of the inverse function (it is observed that a function $I_{(u,v)}$ over $\mathbb{F}_{2^{2m}}$, obtained from the inverse power function by swapping its values at two different points $u \neq 0$ and $v \neq 0$, is a differentially 4-uniform permutation if and only if $tr_{2m}(uv^{-1})tr(u^{-1}v) = 1)$.

- The author, Tang, Tang, and Liao proposed in [325] the following construction, for $n \geq 6$ even, of differentially 4-uniform (n, n)-permutations of algebraic degree $n-1$:

$$(x_1, \ldots, x_{n-1}, x_n) \mapsto \begin{cases} (1/x', f(x')), & \text{if } x_n = 0 \\ (c/x', f(x'/c) + 1), & \text{if } x_n = 1, \end{cases}$$

where $c \in \mathbb{F}_{2^{n-1}} \setminus \mathbb{F}_2$ is such that $tr_{n-1}(c) = tr_{n-1}(1/c) = 1$, $x' \in \mathbb{F}_{2^{n-1}}$ is identified with $(x_1, \ldots, x_{n-1}) \in \mathbb{F}_2^{n-1}$ and f is an arbitrary Boolean function defined on $\mathbb{F}_{2^{n-1}}$. It is shown in [363] that the particular functions corresponding to $f(x') = tr_{n-1}\left(\frac{1}{x'+1}\right)$ have high nonlinearity and are CCZ inequivalent to all known differentially 4-uniform power permutations and to quadratic functions. It is also shown that the functions in the general class are CCZ inequivalent to the inverse function, and for $n = 2k$, $k = 4, \ldots, 7$, to the sums of the inverse function and of Boolean functions.

- Zha et al. [1150] presented two classes of differentially 4-uniform bijections by applying affine transformations to the inverse function on some subfields. Their functions have maximum algebraic degree $n-1$. The lower bounds on the nonlinearity of these functions would need to be worked further. In [1130], another infinite family of differentially 4-uniform permutations with the same "piecewise" method but starting from Gold functions is provided. Inequivalence to known functions needs to be checked. Peng and Tan in [939], Peng et al. in [940], and Xu and Qu in [1132] presented similar transformations.

Tang et al. [1069], for any even $n \geq 6$, introduced a class of subsets U of $\mathbb{F}_{2^n}$ such that the function equal to $(x+1)^{2^n-2}$ if $x \in U$ and to x^{2^n-2} otherwise gives a differentially 4-uniform permutation. For every even n, at least $2^{2^{n-3}-2^{n/2-2}}$ different such sets U are designed. For every even $n \geq 12$, it is proved that if the size of U is such that $0 < |U| < (2^{n-1} - 2^{n/2})/3 - 2$, then the functions are CCZ inequivalent to known differentially 4-uniform power functions and to quadratic functions. A table of comparison with these other functions is given.

- Li et al. in [773] modified the inverse function by cyclically shifting the images of the function over some subset $\{\alpha_0, \alpha_1, \ldots, \alpha_m\}$ of $\mathbb{F}_{2^n}$. Fu and Feng [521] proposed new families with such cycles of length 3.

- Perrin et al. have introduced in [944] the interesting *butterfly construction*, already seen at page 411, generalized by Canteaut et al. in [199]. It is shown in [523, 944] and [199] that the resulting function is differentially 4-uniform with (best-known) nonlinearity $2^{n-1} - 2^{\frac{n}{2}}$ when, respectively, $R_y(x) = (x+ay)^3 + y^3$, with $a \in \mathbb{F}_{2^{\frac{n}{2}}}^*$, $R_y(x) = (x+ay)^{2^i+1} + y^{2^i+1}$, with $a \in \mathbb{F}_{2^{\frac{n}{2}}}^*$, $\gcd(i,n) = 1$, and $R_y(x) = (x+ay)^3 + by^3$, with $a, b \in \mathbb{F}_{2^{\frac{n}{2}}}^*$, $b \neq (1+a)^3$. More differentially 4-uniform permutations with nonlinearity $2^{n-1} - 2^{\frac{n}{2}}$ are obtained with the butterfly construction in [523].

Fu and Feng studied in [521] if some functions among those recalled in the present subsection could be involutions. They obtained the following involutive differentially 4-uniform permutations:

- Functions of the form $x^{2^n-2} + 1_U(x)$ or $(x+1)^{2^n-2}$ if $x \in U$ and to x^{2^n-2} otherwise, where $U = \mathbb{F}_4$ and in the case $n \equiv 2 \pmod 4$, $U = \mathbb{F}_2$ or $U = \mathbb{F}_4 \setminus \mathbb{F}_2$

- The Peng and Tan function [939]: $F(x) = \begin{cases} b(x+1)^{2^n-2} + a & \text{if } x \in \mathbb{F}_{2^t}, \\ x^{2^n-2} & \text{otherwise,} \end{cases}$ where t divides n and $a = b = 1$, or $a = 0, b = 1, t$ even, or $a = 0, b = 1, t = 1, 3, \frac{n}{2}$ odd, or $a = b \in \mathbb{F}_4 \setminus \mathbb{F}_2, t = 2, \frac{n}{2}$ odd, or $a = 1, tr_n(b^{-1}) = 1$ and $\frac{n}{t}$ odd

- The Peng et al. function [940]: $F(x) = \begin{cases} (c\,x)^{2^n-2} & \text{if } x \in U, \\ x^{2^n-2} & \text{otherwise,} \end{cases}$ where $U = \bigcup_{g \in G} g\,\Gamma$, where Γ is the cyclic multiplicative group generated by γ and $\{g^{-1}, g \in G\} = G$ and $tr_n(\gamma) = tr_n(\gamma^{-1})$ and $tr_n\left(\frac{\gamma}{\frac{g}{g'}\gamma^l + \frac{g'}{g}\gamma^{-l}}\right) = 1$ for every $g, g' \in G$ and every l (with l not divisible by $|\Gamma|$ if $g = g'$)

- The particular case given by Fu and Feng [521] of the Li et al. function [773], modifying the inverse function by cyclically shifting a triple $\{\alpha_0, \alpha_1, \alpha_2\}$ of $\mathbb{F}_{2^n}^*$, where $(\alpha_0, \alpha_1, \alpha_2) = (0, \gamma, \gamma^{-1})$ with $\gamma \in \mathbb{F}_{2^n} \setminus \mathbb{F}_2$, $tr_n(\gamma) = tr_n(\frac{1}{\gamma+1}) = 1$ or $(\alpha_0, \alpha_1, \alpha_2) = (1, \gamma, \gamma^{-1})$ with $\gamma \in \mathbb{F}_{2^n} \setminus \mathbb{F}_2$, $tr_n(\gamma) = tr_n(\frac{1}{\gamma}) = tr_n(\frac{1}{\gamma+1}) = 1$, $tr_n(\frac{1}{(\gamma+1)^3}) = 0$

- The functions $F(x_1, \ldots, x_{n-1}, x_n) = \begin{cases} (1/x', f(x')), & \text{if } x_n = 0 \\ (c/x', f(x'/c) + 1) & \text{if } x_n = 1 \end{cases}$ from [325], where $supp(f) = \emptyset$ or $= \{0\}$

It is observed in [967] that the indicators of the graphs of all the known differentially 4-uniform (n,n)-permutations (n even) have algebraic immunity 2. In [1039], the differential uniformity of the composition of two functions is studied, and new differentially 4-uniform permutations from known ones are constructed.

11.6.5 Other differentially 4-uniform (n, n)-functions

There are differentially 4-uniform functions in odd dimension, which we do not list here since they are less interesting, practically. There are also differentially 4-uniform functions in even dimension that are not permutations. These can be obtained from APN functions by adding a Boolean function, or composing them (on the right or on the left) by 2-to-1 affine functions. Differentially 4-uniform functions that are faster and less costly to compute can be obtained by concatenating the outputs of a bent function and of another function [239]:

1. The function $(x, y) \to (xy, (x^3 + w)(y^3 + w'))$, where w, w' and $\frac{w}{w'}$ belong to $\mathbb{F}_{2^{n/2}} \setminus \{x^3, x \in \mathbb{F}_{2^{n/2}}\}$, with $n/2$ even.
2. The function $(x, y) \to (xy, x^3(y^2 + y + 1) + y^3)$, with $n/2$ odd.
3. The function $F : X \in \mathbb{F}_{2^n} \to (X^{2^{n/2}+1}, (X^{2^{n/2}+1})^3 + wX^3 + (wX^3)^{2^{n/2}})$.

Such functions are not bijective but, because of their low implementation complexity, have an advantage when we wish to protect the cryptosystem against side-channel attacks (see Section 12.1, page 425). For instance, Function 1 above has been used in the cryptosystem PICARO [957]. See more in [239]. Other examples of differentially 4-uniform functions are the function $ax^{2^{2s}+1} + bx^{2^s+1} + cx^{2^{2s}+2^s}$ such that $\gcd(s, n) = 1$ as shown in [115], the function $x^{2^{n-1}-1} + ax^5$ (n odd, $a \in \mathbb{F}_{2^n}$) as shown in [120], and several classes given in [243].

Some constructions of differentially 4-uniform functions have been given in [896], in connection with the structure of a commutative semifield already seen in Chapter 6. A semifield is a finite algebraic structure $(E, +, \circ)$ such that (1) $(E, +)$ is an Abelian group, (2) the operation $\circ$ is distributive on the left and on the right with respect to +, (3) there is no nonzero divisor of 0 in E, and (4) E contains an identity element with respect to $\circ$. This structure has been very useful for constructing planar functions in odd characteristic. In characteristic 2, it may lead to new APN functions and differentially 4-uniform permutations by considering, for instance, the function $(x \circ x) \circ x$ in a classical semifield (there are two classes of them, whose underlying Abelian group is the additive group of $\mathbb{F}_{2^n}$: the Albert semifields, in which the multiplication is $x \circ y = xy + \beta(xy)^\sigma$, where $x \to x^\sigma$ is an automorphism of the field $\mathbb{F}_{2^n}$, which is not a generator and $\beta \notin \{x^{\sigma+1}; x \in \mathbb{F}_{2^n}\}$, and the Knuth semifield where the multiplication is $x \circ y = xy + (xtr(y) + ytr(x))^2$, where tr is a trace function from $\mathbb{F}_{2^n}$ to a suitable subfield).

11.6.6 Other differentially uniform (n, n)-functions

Some results have been found on differential uniformities 6 and 8 for (n, n)-functions; see [93, 95, 1129] and the references therein. In [1160], two methods are proposed for constructing balanced (n, m)-functions (with $m < n$ unfortunately) with nonlinearity strictly larger than $2^{n-1} - 2^{n/2}$ and with "good" other parameters.[27]

---

[27] An inappropriate comparison is made in this paper with a permutation – the one used as S-box in the AES – and with the S-box used in PICARO (designed to resist side-channel attacks, and therefore a little weaker with respect to the other features).

11.6.7 On the best differential uniformity of (n, m)-functions

When $m < n$, (n, m)-functions cannot be used in substitution–permutation networks but they can be used in *Feistel ciphers*, like in the DES cipher which has eight S-boxes each mapping 6 bits to 4 bits. When n is even and $m \leq \frac{n}{2}$, these functions can be bent (*i.e.*, PN), which allows them to oppose optimal resistance against differential and linear attacks, but they are then not balanced and the number of their output bits is small. When $\frac{n}{2} < m < n$, little theoretical work has been done on differentially uniform (n, m)-functions. We know that the differential uniformity of such functions is bounded below by $2^{n-m} + 2$. We call this bound *Nyberg's bound*. Characterizing the pairs (n, m) for which this bound is tight is an open question.

- *In the case $m = n - 1$, Nyberg's bound is tight.* There is indeed a simple way of designing differentially 4-uniform $(n, n - 1)$-functions: any function of the form $L \circ F$, where F is an APN (n, n)-function and L is a surjective affine $(n, n - 1)$-function, is indeed differentially 4-uniform. Using such an S-box in a Feistel cipher can be seen as using the APN function itself.

  In [255] an alternate way to construct differentially 4-uniform $(n, n - 1)$-functions by defining their look-up table (LUT) as the concatenation of the LUT of two APN $(n - 1, n - 1)$-functions is studied; the corresponding function $S(x, x_n) = x_n F(x) + (1 + x_n)G(x)$ is a differentially 4-uniform $(n, n - 1)$-function if and only if, for every $a \in \mathbb{F}_{2^{n-1}}$, the function $F(x) + G(x + a)$ is at most 2-to-1 (*i.e.*, each value in the image set has at most two corresponding preimages).

  The particular case where the two APN functions differ by an affine function provides, when one of these functions is a Gold function, the family of quadratic differentially 4-uniform $(n, n - 1)$-functions $(x, x_n) \mapsto x^{2^i+1} + x_n x$, where $x \in \mathbb{F}_{2^{n-1}}$ and $x_n \in \mathbb{F}_2$ with $\gcd(i, n - 1) = 1$, whose Walsh transform and nonlinearity are studied, as well as the CCZ inequivalence to all functions of the form $L \circ F$ above.

- In [259], (n, m)-functions achieving Nyberg's bound with equality are studied in the (Maiorana–McFarland) form $F(x, z) = I(x)\phi(z)$, where $I(x)$ is the (m, m)-*inverse function*[28] and $\phi(z)$ is an $(n - m, m)$-function. An infinite family of differentially $(2^{m-1} + 2)$-uniform $(2m - 1, m)$-functions with $m \geq 3$ is designed (which also have high nonlinearity and not too low algebraic degree). Hence, *Nyberg's bound is tight for $m = \frac{n+1}{2}$, $n \geq 5$ odd*.

  Differentially 4-uniform $(m + 1, m)$-functions in this form are also designed, and a method is proposed to construct infinite families of $(m + k, m)$-functions with low differential uniformity, leading to an infinite family of $(2m - 2, m)$-functions with $\delta \leq 2^{m-1} - 2^{m-6} + 2$ for any $m \geq 8$. But this does not provide functions achieving Nyberg's bound with equality and the existence of such (n, m)-functions for $\frac{n}{2} + 1 \leq m \leq n - 2$ is open.

  In fact, it is even an open problem to determine whether there exist differentially δ-uniform $(n, n - k)$ functions with $k \geq 2$, k significantly smaller than $\frac{n}{2}$, $\delta < 2^{k+1}$, and $n > 5$ ($\delta = 2^{k+1}$ is easily reached with functions $L \circ F$ where F is an APN (n, n)-function and L is an affine surjective $(n, n - k)$-function). In particular, the existence of

---

[28] The only function that returned positive results when we made a computer investigation.

differentially 6-uniform $(n, n - 2)$-functions for $n > 5$ is an open question (differentially 6-uniform $(5, 3)$-functions are known [255]). In [15], Alsalami built more differentially 4-uniform $(n, n - 1)$-functions and differentially 8-uniform $(n, n - 2)$-functions.

In [949], several evolutionary algorithms and problem sizes were explored in order to find such functions. The results of this investigation show that the problem, which is easy in dimensions 4 and 5, is very difficult for larger n.

Recent uses of Boolean and vectorial functions and related problems

Many mathematical problems in computer science result in questions regarding Boolean functions (or vectorial functions). Cryptography has been no exception since the 1950s, and new roles of Boolean functions still emerge nowadays. In this chapter, we give several examples of recent problematics in cryptography that result in new questions about Boolean functions, vectorial functions, and related codes, or that renew the interest of some known notions.

12.1 Physical attacks and related problems on functions and codes

Until the 1990s, cryptographers implicitly considered the *black box attacker model* only, in which the cryptanalyst has access to ciphertexts (in the ciphertext-only attacker model) or to plaintext–ciphertext pairs (in the known-plaintext and the chosen-plaintext models), but has no information beyond input/output. This was realistic when the ciphers were run only on computers, all the more if these were protected (by a Faraday cage, for instance). But nowadays, cryptographic algorithms are run often on mobile devices, on smart cards (which include a part of hardware and work with software implementations), or on light hardware devices (*e.g.*, field-programmable gate arrays [FPGA], application-specific integrated circuits [ASIC]). Side-channel information (through the running-time, power consumption, electromagnetic emanations, etc.) is then accessible.

The *side-channel attacks* (*SCA*) (see [712, 713, 984]) on the implementations of block ciphers[1] in such embedded systems, (see [823]) take advantage of this additional information obtained through the physical environment. They are able to treat this information for extracting the secret parameters of the algorithm and are in practice extremely powerful. They assume an *attacker model* different from classical attacks: the *gray box attacker model*, in which the adversary has also access to leakage. This additional information is all the more usable on block ciphers, which are iterative: each round involves diffusion layers and substitution layers; both kinds are necessary for security, and the diffusion needs several rounds before being effective; the SCA can then be very efficient by attacking the first round (while in the black box model, only the global cipher is attackable) or the last round (the first round of the reverse cipher); see the survey [320].

The exploited *leakage* is a measurable quantity (in the case of a so-called *monovariate attack* or *univariate attack* on a single leakage[2]) depending on the data manipulated by the

---

[1] SCA also exist on asymmetric ciphers, but this is out of the scope of this book, and they have not been as developed for stream ciphers as they were for block ciphers.

[2] Multivariate attacks are more difficult to perform in practice.

algorithm (the key is mixed with the data, and any leakage that depends on this data can be used as an oracle). The important data for SCA are the values of the so-called *sensitive variables* of the algorithm. These are variables whose values are in general stored in registers and which depend on the (varying) input to the algorithm (assumed known by the attacker), and on the (constant) secret key (or better for the attacker, on a part of the secret key, since this allows for a divide-and-conquer approach, where the key is recovered byte by byte, a customary case in block ciphers being when the cipher computes the sum of a public binary vector and of a subsequence of the round key). The length n of such variable is a number depending on the cipher (4 if the cipher works on nibbles, 8 if it works on bytes, 16 if it works on words, etc.).

The attacker records, for instance, the emanations emitted by the register on which the values of the sensitive variable are stored, which can be approximated as a real-valued function $\mathcal{L}$ of the sensitive variable (the register is a micrometric object, whose contents cannot, in general, be measured directly). For instance, in the so-called *Hamming weight leakage model*, $\mathcal{L}(Z)$ equals the Hamming weight of Z; in the *Hamming distance leakage model*, $\mathcal{L}(Z)$ is the Hamming distance between two consecutive values of the register where Z is stored; in more general *linear leakage models*, $\mathcal{L}(Z)$ equals a linear combination with real coefficients of the bits of Z (we speak then of a static linear leakage model, needed to ensure that the leakages corresponding to different shares are independent), or of the differences between the bits at two consecutive states of the register. In what the attacker records, $\mathcal{L}$ is added with inevitable noise $\mathcal{N}$, generally viewed as a white Gaussian variable, due to the activity in the device around the register (an attacker can only measure an aggregated function of each computing element's leakage, such as the total current drawn by the circuit) and depending on the choice of the leakage model (a good choice minimizes the noise). The part independent of the noise in the leak is called the *deterministic leak*. The attacker tests exhaustively all the possible values of the key bits involved in the sensitive variable, computing for each choice the corresponding *modeled leakage* value, the correct key values being those that maximize statistically (for a series of runs with the same key and different plaintexts) the dependency between the modeled leakage (which depends on the tested key value and the plaintext, and also on the leakage model chosen for the attack) and the measured leakage. This dependency can be evaluated by different statistical methods, leading to different SCA. For instance, in *differential power analysis (DPA)* [713] or more general differential analyses, the statistical distinguisher is the difference of means between the two cases (among all plaintexts used) where the leak is larger, resp. smaller, than some fixed value. If the guessed key is correct, then the modeled difference should be close to a nonzero constant, while if it is wrong, it should be close to zero (the two means measuring then a same random variable). In *correlation power analysis (CPA)* or more general correlation analyses, the statistical distinguisher is Pearson's (linear) correlation coefficient (which is more complex to evaluate but more efficient), equal to the covariance between the two values, divided by the product of their standard deviations.

The attacker starts with a first-order attack, in which the leakage is handled as is. It can be proved that this first-order attack is successful if the conditional expectation $\mathbb{E}(\mathcal{L}|Z = z)$ depends on z. If it does not, then the attacker can try successively a second-order attack, which mixes the observations of two leakages (and if these two leakages are the same, the attacker takes then the square of a single leakage[3] in a so-called zero-offset CPA [1100]; we shall consider only this case in the sequel, to simplify the presentation), a third-order attack, etc., increasing the order of the attack until it is successful. The complexity of such *higher-order side-channel attack* (*HO-SCA*) [381, 803, 879, 920, 1047] depends then on the smallest value of the order j such that the conditional expectation $\mathbb{E}(\mathcal{L}^j | Z = z)$ depends on z; see [264]. It is shown in this latter reference that the complexity of the attack (in time and in the number of measuring events – called traces, see below – which is needed) is exponential in the order, essentially because the noise associated to $\mathcal{L}^j$ is exponential in j. Relative to the noise, the leaked information decreases exponentially with the order j; it is proportional to V^{-j}, where V is the variance of the noise $\mathcal{N}$. This is where the choice of the leakage model plays a role: a bad choice will increase the variance of the noise.

SCA are mainly statistical attacks, and the measures are made several times, each time providing a so-called *leakage trace*. Usually, traces are assumed independent and identically distributed.[4] The measure quantifies as we saw above the running time, the power consumption, the electromagnetic radiations of the cryptographic computation, or even the photonic emission. Depending on the execution platform, the part of the leakage due to one bit can be modeled according to its activity (the leakage is observed when the bit changes values; this is the case of complementary metal-oxide-semiconductor [CMOS] technology) or its value (the leakage differs according to the bit's state; this can be viewed as a particular case of the former case). If every bit of a sensitive variable leaks an identical amount, irrespective of its neighbors, we are in the so-called Hamming distance (resp. weight) leakage model (see more in [262]). The measure is inevitably imprecise and noisy as we saw above with HO-SCA, but if the cryptosystem is not protected against SCA, the resulting attack can be devastating (an unprotected AES can be attacked in a few seconds with a few traces while its security against classical attacks is still nowadays of 128 bits, which corresponds to a huge amount of computation time, even for thousands of computers in parallel). In particular, *continuous side-channel attacks* in which the adversary gets information at each invocation of the cryptosystem are especially threatening [713].

SCA are not the only threats on block ciphers, since *fault injection attacks* (*FIA*) can also be performed, which aim at extracting the secret key when the algorithm is running over some device, by injecting some fault in the computation, so as to obtain exploitable differences at the output. For instance, differential fault analysis (DFA) attacks, first proposed by Biham and Shamir [83], use information obtained from an incorrectly functioning implementation of an algorithm to derive the secret information. The AES can be attacked this way (see, *e.g.*, [91]) as well as stream ciphers [606]. These attacks can be noninvasive and perturb internal data (for example, with electromagnetic impulses), without damaging the system, and leaving then no evidence that they have been perpetrated.

Masking. The implementations of cryptosystems need to include countermeasures to *physical attacks* (SCA and FIA). A sound approach against SCA is to use a *secret sharing*

---

[3] This case is more frequent in hardware; two distinct leakages are more exploitable in software because it is easier to determine the exact distinct timings of two leakages than to distinguish them when they happen in parallel; note, however, that the improved capabilities of modern microprocessors more and more allow parallel software computing.

[4] Adaptative adversarial strategies are seldom conferring a significant advantage, compared to nonadaptative strategies.

scheme (see page 145), often called *masking* in the context of side-channel attacks.[5] This method, which aims at amplifying the impact of the noise in the adversary's observations and at randomizing the secret-dependent internal values of the algorithm from one execution to another, is efficient both for implementations in smart cards and FPGA or ASIC (in the former case, the shares are usually manipulated in serial, while in the latter, they are manipulated in parallel). This approach consists, for a given *masking order d*, in splitting each sensitive variable[6] Z of the implementation into $d + 1$ shares $M_0, \ldots, M_d$ such that Z can be recovered from these shares, but no information can be recovered from less than $d + 1$ shares, *i.e.*, Z is a deterministic function of all the M_i, but is independent of $(M_i)_{i \in I}$ if $|I| \leqslant d$. The simplest way (called *Boolean masking*) of achieving this is to draw $M_1, \ldots, M_d$ at random from the space in which lives Z (the M_i are then called *masks* and are redrawn fresh at every encryption) and to take M_0 such that $M_0 + \cdots + M_d$ equals Z, where $+$ is a relevant group operation (in practice, the bitwise XOR). The masks change at every computation. This countermeasure allows resisting the SCA of order d. For instance, for $d = 1$ and if the leakage is the Hamming weight w_H, then instead of having traces corresponding to $w_H(Z)$, the attacker will have traces corresponding to $w_H(Z + M, M) = w_H(Z + M) + w_H(M)$ (note that the individual leak from any of the two shares is useless since it does not give information, being individually random); we assume here that the attacker cannot separate the two leaks (which is more difficult with hardware than with smart cards, as we explained above); if he or she can, the designer needs to take d larger. It can be checked that the first-order attack is then no longer successful. It has been also proposed (see [562, 974]) to use Shamir's $(\ell, d + 1)$ secret sharing scheme (see page 145) rather than Boolean masking (for which the information on the shared data is relatively easy to rebuild from the observed shares, which simplifies the task of the attacker). The advantages of such a masking method are studied in [340], where it is shown that it may be more advantageous for the attacker (in terms of attack complexity) to observe strictly more than $d + 1$ shares (while it could seem natural that observing strictly more than $d + 1$ shares is inappropriate for the attacker since it provides more noise), thanks to the existence of so-called *linear exact repairing codes* (which allow reconstruction from less information than Lagrange's interpolation, thanks to polynomial interpolation formulae that optimize the amount of information which needs to be extracted), and that the choice of the public points (the α_i at page 145) has an impact on the countermeasure strength.

Security. We see with HO-SCA that, since the complexity of mounting a successful side-channel attack increases exponentially with the order of the attack, then when applied against a masked implementation, it grows exponentially with the masking order. Hence, it is always possible, theoretically, to protect a cryptosystem against SCA by masking, but this needs practically to change in the algorithm every function $x \mapsto F(x)$ (that we shall assume to be an (n, n)-function to simplify; the general case is similar) into a function[7] $(m_0, \ldots, m_d) \mapsto (m'_0, \ldots, m'_d)$ such that, if $m_0, \ldots, m_d$ are shares of x, then $m'_0, \ldots, m'_d$ are shares of $F(x)$ (we shall say that such function $(m_0, \ldots, m_d) \mapsto (m'_0, \ldots, m'_d)$ is the *masked version of function F*), and such that the d-th order security property is satisfied. The latter property, which is equivalent to the *probing security model* introduced in [637], states that every tuple

---

[5] Other methods exist: threshold implementations and multiparty computation; see below.
[6] We denote random variables by capital letters.
[7] We denote set or space elements by lower case letters.

of d or less intermediate variables is independent of the secret parameters of the algorithm.[8] When satisfied, it guarantees that no attacker able to learn at most d intermediate results (called *probes*) of a computation can succeed in an attack of order lower than or equal to d. This model, which is a simplified version of the behavior of a device in the real world (in which physical leakages reveal some information on the whole computation), allows thanks to its simplicity to build efficient compilers transforming (at a cost that is quadratic in d) any circuit into a secure one in the probing model (see a survey in the introduction of [49]). A more realistic and more complex model was proposed in [880] , and improved in [973] into the *noisy leakage model*, which was studied further and improved in [487], where the so-called *statistical distance* was introduced, allowing one to show that constructions proved secure in the probing security model are also secure in the noisy leakage model, provided that the probing order is a large enough function of the noisy leakage order. A last improvement can be found in [564].

An a priori weaker notion of d-th order resistance has been introduced in [897] to characterize the security of parallel implementations, for which higher-order probing security can never be achieved because all shares are treated within one single cycle. It is called the *bounded moment security model* and has been studied in several papers (see, *e.g.*, [49]). A masking scheme is secure at order d in this model if no moment of degree d in the intermediate variables depends on the secret. It is more appropriate for hardware. Indeed, the appropriate model and, hence, the kind of masking scheme to be applied depends on the capabilities of the execution platform: embedded software devices such as smart cards can execute operations sequentially, but need to rely on smaller memories (which are constrained resources); therefore, functions such as S-boxes are preferentially *recomputed* [972, section 2.1], while FPGAs are able to execute several operations in parallel, and can leverage on large memory blocks (called Block Random Access Memory [BRAM]); in such a context, masked functions can be simply tabulated, *i.e.*, computed in one clock cycle (such strategy is also referred to as *Global Look-Up Table* [972, section 3.2]). Therefore, masked computations in smart cards require end-to-end security, whereas masked computations in FPGAs can resort to large tabulated functions where only data representation (*i.e.*, tables input and output) shall be secured. Note, however, that if the need in memory appears too important, we can change the algorithm so that, instead of working on $\mathbb{F}_{2^n}$, it works in $\mathbb{F}_{2^{n/k}}$ for some k which provides a time–memory trade-off.

Reductions between the leakage security models seen above are studied in [49] (it is proved in particular that probing security for a serial implementation implies bounded moment security for its parallel counterpart, and that simple refreshing algorithms with linear complexity that are not secure in the continuous probing model are secure in the continuous bounded moment model). When probing and bounded moment security models are considered at the bit level, then they are equivalent [577]. Note that there also exists a parameter quantifying the resistance of S-boxes to DPA, called the (modified) transparency order [343]; we shall not address it here.

Until recently, no method was known for securely composing masked (elementary) functions ensuring d-probing security with a (tight) number $d + 1$ of shares. This problem

---

[8] Note that when the algorithm handles vectors, in $\mathbb{F}_2^n$, there are different ways of interpreting the definition, according to whether it refers to intermediate variables as vectors or as individual bits; we shall then specify *bit-probing security* when needed.

has been solved in [48] thanks to the introduction of the security notions of *t-(strong) noninterference (S)NI* (any set of at most *t* intermediate variables can be perfectly simulated with at most *t* shares of each input, and in the case of strong NI, at most $t - t_{out}$ shares, where t_{out} is the number of output variables among the *t* ones), and optimized in [55] (where is shown that some masked S-boxes may be composed without refreshing).

Security at order one against SCA is nowadays considered insufficient in both models for most practical operational environments. Detecting a single fault is also insufficient. Second-order resistance to both side-channel analysis and fault injection resistance (in a "mask then encode" procedure, which is more efficient than "encode then mask" in terms of variable size growth, but care must be taken on the way the redundancy is applied) may be sufficient[9] (but without a security margin taking into account future improvements of SCA).

Masking functions. If a function F is linear (like diffusion layers – MixColumns and ShiftRows in AES), then we can take $m'_i = F(m_i)$ for designing its masked version. A little more generally, if a function is affine (like the round key addition – AddRoundKey in AES), it can be masked at no extra cost.

If a function F is not affine (which is the case of a substitution layer – SubBytes in AES), then we can design its masked version as follows: assuming that the input to F lives in $\mathbb{F}_{2^n}$ (which is always possible since we assume it lives in a vector space over $\mathbb{F}_2$, and $\mathbb{F}_{2^n}$ is an n-dimensional vector space over $\mathbb{F}_2$), it is a univariate polynomial function (see page 41) and its computation can be decomposed into a sequence of additions and multiplications in the field. The operations of addition, scalar multiplication, and squaring being linear functions, they can be masked at no extra cost (see above). For masking multiplication, there is a method called the *ISW algorithm* (ISW stands for Ishai–Sahai–Wagner), which is introduced in [637] for the case of $\mathbb{F}_2$ and generalized to $\mathbb{F}_{2^n}$ in [996].

Algorithm 3: Higher-order masking scheme ISW for multiplication.

Input : sharings $(a_0, a_1, \ldots, a_d)$ and $(b_0, b_1, \ldots, b_d)$ of a and b in $\mathbb{F}_{2^n}$
Output: a sharing $(c_0, c_1, \ldots, c_d)$ of $c = a \times b$

1 Randomly generate $d(d+1)/2$ elements $r_{ij} \in \mathbb{F}_{2^n}$ indexed such that $0 \leqslant i < j \leqslant d$
2 **for** $i = 0$ **to** d **do**
3   **for** $j = i + 1$ **to** d **do**
4         $r_{j,i} \leftarrow (r_{i,j} + a_i \times b_j) + a_j \times b_i$
5   **end**
6 **end**
7 **for** $i = 0$ **to** d **do**
8     $c_i \leftarrow a_i \times b_i$
9   **for** $j = 0$ **to** d, $j \neq i$ **do**
10         $c_i \leftarrow c_i + r_{i,j}$
11   **end**
12 **end**
13 **return** $(c_0, c_1, \ldots, c_d)$

---

[9] Some palliative countermeasures may then be needed, consisting for instance in desynchronization, random interrupts or dummy operations; such palliative countermeasures are not sufficient on their own.

The time complexity and the amount of random data that needs to be generated for the ISW algorithm are both quadratic in d (see more in [320]).

Other methods[10] exist like in [974] (they are surveyed in [54]; see also [563]), which we do not detail since they do not pose, so far, new questions on Boolean and vectorial functions.

We see that the designer of the block cipher implementation has some advantage over the attacker, because increasing d raises exponentially the complexity of the attack and only quadratically the complexity of the countermeasure. However, countermeasures are costly in terms of running time and program executable file size (in software applications) or of implementation area (in hardware applications). For example, in software with 8-bit AVR architecture, an AES without masking runs in few hundreds of cycles or few thousands, while with masking it needs already about 40,000 cycles for first order; moreover, the program executable file size is also increased because of the need to mask S-boxes (see https://github.com/ANSSI-FR/secAES-ATmega8515/). In hardware, the implementation area is roughly tripled. The cost overhead may be too high for real-world products, all the more when the order of probing security is larger than 1. But the implementation (including masking) must be efficient today, while the SCA can be performed in the future.

We need then to minimize the implementation and memory complexities of the counter-measures. This is where Boolean and vectorial functions can play a role.

12.1.1 A new role of correlation immunity and of the dual distance of codes related to side-channel attack countermeasures

Correlation immune Boolean functions (see Definition 21, page 86), allow reducing in two possible ways the cost overhead due to masking, while keeping the same resistance to dth-order SCA in the bounded moment security model (and possibly the same order of probing security, but this depends on the implementation) when the leak is a linear combination over the reals of the bits of the sensitive variable, added with a Gaussian noise (this assumption on the leak is rather realistic and the assumption on the noise is almost always the case in literature):

- By applying a method called *leakage squeezing*, which allows achieving with one single mask the same protection of registers against higher-order SCA as with d ones, where d is an integer strictly larger than 1 that we shall define. This method, which allows making optimal the representation of the shares and maximizes the resistance order against high-order side-channel attacks, has been introduced in [811] and further studied in [263, 810] (an extremely close countermeasure has been introduced independently in [132]). It uses a bijective vectorial function F that is applied to modify the mask (this is a reason why the method is better adapted to hardware since we need to apply F^{-1} at some point, and in hardware this can be made more easily as we explained, but millions of smart cards built by industry nowadays include leakage squeezing as well). The pair (M_0, M_1) such that $M_0 + M_1 = Z$ is not processed as is in the device, but in the form of $(M_0, F(M_1))$. The condition for achieving resistance to d-th order SCA in the bounded moment security model is proved in [263, 810, 811]: assuming that the

---

[10] One (the threshold implementation) will be seen in Subsection 12.1.4, page 436; its complexity is higher while it addresses a more difficult situation than the ISW algorithm.

leakage model is a pseudo-Boolean function of numerical degree (see Definition 13, page 48) at most d (which is the case of the dth power of a degree 1 leakage), it is that the graph *indicator* of F, that is, the $2n$-variable Boolean function whose support equals the graph $\{(x, y); \; y = F(x)\}$ of F, is d-th order correlation immune. Such graph is a *complementary information set code (CIS)* in the sense that it admits (at least) two *information set*s (see page 314) that are complementary of each other; see [280]. The condition that the indicator of this CIS code is d-th order correlation immune is equivalent to saying that the *dual distance* of this code is at least $d + 1$ (according to Corollary 6, page 88), which is coherent with what was observed by Massey [827] already in 1993. For instance, a rate $\frac{1}{2}$ [16, 8, 5] linear code can be used. But it is shown in [810] that there exists a nonlinear code that achieves better: it is the Nordstrom–Robinson code of parameters $(16, 256, 6)$. A comprehensive study of CIS codes has been made in [280], and it is shown in [264] that the mutual information between the sensitive data and the leakage vanishes exponentially with the noise variance, at a rate that is proportional to the dual distance.

The method of leakage squeezing has been later generalized in [262] to several masks. Compared to first-order leakage squeezing, second-order leakage squeezing is more efficient, since it increments by one unit at least the resistance against high-order attacks, with an appropriate (a priori different) code. In fact, it improves it more, since better improvements have been realized by relevant choices of squeezing bijections. But the optimal solutions are more difficult to find than in the case with one mask. When the masking is applied on bytes (as in AES), optimal leakage squeezing with one mask resists HO-SCA of orders up to 5 (with the Nordstrom–Robinson code), and with two masks, resistance against HO-SCA of order 7 is provided. The study of the corresponding higher-order CIS codes has been made in [277]. A rate $\frac{1}{3}$ [24,8,8] linear code (maximal minimal distance) with three disjoint information sets fulfills the conditions.

- An alternative way of resisting higher-order SCA with one single mask consists in avoiding processing the mask at all: for every sensitive variable Z that is the input to some box S in the block cipher, Z is replaced by $Z + M$, where M is drawn at random, and $Z + M$ is the input to a "masked" box S_M whose output is a masked version of $S(Z)$ (and the process of masking continues similarly during the whole implementation, only the very last step being eventually unmasked to give the result). This method is called *rotating S-box masking* (RSM) [898]. It needs, for each box S in the cipher, to implement a look-up table for each masked box S_M. This is particularly well adapted to hardware: all S-boxes are then addressed in parallel, for a better throughput; the attacker is not able to know which S-box is addressed for a given value of M; he/she is only able to identify that the S-boxes have been looked up, but the order in which they are queried is indistinguishable from his/her standpoint; he/she is limited to collecting an aggregated function of all S-boxes. This being said, many smart cards implement RSM nowadays as well, still more than leakage squeezing.

To reduce the cost, M is not drawn at random in the whole set of binary vectors of the same length as Z, but in a smaller set of such vectors, say E. The condition for achieving resistance to d-th order SCA in the bounded moment security model is that the indicator function 1_E is a d-th order correlation immune function, *i.e.*, that E viewed as a code has dual distance at least $d + 1$ [74, 286]. This is because, for any $j \leq d$, the mean of $w_H^j(Z + M)$ when Z has some fixed value z equals $\frac{1}{|E|} \sum_{m \in E} w_H^j(z + m) = \frac{1}{|E|} \sum_{m \in \mathbb{F}_2^n} 1_E(m) \, w_H^j(z + m) = \frac{1}{|E|} 1_E \otimes w_H^j(z) = \frac{1}{2^n |E|} \widehat{1_E} \times \widehat{w_H^j}(z)$, according to Relation (2.45), page 60, and this mean is independent of z if and only if $\widehat{1_E} \times \widehat{w_H^j}(a) = 0$ for every $a \neq 0_n$, while we know that w_H^j, which has numerical degree j, satisfies that $\widehat{w_H^j}(a) = 0$ if and only if $w_H(a) > j$.

Given d, we wish to choose this d-th order correlation immune function 1_E with lowest possible (nonzero) weight, since the size of the overhead due to the masked look-up tables is proportional to the size of the set.[11]

In [289], it is shown that the security notion (at bit level, *i.e.*, in $\mathbb{F}_2$) corresponds in these two cases to d-probing and d-th order bounded moment security models.

Leakage squeezing and RSM needing correlation immune functions of low weights (with a particular shape in the case of leakage squeezing since the function must then be the graph indicator of a permutation, see more in [244]), this has posed a new problematic on Boolean functions, which we began to address at pages 303 and following (further work is needed). Most of the numerous studies made (mostly in the 1990s) on correlation immune functions in the framework of stream ciphers (see page 86) dealt with *resilient* (balanced) functions and do not apply to low-weight correlation immune functions.

12.1.2 Vectorial functions in univariate form: minimizing the number of nonlinear multiplications for reducing the cost of countermeasures

In [297], properties that an S-box could possess for being more resilient against side-channel attacks, such as the (near) preservation of Hamming weight and a small Hamming distance between input and output are studied; the incidences on the nonlinearity and differential uniformity are determined.

Additional protections, like masking, are in any case unavoidable. We have seen that the complexity of masking additions and linear multiplications (like, for instance, $x \times x$) is negligible compared to that of masking nonlinear multiplications. To efficiently mask an algorithm, we need to minimize the *masking complexity* of each S-box, that is, the minimum number of nonlinear multiplications needed to implement it. This parameter is affine invariant.

When the S-box is a power function $F(x) = x^d$ like in the AES, minimizing the number of nonlinear multiplications results in a variant of the classical problem of minimizing addition chains in a group (see [284]); determining the masking complexity amounts to finding the addition chain for d with the least number of additions that are not doublings. For instance, the *inverse function* $x \to x^{254} = x^{-1}$ in $\mathbb{F}_{2^8}$ can be implemented with four nonlin-

---

[11] Note, however, that if the cipher is made like the AES, with identical substitution boxes up to affine equivalence, the substitution layer can be slightly modified so as to be masked at no extra cost: the affine equivalent boxes are replaced by masked versions of a same box; namely, the 16 byte masks that can be applied to the 16 boxes are the codewords of the $[8, 4, 4]$ self-dual code.

ear multiplications, in many ways (we saw one at page 401; note that the well-known square-and-multiply algorithm for computing the inverse needs more than four multiplications).

When the S-box is a general polynomial, minimizing the number of nonlinear multiplications is a new paradigm. It is proved in [382] that, for every positive integer n, there exists a polynomial $P(x) \in \mathbb{F}_{2^n}[x]$ with masking complexity:

$$\mathcal{MC}(P) \geq \sqrt{\frac{2^n}{n}} - 2. \tag{12.1}$$

There exist several methods for trying to minimize the multiplicative complexity,[12] $\mathcal{MC}(P)$ of polynomials P and allowing their probing secure evaluation at minimized cost. We refer to [284, 320] for more details. The two first methods are provable and the two last are heuristic[13] (and more efficient in practice)

- The *cyclotomic method* consists in rewriting $P(x)$ in the form:

$$P(x) = u_0 + \sum_{i=1}^{q} L_i(x^{\alpha_i}) + u_{2^n-1} x^{2^n-1},$$

where q is a positive integer and $(L_i)_{i \leq q}$ is a family of linear functions. Since the transformations $x \in \mathbb{F}_{2^n} \mapsto x^{2^j}$ are $\mathbb{F}_2$-linear, their masking complexity is null. This implies that the masking complexity of $\sum_{i=1}^{q} L_i(x^{\alpha_i})$ is bounded above by the number of nonlinear multiplications required to evaluate all the monomials x^{α_i}, that is, by $\sum_{\delta | (2^n-1)} \frac{\varphi(\delta)}{\mu(\delta)} - 1$, where $\mu(m)$ denotes the multiplicative order of 2 modulo m and φ the Euler's totient function.

- The *Knuth–Eve method* is based on a recursive use of the observation that any polynomial $P(x)$ of degree t over $\mathbb{F}_{2^n}[x]$ can be written in the form

$$P(x) = P_1(x^2) \oplus P_2(x^2)x,$$

where $P_1(x)$ and $P_2(x)$ have degrees bounded above by $\lfloor t/2 \rfloor$. This implies that the masking complexity of $P(x)$ is at most

$$\begin{cases} 3 \cdot 2^{(n/2)-1} - 2 & \text{if } n \text{ is even,} \\ 2^{(n+1)/2} - 2 & \text{if } n \text{ is odd.} \end{cases}$$

- The *Coron–Roy–Vivek (CRV) method* [382] starts with a union $\mathcal{C}$ of cyclotomic classes $\mathcal{C}_i$ in $\mathbb{Z}/(2^n - 1)\mathbb{Z}$, such that all power functions x^j, $j \in \mathcal{C}$, can be processed with a global small enough number of nonlinear multiplications. This set of monomials x^j spans a subspace $\mathcal{P}$ of $\mathbb{F}_{2^n}[x]$. A polynomial $R \in \mathbb{F}_{2^n}[x_1, \ldots, x_t]$ is searched such that

$$P(x) = R(P_1(x), \ldots, P_t(x)),$$

where the P_i are taken in $\mathcal{P}$. Denoting by μ the number of nonlinear multiplications required to build $\mathcal{C}$, the search tries to minimize $\mathcal{MC}(R) + \mu$. A heuristic approach (in order to speed up the process) is proposed:

---

[12] This term is meant here at the $\mathbb{F}_{2^n}$ field level; it can be also considered at the bit level, in relation with bitsliced implementations; see, *e.g.*, [565] and the references therein.

[13] In the sense of "not proved."

1. Build the union set $\mathcal{C}$ such that all the powers of P's monomials are in $\mathcal{C} + \mathcal{C}$.
2. Choose and fix a set of r polynomials $P_1(x), \ldots, P_r(x)$ in $\mathcal{P}$ and search for $r + 1$ polynomials $P_{r+1}(x), \ldots, P_{2r+1}(x)$ in $\mathcal{P}$ such that

$$P(x) = \sum_{i=1}^{r} P_i(x) \times P_{r+i}(x) + P_{2r+1}(x). \tag{12.2}$$

Thanks to the fact that $P_1(x), \ldots, P_r(x)$ have been fixed, this results in solving a linear system of $n2^n$ Boolean equations in at most $\min(r, |\mathcal{C}|) \times |\mathcal{C}| + |\mathcal{C}|$ unknowns. The condition $2^n \leqslant |\mathcal{C}| \times (1 + \min(r, |\mathcal{C}|))$ ensures then that the method outputs at least one solution. The complexity of the resulting probing secure method is $\mathcal{O}(\sqrt{2^n/n})$, which is asymptotically better than the complexity of Knuth–Eve's method. Moreover, a comparison of Coron's complexity with Inequality (12.1) shows that it is asymptotically optimal.

- The *CPRR method* [321] is more recent and based on another algebraic decomposition heuristic principle (CPRR stands for Carlet–Prouff–Rivain–Roche). It decomposes $P(x)$ by means of functions of low algebraic degree, and designs efficient probing-secure evaluation methods for such low-degree functions. The decomposition step starts by deriving a family of generators: $\begin{cases} G_1(x) = F_1(x) \\ G_i(x) = F_i(G_{i-1}(x)) \end{cases}$, where the F_i are random polynomials of algebraic degree s. Then it randomly generates t polynomials $Q_i = \sum_{j=1}^{r} L_j \circ G_j$, where the L_j are linearized polynomials. Eventually, it searches for t polynomials P_i of algebraic degree s and for $r + 1$ linearized polynomials L_i such that

$$P(x) = \sum_{i=1}^{t} P_i\big(Q_i(x)\big) + \sum_{i=1}^{r} L_i\big(G_i(x)\big) + L_0(x).$$

As in the CRV method, the search for polynomials P_i and L_i amounts to solving a system of linear equations over $\mathbb{F}_{2^n}$.

For masking a function F of algebraic degree at most s, the method uses that for every function from $\mathbb{F}_{2^n}$ to itself of algebraic degree at most s, the mapping

$$\beta_F^{(s)}(a_1, a_2, \ldots, a_s) = \sum_{I \subseteq \{1, \ldots, s\}} F\left(\sum_{i \in I} a_i\right)$$

is multilinear (which is easily seen and has been first observed in [209]), which allows us to prove that, for every $d \geq s$:

$$F\left(\sum_{i=1}^{d} a_i\right) = \sum_{1 \leq i_1 < \cdots < i_s \leq d} \beta_F^{(s)}(a_{i_1}, \ldots, a_{i_s}) + \sum_{j=0}^{s-1} \eta_{d,s}(j) \sum_{\substack{I \subseteq \{1, \ldots, d\} \\ |I| = j}} F\left(\sum_{i \in I} a_i\right),$$

where $\eta_{d,s}(j) = \binom{d-j-1}{s-j-1} \bmod 2$ for every $j \leq s - 1$, and to deduce that

$$F\left(\sum_{i=1}^{d} a_i\right) = \sum_{j=0}^{s} \mu_{d,s}(j) \sum_{\substack{I \subseteq \{1, \ldots, d\} \\ |I| = j}} F\left(\sum_{i \in I} a_i\right),$$

where $\mu_{d,s}(j) = \binom{d-j-1}{s-j} \bmod 2$ for every $j \leq s$. This reduces the complexity of the d-masking of a degree s function to several s-maskings. An alternative (tree-based) method is also proposed. It is shown that the processing of any S-box of dimension $n = 8$ can be split into 11 evaluations of quadratic functions, or into four evaluations of cubic functions.

12.1.3 *Vectorial functions and algebraic side-channel attacks*

In [990], an attack on block ciphers called algebraic side-channel attack is introduced, which combines the two approaches of algebraic attacks and side-channel attacks. In [272], the algebraic phase of this attack is studied. The notion of algebraic immunity is modified to include the information from the leakage on Hamming weight or on Hamming distance, and it is studied how this can allow obtaining enough equations of degree one to be able to solve the algebraic system with Gröbner methods. We refer to these two papers for the technical details.

12.1.4 *Vectorial functions and threshold implementation*

The countermeasures against SCA presented so far suppose, for having good efficiency, that the leakage has some regularity. Building hardware with such property is expensive in practice. In particular, hardware *glitches*, which are transient faults (coming when the input signals of the combinational logic arrive at different moments in time when they should come simultaneously, signal switches then several times when it should switch once) common in CMOS technology, change the leaking into functions $\mathcal{L}$ having numerical degree larger than one, because of the interactions between bits that they cause, and which moreover vary with time. Glitch-free hardware is very expensive. We present here the main known solutions for avoiding needing it.

1. The problem of building implementations secure against d-th order side-channel attacks in the presence of glitches is equivalent to the problem of securing the processing of a function with several semihonest players (see [974]). A related way of masking S-boxes is the so-called *polynomial masking*, introduced separately in [974] and [562], and which gives a solution to this problem without needing sophisticated hardware. The idea is to make the global circuit glitch-free-like by the implementation itself, splitting the circuit implementing the S-box into several subcircuits communicating with each other on the basis of a *multiparty computation* protocol (see page 146), like the one in [59]. The masking operation of a sensitive data $z \in \mathbb{F}_{2^n}$ is based on Shamir's secret sharing seen in Subsection 3.6.1, page 145. It consists in constructing a function $f_z(x) = \sum_{i=1}^{m-1} a_i x^i + z$, where $(a_i)_{1 \leq i \leq m-1}$ are some random secret coefficients, then as in Boolean masking, z can be represented by m shares $(z_0, \ldots, z_{m-1})$, with $z_i = (\alpha_i, f_z(\alpha_i))$ for $0 \leq i \leq m-1$ for some random inputs $(\alpha_i)_{0 \leq i \leq m-1}$. To get z (unmasked), we have to reconstruct f_z by polynomial interpolation,[14] and finally calculate $z = f_z(0)$. The advantage of this method is that it is grounded by a well-studied theory (multiparty computation) and the

---

[14] Better methods have been very recently found; see [340].

security models are clear. Its disadvantage is that it is not very efficient, especially when first-order SCA is considered.

2. Another S-box masking method, also based on ideas of multiparty computation and aiming at solving the problem posed by glitches, is *threshold implementation*[15] (*TI*). Threshold schemes are attractive from an academic viewpoint, because they come with an information-theoretic proof of resistance against first-order DPA while allowing realistic-size circuits.[16] Introduced in [903] and presented more completely in [904], they pose interesting challenges for vectorial functions. In the TI of an (n, m)-*function* F, the shares of the output of F are the outputs of several functions of the shares of the input, each such function being independent of at least one of the shares of the input to F (a different one for each function); these two properties, called correctness and incompleteness, provide first-order probing security (if the implementation is done properly). More precisely:

- The masked version with t masks (*i.e.*, with $t+1$ shares) of each input variable x_i will be denoted by $\mathbf{x_i} = (x_i^{(1)}, \ldots, x_i^{(t+1)}) \in \mathbb{F}_2^{t+1}$. We shall denote the sum $x_i^{(1)} \oplus \ldots \oplus x_i^{(t+1)}$ of the coordinates of $\mathbf{x_i}$ by $s(\mathbf{x_i})$; we have $s(\mathbf{x_i}) = x_i$ for every i. Extending s to a function over $(\mathbb{F}_2^n)^{t+1}$, we have then $s(\mathbf{x}) = x$, for every $x = (x_1, \ldots, x_n)$.

- A t-mask (*i.e.*, $(t+1)$-share) *realization* of an (n, m)-function F is a vector $\mathbf{F} = (F_1, \ldots, F_{t+1})$ of $((t+1)n, m)$-functions, *i.e.*, a function from $(\mathbb{F}_2^n)^{t+1}$ to $(\mathbb{F}_2^m)^{t+1}$, such that, for all $\mathbf{x} \in (\mathbb{F}_2^n)^{t+1}$, denoting also $\sum_{j=1}^{t+1} F_j(\mathbf{x})$ by $s(\mathbf{F}(\mathbf{x}))$, we have

$$\text{if } x = s(\mathbf{x}), \text{ then } F(x) = s(\mathbf{F}(\mathbf{x})).$$

This property is called *correctness*. In practice, the numbers of input and output shares may be different but we take them equal to simplify the presentation. To obtain d-th order security against univariate attacks in a so-called HO-TI, we would need to have td masks and $\binom{td+1}{t}$ shares, and in a so-called consolidated masking scheme, d masks and $(d+1)^t$ output shares later synchronized in a register and compressed back to $d+1$ shares (which is often compared to the ISW multiplication), but with an extra register to protect against glitches; we shall not develop this and refer the reader to [85] and [992].

In terms of function graphs, let $\mathcal{G}_F = \{(x, F(x)); x \in \mathbb{F}_2^n\}$ and $\mathcal{G}_\mathbf{F} = \{(\mathbf{x}, \mathbf{F}(\mathbf{x})); \mathbf{x} \in (\mathbb{F}_2^n)^{t+1}\}$ be the graphs of functions F and $\mathbf{F}$; correctness corresponds to the fact that the linear function

$$(\mathbf{x}, \mathbf{y}) \mapsto (s(\mathbf{x}), s(\mathbf{y}))$$

maps $\mathcal{G}_\mathbf{F}$ to $\mathcal{G}_F$.

Correctness can be characterized by the Walsh transform in the following way:

Proposition 187 *Given a* $((t+1)n, (t+1)m)$-*function:*

$$\mathbf{F} = (F_1, \ldots, F_{t+1}) : \mathbf{x} \in (\mathbb{F}_2^n)^{t+1} \mapsto \mathbf{F}(\mathbf{x}) \in (\mathbb{F}_2^m)^{t+1}$$

and an (n, m)-*function* $F : \mathbb{F}_2^n \mapsto \mathbb{F}_2^m$, *we have*

$$s(\mathbf{F}(\mathbf{x})) = F(s(\mathbf{x}))$$

---

[15] Not to be confused with threshold functions, seen in Subsection 10.1.7.
[16] These can still be attacked by (univariate) mutual information and higher-order analyses.

if and only if

$$\forall u^{(1)}, \dots, u^{(t+1)} \in \mathbb{F}_2^n, \forall v \in \mathbb{F}_2^m, \ W_{\mathbf{F}}((u^{(1)}, \dots, u^{(t+1)}), (v, \dots, v))$$

$$= \begin{cases} 2^{tn} \, W_F(u^{(1)}, v) & \text{if } u^{(1)} = \dots = u^{(t+1)} \\ 0 & \text{otherwise.} \end{cases}$$

Proof We have $(F_1 + \dots + F_{t+1})(x^{(1)}, \dots, x^{(t+1)}) = F(x^{(1)} + \dots + x^{(t+1)})$ if and only if these two functions have the same Walsh transform, that is, if for every $u^{(1)}, \dots, u^{(t+1)} \in \mathbb{F}_2^n$ and $v \in \mathbb{F}_2^m$, $W_{F_1 + \dots + F_{t+1}}((u^{(1)}, \dots, u^{(t+1)}), v)$ equals the value at $((u^{(1)}, \dots, u^{(t+1)}), v)$ of the Walsh transform of function $(x^{(1)}, \dots, x^{(t+1)}) \mapsto F(x^{(1)} + \dots + x^{(t+1)})$, that is,

$$\sum_{(x^{(1)}, \dots, x^{(t+1)}) \in (\mathbb{F}_2^n)^{t+1}} (-1)^{v \cdot F(x^{(1)} + \dots + x^{(t+1)}) + u^{(1)} \cdot x^{(1)} \oplus \dots \oplus u^{(t+1)} \cdot x^{(t+1)}},$$

which, by changing $x^{(1)}$ into $x^{(1)} + \dots + x^{(t+1)}$, equals

$$\sum_{(x^{(1)}, \dots, x^{(t+1)}) \in (\mathbb{F}_2^n)^{t+1}} (-1)^{v \cdot F(x^{(1)}) \oplus u^{(1)} \cdot x^{(1)} \oplus (u^{(1)} + u^{(2)}) \cdot x^{(2)} \oplus \dots \oplus (u^{(1)} \oplus u^{(t+1)}) \cdot x^{(t+1)}}.$$

The rest is straightforward. $\qquad\qquad\qquad\qquad\qquad\qquad\qquad\qquad\qquad\qquad\qquad\square$

A necessary and sufficient condition for a function G to be the realization of some function is then as follows:

Corollary 31 *Given* $G = (G_1, \dots, G_{t+1}) : (\mathbb{F}_2^n)^{t+1} \mapsto (\mathbb{F}_2^m)^{t+1}$, *the function* $(G_1 + \dots + G_{t+1})(x^{(1)}, \dots, x^{(t+1)})$ *depends only on* $x^{(1)} + \dots + x^{(t+1)}$ *if and only if, for every* $u^{(1)}, \dots, u^{(t+1)} \in \mathbb{F}_2^n, v \in \mathbb{F}_2^m$, $W_G((u^{(1)}, \dots, u^{(t+1)}), (v, \dots, v))$ *equals zero when the equalities* $u^{(1)} = \dots = u^{(t+1)}$ *are not all satisfied. Then we have that* $W_G((u^{(1)}, \dots, u^{(t+1)}), (v, \dots, v))$ *is divisible by* 2^{tn} *for every* $u^{(1)}, \dots, u^{(t+1)}$.

Proof The condition that $W_G((u^{(1)}, \dots, u^{(t+1)}), (v, \dots, v))$ equals zero when the equalities $u^{(1)} = \dots = u^{(t+1)}$ are not all satisfied is necessary, according to Proposition 187. It is also sufficient since we have then, according to the *inverse Walsh transform formula* 2.43, page 59:

$$2^{(t+1)n} (-1)^{v \cdot (G_1 + \dots + G_{t+1})(x^{(1)}, \dots, x^{(t+1)})}$$

$$= \sum_{(u^{(1)}, \dots, u^{(t+1)}) \in (\mathbb{F}_2^n)^{t+1}} (-1)^{u^{(1)} \cdot x^{(1)} \oplus \dots \oplus u^{(t+1)} \cdot x^{(t+1)}} W_G((u^{(1)}, \dots, u^{(t+1)}), (v, \dots, v))$$

$$= \sum_{u \in \mathbb{F}_2^n} (-1)^{u \cdot (x^{(1)} + \dots + x^{(t+1)})} W_G((u, \dots, u), (v, \dots, v)) \qquad (12.3)$$

and we have that, for every v, function $v \cdot (G_1 + \dots + G_{t+1})(x^{(1)}, \dots, x^{(t+1)})$ depends then only on $x^{(1)} + \dots + x^{(t+1)}$. It is easily seen that $(G_1 + \dots + G_{t+1})(x^{(1)}, \dots, x^{(t+1)})$ depends then only on $x^{(1)} + \dots + x^{(t+1)}$.

Using now Relation (12.3) with $x^{(2)} = \dots = x^{(t+1)} = 0_n$ and with x instead of $x^{(1)}$ and applying the inverse Walsh transform formula to the resulting function of x, we have

$$2^{tn} \sum_{x \in \mathbb{F}_2^n} (-1)^{v \cdot (G_1 + \cdots + G_{t+1})(x, 0_n, \ldots, 0_n) \oplus u \cdot x} = W_G((u, \ldots, u), (v, \ldots, v)) \text{ and this proves the}$$

divisibility property. $\qquad\qquad\qquad\qquad\qquad\qquad\qquad\qquad\qquad\qquad\qquad\qquad\quad\square$

Correctness is a constraint on the realization $\mathbf{F}$, not really on F itself. But in threshold implementation, a second property is required for $\mathbf{F}$, and a third one is desired too; both also put constraints on F:

- In a threshold implementation $\mathbf{F} = (F_1, \ldots, F_{t+1})$, every function F_j should be independent of the jth coordinate of each $\mathbf{x_i}$ (in the sense that this jth coordinate should not appear at all in the ANF of F_j), i.e. F_j should be independent of the j-th share of $\mathbf{x}$. This property is called *noncompleteness*[17] and implies that the output of F_j, individually, is uncorrelated to any input variable x_i (assuming, as in the subsections above, that any vector of less than $t + 1$ shares of x_i is uncorrelated to x_i). Note that if F has algebraic degree at most t, then it is easy to build such $\mathbf{F}$: starting from the ANF of $F(x)$, replacing each x_i by $x_i^{(1)} \oplus \ldots \oplus x_i^{(t+1)}$ and expanding, we obtain a sum of monomials in each of which at least one upper index is not appearing, and then, starting with $j = 1$ and incrementing j at each step, we store in F_j all those monomials involving variables whose upper indices are different from j and that have not yet been stored. This way guarantees both correctness and noncompleteness.

  For instance, applying this method to the Boolean function $f(x) = x_1 x_2$ gives

$$f_1((x_1^{(1)}, x_1^{(2)}, x_1^{(3)}), (x_2^{(1)}, x_2^{(2)}, x_2^{(3)})) = x_1^{(2)} x_2^{(2)} \oplus x_1^{(2)} x_2^{(3)} \oplus x_1^{(3)} x_2^{(2)}$$
$$f_2((x_1^{(1)}, x_1^{(2)}, x_1^{(3)}), (x_2^{(1)}, x_2^{(2)}, x_2^{(3)})) = x_1^{(3)} x_2^{(3)} \oplus x_1^{(1)} x_2^{(3)} \oplus x_1^{(3)} x_2^{(1)}$$
$$f_3((x_1^{(1)}, x_1^{(2)}, x_1^{(3)}), (x_2^{(1)}, x_2^{(2)}, x_2^{(3)})) = x_1^{(1)} x_2^{(1)} \oplus x_1^{(1)} x_2^{(2)} \oplus x_1^{(2)} x_2^{(1)}.$$

Noncompleteness can be characterized by the Walsh transform in the following way:

Proposition 188 *Given a* $((t + 1)n, (t + 1)m)$*-function*

$$\mathbf{F} = (F_1, \ldots, F_{t+1}) : \mathbf{x} \in (\mathbb{F}_2^n)^{t+1} \mapsto \mathbf{F}(\mathbf{x}) \in (\mathbb{F}_2^m)^{t+1},$$

each function F_j is independent of the jth coordinate of each $\mathbf{x_i}$ if and only if

$$\forall j \in \{1, \ldots, t+1\}, \forall u^{(1)}, \ldots, u^{(t+1)} \in \mathbb{F}_2^n, \forall v^{(1)}, \ldots, v^{(t+1)} \in \mathbb{F}_2^m,$$

$$\left(\begin{array}{l} v^{(k)} = 0_m, \forall k \neq j, \\ and\ u^{(j)} \neq 0_n \end{array} \right) \Rightarrow (W_{\mathbf{F}}((u^{(1)}, \ldots, u^{(t+1)}), (v^{(1)}, \ldots, v^{(t+1)})) = 0). \quad (12.4)$$

Indeed, according to the Walsh and inverse Walsh transform formulae, F_j is independent of $(x_1^{(j)}, \ldots, x_n^{(j)})$ if and only if, for every $(u^{(1)}, \ldots, u^{(t+1)}) \in (\mathbb{F}_2^n)^{t+1}$ such that $u^{(j)} \neq 0_n$, we have $W_{F_j}(u^{(1)}, \ldots, u^{(t+1)}) = 0$.

---

[17] In (univariate) HO-TI of order d, this property becomes: any combination of up to d *component functions* of $\mathbf{F}$ must be independent of at least one input share.

Definition 86 *We call t-mask (i.e., $(t + 1)$-share) TI, or t-th order TI, of an (n, m)-function any function* $\mathbf{F}$ *from* $(\mathbb{F}_2^n)^{t+1}$ *to* $(\mathbb{F}_2^m)^{t+1}$ *satisfying correctness and noncompleteness.*

We shall call F the TI-masked function.

- The following property, called *uniformity (of TI)*, is desired too but is often not included in the very definition of TI: for every $\mathbf{b} = (b^{(1)}, b^{(2)}, \ldots, b^{(t+1)})$ in $(\mathbb{F}_2^m)^{t+1}$, the number of $\mathbf{x}$ in $(\mathbb{F}_2^n)^{t+1}$ for which $\mathbf{F}(\mathbf{x}) = \mathbf{b}$ is equal to $2^{t(n-m)}$ times the number of x in $\mathbb{F}_2^n$ for which $F(x) = s(\mathbf{b})$ (if F is a permutation of $\mathbb{F}_2^n$ then this is equivalent[18] to saying that $\mathbf{F}$ is a permutation of $(\mathbb{F}_2^n)^{t+1}$). This property is needed to make sure that, if the masking of the input to $\mathbf{F}$ is uniform, then the output of $\mathbf{F}$ is also a uniform masking of the output of F. The uniformity property of a TI is then important when the output of the TI is the input to another block (which is always the case in an iterative cryptographic primitive such as a block cipher). If we use a nonuniform TI of a function, we need to add sufficient refreshing (this is how HO-TI can be multivariate secure). Such a possibility is used quite often in practice but is expensive.

Uniformity is the hard property among the three described above. The usual method for trying to achieve it is by adding so-called correction terms to the output of TI when they do not ensure uniformity; these are terms that are added in pairs to shares in a way preserving noncompleteness. The terms in a pair canceling each other when the sum of output shares is made, correctness is preserved as well. But this method is difficult and has to be applied on each S-box; it is not really doable for infinite classes. How many shares are needed for a uniform TI without extra randomness is also currently a question without formal answer. The answer for $(3, 3)$-functions and $(4, 4)$-functions was given in [86, 87] by exhaustive search.

In [904, theorem 1 and corollary 1], the authors observe that correctness, noncompleteness, and the fact that the sharing at input is uniform suffices to ensure that each of the output shares is statistically independent of the input variables and the output variables and that the same holds for all intermediate results. Hence, if the power consumption of each shared sub-circuit implementing one of the functions F_j is independent of the other subcircuits, the implementation resists first-order SCA, even in the presence of glitches. Uniformity ensures additionally that no more information than a possible bias in the output distribution of the TI-masked function is provided. This uses more random values during the setup and this is a disadvantage already acknowledged in [903], but it does not need fresh randomness during the process. We shall specify "TI with uniformity" when needed (that is, when the TI achieves uniformity without additional fresh randomness).

Uniformity can be characterized by means of the Walsh transforms of F and $\mathbf{F}$ as well: the condition is equivalent to $\sum\limits_{\mathbf{x} \in (\mathbb{F}_2^n)^{t+1}, \mathbf{v} \in (\mathbb{F}_2^m)^{t+1}} (-1)^{\mathbf{v} \cdot (\mathbf{F}(\mathbf{x}) + \mathbf{b})} =$

$2^{tn} \sum\limits_{x \in \mathbb{F}_2^n, v \in \mathbb{F}_2^m} (-1)^{v \cdot (F(x) + b)}$, for every $\mathbf{b}$, where $\mathbf{v} = (v^{(1)}, \ldots, v^{(t+1)})$ and $b = s(\mathbf{b})$, that is, $\forall \mathbf{b} \in (\mathbb{F}_2^m)^{t+1}, \sum_{\mathbf{v} \in (\mathbb{F}_2^m)^{t+1}} (-1)^{\mathbf{v} \cdot \mathbf{b}} W_{\mathbf{F}}(0_{n(t+1)}, \mathbf{v}) = 2^{tn} \sum_{v \in \mathbb{F}_2^m} (-1)^{v \cdot s(\mathbf{b})} W_F(0_n, v)$.

---

[18] If the output of F was shared in more shares than the input, it would be equivalent to saying that $\mathbf{F}$ is balanced.

Algebraic degree of functions admitting a t-mask TI

A drawback of threshold implementation is that functions F of algebraic degree t can have TI with at least t masks only[19] (a necessary and sufficient condition for the existence of a t-mask TI with or without uniformity is then that the algebraic degree be at most t). This has been first observed in [903, theorem 1] (with incomplete statement and proof).

Proposition 189 *Let F be any (n, m)-function admitting a t-mask (i.e., a $(t + 1)$-share) TI with or without uniformity. Then $d_{alg}(F) \leq t$.*

Proof Consider the *ANF* of F:

$$F(x) = \sum_{I \subseteq \{1,\ldots,n\}} a_I x^I, \quad a_I \in \mathbb{F}_2^n,$$

where $x^I = \prod_{i \in I} x_i$. Let $\mathbf{F}$ be a t-mask TI of F. Because of correctness, the (unique) ANF of the $((t + 1)n, m)$-function $(s(\mathbf{F}))(\mathbf{x_1}, \ldots, \mathbf{x_n})$ is obtained by expanding:

$$F(s(\mathbf{x_1}), \ldots, s(\mathbf{x_n})) = \sum_{I \subseteq \{1,\ldots,n\}} a_I \prod_{i \in I} (x_i^{(1)} \oplus \ldots \oplus x_i^{(t+1)}). \tag{12.5}$$

Suppose that $d_{alg}(F) \geq t + 1$ and consider a monomial x^I of degree $d_{alg}(F)$. Then the ANF of $F(s(\mathbf{x_1}), \ldots, s(\mathbf{x_n}))$ contains all the monomials of the form $\prod_{i \in I} x_i^{(j_i)}$, where $j_i \in \{1, \ldots, t + 1\}$, with nonzero coefficients. Indeed, two distinct monomials x^I and $x^{I'}$ of degree $d_{alg}(F)$ in the ANF of F provide disjoint sets of monomials in the expansion of (12.5), which cannot then cancel each other. Moreover, none of the monomials of the form $\prod_{i=1}^{k} x_i^{(j_i)}$, where $i \mapsto j_i$ is onto $\{1, \ldots, t+1\}$, can be obtained from $(s(\mathbf{F}))(\mathbf{x_1}, \ldots, \mathbf{x_n})$ because of noncompleteness. A contradiction. $\square$

Hence for instance, the inverse function $F(x) = x^{2^n-2}$ used in the AES, which has algebraic degree $n - 1$, cannot have an $(n - 1)$-share (with $(n - 2)$-masks) TI. A question is: can it have an n-share (with $(n - 1)$-masks) TI with uniformity? Many such questions are open. For instance, recall that, for n odd and $t = \frac{n+1}{2}$, any almost bent function F has algebraic degree at most t. Does any AB function have an $\frac{n+1}{2}$-mask TI with uniformity?

Even for *quadratic functions*, there does not always exist a TI with uniformity of minimum number of masks (that is, with two masks): see [87, corollaries 1 and 2]. In fact, for any $t \geq 2$, we do not know how characterizing the functions for which a t-mask TI exists, despite the theoretical results of [73].

This is a concern since the implementation cost of a function increases then exponentially with its degree: according to Proposition 189, a monomial of degree t results in the sum of $(t + 1)^t$ monomials. This drawback is bypassed by expressing (when it is possible) high algebraic degree functions as the compositions of lower algebraic degree functions for which TI can be found; see [86, 87, 724], and see also [321] and page 435 for a general method (the CPRR method) addressing this problem. Then uniformity can be ensured by introducing (when necessary) fresh randomness when making the composition of two

---

[19] For multivariate first-order security, or td masks for univariate higher-order security.

threshold implementations, that is, by adding to the output of $\mathbf{F}$, a vector $\mathbf{c}$ such that $s(\mathbf{c}) = 0_m$ and such that any subvector of d components is random (this is sometimes called re-masking). Note that when creating a masked implementation of a decomposition, the TI of the lower-degree components have to be separated by a register stage to stop glitches (and reducing the number of these register stages is needed). Of course, it is preferred to minimize the number of the lower algebraic degree functions that are composed for giving the S-box.

The TI of small S-boxes has been studied; see [86, 87, 113] and the references therein. In particular, in [86] the authors designed the threshold implementation with at most four masks for all $(3, 3)$-permutations and $(4, 4)$-permutations.[20] But $n \leq 4$ is interesting for lightweight ciphers only. In [87], the authors studied APN $(5, 5)$-permutations (affine equivalent to the AB power functions x^3, x^5, x^7, x^{11} and x^{15}) and the sole known APN $(6, 6)$-permutation by different methods, in particular by expressing them as the compositions of quadratic functions (which needs remasking and does not provide a TI, properly speaking). But designing TI with uniformity for these functions is an open question, as well as for the multiplicative inverse differentially 4-uniform $(8, 8)$-function used in AES. Note that the *inverse function* plays not only a role in relation with the AES, since we know (see [331, 1184]) that any (n, n)-permutation can be expressed as the composition of functions $x \mapsto ax + b$ and of the inverse permutation.

An alternative approach for designing TI is, given some *secondary construction* of functions, to deduce the TI of the built function from the TI of the used functions. In [1094], the following construction of an $(n + 1, n + 1)$-function H from two (n, n)-functions F and G and two n-variable Boolean functions f and g is studied:

$$H : (x, x_{n+1}) \in \mathbb{F}_2^n \times \mathbb{F}_2 \mapsto x_{n+1}(F(x), f(x)) + (x_{n+1} \oplus 1)(G(x), g(x)) \in \mathbb{F}_2^n \times \mathbb{F}_2.$$

Clearly, every $(n + 1, n + 1)$-function can be obtained this way. Note that H is a permutation if and only if it is injective, that is, if and only if $x \mapsto (F(x), f(x))$ and $x \mapsto (G(x), g(x))$ are injections (which is a necessary and sufficient condition for the fact that two distinct inputs of the same form $(x, 0)$ or of the same form $(x, 1)$ do not give the same output) and have disjoint value sets (which is a necessary and sufficient condition for the fact that an input $(x, 0)$ and an input $(y, 1)$ do not give the same output). If F and G are permutations, then the condition simplifies into $f \circ F^{-1} \oplus g \circ G^{-1} = 1$. It is then shown that if F and f have t-mask TI with uniformity $\mathbf{F}$ and $\mathbf{f}$, and if $G(x_1, \ldots, x_n)$ equals either $F(x_1, \ldots, x_n)$ or $F(x_1, \ldots, x_{i-1}, x_i \oplus 1, x_{i+1}, \ldots, x_n)$ for some $i = 1, \ldots, n$, and g is taken such that $f \circ F^{-1} \oplus g \circ G^{-1} = 1$, then H has a t-mask TI with uniformity. The idea of the proof in the slightly more complex latter case is to decompose $(F(x), f(x))$ in the form $x_i(F_i(x), f_i(x)) + (x_i \oplus 1)(F_i'(x), f_i'(x))$, where $(F_i(x), f_i(x))$ (resp. $(F_i'(x), f_i'(x))$) is the restriction of $(F(x), f(x))$ to the hyperplane of equation $x_i = 0$ (resp. $x_i = 1$) and to observe that $H(x, x_{n+1})$ equals $(x_{n+1} \oplus x_i \oplus 1)(F_i(x), f_i(x)) + (x_{n+1} \oplus x_i)(F_i'(x), f_i'(x))$. It would be nice if less restrictive cases within this general construction could be addressed.

In [105], the authors constructed $(8, 8)$-functions based on a Feistel network, a substitution permutation network, or the (special case of) MISTY network [830], all using quadratic

---

[20] All $(2, 2)$-permutations being affine, they do not need to be studied.

4-bit S-boxes, which admit a TI implementation while still maintaining a good level of differential uniformity and nonlinearity.

A recent general alternative technique, called the *changing of the guards*, and which represents a nice step forward, has been presented in [402] and applied to the Keccak S-box. It builds a $(t + 1)$-share threshold implementation with uniformity of any invertible S-box layer of algebraic degree t, after a transformation (the S-box is subdivided into several stages, separated by registers, and some shares receive additional components; see the details in [402]); each share at the output of S-box i is made uniform by bitwise adding to it one or two shares from the input of S-box $i-1$; this solves the problem of threshold implementation with uniformity (but only after such transformation of the S-box). In a next important step forward, a modification of the changing of the guards has been given in [1056] and applied to the AES S-box, at the cost of a significant extension of the AES S-box design, but ensuring in a nice way uniformity with 3-share TI (while Daemen's method in [402], as is, needs $t + 1$ shares, that is, 8 in the case of the AES S-box). The method includes a generic way to construct a uniform sharing for any function, by changing (by extension and reduction) the function to an invertible one while maintaining its essential functionality unchanged,[21] which can be, in the case of AES S-box, decomposed into quadratic bijections. The extension of an (n, m)-function F is the $(n + m, n + m)$-permutation $(x, y) \mapsto (x, F(x) + y)$. If $\mathbf{F}$ is a 3-share TI of F, then a 3-share TI with uniformity of the extension is, still denoting $\mathbf{x} = (x_1, x_2, x_3)$ and $\mathbf{y} = (y_1, y_2, y_3)$, the function $((x_1, y_1), (x_2, y_2), (x_3, y_3)) \mapsto ((x_2, \mathbf{F}_1(\mathbf{x}) + y_3), (x_3, \mathbf{F}_2(\mathbf{x}) + y_1), (x_1, \mathbf{F}_3(\mathbf{x}) + y_2))$. The reduction of an $(n + m, n + m)$-function G is the $(n + m, n + m)$-function $(x, y) \mapsto (0_n, y)$. If $\mathbf{G}$ is a 3-share TI of G, then a 3-share TI with uniformity of the reduction is the function $((x_1, y_1), (x_2, y_2), (x_3, y_3)) \mapsto ((x_2 + x_3, y_2), (x_3, y_3), (x_2, y_1))$. Composing these two 3-share TI provides a 3-share TI with uniformity of $(x, y) \mapsto (0_n, F(x) + y)$. See more in [1056].

Invariance of the existence of a t-mask TI

The existence of a t-mask TI of $F(x)$ is invariant when changing $F(x)$ into $F(x + a)$ (by changing $\mathbf{F}(\mathbf{x})$ into $\mathbf{F}(\mathbf{x}+\mathbf{a})$ for some $\mathbf{a}$ such that $s(\mathbf{a}) = a$, which also preserves uniformity), and it is also invariant under linear equivalence $F \sim L \circ F \circ L'$ (which preserves uniformity as well), as observed (and proved rather informally) in [86, theorem 2]. Indeed, applying L' on each share of $\mathbf{x}$ and L on each share of the output of $\mathbf{F}$ preserves correctness since L and L' are linear, and it preserves uniformity since L and L' are bijective, and it also preserves noncompleteness, since the applications of L and L' are made separately on each share. Hence the existence of a t-mask TI is an *affine invariant*, as well as the existence of a t-mask TI with uniformity. And the existence of a t-mask TI is also invariant under adding an affine function but it is not clear whether this preserves uniformity (in other words, affine equivalence preserves the existence of a uniform TI, but extended affine equivalence probably does not).

Remark.   Given a permutation F having a t-mask TI, function F^{-1} does not necessarily have a t-mask TI, since there are quadratic functions having 2-mask TI and whose inverses

---

[21] So the success of the method does not contradict Proposition 189.

are not quadratic[22] and therefore do not have a 2-mask TI, according to Proposition 189. In particular, if $\mathbf{F}$ is a t-mask TI of F, function $\mathbf{F}^{-1}$ is not necessarily a t-mask TI of F^{-1}. This is because the condition "for every $j = 1,\ldots,t+1$, the jth coordinate function of $\mathbf{F}$ is independent of the jth coordinate of each $\mathbf{x_i}$" is not equivalent to the condition "for every $j = 1,\ldots,t+1$, the jth coordinate function of $\mathbf{F}^{-1}$ is independent of the jth coordinate of each $\mathbf{x_i}$." This subtle difference can be more easily seen with the characterization by Condition (12.4), which is not the same when applied to $\mathbf{F}$ and to its inverse: the hypothesis "$v_k = 0_n, \forall k \neq j$ and $u_j \neq 0_n$" of the implication, when it is applied to $\mathbf{F}^{-1}$, becomes "$u_k = 0_n, \forall k \neq j$, and $v_j \neq 0_n$," since we know that changing a function into its inverse corresponds for the Walsh transform to swapping the parameter(s) living in the domain and the one (or those) living in the codomain, the same value of the Walsh transform being then kept for this new input.   □

3. A more recent way to protect against SCA in the presence of glitches is domain oriented rather than function oriented; it organizes properly the ISW computations (we described above the methods based on decompositions of polynomials and related masking) and implements the concept of share domains (keeping each domain independent from the others). Each share of a variable is associated with one share domain. This method is called *domain-oriented masking* (see [574, 575]) and is an alternative to threshold implementation requiring less chip area and less randomness, all the more when raising the protection order.   □

12.1.5 Linear complementary dual codes and complementary pairs of codes used for direct sum masking

Direct sum masking has a weaker relationship with Boolean functions than with codes. We briefly describe it, however, since a large number of recent papers deal with the related notions of linear complementary dual codes and complementary pairs of codes, and also, because of the dual distance of codes playing a central role, correlation immune functions are closely related.

The impact of codes on protection against fault injection attacks is well studied; the number of detected faults relates to their minimum distance. The (explicit) use of codes for protecting against SCA is more recent. The *direct sum masking* (*DSM*) countermeasure [131, 288] is a generalization of *Boolean masking* consisting in

*   Encoding (see the definition at pages 5 and 7) the sensitive data, say x, that we consider here as living in $\mathbb{F}_2^k$, into a codeword of a k-dimensional linear subcode C of $\mathbb{F}_2^n$
*   Encoding the mask y drawn at random from $\mathbb{F}_2^{n-k}$ into a codeword of an $(n-k)$-dimensional linear subcode D of $\mathbb{F}_2^n$

The masked version of x equals then the sum of these two codewords. This is only a first-order masking scheme in terms of probing security, if there is a reuse of the mask.

If G is a generator matrix of C and G' a generator matrix of D, we take then

$$z = x \times G + y \times G'; \qquad x \in \mathbb{F}_2^k, y \in \mathbb{F}_2^{n-k}. \tag{12.6}$$

---

[22] This should be checked among quadratic functions with known 2-TI, though.

For allowing the final demasking at the end of the computation, it must be possible to recover x from z (but to avoid leaks, the algorithm should not include a computation of x, unless it has arrived to its end). This means that C and D must have trivial intersection, that is, be supplementary:[23]

$$\mathbb{F}_2^n = C \oplus D.$$

Every vector $z \in \mathbb{F}_2^n$ can then be written in a unique way as in ((12.6)). Note that this provides the possibility of removing the mask without the knowledge of it.

As mentioned above, d-th order masking is a particular case of DSM: we have then $n = (d+1)k$, $C = \mathbb{F}_2^k \times \{0_{dk}\}$, where 0_{dk} is the all-zero vector of length dk, $G = [I_{k,k} : 0_{k,dk}]$, where $I_{k,k}$ is the $k \times k$ identity matrix, and $0_{k,dk}$ is the $k \times dk$ all-zero matrix, $D = \{(y_0, \ldots, y_d); y_i \in \mathbb{F}_2^k, \sum_{i=0}^{d} y_i = 0_k\}$ and, for instance:

$$G' = \begin{bmatrix} I_{k,k} & I_{k,k} & 0_{k,k} & \cdots & 0_{k,k} \\ I_{k,k} & 0_{k,k} & I_{k,k} & \cdots & 0_{k,k} \\ \vdots & \vdots & \vdots & \ddots & \vdots \\ I_{k,k} & 0_{k,k} & \cdots & \cdots & I_{k,k} \end{bmatrix}.$$

But an advantage of DSM is that, when C and D are properly chosen, it can be also a countermeasure against FIA (while classical masking cannot), which helps reduce the cost of the overall countermeasure against SCA and FIA.

A pair (C, D) of supplementary codes is called a *linear complementary pair* (*LCP*) of codes. It is shown in [131] that if the monovariate leak $\mathcal{L}$ (which is a *pseudo-Boolean* function) has numerical degree 1, the encoding with an LCP of codes (C, D) as described above protects against d-th order HO-SCA if and only if the dual distance of D satisfies $d(D^\perp) > d$. Moreover, as shown in [960, section 3.2], d-th order bit-probing security is then ensured, because by definition, less than $d(D^\perp)$ of those equations expressing the coordinates of $z = x \times G + y \times G'$ by means of the coordinates of x and y do not allow to eliminate the coordinates of y since fewer than $d(D^\perp)$ columns of G' are linearly independent. The encoding protects against the injection of faults of Hamming weights at most d if and only if the minimum distance of C satisfies $d(C) > d$. Note that when encoding is made over bits, the ensured security is the so-called *bit-probing security*, whose order can be higher than the probing security order when the attacker can probe symbols belonging to a larger alphabet.

According to the observations above, the security parameter against both HO-SCA and FIA is $\min\{d(C), d(D^\perp)\} - 1$. But taking this minimum as the sole security parameter supposes that the orders of needed protection against SCA and FIA are comparable. This is not always the case. In a safety context like autonomous trains and cars, it is crucial to ensure the detection of faults and side-channel leakage is a lesser risk, while in the context of the internet of things (IoT) or banking, minimizing side-channel leakage is a premium objective. We must then take the pair $(d(C) - 1, d(D^\perp)\} - 1)$ for security parameter.

In the case of *Boolean masking*, the codes, seen above, $C = \mathbb{F}_2^k \times \{0_{dk}\}$ and $D = \{(y_0, \ldots, y_d); y_i \in \mathbb{F}_2^k, \sum_{i=0}^{d} y_i = 0_k\}$ satisfy $d(C) = 1$ and $d(D^\perp) = d + 1$ (since as we saw in a remark at page 17, the dual distance of a linear code equals the minimum

---

[23] We prefer using this term rather than *complementary*, which is ambiguous; we use the classical notation $\oplus$ to denote such direct sum, which needs not to be confused with XOR.

nonzero number of linearly dependent columns in its generator matrix). This confirms that Boolean masking protects against SCA but not FIA.

If D equals the dual $C^\perp$ of C in an LCP of codes, then C and D are so-called *linear complementary dual* (*LCD*) codes. Such codes are well adapted to the cases where the need for protection is the same for SCA and FIA; the security parameter of an LCD code C when used in so-called *orthogonal direct sum masking* (*ODSM*) [131, 288] is simply $d(C) - 1$.

The notion of LCD code is anterior to DSM. In [1134], Yang and Massey introduced it as an optimal linear coding solution for a rather particular problematic: the two user binary adder channel. They provided a necessary and sufficient condition under which a *cyclic code* is LCD. In [75], Bhasin et al. have shown how also using and implementing LCD codes and LCP of codes to strengthen encoded circuits against hardware Trojan horses while minimizing the cost.

Note that $D = C^\perp$ if and only if G' is a parity check matrix of C, that is, $G \times G'^t = 0_{k,k}$, where G'^t is the transposed matrix of matrix G'. We can denote then G' by H and use an orthogonal projection to recover x and y from z: the relation $z = x \times G + y \times H$ implies $z \times H^t = y \times H \times H^t$ and $z \times G^t = x \times G \times G^t$, and this provides x and y since "C is LCD," "the matrix $H \times H^t$ is invertible," and "the matrix $G \times G^t$ is invertible" are equivalent.

Since the introduction of DSM, and the investigation of numerous constructions of LCD codes in [288], many papers have studied constructions of such codes and of LCP of codes; see a description in [295], where a problematic is also described: faults are detected by verifying that masks have not been altered during processing; checking this requires having access to the masks. A possibility is to mask with $z = (x \times G + y \times G', y)$ instead of $z = x \times G + y \times G'$. The leak is then modified. Some *MDS* codes can keep the same protection ability when changing this way the encoding (the code of generator matrix $[G' : I_{n-k}]$, where I_{n-k} is the identity matrix, can have the same dual distance as the code of generator matrix G', which can be MDS).

Remark. A particular case[24] of DSM[25] is *inner product masking* (*IPM*), whose principle for masking a sensitive data $x \in \mathbb{F}_{2^n}$ is to generate a vector over $\mathbb{F}_{2^n}$ whose inner product with some public vector equals x; see [44, 45, 46, 491] (see also [289, 366, 960]; the latter reference expresses the side-channel resistance of IPM in terms of, classically, the minimum distance of $D^\perp$, and less classically, the first nonzero coefficient in its weight enumerator). With the public vector $(1, l_1, \ldots, l_{n-1})$, since we want $x = (x \times G + y \times G') \cdot (1, l_1, \ldots, l_{n-1})$; $x \in \mathbb{F}_{2^n}$, $y \in \mathbb{F}_{2^n}^{n-1}$ as explained above, we can take (as shown in [960]) $G = (1, 0, \ldots, 0)$ (and C has then minimum distance 1, which does not allow detecting FIA) and $y \times G' = (y \cdot (l_1, \ldots, l_{n-1}), y_1, \ldots, y_{n-1})$, and code D has then the generator matrix

---

[24] With a practical difference, though: IPM works over field elements, while DSM often works over bits; hence probing security may not mean the same in both cases. Nevertheless, it is proved in [960] that if the deterministic leaks of the shares are linear functions of their bits, the bounded moment security order of the IPM is equal to the probing security order of the bitwise encoding obtained by decomposing the elements of $\mathbb{F}_{2^n}$ over a basis over $\mathbb{F}_2$.

[25] And also of leakage squeezing, which we saw at page 431, and which is also a particular case of DSM, but only when F is linear.

$$
\begin{bmatrix}
l_1 & 1 & 0 & \cdots & 0 \\
l_2 & 0 & \ddots & \ddots & \vdots \\
\vdots & \vdots & \ddots & \ddots & 0 \\
l_{n-1} & 0 & \cdots & 0 & 1
\end{bmatrix}
$$

(the masked information is $z = (x + \sum_{i=1}^{n-1} l_i y_i, y_1, \ldots, y_{n-1})$, and we have $x = z \cdot (1, l_1, \ldots, l_{n-1})$). Code $D^{\perp}$ has the generator matrix $(1, l_1, \ldots, l_{n-1})$ (and the order of protection against SCA equals the Hamming weight of $(l_1, \ldots, l_{n-1})$).

IPM also contains *Boolean masking* as a particular case (take $(l_1, \ldots, l_{n-1}) = 1_{n-1}$) as well as the methods of masking using secret sharing [974] (see Relation (3.43), page 146). It has been recently modified in [365], so as to allow fault injection detection as well. □

An important issue is to compute (in particular, multiply) efficiently over encodings. In the case of IPM, solutions exist [44, 46], but for DSM, it remains an open challenge, except in a simplified framework addressed in [260].

12.1.6 Robust codes, AMD codes and vectorial functions

In many cases of error detection, the assumption that the most probable errors have low Hamming weight cannot be guaranteed. As shown successively in [664, 666, 667], the classical method of error detection by codes having large enough minimum distance is then often not efficient. In fact, it is in many cases almost impossible to predict the error patterns (*e.g.*, in the case of address decoder errors, or with power glitches, or when data are compressed for transmission and decompressed after). For instance, the error characteristics in silicon devices like memories are changing and in many instances can be unpredictable. This is becoming still more true while embedded systems are becoming ubiquitous, and their roles are becoming more mission critical for sensitive applications. Taking again the example of memories, embedded ones are exposed to unpredictable environments (when for instance moved in a plane from sea level, where cosmic rays are weak, to high sky where the error rate can be large) and their reliability is now a matter of critical importance and safety. This situation of unpredictability is similar to FIA on hardware implementations of cryptographic algorithms (as also observed in the references above): classical methods of error detection are ineffective when the error distribution within a device is controlled by an adversary. For instance, when an attacker induces stress (see [82]) resulting in bits vanishing one after the other in the processed data, this results in the injection of an error on each bit that was equal to 1; when increasing the stress, the error distribution turns to almost uniform. Classical codes (and the codes seen in Subsection 12.1.5) may fail then to detect errors, when the adversary succeeds in producing an error changing a correct codeword into a wrong codeword. The *worst error-masking probability* is the maximal probability that a given error e transforms a codeword into a codeword. In the case of linear codes, the undetectable errors are the codewords themselves, and the attacker only needs, for his or her error injection, to know the code that is used in the device and to be able to inject codewords as errors. The worst error-masking probability being then equal to 1 (worst possible), linear codes are not adapted to minimizing worst error-masking probability.

Codes robust against fault injection with unknown error probability

In [665, 667, 717], the notion of robust code, aiming at providing uniform protection against all errors, without any assumption on the error distribution or on the capabilities of an attacker has been presented:

Definition 87 *Given a positive integer R, an unrestricted (i.e., nonnecessarily linear) code $C \subset \mathbb{F}_q^n$ is called R-robust if the size of the intersection of C and any of its translates $e + C$, where $e \in \mathbb{F}_q^n, e \neq 0_n$, is bounded above by R. Given a code C, the smallest possible value of R having this property shall be denoted by R_C:*

$$R_C = \max_{0_n \neq e \in \mathbb{F}_q^n} |C \cap (e + C)|. \tag{12.7}$$

A binary R-robust code C of length n with $M = |C|$ is denoted by a triple (n, M, R).

The code can be *systematic* (recall that this means there exists a subset I of positions in codewords, called an *information set* of C, such that every possible tuple in $\mathbb{F}_q^I$ occurs in exactly one codeword within the specified coordinates x_i; $i \in I$; this implies that $M = q^{|I|}$). Systematic codes are more practical for error detection in computer hardware thanks to the separation between information bits and check bits. The code equals then, up to a permutation of the codeword coordinates, the graph of a function, $\{(x, F(x)); x \in \mathbb{F}_q^I\}$, for some (not necessarily linear) function F. But we shall see that the code cannot then be perfect robust.

The probability of missing an algebraic manipulation with a code C equals the so-called probability of error masking, which for each possible error e is denoted by $Q(e)$ and is defined as

$$Q(e) = \frac{|C \cap (e + C)|}{|C|}. \tag{12.8}$$

The *worst error-masking probability* $\max_{e \neq 0_n} Q(e)$ equals then $\frac{R_C}{|C|}$. As observed in [666], we have $\max_{e \neq 0_n} Q(e) \geq \frac{|C|-1}{q^n-1}$ (with equality if and only if the code is uniformly robust; see below) for any code of length n over $\mathbb{F}_q$ (which is easily shown by using that the maximum of a sequence of values is always larger than or equal to the arithmetic mean, and equals it if and only if the sequence is constant, and observing that $\sum_{e \neq 0_n} Q(e) = \frac{2}{|C|}\binom{|C|}{2} = |C| - 1$); a little more can be shown by using that the numerator in (12.8) is an integer. Note that there is a slight error in [667] about this result: it is written that for every code, we have $Q(e) \geq \frac{|C|-1}{q^n-1}$ for every $e \neq 0_n$, which is false (suppose that the minimum distance of the code is larger than 1 and let us take e smaller than the minimum distance).

A code is called a *robust code* if its worst error-masking probability is strictly less than 1, and it is called a *uniformly robust code* (or *perfect robust code*) if $Q(e)$ is constant for $e \neq 0_n$, that is, $Q(e) = \frac{|C|-1}{q^n-1}, \forall e \neq 0_n$ (note that the minimum distance of such code is necessarily 1). This is equivalent to saying that C is a *difference set* in $(\mathbb{F}_q^n, +)$, that is, in the case $q = 2$ and assuming that C is neither equal to $\{0_n\}$ nor to $\mathbb{F}_q^n$, that the *indicator* function of C is bent.

Robustness and worst error-masking probability for supports of Boolean functions and graphs of vectorial functions

1. Let C be the support of an n-variable Boolean function. Then if we denote by Δ the symmetric difference between two sets, we have that $|C \Delta (e + C)| = 2|C| - 2|C \cap (e + C)|$ for every $e \in \mathbb{F}_2^n$, and therefore $|C \cap (e + C)| = |C| - \frac{1}{2}|C \Delta (e + C)|$. Let us revisit the case where the function is *bent*: we know then that $|C| = 2^{n-1} + (-1)^\epsilon 2^{\frac{n}{2}-1}$ for some $\epsilon \in \mathbb{F}_2$, and $|C \Delta (e + C)| = 2^{n-1}$, for every $e \neq 0_n$; this gives $|C \cap (e + C)| = 2^{n-2} + (-1)^\epsilon 2^{\frac{n}{2}-1}$, $Q(e) = \frac{2^{n-2}+(-1)^\epsilon 2^{\frac{n}{2}-1}}{2^{n-1}+(-1)^\epsilon 2^{\frac{n}{2}-1}}$ (equal to the optimum $\frac{2^{n-1}+(-1)^\epsilon 2^{\frac{n}{2}-1}-1}{2^n-1}$), and C is uniformly robust (but cannot be systematic since its size is not a power of 2). In [666] (and the references therein), it has been proposed for f the basic Maiorana–McFarland function $f(x, y) = x \cdot y$; $x, y \in \mathbb{F}_2^{\frac{n}{2}}$, n even, but any (binary) bent function would behave the same. In this same reference, it is also proposed to take $C = \{(x, y) \in (\mathbb{F}_q^{\frac{n}{2}})^2; x \cdot y = u\}$, where q is a power of a prime and n is even. This improves $Q(e)$ in some cases (with a different value according to whether u is zero or not). This same reference also investigates codes that are the unions of the codes $\{(x, y) \in (\mathbb{F}_q^{\frac{n}{2}})^2; x \cdot y = u\}$ for some values of u.

2. Let C be now systematic, *i.e.*, the graph of a vectorial function. We have, by slightly completing [717]:

Proposition 190 *Let $C = \{(x, F(x)), x \in \mathbb{F}_2^k\}$ be the graph of a vectorial function F from $\mathbb{F}_2^k$ to $\mathbb{F}_2^r$, with k and r nonnegative. The worst error-masking probability of C equals the differential uniformity of F divided by 2^k. It is then bounded below by 2^{-r} and equals this optimum if and only if F is perfect nonlinear.*

Indeed, denoting $e = (a, b)$, we have

$$|C \cap (e + C)| = \left|\left\{(x, y) \in (\mathbb{F}_2^k)^2; \begin{array}{l} x = y + a \\ F(x) = F(y) + b \end{array}\right\}\right| = \left|(D_a F)^{-1}(b)\right|.$$

For $a = 0_k$ and $b \neq 0_k$, this size is null and $\max_{e \neq 0_{k+r}} |C \cap (e + C)|$ equals then the differential uniformity of F (see Definition 40, page 135). We know from the bound due to Nyberg that it is then bounded below by 2^{k-r} with equality if and only if F is *perfect nonlinear* (in which case the derivatives are balanced). Since C has size 2^k, this gives the result.

Note that for this code, the value $\max_{e \neq 0_{k+r}} Q(e)$, equal to 2^{-r}, is larger than $\frac{|C|-1}{q^n-1} = \frac{2^k-1}{2^n-1}$ (no systematic code can be perfect robust).

Note also that, according to Nyberg's result[26] (Proposition 104, page 269), the best codes C from Proposition 190 can exist only if k is even and $r \leq \frac{k}{2}$, that is, the length $n = k + r$ and the dimension k satisfy $n \leq \frac{3k}{2}$ (*i.e.*, their *transmission rate* is at least $\frac{2}{3}$). If this double condition is not satisfied, we can take F almost perfect nonlinear, and the worst error-masking probability of C is then 2^{-r+1}.

---

[26] The situation is different in odd characteristic; then, PN (n, n)-functions exist for every n.

It is observed in [717] that, thanks to the fact that the robust codes above are nonlinear, the error detection for these codes depends on the encoded data (while for a linear code, the set of missed errors is the same for all encoded data). This makes for the attacker the set of necessary errors harder to determine, all the more when the data depend on the secret key or when randomization is applied. But this makes also, as observed in [304, 690], that the efficiency of these codes depends on the fact that the data are uniformly distributed, which is not reasonable in many situations, in particular when the information bits of messages are also controllable by an attacker. This limitation can be overcome by algebraic manipulation detection (AMD) codes, which we address in the next paragraph.

Codes and algebraic manipulation

A model for error injection has been introduced in [395] under the name of *algebraic manipulation*. This model assumes that the attacker is able to modify the value of some abstract data storage device without having read access to the data. Such a device is denoted by $\sum(G)$ and can hold an element g (corresponding to some secret s), from a public finite Abelian (additive) group G. The attacker is not able to obtain any information about the element g stored in the device $\sum(G)$. However, he can change the stored element g by adding an error $e \in G$ of his choice. After such algebraic manipulation (tampering), the abstract storage device $\sum(G)$ will store the value $g + e$. The attacker can choose the value e only on the basis of what he already knew about g before it was stored in the device (his a priori knowledge of g). This models for instance the situation with *linear secret sharing schemes* (see Subsection 3.6.1, page 145), in which the correctness of the secret s reconstructed from the shares of a qualified coalition of players is guaranteed only if all these shares are correct. If the coalition contains dishonest players and if the honest players in it are not able to reconstruct s on their own (*i.e.*, if they do not constitute a qualified coalition), then the dishonest players can cause the reconstruction of a modified secret s', and they can control the difference between s and s', thanks to the linearity of the secret sharing. In particular, in a minimal qualified coalition of players, a single corrupted player can cause the reconstruction of an incorrect secret.

Two types of fault injection attacks can be considered. In the weaker ones, the adversary cannot choose the input. So, from the attacker's point of view, the source s is uniformly distributed; he can only inject an error e in the storage device $\sum(G)$, but he cannot change value s at his own discretion. In the stronger version, the adversary knows the value s and moreover can choose it, and change it after he got some information from the device (in a kind of adaptive chosen attack). In both types of fault injection attacks, the value g stored in $\sum(G)$ is hidden from the attacker.

The countermeasure against algebraic manipulation consists in using so-called *algebraic manipulation detection codes*, which were introduced in [395] after observations were made in [481]. AMD codes encode an original information $s \in S$ as an element of $g \in G$ in such way that any algebraic manipulation is detected with high probability. No secret key is needed, contrary to the case of message authentication codes.

Definition 88 *An AMD code is a pair of two functions: a probabilistic encoding function $E : S \rightarrow G$ from a set S into a finite Abelian group G, and a deterministic decoding function*

$D : G \to S \cup \{\bot\}$, *where* $\bot \notin S$ *symbolizes that algebraic manipulation has been detected,* *satisfying that* $D(E(s)) = s$ *with probability* 1 *for every* $s \in S$.

The AMD code is called ϵ-*secure for* $\epsilon > 0$ *if, for every* $s \in S$ *and for every* $e \in G$, *the* *probability that* $D(E(s) + e) \notin \{s, \bot\}$ *is at most* ϵ. *It is called weak* ϵ-*secure if, for every* $e \in G$ *and for every* $s \in S$ *sampled from* S *with uniform distribution (independently of* e, *then), the probability that* $D(E(s) + e) \notin \{s, \bot\}$ *is at most* ϵ.

A systematic AMD code is an AMD code in which set S *is a group and the encoding* *function* E *has the form*

$$E : S \to G = S \times G_1 \times G_2$$
$$s \to (s, x, F(x, s)),$$

(12.9)

where G_1 *and* G_2 *are groups,* F *is a function and* x *is randomly chosen with uniform prob-* *ability in* G_1. *The decoding is then* $D(s', x', r') = s'$ *if* $F(x', s') = r'$, *and* $D(s', x', r') = \bot$ *otherwise.*

Given an AMD code, $E(s)$ can safely be stored on $\sum(G)$ (supposed protected from reading) so that the adversary who manipulates the stored value by adding some nonzero e can cause it to decode to some $s' \neq s$ with probability at most ϵ, only. AMD codes also allow the protection of hardware and memories against FIA (seen in Section 12.1), see [1113][27].

Note that if the AMD code is ϵ-secure, then for every $s \in S$, the size $|D^{-1}(s)|$ of the preimage of s by D is necessarily at least $\frac{1}{\epsilon}$ (this property will be used below), since denoting by E_s the set of all possible images of s by E, and choosing e so that there exists in $E_s + e$ an element x of $E_{s'}$ with $s' \neq s$ (and so $D(x) = s' \notin \{s, \bot\}$), the size of E_s needs to be at least $\frac{1}{\epsilon}$ for allowing the probability that $D(E(s) + e) \notin \{s, \bot\}$ to be at most ϵ.

Deterministic weak secure AMD codes are a randomization of systematic robust codes (seen above), with $\max_{e \neq 0} Q(e) = \max_{e \neq 0} \text{Prob} [D(E(s) + e) \notin \{s, \bot\}]$.

Note that, as already seen, every $(|G|, |S|, \lambda)$-difference set D (see page 196) in $(G, +)$, where $G = S \times G_1 \times G_2$ (assuming that S is an additive group and that such a difference set exists) provides then a weak ϵ-secure AMD code with $\epsilon = \frac{\lambda}{|S|}$, by taking for E any bijection between S and D. In fact, it is enough (and necessary) that every nonzero element e in $S \times G_1 \times G_2$ can be written in at most (rather than exactly) λ ways as the difference between two elements of D, that is, $|D \cap (e + D)| \leq \lambda$. The graphs of perfect nonlinear (resp. almost perfect nonlinear) (r, s)-functions have such property with $\lambda = 2^{r-s}$ (resp. $\lambda = 2^{r-s+1}$).

In [395], is proposed the systematic AMD code with $F(x, s) = x^{d+2} + \sum_{i=1}^{d} s_i x^i$, where $s \in \mathbb{F}_q^d$, $x \in \mathbb{F}_q$, which provides a systematic $\frac{d+1}{q}$-secure AMD code, thanks to the fact that, when $e_x \neq 0$, $(x + e_x)^{d+2} - x^{d+2}$ equals a polynomial of degree exactly $d+1$ (which matches any value at most $d+1$ times), and when $e_x = 0$ and $e_s \neq 0$, $\sum_{i=1}^{d} (s_i + [e_s]_i) x^i - \sum_{i=1}^{d} s_i x^i$ is a nonzero polynomial of degree at most d (which matches any value at most d times). This construction is generalized in [396], where it is shown (by extending an idea from [1112], which worked with generalized Reed–Muller codes) how systematic AMD codes can be deduced from classical codes: from any subset S of $G_2^{G_1}$ (*i.e.*, any code of length

---

[27] In this reference, is required for a systematic AMD code that, for any nonzero (e_x, e_s), D_{e_x, e_s} is nonconstant on any section $G_1 \times \{s\}$.

$|G_1|$ over G_2 whose codewords are indexed in G_1), we take for $F(x, s)$ the coordinate of index x in the codeword s; the condition for the ϵ-security of such AMD code is given in [396, 397]. The AMD code from [395] given above corresponds to the case where S equals the subset of a Reed–Solomon code (viewed as in the remark on RS codes at page 45) whose elements correspond to monic polynomials of degree $d + 2$ with no term of degree $d + 1$. Other examples of AMD codes are given in [397, 668, 1112]. In [535], the authors proposed modifications of AMD codes, which can have minimum distances larger than 1, and then not only detect injected faults but also correct errors caused by natural reasons.

It is shown in [916] (which dealt with cheating detection in secret sharing) and recalled in [396] that

- For any ϵ-secure AMD code, we have $|G| \geq \frac{|S|-1}{\epsilon^2} + 1$;

    indeed, given $s \in S$, applying the inequality $|D^{-1}(s')| \geq \frac{1}{\epsilon}$ for each $s' \neq s$, we have that the probability that $D(E(s) + e) \notin \{s, \perp\}$ when e is chosen uniformly at random in $G \setminus \{0\}$ is at least $\frac{|S|-1}{\epsilon(|G|-1)}$, and we have by hypothesis that this probability is at most ϵ.

    - As observed in [396], the inequality $|G| \geq \frac{|S|-1}{\epsilon^2} + 1$ cannot be an equality for systematic codes, since for such codes, the size of E_s (the set of all possible images of s by E) equals $|G_1|$, which is then at least $\frac{1}{\epsilon}$, and we have also $|G_2| \geq \frac{1}{\epsilon}$ because, for every $s \in S$ and $(e_s, e_x) \in S \times G_1 \setminus \{(0, 0)\}$, we have $\max_{e_F \in G_2} \mathrm{Prob}\,[D(E(s) + (e_s, e_x, e_F)) \notin \{s, \perp\}] \geq \frac{1}{|G_2|}$, as this probability equals that of the event $F(x + e_x, s + e_s) - F(x, s) = e_F$, where $F(x + e_x, s + e_s) - F(x, s) \in G_2$; these two inequalities imply $|G| \geq \frac{|S|}{\epsilon^2}$.

    - Moreover, it is shown in [396] (which adapted a proof from [1112] dealing with a different notion of AMD codes) that, for any systematic ϵ-secure AMD code with $\epsilon < 1$, we have $|G_1| \geq \frac{\log |S|}{\epsilon \log |G_2|}$, where log is (for instance) the base 2 logarithm; indeed, the code over G_2 of all functions $x \mapsto F(x, s) + e_F$, where (s, e_F) ranges over $S \times G_2$, contains $|S| |G_2|$ codewords of length $|G_1|$ and has minimum distance at least $|G_1|(1 - \epsilon) > 0$ (since the code is ϵ-secure); the bound is then deduced from the *Singleton bound*[28] (see page 6): $|G_1|(1 - \epsilon) \leq |G_1| - \log_{|G_2|}(|S| |G_2|) + 1$, that is, $|G_1| \epsilon \geq \log_{|G_2|}(|S|)$.

- For weak ϵ-secure AMD codes, we have $|G| \geq \frac{|S|-1}{\epsilon} + 1$; indeed, all that we can then say is that $|D^{-1}(s')| \geq 1$.

A stronger definition of AMD codes has been proposed in [1112, 1113], in which the condition becomes that the probability that $D(E(s) + e) \notin \{\perp\}$ is at most ϵ (hence, in this definition, every undetected algebraic manipulation is treated as a success of the adversary, while in Definition 88, when the source message is unaltered, it is not). This is preferred for some applications (such as nonmalleable secret sharing schemes [558]). More precisely, systematic AMD codes detect algebraic manipulation for errors (e_s, e_x, e_F), under the condition that the information part contains an error, $e_s \neq 0$, while this stronger version

---

[28] Recall that this bound is valid for (unrestricted) codes over any alphabet.

detects errors with zero information part ($e_s = 0, e_x, e_F$); for some secure architectures, the integrity of redundant bits of the codes is indeed also important. The AMD codes described above from [395] satisfy this stronger requirement as well as the main construction in [397]. Lower bounds on the values of ϵ such that such codes can be ϵ-secure are studied in [1113] (with other notation) and constructions are given.

The first domains of application of AMD codes have been, as indicated in [395], robust secret sharing schemes (which ensure that, given a coalition S of players able to reconstruct some secret value s, no subcoalition of (dishonest) players unable on their own to reconstruct s can modify their shares and lead with the other players from S to the reconstruction of some value $s' = s + t$, where $t \neq 0$ could be controlled by the dishonest players; this is achieved by applying a linear secret sharing scheme to an encoding of the secret by an AMD code rather than to the secret itself) and robust fuzzy extractors (enabling to recover a uniformly random key from a noisy and nonuniform secret, such as those obtained by biometrics, in such way that the key can be recovered from any value close to the secret) [395]. Other cryptographic applications are the message authentication codes that remain secure when the adversary can manipulate the key, unconditionally secure *multiparty computation* protocols with a dishonest majority, anonymous message transmission (and quantum communication), and more applications mentioned in [396, 397]. Applications to memory security have been developed in [534, 1114].

12.2 Fully homomorphic encryption and related questions on Boolean functions

We refer to [305, 306, 839] for the present section. We observe nowadays two complementary phenomena: the proliferation of small embedded devices having growing but still limited computing (and data storage) facilities, and the development of cloud services with extensive storage and computing means. The cloud becomes then a more and more unavoidable complement to embedded devices. But the outsourcing of data processing raises new privacy concerns. The users want to prevent the servers from learning about their data, while these servers are needed to help computing values from them. Gentry's *fully homomorphic encryption* (*FHE*) scheme [536, 537] gives a theoretical solution to this problem, by allowing encryption $\mathbf{C}^H$ preserving both operations of addition and multiplication:

$$\mathbf{C}^H(m + m') = \mathbf{C}^H(m) + \mathbf{C}^H(m'); \ \mathbf{C}^H(mm') = \mathbf{C}^H(m)\,\mathbf{C}^H(m'). \tag{12.10}$$

Given a vectorial function F from a finite field to itself (possibly to a subfield), if Alice wants to compute $F(m)$ and needs the help of the cloud for that, she can send $\mathbf{C}^H(m)$ to Claude,[29] who computes $F(\mathbf{C}^H(m))$, which equals $\mathbf{C}^H(F(m))$, thanks to (12.10) and since F has a polynomial representation. After decryption, Alice gets $F(m)$, but the server has not learned anything about m nor about $F(m)$.

But repetitive use of homomorphic encryption requires more computational power and storage capacity than small devices can offer (see more in [305]). A solution to this problem is that Alice uses a *hybrid symmetric-FHE encryption* protocol, which works according to the following phases:

---

[29] The name used now in cryptography to personify the cloud.

1. *Initialization.* Alice sends to Claude her homomorphic public key pk^H and the homomorphic ciphertext of her symmetric key $\mathbf{C}^H(\mathsf{sk}^S)$ (which is much easier to compute than $\mathbf{C}^H(m)$ since sk^S is much shorter than m, and which needs to be computed once for all further communication with Claude).
2. *Storage.* Alice encrypts her data m with the symmetric encryption scheme $\mathbf{C}^S$, and sends $\mathbf{C}^S(m)$ to Claude.
3. *Evaluation.* Claude calculates $\mathbf{C}^H(\mathbf{C}^S(m))$ and homomorphically evaluates the decryption of the symmetric scheme on Alice's data and gets $\mathbf{C}^H(m)$.
4. *Computation.* Claude homomorphically executes the treatment of F on Alice's data, and gets $\mathbf{C}^H(F(m))$.
5. *Result.* Claude sends $\mathbf{C}^H(F(m))$ and Alice gets $F(m)$ by deciphering (deciphering being much less costly than enciphering in FHE).

However, the best-adapted generations of FHE, that is, second and third generations, are noise based (being built on the learning with errors [LWE] problem) and need expensive "bootstrapping" when the noise grows too much. It is then mandatory to reduce the error growth during evaluation-computation, and this is more or less equivalent to reducing the number of multiplications for the second generation (more precisely, to reduce the multiplication depth), and the number of additions for the third generation (in fact, the correct parameter is much more complex; it also depends of multiplications, see [537], but describing it precisely would be too long). The choice of the symmetric cipher $\mathbf{C}^S$ is then central for reducing the cost.

12.2.1 The FLIP cipher

The multiplicative depth of AES being too large (and its additive depth being still larger), other symmetric encryption schemes have been proposed: block ciphers, like *LowMC* [11], *Rasta* and *Agrasta* [480], and the stream cipher *Kreyvium* [192]. These solutions have drawbacks: Kreyvium is expensive (all the more if it needs to be started again, which can happen often), and lowMC has low complexity rounds, but their iteration makes it unadapted, as almost any other block cipher (if we look precisely how they can work with HeLib [584], for instance), except for Rasta and Agrasta, which are also well adapted for *multiparty computation*, but whose originality is not in the choice of the S-box, which is why we do not describe them here.

The filter permutator and the FLIP cipher

The *FLIP cipher* is an encryption scheme described in [839], which tries to minimize the parameters mentioned above (in particular, the multiplicative depth). It is based on a new stream cipher model, called the *filter permutator* (see Figure 12.1 below), consisting in updating at each clock cycle a key register by a permutation of the coordinates, piloted by a pseudorandom number generator (PRNG), and in filtering the resulting permuted key with a Boolean function f, whose input is the whole register[30] and whose output provides the *keystream*. Applying the nonlinear filtering function directly on the key bits allows reducing

---

[30] A future version of FLIP gets rid of this constraint.

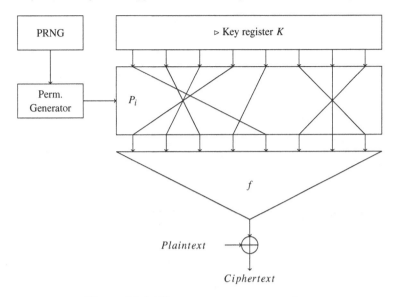

Figure 12.1 Filter permutator construction.

the noise level when used in hybrid symmetric-FHE encryption protocols. In theory, there is no big difference between the filter model seen at page 23 and the filter permutator since the LFSR is simply replaced by a permutator. But in practice, there is much difference since the filter function has hundreds of input bits instead of about 20, and there is another important difference that we shall see in the next subsection.

In the versions of the cipher proposed in [839], function f has $n = n_1 + n_2 + n_3 \geq 500$ variables, where n_2 is even and n_3 equals $\frac{k(k+1)}{2}t$ for some k and t. It is defined as

$$f(x_0, \ldots, x_{n_1-1}, y_0, \ldots, y_{n_2-1}, z_0, \ldots, z_{n_3-1}) = \bigoplus_{i=0}^{n_1-1} x_i \oplus \bigoplus_{i=0}^{n_2/2-1} y_{2i}\, y_{2i+1} \oplus,$$

$$\bigoplus_{j=1}^{t} T_k\left(z_{\frac{(j-1)k(k+1)}{2}}, z_{\frac{(j-1)k(k+1)}{2}+1}, \ldots, z_{\frac{(j-1)k(k+1)}{2}+\frac{k(k+1)}{2}-1} \right),$$

where *triangular function* T_k is defined as

$$T_k(z_0, \ldots, z_{j-1}) = z_0 \oplus z_1 z_2 \oplus z_3 z_4 z_5 \oplus \ldots \oplus z_{\frac{k(k-1)}{2}} \cdots z_{\frac{k(k+1)}{2}-1}.$$

We have seen in Subsection 6.2.6, page 265, how to calculate the nonlinearity of direct sums, in Subsection 9.1.4, page 341, how to calculate their algebraic immunity, and we have calculated in Subsection 10.3.1, page 363, the values of the nonlinearities and algebraic immunities of triangular functions.

Four sets of parameters were proposed for the filtering function. The Hamming weight of the input to the function being forced to $\frac{n}{2}$ where n is the size of the register, the four proposed instances, displayed in Table 12.1, ensure that $\binom{n}{n/2} \geq 2^\lambda$, where λ is a security parameter (the number of elementary operations needed for a cryptanalysis by exhaustive search being 2^λ). There exists a guess and determine attack on a preliminary version of

Table 12.1 n: total number of variables, n_1: linear part, n_2: quadratic part, t: number of triangular functions, k: degree of the triangular functions; λ: resulting security parameter.

Name	n	n_1	n_2	t	k	λ
FLIP-530	530	42	128	8	9	80
FLIP-662	662	46	136	4	15	80
FLIP-1394	1,394	82	224	8	16	128
FLIP-1704	1,704	86	238	5	23	128

FLIP [490]. It is not efficient on the regular versions of FLIP. As checked in [839], FLIP is well suited for reducing the increase of the noise in homomorphic encryption, particularly for the third generation, and even for the second generation.

12.2.2 Boolean functions with restricted inputs

It was asserted in [839] that function f has sufficiently good cryptographic parameters (small balance bias, large algebraic degree, large nonlinearity, large algebraic immunity, and fast algebraic immunity), but by definition in the filter permutator, the input to f has constant Hamming weight (equal to the weight of the secret key), while the study of f was made over the whole space $\mathbb{F}_2^n$. An important question has then been to see if the filtering function proposed in [839] maintains good behavior with respect to classical attacks when its domain is restricted. This has been established in a subsequent paper [306]. The work consisted in

- Reconsidering all classical attacks in the framework of Boolean functions restricted to some generic subset E of $\mathbb{F}_2^n$ (resulting from the specifications of the cryptosystem that uses them, and also possibly of the cryptanalysis performed on it, for instance a guess and determine attack), and in particular to a set of vectors of constant Hamming weight
- Studying how a generic function can contribute to the resistance against each attack in such framework
- Revisiting all related criteria, and studying constructions of functions satisfying the new versions of these criteria
- Studying specifically FLIP's function and seeing if it provides a good trade-off

Set E may change when processing the algorithm or during the cryptanalysis. We may also want the function to be usable in a variety of situations. We are then interested in Boolean functions achieving good trade-off among all important cryptographic criteria, when they are restricted to each set E in some family $\mathcal{E}$. A particular family plays a special role for FLIP, as explained above:

$$\mathcal{E} = \{E_{n,1}, \ldots, E_{n,n-1}\}, \text{ where } E_{n,k} = \{x \in \mathbb{F}_2^n; \ w_H(x) = k\}.$$

These sets are called *slices* in some papers (see, *e.g.,* [504, 505]). Note that symmetric functions (see Section 10.1, page 352), among which are balanced functions, bent functions, and functions with optimal algebraic immunity, are constant on each set $E_{n,k}$ and lose then completely their desirable properties. We shall see other examples of similar degradation.

We recall below from [306] the general study of the most important cryptographic criteria in such general framework and how they particularize when E lives in class $\mathcal{E}$ above.

Note that for the FLIP cipher, Siegenthaler's correlation attack (see page 86) does not seem to apply. We do not study then the resilience of restricted Boolean functions, but such study could be useful for other ciphers and for the resistance to guess and determine attacks.

Remark. A probabilistic and asymptotic study has been made in [504, 507, 508] on the restrictions of Boolean functions to sets of inputs of fixed Hamming weight. We refer the reader interested to these papers (which also contain other interesting results); we deal here with fixed (generic) numbers of variables.

The nonlinearity of Boolean functions under nonuniform input distribution (which is another, possibly more general, way of not reducing the study of Boolean functions to the usual framework) has been also studied in [525], but the chosen distribution is binomial and does not fit with the framework of FLIP nor that of guess and determine attacks. □

Balance We denote by $w_H(f)_k$ the Hamming weight of the restriction of f to $E_{n,k}$:

$$w_H(f)_k = |\{x \in \mathbb{F}_2^n, w_H(x) = k, f(x) = 1\}|.$$

For all $n \geq 2$, there exist balanced Boolean functions that are unbalanced on $E_{n,k}$ for every $k \in [1, n-1]$; these functions can even be $(n-1)$-resilient (and remain then balanced when at most $n-1$ of their variables are arbitrarily fixed): an example is the first elementary symmetric Boolean function $\sigma_1(x) = \bigoplus_{i=1}^n x_i = w_H(x) \pmod 2$. But there exist, for some values of n, balanced functions that are balanced on each $E_{n,k}; k \in [1, n-1]$:

Definition 89 *We call* weightwise perfectly balanced *the functions that are balanced on any $E_{n,k}$ for $k = 1, \ldots, n-1$, that is, such that*

$$\forall k \in [1, n-1], \ w_H(f)_k = \frac{\binom{n}{k}}{2}, \tag{12.11}$$

and such that $f(0_n) = 0$ and $f(1_n) = 1$.

The double condition "$f(0_n) = 0$ and $f(1_n) = 1$" makes f globally balanced and is not restrictive for balanced functions satisfying (12.11), up to the addition of constant 1. Of course, such functions can exist only if $\binom{n}{k}$ is even for every $k = 1, \ldots, n-1$, *i.e.*, n is a power of 2.

Necessary conditions on the algebraic normal form of Boolean functions to be weightwise perfectly balanced are given in [306]. A *secondary construction* based on the "indirect sum" (see Theorem 21, page 300) has been given in this same reference. We recall the proof.

Proposition 191   *[306] Let f, f', and g be weightwise perfectly balanced n-variable functions and let g' be any n-variable Boolean function; then*

$$h(x, y) = f(x) \oplus \prod_{i=1}^{n} x_i \oplus g(y) \oplus (f(x) \oplus f'(x))g'(y); \quad x, y \in \mathbb{F}_2^n$$

is a weightwise perfectly balanced $2n$-variable function.

Proof

- If $w_H(x, y) = 0$, then $h(x, y) = 0$.
- If $k \in \{1, \ldots, n - 1\}$, then the set $\{(x, y) \in \mathbb{F}_2^{2n}; w_H(x, y) = k\}$ equals the disjoint union of the following sets:

  - $\{0_n\} \times \{y \in \mathbb{F}_2^n; w_H(y) = k\}$, on which $h(x, y)$ equals $g(y)$ and is then balanced.
  - $\{x \in \mathbb{F}_2^n; w_H(x) = i\} \times \{y\}$, where $1 \le i \le k$ and $w_H(y) = k - i$, on each of which $h(x, y)$ equals $f(x) \oplus g(y)$ if $g'(y) = 0$ and $f'(x) \oplus g(y)$ if $g'(y) = 1$; in both cases, it is balanced.

- If $k = n$, then the set $\{(x, y) \in \mathbb{F}_2^{2n}; w_H(x, y) = k\}$ equals the disjoint union of the following sets:

  - $\{(0_n, 1_n)\} \cup \{(1_n, 0_n)\}$, on which $h(x, y)$ equals respectively 1 and 0 and is then globally balanced.
  - $\{x \in \mathbb{F}_2^n; w_H(x) = i\} \times \{y\}$, where $1 \le i \le n - 1$ and $w_H(y) = n - i$, on each of which $h(x, y)$ equals $f(x) \oplus g(y)$ if $g'(y) = 0$ and $f'(x) \oplus g(y)$ if $g'(y) = 1$; in both cases, it is balanced.

- If $k \in \{n + 1, \ldots, 2n - 1\}$, then the set $\{(x, y) \in \mathbb{F}_2^{2n}; w_H(x, y) = k\}$ equals the disjoint union of the following sets:

  - $\{1_n\} \times \{y \in \mathbb{F}_2^n; w_H(y) = k - n\}$, on which $h(x, y)$ equals $g(y)$ and is then balanced.
  - $\{x \in \mathbb{F}_2^n; w_H(x) = i\} \times \{y\}$, where $k - n + 1 \le i \le n - 1$ and $w_H(y) = k - i$, on each of which $h(x, y)$ equals $f(x) \oplus g(y)$ if $g'(y) = 0$ and $f'(x) \oplus g(y)$ if $g'(y) = 1$; in both cases, it is balanced.

- If $k = 2n$, then $w_H(x, y) = k$ is equivalent to $x = y = 1_n$, then $h(x, y) = 1$. $\qquad\square$

Noting that $f(x_1, x_2) = x_1$ is weightwise perfectly balanced, we can recursively build weightwise perfectly balanced Boolean functions of 2^ℓ variables, for all ℓ in $\mathbb{N}^*$. For instance, with $f = f'$, we obtain the following class:

$$f(x_1, x_2, \ldots, x_{2^\ell}) = \bigoplus_{a=1}^{\ell} \bigoplus_{i=1}^{2^{\ell-a}} \prod_{j=0}^{2^{a-1}-1} x_{i+j2^{\ell-a+1}}.$$

In [787], another construction is proposed based on the nice idea that if a Boolean function f on $\mathbb{F}_{2^n}$ satisfies $f(0_n) = 0$, $f(1_n) = 1$ and $f(x^2) = f(x) \oplus 1$ for all $x \in \mathbb{F}_{2^n} \setminus \mathbb{F}_2$, the function over $\mathbb{F}_2^n$ obtained by decomposing x over a normal basis is weightwise perfectly balanced. Indeed, the transformation $x \mapsto x^2$ results in a cyclic shift. These functions are invariant under a shift by two positions of the input (we already evoked in Section 10.2, page 360, the interest and risk of such rotation symmetry). The restricted nonlinearities of the functions (see the definition below) are also studied.

In [1073], the authors give a large family of Boolean functions that are weightwise perfectly balanced if n is equal to a power of 2 and weightwise almost perfectly balanced (see below) otherwise, and which have optimal algebraic immunity and keep good algebraic immunity when restricted.

It is possible to extend the construction of Proposition 191 to get for all n *weightwise almost perfectly balanced* functions, satisfying by definition that for all $k \in [1, n-1]$, $w_H(f)_k$ equals $\frac{\binom{n}{k}}{2}$ when $\binom{n}{k}$ is even and $\frac{\binom{n}{k} \pm 1}{2}$ when $\binom{n}{k}$ is odd; see the proof and more results in [306].

The transformation $f \mapsto (g \to \sum_{x \in \mathbb{F}_2^n} (-1)^{f(x)+g(x)})$, where g ranges over the set of all symmetric Boolean functions null at zero input, is introduced in this same reference. This transformation is similar to the Walsh transform, but with symmetric functions playing the role played normally by affine functions. It is shown that, for every n-variable Boolean function f, the quadratic mean of the sequence $k \to \sum_{w_H(x)=k} (-1)^{f(x)}$ equals $\frac{1}{\sqrt{n+1}}$ times the quadratic mean of the sequence $g \to \sum_{x \in \mathbb{F}_2^n} (-1)^{f(x)+g(x)}$.

Nonlinearity The Hamming distance between a function f and a linear function $\ell_a(x) = a \cdot x$ on inputs ranging over some set E equals

$$d_E(f, \ell_a) = \frac{|E|}{2} - \frac{1}{2} \sum_{x \in E} (-1)^{f(x) \oplus a \cdot x}$$

(sum performed in $\mathbb{Z}$). The minimal distance $nl_E(f)$ between f and affine functions over E, which we shall call *nonlinearity with inputs in E*, equals then

$$nl_E(f) = \frac{|E|}{2} - \frac{1}{2} \max_{a \in \mathbb{F}_2^n} \left| \sum_{x \in E} (-1)^{f(x) \oplus a \cdot x} \right|.$$

Since $\sum_{a \in \mathbb{F}_2^n} \left(\sum_{x \in E} (-1)^{f(x) \oplus a \cdot x} \right)^2 = 2^n |E|$, we have then

$$nl_E(f) \leq \frac{|E|}{2} - \frac{\sqrt{|E|}}{2}. \tag{12.12}$$

For $E \subsetneq \mathbb{F}_2^n$, this bound is in general not achievable with equality (contrary to the unrestricted case for n even). In the case of $E = E_{n,k}$, it is never tight, except maybe for two particular pairs (n, k): $(50, 3)$ and $(50, 47)$, since Erdös showed that the binomial coefficient $\binom{n}{k}$ with $3 \leq k \leq n/2$ is the square of an integer for the single case $\binom{50}{3}$.

Bound (12.12) can be improved:

Proposition 192 *[306] Let E be a subset of $\mathbb{F}_2^n$ and f a Boolean function over E. Then:*

$$nl_E(f) \leq \frac{|E|}{2} - \frac{1}{2} \sqrt{|E| + \lambda}$$

where

$$\lambda = \max_{a \in \mathbb{F}_2^n; a \neq 0_n} \left| \sum_{\substack{(x,y) \in E^2 \\ x+y=a}} (-1)^{f(x) \oplus f(y)} \right|.$$

Proof For every nonzero $a \in \mathbb{F}_2^n$, we have

$$\sum_{b \in \mathbb{F}_2^n; a \cdot b = 0} \left(\sum_{x \in E} (-1)^{f(x) \oplus b \cdot x} \right)^2 = \sum_{(x,y) \in E^2} (-1)^{f(x) \oplus f(y)} \sum_{b \in \mathbb{F}_2^n; a \cdot b = 0} (-1)^{b \cdot (x+y)}$$

$$= 2^{n-1} \sum_{\substack{(x,y) \in E^2 \\ x+y \in \{0_n, a\}}} (-1)^{f(x) \oplus f(y)},$$

which implies

$$\max_{b \in \mathbb{F}_2^n; a \cdot b = 0} \left| \sum_{x \in E} (-1)^{f(x) \oplus a \cdot x} \right| \geq \sqrt{|E| + \sum_{\substack{(x,y) \in E^2 \\ x+y=a}} (-1)^{f(x) \oplus f(y)}}.$$

If $\sum_{\substack{(x,y) \in E^2 \\ x+y=a}} (-1)^{f(x) \oplus f(y)}$ is negative, then we can apply this inequality to function $f'(x) = f(x) \oplus v \cdot x$, where $v \cdot a = 1$; we have $\sum_{\substack{(x,y) \in E^2 \\ x+y=a}} (-1)^{f'(x) \oplus f'(y)} = -\sum_{\substack{(x,y) \in E^2 \\ x+y=a}} (-1)^{f(x) \oplus f(y)}$. Relation (3.1), page 79, completes the proof. $\square$

Note that this result applied for $E = \mathbb{F}_2^n$ proves again that the derivatives of bent functions are all balanced.

More observations are made for $E = E_{n,k}$ in [306] and the case of direct sums is studied. Proposition 192 is a particular case of a more general and slightly more complex result given in this same reference, which has been generalized in [878], where the consequences are studied in detail.

The maximal value of $nl_E(f)$ is the covering radius of the punctured first order Reed–Muller code obtained by deleting all the coordinates whose indices lie outside E and is then at least $\frac{d}{2}$, where d is the minimum distance of this code.

For $E = E_{n,k}$, this minimum distance has been determined by Dumer and Kapralova [488]; we have

- For $0 \leq k < n/2, d = \binom{n-1}{k-1}$
- For $k = n/2, d = \binom{n-2}{k-2}$
- For $n/2 < k \leq n-1, d = \binom{n-1}{k}$
- For $k = n, d = 1$.

The maximal value of $nl_{E_{n,k}}(f)$ is then nonzero except for particular values of k.

Nevertheless, fixing the input Hamming weight of some functions may deteriorate their nonlinearity in an extreme way: for every n, there exists f of large nonlinearity such that $nl_k(f) = 0, \forall k = 0, \ldots, n$. For instance, the (bent) elementary symmetric function σ_2 (n even) has this latter property (like any other symmetric function). We leave open the determination of all the bent n-variable Boolean functions such that $nl_k(f) = 0, \forall k = 0, \ldots, n$. Those that are quadratic have been studied in [306], but the proof was incomplete, because the third item of the next technical lemma was viewed as straightforward while it is not.

Lemma 13 *Let n be any positive integer.*

1. *The n-variable Boolean functions such that $nl_k(f) = 0$ for every $k = 1, \ldots, n$ are the functions of the form*

$$f(x) = \bigoplus_{i=1}^{n} x_i \, \varphi_i(x) \oplus \varphi_0(x), \tag{12.13}$$

where $\varphi_0, \varphi_1, \ldots, \varphi_n$ are symmetric Boolean functions.
2. *Up to the addition of an affine function, such a function equals*

$$\bigoplus_{i=1}^{n} \ell_i(x)\sigma_i(x), \tag{12.14}$$

where σ_i is the ith elementary symmetric Boolean function and where the ℓ_i are all affine.
3. *If $n \geq 6$, then f is quadratic if and only if, up to the addition of an affine function, we have*

$$f(x) = \ell(x)\,\sigma_1(x) \oplus \epsilon \, \sigma_2(x), \tag{12.15}$$

where $\epsilon \in \mathbb{F}_2$, and $\ell(x)$ is a linear function.

Proof   1. Any function of the form (12.13) coincides with an affine function on every $E_{n,k}$ since each symmetric function is constant on it, and conversely, if a Boolean function f coincides on every $E_{n,k}$ with an affine function, say with $\ell_k(x) = \sum_{i \in I_k} x_i \oplus \epsilon_k$, then defining, for every $x \in E_{n,k}$ and every $i = 1, \ldots, n$, that $\varphi_i(x) = 1$ if $i \in I_k$ and $\varphi_i(x) = 0$ otherwise, and $\varphi_0(x) = \epsilon_k$, we have $f(x) = \bigoplus_{i=1}^{n} x_i \, \varphi_i(x) \oplus \varphi_0(x)$, where the φ_i are symmetric functions.
2. Expressing each function $\varphi_0, \ldots, \varphi_n$ by means of the elementary symmetric functions $\sigma_1, \ldots, \sigma_n$, we obtain, up to the addition of an affine function, $f(x) = \bigoplus_{i=1}^{n} \ell_i(x)\sigma_i(x)$, where the ℓ_i are all affine.
3. All the terms obtained after expansion of $\bigoplus_{i=3}^{n} \ell_i(x)\sigma_i(x)$ in (12.14) have degree at least 3 and, using the uniqueness of the ANF of a Boolean function, f is quadratic if and only if all those whose degree is at least 4 cancel and those of degree 3 are canceled by those from $\ell_2(x)\sigma_2(x)$ (the expression of the function can then be taken equal to the quadratic part of (12.14) expanded). Let us translate this into explicit conditions on (12.14).
   For every $i, j = 1, \ldots, n$, we have $x_j \, \sigma_i(x) = (\bigoplus_{\substack{I \subseteq \{1, \ldots, n\} \\ |I|=i, j \in I}} x^I) \oplus (\bigoplus_{\substack{I \subseteq \{1, \ldots, n\} \\ |I|=i+1, j \in I}} x^I)$. We deduce that, writing $\ell_i(x) = \bigoplus_{j \in J_i} x_j \oplus \epsilon_i$, we have, for $i < n$:

$$\ell_i(x)\,\sigma_i(x) = \left(\bigoplus_{\substack{I \subseteq \{1, \ldots, n\} \\ |I|=i, |I \cap J_i| \,(\mathrm{mod}\,2) = \epsilon_i \oplus 1}} x^I \right) \oplus \left(\bigoplus_{\substack{I \subseteq \{1, \ldots, n\} \\ |I|=i+1, |I \cap J_i| \,\mathrm{odd}}} x^I \right), \tag{12.16}$$

since each x_j, $j \in J_i$, contributes once for each x^I such that $|I| = i$ and $j \in I$ and once for each x^I such that $|I| = i + 1$ and $j \in I$. And for $i = n$, $\ell_n(x)\,\sigma_n(x)$ equals $\sigma_n(x)$ if $|J_n|$ [mod 2]$= \epsilon_n \oplus 1$ and is zero otherwise. Hence:

- For $i = n$, we have $\ell_n(x)\,\sigma_n(x) = (|J_n|\,[\text{mod 2}] \oplus \epsilon_n)\,\sigma_n(x)$.
- For $1 \le i \le n - 1$, specifying the values of the two subsums in (12.16), we have:

    - If $0 < |J_i| < n$, then $\ell_i(x)\,\sigma_i(x)$ contains terms of degree i but not all of them (since both parities can be achieved by $|I \cap J_i|$ when $|I| = i$) and terms of degree $i + 1$ but, if $i \le n - 2$, not all of them as well, and if $i = n - 1$ the part in $\sigma_{i+1} = \sigma_n$ has coefficient $|J_{n-1}|$ [mod 2].
    - If $|J_i| = 0$, then $\ell_i(x)\,\sigma_i(x) = \epsilon_i\,\sigma_i(x)$ (note that, for $i = n - 1$, the coefficient of σ_{i+1}, which is then 0, takes the same value $|J_{n-1}|$ [mod 2], obtained above for $0 < |J_i| < n$).
    - if $|J_i| = n$, then $\ell_i(x)\,\sigma_i(x) = (\sigma_1(x) \oplus \epsilon_i)\sigma_i(x) = (i\,[\text{mod 2}] \oplus \epsilon_i)\,\sigma_i(x) \oplus (i + 1\,[\text{mod 2}])\sigma_{i+1}(x)$ (and the coefficient $i + 1$ [mod 2] of σ_n for $i = n - 1$ matches the value $|J_{n-1}|$ [mod 2] above as well).

    It cannot then happen, when the function is quadratic, that $0 < |J_i| < n$ for some value of $i \ge 3$ and $|J_i| = 0$ or $|J_i| = n$ for another value of $i \ge 3$.

Then f is quadratic if and only if we have $\epsilon_n = (|J_n| + |J_{n-1}|)$ [mod 2] and, addressing first the two latter cases above and then the first case:

- Either, for every $i = 2, \ldots, n - 1$, we have $|J_i| = \eta_i\,n$ with $\eta_i \in \{0, 1\}$ and for $i \ge 3$, $\epsilon_i = (\eta_i + \eta_{i-1})\,i$ [mod 2].
- Or, for every $i = 3, \ldots, n - 1$, we have $0 < |J_i| < n$ and the two following sets $\{I \subseteq \{1, \ldots, n\}; |I| = i \text{ and } |I \cap J_i|\,[\text{mod 2}] = \epsilon_i \oplus 1\}$ and $\{I \subseteq \{1, \ldots, n\}; |I| = i \text{ and } |I \cap J_{i-1}|\,\text{odd}\}$ are equal. Denoting by z_i the vector of $\mathbb{F}_2^n$ of support J_i, by $B_{\ge 3}$ the set of vectors of $\mathbb{F}_2^n$ of Hamming weight at least 3, by E^0 (rather than $E^\perp$) the orthogonal of an $\mathbb{F}_2$-vector space E and by E^1 its complement, the condition writes $\{0_n, z_i\}^{\epsilon_i \oplus 1} \cap B_{\ge 3} = \{0_n, z_{i-1}\}^1 \cap B_{\ge 3}$, or equivalently $\{0_n, z_i\}^{\epsilon_i} \cap B_{\ge 3} = \{0_n, z_{i-1}\}^0 \cap B_{\ge 3}$.

    If $n \ge 6$ then the linear space $\{0_n, z_{i-1}\}^0$ contains elements of Hamming weight at least 5 and each of its elements of weight at most 2 is then the sum of two elements of $\{0_n, z_{i-1}\}^0 \cap B_{\ge 3}$ (one of weight at least 5 and one of weight at least 3); hence the vector space $\langle \{0_n, z_{i-1}\}^0 \cap B_{\ge 3}\rangle$ spanned by $\{0_n, z_{i-1}\}^0 \cap B_{\ge 3}$ equals $\{0_n, z_{i-1}\}^0$; the same is true for $\{0_n, z_i\}^{\epsilon_i} \cap B_{\ge 3}$ if $\epsilon_i = 0$, in which case we have $z_i = z_{i-1}$, that is, $J_i = J_{i-1}$, and if $\epsilon_i = 1$ then $\{0_n, z_{i-1}\}^0$ equals $\langle \{0_n, z_i\}^{\epsilon_i} \cap B_{\ge 3}\rangle$, which contains $\{0_n, z_i\}^0$ for the same reasons as above and cannot be reduced to a hyperplane, and is then equal to $\mathbb{F}_2^n$, a contradiction.

Summarizing, we have, up to the addition of an affine function:

- We are in the first case above, and $f(x)$ equals the quadratic part of a function of the form $\ell(x)\,\sigma_1(x) \oplus (\eta\,\sigma_1(x) \oplus \epsilon)\,\sigma_2(x)$, where $\epsilon, \eta \in \mathbb{F}_2$, and $\ell(x)$ is a linear function. Since $\eta\,\sigma_1(x)\,\sigma_2(x) = \eta\,\sigma_3(x)$, we can take $\eta = 0$ and we obtain then (12.15).

- Or we are in the second case above with $z_2 = z_3 = \cdots = z_{n-1}$ and $\epsilon_3 = \cdots = \epsilon_{n-1} = 0$, and $f(x)$ is the quadratic part of $\ell(x)\sigma_1(x) \oplus \epsilon\, \sigma_2(x) \oplus \ell'(x)(\bigoplus_{i=2}^{n-1} \sigma_i(x)) \oplus \epsilon_n \sigma_n(x)$, where ℓ and ℓ' are linear and $\epsilon_n = \ell'(1)$, that is, $\ell(x)\sigma_1(x) \oplus \epsilon\, \sigma_2(x) \oplus \ell'(x)(\sigma_1(x) \oplus 1 \oplus \delta_0(x)) = \ell(x)\sigma_1(x) \oplus \epsilon\, \sigma_2(x) \oplus \ell'(x)(\sigma_1(x) \oplus 1)$), and this second case happens then to be equivalent, up to the addition of an affine function, to a particular case of the first. $\qquad\square$

Remark. The same proof shows that a function (12.14) has algebraic degree at most k if and only if all the terms of degree at least $k + 2$ in $\bigoplus_{i=k+1}^{n} \ell_i(x)\sigma_i(x)$ cancel and those of degree $k + 1$ are canceled by those from $\ell_k(x)\sigma_k(x)$. The expression of the function equals then the part of degree at most k in (12.14), which is the part of degree at most k in $\bigoplus_{i=1}^{k-1} \ell_i(x)\sigma_i(x) \oplus (\eta\, \sigma_1(x) \oplus \epsilon)\sigma_k(x)$, where $\ell_i(x)$ is affine for every $i = 1, \ldots k - 1$, and $\epsilon, \eta \in \mathbb{F}_2$. Since the degree k part of $\sigma_1(x)\sigma_k(x)$ equals $\sigma_k(x)$ if k is odd and equals 0 otherwise, we obtain $f(x) = \bigoplus_{i=1}^{k-1} \ell_i(x)\sigma_i(x) \oplus \epsilon\, \sigma_k(x)$, where the ℓ_i are affine and $\epsilon \in \mathbb{F}_2$. $\qquad\square$

Proposition 193 *[306] For every even $n \geq 6$, the quadratic bent functions satisfying $nl_k(f) = 0$ for every k are, up to the addition of an affine function, the functions $f(x) = \ell(x)\,\sigma_1(x) \oplus \sigma_2(x)$, where ℓ is linear and $\ell(1_n) = 0$.*

Proof The symplectic form $(x, y) \rightarrow f(x + y) \oplus f(x) \oplus f(y) \oplus f(0_n)$ associated with the function in (12.15) equals

$$\ell(x)\sigma_1(y) \oplus \ell(y)\sigma_1(x) \oplus \epsilon \left(\bigoplus_{1 \leq j \neq i \leq n} x_j y_i \right).$$

Denoting $\ell(x) = \bigoplus_{i=1}^{n} l_i x_i$, the kernel

$$E = \{x \in F_2^n; \forall y \in F_2^n, f(x + y) \oplus f(x) \oplus f(y) \oplus f(0_n) = 0\}$$

of this symplectic form is the $\mathbb{F}_2$-vector space of the solutions of the equations:

$$(L_i) : \ell(x) \oplus l_i \left(\bigoplus_{j=1}^{n} x_j \right) \oplus \epsilon \left(\bigoplus_{j \neq i} x_j \right) = 0, \quad i = 1, \ldots, n.$$

If $\epsilon = 0$, then since the hyperplane of equation $\bigoplus_{j=1}^{n} x_j = 0$ has nontrivial intersection with the kernel of ℓ (because $n \geq 3$), and since every element in this intersection satisfies all equations, f cannot be bent. We assume then that $\epsilon = 1$. For all those $x \in E$ such that $\bigoplus_{j=1}^{n} x_j = 0$, the equation

$$(L_i + L_{i'}) : (l_i \oplus l_{i'}) \left(\bigoplus_{j=1}^{n} x_j \right) \oplus (x_i \oplus x_{i'}) = 0,$$

valid for every $i \neq i'$, results in $x_i \oplus x_{i'} = 0$ and implies that either all x_i are null (in which case (L_i) is of course satisfied), or all are equal to 1, in which case (L_i) becomes (since n is even) $\ell(1_n) = 1$. Hence, $\epsilon = 1$ and $\ell(1_n) = 0$ is a necessary condition for the function to be bent. It is also sufficient, because for all $x \in E$ such that $\bigoplus_{j=1}^{n} x_j = 1$, according to Equation $(L_i + L_{i'})$ again, all those x_i such that $l_i = 0$ are equal to some value $\eta \in \mathbb{F}_2$

and all those x_i such that $l_i = 1$ are equal to another value, which can be only $\eta \oplus 1$, since $\bigoplus_{j=1}^{n} x_j = 1$, and the number of i such that $l_i = 1$ is odd, that is, $\ell(1_n) = 1$, a contradiction. This completes the proof.   □

It is shown in [306] that for the direct sum of any n-variable function f and any m-variable function g, we have

$$nl_{E_{n+m,k}}(f \oplus g) \geq \sum_{i=0}^{k} \binom{n}{i} nl_{E_{m,k-i}}(g) + \sum_{i=0}^{k} nl_{E_{n,i}}(f) \left(\binom{m}{k-i} - 2nl_{E_{m,k-i}}(g) \right).$$

We refer to this reference for the proof.

Algebraic immunity The majority function being, like every symmetric function, constant on all inputs of the same Hamming weight, and having optimal algebraic immunity, it is an extreme example of degradation of the algebraic immunity when inputs are restricted to $E_{n,k}$. We call *algebraic immunity with inputs in E* of a given Boolean function f the nonnegative integer:

$$AI_E(f) = \min\{\max(d_{alg}(g), d_{alg}((fg)_{|E})); g \not\equiv 0 \text{ on } E\}$$
$$= \min\{d_{alg}(g); (fg)_{|E} \equiv 0 \text{ or } ((f \oplus 1)g)_{|E} \equiv 0; g \not\equiv 0 \text{ on } E\},$$

where $d_{alg}((fg)_{|E})$ equals the minimum algebraic degree of Boolean functions over $\mathbb{F}_2^n$ that coincide with fg over E, and we call annihilators of f over E the functions g such that $(fg)_{|E} \equiv 0$.

The equality between these two minima is shown easily: if g and $h = fg$ achieving the former minimum coincide on E, we have then $g \oplus h = g(f \oplus 1) = 0$ on E, where g has nonzero restriction to E, and if they do not, then after multiplication of equality $h = fg$ by f, we have $(g \oplus h)f = 0$, where $g \oplus h$ has nonzero restriction to E; this proves that the former minimum is bounded below by the latter. The inequality in the other order is still more obvious since the set over which the latter minimum is taken is a subset of the set over which the former is taken.

Remark. Taking the restriction to E may (often) decrease the algebraic immunity (we shall see examples below) since it weakens the condition on g to be an annihilator of f or of $f \oplus 1$, but it may also increase the algebraic immunity, because it strengthens the condition on g to be nonzero. Take for instance an $(n-1)$-variable function f of algebraic immunity at least 2, and define $f'(x, 0) = f(x)$, $f'(x, 1) = 0$, for every $x \in \mathbb{F}_2^{n-1}$. Then the indicator of $\mathbb{F}_2^{n-1} \times \{1\}$ being an annihilator, we have $AI(f') = 1$, while $AI_{\mathbb{F}_2^{n-1} \times \{0\}}(f') = AI(f) \geq 2$. Moreover, for the same reason, we have $AI_k(f') = 1$ for every $k \in \{1, \ldots, n-1\}$, while for some functions f, we can have $AI_k(f) \geq 2$ for some k.   □

The upper bound of Proposition 26, page 92, has been adapted to the algebraic immunity with inputs in E.

Proposition 194 *[306] Let $E \subseteq \mathbb{F}_2^n$ and let f be defined over E. Let d and e be nonnegative integers. Let $M_{d,E}$ be the $(\sum_{i=0}^{d} \binom{n}{i}) \times |E|$ matrix whose term at row indexed by $u \in \mathbb{F}_2^n$ such that $w_H(u) \leq d$, and at column indexed by $x \in E$, equals $\prod_{i=1}^{n} x_i^{u_i}$.*

If $rank(M_{d,E}) + rank(M_{e,E}) > |E|$, *then there exist two Boolean functions* g *and* h *on* E, *such that* g *is not identically null on* E *and*

$$d_{alg}(g) \leq e, \ d_{alg}(h) \leq d \text{ and } fg = h \text{ on } E.$$

We have then

$$AI_E(f) \leq \min \left\{ e; \ rank(M_{e,E}) > \frac{|E|}{2} \right\}. \tag{12.17}$$

Proof By definition, $rank(M_{d,E})$ equals the maximum size of a free family $\mathcal{F}_d$ of restrictions to E of monomials x^u of algebraic degree $w_H(u) \leq d$ (such family generates the restrictions to E of the Boolean functions of algebraic degree at most d) and $|E|$ is the dimension of the $\mathbb{F}_2$-vector space of Boolean functions over E. If $rank(M_{d,E}) + rank(M_{e,E}) > |E|$, the elements of $\mathcal{F}_d$ and the products between f and the elements of a maximum size free family $\mathcal{F}_e$ are necessarily $\mathbb{F}_2$-linearly dependent. Gathering the part of this linear combination dealing with the elements of $\mathcal{F}_d$ and those dealing with $\mathcal{F}_e f$, this linear dependence gives two functions h and g of degrees at most d and e, respectively, such that $(fg)_{|E} = h_{|E}$ and $(g_{|E}, h_{|E}) \not\equiv (0, 0)$, i.e., $g_{|E} \not\equiv 0$. Inequality (12.17) is then straightforward by taking $d = e$. $\qquad\square$

In the case of fixed input weights, a recurring relation on the rank of $M_{d,E_{n,k}}$ has been found in [306] (we refer to this reference for the proof, which is a little too long to be given), where it has been deduced that this rank equals

$$\binom{n}{\min(d, k, n-k)}.$$

For $k \leq n/2$, Relation (12.17) implies then that, for every n-variable Boolean function f:

$$AI_{E_{n,k}}(f) \leq \min \left\{ e; \ 2\binom{n}{e} > \binom{n}{k} \right\}.$$

It is deduced in this same reference (by technical observations dealing with binomial coefficients) that the best possible algebraic immunity of a function with constrained input Hamming weight is lower than for unconstrained functions.

A lower bound exists on the algebraic immunity of the direct sum of two Boolean functions. We recall the proof from [306]:

Proposition 195 *Let* $(f \oplus g)(x, y) = f(x) \oplus g(y)$, $x \in \mathbb{F}_2^n$, $y \in \mathbb{F}_2^m$, *where* $n \leq m$. *Let* k *be such that* $n \leq k \leq m$. *Then the following relation holds:*

$$AI_k(f \oplus g) \geq AI(f) - d_{alg}(g). \tag{12.18}$$

Proof Let $h(x, y)$ be a nonzero annihilator of $f \oplus g$ over $E_{n+m,k}$. Let $(a, b) \in \mathbb{F}_2^{n+m}$ have Hamming weight k and be such that $h(a, b) = 1$. Since (a, b) has Hamming weight k with $n \leq k \leq m$, we may, up to changing the order of the coordinates of b (and without loss of generality), assume that, for every $j = 1, \ldots, n$, we have $b_j = a_j \oplus 1$ and for every $j = n + 1, \ldots k$, we have $b_j = 1$ (so that for every $j = k + 1, \ldots m$, we have

$b_j = 0$). This is possible since $k \geq n$ and in all cases, the last 1 in (a, b) is at position $2n + (k - n) = n + k \leq n + m$. We define the following affine function over $\mathbb{F}_2^n$:

$$L(x) = (x_1 \oplus 1, x_2 \oplus 1, \ldots, x_n \oplus 1, 1, 1, \ldots, 1, 0, \ldots, 0),$$

where the length of the part "$1, \ldots, 1$" equals $k - n$. We have $L(a) = b$. The n-variable function $h(x, L(x))$ is then nonzero and is an annihilator of $f(x) \oplus g(L(x))$ over $\mathbb{F}_2^n$. If $g(b) = 0$, then function $h(x, L(x)) (g(L(x)) \oplus 1)$ is a nonzero annihilator of f and has algebraic degree at most $d_{alg}(h) + d_{alg}(g)$; then we have $d_{alg}(h) + d_{alg}(g) \geq AI(f)$. If $g(b) = 1$, then by applying the same reasoning to $f \oplus 1$ instead of f and $g \oplus 1$ instead of g, we have $d_{alg}(h) + d_{alg}(g) \geq AI(f)$. If $h(x, y)$ is a nonnull annihilator of $f \oplus g \oplus 1$ over $E_{n+m,k}$, we have the same conclusion by replacing f by $f \oplus 1$ or g by $g \oplus 1$. This completes the proof. □

Bound (12.18) may seem loose because of the presence of $-d_{alg}(g)$, but it is not. Let us see with an example (given in [306]) that making the direct sum with some nonconstant Boolean functions g may indeed contribute to a decrease of the algebraic immunity over inputs of fixed Hamming weight: take n odd, $f(x) = 1 \oplus maj(x)$, where maj is the majority function over n variables (which has optimal algebraic immunity $\frac{n+1}{2}$) and $g(y) = maj(y)$ over n variables as well. Then the $2n$-variable function $f \oplus g$ is null at fixed input weight n, because if $w_H(x) + w_H(y) = n$, then either $w_H(x) \leq \frac{n-1}{2}$ and $w_H(y) \geq \frac{n+1}{2}$, and we have then $f(x) = g(y) = 1$, or $w_H(x) \geq \frac{n+1}{2}$ and $w_H(y) \leq \frac{n-1}{2}$, and we have then $f(x) = g(y) = 0$. The algebraic immunity with input weight n equals then 0.

Bound (12.18) also shows that, if $k \geq n$, then taking $g = 0$ (*i.e.*, adding $m \geq k$ virtual variables to f) gives $AI_k(f \oplus 0) \geq AI(f)$; this latter bound is tight (take for f a function whose algebraic immunity equals its algebraic degree). Another example showing the tightness of Bound (12.18) when $d_{alg}(g) = 1$ is also given in this same reference.

It is shown in [306] that for the direct sum of any n-variable function f and any m-variable function g, we have

$$AI_k(f \oplus g) \geq \min_{0 \leq \ell \leq k} (\max[AI_\ell(f), AI_{k-\ell}(g)]).$$

We refer to this reference for the proof.

Impact of Boolean functions with restricted input on FLIP

Balancedness   For given k, let $p_k = Pr_{x \in E_{n,k}}[f(x) = 1] = \frac{1}{2} - \epsilon_k$. The amount of data needed for an attacker to detect the bias ϵ_k is equal to $\frac{1}{\epsilon_k^2}$. In the case of the FLIP cipher, we have $k = \frac{n}{2}$. It has been checked in [306] that the bias is not exploitable, even in the case of guess and determine attacks.

Nonlinearity   In a fast correlation attack (approximating the keystream equations by linear approximation of the filtering function and using a decoding method), the attacker builds a linear system that can be seen as an instance of the learning parity with noise (LPN) problem [99], where the noise parameter is $\eta_k = \frac{nl_{E_{n,k}}}{\binom{n}{k}}$. The data complexity of the attack is $\mathcal{O}(2^h \eta_k^{-2(r+1)})$, where the parameters h and r depend on the algorithm used and on the number of variables. It could be shown in [306] that $nl_{E_{n,\frac{n}{2}}}(f)$ is large enough for allowing the FLIP cipher to resist the fast correlation attack, combined or not with a guess and determine attack.

Algebraic immunity Proposition 195 has allowed to bound $nl_{E_{n,\frac{n}{2}}}(f)$ from below, with the help of the next proposition.

Proposition 196 *Let $f(x)$ be an n-variable Boolean function such that*

$$\forall x \in \mathbb{F}_2^{n-2} \ f(0,0,x) = f(0,1,x) = f(1,0,x).$$

Let $f'(X, x_3, \ldots, x_n)$ be the Boolean function in $n - 1$ variables defined by

$$\forall x \in \mathbb{F}_2^{n-2} \ f'(1,x) = f(1,1,x) \ and \ f'(0,x) = f(0,0,x).$$

If $AI(f) \leq d$, then $AI(f') \leq d$.

This proposition, whose proof can be found in [306], implies that if f is the direct sum of d monomials and if, for every $i \in [k, d]$, f has a monomial of degree i, where k is the smallest degree of all monomials of f, then $AI(f) = d$. This allowed to show that all instances of the FLIP cipher resist the algebraic attack. Determining whether they resist the algebraic attack combined with the guess and determine attack is open. An interesting point observed in [306] is that the high number of triangular functions used in FLIP to prevent the guess and determine attack combined with fast algebraic attack may reduce the algebraic immunity, and there is then a trade-off to be found.

12.3 Local pseudorandom generators and related criteria on Boolean functions

Recall that the principle of *pseudorandom generator*s is to allow expanding short random strings (like private keys), called seeds, into pseudorandom strings, whose length is significantly larger (say, polynomial, that is, in $\mathcal{O}(n^s)$, where n is the length of the seed, with $s > 1$). They are called *local* if each output bit depends on a constant number d of input bits. This property, related to the design of cryptographic primitives that can be evaluated in constant time while using polynomially many cores, allows a wide variety of applications. The only known example of a local pseudorandom generator is the so-called Goldreich's PRG, which applies a simple d-variable Boolean function (Goldreich calls it a d-ary predicate) to public random subsets of size d of the seed.

12.3.1 The Goldreich pseudorandom generator

In [541], Goldreich proposed a *one-way function* (OWF), which is an asymptotic construction aiming at being a "simplest possible function that we do not know how to invert efficiently." This OWF is built as a *random local function* (see below) and was later modified into a *local pseudorandom generator* [543] with nice applications (making possible, with constant computational overhead, a secure two-party computation of any Boolean circuit, and having other applications; see [393, 636]).

Let n and m be two integers, let $(S_1, \ldots, S_m)$ be a list of m subsets of $\{1, \ldots, n\}$ of size d, where d is small compared to n (it can be logarithmic in n or even constant), and let f be a Boolean function in d variables (the so-called predicate). The corresponding *Goldreich's function* $G : \mathbb{F}_2^n \mapsto \mathbb{F}_2^m$ is defined as $G(x) = f(S_1(x)), f(S_2(x)), \ldots, f(S_m(x))$ for every $x \in \mathbb{F}_2^n$, where $S_i(x)$ is a vector made of those bits of x indexed by S_i. Originally, m was of size comparable to n. The one-way property of the function was related to the choice of the predicate and to the fact that $(S_1, \ldots, S_m)$ was an *expander graph*[31] (which corresponds to saying in the particular framework we are in, that for some k, every k subsets cover $k + \Omega(n)$ elements of $\{1, \ldots, n\}$ (which happens to be the case with probability tending to 1 for subsets drawn at random).

Goldreich's pseudorandom generator proposed later takes a larger value of m, polynomial in n. The integer d is called the locality of the PRG, and many works have focused on a framework called "polynomial-stretch local" in which d is constant and $m = n^s$, where $s > 1$ (s is called the *stretch*). For these polynomial-stretch local PRG, the security is considered asymptotically, relative to the class of polynomial adversaries as linear distinguishers. They are conjectured secure under some necessary conditions on the predicate and on the subsets S_i (see the survey [22] and, for a faster overview, [393, section 1.2]). For instance, to avoid an attack by Gaussian elimination, the predicate f must be nonlinear in a basic sense. Moreover, the higher is the algebraic degree, the better, since a random local function with a predicate of algebraic degree s cannot be pseudorandom for a stretch as large as s. The predicate must also be such that, when fixing some number r of input bits to f, its algebraic degree remains large. Note that this has a close relation with algebraic immunity (since if the algebraic degree of f falls down to k when r input bits are fixed, we know that $AI(f) \leq r + k$) and algebraic attacks have been actually further investigated, and the algebraic immunity $AI(f)$ (sometimes called rational degree among people working on Goldreich's PRG) happens to play a direct role and should be large enough (larger than s). There is also an attack [889] when the output of the function is correlated with a number of its input bits smaller than or equal to $\frac{s}{2}$, and f should then be *resilient* with a sufficient order (all the more since this attack has been extended to cases where $m \geq \lambda n$ for large λ); in [915] the authors show that f should be (at least) 2-resilient. The very simple five-variable function $f(x) = x_1 \oplus x_2 \oplus x_3 \oplus x_4 x_5$ (whose structure is similar to that of the FLIP function, but simpler and with considerably smaller parameters) has been proved resisting some attacks based on $\mathbb{F}_2$-linear distinguishers when $m \in \mathcal{O}(n^s)$ with $s < 1.5$ (note that its algebraic degree, resiliency order, and algebraic immunity are all three equal to 2), but of course does not resist the attacks evoked above for larger stretches nor resists algebraic attacks. A general structure has been proposed in [23] for predicates: the direct sum of the full linear function $\bigoplus_{i=1}^k x_i$ and of the *majority function* (see page 335) in $n - k$ variables. No attack is known on such functions when $k \geq 2s$ and $\lceil \frac{n-k}{2} \rceil \geq s$.

Of course, constraints also exist on the choice of the subsets $(S_1, \ldots, S_m)$, more precisely on the hypergraph (see page 70) given by them, which needs to be sufficiently expanding, but in practice, an overwhelming proportion of hypergraphs are sufficiently expanding.

---

[31] A hypergraph whose hyperedges have size d is said to be (α, β)-expanding if, for any choice of $k \leq \alpha m$ edges, their union has size at least $\beta k d$.

As we can see, Goldreich's PRG gives one more example (and an important one) where the classical notions on Boolean functions for cryptography play central roles in frameworks different from stream or block ciphers. An open question is asked in this context by Applebaum and Lovett in [23]: given two positive integers e and k, what is the smallest number of variables (the reference writes "the smallest arity") for which there exists a Boolean function (a predicate) of algebraic immunity (of rational degree) at least e and of resiliency order at least k? The parameters of the direct sum of the full linear function $\bigoplus_{i=1}^{k} x_i$ and of the majority function in $2e - 1$ variables show that this number is at most $k + 2e - 1$ as observed in [838] (Applebaum and Lovett give the bound $k + 2e$ and propose as example the direct sum of function $\bigoplus_{i=1}^{k} x_i$ and of the majority function in $2e$ variables; note that this very function is not k-resilient, at least in the usual sense, because the majority function in $2e$ variables is not balanced, but they probably think of a majority function modified into a balanced function with the same AI). As we can see, the upper bound $k + 2e$ is not optimal, and even $k + 2e - 1$ may not be optimal.

This problem is clearly related to another open question: is there, for $k \leq n - 2$, an upper bound on the algebraic immunity of k-resilient functions that would be sharper than $\min(n-k-1, \lceil \frac{n}{2} \rceil)$ (implied by the *Siegenthaler bound* and the *Courtois–Meier bound*)? We specify $k \leq n - 2$ because for $k = n - 1$, Siegenthealer's bound gives 1 and not 0 (and the two $(n-1)$-resilient functions equal to the full linear n-variable function and its complement have algebraic immunity 1). For very large values of k, the reply to the latter open question is probably no (for instance, for $k = n - 2$, it is clearly no, and for $k = n - 3$, there exist $(n-3)$-resilient functions of algebraic immunity 2, which are easy to obtain with Maiorana–McFarland's construction; an example is the direct sum of the full linear $(n - 2)$-variable function and of the two-variable majority function $x_{n-1}x_n$). Note that many infinite classes of 1-resilient functions of optimal algebraic immunity have been found in even numbers of variables, but as far as we know, none has been found being 2-resilient, nor 1-resilient in odd numbers of variables (recall that, if $f(x)$ is a 1-resilient function with optimal AI in odd number n of variables, then $f(x) \oplus x_{n+1}$ is a 2-resilient function with optimal AI in $n + 1$ variables). So already for $k = 2$, the question is open.

12.4 The Gowers norm on pseudo-Boolean functions

The Gowers uniformity norm has been introduced in 2001 in the paper [568], which provided a new proof of a result originally shown by van der Waerden, on the existence, for any positive integers k, r, of a positive integer M such that, in any r-partition of $\{1, 2, \ldots, M\}$, there exists at least one class containing an arithmetic progression of length k. We shall not try to summarize the content of this rather dense 129-page long paper (available on the internet), in which the norm was defined for functions over $\mathbb{Z}/N\mathbb{Z}$. The Gowers norm can also be expressed, as in [571], in terms of pseudo-Boolean functions (see below). Since 2001, the Gowers norm has been intensively studied and applied in additive combinatorics and in the probabilistic testing of specific properties of Boolean functions (knowing only a few of their values, see the thesis [361], see also [13] where are addressed the Reed–Muller codes and [542]). When applied to the sign function of a Boolean function f, it deals, as we shall see, with the higher-order derivatives of f (whose definition and notation have been given at page 39). It results in a measure related to the higher-order nonlinearity. We shall see with Corollary 32 below that smaller is the Gowers U_k norm of f, higher is then the contribution of f to the resistance to attacks by approximations by Boolean functions of algebraic degree at most $k - 1$ (these attacks are listed after Definition 20, page 83). The definition of the Gowers U_k norm, valid for all pseudo-Boolean functions, is as follows:

Definition 90 *[568, 569, 571] Let k, n be positive integers such that $k < n$. Let $\varphi : \mathbb{F}_2^n \mapsto \mathbb{R}$ be a pseudo-Boolean function. The k-th order Gowers uniformity norm of φ equals:*

$$||\varphi||_{U_k} = \left(\mathbb{E}_{x, x_1, \dots, x_k \in \mathbb{F}_2^n} \left[\prod_{S \subseteq \{1, \dots, k\}} \varphi \left(x + \sum_{i \in S} x_i \right) \right] \right)^{\frac{1}{2^k}},$$

where $\mathbb{E}_{x, x_1, \dots, x_k \in \mathbb{F}_2^n}$ is the notation for arithmetic mean (i.e., for expectation in uniform probability).

Note that, by considering separately the cases where S does not contain k and those where it does, and using that $(x, x_k) \mapsto (x, x + x_k)$ is a permutation of $(\mathbb{F}_2^n)^2$, the expression $\mathbb{E}_{x, x_1, \dots, x_k \in \mathbb{F}_2^n} \left[\prod_{S \subseteq \{1, \dots, k\}} \varphi \left(x + \sum_{i \in S} x_i \right) \right]$ is equal to $\mathbb{E}_{x_1, \dots, x_{k-1} \in \mathbb{F}_2^n} \left[\left(\mathbb{E}_x \left[\prod_{S \subseteq \{1, \dots, k-1\}} \varphi \left(x + \sum_{i \in S} x_i \right) \right] \right)^2 \right]$. Being then always nonnegative, the expression does admit a 2^kth root.

Equality $||\varphi||_{U_k} =$

$$\left(\mathbb{E}_{x_1, \dots, x_{k-1} \in \mathbb{F}_2^n} \left[\left(\mathbb{E}_x \left[\prod_{S \subseteq \{1, \dots, k-1\}} \varphi \left(x + \sum_{i \in S} x_i \right) \right] \right)^2 \right] \right)^{\frac{1}{2^k}} \tag{12.19}$$

has its own interest. For $k = 1$, it shows that

$$||\varphi||_{U_1} = \left| \mathbb{E}_{x \in \mathbb{F}_2^n} [\varphi(x)] \right| = 2^{-n} \left| \sum_{x \in \mathbb{F}_2^n} \varphi(x) \right| \tag{12.20}$$

(which is then not a norm), and for $k = 2$ that

$$||\varphi||_{U_2} = \left(\mathbb{E}_{x_1 \in \mathbb{F}_2^n} \left[\left(\mathbb{E}_x [\varphi(x) \varphi(x + x_1)] \right)^2 \right] \right)^{\frac{1}{4}}.$$

Another identity is also useful:

$$||\varphi||_{U_k} = \mathbb{E}_{x_k \in \mathbb{F}_2^n} \left[\mathbb{E}_{x, x_1, \dots, x_{k-1} \in \mathbb{F}_2^n} \left[\prod_{S \subseteq \{1, \dots, k-1\}} \psi_{x_k} \left(x + \sum_{i \in S} x_i \right) \right] \right], \tag{12.21}$$

where $\psi_{x_k}(x) = \varphi(x) \varphi(x + x_k)$.

Proposition 197 *For every pseudo-Boolean function φ, the sequence $\left(||\varphi||_{U_k} \right)_{k \geq 1}$ is nondecreasing:*

$$||\varphi||_{U_1} \leq ||\varphi||_{U_2} \leq \cdots \leq ||\varphi||_{U_k} \leq \cdots \tag{12.22}$$

This is due to the inequality

$$\mathbb{E}_{x_1,\dots,x_{k-1}\in\mathbb{F}_2^n}\left[\mathbb{E}_{x\in\mathbb{F}_2^n}\left[\prod_{S\subseteq\{1,\dots,k-1\}}\varphi_S\left(x+\sum_{i\in S}x_i\right)\right]\right]\leq$$

$$\left(\mathbb{E}_{x_1,\dots,x_{k-1}\in\mathbb{F}_2^n}\left[\left(\mathbb{E}_{x\in\mathbb{F}_2^n}\left[\prod_{S\subseteq\{1,\dots,k-1\}}\varphi_S\left(x+\sum_{i\in S}x_i\right)\right]\right)^2\right]\right)^{\frac{1}{2}},$$

which is a direct consequence of the Cauchy–Schwarz inequality, since it is equivalent to

inequality $$\left(\sum_{x_1,\dots,x_{k-1}\in\mathbb{F}_2^n}\left(\mathbb{E}_{x\in\mathbb{F}_2^n}\left[\prod_{S\subseteq\{1,\dots,k-1\}}\varphi_S\left(x+\sum_{i\in S}x_i\right)\right]\right)\right)^2$$

$$\leq 2^{(k-1)n}\sum_{x_1,\dots,x_{k-1}\in\mathbb{F}_2^n}\left(\left(\mathbb{E}_{x\in\mathbb{F}_2^n}\left[\prod_{S\subseteq\{1,\dots,k-1\}}\varphi_S\left(x+\sum_{i\in S}x_i\right)\right]\right)^2\right).$$

As shown in [568], for every $k\geq 2$, $||\cdot||_{U_k}$ is a norm. The triangular inequality

$$||\varphi+\psi||_{U_k}\leq||\varphi||_{U_k}+||\psi||_{U_k}$$

can be checked as follows: expanding $\prod_{S\subseteq\{1,\dots,k\}}(\varphi+\psi)\left(x+\sum_{i\in S}x_i\right)$ leads to 2^{2^k} terms of the form $\prod_{S\subseteq\{1,\dots,k\}}\varphi_S\left(x+\sum_{i\in S}x_i\right)$, where each function φ_S is either φ or ψ; for each of these terms, we have, using the Cauchy–Schwarz inequality and Relation (12.19) (in both ways):

$$\left|\mathbb{E}_{x,x_1,\dots,x_k\in\mathbb{F}_2^n}\left[\prod_{S\subseteq\{1,\dots,k\}}\varphi_S\left(x+\sum_{i\in S}x_i\right)\right]\right|$$

$$=\left|\mathbb{E}_{x_1,\dots,x_{k-1}\in\mathbb{F}_2^n}\left[\left(\mathbb{E}_{x\in\mathbb{F}_2^n}\left[\prod_{S\subseteq\{1,\dots,k-1\}}\varphi_S\left(x+\sum_{i\in S}x_i\right)\right]\right)\cdot\right.\right.$$

$$\left.\left.\left(\mathbb{E}_{x'\in\mathbb{F}_2^n}\left[\prod_{S\subseteq\{1,\dots,k-1\}}\varphi_{S\cup\{k\}}\left(x'+\sum_{i\in S}x_i\right)\right]\right)\right]\right|$$

$$\leq\left(\mathbb{E}_{x_1,\dots,x_{k-1}\in\mathbb{F}_2^n}\left[\left(\mathbb{E}_{x\in\mathbb{F}_2^n}\left[\prod_{S\subseteq\{1,\dots,k-1\}}\varphi_S\left(x+\sum_{i\in S}x_i\right)\right]\right)^2\right]\right)^{\frac{1}{2}}\cdot$$

$$\left(\mathbb{E}_{x_1,\dots,x_{k-1}\in\mathbb{F}_2^n}\left[\left(\mathbb{E}_{x\in\mathbb{F}_2^n}\left[\prod_{S\subseteq\{1,\dots,k-1\}}\varphi_{S\cup\{k\}}\left(x+\sum_{i\in S}x_i\right)\right]\right)^2\right]\right)^{\frac{1}{2}}$$

$$=\left(\mathbb{E}_{x,x_1,\dots,x_k\in\mathbb{F}_2^n}\left[\prod_{S\subseteq\{1,\dots,k\}}\varphi_{S\setminus\{k\}}\left(x+\sum_{i\in S}x_i\right)\right]\right)^{\frac{1}{2}}.$$

$$\left(\mathbb{E}_{x,x_1,\ldots,x_k \in \mathbb{F}_2^n}\left[\prod_{S \subseteq \{1,\ldots,k\}} \varphi_{S \cup \{k\}}\left(x + \sum_{i \in S} x_i\right)\right]\right)^{\frac{1}{2}} \leq \cdots$$

$$\leq \prod_{S \subseteq \{1,\ldots,k\}}\left|\mathbb{E}_{x,x_1,\ldots,x_k \in \mathbb{F}_2^n}\left[\prod_{S' \subseteq \{1,\ldots,k\}} \varphi_S\left(x + \sum_{i \in S'} x_i\right)\right]\right|^{\frac{1}{2^k}},$$

resulting in an upper estimate by $\|\varphi\|_{U_k}^r \|\psi\|_{U_k}^{2^k-r}$, where r and $2^k - r$ are the numbers of times that φ_S equals φ and ψ respectively, and this proves that $(\|\varphi + \psi\|_{U_k})^{2^k} \leq \sum_{r=0}^{2^k} \binom{2^k}{r} \|\varphi\|_{U_k}^r \|\psi\|_{U_k}^{2^k-r}$, that is, $\|\varphi + \psi\|_{U_k} \leq \|\varphi\|_{U_k} + \|\psi\|_{U_k}$.

Let now f be an n-variable Boolean function. We can consider the U_k norm of the sign function $f_\chi = (-1)^f$ or that of f itself, viewed as a function from $\mathbb{F}_2^n$ to $\{0, 1\}$. In the former case, which is the most studied one, we have from the very definition:

Proposition 198 *Let k, n be positive integers such that $k < n$. Let f be an n-variable Boolean function. Then $\|f_\chi\|_{U_k}$ equals the 2^kth root of the average value of $2^{-n}\mathcal{F}(D_{a_1} D_{a_2} \ldots D_{a_k} f)$, where $\mathcal{F}(g) = \sum_{x \in \mathbb{F}_2^n}(-1)^{g(x)}$, when $a_1, a_2, \ldots, a_k$ range independently over $\mathbb{F}_2^n$.*

For any $k \geq 1$ and any Boolean function f, according to Proposition 198 and to the fact that, for every n-variable Boolean function g, we have $\mathcal{F}(g) \leq 2^n$ with equality if and only if g is the null function, we have that $\|f_\chi\|_{U_k}$ is bounded above by 1, with equality if and only if all k-th order derivatives of f are null, and we know, according to Proposition 5, page 38, that this is equivalent to saying that f has algebraic degree at most $k - 1$.

Relation (12.21) shows that $\|f_\chi\|_{U_k}$ satisfies the "recurrence" relation:

$$\|f_\chi\|_{U_k} = \left(\mathbb{E}_{h \in \mathbb{F}_2^n}\left[\|(D_h f)_\chi\|_{U_{k-1}}^{2^{k-1}}\right]\right)^{\frac{1}{2^k}}. \tag{12.23}$$

This relation can be iterated and shows then again the role of higher-order derivatives.

Note that, for $k = 2$, according to Proposition 198 and to Relation (3.9), page 98, $\|f_\chi\|_{U_2}$ is related to the second moment $\mathcal{V}(f)$ of the autocorrelation coefficients by

$$(\|f_\chi\|_{U_2})^4 = 2^{-3n}\mathcal{V}(f), \tag{12.24}$$

and all the observations made at page 98 on $\mathcal{V}(f)$ give then corresponding equalities and bounds on $\|f_\chi\|_{U_2}$ (hence, studying the U_2 norm has limited interest).

For instance, we have $nl(f) \leq 2^{n-1} - 2^{n-1}(\|f_\chi\|_{U_2})^2 \leq 2^{n-1} - 2^{\frac{3n}{4}-1}\|f_\chi\|_{U_2}$, with equality on the left-hand side if and only if f is plateaued and overall equality if and only if f is bent. We have also, according to Relations (12.24) and (3.10), page 98, that $\|f_\chi\|_{U_2}$ equals the normalized quartic mean of the Walsh transform of f:

$$\|f_\chi\|_{U_2} = 2^{-n}\left(\sum_{b \in \mathbb{F}_2^n} W_f^4(b)\right)^{\frac{1}{4}}. \tag{12.25}$$

In fact, it is easily shown that, for any pseudo-Boolean function φ, we have

$$||\varphi||_{U_2} = 2^{-n} \left(\sum_{b \in \mathbb{F}_2^n} \widehat{\varphi}^4(b) \right)^{\frac{1}{4}}. \tag{12.26}$$

Relations (12.23) and (12.25) and Relation (6.5), page 198, directly imply that a bent function and its dual have the same U_3 norm (as observed in [528]).

Of course, thanks to Relation (12.23) iterated $k - 2$ times, Relation (12.25) results in a similar relation between $||f_\chi||_{U_k}$ and the average quartic mean of the Walsh transforms of the $(k - 2)$th derivatives of f.

An important property of the Gowers uniformity norm is that $||\varphi||_{U_k}$ is an upper bound for the normalized correlations $\left| \mathbb{E}_{x \in \mathbb{F}_2^n} \varphi(x)(-1)^{g(x)} \right|$ between pseudo-Boolean function φ and the sign functions $(-1)^g$ of all Boolean functions g of algebraic degree at most $k - 1$ (and in fact, between φ and a larger set of pseudo-Boolean functions; see below). This is a direct corollary of Proposition 197:

Corollary 32 *[568, 572] Let k, n be positive integers such that $k < n$. Let φ be an n-variable pseudo-Boolean function and g an n-variable Boolean function of algebraic degree at most $k - 1$. Then:*

$$\left| \mathbb{E}_{x \in \mathbb{F}_2^n} \varphi(x)(-1)^{g(x)} \right| \leq ||\varphi||_{U_k}.$$

Indeed, according to Relation (12.22), we have that $\left| \mathbb{E}_{x \in \mathbb{F}_2^n} \varphi(x)(-1)^{g(x)} \right| = ||\varphi(-1)^g||_{U_1}$ $\leq ||\varphi(-1)^g||_{U_k} = ||\varphi||_{U_k}$.

The result applies more generally when replacing $(-1)^g$ by what is called, in the Gowers norm domain, a "polynomial of degree at most $k - 1$," that is, a pseudo-Boolean function ψ such that $\prod_{S \subseteq \{1,\dots,k\}} \psi \left(x + \sum_{i \in S} x_i \right)$ equals the constant function 1 for every choice of $x_1, \dots, x_k$.

For $\varphi = f_\chi$, we have $\min(d_H(f, g), d_H(f, g \oplus 1)) = 2^{n-1} \left(1 - \left| \mathbb{E}_{x \in \mathbb{F}_2^n} \varphi(x)(-1)^{g(x)} \right| \right)$, and taking the minimum for all Boolean functions g of algebraic degree at most $k - 1$, Corollary 32 implies

$$nl_{k-1}(f) \geq 2^{n-1} \left(1 - ||f_\chi||_{U_k} \right). \tag{12.27}$$

Relation (12.27) means (similarly to what we announced at page 470) that the functions with small U_k norm have large $(k - 1)$-th order nonlinearity. Recall that we have seen at page 83 that, asymptotically and for every $\epsilon > 0$, almost all Boolean functions are such that $nl_{k-1}(f) > 2^{n-1}(1 - \epsilon)$.

The *Gowers inverse conjecture* (GIC) is that if $||\varphi||_{U_k}$ is positive for a given pseudo-Boolean function of absolute value bounded above by 1, then φ correlates (at a level to be determined for each k) with a polynomial of algebraic degree $k - 1$ (as defined above).

This is straightforwardly true for $k = 1$, according to Relation (12.20) (taking constant polynomial 1).

The GIC is also easily checked for $k = 2$: Relation (12.26) gives

$$||\varphi||_{U_2} = 2^{-n} \left(\sum_{b \in \mathbb{F}_2^n} \widehat{\varphi}^4(b) \right)^{\frac{1}{4}}$$

$$\leq 2^{-n} \left(\left(\max_{b \in \mathbb{F}_2^n} \widehat{\varphi}^2(b) \right) \sum_{b \in \mathbb{F}_2^n} \widehat{\varphi}^2(b) \right)^{\frac{1}{4}}$$

$$= 2^{-n} \left(2^n \left(\max_{b \in \mathbb{F}_2^n} \widehat{\varphi}^2(b) \right) \sum_{x \in \mathbb{F}_2^n} \varphi^2(x) \right)^{\frac{1}{4}}$$

$$\leq 2^{-\frac{n}{2}} \left(\max_{b \in \mathbb{F}_2^n} \widehat{\varphi}^2(b) \right)^{\frac{1}{4}},$$

and we observe that $|\widehat{\varphi}(b)|$ measures the correlation between φ and $(-1)^{b \cdot x}$.

The GIC is proved for $\varphi = (-1)^f$ and $k = 3$ in [1010, Appendix A]. The proof is a little too long for being included here.

But for generic values of k, the GIC has been independently refuted by Green and Tao [573] and by Lovett et al. [805] (a counter-example φ for $k = 4$ is the sign function of the elementary symmetric function σ_4: its maximum normalized correlation with the sign functions of cubic Boolean functions tends to 0 when n tends to infinity, but its Gowers U_4 norm is bounded below by a strictly positive number). Bergelson et al. [9] have proposed and proved a modification of the inverse Gowers conjecture valid in low characteristic, but in characteristic 2, their result does not relate to distances, and a better adapted modification needs then to be found.

In [528], the authors studied $||f_\chi||_{U_3}$ for some Maiorana–McFarland bent functions (the value is determined when the permutation involved in the definition of the function, see Relation 6.9, page 209, is APN) and of some cubic monomial functions.

13

Open questions

In this chapter, we list open problems related to the main chapters of this book; some have been already mentioned in [245, 248]. We avoid stating those that seem elusive, such as the determination of all bent functions. Some open questions are, however, quite difficult, while others, more recent, may be easier to address, and some (which have never been proposed until now) may even be easy.

13.1 Questions of general cryptography dealing with functions

1. Generalize the higher-order differential attack to block ciphers using *S-box*es *CCZ equivalent* to *quadratic functions*.
2. Find an expression of the period of general nonlinear-feedback shift register sequences (*NFSR*) by means of the initialization and the feedback function.

13.2 General questions on Boolean functions and vectorial functions

1. Determine, for all values of n, the exact minimum *numerical degree* of n-variable Boolean functions depending on all their variables (this value is near $\log_2 n$, according to Proposition 15, page 67, and to the few lines after its proof); determine the functions having such numerical degree.
2. Determine the set of all possible *coset leaders* of the first order *Reed–Muller code, i.e.,* of those Boolean functions whose *nonlinearity* equals the *Hamming weight*, that is, such that the null function is a best affine approximation, or equivalently such that $W_f(0_n) = \max_{a \in \mathbb{F}_2^n} |W_f(a)|$ (see page 79).
3. Find simple formulae for the number of *balanced quadratic functions* in n variables and for the weight distribution of the dual $RM(n-3, n)$ of the second-order Reed–Muller code.
4. Determine the possible *Hamming weights* in the third-order Reed–Muller code (we know they are diverse, see Section 5.3, page 180); determine the weight distribution of this code.
5. Determine, for all values of n and all $3 \leq k \leq n-2$, those n-variable Boolean functions whose Walsh transform is divisible by 2^k (see the second remark at page 64).
6. Use the numerical normal form (see Definition 12, page 47) to design relevant secondary constructions of Boolean functions (see some ideas of constructions in [248, subsection 4.1]).

7. Determine the best nonlinearities of Boolean functions in odd dimension $n \geq 9$; in particular, find nine-variable Boolean functions having nonlinearity larger than 242 or show they do not exist.

8. Determine the best nonlinearities of *balanced* Boolean functions in dimension $n \geq 8$; in particular, find an eight-variable (resp. ten-variable) balanced Boolean function with nonlinearity 118 (resp. 494) or show they do not exist. Prove or disprove Dobbertin's conjecture for balanced functions (see page 297).

9. Find a better upper bound than the known ones for (n, m)-*functions* when
   - n is odd and $m < n$
   - n is even and $\frac{n}{2} < m < n$

13.3 Bent functions and plateaued functions

1. Characterize all bent functions of *algebraic degree* 3; extend this characterization to plateaued functions for any amplitude.

2. Determine an efficient lower bound on the number of n-variable bent functions (see page 242); same question for plateaued functions of any amplitude.

3. Is any n-variable Boolean function (n even) of *algebraic degree* at most $\frac{n}{2}$ the sum of two *bent* functions? (This is called the *bent sum decomposition problem*; see page 242 as well.)

4. Determine an efficient upper bound on the number of n-variable bent functions (see page 243); same question for plateaued functions of any amplitude.

5. What is the minimum, for all n-variable bent Boolean functions, of the maximal dimension of those affine subspaces of $\mathbb{F}_2^n$ on which they are constant? (We know it is strictly smaller than $n/2$, according to the existence of nonnormal bent functions.) Same question for plateaued functions of any amplitude.

6. Characterize all *self-dual bent functions*; see page 198 (quadratic ones have been determined in [626]).

7. Characterize the *algebraic normal forms* of the elements of class $\mathcal{PS}$ (see page 212) or their trace representations.

8. Investigate the structure of $\mathcal{PS}$, and find a constructive definition of $\mathcal{PS}$ functions.

9. Evaluate the size of $\mathcal{PS}$; determine whether the subclass of those $\mathcal{PS}$ functions that are related to full spreads is a large part of it (as observed by Dillon, the $\mathcal{PS}$ functions related to those partial spreads that can be extended to spreads of larger sizes – in particular, those related to full spreads – have necessarily algebraic degree $n/2$).

10. What are the possible algebraic degrees of $\mathcal{PS}^+$ bent functions?

11. Determine whether all Kasami bent functions $tr_n(ax^{2^{2k}-2^k+1})$ are non-weakly normal for $n \geq 14$ not divisible by 3 and $1 < k < n/2$ coprime with n and $a \in \mathbb{F}_4 \setminus \mathbb{F}_2$ (see page 253 and [270]).

12. Clarify what can be all the *univariate representations* of those Niho bent functions (see page 221) related to known o-polynomials such as Subiaco and Adelaide.

13. Determine the duals of the Niho-bent functions numbers 1 and 3 of pages 221 and foll. (the dual of function number 2 has been determined in [311]).

14. Determine what is the largest possible number of distinct affine *derivatives* of a nonquadratic *bent* n-variable function (n even), which results in determining what

is the maximal dimension of this vector space (it is easy to see that it is at least $n-3$: take a quadratic bent function g in $n-6$ variables and a cubic bent function h in 6 variables; then $g(x)$ has 2^{n-6} affine derivatives and it is easy to see that h can have 2^3 affine derivatives (take for instance the Maiorana McFarland function $x_1y_1 \oplus x_2y_2 \oplus (x_1x_2 \oplus x_3)y_3)$. Then $g(x) \oplus h(y)$, $x \in \mathbb{F}_2^{n-6}, y \in \mathbb{F}_2^6$, has 2^{n-3} distinct affine derivatives.

15. Find codes with the same parameters as the *Kerdock codes* (see page 254) and which are not equivalent to subcodes of the second-order *Reed–Muller code*.

16. Find new simple and general constructions of *perfect nonlinear/bent* (n,m)-functions (see pages 268 and 270).

17. Find *hyper-bent functions* (see page 244) EA inequivalent to $\mathcal{PS}_{ap}$ functions in more than four variables (a sporadic example exists in four variables [278]).

18. Determine if there exist Boolean functions in more than three variables whose second-order *derivatives* $D_a D_b f$ are all *balanced* when a and b are $\mathbb{F}_2$-linearly independent; see page 257.

13.4 Correlation immune and resilient functions

1. Determine an efficient lower bound on the number of n-variable k-resilient functions (see page 311).

2. Determine an efficient upper bound on the number of n-variable k-resilient functions (see page 312).

3. Determine whether there exists any nonaffine 3-*resilient symmetric Boolean function* (see page 356).

4. Determine whether the minimum nonzero *Hamming weight* $\omega_{n,t}$ of n-variable t-th order correlation immune functions satisfies $\omega_{n,t} \leq \omega_{n+1,t}$ for every n and t (see page 305).

5. Determine $\omega_{n,t}$ for every n and t.

13.5 Algebraic immune functions

1. Determine, for n odd and for n even, an efficient lower bound on the number of n-variable functions of maximal algebraic immunity (see page 92).

2. Determine, for n odd and for n even, an efficient upper bound on the number of n-variable functions of maximal algebraic immunity.

3. Determine a lower bound on the *hyper-nonlinearity* of the indicator function of $\{\alpha, \dots, \alpha^{2^{n-1}}\}$ in $\mathbb{F}_{2^n}$ (α *primitive element*), see page 337, which would be not far from the values of the nonlinearity computed for $n \leq 26$.

4. Find a class of Boolean functions that would be as fast to compute as the *hidden weight bit function* (see page 343) and with provably not bad algebraic immunity and fast algebraic immunity, and whose nonlinearity would be good.

5. Determine, for any n, what is the best possible resiliency order of n-variable Boolean functions with optimal algebraic immunity.

6. Determine, for any n, what is the best possible nonlinearity of Boolean functions with optimal algebraic immunity.

13.6 Highly nonlinear vectorial functions with low differential uniformity

1. Determine whether there exist (n, n)-functions with *nonlinearity* strictly larger than $2^{n-1} - 2^{\frac{n}{2}}$ when n is even (see page 371).
2. Determine whether nonquadratic crooked functions exist (see page 278).
3. Find APN functions (see page 137) new up to CCZ equivalence (see page 28), by means of their ANF.
4. Find new APN exponents (see page 390) or prove that all are known.
5. Determine whether *APN* functions with bad nonlinearity exist.
6. Determine whether the APN binomials of Proposition 178, page 405, can be generalized for $t = 4$ to trinomials or quadrinomials.
7. Find simple and general *secondary constructions* of *APN* and *AB* functions (see page 119), and of differentially 4-uniform (n, n)-functions (see page 135) different from the switching construction (see page 407), and if possible more systematic.
8. Find classes of AB functions by using *CCZ equivalence* with Kasami (resp. Welch, Niho) functions (see page 397).
9. Find an example of an AB function CCZ inequivalent to *power function*s and to *quadratic function*s (we have only one APN function known, with $n = 6$, having such property [494]).
10. Find infinite classes of *APN* and *AB* functions CCZ inequivalent to power functions and to quadratic functions.
11. Determine whether there exist *componentwise APN* (*CAPN*) functions (see page 390) that are neither AB nor power permutations.
12. Determine whether there exist APN functions in odd dimension that are not CAPN.
13. Determine whether the CAPNness of permutations is equivalent to the CAPNness of their compositional inverses, and more generally, whether CAPNness is CCZ invariant.
14. Determine whether *Kasami APN functions* are componentwise Walsh uniform (CWU; see page 414).
15. Find a systematic way, given an APN function F, to build another (EA inequivalent) function F' such that $\gamma_{F'} = \gamma_F$ (see Proposition 158, page 375).
16. Find an APN permutation in even dimension $n \geq 8$, or better, an infinite class (this is the so-called "big APN problem"; see observations on this problem in [136, 199, 248] and how to work with CCZ equivalence to reach EA-inequivalent functions in [145]).
17. Derive new simple and general constructions of *APN/AB* functions from *perfect nonlinear* functions (see page 409), and vice versa.
18. If possible, *classify APN* functions, or at least their extended Walsh spectra, or at least their nonlinearities.
19. Determine whether differentially 6-uniform $(n, n - 2)$-functions exist for $n > 5$.
20. Determine the pairs (n, m) for which *Nyberg's bound* (see page 423) is tight.
21. Construct infinite classes of CWU differentially 4-uniform $(n, n - 1)$-functions.

13.7 Recent uses of Boolean and vectorial functions and related problems

1. Characterize for $t \geq 2$ (or at least for $t = 2$) those functions that admit a *threshold implementation* (*TI*) with t masks (*i.e.*, a t-th order TI) and with uniformity; see pages 436 and foll.

2. Can the multiplicative *inverse function* $F(x) = x^{2^n-2}$ have an $(n-1)$-th order TI with uniformity, in particular for $n = 8$?

3. Any *AB* function has it an $\frac{n+1}{2}$th order TI with uniformity?

4. Find generic *primary constructions* of TI with uniformity.

5. Provide cases of secondary constructions of TI with uniformity more general than those exhibited in [1094] (see page 442).

6. Determine all nonquadratic *bent* functions whose restrictions to the set of binary vectors of length n and *Hamming weight* k have null *nonlinearity* (*i.e.,* coincide with an affine function), for every $k = 1, \ldots, n - 1$ (the determination of the quadratic ones is given in Proposition 193, page 463).

7. Determine, for every $1 \le k \le n$, the smallest integer e such that $2\binom{n}{e} > \binom{n}{k}$ (providing an upper bound on algebraic immunity with input restricted to Hamming weight k; see page 465), and study its asymptotic behavior relatively to the standard algebraic immunity upper bound $\lceil n/2 \rceil$.

8. Determine whether the four instances of the FLIP cipher (see Subsection 12.2.1) resist algebraic attacks combined with guess and determine attacks.

9. Given two positive integers e and k, what is the smallest number of variables for which there exists a Boolean function of algebraic immunity at least e and resiliency order at least k (see page 469)?

10. Is there, for $k \le n-2$, an upper bound on the algebraic immunity of k-resilient functions that would be sharper than $\min(n - k - 1, \lceil \frac{n}{2} \rceil)$?

11. Find a modification of the inverse Gowers conjecture (see page 473) that would be true in characteristic 2 and would involve Hamming distances.

14

Appendix: finite fields

We briefly recall the basics on finite fields and the main properties used in the body of the present book. In the limit of this appendix, we are far from complete, and we refer then to the books [775, 890], whose sizes show the extent of the state of the art that we briefly summarize here.

Reminder: A field $(\mathbb{F}, +, *)$ is by definition such that

- $(\mathbb{F}, +)$ is an Abelian group (we denote its neutral element by 0).
- $(\mathbb{F} \setminus \{0\}, *)$ is an Abelian group (we denote its neutral element by 1).
- $*$ is distributive with respect to +.

Notation: $\mathbb{F} \setminus \{0\}$ can be denoted by $\mathbb{F}^*$.

Important property: $\mathbb{F}$ has no nonzero "zero divisor" (we call this way any element α of $\mathbb{F}$ such that there exists $\beta \neq 0$ such that $\alpha * \beta = 0$).

Exercise: Show (by Euclidean division and factorization) that a polynomial of degree n over a field can have at most n zeros in this field.

14.1 Prime fields and fields with four, eight, and nine elements

14.1.1 Characteristic of a finite field

The cardinality of a field is called its *order*. Let $\mathbb{F}$ be a finite field (*i.e.,* a field with a finite order, also called a Galois field). The mapping $m \in \mathbb{N} \to m \cdot 1 = 1 + \cdots + 1 \in \mathbb{F}$ cannot be injective. Hence there exist positive integers m, m' such that $m < m'$ and $m \cdot 1 = m' \cdot 1$. Then we have $(m' - m) \cdot 1 = 0$ and $m' - m > 0$. The smallest positive integer p such that $p \cdot 1 = 0$ is called the *characteristic* of $\mathbb{F}$.

Remark. For every $x \in \mathbb{F}$, we have $p \cdot x = (p \cdot 1) * x = 0$, *i.e.,* the iterated addition of any element with itself is "mod p." $\qquad \square$

Theorem *The characteristic of any finite field is a prime integer.*

Proof Suppose that $p = kl$ for some integers $1 < k < p$ and $1 < l < p$. We have $(kl) \cdot 1 = 0$, then $k \cdot 1$ and $l \cdot 1$ are nonzero divisors of zero. A contradiction. $\qquad\square$

Notation: we will now write p instead of $p \cdot 1$ and the multiplication between field elements will be (classically) represented with a lack of symbol instead of $*$.

14.1.2 Prime fields

For every field $\mathbb{F}$ of characteristic p (prime), we have $\{0, 1, \ldots, p - 1\} \subseteq \mathbb{F}$. As observed already, $0, 1, \ldots, p - 1$ have here to be considered as integers mod p. Hence they belong to $\mathbb{Z}/p\mathbb{Z}$. Hence, more precisely, we have $\mathbb{Z}/p\mathbb{Z} \subseteq \mathbb{F}$.

Theorem *Let p be any prime integer. Every field of characteristic p admits $\mathbb{Z}/p\mathbb{Z}$ as a subfield, and $\mathbb{Z}/p\mathbb{Z}$ does not have a proper subfield (and is then called a prime field).*

Indeed, $\mathbb{Z}/p\mathbb{Z}$ is itself a field (and it is the smallest field of characteristic p): it is a ring (*i.e.*, $(\mathbb{Z}/p\mathbb{Z}, +)$ is an Abelian group and $*$ is associative and distributive with respect to $+$) and every nonzero element a has an inverse, since the mapping $x \in \mathbb{Z}/p\mathbb{Z} \to ax \in \mathbb{Z}/p\mathbb{Z}$ being injective, it is bijective.

If n is not a prime, then $\mathbb{Z}/n\mathbb{Z}$ is not a field, since it has zero divisors.

Remark. According to Bézout's identity, for p prime and $a \in \mathbb{Z}/p\mathbb{Z}^*$, since a and p are coprime, there exist u and v such that $1 = au + pv$ and $(u \bmod p)$ is the inverse of a. It can be calculated by the (extended) Euclidean algorithm. $\qquad\square$

Example: operations in $\mathbb{Z}/7\mathbb{Z}$:

+	0	1	2	3	4	5	6
0	0	1	2	3	4	5	6
1	1	2	3	4	5	6	0
2	2	3	4	5	6	0	1
3	3	4	5	6	0	1	2
4	4	5	6	0	1	2	3
5	5	6	0	1	2	3	4
6	6	0	1	2	3	4	5

*	0	1	2	3	4	5	6
0	0	0	0	0	0	0	0
1	0	1	2	3	4	5	6
2	0	2	4	6	1	3	5
3	0	3	6	2	5	1	4
4	0	4	1	5	2	6	3
5	0	5	3	1	6	4	2
6	0	6	5	4	3	2	1

Notation: Since $\mathbb{Z}/p\mathbb{Z}$ is a field, we shall denote it by $\mathbb{F}_p$.

14.1.3 Possible size of a finite field

Let $\mathbb{F}$ be a finite field of characteristic p. Since $\mathbb{F}_p$ is a subfield, $\mathbb{F}$ *is a vector space over* $\mathbb{F}_p$, and since $\mathbb{F}$ is a finite set, $\mathbb{F}$ must have a finite basis, say of size n. Let $\{b_1, b_2, \ldots, b_n\}$ denote such a basis. Any element of $\mathbb{F}$ can be written uniquely as a linear combination $c_1 b_1 + c_2 b_2 + \cdots + c_n b_n$ and there are then p^n elements in $\mathbb{F}$.

Theorem *A finite field of characteristic p must have size q $= p^n$ for some natural number n.*

Number n is called the *degree*.

14.1.4 Extending prime fields; fields with four, eight, and nine elements

Reminder: $\mathbb{C}$ is an extension field of $\mathbb{R}$ as follows: every element (a_0, a_1) of $\mathbb{R}^2$ is identified to the polynomial $a_0 + a_1 x$; $\mathbb{C}$ equals the set of polynomials $a_0 + a_1 x$ with the usual addition and with multiplication mod $x^2 + 1$; x is written i.

$\mathbb{C}$ has no nonzero zero divisor because the polynomial $x^2 + 1$ is irreducible over $\mathbb{R}$ (*i.e.,* cannot be factored). $\mathbb{C}$ is a field. It is the smallest field containing $\mathbb{R}$ and an additional element i, solution of the equation $x^2 + 1 = 0$.

$\mathbb{C}$ *is an extension field of degree 2 of* $\mathbb{R}$.

The field $\mathbb{F}_4$: It is easily checked that the polynomial $x^2 + x + 1$ is irreducible over $\mathbb{F}_2$. Any element (a_0, a_1) of $\mathbb{F}_2^2$ is identified to the polynomial $a_0 + a_1 x$, and $\mathbb{F}_4$ equals $\mathbb{F}_2^2$ with usual addition and multiplication mod $x^2 + x + 1$.

+	0	1	x	$1+x$
0	0	1	x	$1+x$
1	1	0	$1+x$	x
x	x	$1+x$	0	1
$1+x$	$1+x$	x	1	0

*	0	1	x	$1+x$
0	0	0	0	0
1	0	1	x	$1+x$
x	0	x	$1+x$	1
$1+x$	0	$1+x$	1	x

$\mathbb{F}_4$ has no nonzero zero divisor because $x^2 + x + 1$ is irreducible. The mapping $x \in \mathbb{F}_4 \to ax \in \mathbb{F}_4$ being injective for $a \neq 0$, it is bijective and $\mathbb{F}_4 = \{0, 1, x, 1 + x\}$ is a field. We have also $\mathbb{F}_4 = \{0, 1, x, x^2\}$, that is, x is a generator of $\mathbb{F}_4$, which is related to the fact that $x^2 + x + 1$ is a primitive polynomial (see below).

Notation: x is written α. It is a root in $\mathbb{F}_4$ of the polynomial $x^2 + x + 1$. We have

+	0	1	α	$1+\alpha$
0	0	1	α	$1+\alpha$
1	1	0	$1+\alpha$	α
α	α	$1+\alpha$	0	1
$1+\alpha$	$1+\alpha$	α	1	0

*	0	1	α	$1+\alpha$
0	0	0	0	0
1	0	1	α	$1+\alpha$
α	0	α	$1+\alpha$	1
$1+\alpha$	0	$1+\alpha$	1	α

, that is,

+	0	1	α	α^2
0	0	1	α	α^2
1	1	0	α^2	α
α	α	α^2	0	1
α^2	α^2	α	1	0

*	0	1	α	α^2
0	0	0	0	0
1	0	1	α	α^2
α	0	α	α^2	1
α^2	0	α^2	1	α

The first representation of the elements $0, 1, \alpha, 1+\alpha$ of $\mathbb{F}_4$ is called the additive form and the second one $0, 1, \alpha, \alpha^2$, the multiplicative form.

Exercise: Calculate the tables of + and ∗, in the two representations, for

- $\mathbb{F}_8$, constructed with $\mathbb{F}_2$ and the irreducible (primitive) polynomial $x^3 + x + 1$
- $\mathbb{F}_9$ and $\mathbb{F}_{27}$, constructed with $\mathbb{F}_3$ and the irreducible (primitive) polynomials $x^2 + x + 2$, $x^3 + 2x^2 + 1$

14.2 General finite fields: construction, primitive element

Let p be a prime number, n a positive integer, and $f(x)$ an irreducible polynomial of degree n over $\mathbb{F}_p$ (we shall see below that such polynomial exists for any p and any n). Then Kronecker's construction is to identify $\mathbb{F}_p^n$ with the set of polynomials of degrees at most $n - 1$ over $\mathbb{F}_p$ and to endow it with the usual addition and with the multiplication mod $f(x)$. In precise mathematical terms, we construct $\mathbb{F}_p[x]/(f(x))$, the quotient of the ring $\mathbb{F}_p[x]$, by the ideal $(f(x))$ equal to the set of multiples of $f(x)$. In more practical words, by denoting x by α, we take this symbol and allow it to add and multiply with elements of $\mathbb{F}_p$ and with itself, with the restriction that $f(\alpha) = 0$. We obtain a ring, denoted by $\mathbb{F}_p(\alpha)$, with no nonzero divisor of zero. Since this ring is finite, it is a field: the mapping $x \in \mathbb{F}_p(\alpha) \to ax \in \mathbb{F}_p(\alpha)$ being injective, it is bijective.

Theorem *Let $f(x)$ be an irreducible polynomial over any finite field $\mathbb{K}$ (in practice, a prime field). The set $\mathbb{K}[x]/(f(x))$ obtained from Kronecker's construction is again a field.*

Electronic circuits for calculating in finite fields are based on flip-flops (for storing bits), adders, and multipliers:

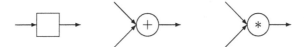

For instance, in $\mathbb{F}_{2^4}$ with irreducible polynomial $X^4 + X + 1$, the operation of multiplication by α results in

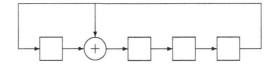

Notation: $\mathbb{F}_p(\alpha)$ is denoted by $\mathbb{F}_{p^n}$ (the same notation[1] for all choices of $f(x)$, for reasons that will appear later).

Remark. Different time/memory trade-offs exist in the literature for implementing multiplications. For hardware implementations and large dimensions n, several works have been published among which are the Omura–Massey method, the Sunar–Koç method, and the

---

[1] But some authors write $GF(p^n)$ instead of $\mathbb{F}_{p^n}$.

Karatsuba algorithm. For software implementations in small dimensions (*e.g.*, $n \leq 10$), the number of pertinent possibilities is reduced. See a survey in [320]. $\qquad\qquad\square$

Remark. In characteristic 2, Newton's formula $(u + v)^k = \sum_{i=0}^{k} \binom{k}{i} u^i v^{k-i}$ has to be applied in conjunction with Lucas' theorem (see page 487), which says that $\binom{k}{i}$ [mod 2] equals 1 if and only if the binary expansion of k covers that of i. $\qquad\qquad\square$

Calculating the inverse: Recall that there is a Euclidean algorithm for polynomials similar to the one for integers. Let $a(x)$, $b(x)$ be a pair of polynomials. The (extended) Euclidean algorithm for polynomials provides their greatest common divisor $d(x)$ and also a pair of polynomials $s(x)$, $t(x)$ such that $s(x)a(x) + t(x)b(x) = d(x)$.

In our situation, one of the polynomials, $b(x) = f(x)$, is irreducible, and the other, $a(x)$ representing a nonzero element of the field, is of degree lower than the irreducible one, so that their greatest common divisor is 1. Then we can find polynomials $s(x)$ and $t(x)$ such that $s(x)a(x) + t(x)f(x) = 1$.

Denoting as usual x by α, we have $f(\alpha) = 0$, then we see that we have found that $s(\alpha)$ is an inverse of $a(\alpha)$.

Example [Euclidean algorithm for $x^2 + 1$ in $\mathbb{F}_{27}$ constructed with the irreducible polynomial $x^3 + 2x^2 + 1$ over $\mathbb{F}_3$]. We detail the operations mathematically, as an illustration. A simpler method will be possible when we arrive at the notion of primitive element (thanks to the multiplicative representation). First we divide $f(x) = x^3 + 2x^2 + 1$ by $a(x) = x^2 + 1$. We get $x^3 + 2x^2 + 1 = (x + 2)(x^2 + 1) + 2x + 2$. The remainder $2x + 2$ is not of degree zero, so we must divide $x^2 + 1$ by $2x + 2$; we get $x^2 + 1 = (2x + 1)(2x + 2) + 2$. Since the remainder is a constant, the Euclidean algorithm stops; the two polynomials are relatively prime with greatest common divisor equal to 1 (after division by 2). Expressing each remainder by its expression obtained in each division, from bottom to top, we have $2 = x^2 + 1 - (2x + 1)(2x + 2) = x^2 + 1 - (2x + 1)[x^3 + 2x^2 + 1 - (x + 2)(x^2 + 1)] = -(2x + 1)(x^3 + 2x^2 + 1) + (2x^2 + 2x)(x^2 + 1)$ and therefore $(2x^2 + 2x)(x^2 + 1) \equiv 2$ [mod $x^3 + 2x^2 + 1$]. If we divide by 2 (*i.e.*, multiply by 2), we conclude that the inverse of $x^2 + 1$ is $x^2 + x$.

14.2.1 *The fundamental equation over finite fields*

Let $\mathbb{F}_q$ be a field of order $q = p^n$, where p is a prime. Consider the multiplicative group $\mathbb{F}_q^*$ of nonzero elements of $\mathbb{F}_q$. It has order $q - 1$. Let β denote an arbitrary element of the multiplicative group. By Lagrange's theorem (saying that, for any finite group G, the order of every subgroup divides the order of G), an element of a group raised to the order of the group equals the identity, that is, $\beta^{q-1} = 1$ (indeed, the set of all powers of β is a subgroup of $\mathbb{F}_q^*$ whose order equals the order of β). This property is called Fermat's little theorem for finite fields.

This equation is valid for any nonzero β. Multiplying through by β yields

$$\beta^q = \beta,$$

which is still valid for nonzero elements and now also valid for zero.

In particular, for all $j \in \mathbb{Z}/p\mathbb{Z}$, we have $j^p = j$.

Another proof of equation $\beta^q = \beta$ (without using Lagrange's theorem) is to say that if $a_1, a_2, \ldots, a_{q-1}$ denote the nonzero elements of $\mathbb{F}_q$ and β is any nonzero element of $\mathbb{F}_q$, the elements $\beta a_1, \beta a_2, \ldots, \beta a_{q-1}$ are all different and are then all nonzero elements of $\mathbb{F}_q$; hence we have $a_1 a_2 \ldots a_{q-1} = \beta a_1 \beta a_2 \ldots \beta a_{q-1} = \beta^{q-1} a_1 a_2 \ldots a_{q-1}$ and therefore $\beta^{q-1} = 1$. The rest is similar.

Exercise: Let $P(x)$ be a polynomial over $\mathbb{F}_q$. Show that $P(x)$ is in fact over $\mathbb{F}_p$ if and only if $(P(x))^p = P(x^p)$.

Note that the polynomial $x^q - x$, having degree q, cannot have more than q zeros (roots), and we know then all its q distinct zeros in $\mathbb{F}_q$, that is, $x^q - x$ factors completely into linear factors in $\mathbb{F}_q$ (i.e., splits): $x^q - x = \prod_{\beta \in \mathbb{F}_q} (x - \beta)$. We say that $\mathbb{F}_q$ is the *splitting field* of $x^q - x$:

$$\mathbb{F}_q = \{x; \ x^q - x = 0\}.$$

Let us now prove that any irreducible polynomial $f(x)$ of degree n over $\mathbb{F}_p$ is a divisor of $x^q - x$. As we saw, this polynomial $f(x)$ does not have any zero in $\mathbb{F}_p$, but Kronecker's construction makes it possible to construct an extension field $\mathbb{F}_q$ in which $f(x)$ does have a zero. We know that in $\mathbb{F}_q$ the polynomial $x^q - x$ has all elements of the field as zeros, so it must have a zero in common with $f(x)$, and since $f(x)$ is irreducible, $\gcd(f(x), x^q - x)$, which is not trivial, equals $f(x)$.

Theorem *Let $q = p^n$ be a power of a prime. Then every irreducible polynomial of degree n over the prime field $\mathbb{F}_p$ divides the polynomial $x^q - x$.*

Moreover, since $x^q - x$ splits in $\mathbb{F}_q$, then $f(x)$ also splits in $\mathbb{F}_q$. Since $f(\beta^p) = (f(\beta))^p$ for every $\beta \in \mathbb{F}_q$, because the Newton formula reduces to $(\beta + \beta')^p = \beta^p + \beta'^p$, and because $j^p = j$ for every $j \in \mathbb{Z}/p\mathbb{Z}$, the elements of the form α^{p^j}, $j = 0, \ldots, n-1$, where α denotes a zero of $f(x)$ in $\mathbb{F}_q$, are zeros of $f(x)$, and they are then all the zeros of $f(x)$ since the degree of this polynomial is assumed equal to n and all the elements α^{p^j} are distinct (otherwise, $f(x)$ would be divisible by a polynomial of degree strictly less than n with coefficients in $\mathbb{F}_p$ and would then not be irreducible). Note that if we do not assume anymore that $f(x)$ has degree n, its degree d is necessarily a divisor of n and $x^{p^d} - x$ divides $x^{p^n} - x$.

14.2.2 Existence of finite fields

Let $q = p^n$ be a power of a prime. If we wish to build $\mathbb{F}_q$, the only thing we need is an irreducible polynomial of degree n over $\mathbb{F}_p$.

Lemma *There exist irreducible polynomials of every degree n over every prime field $\mathbb{F}_p$.*

Proof Let $F_d(x)$ denote the product of all polynomials irreducible over $\mathbb{F}_p$ of degree d. Then since distinct irreducible polynomials are coprime, we have

$$x^q - x = \prod_{d|n} F_d(x).$$

Let N_d denote the number of irreducible polynomials of degree d over $\mathbb{F}_p$. By equating degrees on both sides of this relation, we see that $p^n = \sum_{d|n} d N_d$.

By the Möbius inversion formula [635], denoting by μ the Möbius function $\mu(d) = \begin{cases} 0 \text{ if } d \text{ is divisible by a square} \\ (-1)^{n_d} \text{ otherwise, where } n_d \text{ is the number of primes dividing } d \end{cases}$, we have then

$$n N_n = \sum_{d|n} \mu(d) \, p^{n/d} > 0. \qquad \square$$

Hence, for any power of a prime q, there exists a field with q elements.

Reminder: We have $\sum_{d|n} \mu(d) = \begin{cases} 1 \text{ if } n = 1 \\ 0 \text{ if } n > 1 \end{cases}$, which implies the Möbius inversion formula.

14.2.3 Uniqueness of finite fields

We show now that when building $\mathbb{F}_q$ by Kronecker's construction, any irreducible polynomial of degree n gives the same field up to isomorphism.

Definition *Let $\mathbb{F}$ and $\mathbb{K}$ be two fields, finite or not. An isomorphism between F and $\mathbb{K}$ is a bijective (one-to-one) correspondence ϕ from $\mathbb{F}$ to $\mathbb{K}$ such that for any a and b in $\mathbb{F}$, the following equalities hold:*

$$\phi(a + b) = \phi(a) + \phi(b)$$
$$\phi(ab) = \phi(a)\phi(b).$$

If such an isomorphism exists, the tables of operations $+$ and $*$ are the same in the two *isomorphic* fields, but with different orderings, or names, of the elements. We shall understand this as: the two fields being in fact the same field.

Exercise: Let $q = p^n$ with p prime. Let α be a zero of some irreducible polynomial $f(x)$ over $\mathbb{F}_p$ and let $\mathbb{F}_q = \mathbb{F}_p(\alpha)$. Let $\mathbb{K}$ be a field of the same order q.

1. Show that the image of α by any isomorphism from $\mathbb{F}_q$ to $\mathbb{K}$ must be a zero of $f(x)$.
2. Prove that sending α to a zero of $f(x)$ in $\mathbb{K}$ gives an isomorphism from $\mathbb{F}_q$ to $\mathbb{K}$.

Theorem *All finite fields of the same size are isomorphic and can be obtained with Kronecker's construction.*

Example: Let $\mathbb{F}_{27}$ denote the field obtained by adjoining a zero α of $f(x) = x^3 + 2x^2 + 1$ to $\mathbb{F}_3$, and let $\mathbb{K}_{27}$ be the field obtained by adjoining a zero β of $g(x) = x^3 + 2x + 1$. To find an isomorphism from $\mathbb{F}_{27}$ to $\mathbb{K}_{27}$, we can factor the polynomial $f(x) = x^3 + 2x^2 + 1$ in $\mathbb{K}_{27}$. We know that $f(x)$ must factor completely in $\mathbb{K}_{27}$. So to factor $f(x)$, we need to only look for its three zeros in $\mathbb{K}_{27}$, and there are only 27 elements to try (actually, 24, because no element of $\mathbb{F}_3$ is a zero). We obtain $f(x) = (x + \beta^2 + 2)(x + \beta^2 + \beta)(x + \beta^2 + 2\beta)$, from which we can read that the three zeros are $2\beta^2 + 1, 2\beta^2 + 2\beta$, and $2\beta^2 + \beta$. The isomorphism is now given by sending α into any of the zeros of $f(x)$ in $\mathbb{K}_{27}$.

Exercise: show that $x^{p^n} - x$ divides $x^{p^m} - x$ if and only if n divides m. Deduce that $\mathbb{F}_{p^n}$ is a subfield of $\mathbb{F}_{p^m}$ if and only if n divides m.

14.2.4 *Frobenius automorphism*

In $\mathbb{F}_q$, the mapping $\phi : x \mapsto x^p$ is an automorphism (that we already encountered above), since

-   $(x + y)^p = x^p + y^p, \forall x, y \in \mathbb{F}_q$, since p being a prime $\binom{p}{i} = \frac{p}{i}\binom{p-1}{i-1}$ is divisible by p for every $0 < i < p$.
-   $(xy)^p = x^p y^p$, and $x \mapsto x^p$ is bijective since its (additive or multiplicative) kernel is trivial. It is called the *Frobenius automorphism*.

This implies, for instance, that $(x + y)^{\sum_{i \in I} p^i} = \prod_{i \in I}(x^{p^i} + y^{p^i})$, which for $p = 2$ implies *Lucas' theorem* [809, page 404]: $\binom{n}{j}$ is odd if and only if the binary expansion of j is covered by (*i.e.*, has support included in) that of n.

Exercise: We saw that any polynomial $f(X)$ over $\mathbb{F}_p$ satisfies $f(\phi(\beta)) = \phi(f(\beta))$ for every $\beta \in \mathbb{F}_q$. Show that this is characteristic of polynomials over $\mathbb{F}_p$ among polynomials over $\mathbb{F}_q$.

The automorphisms of $\mathbb{F}_q$ are the powers of the Frobenius automorphism; their set, with the composition operation, is a group, called the Galois group of $\mathbb{F}_q$.

14.2.5 *Primitive element*

When studying $\mathbb{F}_4$, we have seen that the element that we denoted by α is such that $\mathbb{F}_4 = \{0, 1, \alpha, \alpha^2\}$. The lemma below implies that, for every power q of a prime, the multiplicative group $\mathbb{F}_q^*$ is also cyclic, that is, there exists $\alpha \in \mathbb{F}_q$ such that $\mathbb{F}_q = \{0, 1, \alpha, \dots, \alpha^{q-2}\}$ (*i.e.*, $q - 1$ is the smallest possible integer i such that $\alpha^i = 1$). Such α will be called a *primitive element*.

Exercise: Recall that any irreducible polynomial $P(x) \in \mathbb{F}_p[x]$ of degree $n > 1$ is a divisor of $x^{p^n - 1} - 1$. We say that $P(x)$ is primitive if one of its zeros is a primitive element of $\mathbb{F}_{p^n}$ (and then, all its zeros are).

1. Show that if $P(x)$ is a primitive polynomial, then $\min\{m; \ P(x) \mid x^m - 1\} = p^n - 1$.
2. Show conversely that if $P(x)$ is any irreducible polynomial of degree n such that $\min\{m; \ P(x) \mid x^m - 1\} = p^n - 1$, then $P(x)$ is primitive.

Lemma *Let G be a finite multiplicative group with k elements, in which for every $m \leq k$, there are at most m solutions for the equation $x^m = 1$. Then G is a cyclic group.*

Proof Denote by a_m the number of elements of G of order m (that is, satisfying $x^m = 1$ and $x^{m'} \neq 1$ for $m' < m$). Note that, if m does not divide k, then $a_m = 0$, according to Lagrange's theorem. If $a_m \neq 0$, then there exists $g \in G$ of order m. Then, according to the hypothesis that there are at most m solutions for the equation $x^m = 1$, the m powers of g are all solutions of $x^m = 1$. Moreover, g^i has order $\frac{m}{\gcd(i,m)}$. Hence, the group generated by g has $\phi(m)$ generators, where $\phi(m)$ is Euler's totient function (whose value is the number of elements in $\{1, \ldots, m\}$, which are coprime with m). Thus, if a_m is nonzero, then it is precisely $\phi(m)$.

But $\sum_{m|k} \phi(m) = k$ and $\sum_{m|k} a_m = \sum_{m=1}^{k} a_m = k$. Hence $a_m = \phi(m)$ for every m that divides k.

In particular, $a_k = \phi(k) > 0$, so G contains elements of order k, and is cyclic. □

Exercise: We know that every multiplicative subgroup of $\mathbb{F}_q^*$ has for order a divisor of $q - 1$. Show that, for each divisor k of $q - 1$, there exists a unique multiplicative subgroup of $\mathbb{F}_q^*$ of order k. Show that a generator of this subgroup is $\alpha^{\frac{q-1}{k}}$, where α is a primitive element of $\mathbb{F}_q$.

14.3 Representation (additive and multiplicative); trace function

For $q = p^n$, Kronecker's construction with any irreducible polynomial of degree n over $\mathbb{F}_p$ leads for any element $x \in \mathbb{F}_q$ to:

$$x = x_0 + x_1\alpha + x_2\alpha^2 + \cdots + x_{n-1}\alpha^{n-1}; \quad x_0, \ldots, x_{n-1} \in \mathbb{F}_p.$$

This is called the *additive representation* of x

For α primitive, since the fundamental polynomial $x^q - x$ splits in $\mathbb{F}_q$, this α is the zero of an irreducible (a primitive) polynomial over $\mathbb{F}_p$. In other words, for every n, there exists a primitive polynomial of degree n.

Then any nonzero element $x \in \mathbb{F}_q$ can be written

$$x = \alpha^i; \quad \text{for } i \in \mathbb{Z}/(q-1)\mathbb{Z} \text{ that is } i \in \{0, \ldots, q-2\}.$$

This is the *multiplicative representation*.

Remark. Denote by $f_{n,\alpha}(i, j)$ the bivariate function over $\mathbb{Z}/(p^n - 1)\mathbb{Z}$ such that $\alpha^i + \alpha^j = \alpha^{f_{n,\alpha}(i,j)}$. There is no known expression of $f_{n,\alpha}(i, j)$ (see for instance [890, subsection 2.1.7.5, page 27]), but we have $f_{n,\alpha}(i+1, j+1) = f_{n,\alpha}(i, j)+1$, $f_{n,\alpha}(pi, pj) = pf_{n,\alpha}(i, j)$; if k is coprime with $p^n - 1$, then we have $f_{n,\alpha^k}(i, j) = f_{n,\alpha}(ki, kj)$, and if β is a primitive element of $\mathbb{F}_{p^{rn}}$ and $\alpha = \beta^{(p^{rn}-1)/(p^n-1)}$, then we have $f_{rn,\beta}((p^{rn} - 1)i/(p^n - 1), (p^{rn} - 1)j/(p^n - 1)) = (p^{rn} - 1)f_{n,\alpha}(i, j)/(p^n - 1)$. □

Exercise: Show that, for every integer i, we have

$$\{x^i, \ x \in \mathbb{F}_q\} = \{x^{\gcd(i,q-1)}, \ x \in \mathbb{F}_q\}.$$

14.3.1 Absolute trace function

Let $q = p^n$. Recall that the Frobenius automorphism $\Phi : x \to x^p$ satisfies $\Phi^n = Id$ and that $\mathbb{F}_p$ is the set of solutions of equation $\Phi(x) = x$. Two elements are called conjugate if they correspond through Φ^i for some integer i. We have seen that the zeros of any irreducible polynomial over $\mathbb{F}_p$ are conjugate. The function

$$tr_{q/p}(x) = x + \Phi(x) + \Phi^2(x) + \cdots + \Phi^{n-1}(x)$$
$$= x + x^p + x^{p^2} + \cdots + x^{p^{n-1}}$$

is linear over $\mathbb{F}_q$. In the body of our book and below, for $p = 2$ and $q = 2^n$, we simply write tr_n instead of $tr_{q/p}$.

Exercise: Show that

$$tr_{q/p}(\Phi(x)) = \Phi(tr_{q/p}(x)) = tr_{q/p}(x) \text{ for every } x \in \mathbb{F}_q.$$

Hence $tr_{q/p}(x) \in \mathbb{F}_p$ for every element x of $\mathbb{F}_q$ (but not for any element of a superfield of $\mathbb{F}_q$, if we extend the polynomial function $tr_{q/p}$ to this superfield) and $tr_{q/p}$ is an $\mathbb{F}_p$-linear form over the space $\mathbb{F}_q$. It is called the *absolute trace function* over $\mathbb{F}_q$.

Exercise: 1. Show that, for every $a \in \mathbb{F}_q$ the function $tr_{q/p}(ax)$ is identically null on $\mathbb{F}_q$ if and only if $a = 0$.
2. Deduce that the set of all $\mathbb{F}_p$-linear forms over $\mathbb{F}_q$ equals the set of these functions.

Remark. For every nonzero $a \in \mathbb{F}_q$, the set $\{x \in \mathbb{F}_q; \ tr_{q/p}(ax) = 0\}$ is a hyperplane (a vector space of codimension 1) in the vector space $\mathbb{F}_q$ over $\mathbb{F}_p$. If $(\alpha_1, \dots, \alpha_n)$ is a basis of $\mathbb{F}_q$ over $\mathbb{F}_p$ and $(\beta_1, \dots, \beta_n)$ an orthonormal basis (such that $tr_{q/p}(\alpha_i \beta_j) = 1$ if $i = j$ and $tr_{q/p}(\alpha_i \beta_j) = 0$ otherwise) and if $a = \sum_{i=1}^n a_i \beta_i, x = \sum_{i=1}^n x_i \alpha_i$, then the equation of this hyperplane in $\mathbb{F}_p^n$ is $\sum_{i=1}^n a_i x_i = 0$. $\qquad\square$

Exercise: Show that every hyperplane of $\mathbb{F}_q$ (vectorspace over $\mathbb{F}_p$) has this form.

Exercise: Show that, for every $i \in \mathbb{F}_p$, we have

$$tr_{q/p}(X) - i = \prod_{u \in \mathbb{F}_q; tr_{q/p}(u)=i} (X - u).$$

Exercise: 1. Recall why a binary linear recurring sequence

$$s_n = a_1 s_{n-1} \oplus \cdots \oplus a_L s_{n-L} ; \quad a_1, \dots, a_L \in \mathbb{F}_2 \tag{14.1}$$

has ultimate period at most $2^L - 1$.
2. Show that if $a_L \neq 0$, then the sequence is fully periodic.
3. We assume that the polynomial $f(x) = x^L + a_1 x^{L-1} + \cdots + a_L$ is primitive.

a. Show that any sequence of the form $s_n = tr_L(a\alpha^n)$, where $a \in \mathbb{F}_{2^n}^*$ and α is a zero of $f(x)$, satisfies Relation (14.1).

b. Deduce that all the nonzero sequences satisfying Relation (14.1) are of the form $s_n = tr_L(a\alpha^n)$ where $a \in \mathbb{F}_{2^n}^*$. Show that they admit $2^L - 1$ as minimal period.

4. Conversely, we assume that the nonzero sequences s_n satisfying Relation (14.1) admit $2^L - 1$ as minimal period. Show that $f(x)$ is primitive.

These sequences are called *m-sequences*.

Exercise: Determine the kernel of the linear mapping $x \in \mathbb{F}_{2^n} \to x + x^2$ and deduce that, for every $u \in \mathbb{F}_{2^n}$, there exists a solution of the equation $x^2 + x = u$ in $\mathbb{F}_{2^n}$ if and only if $tr_n(u) = 0$.

14.3.2 Subfields and other trace functions

Kronecker's construction can be applied the same way as before to any finite field instead of a prime field: let q be a prime power and $f(x)$ be an irreducible polynomial of degree k over $\mathbb{F}_q$. Then $\mathbb{F}_q[x]/(f(x))$ is a field of order q^k. This implies again that, if n divides m, then (up to isomorphism) $\mathbb{F}_{p^n}$ is a subfield of $\mathbb{F}_{p^m}$. Recall that, conversely, if $\mathbb{F}_{p^n}$ is a subfield of $\mathbb{F}_{p^m}$, then n divides m.

The trace function from $\mathbb{F}_{q^k}$ to $\mathbb{F}_q$ is the function

$$tr_{q^k/q}(x) = x + x^q + x^{q^2} + \cdots + x^{q^{k-1}}.$$

Exercise: Prove that $tr_{q^k/q}$ is a $\mathbb{F}_q$-linear form over $\mathbb{F}_{q^k}$.

Exercise: Check that, if $n \mid m \mid s$, then $tr_{p^s/p^n} = tr_{p^m/p^n} \circ tr_{p^s/p^m}$.

14.4 Permutations on a finite field

Exercise: Show that, for every prime power q, every function $f(x)$ from $\mathbb{F}_q$ to $\mathbb{F}_q$ is a polynomial function of degree at most $q - 1$ over $\mathbb{F}_q$, that is,

$$f(x) = \sum_{i=0}^{q-1} a_i x^i ; \quad a_i \in \mathbb{F}_q$$

and that this representation is unique.

This polynomial is seen as an element of $\mathbb{F}_q[x]/(x^q - x)$. It is called a *permutation polynomial* if the function $f(x)$ is bijective.

14.4.1 Examples of permutation polynomials

Affine polynomials: $P(x) = ax + b, a \neq 0$

Bijective linearized polynomials (or p-polynomials): $P(x) = \sum_{i=0}^{n-1} a_i x^{p^i}, a_i \in \mathbb{F}_q$, such that $ker(P) = \{0\}$. These polynomials being viewed [mod $x^q - x$], the exponents i are viewed in $\mathbb{Z}/n\mathbb{Z}$, where $q = p^n$.

Exercise: Show that the gcd of two linearized polynomials $L(x) = \sum_{i=0}^{n-1} a_i x^{p^i}$, $a_i \in \mathbb{F}_p$, and $L'(x) = \sum_{i=0}^{n-1} b_i x^{p^i}$, $b_i \in \mathbb{F}_p$ (*p-polynomials* over $\mathbb{F}_p$), equals $\sum_{i=0}^{n-1} c_i x^{p^i}$, $c_i \in \mathbb{F}_p$, where $\sum_{i=0}^{n-1} c_i x^i = \gcd(\sum_{i=0}^{n-1} a_i x^i, \sum_{i=0}^{n-1} b_i x^i)$. Deduce that $L(x)$ is a permutation polynomial over $\mathbb{F}_q$ if and only if $\sum_{i=0}^{n-1} a_i x^i$ (its *p*-associate polynomial) is coprime with $x^n - 1$.

This result extends to polynomials $\sum_{i=0}^{n-1} a_i x^{q^i}$, $a_i \in \mathbb{F}_q$, over $\mathbb{F}_{q^n}$ for $q = p^r$.

The sums of such polynomials with constants (affine permutations).

Power (monomial) functions: recall that if α is a primitive element of $\mathbb{F}_q$, then for every $i \in \mathbb{Z}/(q-1)\mathbb{Z}$, α^i is primitive if and only if $\gcd(i, q-1) = 1$.

Exercise: Show that, for every $i \in \mathbb{Z}/(q-1)\mathbb{Z}$, the function $x \to x^i$ is a permutation of $\mathbb{F}_q$ if and only if $\gcd(i, q-1) = 1$.

Exercise: Show for $i = 2^j + 1$ and $q = 2^n$ that $\gcd(i, q-1) = \frac{\gcd(2^{2j}-1, q-1)}{\gcd(2^j - 1, q-1)} = \frac{2^{\gcd(2j,n)}-1}{2^{\gcd(j,n)}-1}$ and that $x \to x^i$ is a permutation of $\mathbb{F}_q$ if and only if $\frac{n}{\gcd(j,n)}$ is odd.

Dickson polynomials

Theorem *For every positive integer k, there exists a polynomial D_k over $\mathbb{Z}$ satisfying the formal equality $D_k\left(x + \frac{1}{x}\right) = x^k + \frac{1}{x^k}$.*

Proof By induction on k: if k is odd then $\left(x + \frac{1}{x}\right)^k = \sum_{i=0}^{\frac{k-1}{2}} \binom{k}{i}\left(x^{2i-k} + x^{k-2i}\right)$ and therefore, assuming the property valid until $k - 1$, it is proved for k and $x^k = \sum_{i=0}^{\frac{k-1}{2}} \binom{k}{i} D_{k-2i}(x)$ and

$$D_k(x) = x^k - \sum_{i=1}^{\frac{k-1}{2}} \binom{k}{i} D_{k-2i}(x)$$

and if k is even, then $\left(x + \frac{1}{x}\right)^k = \sum_{i=0}^{\frac{k}{2}-1} \binom{k}{i}\left(x^{2i-k} + x^{k-2i}\right) + \binom{k}{\frac{k}{2}}$ implies $x^k = \sum_{i=0}^{\frac{k}{2}-1} \binom{k}{i} D_{k-2i}(x) + \binom{k}{\frac{k}{2}}$ and therefore

$$D_k(x) = x^k - \sum_{i=1}^{\frac{k}{2}-1} \binom{k}{i} D_{k-2i}(x) - \binom{k}{\frac{k}{2}}.$$

This completes the proof. $\qquad\square$

Exercise: 1. Let $q = 2^n$. Recall why the equation $x^2 + x = c$ has solutions if and only if $tr_n(c) = 0$. Deduce that, for $a \neq 0$, the equation $x^2 + ax = b$ has solutions if and only if $tr_n\left(\frac{b}{a^2}\right) = 0$.

2. a. Let $q = 2^n$. Show that any element x of $\mathbb{F}_q$ satisfies $tr_{2n}(x) = 0$. Deduce that, for every $x \in \mathbb{F}_q^*$, there exist two elements h of $\mathbb{F}_{q^2}^*$ such that $h + h^{-1} = x$ (by transforming this equation in h into an equation of degree 2 in $\frac{h}{x}$) and that these two elements are inverse of each other.

   b. Show that h belongs to $\mathbb{F}_q$ if and only if $tr_n(x^{-1}) = 0$ and that, otherwise, h belongs to the multiplicative subgroup of order $q + 1$ of $\mathbb{F}_{q^2}$.

3. Let $q = p^n$ with p odd.

   a. Does any element of $\mathbb{F}_q$ have a square root in $\mathbb{F}_q$?

   b. Show that, given a primitive element α of $\mathbb{F}_{q^2}$, every element $x \in \mathbb{F}_q^*$ can be written $\alpha^{i(q+1)}$ and has a square root in $\mathbb{F}_{q^2}$.

   c. Show that, for every $x \in \mathbb{F}_q^*$, there exist two elements h of $\mathbb{F}_{q^2}^*$ such that $h + h^{-1} = x$ and that these two elements are inverse of each other.

Exercise:

1. Show that the Dickson polynomial defines a function from $\mathbb{F}_q$ to $\mathbb{F}_q$.

2. Show that, if $\gcd(k, q^2 - 1) = 1$, then D_k is a permutation polynomial over $\mathbb{F}_q$.

3. To prove the converse, assume that $\gcd(k, q^2 - 1) = d > 1$.

   a. If d is even, show that $D_k(-x) = D_k(x)$ and $-x \neq x$.

   b. If d is odd, then let r be an odd prime dividing d. Show that there exist two distinct elements b, c in $\mathbb{F}_{q^2}^*$ such that $b + \frac{1}{b} \in \mathbb{F}_q$, $c + \frac{1}{c} \in \mathbb{F}_q$, $b \neq \frac{1}{c}$ and $b^r = c^r$ (the two cases where r divides $q - 1$ and r divides $q + 1$ can be distinguished). Check that $D_k(b + \frac{1}{b}) = D_k(c + \frac{1}{c})$ and $b + \frac{1}{b} \neq c + \frac{1}{c}$.

Then D_k is not a permutation polynomial over $\mathbb{F}_q$.

14.4.2 General results on permutation polynomials

Exercise:

1. Show that $\sum_{b \in \mathbb{F}_q} b^t = \begin{cases} 0 \text{ if } t = 0, \ldots, q - 2 \\ -1 \text{ if } t = q - 1 \end{cases}$.

2. Deduce that, for any polynomial $P(x) = \sum_{i=0}^{q-1} p_i x^i$ over $\mathbb{F}_q$, we have $p_{q-1} = -\sum_{b \in \mathbb{F}_q} P(b)$.

Exercise: With the usual convention $0^0 = 1$, show that, given $b \in \mathbb{F}_q$, we have

$$\sum_{t=0}^{q-2} b^t = \begin{cases} 0 \text{ if } b \neq 0, 1 \\ 1 \text{ if } b = 0 \\ -1 \text{ if } b = 1 \end{cases}$$

and

$$\sum_{t=0}^{q-1} b^t = \begin{cases} 1 \text{ if } b \neq 1 \\ 0 \text{ if } b = 1 \end{cases}.$$

Lemma *Let $a_0, \ldots, a_{q-1}$ be elements of $\mathbb{F}_q$. These elements are all distinct if and only if*

$$\sum_{i=0}^{q-1} a_i^t = \begin{cases} 0 \ if \ t = 0, \ldots, q-2 \\ -1 \ if \ t = q-1 \end{cases}.$$

Proof If $a_0, \ldots, a_{q-1}$ are distinct, then $\{a_0, \ldots, a_{q-1}\} = \mathbb{F}_q$ and, denoting by α a primitive element of $\mathbb{F}_q$, we have

$$\sum_{i=0}^{q-1} a_i^t = 0^t + \sum_{j=0}^{q-2} \alpha^{jt} = 0^t + \sum_{j=0}^{q-2} (\alpha^t)^j = \begin{cases} 0 \ if \ t = 0, \ldots, q-2 \\ -1 \ if \ t = q-1 \end{cases}.$$

Conversely, if $\sum_{i=0}^{q-1} a_i^t = \begin{cases} 0 \ if \ t = 0, \ldots, q-2 \\ -1 \ if \ t = q-1 \end{cases}$, then

$$P(x) = \sum_{i=0}^{q-1} \sum_{t=0}^{q-1} a_i^t x^{q-1-t} = -1.$$

For every $b \in \mathbb{F}_q^*$, we have $P(b) = \sum_{i=0}^{q-1} \left(\sum_{t=0}^{q-1} \left(\frac{a_i}{b} \right)^t \right) = |\{i = 0, \ldots, q-1; a_i \neq b\}|$ [mod p], according to the previous exercise. Hence, $|\{i = 0, \ldots, q-1; a_i = b\}| \neq 0$, and the same happens for $b = 0$. This completes the proof. □

Theorem *(Hermite's criterion) A polynomial $P(x)$ over $\mathbb{F}_q$ is a permutation polynomial if and only if the following two conditions hold:*

1. *$P(x)$ has a single root in $\mathbb{F}_q$.*
2. *For each integer $t = 1, \ldots, q-2$ not divisible by p, the polynomial $(P(x))^t$ [mod $x^q - x$] has degree at most $q - 2$.*

Proof Condition 1 is necessary and implies that $\sum_{b \in \mathbb{F}_q} (P(b))^{q-1} = -1$. Condition 2 is equivalent to $\sum_{b \in \mathbb{F}_q} (P(b))^t = 0$ for every $t = 1, \ldots, q-2$ not divisible by p. For $t = pt'$, we have $\sum_{b \in \mathbb{F}_q} (P(b))^t = \left(\sum_{b \in \mathbb{F}_q} (P(b))^{t'} \right)^p$. The lemma above completes the proof. □

Exercise: Show that $\sum_{v \in \mathbb{F}_q} e^{\frac{2i\pi \, tr_{q/p}(va)}{p}} = \begin{cases} q \ if \ a = 0 \\ 0 \ otherwise \end{cases}.$

Theorem *(characterization through* component functions*) A polynomial $P(x)$ over $\mathbb{F}_q$ is a permutation polynomial if and only if, for every $v \in \mathbb{F}_q^*$, the function $tr_{q/p}(vP(x))$ is balanced (that is, takes every value of $\mathbb{F}_p$ the same number of times). Equivalently, for every $v \in \mathbb{F}_q^*$:*

$$\sum_{c \in \mathbb{F}_q} e^{\frac{2i\pi \, tr_{q/p}(vP(c))}{p}} = 0.$$

Proof   If $P(x)$ is a permutation polynomial over $\mathbb{F}_q$, then, for every $v \in \mathbb{F}_q^*$, the function $tr_{q/p}(vP(x))$ is balanced since the function $tr_{q/p}$ is balanced over $\mathbb{F}_q$. This implies that $\sum_{c \in \mathbb{F}_q} e^{\frac{2i\pi tr_{q/p}(vP(c))}{p}}$ is proportional to $\sum_{j=0}^{p-1} (e^{\frac{2i\pi}{p}})^j = 0$.

Conversely, if the condition is satisfied, then for every $b \in \mathbb{F}_q$, we have

$$|\{c \in \mathbb{F}_q; \ P(c) = b\}| = \frac{1}{q} \sum_{c \in \mathbb{F}_q} \sum_{v \in \mathbb{F}_q} e^{\frac{2i\pi tr_{q/p}(vP(c))}{p}} e^{-\frac{2i\pi tr_{q/p}(vb)}{p}} = 1. \qquad \square$$

Remark.   As proved by Carlitz in [330], all permutation polynomials over $\mathbb{F}_q$ with $q > 2$ are generated through composition by the multiplicative inverse monomial x^{q-2} and the degree 1 polynomials $ax + b$ with $a \in \mathbb{F}_q^*, b \in \mathbb{F}_q$. $\qquad \square$

14.5 Equations over finite fields

Fundamental equation and general equations

We have seen that, for every prime power q, the equation $x^q - x = 0$ admits $\mathbb{F}_q$ as set of solutions. Consequently, given a prime p and two positive integers r and s, the equation $x^{p^s} - x = 0$ has for solutions in $\mathbb{F}_{p^r}$ the elements of $\mathbb{F}_{p^r} \cap \mathbb{F}_{p^s} = \mathbb{F}_{p^{\gcd(r,s)}}$, and in $\mathbb{F}_{p'^r}$ with $p' \neq p$, it has solutions $0, 1$.

Important remark. More generally and for the same reason, finding the solutions in $\mathbb{F}_q$ of an equation $P(x) = 0$ over $\mathbb{F}_q$ is equivalent to finding the solutions of the equation $\gcd(P(x), x^q - x) = 0$. Since the polynomial $x^q - x$ splits over $\mathbb{F}_q$, the number of solutions equals the degree of $\gcd(P(x), x^q - x)$.

Equations of degree 1

$ax + b = 0, a \neq 0$, has solution $-b/a$.

Equations of degree 2

$ax^2 + bx + c = 0, a \neq 0$, behaves differently according to whether $p = 2$ or not:

- If $p \neq 2$, then the usual resolution works.
- if $p = 2$ then, if $a \neq 0$ and $b \neq 0$, $ax^2 + bx + c = 0$ is equivalent to $\left(\frac{ax}{b}\right)^2 + \frac{ax}{b} = \frac{ac}{b^2}$. Hence, solving the equation $ax^2 + bx + c = 0$ of degree 2 reduces to solving the equation $x^2 + x = \beta$ for some β. Let $c \in \mathbb{F}_{2^n}$ and $x = \sum_{j=1}^{n-1} \beta^{2^j} \left(\sum_{k=0}^{j-1} c^{2^k} \right)$, then $x +$

$$x^2 = \sum_{j=1}^{n-1} \beta^{2^j} \left(\sum_{k=0}^{j-1} c^{2^k} \right) + \sum_{j=2}^{n} \beta^{2^j} \left(\sum_{k=1}^{j-1} c^{2^k} \right) = \sum_{j=1}^{n-1} \beta^{2^j} \left(\sum_{k=0}^{j-1} c^{2^k} \right) + \sum_{j=2}^{n} \beta^{2^j} \left(\sum_{k=0}^{j-1} c^{2^k} \right) +$$

$$\sum_{j=2}^{n} \beta^{2^j} c = \beta^2 c + \beta \left(\sum_{k=1}^{n-1} c^{2^k} \right) + \sum_{j=2}^{n-1} \beta^{2^j} c = c \, tr_n(\beta) + \beta \, tr_n(c). \text{ This equality and what}$$

we have seen already in an exercise imply:

Theorem *Let n be any positive integer and $\beta \in \mathbb{F}_{2^n}$. A necessary and sufficient condition for the existence of solutions in $\mathbb{F}_{2^n}$ of the equation $x^2 + x = \beta$ is that $tr_n(\beta) = 0$. Assuming that this condition is satisfied, the solutions of the equation are $x = \sum_{j=1}^{n-1} \beta^{2^j} (\sum_{k=0}^{j-1} c^{2^k})$ and $x = 1 + \sum_{j=1}^{n-1} \beta^{2^j} (\sum_{k=0}^{j-1} c^{2^k})$, where c is any (fixed) element such that $tr_n(c) = 1$.*

Note that if $n = 2m$ and $\beta \in \mathbb{F}_{2^m}$, then the condition $tr_n(\beta) = 0$ is satisfied and x simplifies into $x = \beta (\sum_{k=0}^{m-1} c^{2^k}) + \sum_{j=1}^{m-1} \beta^{2^j} (\sum_{k=j}^{m+j-1} c^{2^k}) = \sum_{j=0}^{m-1} (\beta d)^{2^j}$, where $d = \sum_{k=0}^{m-1} c^{2^k}$, and since $tr_n(c) = tr_m^n(d)$, we have that $x = \sum_{j=0}^{m-1} (\beta d)^{2^j}$, where d is any element of $\mathbb{F}_{2^n}$ such that $tr_m^n(d) = 1$. Then, for every $u \neq 0$ and v in $\mathbb{F}_{2^m}$, the equation $x^2 + ux = v$ has for solutions x and $x + u$ in $\mathbb{F}_{2^n}$, where $x = u \sum_{j=0}^{m-1} \left(\frac{vd}{u^2}\right)^{2^j}$, where $d \in \mathbb{F}_{2^n}, tr_m^n(d) = 1$.

Remark. For the more general equation $x + x^{2^k} = b$, where k is odd, $\gcd(k, n) = 1$, and $tr_n(b) = 0$, let $S_{n,k}(x) = \sum_{i=0}^{n-1} x^{2^{ki}}$ and $U = \{\zeta \in \mathbb{F}_{2^{2n}} \mid \zeta^{2^n+1} = 1\}$; let $\zeta \in U \setminus \{1\}$; then, for any $b \in \mathbb{F}_{2^n}^*$, we have $\{x \in \mathbb{F}_{2^n} \mid x + x^{2^k} = b\} = S_{n,k}\left(\frac{b}{\zeta+1}\right) + \mathbb{F}_2$; see [700]. $\square$

Equations of degree 3

Theorem *[64, 1119] Let t_1, t_2 denote the roots of $t^2 + bt + a^3 = 0$ in $\mathbb{F}_{2^{2n}}$, where $a \in \mathbb{F}_{2^n}, b \in \mathbb{F}_{2^n}^*$. Then the factorization of $f(x) = x^3 + ax + b$ over $\mathbb{F}_{2^n}$ is characterized as follows:*

- *f has three zeros in F_{2^n} if and only if $tr_n\left(\frac{a^3}{b^2} + 1\right) = 0$ and t_1, t_2 are cubes in $\mathbb{F}_{2^n}$ (n even), $\mathbb{F}_{2^{2n}}$ (n odd).*
- *f has exactly one zero in $\mathbb{F}_{2^n}$ if and only if $tr_n\left(\frac{a^3}{b^2} + 1\right) = 1$.*
- *f has no zero in $\mathbb{F}_{2^n}$ if and only if $tr_n\left(\frac{a^3}{b^2} + 1\right) = 0$ and t_1, t_2 are not cubes in $\mathbb{F}_{2^n}$ (n even), $\mathbb{F}_{2^{2n}}$ (n odd).*

We refer to [64, 1119] for the proof.

Equation $x^{2^k+1} + x + a = 0$

This equation, first studied in [96, 594, 595], is solved in [700] for $\gcd(k, n) = 1$ (which is a breakthrough).

Power equations

The image set of a power function x^i equals the union of $\{0\}$ and of a multiplicative subgroup of $\mathbb{F}_q^*$ of order $\frac{q-1}{\gcd(i,q-1)}$. The equation $x^i = a$ has one solution if $a = 0$, no solution if a does not belong to this subgroup and $\gcd(i, q-1)$ solutions if a belongs to it, since there exist integers k (coprime with $q-1$) and l (coprime with i), such that $ik + j(q-1) = \gcd(i, q-1)$.

Multivariate method: an example

Hans Dobbertin has developed a method for solving some kinds of equations that play a role when proving that some vectorial functions are APN. The method applies if n is a multiple of a small positive number, say 2 or 3. Assume for instance that n is a multiple of 3, denote $k = n/3$, and assume that we are given some equation in which x appears with exponents that are linear combinations of $1, 2^k$, and 2^{2k}. The idea of the method is then to introduce the two new variables $y = x^{2^k}$ and $z = y^{2^k}$, to express the equation and its 2^k and 2^{2k} powers by means of the unknowns x, y, z and to eliminate (for instance by using resultants) some of these variables from these three equations. Then even if y and z are eliminated, it happens that the resulting equation is different from the original one. We give an example of this method taken from [158].

Let s and k be positive integers with $\gcd(s, 3k) = 1$, and $n = 3k$. Let

$$d = 2^{2k} + 2^{k+s} - (2^s + 1), g_1 = \gcd(2^{3k} - 1, d/(2^k - 1)), g_2 = \gcd(2^k - 1, d/(2^k - 1)),$$

and let $a \in \mathbb{F}_{2^n}^*$ have the order $2^{2k} + 2^k + 1$ (*i.e.* $a = \alpha^{2^k - 1}$ for some primitive element α of $\mathbb{F}_{2^n}^*$). Let

$$\Delta_a(x) = a \left(x^{2^{2k}} + x^{2^{k+s}} \right) + x^{2^s} + x.$$

The equation $\Delta_a(x) = 0$ has $x = 0$ and $x = 1$ for zeros. Let us show that if $g_1 \neq g_2$, then there are no other zeros.

We denote $y = x^{2^k}$, $z = y^{2^k}$ and $b = a^{2^k}$, $c = b^{2^k}$, and so the equation $\Delta_a(x) = 0$ can be rewritten as $a(z + y^{2^s}) + (x^{2^s} + x) = 0$. By definition, a is always a $(2^k - 1)$th power and thus $abc = 1$. Besides, $a \notin \mathbb{F}_2$. Considering also the conjugated equations we derive the following system of equations:

$$\begin{aligned} f_1 = \Delta_a(x) &= a(z + y^{2^s}) + x^{2^s} + x &= 0 \\ f_2 = f_1^{2^k} &= b(x + z^{2^s}) + y^{2^s} + y &= 0 \\ f_3 = f_1^{2^{2k}} &= \tfrac{1}{ab}(y + x^{2^s}) + z^{2^s} + z = 0. \end{aligned}$$

Eliminating y and z from these equations gives an equation in x. It happens that this equation is in general different from the original equation and is often simpler: we compute

$$R_1 = b(f_1)^{2^s} + a^{2^s} f_2 = a^{2^s} b y^{2^{2s}} + a^{2^s} y^{2^s} + a^{2^s} y + b x^{2^{2s}} + b x^{2^s} + a^{2^s} bx$$

$$R_2 = \frac{1}{a(b+1)}(bf_1 + af_2 + abf_3) = y^{2^s} + \frac{a+1}{ab+a} y + \frac{1}{a} x^{2^s} + \frac{ab+b}{ab+a} x$$

to eliminate z. To eliminate $y^{2^{2s}}$, we compute

$$\begin{aligned} R_3 &= R_1 + a^{2^s} b(R_2)^{2^s} \\ &= \frac{a^{2^s}(b+1)^{2^s} + (a+1)^{2^s} b}{(b+1)^{2^s}} y^{2^s} + a^{2^s} y + \frac{a^{2^s} b^{2^s+1} + b}{b^{2^s} + 1} x^{2^s} + a^{2^s} bx. \end{aligned}$$

Using equations R_2 and R_3, we can eliminate y^{2^s} by computing

$$R_4 = R_3 + \frac{a^{2^s}(b+1)^{2^s} + (a+1)^{2^s} b}{(b+1)^{2^s}} R_2 = P(a)(y + (b+1)x^{2^s} + bx),$$

where

$$P(a) = \frac{(ab)^{2^s+1} + (ab)^{2^s} + a^{2^s}b + a^{2^s} + ab + b}{(b+1)^{2^s+1}a}.$$

Computing

$$R_5 = (R_4)^{2^s} + P(a)^{2^s} R_2 = P(a)^{2^s}$$
$$\times \left(\frac{a+1}{ab+a}y + (b^{2^s}+1)x^{2^{2s}} + \frac{ab^{2^s}+1}{a}x^{2^s} + \frac{ab+b}{ab+a}x \right)$$

we finally get our desired equation by

$$R_6 = \frac{a+1}{ab+a}P(a)^{2^s-1}R_4 + R_5 = P(a)^{2^s}(b+1)^{2^s}\left(x^{2^{2s}} + x^{2^s}\right).$$

Obviously if x is a solution of $\Delta_a(x) = 0$, then $R_6(x) = 0$. For $P(a)^{2^s}(b+1) \neq 0$, this is equivalent to $x = 0, 1$. Thus to prove the result, it is sufficient to show that $P(a)$ does not vanish for elements a fulfilling the equation

$$a = \left(\alpha v^{2^k+2^s+1}\right)^{2^k-1} \tag{14.2}$$

Note that, if a satisfies (14.2), then a is not a $(2^k + 2^s + 1)$th power, since α^{2^k-1} is not: $g_2 = \gcd(2^k - 1, 2^k + 2^s + 1)$ is by hypothesis a strict divisor of $g_1 = \gcd(2^n - 1, 2^k + 2^s + 1)$ and α being a primitive element, it cannot be a (g_1/g_2)th power.

Consequently, it is sufficient to show that if $P(a) = 0$, then a is a $(2^k + 2^s + 1)$th power. For $a \notin \mathbb{F}_2$ the equation $P(a) = 0$ is equivalent to

$$a = \left(\frac{a+1}{c+1}\right)^{2^s+1} c^{2^s+1} \left(\frac{b+1}{a+1}\right) \quad a = \left(\frac{a+1}{c+1}c\right)^{2^k+2^s+1},$$

as can be easily seen by dividing this equality by a, simplifying it by $(a + 1)$, and then expanding it, using that $c = 1/ab$. Note that the right-hand side is always a $(2^k + 2^s + 1)$-th power. This proves the property.

References

[1] E. Abbe, A. Shpilka, and A. Wigderson. Reed–Muller codes for random erasures and errors. *IEEE Transactions on Information Theory* 61 (10), pp. 5229–5252, 2015. See page 151.

[2] K. Abdukhalikov. Bent functions and line ovals. *Finite Fields and Their Applications* 47, pp. 94–124, 2017. See pages 220 and 221.

[3] K. Abdukhalikov. Hyperovals and bent functions. *European J. Combin.* 79, pp. 123–139, 2019. See page 220.

[4] K. Abdukhalikov and S. Mesnager. Explicit constructions of bent functions from pseudo-planar functions. *Advances in Mathematics of Communications* 11 (2), pp. 293–299, 2017. See page 217.

[5] K. Abdukhalikov and S. Mesnager. Bent functions linear on elements of some classical spreads and presemifields spreads. *Cryptography and Communications* 9 (1), pp. 3–21, 2017. See page 227.

[6] C. M. Adams. Constructing symmetric ciphers using the cast design procedure. *Designs, Codes and Cryptography* 12 (3), pp. 283–316, 1997. See page 26.

[7] C. M. Adams and S. E. Tavares. Generating and counting binary bent sequences. *IEEE Transactions on Information Theory* 36 (5), pp. 1170–1173, 1990. See pages 234 and 293.

[8] S. Agievich. On the representation of bent functions by bent rectangles. *Proceedings of Probabilistic Methods in Discrete Mathematics: Fifth International Conference*, pp. 121–135, 2002, and arXiv /0502087, 2005. See pages 237 and 239.

[9] S. Agievich. On the affine classification of cubic bent functions. *IACR Cryptology ePrint Archive* (http://eprint.iacr.org/) 2005/44, 2005. See page 208.

[10] S. Agievich. Bent rectangles. *NATO Science for Peace and Security Series – D: Information and Communication Security*, Vol 18: Boolean Functions in Cryptology and Information Security, IOS Press, pp. 3–22, 2008. See page 239.

[11] M. R. Albrecht, C. Rechberger, T. Schneider, T. Tiessen, and M. Zohner. Ciphers for MPC and FHE. *Proceedings of EUROCRYPT (1) 2015, Lecture Notes in Computer Science* 9056, pp. 430–454, 2015. See page 454.

[12] N. Alon, O. Goldreich, J. Hastad, and R. Peralta. Simple constructions of almost k-wise independent random variables. *Random Stuctures and Algorithms* 3 (3), pp. 289–304, 1992. See page 105.

[13] N. Alon, T. Kaufman, M. Krivelevich, S. Litsyn, and D. Ron. Testing Reed–Muller codes. *IEEE Transactions on Information Theory* 51 (11), pp. 4032–4039, 2005. See page 469.

[14] N. Alon and J. H. Spencer. *The Probabilistic Method*. Wiley-VCH, 2000 (second edition). See page 84.

[15] Y. Alsalami. Constructions with high algebraic degree of differentially 4-uniform $(n, n-1)$-functions and differentially 8-uniform $(n, n-2)$-functions. *Cryptography and Communications* 10 (4), pp. 611–628, 2018. See page 424.

[16] A. S. Ambrosimov. Properties of bent functions of q-valued logic over finite fields. *Discrete Mathematics and Applications* 4 (4), pp. 341–350, 1994. See page 193.

[17] N. Anbar and W. Meidl. Bent and bent$_4$ spectra of Boolean functions over finite fields. *Finite Fields and Their Applications* 46, 163–178, 2017. See pages 266 and 268.

[18] N. Anbar and W. Meidl. Modified planar functions and their components. *Cryptography and Communications* 10 (2), pp. 235–249, 2018. See pages 266, 267, 268, and 274.

[19] N. Anbar, W. Meidl, and A. Topuzoğlu. On the nonlinearity of idempotent quadratic functions and the weight distribution of subcodes of Reed–Muller codes. *Proceedings of the 9th International Workshop on Coding and Cryptography 2015 WCC2015*, (https://hal.archives-ouvertes.fr/WCC2015browse/latest-publications), 2015. See page 178.

[20] R. J. Anderson. Searching for the optimum correlation attack. *Proceedings of Fast Software Encryption FSE 1994, Lecture Notes in Computer Science* 1008, pp. 137–143, 1994. See page 89.

[21] B. Applebaum. Pseudorandom generators with long stretch and low locality from random local one-way functions. *Proceedings of ACM STOC 2012*, pp. 805–816. ACM Press, 2012.

[22] B. Applebaum. Cryptographic hardness of random local functions-survey. *Computational Complexity* 25 (3), pp. 667–722, 2013. See page 468.

[23] B. Applebaum and S. Lovett. Algebraic attacks against random local functions and their countermeasures. *Proceedings of ACM STOC 2016*, pp. 1087–1100, 2016. See pages 468 and 469.

[24] R. Aragona, M. Calderini, D. Maccauro, and M. Sala. On some differential properties of Boolean functions. *Applicable Algebra in Engineering, Communication and Computing* 27 (5), pp. 359–372, 2016. See pages 373, 383, and 411.

[25] F. Armknecht. Improving fast algebraic attacks. *Proceedings of Fast Software Encryption FSE 2004, Lecture Notes in Computer Science* 3017, pp. 65–82, 2004. See page 94.

[26] F. Armknecht and G. Ars. Introducing a new variant of fast algebraic attacks and minimizing their successive data complexity. *Proceedings of International Conference on Cryptology in Malaysia Mycrypt 2005, Lecture Notes in Computer Science* 3715, pp. 16–32, 2005. See page 94.

[27] F. Armknecht, C. Carlet, P. Gaborit, S. Künzli, W. Meier, and O. Ruatta. Efficient computation of algebraic immunity for algebraic and fast algebraic attacks. *Proceedings of EUROCRYPT 2006, Lecture Notes in Computer Science* 4004 , pp. 147–164, 2006. See pages 92, 321, 334, 335, 336, and 338.

[28] F. Armknecht and M. Krause. Algebraic attacks on combiners with memory. *Proceedings of CRYPTO 2003, Lecture Notes in Computer Science* 2729, pp. 162–175, 2003. See page 91.

[29] F. Armknecht and M. Krause. Constructing single- and multi-output Boolean functions with maximal algebraic immunity. *Proceedings of ICALP 2006, Lecture Notes of Computer Science* 4052, pp. 180–191, 2006. See pages 127, 128, 344, 345, 346, and 348.

[30] F. Arnault and T. P. Berger. Design and properties of a new pseudorandom generator based on a filtered FCSR automaton. *IEEE Transactions on Computers* 54 (11), pp. 1374–1383, 2005. See page 23.

[31] S. Arora and B. Barak. *Computational Complexity : A Modern Approach*. Cambridge University Press, 2009. See page 19.

[32] G. Ars and J.-C. Faugère. Algebraic immunities of functions over finite fields. *Proceedings of the Conference BFCA 2005*, Publications des universités de Rouen et du Havre, pp. 21–38, 2005. See pages 127 and 344.

[33] A. Ashikhmin and A. Barg. Minimal vectors in linear codes. *IEEE Transactions on Information Theory* 44 (5), pp. 2010–2017, 1998. See pages 148 and 149.

[34] E. F. Assmus. On the Reed–Muller codes. *Discrete Mathematics* 106/107, pp. 25–33, 1992. See page 154.

[35] E. F. Assmus and J. D. Key. *Designs and Their Codes*. Cambridge University Press, 1992.

[36] E. F. Assmus Jr. and H. F. Mattson Jr. New 5-designs. *Journal of Combinatorial Theory, Series A* 6 (2), pp. 122–151, 1969. See page 270.

[37] E. F. Assmus Jr. and H. F. Mattson Jr. The weight-distribution of a coset of a linear code. *IEEE Transactions on Information Theory* 24 (4), p. 497, 1978. See page 15.

[38] Y. Aubry, D. J. Katz, and P. Langevin. Cyclotomy of Weil sums of binomials. *Journal of Number Theory* 154, pp. 160–178, 2015. See page 73.

[39] Y. Aubry and P. Langevin. On a conjecture of Helleseth. *Proceedings of Algebraic informatics CAI 2013, Lecture Notes in Comput. Science* 8080, pp. 113–118, 2013. See page 73.

[40] Y. Aubry, G. McGuire, and F. Rodier. A few more functions that are not APN infinitely often. *Proceedings of Fq9, Contemporary Mathematics* 518, 2010. ArXiv 0909.2304. See page 404.

[41] J. Ax. Zeroes of polynomials over finite fields. *American Journal on Mathematics* 86, pp. 255–261, 1964. See page 156.

[42] T. Baignères, P. Junod, and S. Vaudenay. How far can we go beyond linear cryptanalysis? *Proceedings of ASIACRYPT 2004, Lecture Notes in Computer Science* 3329, pp. 432–450, 2004. See page 191.

[43] R. D. Baker, J. H. Van Lint, and R. M. Wilson. On the Preparata and Goethals codes. *IEEE Transactions on Information Theory* 29, pp. 342–345, 1983. See page 255.

[44] J. Balasch, S. Faust, and B. Gierlichs. Inner product masking revisited. *Proceedings of EURO-CRYPT 2015, Lecture Notes in Computer Science* 9056, pp. 486–510, 2015. See pages 446 and 447.

[45] J. Balasch, S. Faust, B. Gierlichs, C. Paglialonga, and F.-X. Standaert. Consolidating inner product masking. *Proceedings of ASIACRYPT 2017, Lecture Notes in Computer Science* 10624, pp. 724–754, 2017. See page 446.

[46] J. Balasch, S. Faust, B. Gierlichs, and I. Verbauwhede. Theory and practice of a leakage resilient masking scheme. *Proceedings of ASIACRYPT 2012, Lecture Notes in Computer Science* 7658, pp. 758–775, 2012. See pages 446 and 447.

[47] B. Barak, G. Kindler, R. Shaltiel, B. Sudakov, and A. Wigderson. Simulating Independence: new constructions of condensers, Ramsey graphs, dispersers, and extractors. *Proceedings of ACM STOC 2005*, 2005. See page 108.

[48] G. Barthe, S. Belaïd, F. Dupressoir, et al. Strong non-interference and type-directed higher-order masking. *Proceedings of ACM CCS 16, ACM Press*, pp. 116–129, 2016. See page 430.

[49] G. Barthe, F. Dupressoir, S. Faust, B. Grégoire, F.-X. Standaert, and P.-Y. Strub. Parallel implementations of masking schemes and the bounded moment leakage model. *Proceedings of EUROCRYPT 2017, Lecture Notes in Computer Science* 10210, pp. 535–566, 2017. See page 429.

[50] L. A. Bassalygo, G. V. Zaitsev, and V. A. Zinoviev. Uniformly packed codes. *Problems of Information Transmission* 10, No. 1, pp. 9–14, 1974. See page 10.

[51] L. A. Bassalygo and V. A. Zinoviev. Remarks on uniformly packed codes. *Problems of Information Transmission* 13, No 3, pp. 22–25, 1977. See page 10.

[52] L. M. Batten. Algebraic attacks over $GF(q)$. *Proceedings of INDOCRYPT 2004, Lecture Notes in Computer Science* 3348, pp. 84–91, 2004. See page 91.

[53] P. Beelen and G. Leander. A new construction of highly nonlinear S-boxes. *Cryptography and Communications* 4(1), pp. 65–77, 2012. See pages 122 and 160.

[54] S. Belaïd, F. Benhamouda, A. Passelègue, E. Prouff, A. Thillard, and D. Vergnaud. Private multiplication over finite fields. *Proceedings of CRYPTO 2017, Lecture Notes in Computer Science* 10403, pp. 397–426, 2017. See page 431.

[55] S. Belaïd, D. Goudarzi, and M. Rivain. Tight private circuits: achieving probing security with the least refreshing. *Proceedings of ASIACRYPT 2018, Lecture Notes in Computer Science* 11273, pp. 343–372, 2018. See page 430.

[56] T. D. Bending. Bent functions, SDP designs and their automorphism groups. *Ph.D. thesis, Queen Mary and Westfield College*, 1993. See page 192.

[57] T. Bending and D. Fon-Der-Flaass. Crooked functions, bent functions and distance regular graphs. *Electron. J. Comb.* 5, Research paper 34 (electronic), 14 pages, 1998. See pages 231, 278, 279, and 373.

[58] C. H. Bennett, G. Brassard, and J. M. Robert. Privacy amplification by public discussion. *SIAM Journal on Computing* 17, pp. 210–229, 1988. See pages 129, 292, and 314.

[59] M. Ben-Or, S. Goldwasser, and A. Wigderson. Completeness theorems for non- cryptographic fault-tolerant distributed computation. *Proceedings of ACM STOC 1988*, pp. 1–10, 1988. See page 436.

[60] C. Berbain, O. Billet, A. Canteaut, et al.. Decim v2. *New Stream Cipher Designs – The eSTREAM Finalists, Lecture Notes in. Computer Science* 4986, pp. 140–151, 2008. See page 318.

[61] C. Berbain, H. Gilbert, and J. Patarin. QUAD: a practical stream cipher with provable security. *Proceedings of EUROCRYPT 2006, Lecture Notes in Computer Science* 4004, pp 109–128, 2006. See page 4.

[62] T. Berger, A. Canteaut, P. Charpin, and Y. Laigle-Chapuy. On almost perfect nonlinear functions. *IEEE Transactions on Information Theory* 52 (9), pp. 4160–4170, 2006. See pages 385, 386, 391, and 411.

[63] E. Berlekamp, *Algebraic Coding Theory,* McGraw-Hill, 1968. See page 4.

[64] E. R. Berlekamp, H. Rumsey, and G. Solomon. On the solution of algebraic equations over finite fields. *Information and Control* 10, pp. 553–564, 1967. See page 495.

[65] E. R. Berlekamp and N. J. A. Sloane. Restrictions on the weight distributions of the Reed–Muller codes. *Information and Control* 14, pp. 442–446, 1969. See page 157.

[66] E. R. Berlekamp and L. R. Welch. Weight distributions of the cosets of the (32,6) Reed–Muller code. *IEEE Transactions on Information Theory*, 18 (1), pp. 203–207, 1972. See pages 143 and 156.

[67] S. D. Berman. On the theory of group codes. *Kibernetica* 1 (1), pp. 31–39, 1967. See page 152.

[68] A. Bernasconi and B. Codenotti. Spectral analysis of Boolean functions as a graph eigenvalue problem. *IEEE Transactions on Computers* 48 (3), pp. 345–351, 1999. See pages 70 and 193.

[69] A. Bernasconi, B. Codenotti, and J. M. Vanderkam. A characterization of bent functions in terms of strongly regular graphs. *IEEE Transactions on Computers* 50 (9), pp. 984–985, 2001. See page 70.

[70] D. J. Bernstein. Post-quantum cryptography. *Encyclopedia of Cryptography and Security*, pp. 949–950, 2011. See page 1.

[71] T. Beth and C. Ding. On almost perfect nonlinear permutations. *Proceedings of EUROCRYPT 93, Lecture Notes in Computer Science* 765, pp. 65–76, 1994. See pages 137, 373, 374, and 400.

[72] C. Bey and G. M. Kyureghyan. On Boolean functions with the sum of every two of them being bent. *Designs, Codes and Cryptography* 49, pp. 341–346, 2008. See page 255.

[73] T. Beyne and B. Bilgin. Uniform first-order threshold implementations. *Proceedings of SAC 2016, Lecture Notes in Computer Science* 10532, pp. 79–98, 2016. See page 441.

[74] S. Bhasin, C. Carlet, and S. Guilley. Theory of masking with codewords in hardware: low-weight dth-order correlation-immune Boolean functions. *IACR Cryptology ePrint Archive* (http://eprint .iacr.org/) 2013/303, 2013. See pages 144, 304, 306, and 433.

[75] S. Bhasin, J.-L. Danger, S. Guilley, Z. Najm, and X. T. Ngo. Linear complementary dual code improvement to strengthen encoded circuit against hardware Trojan horses. *IEEE International Symposium on Hardware Oriented Security and Trust (HOST)*, May 5–7, 2015. See page 446.

[76] A. Bhattacharyya, S. Kopparty, G. Shoenebeck, M. Sudan, and D. Zuckerman. Optimal testing of Reed–Muller codes. *Proceedings of Electronic Colloquium on Computational Complexity*, report no. 86, 2009.

[77] J. Bierbrauer. New semifields, PN and APN functions. *Designs, Codes and Cryptography* 54, pp. 189–200, 2010. See page 394.

[78] J. Bierbrauer, K. Gopalakrishnan, and D. R. Stinson. Bounds for resilient functions and orthogonal arrays. *Proceedings of CRYPTO 1994, Lecture Notes in Computer Science* 839, pp. 247–256, 1994. See pages 313 and 357.

[79] J. Bierbrauer, K. Gopalakrishnan, and D. R. Stinson. Orthogonal arrays, resilient functions, error-correcting codes, and linear programming bounds. *SIAM Journal on Discrete Mathematics* 9 (3), pp. 424–452, 1996. See page 129.

[80] J. Bierbrauer and G. Kyureghyan. Crooked binomials. *Designs Codes Cryptography* 46(3), pp. 269–301, 2008. See pages 278, 373, and 393.

[81] A. Biere, M. Heule, H. van Maaren, and T. Walsh, eds. *Handbook of Satisfiability*. IOS Press, 2009. See page 19.

[82] E. Biham and A. Shamir. Differential cryptanalysis of DES-like cryptosystems. *Journal of Cryptology* 4 (1), pp. 3–72, 1991. See pages 134 and 447.

[83] E. Biham and A. Shamir. Differential fault analysis of secret key cryptosystems. *Proceedings of CRYPTO 1997, Lecture Notes in Computer Science* 1294, 1997, pp. 513–525. See page 427.

[84] B. Bilgin, A. Bogdanov, M. Knezevic, F. Mendel, and Q. Wang. Fides: lightweight authenticated cipher with side-channel resistance for constrained hardware. *Proceedings of International Workshop Cryptographic Hardware and Embedded Systems CHES 2013, Lecture Notes in Computer Science* 8086, pp. 142–158, 2013. See page 411.

[85] B. Bilgin, B. Gierlichs, S. Nikova, V. Nikov, and V. Rijmen. Higher-order threshold implementations. *Proceedings of ASIACRYPT 2014, Lecture Notes in Computer Science* 8874, pp. 326–343, 2014. See page 437.

[86] B. Bilgin, S. Nikova, V. Nikov, V. Rijmen, and G. Stütz. Threshold implementations of all 3×3 and 4×4 S-boxes. *Proceedings of International Workshop Cryptographic Hardware and Embedded Systems CHES 2012, Lecture Notes in Computer Science* 7428, pp. 76–91, 2012. See pages 440, 441, 442, 443, and 502.

[87] B. Bilgin, S. Nikova, V. Nikov, V. Rijmen, N. N. Tokareva, and V. Vitkup. Threshold implementations of small S-boxes. *Cryptography and Communications* 7(1), pp. 3–33, 2015 (extended version of [86]). See pages 440, 441, and 442.

[88] A. Biryukov and C. De Cannière. Data Encryption Standard (DES). Encyclopedia of cryptography and security; Editors: H. C. A. van Tilborg, S. Jajodia, pp. 295–301, 2011. See page 25.

[89] A. Biryukov and D. Wagner. Slide attacks. *Proceedings of Fast Software Encryption FSE 1999, Lecture Notes in Computer Science* 1636, pp. 245–259, 1999. See page 142.

[90] G. Blakely. Safeguarding cryptographic keys. *National Comp. Conf.* 48, pp. 313–317, New York, June 1979. AFIPS Press. See page 145.

[91] J. Blömer and J.-P. Seifert. Fault based cryptanalysis of the Advanced Encryption Standard (AES). *Proceedings of Financial Cryptography, Lecture Notes in Computer Science* 2742, pp. 162–181, 2003. See page 427.

[92] C. Blondeau, A. Canteaut, and P. Charpin. Differential properties of power functions. *International Journal of Information and Coding Theory* 1 (2), pp. 149–170, 2010. See also the *Proceedings of the 2010 IEEE International Symposium on Information Theory (ISIT)*, pp. 2478–2482, 2010. See page 418.

[93] C. Blondeau, A. Canteaut, and P. Charpin. Differential properties of $x \mapsto x^{2^t - 1}$. *IEEE Transactions on Information Theory* 57 (12), pp. 8127–8137, 2011. See pages 401 and 422.

[94] C. Blondeau and K. Nyberg. Perfect nonlinear functions and cryptography. *Finite Fields and Their Applications* 32, pp. 120–147, 2015. See pages 369 and 373.

[95] C. Blondeau and L. Perrin. More differentially 6-uniform power functions. *Designs, Codes and Cryptography* 73(2), pp. 487–505, 2014. See page 422.

[96] A. W. Bluher. On $x^{q+1} + ax + b$. *Finite Fields and Their Applications* 10(3), pp. 285–305, 2004. See page 495.

[97] A. W. Bluher. On existence of Budaghyan–Carlet APN hexanomials. *Finite Fields and Their Applications* 24, pp. 118–123, 2013. See pages 408 and 409.

[98] L. Blum, M. Blum, and M. Shub. A simple unpredictable pseudo-random number generator. *SIAM Journal on Computing* 15 (2), pp. 364–383, 1986. See page 4.

[99] A. Blum, A. Kalai, and H. Wasserman. Noise-tolerant learning, the parity problem, and the statistical query model. *Journal ACM* 50(4), pp. 506–519, 2003. See page 466.

[100] A. Bogdanov, L. R. Knudsen, G. Leander, C. Paar, A. Poschmann, M. J. Robshaw, Y. Seurin, and C. Vikkelsoe. PRESENT: An ultra-lightweight block cipher. *Proceedings of 9th International Workshop Cryptographic Hardware and Embedded Systems CHES 2007, Lecture Notes in Computer Science* 4727, pp. 450–466, 2007. See page 26.

[101] Y. Borissov, A. Braeken, S. Nikova, and B. Preneel. On the covering radii of binary Reed–Muller codes in the set of resilient Boolean functions. *IEEE Transactions on Information Theory* 51 (3), pp. 1182–1189, 2005. See page 287.

[102] Y. Borissov, A. Braeken, S. Nikova, and B. Preneel. Classification of the cosets of RM(1, 7) in RM(3, 7) revisited. *NATO Science for Peace and Security Series – D: Information and Communication Security*, Vol 18: Boolean Functions in Cryptology and Information Security, IOS Press, pp. 58–72, 2008. See page 144.

[103] Y. Borissov, N. Manev, and S. Nikova. On the non-minimal codewords of weight $2d_{min}$ in the binary Reed–Muller code. *Proceedings of the Workshop on Coding and Cryptography* 2001, *Electronic Notes in Discrete Mathematics*, Elsevier, vol. 6, pp. 103–110, 2001. Revised version in *Discrete*

Applied Mathematics 128 (Special Issue "Int. Workshop on Coding and Cryptography (2001)"), pp. 65–74, 2003. See page 148.

[104] Y. Borissov, N. Manev, and S. Nikova. On the non-minimal codewords in binary Reed–Muller codes. *Discrete Applied Mathematics* 128, pp. 65–74, 2003. See page 148.

[105] E. Boss, V. Grosso, T. Güneysu, G. Leander, and A. Moradi, and Tobias Schneider. Strong 8-bit Sboxes with efficient masking in hardware extended version. *Journal of Cryptographic Engineering JCEN* 7 (2), pp. 149–165, 2017 and *IACR Cryptology ePrint Archive* (http://eprint.iacr.org/) 2016/647. See page 442.

[106] C. Boura and A. Canteaut. On the influence of the algebraic degree of F^{-1} on the algebraic degree of $G \circ F$. *IEEE Transactions on Information Theory* 59 (1), pp. 691–702, 2013. See pages 40, 41, 114, and 115.

[107] C. Boura and A. Canteaut. On the boomerang uniformity of cryptographic Sboxes. *IACR Transactions on Symmetric Cryptology* 2018 (3), pp. 290–310, 2018. See pages 141 and 142.

[108] C. Boura, A. Canteaut, and C. Cannière. Higher-order differential properties of Keccak and Luffa. *Proceedings of Fast Software Encryption FSE 2011, Lecture Notes in Computer Science* 6733, pp. 252–269, 2011. See page 115.

[109] C. Boura, A. Canteaut, J. Jean, and V. Suder. Two notions of Differential equivalence on Sboxes. *Designs, Codes and Cryptography* 87 (2–3), pp. 185–202, 2019 and *IACR Cryptology ePrint Archive* (http://eprint.iacr.org/) 2018/617. See page 376.

[110] J. Bourgain. On the construction of affine extractors. *Geometric & Functional Analysis GAFA* 17 (1), pp. 33–57, 2007. See page 105.

[111] J. Boyar and M. G. Find. Constructive relationships between algebraic thickness and normality. *Proceedings of International Symposium on Fundamentals of Computation Theory*, pp. 106–117, 2015. See page 109.

[112] P. Boyvalenkov, T. Marinova, and M. Stoyanovac. Nonexistence of a few binary orthogonal arrays. *Discrete Applied Mathematics* 217, Part 2, pp. 144–150, 2017. See page 305.

[113] D. Bozilov, B. Bilgin, and H. Sahin. A note on 5-bit quadratic permutations classification. *IACR Transactions on Symmetric Cryptology* 2017 1, pp. 398–404, 2017. See page 442.

[114] C. Bracken, E. Byrne, N. Markin, and G. McGuire. On the Walsh spectrum of a new APN function. *Proceedings of IMA Conference on Cryptography and Coding 2007, Lecture Notes in Computer Science* 4887, pp. 92–98, 2007. See page 406.

[115] C. Bracken, E. Byrne, N. Markin, and G. McGuire. Determining the nonlinearity of a new family of APN functions. *Proceedings of AAECC-17 Conference, Lecture Notes in Computer Science* 4851, pp. 72–79, 2007. See page 422.

[116] C. Bracken, E. Byrne, N. Markin, and G. McGuire. New families of quadratic almost perfect nonlinear trinomials and multinomials. *Finite Fields and Their Applications* 14, pp. 703–714, 2008. See pages 231, 398, 406, and 407.

[117] C. Bracken, E. Byrne, N. Markin, and G. McGuire. On the Fourier spectrum of binomial APN functions. *SIAM Journal on Discrete Mathematics* 23 (2), pp. 596–608, 2009. See pages 398 and 412.

[118] C. Bracken, E. Byrne, N. Markin, and G. McGuire. A few more quadratic APN functions. *Cryptography and Communications* 3 (1), pp. 43–53, 2011. See pages 398, 405, and 406.

[119] C. Bracken, E. Byrne, G. McGuire, and G. Nebe. On the equivalence of quadratic APN functions. *Designs, Codes and Cryptography* 61 (3), pp. 261–272, 2011. See page 30.

[120] C. Bracken and G. Leander. A highly nonlinear differentially 4 uniform power mapping that permutes fields of even degree. *Finite Fields and Their Applications* 16(4), pp. 231–242, 2010. See pages 418 and 422.

[121] C. Bracken, C. Tan, and Y. Tan. Binomial differentially 4 uniform permutations with high nonlinearity. *Finite Fields and Their Applications* 18(3), pp. 537–546, 2012. See page 418.

[122] C. Bracken, C. H. Tan, and Y. Tan. On a class of quadratic polynomials with no zeros and its application to APN functions. *Finite Fields and Their Applications* 25, pp. 26–36, 2014. See pages 408 and 409.

[123] C. Bracken and Z. Zha. On the Fourier spectra of the infinite families of quadratic APN functions. *Advances in Mathematics of Communications* 3 (3), pp. 219–226, 2009. See pages 406 and 412.

[124] A. Braeken, Y. Borisov, S. Nikova, and B. Preneel. Classification of Boolean functions of 6 variables or less with respect to cryptographic properties. *Proceedings of ICALP 2005, Lecture Notes in Computer Science* 3580, pp. 324–334, 2005. See pages 143 and 208.

[125] A. Braeken, Y. Borisov, S. Nikova, and B. Preneel. Classification of cubic $(n − 4)$-resilient boolean functions. *IEEE Transactions on Information Theory* 52 (4), pp. 1670–1676, 2006. See page 312.

[126] A. Braeken, V. Nikov, S. Nikova, and B. Preneel. On Boolean functions with generalized cryptographic properties. *Proceedings of INDOCRYPT 2004, Lecture Notes in Computer Science* 3348, pp. 120–135, 2004. See page 290.

[127] A. Braeken and B. Preneel. On the algebraic immunity of symmetric Boolean functions. *Proceedings of Indocrypt 2005, Lecture Notes in Computer Science* 3797, pp. 35–48, 2005. Some false results of this reference are corrected in Braeken's PhD thesis "Cryptographic properties of Boolean functions and S-boxes." See pages 335, 336, and 358.

[128] A. Braeken and B. Preneel. Probabilistic algebraic attacks. *Proceedings of IMA Conference on Cryptography and Coding 2005, Lecture Notes in Computer Science* 3796, pp. 290–303, 2005. See page 324.

[129] N. Brandstätter, T. Lange, and A. Winterhof. On the non-linearity and sparsity of Boolean functions related to the discrete logarithm in finite fields of characteristic two. *Proceedings of International Workshop on Coding and Cryptography WCC 2005, Lecture Notes in Computer Science* 3969, pp. 135–143, 2006. See page 338.

[130] E. Brier and P. Langevin. Classification of cubic Boolean functions of 9 variables. *Proceedings of the IEEE Information Theory Workshop ITW 2003*, Paris, France, 2003. See page 155.

[131] J. Bringer, C. Carlet, H. Chabanne, S. Guilley, and H. Maghrebi. Orthogonal direct sum masking – a smartcard friendly computation paradigm in a code, with builtin protection against side-channel and fault attacks. *Proceedings of WISTP*, Springer, Heraklion, 2014, 40–56. See pages 444, 445, and 446.

[132] J. Bringer, H. Chabanne, and T. Ha Le. Protecting AES against side-channel analysis using wire-tap codes. *Journal of Cryptographic Engineering JCEN* 2 (2), pp. 129–141, 2012. See page 431.

[133] J. Bringer, V. Gillot, and P. Langevin. Exponential sums and Boolean functions. *Proceedings of the Conference BFCA 2005*, Publications des universités de Rouen et du Havre, pp. 177–185, 2005. See page 81.

[134] M. Brinkmann and G. Leander. On the classification of APN functions up to dimension five. *Designs, Codes and Cryptography* 49, Issue 1–3, pp. 273–288, 2008. Revised and extended version of a paper with the same title in the *Proceedings of the Workshop on Coding and Cryptography WCC 2007*, pp. 39–48, 2007 See pages 138, 144, 399, 402, and 408.

[135] K. Browning, J. F. Dillon, R. E. Kibler, and M. McQuistan. APN polynomials and related codes. *Special Volume of Journal of Combinatorics, Information and System Sciences, Honoring the 75-th Birthday of Prof. D.K. Ray-Chaudhuri* 34, Issue 1–4, pp. 135–159, 2009. See pages 144, 379, 380, 392, 399, 403, 404, and 411.

[136] K. Browning, J. F. Dillon, M. McQuistan, and A. J. Wolfe. An APN permutation in dimension 6. *Proceedings of Conference Finite Fields and Applications Fq9*, Contemporary Mathematics 518, pp. 33–42, 2009. See pages 10, 399, 411, 417, and 478.

[137] R. A. Brualdi, N. Cai, and V. S. Pless. Orphans of the first order Reed–Muller codes. *IEEE Transactions on Information Theory* 36, pp. 399–401, 1990. See page 262.

[138] J. O. Brüer. On pseudorandom sequences as crypto generators. *Proceedings of International Zurich Seminar on Digital Communications*, pp. 157–161, 1984. See page 356.

[139] L. Budaghyan. The equivalence of almost bent and almost perfect nonlinear functions and their generalizations. PhD thesis. Otto-von-Guericke-University, 2005.

[140] L. Budaghyan. The simplest method for constructing APN polynomials EA-inequivalent to power functions. *Proceedings of the International Workshop on the Arithmetic of Finite Fields, WAIFI 2007, Lecture Notes in Computer Science* 4547, pp. 177–188, 2007. See page 397.

[141] L. Budaghyan. *Construction and Analysis of Cryptographic Functions*. Springer, 2014. See page 369.

[142] L. Budaghyan, M. Calderini, C. Carlet, R. S. Coulter and I. Villa. Constructing APN Functions through isotopic shifts. To appear in IEEE Transactions on Information Theory. See also "On isotopic construction of APN functions", IACR Cryptology ePrint Archive (http://eprint.iacr.org/) 2018/769, 2018. Presented at SETA 2018. See pages 398 and 407.

[143] L. Budaghyan, M. Calderini, C. Carlet, R. S. Coulter, and I. Villa. Generalized isotopic shift of Gold functions. *Proceedings of International Workshop on Coding and Cryptography WCC 2019*, 2019. See page 399.

[144] L. Budaghyan, M. Calderini, C. Carlet, and N. Kaleyski. On a relationship between Gold and Kasami functions and its generalization for other power APN functions. *Boolean Functions and Application*, Florence, Italy, June 16–21, 2019. See page 395.

[145] L. Budaghyan, M. Calderini, and I. Villa. On relations between CCZ- and EA-equivalences. *Cryptography and Communications* 12 (1), pp. 85–100, 2020 See also *IACR Cryptology ePrint Archive* (http://eprint.iacr.org/) 2018/796, 2018. See pages 397 and 478.

[146] L. Budaghyan, M. Calderini and I. Villa. On equivalence between known families of quadratic APN functions. To appear in *Finite Fields and Their Applications*. See also "On equivalence between some families of APN functions", *Proceedings of International Workshop on Coding and Cryptography WCC* 2019. See pages 406, 408, and 409.

[147] L. Budaghyan and C. Carlet. Classes of quadratic APN trinomials and hexanomials and related structures. *IEEE Transactions on Information Theory* 54 (5), pp. 2354–2357, 2008. See pages 393, 407, and 408.

[148] L. Budaghyan and C. Carlet. On CCZ-equivalence and its use in secondary constructions of bent functions. *Proceedings of International Workshop on Coding and Cryptography WCC 2009* and *IACR Cryptology ePrint Archive* (http://eprint.iacr.org/) 2009/42, 2009. See pages 30 and 269.

[149] L. Budaghyan and C. Carlet. CCZ-equivalence of single and multi output Boolean functions. *AMS Contemporary Math. 518, Post-Proceedings of the Conference Fq9*, pp. 43–54, 2010. See pages 29, 30, and 192.

[150] L. Budaghyan and C. Carlet. CCZ-equivalence of bent vectorial functions and related constructions. *Designs, Codes and Cryptography* 59(1–3), pp. 69–87, 2011. See pages 30, 192, 231, 269, and 272.

[151] L. Budaghyan, C. Carlet, P. Felke, and G. Leander. An infinite class of quadratic APN functions which are not equivalent to power functions. *Proceedings of IEEE International Symposium on Information Theory (ISIT) 2006*, 2006. See pages 373, 393, 397, 398, and 506.

[152] L. Budaghyan, C. Carlet, and T. Helleseth. On bent functions associated to AB functions. *Proceedings of the IEEE Information Theory Workshop ITW 2011*, 2011. See pages 228 and 376.

[153] L. Budaghyan, C. Carlet, T. Helleseth, and N. Kaleyski. Changing values in APN functions. To appear in *IEEE Transactions on Information Theory*. See also Changing points in APN functions. ACR Cryptology ePrint Archive (http://eprint.iacr.org/) 2018/1217. Preprint, 2019. See pages 373 and 403.

[154] L. Budaghyan, C. Carlet, T. Helleseth, and A. Kholosha. On o-equivalence of Niho bent functions. *Proceedings of International Workshop on the Arithmetic of Finite Fields* pp. 155–168, 2014. See pages 219 and 220.

[155] L. Budaghyan, C. Carlet, T. Helleseth, A. Kholosha, and S. Mesnager. Further results on Niho bent functions. *IEEE Transactions on Information Theory* 58, No. 11, pp. 6979–6985, 2012. See page 222.

[156] L. Budaghyan, C. Carlet, T. Helleseth, N. Li, and B. Sun. On upper bounds for algebraic degrees of APN functions. *IEEE Transactions on Information Theory* 64 (6), pp. 4399–4411, 2018. See page 373.

[157] L. Budaghyan, C. Carlet, and G. Leander. Another class of quadratic APN binomials over $\mathbb{F}_{2^n}$: the case n divisible by 4. *Proceedings of the Workshop on Coding and Cryptography, WCC 2007*, pp. 49–58, 2007. See pages 393, 405, and 506.

[158] L. Budaghyan, C. Carlet, and G. Leander. Two classes of quadratic APN binomials inequivalent to power functions. *IEEE Transactions on Information Theory* 54 (9), pp. 4218–4229, 2008. This

paper is a completed and merged version of [151] and [157]. See pages 373, 393, 396, 397, 398, 403, 405, 407, and 496.

[159] L. Budaghyan, C. Carlet, and G. Leander. On inequivalence between known power APN functions. *Proceedings of the conference BFCA 2008*, 2008. See pages 396, 402, and 403.

[160] L. Budaghyan, C. Carlet, and G. Leander. Constructing new APN functions from known ones. *Finite Fields and Their Applications* 15, pp. 150–159, 2009. See pages 393, 398, 403, 406, and 407.

[161] L. Budaghyan, C. Carlet, and G. Leander. On a construction of quadratic APN functions. *Proceedings of the IEEE Information Theory Workshop ITW 2009*, pp. 374–378, 2009. See pages 398, 406, and 407.

[162] L. Budaghyan, C. Carlet, and A. Pott. New classes of almost bent and almost perfect nonlinear polynomials. *Proceedings of the Workshop on Coding and Cryptography 2005*, pp. 306–315, 2005. See pages 29, 36, 138, 396, 397, 404, 405, and 506.

[163] L. Budaghyan, C. Carlet, and A. Pott. New classes of almost bent and almost perfect nonlinear functions. *IEEE Transactions on Information Theory* 52 (3), pp. 1141–1152, 2006. This is a completed version of [162]. See pages 28, 29, 36, 138, 272, 396, 397, 404, and 405.

[164] L. Budaghyan and T. Helleseth. New commutative semifields defined by new PN multinomials. *Cryptography and Communications* 3 (1), pp. 1–16, 2011. See page 30.

[165] L. Budaghyan, T. Helleseth and N. Kaleyski. A new family of APN quadrinomials. *IACR Cryptology ePrint Archive* (http://eprint.iacr.org/) 2019/994 See pages 407 and 410.

[166] L. Budaghyan, T. Helleseth, N. Li, and B. Sun. Some results on the known classes of quadratic APN functions. *Proceedings of C2SI 2017, Lecture Notes in Computer Science* 10194, pp. 3–16, 2017. See pages 406 and 408.

[167] L. Budaghyan, N. Kaleyski, S. Kwon, C. Riera, and P. Stănică. Partially APN Boolean functions and classes of functions that are not APN infinitely often. To appear in the *Special Issue on Boolean Functions and Their Applications 2018, Cryptography and Communications*. See page 373.

[168] L. Budaghyan, A. Kholosha, C. Carlet, and T. Helleseth. Univariate Niho bent functions from o-polynomials. *IEEE Transactions on Information Theory* 62 (4), pp. 2254–2265, 2016. Extended version of "Niho Bent functions from quadratic o-monomials." *Proceedings of IEEE International Symposium on Information Theory (ISIT) 2014*, pp. 1827–1831, 2014. See pages 220 and 222.

[169] L. Budaghyan and A. Pott. On differential uniformity and nonlinearity of functions. *Discrete Mathematics, Special Issue "Combinatorics 2006"* 309 (2), pp. 371–384, 2009.

[170] L. Burnett, G. Carter, E. Dawson, and W. Millan. Efficient methods for generating MARS-like S-boxes. *Proceedings of Fast Software Encryption FSE 2000, Lecture Notes in Computer Science* 1978, pp. 300–314, 2000. See page 145.

[171] W. Burnside. *Theory of Groups of Finite Order*. Cambridge University Press, 1897. See page 144.

[172] E. Byrne and G. McGuire. On the non-existence of crooked functions on finite fields. *Proceedings of the Workshop on Coding and Cryptography, WCC 2005*, pp. 316–324, 2005. See page 373.

[173] J. Cai, F. Green, and T. Thierauf. On the correlation of symmetric functions. *Math. Systems Theory* 29, pp. 245–258, 1996. See page 354.

[174] A. R. Calderbank, G. McGuire, B. Poonen, and M. Rubinstein. On a conjecture of Helleseth regarding pairs of binary m-sequences. *IEEE Transactions on Information Theory* 42, pp. 988–990, 1996. See pages 73, 275, and 384.

[175] A. R. Calderbank and W. M. Kantor. The geometry of two-weight codes. *Bull. Lond. Math. Soc.* 18 (2), pp. 97–122, 1986.

[176] M. Calderini, M. Sala, and I. Villa. A note on APN permutations in even dimension. *Finite Fields and Their Applications* 46, pp. 1–16, 2017. See page 411.

[177] P. J. Cameron and J. H. van Lint. *Designs, Graphs, Codes and Their Links*. Cambridge University Press, 1991. See page 254.

[178] P. Camion and A. Canteaut. Construction of t-resilient functions over a finite alphabet. *Proceedings of EUROCRYPT 1996, Lecture Notes in Computer Sciences* 1070, pp. 283–293, 1996. See page 284.

[179] P. Camion and A. Canteaut. Generalization of Siegenthaler inequality and Schnorr–Vaudenay multipermutations. *Proceedings of CRYPTO 1996, Lecture Notes in Computer Science* 1109, pp. 372–386, 1996. See page 129.

[180] P. Camion and A. Canteaut. Correlation-immune and resilient functions over finite alphabets and their applications in cryptography. *Designs, Codes and Cryptography* 16, 1999. See pages 314 and 317.

[181] P. Camion, C. Carlet, P. Charpin, and N. Sendrier. On correlation-immune functions. *Proceedings of CRYPTO 1991, Lecture Notes in Computer Science* 576, pp. 86–100, 1991. See pages 86, 165, 210, 284, 293, 298, 312, and 314.

[182] E. R. Canfield, Z. Gao, C. Greenhill, B. D. McKay, and R. W. Robinson. Asymptotic enumeration of correlation-immune boolean functions. *Cryptography and Communications* 2 (1), pp. 111–126, 2010. See page 312.

[183] C. De Cannière. Analysis and design of symmetric encryption algorithms. PhD thesis, KU Leuven, 2007. See pages 144 and 417.

[184] A. Canteaut. Differential cryptanalysis of Feistel ciphers and differentially uniform mappings. *Proceedings of Selected Areas on Cryptography, SAC 1997*, pp. 172–184, 1997. See page 411.

[185] A. Canteaut. On the weight distributions of optimal cosets of the first-order Reed–Muller code. *IEEE Transactions on Information Theory*, 47(1), pp. 407–413, 2001. See page 157.

[186] A. Canteaut. Cryptographic functions and design criteria for block ciphers. *Proceedings of INDOCRYPT 2001, Lecture Notes in Computer Science* 2247, pp. 1–16, 2001. See page 382.

[187] A. Canteaut. On the correlations between a combining function and functions of fewer variables. *Proceedings of the IEEE Information Theory Workshop ITW 2002* pp. 78–81, 2002. See pages 87, 102, 290, and 319.

[188] A. Canteaut. Open problems related to algebraic attacks on stream ciphers. *Proceedings of Workshop on Coding and Cryptography WCC* 2005, pp. 1–10, 2005. See also a revised version in *Lecture Notes in Computer Science* 3969, pp. 120–134, 2006. See pages 96 and 328.

[189] A. Canteaut. Analysis and design of symmetric ciphers. Habilitation for Directing Theses, University of Paris 6, 2006. See pages 89, 194, 344, and 386.

[190] A. Canteaut, C. Carlet, P. Charpin, and C. Fontaine. Propagation characteristics and correlation-immunity of highly nonlinear Boolean functions. *Proceedings of EUROCRYPT 2000, Lecture Notes in Computer Science* 187, pp. 507–522, 2000. See pages 58, 100, and 192.

[191] A. Canteaut, C. Carlet, P. Charpin, and C. Fontaine. On cryptographic properties of the cosets of $R(1,m)$. *IEEE Transactions on Information Theory* 47 (4), pp. 1494–1513, 2001. See pages 58, 62, 98, 106, 153, 192, 232, 240, 241, 259, 262, and 263.

[192] A. Canteaut, S. Carpov, C. Fontaine, T. Lepoint, M. Naya-Plasencia, P. Paillier, and R. Sirdey. Stream ciphers: a practical solution for efficient homomorphic-ciphertext compression. *Proceedings of Fast Software Encryption FSE 2016, Lecture Notes in Computer Science* 9783, pp. 313–333, 2016. See page 454.

[193] A. Canteaut and P. Charpin. Decomposing bent functions. *IEEE Transactions on Information Theory* 49, pp. 2004–2019, 2003. See pages 100, 198, 203, 208, and 241.

[194] A. Canteaut, P. Charpin, and H. Dobbertin. A new characterization of almost bent functions. *Proceedings of Fast Software Encryption 99, Lecture Notes in Computer Science* 1636, pp. 186–200, 1999. See pages 73, 276, and 382.

[195] A. Canteaut, P. Charpin, and H. Dobbertin. Binary m-sequences with three-valued crosscorrelation: a proof of Welch's conjecture. *IEEE Transactions on Information Theory* 46 (1), pp. 4–8, 2000. See pages 382, 388, and 395.

[196] A. Canteaut, P. Charpin, and H. Dobbertin. Weight divisibility of cyclic codes, highly nonlinear functions on $GF(2^m)$ and crosscorrelation of maximum-length sequences. *SIAM Journal on Discrete Mathematics*, 13(1), pp. 105–138, 2000. See pages 73, 276, 382, 395, 401, 402, and 412.

[197] A. Canteaut, P. Charpin, and G. Kyureghyan. A new class of monomial bent functions. *Finite Fields and Their Applications* 14(1), pp. 221–241, 2008. See page 230.

[198] A. Canteaut, M. Daum, H. Dobbertin, and G. Leander. Finding nonnormal bent functions. *Discrete Applied Mathematics* 154, pp. 202 - 218, 2006. See also "Normal and Non-Normal Bent Functions." *Proceedings of the Workshop on Coding and Cryptography 2003*, pp. 91–100, 2003. See pages 203, 211, 241, and 252.

[199] A. Canteaut, S. Duval, and L. Perrin. A generalisation of Dillon's APN permutation with the best known differential and nonlinear properties for all fields of size 2^{4k+2}. *IEEE Transactions on Information Theory* 63 (11), pp. 7575–7591, 2017. See pages 411, 421, and 478.

[200] A. Canteaut and M. Naya-Plasencia. Structural weaknesses of permutations with a low differential uniformity and generalized crooked functions. *Contemporary Mathematics* 518, pp. 55–71, 2010. See page 279.

[201] A. Canteaut and L. Perrin. On CCZ-equivalence, extended-affine equivalence, and function twisting. *Finite Fields and Their Applications* 56, pp. 209–246, 2019. Preliminary version available in *IACR Cryptology ePrint Archive* (http://eprint.iacr.org/) 2018/713. See pages 72 and 136.

[202] A. Canteaut and Y. Rotella. Attacks against filter generators exploiting monomial mappings. *Proceedings of Fast Software Encryption FSE 2016, Lecture Notes in Computer Science* 9783, pp. 78–98, 2016. See page 243.

[203] A. Canteaut and M. Trabbia. Improved fast correlation attacks using parity-check equations of weight 4 and 5, *Proceedings of EUROCRYPT 2000. Lecture Notes in Computer Science* 1807, pp. 573–588, 2000. See pages 78, 87, 194, and 290.

[204] A. Canteaut and M. Videau. Degree of composition of highly nonlinear functions and applications to higher order differential cryptanalysis. *Proceedings of EUROCRYPT 2002, Lecture Notes in Computer Science* 2332, pp. 518–533, 2002. See pages 57, 64, 114, 115, 295, and 371.

[205] A. Canteaut and M. Videau. Symmetric Boolean functions. *IEEE Transactions on Information Theory* 51 (8), pp. 2791–2811, 2005. See pages 354, 355, 356, and 357.

[206] X. Cao, H. Chen, and S. Mesnager. Further results on semi-bent functions in polynomial form. *Advances in Mathematics of Communications* 10 (4), pp. 725–741, 2016. See page 263.

[207] J. R. du Carlet. La Cryptographie, contenant une très subtile manière d'escrire secrètement, composée par Maistre Jean Robert Du Carlet, 1644. A manuscript exists at the Bibliothèque Nationale (Très Grande Bibliothèque), Paris, France. See page 1.

[208] C. Carlet. A simple description of Kerdock codes. *Proceedings of Coding Theory and Applications 1988, 3rd International Colloquium, Lecture Notes in Computer Science* 388, pp. 202–208, 1989. See page 255.

[209] C. Carlet. Codes de Reed–Muller, codes de Kerdock et de Preparata. PhD thesis. Publication of LITP, Institut Blaise Pascal, Université Paris 6, 90.59, 1990. See pages 46, 171, 197, and 435.

[210] C. Carlet. A transformation on Boolean functions, its consequences on some problems related to Reed–Muller codes. *Proceedings of EUROCODE 1990, Lecture Notes in Computer Science* 514, pp. 42–50, 1991. See pages 157, 180, 203, and 204.

[211] C. Carlet. Partially-bent functions. *Designs Codes and Cryptography*, 3, pp. 135–145, 1993, and *Proceedings of CRYPTO 1992, Lecture Notes in Computer Science* 740, pp. 280–291, 1993. See pages 62, 190, 256, and 257.

[212] C. Carlet. Two new classes of bent functions. *Proceedings of EUROCRYPT 1993, Lecture Notes in Computer Science* 765, pp. 77–101, 1994. See pages 58, 63, 197, 200, 202, 208, 210, 211, 215, and 252.

[213] C. Carlet. Generalized partial spreads. *IEEE Transactions on Information Theory* 41 (5), pp. 1482–1487, 1995. See pages 241 and 242.

[214] C. Carlet. Hyper-bent functions. PRAGOCRYPT 1996, Czech Technical University Publishing House, pp. 145–155, 1996. See page 244.

[215] C. Carlet. A construction of bent functions. *Finite Fields and Applications, London Mathematical Society*, Lecture Series 233, Cambridge University Press, pp. 47–58, 1996. See pages 234 and 235.

[216] C. Carlet. More correlation-immune and resilient functions over Galois fields and Galois rings. *Proceedings of EUROCRYPT 1997, Lecture Notes in Computer Science* 1233, pp. 422–433, 1997. See pages 295 and 303.

[217] C. Carlet. On Kerdock codes, American Mathematical Society. *Proceedings of the Conference Finite Fields and Applications Fq4, Contemporary Mathematics* 225, pp. 155–163, 1999. See page 255.

[218] C. Carlet. On the propagation criterion of degree ℓ and order k. *Proceedings of EUROCRYPT 1998, Lecture Notes in Computer Science* 1403, pp. 462–474, 1998. See pages 318, 319, and 320.

[219] C. Carlet. On cryptographic propagation criteria for Boolean functions. *Information and Computation* 151, Academic Press, pp. 32–56, 1999. See pages 97, 198, 318, 319, and 320.

[220] C. Carlet. On the coset weight divisibility and nonlinearity of resilient and correlation-immune functions. *Proceedings of International Conference on Sequences and Their Applications SETA 2001, Discrete Mathematics and Theoretical Computer Science*, pp. 131–144, 2001. See pages 47, 286, 287, and 289.

[221] C. Carlet. A larger class of cryptographic Boolean functions via a study of the Maiorana–McFarland construction. *Proceedings of CRYPT0 2002, Lecture Notes in Computer Science* 2442, pp. 549–564, 2002. See pages 179, 293, 294, and 295.

[222] C. Carlet, On cryptographic complexity of Boolean functions. *Finite Fields with Applications to Coding Theory, Cryptography and Related Areas* (Proceedings of the Conference Fq6), Springer-Verlag, Berlin, pp. 53–69, 2002. See pages 103, 104, 105, 107, 108, 328, and 509.

[223] C. Carlet. On the confusion and diffusion properties of Maiorana–McFarland's and extended Maiorana–McFarland's functions. *Special Issue "Complexity Issues in Coding and Cryptography", Dedicated to Prof. Harald Niederreiter on the Occasion of his 60th Birthday, Journal of Complexity* 20, pp. 182–204, 2004. See pages 211, 264, 293, and 296.

[224] C. Carlet. On the degree, nonlinearity, algebraic thickness and non-normality of Boolean functions, with developments on symmetric functions. Extended version of [222]. *IEEE Transactions on Information Theory* 50, pp. 2178–2185, 2004. See pages 80, 103, 104, 105, 107, 328, and 356.

[225] C. Carlet. On the secondary constructions of resilient and bent functions. *Proceedings of the Workshop on Coding, Cryptography and Combinatorics 2003, Published by Birkhäuser Verlag*, pp. 3–28, 2004. See pages 233, 300, 301, and 317.

[226] C. Carlet. Concatenating indicators of flats for designing cryptographic functions. *Designs, Codes and Cryptography* 36 (2), pp. 189–202, 2005. See pages 181, 182, and 295.

[227] C. Carlet. On bent and highly nonlinear balanced/resilient functions and their algebraic immunities. *Proceedings of AAECC-16 Conference, Lecture Notes in Computer Science* 3857, pp. 1–28, 2006. Extended version of "Improving the algebraic immunity of resilient and nonlinear functions and constructing bent function", *IACR Cryptology ePrint Archive* (http://eprint.iacr.org/) 2004/276, 2004, and of "Designing bent functions and resilient functions from known ones, without extending their number of variables," *Proceedings of IEEE International Symposium on Information Theory (ISIT) 2005*, pp. 1096–1100, 2005. See pages 231, 236, 237, 238, 302, 303, 332, and 341.

[228] C. Carlet. On the higher order nonlinearities of algebraic immune functions. *Proceedings of CRYPTO 2006, Lecture Notes in Computer Science* 4117, pp. 584–601, 2006. See pages 323 and 331.

[229] C. Carlet. The complexity of Boolean functions from cryptographic viewpoint. *Dagstuhl Seminar Proceedings 06111 Complexity of Boolean Functions*, 2006 (http://drops.dagstuhl.de/opus/volltexte/) 2006/604 See pages 80, 83, and 103.

[230] C. Carlet. A method of construction of balanced functions with optimum algebraic immunity. *Proceedings of the International Workshop on Coding and Cryptography 2007, World Scientific Publishing, Series of Coding and Cryptology*, pp. 25–43, 2008. Preliminary version available in *IACR Cryptology ePrint Archive* (http://eprint.iacr.org/) 2006/149, pp. 25–43 2006. See page 336.

[231] C. Carlet. Partial covering sequences: a method for designing classes of cryptographic functions. *Proceedings of "The First Symposium on Algebraic Geometry and Its Applications" Dedicated to Gilles Lachaud (SAGA'07), Tahiti, 2007, World Scientific, Series on Number Theory and its Applications* 5, pp. 366–387, 2008. See pages 183 and 184.

[232] C. Carlet. Recursive lower bounds on the nonlinearity profile of Boolean functions and their applications. *IEEE Transactions on Information Theory* 54 (3), pp. 1262–1272, 2008. See pages 84, 85, and 125.

[233] C. Carlet. On the higher order nonlinearities of Boolean functions and S-boxes, and their generalizations. *Proceedings of International Conference on Sequences and Their Applications SETA 2008, Lecture Notes in Computer Science* 5203, pp. 345–367, 2008. See pages 122, 123, 124, 125, 348, and 349.

[234] C. Carlet. On almost perfect nonlinear functions. *Special Section on Signal Design and Its Application in Communications, IEICE Trans. Fundamentals* E91-A (12), pp. 3665–3678, 2008. See pages 122 and 273.

[235] C. Carlet. On the algebraic immunities and higher order nonlinearities of vectorial Boolean functions. *NATO Science for Peace and Security Series, D: Information and Communication Security – Vol 23; Enhancing Cryptographic Primitives with Techniques from Error Correcting Codes*, pp. 104–116, 2009. See pages 128, 129, 344, 345, 346, 347, and 348.

[236] C. Carlet. Boolean functions for cryptography and error correcting codes. Chapter of the monography *Boolean Models and Methods in Mathematics, Computer Science, and Engineering*, Y. Crama and P. Hammer, eds., Cambridge University Press, pp. 257–397, 2010. See pages ix, 198, 207, and 338.

[237] C. Carlet. Vectorial Boolean functions for cryptography. Chapter of the monography *Boolean Models and Methods in Mathematics, Computer Science, and Engineering*, Y. Crama and P. Hammer, eds., Cambridge University Press, pp. 398–469, 2010. See pages ix, 138, and 381.

[238] C. Carlet. Comment on "constructions of cryptographically significant Boolean functions using primitive polynomials." *IEEE Transactions on Information Theory* 57 (7), pp. 4852–4853, 2011. See pages 337 and 339.

[239] C. Carlet. Relating three nonlinearity parameters of vectorial functions and building APN functions from bent. *Designs, Codes and Cryptography* 59 (1), pp. 89–109, 2011. See pages 119, 120, 138, 140, 141, 393, 406, 408, 409, and 422.

[240] C. Carlet. More vectorial Boolean functions with unbounded nonlinearity profile. *Special Issue on Cryptography of International Journal of Foundations of Computer Science* 22 (6), pp. 1259–1269, 2011. See page 85.

[241] C. Carlet. On known and new differentially uniform functions. *Proceedings of the 16th Australasian Conference on Information Security and Privacy ACISP 2011, Lecture Notes in Computer Science* 6812, pp. 1–15, 2011. See pages 418 and 419.

[242] C. Carlet. A survey on nonlinear Boolean functions with optimal algebraic immunity suitable for stream ciphers. Proceedings of the SMF-VMS conference, Hué, Vietnam, August 20–24, 2012. *Special Issue of the Vietnam Journal of Mathematics* 41 (4), pp. 527–541, 2013. See pages 3, 337, 338, and 340.

[243] C. Carlet. More constructions of APN and differentially 4-uniform functions by concatenation. *Science China Mathematics* 56 (7), pp. 1373–1384, 2013. See pages 410 and 422.

[244] C. Carlet. Correlation-immune Boolean functions for leakage squeezing and rotating S-box masking against side channel attacks. *Proceedings of SPACE 2013, Lecture Notes in Computer Science* 8204, pp. 70–74, 2013. See page 433.

[245] C. Carlet. Open problems on binary bent functions. *Proceedings of the Conference Open Problems in Mathematical and Computational Sciences*, September 18–20, 2013, in Istanbul, Turkey, Springer, pp. 203–241, 2014. See pages 47, 234, 249, 250, 251, 361, 362, and 475.

[246] C. Carlet. More PS and H-like bent functions. *IACR Cryptology ePrint Archive* (http://eprint.iacr.org/) 2015/168, 2015. See pages 216, 223, 224, and 225.

[247] C. Carlet. Boolean and vectorial plateaued functions, and APN functions. *IEEE Transactions on Information Theory* 61 (11), pp. 6272–6289, 2015. See pages 190, 258, 260, 261, 263, 265, 266, 275, 276, 277, 278, 279, 280, 281, 282, 392, 393, 394, and 402.

[248] C. Carlet. Open questions on nonlinearity and on APN functions. *Proceedings of Arithmetic of Finite Fields 5th International Workshop, WAIFI 2014, 2014, Lecture Notes in Computer Science* 9061, pp. 83–107, 2015. See pages 82, 272, 338, 475, and 478.

[249] C. Carlet. On the nonlinearity of monotone Boolean functions. Special Issue SETA 2016 of *Cryptography and Communications* 10 (6), pp. 1051–1061, 2018. See pages 364, 366, 367, and 368.

[250] C. Carlet. Characterizations of the differential uniformity of vectorial functions by the Walsh transform, *IEEE Transactions on Information Theory* 64 (9), pp. 6443–6453, 2018. (Preliminary version available in *IACR Cryptology ePrint Archive* (http://eprint.iacr.org/) 2017/516, 2017. See pages 386, 387, 412, 413, and 414.

[251] C. Carlet. Componentwise APNness, Walsh uniformity of APN functions and cyclic-additive difference sets. *Finite Fields and Their Applications* 53, pp. 226–253, 2018. (Preliminary version available in *IACR Cryptology ePrint Archive* (http://eprint.iacr.org/) 2017/528, 2017. See pages 390, 391, 414, 415, and 416.

[252] C. Carlet. On APN exponents, characterizations of differentially uniform functions by the Walsh transform, and related cyclic-difference-set-like structures. *Designs, Codes and Cryptography* 87 (2) (Postproceedings of WCC 2017), pp. 203–224, 2018. See pages 278, 389, 412, 414, 415, and 416.

[253] C. Carlet. Handling vectorial functions by means of their graph indicators, To appear in *IEEE Transactions on Information Theory*, 2020. See pages 35, 40, and 47.

[254] C. Carlet. Graph indicators of S-boxes and related bounds on the algebraic degree of composite functions. Preprint, 2020. See pages 35, 39, 40, 41, 47, 64, and 115.

[255] C. Carlet and Y. Alsalami. A new construction of differentially 4-uniform $(n, n - 1)$-functions. *Advances in Mathematics of Communications* 9 (4), pp. 541–565, 2015. See pages 423 and 424.

[256] C. Carlet and P. Charpin. Cubic Boolean functions with highest resiliency. *IEEE Transactions on Information Theory* 51 (2), pp. 562–571, 2005. See page 312.

[257] C. Carlet, P. Charpin, and V. Zinoviev. Codes, bent functions and permutations suitable for DES-like cryptosystems. *Designs, Codes and Cryptography*, 15 (2), pp. 125–156, 1998. See pages 28, 160, 370, 372, 375, 376, 378, 380, 381, 382, 385, 387, 396, and 398.

[258] C. Carlet and X. Chen. Constructing low-weight dth-order correlation-immune Boolean functions through the Fourier–Hadamard transform. *IEEE Transactions on Information Theory* 64 (4) (Special Issue in honor of Solomon Golomb), pp. 2969–2978, 2018. See pages 291, 304, 305, 306, 307, 308, 309, 310, and 311.

[259] C. Carlet, X. Chen, and L. Qu. Constructing infinite families of low differential uniformity (n, m)-functions with $m > n/2$. *Designs, Codes and Cryptography* 87 (7), pp. 1577–1599, 2019. Preliminary version available in *IACR Cryptology ePrint Archive* (http://eprint.iacr.org/) 2018/1046. See page 423.

[260] C. Carlet, A. Daif, S. Guilley, and C. Tavernier. Polynomial direct sum masking to protect against both SCA and FIA. *Journal of Cryptographic Engineering JCEN*, 9 (3), pp. 303–312, 2019. Preliminary version available in *IACR Cryptology ePrint Archive* (http://eprint.iacr.org/) 2018/531, 2018. See page 447.

[261] C. Carlet, D. Dalai, K. Gupta, and S. Maitra. Algebraic immunity for cryptographically significant Boolean functions: analysis and construction. *IEEE Transactions on Information Theory* 52 (7), pp. 3105–3121, 2006. See pages 323, 330, 331, 336, 342, 343, and 344.

[262] C. Carlet, J.-L. Danger, S. Guilley, and H. Maghrebi. Leakage squeezing of order two. *Proceedings of INDOCRYPT 2012, Lecture Notes in Computer Science* 7668, pp. 120–139, 2012. See pages 427 and 432.

[263] C. Carlet, J.-L. Danger, S. Guilley, and H. Maghrebi. Leakage squeezing: optimal implementation and security evaluation. *Journal of Mathematical Cryptology* 8 (3), pp. 249–295, 2014. See page 431.

[264] C. Carlet, J.-L. Danger, S. Guilley, H. Maghrebi, and E. Prouff. Achieving side-channel high-order correlation immunity with leakage squeezing. *Journal of Cryptographic Engineering JCEN* 4(2), pp. 107–121, 2014. See pages 427 and 432.

[265] C. Carlet, L. E. Danielsen, M. G. Parker, and P. Solé. Self-dual bent functions. Special Issue of the *International Journal of Information and Coding Theory (IJICoT) dedicated to Vera Pless* 1 (4), pp. 384–399, 2010. A preliminary version appeared in the proceedings of the BFCA 2008 conference. See pages 198 and 199.

[266] C. Carlet and C. Ding. Highly nonlinear mappings. *Special Issue "Complexity Issues in Coding and Cryptography," dedicated to Prof. Harald Niederreiter on the Occasion of his 60th Birthday, Journal of Complexity* 20, pp. 205–244, 2004. See pages 122 and 193.

[267] C. Carlet and C. Ding. Nonlinearities of S-boxes. *Finite Fields and Their Applications* 13 (1), pp. 121–135, 2007. See pages 114, 122, 138, and 140.

[268] C. Carlet, C. Ding, and H. Niederreiter. Authentication schemes from highly nonlinear functions. *Designs, Codes and Cryptography* 40 (1), pp. 71–79, 2006. See page 150.

[269] C. Carlet, C. Ding, and J. Yuan. Linear codes from perfect nonlinear mappings and their secret sharing schemes. *IEEE Transactions on Information Theory* 51 (6), pp. 2089–2102, 2005. See pages 147 and 160.

[270] C. Carlet, H. Dobbertin, and G. Leander. Normal extensions of bent functions. *IEEE Transactions on Information Theory* 50 (11), pp. 2880–2885, 2004. See pages 235, 253, and 476.

[271] C. Carlet and S. Dubuc. On generalized bent and q-ary perfect nonlinear functions. *Proceedings of Finite Fields and Applications Fq5*, Springer, pp. 81–94, 2000. See page 193.

[272] C. Carlet, J.-C. Faugère, C. Goyet, and G. Renault. Analysis of the algebraic side channel attack. *Journal of Cryptographic Engineering JCEN* 2(1), pp. 45–62, 2012. See page 436.

[273] C. Carlet and K. Feng. An infinite class of balanced functions with optimum algebraic immunity, good immunity to fast algebraic attacks and good nonlinearity. *Proceedings of ASIACRYPT 2008, Lecture Notes in Computer Science* 5350, pp. 425–440, 2008. See pages 321, 336, 337, 338, and 348.

[274] C. Carlet and K. Feng. An infinite class of balanced vectorial Boolean functions with optimum algebraic immunity and good nonlinearity. *Proceedings of IWCC 2009, Lecture Notes in Computer Science* 5557, pp. 1–11, 2009. See page 350.

[275] C. Carlet and S. Feukoua. Three basic questions on Boolean functions. *Advances in Mathematics of Communications* 11 (4), pp. 837–855, 2017. See pages 38, 257, and 258.

[276] C. Carlet and S. Feukoua. Three parameters of Boolean functions related to their constancy on affine spaces. To appear in *Advances in Mathematics of Communications*. See page 105.

[277] C. Carlet, F. Freibert, S. Guilley, M. Kiermaier, J.-L. Kim, and P. Solé. Higher-order CIS codes. *IEEE Transactions on Information Theory* 60 (9), pp. 5283–5295, 2014. See page 432.

[278] C. Carlet and P. Gaborit. Hyper-bent functions and cyclic codes. *Journal of Combinatorial Theory, Series A* 113 (3), 466–482, 2006. See pages 189, 216, 243, 244, 245, 246, 253, and 477.

[279] C. Carlet and P. Gaborit. On the construction of balanced Boolean functions with a good algebraic immunity. *Proceedings of IEEE International Symposium on Information Theory (ISIT)* 2005. Longer version in the *Proceedings of the Conference BFCA 2005*, Publications des universités de Rouen et du Havre, pp. 1–20, 2005. See pages 324, 335, 342, and 363.

[280] C. Carlet, P. Gaborit, J.-L. Kim, and P. Solé. A new class of codes for Boolean masking of cryptographic computations. *IEEE Transactions on Information Theory* 58 (9), pp. 6000–6011, 2012. See page 432.

[281] C. Carlet and G. Gao. A secondary construction and a transformation on rotation symmetric functions, and their action on bent and semi-bent functions. *Journal of Combinatorial Theory, Series A* 127 (1), pp. 161–175, 2014. See pages 249, 251, 252, 361, and 362.

[282] C. Carlet, G. Gao, and W. Liu. Results on constructions of rotation symmetric bent and semi-bent functions. *Proceedings of International Conference on Sequences and Their Applications SETA 2014, Lecture Notes in Computer Science* 8865, pp. 21–33, 2014. See pages 251, 252, and 263.

[283] C. Carlet, G. Gong, and Y. Tan. Quadratic zero-difference balanced functions, APN functions and strongly regular graphs. *Designs, Codes and Cryptography* 78 (3), pp. 629–654, 2016. See pages 153, 393, and 394.

[284] C. Carlet, L. Goubin, E. Prouff, M. Quisquater, and M. Rivain. Higher-order masking schemes for S-boxes. *Proceedings of Fast Software Encryption FSE 2012, Lecture Notes in Computer Science* 7549 , pp. 366–384, 2012. See pages 433 and 434.

[285] C. Carlet and A. Gouget. An upper bound on the number of m-resilient Boolean functions. *Proceedings of ASIACRYPT 2002, Lecture Notes in Computer Science* 2501, pp. 484–496, 2002. See page 312.

[286] C. Carlet and S. Guilley. Side-channel indistinguishability. *Proceedings of HASP 2013, 2nd International Workshop on Hardware and Architectural Support for Security and Privacy*, ACM, pp. 9:1–9:8 2013. See pages 284 and 433.

[287] C. Carlet and S. Guilley, Correlation-immune Boolean functions for easing counter-measures to side channel attacks. *Proceedings of the Workshop "Emerging Applications of Finite Fields", Algebraic Curves and Finite Fields*, Radon Series on Computational and Applied Mathematics, de Gruyter, pp. 41–70, 2014. See pages 304 and 306.

[288] C. Carlet and S. Guilley. Complementary dual codes for counter-measures to side-channel attacks. *Advances in Mathematics of Communications* 10 (1), pp. 131–150, 2016. See pages 444 and 446.

[289] C. Carlet and S. Guilley. Statistical properties of side-channel and fault injection attacks using coding theory. *Cryptography and Communications* 10 (5), pp. 909–933, 2018. See pages 433 and 446.

[290] C. Carlet and P. Guillot. A characterization of binary bent functions. *Journal of Combinatorial Theory, Series A* 76 (2), pp. 328–335, 1996. See page 241.

[291] C. Carlet and P. Guillot. An alternate characterization of the bentness of binary functions, with uniqueness. *Designs, Codes and Cryptography* 14, pp. 133–140, 1998. See page 242.

[292] C. Carlet and P. Guillot. A new representation of Boolean functions. *Proceedings of AAECC-13 Conference, Lecture Notes in Computer Science* 1719, pp. 94–103, 1999. See pages 47, 48, 49, 50, 51, 66, 156, 157, 195, and 201.

[293] C. Carlet and P. Guillot. Bent, resilient functions and the numerical normal form. *DIMACS Series in Discrete Mathematics and Theoretical Computer Science,* 56, pp. 87–96, 2001. See pages 47, 48, 51, 195, and 286.

[294] C. Carlet, P. Guillot, and S. Mesnager. On immunity profile of Boolean functions. *Proceedings of International Conference on Sequences and Their Applications SETA 2006, Lecture Notes in Computer Science* 4086, pp. 364–375, 2006. See page 290.

[295] C. Carlet, C. Güneri, S. Mesnager, and F. Özbudak. Construction of codes suitable for both SCA and FIA. *Proceedings of WAIFI 2018, Lecture Notes in Computer Science* 11321, pp. 95–107, 2018. See page 446.

[296] C. Carlet, T. Helleseth, A. Kholosha, and S. Mesnager. On the duals of bent functions with 2^r Niho exponents. *Proceedings of IEEE International Symposium on Information Theory (ISIT) 2011*, pp. 703–707, 2011. See page 222.

[297] C. Carlet, A. Heuser, and S. Picek. Trade-offs for S-boxes: cryptographic properties and side-channel resilience. *Proceedings of ACNS 2017, Lecture Notes in Computer Science* 10355, pp. 393–414, 2017. See pages 145 and 433.

[298] C. Carlet, D. Joyner, P. Stănică, and D. Tang. Cryptographic properties of monotone Boolean functions. *Journal of Mathematical Cryptology* 10 (1), pp. 1–14, 2016. See pages 364 and 368.

[299] C. Carlet, K. Khoo, C.-W. Lim, and C.-W. Loe. Generalized correlation analysis of vectorial Boolean functions. *Proceedings of Fast Software Encryption FSE 2007, Lecture Notes in Computer Science* 4593, pp. 382–398, 2007. See pages 131 and 132.

[300] C. Carlet, K. Khoo, C.-W. Lim, and C.-W. Loe. On an improved correlation analysis of stream ciphers using multi-output Boolean functions and the related generalized notion of nonlinearity. *Advances in Mathematics of Communications* 2 (2), pp. 201–221, 2008. See page 133.

[301] C. Carlet and A. Klapper. Upper bounds on the numbers of resilient functions and of bent functions. This paper was meant to appear in an issue of *Lecture Notes in Computer Sciences* dedicated to Philippe Delsarte, Editor Jean-Jacques Quisquater, which never appeared. Shorter version in the *Proceedings of the 23rd Symposium on Information Theory in the Benelux*, Louvain-La-Neuve, Belgium, 2002. See pages 67, 195, 243, and 312.

[302] C. Carlet and A. Klapper. On the arithmetic Walsh coefficients of Boolean functions. *Designs, Codes and Cryptography* 73 (2), pp. 299–318, 2014. See page 57.

[303] C. Carlet, J. C. Ku-Cauich, and H. Tapia-Recillas. Bent functions on a Galois ring and systematic authentication codes. *Advances in Mathematics of Communications* 6 (2), pp. 249–258, 2012. See page 150.

[304] C. Carlet, A.B. Levina, and S. V. Taranov. Algebraic manipulation detection codes with perfect nonlinear functions under non-uniform distribution. *Scientific and Technical Journal of Information Technologies, Mechanics and Optics* 17, 6 (112), pp. 1052–1062, 2017. See page 450.

[305] C. Carlet and P. Méaux. Boolean functions for homomorphic-friendly stream ciphers. *Proceedings of the Conference on Algebra, Codes and Cryptology (A2C), Lecture Notes in Computer Science*, pp. 166–182, Springer, Cham 2019 2019 (this version does not include proofs; a full paper is to come later). See pages 341, 342, 360, 363, and 453.

[306] C. Carlet, P. Méaux, and Y. Rotella. Boolean functions with restricted input and their robustness; application to the FLIP cipher. *IACR Transactions on Symmetric Cryptology* 2017 (3), pp. 192–227, 2017. See pages 321, 363, 453, 456, 457, 458, 459, 460, 461, 463, 464, 465, 466, and 467.

[307] C. Carlet and B. Merabet. Asymptotic lower bound on the algebraic immunity of random balanced multi-output Boolean functions. *Advances in Mathematics of Communications* 7 (2), pp. 197–217, 2013. See page 93.

[308] C. Carlet and S. Mesnager. On the supports of the Walsh transforms of Boolean functions. *Proceedings of the Conference BFCA 2005*, Publications des universités de Rouen et du Havre, pp. 65–82, 2005. See pages 57 and 183.

[309] C. Carlet and S. Mesnager. Improving the upper bounds on the covering radii of binary Reed–Muller codes. *IEEE Transactions on Information Theory* 53, pp. 162–173, 2007. See pages 83, 158, and 159.

[310] C. Carlet and S. Mesnager. On the construction of bent vectorial functions. Special Issue of the *International Journal of Information and Coding Theory* (IJICoT) 1 (2), dedicated to Vera Pless, pp. 133–148, 2010. See pages 269, 270, 271, and 274.

[311] C. Carlet and S. Mesnager. On Dillon's class H of bent functions, Niho bent functions and o-polynomials. *Journal of Combinatorial Theory, Series A* 118, pp. 2392–2410, 2011. See pages 168, 199, 217, 218, 219, 220, 222, 362, and 476.

[312] C. Carlet and S. Mesnager. On semi-bent Boolean functions. *IEEE Transactions on Information Theory* 58, pp. 3287–3292, 2012. See pages 61, 263, and 362.

[313] C. Carlet and S. Mesnager. Four decades of research on bent functions. *Designs, Codes and Cryptography* 78 (1), pp. 5–50, 2016. See pages 190, 201, 222, 266, and 270.

[314] C. Carlet and S. Mesnager. Characterizations of o-polynomials by the Walsh transform, arXiv:1709.03765, 2017 https://arxiv.org/abs/1709.03765. See page 414.

[315] C. Carlet and S. Mesnager. On those multiplicative subgroups of $\mathbb{F}_{2^n}^*$ which are Sidon sets and/or sum-free sets. Preprint 2019. See page 390.

[316] C. Carlet and S. Picek. On the exponents of APN power functions and Sidon sets, sum-free sets, and Dickson polynomials. *IACR Cryptology ePrint Archive* (http://eprint.iacr.org/) 2017/1179, 2017. See pages 388, 389, and 390.

[317] C. Carlet and E. Prouff. On plateaued functions and their constructions. *Proceedings of Fast Software Encryption FSE 2003, Lecture Notes in Computer Science* 2887, pp. 54–73, 2003. See pages 180, 193, 258, 260, 264, 265, and 295.

[318] C. Carlet and E. Prouff. On a new notion of nonlinearity relevant to multi-output pseudo-random generators. *Proceedings of Selected Areas in Cryptography 2003, Lecture Notes in Computer Science* 3006, pp. 291–305, 2004. See pages 131 and 133.

[319] C. Carlet and E. Prouff. Vectorial functions and covering sequences. *Proceedings of Finite Fields and Applications, Fq7, Lecture Notes in Computer Science* 2948, pp. 215–248, 2004. See pages 184, 186, 187, and 316.

[320] C. Carlet and E. Prouff. Polynomial evaluation and side channel analysis. *The New Codebreakers, Dedicated to David Kahn on the Occasion of His 85th Birthday*, pp. 315–341, 2016. See pages 74, 425, 431, 434, and 484.

[321] C. Carlet, E. Prouff, M. Rivain, and T. Roche. Algebraic decomposition for probing security. *Proceedings of CRYPTO 2015, Lecture Notes in Computer Science* 9215, pp. 742–763, 2015. See pages 435 and 441.

[322] C. Carlet and P. Sarkar. Spectral domain analysis of correlation immune and resilient Boolean functions. *Finite Fields and Their Applications* 8, pp. 120–130, 2002. See pages 287, 289, and 290.

[323] C. Carlet and Y. Tan. On group rings and some of their applications to combinatorics and cryptography. *International Journal of Group Theory* 4 (4), pp. 61–74, 2015. See page 153.

[324] C. Carlet and D. Tang. Enhanced Boolean functions suitable for the filter model of pseudo-random generator. *Designs, Codes and Cryptography* 76 (3), pp. 571–587, 2015. See pages 94, 322, 343, and 344.

[325] C. Carlet, D. Tang, X. Tang, and Q. Liao. New construction of differentially 4-uniform bijections. *Proceedings of INSCRYPT 2013, 9th International Conference, Guangzhou, China, November 27–30, 2013, Lecture Notes in Computer Science* 8567, pp. 22–38, 2014. See pages 420 and 421.

[326] C. Carlet and Y. V. Tarannikov. Covering sequences of Boolean functions and their cryptographic significance. *Designs, Codes and Cryptography*, 25, pp. 263–279, 2002. See pages 182, 290, and 291.

[327] C. Carlet and J. L. Yucas. Piecewise constructions of bent and almost optimal Boolean functions. *Designs, Codes and Cryptography* 37 (3), pp. 449–464, 2005. See pages 237 and 255.

[328] C. Carlet, X. Zeng, C. Lei, and L. Hu. Further properties of several classes of Boolean functions with optimum algebraic immunity. *Proceedings of the First International Conference on Symbolic Computation and Cryptography* SCC 2008, LMIB, pp. 42–54, 2008. See pages 336 and 355.

[329] C. Carlet, F. Zhang, and Y. Hu. Secondary constructions of bent functions and their enforcement. *Advances in Mathematics of Communications* 6 (3), pp. 305–314, 2012. See page 233.

[330] L. Carlitz. Permutations in a finite field. *Proc. Amer. Math. Soc.* 4, p. 538, 1953. See page 494.

[331] L. Carlitz. A note on permutation functions over a finite field. *Duke Math. Journal* 29 (2), pp. 325–332, 1962. See page 442.

[332] L. Carlitz. Explicit evaluation of certain exponential sums. *Math. Scand.*, **44**, pp. 5–16, 1979. See page 177.

[333] L. Carlitz and S. Uchiyama. Bounds for exponential sums. *Duke Math. Journal* 1, pp. 37–41, 1957. See pages 188 and 401.

[334] F. N. Castro, and L. A. Medina. Linear recurrences and asymptotic behavior of exponential sums of symmetric Boolean functions. *The Electronic Journal of Combinatorics* 18 (2), p. 8, 2011. See page 355.

[335] A. Çeşmelioglu, W. Meidl, and A. Pott. Bent functions, spreads and o-polynomials. *SIAM Journal on Discrete Mathematics* 29 (2), pp. 854–867, 2015. See page 224.

[336] A. Çeşmelioglu, W. Meidl, and A. Pott. There are infinitely many bent functions for which the dual is not bent. *IEEE Transactions on Information Theory* 62 (9), pp. 5204–5208, 2016. See page 234.

[337] A. Çeşmelioglu, W. Meidl, and A. Pott. Vectorial bent functions and their duals. *Linear Algebra and Its Applications* 548, pp. 305–320, 2018. See page 269.

[338] A. Çeşmelioglu, W. Meidl, and A. Topuzoğlu. Partially bent functions and their properties. *Applied Algebra and Number Theory* 2014, pp. 22–38, 2014. See page 256.

[339] H. Chabanne, G. D. Cohen, and A. Patey. Towards secure two-party computation from the wire-tap channel. *Proceedings of ICISC 2013, Lecture Notes in Computer Science* 8565, pp. 34–46, 2013. See page 149.

[340] H. Chabanne, H. Maghrebi, and E. Prouff. Linear repairing codes and side-channel attacks. *IACR Transactions on Cryptographic Hardware and Embedded Systems* 2018 (1), pp. 118–141, 2018. See pages 428 and 436.

[341] F. Chabaud and S. Vaudenay. Links between differential and linear cryptanalysis. *Proceedings of EUROCRYPT 1994, Lecture Notes in Computer Science* 950, pp. 356–365, 1995. See pages 117, 118, 119, and 372.

[342] C. Chaigneau, T. Fuhr, H. Gilbert, J. Guo, J. Jean, J.-R. Reinhard, and L. Song. Key-recovery attacks on full Kravatte. *IACR Transactions on Symmetric Cryptology* 2018 (1), pp. 5–28, 2018. See page 96.

[343] K. Chakraborty, S. Sarkar, S. Maitra, B. Mazumdar, D. Mukhopadhyay, and E. Prouff. Redefining the transparency order. *Designs, Codes and Cryptography* 82 (1–2), pp. 95–115, 2017. See page 429.

[344] A. H. Chan and R. A. Games. On the quadratic spans of De Bruijn sequences. *IEEE Transactions on Information Theory* 36 (4), pp. 822–829, 1990. See page 23.

[345] S. Chang and J. Y. Hyun. Linear codes from simplicial complexes. *Designs, Codes and Cryptography* 86 (10), pp. 2167–2181, 2018. See page 149.

[346] S. Chanson, C. Ding, and A. Salomaa. Cartesian authentication codes from functions with optimal nonlinearity. *Theoretical Computer Science* 290, pp. 1737–1752, 2003. See page 370.

[347] C. Charnes, M. Rötteler, and T. Beth. Homogeneous bent functions, invariants, and designs. *Designs, Codes and Cryptography*, 26, pp. 139–154, 2002. See pages 209 and 248.

[348] P. Charpin. Open Problems on Cyclic Codes. In *Handbook of Coding Theory*, Part 1, chapter 11, V. S. Pless and W. C. Huffman, eds., R. A. Brualdi, assistant editor. Elsevier, part 1, chapter 11, pp. 963–1063, 1998. See page 6.

[349] P. Charpin. Normal Boolean functions. *Special Issue "Complexity Issues in Coding and Cryptography," Dedicated to Prof. Harald Niederreiter on the Occasion of His 60th Birthday, Journal of Complexity* 20, pp. 245–265, 2004. See pages 241 and 253.

[350] P. Charpin and G. Gong. Hyperbent functions, Kloosterman sums and Dickson polynomials. *IEEE Transactions on Information Theory* 54 (9), pp. 4230–4238, 2008. See pages 215, 231, 246, and 247.

[351] P. Charpin, T. Helleseth, and V. Zinoviev. Propagation characteristics of $x \rightarrow 1/x$ and Kloosterman sums. *Finite Fields and Their Applications* 13 (2), pp. 366–381, 2007. See page 401.

[352] P. Charpin and G. Kyureghyan. Cubic monomial bent functions: a subclass of $\mathcal{M}$. *SIAM Journal on Discrete Mathematics* 22 (2), pp. 650–665, 2008. See pages 230 and 231.

[353] P. Charpin and G. Kyureghyan. On sets determining the differential spectrum of mappings. *International Journal of Information and Coding Theory (IJICoT)* 4 (2/3), pp. 170–184, 2017. See also: A note on verifying the APN property. *IACR Cryptology ePrint Archive* (http://eprint.iacr.org/) 2013/475, 2013. See pages 192 and 373.

[354] P. Charpin and E. Pasalic. On propagation characteristics of resilient functions. *Proceedings of SAC 2002, Lecture Notes in Computer Science* 2595, pp. 356–365, 2002. See pages 101, 290, and 292.

[355] P. Charpin, E. Pasalic, and C. Tavernier. On bent and semi-bent quadratic Boolean functions. *IEEE Transactions on Information Theory* 51 (12), pp. 4286–4298, 2005. See pages 178, 206, 230, and 263.

[356] P. Charpin and J. Peng. New links between nonlinearity and differential uniformity. *Finite Fields and Their Applications* 56, pp. 188–208, 2019. See pages 387 and 418.

[357] S. Chee, S. Lee, and K. Kim. Semi-bent functions. *Proceedings of ASIACRYPT 1994, Lecture Notes in Computer Science 917*, pp. 107–118, 1994. See page 263.

[358] S. Chee, S. Lee, K. Kim, and D. Kim. Correlation immune functions with controlable nonlinearity. *ETRI Journal* 19, (4), pp. 389–401, 1997. See page 294.

[359] S. Chee, S. Lee, D. Lee, and S. H. Sung. On the correlation immune functions and their nonlinearity. *Proceedings of ASIACRYPT 1996, Lecture Notes in Computer Science* 1163, pp. 232–243, 1997. See page 294.

[360] L. Chen, S. Jordan, Y.-K. Liu, D. Moody, R. Peralta, R. Perlner, and D. Smith-Tone. Report on post-quantum cryptography. US Department of Commerce, National Institute of Standards and Technology, NISTIR 8105. See page 1.

[361] V. Y.-W. Chen. The Gowers' norm in the testing of Boolean functions. PhD thesis, Massachusetts Institute of Technology, 2009. See page 469.

[362] X. Chen, Y. Deng, M. Zhu, and L. Qu. An equivalent condition on the switching construction of differentially 4-uniform permutations on from the inverse function. *International Journal of Computer Mathematics* 94 (6), pp. 1252–1267, 2017. See page 420.

[363] X. Chen, L. Qu, C. Li, and J. Du. A new method to investigate the CCZ-equivalence between functions with low differential uniformity. *Finite Fields and Their Applications* 42, pp. 165–186, 2016. See page 420.

[364] Y. Chen and P. Lu. Two classes of symmetric Boolean functions with optimum algebraic immunity: construction and analysis. *IEEE Transactions on Information Theory* 57, pp. 2522–2538, 2011. See page 358.

[365] W. Cheng, C. Carlet, K. Goli, S. Guilley, and J.-L. Danger. Detecting faults in inner product masking scheme. *IACR Cryptology ePrint Archive* (http://eprint.iacr.org/) 2019/919. Presented at PROOFS 2019, 8th International Workshop on Security Proofs for Embedded Systems, Atlanta, USA, 2019 (https://easychair.org/publications/paper/HTzP). See page 447.

[366] W. Cheng, S. Guilley, C. Carlet, J.-L. Danger, and A. Schaub. Optimal codes for inner product masking. *17th CryptArchi Workshop*, Prague 2019. See page 446.

[367] J. H. Cheon. Nonlinear vector resilient functions. *Proceedings of CRYPTO 2001, Lecture Notes in Computer Science* 2139, pp. 458–469, 2001. See page 317.

[368] J. H. Cheon and D. H. Lee. Resistance of S-boxes against algebraic attacks. *Proceedings of Fast Software Encryption FSE 2004, Lecture Notes in Computer Science* 3017, pp. 83–94, 2004. See page 345.

[369] V. Chepyzhov and B. Smeets. On a fast correlation attack on certain stream ciphers. *Proceedings of EUROCRYPT 1991, Lecture Notes in Computer Science* 547, pp. 176–185, 1992. See page 78.

[370] B. Chor, O. Goldreich, J. Hastad, S. Freidmann, S. Rudich, and R. Smolensky. The bit extraction problem or t-resilient functions. *Proceedings of the 26th IEEE Symposium on Foundations of Computer Science*, pp. 396–407, 1985. See pages 86, 129, 284, 314, and 356.

[371] C. Cid, T. Huang, T. Peyrin, Y. Sasaki, and L. Song. Boomerang connectivity table: a new cryptanalysis tool. *Proceedings of EUROCRYPT (2) 2018, Lecture Notes in Computer Science* 10821, pp. 683–714, 2018. See page 141.

[372] J. A. Clark, J. L. Jacob, and S. Stepney. The design of S-boxes by simulated annealing. *New Generation Computing* 23 (3), pp. 219–231, 2005. See page 145.

[373] E. M. Clarke, K. L. McMillan, X. Zhao, M. Fujita, and J. Yang. Spectral transforms for large Boolean functions with applications to technology mapping. *Proceedings of 30th ACM/IEEE Design Automation Conference, IEEE*, pp. 54–60, 1993. See page 57.

[374] G. Cohen and J. P. Flori. On a generalized combinatorial conjecture involving addition mod $2^k - 1$. *IACR Cryptology ePrint Archive* (http://eprint.iacr.org/) 2011/400, 2011. See page 340.

[375] G. Cohen, I. Honkala, S. Litsyn, and A. Lobstein. *Covering Codes*. North-Holland, 1997. See pages 7 and 158.

[376] G. Cohen and S. Mesnager. On constructions of semi-bent functions from bent functions. *Journal Contemporary Mathematics* 625, Discrete Geometry and Algebraic Combinatorics, American Mathematical Society, pp. 141–154, 2014. See page 263.

[377] G. Cohen and A. Tal. Two structural results for low degree polynomials and applications. *18th International Workshop on Approximation Algorithms for Combinatorial Optimization Problems, APPROX 2015, and 19th International Workshop on Randomization and Computation, RANDOM 2015 – Princeton, United States. CoRR*, abs/1404.0654, 2014. See page 109.

[378] G. D. Cohen, M. G. Karpovsky, H. F. Mattson Jr., and J. R. Schatz. Covering radius – survey and recent results. *IEEE Transactions on Information Theory* 31 (3), pp. 328–343, 1985. See page 158.

[379] G. D. Cohen and S. Litsyn. On the covering radius of Reed–Muller codes. *Discrete Mathematics* 106–107, pp. 147–155, 1992. See page 158.

[380] S. D. Cohen and R. W. Matthews. A class of exceptional polynomials. *Transactions of the AMS* 345, pp. 897–909, 1994. See page 400.

[381] J.-S. Coron, E. Prouff, M. Rivain, and T. Roche. Higher-order side channel security and mask refreshing. *Proceedings of Fast Software Encryption FSE 2013, Lecture Notes in Computer Science* 8424, pp. 410–424, 2013, and *IACR Cryptology ePrint Archive* (http://eprint.iacr.org/) 2015/359, 2015. See page 427.

[382] J.-S. Coron, A. Roy, and S. Vivek. Fast evaluation of polynomials over binary finite fields and application to side-channel countermeasures. *Proceedings of International Workshop Cryptographic Hardware and Embedded Systems CHES 2014, Lecture Notes in Computer Science* 8731, pp. 170–187, 2014. See page 434.

[383] A. Coşgun and F. Özbudak. A correction and improvements of some recent results on Walsh transforms of Gold type and Kasami–Welch type functions. *Proceedings of WAIFI 2016, Lecture Notes in Computer Science* 10064, pp. 243–257, 2016. See page 178.

[384] R. S. Coulter. On the evaluation of a class of Weil sums in characteristic 2, *New Zealand J. Math.* 28, pp. 171–184, 1999. See page 178.

[385] R. S. Coulter. The number of rational points of a class of Artin–Schreier curves. *Finite Fields and Their Applications* 8, pp. 397–413, 2002. See page 178.

[386] R. S. Coulter and S. Mesnager. Bent functions from involutions over $\mathbb{F}_{2^n}$. *IEEE Transactions on Information Theory* 64 (4), pp. 2979–2986, 2018. See page 237.

[387] N. Courtois. Higher order correlation attacks, XL algorithm and cryptanalysis of Toyocrypt. *Proceedings of ICISC 2002, Lecture Notes in Computer Science* 2587, pp. 182–199, 2003. See pages 3 and 83.

[388] N. Courtois. Fast algebraic attacks on stream ciphers with linear feedback. *Proceedings of CRYPTO 2003, Lecture Notes in Computer Science* 2729, pp. 177–194, 2003. See pages 76, 89, 93, and 284.

[389] N. Courtois. Algebraic attacks on combiners with memory and several outputs. *Proceedings of ICISC 2004, Lecture Notes in Computer Science* 3506, pp. 3–20, 2005. See page 91.

[390] N. Courtois. Cryptanalysis of SFINKS. *Proceedings of ICISC 2005*. Preliminary version available in *IACR Cryptology ePrint Archive* (http://eprint.iacr.org/) pp. 261–269, 2005/243, 2005. See page 93.

[391] N. Courtois and W. Meier. Algebraic attacks on stream ciphers with linear feedback. *Proceedings of EUROCRYPT 2003, Lecture Notes in Computer Science* 2656, pp. 346–359. See pages 76, 89, 91, 92, and 93.

[392] N. Courtois and J. Pieprzyk. Cryptanalysis of block ciphers with overdefined systems of equations. *Proceedings of ASIACRYPT 2002, Lecture Notes in Computer Science* 2501, pp. 267–287, 2003. See pages 125, 126, 127, and 345.

[393] G. Couteau, A. Dupin, P. Méaux, M. Rossi, and Y. Rotella. On the concrete security of Goldreich's pseudorandom generator. *Proceedings of ASIACRYPT 2018, Part I, Lecture Notes in Computer Science*, 11273, pp. 96–124, 2018. See pages 467 and 468.

[394] Y. Crama and P. L. Hammer. *Boolean Models and Methods in Mathematics, Computer Science, and Engineering*. Cambridge University Press, 2010 Cambridge University Press, 2010. See page ix.

[395] R. Cramer, Y. Dodis, S. Fehr, C. Padro, and D. Wichs. Detection of algebraic manipulation with application to robust secret sharing and fuzzy extractors. *Proceedings of EUROCRYPT 2008, Lecture Notes in Computer Science* 4965, pp. 471–488, 2008 (preliminary version available in *IACR Cryptology ePrint Archive* http://eprint.iacr.org/ 2008/030). See pages 450, 451, 452, and 453.

[396] R. Cramer, S. Fehr, and C. Padro. Algebraic manipulation detection codes. *Science China Mathematics* 56 (7), pp. 1349–1358, 2013. See pages 451, 452, and 453.

[397] R. Cramer, C. Padr, and C. Xing. Optimal algebraic manipulation detection codes in the constant-error model. *Proceedings of TCC (1) 2015, Lecture Notes in Computer Science* 9014, pp. 481–501, 2015. See pages 452 and 453.

[398] T. W. Cusick. On constructing balanced correlation immune functions. *Proceedings of International Conference on Sequences and Their Applications SETA 1998, Discrete Mathematics and Theoretical Computer Science*, pp. 184–190, 1999. See page 293.

[399] T. W. Cusick. Weight recursions for any rotation symmetric Boolean functions. *IEEE Transactions on Information Theory* 64 (4), pp. 2962–2968, 2018. See page 362.

[400] T. W. Cusick, C. Ding, and A. Renvall. *Stream Ciphers and Number Theory,* North-Holland Mathematical Library 55. North-Holland/Elsevier, 1998.

[401] T. W. Cusick and P. Stănică. *Cryptographic Boolean Functions and Applications* (second edition), Elsevier, 2017. See page 76.

[402] J. Daemen. Changing of the guards: a simple and efficient method for achieving uniformity in threshold sharing. *Proceedings of International Workshop Cryptographic Hardware and Embedded Systems CHES 2017, Lecture Notes in Computer Science* 10529, pp. 137–153, 2017. See page 443.

[403] J. Daemen and V. Rijmen. AES proposal: Rijndael, 1999. See www.quadibloc.com/crypto/co040401.htm. See page 3.

[404] J. Daemen and V. Rijmen, *The Design of Rijndael: AES – The Advanced Encryption Standard.* Springer, 2002. See pages 3 and 25.

[405] J. Daemen and V. Rijmen. Probability distributions of correlation and differentials in block ciphers. *Journal of Mathematical Cryptology (JMC)* 1 (3), pp. 221–242, 2007. See page 136.

[406] D. Dalai. On 3-to-1 and power APN S-boxes. *Proceedings of International Conference on Sequences and Their Applications SETA 2008, Lecture Notes in Computer Science* 5203, pp. 377–389, 2008. See pages 385 and 386.

[407] D. K. Dalai, K. C. Gupta, and S. Maitra. Results on algebraic immunity for cryptographically significant Boolean functions. *Proceedings of Indocrypt 2004, Lecture Notes in Computer Science* 3348, pp. 92–106, 2004. See pages 324, 334, and 343.

[408] D. K. Dalai, K. C. Gupta, and S. Maitra. Cryptographically significant Boolean functions: construction and analysis in terms of algebraic immunity. *Proceedings of Fast Software Encryption FSE 2005, Lecture Notes in Computer Science* 3557, pp. 98–111, 2005. See page 336.

[409] D. K. Dalai, S. Maitra, and S. Sarkar. Basic theory in construction of Boolean functions with maximum possible annihilator immunity. *Designs, Codes and Cryptography* 40 (1) pp, 41–58, 2006 (preliminary version available in *IACR Cryptology ePrint Archive*, http://eprint.iacr.org/ 2005/229, 2005). See pages 334, 335, and 360.

[410] E. R. van Dam and D. Fon-Der-Flaass. Codes, graphs, and schemes from nonlinear functions. *European Journal of Combinatorics* 24 (1), pp. 85–98, 2003. See pages 373 and 376.

[411] E. R. van Dam and M. Muzychuk. Some implications on amorphic association schemes. *Journal of Combinatorial Theory, Series A* 117 (2), pp. 111–127, 2010. See page 162.

[412] M. Daum, H. Dobbertin, and G. Leander. An algorithm for checking normality of Boolean functions. *Proceedings of the Workshop on Coding and Cryptography 2003*, pp. 133–142, 2003. See page 252.

[413] M. Daum, H. Dobbertin, and G. Leander. Short description of an algorithm to create bent functions. Private communication. See page 243.

[414] D. Davidova. Magic action of o-polynomials and EA equivalence of Niho bent functions. *BFA 2018*, June 2018, Loen, Norway (https://people.uib.no/chunlei.li/workshops/BFA2018/Slides/ Davidova.pdf). See page 221.

[415] J. A. Davis and J. Jedwab. A unifying construction for difference sets. *Journal of Combinatorial Theory Series A* 80, pp. 13–78, 1997. See page 235.

[416] J. A. Davis and J. Jedwab. Peak-to-mean power control in OFDM, Golay complementary sequences and Reed–Muller codes. *IEEE Transactions on Information Theory* 45 (7), pp. 2397–2417, 1999. See page 189.

[417] E. Dawson and C.-K. Wu. Construction of correlation immune Boolean functions. *Proceedings of ICICS 1997*, pp. 170–180, 1997. See page 292.

[418] M. Delgado. The state of the art on the conjecture of exceptional APN functions. *Note Mat.* 37 (1), pp. 41–51, 2017. See page 404.

[419] M. Delgado and H. Janwa. On the conjecture on APN functions and absolute irreducibility of polynomials. *Designs, Codes and Cryptography* 82 (3), pp. 617–627, 2017. See page 404.

[420] P. Delsarte. A geometrical approach to a class of cyclic codes. *Journal of Combinatorial Theory* 6 (4), pp. 340–358, 1969. See page 154.

[421] P. Delsarte. Bounds for unrestricted codes, by linear programming. *Philips Research Reports* 27, pp. 272–289, 1972. See page 129.

[422] P. Delsarte. An algebraic approach to the association schemes of coding theory. PhD thesis. Université Catholique de Louvain, 1973. See pages 88, 254, 304, and 314.

[423] P. Delsarte. Four fundamental parameters of a code and their combinatorial significance. *Information and Control* 23 (5), pp. 407–438, 1973. See page 88.

[424] P. Delsarte and V. I. Levenshtein. Association schemes and coding theory. *IEEE Transactions on Information Theory* 44 (6), pp. 2477–2504, 1998. See page 162.

[425] P. Dembowski. *Finite Geometries*. Springer, 1968. See pages 224 and 225.

[426] U. Dempwolff. Automorphisms and equivalence of bent functions and of difference sets in elementary Abelian 2-groups. *Comm. Algebra* 34 (3), pp. 1077–1131, 2006. See page 192.

[427] U. Dempwolff and T. Neumann. Geometric and design-theoretic aspects of semi-bent functions I. *Designs, Codes and Cryptography* 57 (3), pp. 373–381, 2010. See page 262.

[428] U. Dempwolff. Dimensional doubly dual hyperovals and bent functions. *Innov. Incidence Geom.* 13 (1), pp. 149–178, 2013. See page 197.

[429] U. Dempwolff. CCZ equivalence of power functions. *Designs, Codes and Cryptography* 86 (3), pp. 665–692, 2018. See page 396.

[430] U. Dempwolff and Y. Edel. Isomorphisms and automorphisms of extensions of bilinear dimensional dual hyperovals and quadratic APN functions. *Journal of Group Theory* 19 (2), pp. 249–322, 2016. See page 383.

[431] U. Dempwolff and P. Müller. Permutation polynomials and translation planes of even order. *Adv. Geom.* 13, pp. 293–313, 2013. See page 225.

[432] J. D. Denev and V. D. Tonchev. On the number of equivalence classes of Boolean functions under a transformation group. *IEEE Transactions on Information Theory* 26 (5), pp. 625–626, 1980 See page 29.

[433] O. Denisov. An asymptotic formula for the number of correlation-immune of order k Boolean functions. *Discrete Mathematics and Applications* 2 (4), pp. 407–426, 1992. Translation of a Russian article in *Diskretnaya Matematika* 3, pp. 25–46, 1990. See page 312.

[434] O. Denisov. A local limit theorem for the distribution of a part of the spectrum of a random binary function. *Discrete Mathematics and Applications* 10 (1), pp. 87–102, 2000. See page 312.

[435] S. Dib. Distribution of Boolean functions according to the second-order nonlinearity. *Proceedings of Arithmetic of Finite Fields WAIFI 2010, Lecture Notes in Computer Science* 6087, pp. 86–96, 2010. See page 84.

[436] S. Dib. Asymptotic nonlinearity of vectorial Boolean functions. *Cryptography and Communications* 6 (2), pp. 103–115, 2013. See pages 117 and 369.

[437] F. Didier. A new upper bound on the block error probability after decoding over the erasure channel. *IEEE Transactions on Information Theory* 52, pp. 4496–4503, 2006. See pages 93 and 334.

[438] F. Didier. Using Wiedemann's algorithm to compute the immunity against algebraic and fast algebraic attacks. *Proceedings of Indocrypt 2006, Lecture Notes in Computer Science* 4329, pp. 236–250, 2006. See page 334.

[439] F. Didier and J.-P. Tillich. Computing the algebraic immunity efficiently. *Proceedings of Fast Software Encryption FSE 2006, Lecture Notes in Computer Science* 4047, pp. 359–374, 2006. See page 334.

[440] J. F. Dillon. A survey of bent functions. *NSA Technical Journal Special Issue*, pp. 191–215, 1972. See pages 196, 208, 210, and 230.

[441] J. F. Dillon. Elementary Hadamard difference sets. Ph. D. Thesis, University of Maryland, 1974. See pages 165, 167, 197, 198, 200, 201, 209, 212, 213, 216, 217, 218, 227, 231, 232, and 246.

[442] J. F. Dillon. Elementary Hadamard difference sets. *Proceedings of the Sixth S-E Conf. Comb. Graph Theory and Comp.*, Winnipeg Utilitas Math, pp. 237–249, 1975. See pages 214, 215, and 232.

[443] J. F. Dillon. Multiplicative difference sets via additive characters. *Designs, Codes and Cryptography* 17, pp. 225–235, 1999. See pages 394, 395, and 416.

[444] J. F. Dillon. Geometry, codes and difference sets: exceptional connections. *Codes and Designs, Proceedings of a Conference Honoring Professor D. K. Ray-Chaudury, Columbus, OH, 2000, Ohio State University*, volume 10, pp. 73–85, 2002. See page 404.

[445] J. F. Dillon. APN polynomials and related codes. *Banff Conference*, November 2006. See pages 408 and 412.

[446] J. F. Dillon. More DD difference sets. *Designs, Codes and Cryptography* 49 (1–2), pp. 23–32, 2008.

[447] J. F. Dillon. On the dimension of an APN code. *Cryptography and Communications* 3 (4) (Special issue in honor of Jacques Wolfmann), pp. 275–279, 2011. See page 379.

[448] J. F. Dillon and H. Dobbertin. New cyclic difference sets with Singer parameters. *Finite Fields and Their Applications* 10, pp. 342–389, 2004. See pages 173, 178, 230, 231, 252, 382, 395, 400, 415, and 416.

[449] J. F. Dillon and G. McGuire. Near bent functions on a hyperplane. *Finite Fields and Their Applications* 14 (3), pp. 715–720, 2008. See page 232.

[450] J. F. Dillon and J. R. Schatz. Block designs with the symmetric difference property. *Proc. NSA Mathematical Sciences Meetings* (R. L. Ward, ed.), pp. 159–164, U.S. Govt. Printing Office, 1987. www.openmathtexts.org/papers/dillon-shatz-designs.pdf. See page 201.

[451] C. Ding. Optimal constant composition codes from zero-difference balanced functions. *IEEE Transactions on Information Theory* 54 (12), pp. 5766–5770, 2008. See page 394.

[452] C. Ding. Cyclic codes from some monomials and trinomials. *SIAM Journal on Discrete Mathematics* 27 (4), pp. 1977–1994, 2013. See page 161.

[453] C. Ding. Linear codes from some 2-designs. *IEEE Transactions on Information Theory* 60 (6), pp. 3265–3275, 2015. See pages 160, 189, and 263.

[454] C. Ding. A construction of binary linear codes from Boolean functions. *Discrete Mathematics* 339 (9), pp. 2288–2303, 2016. See page 159.

[455] C. Ding. A sequence construction of cyclic codes over finite fields. *Cryptography and Communications* 10 (2), pp. 319–341, 2018. See page 159.

[456] C. Ding, Z. Heng, and Z. Zhou. Minimal binary linear codes. *IEEE Transactions on Information Theory* 64 (10), pp. 6536–6545, 2018. See pages 147 and 149.

[457] C. Ding, C. Li, and Y. Xia. Another generalisation of the binary Reed–Muller codes and its applications. *Finite Fields and Their Applications* 53, pp. 144–174, 2018. See page 151.

[458] C. Ding, S. Mesnager, C. Tang, and M. Xiong. Cyclic bent functions and their applications in codes, codebooks, designs, MUBs and sequences. arXiv:1811.07725, 2019. See page 207.

[459] C. Ding, A. Munemasa, and V. D. Tonchev. Bent vectorial functions, codes and designs. *Transactions on Information Theory* 65 (11), pp. 7533–7541, 2019. https://arxiv.org/abs/1808.08487. See page 270.

[460] C. Ding and H. Niederreiter. Systematic authentication codes from highly nonlinear functions. *IEEE Transactions on Information Theory* 50 (10), pp. 2421–2428, 2004. See page 150.

[461] C. Ding, D. Pei, and A. Salomaa. *Chinese Remainder Theorem: Applications in Computing, Coding, Cryptography*. World Scientific, 1996. See pages 147 and 284.

[462] C. Ding and Y. Tan. Zero-difference balanced functions with applications. *Journal of Statistical Theory and Practice* 6 (1), pp. 3–19, 2012. See page 394.

[463] C. Ding, G. Z. Xiao, and W. Shan. *The Stability Theory of Stream Ciphers, Lecture Notes in Computer Science* 561, 1991. See page 3.

[464] C. Ding and Z. Zhou. Binary cyclic codes from explicit polynomials over $GF(2^m)$. *Discrete Mathematics* 321, pp. 76–89, 2014. See page 161.

[465] I. Dinur and A. Shamir. Breaking Grain-128 with dynamic cube attacks. *Proceedings of Fast Software Encryption FSE 2011, Lecture Notes in Computer Science* 6733, pp. 167–187, 2011. See pages 97 and 114.

[466] H. Dobbertin. Construction of bent functions and balanced Boolean functions with high nonlinearity. *Proceedings of Fast Software Encryption FSE 1995, Lecture Notes in Computer Science* 1008, pp. 61–74, 1995. See pages 81, 105, 228, and 388.

[467] H. Dobbertin. one-to-one highly nonlinear power functions on $GF(2^n)$. *Applicable Algebra in Engineering, Communication and Computing (AAECC)* 9 (2), pp. 139–152, 1998. See pages 402 and 418.

[468] H. Dobbertin. Kasami power functions, permutation polynomials and cyclic difference sets. *Proceedings of the NATO-A.S.I. Workshop "Difference Sets, Sequences and Their Correlation Properties,"* Bad Windsheim, Kluwer Verlag, pp. 133–158, 1998. See page 400.

[469] H. Dobbertin. Private communication, 1998. See page 385.

[470] H. Dobbertin. Another proof of Kasami's theorem. *Designs, Codes and Cryptography* 17, pp. 177–180, 1999. See pages 229 and 394.

[471] H. Dobbertin, Almost perfect nonlinear power functions on $GF(2^n)$: the Welch case. *IEEE Transactions on Information Theory* 45 (4), pp. 1271–1275, 1999. See page 395.

[472] H. Dobbertin. Almost perfect nonlinear power functions on $GF(2^n)$: The Niho case. *Information and Computation* 151, pp. 57–72, 1999. See page 395.

[473] H. Dobbertin. Almost perfect nonlinear power functions on GF(2^n): a new case for n divisible by 5. *Proceedings of Finite Fields and Applications* Fq5, Augsburg, Germany. Springer, pp. 113–121, 2000. See page 401.

[474] H. Dobbertin. Uniformly representable permutation polynomials. *Proceedings of International Conference on Sequences and Their Applications SETA 2001 (International Conference on Sequences and Their Applications), Discrete Mathematics and Theoretical Computer Science.* Springer, pp. 1–22, 2002. See pages 395 and 400.

[475] H. Dobbertin, P. Felke, T. Helleseth, and P. Rosenthal. Niho type cross-correlation functions via Dickson polynomials and Kloosterman sums. *IEEE Transactions on Information Theory* 52 (2), pp. 613–627, 2006. See pages 222 and 247.

[476] H. Dobbertin and G. Leander. Cryptographer's toolkit for construction of 8-bit bent functions, *IACR Cryptology ePrint Archive* (http://eprint.iacr.org/) 2005/089, 2005. See page 239.

[477] H. Dobbertin and G. Leander. Bent functions embedded into the recursive framework of $\mathbb{Z}$-bent functions. *Designs, Codes and Cryptography* 49 (1–3), pp. 3–22, 2008. See pages 232, 239, and 240.

[478] H. Dobbertin and G. Leander. A survey of some recent results on bent functions. *Proceeding of International Conference on Sequences and Their Applications SETA 2004, Lecture Notes in Computer Science* 3486, pp. 1–29, 2005. See page 231.

[479] H. Dobbertin, G. Leander, A. Canteaut, C. Carlet, P. Felke, and P. Gaborit. Construction of bent functions via Niho power functions. *Journal of Combinatorial Theory, Series A* 113 (5), pp. 779–798, 2006. See pages 221, 222, 231, and 271.

[480] C. Dobraunig, M. Eichlseder, L. Grassi, et al. Rasta: a cipher with low ANDdepth and few ANDs per Bit. *Proceedings of CRYPTO 2018 (1), Lecture Notes in Computer Science* 10991, pp. 662–692, 2018. See page 454.

[481] Y. Dodis, J. Katz, L. Reyzin, and A. Smith. Robust fuzzy extractors and authenticated key agreement from close secrets. *Proceedings of CRYPTO 2006, Lecture Notes in Computer Science* 4117, pp. 232–250, 2006. See page 450.

[482] S. M. Dodunekov and V. A. Zinoviev. A note on Preparata codes. *Proceedings of Sixth Intern. Symp. on Information Theory, Moscow – Tashkent Part 2*, pp. 78–80, 1984. See pages 379 and 380.

[483] D. Dong, X. Zhang, L. Qu and S. Fu. A note on vectorial bent functions. *Information Processing Letters* 113 (22–24), pp. 866–870, 2013. See page 272.

[484] B. Dravie, J. Parriaux, P. Guillot, and G. Millérioux. Matrix representations of vectorial Boolean functions and eigenanalysis. *Cryptography and Communications* 8 (4), pp. 555–577, 2016. See pages 51 and 52.

[485] Y. Du and F. Zhang. On the existence of Boolean functions with optimal resistance against fast algebraic attacks. *IACR Cryptology ePrint Archive* (http://eprint.iacr.org/) 2012/210, 2012. See page 322.

[486] S. Dubuc. Characterization of linear structures. *Designs, Codes and Cryptography* 22, pp. 33–45, 2001. See page 100.

[487] A. Duc, S. Dziembowski, and S. Faust. Unifying leakage models: from probing attacks to noisy leakage. *Proceedings of EUROCRYPT 2014, Lecture Notes in Computer Science* 8441, pp. 423–440, 2014 See page 429.

[488] I. Dumer and O. Kapralova. Spherically punctured Reed–Muller Codes. *IEEE Transactions on Information Theory* 63 (5), pp. 2773–2780, 2017. See page 460.

[489] O. Dunkelman and S. Huang. Reconstructing an S-box from its difference distribution table. *IACR Transactions on Symmetric Cryptology* 2019 (2), pp. 193–217, 2019. See also *IACR Cryptology ePrint Archive* (http://eprint.iacr.org/) 2018/811. See page 376.

[490] S. Duval, V. Lallemand, and Y. Rotella. Cryptanalysis of the FLIP family of stream ciphers. *Proceedings of CRYPTO (1) 2016, Lecture Notes in Computer Science* 9814, pp. 457–475, 2016. See page 456.

[491] S. Dziembowski and S. Faust. Leakage-resilient cryptography from the inner-product extractor. *Proceedings of ASIACRYPT 2011, Lecture Notes in Computer Science* 7073, pp. 702–721, 2011. See page 446.

[492] Y. Edel. Quadratic APN functions as subspaces of alternating bilinear forms. *Proceedings of the Contact Forum Coding Theory and Cryptography III*, Belgium 2009, pp. 11–24, 2011. See page 399.

[493] Y. Edel, G. Kyureghyan, and A. Pott. A new APN function which is not equivalent to a power mapping. *IEEE Transactions on Information Theory* 52 (2), pp. 744–747, 2006. See pages 397, 399, and 405.

[494] Y. Edel and A. Pott. A new almost perfect nonlinear function which is not quadratic. *Advances in Mathematics of Communications* 3 (1), pp. 59–81, 2009. See pages 399, 402, 403, 407, 408, and 478.

[495] eSTREAM Project. www.ecrypt.eu.org/stream/. See pages 3, 22, 23, and 93.

[496] J. H. Evertse. Linear structures in block ciphers. *Proceedings of EUROCRYPT 1987, Lecture Notes in Computer Science* 304, pp. 249–266, 1988. See page 99.

[497] J.-C. Faugère and G. Ars. An algebraic cryptanalysis of nonlinear filter generators using Gröbner bases. *Rapport de Recherche INRIA* 4739, 2003. See pages 89 and 90.

[498] X. Feng and G. Gong. On algebraic immunity of trace inverse functions over finite fields with characteristic two. *Journal of Systems Science and Complexity* 29 (1), pp. 272–288, 2016 and *IACR Cryptology ePrint Archive* (http://eprint.iacr.org/) 2013/585, 2013. See page 324.

[499] T. Feng, K. Leung, and Q. Xiang. Binary cyclic codes with two primitive nonzeros. *Science China Mathematics* 56 (7), pp. 1403–1412, 2013.

[500] K. Feng, Q. Liao, and J. Yang. Maximal values of generalized algebraic immunity. *Designs, Codes and Cryptography* 50, pp. 243–252, 2009. See pages 128, 337, 346, 348, and 350.

[501] K. Feng and J. Yang. Vectorial Boolean functions with good cryptographic properties. *International Journal of Foundations of Computer Science* 22 (6), pp. 1271–1282, 2011. See page 340.

[502] T. Feulner, L. Sok, P. Solé, and A. Wassermann. Towards the classification of self-dual bent functions in eight variables. *Designs, Codes and Cryptography* 68 (1–3), pp. 395–406, 2013. See page 198.

[503] E. Filiol and C. Fontaine. Highly nonlinear balanced Boolean functions with a good correlation-immunity. *Proceedings of EUROCRYPT 1998, Lecture Notes in Computer Science* 1403, pp. 475–488, 1998. See pages 248, 292, and 360.

[504] Y. Filmus. Friedgut-kalai-naor theorem for slices of the Boolean cube. *Chicago J. Theor. Comput. Sci.*, 2016. See pages 456 and 457.

[505] Y. Filmus. An orthogonal basis for functions over a slice of the Boolean hypercube. *The Electronic Journal of Combinatorics* 23 (1), p. P1. 23, 2016. See page 456.

[506] Y. Filmus and F. Ihringer. Boolean degree 1 functions on some classical association schemes. *Journal of Combinatorial Theory, Series A* 162, pp. 241–270, 2019. See page 163.

[507] Y. Filmus, G. Kindler, E. Mossel, and K. Wimmer. Invariance principle on the slice. *31st Conference on Computational Complexity, CCC 2016*, pp. 15:1–15:10, 2016. See page 457.

[508] Y. Filmus and E. Mossel. Harmonicity and invariance on slices of the Boolean cube. *31st Conference on Computational Complexity, CCC 2016*, pp. 16:1–16:13, 2016. See page 457.

[509] S. Fischer and W. Meier. Algebraic immunity of S-boxes and augmented functions. *Proceedings of Fast Software Encryption FSE 2007. Lecture Notes in Computer Science* 4593, pp. 366–381, 2007. See page 95.

[510] R. W. Fitzgerald. Trace forms over finite fields of characteristic 2 with prescribed invariants. *Finite Fields and Their Applications* 15 (1), pp. 69–81, 2009. See page 178.

[511] J. P. Flori and S. Mesnager. Dickson polynomials, hyperelliptic curves and hyper-bent functions. *Proceedings of International Conference on Sequences and Their Applications SETA 2012, Lecture Notes in Computer Science 7780*, pp. 40–52, Springer, 2012. See page 247.

[512] J.-P. Flori and S. Mesnager. An efficient characterization of a family of hyper-bent functions with multiple trace terms. *Journal of Mathematical Cryptology* 7 (1), pp. 43–68, 2013. See also *IACR Cryptology ePrint Archive* (http://eprint.iacr.org/) 2011/373. See page 247.

[513] J. P. Flori H. Randriambololona, G. Cohen, and S. Mesnager. On a conjecture about binary strings distribution. *Proceedings of International Conference on Sequences and Their Applications SETA 2010, Lecture Notes in Computer Science* 6338, pp. 346–358, 2010. See page 339.

[514] D. G. Fon-Der-Flaass. A bound on correlation immunity. *Sib. Elektron. Mat. Izv.* 4, pp. 133–135, 2007. (http://semr.math.nsc.ru/v4/p133-135.pdf). See page 285.

[515] C. Fontaine. On some cosets of the first-order Reed–Muller code with high minimum weight. *IEEE Transactions on Information Theory* 45 (4), pp. 1237–1243, 1999. See pages 81, 248, and 292.

[516] R. Forré. The strict avalanche criterion: spectral properties of Boolean functions and an extended definition. *Proceedings of CRYPTO 1988, Lecture Notes in Computer Science* 403, pp. 450–468, 1989. See pages 97 and 318.

[517] R. Forré. A fast correlation attack on nonlinearly feedforward filtered shift register sequences. *Proceedings of EUROCRYPT 1989, Lecture Notes in Computer Science* 434, pp. 586–595, 1990. See page 78.

[518] R. Fourquet and C. Tavernier. List decoding of second order Reed–Muller and its covering radius implications. *Proceedings of Workshop on Coding and Cryptography WCC 2007*, pp. 147–156, 2007. See page 84.

[519] E. Friedgut. Boolean functions with low average sensitivity depend on few coordinates. *Combinatorica* 18 (1), pp. 27–36, 1998 See page 102.

[520] J. Friedman. On the bit extraction problem. *Proceedings of the 33rd IEEE Symposium on Foundations of Computer Science*, pp. 314–319, 1992. See pages 87, 312, and 313.

[521] S. Fu and X. Feng. Involutory differentially 4-uniform permutations from known constructions. *Designs, Codes and Cryptography* 87 (1), pp. 31–56, 2018. See also *IACR Cryptology ePrint Archive* (http://eprint.iacr.org/) 2017/292. See pages 417 and 421.

[522] S. Fu, X. Feng, Q. Wang, and C. Carlet. On the derivative imbalance and ambiguity of functions. *IEEE Transactions on Information Theory* 65 (9), pp. 5833–5845, 2019. See pages 138 and 139.

[523] S. Fu, X. Feng, and B. Wu. Differentially 4-uniform permutations with the best known nonlinearity from butterflies. *IACR Transactions on Symmetric Cryptology*, 2017 (2), pp. 228–249, 2017. See page 421.

[524] R. G. Gallager. *Low Density Parity Check Codes*. MIT Press, 1963. See page 78.

[525] S. Gangopadhyay, A. K. Gangopadhyay, S. Pollatos, and P. Stănică. Cryptographic Boolean functions with biased inputs. *Cryptography and Communications* 9(2), pp. 301–314, 2017. See page 457.

[526] S. Gangopadhyay, A. Joshi, G. Leander, and R. K. Sharma. A new construction of bent functions based on $\mathbb{Z}$-bent functions. *Designs, Codes and Cryptography* 66, (1–2), pp. 243–256, 2013. See page 240.

[527] S. Gangopadhyay, P. H. Keskar, and S. Maitra. Patterson–Wiedemann construction revisited. *Discrete Mathematics* 306, pp. 1540–1556, 2002 (selected papers from R. C. Bose Centennial Symposium on Discrete Mathememations and Applications). See page 320.

[528] S. Gangopadhyay, B. Mandal, and P. Stănică. Gowers U_3 norm of some classes of bent Boolean functions. *Designs, Codes and Cryptography* 86 (5), pp. 1131–1148, 2018. See pages 473 and 474.

[529] S. Gangopadhyay, E. Pasalic, and P. Stănică. A note on generalized bent criteria for Boolean functions. *IEEE Transactions on Information Theory* 59 (5), 3233–3236, 2013. See page 266.

[530] G. Gao, Y. Guo, and Y. Zhao. Recent results on balanced symmetric Boolean functions. *IEEE Transactions on Information Theory* 62 (9), pp. 5199–5203, 2015. See page 354.

[531] G. Gao, X. Zhang, W. Liu, and C. Carlet. Constructions of quadratic and cubic rotation symmetric bent functions. *IEEE Transactions on Information Theory* 58, 4908–4913, 2012. See pages 249 and 251.

[532] J. von zur Gathen and J. R. Roche. Polynomials with two values. *Combinatorica* 17 (3), pp. 345–362, 1997. See pages 354 and 357.

[533] J. von zur Gathen and J. Gerhard. *Modern Computer Algebra*. Cambridge University Press, 2013 (third edition). See page 21.

[534] S. Ge, Z. Wang, P. Luo, and M. Karpovsky. Reliable and secure memories based on algebraic manipulation detection codes and robust error correction. *Proceedings of Int. Depend Symp. Citeseer*, 2013. See page 453.

[535] S. Ge, Z. Wang, P. Luo, and M. Karpovsky. Secure memories resistant to both random errors and fault injection attacks using nonlinear error correction codes. *Proceedings of HASP 2013, ACM 2013*, pp. 1–8, 2013. See page 452.

[536] C. Gentry. Fully homomorphic encryption using ideal lattices. *Proceedings of ACM STOC 2009*, pp. 169–178, 2009. See page 453.

[537] C. Gentry, A. Sahai, and B. Waters. Homomorphic encryption from learning with errors: conceptually-simpler, asymptotically-faster, attribute-based. *Proceedings of CRYPTO 2013, Part I, Lecture Notes in Computer Science* 8042, pp. 75–92, 2013. See pages 453 and 454.

[538] R. Gode and S. Gangopadhyay. Third-order nonlinearities of a subclass of Kasami functions. *Cryptography and Communications* 2, pp. 69–83, 2010. See page 85.

[539] C. Godsil and A. Roy. Two characterizations of crooked functions. *IEEE Transactions on Information Theory* 54 (2), pp. 864–866, 2008. See page 279.

[540] R. Gold. Maximal recursive sequences with 3-valued recursive crosscorrelation functions. *IEEE Transactions on Information Theory* 14, pp. 154–156, 1968. See pages 394, 400, and 401.

[541] O. Goldreich. Candidate one-way functions based on expander graphs. *Electronic Colloquium on Computational Complexity (ECCC)* 7(90), 2000. See also *IACR Cryptology ePrint Archive* (http://eprint.iacr.org/) 2000/063, 2000. See page 467.

[542] O. Goldreich. *Introduction to Property Testing*. Cambridge University Press, 2017. See page 469.

[543] O. Goldreich and R. Izsak. Monotone circuits: one-way functions versus pseudorandom generators. *Theory of Computing* 8 (1), pp. 231–238, 2012. See page 467.

[544] J. Golić. Fast low order approximation of cryptographic functions. *Proceedings of EUROCRYPT 1996, Lecture Notes in Computer Science* 1070, pp. 268–282, 1996. See page 83.

[545] J. Golić. On the security of nonlinear filter generators. *Proceedings of Fast Software Encryption FSE 1996, Lecture Notes in Computer Science* 1039, pp. 173–188, 1996. See pages 89 and 344.

[546] F. Göloglŭ. Almost bent and almost perfect nonlinear functions, exponential sums, geometries and sequences. PhD dissertation, University of Magdeburg, 2009. See page 247.

[547] F. Göloglŭ. Almost perfect nonlinear trinomials and hexanomials. *Finite Fields and Their Applications* 33, pp. 258–282, 2015. See pages 168 and 408.

[548] F. Göloglu and A. Pott. Results on the crosscorrelation and autocorrelation of sequences. *Proceedings of International Conference on Sequences and Their Applications SETA 2008, Lecture Notes in Computer Science* 5203, pp. 95–105, 2008. See pages 178, 232, and 396.

[549] S. W. Golomb. On the classification of Boolean functions. *IEEE Transactions on Information Theory* 5 (5), pp. 176–186, 1959. See pages 52, 87, and 143.

[550] S. W. Golomb. *Shift Register Sequences*. Aegean Park Press, 1982. See pages 20 and 384.

[551] S. W. Golomb. Shift register sequences – a retrospective account. *Proceedings of International Conference on Sequences and Their Applications SETA 2006, Lecture Notes in Computer Science* 4086, pp. 1–4, 2006. See page 384.

[552] S. W. Golomb and G. Gong. *Signal Design for Good Correlation*. Cambridge University Press, 2005. See page 384.

[553] G. Gong. Sequences, DFT and resistance against fast algebraic attacks. *Proceedings of International Conference on Sequences and Their Applications SETA 2008, Lecture Notes in Computer Science* 5203, pp. 197–218, 2008. See page 94.

[554] G. Gong and S. W. Golomb. Transform domain analysis of DES. *IEEE Transactions on Information Theory* 45 (6), pp. 2065–2073, 1999. See pages 243 and 244.

[555] G. Gong, T. Helleseth, and P. V. Kumar. Solomon W. Golomb – mathematician, engineer and pioneer. *IEEE Transactions on Information Theory* 64 (4), pp. 2844–2857, 2018 See pages 52 and 384.

[556] G. Gong, S. Rønjom, T. Helleseth, and H. Hu. Fast discrete Fourier spectra attacks on stream ciphers. *IEEE Transactions on Information Theory* 57 (8), pp. 5555–5565, 2011. See pages 95 and 96.

[557] K. Gopalakrishnan, D. G. Hoffman and D. R. Stinson. A note on a conjecture concerning symmetric resilient functions. *Information Processing Letters* 47 (3), pp. 139–143, 1993. See pages 356 and 357.

[558] S. D. Gordon, Y. Ishai, T. Moran, R. Ostrovsky, and A. Sahai. On complete primitives for fairness. *Proceedings of Theory of Cryptography, TCC 2010, Lecture Notes in Computer Science* 5978, pp. 91–108, 2010. See page 452.

[559] M. Goresky and A. Klapper. Fibonacci and Galois representation of feedback with carry shift registers. *IEEE Transactions on Information Theory* 48, pp. 2826–2836, 2002. See page 23.

[560] M. Goresky and A. Klapper. Periodicity and distribution properties of combined FCSR sequences. *Proceedings of International Conference on Sequences and Their Applications SETA 2006, Lecture Notes in Computer Science* 4086, pp. 334–341, 2006. See page 23.

[561] A. Gorodilova. On differential equivalence of APN functions. *Cryptography and Communications* 11 (4), pp. 793–813, 2019. Preliminary version in *IACR Cryptology ePrint Archive* (http://eprint .iacr.org/) 2017/907. See also: On a remarkable property of APN Gold functions, *IACR Cryptology ePrint Archive* (http://eprint.iacr.org/) 2016/286. See page 376.

[562] L. Goubin and A. Martinelli. Protecting AES with Shamir's secret sharing scheme. *Proceedings of International Workshop Cryptographic Hardware and Embedded Systems CHES 2011, Lecture Notes in Computer Science* 6917, pp. 79–94, 2011. See pages 428 and 436.

[563] D. Goudarzi, A. Joux, and M. Rivain. How to securely compute with noisy leakage in quasi-linear complexity. *Proceedings of ASIACRYPT 2018, Lecture Notes in Computer Science* 11273, pp. 547–574, 2018. See page 431.

[564] D. Goudarzi, A. Martinelli, A. Passelegue, and T. Prest. Unifying leakage models on a Rényi day. *IACR Cryptology ePrint Archive* (http://eprint.iacr.org/) 2019/138. See page 429.

[565] D. Goudarzi and M. Rivain. On the multiplicative complexity of Boolean functions and bitsliced higher-order masking. *Proceedings of International Workshop Cryptographic Hardware and Embedded Systems CHES 2016, Lecture Notes in Computer Science* 9813, pp. 457–478, 2016. See page 434.

[566] A. Gouget. On the propagation criterion of Boolean functions. *Proceedings of the Workshop on Coding, Cryptography and Combinatorics 2003, Birkhäuser Verlag*, pp. 153–168, 2004. See page 355.

[567] A. Gouget and H. Sibert. Revisiting correlation-immunity in filter generators. *Proceedings of SAC 2007, Lecture Notes in Computer Science* 4876, pp. 378–395, 2007. See page 89.

[568] W. T. Gowers. A new proof of Szemerédi's theorem. *Geom. Funct. Anal.* 11 (3), pp. 465–588, 2001. See pages 469, 470, 471, and 473.

[569] W. T. Gowers and L. Milicevic. A quantitative inverse theorem for the U4 norm over finite fields, 2017 (https://arxiv.org/pdf/1712.00241.pdf). See page 470.

[570] M. Grassl. Code tables: bounds on the parameters of various types of codes. Available at www .codetables.de/, Universitat Karlsruhe. See pages 6 and 316.

[571] B. Green. Finite field models in additive combinatorics. *Proceedings of British Combinatorial Conference 2005, Surveys in Combinatorics*, pp. 1–27, https://arxiv.org/pdf/math/0409420.pdf, 2005. See pages 469 and 470.

[572] B. Green and T. Tao. An inverse theorem for the Gowers U_3 norm (arXiv:math/0503014 [math.NT]), 2006. See page 473.

[573] B. Green and T. Tao. The distribution of polynomials over finite fields, with applications to the Gowers norms. arXiv/0711.3191, 2007. See page 474.

[574] H. Gross and S. Mangard Reconciling $d + 1$ masking in hardware and software. *Proceedings of International Workshop Cryptographic Hardware and Embedded Systems CHES 2017, Lecture Notes in Computer Science* 10529, pp. 115–136, 2017. See page 444.

[575] H. Gross, S. Mangard, and T. Korak. Domain-oriented masking: compact masked hardware implementations with arbitrary protection order. *Proceedings of the 2016 ACM Workshop on Theory of Implementation Security (TIS)* and *IACR Cryptology ePrint Archive* (http://eprint.iacr .org/) 2016/486, 2016. See page 444.

[576] L. Grover. A fast quantum mechanical algorithm for database search. *Proceedings of ACM STOC 1996*, pp. 212–219, 1996 (also Bell Labs, New Jersey, Tech. Rep., 1996). See page 3.

[577] S. Guilley, A. Heuser, and O. Rioul. Codes for side-channel attacks and protections. *Proceedings of C2SI, Lecture Notes in Computer Science* 10194, pp. 35–55, 2017. See page 429.

[578] P. Guillot. Partial bent functions. *Proceedings of the World Multiconference on Systemics, Cybernetics and Informatics, SCI 2000*, 2000. See page 258.

[579] P. Guillot. Completed GPS covers all bent functions. *Journal of Combinatorial Theory*, Series A 93, pp. 242–260, 2001. See pages 69 and 242.

[580] K. Gupta and P. Sarkar. Improved construction of nonlinear resilient S-boxes. *Proceedings of ASIACRYPT 2002, Lecture Notes in Computer Science* 2501, pp. 466–483, 2002. See pages 315 and 316.

[581] K. Gupta and P. Sarkar. Construction of perfect nonlinear and maximally nonlinear multiple-output Boolean functions satisfying higher order strict avalanche criteria. *IEEE Transactions on Information Theory* 50, pp. 2886–2894, 2004. See page 318.

[582] K. C. Gupta and P. Sarkar. Computing partial Walsh transform from the algebraic normal form of a Boolean function. *IEEE Transactions on Information Theory* 55 (3), pp. 1354–1359, 2009. See page 57.

[583] V. Guruswami and M. Wootters. Repairing Reed–Solomon codes. *IEEE Transactions on Information Theory* 63 (9), pp. 5684–5698, 2017. See page 146.

[584] S. Halevi and V. Shoup. Algorithms in HeLib. *Proceedings of CRYPTO 2014, Lecture Notes in Computer Science* 8616, pp. 554–571, 2014. See page 454.

[585] R. W. Hamming. Error detecting and error correcting codes. *The Bell System Technical Journal* 29 (2), pp. 147–160, 1950. See page 5.

[586] A. R. Hammons Jr., P. V. Kumar, A. R. Calderbank, N. J. A. Sloane, and P. Solé. The $\mathbb{Z}_4$-linearity of Kerdock, Preparata, Goethals and related codes. *IEEE Transactions on Information Theory* 40, pp. 301–319, 1994. See page 255.

[587] H. Han and C. Tang. New classes of even-variable Boolean functions with optimal algebraic immunity and very high nonlinearity. *International Journal of Advanced Computer Technology* 5 (2), pp. 419–428, 2013. See page 340.

[588] M. A. Harrison. On the classification of Boolean functions by the general linear and affine groups. *Journal of the Society for Industrial and Applied Mathematics* 12 (2), pp. 285–299, 1964. See page 143.

[589] P. Hawkes and L. O'Connor. XOR and Non-XOR differential probabilities. *Proceedings of EUROCRYPT 1999, Lecture Notes in Computer Science* 1592, pp. 272–285, 1999. See page 136.

[590] P. Hawkes and G. Rose. Rewriting variables: the complexity of fast algebraic attacks on stream ciphers. *Proceedings of CRYPTO 2004, Lecture Notes in Computer Science* 3152, pp. 390–406, 2004. See page 94.

[591] A. S. Hedayat, N. J. A. Sloane, and J. Stufken. *Orthogonal Arrays, Theory and Applications.* Springer Series in Statistics, 1999. See pages 87, 303, and 304.

[592] T. Helleseth. Some results about the cross-correlation function between two maximal linear sequences. *Discrete Mathematics* 16 (3), pp. 209–232, 1976. See pages 72 and 372.

[593] T. Helleseth. Open problems on the cross-correlation of m-sequences. *Proceeding of the Conference Open Problems in Mathematical and Computational Sciences*, September 18–20, 2013, Istanbul, Turkey. Springer, pp. 163–179, 2014. See page 384.

[594] T. Helleseth and A. Kholosha. On the equation $x^{2^l+1} + x + a = 0$ over $GF(2^k)$. *Finite Fields and Their Applications* 14 (1), pp. 159–176, 2008. See page 495.

[595] T. Helleseth and A. Kholosha. $x^{2^l+1} + x + a$ and related affine polynomials over $GF(2^k)$. *Cryptography and Communications* 2 (1), pp. 85–109, 2010. See page 495.

[596] T. Helleseth, A. Kholosha, and S. Mesnager. Niho bent functions and Subiaco hyperovals. *Proceedings of the 10-th International Conference on Finite Fields and Their Applications (Fq'10), Contemporary Mathematics*, 579, pp. 91–101, 2012. See pages 221 and 222.

[597] T. Helleseth, T. Kløve, and J. Mykkelveit. On the covering radius of binary codes. *IEEE Transactions on Information Theory* 24 (5), pp. 627–628, 1978. See page 81.

[598] T. Helleseth and P. V. Kumar. Sequences with low correlation. *Handbook of Coding Theory*, V. Pless and W. C. Huffman, eds. Elsevier, vol. II, pp. 1765–1854, 1998. See page 384.

[599] T. Helleseth and H. F. Mattson Jr. On the cosets of the simplex code. *Discrete Mathematics* 56, pp. 169–189, 1985. See page 262.

[600] T. Helleseth and S. Rønjom. Simplifying algebraic attacks with univariate analysis. *Proceedings of Information Theory and Applications Workshop, ITA 2011, San Diego, California, USA, February 6–11, 2011*, pp. 153–159, 2011. See pages 95, 326, and 327.

[601] T. Helleseth and V. Zinoviev. On $\mathbb{Z}_4$-linear Goethals codes and Kloosterman sums. *Designs, Codes and Cryptography* 17, pp. 269–288, 1999. See page 402.

[602] Z. Heng, C. Ding, and Z. Zhou. Minimal linear codes over finite fields. *Finite Fields and Their Applications* 54, pp. 176–196, 2018. See page 149.

[603] F. Hernando and G. McGuire. Proof of a conjecture on the sequence of exceptional numbers, classifying cyclic codes and APN functions. *Journal of Algebra* 343 (1), pp. 78–92, 2011. See page 404.

[604] D. Hertel and A. Pott, Two results on maximum nonlinear functions, *Designs, Codes and Cryptography* 47 (1–3), pp. 225–235, 2008. See page 418.

[605] S. Hirose and K. Ikeda. Complexity of Boolean functions satisfying the propagation criterion. *IEICE Transactions on Fundamentals of Electronics, Communications and Computer Sciences* 78 (4), pp. 470–478, 1995. Presented at 1995 Symposium on Cryptography and Information Security, SCIS95-B3.3, 1995. See page 318.

[606] J. J. Hoch and A. Shamir. Fault analysis of stream ciphers. *Proceedings of International Workshop Cryptographic Hardware and Embedded Systems CHES 2004, Lecture Notes in Computer Science* 3156, Springer, pp. 240–253, 2004. See page 427.

[607] R. Hofer and A. Winterhof. r-th order nonlinearity, correlation measure and least significant bit of the discrete logarithm. *Cryptography and Communications* 11 (5), pp. 993–998, 2019. See page 85.

[608] H. Hollmann and Q. Xiang. A proof of the Welch and Niho conjectures on crosscorrelations of binary m-sequences. *Finite Fields and Their Applications* 7, pp. 253–286, 2001. See page 395.

[609] K. Horadam. *Hadamard Matrices and Their Applications*. Princeton University Press, 2006. See page 53.

[610] X.-D. Hou. Some results on the covering radii of Reed–Muller codes. *IEEE Transactions on Information Theory* 39 (2), pp. 366–378, 1993. See page 158.

[611] X.-D. Hou. Classification of cosets of the Reed–Muller code $R(m - 3, m)$. *Discrete Mathematics*, 128, pp. 203–224, 1994. See page 155.

[612] X.-D. Hou. The covering radius of $R(1, 9)$ in $R(4, 9)$. *Designs, Codes and Cryptography* 8 (3), pp. 285–292, 1995. See page 158.

[613] X.-D. Hou. $AGL(m, 2)$ acting on $R(r, m)/R(s, m)$. *Journal of Algebra* 171, pp. 921–938, 1995. See pages 144 and 155.

[614] X.-D. Hou. Covering radius of the Reed–Muller code $R(1, 7)$ – a simpler proof. *Journal of Combinatorial Theory*, Series A 74, pp. 337–341, 1996. See page 158.

[615] X.-D. Hou. $GL(m, 2)$ acting on $R(r, m)/R(r - 1, m)$. *Discrete Mathematics* 149, pp. 99–122, 1996. See page 155.

[616] X.-D. Hou. On the covering radius of $R(1, m)$ in $R(3, m)$. *IEEE Transactions on Information Theory* 42 (3), pp. 1035–1037, 1996. See pages 108 and 158.

[617] X.-D. Hou. On the norm and covering radius of the first-order Reed–Muller codes. *IEEE Transactions on Information Theory* 43 (3), pp. 1025–1027, 1997. See pages 81 and 157.

[618] X.-D. Hou. Cubic bent functions. *Discrete Mathematics* 189, pp. 149–161, 1998. See page 208.

[619] X.-D. Hou. On the coefficients of binary bent functions. *Proc. Amer. Math. Soc.* 128 (4), pp. 987–996, 2000. See page 200.

[620] X.-D. Hou. New constructions of bent functions. *Proceedings of the International Conference on Combinatorics, Information Theory and Statistics; Journal of Combinatorics, Information and System Sciences* 25 (1–4), pp. 173–189, 2000. See pages 200, 234, and 236.

[621] X.-D. Hou. On binary resilient functions. *Designs, Codes and Cryptography* 28 (1), pp. 93–112, 2003. See page 287.

[622] X.-D. Hou. Group actions on binary resilient functions. *Applicable Algebra in Engineering, Communication and Computing (AAECC)* 14 (2), pp. 97–115, 2003. See page 88.

[623] X.-D. Hou. A note on the proof of a theorem of Katz. *Finite Fields and Their Applications* 11, pp. 316–319, 2005. See page 156.

[624] X.-D. Hou. Affinity of permutations of $\mathbb{F}_2^n$. *Proceedings of Workshop on Coding and Cryptography WCC 2003*, pp. 273–280, 2003. Completed version in *Discrete Applied Mathematics* 154 (2), pp. 313–325, 2006. See page 411.

[625] X.-D. Hou. Explicit evaluation of certain exponential sums of binary quadratic functions. *Finite Fields and Their Applications* 13, pp. 843–868, 2007. See pages 173, 174, 176, and 178.

[626] X.-D. Hou. Classification of self dual quadratic bent functions. *Designs, Codes and Cryptography* 63 (2), pp. 183–198, 2012. See pages 198, 199, and 476.

[627] X.-D. Hou and P. Langevin. Results on bent functions. *Journal of Combinatorial Theory, Series A* 80, pp. 232–246, 1997. See pages 195 and 235.

[628] X.-D. Hou, G. L. Mullen, J. A. Sellers, and J. Yucas. Reversed Dickson polynomials over finite fields. *Finite Fields and Their Applications* 15, pp. 748–773, 2009. See page 389.

[629] H. Hu and D. Feng. On quadratic bent functions in polynomial forms. *IEEE Transactions on Information Theory* 53, pp. 2610–2615, 2007. See pages 178, 206, 230, and 231.

[630] H. Hu and G. Gong. Periods on two kinds of nonlinear feedback shift registers with time varying feedback functions. *International Journal of Foundations of Computer Science* 22 (6), pp. 1317–1329, 2011. See page 23.

[631] H. Huang. Induced subgraphs of hypercubes and a proof of the sensitivity conjecture. *Annals of Mathematics* 190 (3), pp. 949–955, 2019. See also arXiv preprint arXiv:1907.00847, 2019. See page 320.

[632] D. Huang, C. Tang, Y. Qi, and M. Xu. New quadratic bent functions in polynomial forms with coefficients in extension fields. *Applicable Algebra in Engineering, Communication and Computing (AAECC)* 30, pp. 333–347, 2019. See also C. Tang, Y. Qi and M. Xu, *IACR Cryptology ePrint Archive* (http://eprint.iacr.org/) 2013/405, 2013. See page 206.

[633] J.Y. Hyun, H. Lee, and Y. Lee. MacWilliams duality and Gleason-type theorem on self-dual bent functions. *Designs, Codes and Cryptography* 63 (3), pp. 295–304, 2012. See page 196.

[634] J.Y. Hyun, H. Lee, and Y. Lee. Boolean functions with MacWilliams duality. *Designs, Codes and Cryptography* 72 (2), pp. 273–287, 2014. See page 196.

[635] K. Ireland and M. Rosen. *A Classical Introduction to Modern Number Theory*. Graduate Texts in Mathematics (Book 84) (second edition). Springer-Verlag, 2010. See page 486.

[636] Y. Ishai, E. Kushilevitz, R. Ostrovsky, and A. Sahai. Cryptography with constant computational overhead. *Proceedings of ACM STOC 2008*, pp. 433–442, ACM Press, 2008. See page 467.

[637] Y. Ishai, A. Sahai, and D. Wagner. Private circuits: securing hardware against probing attacks. *Proceedings of CRYPTO 2003, Lecture Notes in Computer Science* 2729, pp. 463–481, 2003. See pages 428 and 430.

[638] T. Iwata and K. Kurosawa. Probabilistic higher order differential attack and higher order bent functions. *Proceedings of ASIACRYPT 1999, Lecture Notes in Computer Science* 1716, pp. 62–74, 1999. See pages 83, 85, and 114.

[639] T. Jakobsen and L. R. Knudsen. The interpolation attack on block ciphers. *Proceedings of Fast Software Encryption FSE 1997, Lecture Notes in Computer Science* 1267, pp. 28–40, 1997. See page 142.

[640] C. J. A. Jansen and D. E. Boekee. The shortest feedback shift register that can generate a given sequence. *Proceedings of CRYPTO 1989, Lecture Notes in Computer Science* 435, pp. 90–99, 1990. See page 23.

[641] H. Janwa and R. Wilson. Hyperplane sections of Fermat varieties in P^3 in char. 2 and some applications to cyclic codes. *Proceedings of AAECC-10 Conference, Lecture Notes in Computer Science* 673, pp. 180–194, 1993. See pages 378 and 400.

[642] H. Janwa, G. McGuire, and R. Wilson. Double-error-correcting codes and absolutely irreducible polynomials over $GF(2)$. *Journal of Algebra* 178, pp. 665–676, 1995. See pages 378 and 404.

[643] D. Jedlicka. APN monomials over $GF(2^n)$ for infinitely many n. *Finite Fields and Their Applications* 13, pp. 1006–1028, 2007. See page 136.

[644] Q. Jin, Z. Liu, B. Wu, and X. Zhang. A general conjecture similar to T-D conjecture and its applications in constructing Boolean functions with optimal algebraic immunity. *IACR Cryptology ePrint Archive* (http://eprint.iacr.org/) 2011/515, 2011. See page 340.

[645] T. Johansson and F. Jönsson. Improved fast correlation attack on stream ciphers via convolutional codes. *Proceedings of EUROCRYPT 1999, Lecture Notes in Computer Science* 1592, pp. 347–362, 1999. See page 78.

[646] T. Johansson and F. Jönsson. Fast correlation attacks based on turbo code techniques. *Proceedings of CRYPTO 1999, Lecture Notes in Computer Science* 1666, pp. 181–197, 1999. See page 78.

[647] T. Johansson and F. Jönsson. Fast correlation attacks through reconstruction of linear polynomials. *Proceedings of CRYPTO 2000, in Lecture Notes in Computer Science* 1880, pp. 300–315, 2000. See page 78.

[648] T. Johansson and E. Pasalic. A construction of resilient functions with high nonlinearity. *Proceedings of the IEEE International Symposium on Information Theory*, Sorrento, Italy, pp. 494–501, 2000. See pages 314 and 316.

[649] N. Johnson, V. Jha, and M. Biliotti. *Handbook of Finite Translation Planes*. Pure and Applied Mathematics 289. Chapman & Hall/CRC, 2007. See pages 224 and 225.

[650] F. Jönsson. Some results on fast correlation attacks. PhD thesis, Lund University, 2002. See page 80.

[651] D. Jungnickel and A. Pott. Difference sets: an introduction. In *Difference Sets, Sequences and Their Autocorrelation Properties*. A. Pott, P. V. Kumar, T. Helleseth, and D. Jungnickel, eds. Kluwer, pp. 259–295, 1999. See page 190.

[652] J. Kahn, G. Kalai, and N. Linian. The influence of variables on Boolean functions. *Proceedings of 29th Annual Symposium on Foundations of Computer Science (IEEE)*, pp. 68–80, 1988. See page 68.

[653] G. Kalai. Boolean functions: influence, threshold and noise. *European Congress of Mathematics*, pp. 85–110, 2018. See page 68.

[654] N. Kaleyski. Changing APN functions at two points. *Special Issue on Boolean Functions and Their Applications 2018, Cryptography and Communications* 11 (6), pp. 1165–1184, 2019 See page 373.

[655] N. Kaleyski. An update on known invariants of vectorial Boolean functions. *Proceedings of International Workshop on Signal Design and its Applications in Communications (IWSDA) 2019*, pp. 1–3, 2019. See page 392.

[656] W. M. Kantor. Symplectic groups, symmetric designs, and line ovals. *Journal of Algebra* 33, pp. 43–58, 1975. See page 201.

[657] W. M. Kantor. An exponential number of generalized Kerdock codes. *Information and Control* 53, pp. 74–80, 1982. See page 255.

[658] W. M. Kantor. Spreads, translation planes and Kerdock sets II. *SIAM Journal on Algebraic and Discrete Methods* 3, pp. 308–318, 1982. See page 255.

[659] W. M. Kantor. Exponential numbers of two-weight codes, difference sets and symmetric designs. *Discrete Mathematics* 46 (1), pp. 95–98, 1983. See pages 192 and 226.

[660] W. M. Kantor. Commutative semifields and symplectic spreads. *Journal of Algebra* 270, pp. 96–114, 2003. See page 217.

[661] W. M. Kantor. Finite semifields. *Finite Geometries, Groups, and Computation (Proc. of Conf. at Pingree Park, CO Sept. 2005)*, pp. 103–114, de Gruyter, 2006. See pages 224 and 225.

[662] W. M. Kantor. Bent functions generalizing Dillon's partial spread functions. arXiv:1211.2600, 2012. See page 225.

[663] W. M. Kantor. Bent functions and spreads. (https://pages.uoregon.edu/kantor/PAPERS/Bent+spreads Final.pdf), (not meant to be published), 2015. See page 217.

[664] M. G. Karpovsky, K. J Kulikowski, and Z. Wang. Robust error detection in communication and computational channels. *Proceedings of Spectral Methods and Multirate Signal Processing, SMMSP2007*. Citeseer, 2007. See page 447.

[665] M. G. Karpovsky , K. J. Kulikowski, and Z. Wang. On-line self error detection with equal protection against all errors. *Int. J. High. Reliab. Electron. Syst. Des.*, 2008. See page 448.

[666] M. G. Karpovsky and P. Nagvajara. Optimal codes for the minimax criterion on error detection. *IEEE Transactions on Information Theory* 35 (6), pp. 1299–1305, 1989. See pages 447, 448, and 449.

[667] M. G. Karpovsky and A. Taubin. A new class of nonlinear systematic error detecting codes. *IEEE Transactions on Information Theory* 50 (8), pp. 1818–1820, 2004. See pages 447 and 448.

[668] M. Karpovsky and Z. Wang. Design of strongly secure communication and computation channels by nonlinear error detecting codes. *IEEE Transactions on Computers* 63 (11), pp. 2716–2728, 2014. See page 452.

[669] T. Kasami. The weight enumerators for several classes of subcodes of the second order binary Reed–Muller codes. *Information and Control* 18, pp. 369–394, 1971. See pages 230, 394, 401, and 418.

[670] T. Kasami and N. Tokura. On the weight structure of the Reed–Muller codes, *IEEE Transactions on Information Theory* 16, pp. 752–759, 1970. See pages 157 and 181.

[671] T. Kasami, N. Tokura, and S. Azumi. On the weight enumeration of weights less than 2.5d of Reed–Muller Codes. *Information and Control*, 30:380–395, 1976. See page 157.

[672] C. Kaşıkcı, W. Meidl, and A. Topuzoğlu. Spectra of a class of quadratic functions: average behavior and counting functions. *Cryptography and Communications* 8 (2), pp. 191–214, 2016. See page 178.

[673] D. J. Katz. Weil sums of binomials, three-level cross-correlation, and a conjecture of Helleseth. *Journal of Combinatorial Theory, Series A* 119 (8), pp. 1644–1659, 2012. See page 73.

[674] D. J. Katz. Divisibility of Weil sums of binomials. *Proc. Amer. Math. Soc.* 143 (11), pp. 4623–4632, 2015. See page 65.

[675] D. J. Katz and P. Langevin. New open problems related to old conjectures by Helleseth. *Cryptography and Communications* 8 (2), pp. 175–189, 2016. See page 73.

[676] D. J. Katz, P. Langevin, S. Lee, and Y. Sapozhnikov. The p-adic valuations of Weil sums of binomials. *Journal of Number Theory* 181, pp. 1–26, 2017. See page 65.

[677] N. Katz. On a theorem of Ax. *American Journal of Mathematics* 93, pp. 485–499, 1971. See page 156.

[678] T. Kaufman and S. Lovett. New extension of the Weil bound for character sums with applications to coding. *Proceedings of IEEE 52nd Annual Symposium on Foundations of Computer Science*, pp. 788–796, 2011. See page 188.

[679] T. Kaufman, S. Lovett, and E. Porat. Weight distribution and list-decoding size of Reed–Muller codes. *IEEE Transactions on Information Theory* 58 (5), pp. 2689–2696, 2012. See page 156.

[680] S. Kavut. Results on rotation-symmetric s-boxes. *Information Sciences* 201, pp. 93–113, 2012. See page 362.

[681] S. Kavut. Correction to the paper: Patterson–Wiedemann construction revisited. *Discrete Applied Mathematics* 202, pp. 185–187, 2016. See page 320.

[682] S. Kavut and S. Baloğlu. Results on symmetric S-boxes constructed by concatenation of RSSBs. *Cryptography and Communications* 11 (4), pp. 641–660, 2019. See page 145.

[683] S. Kavut, S. Maitra, and D. Tang. Searching balanced boolean functions on even number of variables with excellent autocorrelation profile. *Designs, Codes and Cryptography* 87 (2–3), pp. 261–276, 2019. See page 320.

[684] S. Kavut, S. Maitra, and M. D. Yücel. Search for Boolean functions with excellent profiles in the rotation symmetric class. *IEEE Transactions on Information Theory* 53 (5), pp. 1743–1751, 2007. See pages 81, 157, 320, and 360.

[685] S. Kavut and M. D. Yücel. Generalized rotation symmetric and dihedral symmetric Boolean functions–9 variable Boolean functions with nonlinearity 242. *Applied Algebra, Algebraic Algorithms and Error-Correcting Codes*. Springer Berlin Heidelberg, pp. 321–329, 2007. See pages 82 and 362.

[686] S. Kavut and M. D. Yücel. 9-variable Boolean functions with nonlinearity 242 in the generalized rotation symmetric class. *Information and Computation* 208 (4), pp. 341–350, 2010. See pages 81, 157, 158, and 360.

[687] European Telecommunications Standards Institute. Technical Specification 135 202 V9.0.0: universal mobile telecommunications system (UMTS); LTE; specification of the 3GPP confidentiality and integrity algorithms; Document 2: KASUMI specification (3GPP TS 35.202 V9.0.0 Release 9). See page 410.

[688] A. Kerckhoffs. La Cryptographie Militaire. *Journal des Sciences Militaires*, 1883. See page 1.

[689] A. M. Kerdock. A class of low-rate non linear codes. *Information and Control* 20, pp. 182–187, 1972. See pages 177 and 254.

[690] O. Keren, I. Shumsky, and M. G. Karpovsky. Robustness of security- oriented binary codes under non-uniform distribution of codewords. *Proceedings of 6th Int. Conf. on Dependability 2013*, pp. 25–30, 2013. See page 450.

[691] J. D. Key, T. P. McDonough, and V. C. Mavron. Information sets and partial permutation decoding for codes from finite geometries. *Finite Fields and Their Applications* 12 (2), pp. 232–247, 2006. See page 335.

[692] A. V. Khalyavin, M. S. Lobanov and Y. V. Tarannikov. On plateaued Boolean functions with the same spectrum support. *Sib. Elektron. Mat. Izv.* 13, pp. 1346–1368, 2016. See pages 259 and 264.

[693] J. Khan, G. Kalai, and N. Linial. The influence of variables on Boolean functions. *IEEE 29th Symp. on Foundations of Computer Science*, pp. 68–80, 1988. See page 59.

[694] M. A. Khan and F. Özbudak. Improvement in non-linearity of Carlet–Feng infinite class of Boolean functions. *Cryptology and Network Security,Lecture Notes in Computer Science* 7712, pp 280–295, 2012. See pages 144 and 335.

[695] A. Kholosha and A. Pott. Bent and related functions. *Handbook of Finite Fields*, CRC Press Book, Subsection 9.3, pp. 262–273, 2013. See page 197.

[696] K. Khoo and G. Gong. New constructions for resilient and highly nonlinear Boolean functions. *Proceedings of 8th Australasian Conference, ACISP 2003, Lecture Notes in Computer Science* 2727, pp. 498–509, 2003. See pages 81, 299, and 317.

[697] K. Khoo, G. Gong, and D. R. Stinson. A new family of Gold-like sequences. *Proceedings of IEEE International Symposium on Information Theory (ISIT) 2002*, p. 181, 2002. See page 178.

[698] K. Khoo, G. Gong, and D. Stinson. Highly nonlinear S-boxes with reduced bound on maximum correlation. *Proceedings of 2003 IEEE International Symposium on Information Theory*. 2003. www.cacr.math.uwaterloo.ca/techreports/2003/corr2003-12.ps. See page 133.

[699] K. Khoo, G. Gong, and D. Stinson. A new characterization of semi-bent and bent functions on finite fields. *Designs, Codes and Cryptography* 38 (2), pp. 279–295, 2006. See pages 178, 206, 230, and 362.

[700] K. H. Kim and S. Mesnager. Solving $x^{2^k+1}+x+a = 0$ in $\mathbb{F}_{2^n}$ with $\gcd(n, k) = 1$. *IACR Cryptology ePrint Archive* (http://eprint.iacr.org/) 2019/307, 2019. See page 495.

[701] S. H. Kim and J. S. No. New families of binary sequences with low correlation. *IEEE Transactions on Information Theory* 49 (11), pp. 3059–3065, 2003. See page 230.

[702] K. Kjeldsen. On the cycle structure of a set of nonlinear shift registers with symmetric feedback functions. *Journal of Combinatorial Theory, Series A* 20 (2), pp. 154–169, 1976. See page 23.

[703] A. Klapper and M. Goresky. Feedback shift registers, 2-adic span, and combiners with memory. *Journal of Cryptology* 10, pp. 111–147. 1997. See page 23.

[704] A. Klapper and M. Goresky. Arithmetic correlations and Walsh transforms. *IEEE Transactions on Information Theory* 58 (1), pp. 479–492, 2012. See page 57.

[705] A. Klimov and A. Shamir. Cryptographic applications of T-functions. *Proceedings of Selected Areas in Cryptography 2003, Lecture Notes in Computer Science* 3006, pp. 248–261, 2004. See page 26.

[706] L. Knudsen. Truncated and higher order differentials. *Proceedings of Fast Software Encryption FSE 1995, Lecture Notes in Computer Science* 1008, pp. 196–211, 1995. See pages 114, 136, and 142.

[707] L. R. Knudsen and M. P. J. Robshaw. Non-linear approximations in linear cryptanalysis. *Proceedings of EUROCRYPT 1996, Lecture Notes in Computer Science* 1070, pp. 224–236, 1996. See page 83.

[708] L. R. Knudsen and M. P. J. Robshaw. *The Block Cipher Companion*. Information Security and Cryptography. Springer, 2011. See page 26.

[709] L. R. Knudsen and D. Wagner. Integral cryptanalysis. *Proceedings of Fast Software Encryption FSE 2002, Lecture Notes in Computer Science* 2365, pp. 112–127, 2002. See page 114.

[710] D. E. Knuth. Finite semifields and projective planes. *Journal of Algebra* 2, pp. 182–217, 1965. See page 226.

[711] N. Koçak, S. Mesnager, and F. Özbudak. Bent and semi-bent functions via linear translators. *Proceedings of IMA Conference on Cryptography and Coding 2015, Lecture Notes in Computer Science* 9496, pp. 205–224, 2015. See pages 237 and 263.

[712] P. Kocher. Timing attacks on implementations of Diffie–Hellman, RSA, DSS, and other systems. *Proceedings of CRYPTO 1996, Lecture Notes in Computer Science* 1109, pp. 104–113, 1996. See page 425.

[713] P. Kocher, J. Jaffe, and B. Jun. Differential power analysis. *Proceedings of CRYPTO 1999, Lecture Notes in Computer Science* 1666, pp. 388–397, 1999. See pages 425, 426, and 427.

[714] N. Kolokotronis and K. Limniotis. Maiorana–McFarland Functions with high second-order nonlinearity. *IACR Cryptology ePrint Archive* (http://eprint.iacr.org/) 2011/212. See pages 85 and 158.

[715] N. Kolokotronis, K. Limniotis, and N. Kalouptsidis. Best affine and quadratic approximations of particular classes of Boolean functions. *IEEE Transactions on Information Theory* 55 (11), pp. 5211–5222, 2009. See pages 157 and 158.

[716] N. A. Kolomeec. The graph of minimal distances of bent functions and its properties. *Designs, Codes and Cryptography* 85 (3), pp. 1–16, 2017. See page 205.

[717] K. J. Kulikowski, M. G. Karpovsky, and A. Taubin. Robust codes and robust, fault-tolerant architectures of the advanced encryption standard. *Journal of Systems Architecture* 53 (2–3), pp. 139–149, 2007. See pages 448, 449, and 450.

[718] P. V. Kumar, R. A. Scholtz and L. R. Welch. Generalized bent functions and their properties. *Journal of Combinatorial Theory, Series A* 40, pp. 90–107, 1985. See page 193.

[719] K. Kurosawa, T. Iwata, and T. Yoshiwara. New covering radius of Reed–Muller codes for t-resilient functions. *Proceedings of Selected Areas in Cryptography, 8th Annual International Workshop, Lecture Notes in Computer Science* 2259, pp. 75 ff, 2001, and *IEEE Transactions on Information Theory* 50, pp. 468–475, 2004. See page 287.

[720] K. Kurosawa, T. Johansson, and D. Stinson. Almost k-wise independent sample spaces and their applications. *Journal of Cryptology* 14 (4), pp. 231–253, 2001. See page 290.

[721] K. Kurosawa and R. Matsumoto. Almost security of cryptographic Boolean functions. *IEEE Transactions on Information Theory* 50 (11), pp. 2752–2761, 2004. See pages 97 and 290.

[722] K. Kurosawa and T. Satoh. Design of $SAC/PC(\ell)$ of order k Boolean functions and three other cryptographic criteria. *Proceedings of EUROCRYPT 1997, Lecture Notes in Computer Science* 1233, pp. 434–449, 1997. See pages 319 and 320.

[723] K. Kurosawa, T. Satoh, and K. Yamamoto. Highly nonlinear t-resilient functions. *Journal of Universal Computer Science* 3 (6), pp. 721–729, 1997. See pages 314 and 316.

[724] S. Kutzner, P. Ha Nguyen, and A. Poschmann. Enabling 3-share threshold implementations for all 4-bit s-boxes. *Proceedings of ICISC 2013, Lecture Notes in Computer Science* 8565, pp. 91–108, 2013. See page 441.

[725] A. S. Kuzmin, V. T. Markov, A. A. Nechaev and A. B. Shishkov. Approximation of Boolean functions by monomial ones. *Discrete Mathematics and Applications* 16 (1), pp. 7–28, 2006. See page 246.

[726] G. Kyureghyan. Differentially affine maps. *Proceedings of the Workshop on Coding and Cryptography, WCC 2005*, pp. 296–305, 2005. See page 373.

[727] G. Kyureghyan. Crooked maps in finite fields. *2005 European Conference on Combinatorics, Graph Theory and Applications (EuroComb '05), Discrete Mathematics & Theoretical Computer Science* Proceedings, pp. 167–170, 2005. See pages 278 and 373.

[728] G. Kyureghyan. The only crooked power functions are $x^{2^k+2^l}$. *European Journal of Combinatorics* 28 (4), pp. 1345–1350, 2007. See pages 278 and 373.

[729] G. Kyureghyan. Crooked maps in $\mathbb{F}_{2^n}$. *Finite Fields and Their Applications* 13 (3), pp. 713–726, 2007. See pages 278 and 373.

[730] G. Kyureghyan. Special mappings of finite fields. *Finite Fields and Their Applications, Radon Ser. Comput. Appl. Math.* 11, pp. 117–144, De Gruyter, Berlin, 2013. See page 278.

[731] G. Kyureghyan and V. Suder. On inversion in $\mathbb{Z}_{2^n-1}$. *Finite Fields and Their Applications* 25, pp. 234–254, 2014. See pages 177 and 394.

[732] P. Lacharme. Post processing functions for a physical random number generator. *Proceedings of Fast Software Encryption FSE 2008, Lecture Notes in Computer Science* 5086, pp 334–342, 2008. See page 290.

[733] G. Lachaud and J. Wolfmann. The weights of the orthogonals of the extended quadratic binary goppa codes. *IEEE Transactions on Information Theory* 36, pp. 686–692, 1990. See pages 72, 215, and 402.

[734] J. Lahtonen, G. McGuire, and H. Ward. Gold and Kasami–Welch functions, quadratic forms and bent functions. *Advances in Mathematics of Communications* 1, pp. 243–250, 2007. See pages 178, 231, 395, and 396.

[735] X. Lai. Higher order derivatives and differential cryptanalysis. *Proceedings of the "Symposium on Communication, Coding and Cryptography", in honor of J. L. Massey on the Occasion of his 60'th birthday*, pp. 227–233, 1994. See pages 38, 114, and 142.

[736] X. Lai. Additive and linear structures of cryptographic functions. *Proceedings of Fast Software Encryption FSE 1995, Lecture Notes in Computer Science* 1008, pp. 75–85, 1995. See page 100.

[737] P. Langevin. Covering radius of $RM(1,9)$ in $RM(3,9)$. *Eurocode 1990, Lecture Notes in Computer Science* 514, pp. 51–59, 1991. See page 63.

[738] P. Langevin. On the orphans and covering radius of the Reed–Muller codes. *Proceedings of AAECC-9 Conference, Lecture Notes in Computer Science* 539, pp. 234–240, 1991. See page 262.

[739] P. Langevin and G. Leander. Classification of Boolean quartic forms in eight variables. *NATO Science for Peace and Security Series – D: Information and Communication Security*, IOS Press, vol. 18: Boolean Functions in Cryptology and Information Security, pp. 139–147, 2008. See page 144.

[740] P. Langevin and G. Leander. Monomial bent functions and Stickelberger's theorem. *Finite Fields and Their Applications* 14 (3), pp. 727–742, 2008. See page 156.

[741] P. Langevin and G. Leander. Counting all bent functions in dimension eight 99270589265934370305785861242880. *Designs, Codes and Cryptography* 59 (1–3), pp. 193–205, 2011 (see also the proceedings of WCC 2009). See pages 144 and 208.

[742] P. Langevin, G. Leander, G. McGuire, and E. Zalinescu. Analysis of Kasami–Welch functions in odd dimension using Stickelberger's theorem. *Journal of Combinatorics and Number Theory* 2 (1), pp. 55–72, 2010. See page 396.

[743] P. Langevin, G. Leander, P. Rabizzoni, P. Veron, and J.-P. Zanotti. Webpage http://langevin.univ-tln.fr/project/quartics/. See pages 208 and 243.

[744] P. Langevin, P. Rabizzoni, P. Veron, and J.-P. Zanotti. On the number of bent functions with 8 variables. *Proceedings of the Conference BFCA 2006*, Publications des universités de Rouen et du Havre, pp. 125–136, 2007. See page 243.

[745] P. Langevin and P. Solé. Kernels and defaults. (*Proceedings of the Conference Finite Fields and Applications* Fq4) *Contemporary Mathematics* 225, pp. 77–85, 1999. See page 181.

[746] P. Langevin and P. Véron. On the nonlinearity of power functions. *Designs, Codes and Cryptography* 37 (1), pp. 31–43, 2005. See pages 73 and 156.

[747] P. Langevin and J.-P. Zanotti. Nonlinearity of some invariant Boolean functions. *Designs, Codes and Cryptography* 36, pp. 131–146, 2005. See page 81.

[748] C. Lauradoux and M. Videau. Matriochka symmetric Boolean functions. *Proceedings of IEEE International Symposium on Information Theory (ISIT) 2008* pp. 1631–1635, 2008. See page 362.

[749] G. Leander. Bent functions with 2^r Niho exponents. *Proceedings of the Workshop on Coding and Cryptography 2005*, pp. 454–461, 2005. See pages 221 and 231.

[750] G. Leander. Monomial bent functions. *Proceedings of the Workshop on Coding and Cryptography* 2005, Bergen, pp. 462–470, 2005. And *IEEE Transactions on Information Theory* 52 (2), pp. 738–743, 2006. See pages 215, 230, and 246.

[751] G. Leander. Another class of non-normal bent functions. *Proceedings of the Conference BFCA 2006*, Publications des universités de Rouen et du Havre, pp. 87–98, 2006.

[752] G. Leander and A. Kholosha. Bent functions with 2^r Niho exponents. *IEEE Transactions on Information Theory*. 52 (12), pp. 5529–5532, 2006. See pages 221 and 231.

[753] G. Leander and P. Langevin. On exponents with highly divisible Fourier–Hadamard coefficients and conjectures of Niho and Dobbertin. *Proceedings of "The First Symposium on Algebraic Geometry and Its Applications" Dedicated to Gilles Lachaud (SAGA'07), 2007, World Scientific, Series on Number Theory and Its Applications* 5, pp. 410–418, 2008. See page 390.

[754] G. Leander and G. McGuire. Spectra of functions, subspaces of matrices, and going up versus going down. *Proceedings of AAECC-17 Conference, Lecture Notes in Computer Science* 4851, pp. 51–66, 2007. See page 232.

[755] G. Leander and G. McGuire. Construction of bent functions from near-bent functions. *Journal of Combinatorial Theory, Series A* 116, pp. 960–970, 2009. See page 232.

[756] G. Leander and A. Poschmann. On the classification of 4 bit S-boxes. *Proceedings of International Workshop on the Arithmetic of Finite Fields WAIFI 2007, Lecture Notes in Computer Science* 4547, pp. 159–176, 2007. See pages 144 and 417.

[757] G. Leander and F. Rodier. Bounds on the degree of APN polynomials: the case of $x^{-1} + g(x)$. *Designs, Codes and Cryptography* 59 (1–3), pp. 207–222, 2011. See page 401.

[758] J.-M. Le Bars and A. Viola. Equivalence classes of Boolean functions for first-order correlation. *IEEE Transactions on Information Theory* 56 (3), pp. 1247–1261, 2010. See page 313.

[759] R. J. Lechner. Harmonic analysis of switching functions. *Recent Developments in Switching Theory*, Academic Press, pp. 121–228, 1971. See page 58.

[760] V. I. Levenshtein. Split orthogonal arrays and maximum independent resilient systems of functions. *Designs, Codes and Cryptography* 12 (2), pp. 131–160, 1997. See page 129.

[761] J. Li, C. Carlet, X. Zeng, C. Li, L. Hu, and J. Shan. Two constructions of balanced Boolean functions with optimal algebraic immunity, high nonlinearity and good behavior against fast algebraic attacks. *Designs, Codes and Cryptography* 76 (2), pp. 279–305, 2015. See page 340.

[762] K. Li, L. Qu, B. Sun, and C. Li. New results about the boomerang uniformity of permutation polynomials. *IEEE Transactions on Information Theory* 65 (11), pp. 7542–7553, 2019. Also: arXiv preprint arXiv:1901.10999, 2019 – arxiv.org. See page 142.

[763] N. Li, T. Helleseth, A. Kholosha, and X. Tang. On the Walsh transform of a class of functions from Niho exponents. *IEEE Transactions on Information Theory* 59 (7), pp. 4662–4667, 2013. See page 222.

[764] N. Li, T. Helleseth, X. Tang and A. Kholosha. Several new classes of bent functions from Dillon exponents. *IEEE Transactions on Information Theory* 59 (3), pp. 1818–1831, 2013. See pages 231 and 247.

[765] N. Li and W.-F. Qi. Symmetric Boolean functions depending on an odd number of variables with maximum algebraic immunity. *IEEE Transactions on Information Theory* 52 (5), pp. 2271–2273, 2006. See page 357.

[766] N. Li and W.-F. Qi. Construction and analysis of Boolean functions of $2t + 1$ variables with maximum algebraic immunity. *Proceedings of ASIACRYPT 2006, Lecture Notes in Computer Science* 4284, pp. 84–98, 2006. See page 336.

[767] N. Li, L. Qu, W.-F. Qi, G. Feng, C. Li, and D. Xie. On the construction of Boolean functions with optimal algebraic immunity. *IEEE Transactions on Information Theory* 54 (3), pp. 1330–1334, 2008. See page 336.

[768] N. Li, X. Tang and T. Helleseth. New Constructions of Quadratic Bent Functions in Polynomial Form. *IEEE Transactions on Information Theory* 60 (9), pp. 5760–5767, 2014. See page 206.

[769] N. Li and X. Zeng. A survey on the applications of Niho exponents. *Cryptography and Communications* 11 (3), pp. 1–40, 2018. See pages 169, 220, and 222.

[770] Y. Li. Characterization of robust immune symmetric boolean functions. *Cryptography and Communications* 7 (3), pp. 297–315, 2015. See page 91.

[771] Y. Li and M. Wang. The nonexistence of permutations EA-equivalent to certain AB functions. *IEEE Transactions on Information Theory* 59 (1), pp. 672–679, 2013. See pages 30 and 397.

[772] Y. Li and M. Wang. Constructing differentially 4-uniform permutations over $GF(2^{2m})$ from quadratic APN permutations over $GF(2^{2m+1})$. *Designs, Codes and Cryptography* 72 (2), pp. 249–264, 2014. See page 419.

[773] Y. Li, M. Wang, and Y. Yu. Constructing differentially 4-uniform permutations over $GF(2^{2k})$ from the inverse function revisited. *IACR Cryptology ePrint Archive* (http://eprint.iacr.org/) 2013/731, 2013. See page 421.

[774] Q. Liao, F. Liu, and K. Feng. On $(2^m + 1)$-variable symmetric Boolean functions with submaximum algebraic immunity 2^{m-1}. *Science China Mathematics* 52(1), pp. 17–28, 2009. See page 358.

[775] R. Lidl and H. Niederreiter. *Finite Fields*. Cambridge University Press, vol. 20, 1997 See pages 41, 112, 187, 248, 254, and 480.

[776] K. Limniotis and N. Kolokotronis. Boolean functions with maximum algebraic immunity: further extensions of the Carlet–Feng construction. *Designs, Codes and Cryptography* 86 (8), pp. 1685–1706, 2018. See page 341.

[777] K. Limniotis, N. Kolokotronis, and N. Kalouptsidis. Secondary constructions of Boolean functions with maximum algebraic immunity. *Cryptography and Communications* 5, pp. 179–199, 2013. See page 340.

[778] S. J. Lin, Y. S. Han and N. Yu. New Locally Correctable Codes Based on Projective Reed-Muller Codes. *IEEE Transactions on Information Theory* 67 (6), pp. 3834–3841, 2019. See page 151.

[779] N. Linial, Y. Mansour, and N. Nisan. Constant depth circuits, Fourier transform, and learnability. *Journal of the Association for Computing Machinery* 40 (3), pp. 607–620, 1993. See pages 59 and 62.

[780] J. H. van Lint. *Introduction to Coding Theory*. Springer, 1982. See page 4.

[781] P. Lisoněk. On the connection between Kloosterman sums and elliptic curves. *Proceedings of International Conference on Sequences and Their Applications SETA 2008, Lecture Notes in Computer Science* 5203, pp. 182–187, 2008. See page 215.

[782] P. Lisoněk. An efficient characterization of a family of hyperbent functions. *IEEE Transactions on Information Theory* 57 (9), pp. 6010–6014, 2011. See page 247.

[783] P. Lisoněk and M. Marko. On zeros of Kloosterman sums. *Designs, Codes and Cryptography* 59, pp. 223–230, 2011. See page 251.

[784] S. Litsyn and A. Shpunt. On the distribution of Boolean function nonlinearity. *SIAM Journal on Discrete Mathematics* 23 (1), pp. 79–95, 2008. See page 80.

[785] F. Liu and K. Feng. On the 2^m-variable symmetric Boolean functions with maximum algebraic immunity 2^{m-1}. *Proceedings of Workshop on Coding and Cryptography WCC 2007*, pp. 225–232, 2007. See page 358.

[786] F. Liu and K. Feng. Efficient computation of algebraic immunity of symmetric Boolean functions. *Proceedings of TAMC 2007, Lecture Notes in Computer Science* 4484, pp. 318–329, 2007. See page 358.

[787] J. Liu and S. Mesnager. Weightwise perfectly balanced functions with high weightwise nonlinearity profile. *Designs, Codes and Cryptography* 87 (8), pp. 1797–1813, 2019; see also CoRR abs/1709.02959 (2017). See page 458.

[788] J. Liu, S. Mesnager, and L. Chen. On the nonlinearity of S-boxes and linear codes. *Cryptography and Communications* 9 (3), pp. 345–361, 2017. See pages 122 and 161.

[789] M. Liu and D. Lin. Almost perfect algebraic immune functions with good nonlinearity. *Proceedings of IEEE International Symposium on Information Theory (ISIT) 2014*, pp. 1837–1841, 2014, and *IACR Cryptology ePrint Archive* (http://eprint.iacr.org/) 2012/498. See pages 322 and 340.

[790] M. Liu and D. Lin. Results on highly nonlinear Boolean functions with provably good immunity to fast algebraic attacks. *Information Sciences* 421, pp. 181–203, 2017. See page 340.

[791] M. Liu, D. Lin, and D. Pei. Fast algebraic attacks and decomposition of symmetric Boolean functions. *IEEE Transactions on Information Theory* 57, pp. 4817–4821, 2011. See also ArXiv: 0910.4632v1 [cs.CR] (http://arxiv.org/abs/0910.4632). See pages 94, 322, and 358.

[792] M. Liu, D. Lin, and D. Pei. Results on the immunity of Boolean functions against probabilistic algebraic attacks. *Proceedings of ACISP 2011, Lecture Notes in Computer Science* 6812, pp. 34–46, 2011. See page 331.

[793] M. Liu, Y. Zhang, and D. Lin. Perfect algebraic immune functions. *Proceedings of ASIACRYPT 2012, Lecture Notes in Computer Science* 7658, pp. 172–189, 2012. See pages 322, 331, and 338.

[794] M. Liu, Y. Zhang, and D. Lin. On the immunity of Boolean functions against fast algebraic attacks using bivariate polynomial representation. *IACR Cryptology ePrint Archive* (http://eprint.iacr.org/) 2012/498, 2012. See pages 334 and 340.

[795] Y. Liu, V. Rijmen, and G. Leander. Nonlinear diffusion layers. *Designs, Codes and Cryptography* 86 (11), pp. 2469–2484, 2018. See page 162.

[796] Z. Liu and B. Wu. Recent results on constructing Boolean functions with (potentially) optimal algebraic immunity based on decompositions of finite fields. *J. Systems Science & Complexity* 32 (1), pp. 356–374, 2019. See page 340.

[797] S. Lloyd. Properties of binary functions. *Proceedings of EUROCRYPT 1990, Lecture Notes in Computer Science* 473, pp. 124–139, 1991. See pages 58 and 320.

[798] M. Lobanov. Tight bound between nonlinearity and algebraic immunity. *IACR Cryptology ePrint Archive* (http://eprint.iacr.org/) 2005/441, 2005. See page 331.

[799] M. Lobanov. Exact relation between nonlinearity and algebraic immunity. *Discrete Mathematics and Applications* 16 (5), pp. 453–460, 2006. See page 331.

[800] M. Lobanov. Tight bounds between algebraic immunity and nonlinearities of high orders. *NATO Science for Peace and Security Series – D: Information and Communication Security*, IOS Press, vol 18: Boolean Functions in Cryptology and Information Security, pp. 296–306, 2008, and *IACR Cryptology ePrint Archive* (http://eprint.iacr.org/) 2007/444, 2007 and *Journal of Applied and Industrial Mathematics* 3 (3), pp. 367–376, 2009 (title: Exact relations between nonlinearity and algebraic immunity) and private communication. See pages 328, 329, and 331.

[801] M. Lobanov. A method for obtaining lower bounds on the higher order nonlinearity. *IACR Cryptology ePrint Archive* (http://eprint.iacr.org/) 2013/332, 2013. See pages 329 and 332.

[802] O. A. Logachev, A. A. Salnikov and V. V. Yashchenko. Bent functions on a finite Abelian group. *Discrete Mathematics and Applications* 7 (6), pp. 547–564, 1997. See pages 193 and 212.

[803] V. Lomné, E. Prouff, and T. Roche. Behind the scene of side channel attacks. *Proceedings of ASIACRYPT 2013, Lecture Notes in Computer Science* 8269, pp. 506–525, 2013. See page 427.

[804] Y. Lou, H. Han, C. Tang, Z. Wu, and M. Xu. Constructing vectorial Boolean functions with high algebraic immunity based on group decomposition. *International Journal of Computer Mathematics* 92 (3), pp. 451–462, 2015 (preliminary version by Y. Lou, H. Han, C. Tang, and M. Xu, *IACR Cryptology ePrint Archive* http://eprint.iacr.org/, 2012/335, 2012). See pages 168, 271, and 351.

[805] S. Lovett, R. Meshulam, and A. Samorodnitsky. Inverse conjecture for the Gowers norm is false. *Proceedings of ACM STOC 2008*, pp. 547–556, 2008. See page 474.

[806] G. Luo, X. Cao, and S. Mesnager. Several new classes of self-dual bent functions derived from involutions. *Special Issue on Boolean Functions and Their Applications 2018, Cryptography and Communications* 11 (6), pp. 1261–1273, 2019. See page 199.

[807] O. B. Lupanov. On circuits of functional elements with delay. *Probl. Kibern.* 23, pp. 43–81, 1970. See page 103.

[808] W. Ma, M. Lee, and F. Zhang. A new class of bent functions. *EICE Trans. Fundamentals* E88-A (7), pp. 2039–2040, 2005. See pages 230 and 250.

[809] F. J. MacWilliams and N. J. Sloane. *The Theory of Error-Correcting Codes*. North Holland, 1977. See pages 4, 7, 12, 13, 14, 15, 16, 44, 105, 107, 124, 128, 152, 153, 155, 156, 172, 173, 289, 333, 347, 353, 355, 359, 388, and 487.

[810] H. Maghrebi, C. Carlet, S. Guilley, and J.-L. Danger. Optimal first-order masking with linear and non-linear bijections. *Proceedings of AFRICACRYPT, Lecture Notes in Computer Science* 7374, pp. 60–377, 2012. See pages 431 and 432.

[811] M. Maghrebi, S. Guilley, and J.-L. Danger. Leakage squeezing countermeasure against high-order attacks. *Proceedings of WISTP, Lecture Notes in Computer Science* 6633, pp. 208–223, 2011. See page 431.

[812] J. A. Maiorana. A classification of the cosets of the Reed–Muller code $R(1, 6)$. *Mathematics of Computation* 57 (195), pp. 403–414, 1991. See pages 144 and 155.

[813] S. Maitra. Highly nonlinear balanced Boolean functions with very good autocorrelation property. *Proceedings of the Workshop on Coding and Cryptography 2001*, Electronic Notes in Discrete Mathematics, Elsevier, vol. 6, pp. 355–364, 2001. See page 99.

[814] S. Maitra. Autocorrelation properties of correlation immune Boolean functions. *Proceedings of INDOCRYPT 2001, Lecture Notes in Computer Science* 2247, pp. 242–253, 2001. See pages 288, 290, and 292.

[815] S. Maitra. Boolean functions on odd number of variables having nonlinearity greater than the bent concatenation bound. *NATO Science for Peace and Security Series – D: Information and Communication Security*, IOS Press, vol 18: Boolean Functions in Cryptology and Information Security, pp. 173–182, 2008. See pages 81 and 82.

[816] S. Maitra, S. Kavut, and M. Yücel. Balanced Boolean function on 13-variables having nonlinearity greater than the Bent concatenation bound. *Proceedings of the Conference BFCA 2008, Copenhagen*, pp. 109–118, 2008. See pages 81 and 82.

[817] S. Maitra and E. Pasalic. Further constructions of resilient Boolean functions with very high nonlinearity. *IEEE Transactions on Information Theory* 48 (7), pp. 1825–1834, 2002. See page 295.

[818] S. Maitra and P. Sarkar. Maximum nonlinearity of symmetric Boolean functions on odd number of variables. *IEEE Transactions on Information Theory* 48, pp. 2626–2630, 2002. See page 356.

[819] S. Maitra and P. Sarkar. Highly nonlinear resilient functions optimizing Siegenthaler's inequality. *Proceedings of CRYPTO 1999, Lecture Notes in Computer Science* 1666, pp. 198–215, 1999. See page 292.

[820] S. Maitra and P. Sarkar. Modifications of Patterson–Wiedemann functions for cryptographic applications. *IEEE Transactions on Information Theory* 48, pp. 278–284, 2002. See pages 81 and 320.

[821] S. Maity and S. Maitra. Minimum distance between bent and 1-resilient Boolean functions. *Proceedings of Fast Software Encryption FSE 2004, Lecture Notes in Computer Science* 3017, pp. 143–160, 2004. See page 297.

[822] B. Mandal, P. Stănică, S. Gangopadhyay, and E. Pasalic. An analysis of the C class of bent functions. *Fundamenta Informaticae* 146 (3), pp. 271–292, 2016. See page 211.

[823] S. Mangard, E. Oswald, and T. Popp. *Power Analysis Attacks: Revealing the Secrets of Smart Cards*. Springer, 2006. www.dpabook.org/. See page 425.

[824] H. B. Mann. *Addition Theorems*. Inderscience, 1965. See page 197.

[825] A. Maschietti. Difference sets and hyperovals. *Designs, Codes and Cryptography* 14 (1), pp. 89–98, 1998. See page 416.

[826] J. L. Massey. Shift-register analysis and BCH decoding. *IEEE Transactions on Information Theory* 15, pp. 122–127, 1969. See pages 21 and 76.

[827] J. L. Massey. Minimal codewords and secret sharing. *Proceedings of 6th Joint Swedish–Russian Workshop on Information Theory*, Mlle, Sweden, August 22–27, 1993 See pages 146, 148, and 432.

[828] J. L. Massey. Randomness, arrays, differences and duality. *IEEE Transactions on Information Theory* 48, pp. 1698–1703, 2002. See page 88.

[829] M. Matsui. Linear cryptanalysis method for DES cipher. *Proceedings of EUROCRYPT 1993, Lecture Notes in Computer Science* 765, pp. 386–397, 1994. See pages 79, 115, and 121.

[830] M. Matsui. Block encryption algorithm MISTY. *Proceedings of Fast Software Encryption FSE 1997, Lecture Notes in Computer Science* 1267, pp. 54–68, 1997. See pages 410 and 442.

[831] U. M. Maurer. New approaches to the design of self-synchronizing stream ciphers. *Proceedings of EUROCRYPT 1991, Lecture Notes in Computer Science* 547, pp. 458–471, 1991. See page 83.

[832] V. Mavroudis, K. Vishi, M. D. Zych, and A. Jøsang. The impact of quantum computing on present cryptography. *International Journal of Advanced Computer Science and Applications* 9 (3) (https://arxiv.org/pdf/1804.00200), 2018. See page 1.

[833] R. J. McEliece. Weight congruence for p-ary cyclic codes. *Discrete Mathematics*, 3, pp. 177–192, 1972. See pages 13 and 156.

[834] R. L. McFarland. A family of noncyclic difference sets. *Journal of Combinatorial Theory, Series A* 15, pp. 1–10, 1973. See pages 165 and 209.

[835] G. McGuire and A. R. Calderbank. Proof of a conjecture of Sarwate and Pursley regarding pairs of binary m-sequences. *IEEE Transactions on Information Theory* 41 (4), pp. 1153–1155, 1995. See page 275.

[836] J. McLaughlin and J. A. Clark. Evolving balanced Boolean functions with optimal resistance to algebraic and fast algebraic attacks, maximal algebraic degree, and very high nonlinearity. *IACR Cryptology ePrint Archive* (http://eprint.iacr.org/) 2013/011, 2013. See page 335.

[837] A. McLoughlin. The covering radius of the $(m - 3)$rd-order Reed–Muller codes and a lower bound on the $(m-4)$th-order Reed–Muller codes. *SIAM Journal on Applied Mathematics* 37, pp. 419–422, 1979. See page 158.

[838] P. Méaux, C. Carlet, A. Journault, and F.-X. Standaert. Improved filter permutators for efficient FHE: better instances and implementations. *Proceedings of Indocrypt 2019, Lecture Notes in Computer Science* 11898, pp. 68–91, 2019. See page 469.

[839] P. Méaux, A. Journault, F.-X. Standaert, and C. Carlet. Towards stream ciphers for efficient FHE with low-noise ciphertexts. *Proceedings of EUROCRYPT 2016, Lecture Notes in Computer Science* 9665, pp. 311–343, 2016. See pages 232, 321, 363, 453, 454, 455, and 456.

[840] W. Meidl, S. Roy and A. Topuzoğlu. Enumeration of quadratic functions with prescribed Walsh spectrum. *IEEE Transactions on Information Theory* 60, pp. 6669–6680, 2014. See page 178.

[841] W. Meidl and A. Topuzoğlu. Quadratic functions with prescribed spectra. *Designs, Codes and Cryptography* 66, pp. 257–273, 2013. See page 178.

[842] W. Meier, E. Pasalic, and C. Carlet. Algebraic attacks and decomposition of Boolean functions. *Proceedings of EUROCRYPT 2004, Lecture Notes in Computer Science* 3027, pp. 474–491, 2004. See pages 76, 90, and 91.

[843] W. Meier and O. Staffelbach. Fast correlation attacks on stream ciphers. *Proceedings of EURO-CRYPT 1988, Lecture Notes in Computer Science* 330, pp. 301–314, 1988. See pages 76, 78, 103, and 115.

[844] W. Meier and O. Staffelbach. Nonlinearity criteria for cryptographic functions. *Proceedings of EUROCRYPT 1989, Lecture Notes in Computer Science* 434, pp. 549–562, 1990. See pages 76, 101, and 103.

[845] W. Meier and O. Staffelbach. Correlation properties of combiners with memory in stream ciphers. *Proceedings of EUROCRYPT 1990, Lecture Notes in Computer Science* 473, pp. 204–213, 1990. See page 286.

[846] A. Menezes, P. van Oorschot, and S. Vanstone. *Handbook of Applied Cryptography*. CRC Press Series on Discrete Mathematics and Its Applications, 1996. See page 2.

[847] Q. Meng, L. Chen, and F.-W. Fu. On homogeneous rotation symmetric bent functions. *Discrete Applied Mathematics* 158 (10), pp. 111–1117, 2010. See page 248.

[848] Q. Meng, H. Zhang, M. Yang, and J. Cui. On the degree of homogeneous bent functions. *Discrete Applied Mathematics* 155 (5), pp. 665–669, 2007. See page 248.

[849] S. Mesnager. Improving the lower bound on the higher order nonlinearity of Boolean functions with prescribed algebraic immunity. *IEEE Transactions on Information Theory* 54 (8), pp. 3656–3662, 2008. Preliminary version available in *IACR Cryptology ePrint Archive* (http://eprint.iacr.org/) 2007/117, 2007. See page 331.

[850] S. Mesnager. On the number of resilient Boolean functions. *Proceedings of "The First Symposium on Algebraic Geometry and Its Applications" Dedicated to Gilles Lachaud (SAGA'07), Tahiti, 2007, Published by World Scientific, Series on Number Theory and Its Applications* 5, pp. 419–433, 2008. See page 312.

[851] S. Mesnager. A new family of hyper-bent Boolean functions in polynomial form. *Proceedings of IMA Conference on Cryptography and Coding 2009, Lecture Notes in Computer Science* 5921, pp. 402–417, 2009. See pages 231 and 246.

[852] S. Mesnager. Hyper-bent Boolean functions with multiple trace terms. *Proceedings of International Workshop on the Arithmetic of Finite Fields WAIFI 2010, Lecture Notes in Computer Science* 6087, pp. 97–113, 2010. See pages 231 and 247.

[853] S. Mesnager. A new class of bent and hyper-bent Boolean functions in polynomial forms. *Designs, Codes and Cryptography* 59 (1–3), pp. 265–279, 2011. See pages 231 and 246.

[854] S. Mesnager. Bent and hyper-bent functions in polynomial form and their link with some exponential sums and Dickson polynomials. *IEEE Transactions on Information Theory* 57 (9), pp. 5996–6009, 2011. See pages 189 and 272.

[855] S. Mesnager. Semi-bent functions from Dillon and Niho exponents, Kloosterman sums, and Dickson polynomials. *IEEE Transactions on Information Theory* 57, pp. 7443–7458, 2011. See page 263.

[856] S. Mesnager. Semi-bent functions with multiple trace terms and hyperelliptic curves. *Proceeding of International Conference on Cryptology and Information Security in Latin America (IACR), Latincrypt 2012, Lecture Notes in Computer Science 7533.* CpbfcCPM, pp. 18–36, 2012. See page 263.

[857] S. Mesnager. Semi-bent functions from oval polynomials. *Proceedings of IMA Conference on Cryptography and Coding 2013, Lecture Notes in Computer Science* 8308, pp. 1–15, 2013. See page 263.

[858] S. Mesnager. Characterizations of plateaued and bent functions in characteristic p. *Proceedings of International Conference on Sequences and Their Applications SETA 2014, Lecture Notes in Computer Science* 8865, pp. 72–82, 2014. See pages 258, 261, and 281.

[859] S. Mesnager. On semi-bent functions and related plateaued functions over the Galois field F_{2^n}. *Proceedings of the Conference Open Problems in Mathematical and Computational Sciences*, September 18–20, 2013, in Istanbul, Turkey, Springer, pp. 243–273, 2014. See pages 262 and 263.

[860] S. Mesnager. Several new infinite families of bent functions and their duals. *IEEE Transactions on Information Theory* 60 (7), pp. 4397–4407, 2014. See page 237.

[861] S. Mesnager. Bent functions from spreads. *Proceedings of the 11th International Conference on Finite Fields and Their Applications (Fq'11), Journal of the American Mathematical Society (AMS), Contemporary Mathematic* 632, pp. 295–316, 2015. See page 223.

[862] S. Mesnager. Bent vectorial functions and linear codes from o-polynomials. *Designs, Codes and Cryptography.* 77 (1), pp. 99–116, 2015. See pages 149, 161, and 271.

[863] S. Mesnager. A note on constructions of bent functions from involutions. *IACR Cryptology ePrint Archive* (http://eprint.iacr.org/) 2015/982, 2015. See page 237.

[864] S. Mesnager. Further constructions of infinite families of bent functions from new permutations and their duals. *Cryptography and Communications* 8 (2), pp. 229–246, 2016. See page 237.

[865] S. Mesnager. *Bent functions: Fundamentals and Results.* Springer, pp. 1–544, 2016. See pages 189 and 190.

[866] S. Mesnager. Linear codes with few weights from weakly regular bent functions based on a generic construction. *Cryptography and Communications* 9 (1), pp. 71–84, 2017 (preliminary version available in *IACR Cryptology ePrint Archive*, http://eprint.iacr.org/2015/1103). See page 189.

[867] S. Mesnager. Linear codes with few weights from weakly regular bent functions based on a generic construction. *Cryptography and Communications* 9 (1), pp. 71–84, 2017. See page 147.

[868] S. Mesnager and G. Cohen. On the link of some semi-bent functions with Kloosterman sums. *Proceedings of International Workshop on Coding and Cryptology, IWCC 2011, Lecture Notes in Computer Science 6639*, Springer, pp. 263–272, 2011. See page 263.

[869] S. Mesnager and G. Cohen. Cyclic codes and algebraic immunity of Boolean functions. *Proceedings of ITW 2015*, pp. 1–5, 2015. See page 327.

[870] S. Mesnager and G. Cohen. Fast algebraic immunity of Boolean functions. *Advances in Mathematics of Communications* 11 (2), pp. 373–377, 2017. See pages 94 and 323.

[871] S. Mesnager and J. P. Flori. Hyper-bent functions via Dillon-like exponents. *IEEE Transactions on Information Theory* 59 (5), pp. 3215–3232, 2013. See pages 231, 247, and 362.

[872] S. Mesnager, G. McGrew, J. Davis, D. Steele, and K. Marsten. A comparison of Carlet's second-order nonlinearity bounds. *International Journal of Computer Mathematics* 94 (3), pp. 427–436, 2017. See page 86.

[873] S. Mesnager, P. Ongan, and F. Özbudak. New bent functions from permutations and linear translators. *Proceedings of C2SI 2017, Lecture Notes in Computer Science* 10194, pp. 282–297, 2017. See page 237.

[874] S. Mesnager, F. Özbudak, and A. Sınak. Linear codes from weakly regular plateaued functions and their secret sharing schemes. *Designs, Codes and Cryptography* 87 (2–3), pp. 463–480, 2019. See pages 147 and 262.

[875] S. Mesnager, C. Tang, and M. Xiong. On the boomerang uniformity of quadratic permutations over $\mathbb{F}_{2^n}$. *IACR Cryptology ePrint Archive* (http://eprint.iacr.org/2019/277 and arXiv preprint arXiv:1903.00501, 2019 – arxiv.org). See page 142.

[876] S. Mesnager and F. Zhang. On constructions of bent, semi-bent and five valued spectrum functions from old bent functions. *Advances in Mathematics of Communications* 11 (2), pp. 339–345, 2017. See pages 233 and 263.

[877] S. Mesnager, F. Zhang, C. Tang, and Y. Zhou. Further study on the maximum number of bent components of vectorial functions. *Designs, Codes and Cryptography* 87 (11), pp. 2597–2610, 2019. Also: arXiv:1801.06542. See page 243.

[878] S. Mesnager, Z. Zhou, and C. Ding. On the nonlinearity of Boolean functions with restricted input. *Cryptography and Communications* 11 (1), pp. 63–76, 2019. See page 460.

[879] T.S. Messerges. Using Second-order Power Analysis to Attack DPA Resistant software. *Proceedings of International Workshop Cryptographic Hardware and Embedded Systems CHES 2000, Lecture Notes in Computer Science* 1965, pp. 238–251, 2000. See page 427.

[880] S. Micali and L. Reyzin. Physically observable cryptography (extended abstract). *Proceedings of TCC, Lecture Notes in Computer Science* 2951, pp. 278–296, 2004. See page 429.

[881] M. J. Mihaljevic, S. Gangopadhyay, G. Paul, and H. Imai. Generic cryptographic weakness of k-normal boolean functions in certain stream ciphers and cryptanalysis of grain-128. *Periodica Mathematica Hungarica* 65 (2), pp. 205–227, 2012. See page 105.

[882] W. Millan. Low order approximation of cipher functions. *Proceedings of Cryptographic Policy and Algorithms, Lecture Notes in Computer Science* 1029, pp. 144–155, 1996. See page 83.

[883] W. Millan, L. Burnett, G. Carter, A. Clark, and E. Dawson. Evolutionary heuristics for finding cryptographically strong S-boxes. *Proceedings of Information and Communication Security, Lecture Notes in Computer Science* 1726, pp. 263–274, 1999. See page 145.

[884] W. Millan, A. Clark and E. Dawson. An effective genetic algorithm for finding highly nonlinear boolean functions. *Proceedings of ICICS 1997, Lecture Notes in Computer Science* 1334, pp. 149–158, 1997. See page 144.

[885] W. Millan, A. Clark, and E. Dawson. Heuristic design of cryptographically strong balanced Boolean functions. *Proceedings of EUROCRYPT 1998, Lecture Notes in Computer Science* 1403, pp. 489–499, 1998.

[886] M. Minsky and S. A. Papert. *Perceptrons: An Introduction to Computational Geometry.* Reissue of the 1988 Expanded Edition. MIT Press, 2017. See page 47.

[887] C. J. Mitchell. Enumerating Boolean functions of cryptographic signifiance. *Journal of Cryptology* 2 (3), pp. 155–170, 1990. See pages 356 and 357.

[888] A. Moradi, A. Poschmann, S. Ling, C. Paar, and H. Wang. Pushing the limits: a very compact and a threshold implementation of AES. *Proceedings of EUROCRYPT 2011, Lecture Notes in Computer Science* 6632, pp. 69–88, 2011.

[889] E. Mossel, A. Shpilka, and L. Trevisan. On e-biased generators in NC0. *Proceedings of 44th FOCS*, pp. 136–145. IEEE Computer Society Press, 2003. See page 468.

[890] G. Mullen and D. Panario. *Handbook of Finite Fields.* CRC Press Book, 2013. See pages 20, 41, 76, 248, 254, 389, 480, and 488.

[891] D. E. Muller. Application of boolean algebra to switching circuit design and to error detection. *Trans. I.R.E. Prof. Group on Electronic Computers*, 3 (3), pp. 6–12, 1954. See page 151.

[892] A. Muratović-Ribić, E. Pasalic, and S. Bajrić. Vectorial bent functions from multiple terms trace Functions. *IEEE Transactions on Information Theory* 60 (2), pp. 1337–1347, 2014. See page 272.

[893] A. Muratović-Ribić, E. Pasalic, and S. Bajrić. Vectorial hyperbent trace functions from the PS_{ap} Class – Their Exact Number and Specification. *IEEE Transactions on Information Theory* 60 (7), pp. 4408–4413, 2014. See page 272.

[894] J. Mykkelveit. The covering radius of the [128,8] Reed–Muller code is 56. *IEEE Transactions on Information Theory* 26 (3), pp. 359–362, 1980. See pages 81 and 157.

[895] N. Nakagawa. On equations of finite fields of characteristic 2 and APN functions. *AKCE International Journal of Graphs and Combinatorics* 12, pp. 75–93, 2015. See page 383.

[896] N. Nakagawa and S. Yoshiara. A construction of differentially 4-uniform functions from commutative semifields of characteristic 2. *Proceedings of International Workshop on the Arithmetic of Finite Fields WAIFI 2007, Lecture Notes in Computer Science* 4547, pp. 134–146, 2007. See pages 394 and 422.

[897] M. Nassar, S. Guilley, and J.-L. Danger. Formal analysis of the entropy/security trade-off in first-order masking countermeasures against side-channel attacks. *Proceedings of INDOCRYPT 2011, Lecture Notes in Computer Science* 7107, pp. 22–39, 2011. See page 429.

[898] M. Nassar, Y. Souissi, S. Guilley, and J.-L. Danger. RSM: a small and fast countermeasure for AES, secure against 1st and 2nd-order zero-offset SCAs. *Proceedings of 2012 Design, Automation & Test in Europe Conference & Exhibition (DATE 2012)* IEEE 2012, pp. 1173–1178, 2012. See page 432.

[899] Y. Nawaz, G. Gong, and K. Gupta. Upper bounds on algebraic immunity of power functions. *Proceedings of Fast Software Encryption FSE 2006, Lecture Notes in Computer Science* 4047, pp. 375–389, 2006. See page 323.

[900] Y. Nawaz, K. Gupta, and G. Gong. Algebraic immunity of S-boxes based on power mappings: analysis and construction. *IEEE Transactions on Information Theory* 55 (9), pp. 4263–4273, 2009 (preliminary version available in *IACR Cryptology ePrint Archive* http://eprint.iacr.org/2006/322). See page 323.

[901] NESSIE Project. www.cosic.esat.kuleuven.be/nessie/. See pages 3 and 23.

[902] Y. Niho. Multi-valued cross-correlation functions between two maximal linear recursive sequences. PhD dissertation, University of Southern California, Los Angeles, 1972. See page 169.

[903] S. Nikova, C. Rechberger, and V. Rijmen. Threshold implementations against side-channel attacks and glitches. *Proceedings of ICICS 2006, Lecture Notes in Computer Science* 4307, pp. 529–545, 2006. See pages 437, 440, and 441.

[904] S. Nikova, V. Rijmen, and M. Schläffer. Secure hardware implementation of nonlinear functions in the presence of glitches. *Journal of Cryptology* 24 (2), pp. 292–321, 2011. See pages 437 and 440.

[905] N. Nisan and M. Szegedy. On the degree of Boolean functions as real polynomials. *Comput. Complexity* 4, pp. 301–313, 1994. See pages 47, 48, 62, 67, 68, and 320.

[906] K. Nyberg. Perfect non-linear S-boxes. *Proceedings of EUROCRYPT 1991, Lecture Notes in Computer Science* 547, pp. 378–386, 1992. See pages 135, 190, 269, 270, and 314.

[907] K. Nyberg. On the construction of highly nonlinear permutations. *Proceedings of EUROCRYPT 1992, Lecture Notes in Computer Science* 658, pp. 92–98, 1993. See pages 28, 117, 135, 177, and 316.

[908] K. Nyberg. Differentially uniform mappings for cryptography. *Proceedings of EUROCRYPT 1993, Lecture Notes in Computer Science* 765, pp. 55–64, 1994. See pages 135, 137, 394, 395, 400, 401, and 417.

[909] K. Nyberg. New bent mappings suitable for fast implementation. *Proceedings of Fast Software Encryption FSE 1993, Lecture Notes in Computer Science* 809, pp. 179–184, 1994. See page 270.

[910] K. Nyberg. S-boxes and round functions with controllable linearity and differential uniformity. *Proceedings of Fast Software Encryption FSE 1994, Lecture Notes in Computer Science* 1008, pp. 111–130, 1995. See pages 136, 372, 391, and 411.

[911] K. Nyberg. Multidimensional Walsh transform and a characterization of bent functions. *Proceedings of the IEEE Information Theory Workshop ITW 2007*, pp. 1–4, 2007. See page 74.

[912] K. Nyberg and L. R. Knudsen. Provable security against differential cryptanalysis. *Journal of Cryptology* 8 (1), pp. 27–37, 1995, (extended version of the *Proceedings of CRYPTO' 92, Lecture Notes in Computer Science* 740, pp. 566–574, 1993). See pages 135 and 137.

[913] L. O'Connor. On the distribution of characteristics in bijective mappings. *Proceedings of EUROCRYPT 1993, Lecture Notes in Computer Science* 765, pp. 360–370, 1993. See page 136.

[914] R. O'Donnell. *Analysis of Boolean Functions.* Cambridge University Press, 2014. See pages 37, 59, 68, 102, and 358.

[915] R. O'Donnell and D. Witmer. Goldreich's PRG: evidence for near-optimal polynomial stretch. *IEEE Conference on Computational Complexity 2014*, pp. 1–12, 2014. See page 468.

[916] W. Ogata and K. Kurosawa. Optimum secret sharing scheme secure against cheating. *Proceedings of EUROCRYPT 1996, Lecture Notes in Computer Science* 1070, pp. 200–211, 1996. See page 452.

[917] D. Olejár and M. Stanek. On cryptographic properties of random Boolean functions. *Journal of Universal Computer Science* 4 (8), pp. 705–717, 1998. See page 80.

[918] O. Olmez. Plateaued functions and one-and-half difference sets. *Designs, Codes and Cryptography* 76 (3), pp. 537–549, 2015. See page 259.

[919] J. D. Olsen, R. A. Scholtz, and L. R. Welch. Bent-function sequences. *IEEE Transactions on Information Theory* 28 (6), pp. 858–864, 1982. See page 189.

[920] E. Oswald, S. Mangard, C. Herbst, and S. Tillich. Practical second-order DPA attacks for masked smart card implementations of block ciphers. *Proceedings of CT-RSA 2006, Lecture Notes in Computer Science* 3860, pp. 192–207, 2006. See page 427.

[921] D. Panario, A. Sakzad, B. Stevens, D. Thomson, and Qiang Wang. Ambiguity and deficiency of permutations over finite fields with linearized difference map. *IEEE Transactions on Information Theory* 59 (9), pp. 5616–5626, 2013. See page 139.

[922] D. Panario, A. Sakzad, B. Stevens, and Q. Wang. Two new measures for permutations: ambiguity and deficiency. *IEEE Transactions on Information Theory* 57 (11), pp. 7648–7657, 2011. See page 139.

[923] D. Panario, A. Sakzad, and D. Thomson. Ambiguity and deficiency of reversed Dickson permutations. *Proceedings of Fq13, Contemporary Mathematics: Topics in Finite Fields* 632, pp. 347–358, 2013. See page 139.

[924] D. Panario, D. Santana, and Q. Wang. Ambiguity, deficiency and differential spectrum of normalized permutation polynomials over finite fields. *Finite Fields and Their Applications* 47, pp. 330–350, 2017. See page 139.

[925] D. Panario, B. Stevens, and Q. Wang. Ambiguity and deficiency in Costas arrays and APN permutations. *Proceedings of LATIN 2010, Lecture Notes in Computer Science* 6034, pp. 397–406, 2010. See page 139.

[926] S. M. Park, S. Lee, S. H. Sung, and K. Kim. Improving bounds for the number of correlation-immune Boolean functions. *Information Processing Letters* 61, pp. 209–212, 1997. See page 312.

[927] M. G. Parker and A. Pott. On Boolean functions which are bent and negabent. *Sequences, Subsequences, and Consequences, Lecture Notes in Computer Science* 4893, pp. 9–23, 2007. See pages 266 and 267.

[928] E. Pasalic. Maiorana–McFarland class: degree optimization and algebraic properties. *IEEE Transactions on Information Theory* 52 (10), pp. 4581–4594, 2006. See page 295.

[929] E. Pasalic. Almost fully optimized infinite classes of Boolean functions resistant to (fast) algebraic cryptanalysis. *Proceedings of ICISC 2008, Lecture Notes in Computer Science* 5461, pp. 399–414, 2008. See pages 322 and 336.

[930] E. Pasalic. A note on nonexistence of vectorial bent functions with binomial trace representation in the PS- class. *Information Processing Letters* 115 (2), pp. 139–140, 2015. See page 272.

[931] E. Pasalic. Corrigendum to "a note on nonexistence of vectorial bent functions with binomial trace representation in the PS- class" [*Information Processing Letters* 115 (2) (2015) 139–140]. *Information Processing Letters* 115 (4): 520, 2015. See page 272.

[932] E. Pasalic, S. Hodžić, F. Zhang, and Y. Wei. Bent functions from nonlinear permutations and conversely. *Cryptography and Communications* 11 (2), pp. 207–225, 2019. See page 236.

[933] E. Pasalic and S. Maitra. Linear codes in generalized construction of resilient functions with very high nonlinearity. *IEEE Transactions on Information Theory* 48, pp. 2182–2191, 2002, completed version of a paper published in the *Proceedings of Selected Areas in Cryptography, SAC 2001, Lecture Notes in Computer Science* 2259, pp. 60–74, 2002. See pages 315 and 316.

[934] E. Pasalic, S. Maitra, T. Johansson, and P. Sarkar. New constructions of resilient and correlation immune Boolean functions achieving upper bound on nonlinearity. *Proceedings of the Workshop on Coding and Cryptography* 2001, published by *Electronic Notes in Discrete Mathematics*, Elsevier, vol. 6, pp. 425–434, 2001. See pages 291, 295, and 300.

[935] E. Pasalic and W.-G. Zhang. On multiple output bent functions. *Information Processing Letters* 112 (21), pp. 811–815, 2012. See page 272.

[936] N. J. Patterson and D. H. Wiedemann. The covering radius of the $[2^{15}, 16]$ Reed–Muller code is at least 16276. *IEEE Transactions on Information Theory* 29, pp. 354–356, 1983. See pages 81, 157, and 543.

[937] N. J. Patterson and D. H. Wiedemann. Correction to [936]. *IEEE Transactions on Information Theory* 36 (2), pp. 443, 1990. See pages 81 and 157.

[938] J. Peng and C. H. Tan. New explicit constructions of differentially 4-uniform permutations via special partitions of $\mathbb{F}_{2^{2k}}$. *Finite Fields and Their Applications* 40, pp. 73–89, 2016. See page 420.

[939] J. Peng and C. H. Tan. New differentially 4-uniform permutations by modifying the inverse function on subfields. *Cryptography and Communications* 9 (3), pp. 363–378, 2017. See pages 420 and 421.

[940] J. Peng, C. H. Tan, and Q. Wang. A new family of differentially 4-uniform permutations over $\mathbb{F}_{2^k}$ for odd k. *Science China Mathematics* 59 (6), pp. 1221–1234, 2016. See pages 420 and 421.

[941] J. Peng, Q. Wu, and H. Kan. On symmetric Boolean functions with high algebraic immunity on even number of variables. *IEEE Transactions on Information Theory* 57 (10), pp. 7205–7220, 2011. See page 358.

[942] T. Penttila (Joint work with L. Budaghyan, C. Carlet, T. Helleseth, and A. Kholosha). Projective equivalence of ovals and EA-equivalence of Niho bent functions. Invited talk at the Finite Geometries Fourth Irsee Conference (2014). See pages 220 and 221.

[943] L. Perrin, A. Canteaut, and S. Tian. If a generalised butterfly is APN then it operates on 6 bits. *Special Issue on Boolean Functions and Their Applications 2018, Cryptography and Communications* 11 (6), pp. 1147–1164, 2019. See page 411.

[944] L. Perrin, A. Udovenko, and A. Biryukov. Cryptanalysis of a theorem: decomposing the only known solution to the big APN problem. *Proceedings of CRYPTO 2016, Lecture Notes in Computer Science* 9815, part II, pp. 93–122, 2016. See pages 411 and 421.

[945] S. Picek, C. Carlet, S. Guilley, J. F. Miller, and D. Jakobovic. Evolutionary algorithms for Boolean functions in diverse domains of cryptography. *Evolutionary Computation* 24 (4), pp. 667–694, 2016. See page 144.

[946] S. Picek, S. Guilley, C. Carlet, D. Jakobovic, and J. F. Miller. Evolutionary approach for finding correlation immune Boolean functions of order t with minimal hamming weight. *Proceedings of TPNC 2015, Lecture Notes in Computer Science* 9477, pp. 71–82, 2015. See pages 144 and 305.

[947] S. Picek and D. Jakobovic. Evolving algebraic constructions for designing bent Boolean functions. *Proceedings of the Genetic and Evolutionary Computation Conference GECCO 2016*, pp. 781–788, 2016. See page 144.

[948] S. Picek, K. Knezevic, and D. Jakobovic. On the evolution of bent (n, m) functions. *Proceedings of CEC 2017*, pp. 2137–2144, 2017. See page 145.

[949] S. Picek, K. Knezevic, D. Jakobovic, and C. Carlet. A search for differentially-6 uniform $(n, n-2)$ functions. *Proceedings of IEEE CEC 2018*. See pages 145 and 424.

[950] S. Picek, L. Mariot, B. Yang, D. Jakobovic, and N. Mentens. Design of S-boxes defined with cellular automata rules. *Proceedings of the Computing Frontiers Conference, CF'17*, pp. 409–414, 2017. See page 145.

[951] S. Picek, R. I. McKay, R. Santana, and T. Gedeon. Fighting the symmetries: the structure of cryptographic Boolean function spaces. *Proceedings of the Conference on Genetic and Evolutionary Computation GECCO 2015*, pp. 457–464, 2015. See page 144.

[952] S. Picek, D. Sisejkovic, and D. Jakobovic. Immunological algorithms paradigm for construction of Boolean functions with good cryptographic properties. *Engineering Applications of Artificial Intelligence* 62, pp. 320–330, 2017. See page 144.

[953] S. Picek, B. Yang, V. Rozic, and N. Mentens. On the construction of hardware-friendly 4×4 and 5×5 S-boxes. *Proceedings of Selected Areas in Cryptography – SAC 2016, Lecture Notes in Computer Science* 10532, pp. 161–179, 2016. See page 145.

[954] J. Pieprzyk and C. Qu. Fast hashing and rotation symmetric functions, *Journal of Unversal Computer Science* 5, pp. 20–31, 1999. See page 248.

[955] J. Pieprzyk and X.-M. Zhang. Computing Möbius transforms of Boolean functions and characterizing coincident Boolean functions. *Proceedings of the Conference BFCA 2007*, Publications des universités de Rouen et du Havre, 2007. See page 37.

[956] G. Pirsic and A. Winterhof. Boolean functions derived from pseudorandom binary sequences. *Proceedings of International Conference on Sequences and Their Applications SETA 2012, Lecture Notes in Computer Science* 7280, pp. 101–109, 2012. See page 104.

[957] G. Piret, T. Roche, and C. Carlet. PICARO – a block cipher allowing efficient higher-order side-channel resistance. *Proceedings of ACNS 2012, Lecture Notes in Computer Science* 7341, pp. 311–328, 2012. See pages 26, 112, 142, 189, and 422.

[958] V. Pless. Power moment identities on weight distributions in error-correcting codes. *Information and Control* 6, pp. 147–152, 1963. See page 381.

[959] V. S. Pless, W. C. Huffman, eds., R. A. Brualdi, assistant editor. *Handbook of Coding Theory*. Elsevier, 1998. See pages 20, 21, and 156.

[960] R. Poussier, Q. Guo, F.-X. Standaert, C. Carlet, and S. Guilley. Connecting and improving direct sum masking and inner product masking. *Proceedings of CARDIS 2017, Lecture Notes in Computer Science* 10728, pp. 123–141, 2017. See pages 445 and 446.

[961] A. Pott, E. Pasalic, A. Muratović-Ribić, and S. Bajrić. Vectorial quadratic bent functions as a product of two linearized polynomials. *Proceedings of Workshop on Coding and Cryptography WCC*, 2015. See page 272.

[962] A. Pott, E. Pasalic, A. Muratović-Ribić, and S. Bajrić. On the maximum number of bent components of vectorial functions. *IEEE Transactions on Information Theory* 64 (1), pp. 403–411, 2018. See page 243.

[963] A. Pott, K.-U. Schmidt, and Y. Zhou. Semifields, relative difference sets, and bent functions. *Proceedings of the Workshop "Emerging Applications of Finite Fields", Algebraic Curves and Finite Fields*, Radon Series on Computational and Applied Mathematics, de Gruyter, pp. 161–177, 2014. See pages 217 and 269.

[964] A. Pott, Y. Tan, T. Feng, and S. Ling. Association schemes arising from bent functions. *Designs, Codes and Cryptography* 59 (1–3), pp. 319–331, 2011. See page 163.

[965] A. Pott, Q. Wang, and Y. Zhou. Sequences and functions derived from projective planes and their difference sets. *Proceedings of International Workshop on the Arithmetic of Finite Fields WAIFI 2012, Lecture Notes in Computer Science* 7369, pp. 64–80, 2012. See page 197.

[966] A. Pott and Y. Zhou. CCZ and EA equivalence between mappings over finite Abelian groups. *Designs, Codes and Cryptography* 66 (1–3), pp. 99–109, 2013. See page 29.

[967] T. F. Prabowo and C. H. Tan. Implicit quadratic property of differentially 4-uniform permutations. *Proceedings of INDOCRYPT 2016, Lecture Notes in Computer Science* 10095, pp 364–379, 2016. See page 421.

[968] B. Preneel. *Analysis and Design of Cryptographic Hash Functions*, PhD thesis, Katholieke Universiteit Leuven, K. Mercierlaan 94, 3001 Leuven, Belgium, U.D.C. 621.391.7, 1993. See pages 97, 109, 208, 243, and 319.

[969] B. Preneel, R. Govaerts, and J. Vandevalle. Boolean functions satisfying higher order propagation criteria. *Proceedings of EUROCRYPT 1991, Lecture Notes in Computer Sciences* 547, pp. 141–152, 1991. See pages 97 and 256.

[970] B. Preneel, W. Van Leekwijck, L. Van Linden, R. Govaerts, and J. Vandevalle. Propagation characteristics of Boolean functions. *Proceedings of EUROCRYPT 1990, Lecture Notes in Computer Sciences* 473, pp. 161–173, 1991. See pages 76, 97, and 320.

[971] E. Prouff. DPA attacks and S-boxes. *Proceedings of Fast Software Encryption FSE 2005, Lecture Notes in Computer Science* 3557, pp. 424–442, 2005.

[972] E. Prouff and M. Rivain. A generic method for secure Sbox implementation. *Proceedings of WISA 2007, Lecture Notes in Computer Science* 4867, pp. 227–244, 2007. See page 429.

[973] E. Prouff and M. Rivain. Masking against side-channel attacks: a formal security proof. *Proceedings of EUROCRYPT 2013, Lecture Notes in Computer Science* 7881, pp. 142–159, 2013. See page 429.

[974] E. Prouff and T. Roche. Higher-order glitches free Implementation of the AES using secure multi-party computation protocols. *Proceedings of International Workshop Cryptographic Hardware and Embedded Systems CHES 2011, Lecture Notes in Computer Science* 6917, pp. 63–78, 2011. Extended version (T. Roche and E. Prouff): *Journal of Cryptographic Engineering JCEN* 2 (2), pp. 111–127, 2012. See pages 428, 431, 436, and 447.

[975] C. Qu, J. Seberry, and J. Pieprzyk. Homogeneous bent functions. *Discrete Applied Mathematics* 102 (1–2), pp. 133–139, 2000. See page 248.

[976] L. Qu, K. Feng, L. Feng, and L. Wang. Constructing symmetric Boolean functions with maximum algebraic immunity. *IEEE Transactions on Information Theory* 55, pp. 2406–2412, 2009. See page 358.

[977] L. Qu, S. Fu, Q. Dai, and C. Li. When a Boolean function can be expressed as the sum of two bent functions. *IACR Cryptology ePrint Archive* (http://eprint.iacr.org/) 2014/48, 2014. See page 242.

[978] L. Qu and C. Li. Weight support technique and the symmetric Boolean functions with maximum algebraic immunity on even number of variables. *Proceedings of INSCRYPT 2007, Lecture Note in Computer Science* 4990, pp. 271–282. See page 358.

[979] L. Qu, C. Li, and K. Feng. A note on symmetric Boolean functions with maximum algebraic immunity in odd number of variables. *IEEE Transactions on Information Theory* 53, pp. 2908–2910, 2007. See pages 357 and 358.

[980] L. Qu, Y. Tan, and C. Li. On the Walsh spectrum of a family of quadratic APN functions with five terms. *Science China Information Sciences* 57 (2), pp. 1–7, 2014. See page 409.

[981] L. Qu, Y. Tan, C. Li, and G. Gong. More constructions of differentially 4-uniform permutations on $\mathbb{F}_{2^{2k}}$. *Designs, Codes and Cryptography* 78 (2), pp. 391–408, 2016. See page 420.

[982] L. Qu, Y. Tan, C. H. Tan, and C. Li. Constructing differentially 4-uniform permutations over $\mathbb{F}_{2^{2k}}$ via the switching method. *IEEE Transactions on Information Theory* 59 (7), pp. 4675–4686, 2013. See page 420.

[983] L. Qu, H. Xiong, and C. Li. A negative answer to Bracken–Tan–Tan's problem on differentially 4-uniform permutations over $\mathbb{F}_{2^n}$. *Finite Fields and Their Applications* 24, pp. 55–65, 2013. See page 418.

[984] J.-J. Quisquater and D. Samyde. ElectroMagnetic Analysis (EMA): measures and countermeasures for smart cards. *Proceedings of E-smart 2001, Lecture Notes in Computer Science* 2140, pp. 200–210, 2001. See page 425.

[985] M. Quisquater. Applications of character theory and the Möbius inversion principle to the study of cryptographic properties of Boolean functions. PhD thesis, Katholieke Universiteit Leuven, 2004. See page 69.

[986] M. Quisquater, B. Preneel, and J. Vandewalle. A new inequality in discrete Fourier–Hadamard theory. *IEEE Transactions on Information Theory* 49, pp. 2038–2040, 2003. See page 256.

[987] M. Quisquater, B. Preneel, and J. Vandewalle. Spectral characterization of cryptographic Boolean functions satisfying the (extended) propagation criterion of degree 1 and order k. *Information Processing Letters* 93 (1), pp. 25–28, 2005. See page 320.

[988] C. R. Rao. Factorial experiments derivable from combinatorial arrangements of arrays. *J. Royal Statist. Soc.* 9, pp. 128–139, 1947. See pages 86, 87, and 129.

[989] I. S. Reed. A class of multiple-error-correcting codes and the decoding scheme. *Transactions of the IRE Professional Group on Information Theory* 4 (4), pp. 38–49, 1954. See page 151.

[990] M. Renauld, F.-X. Standaert, and N. Veyrat-Charvillon. Algebraic side-channel attacks on the AES: why time also matters in DPA. *Proceedings of International Workshop Cryptographic Hardware and Embedded Systems CHES 2009, Lecture Notes in Computer Science* 5747, pp. 97–111, 2009. See page 436.

[991] S. Renner. Protection des algorithmes cryptographiques embarqués. Thesis, Bordeaux. (https://tel.archives-ouvertes.fr/tel-01149061/document). See page 147.

[992] O. Reparaz, B. Bilgin, S. Nikova, B. Gierlichs, and I. Verbauwhede. Consolidating Masking Schemes. *Proceedings of CRYPTO (1) 2015, Lecture Notes in Computer Science* 9215, pp. 764–783, 2015. See page 437.

[993] C. Riera and M. G. Parker. Generalised bent criteria for Boolean functions. *IEEE Transactions on Information Theory* 52 (9), pp. 4142–4159, 2006. See pages 191 and 266.

[994] V. Rijmen, P. S. L. M. Barreto, and D. L. G. Filho. Rotation symmetry in algebraically generated cryptographic substitution tables. *Information Processing Letters* 106 (6), pp. 246–250, 2008. See page 362.

[995] V. Rijmen, B. Preneel, and E. De Win. On weaknesses of non-surjective round functions. *Designs, Codes and Cryptography* 12 (3), pp. 253–266, 1997. See page 142.

[996] M. Rivain and E. Prouff. Provably secure higher-order masking of aes. *Proceedings of International Workshop Cryptographic Hardware and Embedded Systems CHES 2010, Lecture Notes in Computer Science* 6225, pp. 413–427, 2010. See page 430.

[997] P. Rizomiliotis. On the resistance of Boolean functions against algebraic attacks using univariate polynomial representation. *IEEE Transactions on Information Theory* 56, pp. 4014–4024, 2010. See pages 334, 339, and 340.

[998] P. Rizomiliotis. Improving the higher order nonlinearity lower bound for Boolean functions with given algebraic immunity. *Discrete Applied Mathematics* 158 (18), pp. 2049–2055, 2010. See page 331.

[999] P. Rizomiliotis. On the security of the Feng–Liao–Yang Boolean functions with optimal algebraic immunity against fast algebraic attacks. *Designs, Codes and Cryptography* 57 (3), pp. 283–292, 2010. See page 334.

[1000] F. Rodier. Asymptotic nonlinearity of Boolean functions. *Designs, Codes and Cryptography* 40 (1), pp 59–70, 2006 (preliminary version: *Proceedings of WCC 2003, Workshop on Coding and Cryptography*, pp. 397–405, 2003). See pages 80, 84, and 334.

[1001] S. Rønjom. Improving algebraic attacks on stream ciphers based on linear feedback shift register over $\mathbb{F}_{2^k}$. *Designs, Codes and Cryptography* 82, pp. 27–41, 2017. See pages 95 and 96.

[1002] S. Rønjom, G. Gong, and T. Helleseth. On attacks on filtering generators using linear subspace structures. *Proceedings of Sequences, Subsequences, and Consequences, Lecture Notes in Computer Science* 4893, pp. 204–217, 2007. See page 95.

[1003] S. Rønjom and T. Helleseth. A new attack on the filter generator. *IEEE Transactions on Information Theory* 53 (5), pp. 1752–1758, 2007. See pages 95 and 284.

[1004] S. Rønjom and T. Helleseth. Attacking the filter generator over $GF(2^m)$. *Proceedings of International Workshop on the Arithmetic of Finite Fields WAIFI 2007, Lecture Notes in Computer Science* 4547, pp. 264–275, June 2007. See page 95.

[1005] O. S. Rothaus. On "bent" functions. *Journal of Combinatorial Theory, Series A* 20, pp. 300–305, 1976. See pages 144, 190, 197, 200, 208, and 232.

[1006] R. A. Rueppel. *Analysis and Design of Stream Ciphers*. Com. and Contr. Eng. Series. Springer, 1986. See pages 21 and 77.

[1007] R. A. Rueppel and O. J. Staffelbach. Products of linear recurring sequences with maximum complexity. *IEEE Transactions on Information Theory* 33 (1), pp. 124–131, 1987. See page 77.

[1008] B.V. Ryazanov. On the distribution of the spectral complexity of Boolean functions. *Discrete Mathematics and Applications* 4 (3), pp. 279–288, 1994. See pages 109 and 110.

[1009] M.-J. O. Saarinen. Cryptographic analysis of all 4×4-bit S-boxes. *Proceedings of SAC 2011, Lecture Notes in Computer Science* 7118, pp. 118–133, 2011. See page 144.

[1010] A. Samorodnitsky. Low-degree tests at large distances. *Proceedings of ACM STOC 2007*, pp. 506–515 (https://arxiv.org/pdf/math/0604353.pdf), 2007. See page 474.

[1011] P. Sarkar and S. Maitra. Construction of nonlinear Boolean functions with important cryptographic properties. *Proceedings of EUROCRYPT 2000, Lecture Notes in Computer Science* 1807, pp. 485–506, 2000. See pages 291, 292, and 320.

[1012] P. Sarkar and S. Maitra. Nonlinearity bounds and constructions of resilient Boolean functions. *Proceedings of CRYPTO 2000, Lecture Notes in Computer Science* 1880, pp. 515–532, 2000. See pages 287, 288, and 291.

[1013] P. Sarkar and S. Maitra. Construction of nonlinear resilient Boolean functions using "small" affine functions. *IEEE Transactions on Information Theory* 50 (9), pp. 2185–2193, 2004. See page 295.

[1014] P. Sarkar and S. Maitra. Balancedness and correlation immunity of symmetric Boolean functions. *Discrete Mathematics* 307, pp. 2351–2358, 2007. See page 357.

[1015] P. Sarkar and S. Maitra. Construction of rotation symmetric Boolean functions on odd number of variables with maximum algebraic immunity. *Proceedings of AAECC 2007, Lecture Notes in Computer Science* 4851, pp. 271–280, 2007. See page 362.

[1016] S. Sarkar and S. Maitra. Idempotents in the neighbourhood of Patterson–Wiedemann functions having Walsh spectra zeros. *Designs, Codes and Cryptography,* 49, pp. 95–103, 2008. See pages 81 and 82.

[1017] D. V. Sarwate and M. B. Pursley. Crosscorrelation properties of pseudorandom and related sequences. *Proceedings of the IEEE* 68 (5), pp. 593–619 (1980). Correction in *Proceedings of the IEEE* 68 (12), pp. 1554, 1980.

[1018] T. Satoh, T. Iwata, and K. Kurosawa. On cryptographically secure vectorial Boolean functions. *Proceedings of ASIACRYPT 1999, Lecture Notes in Computer Science* 1716, pp. 20–28, 1999. See page 270.

[1019] P. Savicky. On the bent Boolean functions that are symmetric. *European Journal of Combinatorics* 15, pp. 407–410, 1994. See page 355.

[1020] J. Schatz. The second-order Reed–Muller code of length 64 has covering radius 18. *IEEE Transactions in Information Theory* 27 (4), pp. 529–530, 1981. See page 158.

[1021] K.-U. Schmidt. Nonlinearity measures of random Boolean functions. *Cryptography and Communications* 8 (4), pp. 637–645, 2016. See pages 84 and 159.

[1022] K.-U. Schmidt. Asymptotically optimal Boolean functions. *Journal of Combinatorial Theory, Series A* 164, pp. 50–59, 2019. See page 157.

[1023] K.-U. Schmidt and Y. Zhou. Planar functions over fields of characteristic two. CoRR abs/1301.6999, 2013. See page 269.

[1024] M. Schneider. A note on the construction and upper bounds of correlation-immune functions. *Proceedings of IMA Conference on Cryptography and Coding 1997, Lecture Notes In Computer Science* 1355, pp. 295–306, 1997. An extended version appeared under the title "On the construction and upper bounds of balanced and correlation-immune functions," *Selected Areas in Cryptography (SAC)*, pp. 73–87, 1997. See page 312.

[1025] J. Seberry and X-.M. Zhang. Constructions of bent functions from two known bent functions. *Australasian Journal of Combinatorics* 9, pp. 21–35, 1994. See page 234.

[1026] J. Seberry, X-.M. Zhang, and Y. Zheng. On constructions and nonlinearity of correlation immune Boolean functions. *Proceedings of EUROCRYPT 1993, Lecture Notes in Computer Science* 765, pp. 181–199, 1994. See page 294.

[1027] J. Seberry, X-.M. Zhang, and Y. Zheng. Nonlinearly balanced Boolean functions and their propagation characteristics. *Proceedings of CRYPTO 1993, Lecture Notes in Computer Science* 773, pp. 49–60, 1994. See page 81.

[1028] J. Seberry, X.-M. Zhang, and Y. Zheng. Nonlinearity characteristics of quadratic substitution boxes. *Proceedings of Selected Areas in Cryptography (SAC 1994)*. This paper appeared under the title "Relationship among nonlinearity criteria" in the *Proceedings of EUROCRYPT 1994, Lecture Notes in Computer Science*, 950 pp. 376–388, 1995. See page 391.

[1029] N. V. Semakov and V. A. Zinoviev. Balanced codes and tactical configurations. *Problems of Information Transmission* 5 (3), pp. 22–28 (1969) See page 255.

[1030] A. Shamir. How to share a secret. *Commun. ACM* 22 (11), pp. 612–613, 1979. See page 145.

[1031] J. Shan, L. Hu, and X. Zeng. Cryptographic properties of nested functions and algebraic immunity of the Boolean function in Hitag2 stream cipher. *Cryptography and Communications* 6 (3), pp. 233–254, 2014. See page 335.

[1032] A. Shanbhag, V. Kumar, and T. Helleseth. An upper bound for the extended Kloosterman sums over Galois rings. *Finite Fields and Their Applications* 4, pp. 218–238, 1998. See page 188.

[1033] C. E. Shannon. A mathematical theory of communication. *Bell System Technical Journal*, 27, pp. 379–423, 1948. See page 4.

[1034] C. E. Shannon. Communication theory of secrecy systems. *Bell System Technical Journal*, 28, pp. 656–715, 1949. See pages 19, 76, and 89.

[1035] C. E. Shannon. The synthesis of two-terminal switching circuits. *Bell System Technical Journal*, 28, pp. 59–98, 1949. See page 103.

[1036] R. Shaltiel. Dispersers for affine sources with sub-polynomial entropy. *Proceedings of 52nd Annual Symposium on Foundations of Computer Science, FOCS 2011*, pp. 247–256, 2011. See pages 105 and 108.

[1037] T. Shimoyama and T. Kaneko. Quadratic relation of S-box and its application to the linear attack of full round DES. *Proceedings of CRYPTO 1998, Lecture Notes in Computer Science* 1462, pp. 200–211, 1998. See page 122.

[1038] I. Shparlinski. On the singularity of generalised Vandermonde matrices over finite fields. *Finite Fields and Their Applications* 11, pp. 193–199, 2005. See page 96.

[1039] L. Shuai, L. Wang, L. Miao, and X. Zhou. Differential uniformity of the composition of two functions. *Cryptography and Communications* 12 (2), pp. 205–220, 2020. See page 421.

[1040] V. M. Sidelnikov. On the mutual correlation of sequences. *Soviet Math. Dokl.* 12, pp. 197–201, 1971. See page 118.

[1041] T. Siegenthaler. Correlation-immunity of nonlinear combining functions for cryptographic applications. *IEEE Transactions on Information Theory* 30 (5), pp. 776–780, 1984. See pages 76, 86, 284, 285, 297, and 298.

[1042] T. Siegenthaler. Decrypting a Class of stream ciphers using ciphertext only. *IEEE Transactions on Computer* C-34 (1), pp. 81–85, 1985. See pages 76 and 87.

[1043] R. Singh, B. Sarma, and A. Saikia. Public key cryptography using permutation p-polynomials over finite fields. *IACR Cryptology ePrint Archive* (http://eprint.iacr.org/) 2009/208, 2009. See page 250.

[1044] S. Smyshlyaev. Perfectly balanced Boolean functions and Golić conjecture. *Journal of Cryptology* **25**, pp. 464–48, 2012. See page 344.

[1045] J. Søreng. The periods of the sequences generated by some symmetric shift registers. *Journal of Combinatorial Theory, Series A* 21 (2), pp. 164–187, 1976. See page 23.

[1046] J. Søreng. Symmetric shift registers. *Pacific J. Math.* 85 (1), pp. 201–229, 1979. See page 23.

[1047] F.-X. Standaert, N. Veyrat-Charvillon, E. Oswald, etc. The world is not enough: another look on second-order dpa. *IACR Cryptology ePrint Archive* (http://eprint.iacr.org/) 2010/180, 2010. See page 427.

[1048] P. Stănică, S. Maitra, and J. Clark. Results on rotation symmetric bent and correlation immune Boolean functions. *Proceedings of Fast Software Encryption FSE 2004, Lecture Notes in Computer Science* 3017, pp. 161–177, 2004. See page 360.

[1049] D. R. Stinson. Resilient functions and large sets of orthogonal arrays. *Congressus Numer.* 92, pp. 105–110, 1993. See page 314.

[1050] D. R. Stinson and J. L. Massey. An infinite class of counterexamples to a conjecture concerning nonlinear resilient functions. *Journal of Cryptology* 8, n° 3, pp. 167–173, 1995. See page 314.

[1051] K. Stoffelen. Optimizing S-box implementations for several criteria using SAT solvers. *Proceedings of Fast Software Encryption FSE 2016, Lecture Notes in Computer Science* 9783, pp. 140–160, 2016. See page 144.

[1052] V. Strassen. Gaussian elimination is not optimal. *Numerische Math.* 13, pp. 354–356, 1969. See page 90.

[1053] I. Strazdins. Universal affine classification of Boolean functions. *Acta Applicandae Mathematicae* 46, pp. 147–167, 1997. See page 155.

[1054] S. Su and X. Tang. Systematic constructions of rotation symmetric bent functions, 2-rotation symmetric bent functions, and bent idempotent functions. *IEEE Transactions on Information Theory* 63 (7), pp. 4658–4667, 2017. See also: On the systematic constructions of rotation symmetric bent functions with any possible algebraic degrees. *IACR Cryptology ePrint Archive* (http://eprint.iacr.org/) 2015/451, 2015. See page 252.

[1055] W. Su, X. Zeng, and L. Hu. Construction of 1-resilient Boolean functions with optimum algebraic immunity. *International Journal of Computer Mathematics* 88 (2), pp. 222–238, 2011. See page 344.

[1056] T. Sugawara. 3-share threshold implementation of AES S-box without fresh randomness. *IACR Transactions on Cryptographic Hardware and Embedded Systems* 2019 (1), pp. 123–145, 2019. See page 443.

[1057] T. Sugita, T. Kasami, and T. Fujiwara. Weight distributions of the third and fifth order Reed–Muller codes of length 512. *Nara Inst. Sci. Tech. Report*, 1996. See page 155.

[1058] T.-F. Sun, B. Hu, Y. Liu, and L.-P. Xu. On primary construction of plateaued functions. *Proceedings of 3rd International Conference on Material, Mechanical and Manufacturing Engineering IC3ME 2015*, Atlantis Press, 2015. See page 265.

[1059] S. H. Sung, S. Chee, and C. Park. Global avalanche characteristics and propagation criterion of balanced Boolean functions. *Information Processing Letters* 69, pp. 21–24, 1999.

[1060] Y. Tan, G. Gong, and B. Zhu. Enhanced criteria on differential uniformity and nonlinearity of cryptographically significant functions. *Cryptography and Communications* 8 (2), pp. 291–311, 2016. See page 136.

[1061] Y. Tan, L. Qu, S. Ling, and C. H. Tan. On the Fourier spectra of new APN functions. *SIAM Journal on Discrete Mathematics* 27 (2), pp. 791–801, 2013. See page 412.

[1062] C. Tang and Y. Qi. Constructing Hyper-Bent Functions from Boolean Functions with the Walsh Spectrum Taking the Same Value Twice. *Proceedings of International Conference on Sequences and Their Applications SETA 2014, Lecture Notes in Computer Science*, pp. 60–71, 2014. See page 247.

[1063] C. Tang and Y. Qi. A class of hyper-bent functions and Kloosterman sums. *Cryptography and Communications* 9 (5), pp. 647–664, 2017. See page 247.

[1064] C. Tang, Y. Qi, and M. Xu. Multiple output bent functions characterized by families of bent functions. *Journal of Cryptologic Research* 1 (4), pp. 321–326, 2014. See page 272.

[1065] C. Tang, Y. Qi, Z. Zhou, and C. Fan. Two infinite classes of rotation symmetric bent functions with simple representation. *Applicable Algebra in Engineering Communication and Computing* (AAECC) 29 (3), pp. 197–208, 2018. See pages 249 and 251.

[1066] D. Tang, C. Carlet, and X. Tang. On the second-order nonlinearities of some bent functions. *Information Sciences* 223, pp. 322–330, 2013. See page 85.

[1067] D. Tang, C. Carlet, and X. Tang. Highly nonlinear Boolean functions with optimal algebraic immunity and good behavior against fast algebraic attacks. *IEEE Transactions on Information Theory* 59 (1), pp. 653–664, 2013 (preliminary version available in *IACR Cryptology ePrint Archive*, http://eprint.iacr.org/2011/366, 2011). See pages 332 and 340.

[1068] D. Tang, C. Carlet, and X. Tang. A class of 1-resilient Boolean functions with optimal algebraic immunity and good behavior against fast algebraic attacks. *International Journal of Foundations of Computer Science* 25 (6), pp. 763–780, 2014. See page 340.

[1069] D. Tang, C. Carlet, and X. Tang. Differentially 4-uniform bijections by permuting the inverse function. *Designs, Codes and Cryptography* 77 (1), pp. 117–141, 2015. See page 421.

[1070] D. Tang, C. Carlet, X. Tang, and Z. Zhou. Construction of highly nonlinear 1-resilient Boolean functions with optimal algebraic immunity and provably high fast algebraic immunity. *IEEE Transactions on Information Theory* 63 (9), pp. 6113–6125, 2017. See page 344.

[1071] D. Tang, C. Carlet, and Z. Zhou. Binary linear codes from vectorial Boolean functions and their weight distribution. *Discrete Mathematics* 340 (12), pp. 3055–3072, 2017. See page 161.

[1072] D. Tang, S. Kavut, B. Mandal, and S. Maitra. Modifying Maiorana–McFarland type bent functions for good cryptographic properties and efficient implementation. *SIAM Journal of Discrete Mathematics* 33 (1), pp. 238–256, 2019. See page 99.

[1073] D. Tang and J. Liu. A family of weightwise (almost) perfectly balanced Boolean functions with optimal algebraic immunity. *Special Issue on Boolean Functions and Their Applications 2018, Cryptography and Communications* 11 (6), pp. 1185–1197, 2019. See page 459.

[1074] D. Tang and S. Maitra. Construction of n-variable ($n \equiv 2 \bmod 4$) balanced Boolean functions with maximum absolute value in autocorrelation spectra $< 2^{\frac{n}{2}}$. *IEEE Transactions on Information Theory* 64 (1), pp. 393–402, 2018. See page 320.

[1075] C. Tang, Z. Zhou, Y. Qi, X. Zhang, C. Fan, and T. Helleseth. Generic construction of bent functions and bent idempotents with any possible algebraic degrees. *IEEE Transactions on Information Theory* 63 (10), pp. 6149–6157, 2017. See page 251.

[1076] X. H. Tang, D. Tang, X. Zeng, and L. Hu. Balanced Boolean functions with (almost) optimal algebraic immunity and very high nonlinearity. *IACR Cryptology ePrint Archive* (http://eprint.iacr.org/) 2010/443, 2010. See pages 340 and 344.

[1077] H. Taniguchi. On some quadratic APN functions. *Designs, Codes and Cryptography* 87 (9), pp. 1973–1983, 2019. See pages 407 and 410.

[1078] T. Tao. Structure and randomness in combinatorics. *Proceedings of FOCS 2007*, pp. 3–15 (also arXiv:0707.4269v2[math.CO], 2007).

[1079] H. Tapia-Recillas and G. Vega. An upper bound on the number of iterations for transforming a Boolean function of degree greater than or equal than 4 to as function of degree 3. *Designs, Codes and Cryptography* 24, pp. 305–312, 2001.

[1080] Y. V. Tarannikov. On resilient Boolean functions with maximum possible nonlinearity. *Proceedings of INDOCRYPT 2000, Lecture Notes in Computer Science* 1977, pp. 19–30, 2000. See pages 287, 288, 291, and 300.

[1081] Y. V. Tarannikov. New constructions of resilient Boolean functions with maximum nonlinearity. *Proceedings of Fast Software Encryption FSE 2001, Lecture Notes in Computer Science* 2355, pp. 66–77, 2001. See pages 287 and 291.

[1082] Y. V. Tarannikov and D. Kirienko. Spectral analysis of high order correlation immune functions. *Proceedings of 2001 IEEE International Symposium on Information Theory*, p. 69, 2001. Preliminary version available in *IACR Cryptology ePrint Archive* (http://eprint.iacr.org/) 2000/050, 2000. See pages 101 and 313.

[1083] Y. V. Tarannikov, P. Korolev, and A. Botev. Autocorrelation coefficients and correlation immunity of Boolean functions. *Proceedings of ASIACRYPT 2001, Lecture Notes in Computer Science* 2248, pp. 460–479, 2001 See pages 287, 290, and 313.

[1084] A. Tardy-Corfdir and H. Gilbert. A known plaintext attack on feal-4 and feal-6. *Proceedings of CRYPTO 1991, Lecture Notes in Computer Science* 576, pp. 172–181, 1991. See page 115.

[1085] E. Thomé. Subquadratic computation of vector generating polynomials and improvement of the block Wiedemann algorithm. *Journal of Symbolic Computation* 33 (5), pp. 757–775, 2002. See page 21.

[1086] Y. Todo. Structural evaluation by generalized integral property. *Proceedings of EUROCRYPT 2015, Part I. Lecture Notes in Computer Science* 9056, pp. 287–314, 2015. See page 114.

[1087] N. Tokareva. On the number of bent functions from iterative constructions: lower bounds and hypotheses. *Advances in Mathematics of Communications* 5 (4), pp., 609–621, 2011. See page 242.

[1088] N. Tokareva. Duality between bent functions and affine functions. *Discrete Mathematics* 312, pp. 666–670, 2012. See page 191.

[1089] N. Tokareva. *Bent Functions, Results and applications to cryptography*. Elsevier, 2015. See page 190.

[1090] S. Tsai. Lower bounds on representing Boolean functions as polynomials in $\mathbb{Z}_m^*$. *SIAM Journal on Discrete Mathematics* 9 (1), pp. 55–62, 1996. See page 37.

[1091] Z. Tu and Y. Deng. A conjecture on binary string and its applications on constructing Boolean functions of optimal algebraic immunity. *Designs, Codes and Cryptography* 60 (1), pp. 1–14, 2011. See pages 332, 337, and 339.

[1092] Z. Tu and Y. Deng. Boolean functions optimizing most of the cryptographic criteria. *Discrete Applied Mathematics* 160 (4), pp. 427–435, 2012. See page 344.

[1093] Z. Tu, D. Zheng, X. Zeng, and L. Hu. Boolean functions with two distinct Walsh coefficients. *Applicable Algebra in Engineering, Communication and Computing AAECC* 22 (5–6), pp. 359–366, 2011. See page 190.

[1094] K. Varici, S. Nikova, V. Nikov, and V. Rijmen. Constructions of S-boxes with uniform sharing. *Cryptography and Communications* 11 (3), pp. 385–398, 2019. Preliminary version in *IACR Cryptology ePrint Archive* (http://eprint.iacr.org/) 2018/92, 2018. See pages 442 and 479.

[1095] S. Vaudenay. On the need for multipermutations: cryptanalysis of MD4 and SAFER. *Proceedings of Fast Software Encryption FSE 1995, Lecture Notes in Computer Science* 1008, pp. 286–297, 1995. See page 129.

[1096] I. Villa. On APN functions $L_1(x^3) + L_2(x^9)$ with linear L_1 and L_2. *Cryptography and Communications* 11 (1), pp. 3–20, 2019. See page 406.

[1097] S. F. Vinokurov and N. A. Peryazev. An expansion of Boolean function into a sum of products of subfunctions. *Discrete Mathematics and Applications* 3 (5), pp. 531–533, 1993.

[1098] J. F. Voloch. Symmetric cryptography and algebraic curves. *Proceedings of "The First Symposium on Algebraic Geometry and Its Applications" Dedicated to Gilles Lachaud (SAGA'07), Tahiti, 2007, Published by World Scientific, Series on Number Theory and Its Applications* 5, pp. 135–141, 2008. See pages 136 and 369.

[1099] T. Wadayama, T. Hada, K. Wagasugi, and M. Kasahara. Upper and lower bounds on the maximum nonlinearity of n-input m-output Boolean functions. *Designs, Codes and Cryptography* 23, pp. 23–33, 2001. See pages 160, 370, and 378.

[1100] J. Waddle and D. Wagner. Towards efficient second-order power analysis. *Proceedings of International Workshop Cryptographic Hardware and Embedded Systems CHES 2010, Lecture Notes in Computer Science* 3156, pp. 1–15, 2004. See page 427.

[1101] D. Wagner. The boomerang attack. *Proceedings of Fast Software Encryption FSE 1999, Lecture Notes in Computer Science* 1636, pp. 156–170, 1999. See page 141.

[1102] Q. Wang. The covering radius of the Reed–Muller code RM (2, 7) is 40. *Discrete Mathematics* 342 (12), p. 111625, 2019. See pages 157 and 158.

[1103] H. Wang, J. Peng, Y. Li, and H. Kan. On $2k$-variable symmetric Boolean functions with maximum algebraic immunity k. *IEEE Transactions on Information Theory* 58 (8), pp. 5612–5624, 2012. See page 358.

[1104] Q. Wang. Hadamard matrices, d-linearly independent sets and correlation-immune Boolean functions with minimum hamming weights. *Designs, Codes and Cryptography* 87 (10), pp. 2321–2333, 2019 . See also *IACR Cryptology ePrint Archive* (http://eprint.iacr.org/) 2018/284. See pages 291, 304, 305, and 306.

[1105] Q. Wang, C. Carlet, P. Stănică, and C. H. Tan. Cryptographic properties of the hidden weighted bit function. *Discrete Applied Mathematics* 174, pp. 1–10, 2014. See page 343.

[1106] Q. Wang and T. Johansson. A note on fast algebraic attacks and higher order nonlinearities. *Proceedings of INSCRYPT 2010, Lecture Notes in Computer Science* 6584, pp. 84–98, 2010. See pages 94, 332, and 340.

[1107] Q. Wang and H. Kan. A note on the construction of differentially uniform permutations using extension fields. *IEICE Transactions* 95-A (11), pp. 2080–2083, 2012. See page 419.

[1108] Q. Wang and P. Stănică. A trigonometric sum sharp estimate and new bounds on the nonlinearity of some cryptographic Boolean functions. *Designs, Codes and Cryptography* 87 (8), pp. 1749–1763, 2019. See page 340.

[1109] Q. Wang, C. H. Tan, and T. F. Prabowo. On the covering radius of the third order Reed–Muller code RM (3, 7). *Designs, Codes and Cryptography* 86 (1), pp. 151–159, 2018. See page 158.

[1110] Z. Wang and G. Gong. Discrete Fourier transform of Boolean functions over the complex field and its applications. *IEEE Transactions on Information Theory* 64 (4) (Special Issue in Honor of Solomon Golomb), pp. 3000–3009, 2018. See pages 44, 52, 53, and 88.

[1111] T. Wang, M. Liu, and D. Lin. Construction of resilient and nonlinear Boolean functions with almost perfect immunity to algebraic and fast algebraic attacks. *Information Security and Cryptology. Inscrypt 2012*, M. Kutyłowski and M. Yung, eds. Lecture Notes in Computer Science, vol. 7763, Springer, pp. 276–293, 2013. See page 344.

[1112] Z. Wang and M. Karpovsky. Algebraic manipulation detection codes and their applications for design of secure cryptographic devices. *Proceedings of On-Line Testing Symposium (IOLTS), 2011*, pp. 234–239, 2011. See pages 451 and 452.

[1113] Z. Wang and M. Karpovsky. New error detecting codes for the design of hardware resistant to strong fault injection attacks. *Proceedings of International Conference on Security and Management, SAM*, 2012. See pages 451, 452, and 453.

[1114] Z. Wang, M. Karpovsky, and K. J Kulikowski. Design of memories with concurrent error detection and correction by nonlinear SEC-DED codes. *Journal of Electronic Testing* 26 (5), pp. 559–580, 2010. See page 453.

[1115] Z. Wang, X. Zhang, S. Wang, Z. Zheng, and W. Wang. Construction of Boolean functions with excellent cryptographic criteria using bivariate polynomial representation. *International Journal of Computer Mathematics*, 93 (3), pp. 425–444, 2016. See page 344.

[1116] A. F. Webster and S. E. Tavares. On the design of S-boxes. *Proceedings of CRYPTO 1985, Lecture Notes in Computer Science* 219, pp. 523–534, 1985. See page 97.

[1117] I. Wegener, *The Complexity of Boolean Functions*, John Wiley & Sons, 1987. See pages 19 and 352.

[1118] G. Weng, Y. Tan, and G. Gong. On almost perfect nonlinear functions and their related algebraic objects. *Proceedings of International Workshop on Coding and Cryptography*, pp. 48–57, 2013. See pages 393 and 399.

[1119] K. S. Williams, Note on cubics over $GF(2^n)$ and $GF(3^n)$. *Journal of Number Theory* 7 (4), pp. 361–365, 1975. See page 495.

[1120] J. Wolfmann. Bent functions and coding theory. *Difference Sets, Sequences and their Correlation Properties*, A. Pott, P. V. Kumar, T. Helleseth, and D. Jungnickel, eds., Kluwer, pp. 393–417. 1999. See pages 160, 195, and 196.

[1121] J. Wolfmann. Cyclic code aspects of bent functions. Finite Fields Theory and Applications, Contemporary Mathematics Series of the AMS, Amer. Math Soc., vol. 518, pp. 363–384, 2010. See page 262.

[1122] J. Wolfmann. Sequences of bent and near-bent functions. *Cryptography and Communications* 9 (6), pp. 729–736, 2017. See page 240.

[1123] B. Wu. $\mathcal{PS}$ bent functions constructed from finite pre-quasifield spreads. http://arxiv.org/abs/1308 .3355, 2013. See pages 217, 225, and 226.

[1124] B. Wu, J. Zheng and D. Lin: Constructing Boolean functions with (potentially) optimal algebraic immunity based on multiplicative decompositions of finite fields. *Proceedings of IEEE International Symposium on Information Theory (ISIT) 2015*, pp. 491–495, 2015. See page 340.

[1125] C.-K. Wu and D. Feng. *Boolean Functions and Their Applications in Cryptography*. Springer, 2016. See page 76.

[1126] T. Xia, J. Seberry, J. Pieprzyk, and C. Charnes. Homogeneous bent functions of degree n in $2n$ variables do not exist for $n > 3$. *Discrete Applied Mathematics* 142 (1–3), pp. 127–132, 2004. See page 248.

[1127] Y. Xia, N. Li, X. Zeng, and T. Helleseth. An open problem on the distribution of a Niho type cross-correlation function. *IEEE Transactions on Information Theory* 62 (12), pp. 7546–7554, 2016. See page 384.

[1128] G.-Z. Xiao and J. L. Massey. A spectral characterization of correlation-immune combining functions. *IEEE Transactions on Information Theory* 34 (3), pp. 569–571, 1988. See page 87.

[1129] M. Xiong, H. Yan, and P. Yuan. On a conjecture of differentially 8-uniform power functions. *Designs, Codes and Cryptography* 86 (8), pp. 1601–1621, 2018. See page 422.

[1130] G. Xu and X. Cao. Constructing new piecewise differentially 4-uniform permutations from known APN functions. *International Journal of Foundations of Computer Science* 26 (5), pp. 599–609, 2015. See page 420.

[1131] G. Xu, X. Cao, and S. Xu. Several new classes of Boolean functions with few Walsh transform values. *Applicable Algebra in Engineering Communication and Computing* (AAECC) 28 (2), pp. 155–176, 2017. See pages 231 and 263.

[1132] G. Xu and L. Qu. Two classes of differentially 4-uniform permutations over $\mathbb{F}_2^n$ with n even. To appear in *Advances in Mathematics of Communications* 14 (1), 2020. See page 420.

[1133] Y. Xu, C. Carlet, S. Mesnager, and C. Wu. Classification of bent monomials, constructions of bent multinomials and upper bounds on the nonlinearity of vectorial functions. *IEEE Transactions on Information Theory* 64 (1), pp. 367–383, 2018. See pages 122, 140, and 272.

[1134] X. Yang and J. L. Massey. The condition for a cyclic code to have a complementary dual. *Discrete Mathematics* 126, pp. 391–393, 1994. See page 446.

[1135] Y. X. Yang and B. Guo. Further enumerating Boolean functions of cryptographic signifiance. *Journal of Cryptology* 8 (3), pp. 115–122, 1995. See pages 356 and 357.

[1136] A. C. Yao. Protocols for secure computations (extended abstract). *Proceedings of FOCS 1982*, pp. 160–164, 1982. See page 146.

[1137] R. Yarlagadda and J. E. Hershey. Analysis and synthesis of bent sequences, *IEE Proceedings. Part E. Computers and Digital Techniques* 136, pp. 112–123, 1989. See pages 231 and 293.

[1138] K. Yasunaga and T. Fujiwara. On correctable errors of binary linear codes. *IEEE Transactions on Information Theory* 56 (6), pp. 2537–2548, 2010. See page 79.

[1139] S. Yoshiara. Equivalences of quadratic APN functions. *Journal of Algebraic Combinatorics* 35, pp. 461–475, 2012. See pages 30 and 281.

[1140] S. Yoshiara. Equivalences of power APN functions with power or quadratic APN functions. *Journal of Algebraic Combinatorics* 44 (3), pp. 561–585, 2016. See pages 281, 396, 398, 402, 405, and 406.

[1141] S. Yoshiara. Equivalences among plateaued APN functions. *Designs, Codes and Cryptography* 85 (2), pp. 205–217, 2017. See pages 281 and 402.

[1142] S. Yoshiara. Plateaudness of Kasami APN functions. *Finite Fields and Their Applications* 47, pp. 11–32, 2017. See pages 382 and 400.

[1143] A. M. Youssef and G. Gong. Hyper-bent functions. *Proceedings of EUROCRYPT 2001, Lecture Notes in Computer Science* 2045, Berlin, pp. 406–419, 2001. See pages 244 and 272.

[1144] N. Y. Yu and G. Gong. Constructions of quadratic bent functions in polynomial forms. *IEEE Transactions on Information Theory* 52 (7), pp. 3291–3299, 2006. See pages 206, 230, 231, and 250.

[1145] Y. Yu, M. Wang, and Y. Li. A matrix approach for constructing quadratic APN functions. *Proceedings of International Workshop on Coding and Cryptography*, pp. 39–47, 2013, and *Designs, Codes and Cryptography* 73 (2), pp 587–600, 2014. See pages 392, 393, and 399.

[1146] Y. Yu, M. S. Wang, and Y. Q. Li. Constructing low differential uniformity functions from known ones. *Chinese Journal of Electronics* 22 (3), pp. 495–499, 2013. See also *IACR Cryptology ePrint Archive* (http://eprint.iacr.org/) 2011/47, entitled "Constructing differential 4-uniform permutations from known ones." See page 420.

[1147] J. Yuan, C. Carlet, and C. Ding. The weight distribution of a class of linear codes from perfect nonlinear functions. *IEEE Transactions on Information Theory* 52 (2), pp. 712–717, 2006. See page 160.

[1148] X. Zeng, C. Carlet, J. Shan, and L. Hu. More balanced Boolean functions with optimal algebraic immunity and good nonlinearity and resistance to fast algebraic attacks. *IEEE Transactions on Information Theory* 57 (9), pp. 6310–6320, 2011. See pages 337 and 339.

[1149] X. Zeng and L. Hu. Constructing Boolean functions by modifying Maiorana–McFarland's superclass functions. *IEICE Transactions on Fundamentals of Electronics, Communications and Computer Sciences* 88-A (1), pp. 59–66, 2005. See page 340.

[1150] Z. Zha, L. Hu, and S. Sun. Constructing new differentially 4-uniform permutations from the inverse function. *Finite Fields and Their Applications* 25, pp. 64–78, 2014. See page 420.

[1151] Z. Zha, L. Hu, S. Sun, and J. Shan. Further results on differentially 4-uniform permutations over $\mathbb{F}_{2^{2m}}$. *Science China Mathematics* 58 (7), pp. 1577–1588, 2015. See page 420.

[1152] F. Zhang, C. Carlet, Y. Hu, and T.-J. Cao. Secondary constructions of highly nonlinear Boolean functions and disjoint spectra plateaued functions. *Information Sciences* 283, pp. 94–106, 2014. See page 266.

[1153] F. Zhang, C. Carlet, Y. Hu, and W. Zhang. New secondary constructions of bent functions. *Applicable Algebra in Engineering, Communication and Computing (AAECC)* 27 (5), pp. 413–434, 2016. See page 234.

[1154] F. Zhang, E. Pasalic, N. Cepak, and Y. Wei. Bent functions in $\mathcal{C}$ and $\mathcal{D}$ Outside the completed Maiorana–McFarland class. *Proceedings of C2SI 2017, Lecture Notes in Computer Science* 10194, pp. 298–313, 2017. See page 211.

[1155] M. Zhang. Maximum correlation analysis of nonlinear combining functions in stream ciphers. *Journal of Cryptology* 13 (3), pp. 301–313, 2000. See pages 101 and 290.

[1156] M. Zhang and A. Chan. Maximum correlation analysis of nonlinear S-boxes in stream ciphers. *Proceedings of CRYPTO 2000, Lecture Notes in Computer Science* 1880, pp. 501–514, 2000. See pages 131 and 132.

[1157] W. Zhang. High-meets-low: construction of strictly almost optimal resilient Boolean functions via fragmentary Walsh spectra. *IEEE Transactions on Information Theory* 65 (9), pp. 5856–5864, 2019. See page 317.

[1158] W. Zhang, Z. Bao, V. Rijmen, and M. Liu. A new classification of 4-bit optimal S-boxes and its application to PRESENT, RECTANGLE and SPONGENT. *Proceedings of Fast Software Encryption FSE 2015, Lecture Notes in Computer Science* 9054, pp. 494–515, 2015; see also https://eprint.iacr.org/2015/433. See page 144.

[1159] W. Zhang, L. Li, and E. Pasalic. Construction of resilient S-boxes with higher-dimensional vectorial outputs and strictly almost optimal non-linearity. *IET Information Security* 11 (4), pp. 199–203, 2017. See page 317.

[1160] W. Zhang and E. Pasalic. Highly nonlinear balanced S-boxes with good differential properties. *IEEE Transactions on Information Theory* 60 (12), pp. 7970–7979, 2014. See page 422.

[1161] W. Zhang and E. Pasalic. Constructions of resilient S-Boxes with strictly almost optimal nonlinearity through disjoint linear codes. *IEEE Transactions on Information Theory* 60 (3), pp. 1638–1651, 2014. See page 317.

[1162] W. Zhang, Z. Xing, and K. Feng. A construction of bent functions with optimal algebraic degree and large symmetric group. *Advances in Mathematics of Communications* 14 (1), pp. 23–33, 2020. See also *IACR Cryptology ePrint Archive* (http://eprint.iacr.org/) 2017/197. See page 192.

[1163] W.-G. Zhang and E. Pasalic. Generalized Maiorana–McFarland construction of resilient Boolean functions with high nonlinearity and good algebraic properties. *IEEE Transactions on Information Theory* 60 (10), pp. 6681–6695, 2014. See page 295.

[1164] W. G. Zhang and G. Z. Xiao. Constructions of almost optimal resilient Boolean functions on large even number of variables. *IEEE Transactions on Information Theory* 55 (12), pp. 5822–5831, 2009. See page 295.

[1165] X. Zhang, X. Cao, and R. Feng. A method of evaluation of exponential sum of binary quadratic functions. *Finite Fields and Their Applications* 18, pp. 1089–1103, 2012. See page 179.

[1166] X. Zhang and M. Zhou. Construction of CCZ transform for quadratic APN functions. *Cognitive Systems Research* 57, pp. 41–45, 2019. See page 404.

[1167] X.-M. Zhang and Y. Zheng. GAC – the criterion for global avalanche characteristics of cryptographic functions. *Journal of Universal Computer Science*, 1 (5), pp. 320–337, 1995. See pages 97 and 320.

[1168] X.-M. Zhang and Y. Zheng. On nonlinear resilient functions. *Proceedings of EUROCRYPT 1995, Lecture Notes in Computer Science* 921, pp. 274–288, 1995. See pages 129 and 317.

[1169] X.-M. Zhang and Y. Zheng. Auto-correlations and new bounds on the nonlinearity of Boolean functions. *Proceedings of EUROCRYPT 1996, Lecture Notes in Computer Science* 1070, pp. 294–306, 1996. See pages 81, 98, and 318.

[1170] X.-M. Zhang and Y. Zheng. Cryptographically resilient functions. *IEEE Transactions on Information Theory* 43, pp. 1740–1747, 1997. See page 317.

[1171] X.-M. Zhang and Y. Zheng. The nonhomomorphicity of Boolean functions. *Proceedings of SAC 1998, Lecture Notes in Computer Science* 1556, pp. 280–295, 1999. See page 111.

[1172] J. Zheng, B. Wu, Y. Chen, and Z. Liu. Constructing $2m$-variable Boolean functions with optimal algebraic immunity based on polar decomposition of $\mathbb{F}_{2^{2m}}^*$. *International Journal of Foundations of Computer Science* 25 (5), pp. 537–552, 2014. See page 340.

[1173] Y. Zheng and X. M. Zhang. Plateaued functions. *Proceedings of ICICS 1999, Lecture Notes in Computer Science* 1726, pp. 284–300, 1999. See pages 81, 98, 190, 258, 259, and 264.

[1174] Y. Zheng and X. M. Zhang. Relationships between bent functions and complementary plateaued functions. *Lecture Notes in Computer Science* 1787, pp. 60–75, 1999. See page 258.

[1175] Y. Zheng and X.-M. Zhang. On relationships among avalanche, nonlinearity and correlation immunity. *Proceedings of ASIACRYPT 2000, Lecture Notes in Computer Science* 1976, pp. 470–483, 2000. See page 290.

[1176] Y. Zheng and X. M. Zhang. On plateaued functions. *IEEE Transactions on Information Theory* 47 (3), pp. 1215–1223, 2001. See page 258.

[1177] Y. Zheng and X.-M. Zhang. Improving upper bound on the nonlinearity of high order correlation immune functions. *Proceedings of Selected Areas in Cryptography 2000, Lecture Notes in Computer Science* 2012, pp. 262–274, 2001. See page 287.

[1178] Y. Zheng and X.-M. Zhang. On balanced nonlinear Boolean functions. *NATO Science for Peace and Security Series – D: Information and Communication Security*, IOS Press, Vol 18: Boolean Functions in Cryptology and Information Security, pp. 243–282, 2008. See pages 257, 258, and 320.

[1179] Y. Zheng, X.-M. Zhang, and H. Imai. Restriction, terms and nonlinearity of Boolean functions. *Theoretical Computer Science*, 226 (1–2), pp. 207–223, 1999. See pages 71, 106, and 153.

[1180] Y. Zhou. On the distribution of auto-correlation value of balanced Boolean functions. *Advances in Mathematics of Communications* 7 (3), pp. 335–347, 2013. See page 98.

[1181] Y. Zhou and C. Li. The Walsh spectrum of a new family of APN functions. *Proceedings of WSPC*, 2008. See also *IACR Cryptology ePrint Archive* (http://eprint.iacr.org/) 2008/154. See page 408.

[1182] Y. Zhou and A. Pott. A new family of semifields with 2 parameters. *Advances in Mathematics* 234, pp. 43–60, 2013. See pages 407 and 410.

[1183] N. Zierler and W. H. Mills. Products of linear recurring sequences. *Journal of Algebra* 27, pp. 147–157, 1973. See page 77.

[1184] M. Zieve. On a theorem of Carlitz. *Journal of Group Theory* 17, pp. 667–669, 2014. See page 442.

Index

557

Printed in the United States
by Baker & Taylor Publisher Services